Key to ...

🐎 Children welcome (from age shown in brackets, if specified)

🅿 Off-street car parking (number of places shown in brackets)

✘ No smoking

📺 Television (either in every room or in a TV lounge)

🐕 Pets accepted (by prior arrangement)

✕ Evening meal available (by prior arrangement)

Ⓥ Special diets catered for (by prior arrangement - please check with owner to see if your particular requirements are catered for)

♨ Coffee/Tea making facilities

▲ Youth Hostel

🛖 Camping Barn

▲ Camping facilities

🔋 Packed lunches available

✦ Drying facilities for wet clothes and boots

🚐 Vehicle back-up service (pick-up from path drop-off next day)

The location heading - every hamlet, village, town and city mentioned in this directory is represented on the local path map at the head of each chapter.

Use the National Grid reference with Ordnance Survey maps and any atlas that uses the National Grid. The letters refer to a 100 kilometre grid square. The first two numbers refer to a North/South grid line and the last two numbers refer to an East/West grid line. The grid reference indicates their intersection point.

Local pubs - these are the names of nearby pubs that serve food in the evening, as suggested by local B&Bs

Penny Hassett　　12

National Grid Ref: PH2096.

🍴 ♨ Cat & Fiddle, The Bull

Map reference (in the order that the location appears along the route).

Distance from paths in miles

(On Path 🚐) *The Old Rectory, Main Street, Penny Hassett, Borchester, Borsetshire, BC2 3QT.*
C18th former rectory, lovely garden.
Grades: ETB 2 Cr, Comm.
Tel: **01048 598464.** Mrs Smythe.
Rates fr: *£14.00*-**£16.00**.
Open: All Year
Beds: 1F 1D 1T
Baths: 1 Private 2 Shared
🐎(4) 🅿(2) ✘ 📺 🐕 ✕ 🔋 Ⓥ ♨ ✦ 🚐

The figure in *italics* is the lowest 1996 double or twin rate per person per night. The figure in **bold** is the lowest 1996 single rate. Some establishments do not accept single bookings.

Bedrooms
F = Family
D = Double
T = Twin
S = Single

Grades - the English, Scottish and Welsh Tourist Boards (**ETB**, **STB** and **WTB**) have the national Crown rating (**Cr**), in which the range of facilities and services an establishment provides is indicated by "Listed" or 1 to 5 Crowns in ascending order of merit. Northern Ireland has a simple approved system (**Approv**). An optional quality grading, using the terms Approved (**Approv**), Commended (**Comm**), Highly Commended (**High Comm**) and De Luxe is also used. More details of the national Crown rating and the quality grading can be had from any Tourist Information Centre. The Automobile Association (**AA**) employs two grading systems: the one for hotels uses 1 to 5 Stars (**St**) in ascending order of merit; there is also a B&B rating that uses the letter **Q** (for quality) on a scale of 1 to 4; the highest have 4 Qs and a Selected award (**Select**). For more details, telephone the AA on 01256 20123. The Royal Automobile Club (**RAC**) also uses a Star (**St**) system for large hotels; small hotels and B&Bs obtain the ratings 'Acclaimed' (**Acclaim**) or 'Highly Acclaimed' (**High Acclaim**). For more details, telephone the RAC on 0181-686 0088.

NATIONAL
TRAIL COMPANION
1996

EDITED BY TIM STILWELL
& DEAN CONWAY

STILWELL

Publishing Ltd

Distributed in Great Britain, Europe & the Commonwealth by Bailey Distribution Ltd, Learoyd Road, New Romney, Kent, TN28 8XU (Tel: 01797 366905) and available from all good bookshops. Distributed in North America by Seven Hills Book Distributors, 49 Central Ave, Cincinatti, Ohio 45202, U.S.A (Tel: (513) 3813881).

ISBN 0-9521909-4-X.

Published by Stilwell Publishing Ltd,
59 Charlotte Road, Shoreditch, London, EC2A 3QT.
Tel: 0171-739 7179. Fax: 0171 739 7191. E-mail: stilwell@cityscape.co.uk

Editor: Tim Stilwell
Assistant Editor: Dean Conway
Design and Maps: Nigel Simpson
Cover Photograph: Walking near Tintagel on the Cornwall section of the South West Coast Path. Keith Daniels, courtesy of Johnson Photography & Publishing, tel: 01623 645471

Typesetting by ITM Graphics Ltd, Hoxton, , London N7.

Printed in Great Britain by the Guernsey Press Company, Guernsey, Channel Islands.

Contents

Introduction

I said in last year's introduction that this annual directory had been a long time coming. This year's edition has taken just as long, too, with 18 paths added to the last year's 21. Such hard work has its rewards in unexpected ways. The original concept had been to come up with a book that any long-distance walker could rely on when planning the next walk. By happy accident, we seem to have created something else. The book actually fosters choice for walkers in a manner that we never envisaged, pushes the reader to travel and discover by the extent of its coverage. This is no bad thing. The variety that the British landscape offers to walkers remains largely undiscovered by the British themselves (the circulation of our largest walking magazine is around 30,000; our population is 56 million). Instead, the great outdoors is experienced vicariously through our newspapers, magazines, books and television. The 200 or so members of the Guild of Outdoor Writers who provide most of this material for the media are lucky indeed. They traverse the length and breadth of our country, year in, year out, for a living (a privilege shared only with itinerants, sales representatives and politicians). Only mundane practicalities prevent the rest of us from setting out for the hills beside them - lack of time, money and information. The National Trail Companion can do nothing about the first two. But if this book provides clear, useful information about a few paths, then surely more people will find my belief confirmed: that walking is a unbeatable way of getting to know the country - a irresistible combination of exercise, contemplation and the extraordinary British landscape.

The story behind the book is simple. My wife and I walked the North Downs Way over several weekends in the summer of 1991. Neither of us are born to camping, nor could we afford to stay in expensive hotels. We decided on B&Bs and found a problem straightaway. One could not find good value bed and breakfast accommodation along the route without going to a lot of trouble. Local libraries, directory enquiries, six different Tourist Information Centres and a large pile of brochures yielded nothing but a hotchpotch of B&B addresses, most of them miles out of our way. We abandoned the research and did the walk in one-day stretches, high-tailing it back to our London home each evening on the train.

The point is that we didn't really want to take the train back, especially when the time spent in waiting and travelling matched the time spent walking. A good weekend's walk would have been ideal, but we didn't know where to stay. Murphy's Law dictates that wherever you choose to finish your day's walk, there is either nothing in sight or a large country house hotel charging £100 for a one night stay. The train proved the logical option.

We did the South Downs Way like this, too in 1992. In 1993 we set out to spend a week walking the first half of Offa's Dyke and realised that we were hooked. Once you have walked one trail, you tend to want to walk another one fairly soon. Is there a collective noun for these poor obsessives? Anyway, as most trails are not a short train journey from home, the accommodation problem now loomed much larger. We eventually found out about the Offa's Dyke Association's excellent accommodation pamphlet. Planning walks along other paths I soon realised that a path has an accommodation list only if it has a strong Association behind it or proper commitment from a local County Council, and that even then, publishing standards vary. Many of you will know that when a path crosses a county boundary the standard and quality of signposting can change dramatically. This is true of all support services for a path and accommodation lists are no exception.

So we set out to create a directory that, for the price of the average compass, publishes accommodation details for all the National Trails in the order that they appear along the path. Why? Well, when I consider walking a long distance path, I wish to seize the moment, to book my room now. 'Next weekend, please', is the cry that goes up in this household. This book helps the armchair walker to achieve his or her desire in precisely that respect. No more accommodation research, no more long distance telephone calls to tourist information centres, no more sending off cheques for £1.85 for leaflets that arrive a week later. Moreover, the reader is now more at leisure to conceive of a path as a series of weekend walks rather than a 10-day procession. Itineraries are easier to work out, any pressure to complete a walk inside an allotted time begins to fade and paths previously thought difficult become a distinct possibility.

One issue should be set straight before anything else. This book is not intended as a map guide. It is no substitute for one at all. Aurum Press, Constable, Cicerone and several small publishers have brought out guides dedicated to describing routes on foot (details of which can be found in the chapter introduction for each path). These provide invaluable information regarding mileage, history, sights and navigation; they also include maps of a scale more suited to a walker's needs. That said, these guides should still be used with proper maps such as the Ordnance Survey's Landranger or Pathfinder series - or the specialist path maps published by Footprint of Stirling. In general, a guide does not include accommodation details, because the edition is meant to last several years; such details will change radically over this time. The National Trail Companion is intended to be used alongside these guides - hence the title.

All the National Trails as set out by the Countryside Commission and Scottish Heritage are represented in this book, plus some of the more famous long distance footpaths, many of which are up for recognition as National Trails. That we have been able to publish this book at all is down to new technology, which enables us to track any given path through the geographic information held in our database of B&Bs. The information published in these pages has been collected over one year and provided by the owners themselves. The vast majority offer bed and breakfast at well under £25 per person per night, which we consider near the limit a walker would wish to pay. The pink highlight boxes are advertisements. Once again, we should make it clear that inclusion in these pages does not imply personal recommendation - we have not visited them all, merely written to them or phoned them. A simple glance over the salient details on any page, however, and the reader will be his or her own guide.

Owners were asked to provide their lowest rates per person per night for the year in question. The rates are thus forecasts and are in any case always subject to fluctuation in demand. Of course, some information may already be out of date. Grades may go up or down, or be removed altogether. British Telecom may alter exchange numbers. Proprietors may decide on a whim to move out of the business altogether. That is why the National Trail Companion has to be a yearbook; in general, though, the information published here will be accurate, pertinent and useful for a while to come.

One of the most important considerations for any walker planning a night's rest at a hostel or B&B is 'how far off the path is it?' Our concern has been, of course, to research Youth Hostels and B&Bs that are at least close to a given path; the reader can gauge at a glance how far one village is from the path compared with another by looking at the map. At the beginning of each entry, the reader will also see a figure in brackets, showing how many miles the premises are from the path. Where it says 'On Path', this means that the premises are either directly on the path or within 200 yards of it. Some also show a car sign, indicating a valuable service indeed. The owners will pick you up by car from the path and drop you off again in the morning. I should stress that this service is provided within reason - ie., from the closest possible point with vehicle access. It is also subject to such mundane matters as afternoon shopping trips, school collections and even flat tyres, so please have some understanding for the owner's needs.

The accommodation lists are published in the order in which they appear along the path. This year we have numbered the locations to make cross-referencing easier. We have also included pubs and inns that serve food in the evenings. For many walkers, the promise of an evening meal will be of prime importance in deciding where to stay. The direction in which the locations are listed is determined by popular choice and not by personal preference. If you wish to walk Offa's Dyke from North to South or the Thames Path from Kemble to London, then you will simply have to flick backwards through the chapter's pages rather than forwards. As far as mapping is concerned, I have omitted giving Landranger map numbers, except in the introduction to each path. The Ordnance Survey's national grid references are more important; to this end we have indicated grid labels and lines at the edge of each map.

Throughout the book you will find boxes offering advice to walkers staying at B&Bs. Some of you may think these a waste of time. Their pompous tone made one reviewer feel tempted to tread mud into carpets at the first opportunity and to order impossible sandwiches at the very last minute. I apologise for this! In fact, these boxes are a publishing device. They fill space and tidy the page up. But we really have heard horror stories about walkers from B&B owners, mainly concerning disregard for other people's property. Much of this is done through thoughtlessness and not by intent. If a few words can remind someone of his or her obligations, then these boxes, however pompous, will have done the trick.

Some readers will be disappointed - the path that they wished to walk is not included. I can offer some consolation here. By March 1996, we should have the technology to provide accommodation lists immediately for *any path in the UK* and probably in Ireland too - even paths that walkers devise for themselves, long or short. The presentation may not be as professional and we would make a small charge, depending on the nature of the task. If anyone wishes to make use of this facility, please contact us at the address at the front of the book. Lastly, over the past year we have had letters from readers making suggestions for this 1996 edition and we have acted on them. We still wish to improve the scope and coverage with each edition. If any readers have criticisms or wish to make suggestions regarding forthcoming editions, please write in to us - again, at the address published at the front of the book. Happy walking!

Path Locations

Cambrian Way	1	Pennine Way	20
Cleveland Way &		Ribble Way	21
Tabular Hills Link	2	The Ridgeway	22
Coast to Coast Path	3	Shropshire Way	23
Cotswold Way	4	South Downs Way	24
Cumbria Way	5	Southern Upland Way	25
Dales Way	6	South West Coast Path	26
Essex Way	7	Speyside Way	27
Fife Coastal Path	8	Staffordshire Way	28
Glyndwr's Way	9	Thames Path	29
Greensand Way	10	Two Moors Way	30
Hadrian's Wall	11	Ulster Way	31
Heart of England Way	12	Vanguard Way	32
Hereward Way	13	Viking Way	33
Icknield Way	14	Wayfarer's Walk	34
North Downs Way	15	Wealdway 1996	35
Offa's Dyke Path	16	Wessex Ridgeway	36
Oxfordshire Way	17	West Highland Way	37
Peddars & Norfolk Coast Path	18	Wolds Way	38
Pembrokeshire Coast Path	19	Wye Valley Walk	39

Cambrian Way

Tony Drake, author of the only in-print guide to the **Cambrian Way**, calls this path the 'mountain connoisseur's walk'. How right he is. Three-fifths of this route runs above 800 feet, over the greatest mountains these islands offer outside Scotland. For the Cambrian Way is quite deliberately a 'designed' path. Devised 27 years ago by Tony Drake himself, its very raison d'etre is the magnificent scenery it traverses. Mr Drake and the **Ramblers Association** originally had official recognition in mind, but sadly, opposition was successful and the **Cambrian Way** never got the go-ahead as a National Trail.

Clearly that first idea was too good to be killed off. By a combination of strong wills and growing demand, the path has slowly taken a correct and proper shape despite the setbacks. And what better way is there to meet the major challenges of walking in Wales? This is God-given walking country - dramatic, remote and testing. This path is certainly for experienced or at least supervised walkers, preferably those with some knowledge of rock-scrambling and adverse conditions. Although only 24 miles longer than the Pennine Way, the ascent involved is almost double. Impeccable map-reading skills are essential. Bad weather brings obvious dangers: wind and rain at high altitudes require the proper outdoor clothing and nothing less. Accommodation can be sparse; there is none in the central Rhinogs at all. Like the Southern Upland Way, this is a tough one - with access to public transport limited. But with good planning the route can certainly be done without camping gear - ask yourself, is the extra freedom of a tent worth the extra weight, given the great distance and ascent?

That said, the walking is memorable, the views unbeatable and the peace and quiet defy superlatives. In mid-Wales you may go for a day without meeting a soul. The 274 miles are split into three natural sections - from Cardiff, skirting the edge of the South Wales Valleys, then a splendid circuit of the Black Mountains before crossing the bleak Brecon Beacons to Llandovery; then along the Cambrian Mountains, with their rare red kites, eventually curving round through Dinas Mawddwy to the stunning Cadair Idris. The path then crosses the Mawddach to Barmouth on the coast before heading over the Rhinogs (the roughest but most magnificent part of the whole walk) for the final and superb Snowdon range. This is definitely one worth travelling a long way for, as testified by the increasing number of European visitors walking all or part of this route each year.

There is a solution for those of us (perhaps the majority) who love the idea of the Cambrian Way but are wise enough to know our limitations. The **Cambrian Way Walkers Association** is a consortium of accommodation providers offering a service to those wishing to complete the walk in set stages. They have split the walk into five sections, with each section having an organiser. The organisers provide laminated marked maps, stage notes, handbook and compass. Three sections (Cardiff to Strata Florida) even have mobile phones and a GBS satellite system to help walkers. Each day the organisers arrange transport, taking you out to the path and picking you up at the end of the day. For further details contact Nick Bointon, **Cambrian Way Walkers Association**, Llandovery, SA20 0NB. Tel: 01550 750274.

Guides: *Cambrian Way* by A.J. Drake (ISBN 0-9509580-3-4), available from all good map shops or by post from the Rambler's Association, 1-5 Wandsworth Road, London, SW8 2XX (tel: 0171 582 6878) for £4.50 + 70p p&p.

Maps: 1:50000 Ordnance Survey Landranger Series: 115, 124, 135, 147, 160, 161 and 171.

Cardiff   1

National Grid Ref: ST1677

⏻ 🍴 Robin Hood, The Beverley, Hayes Court Hotel, Halfway House

(▲ 1m) *Cardiff Youth Hostel,* Ty Croeso, 2 Wedal Road, Roath Park, Cardiff, South Glamorgan, *CF2 5PG.*
Actual grid ref: ST185788
Warden: Ms Hilary Davis.
Tel: **01222 464571**
Under 18: £6.15 **Adults:** £9.10
Family Rooms, Evening Meal (7pm), Table Licence, Centrally Heated, Facilities for Disabled, Laundry Room, Secure Lockers Available, Shop, Parking
Conveniently located hostel near the city centre and Roath Park lake, with cycling and sailing facilities

(0.25m) *Rambler Court Hotel,* 188 Cathedral Road, Cardiff, *S Glam, CF1 9JE.*
Large Victorian house.
Grades: WTB 2 Cr
Tel: **01222 221187** Mr Cronin.
Rates fr: *£13.00*-£16.00.
Open: All Year
Beds: 3F 4D 2T 1S
Baths: 4 Ensuite 5 Shared
🛏 (5) 🅿 (2) ✒ 🗙 🛏 ♿ ✦

(0.5m) *Wynford Hotel, Clare Street, Cardiff, S Glam, CF1 8SD.*
Central private hotel/security carpark.
Grades: WTB 2 Cr
Tel: **01222 371983** Mr Popham.
Rates fr: *£17.00*-£23.00.
Open: All Year (not Xmas)
Beds: 4F 3D 11T 2S
Baths: 16 Ensuite 4 Shared
🛏 🅿 (20) 🗙 🛏 Ⓥ 🛡 ✦

The lowest *double* rate per person is shown in *italics*.

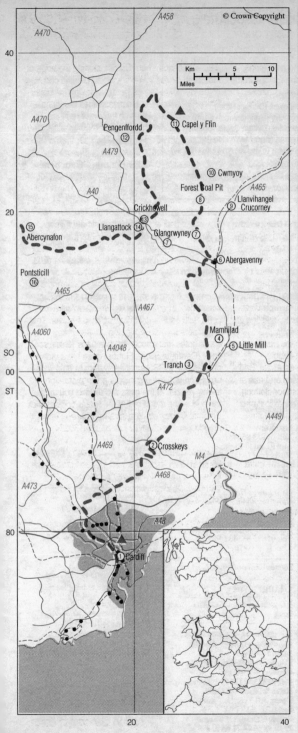

© Crown Copyright

(1m) *Maxines Guest House,*
150 Cathedral Road, Pontcanna,
Cardiff, S Glam, CF1 9JB.
Large Victorian guesthouse.
Grades: WTB 2 Cr
Tel: 01222 220288 Mr Barrett.
Rates fr: *£17.00-£18.00.*
Open: All Year (not Xmas)
Beds: 1F 3D 3T 3S
Baths: 4 Ensuite 2 Shared
🛏 (5) 🅿 (4) 🕮 🛏 🌑 Ⓥ

(0.25m) *Preste Garden Hotel, 181*
Cathedral Road, Pontcanna,
Cardiff, S Glam, CF1 9PN.
Comfortable, ex-Norwegian con-
sulate.
Grades: WTB 2 Cr, Comm
Tel: 01222 228607 Mr Nicholls.
Rates fr: *£15.00-£18.00.*
Open: All Year (not Xmas)
Beds: 2F 3D 2T 3S
Baths: 10 Ensuite
🛏 🅿 (2) 🛏 🌑 Ⓥ ♣

(0.5m) *Austins, 11 Coldstream*
Terrace, Cardiff, S Glam, CF1 8LJ.
Small friendly city centre hotel.
Grades: WTB 2 Cr
Tel: 01222 377148 Mr Hopkins.
Rates fr: *£13.00-£14.00.*
Open: All Year
Beds: 1F 5T 5S
Baths: 3 Ensuite 2 Shared
🛏 🛏 🐾 🌑

Crosskeys   2

National Grid Ref: ST2291

🍴 🍺 The Sebastopol

(1m 🚌) *Westwood Guest House,*
59 Risca Road, Crosskeys,
Newport, Gwent, NP1 7BT.
A warm welcome assured.
Grades: WTB 2 Cr, Highly Comm
Tel: 01495 270336
Rates fr: *£20.00-£20.00.*
Open: All Year
Beds: 1F 2D 1T 1S
Baths: 2 Ensuite
🛏 🅿 (6) 🛏 🐾 ✕ 🌑 Ⓥ ♣ ⚡

Tranch   3

National Grid Ref: SO2600

🍴 🍺 The Horseshoe

(On Path) *Ty Shon Jacob Farm,*
Tranch, Pontypool, Gwent, NP4 6BP.
Peaceful retreat with panoramic
views.
Grades: WTB 2 Cr, Comm
Tel: 01495 757536 Mrs Harris.
Rates fr: *£16.00-£16.00.*
Open: All Year
Beds: 2D 1T
Baths: 3 Ensuite
🛏 🅿 (10) 🛏 🐾 ✕ 🌑 Ⓥ ♣ ⚡

The *lowest* single

rate *is shown in* bold.

CAMBRIAN WAY WALKERS ASSOCIATION

CARDIFF - 274 miles - CONWY

The Association's members below offer a chain of co-ordinated comfortable accommodation with daily transport to and from each stage. Guides, maps, handbooks and logbooks available covering the whole length of Wales's longest long distance footpath

SEE UNDER

SOUTHERN	Crickhowell (Dragon Hotel)
SOUTH CENTRAL	Llandovery (Llanerchindda Farm)
CENTRAL	Ponterwyd (Dyffryn Castell Hotel)
NORTH CENTRAL	Barmouth (Bryn Melyn Hotel)
NORTH	Beddgelert (Plas Colwyn Guest House)

Information pack and free log book from:
Cambrian Way Walkers Association, Llandovery, SA20 0NB
Tel (01550 750274) Tel (01550 750300)

Mamhilad 4

National Grid Ref: SO3003

� ⬛ Horseshoe Inn

(0.5m) *Ty'r Ywen Farm, Lasgarn Lane, Mamhilad, Trevethin, Pontypool, Gwent, NP4 8TT.*
Actual grid ref: SO296047
Remote C16th hill farm.
Tel: **01495 785200** Mrs Armitage.
Rates fr: *£19.00-£25.00*.
Open: All Year (not Xmas)
Beds: 3D 1T
Baths: 4 Ensuite
⛺ (14) ⬛ (6) ⚲ ⬜ ⭥ ✕ ⬛ Ⓥ ⬩

(0.5m 🚌) *Ty-Cooke Farm, Mamhilad, Pontypool, Gwent, NP4 8QZ.*
Actual grid ref: SO308052
Spacious C18th farmhouse.
Grades: WTB Listed, Comm, AA 2 Q
Tel: **01873 880382** Mrs Price.
Rates fr: *£16.00-£18.00*.
Open: All Year (not Xmas)
Beds: 1F 1D 1T **Baths:** 1 Shared
⛺ ⬛ ⬜ Ⓥ ⬩ ⬩

Little Mill 5

National Grid Ref: SO3202

(2m 🚌) *Pentwyn Farm, Little Mill, Pontypool, Gwent, NP4 0HQ.*
Pretty Welsh longhouse charmingly converted.
Grades: WTB 3 Cr, High Comm
Tel: **01495 785249** Mrs Bradey.
Rates fr: *£15.00-£20.00*.
Open: All Year (not Xmas)
Beds: 2D 2T
Baths: 2 Ensuite 2 Shared
⛺ (4) ⬛ ⬜ ✕ ⬛ Ⓥ ⬩

Bringing children with you? Always ask for any special rates.

Abergavenny 6

National Grid Ref: SO2914

⛽ ⬛ Somerset Arms

(4m 🚌) *Ty'r Morwydd House, Pen-y-Pound, Abergavenny, Gwent, NP7 5UD.*
Actual grid ref: SO297147
Georgian house with modern accommodation. **Grades:** WTB 1 Cr
Tel: **01873 855959** Mrs Senior.
Rates fr: *£12.50-£17.00*.
Open: All Year (not Xmas)
Beds: 18T 31S **Baths:** 17 Shared
⛺ ⬛ (30) ⚲ ⬜ ⭥ ✕ ⬛ Ⓥ ⬩ ⬩

(On Path 🚌) *Pentre House, Brecon Road, Abergavenny, Gwent, NP7 7EW.*
Actual grid ref: SO283151
Delightful small Georgian country house.
Grades: WTB 1 Cr, High Comm
Tel: **01873 853435**
Mrs Reardon-Smith.
Rates fr: *£15.00-£18.00*.
Open: All Year **Beds:** 3F 2D 1T
⛺ ⬛ ⬜ ⭥ ✕ ⬛ Ⓥ ⬩ ⬩

(1m) *Lower House Farm, Old Hereford Road, Abergavenny, Gwent, NP7 7HR.*
Actual grid ref: SO304178
Recently converted bunk house.
Tel: **01873 853432** Mrs Smith.
Also ⛺ *£3.00 per tent.* Also bunkhouse, £3.00 per bunk,
Open: All Year ⛺ Ⓣ ✕ ♿

Glangrwyney 7

National Grid Ref: SO2416

⛽ ⬛ The Bell Hotel

(2m) *White Hall, Glangrwyney, Crickhowell, Powys, NP8 1EW.*
Actual grid ref: SO240163
Comfortable Georgian house.
Grades: WTB 2 Cr
Tel: **01873 811155** Ms Llewelyn.
Rates fr: *£15.00-£13.00*.
Open: All Year (not Xmas)
Beds: 1F 2D 1T 1S
Baths: 2 Ensuite 1 Shared
⛺ ⬛ (4) ⚲ ⬜ ⭥ ⬛ Ⓥ ⬩ ⬩

Forest Coal Pit 8

National Grid Ref: SO2821

(On Path) *The Farm, Forest Coal Pit, Abergavenny, Monmouthshire, NP7 7LH.*
Typical Welsh working farm house.
Grades: WTB Listed
Tel: **01873 890413** Mrs Morgan.
Rates fr: *£12.50-£13.50*.
Open: All Year (not Xmas)
Beds: 1F
⛺ ⬛ ⬜ ⭥ ⬛

Llanvihangel Crucorney 9

National Grid Ref: SO3220

⛽ ⬛ Skirrid Mountain Inn, Crown Inn

(2.25m) *Penyclawdd Farm, Llanvihangel Crucorney, Abergavenny, Monmouthshire, NP7 7LB.*
Comfortable farmhouse in Black Mountains.
Grades: WTB Listed, Comm, AA 3 Q, Recomm
Tel: **01873 890591** Mrs Davies.
Rates fr: *£15.00-£15.00*.
Open: All Year
Beds: 1F 1D
Baths: 1 Shared
⛺ (4) ⬛ (4) ⚲ ⬜ ⭥ ⬛ Ⓥ

(2.25m) *The Skirrid Mountain Inn, Llanvihangel Crucorney, Abergavenny, NP7 8DH.*
Historic C12th country inn.
Grades: WTB 3 Cr, Comm
Tel: **01873 890258** Mrs Gant.
Rates fr: *£20.00-£25.00*.
Open: All Year
Beds: 1F 2D
Baths: 3 Private
⛺ ⬛ (20) ⬜ ⭥ ✕ ⬛ Ⓥ

Cwmyoy 10

National Grid Ref: SO2923

⛽ ⬛ Skirrid Mountain Inn

(1m) *Gaer Farm, Cwmyoy, Abergavenny, Monmouthshire, NP7 7NE.*
Peaceful, spectacular views.
Grades: WTB 2 Cr
Tel: **01873 890345** Mrs Judd.
Rates fr: *£18.00-£20.00*.
Open: All Year (not Xmas)
Beds: 1D 1T
Baths: 2 Ensuite
⛺ (10) ⬛ (4) ⚲ ⬜ ⭥

Planning a longer stay? Always ask for any special rates.

Capel-y-Ffin 11

National Grid Ref: SO2531

(▲ 0.75m) *Capel-y-Ffin Youth Hostel*, Capel-y-Ffin, Abergavenny, Gwent, NP7 7NP.
Actual grid ref: SO250328
Warden: Ms D Evans.
Tel: **01873 890650**
Under 18: £4.60 **Adults:** £6.75
Evening Meal (no meals on Weds July/August), Self Catering Facilities, Camping, No Smoking, Grounds Available for Games, Shop, Parking
Converted farmhouse in the beautiful and peaceful Llanthony Valley, offering traditional hostel accomodation

(0.75m 🚉) *The Grange*, Capel-y-Ffin, Abergavenny, Gwent, NP7 7NP.
Actual grid ref: SO251315
Small farm family guesthouse.
Grades: WTB 1 Cr
Tel: **01873 890215** Miss Griffiths.
Rates fr: £20.00-£20.00.
Open: Easter to Oct
Beds: 1F 1D 1T 1S
Baths: 1 Shared
🍼 (5) 🅿 (10) 🛏 ✕ 🖳 🕭 Ⓥ ⓐ ✦

Pengenffordd 12

National Grid Ref: SO1730

🍴 🍺 Castle Inn

(1.5m) *Castle Inn*, Pengenffordd, Talgarth, Brecon, Powys, LD3 0EP.
Actual grid ref: SO174296
Traditional inn, former hill farm.
Grades: WTB 3 Cr, AA 3 Q
Tel: **01874 711353** Mr Mountjoy.
Rates fr: £18.00-£18.00.

Open: All Year (not Xmas)
Beds: 1F 2D 1T 1S
Baths: 2 Ensuite 1 Shared
🍼 🅿 (50) ⧠ ✕ 🖳 Ⓥ ⓐ
Also ▲ £3.00 per tent. Also bunkhouse, £3.00 per bunk,
Open: All Year 🕭 🖵 ✕ 🕭

(0.5m 🚉) *Cwmfforest Guest House*, Pengenffordd, Talgarth, Brecon, Powys, LD3 0EU.
Actual grid ref: SO183292
Traditional Welsh farmhouse. Bavarian cooking.
Grades: WTB 2 Cr
Tel: **01874 711398** Mrs Turner.
Rates fr: £17.50-£17.50.
Open: All Year **Beds:** 2T 2S
Baths: 2 Ensuite 1 Shared
🅿 (10) ⧗ ✕ Ⓥ ⓐ ✦

Crickhowell 13

National Grid Ref: SO2118

🍴 🍺 Dragon Hotel, Bell Inn

(On Path 🚉) *Dragon Hotel*, High Street, Crickhowell, Powys, NP8 1BE.
Actual grid ref: SO217183
Grades: WTB 3 Cr, Comm, AA 3 Q, RAC Acclaim
Tel: **01873 810362**
Mr & Mrs Thomas.
Rates fr: £25.00-£25.00.
Open: All Year **Beds:** 2F 5D 6T 2S
Baths: 14 Ensuite, 1 Shared
🍼 🅿 (15) ⧗ ⧠ 🛏 ✕ 🖳 Ⓥ ⓐ ✦
Character C18th hotel in picturesque Crickhowell. Marvellous atmosphere, excellent food/accommodation. Organiser of Southern section of 'The Cambrian Way Walkers Association'. Good value walking breaks programme.

(0.25m 🚉) *Hafod Swn-Y-Dwr*, The Dardy, Crickhowell, Powys, NP8 1PU.
Actual grid ref: SO206184
Canalside C18th house - superb views.
Grades: WTB 2 Cr, High Comm
Tel: **01873 810821** Mr Williams.
Rates fr: £17.00-£25.00.
Open: All Year
Beds: 1F 2D **Baths:** 3 Ensuite
🍼 (3) 🅿 (6) ⧗ ⧠ 🛏 ✕ 🖳 🕭 Ⓥ ⓐ ✦

Llangattock 14

National Grid Ref: SO2117

🍴 🍺 The Horseshoe Inn (Llangattock)

(On Path) *The Horseshoe Inn*, Beaufort Ave, Llangattock, Crickhowell, Powys, NP8 1PN.
Actual grid ref: SO218172
C17th coaching inn.
Tel: **01873 810393** Mrs Groves.
Rates fr: £14.50-£15.00.
Beds: 1D 2T **Baths:** 1 Shared
🍼 🅿 🛏 ✕ 🖳 ⓐ

Abercynafon 15

National Grid Ref: SO0817

🍴 🍺 Travellers Rest, Usk Hotel, White Hart, The Star

(1.5m) *Abercynafon Lodge*, Abercynafon, Talybont-on-Usk, Brecon, Powys, LD3 7YT.
Family home, quiet, idyllic situation.
Grades: WTB 2 Cr
Tel: **01874 676342** Mrs Carr.
Rates fr: £15.00-£17.00.
Open: All Year **Beds:** 1D 2T
Baths: 1 Private 2 Shared
🍼 (3) 🛏 ✕ 🖳 🕭 Ⓥ

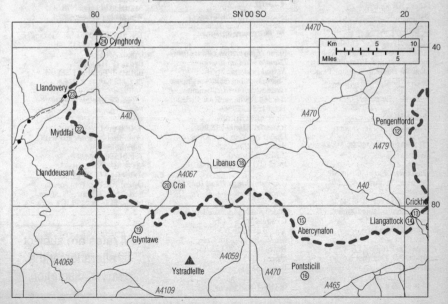

Pontsticill   16

National Grid Ref: SO0511

🍴⛉Butcher's Arms, Red Cow

(2m) *Penrhadw Farm, Pontsticill,*
Merthyr Tydfil, M Glam, CF48 2TU.
Situated in the Beacons.
Tel: **01685 723481** Mrs Gillman.
Rates fr: £15.00-£15.00.
Open: All Year
Beds: 2D 2S
Baths: 3 Shared
🛏 (0) 🅿 (10) ⊬⟋ ☐ 🎟. 🛈 ⚡

Ystradfellte   17

National Grid Ref: SN9213

(▲4m) *Ystradfellte Youth Hostel,*
Tai'r Heol, Ystradfellte, Aberdare,
Mid Glamorgan, CF44 9JF.
Actual grid ref: SN925127
Warden: Mr D Jenkins.
Tel: **01639 720301**
Under 18: £4.15 **Adults:** £6.10
Family Rooms, Self Catering
Facilities, Parking
Charming mixture of three C17th
cottages close to the Nedd and
Melte river systems in the Brecon
Beacons National Park

Libanus   18

National Grid Ref: SN9925

🍴⛉Tair Bull Inn

(2.5m) *Tair Bull Inn, Libanus,*
Brecon, Powys, LD3 8EL.
Actual grid ref: SN9925
Grades: WTB 3 Cr, Comm,
RAC 1 St
Tel: **01874 625849** Mrs Williams.
Rates fr: £17.00-£20.00.
Open: All Year
Beds: 1F 3D 1T
Baths: 5 Ensuite
🛏 🅿 (12) ☐ ✗ 🎟. 🔲 🛈
Ideal walking base, climb Pen-y-
fan from our front door. Close to
mountain centre. Winter breaks
from 1st November. Packed lunch-
es on request. Meals available
seven nights.

Glyntawe   19

National Grid Ref: SN8416

🍴⛉Tafarn-Y-Garreg, Gwyn
Arms

(2m) *Dderi Farm, Glyntawe,*
Penycae, Swansea, W. Glam,
SA9 1GT.
Actual grid ref: SN851175
C15th comfortable farmhouse.
Grades: WTB 2 Cr
Tel: **01639 730458**
Mrs Williams.
Rates fr: £16.00-£17.00.
Open: All Year (not Xmas)
Beds: 1F
Baths: 1 Ensuite
🅿 ⊬⟋ ☐ 🎟. 🛈 ⚡

Crai   20

National Grid Ref: SN8924

(3m) *Llwynhir Farm, Crai,*
Brecon, Powys, LD3 8YW.
500-acre mixed working farm.
Grades: WTB Listed
Tel: **01874 636563**
Rates fr: £15.00-£16.00.
Open: Mar to Oct
Beds: 2D 1S
🛏 🅿 ☐ 🎟 🔲

Llanddeusant   21

National Grid Ref: SN7724

(▲On Path) *Llanddeusant Youth*
Hostel, The Old Red Lion,
Llanddeusant, Llangadog, Dyfed,
SA19 6UL.
Actual grid ref: SN776245
Warden: Ms C Spackman.
Tel: **01550 740634 / 740619**
Under 18: £4.15 **Adults:** £6.10
Self Catering, Centrally Heated,
Camping, Parking (No coaches)
A simple traditional hostel convert-
ed from an inn, overlooking
Sawdde Valley

Myddfai   22

National Grid Ref: SN7730

(On Path) *Erwlas, Myddfai,*
Llandovery, Dyfed, SA20 0JB.
Modern, comfortable bungalow,
quiet location.
Tel: **01550 720797** Mrs Holloway.
Rates fr: £13.00-£13.00.
Open: All Year (not Xmas)
Beds: 1D 1T
Baths: 1 Shared
🛏 🅿 ⊬⟋ ☐ 🎟 ✗ 🎟. 🔲 🛈 ⚡

Llandovery   23

National Grid Ref: SN7634

🍴⛉Drovers Restaurant

(0.5m) *Llwyncelyn Guest House,*
Llandovery, Dyfed, SA20 0EP.
Actual grid ref: SN761347
Charming stone built guesthouse.
Grades: WTB 1 Cr, Comm,
AA 3Q, Recomm, RAC Listed
Tel: **01550 720566**
Mr & Mrs Griffiths.
Rates fr: £16.00-£18.00.
Open: All Year (not Xmas)
Beds: 1F 2D 2T 1S
Baths: 2 Shared
🛏 🅿 (12) ☐ ✗ 🎟. 🔲 🛈 ⚡

(On Path) *Kings Head Inn, Market*
Square, Llandovery, Dyfed,
SA20 0AB.
Olde worlde inn, excellent food.
Grades: WTB 3 Cr
Tel: **01550 720393**
Mr & Mrs Madeira Cole.
Rates fr: £22.00-£26.00.
Open: All Year
Beds: 2D 2T
Baths: 4 Ensuite
🅿 (4) ☐ 🎟 ✗ 🎟. 🛈 ⚡

Cynghordy   24

National Grid Ref: SN8039

(0.5m 🚗) *Llanerchindda Farm,*
Cynghordy, Llandovery, Dyfed,
SA20 0NB.
Actual grid ref: SN808428
Grades: WTB 2 Cr, Comm
Tel: **01550 750274** Mr Bointon.
Rates fr: £21.00-£21.00.
Open: All Year
Beds: 2F 3D 3T 1S
Baths: 9 Ensuite
🛏 🅿 (14) ☐ 🎟 ✗ 🎟. 🔲 🛈 ⚡
The perfect venue for walkers,
large comfortable farmhouse,
underfloor heating, log-fires, bar,
famous food. Area organiser of the
Cambrian Way 'Black to Black' and
'The 5 Rivers Walk'. Daily trans-
port to stages 8-14 of the Cambrian
Way.

(▲On Path) *Bryn Poeth Uchaf*
Youth Hostel, Hafod-y-pant,
Cynghordy, Llandovery, SA20 0NB.
Actual grid ref: SN796439
Warden: Mr Lodge.
Tel: **01550 750235**
Under 18: £3.75 **Adults:** £5.50
Family Rooms, Self Catering,
Parking (No Coaches)
Formerly an old farmhouse, this
hostel is quite simple and isolated,
but provides great views back to
Brecon Beacons

Rhandirmwyn   25

National Grid Ref: SN7843

🍴⛉Royal Oak

(1m 🚗) *Royal Oak Inn,*
Rhandirmwyn, Llandovery, Dyfed,
SA20 0NY.
Actual grid ref: SN781435
Welcoming village inn.
Grades: WTB 1 Cr, AA Listed
Tel: **01550 760201** Mr Alexander.
Rates fr: £20.00-£18.00.
Open: All Year
Beds: 1F 1D 1T 2S
Baths: 3 Ensuite, 1 Shared
🛏 (3) 🅿 (20) 🎟 ✗ 🔲 🛈 ⚡

(2.5m 🚗) *Bwlch-Y-Ffin,*
Rhandirmwyn, Llandovery, Dyfed,
SA20 0PG.
Actual grid ref: SN795481
Comfortable farmhouse with
incredible views.
Tel: **01550 760311**
Mr & Mrs Williams.
Rates fr: £15.00-£15.00.
Open: All Year (not Xmas)
Beds: 1D 2T **Baths:** 1 Shared
🛏 (12) 🅿 ⊬⟋ 🎟 ✗ 🎟. 🔲 🛈 ⚡

All rates are subject
to alteration at the
owners' discretion.

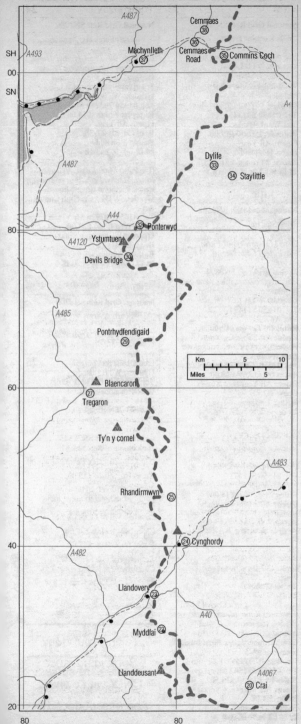

Ty'n-y-cornel 26

National Grid Ref: SN7553

(🔺 On Path) *Ty'n-y-cornel Youth Hostel*, *Ty'n-y-cornel, Llanddewi Brefi, Tregaron, Dyfed*, *SY25 6PH*.
Actual grid ref: SN7553
Tel: **01222 222122**
Under 18: £3.75 **Adults:** £5.50
Self Catering, Camping, Parking (No Coaches)
Very simple former farmhouse in a very isolated next-to-nature setting at the head of Doethie valley, lit solely by gas

Tregaron 27

National Grid Ref: SN6759

(On Path 🚐) *Glanbrennig Guest House*, *Tregaron, Dyfed*, *SY25 6QS*.
Tranquil, in own grounds.
Grades: WTB 3 Cr
Tel: **01974 298825** Mrs Cutter.
Rates fr: *£16.50*-**£18.50**.
Open: All Year (not Xmas)
Beds: 1F 1D 1T 1S
Baths: 4 Ensuite
🛇 🅿 🍴 ✕ 🖾 ♿ 🆅 🛆 🖋

(On Path 🚐) *Talbot Hotel*, *The Square, Tregaron, Dyfed*, *SY25 6JL*.
Olde worlde comfortable family atmosphere.
Grades: WTB 2 CrRAC 1 St
Tel: **01974 298208**
Mr Williams.
Rates fr: *£21.00*-**£25.00**.
Open: All Year (not Xmas)
Beds: 1F 6D 7T
Baths: 4 Ensuite 4 Shared
🛇 🅿 ◻ 🍴 ✕ 🖾 🆅 🛆 🖋

Blaencaron 28

National Grid Ref: SN7160

(🔺 2.5m) *Blaencaron Youth Hostel*, *Blaencaron, Tregaron, Dyfed*, *SY25 6HL*.
Actual grid ref: SN7160
Tel: **01974 298441**
Under 18: £3.75
Adults: £5.50
Family Rooms, Self Catering, Camping, Parking
Old village school set in the unspoilt Afon Groes Valley, west of the Cambrian mountains

Pontrhydfendigaid 29

National Grid Ref: SN7366

(On Path) *Black Lion Hotel*, *Pontrhydfendigaid, Ystrad Meurig, Dyfed*, *SY25 6BE*.
Actual grid ref: SN731665
Traditional village inn.
Tel: **01974 831626**
Mr Quesnel.
Rates fr: *£17.50*-**£20.00**.
Open: All Year
Beds: 1D 3T
Baths: 4 Ensuite
🛇 🅿 (10) 🖋 ◻ 🍴 ✕ 🖾 🆅 🛆 🖋

Devils Bridge · 30

National Grid Ref: SN7376

¶ Mount Pleasant

(On Path) *Mount Pleasant*, Devils
Bridge, Aberystwyth, Dyfed,
SY23 4QY.
Actual grid ref: SN736769
Family run licensed guesthouse.
Grades: WTB 3 Cr, High Comm
Tel: **01970 890219**
Mr & Mrs Sherlock.
Rates fr: *£18.00*-**£17.50**.
Open: All Year
Beds: 1F 2D 2T 1S
Baths: 2 Ensuite 3 Shared
ひ (10) ▣ (6) ⊡ ✕ ▥ Ⓥ ♦

(On Path) *Erwbarfe Farm*, Devils
Bridge, Aberystwyth, Dyfed, *SY23 3JR*
Comfortable farmhouse in spectac-
ular countryside.
Grades: WTB Listed
Tel: **01970 890251** Mrs Lewis.
Rates fr: *£16.00*-**£20.00**.
Open: Easter to Oct
Beds: 1F 1D **Baths:** 1 Shared
ひ ▣ (4) ⊡ ✕ ▥ Ⓥ ▪

Ystumtuen · 31

National Grid Ref: SN7378

(▲On Path) *Ystumtuen Youth
Hostel*, Glantuen, Ystumtuen,
Aberystwyth, Dyfed, *SY23 3AE.*
Actual grid ref: SN735786
Warden: Ms S Pugh.
Tel: **01970 890693**
Under 18: £3.75 **Adults:** £5.50
Family Rooms, Self catering,
Parking
*A former school, this traditional,
self catering Hostel is set in a
quiet, old lead mining village at the
north end of the Elenith and only
10m from Aberystwyth*

Ponterwyd · 32

National Grid Ref: SN7480

¶ Dyffryn Castell Hotel

(On Path 🐾) *Dyffryn Castell
Hotel*, Ponterwyd, Devils Bridge,
Aberystwyth, Dyfed, *SY23 3LB.*
Actual grid ref: SN817773
Old coaching inn 'Cambrian Way'
(central stage organizers).
Grades: WTB 3 Cr, Comm,
AA 2 St
Tel: **01970 890237**
Rates fr: *£20.00*-**£22.00**.
Open: All Year (not Xmas)
Beds: 6F 2D 1T
Baths: 6 Ensuite, 1 Shared
ひ ▣ (60) ⊁ ⊡ ★ ✕ ▥ ▪ ♦

Please take muddy
boots off before
entering premises

Dylife · 33

National Grid Ref: SN8694

¶ Star Inn (Dylife)

(On Path) *Star Inn*, Dylife,
Staylittle, Llanbrynmair, Powys,
SY19 7BW.
Traditional country inn, log fires,
real ales.
Grades: WTB 2 Cr, Approv
Tel: **01650 521345**
Mrs Ward -Banks.
Rates fr: *£17.00*-**£17.00**.
Open: All Year
Beds: 1F 3D 1T 2S
Baths: 2 Private 1 Shared
ひ ▣ ⊁ ⊡ ★ ✕ ▥ Ⓥ ♦

Staylittle · 34

National Grid Ref: SN8892

¶ Star Inn

(1m) *Maesmedrisiol Farm*,
Staylittle, Llanbrynmair, Powys,
SY19 7BN.
Actual grid ref: SN8894
Friendly, comfortable, stone-built
farmhouse.
Grades: WTB 1 Cr
Tel: **01650 521494**
Mrs Anwyl.
Rates fr: *£14.00*-**£14.00**.
Open: All Year (not Xmas)
Beds: 2F 2D 1T 2S
Baths: 1 Private
ひ (1) ▣ (8) ⊡ ✕ ▥ Ⓥ ♦

Commins Coch · 35

National Grid Ref: SH8403

¶ Penrhos Arms

(On Path) *Gwalia*, Commins Coch,
Machynlleth, Powys, *SY20.*
Actual grid ref: SH853048
Peaceful family smallholding.
Tel: **01650 511377**
Mrs Chandler.
Rates fr: *£14.00*-**£14.00**.
Open: All Year (not Xmas)
Beds: 1F 1T
Baths: ! Shared
ひ ▣ ⊁ ⊡ ✕ Ⓥ ♦

Cemmaes Road · 36

National Grid Ref: SH8204

¶ Penrhos Arms

(On Path 🐾) *Cefn Coch Uchaf*,
Cemmaes Road, Machynlleth,
Powys, *SY20 8LU.*
Actual grid ref: SH835033
C14th Dovey Valley farmhouse,
lovely views.
Grades: WTB Listed, Comm
Tel: **01650 511552** Mrs Harris.
Rates fr: *£14.50*-**£14.50**.
Open: All Year (not Xmas)
Beds: 2D 1T
Baths: 1 Private 1 Shared
ひ ▣ ★ ✕ ▥ Ⓥ ♦

Machynlleth · 37

National Grid Ref: SH7400

¶ Dyfi Forester, Glyndwr

(On Path 🐾) *The Glyndwr Hotel*,
Doll Street, Machynlleth, Powys,
SY20 8BQ.
Small family-run hotel.
Grades: WTB Listed
Tel: **01654 703989** Mr Duckett.
Rates fr: *£14.00*-**£14.00**.
Open: All Year
Beds: 2F 3D 2T 2S
Baths: 4 Shared
ひ ▣ (25) ✕ ▥ ▪ ♦

(On Path) *Maenllwyd*, Newtown
Road, Machynlleth, Powys, *SY20 8EY.*
Large Victorian private house.
Grades: WTB 3 Cr, High Comm,
AA 3 Q
Tel: **01654 702928** Mr Vince.
Rates fr: *£17.50*-**£23.00**.
Open: All Year (not Xmas)
Beds: 2F 4D 2T
Baths: 8 Ensuite
ひ ▣ (10) ⊁ ⊡ ★ ✕ ▥ Ⓥ ▪

Cemmaes · 38

National Grid Ref: SH8306

¶ Penrhos Arms

(4.25m) *Penrhos Arms Hotel*,
Cemmaes, Machynlleth, Powys,
SY20 9PR.
Late C18th coaching inn.
Grades: WTB Listed
Tel: **01650 511243** Mr Astley.
Rates fr: *£12.00*-**£12.00**.
Open: Easter to Oct **Beds:** 1F 2D
ひ ▣ ⊁ ⊡ ✕ Ⓥ

Minllyn · 39

National Grid Ref: SH8513

(On Path) *Buckley Pines Hotel*,
Minllyn, Dinas Mawddwy,
Machynlleth, Powys, *SY20 9LP.*
Actual grid ref: SH860139
Family-run hotel in Snowdonia
National Park.
Grades: WTB 3 Cr, AA 2 St,
RAC 2 St
Tel: **01650 531261** Mrs Farr.
Rates fr: *£20.00*-**£25.00**.
Open: All Year (not Xmas)
Beds: 1F 5D 4T 1S
Baths: 5 Ensuite 2 Shared
ひ (1) ▣ (40) ⊡ ★ ✕ ▥ Ⓥ ▪ ♦

Taking your dog?
Book *in advance*
ONLY with owners
who accept dogs (★)

All rates are subject to alteration at the owners' discretion.

Dinas Mawddwy 40

National Grid Ref: SH8514

⑩🍴 Red Lion Inn

(On Path 🚍) *The Dolbrodmaeth Inn*, Dinas Mawddwy, Machynlleth, Powys, *SY20 9LP*.
Tranquil riverside setting. Interesting menus.
Grades: WTB 3 Cr
Tel: **01650 531333**
Mr & Mrs Williams
Rates fr: £15.00-£20.00.
Open: All Year **Beds:** 1F 3D 3T
Baths: 5 Ensuite 2 Shared
🐾🖪🗈🏄🗶🟩🖳🔲🛢✦
Also ▲ *£1.50 per person.,*
Open: All Year 🏠🗊🗶🕭

(On Path) *Gwelafon*, Dinas Mawddwy, Machynlleth, Powys, *SY0 9LL*.
Modern, homely, good food, comfortable.
Tel: **01650 531287** Mrs Evans.
Rates fr: £13.50-£13.50.
Open: Easter to Oct
Beds: 2D 1S **Baths:** 1 Shared
🐾🖪 (3) 🔗🖳🔲🛢✦

Dolffanog 41

National Grid Ref: SH7210

(On Path) *Dolffanog Fawr*, Dolffanog, Talyllyn, Tywyn, Gwynedd, *LL36 9AJ*.
Beautifully furnished with many extras.
Grades: WTB 3 Cr, Highly Comm, AA 4 Q.
Tel: **01654 761247** Mr/Mrs Coulter
Rates fr: £21.00-£36.00.
Open: All Year (not Xmas)
Beds: 2D 2T **Baths:** 4 Ensuite
🖪 (6) 🔗🗶🖳🔲🛢✦

Talyllyn 42

National Grid Ref: SH7109

⑩🍴 Penybont Hotel

(0.25m) *Dolffanog Fach*, Talyllyn, Tywyn, Gwynedd, *LL36 9AJ*.
Stone-built with modern conveniences.
Grades: WTB 2 Cr, RAC Listed
Tel: **01654 761235** Mrs Pughe.
Rates fr: £15.00-£15.00.
Open: All Year (not Xmas)
Beds: 1F 1D 1T
Baths: 1 Ensuite 2 Shared
🐾🖪 (6) 🔗🖳🏄🗶🖳🔲🛢✦

Abergynolwyn 43

National Grid Ref: SH6707

⑩🍴 Railway Hotel

(4m) *Tanycoed Uchaf*, Abergynolwyn, Tywyn, Gwynedd, *LL36 9UP*.
Actual grid ref: SH666124
Grades: WTB Listed
Tel: **01654 782228** Mrs Pugh.
Rates fr: £13.50-£13.50.
Open: All Year
Beds: 1D 1T 1S
Baths: 1 Shared
🐾🖪🏄🗶🖳🔲🛢✦
Tanycoed is situated within easy reach of Dolgoch Falls, Bird Rock, Bere Castle, and Cader Idris Ranges. Lovely walking area.

(4m 🚍) *Riverside Guest House and Campsite*, Abergynolwyn, Tywyn, Gwynedd, *LL36 9YR*.
Actual grid ref: SH676072
Victorian family house on riverside.
Tel: **01654 782235** Mr Bott.
Rates fr: £13.00-£15.00.
Open: All Year (not Xmas)
Beds: 2F 1D
Baths: 2 Shared
🐾🖪 (3) 🔗🖳🏄🖳🔲🛢✦
Also ▲ *£5.00 per tent.£2.50 per person.,*
Open: All Year (not Xmas) 🏠🗊▨
🗶✦🕭

Islaw'r Dref 44

National Grid Ref: SH6815

⑩🍴 Gwernan Lake Hotel

(▲ 0.75m) *Kings Youth Hostel*, Islaw'r Dref, Penmaenpool, Dolgellau, Gwynedd, *LL40 1TB*.
Actual grid ref: SH6816
Warden: Mr C Malyon.
Tel: **01341 422392**
Under 18: £4.60 **Adults:** £6.75
Evening Meal, Self Catering Facilities, Centrally Heated, Camping, Grounds Availalbe for Games, Shop, Parking
Traditional Hostel set in idyllic wooded valley, with magnificent views upto Cader Idris and Rhinog mountain ranges

(1m) *Gwernan Lake Hotel*, Islaw'r Dref, Dolgellau, Gwynedd, *LL40 1TL*.
Actual grid ref: SH704159
Fully licensed hotel.
Tel: **01341 422488** Ms Lathaen.
Rates fr: £18.00-£20.00.
Open: All Year **Beds:** 3D 2T 3S
Baths: 1 Ensuite 2 Shared
🖪 (15) 🔲🗶🖳🔲🛢✦

Arthog 45

National Grid Ref: SH6414

(1m 🚍) *Cyfannedd Uchaf Guest House*, Arthog, Gwynedd, *LL39 1LX*.
Actual grid ref: SH635127
Peace, tranquillity, a hidden place.
Grades: WTB 1 Cr, High Comm
Tel: **01341 250526** Mrs Tovey.
Rates fr: £16.00-£16.00.
Open: Easter to Sep
Beds: 2D 1T
Baths: 1 Ensuite 1 Shared
🖪 (4) 🔗🗶🖳🛢✦

All details shown are as supplied by B&B owners in Autumn 1995.

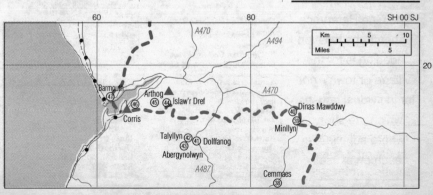

(On Path) *Craig Wen Guest House, Arthog, Gwynedd, LL39 1BQ.*
Actual grid ref: SH6414
Quiet, overlooking Mawddach Estuary. **Grades:** WTB 3 Cr
Tel: **01341 250482** Mrs Ameson.
Rates fr: *£14.50*-**£18.00**.
Open: All Year
Beds: 1F 2T 1S
Baths: 3 Ensuite
⇘▣⌷✕🏠&Ⓥ🛈⚡
Also ▲ *£2 per person.,*
Open: All Year ⇘Ⓣ🛆

Corris   46

National Grid Ref: SH7508

🍴🍺Braich Goch Hotel

(▲4.5m) *Corris Youth Hostel, Old School, Old Road, Corris, Machynlleth, Powys, SY20 9QT.*
Actual grid ref: SH7508
Tel: **01654 761686**
Under 18: £5.00 **Adults:** £7.45
Family Rooms, Evening Meal, Self Catering Facilities, Centrally Heated, Laundry Facilities, Secure Lockers Available, No Smoking, Study Room Available, Parking
Picturesque former village school, recently renovated, with panoramic views of Corris

Barmouth   47

National Grid Ref: SH6115

🍴🍺Tal-Y-Don Hotel, Halfway House, Last Inn

(On Path 🚗) *Bryn Melyn Hotel, Panorama Road, Barmouth, Gwynedd, LL42 1DQ.*
Delightful hotel with magnificent views.
Grades: WTB 3 Cr, High Comm, AA 2 St
Tel: **01341 280556** Mr Clay.
Rates fr: *£24.00*-**£29.00**.
Open: Feb to Nov
Beds: 2F 4D 3T
Baths: 9 Ensuite
⇘(5)▣(9)⌷🛏✕🏠Ⓥ🛈⚡

The Grid Reference beneath the location heading is for the village or town - *not* for individual houses, which are shown (where supplied) in each entry itself.

The lowest *double* rate per person is shown in *italics*.

(On Path) *Tal-Y-Don Hotel, High Street, Barmouth, Gwynedd, LL42 1DL.*
Small comfortable friendly hotel.
Grades: WTB 2 Cr
Tel: **01341 280508** Mrs Davies.
Rates fr: *£20.00*.
Open: All Year (not Xmas)
Beds: 2F 2D 4T
Baths: 4 Ensuite 2 Shared
⇘▣(6)🗷⌷✕🏠Ⓥ🛈

(0.25m) *Cranbourne Hotel, 9 Marine Parade, Barmouth, Gwynedd, LL42 1NA.*
Seafront family run hotel.
Grades: WTB 3 Cr
Tel: **01341 280202** Mr Tomlinson.
Rates fr: *£17.50*-**£15.50**.
Open: All Year (not Xmas)
Beds: 3F 4D 1T 2S
Baths: 7 Ensuite 2 Shared
⇘⌷✕🏠Ⓥ🛈

(0.5m) *The Sandpiper, 7 Marine Parade, Barmouth, Gwynedd, LL42 1NA.*
Seafront guesthouse.
Grades: WTB 2 Cr, High Comm
Tel: **01341 280318**
Mr & Mrs Palmer.
Rates fr: *£12.50*-**£14.00**.
Open: Easter to Oct
Beds: 4F 5D 2S
Baths: 6 Ensuite 2 Shared
⇘⌷🏠&

(On Path) *Pen Parc Guest House, Park Road, Barmouth, Gwynedd, LL42 1PH.*
Actual grid ref: SH6115
Victorian manse.
Grades: WTB 1 Cr, High Comm
Tel: **01341 280150** Mrs Robey.
Rates fr: *£15.00*-**£15.00**.
Open: Easter to Nov
Beds: 2D 1T 1S
Baths: 1 Shared
⇘(8)▣(1)🗷⌷✕🏠Ⓥ🛈⚡

Trawsfynydd   48

National Grid Ref: SH7035

🍴🍺Rhiw Goch Hotel

(0.25m) *Bryn Celynog Farm, Cwmprysor, Trawsfynydd, Blaenau Ffestiniog, Gwynedd, LL41 4TR.*
Actual grid ref: SH744354
Comfortable farmhouse on working farm.
Grades: WTB 2 Cr, High Comm
Tel: **01766 540378**
Mrs Hughes.
Rates fr: *£16.00*-**£16.00**.
Open: All Year (not Xmas)
Beds: 1F 1D 1T
Baths: 1 Ensuite 1 Shared
⇘▣(6)⌷🛏✕🏠Ⓥ🛈⚡

(On Path) *Fron Olau Farm, Trawsfynydd, Blaenau Ffestiniog, Gwynedd, LL41 4UN.*
Actual grid ref: SH7135
Ensuite bedrooms in converted mill buildings.
Grades: WTB 2 Cr, RAC Listed
Tel: **01766 540397** Mrs Bain.
Rates fr: *£18.00*-**£20.00**.
Open: All Year
Beds: 2F 3D 2T
Baths: 7 Ensuite
⇘▣(8)🗷⌷🛏✕🏠&Ⓥ

(On Path 🚗) *Old Mill Farm House, Fron Oleu, Trawsfynydd, Blaenau Ffestiniog, Gwynedd, LL41 4UN.*
Actual grid ref: SH7135
Farm building conversion, ensuite bedrooms.
Grades: WTB 2 Cr, RAC Listed
Tel: **01766 540397**
Rates fr: *£18.00*-**£18.00**.
Open: All Year
Beds: 2F 3D 2T
Baths: 7 Ensuite
⇘▣⌷🛏✕🏠Ⓥ🛈⚡

Gellilydan   49

National Grid Ref: SH6839

🍴🍺The Bryn Arms

(On Path 🚗) *Gwynfryn, Gellilydan, Blaenau Ffestiniog, Gwynedd, LL41 4EA.*
Actual grid ref: SH685398
Detached comfortable period house.
Grades: WTB 1 Cr
Tel: **01766 590225** Mrs Jones.
Rates fr: *£13.00*-**£13.00**.
Open: Jan to Nov
Beds: 1D 1T 1S **Baths:** 1 Shared
⇘▣🗷⌷✕🏠Ⓥ🛈⚡

(0.25m 🚗) *Tyddyn Du Farm, Gellilydan, Blaenau Ffestiniog, Gwynedd, LL41 4RB.*
Actual grid ref: SH691398
Grades: WTB 3 Cr, High Comm, AA 4 Q
Tel: **01766 590281** Mrs Williams.
Rates fr: *£16.00*.
Open: All Year (not Xmas)
Beds: 2F 2D 1T 1S
Baths: 2 Ensuite 2 Shared
⇘▣(10)🗷⌷✕🏠Ⓥ🛈⚡

Maentwrog   50

National Grid Ref: SH6640

🍴🍺Grapes Hotel (Maentwrog)

(2.5m) *The Old Rectory Hotel, Maentwrog, Blaenau Ffestiniog, Gwynedd, LL41 4HN.*
C18th stone rectory.
Grades: WTB 2 Cr
Tel: **01766 590305** Ms Herbert.
Rates fr: *£18.00*-**£25.00**.
Open: All Year
Beds: 3F 7D 1T 1S
Baths: 12 Ensuite
⇘▣⌷🛏✕🏠Ⓥ🛈⚡

Ffestiniog 51

National Grid Ref: SH7041

🍽 🍺 The Grapes

(▲ On Path) *Ffestiniog Youth Hostel, Caerblaidd, Ffestiniog, Blaenau Ffestiniog, Gwynedd, LL41 4PH.*
Actual grid ref: SH704427
Warden: Mr C Jones.
Tel: **01766 762765**
Under 18: £4.60 **Adults:** £6.75
Family Rooms, Self Catering,Grounds Available for Games, Shop, Parking (no coaches) *Large house situated on the northern edge of the picturesque village of Llan Ffestiniog, at the centre of the Snowdonia National Park*

(On Path) *Tyddyn Pant Glas, Ffestiniog, Blaenau Ffestiniog, Gwynedd, LL41 4PU.*
Self-contained annexe - superb views.
Grades: WTB 2 Cr
Tel: **01766 762442**
Mrs Langdale-Pope.
Rates fr: *£15.00-£20.00.*
Open: All Year (not Xmas)
Beds: 1D
Baths: 1 Ensuite
🅿 ⌫ 🛏 🔳

(On Path) *Morannedd Guest House, Blaenau Road, Ffestiniog, Blaenau Ffestiniog, Gwynedd, LL41 4LG.*
Comfortable guesthouse with mountain views.
Grades: WTB 2 Cr, Comm
Tel: **01766 762734**
Mrs Lethbridge.
Rates fr: *£15.50-£15.50.*
Open: Easter to Oct
Beds: 1F 1D 2T 1S
Baths: 2 Private 2 Shared
🛏 (1) 🅿 (4) ⌫ 🛏 🕿 ✗ �

(On Path) *Ty Clwb, The Square, Ffestiniog, Blaenau Ffestiniog, Gwynedd, LL41 4LS.*
Modernised C18th guesthouse.
Grades: WTB 1 Cr, High Comm
Tel: **01766 762658** Mrs Mobbs.
Rates fr: *£13.00-£18.00.*
Open: All Year (not Xmas)
Beds: 2D 1T
Baths: 3 Private
🛏 ⌫ 🛏 🕿 🔳 byte

Please order your packed lunch the evening before you need them. Not at breakfast!

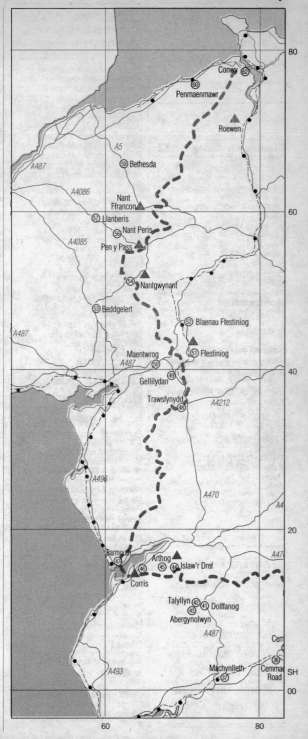

Please don't camp on anyone's land without first obtaining their permission.

Blaenau Ffestiniog 52

National Grid Ref: SH7045

(2m) *Afallon Guest House, Manod Road, Blaenau Ffestiniog, Gwynedd, LL41 4AE.*
Comfortable family-run guesthouse.
Grades: WTB 1 Cr, High Comm
Tel: 01766 830468 Mrs Griffiths.
Rates fr: *£12.00-***£12.00**.
Open: All Year (not Xmas)
Beds: 1D 1T 1S
Baths: 1 Shared
⛉ 🄿 (4) ⏀ ⏃ ⨯ ▥ Ⓥ

Beddgelert 53

National Grid Ref: SH5948

🍴 🍺 Plas Colwyn

(2.5m 🚌) *Plas Colwyn Guest House, Beddgelert, Caernarfon, Gwynedd, LL55 4UY.*
Actual grid ref: SH589482
Stone built house overlooking river.
Grades: WTB 3 Cr
Tel: 01766 890458 Mrs Osmond.
Rates fr: *£15.00-***£15.00**.
Open: All Year (not Xmas)
Beds: 2F 2D 1T 1S
Baths: 3 Ensuite 3 Shared
⛉ 🄿 (5) ⏀ ⏃ ⨯ ▥ Ⓥ ⸙

(2.25m) *Ael-Y-Bryn, Caerarfon Road, Beddgelert, Caernarfon, Gwynedd, LL55 4UY.*
Large detached house, splendid views.
Grades: WTB 1 Cr
Tel: 01766 890310 Mrs Duffield.
Rates fr: *£15.00-***£20.00**.
Open: All Year (not Xmas)
Beds: 1D 1T
Baths: 1 Ensuite
⛉ (14) 🄿 (8) ⏀ ⏃ ⨯ ▥ Ⓥ ⸙

All rooms full and nowhere else to stay? Ask the owner if there's anywhere nearby

Nantgwynant 54

National Grid Ref: SH6250

(▲On Path) *Bryn Gwynant Youth Hostel, Nantgwynant, Caernarfon, Gywnedd, LL55 4NP.*
Actual grid ref: SH641513
Warden: Mr N Warner.
Tel: 01766 890251
Under 18: £5.55 **Adults:** £8.25
Family Rooms, Evening Meal, Self Catering Facilities, Centrally Heated, Camping, Games Room, Grounds Available for Games, Shop, Parking, Study Room
Recently refurbished impressive former mansion with 40 acres of grounds, overlooking Llyn Gwynant lake

(1m) *Pen-Y-Gwryd Hotel, Nantgwynant, Caernarfon, Gwynedd, LL55 4NT.*
Actual grid ref: SH660558
Small mountain hotel.
Tel: 01286 870211
Rates fr: *£20.00-***£20.00**.
Open: Mar to Nov
⛉ 🄿 (30) ⏄ ⨯ ▥ Ⓥ ⸙

(1m) *Glan Gwynant, Country Guest House, Nantgwynant, Caernarfon, Gwynedd, LL55 4NW.*
Actual grid ref: SH638514
Lakeside Victorian house, unrivalled situation.
Grades: WTB 2 Cr
Tel: 01766 890440
Mr & Mrs Harper.
Rates fr: *£16.00-***£16.00**.
Open: Feb to Dec
Beds: 1D 1T 1S
Baths: 1 Ensuite 1 Shared
⛉ (12) 🄿 (6) ⨯ ▥ Ⓥ ⸙

Pen-y-Pass 55

National Grid Ref: SH6455

🍴 🍺 Pen-y-Gwryd Hotel

(▲On Path) *Pen-y-Pass Youth Hostel, Pen-y-Pass, Nantgwynant, Caernarfon, Gwynedd, LL55 4NY.*
Actual grid ref: SH647556
Warden: Mr H Lloyd.
Tel: 01286 870428
Under 18: £6.15 **Adults:** £9.10
Family Rooms, Evening Meal, Self Catering Facilities, Games Room, Facilities for the Disabled, Shop, Study Room Available, Parking
A converted pub that has become the largest Hostel in Snowdonia, situated right at the head of the Llanberis Pass

Nant Peris 56

National Grid Ref: SH6058

🍴 🍺 Vaynol Arms

(3m) *3 Gwastadnant, Nant Peris, Caernarfon, Gwynedd, LL55 4UL.*
Friendly welcome in magnificent scenery.

Grades: WTB Listed
Tel: 01286 870356 Mr Cumberton.
Rates fr: *£13.00-***£13.00**.
Open: All Year
Beds: 3D 1T 1S
Baths: 1 Shared
⛉ 🄿 (16) ▥ Ⓥ

Llanberis 57

National Grid Ref: SH5760

🍴 🍺 Ye Olde Bull Inn, Gallt Y Glyn, Padarn Lake Hotel, Mount Pleasant Hotel

(4m) *Gallt Y Glyn Hotel, Llanberis, Caernarfon, Gwynedd, LL55 4EL.*
Actual grid ref: SH5756
Comfortable hotel magnificent views.
Grades: WTB 1 St, AA 2 Cr
Tel: 01286 870370 Mrs Rayment.
Rates fr: *£16.50-***£18.50**.
Open: All Year (not Xmas)
Beds: 1F 5D 3T
Baths: 5 Ensuite 2 Shared
⛉ 🄿 (12) ⏀ ⨯ ▥ Ⓥ

Nant Ffrancon 58

National Grid Ref: SH6460

(▲0.25m) *Idwal Cottage Youth Hostel, Nant Ffrancon, Bethesda, Bangor, Gwynedd, LL57 3LZ.*
Actual grid ref: SH648603
Warden: Mr C Drake.
Tel: 01341 422392
Under 18: £4.60 **Adults:** £6.75
Family Rooms, Evening Meal, Self Catering Facilities, Camping, Grounds Available for Games, Shop, Parking
Originally a quarry manager's cottage, set in a small wood near Ogwen Lake below the impressive Glyder mountains, overlooking the Nant Ffrancon pass

Bethesda 59

National Grid Ref: SH6266

(5m) *Joys of Life Country Park, Bethesda, Bangor, Gwynedd, LL57 4YW.*
Actual grid ref: SH6266
Modern luxury house in Snowdonia.
Grades: WTB Listed
Tel: 01248 602122 Mrs Robinson.
Rates fr: *£15.00-***£20.00**.
Open: All Year (not Xmas)
Beds: 1F 1D 1T **Baths:** 1 Shared
⛉ 🄿 (6) ⏀ ⨯ ▥

Many rates vary according to season - the lowest only are shown here

Penmaenmawr 60

National Grid Ref: SH7176

⭑◀ Legend Inn, Fairy Glen

(3m) *Arosfa, Conway Road, Penmaenmawr, Gwynedd, LL34 6BL.*
Large Victorian private house.
Tel: **01492 622420** Mrs Newbound.
Rates fr: *£11.50*-**£12.50**.
Open: All Year
Beds: 1D 1T 1S
Baths: 2 Shared
⌂ ☷ (4) ⌧ ⌖ ✗ ▥.

(3m) *Glyn, Old Mill Road, Capelulo, Penmaenmawr, Gwynedd, LL34 6TB.*
Historic ex-country gentleman's residence.
Tel: **01492 622889** Mr Godsave.
Rates fr: *£14.00*-**£14.00**.
Open: All Year
Beds: 1F 1T 1S
Baths: 1 Shared
⌂ ☷ ⌲ ⌧ ✗ ▥. Ⓥ

Planning a longer stay? Always ask for any special rates.

Roewen 61

National Grid Ref: SH7472

⭑◀ Ty Gwyn Hotel

(▲ 1.25m) *Roewen Youth Hostel, Rhiw Farm, Roewen, Conwy, Gwynedd, LL32 8YW.*
Actual grid ref: SH747721
Tel: **01492 530627**
Under 18: £3.75 **Adults:** £5.50
Family Rooms, Self Catering Facilities, Camping, Grounds Available for Games, Shop, Parking
Simple, remote Welsh hill farmhouse set high above Roewen village with panoramic views of Conwy Valley

(1.5m) *Gwern Borter Country Manor, Roewen, Conwy, Gwynedd, LL32 8YL.*
Idyllic mountain setting, beautiful grounds.
Grades: WTB 3 Cr, High Comm, AA 4 Q, Select
Tel: **01492 650360** Mr Powell.
Rates fr: *£17.00*-**£24.00**.
Open: All Year
Beds: 1F 2D **Baths:** 3 Private
⌂ ☷ (20) ⌧ ⌖ ✗ ▥. Ⓥ

Conwy 62

National Grid Ref: SH7777

(1m 🚐) *Glan Heulog Guest House, Llanrwst Road, Conwy, Gwynedd, LL32 8LT.*
Large Victorian house.
Grades: WTB 3 Cr, AA 3 Q
Tel: **01492 593845** Mr Round.
Rates fr: *£13.00*-**£13.00**.
Open: All Year
Beds: 1F 3D 2T 1S
Baths: 4 Ensuite 3 Shared
⌂ ☷ (8) ⌧ ✗ ▥. Ⓥ ⌑

Cleveland Way & Tabular Hills Walk

The **Cleveland Way** is a waymarked National Trail, consisting of 100 miles of heather moorland and coastal path, starting at the little Yorkshire market town of Helmsley, skirting the western and northern edges of the North York Moors National Park (where it coincides for a few miles with the **Coast to Coast Path**), before leaving to head south-east on a magnificent and famous stretch of North Sea coastline with superb, towering cliffs, passing Whitby, Scarborough and ending in Filey. There is also a link called the **Tabular Hills Walk** which connects Scarborough wih Helmsley, along the southern side of the National Park, turning a linear path into a 148-mile circular route. This one can be wet; you are well-advised therefore to dress accordingly.

Maps: 1:50000 Ordnance Survey Landranger Series: 93, 94, 99, 100 and 101. *The Cleveland Way (4-colour linear route map)*, ISBN 1 8711490 9 6, published by Footprint, Unit 87, Stirling Enterprise Park, Stirling, FK7 7RP, price £2.95 (+ 40p p&p).

Guides (all available from good map shops unless stated):
Cleveland Way by Ian Sampson (ISBN 1 8541002 1 1), published by Aurum Press in association with the Countryside Commission and Ordnance Survey, price £9.99

The Cleveland Way by W. Cowley (ISBN 0 8520690 6 5), published by Dalesman Publishing Co Ltd, Clapham, Lancaster, LA2 8EB, (tel. 015242 51225), price £3.95 (+70p p&p)

Walking the Cleveland Way and the Missing Link by Malcolm Boyes (ISBN 1 8528401 4 5), published by Cicerone Press, 2 Police Square, Milnthorpe, Cumbria, LA7 7PY, (tel. 01539 562069), price £5.99 (+ 75p p&p)

Cleveland Way Companion by Paul Hannon (ISBN 1 8701411 7 2), published by Hillside Publications, 11 Nessfield Grove, Exley Head, Keighley, W. Yorks, BD22 6NU, (tel. 01535 681505), price £5.50 (+50p p&p)

The Cleveland Way by John Merrill (ISBN 0 9074967 0 6), published by Footprint Press Ltd,19 Moseley Street, Ripley, Derbyshire, DE5 3DA, (tel. 01773 512143), price £4.95 (+50p p&p)

The Link through the Tabular Hills Walk, published by the North York Moors National Park Authority and available only by post: write to The Old Vicarage, Bondgate, Helmsley, York, YO6 5BP, (tel. 01439 770657), price £3.95 (+50p p&p)

Comments on the path to: **Malcolm Hodgson**, Cleveland Way Project, North Yorks Moors National Park, The Old Vicarage, Bondgate, Helmsley, N. Yorks, YO6 5BP (tel. 01439 770657).

Helmsley   1

National Grid Ref: SE6184

🍴 🍺 Royal Oak, Crown Hotel, Feathers Hotel, Malt Shovel, White Swan

(▲ On Path) **Helmsley Youth Hostel**, Carlton Lane, Helmsley, York, *YO6 5HB*.
Actual grid ref: SE6184
Warden: Ms H Yardley.
Tel: **01439 770433**
Under 18: £5.00
Adults: £7.45
Family Bunk Room, Full Central Heating, Showers, Evening Meal (7.00 pm), Shop, Car Parking *Conveniently located in the small market town of Helmsley, this hostel is a great base from which to start your walk*

(On Path) **Stilworth House,** *1 Church Street, Helmsley, York, YO6 5AD*.
Relaxing house just off Market Square.
Grades: ETB 2 Cr
Tel: **01439 771072**
Mrs Swift.
Rates fr: *£22.50-£35.00*.
Open: All Year
Beds: 1F 2D 1T
Baths: 4 Ensuite 1 Shared
🅿 (4) 🛏 🍽 📺

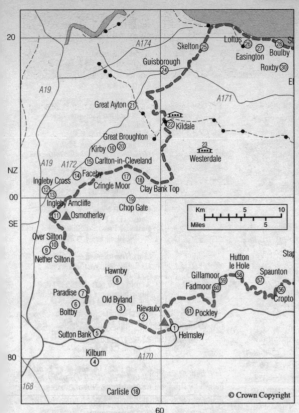

© Crown Copyright

Rievaulx 2

National Grid Ref: SE5785

(On Path 🚌) *Barn Close Farm, Rievaulx, Helmsley, York, YO6 5LH.*
Highly commended farmhouse.
Grades: ETB 3 Cr, RAC Acclaim
Tel: 01439 798321 Mrs Milburn.
Rates fr: *£18.00-£25.00.*
Open: All Year
Beds: 1F 1D **Baths:** 2 Ensuite
🛇 🅿 🖵 ⊁ ✕ 🎹 Ⅴ 🛦 ✔

Old Byland 3

National Grid Ref: SE5485

(2m 🚌) *Valley View Farm, Old Byland, Helmsley, York, N. Yorks, YO6 5LG.*
Actual grid ref: SE5384
Warm, friendly farmhouse.
Grades: ETB 2 Cr, High Comm
Tel: 01439 798221 Mrs Robinson.
Rates fr: *£24.00-£27.00.*
Open: All Year
Beds: 4F 1D 2T
Baths: 4 Private
🛇 🅿 🖵 ⊁ ✕ 🎹 Ⅴ 🛦 ✔

Kilburn 4

National Grid Ref: SE5179

(1.5m) *Village Farmhouse, Kilburn, York, YO6 4AG.*
Comfortable farmhouse in picturesque village.
Grades: ETB Listed
Tel: 01347 868562 Mrs Thompson.
Rates fr: *£14.00.*
Open: All Year (not Xmas)
Beds: 1F 1D
Baths: 1 Shared
🛇 🅿 🖵 🎹 🛦

Sutton Bank 5

National Grid Ref: SE5182

🍽 🍲 Hambleton Inn

(On Path) *Cote Faw, Hambleton Cottages, Sutton Bank, Thirsk, N. Yorks, YO7 2EZ.*
Actual grid ref: SE522830
Comfortable cottage in National Park.
Tel: 01845 597363 Mrs Jeffray.
Rates fr: *£14.00-£14.00.*
Open: All Year (not Xmas)
Beds: 1F 1D 1S
Baths: 1 Shared
🅿 (3) 🖵 🎹 Ⅴ 🛦 ✔

(0.25m 🚌) *High House Farm, Sutton Bank, Thirsk, N. Yorks, YO7 2HA.*
Actual grid ref: SE523830
Comfortable with home produced food.
Grades: ETB 1 Cr
Tel: 01845 597557 Mrs Hope.
Rates fr: *£18.00-£36.00.*
Open: Easter to Nov
Beds: 1F 1D
Baths: 1 Shared
🛇 🅿 (4) 🖵 🛏 ✕ 🎹 Ⅴ 🛦 ✔

().25m) *Castle View Guest House, 19 Bridge Street, Helmsley, York, YO6 5BG.*
Comfortable relaxed atmosphere, centrally located.
Tel: 01439 770618
Mrs Dyson.
Rates fr: *£17.50-£17.50.*
Open: Mar to Jan (not XMas)
Beds: 3D **Baths:** 2 shared
🛇 🅿 ⊁ 🖵 🛏 ✕ 🎹 Ⅴ 🛦 ✔

(0.5m) *14 Elmslac Road, Helmsley, York, YO6 5AP.*
Pleasant situation, quiet house.
Grades: ETB Reg
Tel: 01439 770287
Mrs Holding.
Rates fr: *£11.50-£12.00.*
Open: All Year
Beds: 1D
Baths: 1 Private
⊁ Ⅴ

(0.5m) *4 Ashdale Road, Helmsley, York, YO6 5DD.*
Quiet private house.
Tel: 01439 770375 Mrs Barton.
Rates fr: *£12.50.*
Open: All Year (not Xmas)
Beds: 1D 1T
Baths: 1 Shared
🅿 (2) ⊁ 🖵 🛏 Ⅴ

(On Path 🚌) *Black Swan Hotel, Market Place, Helmsley, York, YO6 5BJ.*
Actual grid ref: SE613839
Very comfortable with first-class food.
Grades: ETB 4 Cr, AA 3 St, 1 Rosette, RAC 3 St
Tel: 01439 770466
Rates fr: *£54.00-£54.00.*
Open: All Year
Beds: 4F 19D 17T 4S
Baths: 44 Ensuite
🛇 🅿 (60) ⊁ 🖵 🛏 ✕ 🎹 Ⅴ 🛦 ✔

(0.5m) *Ashberry, 41 Ashdale Road, Helmsley, York, YO6 5DE.*
Friendly atmosphere in comfortable home.
Tel: 01439 770488 Mrs O'Neil.
Rates fr: *£15.00-£15.00.*
Open: All Year (not Xmas)
Beds: 1D 1T 1S
Baths: 1 Shared
🛇 🅿 (2) 🖵 🛏 🎹 Ⅴ 🛦 ✔

The *lowest* **single**
rate *is shown in* **bold.**

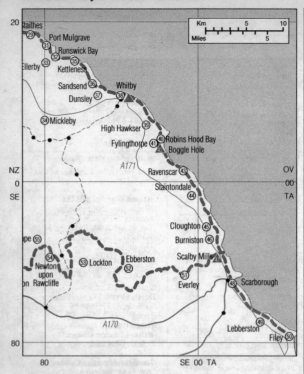

Tel: **01609 883495** Mrs Martin.
Rates fr: *£14.00*-**£15.00**.
Open: All Year (not Xmas)
Beds: 2D 1T
Baths: 1 Shared
🛏 (10) 🅿 (4) ⅙⊡✗▥ Ⅴ ⓐ ✦

Osmotherley 11

National Grid Ref: SE4597

🍽 🍺 Golden Lion Inn, Queen
Catherine

(0.75m 🚍) *Foxton Mill,*
Osmotherley, Northallerton,
N. Yorks, DL6 3PZ.
Actual grid ref: SE452965
Converted 17th Century water mill.
Tel: **01609 883377** Mrs Russell.
Rates fr: *£20.00*-**£20.00**.
Open: All Year (not Xmas)
Beds: 1D 1T
Baths: 1 Private 1 Shared
🛏 (10) 🅿 (6) ⅙⊡♁✗▥ Ⅴ ⓐ ✦

(1m) *Hemmelstones, Clack Lane,*
Osmotherley, Northallerton,
N. Yorks, DL6 3PP.
Actual grid ref: SE449971
Stone bungalow on small holding.
Tel: **01609 883313**
Mrs Gardner.
Rates fr: *£14.50*-**£14.50**.
Open: All Year (not Xmas)
Beds: 1D 1T
🛏 (4) ⊡♁▥ ⓐ ✦

(▲ On Path) *Osmotherley Youth*
Hostel, Cote Ghyll, Osmotherley,
Northallerton, N. Yorks, DL6 3AH.
Actual grid ref: SE461981
Warden: Ms H Ward.
Tel: **01609 883575**
Under 18: £5.00 **Adults:** £7.45
Family Bunk Room, Central
Heating, Showers, Evening Meal
(7.00 pm), Shop, Television,
Games Room
Surrounded by woodland, the
Youth Hostel is fully modernised
with excellent facilities, right on
the edge of the North Yorks Moors
National Park.

(On Path) *Quintana House, Back*
Lane, Osmotherley, Northallerton,
N. Yorks, DL6 3BJ.
Actual grid ref: SE457974
Detached stone house near village
centre.
Grades: ETB Listed, Comm
Tel: **01609 883258**
Dr Bainbridge.
Rates fr: *£15.00*.
Open: All Year (not Xmas)
Beds: 1D 1T **Baths:** 1 Shared
🛏 🅿 (4) ⅙⊡✗▥ Ⅴ ⓐ ✦

Boltby 6

National Grid Ref: SE4986

(1m 🚍) *Town Pasture Farm,*
Boltby, Thirsk, N. Yorks, YO7 2DY.
Actual grid ref: SE494866
Comfortable farmhouse in beauti-
ful village. **Grades:** ETB Listed
Tel: **01845 537298** Mrs Fountain.
Rates fr: *£13.50*-**£13.50**.
Open: All Year
Beds: 1F 1D 1T **Baths:** 1 Shared
🛏 🅿 (3) ⊡♁✗▥ Ⅴ ⓐ ✦

Paradise 7

National Grid Ref: SE5088

(0.25m) *Lower Paradise Farm,*
Paradise, Boltby, Thirsk, N. Yorks,
YO7 2HS.
Actual grid ref: SE502882
C17th oak-beamed farmhouse.
Grades: ETB Listed, Comm
Tel: **01845 537253** Mrs Todd.
Rates fr: *£16.00*-**£20.00**.
Open: Feb to Nov
Beds: 2D 2T **Baths:** 1Shared
🛏 🅿 ⅙⊡✗▥ Ⅴ ⓐ ✦

Hawnby 8

National Grid Ref: SE5489

(3m 🚍) *Laskill Farm, Hawnby,*
Helmsley, York, YO6 5NB.
Actual grid ref: SE564908
Lovely country farmhouse with
own lake.
Grades: ETB 3 Cr, AA 3 Q
Tel: **01439 798268** Mrs Smith.
Rates fr: *£17.50*-**£17.50**.
Open: All Year **Beds:** 4D 3T 1S
Baths: 6 Private 1 Shared
🛏 🅿 (15) ⊡♁✗▥ Ⅴ ⓐ ✦

Nether Silton 9

National Grid Ref: SE4592

(2.5m) *The Gold Cup Inn, Nether*
Silton, Thirsk, N. Yorks, YO7 2JZ.
Actual grid ref: SE455924
Quiet country inn.
Tel: **01609 883416** Mr Makin.
Rates fr: *£17.50*-**£17.50**.
Open: All Year
Beds: 1D **Baths:** 1 Ensuite
🅿 ⅙✗▥ Ⅴ ⓐ

Over Silton 10

National Grid Ref: SE4593

(2.5m 🚍) *Thistle Garth, Over*
Silton, Thirsk, N. Yorks, YO7 2LJ.
Actual grid ref: SE452932
Modern, comfortable, large private
house.

The lowest *double* rate per

person is shown in *italics*.

Pay B&Bs by cash or

cheque and be prepared

to pay up front.

(0.75m ⊕) *The Queen Catherine Inn*, 7 West End, Osmotherley, Northallerton, N. Yorks, *DL6 3AG*.
Family-run warm, friendly, comfortable inn.
Tel: **01609 883209** Mrs Bell.
Rates fr: *£19.97*-**£19.97**.
Open: All Year
Beds: 1D 3T 1S
🛏✕⌷🛏✕🏧Ⅴ🛆↯

Ingleby Cross 12

National Grid Ref: SE4400

¶⊛⚑Blue Bell Inn

(On Path ⊕) *Blue Bell Inn*, Ingleby Cross, Northallerton, N. Yorks, *DL6 3NF*.
Comfortably friendly village inn.
Tel: **01609 882272**
Mr Kinsella.
Rates fr: *£15.00*-**£15.00**.
Open: All Year
Beds: 2D 3T
Baths: 5 Ensuite
🛏 ⓟ(20) ✕Ⅴ🛆↯
Also ⚑ *£2.00 per tent.,*
Open: All Year ⟨⊛Ⓣ🏧✕↯⟩

(0.25m ⊕) *North York Moors Adventure Ctr*, Park House, Ingleby Cross, Northallerton, N. Yorks, *DL6 3PE*.
Actual grid ref: SE453995
Comfortable sandstone farmhouse in woodland.
Tel: **01609 882571**
Mr Bennett.
Rates fr: *£12.00*-**£12.00**.
Open: All Year (not Xmas)
Beds: 2F 1D 1T 2S
Baths: 2 Shared
🛏(1) ⓟ(10)⌷🛏✕🏧Ⅴ🛆↯
Also ⚑ *£1.00 per tent.,*
Open: All Year ⟨⊛Ⓣ🏧⟩

Ingleby Arncliffe 13

National Grid Ref: NZ4400

¶⊛⚑The Blue Bell (Ingleby Arncliffe)

(On Path) *Monks House*, Ingleby Arncliffe, Northallerton, N. Yorks, *DL6 3ND*.
Actual grid ref: NZ4400
Unique, comfortable, atmospheric C14th residence.
Tel: **01609 882294**
Mrs Backhouse.
Rates fr: *£15.00*-**£15.00**.
Open: Easter to Oct
Beds: 1D 1S
Baths: 1 shared
🛏(8)✕⌷🛏🏧🛆↯

Faceby 14

National Grid Ref: NZ4903

(1.25m ⊕) *Four Wynds*, Whorl Hill, Faceby, Middlesbrough, *TS9 7BZ*.
Actual grid ref: NZ487033
Modern, comfortable farmhouse - ideally situated.
Grades: ETB Listed
Tel: **01642 701315** Mr Barnfather.
Rates fr: *£15.00*-**£15.00**.
Open: All Year
Beds: 1F 1D 1T
Baths: 1 Ensuite 1 Shared
🛏 ⓟ(8)⌷🛏✕🏧Ⅴ🛆↯

Carlton-in-Cleveland 15

National Grid Ref: NZ3921

¶⊛⚑Blackwell Ox Inn

(1m ⊕) *Hill Rise*, Carlton-in-Cleveland, Stokesley, Middlesbrough, *TS9 7DD*.
Modernn comfortable farmhouse.
Tel: **01642 712212** Mrs Leng.
Rates fr: *£14.00*-**£14.00**.
Open: Easter to Nov
Beds: 1D 1T **Baths:** 1 Shared
🛏(3) ⓟ(3) 🏧Ⅴ

Kirkby 16

National Grid Ref: NZ5208

(1m ⊕) *Dromonby Grange Farm*, Kirkby, Middlesbrough, *TS9 7AR*.
Actual grid ref: NZ529051
C18th working farmhouse.
Tel: **01642 712227** Mrs Hugill.
Rates fr: *£15.00*-**£15.00**.
Open: Easter to Oct
Beds: 1D 2T **Baths:** 1 Shared
🛏(13) ⓟ✕⌷🛏✕🏧Ⅴ🛆↯

(1.5m ⊕) *Dromonby Hall Farm*, Busby Lane, Kirkby, Stokesley, Middlesbrough, Cleveland, *TS9 7AP*.
Spacious modern farmhouse.
Grades: ETB 1 Cr, Comm
Tel: **01642 712312** Mrs Weighell.
Rates fr: *£15.00*-**£17.50**.
Open: All Year (not Xmas)
Beds: 1D 2T
Baths: 1 Ensuite 1 Shared
🛏(2) ⓟ(6)✕⌷🛏🏧🛆🛆↯

Cringle Moor 17

National Grid Ref: NZ5302

¶⊛⚑Buck Inn Hotel

(0.5m ⊕) *Beakhills Farm*, Cringle Moor, Chop Gate, Stokesley, Middlesbrough, Cleveland, *TS9 7JJ*.
Actual grid ref: NZ545024
Comfortable farmhouse.
Tel: **01642 778371** Mrs Cook.
Rates fr: *£14.00*-**£14.00**.
Open: All Year (not Xmas)
Beds: 1F 1D 1T 1S
🛏⌷🛏✕Ⅴ🛆↯
Also ⚑ *£1.00 per person.,*
Open: All Year Ⓣ🛆

Clay Bank Top 18

National Grid Ref: NZ5701

(1m ⊕) *Maltkiln House*, Clay Bank Top, Bilsdale, Middlesbrough, *TS9 7HZ*.
Actual grid ref: NZ571017
Stone farmhouse in magnificent location.
Tel: **01642 778216**
Mr & Mrs Broad.
Rates fr: *£16.00*-**£16.00**.
Open: All Year
Beds: 1D 2T
Baths: 2 Shared
🛏 (8) ⓟ (3)✕⌷✕Ⅴ🛆↯

Chop Gate 19

National Grid Ref: SE5599

¶⊛⚑The Buck Inn (Chop Gate)

(1.75m ⊕) *Hill End Farm*, Chop Gate, Bilsdale, Middlesbrough, Cleveland, *TS9 7JR*.
Actual grid ref: NZ576978
Comfortable farmhouse with beautiful view.
Grades: ETB 2 Cr
Tel: **01439 798278** Mrs Johnson.
Rates fr: *£15.00*-**£20.00**.
Open: Easter to Nov
Beds: 1F 1D
Baths: 1 Ensuite 1 Shared
🛏 ⓟ(3)⌷✕🏧🛆

(2m ⊕) *1 Foresters Cottage*, Chop Gate, Stokesley, Middlesbrough, *TS9 7JD*.
Actual grid ref: NZ562006
Semi-detached forester's cottage.
Tel: **01642 778368** Mrs Cook.
Rates fr: *£14.00*-**£14.00**.
Open: All Year (not Xmas)
Beds: 1F 1D
Baths: 1 Shared
🛏 ⓟ(2)✕🛏✕🏧🛆↯

Great Broughton 20

National Grid Ref: NZ5406

¶⊛⚑Jet Miners Inn, Bay Horse, Wainstenes Hotel

(2m ⊕) *Ingle Hill*, Ingleby Road, Great Broughton, Middlesbrough, Cleveland, *TS9 7ER*.
Actual grid ref: NZ548063
Comfortable accommodation viewing Yorkshire Moors.
Tel: **01642 712449** Mrs Sutcliffe.
Rates fr: *£16.00*-**£16.00**.
Open: All Year (not Xmas)
Beds: 1F 1D 1T
Baths: 2 Ensuite 1 Shared
🛏 ⓟ(4)✕⌷🛏🏧Ⅴ🛆↯

All paths are popular: you are well-advised to book ahead

All rates are subject to alteration at the owners' discretion.

(1.75m) *Jet Miners Inn*, *61 High Street, Great Broughton, Middlesbrough, TS9 7EF.*
Actual grid ref: NZ547063
Inn/camp site/shower block.
Tel: **01642 712427** Mr Willis.
Also ⚑ *£1.00 per person.,*
Open: All Year 🏠 🖵 ♨ ✕ ⚡ ⚹

(2m ☂) *Hilton House*, *52 High Street, Great Broughton, Middlesbrough, Cleveland, TS9 7EG.*
C18th Yorkshire sandstone house.
Grades: ETB Listed
Tel: **01642 712526** Mrs Mead.
Rates fr: *£16.50-£16.50.*
Open: All Year (not Xmas)
Beds: 1D 2T
Baths: 1 Ensuite 1 Shared
🛏 🅿 (3) ⚹ ✕ 🖵 Ⅴ 🖤 ⚡

(2m ☂) *Holme Farm*, *12 The Holme, Great Broughton, Stokesley, Middlesbrough, Cleveland, TS9 7HF.*
Actual grid ref: NZ546062
Quaint.
Tel: **01642 712345** Mr Robinson.
Rates fr: *£16.00-£16.00.*
Open: All Year
Beds: 2D 2T **Baths:** 2 Shared
🛏 🅿 (4) ⚹ 🖵 🖤 Ⅴ 🖤 ⚡

Great Ayton 21

National Grid Ref: NZ5611

🍽 🍺 The Buck Hotel, The Royal Oak Hotel

(2m ☂) *1 Park Rise*, *Great Ayton, Middlesbrough, Cleveland, TS9 6ND.*
Actual grid ref: NZ5611
Comfortable homely bungalow (central).
Grades: ETB 2 Cr, Comm
Tel: **01642 722436** Mrs Petch.
Rates fr: *£14.00-£16.00*
Open: All Year (not Xmas)
Beds: 1F 1T **Baths:** 2 Ensuite
🅿 (2) ⚹ 🖵 🖵 Ⅴ 🖤 ⚡

(1.5m ☂) *Eskdale Cottage*, *31 Newton Road, Great Ayton, Middlesbrough, Cleveland, TS9 6DT.*
Actual grid ref: NZ564115
100-year-old cottage near centre of picturesque village.
Grades: ETB 1 Cr, Comm
Tel: **01642 724306**
Mrs Houghton.
Rates fr: *£15.00-£15.00.*
Open: All Year (not Xmas)
Beds: 2T **Baths:** 1 Shared
🛏 (1) 🅿 (2) ⚹ 🖵 ✕ 🖵 Ⅴ 🖤 ⚡

(1.5m ☂) *Travellers Rest*, *97 High Street, Great Ayton, Middlesbrough, Cleveland, TS9 6NF.*
Delightful ivy-covered cottage.
Tel: **01642 723409**
Mrs Weatherley.
Rates fr: *£15.00-£15.00.*
Open: All Year
Beds: 2D 1T
Baths: 1 Private 2 Shared
🛏 🖵 🐾 🖵 🖤 ⚡

Kildale 22

National Grid Ref: NZ6009

(On Path) *Bankside Cottage*, *Kildale, Whitby, N. Yorks, YO21 2RT.*
Actual grid ref: NZ605101
Comfortable cottage with lovely view.
Tel: **01642 723259** Mrs Addison.
Rates fr: *£14.00-£14.00.*
Open: All year (not Xmas)
Beds: 1F 1T 1D **Baths:** 1 Shared
🛏 (0) 🅿 (4) ⚹ 🖵 🖵 Ⅴ 🖤 ⚡

(⛺ On Path) *Kildale Camping Barn*, *Park Farm, Kildale, Whitby, N. Yorksire, .*
Actual grid ref: NZ602085
Tel: **01629 825650** *Simple barn, sleeps 12. A listed building, superbly located on the North York Moors Mr & Mrs Cook.*
£3.00 per person. ADVANCE BOOKING ESSENTIAL.

Westerdale 23

National Grid Ref: NZ6704

(⛺ 3.5m) *Westerdale Camping Barn*, *Broadgate Farm, Westerdale, Whitby, N. Yorkshire, .*
Actual grid ref: NZ6704
Tel: **01629 825650** *Simple barn, sleeps 12. Lovely views of Westerdale Moor and Castleton Rigg Mr & Mrs Alderson*
£3.00 per person. ADVANCE BOOKING ESSENTIAL.

Guisborough 24

National Grid Ref: NZ6115

(1.25m ☂) *Three Fiddles Hotel*, *34 Westgate, Guisborough, Cleveland, TS14 6ND.*
B&B and pub.
Tel: **01287 632417**
Rates fr: *£18.00-£18.00.*
Open: All Year (not Xmas)
Beds: 2D 3T
🛏 🖵 🐾 ✕ 🖵 🖤 ⚡

Skelton 25

National Grid Ref: NZ6518

🍽 🍺 Lingdale Tavern

(On Path ☂) *Westerlands Guest House*, *27 East Parade, Skelton, Saltburn-by-the-Sea, Cleveland, TS12 2BJ.*
Modern, large detached country house. **Grades:** ETB Listed
Tel: **01287 650690** Mr Bull.
Rates fr: *£13.00-£13.00.*
Open: Mar to Oct **Beds:** 3D 3S
Baths: 2 Private 4 Shared
🛏 🅿 (5) ⚹ 🖵 🐾 ✕ 🖵 Ⅴ 🖤 ⚡

(0.5m ☂) *Wharton Arms Hotel*, *High Street, Skelton, Saltburn-by-the-Sea, Cleveland, TS12 2DY.*
Midway between coast and moors.
Tel: **01287 650618**
Miss Cummings.

Rates fr: *£18.00-£17.50.*
Open: All Year
Beds: 1F 1D 2T 1S
Baths: 5 Ensuite
🛏 🅿 (15) 🖵 🐾 🖵 ⚡

Loftus 26

National Grid Ref: NZ7118

(1m ☂) *Station Hotel*, *Station Road, Loftus, Saltburn-by-the-Sea, Cleveland, TS13 4QB.*
Tel: **01287 640373**
Mr Fitzpatrick.
Rates fr: *£11.00-£14.00.*
Open: All Year
Beds: 2F 3T 2S
Baths: 2 Ensuite 3 Shared
🛏 🅿 🖵 ✕ 🖵 🐾 🖵 ⚡
North Yorks Cleveland border. Surrounded by woodland walks. One mile from coast. Good beer, music and food. Traditional quiet bar and music lounge. Good touring base.

Easington 27

National Grid Ref: NZ7417

🍽 🍺 Elterby Hotel

(On Path ☂) *Boulby Barns Farm*, *Easington, Loftus, Saltburn-by-the-Sea, Cleveland, TS13 4UT.*
Actual grid ref: NZ753192
Traditional stone farmhouse.
Grades: ETB Listed
Tel: **01287 641306** Mr/Mrs Blyth.
Rates fr: *£17.50-£17.50.*
Open: Apr to Nov
Beds: 1D 2T **Baths:** 2 Shared
🛏 (5) 🅿 (8) ⚹ 🖵 🐾 🖵 ⚡

Boulby 28

National Grid Ref: NZ7618

🍽 🍺 Ellerley Hotel

(On Path ☂) *Old Stables*, *Boulby, Saltburn-by-the-Sea, Cleveland, TS13 4UR.*
Actual grid ref: NZ761180
Grades: ETB Reg
Tel: **01287 641109**
Mrs Yeomans.
Rates fr: *£13.50-£15.00.*
Open: All Year
Beds: 1F 3D 1T
Baths: 3 Ensuite 2 Private
🛏 (3) 🅿 (5) ⚹ 🖵 🐾 ✕ 🖵 Ⅴ 🖤 ⚡
C17th building set in 2.5 acres. Stunning coastal views. Quiet and restful yet only short walk to the old fishing village of Staithes

(On Path ☂) *Boulby Barns Farm*, *Boulby, Easington, Saltburn-by-the-Sea, Cleveland, TS13 4UT.*
Grades: ETB Listed
Tel: **01287 641306** Mr Blyth.
Rates fr: *£15.00-£15.00.*
Open: Apr to Nov
Beds: 1D 2T
Baths: 2 Shared
🛏 (5) 🅿 (8) ⚹ 🖵 🐾 🖵 ⚡

Staithes 29

National Grid Ref: NZ7818

⭑⬛ Cod & Lobster, Royal George

(On Path) *Endeavour Restaurant,*
1 High Street, Staithes, Saltburn-
by-the-Sea, Cleveland, TS13 5BH.
Seafood restaurant with accommodation.
Tel: **01947 840825** Ms Chapman.
Rates fr: *£19.00-***£18.00.**
Open: Mar to Jan
Beds: 1D 1T 1S
Baths: 1 Private 1 Shared
🛏 ⬜ 🍴 ✕ ▥ Ⓥ ⬧

(On Path) *Harbour Side Guest*
House, Staithes, Saltburn-by-the-
Sea, Cleveland, TS13 5.
Friendly seafront guesthouse.
Tel: **01947 841296** Mr Tatham.
Rates fr: *£19.50-***£20.00.**
Open: All Year (not Xmas)
Beds: 1F 2D 1T
Baths: 1 Shared
🛏 ⬜ 🍴 ✕ ▥ Ⓥ ⬧ ✦

Roxby 30

National Grid Ref: NZ7616

(2.5m 🚍) *Fox Inn, Roxby,*
Staithes, Saltburn-by-the-Sea,
Cleveland, TS13 5EB.
Family-run village inn.
Grades: ETB Registered
Tel: **01947 840335** Mrs Stevenson.
Rates fr: *£15.00-***£18..00.**
Open: All Year (not Xmas)
Beds: 1D 1T **Baths:** 1 Shared
🛏 (5) ⬜ (12) ⬜ 🍴 ✕ ▥ Ⓥ ⬧ ✦

Port Mulgrave 31

National Grid Ref: NZ7917

(0.5m) *The Ship Inn, Port*
Mulgrave, Hinderwell, Saltburn-
by-the-Sea, Cleveland, TS13 5JZ.
Traditional family run village pub.
Tel: **01947 840303** Mrs Nedley.
Rates fr: *£15.00-***£15.00.**
Open: All Year
Beds: 2F 2S **Baths:** 2 Shared
🛏 ⬜ (10) ⬜ 🍴 ✕ ▥ Ⓥ ⬧ ✦

Runswick Bay 32

National Grid Ref: NZ8016

⭑⬛ Runswick Bay Hotel, Royal Hotel

(On Path) *Cockpit House, The Old*
Village, Runswick Bay, Saltburn-
by-the-Sea, Cleveland, TS13 5HU.
Large seafront house, sea views.
Tel: **01947 840504/603047**
Mrs Smith.
Rates fr: *£15.00-***£15.00.**
Open: All Year (not Xmas)
Beds: 2T **Baths:** 1 Shared
🛏 (5) ⬜ 🍴 ▥ Ⓥ ⬧ ✦

(On Path) *10 Hinderwell Lane,*
Runswick Bay, Saltburn-by-the-
Sea, Cleveland, TS13 5HR.
Comfortable homely guest house.
Tel: **01947 840758** Mrs Smith.
Rates fr: *£11.00.*
Open: Easter to Oct
Beds: 2F 1D
🛏 ⬜ (2) ⬜ 🍴

(On Path) *Cornforth Guest House,*
Corner Cottage, Runswick Bay,
Saltburn-by-the-Sea, Cleveland,
TS13 5HU.
People come first. Established 30
years.
Tel: **01947 840597**
Mr & Mrs Cornforth.
Rates fr: *£16.00-***£16.00.**
Open: Easter to Oct
Beds: 1F 1D 1T 1S
Baths: 1 Ensuite 1 Shared
🛏 (10) ⬜ (2) ✕ ▥ Ⓥ ⬧ ✦

Ellerby 33

National Grid Ref: NZ7914

⭑⬛ Ellerby Hotel (Ellerby)

(1m) *Ellerby Hotel, Ellerby,*
Saltburn-by-the-Sea, Cleveland,
TS13 5LP.
Residential country inn.
Grades: ETB 4 Cr, Comm
Tel: **01947 840342** Mr Alderson.
Rates fr: *£22.00-***£30.00.**
Open: All Year
Beds: 2F 5D 2T
Baths: 9 Private
🛏 ⬜ (50) ⬜ 🍴 ✕ ▥ ♿ Ⓥ ⬧

Mickleby 34

National Grid Ref: NZ8012

(5m) *Northfield Farm, Mickleby,*
Saltburn-by-the-Sea, Cleveland,
TS13 5NE.
Actual grid ref: NZ808142
Quiet, friendly, comfortable farmhouse.
Tel: **01947 840343**
Mrs Prudom.
Rates fr: *£14.00-***£14.00.**
Open: May to Oct
Beds: 1F 1D 1T
Baths: 1 Ensuite 1 Shared
🛏 ⬜ ✕ ✕ ▥ Ⓥ ⬧ ✦

Kettleness 35

National Grid Ref: NZ8315

⭑⬛ Fox and Hounds, Goldsborough

(On Path 🚍) *The Anchorage,*
Kettleness, Whitby, N. Yorks,
YO21 3RY.
Actual grid ref: NZ832156
C17th cliff-top cottage.
Tel: **01947 893386** Mrs Radford.
Rates fr: *£12.50-***£12.50.**
Open: All Year (not Xmas)
Beds: 1F 1D
Baths: 1 Shared
🛏 ⬜ (3) ⬜ 🍴 ✕ ⬧ ✦

Sandsend 36

National Grid Ref: NZ8612

(On Path) *Estbek House,*
Sandsend, Whitby, N. Yorks, YO21
3SU.
Actual grid ref: NZ8612
Small family run hotel.
Tel: **01947 893424**
Mr & Mrs Cooper.
Rates fr: *£22.00-***£26.00.**
Open: All Year
Beds: 1D 2D 1T
Baths: 4 Ensuite
🛏 (1) ⬜ (4) ✕ ⬜ ✕ ▥ Ⓥ ⬧ ✦

Dunsley 37

National Grid Ref: NZ8511

(1m 🚍) *Dunsley Hall, Dunsley,*
Whitby, N. Yorks, YO21 3TL.
Actual grid ref: NZ858104
Grades: ETB 3 Cr, Comm, AA
Recomm, RAC High Acclaim
Tel: **01947 893437** Mr Ward.
Rates fr: *£36.50-***£36.50.**
Open: All Year
Beds: 11T **Baths:** 11 Ensuite
🛏 ⬜ (30) ⬜ 🍴 ✕ ▥ Ⓥ ⬧ ✦
19th Century country hall - highly
acclaimed restaurant, indoor swimming pool, gymnasium, tennis
courts - two miles Whitby. In four
acres. Guaranteed Yorkshire welcome

(1.5m 🚍) *Low Farm, Dunsley,*
Whitby, N. Yorks, YO21 3TL.
Working farm, large comfortable
farmhouse.
Tel: **01947 893218** Mrs Hodgson.
Rates fr: *£14.00-***£14.00.**
Open: Jun to Oct
Beds: 1D 1T **Baths:** 1 Shared
⬜ ⬜ 🍴 ✕ ▥ Ⓥ ⬧ ✦

Whitby 38

National Grid Ref: NZ8910

⭑⬛ Buck Inn, Duke of York,
Granby Inn

(0.5m) *Falcon Guest House,*
29 Falcon Terrace, Whitby,
N. Yorks, YO21 1EH.
Quiet private house near centre.
Tel: **01947 603507** Mr Lyth.
Rates fr: *£13.00-***£13.00.**
Open: All Year
Beds: 2F **Baths:** 1 Shared
🛏 ⬜ Ⓥ ⬧ ✦

(0.25m) *Abbey House, East Cliff, Whitby, N. Yorks, YO22 4JT.*
Actual grid ref: NZ902111
Manor house beside historic abbey.
Tel: **01947 600557**
Mr & Mrs Blount.
Rates fr: *£18.00-£18.00*.
Open: All Year
Beds: 6F 19T 6S
Baths: 7 Shared
☼ **P** (30) ⟡ ⟡ **X** 📺 ❚ ✦

(▲ On Path) *Whitby Youth Hostel, East Cliff, Whitby, N. Yorks, YO22 4JT.*
Warden: S & C Pattinson.
Tel: **01947 602878**
Under 18: £4.60 **Adults:** £6.75
Partially Heated, Showers, Evening Meal (7.00 pm)
Converted stable range near Abbey at top of 199 steps above the harbour of this ancient fishing town.

(On Path) *Leeway Guest House, 1 Havelock Place, Whitby, N. Yorks, YO21 3ER.*
Actual grid ref: NZ896112
Large Victorian guest house.
Grades: ETB 3 Cr, Comm
Tel: **01947 602604**
Mr & Mrs Wan.
Rates fr: *£15.00-£15.00*.
Open: Mar to Nov
Beds: 5F 5D 4T 3S
Baths: 4 Ensuite 2 Shared
☼ ⟡ **X** 📺 ❚ ✦

(0.5m) *Haven Guest House, 4 East Crescent, Whitby, N. Yorks, YO21 3HD.*
Comfortable, homely house, overlooking sea.
Grades: AA 3 Q
Tel: **01947 603842** Mrs Smith.
Rates fr: *£15.00-£18.00*.
Open: Mar to Oct
Beds: 1F 5D 2S
Baths: 5 Private 1 Shared
☼ (5) ⟡ 📺 ✦

High Hawsker 39

National Grid Ref: NZ9207

🍴 🍺 Hare & Hound Public House

(0.5m) *Old Blacksmiths Arms, High Hawsker, Whitby, N. Yorks, YO22 4LH.*
Actual grid ref: NZ947075
Converted C17th village pub.
Tel: **01947 880800** Mrs Stubbs.
Rates fr: *£15.50-£15.50*.
Open: Mar to Oct
Beds: 1D 2T 1S
Baths: 2 Shared
☼ **P** (4) ⟡ 🍺 📺 ❚ ✦

(On Path) *York House Private Hotel, High Hawsker, Whitby, N. Yorks, YO22 4LW.*
Small modernised Edwardian private hotel.
Grades: ETB 3 CrRAC High Acclaim

Tel: **01947 880314**
Mr & Mrs Walley.
Rates fr: *£22.00-£22.00*.
Open: Easter to Oct
Beds: 4T **Baths:** 4 Ensuite
P (6) ⟡ ⟡ **X** 📺 ❚ ✦

Robin Hood's Bay 40

National Grid Ref: NZ9504

🍴 🍺 Dolphin, Victoria Hotel, Bay Hotel, Grosvenor Hotel

(On Path) *Wayfarer Restaurant, Robin Hood's Bay, Whitby, N. Yorks, YO22 4.*
Actual grid ref: 94952067
Tel: **01947 880240** Mrs Gray.
Rates fr: *£15.00-£20.00*.
Open: All Year (not Xmas)
Beds: 2F 1D 1T
Baths: 3 Ensuite, 1 Shared
☼ (3) **P** (3) ⟡ ⟡ 🍺 ❚ ✦
Cliff top on the Cleveland Way. Adjacent to main bus route. 50 yards from good beer and food. Treat yourself to the best. You deserve it.

(On Path) *Rosegarth, Thorpe Lane, Robin Hood's Bay, Whitby, N. Yorks, YO22 4RN.*
Modern comfortable semi detached house.
Grades: ETB Listed
Tel: **01947 880578** Mrs Stubbs.
Rates fr: *£15.00-£17.00*.
Open: Easter to Oct
Beds: 1D 1T 1S **Baths:** 1 Shared
☼ (11) **P** (4) ⟡ 🍺 📺 ✦

(On Path) *The White Owl, Station Road, Robin Hood's Bay, Whitby, N. Yorks, YO22 4RL.*
Large interesting house.
Tel: **01947 880879**
Mr & Mrs Higgins.
Rates fr: *£14.50-£15.00*.
Open: All Year
Beds: 1F 1D 1T **Baths:** 3 Private
☼ **P** (3) ⟡ 🍺 📺 ❚ ✦

(On Path) *Devon House, Station Road, Robin Hood's Bay, Whitby, N. Yorks, YO22 4RL.*
Actual grid ref: NZ952054
Small family-run B&B, clean delightful accommodation.
Tel: **01947 880197**
Mrs Duncalfe.
Rates fr: *£14.00-£14.00*.
Open: All Year (not Xmas)
Beds: 3D
Baths: 2 Shared
☼ **P** ⟡ ⟡ 📺 ❚ ✦

(On Path) *Meadowfield, Mount Pleasant North, Robin Hood's Bay, Whitby, N. Yorks, YO22 4RE.*
Large Victorian house.
Tel: **01947 880564** Mrs Luker.
Rates fr: *£13.00-£17.50*.
Open: All Year
Beds: 2D 2T 1S
Baths: 1 Ensuite 1 Shared
⟡ 📺 ❚ ✦

(On Path) *Victoria Hotel, Robin Hood's Bay, Whitby, N. Yorks, YO22 4RL.*
Victorian hotel overlooking sea.
Grades: ETB 2 Cr
Tel: **01947 880205**
Mr Gibson.
Rates fr: *£27.00-£25.00*.
Open: All Year (not Xmas)
Beds: 2F 6D 2T 1S
Baths: 9 Ensuite 2 Shared
☼ **P** **X** 📺 ❚

(On Path) *Muir-Lea Stores, Robin Hood's Bay, Whitby, N. Yorks, YO22 4UQ.*
Actual grid ref: NZ952052
C17th smugglers retreat.
Grades: ETB Reg
Tel: **01947 880316** Mrs Leaf.
Rates fr: *£13.00-£15.00*.
Open: All Year **Beds:** 3D 1S
⟡ 🍺 📺

(0.25m) *Streonshalh, Mount Pleasant South, Robin Hood's Bay, Whitby, N. Yorks, YO22 4RQ.*
Large Victorian house, tastefully decorated.
Tel: **01947 880619**
Mrs Paxton.
Rates fr: *£14.50*.
Open: Easter to Oct
Beds: 1F 2D 1T
☼ ⟡ ⟡ 📺 ❚

Fylingthorpe 41

National Grid Ref: NZ9404

🍴 🍺 Fylingdales Inn, Victoria Hotel, Grosvenor Hotel

(1m) *Croft Farm, Fylingthorpe, Whitby, N. Yorks, YO22 4PW.*
Farmhouse and cottage. Panoramic views.
Grades: ETB 2 Cr, Comm
Tel: **01947 880231**
Mrs Featherstone.
Rates fr: *£16.00-£16.00*.
Open: Easter to Oct
Beds: 1F 1D 1S
Baths: 1 Private 1 Shared
☼ (5) **P** (4) ⟡ ⟡ 📺 ❚ ✦

Boggle Hole 42

National Grid Ref: NZ9504

(▲ On Path) *Boggle Hole Youth Hostel, Mill Beck, Boggle Hole, Robin Hood's Bay, Whitby, N. Yorks, YO22 4UQ.*
Actual grid ref: NZ9504
Warden: Mr P Hobson/Ms P Saunders.
Tel: **01947 880352**
Under 18: £5.55 **Adults:** £8.25
Family Bunk Rooms, Centrally Heated, Showers, Evening Meal (7.00 pm), Shop, Security Lockers, Television, Games Room
A former mill in a wooded ravine, Boggle Hole has the North Sea tide coming up to the doorstep and the North York Moors behind

Ravenscar 43

National Grid Ref: NZ9801

⊯ ◗Raven Hall Hotel

(1m) *Smugglers Rock, Country Guest House, Ravenscar, Scarborough, N. Yorks, YO13 0ER.*
Georgian country house (renovated).
Grades: ETB 2 Cr, AA 3 Q
Tel: 01723 870044
Mr Greenfield.
Rates fr: £20.00-£20.00.
Open: All Year (not Xmas)
Beds: 1F 3D 2T 2S
Baths: 8 Ensuite, 1 Shared
⛵ (3) ❷ (10) ❐ ❒ ✕ ⅏ ✐

(On Path) *Bide-A-While, 3 Lorings Road, Ravenscar, Scarborough, N. Yorks, YO13 0LY.*
Grades: ETB Listed, Approv
Tel: 01723 870643
Mrs Leach.
Rates fr: £16.50-£18.50.
Open: All Year (not Xmas)
Beds: 2F 2D
⛵ ❐ ✕ ⅏ Ⅴ ▮ ✐

(On Path 🚐) *Dunelm, Raven Hall Road, Ravenscar, Scarborough, N. Yorks, YO13 0NA.*
Actual grid ref: NZ980014
Comfortable accommodation, splendid view.
Tel: 01723 870430
Ms Bartlet.
Rates fr: £13.00-£13.00.
Open: All Year (not Xmas)
Beds: 1D 1T 2S
Baths: 2 Shared
⛵ ❷ ⅍ ❒ ❒ ✕ ⅏ Ⅴ ▮ ✐

(On Path 🚐) *Crag Hill, Ravenscar, Scarborough, N. Yorks, YO13 0NA.*
Actual grid ref: NZ949901
Large Victorian private licensed hotel.
Grades: ETB 3 Cr
Tel: 01723 870925
Mr & Mrs Kirkham.
Rates fr: £16.00-£20.00.
Open: All Year (not Xmas)
Beds: 2F 3D 2T
Baths: 4 Ensuite 1 Shared
⛵ ❷ (12) ⅍ ❒ ❒ ✕ ⅏ ▮ ✐

Staintondale 44

National Grid Ref: SE9998

(1m) *Tofta Farm, Staintondale, Scarborough, N. Yorks, YO13 0EB.*
Actual grid ref: SE982985
Modernised C17th farmhouse.
Grades: RAC Listed
Tel: 01723 870298
Mrs Dobson.
Rates fr: £15.00-£16.00.
Open: All Year (not Xmas)
Beds: 1F 3D
Baths: 1 Private 1 Shared
⛵ ❷ ❐ ❒ ❒ ✕ ⅏ Ⅴ

Cloughton 45

National Grid Ref: TA0094

(0.5m) *Red Lion Hotel, High Street, Cloughton, Scarborough, N. Yorks, YO13 0AE.*
Actual grid ref: TA009946
Good food, clean, friendly atmosphere.
Tel: 01723 870702
Mr Culling.
Rates fr: £15.00-£15.00.
Open: All Year
Beds: 1F 1D 1T 1S
Baths: 1 Shared
⛵ ❷ (14) ❐ ✕ ⅏ Ⅴ ▮

Burniston 46

National Grid Ref: TA0193

⊯ ◗The Oak Wheel, Three Jolly Sailors

(1.5m) *Cherry Tree Cottage, South End, Burniston, Scarborough, N. Yorks, YO13 0HP.*
Actual grid ref: TA014927
Comfortable village cottage, pleasant garden.
Tel: 01723 870407
Mrs Rimington.
Rates fr: £12.00-£12.00.
Open: All Year
Beds: 1D 1S
Baths: 1 Shared
❷ (1) ❐ ▮ ✐

Scalby Mills 47

National Grid Ref: TA0290

(🔺0.5m) *Scarborough Youth Hostel, The White House, Burniston Road, Scalby Mills, Scarborough, N. Yorks, YO13 0DA.*
Actual grid ref: TA0290
Warden: Mr A Halston.
Tel: 01723 361176
Under 18: £4.60
Adults: £6.75
Family Bunk Rooms, Centrally Heated, Showers, Evening Meal (7.00 pm)
A converted water mill by a bridge on the Sea Cut, just outside Scarborough, 10 minutes' walk from the Cleveland Way

---

🚐 sign means that, *given due notice,* owners will pick you up from the path and drop you off *within reason.*

Scarborough 48

National Grid Ref: TA0388

⊯ ◗Scalby Manor, Jolly Sailors, The Cask, Gridley's Carvery, The Crescent, Green Lizard Restaurant, Tricolos's Restaurant

(0.25m 🚐) *Attenborough Hotel, 28-29 Albemarle Crescent, Scarborough, N. Yorks, YO11 1XX.*
Tel: 01723 360857 Mr & Mrs Snow.
Rates fr: £14.50-£14.50.
Open: All Year
Beds: 7F 7D 5T 4S
Baths: 6 Ensuite, 4 Shared
⛵ ❷ (7) ❐ ✕ ⅏ Ⅴ ▮ ✐
A welcoming family owned hotel, forming part of a Victorian crescent. Quiet central location, ideal base for Cleveland Way, Lyke Wake, etc.

(On Path) *Premier Hotel, 66 Esplanade, South Cliff, Scarborough, N. Yorks, YO11 2UZ.*
Victorian sea-view licensed hotel.
Grades: ETB 3 Cr, AA Listed, RAC High Acclaim
Tel: 01723 501062 Mr Jacques.
Rates fr: £25.00-£28.00.
Open: Easter to Nov
Beds: 3F 8D 5T 3S
Baths: 19 Ensuite
⛵ ❷ (6) ❐ ❒ ✕ ⅏ Ⅴ ▮

(1m) *Stewart Hotel, St Nicholas Cliff, Scarborough, N. Yorks, YO11 2ES.*
Tel: 01723 361095 Mr Pummell.
Rates fr: £20.00-£20.00.
Open: All Year
Beds: 3F 10D 2T 1S
Baths: 9 Ensuite 7 Shared
⛵ ⅏.
Hotel built in 1793. Grade II Listed Georgian building - unique position overlooking South Bay. The perfect setting for pleasure, leisure, conferences and business.

(0.25m) *The Girvan Hotel, 61 Northstead Manor Drive, Scarborough, N. Yorks, YO12 6AF.*
Welcoming detached house overlooking park.
Tel: 01723 364518
Mrs Hurrell.
Rates fr: £14.00-£14.00.
Open: All Year
Beds: 4F 5D 1T 2S
Baths: 12 Ensuite
⛵ ❷ (11) ❐ ❒ ✕ ⅏ Ⅴ ▮ ✐

(0.25m) *Ashburton Hotel, 43 Valley Road, Scarborough, N. Yorks, YO11 2LX.*
Small, clean and friendly hotel.
Tel: 01723 374382
Mr & Mrs Hindhaugh.
Rates fr: £15.50-£15.50.
Open: All Year
Beds: 4F 3D 1T 1S
Baths: 3 Ensuite, 2 Shared
⛵ ❷ (8) ❐ ✕ ⅏ Ⅴ ▮ ✐

All rates are subject to alteration at the owners' discretion.

(0.25m) *The Terrace Hotel*, 69 Westborough, Scarborough, N. Yorks, YO11 1TS. Friendly family-run small hotel. Tel: **01723 374937** Mr/Mrs Kirk. **Rates fr:** £14.00-**£14.00**. **Open:** All Year (not Xmas) **Beds:** 3F 3D 1S **Baths:** 2 Ensuite, 1 Private, 1 Shared ☎ 🏱 (4) 🗔 ✕ 🎥,

(0.25m) *Highbank Hotel*, 5 Givendale Road, Scarborough, N. Yorks, YO12 6LE. **Actual grid ref:** TA031898 Quite North Bay Hotel. **Grades:** ETB Listed, Comm Tel: **01723 365265** Mr Marsh. **Rates fr:** £17.50-**£18.50**. **Open:** All Year **Beds:** 3D 2T 2S **Baths:** 7 Ensuite ☎ (5) 🏱 (10) ✟🗔 🛏 ✕ 🎥 🗥 🖳 ♨ ✦

(On Path) *Brincliffe Edge Hotel*, 105 Queens Parade, Scarborough, N. Yorks, YO12 7HY. Family run hotel overlooking sea. Tel: **01723 364834** Mr & Mrs Sutcliffe. **Rates fr:** £16.50-**£16.50**. **Open:** Easter to Oct **Beds:** 2F 7D 1T 1S **Baths:** 9 Ensuite, 2 Shared ☎ 🏱 (7) 🗔 ✕ 🎥 🖳 🖳 ♨ ✦

(On Path) *Sylvern Hotel*, 25 New Queen Street, Scarborough, N. Yorks, YO12 7HJ. Small friendly family run hotel. Tel: **01723 360952** Mr Wheeler. **Rates fr:** £14.00-**£14.00**. **Open:** All Year **Beds:** 3F 2D 2T 2S **Baths:** 4 Ensuite, 2 Shared ☎ 🗔 🛏 ✕ 🖳

(On path) *Derwent House Hotel*, 6 Rutland Terrace, Queens Parade, Scarborough, N. Yorks, YO12 7JB. Seaview hotel. No smoking. Tel: **01723 373880** Mr & Mrs Greenhough. **Rates fr:** £16.50-**£18.00**. **Open:** All Year **Beds:** 4F 4D 2T 2S **Baths:** 6 Private 6 Shared ☎ ✟🗔 ✕ 🎥 🖳 ♨

(0.25m) *Meadow Court Hotel*, Queens Terrace, Scarborough, N. Yorks, YO12 7HJ. Family-run licensed hotel. **Grades:** AA 2 Q Tel: **01723 360839** Mr Buckle. **Rates fr:** £13.00-**£13.00**. **Open:** All Year **Beds:** 2F 4D 2T 2S **Baths:** 2 Shared ☎ ✟🛏 ✕ 🎥 🖳 ♨

(0.25m) *Glenderry Non-Smoking Guest House*, 26 The Dene, Scarborough, N. Yorks, YO12 7NJ. **Actual grid ref:** TA035891 Small, friendly select guest house. **Grades:** ETB 2 Cr, Comm Tel: **01723 36 2546** Mr & Mrs Harrison. **Rates fr:** £12.50-**£12.50**. **Open:** All Year (not Xmas) **Beds:** 3F 1D 1S **Baths:** 2 Private 1 Shared ☎ (2) ✟🗔 🛏 ✕ 🎥 🖳

Lebberston 49

National Grid Ref: TA0782

🍴 🍺 Blacksmiths Arms

(1m) *Manor Farm*, Lebberston, Scarborough, N. Yorks, YO11 3PA. Comfortable farmhouse on dairy farm. Tel: **01723 584624** Mrs Green. **Rates fr:** £13.50-**£15.00**. **Open:** May to Sep **Beds:** 1D **Baths:** 1 Private 🏱 (2) ✟🗔 🎥,

Filey 50

National Grid Ref: TA1180

(0.5m) *Abbots Leigh Guest House*, 7 Rutland Street, Filey, N. Yorks, YO14 9JA. Comfortable Victorian terrace house. **Grades:** ETB 3 Cr, Comm, AA 3 Q Tel: **01723 513334** Mr & Mrs Carter. **Rates fr:** £18.00-**£20.00**. **Open:** All Year (not Xmas) **Beds:** 2F 2D 2T **Baths:** 6 Ensuite ☎ (3) 🏱 (4) ✟🗔 ✕ 🎥 🖳

> For those wishing to walk back to Helmsley, this is the Tabular Hills Walk.

Everley 51

National Grid Ref: SE9888

🍴 🍺 The Everley

(On Path) *Mowthorpe Farm*, Everley, Scarborough, N. Yorks, YO12 5TB. **Actual grid ref:** SE981883 Georgian, Grade II Listed. Tel: **01723 882249** **Rates fr:** £14.00-**£14.00**. **Open:** All Year (not Xmas/New Year) **Beds:** 1F 1D **Baths:** 1 Shared 🏱 (6) ✟🛏 🖳 ♨ ✦

Ebberston 52

National Grid Ref: SE9089

(0.25m) *Givendale Head Farm*, Ebberston, Scarborough, N. Yorks, YO13 9PU. Tel: **01723 859383** **Rates fr:** £15.00-**£15.00**. **Open:** All Year (not Xmas) **Beds:** 2D **Baths:** 1 Ensuite 1 Shared 🏱 ✟ ✕ 🎥 🖳 ♨ ✦

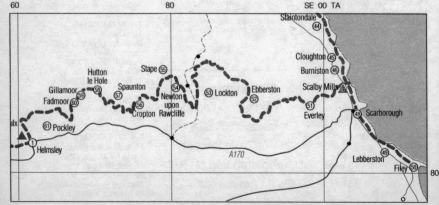

Lockton 53

National Grid Ref: SE8489

⑩ ◲ Horseshoe Inn, Fox & Rabbit Inn

(0.25m 🚐) *Ivy Cottage, Lockton, Pickering, N. Yorks, YO18 7PY.*
Cosy 17th Century beamed cottage.
Tel: **01751 460325** Mr & Mrs Fisk.
Rates fr: *£14.00-£20.00.*
Open: All Year (not Xmas)
Beds: 1F 1D
Baths: 1 Shared
⛺ (A) ▣ (4) ⊁ ⊡ ⋔ ⠿ 🛆 ⚡

Newton-upon-Rawcliffe 54

National Grid Ref: SE8190

⑩ ◲ White Swan Pub

(On Path 🚐) *Swan Cottage, Newton-upon-Rawcliffe, Pickering, N. Yorks, YO18 8QA.*
Actual grid ref: SE813906
Comfortable, homely C18th cottage.
Tel: **01751 472502** Mrs Heaton.
Rates fr: *£14.00-£14.00.*
Open: All Year (not Xmas)
Beds: 1D 1T 1S
Baths: 1 Shared
(A) ▣ (2) ⊡ ⋔ ✗ ⠿ Ⓥ 🛆 ⚡

Stape 55

National Grid Ref: SE7993

(On Path) *Seavy Slack Farm, Stape, Pickering, N. Yorks, YO18 8HZ.*
Actual grid ref: SE799922
Comfortable farmhouse on working farm.
Grades: ETB Listed, Approv
Tel: **01751 473131** Mrs Barrett.
Rates fr: *£15.00-£15.00.*
Open: Easter to Oct
Beds: 1F 1D
Baths: 1 Shared
(A) ▣ (6) ⊡ ⋔ ✗ Ⓥ 🛆 ⚡

Cropton 56

National Grid Ref: SE7589

⑩ ◲ New Inn

(On Path) *High Farm, Cropton, Pickering, N. Yorks, YO18 8HL.*
Actual grid ref: SE758950
Large Victorian farmhouse, own grounds.
Grades: ETB 2 Cr, Comm
Tel: **01751 417461** Mrs Feaster.
Rates fr: *£18.50-£25.00.*
Open: All Year
Beds: 3D **Baths:** 3 Ensuite
⛺ (A) ▣ (10) ⊡ ⠿ Ⓥ

Spaunton 57

National Grid Ref: SE7390

(On Path 🚐) *Holywell House, Spaunton Bank Foot, Spaunton, Appleton Le Moors, York, YO6 6TR.*
Actual grid ref: SE723904
Country house with large garden.
Grades: ETB Listed, High Comm
Tel: **01751 417624**
Mrs Makepeace.
Rates fr: *£15.00-£15.00.*
Open: All Year
Beds: 1D 1T 1S
Baths: 1 Shared
(A) ▣ (4) ⊁ ⊡ ⠿ Ⓥ 🛆 ⚡

Hutton-le-Hole 58

National Grid Ref: SE7089

(On Path 🚐) *Hammer & Hand Country Guest House, Hutton-le-Hole, York, YO6 6UA.*
Actual grid ref: SE706902
Former beerhouse 1784, character features.
Grades: ETB 2 Cr, Comm,
RAC Highly Acclaimed
Tel: **01751 417300** Mrs Wilkins.
Rates fr: *£18.00-£25.00.*
Open: All Year (not Xmas)
Beds: 2D 1T **Baths:** 3 Private
⛺ (A) ▣ (6) ⊁ ⊡ ⋔ ✗ ⠿ Ⓥ 🛆 ⚡

Gillamoor 59

National Grid Ref: SE6889

(2.75m) *The Royal Oak Inn, Gillamoor, Kirkbymoorside, York, YO6 6HX.*
Traditional inn, olde-worlde charm.
Grades: ETB 2 Cr, Comm
Tel: **01751 431414**
Mr & Mrs Pickard.
Rates fr: *£22.00-£35.00.*
Open: All Year (not Xmas)
Beds: 5D 1T
Baths: 6 Ensuite
▣ (6) ⊁ ⊡ ✗ ⠿ Ⓥ 🛆

Fadmoor 60

National Grid Ref: SE6789

(On Path) *The Plough Inn, Fadmoor, Kirkbymoorside, York, YO6 6HY.*
Actual grid ref: SE674894
C18th country inn.
Grades: ETB Listed
Tel: **01751 431515**
Mr O'Connell.
Rates fr: *£14.50-£14.50.*
Open: All Year (not Xmas)
Beds: 1D 1T 2S
Baths: 1 Shared
⛺ (A) ▣ (15) ✗ ⠿

Pockley 61

National Grid Ref: SE6385

(On Path 🚐) *High Farm, Beadlam Rigg, Pockley, York, YO6 5TG.*
Peacefully situated mixed working farm.
Tel: **01439 771268**
Mrs Teasdale.
Rates fr: *£13.00-£13.00.*
Open: All Year
Beds: 1F 1D 1T
Baths: 2 Shared
⛺ (A) ▣ (6) ⊡ ✗ ⠿ Ⓥ 🛆 ⚡

Coast to Coast

Passing through three National Parks - the Lake District, the Yorkshire Dales and the North York Moors - the Coast to Coast Path was the special creation of A. Wainwright, the man whose sketches and guidebooks mean so much to fellwalkers old and young. Featured on the television, the radio and in countless books, the Coast to Coast is now probably as famous as the Pennine Way itself. Running from the Cumbrian Coast to the North Sea, it is the most popular long distance path as yet unrecognised by the **Countryside Commission**. Despite this fame, there are still some debatable stretches which do not follow rights of way as defined at present. Please therefore take care in these areas and pay attention to diversion signs where they appear - local goodwill depends on walkers' behaviour. With regard to accommodation, although there is plenty of it, you are well advised to book ahead - don't just expect to turn up and find a place waiting for you.

The **Youth Hostel Association** run a useful **Accommodation Booking Bureau** for the **Coast to Coast Path**, based on their hostels and local B&Bs along the path. Ring 01629 825850 and ask for the Coast to Coast Booking Bureau Pack form and they can sort out your entire itinerary without further ado. There are also a couple of passenger minibus or taxi services handling luggage delivery, safe car-parking and back-up; **White Knight** (flexible backup service - tel 01903 766475, please see advertisement) and **Coast to Coast Packhorse** (fixed bus service - tel 01768 371680). Both provide a useful fallback for weary or injured walkers or just those who do not wish to carry a large pack (most of us, probably).

Maps: 1:50000 Ordnance Survey Landranger Series: 89, 90, 91, 92, 93, 94, 98, 99. *Coast to Coast, Part One - West*, ISBN 1 871149 11 8 and *Coast to Coast, Part Two* - East, ISBN 1 871149 12 6, both 4-colour linear route maps, published by Footprint and available from all good map shops or directly from their offices (Unit 87, Stirling Enterprise Park, Stirling, FK7 7RP), £2.95 (+ 40p p&p)

Guides: *The Coast to Coast Walk* by Paul Hannon (ISBN 1 870141 18 0), published by Hillside Publications and available from all good map shops or directly from the publishers (11 Nessfield Grove, Exley Head, Keighley, W. Yorks, BD22 6NU, tel. 01535 681505), £7.99 (+50p p&p)

A Coast to Coast Walk by A. Wainwright is still available, but readers should be reminded that significant changes have taken place since the path's creator put down his pen. You can obtain an updated version from the Rambler's Association National Office (1/5 Wandsworth Road, London, SW8 2XX, tel. 0171 582 6878), £9.99 (+ £1 p&p)

The lowest *double* rate per person is shown in *italics*.

St Bees   1

National Grid Ref: NX9711

ꗽ 🍴 Queens Hotel, Manor House Hotel, Oddfellows Pub

(0.5m 🚌) *Stonehouse Farm, Main St, St Bees, Cumbria, CA27 0DE*
Actual grid ref: NX972119
Modern comfortable farmhouse, centre village.
Grades: ETB Listed, Approv
Tel: **01946 822224** Mrs Smith.
Rates fr: *£15.00*-£18.00.
Open: All Year **Beds:** 1F 2D 3T 1S
ꗽ ⓟ (10) ❏ ⌹ ✕ ⅏ Ⓥ 🛈 ☕ ⚕
Also ▲ £2 per tent. ⌂ Ⓣ ⚕ ♿

(0.5m) *Fairladies Barn Guest House, Main Street, St Bees, Cumbria, CA27 0AD.*
Converted barn in quiet area.
Tel: **01946 822718** Mrs Blakeley.
Rates fr: *£14.00*-£14.00.
Open: All Year (not Xmas)
Beds: 1F 3D 3T 1S
Baths: 1 Shared
ꗽ ⓟ (8) ❏ ⌹ ⅏ 🛈 ☕ ⚕

(0.25m) *Tomlin Guest House, 1 Tomlin House, St Bees, Cumbria, CA27 0EN.*
Actual grid ref: NX963118
Comfortable Victorian house with warm welcome.
Tel: **01946 822284**
Mrs Whitehead.
Rates fr: *£13.50*-£15.50.
Open: All Year (not Xmas)
Beds: 1F 1D 2T
Baths: 2 Private 2 Shared
ꗽ ⓟ (2) ⚲ ❏ ⌹ ✕ ⅏ Ⓥ 🛈 ☕ ⚕

The White Knight Luggage Link

Coast to Coast
Safe • Flexible • Door to Door • Any Direction
Tel: 0193 766 475
Mobile: 0850 007 062

(0.75m) *Outrigg House*, St Bees, Cumbria, CA27 0AN.
Large, homely, Georgian private house.
Grades: ETB Reg
Tel: **01946 822348** Mrs Moffat.
Rates fr: *£15.00*-**£15.00**.
Open: All Year (not Xmas)
Beds: 1F 1T 1S **Baths:** 1 Shared

Sandwith 2

National Grid Ref: NX9614

Lowther Arms, Dog & Partridge

(On Path) *Tarn Flatt Hall*, Sandwith, Whitehaven, Cumbria, CA28 9UX.
Actual grid ref: NX947146
Comfortable 18th Century working farmhouse.
Tel: **01946 692162** Mrs Telfer.
Rates fr: *£13.50*-**£13.50**.
Open: All Year
Beds: 2T
Baths: 1 Shared
Also £1.50 per person. Also bunkhouse, £3 per bunk,
Open: All Year

(On Path) *Aikbank House*, Sandwith, Whitehaven, Cumbria, CA28 9UG.
C17th cottage and Post Office.
Tel: **01946 695771** Mr Urwin.
Rates fr: *£14.00*-**£14.00**.
Open: All Year (not Xmas)
Beds: 1D 1T
Baths: 1 Shared
Also £2.00 per tent.,
Open: All Year

Whitehaven 3

National Grid Ref: NX9718

Ewe & Lamb, The Chase Hotel, Golden Fleece

(1.25m) *The Cross Georgian Guest House*, Sneckyeat Road, Hensingham, Whitehaven, Cumbria, CA28 8JQ.
In private ground, spectacular views.
Tel: **01946 63716** Mrs Bailey.
Rates fr: *£15.00*-**£15.00**.
Open: All Year
Beds: 2T 2S
Baths: 2 Private 1 Shared

Cleator 4

National Grid Ref: NY0113

Shepherd's Arms (Cleator), Grove Court Hotel

(On Path) *Fell View*, 3 Cleator Gate, Cleator, Cumbria, CA23 3DN.
Actual grid ref: NY015135
Comfortable Georgian house. Home cooking.
Tel: **01946 813394** Mrs Fowler.
Rates fr: *£14.00*-**£14.00**.
Open: Apr to Oct
Beds: 1F 1T 1S
Baths: 1 Shared

(On Path) *Inglenook Cottage*, 37 Main Street, Cleator, Cumbria, CA23 3BU.
Charming, olde worlde, comfortable cottage.
Tel: **01946 813156** Mrs Bradshaw.
Rates fr: *£14.00*-**£14.00**.
Open: All Year (not Xmas)
Beds: 1D 2T 1S
Baths: 2 Shared

(On Path) *Routen Llama Farm*, Cleator, Cumbria, CA23 3AU.
Comfortable farmhouse overlooking Ennerdale Water.
Tel: **01946 861270** Mrs Wakem.
Rates fr: *£18.00*-**£18.00**.
Open: All Year
Beds: 1D **Baths:** 1 Private

Ennerdale Bridge 5

National Grid Ref: NY0715

Fox & Hounds, Shepherds Arms

(On Path) *The Shepherds Arms Hotel*, Ennerdale Bridge, Cleator, Cumbria, CA23 3AR.
Grades: ETB 3 Cr
Tel: **01946 861249**
Mr Whitfield Bott.
Rates fr: *£21.50*-**£21.50**.
Open: All Year
Beds: 3D 2T 1S
Baths: 3 Ensuite 1 Shared
Village centre hotel. Dinner and bar meals. Two day rates with free car park for duration of walk. Luggage transfer arranged.

(On Path) *Low Moor End Farm*, Ennerdale Bridge, Cleator, Cumbria, CA23 3AS.
Actual grid ref: NY075156
Working C17th fell farm.
Tel: **01946 861388**
Mrs Hinde.
Rates fr: *£12.50*-**£15.00**.
Open: Easter to October
Beds: 1D 1T
Baths: 1 Shared
Also £3.00 per tent.,
Open: Easter to October

Ennerdale 6

National Grid Ref: NY0515 to NY1015

Shepherds Arms, Fox & Hounds

(On Path) *The Old Vicarage*, Ennerdale, Cleator, Cumbria, CA23 3AG.
Actual grid ref: NY065156
Lovely old former vicarage.
Grades: ETB Registered
Tel: **01946 861107**
Mrs Lake.
Rates fr: *£16.00*-**£16.00**.
Open: All Year (not Xmas)
Beds: 1F 1D 2T 1S
Baths: 2 Shared

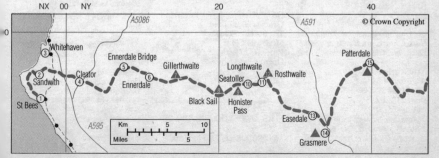

(On Path (other shore) *Beckfoot,* *Ennerdale, Cleator, Cumbria,* *CA23 3AU.*
Actual grid ref: NY102162
Comfortable accommodation, overlooking Ennerdale Lake.
Tel: **01946 861235** Mrs Loxham.
Rates fr: *£15.00*-**£21.00**.
Open: All Year (not Xmas)
Beds: 1F 1D 1T
Baths: 1 Shared
♿ (3) **P** (3) ⊬ ⟷ × ▦ Ⓥ ● ⚡

(0.5m) *How Hall Farm,* *Ennerdale, Cleator, Cumbria,* *CA23 3AU.*
Actual grid ref: NY091164
Traditional Lakeland farm, peaceful location.
Tel: **01946 861266**
Mrs Hardisty.
Rates fr: *£15.00*-**£17.00**.
Open: Mar to Nov
Beds: 1F 1D 1T
Baths: 2 Shared
♿ **P** (3) ⟷ × ▦ Ⓥ ● ⚡

Gillerthwaite 7

National Grid Ref: NY1314

(▲ On Path) *Ennerdale Youth Hostel, Cat Crag, Gillerthwaite,* *Ennerdale, Cleator, Cumbria,* *CA23 2AX.*
Actual grid ref: NY1414
Warden: Ms E Leibowitz.
Tel: **01946 861237**
Under 18: £4.60
Adults: £6.75
Family Bunk Room, Centrally Heated, Showers, Evening Meal (7.00 pm)
Two converted forest cottages, with real log fire, dramatically situated in the peaceful valley, 1 mile East of Ennerdale Water

(On Path 🐾) *High Gillerthwaite Farm, Gillerthwaite, Ennerdale Bridge, Cleator, Cumbria, CA23 3AX.*
Actual grid ref: NY143141
Ideal for walkers and climbers.
Tel: **01946 861673** Mrs Thompson.
Rates fr: *£14.00*-**£15.00**.
Open: All Year (not Xmas)
Beds: 1D 2S
Baths: 1 Shared
♿ (7) **P** (4) 🛏 × ▦ ● ⚡

Black Sail 8

National Grid Ref: NY1912

(▲ On Path) *Black Sail Youth Hostel, Black Sail Hut, Black Sail,* *Ennerdale, Cleator, Cumbria,* *CA23 3AY.*
Actual grid ref: NY1912
Warden: Mr M McIver.
Tel: **01434 381509**
Under 18: £3.75
Adults: £5.50
Showers, Evening Meal (7.00 pm)
A former shepherd's bothy, this is the most isolated, excitingly situated hostel in England!

Honister Pass 9

National Grid Ref: NY2213

(▲ On Path) *Honister Hause Youth Hostel, Honister Pass,* *Seatoller, Keswick, Cumbria,* *CA12 5XN.*
Actual grid ref: NY2213
Warden: Mr A Gibson.
Tel: **017687 77267**
Under 18: £4.60 **Adults:** £6.75
Family Bunk Room, Centrally Heated, Showers, Evening Meal (7.00 pm)
A purpose-built hostel dramatically situated at the summit of Honister Pass, with superb views of Honister Crag. Hearty and substantial food.

Seatoller 10

National Grid Ref: NY2413

(On Path) *Glaramara, Seatoller,* *Keswick, Cumbria, CA12 5XQ.*
Actual grid ref: NY247138
Ideally located country guesthouse.
Tel: **017687 77222** Mrs Moreno.
Rates fr: *£15.00*-**£15.00**.
Open: All Year
Beds: 14T 19S **Baths:** 10 Shared
♿ **P** (40) ⟷ × ▦ Ⓥ ● ⚡

Longthwaite 11

National Grid Ref: NY2514

(▲ On Path) *Longthwaite Youth Hostel, Longthwaite, Borrowdale,* *Keswick, Cumbria, CA12 5XE.*
Actual grid ref: NY2514
Warden: I & S Baker.
Tel: **017687 77257**
Under 18: £5.00 **Adults:** £7.45
Family Bunk Room, Centrally Heated, Showers, Evening Meal (7.00 pm)
Purpose-built hotel constructed from Canadian Red Cedar wood in extensive riverside grounds in the beautiful Borrowdale valley.

Rosthwaite 12

National Grid Ref: NY2514

🍴 ⊞ Langstrath Hotel, Scafell Hotel, Riverside Bar

(0.25m) *Yew Craggs, Rosthwaite,* *Borrowdale, Keswick, Cumbria,* *CA12 5XB.*
H&C all rooms, drying facilities.
Grades: ETB Listed
Tel: **017687 77260**
Mr & Mrs Crofts.
Rates fr: *£15.00*-**£25.00**.
Open: Feb to Nov
Beds: 2F 3D
♿ (6) **P** (6) ⊬ ● ⚡

The lowest *double* rate per person is shown in *italics*.

(On Path) *Gillercombe,* *Stonethwaite Road End,* *Rosthwaite, Borrowdale, Keswick,* *Cumbria, CA12 5XG.*
Actual grid ref: NY257142
Comfortable, homely, clean and good views.
Tel: **017687 77602** Mrs Dunkley.
Rates fr: *£15.00*-**£15.00**.
Open: Feb to Nov
Beds: 1D 3T 1S
Baths: 1 Shared
P (5) ⊬ ▦ ● ⚡
Also ▲ £1.00 per person.
Open: All Year 🔥 Ⓣ ♿

(On Path) *Royal Oak Hotel,* *Rosthwaite, Keswick, Cumbria,* *CA12 5XB.*
Cosy family-run walker's hotel.
Grades: ETB 3 Cr, Comm
Tel: **017687 77214** Mr Dowie.
Rates fr: *£18.00*-**£24.00**.
Open: All Year (not Xmas)
Beds: 4F 4D 2T 2S
Baths: 8 Private 4 Shared
♿ **P** (12) ⟷ 🛏 × ▦ Ⓥ ● ⚡

Easedale 13

National Grid Ref: NY3208

🍴 ⊞ Travellers Rest, Tweedies Bar

(On Path) *Roundhill, Easedale,* *Grasmere, Ambleside, Cumbria,* *LA22 9QR.*
Traditional detached Lakeland stone house.
Grades: ETB Listed
Tel: **015394 35233** Mrs McGlasson
Rates fr: *£17.50*-**£20.00**.
Open: Mar to Dec
Beds: 1F 1D 1T **Baths:** 1 Shared
♿ (3) **P** (6) ⊬ ⟷ ▦ Ⓥ ⚡

(On Path) *Lancrigg Vegetarian Guest House, Easedale, Grasmere,* *Ambleside, Cumbria, LA22 9QN.*
Magnificent view. Delicious vegetarian cuisine. **Grades:** ETB 3 Cr
Tel: **015394 35317** Mr Allen.
Rates fr: *£18.50*-**£18.50**.
Open: All Year
Beds: 2F 15D 2T 2S
Baths: 13 Private
♿ **P** (15) ⟷ 🛏 × Ⓥ ● ⚡

Grasmere 14

National Grid Ref: NY3307

🍴 ⊞ Travellers Rest, Tweedies Bar

(On Path) *Oak Lodge, Easedale* *Road, Grasmere, Ambleside,* *Cumbria, LA22 9QJ.*
Actual grid ref: NY331081
Quietly located stone bungalow.
Grades: ETB Listed
Tel: **015394 35527** Mrs Dixon.
Rates fr: *£17.00*.
Open: Easter to Nov
Beds: 1D 1T
Baths: 1 Shared
♿ (7) **P** (2) ⊬ ⟷ ▦ ♿ Ⓥ ●

(On Path) *Forest Side, Grasmere, Ambleside, Cumbria, LA22 9RN.*
Actual grid ref: NY342081
Elegant refurbished Victorian mansion.
Tel: **015394 35250** Mrs Samson.
Rates fr: *£18.00-£18.00.*
Open: All Year
Beds: 6D 16T 10S
Baths: 24 Private 2 Shared
🛏 🅿 (30) ⅋ 🛏 ✕ 🎹 Ⅴ 🛄 ⚡

(▲ On Path) *Thorney How Youth Hostel, Grasmere, Ambleside, Cumbria, LA22 9QW.*
Actual grid ref: NY3308
Warden: Mr R Wilson.
Tel: **015394 35591**
Under 18: £5.55
Adults: £8.25
Family Bunk Room, Centrally Heated, Showers, Evening Meal (7.00 pm). Parking
An old Lakeland farmhouse, full of character, open as a hostel since 1932 - 1m from centre of Grasmere.

(▲ On Path) *Butterlip How Youth Hostel, Butterlip How, Grasmere, Ambleside, Cumbria, LA22 9QG.*
Actual grid ref: NY3307
Warden: R & A Hamshaw.
Tel: **015394 35316**
Under 18: £5.55
Adults: £8.25
Family Bunk Room, Centrally Heated, Showers, Evening Meal (7.00 pm), Shop, Television, Games Room
Victorian Lakeland stone house in large grounds with rhododendrons and azaleas. Impressive views of the surrounding fells

(0.5m) *Moss Grove Hotel, Grasmere, Ambleside, Cumbria, LA22 9SW.*
Actual grid ref: NY337075
Refurbished Victorian hotel in village centre.
Grades: ETB 3 Cr, Comm, RAC 2 St

Tel: **015394 35251** Mr Wood.
Rates fr: *£24.00-£24.00.*
Open: Feb to Dec
Beds: 3F 5D 4T 2S
Baths: 13 Ensuite 1 Shared
🛏 🅿 (16) 🛄 ✕ 🎹 Ⅴ 🛄 ⚡

(On Path) *Titteringdales, Pye Lane, Grasmere, Ambleside, Cumbria, LA22 9RQ.*
Quietly situated with good views.
Grades: ETB 2 Cr, Comm
Tel: **015394 35439**
Mr Scott.
Rates fr: *£16.00-£18.00.*
Open: All Year
Beds: 6D 1T 1S **Baths:** 6 Private
🛏 (12) 🅿 (7) 🛄 ✕ 🎹

Patterdale   15

National Grid Ref: NY3915

🍴 🍺 White Lion

(On Path) *Patterdale Hotel, Patterdale, Penrith, Cumbria, CA11 0NN.*
Large comfortable hotel.
Grades: ETB 3 Cr, AA 2 St, RAC 2 St
Tel: **017684 82231**
Mr Tonkin.
Rates fr: *£22.50-£22.50.*
Open: Mar to Dec
Beds: 3F 21D 21T 12S
Baths: 57 Ensuite
🛏 🅿 (50) 🛄 🛏 ✕ 🎹 Ⅴ 🛄 ⚡

(▲ On Path) *Patterdale Youth Hostel, Goldrill House, Patterdale, Penrith, Cumbria, CA11 0NW.*
Actual grid ref: NY3915
Warden: Ms M Boothroyd.
Tel: **017684 82394**
Under 18: £6.15
Adults: £9.10
Family Bunk Room, Centrally Heated, Showers, Evening Meal (7.00 pm), Parking
Purpose-built hostel open all day, skilfully designed to blend with the fine scenery to the south of Ullswater

(On Path) *Home Farm, Patterdale, Penrith, Cumbria, CA11 0PU.*
Working hill farm.
Tel: **017684 82370** Mrs Beatty.
Rates fr: *£14.50-£14.50.*
Open: Mar to Nov
Beds: 1D 1T
Baths: 1 Shared
🛏 (10) 🅿 🛏 🎹 Ⅴ 🛄 ⚡

(On Path) *The White Lion Inn, Patterdale, Penrith, Cumbria, CA11 0NN.*
Comfortable, family-run C17th inn.
Grades: ETB Listed
Tel: **017684 82214**
Mr & Mrs McDowall.
Rates fr: *£25.00-£25.00.*
Open: All Year (not Xmas)
Beds: 7 **Baths:** 7 Ensuite
🛏 🅿 🛄 🛏 ✕ 🎹 🛄 ⚡

Burnbanks   16

National Grid Ref: NY5016

(On Path) *Thornthwaite Hall, Burnbanks, Bampton, Penrith, Cumbria, CA10 2RJ.*
C14th working sheep farm - former monastery.
Tel: **01931 713246**
Mrs Lightburn.
Rates fr: *£15.00-£15.00.*
Open: All Year
Beds: 3D **Baths:** 1 Shared
🛏 🅿 🛄 🛏 ✕ 🎹 Ⅴ 🛄 ⚡

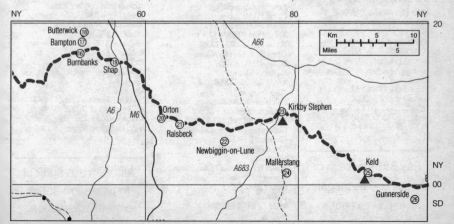

High season,
bank holidays and
special events mean
low availability
everywhere.

Bampton 17

National Grid Ref: NY5118

ᴪ⬛ St Patricks Well Inn, Crown
& Mitre

(On Path 🔴) *St Patricks Well Inn,*
Bampton, Penrith, Cumbria,
CA10 2RQ.
Old Country Inn, coal fires.
Grades: ETB Registered
Tel: **01931 713244** Mrs Barry.
Rates fr: *£17.50-£17.50.*
Open: All Year (not Xmas)
Beds: 1D 2T
Baths: 1Shared
🛇 (14) 🅿 (3) ⬜ ✕ ▥ ⓥ ∎ ✦

Butterwick 18

National Grid Ref: NY5119

(0.5m 🔴) *Fell End Farm,*
Butterwick, Penrith, Cumbria,
CA10 2QQ.
Actual grid ref: NY510195
Comfortable friendly family-run
farmhouse.
Grades: ETB Registered
Tel: **01931 713269** Mrs Sandells.
Rates fr: *£16.50-£18.00.*
Open: All Year
Beds: 1D 1T **Baths:** 1 Shared
🛇 🅿 (4) ⬜ ↟ ▥ ⓥ ∎ ✦

Shap 19

National Grid Ref: NY5615

ᴪ⬛ Greyhound, The Bull, The
Crown

(On Path) *New Ing Farm,* Shap,
Penrith, Cumbria, CA10 3LX.
Actual grid ref: NY562156
Homely, spacious former coaching
inn.
Tel: **01931 716661** Mrs Kirkby.
Rates fr: *£14.50-£15.00.*
Open: Easter to October
Beds: 2F 3D 3T **Baths:** 3 Shared
🛇 (10) 🅿 (10) ⬜ ▥ ⓥ ∎ ✦

Pay B&Bs by cash or
cheque and be prepared
to pay up front.

(On Path) *Bulls Head Inn,* Main
Street, Shap, Penrith, Cumbria,
CA10 3NG.
Comfortable friendly pub.
Tel: **01931 716678**
Mrs Humphries.
Rates fr: *£17.00-£17.00.*
Open: All Year
Beds: 1F 1T
Baths: 1 Shared
🛇 🅿 (3) ↟ ✕ ▥ ⓥ ✦
Also ⛺ *£2.50 per person.*
Open: All Year ⊤ ⬛ ✕ ᕱ

(0.5m) *Brookfield,* Shap, Penrith,
Cumbria, CA10 3PZ.
Good food. Comfortable. Personal
attention.
Grades: AA 3 Q, Recomm
Tel: **01931 716397**
Mrs Brunskill.
Rates fr: *£16.00-£16.00.*
Open: All Year (not Xmas)
Beds: 3F 1D 1T
Baths: 1 Private 1 Shared
🛇 🅿 (20) ⬜ ✕ ▥ ⓥ ∎ ✦

(On Path 🔴) *Fell House,* Shap,
Penrith, Cumbria, CA10 3NY.
Victorian house incorporating
General Store.
Tel: **01931 716343**
Mr & Mrs Farmer.
Rates fr: *£13.50-£15.50.*
Open: All Year
Beds: 2F 1D 2T 1S
Baths: 3 Shared
🅿 (5) ⬜ ↟ ▥ ∎ ✦

(On Path) *King Arms Hotel,* Main
Street, Shap, Penrith, Cumbria,
CA10 3NU.
Comfortable and friendly accom-
modation.
Grades: ETB Listed
Tel: **01931 716277**
Mrs Collins.
Rates fr: *£18.00-£20.00.*
Open: All Year
Beds: 2F 2D 2T
🛇 🅿 (15) ⬜ ↟ ✕ ⓥ

(On Path 🔴) *Pleasant View,* Shap,
Penrith, Cumbria, CA10 3PD.
Comfortable homely accommoda-
tion, period house.
Tel: **01931 716336** Mrs Rylands.
Rates fr: *£13.00-£13.00.*
Open: All Year (not Xmas)
Beds: 1F 1D 1T 1S
Baths: 1 Shared
🛇 (5) 🅿 (3) ↲ ⬜ ▥ ⓥ ✦

(On Path) *1 The Rockery,* Shap,
Penrith, Cumbria, CA10 3LY.
Actual grid ref: NY564157
Converted C18th coaching inn.
Grades: ETB Reg
Tel: **01931 716340**
Mrs Hicks.
Rates fr: *£15.00-£15.00.*
Open: All Year (not Xmas)
Beds: 1F 1D
Baths: 2 shared
🛇 🅿 (5) ↲ ⬜ ▥ ⓥ
Also ⛺

Orton 20

National Grid Ref: NY6208

ᴪ⬛ The George Hotel

(On Path 🔴) *Berwyn House,*
Orton, Penrith, Cumbria, CA10 3RQ.
Victorian private house.
Tel: **015396 24345** Mrs Dunford.
Rates fr: *£15.00-£15.00.*
Open: All Year
Beds: 1D 2T **Baths:** 1 Shared
🛇 ⬜ ↟ ✕ ⓥ ∎ ✦

(On Path) *The Vicarage,* Orton,
Penrith, Cumbria, CA10 3RQ.
Actual grid ref: NY624084
Comfortable, good food, working
vicarage.
Grades: ETB Listed, Comm
Tel: **015396 24873** Mrs Levey.
Rates fr: *£15.00-£15.00.*
Open: All Year
Beds: 1D 2T
Baths: 1 Shared
🛇 🅿 (3) ↲ ⬜ ↟ ✕ ▥ ⓥ ∎ ✦

Raisbeck 21

National Grid Ref: NY6407

(On Path) *New House Farm,*
Raisbeck, Orton, Penrith, Cumbria,
CA10 3SD.
Actual grid ref: NY641077
Modern comfortable farmhouse.
Tel: **015396 24324** Mrs Winder.
Rates fr: *£14.00-£14.00.*
Open: All Year
Beds: 2T
Baths: 1 Shared
🛇 🅿 ↲ ⬜ ↟ ✕ ▥ ∎ ✦
Also ⛺ *£2.00 per person.,*
Open: All Year ⊤ ✕ ᕱ

Newbiggin-on-Lune 22

National Grid Ref: NY7005

ᴪ⬛ The Kings Head

(On Path) *Bents Farm,* Newbiggin-
on-Lune, Kirkby Stephen, Cumbria,
CA17 4NX.
Actual grid ref: NY7005
Tel: **015396 23681** Mrs Ousby.
Rates fr: *£14.00-£15.00.*
Open: All Year
Beds: 2F 1D
Baths: 2 Shared
🛇 🅿 ⬜ ↟ ✕ ⓥ ∎ ✦
Also ⛺ *Also bunkhouse,*
£3 per bunk,
Open: All Year ⊤ ᕱ
Working farm on Coast to Coast
walk. Views of Howgill Fells.
Home cooking. One mile from vil-
lage. Excellent walking. Camping
barn for groups, sleeps 12.

All rates are subject
to alteration at the
owners' discretion.

(0.75m) *Tranna Hill, Newbiggin-on-Lune, Kirkby Stephen, Cumbria, CA17 4NY.*
Large, comfortable, Victorian private house.
Grades: ETB Listed
Tel: 015396 23227 Mrs Boustead.
Rates fr: *£16.00-£16.00.*
Open: All Year (not Xmas)
Beds: 1D 1T 1S
Baths: 1 Ensuite 1 Shared
ॐ 🅿 (6) ⌇ 🖵 ✗ Ⅲ. Ⅴ ⓘ ⌁

(0.75m) *Church View Farmhouse, Newbiggin-on-Lune, Kirkby Stephen, Cumbria, CA17 4NS.*
Actual grid ref: NY705053
Charming C17th ex-farmhouse.
Tel: 015396 23283
Mrs Young.
Rates fr: *£14.00-£14.00.*
Open: All Year
Beds: 1F 1D
Baths: 1 Shared
ॐ ⌇ 🖵 ⻌ ✗ Ⅲ. Ⅴ ⓘ ⌁

Kirkby Stephen   23

National Grid Ref: NY7708

|●| 🍺 Kings Arms, Whoop Hall Inn, The Pheasant, The Old Forge Restaurant

(On Path) *Redmayne House, Kirkby Stephen, Cumbria, CA17 4RB.*
Actual grid ref: NY774088
Spacious Georgian home, quiet situation.
Tel: 017683 71441
Mrs Prime.
Rates fr: *£15.00-£15.00.*
Open: All Year
Beds: 1F 1D 1T 1S
Baths: 2 Shared
ॐ 🅿 (2) ⌇ 🖵 ⻌ Ⅲ. Ⅴ ⓘ ⌁

(On Path) *The Old Court House, High Street, Kirkby Stephen, Cumbria, CA17 4SH.*
Converted court house near market square.
Grades: ETB 2 Cr, Comm
Tel: 017683 71061
Mrs Claxton.
Rates fr: *£15.00-£20.00.*
Open: All Year
Beds: 1F 1D 1T
Baths: 2 Private
ॐ (10) 🅿 (2) 🖵 ⻌ ✗ Ⅲ. Ⅴ

(▲ On Path) *Kirkby Stephen Youth Hostel, Fletcher Hill, Market Street, Kirkby Stephen, Cumbria, CA17 7QQ.*
Actual grid ref: NY7708
Warden: Ms C Seddon.
Tel: 017683 71793
Under 18: £5.00
Adults: £7.45
Family Bunk Rooms, Centrally Heated, Showers, Evening Meal (7.00 pm)
Attractive converted chapel, just south of the town square in this interesting old market town in the Upper Eden Valley.

(On Path) *Lyndhurst, 46 South Road, Kirkby Stephen, Cumbria, CA17 4SN.*
Actual grid ref: NY772078
Comfortable Victorian family home.
Grades: ETB Registered
Tel: 017683 71448 Mrs Bell.
Rates fr: *£15.00-£18.00.*
Open: Mar to Nov
Beds: 1F 1D 1T
Baths: 1 Private 1 Shared
ॐ 🅿 (3) ⌇ 🖵 ⻌ Ⅲ. Ⅴ ⌁

(0.25m) *Cold Keld, Fell End, Kirkby Stephen, Cumbria, CA17 4LN.*
Farmhouse offering guided walking holidays.
Grades: ETB 2 Cr
Tel: 015396 23273
Mr & Mrs Trimmer.
Rates fr: *£16.00-£19.00.*
Open: All Year (not Xmas)
Beds: 1F 3D 1T
Baths: 5 Private
ॐ 🅿 (12) ⌇ 🖵 ⻌ Ⅲ. Ⅴ

Mallerstang   24

National Grid Ref: NY7901

|●| 🍺 White Lion

(4m 🚗) *Dalefoot, Mallerstang, Kirkby Stephen, Cumbria, CA17 4JT.*
Actual grid ref: NY7905
C17th farmhouse on working farm.
Grades: ETB Listed
Tel: 017684 72519
Mrs Halliday.
Rates fr: *£15.00-£15.00.*
Open: All Year (not Xmas)
Beds: 1F 1S
Baths: 1 Shared
ॐ 🅿 (2) ⌇ 🖵 ✗ Ⅴ ⓘ ⌁

Keld   25

National Grid Ref: NY8901

|●| 🍺 Tan Hill Inn

(0.25m) *Tan Hill Inn, Keld, Richmond, N. Yorks, DL11 6ED.*
Highest inn in Great Britain.
Tel: 01833 628246
Mrs Baines.
Rates fr: *£19.50-£25.00.*
Open: All Year (not Xmas)
Beds: 2D 5T
Baths: 7 Private
ॐ 🅿 (20) 🖵 ✗ Ⅲ. Ⅴ ⓘ

(▲ 0.25m) *Keld Youth Hostel, Keld Lodge, Keld, Upper Swaledale, Richmond, N. Yorks, DL11 6LL.*
Actual grid ref: NY8900
Warden: Mr L Roe.
Tel: 01748 886259
Under 18: £4.60
Adults: £6.75
Family Bunk Rooms, Centrally Heated, Showers, Evening Meal (7.00 pm), Shop, Television
Former shooting lodge located at the head of Swaledale, surrounded by moorland and waterfalls

(0.75m) *Frith Lodge, Keld, Richmond, N. Yorks, DL11 6EB.*
Actual grid ref: NY891031
Family-run farmhouse accommodation.
Tel: 01748 886489
Mrs Pepper.
Rates fr: *£14.00-£14.00.*
Open: All Year
Beds: 2T
Baths: 1 Shared
ॐ 🖵 ⻌ ✗ Ⅲ. Ⅴ ⓘ ⌁

Gunnerside   26

National Grid Ref: SD9598

|●| 🍺 Kings Head

(On Path) *Rogans Country House, Satron, Gunnerside, Richmond, N. Yorks, DL11 6JW.*
Actual grid ref: SD940977
Exceptional accommodation for the discerning.
Tel: 01748 886414
Mrs Trafford.
Rates fr: *£20.00-£25.00.*
Open: All Year (not Xmas)
Beds: 2D 1T
Baths: 3 Private
ॐ 🅿 (6) ⌇ 🖵 Ⅲ. Ⅴ ⓘ ⌁

Blades   27

National Grid Ref: SD9898

(0.25m 🚗) *Glory Be, Blades, Low Row, Richmond, N. Yorks, DL11 6PS.*
Actual grid ref: SD980985
Luxury, period accommodation, magnificent views.
Tel: 01748 886361
Mrs Jutsum.
Rates fr: *£18.00-£24.00.*
Open: All Year (not Xmas)
Beds: 1T 1S
Baths: 1 Ensuite, 1 Shared
🅿 ⌇ 🖵 Ⅲ. Ⅴ ⓘ ⌁

Low Row   28

National Grid Ref: SD9897

|●| 🍺 Punch Bowl Inn

(🛏 1m) *Low Row Camping Barn, Low Whita Farm, Low Row, Richmond, N. Yorks.*
Actual grid ref: SE003983
Tel: 01629 825850 *Simple barn, sleeps 15. Heart of the fantastic Dales* Mr & Mrs Clarkson.
£3 per person.

(1m) *Punch Bowl Inn, Low Row, Richmond, N. Yorks, DL11 6PF.*
Actual grid ref: SD987984
Informal, hospitable C17th inn.
Tel: 01748 886233
Mr Roe.
Rates fr: *£15.00-£19.00.*
Open: All Year
Beds: 4F 3D 5T 2S
Baths: 5 Private
ॐ 🅿 (20) ✗ Ⅲ. Ⅴ ⓘ ⌁
Also ▲ *£6.00 per person.*

Reeth 29

National Grid Ref: SE0499

|O| ⬛Kings Arms, Black Bull, Buck Hotel

(On Path) *The Olde Temperance,*
Reeth, Richmond, N. Yorks,
DL11 6TB.
Tel: **01748 84401**
Mrs Lord.
Rates fr: *£16.00-£17.00.*
Open: All Year (not Xmas)
Beds: 1D 1T 1S
Baths: 1 Shared
�Ⓟ(2)🛏🍽✕🛁🖥☑🚭♿
Fully modernised guesthouse providing a good range of facilities for walkers in the centre of village. Home cooked food. We always aim to please.

(On Path 🚐**)** *Hackney House,*
Bridge Terrace, Reeth, Richmond,
N. Yorks, DL11 6TW.
Actual grid ref: SE039992
Large Edwardian guesthouse.
Tel: **01748 884302**
Mrs Plant.
Rates fr: *£15.00-£15.00.*
Open: All Year (not Xmas)
Beds: 1F 3D 2T 1S
Baths: 2 Ensuite 1 Shared
♿Ⓟ(4)✖🛁✕🖥☑🚭♿

(On Path) *Arkle House, Mill Lane,*
Reeth, Richmond, N. Yorks,
DL11 6SJ.
Actual grid ref: SE038994
Large Georgian private house.
Tel: **01748 884815**
Mr Simpson.
Rates fr: *£15.00-£20.00.*
Open: All Year (not Xmas)
Beds: 1D 2T
Baths: 2 Private 1 Shared
♿(6)Ⓟ(3)🛁🖥☑🚭♿

(On Path) *The Black Bull, Reeth,*
Richmond, N. Yorks, DL11 6SZ.
C17th coaching inn.
Grades: ETB 2 Cr, Approv
Tel: **01748 884213**
Mrs Sykes.
Rates fr: *£16.00-£16.00.*
Open: All Year
Beds: 3F 5D 1T 1S
Baths: 3 Private 3 Shared
♿🛏✕🖥☑🚭♿

(On Path) *2 Bridge Terrace, Reeth,*
Richmond, N. Yorks, DL11 6TP.
Actual grid ref: SD041991
A welcoming, friendly home.
Tel: **01748 884572** Mrs Davies.
Rates fr: *£14.50-£17.00.*
Open: Easter to Oct
Beds: 1D 1T **Baths:** 1 Shared
♿✖🖥☑🚭♿

Grinton 30

National Grid Ref: SE0498

(▲1.25m) *Grinton Lodge Youth Hostel, Grinton, Richmond, N. Yorks, DL11 6HS.*
Actual grid ref: SD0497
Warden: D & V Lawson.
Tel: **01748 884206**
Under 18: £4.60 **Adults:** £6.75
Family Bunk Room, Centrally Heated, Showers, Evening Meal (7.00 pm), Shop, Television, Games Room, Parking
Originally built as a shooting lodge, high on the moors above Grinton village, with great views of Swaledale and Arkengarthdale

---

All paths are
popular: you are
well-advised to
book ahead

Marrick 31

National Grid Ref: SE0798

(On Path 🚐**)** *Helmsley House,*
Marrick, Richmond, N. Yorks,
DL11 7LQ.
Actual grid ref: SE077979
Quiet C18th Dales farmhouse.
Grades: ETB Listed
Tel: **01748 884351**
Mrs Sutcliffe.
Rates fr: *£15.00-£20.00.*
Open: All Year (not Xmas)
Beds: 2F 1D 1T
Baths: 1 Shared
♿Ⓟ(4)✖🛏✕🖥☑🚭♿
Also ▲ *£2.00 per tent.,*
Open: All Year 🅿🅃🏕✕♿⚲

Hudswell 32

National Grid Ref: NZ1400

|O| ⬛The George & Dragon

(1m 🚐**)** *Holme Farm Cottage,*
Hudswell, Richmond, N. Yorks, DL11 6BJ
Actual grid ref: NZ147002
Peaceful country cottage.
Richmond 2.5 miles.
Tel: **01748 824514** Mrs Farrar.
Rates fr: *£14.50-£15.00.*
Open: All Year
Beds: 1D 1T 1S **Baths:** 2 Shared
Ⓟ(3)✖🖥☑🚭♿

Richmond 33

National Grid Ref: NZ1701

|O| ⬛Black Lion, Turf Hotel, Bishop Blaize, The Castle Hill Restaurant, Holly Hill

(On Path) *Kimber House,*
Lombards Wynd, Richmond,
N. Yorks, DL10 4JY.
Self-contained annexe with patio, garden furniture.
Grades: ETB Listed
Tel: **01748 824105** Mrs Collingburn
Rates fr: *£17.00-£18.00.*
Open: All Year
Beds: 1D 1T **Baths:** 2 Private
♿(0)Ⓟ(3)🛏🖥☑🚭♿

(On Path) *58 Frenchgate,*
Richmond, N. Yorks, DL10 7AG.
Grades: ETB Listed
Tel: **01748 823227** Mrs Fifoot.
Rates fr: *£18.00.*
Open: Easter to Oct
Beds: 1D **Baths:** 1 Private
Ⓟ(1)✖🖥☑🚭♿
Beautiful Georgian house in elegant Frenchgate. Spacious room, comfortable brass bed with cotton sheets. Delicious breakfast served in the conservatory. Breathtaking views and lovely gardens.

(On Path 🚐**)** *The Black Lion Hotel, 12 Finkle Street, Richmond, N. Yorks, DL10 4QB.*
C16th family-run coaching inn, log fires. **Grades:** ETB Reg
Tel: **01748 823121** Mr Foster.
Rates fr: *£19.00-£20.00.*
Open: All Year
Beds: 1F 6D 4T 3S
Baths: 4 Shared
♿Ⓟ(12)🛏🍽✕🖥☑🚭♿

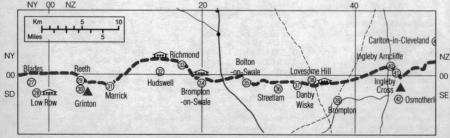

(0.5m) *47 Maison Dieu,*
Richmond, N. Yorks, *DL10 7AU*.
Actual grid ref: NZ176013
Large comfortable Yorkshire
family house.
Tel: **01748 825982** Mr Press.
Rates fr: *£15.00*-**£15.00**.
Open: All Year (not Xmas)
Beds: 1F 1D 1T 1S
Baths: 1 Ensuite 1 Shared
🛏 🅿 (5) ⬜ ☎ 🖤 Ⓥ ⓐ ∜

(On Path) *27 Hurgill Road,*
Richmond, N. Yorks, *DL10 4AR*.
Small, friendly guesthouse.
Grades: ETB Listed
Tel: **01748 824092** Mrs Lee.
Rates fr: *£17.00*-**£20.00**.
Open: All Year (not Xmas)
Beds: 2D 2T 1S
🛏 (10) 🅿 ⬜ 🖤 ⓐ ∜

(🏠 1m) *Richmond Camping
Barn,* East Applegarth Farm,
Richmond, N Yorks, .
Actual grid ref: NZ133016
Tel: **01629 825850**
*Simple barn, sleeps 12, magnifi-
cent views across Swaledale*
Mr & Mrs Atkinson.
£3.00 per person

(On Path) *Hillcrest,* Sleegill,
Richmond, N. Yorks, *DL10 4RH*.
Country Victorian house, large
garden. Tel: **01748 823280**
Mrs Irwin.
Rates fr: *£15.00*-**£15.00**
Open: All Year (not Xmas)
Beds: 1D 1T 1S **Baths:** 1 Shared
🛏 🅿 ⬚ ⬜ ☎ 🖤 Ⓥ ⓐ ∜

(On Path) *West Cottage,* Victoria
Road, Richmond, N. Yorks, *DL10 4AS*.
Large Victorian private house.
Tel: **01748 824046** Mrs Gibson.
Rates fr: *£15.00*-**£18.00**.
Open: Easter to Nov
Beds: 1D 1T
Baths: 1 Ensuite 1 Shared
🅿 (2) ⬚ ⬜ 🖤 ⓐ ⓥ

(On Path) *The Restaurant On The
Green,* 5-7 Bridge Street,
Richmond, N. Yorks, *DL10 4RW*.
Actual grid ref: NZ169007
William and Mary town house.
Grades: ETB Listed, Comm

Tel: **01748 826229**
Mr/Mrs Bennett
Rates fr: *£17.50*-**£29.00**.
Open: All Year
Beds: 1D 1T
🛏 (10) ⬚ ✕ 🖤 Ⓥ ⓐ ∜

Brompton-on-Swale   34

National Grid Ref: SE2199

🍴 🍺 The Tudor Inn

(0.75m) *Holly Villa, Gatherley
Road, Brompton-on-Swale,
Richmond, N. Yorks, *DL10 7JF*.
Modernised, comfortable Georgian
farmhouse.
Tel: **01748 811183**
Mr Coventry.
Rates fr: *£16.00*-**£20.00**.
Open: All Year
Beds: 2T
Baths: 2 Ensuite
🛏 🅿 (8) ⬚ ⬜ ☎ 🖤 Ⓥ

(🏠 0.5m) *Brompton-on-Swale
Camping Barn,* Village Farm,
Brompton-on-Swale, Richmond,
N. Yorkshire, .
Actual grid ref: SE216997
Tel: **01629 825850**
*Simple barn, sleeps 12. A former
byre in the famyard*
Mr & Mrs Wilkin.
£3.00 per person

Bolton-on-Swale   35

National Grid Ref: SE2599

(On Path) *School House,* Bolton-
on-Swale, Richmond, N. Yorks,
DL10 6AQ.
Converted village school.
Tel: **01748 818532**
Mrs Robinson.
Rates fr: *£15.00*-**£15.00**.
Open: Mar to Oct **Beds:** 2T
Baths: 1 Shared ⬚ ⬜ ✕ Ⓥ ⓐ

Streetlam   36

National Grid Ref: SE3198

(0.75m) *Middle Brockholme
Farm,* Streetlam, Northallerton,
N. Yorks, *DL7 0AJ*.
Actual grid ref: SE317978

Comfortable farmhouse, good
food. Tel: **01609 780456**
Mrs Robertshaw.
Rates fr: *£15.00*-**£15.00**.
Open: Easter to Oct
Beds: 1D 2T 1S
Baths: 1 Shared
🛏 🅿 (4) ⬚ ✕ 🖤 ⓐ ∜

Danby Wiske   37

National Grid Ref: SE3398

🍴 🍺 White Swan

(On Path) *The Manor House,*
Danby Wiske, Northallerton, N.
Yorks, *DL7 0LZ*.
Actual grid ref: SE338986
C17th hand-made brick long house.
Grades: ETB Registered
Tel: **01609 774662**
Mrs Sanders.
Rates fr: *£15.00*-**£15.00**.
Open: All Year (not Xmas)
Beds: 1D 1T
Baths: 1 Shared
🛏 🅿 (2) ☎ 🖤 Ⓥ ⓐ ∜

Lovesome Hill   38

National Grid Ref: SE 3699

(🏠 0.3m) *Lovesome Hill
Camping Barn,* Lovesome Hill
Farm, Lovesome Hill,
Northallerton,
N. Yorks, *DL6 2PB*.
Actual grid ref: SE361998
Tel: **01629 825850**
*Simple barn, sleeps 15, former
cornstore in the farmyard*
Mr & Mrs Pearson.
£3.00 per person

(0.25m 🚐) *Lovesome Hill Farm,*
(on A167), Lovesome Hill,
Northallerton, N. Yorks, *DL6 2PB*.
Lovely farmhouse with camping barn
Grades: ETB 2 Cr, Comm
Tel: **01609 772311**
Mrs Pearson.
Rates fr: *£18.00*-**£20.00**.
Open: Easter to Nov
Beds: 1F 1D 1T 1S
Baths: 4 Private
🛏 🅿 ⬚ ✕ 🖤 Ⓥ ⓐ ∜
Also ⛺ *£2.75 per person.,*
Open: All Year ⓡ Ⓣ ♿

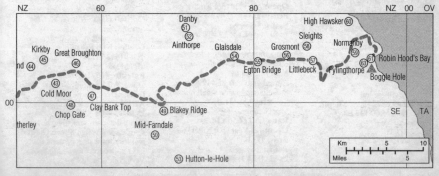

Brompton 39

National Grid Ref: SE3796

⑩ ⌕ Green Tree Inn

(1m ⊕) *Hallikeld House, Long Lane, Brompton, Northallerton, N. Yorks, DL6 2UE.*
Comfortable country setting.
Grades: ETB Registered
Tel: **01609 773613** Mrs Saxby.
Rates fr: £14.00-£14.00.
Open: Easter to Oct
Beds: 1F 1D
ⵎ (0) ⌀ (4) ⌿ ⌸ ⊞ ▯ ∅

(1m) *Hallikeld House, Brompton, Northallerton, N. Yorks, DL6 2UE.*
Comfortable country setting.
Tel: **01609 773613** Mrs Saxby.
Rates fr: £14.00-£14.00.
Open: Easter to Oct
Beds: 1F 1D **Baths:** 1 Shared
ⵎ ⌀ (2) ⊞

Ingleby Arncliffe 40

National Grid Ref: NZ4400

⑩ ⌕ Bluebell Inn

(On Path) *Monks House, Ingleby Arncliffe, Northallerton, N. Yorks, DL6 3ND.*
Unique, comfortable, atmospheric C14th residence.
Tel: **01609 882294** Mrs Backhouse.
Rates fr: £15.00-£15.00.
Open: Easter to Oct
Beds: 1D 1S **Baths:** 1 shared
ⵎ (8) ⌿ ⌸ ⌇ ⊞ ▯ ∅

Ingleby Cross 41

National Grid Ref: NZ4500

⑩ ⌕ The Bluebell Inn

(On Path ⊕) *North York Moors Adventure Ctr, Park House, Ingleby Cross, Northallerton, N. Yorks, DL6 3PE.*
Comfortable sandstone farmhouse set in woodland.
Tel: **01609 882571** Mr Bennett.
Rates fr: £12.00-£12.00.
Open: All Year (not Xmas)
Beds: 2F 1D 1T 2S
Baths: 2 Shared
ⵎ (1) ⌀ (10) ⌸ ⌇ ⌇ ⊞ ▯ ∅
Also ▲ *£1.00 per tent.,*
Open: All Year ⌖ ⏏ ⌘

(On Path) *Blue Bell Inn, Ingleby Cross, Northallerton, N. Yorks, DL6 3NF.*
Friendly village inn.
Tel: **01609 882272** Mr Kinsella.
Rates fr: £15.00-£15.00.
Open: All Year
Beds: 2D 3T
ⵎ ⌀ (20) ⌇ ▯ ∅
Also ▲ *£2.00 per tent.,*
Open: All Year

Osmotherley 42

National Grid Ref: SE4597

⑩ ⌕ Queen Catherine, Golden Lion

(▲ 1m) *Osmotherley Youth Hostel, Cote Ghyll, Osmotherley, Northallerton, N. Yorks, DL6 3AH.*
Actual grid ref: SE4698
Warden: Ms H Ward.
Tel: **01609 883575**
Under 18: £5.00
Adults: £7.45
Family Bunk Room, Central Heating, Showers, Evening Meal (7.00 pm), Shop, Television, Games Room
Surrounded by woodland, the Youth Hostel is fully modernised with excellent facilities, right on the edge of the North Yorks Moors National Park.

(0.75m ⊕) *Foxton Mill, Osmotherley, Northallerton, N. Yorks, DL6 3PZ.*
Actual grid ref: SE452965
Converted C17th water mill.
Tel: **01609 883377** Mrs Russell.
Rates fr: £20.00-£20.00.
Open: All Year (not Xmas)
Beds: 1D 1T
Baths: 1 Private 1 Shared
ⵎ (10) ⌀ (6) ⌿ ⌸ ⌇ ⌇ ⊞ ▯ ∅

(0.75m ⊕) *The Queen Catherine Inn, 7 West End, Osmotherley, Northallerton, N. Yorks, DL6 3AG.*
Family-run warm, friendly, comfortable inn.
Tel: **01609 883209**
Mrs Bell.
Rates fr: £19.97-£19.97.
Open: All Year
Beds: 1D 3T 1S
ⵎ ⌿ ⌸ ⌇ ⌇ ⊞ ▯ ∅

(1m) *Quintana House, Back Lane, Osmotherley, Northallerton, N. Yorks, DL6 3BJ.*
Actual grid ref: SE457974
Detached stone cottage-style residence.
Grades: ETB Listed, Comm
Tel: **01609 883258**
Dr Bainbridge.
Rates fr: £15.00.
Open: All Year (not Xmas)
Beds: 1D 1T
Baths: 1 Shared
ⵎ ⌀ (4) ⌿ ⌸ ⌇ ⊞ ▯ ∅

(1m) *Hemmelstones, Clack Lane, Osmotherley, Northallerton, N. Yorks, DL6 3PP.*
Actual grid ref: SE449971
Stone bungalow on small holding.
Tel: **01609 883313**
Mrs Gardner.
Rates fr: £14.50-£14.50.
Open: All Year (not Xmas)
Beds: 1D 1T
Baths: 2 Shared
ⵎ ⌀ (4) ⌸ ⌇ ⊞ ▯ ∅

Cold Moor 43

National Grid Ref: SE5402

(0.5m ⊕) *Beakhills Farm, Cold Moor, Chop Gate, Stokesley, Middlesbrough, Cleveland, TS9 7JJ.*
Actual grid ref: NZ545024
Comfortable farmhouse.
Tel: **01642 778371**
Mrs Cook.
Rates fr: £14.00-£14.00.
Open: All Year
Beds: 1F 1D 1T
ⵎ ⌀ ⌸ ⌇ ⌇ ⌇ ▯ ∅
Also ▲ *£1.00 per person.,*
Open: All Year ⏏ ⌘

Carlton-in-Cleveland 44

National Grid Ref: NZ3921

⑩ ⌕ Blackwell Ox Inn

(1.25m) *Hill Rise, Carlton-in-Cleveland, Stokesley, Middlesbrough, TS9 7DD.*
Modern comfortable farmhouse.
Tel: **01642 712212**
Mrs Leng.
Rates fr: £14.00-£14.00.
Open: Easter to Nov
Beds: 1D 1T
Baths: 1 Shared
ⵎ (3) ⌀ (3) ⊞ ▯

Kirkby 45

National Grid Ref: NZ5306

(1m ⊕) *Dromonby Hall Farm, Busby Lane, Kirkby, Stokesley, Middlesbrough, Cleveland, TS9 7AP.*
Actual grid ref: NZ532059
Modern, spacious farmhouse.
Grades: ETB 1 Cr, Comm
Tel: **01642 712 312**
Mrs Weighell.
Rates fr: £15.00-£17.50.
Open: All Year (not Xmas)
Beds: 1D 2T
Baths: 1 Ensuite 1 Shared
ⵎ ⌀ (6) ⌿ ⌸ ⊞ ⌘ ▯ ∅

Great Broughton 46

National Grid Ref: NZ5406

⑩ ⌕ Jet Miners, Bay Horse, Wainstones

(2m ⊕) *Hilton House, 52 High Street, Great Broughton, Middlesbrough, Cleveland, TS9 7EG.*
Grades: ETB Listed
Tel: **01642 712526**
Mrs Mead.
Rates fr: £16.50-£16.50.
Open: All Year (not Xmas)
Beds: 1D 2T
Baths: 1 Ensuite, 1 Shared
ⵎ ⌀ (3) ⌿ ⌸ ⊞ ▯ ∅
C18th detached sandstone house set back from High Street. Our full facilities for walkers extend to large collection of walking books. Very comfortable.

(2m) *Ingle Hill, Ingleby Road, Great Broughton, Middlesbrough, Cleveland,* TS9 7ER.
Actual grid ref: NZ548063
Comfortable accommodation viewing Yorkshire Moors.
Tel: **01642 712449** Mrs Sutcliffe.
Rates fr: *£16.00-£16.00.*
Open: All Year (not Xmas)
Beds: 1F 1D 1T
Baths: 2 Ensuite 1 Shared
🅿 (4) ⌇ ⎵ ⊁ 🎁 🗏 🆅 🖊 ✦

(2m 🐾) *Holme Farm, 12 The Holme, Great Broughton, Stokesley, Middlesbrough, Cleveland,* TS9 7HF.
Actual grid ref: NZ546062
Quaint old farmer.
Tel: **01642 712345** Mr Robinson.
Rates fr: *£16.00-£16.00.*
Open: All Year
Beds: 2D 2T **Baths:** 2 Shared
🐾 🅿 ⌇ ⎵ 🗏 🖊 ✦

Clay Bank Top　　47

National Grid Ref: NZ5701

(1m 🐾) *Maltkiln House, Clay Bank Top, Bilsdale, Middlesbrough,* TS9 7HZ.
Actual grid ref: NZ571017
Stone farmhouse in magnificent location.
Tel: **01642 778216**
Mr & Mrs Broad.
Rates fr: *£16.00-£16.00.*
Open: All Year
Beds: 1D 2T **Baths:** 2 Shared
🐾 (8) 🅿 (3) ⌇ ⎵ 🗙 🆅 🖊 ✦

Chop Gate　　48

National Grid Ref: SE5599

⦿❘ 🍴 Buck Inn Hotel

(2m 🐾) *Buck Inn Hotel, Chop Gate, Stokesley, Middlesbrough, Cleveland,* TS9 7JL.
Tel: **01642 778334** Mrs Stewart.
Rates fr: *£21.00.*
Open: All Year
Beds: 1F 1D 4T **Baths:** 6 Private
🐾 🅿 (60) ⎵ 🗙 🗏 🆅 🖊 ✦
Relax in a warm friendly atmosphere. Superb accommodation, all ensuite bedrooms. Panoramic views of beautiful Bilsdale Valley.

Blakey Ridge　　49

National Grid Ref: SE6897

⦿❘ 🍴 The Lion Inn

(On Path) *The Lion Inn, Blakey Ridge, Kirkbymoorside, York, N. Yorks,* YO6 6LQ.
Actual grid ref: SE679997
C16th inn. Breathtaking views.
Tel: **01751 417320** Mr Croosland.
Rates fr: *£15.50-£15.50.*
Open: All Year **Beds:** 3F 6D 1T
Baths: 7 Private 3 Shared
🐾 🅿 (150) ⌇ ⎵ ⊁ 🗙 🗏 🖐 🆅 🖊 ✦
Also ▲ *£1.00 per tent.*

(On Path) *High Blakey House, Blakey Ridge, Kirkbymoorside, York, N. Yorks,* YO6 6LQ.
Actual grid ref: SE679997
Unique stonebuilt house - restored ruin.
Tel: **01751 417641** Mrs Ellerington.
Rates fr: *£18.00-£18.00.*
Open: Mar to Nov
Beds: 1D 2T **Baths:** 2 Shared
🅿 (2) ⌇ ⎵ 🗏 🆅 🖊 ✦

Mid-Farndale　　50

National Grid Ref: SE6694

(2m 🐾) *Keysbeck Farm, Mid-Farndale, Kirkbymoorside, York, N. Yorks,* YO6 6UZ.
Old beamed farmhouse.
Tel: **01751 433221**
Mrs Featherstone
Rates fr: *£11.00-£11.00.*
Open: All Year **Beds:** 2D 1T 1S
🐾 🅿 (4) ⊁ 🗙 🆅 🖊

Danby　　51

National Grid Ref: NZ7008

⦿❘ 🍴 Duke of Wellington

(2.5m) *Duke of Wellington, 2 West Lane, Danby, Whitby, N. Yorks,* YO21 2LY.
Grades: ETB 2 Cr, Comm
Tel: **01287 660351** Mr Howat.
Rates fr: *£20.00-£20.00.*
Open: All Year **Beds:** 2F 4D 1T 2S
Baths: 8 Private
🐾 🅿 ⌇ ⎵ ⊁ 🗙 🗏 🆅 🖊 ✦
C18th coaching inn set in tranquil village in the heart of North York Moors. Restaurant open every evening. Access by road or rail

---

The Country Code

Enjoy the countryside and respect its life and work

Guard against all risk of fire

Fasten all gates

Keep your dogs under close control

Keep to public paths across farmland

Use gates and stiles to cross fences, hedges and walls

Leave livestock, crops and machinery alone

Take your litter home

Help to keep all water clean

Protect wild-life, plants and trees

Take special care on country roads

Make no unnecessary noise

Planning a longer stay? Always ask for any special rates.

(2.5m 🐾) *Sycamore House, Danby, Whitby, N. Yorks,* YO21 2NW.
Actual grid ref: NZ688058
C17th farmhouse. Stunning views.
Tel: **01287 660125** Mr Lowson.
Rates fr: *£16.00-£16.00.*
Open: All Year (not Xmas)
Beds: 1F 1D 1T 1S
Baths: 2 Shared
🐾 🅿 (6) ⌇ ⎵ ⊁ 🗙 🗏 🆅 🖊 ✦

(2.5m) *Crag Farm, Danby, Whitby, N. Yorks,* YO21 2LQ.
Warm, comfortable, old farmhouse.
Grades: ETB 2 Cr
Tel: **01287 660279** Mrs Smith.
Rates fr: *£12.00-£20.00.*
Open: Mar to Oct
Beds: 1D
Baths: 1 Private
🐾 🅿 (3) ⌇ ⎵ 🗏 🆅 🖊 ✦

(2.5m) *Botton Grove Farm, Danby Head, Danby, Whitby, N. Yorks,* YO21 2NH.
Large, comfortable, stone-built farmhouse.
Tel: **01287 660284** Mrs Tait.
Rates fr: *£13.00-£13.00.*
Open: May to Feb
Beds: 1D 1T 2S
Baths: 1 Shared
🐾 🅿 (3) ⎵ ⊁ 🗏 🆅 🖊 ✦

Ainthorpe　　52

National Grid Ref: NZ7007

(3.5m 🐾) *Fox & Hounds Inn, Ainthorpe, Danby, Whitby, N. Yorks,* YO21 2LD.
C16th coaching inn.
Tel: **01287 660218** Mrs Dickinson.
Rates fr: *£18.00-£20.00.*
Open: All Year
Beds: 2F 4D 2T 1S
Baths: 2 Shared
🐾 🅿 (40) ⌇ ⎵ 🗏 🆅 🖊 ✦

Hutton-le-Hole　　53

National Grid Ref: SE7089

(6.5m 🐾) *Hammer & Hand Country Guest Hs, Hutton-le-Hole, Kirkbymoorside, York, N. Yorks,* YO6 6UA.
Actual grid ref: SE7190
Georgian house, character and comfort.
Grades: ETB Comm,
RAC High Acclaim
Tel: **01751 417300** Mrs Wilkins.
Rates fr: *£16.00-£18.00.*
Open: All Year (not Xmas)
Beds: 3D 2T
Baths: 3 Ensuite 1 Shared
🐾 (5) 🅿 (3) ⌇ ⎵ ⊁ 🗙 🗏 🆅 🖊 ✦

Glaisdale 54

National Grid Ref: NZ7603

⦿ ◗ Anglers Rest, Ancliffe Arms, Mitre Tavern

(On Path 🐾) Arncliffe Arms Hotel, *Glaisdale, Whitby, N. Yorks,* YO21 2QL.
Actual grid ref: NZ782055
Tel: **01947 897209**
Mr Westwood.
Rates fr: £15.00-**£15.00**.
Open: All Year
Beds: 1F 2D 2T 1S
Baths: 2 Shared
🛏 🅿 ⽥ ⾕ ✕ 🎇 🌣 ⍝ ⚡
Situated on the scenic River Esk, with the railway station and historic Beggars' Bridge nearby. Excellent local walks. Good food - renowned for delicious curries.

(On Path) *The Mitre Tavern,* *Glaisdale, Whitby, N. Yorks,* YO21 2PL.
Actual grid ref: NZ775055
Comfortable quiet inn.
Tel: **01947 897315**
Mrs Brown.
Rates fr: £15.00-**£18.00**.
Open: All Year (not Xmas)
Beds: 1F 1D 1S
Baths: 1 Shared
🛏 (8) 🅿 (18) ✕ 🎇 Ⓥ ⍝ ⚡

(On Path 🐾) *Anglers Rest Inn,* *Glaisdale, Whitby, N. Yorks,* YO21 2QH.
Cosy country inn.
Tel: **01947 897261**
Mrs Baker.
Rates fr: £18.50-**£18.50**.
Open: All Year
Beds: 1F 1D 1T 1S
Baths: 1 Shared
🛏 🅿 (40) ⽥ ⾕ ✕ Ⓥ ⍝ ⚡
Also 🔺 *£3 per person.,*
Open: All Year ⦿ Ⓣ 🎇 ✕ ⚡ 🐌

(On Path 🐾) *The Railway Station,* *Glaisdale, Whitby, N. Yorks,* YO21 2QL.
Working railway station, Esk Valley.
Tel: **01947 987533**
Messrs Silkstone.
Rates fr: £15.00.
Open: Easter to Oct
Beds: 1T
Baths: 1 Ensuite
🅿 (2) ⽥ ⾕ 🎇 Ⓥ ⍝ ⚡

(0.25m) *Hollins Farm, Glaisdale,* *Whitby, N. Yorks,* YO21 2PZ.
Actual grid ref: NZ753042
Comfortable farmhouse B&B.
Tel: **01947 897516**
Mrs Mortimer.
Rates fr: £13.00-**£13.00**.
Open: All Year (not Xmas)
Beds: 1F 1D 1T
Baths: 2 Shared
🛏 🅿 (6) ⽥ ⾕ ✕ Ⓥ ⍝ ⚡
Also 🔺 ,
Open: Mar to Oct ⦿ Ⓣ 🐌

(On Path) *Red House Farm,* *Glaisdale, Whitby, N. Yorks,* YO21 2PZ.
Actual grid ref: NZ773048
Listed Georgian farmhouse, tastefully refurbished.
Tel: **01947 87242** Mr Spashett.
Rates fr: £18.00-**£18.00**.
Open: All Year
Beds: 1F 2D 1T 1S
Baths: 4 Private 1 Shared
🛏 (5) 🅿 (4) ✕ ⽥ ⾕ ✕ 🎇 ⍝ ⚡

(0.25m) *Sycamore Dell, Glaisdale,* *Whitby, N. Yorks,* YO21 2PZ.
Actual grid ref: NZ769047
Comfortable converted C17th barn.
Tel: **01947 87345** Mr & Mrs Hogben.
Rates fr: £14.00-**£14.00**.
Open: Mar to Oct
Beds: 1F 2D 1S
Baths: 1 Shared
🛏 (11) 🅿 (3) ✕ ⽥ 🎇 ⍝ ⚡

Please respect
a B&B's wishes
regarding children,
animals & smoking.

Egton Bridge 55

National Grid Ref: NZ8005

⦿ ◗ Horseshoe Hotel, Postgate Inn

(On Path) *Horseshoe Hotel, Egton* *Bridge, Whitby, N. Yorks,* YO21 1XE.
Comfortable, family-run riverside hotel.
Grades: ETB 3 Cr
Tel: **01947 895245**
Mr & Mrs Mullins.
Rates fr: £19.00-**£26.00**.
Open: All Year (not Xmas)
Beds: 4D 2T
Baths: 3 Private 2 Shared
🛏 🅿 ⽥ ✕ 🎇 Ⓥ ⍝

Grosmont 56

National Grid Ref: NZ8205

⦿ ◗ Station Tavern, Horseshoe

(On Path) *Eskdale, Grosmont,* *Whitby, N. Yorks,* YO22 5PT.
Actual grid ref: NZ825054
Detached Georgian house.
Grades: ETB Listed, Comm
Tel: **01947 895385**
Mrs Counsell.
Rates fr: £15.50-**£15.50**.
Open: Easter to Nov
Beds: 2D 2S
Baths: 1 Shared
🛏 🅿 (4) ⽥ ⾕ 🎇 ⍝ ⚡

(On Path) *Woodside, Front Street,* *Grosmont, Whitby, N. Yorks,* YO22 5PF.
Actual grid ref: NZ830052
Friendly family home. Delightful views.
Tel: **01947 85205** Mrs Beesley.
Rates fr: £16.00-**£16.00**.
Open: All Year
Beds: 2T 1S
Baths: 1 Shared
🛏 🅿 (3) ⽥ ⾕ 🎇 ⍝ ⚡
Also 🔺 ,
Open: All Year ⦿ Ⓣ 🎇 ✕ ⚡ 🐌

Littlebeck 57

National Grid Ref: NZ8805

⦿ ◗ Plough Inn

(On Path 🐾) *The Old Mill,* *Littlebeck, Whitby, N. Yorks,* YO22 5HA.
Actual grid ref: NZ879050
Converted mill house.
Tel: **01947 810442** Mrs Hall.
Rates fr: £16.00-**£16.00**.
Open: Easter to Oct
Beds: 1D 1T
Baths: 1 Shared
🛏 🅿 (4) ✕ ⽥ ✕ 🎇 Ⓥ ⍝ ⚡

Sleights 58

National Grid Ref: NZ8607

⦿ ◗ Plough Inn (Sleights)

(0.5m) *Inkwells Guest House,* *1 Eskdaleside, Sleights, Whitby,* *N. Yorks,* YO22 5EP.
Actual grid ref: NZ865068
Stone-built converted village school..
Tel: **01947 810959**
Mr & Mrs Thompson.
Rates fr: £15.00-**£15.00**.
Open: All Year
Beds: 2D 1T 1S
Baths: 1 Shared
🛏 (4) 🅿 (3) ✕ ⽥ ⾕ 🎇 Ⓥ ⚡

Normanby 59

National Grid Ref: NZ9206

(On Path) *The Ridings, Normanby,* *Whitby, N. Yorks,* YO22 4PS.
Comfortable country guesthouse, superb views.
Grades: ETB Registered
Tel: **01947 880016** MrS Cook.
Rates fr: £17.50-**£17.50**.
Open: All Year (not Xmas)
Beds: 2D 1T
Baths: £ Private
🛏 (5) 🅿 (10) ⽥ 🎇 ⍝ ⚡

---

taking your dog?
book in advance only
with owners who
accept dogs (🐾)

High Hawsker 60

National Grid Ref: NZ9207

🍴 🍺 Hare & Hounds Pub

(On Path) **York House Private Hotel**, High Hawsker, Whitby, N. Yorks, *YO22 4LW*.
Small modernised Edwardian private hotel.
Grades: ETB 3 Cr, RAC High Acclaim
Tel: 01947 880314
Mr & Mrs Walley.
Rates fr: *£22.00*-**£22.00**.
Open: Easter to Oct
Beds: 4T
Baths: 4 Ensuite
🅿 (6) ⊬ 🛏 ✕ 🖵 🎥 🛆 ⬧

(0.5m) **Old Blacksmiths Arms**, High Hawsker, Whitby, N. Yorks, *YO22 4LH*.
Actual grid ref: NZ927075
Converted C17th village inn.
Tel: 01947 880800 Mrs Stubbs.
Rates fr: *£15.50*-**£15.50**.
Open: Easter to Oct
Beds: 1D 1T 1S
Baths: 2 Shared
🖙 (10) 🅿 (4) 🛏 🛏 🖵 🛆 ⬧

Robin Hood's Bay 61

National Grid Ref: NZ9505

🍴 🍺 Bay Hotel, Dolphin Hotel, Victoria Hotel, Grosvenor Hotel

(On Path) **Wayfarer Restaurant**, Robin Hood's Bay, Whitby, N. Yorks, *YO22 4*.
Actual grid ref: NZ952067
Tel: 01947 880240 Mrs Gray.
Rates fr: *£15.00*-**£20.00**.
Open: All Year (not Xmas)
Beds: 2F 1D 1T
Baths: 3 Ensuite, 1 Shared
🖙 (3) 🅿 (3) ⊬ 🛏 🛏 🖵 🛆 ⬧
Cliff top at finish of C/C. Adjacent to main bus route. 50 yards from good beer and food. Treat yourself to the best. You deserve it.

(On Path) **The White Owl**, Station Road, Robin Hood's Bay, Whitby, N. Yorks, *YO22 4RL*.
Large interesting house.
Tel: 01947 880879 Mr & Mrs Higgins.
Rates fr: *£14.50*-**£15.00**.
Open: All Year
Beds: 1F 1D 1T
Baths: 3 Private
🖙 🅿 (3) 🛏 🛏 🖵 🎥 🛆 ⬧

(On Path) **Victoria Hotel**, Robin Hood's Bay, Whitby, N. Yorks, *YO22 4RL*.
Victorian hotel overlooking sea.
Grades: ETB 2 Cr
Tel: 01947 880205 Mr Gibson.
Rates fr: *£27.00*-**£25.00**.
Open: All Year (not Xmas)
Beds: 2F 6D 2T 1S
Baths: 9 Ensuite 2 Shared
🖙 🅿 ✕ 🖵 🎥 🛆

(On Path) **Rosegarth**, Thorpe Lane, Robin Hood's Bay, Whitby, N. Yorks, *YO22 4RN*.
Modern comfortable semi-detached house.
Grades: ETB Listed
Tel: 01947 880578 Mrs Stubbs.
Rates fr: *£15.00*-**£17.00**.
Open: Easter to Nov
Beds: 1D 1T 1S
Baths: 1 Shared
🖙 (11) 🅿 (4) 🛏 🛏 🖵 ⬧

(0.25m) **Streonshalh**, Mount Pleasant South, Robin Hood's Bay, Whitby, N. Yorks, *YO22 4RL*.
Large Victorian house, tastefully decorated.
Tel: 01947 880619 Mrs Paxton.
Rates fr: *£14.50*.
Open: Easter to Oct
Beds: 1F 2D 1T
🖙 ⊬ 🛏 🛏 🖵 🎥 🛆

(On Path) **Meadowfield**, Mount Pleasant North, Robin Hood's Bay, Whitby, N. Yorks, *YO22 4RE*.
Large Victorian house.
Tel: 01947 880564 Mrs Luker.
Rates fr: *£13.00*-**£17.50**.
Open: All Year
Beds: 2D 2T 1S
Baths: 1 Ensuite 1 Shared
🖵 🖵 🎥 🛆 ⬧

(On Path) **Devon House**, Station Road, Robin Hood's Bay, Whitby, N. Yorks, *YO22 4RL*.
Actual grid ref: NZ952054
Small family-run B&B, clean delightful accommodation.
Tel: 01947 880197 Mrs Duncalfe.
Rates fr: *£14.00*-**£14.00**.
Open: All Year (not Xmas)
Beds: 3D **Baths:** 2 Shared
🖙 🅿 ⊬ 🖵 🖵 🛆 ⬧

The lowest *double* rate per person is shown in *italics*.

High season, bank holidays and special events mean low availability *anywhere*.

(On Path) **Muir-Lea Stores**, Robin Hood's Bay, Whitby, N. Yorks, *YO22 4UQ*.
Actual grid ref: NZ952052
C17th smugglers retreat.
Grades: ETB Reg
Tel: 01947 880316 Mrs Leaf.
Rates fr: *£13.00*-**£15.00**.
Open: All Year **Beds:** 3D 1S
🖵 🛏 🖵.

Boggle Hole 62

National Grid Ref: NZ9504

(⛺ On Path) **Boggle Hole Youth Hostel**, Mill Beck, Boggle Hole, Robin Hood's Bay, Whitby, N. Yorks, *YO22 4UQ*.
Actual grid ref: NZ9504
Warden: Mr P Hobson/Ms P Saunders.
Tel: 01947 880352
Under 18: £5.55
Adults: £8.25
Family Bunk Rooms, Centrally Heated, Showers, Evening Meal (7.00 pm), Shop, Security Lockers, Television, Games Room
A former mill in a wooded ravine, Boggle Hole has the North Sea tide coming up to the doorstep and the North York Moors behind

Fylingthorpe 63

National Grid Ref: NZ9404

🍴 🍺 Fylingdales Inn, Victoria Hotel, Grosvenor Hotel

(0.5m) **Croft Farm**, Fylingthorpe, Whitby, N. Yorks, *YO22 4PW*.
Farmhouse and cottage. Panoramic views.
Grades: ETB 2 Cr, Comm
Tel: 01947 880231 Mrs Featherstone.
Rates fr: *£16.00*-**£16.00**.
Open: Easter to Oct
Beds: 1F 1D 1S
Baths: 1 Private 1 Shared
🖙 (5) 🅿 (4) ⊬ 🖵 🖵 🎥

Cotswold Way

Officially 97 miles, the **Cotswold Way** leads south west along the Cotswold escarpment from Chipping Campden in North Gloucestershire to glorious Bath in North Somerset. The steepness of the scarp gives the impression of a coastal rather than an inland path, with wide views over the Severn Vale. The Cotswolds are rightly famous for their English beauty; this route takes in many pretty little villages and interesting historic sites, so be prepared to take detours. Although the **Cotswold Way** is some way off from becoming a National Trail, the voluntary wardens who look after the Cotswold Area of Outstanding Natural Beauty have made sure that the path is well way-marked. Much of the path is across cultivated land, so the usual care must be taken with dogs and gates. This also means that it can be very muddy in wet weather.

Guides (all available from good map shops unless stated):
The Cotswold Way by Richard Sale (ISBN 009 469 1304), published by Constable & Co, £8.99

The Cotswold Way by Anthony Burton (ISBN 1 85410 3172), published by Aurum Press in association with Ordnance Survey, £9.99
The Cotswold Way by Mark Richards (ISBN 01404691 6 8), published by Penguin Books, £5.99

Cotswold Way - a Walker's Guide by Mark Richards, published by Thornhill Press and available only from the RA National office (1/5 Wandsworth Road, London, SW8 2XX, tel. 0171 582 6878), £1.50 (+70p p&p)

Cotswold Way Handbook by RA Glos area (ISBN 0 900613 858), published by the Rambler's Association and available only by post from the Rambler's Association National Office (1/5 Wandsworth Road, London, SW8 2XX, tel. 0171 582 6878), £1.20 (+70p p&p)

Comments on the path to: **Elaine Fletcher**, Cotswold Countryside Service, Planning Dept, Shire Hall, Gloucester, GL1 2TN.

Maps: 1:50000 Ordnance Survey Landranger Series: 150, 151, 162, 163, 172, 173

Chipping Campden   1

National Grid Ref: SP1539

🍴 🍺 The Eight Bells, The Lygon Arms, The Volunteer, The Red Lion, Green Stocks, The Noel Arms, King Arms, Butcher Arms

(0.25m 🚌) *The Bank House*, Mickleton, Chipping Campden, Glos, GL55 6RX.
Period stone built village house.
Grades: ETB 2 Cr, Comm
Tel: 01386 438302 Mrs Billington.
Rates fr: *£17.50-£27.00*.

Open: All Year (not Xmas)
Beds: 1D 2T **Baths:** 3 Ensuite
🅿 (3) 🛏 ❐ 🛋 ✗

(On Path) *Haydon House, Church Street, Chipping Campden, Glos*, GL55 6JG.
Converted dairy/bakehouse, vine-hung courtyard.
Grades: ETB 2 Cr, Comm
Tel: 01386 840275 Mrs Gilmour.
Rates fr: *£22.00-£22.00*.
Open: Apr to Nov **Beds:** 1D 1T 1S
Baths: 2 Ensuite 1 Private
🛏 ❐ 🛋 Ⅴ 🎗 ✗

(On Path) *Sandalwood House, Back Ends, Chipping Campden, Glos*, GL55 6AU.
Actual grid ref: SP143387
Traditional Cotswold house. Peacefully located.
Grades: ETB 2 Cr, Approv
Tel: 01386 840091 Mrs Bendall.
Rates fr: *£20.00-£25.00*.
Open: All Year (not Xmas)
Beds: 1F 1T **Baths:** 2 Private
🐾 (6) 🅿 (5) 🛏 ❐ 🛋 Ⅴ ✗

(On Path) *Weston Park Farm, Dovers Hill, Chipping Campden, Glos*, GL55 6UW.
Traditional Cotswold stone beamed farmhouse.
Grades: ETB 2 Cr

Tel: 01386 840835
Mr Whitehouse.
Rates fr: *£19.00-£25.00*.
Open: All Year **Beds:** 1F 1D
Baths: 2 Ensuite
🐾 🅿 ❐ 🛋 Ⅴ ✗

Broad Campden   2

National Grid Ref: SP1537

🍴 🍺 Bakers Arms

(1m) *The Malt House, Broad Campden, Chipping Campden, Glos*, GL55 6UU.
C16th Cotswold home.
Grades: AA 5 Q, Prem
Tel: 01386 840295 Mr Brown.
Rates fr: *£39.50*.
Open: All Year
Beds: 1F 4D **Baths:** 5 Ensuite
🅿 (8) ❐ 🛏 ✗ 🛋 Ⅴ 🎗 ✗

(1m) *Wyldlands, Broad Campden, Chipping Campden, Glos*, GL55 6UR.
Warm welcome in recommended accommodation.
Grades: ETB Listed, Comm
Tel: 01386 840478 Mrs Wadey.
Rates fr: *£17.00-£20.00*.
Open: All Year (not Xmas)
Beds: 2D 1T
Baths: 1 Private 1 Shared
🐾 🅿 (4) 🛏 ❐ 🛋 Ⅴ 🎗 ✗

Taking your dog?
Book in advance
only with owners who
accept dogs (🐕)

(0.25m) *Marnic, Broad Campden,
Chipping Campden, Glos, GL55 6UR.*
Actual grid ref: SP159378
Family cottage in Cotswold village.
Grades: ETB 2 Cr, High Comm
Tel: 01386 840014
Mrs Rawlings.
Rates fr: *£17.00-£20.00.*
Open: All Year (not Xmas)
Beds: 1F 1D 1T **Baths:** 2 Ensuite
🐕 (5) 🅿 (4) ⊁ 🖵 📺 📟 ✦

Dovers Hill 3

National Grid Ref: SP1339

(On Path 🐕) *Weston Park Farm,
Dovers Hill, Chipping Campden,
Glos, GL55 6UW.*
Farmhouse in magnificent setting.
Grades: ETB 2 Cr
Tel: 01386 840835
Mr Whitehouse.
Rates fr: *£19.00-£25.00.*
Open: All Year (not Xmas)
Beds: 1F **Baths:** 1 Private
🐕 🅿 (20) 🖵 📺 📟 ✦

Broadway 4

National Grid Ref: SP0937

🍴 🍺 Crown & Trumpet, Horse &
Hounds, Broadway Hotel, Swan
Inn, Goblets Wine Bar

(0.75m) *Pennylands, Evesham
Road, Broadway, Worcs, WR12 7DG.*
Actual grid ref: SP0937
Spacious comfortable accommoda-
tion, super breakfasts.

Grades: ETB 1 Cr, AA 3 Q
Tel: 01386 858437
Mrs Brazier.
Rates fr: *£16.00.*
Open: All Year (not Xmas)
Beds: 2D 1T **Baths:** 3 Private
🐕 🅿 (5) ⊁ 🖵 ✕ 📺 🔥 📺 📟 ✦

(0.25m) *The Mill, Snowshill Road,
Broadway, Worcs, WR12 7JS.*
Actual grid ref: SP094365
View over garden, spacious, warm.
Grades: ETB 2 Cr
Tel: 01386 858298 Mrs Verney.
Rates fr: *£25.00-£37.00.*
Open: All Year (not Xmas)
Beds: 1F 2D **Baths:** 3 Ensuite
🐕 (8) 🅿 (3) 📺 📺 ✦

(On Path) *Crown & Trumpet Inn,
Church Street, Broadway, Worcs,
WR12 7AE.*
C17th Cotswold Inn, CAMRA rec-
ommended.
Grades: ETB 3 Cr, Approv
Tel: 01386 853202 Mr Scott.
Rates fr: *£20.00.*
Open: All Year
Beds: 3D 1T **Baths:** 4 Private
🐕 🅿 🖵 🐕 ✕ 📺 📺

(0.25m) *Pye Corner Farm, West
End, Broadway, Worcs, WR12 7JP.*
Working family sheep farm.
Tel: 01386 853740 Mrs James.
Rates fr: *£17.00.*
Open: Easter to Nov
Beds: 1F 1T **Baths:** 2 Private
🐕 (5) 🅿 (4) ⊁ 📺

(On Path) *Olive Branch Guest
House, 78 High Street, Broadway,
Worcs, WR12 7AJ.*
C16th friendly former coaching
inn.
Grades: ETB 3 Cr, AA Recomm,
RAC Acclaim
Tel: 01386 853440 Mr Riley.
Rates fr: *£20.00-£19.50.*
Open: All Year
Beds: 2F 2D 2T 3S
Baths: 6 Ensuite 3 Shared
🐕 🅿 (9) 🖵 📺 📟 ✦

(0.5m) *Whiteacres Guest House,
Station Road, Broadway, Worcs,
WR12 7DE.*
Large Victorian private house.
Grades: ETB 2 Cr, Comm
Tel: 01386 852320
Mrs Richardson.
Rates fr: *£19.00.*
Open: Mar to Oct
Beds: 5D 1T **Baths:** 6 Ensuite
🅿 (8) ⊁ 🖵 📺 ✦

(0.25m 🐕) *Southwold House,
Station Road, Broadway, Worcs,
WR12 7DE.*
Actual grid ref: SP092377
Welcoming Edwardian family
house.
Grades: ETB 2 Cr, Comm
Tel: 01386 853681
Mr & Mrs Price.
Rates fr: *£17.00-£17.00.*
Open: All Year (not Xmas)
Beds: 5D 2T 1S
Baths: 5 Private 2 Shared
🐕 🅿 (8) 🖵 🐕 📺 📺 ✦

(0.5m 🐕) *West Bank, Station
Road, Broadway, Worcs, WR12 7DE.*
Actual grid ref: SP095375
Large Edwardian private house.
Grades: ETB Listed
Tel: 01386 852372 Mrs Renfrew.
Rates fr: *£14.00-£15.00.*
Open: Easter to Nov
Beds: 1F 1T **Baths:** 1 Shared
🐕 🅿 (2) ⊁ 🖵 📺 📺 📟 ✦

Childswickham 5

National Grid Ref: SP0738

(2.5m) *Mount Pleasant Farm,
Childswickham, Broadway, Worcs,
WR12 7HZ.*
Farmhouse set in 350 acres, near
Broadway.
Grades: ETB High Comm
Tel: 01386 853424 Mrs Perry.
Rates fr: *£17.50-£22.00.*
Open: All Year
Beds: 2D 1T 1S **Baths:** 4 Private
🐕 (5) 🅿 (12) ⊁ 🖵 📺

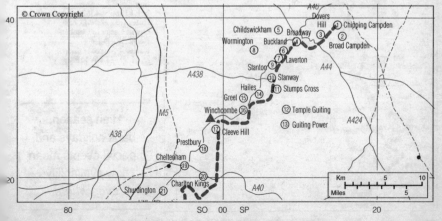

© Crown Copyright

The lowest *double* rate per person is shown in *italics*.

Buckland 6

National Grid Ref: SP0836

¶◄ Crown & Trumpet (Buckland), Swan Inn (Buckland)

(0.25m) *Garretts Farm, Buckland, Broadway, Worcs, WR12 7LY.*
Small Victorian farmhouse in village setting.
Tel: **01386 858699** Mrs Smith.
Rates fr: *£16.00*-**£20.00**.
Open: Mar to Jul & Sep to Dec
Beds: 1T
Baths: 1 Ensuite
ॐ 🅿 (2) ⅙ 🖵 🛏 🛏 🛒 🗓 ⚡

Laverton 7

National Grid Ref: SP0735

¶◄ Snowshill Arms

(0.5m) *Gunners Orchard, Laverton, Broadway, Glos, WR12 7NA.*
Comfortable private house, personal attention.
Tel: **01386 584213** Mrs Stephenson
Rates fr: *£16.00*-**£25.00**.
Open: All Year (not Xmas)
Beds: 1D 1T **Baths:** 1 Shared
ॐ (10) 🅿 (6) ⅙ 🖵 🛒 🗓 ⓥ

Wormington 8

National Grid Ref: SP0336

(3m) *Manor Farm, Wormington, Broadway, Worcs, WR12 7NL.*
Black and white Tudor farmhouse.
Grades: ETB 2 Cr, Comm

Tel: **01386 584302** Mrs Russell.
Rates fr: *£15.00*-**£17.00**.
Open: All Year
Beds: 2D 1T
Baths: 3 Ensuite
ॐ (5) 🅿 (4) 🖵 🛏 🛒

Stanton 9

National Grid Ref: SP0634

¶◄ The Mount Inn (Stanton)

(On Path 🚌) *Shenberrow Hill, Stanton, Broadway, Worcs, WR12 7NE.*
Charming country house, peaceful, comfortable.
Grades: ETB Listed
Tel: **01386 584468**
Mr & Mrs Neilan.
Rates fr: *£18.00*-**£25.00**.
Open: All Year (not Xmas)
Beds: 1F 1D 1T
Baths: 3 Private
ॐ (5) 🅿 (6) 🖵 🛏 ✕ 🛒 ⓥ 🗓 ⚡

Stanway 10

National Grid Ref: SP0632

¶◄ Pheasant Inn, Mount Inn

(On Path) *The Old Bakehouse, Stanway, Cheltenham, Glos, GL54 5PH.*
Lovely family home. Outstanding views.
Tel: **01386 584204** Mrs Garwood.
Rates fr: *£14.00*-**£17.00**.
Open: All Year (not Xmas)
Beds: 2D 1T
Baths: 1 Shared
ॐ 🅿 (12) 🖵 🛒 ⓥ ⚡

Stumps Cross 11

National Grid Ref: SP0730

¶◄ Snowshill Arms

(On Path 🚌) *Stumps Cross Cottage, Stumps Cross, Stanway Hill, Cheltenham, Glos, GL54 5SB.*
Actual grid ref: SP075303
Comfortable country accomodation.
Tel: **01386 584362** Mr Abbott.
Rates fr: *£17.50*-**£17.50**.
Open: Easter to October
Beds: 2F 1D 1S
Baths: 1 Shared
ॐ 🅿 (3) ⅙ 🖵 🛏 ✕ 🛒 ⚡

High season, bank holidays and special events mean low availability *everywhere*.

Temple Guiting 12

National Grid Ref: SP0928

🍴 🍺 Farmers Arms, Ye Old Inn

(1.25m 🚗) *New Barn Farm,*
Temple Guiting, Cheltenham, Glos,
GL54 5RW.
Centrally-heated Cotswold farm-
house.
Grades: ETB Listed
Tel: **01451 850367**
Mr & Mrs Ridout.
Rates fr: £15.00-£17.00.
Open: Feb to Dec
Beds: 2T 1S **Baths:** 2 Shared
🛇 🅿 (3) 🗗 🗯 🛏 ⬛ ♨ ✦

Guiting Power 13

National Grid Ref: SP0924

🍴 🍺 Ye Olde Inne (Guiting
Power)

(1.25m) *The Old Vicarage, Tally*
Ho Lane, Guiting Power,
Cheltenham, Glos, GL54 5TY.
Comfortable Edwardian private
house. **Grades:** ETB 2 Cr
Tel: **01451 850596** Mrs Burrough.
Rates fr: £23.00-£14.00.
Open: Mar to Oct
Beds: 2T **Baths:** 2 Private
🛇 (5) 🅿 (2) ⬛

Hailes 14

National Grid Ref: SP0430

🍴 🍺 Harvest Home

(On Path) *Pilgrim House, Hailes,*
Winchcombe, Cheltenham, Glos,
GL54 5PB.
Early C18th Cotswold stone farm-
house.
Tel: **01242 603011** Mrs Cooper.
Rates fr: £15.00-£20.00.
Open: All Year (not Xmas)
Beds: 2T **Baths:** 1 Shared
🛇 🅿 (6) ⚡ 🗗 ✕ ⬛ ⬛ ✦

(0.5m 🚗) *Ireley Farm, Ireley*
Road, Hailes, Winchcombe,
Cheltenham, Glos, GL54 5PA.
Actual grid ref: SP037304
Tranquil homely old farmhouse.
Grades: ETB Listed
Tel: **01242 602445** Mrs Warmington
Rates fr: £15.00-£15.00.
Open: Easter to Nov
Beds: 1F 1D 1T
Baths: 1 Private 1 Shared
🅿 (4) 🗗 🗯 🛏 ⬛ ♨ ✦

Greet 15

National Grid Ref: SP0230

🍴 🍺 The Harvest Home (Greet)

(1m) *The Homestead, Smithy*
Lane, Greet, Winchcombe,
Cheltenham, Glos, GL54 5BP.
Large private country house.
Tel: **01242 603808** Mrs Bloom.

Rates fr: £15.00-£20.00.
Open: Easter to Nov
Beds: 1F 1D 1T
Baths: 2 Ensuite 1 Shared
🛇 (7) 🅿 (4) 🗗 🗯 🛏 ⬛ ✦

Winchcombe 16

National Grid Ref: SP0228

🍴 🍺 Plaisterers Arms, White Hart,
White Lion, Pilgrims Bistro

(On Path 🚗) *Cleevely Cottage,*
Wadfield Farm, Corndean Lane,
Winchcombe, Cheltenham, Glos,
GL54 5AL.
Actual grid ref: SP022266
Grades: ETB Listed
Tel: **01242 602059** Mrs Rand.
Rates fr: £15.00-£16.00.
Open: All Year (not Xmas)
Beds: 1F 1D 1T
Baths: 1 Shared
🛇 🅿 (4) 🗗 🗯 ✕ ⬛ ⬛ ♨ ✦
Half timbered Cotswold stone
house on working 350 acre fam
overlooking Winchcombe and
Sudeley. Cotswold Way. B&B.
E.Meal, ETB and Rambler's
Recommended. TV Lounge.

(On Path) *Gower House,*
16 North Street, Winchcombe,
Cheltenham, Glos, GL54 5LH.
C17th town house near shops.
Grades: ETB 2 Cr
Tel: **01242 602616** Mrs Simmonds.
Rates fr: £16.00-£20.00.
Open: All Year (not Xmas)
Beds: 1D 2T
Baths: 2 Shared
🛇 🅿 (3) 🗗 ⬛ ⬛ ♨ ✦

(On Path 🚗) *The Plaisterers*
Arms, Abbey Terrace,
Winchcombe, Cheltenham, Glos,
GL54 5U.
Grades: ETB 2 Cr, Comm
Tel: **01242 602358** Mr Gould.
Rates fr: £15.00-£18.00.
Open: All Year
Beds: 1F 2D 1T 1S
Baths: 5 Private
🛇 🗗 🗯 ✕ ⬛ ⬛ ♨ ✦
Also 🅰
Traditional stone Cotswold inn,
beautiful gardens. Extensive menu
(bar snacks, pub lunches, evening
meals) supplemented with daily
specials. Comfortable ensuite
accommodation, range of tradition-
al ales.

(0.25m) *Hill View, Farmcote,*
Winchcombe, Cheltenham, Glos,
GL54 5AU.
Actual grid ref: SP062292
Rural farm cottage. Magnificent
views.
Tel: **01242 603860 / 602304**
Miss Eayrs.
Rates fr: £16.00-£18.00.
Open: All Year (not Xmas)
Beds: 1D 1T
Baths: 1 Shared
🛇 🅿 (2) ⚡ 🗗 ✕ ⬛ ⬛ ♨ ✦

(1.25m 🚗) *The Dairy Farm*
House, Rushley Lane,
Winchcombe, Cheltenham, Glos,
GL54 5.
Actual grid ref: SP032280
Comfortable converted C18th
Cotswold farmhouse.
Grades: ETB Reg
Tel: **01242 603496** Mrs Fisher.
Rates fr: £16.50-£17.50.
Open: All Year (not Xmas)
Beds: 2T
Baths: 2 Private
🛇 (5) 🅿 (4) ⚡ 🗗 🗯 ⬛ ⓥ ♨ ✦

(1m 🚗) *Manor Farm,*
Winchcombe, Cheltenham, Glos,
GL54 5BJ.
Modernised Cotswold manor on
family farm.
Grades: ETB 2 Cr
Tel: **01242 602423** Messrs Day.
Rates fr: £20.00-£20.00.
Open: All Year (not Xmas)
Beds: 2D 1T
Baths: 3 Ensuite
🛇 🅿 (20) 🗗 ⬛ ✦
Also 🅰 *£5 per tent.,*
Open: All Year 🏠 🛈 💺 ✦ ♿

(On Path 🚗) *Mercia, Hailes*
Street, Winchcombe, Cheltenham,
Glos, GL54 5HU.
500-year-old cottage, lovely views
and garden.
Grades: ETB 2 Cr, Comm
Tel: **01242 602251** Mrs Upton.
Rates fr: £18.00-£20.00.
Open: All Year (not Xmas)
Beds: 2D 1T
Baths: 3 Private
🛇 🅿 (3) 🗗 🗯 ⬛ ⓥ ♨ ✦

(0.5m) *Sudeley Hill Farm,*
Winchcombe, Cheltenham, Glos,
GL54 5JB.
Actual grid ref: SP0427
Comfortably furnished C15th farm-
house.
Grades: ETB 2 Cr, High Comm
Tel: **01242 602344** Mrs
Scudamore:
Rates fr: £20.00-£25.00.
Open: All Year (not Xmas)
Beds: 1F 1D 1T
Baths: 3 Private
🛇 🅿 (10) 🗗 ⬛ ⓥ

Cleeve Hill 17

National Grid Ref: SO9726

🍴 🍺 Delabere, Rising Sun

(1.75m 🚗) *Cleyne Hage, Southam*
Lane, Cleeve Hill, Southam,
Cheltenham, Glos, GL52 3NY.
Cotswold stone chalet-style guest-
house.
Grades: ETB 2Cr, Approv
Tel: **01242 518569 / 0850 285338**
Mrs Blankenspoor.
Rates fr: £16.00-£18.00.
Open: All Year
Beds: 1F 1D 1T 2S
Baths: 2 Ensuite
🛇 🅿 (6) ⚡ 🗗 🗯 ⬛ ♿ ♨ ✦

(0.25m 🚌**) *Inglecroft*, *Post Office Lane, Cleeve Hill, Cheltenham, Glos*, GL54 4.**
Large Edwardian private house.
Tel: 01242 673558
Mrs Carter.
Rates fr: *£15.00*-**£15.00**.
Open: All Year
Beds: 2F 1T
Baths: 1 Shared
🛇 🅿 (4) ⌁ ⌂ 🏢 Ⅴ 🏚 ✦

Prestbury   18

National Grid Ref: SO9723

🍴 🍺 Kings Arms

(1.5m 🚌**) *Craven House*, *7 High Street, Prestbury, Cheltenham, Glos*, GL52 3AR.**
Actual grid ref: SO970239
A warm welcome awaits you.
Grades: ETB 2 Cr
Tel: 01242 262377
Mrs Chatterley.
Rates fr: *£16.00*-**£18.50**.
Open: All Year
Beds: 2F 1D 1T
Baths: 2 Private 1 Shared
🛇 🅿 (4) ⌁ ⌂ 🏠 ✕ 🏢 Ⅴ 🏚 ✦

Cheltenham   19

National Grid Ref: SO9422

🍴 🍺 Beamont Arms, London Inn, Malvern Inn, Norwood Arms, Suffolk Arms

(4m) *Hamilton*, *46 All Saints Road, Cheltenham, Glos*, GL52 2HA.
Victorian town house: walking distance of town centre.
Grades: ETB 1 Cr
Tel: 01242 582845
Mrs Lammiman.
Rates fr: *£16.00*-**£18.00**.
Open: All Year (not Xmas)
Beds: 1D 1T
⌁ ⌂ 🏢

(2m) *The Bowler Hat Hotel*, *130 London Road, Cheltenham, Glos*, GL52 6HJ.
Actual grid ref: SO957216
Regency house close to town.
Grades: ETB 2 Cr
Tel: 01242 523614
Mr Barton.
Rates fr: *£15.50*-**£18.00**.
Open: All Year
Beds: 1F 2D 1T 2S
Baths: 2 Private 1 Shared
🛇 (8) 🅿 (8) ⌂ 🏢

(1m) *Crossways Guest House*, *Oriel Place, 57 Bath Road, Cheltenham, Glos*, GL51 7LH.
Grades: ETB 1 Cr, Approv, AA 2 Q
Tel: 01242 527683
Mr Johnson.
Rates fr: *£17.00*-**£17.00**.
Open: All Year
Beds: 3F 1T 2S
Baths: 3 Private 1 Shared
🛇 ⌂ 🏠 🏢 Ⅴ 🏚 ✦

(3m 🚌**) *The Spinney*, *137 Old Bath Road, Cheltenham, Glos*, GL53 7DN.**
Comfortable accommodation in Edwardian house.
Grades: ETB Listed
Tel: 01242 513644 Mrs Brooks.
Rates fr: *£13.00*-**£13.00**.
Open: All Year (not Xmas)
Beds: 3T 1S
Baths: 1 Shared
🛇 🅿 (2) ⌂ 🏠 Ⅴ

Charlton Kings   20

National Grid Ref: SO9620

🍴 🍺 Ryeworth Inn, Reservoir Inn, Duke of York, London Inn, Little Owl

(1m) *Old Stables*, *239a London Road, Charlton Kings, Cheltenham, Glos*, GL52 6YE.
Actual grid ref: SO965209
Former coach house and stables.
Grades: ETB Listed
Tel: 01242 583660
Mr Seeley.
Rates fr: *£14.00*-**£15.00**.
Open: All Year
Beds: 1F 1D 1T
Baths: 1 Ensuite 1 Shared
🛇 🅿 (3) ⌁ ⌂ 🏠 🏢 Ⅴ ✦

(On Path 🚌**) *Langett*, *Dowdeswell Reservoir, Charlton Kings, Cheltenham, Glos*, GL54 4HG.**
Actual grid ref: SO986198
Large bungalow.
Tel: 01242 820192 Mrs Cox.
Rates fr: *£16.00*-**£16.00**.
Open: All Year (not Xmas)
Beds: 1D 1T
Baths: 2 Shared
🛇 (5) 🅿 (10) ⌁ ⌂ 🏠 🏢 Ⅴ 🏚 ✦

Shurdington   21

National Grid Ref: SO9218

🍴 🍺 Bell

(1m) *Allards Hotel*, *Shurdington, Cheltenham, Glos*, GL51 5XA.
Actual grid ref: SO9218
Modern hotel in 3 acres.
Grades: ETB 3 Cr, AA 2 St, RAC 2 St
Tel: 01242 862498 Mr Castle.
Rates fr: *£22.50*-**£37.00**.
Open: All Year
Beds: 2F 5D 4T 1S
Baths: 12 Ensuite
🛇 (1) 🅿 (40) ⌂ ✕ 🏢 Ⅴ 🏚 ✦

The lowest *double*

rate per person is

shown in *italics*.

Cowley   22

National Grid Ref: SO9614

🍴 🍺 Green Dragon Inn

(2m 🚌**) *Manor Barn*, *Cowley, Cheltenham, Glos*, GL53 9NN.**
Converted C19th granary & stables.
Grades: ETB 2 Cr Comm, AA 3 Q
Tel: 01242 870229
Mr & Mrs Roff.
Rates fr: *£15.00*-**£15.00**.
Open: All Year
Beds: 2D 1T
Baths: 1 Ensuite 1 Shared
🛇 (7) 🅿 (6) ⌁ ⌂ 🏠 ✕ 🏢 Ⅴ 🏚 ✦

Little Witcombe   23

National Grid Ref: SO9115

🍴 🍺 Twelve Bells Inn

(0.5m) *Springfield Farm*, *Crickley Hill, Little Witcombe, Gloucester, Glos*, GL3 4TU.
Farmhouse - home produce, guests' lounge.
Grades: ETB Listed
Tel: 01452 863532
Mrs Bickell.
Rates fr: *£26.00*-**£13.50**.
Open: All Year (not Xmas)
Beds: 1F 2D 1S
Baths: 1 Shared
🅿 (8) ⌁ ⌂ 🏢 Ⅴ 🏚 ✦
Also 🏕 **£2.00 per tent.**,
Open: Apr to Oct 🅣 ░ ✦ ♿

Birdlip   24

National Grid Ref: SO9214

(0.25m) *Beechmount*, *Birdlip, Gloucester, Glos*, GL4 8JH.
Family guesthouse, competitive rates.
Grades: ETB 2 Cr, Comm
Tel: 01452 862262
Mrs Carter.
Rates fr: *£14.00*-**£14.50**.
Open: All Year
Beds: 2F 2D 2T 1S
Baths: 2 Ensuite, 1 Shared
🛇 🅿 ⌂ 🏠 🏢 Ⅴ 🏚 ✦

Coopers Hill   25

National Grid Ref: SO8914

🍴 🍺 Royal William

(On Path 🚌**) *The Haven Tea Garden*, *Coopers Hill, Gloucester, Glos*, GL3 4SB.**
Cute little green bungalow.
Tel: 01452 863213
Mrs Hellerman.
Rates fr: *£15.00*-**£15.00**.
Open: Easter to Oct
Beds: 1F 1T
Baths: 1 Shared
🛇 🅿 (2) ⌂ 🏠 Ⅴ 🏚 ✦

Upton St Leonards 26

National Grid Ref: SO8614

🍴 🍺 Kings Head

(1m) *Bullens Manor Farm,*
Portway, Upton St Leonards,
Gloucester, Glos, GL4 8DL.
Comfortable C17th farmhouse.
Grades: ETB 2 Cr
Tel: 01452 616463 Mrs Warner.
Rates fr: *£16.50-£20.00.*
Open: All Year
Beds: 1D 2T
Baths: 3 Private
🛏 🅿 🍽 🛇 🖵 🛋 Ⓥ 🛎 ⚡
Also Ⓐ

When booking,

please mention

Stilwell's National

Trail Companion.

Prinknash 27

National Grid Ref: SO8713

🍴 🍺 Royal Oak, Royal William
(Prinknash), Black Horse

(On Path 🚌) *Castle Lodge, The*
Beacon, Prinknash, Painswick,
Stroud, Glos, GL6 6TU.
Actual grid ref: SO877127
Traditional manor house.
Charming position.
Grades: ETB 2 Cr
Tel: 01452 813603
Mr Cooke.
Rates fr: *£20.00-£25.00.*
Open: All Year
Beds: 1F 1D 1T
Baths: 5 Private
🛏 🅿 🍽 🖵 🛏 🛋 Ⓥ 🛎 ⚡
Also Ⓐ *£2.00 per tent.*
Open: All Year Ⓣ 🏕 ⚡ 🛁

The Camp 28

National Grid Ref: SO9109

🍴 🍺 The Butchers Arms

(3m 🚌) *Bidfield Farmhouse, The*
Camp, Stroud, Glos, GL6 7ET.
Actual grid ref: SO901117
Large, comfortable C17th
Cotswold farmhouse.
Tel: 01285 821263
Mrs Baird.
Rates fr: *£15.00-£18.00.*
Open: Mar to Nov
Beds: 1F 1T
Baths: 2 Ensuite
🛏 🅿 (10) 🖵 🛏 🛋 Ⓥ 🛎 ⚡

Duntisbourne Abbots 29

National Grid Ref: SO9707

🍴 🍺 Highwayman Inn, Golden
Hart Inn, Stirrup Cup

(🔺 4.5m) *Duntisbourne Abbots*
Youth Hostel, Duntisbourne
Abbots, Cirencester, Glos, GL7 7JN.
Actual grid ref: SO9708
Warden: Ms A Harvey.
Tel: 01285 821682
Under 18: £5.00 **Adults:** £7.45
Family Bunk Rooms, Centrally
Heated, Showers, Evening Meal
(7.00 pm), Shop, Games Room
Viotorian rectory in 2-acre
grounds, set in the steep banks of a
Cotswold hillside village. Home
cooking and kitchen garden has
won national acclaim

(4.25m) *Dixs Barn, Duntisbourne*
Abbots, Cirencester, Glos, GL7 7NJ.
Converted barn with lovely views.
Grades: ETB 2 Cr
Tel: 01285 821249 Mrs Wilcox.
Rates fr: *£16.00-£16.00.*
Open: All Year **Beds:** 1D 1T
Baths: 1 Ensuite 1 Private
🛏 🅿 🖵 🛏 🛋 Ⓥ

Brookthorpe 30

National Grid Ref: SO8312

🍴 🍺 Four Mile House

(2m 🚌) *Gilberts, Gilberts Lane,*
Brookthorpe, Gloucester, Glos, GL4
0UH.
Actual grid ref: SO836128
Outstanding Listed half-timbered
manor house.
Grades: ETB 2 Cr, Highly Comm,
RAC High Acclaim
Tel: 01452 812364 Mrs Beer.
Rates fr: *£23.00-£23.00.*
Open: All Year
Beds: 2D 1T 1S
Baths: 4 Private
🅿 (6) 🍽 🖵 🛋 Ⓥ 🛎 ⚡

Painswick 31

National Grid Ref: SO8609

🍴 🍺 Royal Oak (Painswick),
Royal William (Painswick), Black
Horse (Painswick)

(On Path) *Hambutts Mynd, Edge*
Road, Painswick, Stroud, Glos, GL6.
Converted 1700 corn mill.
Grades: ETB 2 C, rRAC Acclaim
Tel: 01452 812352 Mr Warland
Rates fr: *£38.00-£20.00.*
Open: All Year
Beds: 1D 1T 1S
🅿 (3) 🖵 🛏 🛋 Ⓥ ⚡

(On Path) *Thorne, Friday Street,*
Painswick, Stroud, Glos, GL6 6QJ.
Actual grid ref: SO8609
Tudor weaver's house halfway
along Cotswold Way.
Grades: ETB 2 Cr

Tel: 01452 812476 Mrs Blatchley.
Rates fr: *£18.00-£20.00.*
Open: Easter to Oct
Beds: 2T
Baths: 2 Private
🅿 🖵 🛏 🛋 Ⓥ ⚡

(0.25m 🚌) *Upper Doreys Mill,*
Edge, Painswick, Stroud, Glos,
GL6 6NF.
C18th cloth mill by stream.
Grades: ETB 2 Cr
Tel: 01452 812459 Mrs Marden.
Rates fr: *£19.00-£25.00.*
Open: All Year
Beds: 2D 1T
Baths: 3 Private
🛏 🅿 (6) 🍽 🖵 Ⓥ ⚡

(On Path 🚌) *Armany, Golf*
Course Road, Painswick, Stroud,
Glos, GL6 6TJ.
Actual grid ref: SO868107
Quiet family house.
Grades: ETB Listed
Tel: 01452 812242 Mrs Dean.
Rates fr: *£18.00-£20.00.*
Open: All Year (not Xmas)
Beds: 1D 1T
Baths: 1 Private 1 Shared
🛏 (1) 🅿 (5) 🖵 🍽 🛋 Ⓥ 🛎

Edge 32

National Grid Ref: SO8509

🍴 🍺 Edgemoor Inn

(0.5m 🚌) *Wild Acre, Back Edge*
Lane, Edge, Stroud, Glos, GL6 6PE.
Actual grid ref: SO849099
Rural location, ground floor
accommodation.
Tel: 01452 813077 Mrs Sanders.
Rates fr: *£15.00-£18.00.*
Open: Easter to Oct
Beds: 1D 1T
Baths: 1 Private 1 Shared
🛏 🅿 🍽 🖵 🛏 🛋 🛎 ⚡

Haresfield 33

National Grid Ref: SO8110

🍴 🍺 Beacon Hotel

(1m) *Lower Green Farmhouse,*
Haresfield, Stonehouse, Glos,
GL10 3DS.
Actual grid ref: SO811097
C17th Cotswold stone farmhouse.
Grades: ETB 1 Cr
Tel: 01452 728264 Mrs Reed.
Rates fr: *£15.50-£18.00.*
Open: All Year (not Xmas)
Beds: 1F 1D 1T **Baths:** 2 Shared
🛏 🅿 (6) 🖵 🛏 🛋 Ⓥ 🛎 ⚡

Pay B&Bs by
cash or cheque and
be prepared to
pay up front.

Slad   34

National Grid Ref: SO8707

|❍| 🍴 The Woolpack

(3m) *The Old Chapel*, *Slad*,
Stroud, Glos, GL6 7QD.
Converted Victorian old chapel.
Grades: ETB Listed
Tel: **01452 812457**
Mr & Mrs Zajac.
Rates fr: *£17.50*-**£25.00**.
Open: All Year (not Xmas)
Beds: 1D 1T
Baths: 1 Shared
🛌 (10) 🅿 (3) 🖵 🏊

Pitchcombe   35

National Grid Ref: SO8508

|❍| 🍴 Edgemoor Inn

(1m 🚐) *Gable End*, *Pitchcombe*,
Stroud, Glos, GL6 6LN.
C17th cottages overlooking
Pitchcombe village.
Grades: ETB Listed
Tel: **01452 812166** Mrs Partridge.
Rates fr: *£17.50*-**£25.00**.
Open: All Year
Beds: 1F 1D
Baths: 2 Ensuite
🛌 (7) 🅿 (6) 🖵 🗙 🛢 Ⓥ 🔒 ⌀

Randwick   36

National Grid Ref: SO8206

(0.5m 🚐) *Court Farm*, *Randwick*,
Stroud, Glos, GL6 6HH.
Actual grid ref: SO8307
Cotswold C17th beamed farm-
house.
Grades: ETB Listed
Tel: **01453 764210** Mr Taylor.
Rates fr: *£16.00*-**£16.00**.
Open: All Year
Beds: 1F 1D 2T
Baths: 2Shared
🛌 🅿 (6) 🖵 🏊 🗙 🛢 Ⓥ 🔒 ⌀

Stonehouse   37

National Grid Ref: SO8005

|❍| 🍴 Barnaby's Carvery

(On Path 🚐) *Merton Lodge*,
*8 Ebley Road, Stonehouse, Glos,
GL10 2LQ*.
Spacious, impressive 100-year-old
house.
Grades: ETB 2 Cr
Tel: **01453 822018** Mrs Hodge.
Rates fr: *£14.00*-**£14.00**.
Open: All Year (not Xmas)
Beds: 1F 2D
Baths: 1 Private 1 Shared
🛌 🅿 ⌀ 🖵 🛢 Ⓥ

The lowest *double* rate per
person is shown in *italics*.

Stroud   38

National Grid Ref: SO8405

|❍| 🍴 Stirrup Cup, Pelican

(2m) *Downfield Hotel*, *Cainscross
Road, Stroud, Glos, GL5 4HN*.
Imposing comfortable Georgian
house.
Grades: ETB 3 Cr, AA 3 Q,
RAC Acclaim
Tel: **01453 764496** Mr Spandler.
Rates fr: *£14.50*-**£23.00**.
Open: All Year (not Xmas)
Beds: 4F 7D 6T 4S
Baths: 11 Ensuite
🛌 🅿 (21) 🖵 🏊 🗙 🛢 Ⓥ 🔒 ⌀

(4m) *Cairngall Guest House*,
*65 Bisley Old Road, Stroud, Glos,
GL5 1NF*.
Listed Georgian house. Warm,
comfortable.
Grades: ETB 1 Cr, Comm
Tel: **01453 764595**
Mrs Thacker.
Rates fr: *£15.00*-**£16.00**.
Open: Easter to Sep
Beds: 1F 1T
Baths: 1 Shared
🛌 (1) 🅿 (3) 🖵 🛢 ⌀

(2.5m) *Fir Tree House*,
Rodborough, Stroud, Glos, GL5 3UG.
Old Cotswold stone house.
Grades: ETB Listed
Tel: **01453 762591**
Mrs Walwin.
Rates fr: *£13.50*-**£12.50**.
Open: All Year (not Xmas)
Beds: 1D 1T 1S
Baths: 1 Private 1 Shared
🛌 (10) 🅿 (3) 🖵 🛢

Kings Stanley   39

National Grid Ref: SO8103

|❍| 🍴 Kings Head

(0.25m 🚐) *Old Chapel House*,
*Broad Street, Kings Stanley,
Stonehouse, Glos, GL10 3PN*.
Actual grid ref: SO813033
Converted chapel on Cotswold
Way.
Tel: **01453 826289**
Ms Richards Hanna.
Rates fr: *£20.00*-**£20.00**.
Open: All Year (not Xmas)
Beds: 1F 1D 2T 1S
Baths: 2 Ensuite 1 Shared
🛌 (5) 🅿 (4) 🖵 🗙 🛢 Ⓥ 🔒 ⌀

(0.25m) *Nurashell*, *Bath Road,
Kings Stanley, Stonehouse, Glos,
GL10 3JG*.
Actual grid ref: SO811034
Victorian private house. Village
centre..
Tel: **01453 823642** Mrs Rollins.
Rates fr: *£16.00*-**£16.00**.
Open: All Year (not Xmas)
Beds: 1D 1T
Baths: 1Shared
🛌 ⌀ 🏊 🛢 🔒 ⌀

Woodchester   40

National Grid Ref: SO8402

|❍| 🍴 Ram Inn, Royal Oak

(2.5m) *Southfield House*,
Woodchester, Stroud, Glos, GL5 5PA.
Historic mill house.
Grades: ETB 1 Cr
Tel: **01453 873437**
Mrs Richardson.
Rates fr: *£20.00*-**£20.00**.
Open: All Year
Beds: 2T 1S
Baths: 2 Private
🅿 (8) ⌀ 🖵 🛢.

Nympsfield   41

National Grid Ref: SO8000

|❍| 🍴 Rose & Crown Inn

(1m) *Rose & Crown Inn*,
*Nympsfield, Stonehouse, Glos,
GL10 3TU*.
Busy Cotswold village pub.
Grades: ETB 3 Cr, Comm,
AA 3 Q, RAC Acclaim
Tel: **01453 860240**
Mr Smith.
Rates fr: *£24.00*-**£28.00**.
Open: All Year
Beds: 3F 1D
🛌 🅿 🖵 🗙 🛢 Ⓥ ⌀
Also 🔺 Free of charge.,
Open: All Year 🗙 🛌

Nailsworth   42

National Grid Ref: ST8499

(3m) *Windsoredge House*,
*Windsoredge Lane, Nailsworth,
Stroud, Glos, GL6 0NP*.
Actual grid ref: SO841005
Grades: ETB 2 Cr
Tel: **01453 833626**
Mrs Butcher.
Rates fr: *£16.00*-**£21.00**.
Open: All Year
Beds: 1F 1D 1T
Baths: 2 Ensuite, 1 Private
🛌 🅿 (4) ⌀ 🖵 🗙 🛢 Ⓥ ⌀
Clean comfortable accommodation.
Widely acclaimed hospitality and
home cooking. Set in a quiet
secluded hamlet with wonderful
views over Woodchester Park and
the Nailsworth Valley.

🚐 sign means that,
given due notice,
owners will pick you
up from the path
and drop you off with-
in reason.

Crawley Hill 43

National Grid Ref: ST7899

🍴 🍺 Old Crown, Rose & Crown

(0.25m 🚍) **Hill House**, *Crawley Hill, Uley, Dursley, Glos, GL11 5BH.* Quiet beautiful views, Cotswold house.
Tel: **01453 860267** Mrs Kent.
Rates fr: **£16.50-£20.00**.
Open: All Year (not Xmas)
Beds: 1F 1T
Baths: 2 Private
🛏 🅿 ⤢ 🗹 ✕ 🎟 �V 🔌 ✻

Uley 44

National Grid Ref: ST7898

🍴 🍺 The Old Crown Inn, The Green

(0.75m 🚍) **57 The Street**, *Uley, Dursley, Glos, GL11 5SL.* Modernised Cotswold stone house.
Tel: **01453 860305** Mrs Strain.
Rates fr: **£17.50-£20.00**.
Open: All Year (not Xmas)
Beds: 2D 1T
Baths: 1 Ensuite 1 Shared
🅿 (2) ⤢ 🗹 🎟 �V 🔌 ✻

(0.25m) **The Old Crown Inn**, *Uley, Dursley, Glos, GL11 5SN.* Traditional C17th village pub, homecooking.
Grades: ETB 2 Cr
Tel: **01453 860502** Mrs Barrell.
Rates fr: **£20.00-£25.00**.
Open: All Year (not Xmas)
Beds: 1F 2D
Baths: 3 Private
🛏 🅿 (30) 🗹 ✕ 🎟 �V 🔌

Slimbridge 45

National Grid Ref: ST7303

🍴 🍺 Tudor Arms

(⚠ 4m) **Slimbridge Youth Hostel**, *Shepherd's Patch, Slimbridge, Gloucester, Glos, GL2 7BP.*
Actual grid ref: ST730043
Warden: Mr Parsons.
Tel: **01453 890275**
Under 18: **£6.00** Adults: **£9.00**
Family bunk rooms, centrally heated, Showers, Evening Meal (7.00 pm), Shop, Games Room, Car Park *Purpose-built Youth Hostel, with its own pond and wildfowl collection, next to the Sharpness Canal and Sir Peter Scott's famous wildfowl reserve*

All rates are subject to alteration at the owners' discretion.

Cam 46

National Grid Ref: ST7499

(0.5m 🚍) **Green Street Farm**, *Cam Green, Cam, Dursley, Glos, GL11 5HW.*
Actual grid ref: SO761005
1680 farmhouse with indoor pool.
Tel: **01453 542845** Mrs Purnell.
Rates fr: **£17.00-£18.50**.
Open: All Year (not Xmas)
🛏 🅿 (5) ⤢ 🗹 ✕ 🎟 ✻

Dursley 47

National Grid Ref: ST7598

🍴 🍺 Kings Head, The Inn Place

(On Path) **Highlands**, *Stinchcombe Hill Golf Course, Dursley, Glos, GL11 6AQ.*
Grades: ETB 2 Cr
Tel: **01453 542539** Mrs Daley.
Rates fr: **£20.00-£22.00**.
Open: All Year (not Xmas)
Beds: 2D 1T
Baths: 3 Ensuite
🛏 (14) 🅿 (7) ⤢ ✕ 🎟 �V 🔌 ✻

(0.25m) **Claremont House**, *66 Kingshill Road, Dursley, Glos, GL11 4EG.*
Large Victorian family house.
Grades: ETB 2 Cr
Tel: **01453 542018** Mrs Williams.
Rates fr: **£16.00-£15.00**.
Open: All Year (not Xmas/New Year)
Beds: 1F 2D 1T
Baths: 2 Private 1 Shared
🛏 🅿 (8) 🗹 ✕ 🎟 �V 🔌 ✻

(0.25m) **Drakestone House**, *Dursley, Glos, GL11 6AS.*
Charming Listed house, beautifully situated.
Tel: **01453 542140**
Mr & Mrs St John Mildmay.
Rates fr: **£25.00-£30.00**.
Open: Easter to Oct
Beds: 2D 1T
🛏 🅿 (4) ⤢ 🐾 ✕ 🎟 �V ✻

(0.25m) **Stanthill House**, *Uley Road, Dursley, Glos, GL11 4PF.*
Actual grid ref: ST759979
Georgian town house. Large, central.
Tel: **01453 545186** Mrs Waterson.
Rates fr: **£16.50-£16.50**.
Open: All Year (not Xmas)
Beds: 1D 2T
🛏 (12) 🅿 (2) ⤢ 🗹 ✕ 🎟 ✻

North Nibley 48

National Grid Ref: ST7395

🍴 🍺 Black Horse

(On Path 🚍) **Nibley House**, *North Nibley, Dursley, Glos, GL11 6DL.*
Actual grid ref: ST736958
Spacious C17th Georgian manor house.

Tel: **01453 543108** Mrs Eley.
Rates fr: **£16.00-£16.00**.
Open: All Year (not Xmas)
Beds: 1F 1D 1T
Baths: 3 Private
🛏 🅿 (12) ⤢ 🗹 🐾 🎟 🔌 ✻
Also ⚠ £3.00 per person.,
Open: All Year 🏠 🎟 ♨ ✻ ♿

(On Path) **Nibley Cottage**, *40 The Street, North Nibley, Dursley, Glos, GL11 6DW.*
Georgian Listed private house.
Tel: **01453 542794** Mrs Mizen.
Rates fr: **£16.00-£16.00**.
Open: All Year (not Xmas)
Beds: 1D 1T 2S
Baths: 1 Private 1 Shared
🛏 (2) 🅿 (6) ⤢ 🗹 🐾 ✕ 🎟 🔌 ✻

(On Path) **Black Horse Inn**, *North Nibley, Dursley, Glos, GL11 6DT.*
Traditional C16th village inn.
Grades: ETB 2 Cr, Approv
Tel: **01453 546841** Mr & Mrs Hamston.
Rates fr: **£20.00-£27.50**.
Open: All Year
Beds: 1F 2D 3T
Baths: 4 Ensuite 1 Shared
🛏 🅿 🗹 ✕ 🎟 🔌

Wotton-under-Edge 49

National Grid Ref: ST7692

🍴 🍺 Royal Oak

(On Path 🚍) **Church Street Bed & Breakfast**, *3 Church Street, Old Town, Wotton-under-Edge, Glos, GL12 7HB.*
Actual grid ref: ST759934
C16th Grade II Listed accommodation.
Tel: **01453 843272 / 521650**
Ms McIlroy.
Rates fr: **£19.00-£25.00**.
Open: All Year
Beds: 1D 2T
Baths: 2 Shared
⤢ 🗹 🎟 🔌 ✻

(0.25m) **Under-The-Hill-House**, *Adeys Lane, Wotton-under-Edge, Glos, GL12 7LY.*
Grade II Listed Queen Anne house.
Tel: **01453 842557** Mrs Forster.
Rates fr: **£18.00-£18.00**.
Open: Easter to Oct
Beds: 1D 1T
Baths: 1 Shared
🛏 (12) 🅿 (2) ⤢ 🗹 🎟 �& 🔌 ✻

(0.25m 🚍) **Coombe Lodge**, *Wotton-under-Edge, Glos, GL12 7NB.*
Actual grid ref: ST766941
Georgian country house, South Cotswolds.
Grades: ETB 1 Cr, High Comm
Tel: **01453 845057** Mrs Mayo.
Rates fr: **£18.00-£24.00**.
Open: All Year (not Xmas)
Beds: 2D 1T
Baths: 1 Shared
🛏 🅿 (6) ⤢ 🗹 🐾 ✕ 🎟 🔌 ✻

Wortley 50

National Grid Ref: ST7691

(0.25m 🚗) *The Thatched Cottage, Wortley, Wotton-under-Edge, Glos, GL12 7QP.*
Actual grid ref: ST766916
Thatched C14th cottage.
Grades: ETB Registered
Tel: **01453 842776** Mrs Cory.
Rates fr: *£16.00*-**£19.00**.
Open: All Year
Beds: 1D 2T
Baths: 1 Private 1 Shared
ち ☻ (6) ☐ Ⓥ 🏠 ✤

Hillesley 51

National Grid Ref: ST7689

†⊙† ◖ Fleece Inn

(0.25m 🚗) *Fleece Inn, Hillesley, Wotton-under-Edge, Glos, GL12 7RD.*
Grade 2 Listed Country Inn.
Tel: **01453 843189**
Mrs Rollo.
Rates fr: *£15.00*-**£15.00**.
Open: All Year
Beds: 2D 1T
Baths: 1 Shared
ち ☻ (30) ⊬ ☐ 🏠 ✕ 🎞 Ⓥ 🏠 ✤

Old Sodbury 52

National Grid Ref: ST7581

†⊙† ◖ The Bell, The Dog

(On Path) *Dornden Guest House, Church Lane, Old Sodbury, Bristol, Avon, BS17 6NB.*
Actual grid ref: ST756818
Former vicarage, beautiful setting, quiet.
Grades: ETB 2 Cr
Tel: **01454 313325** Mrs Paz.
Rates fr: *£20.00*-**£24.50**.
Open: All Year (not Xmas)
Beds: 5F 2T 2S
Baths: 5 Ensuite, 2 Shared
ち ☻ (15) ☐ 🏠 ✕ 🎞 Ⓥ 🏠 ✤

(On Path) *Crofton, 8 Chapel Lane, Old Sodbury, Bristol, Avon, BS17 6NG.*
Artist's C18th cottage.
Tel: **01454 314288**
Mrs Ford.
Rates fr: *£16.00*-**£17.50**.
Open: Easter to October
Beds: 1F 1D
Baths: 1 Shared
ち (8) ☐ 🏠 🎞 Ⓥ ✤

(On Path) *1 The Green, Old Sodbury, Bristol, Avon, BS17 6LY.*
Actual grid ref: ST753816
Converted C18th Cotswold cottages.
Tel: **01454 314688**
Mr & Mrs Rees.
Rates fr: *£17.00*-**£17.00**.
Open: All Year (not Xmas)
Beds: 1D 1T 3S
Baths: 1 Shared
☻ (4) ⊬ ☐ 🎞 ᴪ ✤

(On Path 🚗) *Dog Inn, Old Sodbury, Bristol, Avon, BS17 6LZ.*
Large cottage.
Tel: **01454 317053**
Mr & Mrs Harris.
Rates fr: *£15.00*-**£17.50**.
Open: All Year
Beds: 2F 1D 1T
Baths: 1 Ensuite 2 Shared
ち ☻ Ⓥ ☐ 🏠 ✕ 🎞 ᴪ
Also ▲ 🏠 Ⓣ 👽 ✕ ✤ ᴪ

(1m 🚗) *Elmgrove, Badminton Road, Old Sodbury, Bristol, Avon, BS17 6LL.*
Large family home with gardens.
Tel: **01454 313276** Mrs Arney.
Rates fr: *£13.00*-**£13.00**.
Open: All Year
Beds: 2T 2S
Baths: 1 Shared
ち ☻ (8) ☐ 🏠 🎞 🏠 ✤

Tormarton 53

National Grid Ref: ST7678

†⊙† ◖ Compass Inn

(0.25m) *Chestnut Farm, Tormarton, Badminton, Avon, GL9 1HS.*
Small Georgian farmhouse.
Tel: **01454 218563** Ms Cadei.
Rates fr: *£19.50*-**£25.00**.
Open: All Year
Beds: 2D 3T
Baths: 3 Private
ち ☻ (8) ☐ 🏠 ✕ 🎞 Ⓥ 🏠 ✤

Cold Ashton 54

National Grid Ref: ST7472

†⊙† ◖ White Hart Inn, The Swan Inn

(On Path) *Whittington Farmhouse, Cold Ashton, Chippenham, Wilts, SN14 8JS.*
Actual grid ref: ST749726
Grades: ETB High Comm
Tel: **01225 891628**
Mrs Hacker.
Rates fr: *£17.50*-**£25.00**.
Open: Feb to Nov
Beds: 2D
Baths: 1 Ensuite
☻ (10) ☐ 🏠 Ⓥ
A peaceful Cotswold farmhouse (circa 1700) on the Cotswold Way. Two double bedrooms with private facilities, tea/coffee tray, colour TV in each room.

(On Path) *High Lanes, Cold Ashton, Chippenham, Wilts, SN14 8JU.*
Actual grid ref: ST7472
C17th 'Cotswold Way' cottage.
Grades: ETB Reg
Tel: **01225 891255**
Mrs Williamson.
Rates fr: *£17.00*-**£20.00**.
Open: Feb to Nov
Beds: 1T 1S
Baths: 1 Shared
ち (8) ⊬ 🎞 ✤

(1m) *Toghill House Farm, Cold Ashton, Wick, Bristol, Avon, BS15 5RT.*
Actual grid ref: ST725730
Warm and cosy C17th farmhouse.
Grades: ETB Listed, Comm
Tel: **01225 891261** Mrs Bishop.
Rates fr: *£19.50*-**£25.00**.
Open: All Year
Beds: 2F 1D
Baths: 3 Private
ち ☻ (20) ☐ 🏠 🎞 Ⓥ 🏠 ✤

(0.5m 🚗) *Whiteways, Tormarton Road, Cold Ashton, Chippenham, Wilts, SN14 8JY.*
Actual grid ref: ST747716
Modern comfortable smallholding.
Tel: **01225 891333** Mrs Pike.
Rates fr: *£17.00*-**£20.00**.
Open: All Year (not Xmas)
Beds: 1F 1D 1T
Baths: 2 Shared
ち ☻ ⊬ ☐ 🎞 🏠 ✤

Marshfield 55

National Grid Ref: ST7773

(3m 🚗) *Knowle Hill Farm, Beeks Lane, Marshfield, Chippenham, Wilts, SN14 8AA.*
Modern,comfortable farmhouse.
Tel: **01225 891503** Mrs Bond.
Rates fr: *£15.00*-**£15.00**.
Open: All year(not Xmas/N. Year)
Beds: 1F 1D 1T
Baths: 1 Ensuite 1 Shared
ち ☻ (3) ☐ 🏠 ✕ 🏠 ✤

Saltford 56

National Grid Ref: ST6866

†⊙† ◖ Crown

(1.5m 🚗) *Prospect Villa, 570 Bath Road, Saltford, Bristol, Avon, BS18 3JN.*
Pleasant, friendly, Victorian guesthouse.
Tel: **01225 873211** Mrs Bryan.
Rates fr: *£15.00*-**£17.00**.
Open: All Year
Beds: 2F 4D 3T 2S
Baths: 1Private 2 Shared
ち ☐ 🏠 🎞 Ⓥ 🏠 ✤

The Grid Reference beneath the location heading is for the village or town - *not* for individual houses, which are shown (where supplied) in each entry itself.

Bath 57

National Grid Ref: ST7464

⛺️ Royal Oak, The Bear, Huntsman, Golden Fleece, Green Park Tavern, The Old Crown

(0.25m) *The Terrace Guest House, 3 Pulteney Terrace, Bath, Avon, BA2 4HJ.*
Small house close to city centre.
Grades: ETB Listed
Tel: 01225 316578 Mrs Gould.
Rates fr: *£15.00*-**£18.00**.
Open: All Year (not Xmas)
Beds: 1F 1D 1S
Baths: 2 Shared
ॐ (6) ☐ ▥ ♥ ✦

(▲ On Path) *Bath Youth Hostel, Bathwick Hill, Bath, Avon, BA2 6JZ.*
Actual grid ref: ST7664
Warden: Mr R Newsun.
Tel: 01225 465674
Under 18: £5.55 **Adults:** £8.25
Family Bunk Rooms, Centrally Heated, Showers, Evening Meal (6.45 pm), Shop, Security Lockers, Television, Games Room
Handsome Italianate mansion, set in beautiful, secluded gardens, with views of historic city and surrounding hills

(On Path) *14 Raby Place, Bathwick Hill, Bath, Avon, BA2 4EH.*
Georgian terrace house. Fine views.
Grades: ETB 1 Cr
Tel: 01225 465120 Mrs Guy.
Rates fr: *£17.50*-**£16.00**.
Open: All Year
Beds: 1F 2D 2T 1S
Baths: 2 Private 2 Shared
ॐ ⊁ ☐ ★ ▥ ♥

(0.25m) *Ashley House, 8 Pulteney Gardens, Bath, Avon, BA2 4HG.*
Actual grid ref: ST757646
Victorian house in quiet location.
Grades: ETB 1 Cr
Tel: 01225 425027 Mrs Pharo.
Rates fr: *£15.00*-**£20.00**.
Open: All Year
Beds: 2F 2D 1T 3S
Baths: 5 Private 2 Shared
ॐ ⊁ ☐ ▥ ♥ ♠

(0.25m) *Wentworth House Hotel, 106 Bloomfield Road, Bath, Avon, BA2 2AP.*
Victorian mansion in own grounds.
Grades: ETB 3 Cr, AA 3 Q, RAC Acclaim
Tel: 01225 339193 Mrs Kitching.
Rates fr: *£23.00*-**£30.00**.
Open: All Year (not Xmas)
Beds: 2F 11D 5T
Baths: 16 Ensuite 2 Shared
ॐ (5) ☐ ★ ✕ ▥

(5m) *Wellsway Guest House, 51 Wellsway, Bath, Avon, BA2 4RS.*
Edwardian house; close shops, laundrette.
Grades: ETB 1 Cr
Tel: 01225 423434 Mrs Strong.
Rates fr: *£14.00*-**£18.00**.
Open: All Year
Beds: 1F 1D 1S
Baths: 1 Shared
ॐ ☐ (2) ☐ ★ ▥ ♥

(0.25m) *Sarnia, 19 Combe Road, Weston, Bath, Avon, BA1 3NR.*
Actual grid ref: ST730656
Superb accommodation, large Victorian home.
Grades: ETB 2 Cr, High Comm, AA 4 Q, Select
Tel: 01225 424159
Mr & Mrs Fradley.

Rates fr: *£19.00*-**£20.00**.
Open: All Year (not Xmas)
Beds: 1F 2D 1T
Baths: 2 Ensuite 2 Private
ॐ ☐ (4) ⊁ ☐ ▥ ♥ ♠ ✦

(1.25m) *The Gardens Guest House, 7 Pulteney Gardens, Bath, Avon, BA2 4HG.*
Large central Victorian guesthouse with parking.
Grades: ETB Listed
Tel: 01225 337642
Mr & Mrs Moore.
Rates fr: *£15.00*-**£20.00**.
Open: All Year
Beds: 2F 3D 3T
Baths: 8 Ensuite
ॐ ☐ (4) ☐ ★ ▥

(1m) *21 Newbridge Road, Bath, Avon, BA1 3HE.*
Actual grid ref: ST731652
Spacious house, informative, friendly hosts.
Grades: ETB 1 Cr
Tel: 01225 314694
Mr & Mrs Shepherd.
Rates fr: *£16.00*-**£18.000**.
Open: Mar to Dec
Beds: 1D 1T 1S **Baths:** 1 Shared
ॐ ⊁ ☐ ▥ ♥ ✦
Also ▲

(On Path) *Lynwood Guest House, 6 Pulteney Gardens, Bath, Avon, BA2 4HG.*
Large Victorian private house.
Grades: ETB 2 Cr, RAC Listed
Tel: 01225 426410 Mrs Cullen.
Rates fr: *£20.00*-**£23.00**.
Open: All Year
Beds: 1F 2D 1T 2S
Baths: 2 Private 1 Shared
☐ (1) ☐ ★ ▥ ✦

Cumbria Way

The **Cumbria Way** provides a great introduction to Lakeland walking for the first-time visitor. So many people first see the Lakes from a car window - this path is the ideal alternative. Most of the path lies in the valleys rather than over the mountains, so the walker is sheltered from the worst of bad weather; and at 70 miles it's one that can be done inside a week. There is a link with the **Coast to Coast Path** as they cross in the Borrowdale Fells.

From the old textile centre of Ulverston, close to the shores of Morecambe Bay, the path meanders northwards, skirting the west side of Coniston Water. At Great Langdale you stroll among the moraines before reaching the craggy slopes that lead to Stake Pass. You come down by Langstrath Beck through the Borrowdale villages to Derwent Water and then Keswick, before crossing to Skiddaw Forest, curving around its eastern base. At this point two alternative routes can be taken, either north westerly to Orthwaite or north easterly up to the Caldbeck Fells and descending to Caldbeck. The concluding walk to historic Carlisle is pleasantly relaxed.

Maps: 1:50000 Ordnance Survey Landranger Series: 85, 90, 97

Guides: *The Cumbria Way* by John Trevelyan (ISBN 1 85568 000 9), published by Dalesman Publishing Co Ltd and also available by post from their offices Clapham, Lancaster, LA2 8EB, (tel. 015242 51225), £3.95 (+ 70p p&p)

Ulverston   1

National Grid Ref: SD2878

¶◀ Rose & Crown

(0.5m 🚌) *Sefton House Hotel,* Queen Street, Ulverston, Cumbria, *LA12 7AF.*
Georgian town house.
Grades: RAC 2 St
Tel: 01229 582190 Mrs Glaister.
Rates fr: *£15.00*-*£20.00.*
Open: All Year (not Xmas)
Beds: 1F 4D 3T 6S
Baths: 10 Ensuite 2 Shared
🛇 🅿 (15) ⌷ ✕ 🎬 Ⓥ ♿ ⌀

The lowest *double* rate per person is shown in *italics*.

Lowick   2

National Grid Ref: SD2986

¶◀ Red Lion, Lowick Bridge

(1m 🚌) *Garth Row, Lowick Green, Lowick, Ulverston, Cumbria, LA12 8EB.*
Traditional Lakeland cottage. Friendly, comfortable.
Grades: ETB Listed
Tel: 01229 885633
Mrs Wickens.
Rates fr: *£12.50*-*£12.50.*
Open: All Year (not Xmas)
Beds: 1F 1D
Baths: 1 Shared
🛇 🅿 (4) ⌷ 🛏 🎬 Ⓥ ♿ ⌀

Subberthwaite   3

National Grid Ref: SD2687

(0.25m) *Crooked Birch Farm House, Subberthwaite, Ulverston, Cumbria, LA12 8EP.*
Actual grid ref: SD265871
Comfortable lakeland farmhouse.
Tel: 01229 885317
Mrs Thorne.
Rates fr: *£16.50*-*£18.00.*
Open: All Year (not Xmas)
Beds: 1F 1D 1T
Baths: 2 Ensuite 1 Shared
🛇 🅿 (4) ⌷ 🛏 ✕ 🎬 Ⓥ ♿ ⌀

Water Yeat   4

National Grid Ref: SD2889

(0.75m 🚌) *Water Yeat Country Guest House, Water Yeat, Ulverston, Cumbria, LA12 8DJ.*
Actual grid ref: SD2888
Converted Lakeland farmhouse, fine cuisine.
Tel: 01299 885306
Mrs Labat.
Rates fr: *£20.00*-*£20.50.*
Open: Feb to Dec
Beds: 1F 2D 2T 2S
Baths: 3 Ensuite 2 Shared
🛇 (4) 🅿 (10) ⌷ ✕ 🎬 Ⓥ ♿ ⌀

Torver   5

National Grid Ref: SD2894

¶◀ Wilson Arms, Torver Inn, Church House Inn

(On Path) *Old Rectory Hotel, Torver, Coniston, Cumbria, LA21 8AX.*
Actual grid ref: SD288946
Beautifully converted Victorian rectory.
Grades: ETB 3 Cr, High Comm, AA 1 St
Tel: 015394 41353
Mr Fletcher.
Rates fr: *£16.50*-*£16.50.*
Open: All Year
Beds: 2F 2D 2T 1S
Baths: 8 Ensuite
🛇 🅿 (10) ⌷ 🛏 ✕ 🎬 Ⓥ ♿ ⌀

(1m) *Brigg House, Torver, Coniston, Cumbria, LA21 8AY.*
Actual grid ref: SD286945
Country house in beautiful setting.
Grades: ETB 2 Cr, High Comm
Tel: 015394 41592
Mrs Newport.
Rates fr: *£19.00*-*£21.00.*
Open: Easter to Nov
Beds: 2D 1T
Baths: 3 Ensuite
🛇 (8) 🅿 (4) ⌷ 🛏 🎬 Ⓥ ♿ ⌀

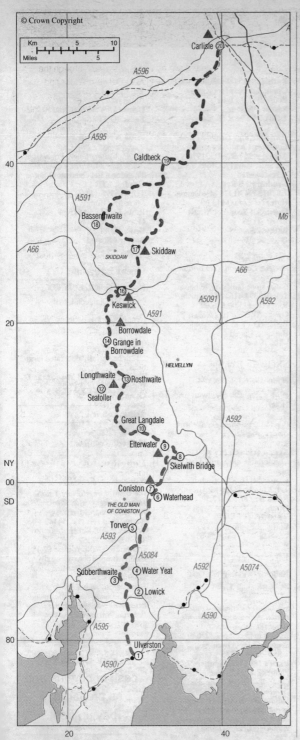

© Crown Copyright

Km 5 10
Miles 5

Carlisle 20

A596

A595

Caldbeck 19

A591

Bassenthwaite 18

A66

A595

A66

17 Skiddaw

SKIDDAW

A5091 A592

16

Keswick A591

Borrowdale

14 Grange in
Borrowdale

HELVELLYN

Longthwaite 13 Rosthwaite

12
Seatoller

Great Langdale
10

Elterwater 9

8

Skelwith Bridge

A592

Coniston 7

THE OLD MAN
OF CONISTON

6 Waterhead

Torver 5

A593

A5084

4 Water Yeat A592 A5074

Subberthwaite
3

2 Lowick

A595

Ulverston 1

A590

M6

A592

A590

20 40

Waterhead   6

National Grid Ref: SD3197

🍴 🍺 The Sun

(0.25m) *Thwaite Cottage,*
Waterhead, Coniston, Cumbria,
LA21 8AJ.
Actual grid ref: SD311977
Beautiful, peaceful character-full
C17th cottage.
Grades: ETB 1 Cr, Comm
Tel: **015394 41367**
Mrs Aldridge.
Rates fr: *£17.00*-**£17.00**.
Open: All Year (not Xmas)
Beds: 1F 2D
🛏 🅿 (3) ✂ 🖵 🍴 🛖 Ⅴ ✦

Coniston   7

National Grid Ref: SD3097

🍴 🍺 Black Bull, Sun Inn, Yewdale
Inn

(On Path) *Yewdale Hotel,*
Coniston, Cumbria, LA21 8LU.
Actual grid ref: SD303975
Grades: ETB 3 Cr, AA 2 St,
RAC 2 St
Tel: **015394 41280**
Mr Barrow.
Rates fr: *£21.95*-**£28.70**.
Open: All Year
Beds: 4F 3D 5T
Baths: 12 Ensuite
🛏 🅿 (6) ✂ 🖵 🍴 ✕ 🛖 Ⅴ 🗋 ✦
Owners long distance walkers.
Family run. Now in 21st year.
Caring, comfortable. Residents
lounge. Well stocked bar. Fresh
cooked meals. Also restaurant
facilities.

(0.25m 🚐) *Black Bull Inn &*
Hotel, 1 Yewdale Road, Coniston,
Cumbria, LA21 8DU.
Traditional C16th olde coaching
inn.
Grades: ETB 3 Cr, High Comm,
AA 2 St, Recomm, RAC 2 St,
Acclaim
Tel: **015394 41335**
Rates fr: *£25.00*-**£25.00**.
Open: All Year
Beds: 2F 10D 3T 2S
Baths: 15 Ensuite
🛏 🅿 (15) 🖵 🍴 ✕ 🛖 Ⅴ 🗋 ✦

🚐 sign means that,
given due notice,
owners will pick you
up from the path

and drop you off

within reason.

(On Path 🐾) *Crown Hotel,*
Coniston, Cumbria, LA21 8EA.
Grades: ETB 1 CrRAC Listed
Tel: 015394 41243 Mr Tiidus.
Rates fr: *£18.00-£20.00.*
Open: All Year (not Xmas)
Beds: 3F 3D 2T
Baths: 1 Ensuite 2 Shared
🛏 (1) 🅿 (30) ❑ ✕ 🔲 Ⓥ 🍴 ⚡
The Crown Hotel is situated in the
picturesque village of Coniston
within easy reach of the famous
lake and the mountains, including
Coniston Old Man (2,633 feet).

(▲ 0.25m) *Coniston (Holly How)*
Youth Hostel, Holly How, Far
End, Coniston, Cumbria, LA21 8DD.
Actual grid ref: SD302980
Warden: Mr S Kruger.
Tel: 015394 41323
Under 18: £5.00 **Adults:** £7.45
Family Rooms, Evening Meal,
Centrally Heated, Grounds
Available for Games, Shop,
Parking
Coniston Holly How is a tradition-
al Lakeland slate building in its
own attractive gardens, dominated
in the distance by the 'Old Man of
Coniston'

(▲ 1m) *Coniston Coppermines*
Youth Hostel, Coppermine House,
Coniston, Cumbria, LA21 8HP.
Actual grid ref: SD289986
Warden: Mr M Blamires.
Tel: 015394 41261
Under 18: £4.60 **Adults:** £6.75
Evening Meal, Shop, Parking (no
coaches), Wet Weather Shelter
Available During Daytime
Small Hostel close to Coniston yet
distant enough to feel isolated, sur-
rounded by Coniston fells, and
once the home of the manager of
the old coppermines

The Country Code

Enjoy the countryside and
respect its life and work

Guard against all risk of fire

Fasten all gates

Keep your dogs under close
control

Keep to public paths across
farmland

Use gates and stiles to cross
fences, hedges and walls

Leave livestock, crops and
machinery alone

Take your litter home

Help to keep all water clean

Protect wild-life, plants and
trees

Take special care on country
roads

Make no unnecessary noise

(0.25m) *Lakeland House,*
Tilberthwaite Avenue, Coniston,
Cumbria, LA21 8ED.
Friendly, family run guesthouse.
Grades: ETB Listed
Tel: 015394 41303
Mr Heywood.
Rates fr: *£15.00-£15.00.*
Open: All Year (not Xmas)
Beds: 2F 2D 1T 1S
Baths: 1 Ensuite 2 Shared
🛏 🅿 (2) ❑ 🕇 ✕ 🔲 Ⓥ 🍴 ⚡

(1m 🐾) *Knipe Ground Farm,*
Coniston, Cumbria, LA21 8AE.
Actual grid ref: SD321976
Peaceful, homely, C16th, sensitive-
ly rejuvenated.
Grades: ETB Reg, AA Listed
Tel: 015394 41221 Mrs Dutton.
Rates fr: *£14.00-£13.00.*
Open: All Year (not Xmas)
Beds: 2D 2S
Baths: 2 Shared
🛏 (6) 🅿 (4) ✂ Ⓥ 🛆 ⚡

(m) *Southview, Tilberthwaite*
Avenue, Coniston, Cumbria,
LA21 8EE.
Large stone built private house.
Tel: 015394 41642 Mr Brown.
Rates fr: *£15.00-£16.00.*
Open: All Year (not Xmas)
Beds: 1D 1T 1S
Baths: 1 Shared
❑ 🔲 Ⓥ 🛆 ⚡

Skelwith Bridge   8

National Grid Ref: NY3403

🍴 🍺 Talbot Bar (Skelwith Bridge
Hotel)

(On Path) *Greenbank,* Skelwith
Bridge, Ambleside, Cumbria, LA22
9NW.
Actual grid ref: NY345033
Comfortable modernised Lakeland
home.
Grades: ETB 2 Cr, Comm
Tel: 015394 33236 Mr Green.
Rates fr: *£17.50-£17.50.*
Open: All Year (not Xmas)
Beds: 2D 1T
Baths: 3 Ensuite
🛏 (5) 🅿 (5) ✂ 🕇 🔲 Ⓥ 🛆 ⚡

Elterwater   9

National Grid Ref: NY3204

🍴 🍺 Britannia Inn

(▲ 0.2m) *Elterwater Youth*
Hostel, Elterwater, Ambleside,
Cumbria, LA22 9HX.
Actual grid ref: NY327046
Warden: Mr N Owen.
Tel: 015394 37245
Under 18: £5.00 **Adults:** £7.45
Family Rooms, Evening Meal,
Centrally Heated, Shop, Parking
Originally converted from farm
buildings, this Hostel is on the edge
of the tiny hamlet of Elterwater -
heart of the classic Lakeland
scenery, and close to the fells

(On Path) *Britannia Inn,*
Elterwater, Langdale, Ambleside,
Cumbria, LA22 9HP.
Actual grid ref: NY328048
400-year-old traditional lakeland
inn.
Grades: ETB 3 Cr, Comm,
AA 3 Q
Tel: 015394 37210
Rates fr: *£17.00-£17.00.*
Open: All Year (not Xmas)
Beds: 9D 3T 1S
Baths: 9 Ensuite 2 Shared
🛏 ❑ 🕇 ✕ 🔲 Ⓥ 🛆 ⚡

(On Path) *Barnhowe, Elterwater,*
Ambleside, Cumbria, LA22 9HU.
Traditional Lakeland stone house.
Grades: ETB 1 Cr, Comm
Tel: 015394 37346
Mr & Mrs Riley.
Rates fr: *£15.50-£15.50.*
Open: Easter to Nov
Beds: 1D 1T 1S
Baths: 1 Shared
🛏 🅿 (7) ✂ 🔲 Ⓥ ⚡

Great Langdale   10

National Grid Ref: NY3006

🍴 🍺 Old Dungeon Ghyll

(0.5m) *Baysbrown Farm,* Great
Langdale, Ambleside, Cumbria,
LA22 9JZ.
Actual grid ref: NY3006
C12th beautifully decorated farm-
house.
Tel: 015394 37300 Mrs Rowand.
Rates fr: *£17.00-£17.00.*
Open: Mar to Oct
Beds: 1F 1D 1T
Baths: 1 Shared
🛏 🅿 (6) ❑ 🕇 ✕ Ⓥ 🛆 ⚡
Also ▲ *£1.80 per person.,*
Open: All Year Ⓣ ♿

Longthwaite   11

National Grid Ref: NY2514

(▲ 0.5m) *Longthwaite Youth*
Hostel, Longthwaite, Borrowdale,
Keswick, Cumbria, CA12 5XE.
Actual grid ref: NY254142
Warden: I & S Baker.
Tel: 017687 77257
Under 18: £5.00 **Adults:** £7.45
Family Bunk Room, Centrally
Heated, Showers, Evening Meal
(7.00 pm)
Purpose-built hotel constructed
from Canadian Red Cedar wood in
extensive riverside grounds in the
beautiful Borrowdale valley.

Pay B&Bs by
cash or cheque and
be prepared to
pay up front.

Seatoller 12

National Grid Ref: NY2413

(On Path) *Glaramara, Seatoller, Keswick, Cumbria, CA12 5XQ.*
Actual grid ref: NY247138
Ideally located country guest house.
Tel: 017687 77222
Mrs Moreno.
Rates fr: *£15.00-***£15.00**.
Open: All Year
Beds: 14T 19S
Baths: 10 Shared
🛇 🅿 (40) ⅙ ✕ 🎟 Ⅵ 🛈 ⚡

Rosthwaite 13

National Grid Ref: NY2514

🍴 🍺 Scafell Hotel, Riverside Bar, Langstrath Inn

(On Path) *Royal Oak Hotel, Rosthwaite, Keswick, Cumbria, CA12 5XB.*
Actual grid ref: NY259148
Traditional friendly walkers' hotel.
Grades: ETB 3 Cr, Comm
Tel: 017687 77214 Mr Dowie.
Rates fr: *£17.00-***£19.00**.
Open: All Year (not Xmas)
Beds: 4F 4D 2T 2S
Baths: 8 Ensuite, 4 Shared
🛇 🅿 (12) 🗗 ✕ 🎟 Ⅵ 🛈 ⚡

(0.25m) *Yew Craggs, Rosthwaite, Borrowdale, Keswick, Cumbria, CA12 5XB.*
H&C all rooms, drying facilities.
Grades: ETB Listed
Tel: 017687 77260
Mr & Mrs Crofts.
Rates fr: *£15.00-***£25.00**.
Open: Feb to Nov
Beds: 2F 3D
🛇 (6) 🅿 (6) ⅙ 🛈 ⚡

(On Path) *Gillercombe, Stonethwaite Road End, Rosthwaite, Borrowdale, Keswick, Cumbria, CA12 5XG.*
Actual grid ref: NY257142
Comfortable, homely, clean and good views.
Tel: 017687 77602
Mrs Dunkley.
Rates fr: *£15.00-***£15.00**.
Open: Feb to Nov
Beds: 1D 3T 1S
Baths: 1 Shared
🅿 (5) ⅙ 🎟 🛈 ⚡
Also ⛺ *£1.00 per person.,*
Open: All Year 🏠 🅣 ♿

(On Path) *Royal Oak Hotel, Rosthwaite, Keswick, Cumbria, CA12 5XB.*
Cosy family-run walker's hotel.
Grades: ETB 3 Cr, Comm
Tel: 017687 77214 Mr Dowie.
Rates fr: *£18.00-***£24.00**.
Open: All Year (not Xmas)
Beds: 4F 4D 2T 2S
Baths: 8 Private 4 Shared
🛇 🅿 (12) 🗗 ✕ 🎟 Ⅵ 🛈 ⚡

Grange-in-Borrowdale 14

National Grid Ref: NY2517

🍴 🍺 Grange Bridge Cottage, Grange Cafe

(0.33m) 🐄 *Scawdel, Grange-in-Borrowdale, Keswick, Cumbria, CA12 5UQ.*
Actual grid ref: NY252175
Modern, friendly, comfortable private house.
Tel: 017687 77271 Mr Reinecke.
Rates fr: *£15.50-***£16.50**.
Open: All Year
Beds: 2D 1T
Baths: 1 Shared
🛇 (7) 🅿 (4) ⅙ 🛏 🐾 🎟 Ⅵ 🛈 ⚡

Borrowdale 15

National Grid Ref: NY2726

(⛰ 1m) *Derwent Water Youth Hostel, Barrow House, Borrowdale, Keswick, Cumbria, CA12 5UR.*
Tel: 017687 77246
Under 18: £5.95 **Adults:** £8.80
Family Rooms, Evening Meal, Licenced, Self Catering Facilities, Laundry Facilities, Shop, Parking, Grounds available for Games, Games, Central Heating
Magnificent 200-year-old mansion overlooking beautiful Derwent Water in lovely Borrowdale

Keswick 16

National Grid Ref: NY2623

🍴 🍺 Two Dogs, Dog & Gun, Skiddaw Hotel, Four in Hand, Pheasant Inn, George Hotel, Farmers Arms

(⛰ 0.25m) *Keswick Youth Hostel, Station Road, Keswick, Cumbria, CA12 5LH.*
Actual grid ref: NY267235
Warden: Mr C Williams.
Tel: 017687 72484
Under 18: £6.15 **Adults:** £9.10
Family Rooms, Evening Meal, Centrally Heated, Games Room, Laundry Facilities, Grounds Available for Games, Shop, Parking
Standing above the River Greta, this Hostel is ideally placed in Keswick - the northern hub of the Lake District - for superb views across the park to Skiddaw

---

Taking your dog?

Book in advance

only with owners who

accept dogs (🛏)

(0.25m) *Acorn House Hotel, Ambleside Road, Keswick, Cumbria, CA12 4DL.*
Grades: ETB 2 Cr, High Comm, AA 4 Q, Select, RAC High Acclaim
Tel: 017687 72553 Mrs Miller.
Rates fr: *£22.50-***£35.00**.
Open: Feb to Nov
Beds: 3F 6D 1T **Baths:** 10 Ensuite
🛇 (8) 🅿 (10) 🎟 Ⅵ 🛈 ⚡
Excellent hotel with colourful garden and flowers. Close to town and lake. Bedrooms furnished and decorated to a high standard; some with 4 poster beds. Private parking.

(0.5m 🐄) *Daresfield, Chestnut Hill, Keswick, Cumbria, CA12 4LS.*
Actual grid ref: NY280236
Comfortable friendly accommodation, superb outlook.
Tel: 017687 72531 Mrs Spencer.
Rates fr: *£14.00-***£15.00**.
Open: All Year (not Xmas)
Beds: 1F **Baths:** 1 Shared
🛇 🅿 (3) ⅙ 🗗 🛏 🎟 ♿ Ⅵ 🛈 ⚡

(0.5m) *14 Eskin Street, Keswick, Cumbria, CA12 4DQ.*
Victorian house with modern facilities.
Grades: ETB 2 Cr, Comm, AA 3 Q, Listed
Tel: 017687 73186 Mrs Raine.
Rates fr: *£20.00-***£20.00**.
Open: All Year (not Xmas)
Beds: 4D 4T 1S
Baths: 8 Ensuite, 1 Shared
🛇 (5) ⅙ 🎟 🛈 ⚡

(5.5m) *The Great Little Tea Shop, Lake Road, Keswick, Cumbria, CA12 5DQ.*
Cosy, traditional slate building.
Grades: ETB 3 Cr
Tel: 017687 73545 Mr Jones.
Rates fr: *£19.00-***£23.00**.
Open: All Year
Beds: 1F 4D 2T **Baths:** 7 Ensuite
🛇 (3) ⅙ 🗗 🛏 🎟 Ⅵ 🛈 ⚡

(0.25m) *Dalkeith House, 1 Leonards Street, Keswick, Cumbria, CA12 4EJ.*
Victorian house close to town centre.
Grades: ETB 1 Cr
Tel: 017687 72696
Mr & Mrs Seymour.
Rates fr: *£14.00-***£14.00**.
Open: All Year (not Xmas)
Beds: 1F 3D 1T 2S
Baths: 2 Shared
🛇 ⅙ 🗗 ✕ 🎟 🛈 ⚡

(0.75m) *Goodwin House, 29 Southey Street, Keswick, Cumbria, CA12 4EE.*
Imposing Victorian private house.
Grades: AA 3 Q, Recomm
Tel: 017687 74634 Mr Dawson.
Rates fr: *£12.00-***£12.00**.
Open: All Year (not Xmas)
Beds: 1F 3D 1T 1S
Baths: 4 Ensuite 2 Shared
🛇 🅿 (10) 🗗 ✕ 🎟 Ⅵ 🛈 ⚡

(0.5m) *Cumbria Hotel,*
1 Derwentwater Place, Keswick,
Cumbria, *CA12 4DR.*
Large Victorian private house.
Grades: ETB 2 Cr, Comm
Tel: **017687 73171**
Mr Arnold.
Rates fr: *£17.00*-**£18.00**.
Open: All Year (not Xmas)
Beds: 2F 4D 3S
Baths: 4 Ensuite 2 Shared
🛇 🅿 (8) ⅙ ⛌ 🛉 ✕ 🎹 Ⓥ 🛆 ⚡

(0.25m) *Rivendell, 23 Helvellyn
Street, Keswick, Cumbria,* CA12 4EN.
Actual grid ref: NY271233
Warm comfortable family guest-
house.
Grades: ETB Reg
Tel: **017687 73822**
Mrs Knox.
Rates fr: *£15.00*-**£15.00**.
Open: All Year (not Xmas)
Beds: 1F 4D 1T 1S
Baths: 3 Ensuite 1 Shared
🛇 ⅙ ⛌ 🛉 ✕ 🎹 Ⓥ 🛆 ⚡

(0.25m) *Derwentdale Guest Hotel,*
8 Blencathra Street, Keswick,
Cumbria, *CA12 4HP.*
Warm friendly comfortable guest-
house.
Grades: ETB Listed, Comm
Tel: **017687 74187**
Mrs Riding.
Rates fr: *£14.50*-**£14.50**.
Open: All Year
Beds: 3D 1T 2S
Baths: 1 Ensuite 2 Shared
🛇 ⅙ ⛌ ✕ 🎹 Ⓥ 🛆

(0.25m) *Bonshaw Guest House,*
20 Eskin Street, Keswick, Cumbria,
CA12 4DG.
Small friendly guesthouse, good
homecooking.
Grades: ETB Listed, Comm
Tel: **017687 73084**
Mr Attwood.
Rates fr: *£13.00*-**£15.00**.
Open: All Year
Beds: 2D 1T 3S
Baths: 2 Ensuite
🛇 (8) 🅿 (6) ⅙ 🛉 ✕ 🎹 Ⓥ 🛆

The Grid Reference
beneath the location
heading is for the
village or town - *not*
for individual houses,
which are shown
(where supplied) in
each entry itself.

The lowest *double*
rate per person is
shown in *italics.*

(0.5m) *Glaramara Guest House,*
9 Acorn Street, Keswick, Cumbria,
CA12 4EA.
Victorian, family run, home cook-
ing.
Tel: **017687 73216**
Mrs Lathan.
Rates fr: *£14.50*-**£14.50**.
Open: All Year (not Xmas)
Beds: 2F 2D 1T 1S
Baths: 2 Ensuite 1 Shared
🛇 🅿 (2) ⛌ 🛉 ✕ 🎹 🛆

(1m) *Greystoke House, 9 Leonard
Street, Keswick, Cumbria,* CA12 4EL.
Centrally situated town house.
Grades: ETB 2 Cr, RAC Acclaim
Tel: **017687 72603**
Mrs Robinson.
Rates fr: *£15.00*-**£15.00**.
Open: All Year
Beds: 5D 1S
Baths: 4 Ensuite 2 Shared
🛇 (10) 🅿 (4) ⛌ 🛉 ✕ 🎹 Ⓥ 🛆 ⚡

(0.5m) *Beckside, 5 Wordsworth
Street, Keswick, Cumbria,* CA12 4HU.
Actual grid ref: NY270235
Small, very comfortable guest
house.
Grades: ETB 2 Cr, Comm,
AA 3 Q, RAC High Acclaim
Tel: **017687 73093**
Mrs Wraight.
Rates fr: *£17.00*.
Open: All Year (not Xmas)
Beds: 1F 2D 1T
Baths: 4 Ensuite
🛇 ⅙ ⛌ ✕ 🎹 Ⓥ 🛆 ⚡

(0.25m) *Maharg, 12 Stanger
Street, Keswick, Cumbria,* CA12 5JU.
Small, homely, good food.
Grades: ETB Reg
Tel: **017687 73833**
Mrs Graham.
Rates fr: *£13.00*.
Open: All Year (not Xmas)
Beds: 1D
Baths: 1
🅿 (1) ⛌ 🎹.

Skiddaw   17

National Grid Ref: NY2629

(▲ On Path) *Skiddaw House
Youth Hostel, Skiddaw,
Bassenthwaite, Keswick, Cumbria,*
CA12 4QX.
Actual grid ref: NY288291
Warden: Mr M Webster.
Tel: **016974 78325**
Under 18: £3.75 **Adults:** £5.50
Family Rooms, Self Catering
Facilities, Games Room, Grounds

Available for Games, Shop
*At 1550ft this is one of the highest,
most remote and isolated hostels in
the UK - with no sign of civilization
in any direction, beneath the summit of Skiddaw*

Bassenthwaite   18

National Grid Ref: NY2332

🍴 🍺 Sun Inn

(2m) *Bassenthwaite Hall Farm,
Bassenthwaite, Keswick, Cumbria,*
CA12 4QP.
C17th modernised comfortable
farmhouse, bunkhouse.
Tel: **017687 76393** Mrs Trafford.
Rates fr: *£15.00*-**£20.00**.
Open: All Year
Beds: 2D
Baths: 1 Shared
🛇 (10) 🅿 (3) ⅙ 🛉 🎹 ⚡

All rooms full and
nowhere else to stay?
Ask the owner if there's
anywhere nearby

Caldbeck   19

National Grid Ref: NY3239

🍴 🍺 Oddfellows Arms

(On Path) *Friar Hall, Caldbeck,
Wigton, Cumbria,* CA7 8DS.
Modern house and working farm.
Grades: ETB 1 Cr
Tel: **016974 78633** Mrs Coulthard.
Rates fr: *£16.50*-**£18.00**.
Open: Easter to Nov
Beds: 1D 1T 1S
Baths: 1 Ensuite 1 Shared
🛇 🅿 (4) ⛌ 🛉

Carlisle   20

National Grid Ref: NY3955

🍴 🍺 Lordy's, Gianni's, Coach and
Horses

(0.25m) *Craighead, 6 Hartington
Place, Carlisle, Cumbria,* CA1 1HL.
Grades: ETB 1 Cr, Comm
Tel: **01228 596767** Mrs Smith.
Rates fr: *£15.50*-**£14.00**.
Open: All Year (not Xmas)
Beds: 1F 1D 1T 2S
Baths: 2 Shared
🛇 🅿 🛉 🎹 Ⓥ ⅙
Grade II Listed Victorian town-
house with spacious rooms and
original features. CTV, tea/coffee
tray - all rooms. Minutes walk city
centre bus/rail station, all
amenities.

(0.25m) *Howard House,*
27 Howard Place, Carlisle,
Cumbria, CA1 1HR.
Elegant Victorian town house.
Grades: ETB 3 Cr, High Comm,
AA 3 Q, Select
Tel: 01228 29159 / 512550
Mrs Fisher.
Rates fr: *£15.00-***£15.00**.
Open: All Year
Beds: 2F 1D 1T 2S
Baths: 2 Ensuite, 2 Shared
ᗡ ◻ ↟ ✕ ▦ Ⓥ 🛢 ⌀

(0.25m) *Chatsworth Guest House,*
22 Chatsworth Square, Carlisle,
Cumbria, CA1 1HF.
Large Victorian town house.
Grades: ETB 2 Cr, Comm
Tel: 01228 24023
Mrs Irving.
Rates fr: *£14.00-***£15.00**.
Open: All Year (not Xmas)
Beds: 2F 3T 1S
Baths: 2 Ensuite 1 Shared
ᗡ (2) ◻ ✕ ▦ ⌀

(0.25m) *Cornerways Guest House,*
107 Warwick Road, Carlisle,
Cumbria, CA1 1EA.
Large Victorian town house.
Grades: ETB 1 Cr
Tel: 01228 21733
Mrs Fisher.
Rates fr: *£12.50-***£13.00**.
Open: All Year (not Xmas)
Beds: 1F 2D 4T 3S
Baths: 1 Ensuite 2 Shared
ᗡ 🅿 (5) ◻ ↟ ✕ ▦ Ⓥ 🛢

(0.25m) *East View Guest House,*
110 Warwick Road, Carlisle,
Cumbria, CA1 1JU.
Actual grid ref: NY407560
Victorian family run guesthouse.
Grades: ETB 1 Cr, AA 3 Q,
RAC Acclaim
Tel: 01228 22112 Mrs MacKin.
Rates fr: *£16.00-***£18.00**.
Open: All Year
Beds: 3F 3D 1T 1S
Baths: 8 Ensuite
ᗡ 🅿 (4) ◻ ▦ ⌀

(▲ 0.25m) *Carlisle Youth Hostel,*
Etterby House, Etterby, Carlisle,
Cumbria, CA3 9QS.
Actual grid ref: NY386569
Warden: Ms L Rhind.
Tel: 01228 23934
Under 18: £4.15 **Adults:** £6.10
Family Rooms, Evening Meal, Self
Catering Facilities, Laundry
Facilities, Shop, Parking
*The Hostel is a Victorian house in
a quiet suburb standing on the
banks of River Eden, in close prox-
imity to the historic city of Carlisle*

When booking,
please mention
*Stilwell's National
Trail Companion.*

Dales Way

The 84-mile **Dales Way** is another good one for walkers to cut their teeth on, especially those new to walking in Northern England. The path splits naturally into two halves - the slow ascent to Ribblehead to cross the Pennines and the gradual descent from Newby Head. The route links the **Yorkshire Dales** and the **Lake District National Parks** in almost a straight line from Ilkley Moor to Lake Windermere through Wharfedale and Dentdale and the views over the fells and dales are spectacular. It is relatively short, with good transport links at Ilkley, Ribblehead, Kendal and Windermere and thus a good candidate for doing in stages over a couple of long weekends.

Guides (available from all good map shops):
Dales Way Companion by Paul Hannon (ISBN 1 870141 09 1), published by Hillside Publications and available from all good map shops or directly from the publishers (11 Nessfield Grove, Exley Head, Keighley, W. Yorks, BD22 6NU, tel. 01535 681505), £5.50 (+50p p&p)

The Dales Way (Ilkley-Windermere) by Colin Speakman, published by Dalesman Publishing Ltd and available from the Rambler's Association National Office (1/5 Wandsworth Road, London, SW8 2XX, tel. 0171 582 6878), £4.95 (+70p p&p)

The Dales Way by Anthony Burton (ISBN 1 85410 3148), published by Aurum Press in association with Ordnance Survey and available from all major bookshops, £9.99

The Dales Way by Terry Marsh, published by Cicerone Press and available from all good map shops or directly from the publishers (2 Police Square, Milnthorpe, Cumbria, LA7 7PY, 01539 562069), £5.99 (+75p p&p)

Dalesway Route Guide by Arthur Gemmell & Colin Speakman, published by Stile Publications and available from by post from the RA National Office or from the publishers (24 Lisker Drive, Otley, W. Yorks, LS21 1DQ, tel. 01943 466326), £2.80 (+50p p&p)

Maps: 1:50000 Ordnance Survey Landranger Series: 97, 98, 104.
The Dales Way (4-colour linear route map), ISBN 1 871149 05 3, published by Footprint and available in all good map shops or by post from their offices (Unit 87, Stirling Enterprise Park, Stirling, FK7 7RP), £2.95 (+ 40p p&p)

Ilkley   1

National Grid Ref: SE1147

🍴 🍺 La Sila Restaurant, Wharfedale Gate, Brewers Fayre

(On Path 🐾) *Archway Cottage*, *24 Skipton Road, Ilkley, W. Yorks, LS29 9EP.*
Tel: **01943 603399** Mrs Below.
Rates fr: *£15.00-£15.00.*
Open: All Year (not Xmas)
Beds: 4D 2T
🅿 (2) 🖵 🎞 Ⅵ 🛆 ⚡
Modernised comfortable accommodation in central Ilkley, offering a friendly welcome and an excellent breakfast. Phone Pat Below or fax 01943 817946.

(On Path) *Hollygarth House*, *293 Leeds Road, Ilkley, W. Yorks, LS29 8LL.*
Large house, garden to river.
Tel: **01943 609223** Mrs Taylor.
Rates fr: *£14.00-£14.00.*
Open: Easter to Oct
Beds: 1F 1D 1T 1S
Baths: 1 Shared
🛏 (5) 🅿 (5) 🖵 🕇 🎞 Ⅵ

(On Path) *Moorview House Hotel*, *104 Skipton Road, Ilkley, W. Yorks, LS29 9HE.*
Grades: ETB 2 Cr, AA 1 St
Tel: **01943 600156**
Mrs Head.
Rates fr: *£19.00-£25.00.*
Open: All Year
Beds: 3F 4D 4T 1S
Baths: 7 Ensuite 3 Shared
🛏 🅿 (10) 🖵 🕇 🎞 ✕ 🎞 Ⅵ 🛆 ⚡
Large, comfortable rooms, wonderful views of river and moors. Log fires, close to Ilkley shops and restaurants. The start of the Dales Way!

(0.5m) *The Grove Hotel*, 66 The Grove, Ilkley, W. Yorks, LS29 9PA.
Spacious, well-appointed Victorian townhouse.
Grades: ETB 3 Cr, Comm, AA 1 St
Tel: **01943 600298**
Mr Emslie.
Rates fr: *£20.00-£30.00.*
Open: All Year (not Xmas)
Beds: 2F 1D 2T 1S
Baths: 6 Private 1 Shared
🛏 🅿 (5) 🖵 🕇 ✕ 🎞 Ⅵ 🛆

(On Path 🐾) *Riverside Hotel*, *Bridge Lane, Ilkley, W. Yorks, LS29 9HN.*
Licensed hotel.
Tel: **01943 607338** Mrs Dobson.
Rates fr: *£20.00-£25.00.*
Open: All Year
Beds: 1F 4D 4T 1S
Baths: 8 Ensuite 2 Shared
🛏 🅿 (30) 🖵 🕇 ✕ 🎞 Ⅵ 🛆 ⚡

(0.25m) *Poplar View Guest House,*
8 Bolton Bridge Road, Ilkley, W.
Yorks, LS29 9AA.
Victorian house near town centre.
Tel: 01943 608436 Mrs O'Neill.
Rates fr: £15.00-£18.00.
Open: All Year (not Xmas)
Beds: 1D 1T
Baths: 1 Shared
🛇🛏🏠🖚📷 V

(0.5m 🚗) *63 Skipton Road, Ilkley,*
W. Yorks, LS29 9HF.
Modern detached house.
Tel: 01943 817542 Mrs Roberts.
Rates fr: £15.00-£15.00.
Open: All Year
Beds: 1F 1D 1S **Baths:** 1 Shared
🛇 P (5) ⚡🖚🗙📷 V ✦

(0.25m) *126 Skipton Road, Ilkley,*
W. Yorks, LS29 9BQ.
Modern house overlooking the
Dales Way.
Grades: ETB Reg
Tel: 01943 600635 Mrs Read.
Rates fr: £16.50-£18.00.
Open: All Year (not Xmas)
Beds: 1T **Baths:** 1 Ensuite
🛇 (10) P (2) ⚡🖚📷 ✦

(0.25m) *Osbourne House, 1 Tivoli*
Place, Ilkley, W. Yorks, LS29 8SU.
Large Victorian guesthouse.
Tel: 01943 609483
Mr & Mrs Bradbury.
Rates fr: £14.00-£14.00.
Open: All Year **Beds:** 1F 1D 2T
🛇⚡🖚📷 V 🔒✦

(0.25m) *Belvedere, 2 Victoria*
Avenue, Ilkley, W. Yorks, LS29 9BL.
Large Victorian house overlooking
valley.
Tel: 01943 607598 Mrs Terry.
Rates fr: £13.00-£14.00.
Open: All Year
Beds: 1F 1D 1T 1S
Baths: 1 Shared
🛇 (1) ⚡🖚📷 V 🔒✦

Addingham 2

National Grid Ref: SE0749

(On Path) *Olicana Cottage, High*
Mill Lane, Addingham, Ilkley,
W. Yorks, LS29 0RD.
Olde worlde riverside cottage.
Tel: 01943 830500 Mrs Pape.
Rates fr: £16.00-£16.00.
Open: All Year (not Xmas)
Beds: 2D 2S **Baths:** 1 Shared
🛇 P (3) ⚡🖚📷 V 🔒✦

Bolton Abbey 3

National Grid Ref: SE0753

(On Path) *Devonshire Arms Hotel,*
Bolton Abbey, Skipton,
N. Yorks, BD23 6AJ.
Actual grid ref: SE071533
C17th coaching inn.
Grades: ETB 5 Cr, De Luxe,
AA 3 St, RAC 4 St
Tel: 01756 710441
Rates fr: £65.00-£95.00.

Open: All Year
Beds: 20D 21T **Baths:** 41 Ensuite
🛇 P (150) ⚡🖚🗙📷 V ✦

(0.75m) *Hesketh House, Bolton*
Abbey, Skipton, N. Yorks, BD23 6HA.
Large working hill/sheep farm.
Tel: 01756 710332 Mrs Heseltine.
Rates fr: £14.00-£14.00.
Open: Easter to Oct
Beds: 2D 1T **Baths:** 2 Shared
🛇 P (6) 🖚📷 ✦

Barden 4

National Grid Ref: SE0557

🍴 🍺 Craven Arms (Barden)

(0.25m) *Howgill Lodge, Barden,*
Skipton, N. Yorks, BD23 6DJ.
Actual grid ref: SE065953
Quiet C17th barn, lovely views.
Tel: 01756 720655 Mrs Foster.
Rates fr: £22.00-£28.00.
Open: All Year (not Xmas)
Beds: 1F 2D 1T
Baths: 4 Private
🛇 P 📷 V 🔒✦
Also ⛺ *£2.00 per person.*
Open: Apr to Oct 🔘 T ♨✦♿

Appletreewick 5

National Grid Ref: SE0560

🍴 🍺 Craven Arms

(0.25m 🚗) *Blundellstead,*
Appletreewick, Skipton, N. Yorks,
BD23 6DB.
Actual grid ref: SE054602
Comfortable, quiet, Dales country
home.

Grades: ETB Listed
Tel: 01756 720632 Ms Coney.
Rates fr: £14.00-£14.00.
Open: All Year (not Xmas)
Beds: 1D 2S **Baths:** 1 Shared
🛇 P (2) ⚡🖚🗙📷 V ✦

Burnsall 6

National Grid Ref: SE0361

🍴 🍺 Red Lion, Fell Hotel

(On Path 🚗) *Red Lion Hotel,*
Burnsall, Skipton, N. Yorks,
BD23 6BU.
Actual grid ref: SE033612
Grades: ETB 3 Cr, Comm,
AA 2 St, RAC 2 St
Tel: 01756 720204 Mrs Grayshon.
Rates fr: £32.00-£32.00.
Open: All Year
Beds: 2F 4D 4T 1S
Baths: 12 Private
🛇 P (40) 🗙📷 V 🔒✦
Family-run C17th Ferryman's Inn
on bank of R.Wharfe. Excellent
restaurant, superb range of bar
food, real ales, log fires and
extremely comfortable accommo-
dation.

(On Path) *Conistone House,*
Burnsall, Skipton, N. Yorks,
BD23 6BN.
Comfortable, friendly, family
house.
Tel: 01756 720650 Mrs Mason.
Rates fr: £18.00-£23.00.
Open: Easter to Oct
Beds: 1D 2T
Baths: 1 Shared
🛇 P (3) 📷 ✦

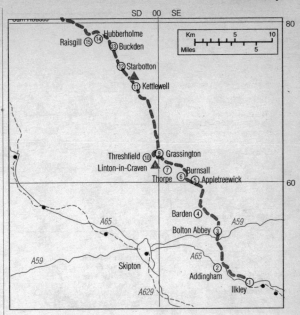

SD 00 SE

Km | 5 | 10
Miles | 5

Hubberholme
Raisgill ⑮ ⑭
⑬ Buckden
⑫ Starbotton
⑪ Kettlewell
Threshfield ⑩ ⑨ Grassington
Linton-in-Craven Burnsall
Thorpe ⑥ ⑤ Appletreewick
Barden ④
A65 A59
Bolton Abbey ③
A65 ②
Skipton Addingham
A59 ①
Ilkley
A629

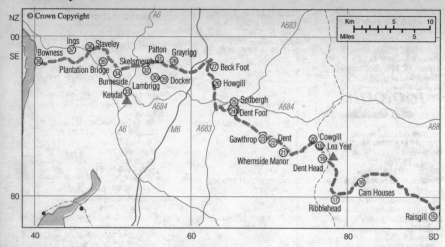

Thorpe 7

National Grid Ref: SE0161

|⊙| ◫ Fountain

(1m 🚍) *Holly Tree Farm*, Thorpe, Skipton, N. Yorks, *BD23 6BJ*.
Actual grid ref: SE014617
Quiet homely Dales sheep farm.
Tel: **01756 720604** Mrs Hall.
Rates fr: *£15.00-£15.00*.
Open: All Year
Beds: 1D 1S **Baths:** 1 Shared
🖢⊬◻

Linton-in-Craven 8

National Grid Ref: SD9962

|⊙| ◫ Fountain (Linton-in-Craven)

(▲ 0.25m) *Linton Youth Hostel*, The Old Rectory, Linton-in-Craven, Skipton, N. Yorks, *BD23 5HH*.
Actual grid ref: SD9962
Warden: Mr R Suddaby.
Tel: **01756 752400**
Under 18: £5.55 **Adults:** £8.25
Family Bunk Rooms, Partially Heated, Showers, Evening Meal (7.00 pm), Parking
C17th former rectory in own grounds, across the stream from the village green in one of Wharfedale's most picturesque and unspoilt villages

Grassington 9

National Grid Ref: SE0064

|⊙| ◫ Foresters, Black Horse, Devonshire Hotel, Paul & Cheryls

(0.25m) *Foresters Arms*, Grassington, Skipton, N. Yorks, *BD23 5AA*.
Friendly family-run pub.
Grades: ETB Listed
Tel: **01756 752349**

Mrs Richardson.
Rates fr: *£18.00-£18.00*.
Open: All Year (not Xmas)
Beds: 2F 4D 1S
Baths: 1 Private 2 Shared
🖢⊉(2)◻►✗▥Ⅵ⊬

(0.5m) *The Lodge*, 8 Wood Lane, Grassington, Skipton, N. Yorks, *BD23 5LU*.
Large Victorian stone built house.
Grades: ETB 2 Cr, AA 3 Q, Recomm
Tel: **01756 752518** Mr Lingard.
Rates fr: *£16.00-£22.00*.
Open: Mar to Nov **Beds:** 3D 4T
Baths: 2 Ensuite, 3 Shared
🖢⊉(7)◻►✗▥Ⅵ⊬

(0.5m) *Town Head Guest House*, 1 Low Lane, Grassington, Skipton, N. Yorks, *BD23 5AU*.
Modern guesthouse.
Grades: ETB 2 Cr, Comm
Tel: **01756 752811** Mrs Lister.
Rates fr: *£16.50-£25.00*.
Open: All Year (not Xmas)
Beds: 4D 1T
Baths: 3 Private 2 Shared
⊉(3)⊬◻✗▥ê

(On Path) *Springroyd House*, 8a Station Road, Grassington, Skipton, N. Yorks, *BD23 5NQ*.
Actual grid ref: SD980163
Warm welcome, homely relaxing atmosphere.
Grades: ETB Reg
Tel: **01756 752473**
Mr Berry.
Rates fr: *£15.00-£20.00*.
Open: All Year (not Xmas)
Beds: 1D 1T
Baths: 1 Shared
🖢(5)⊉(2)◻▥ê⊬

(On Path) *Kirkfield*, Hebden Road, Grassington, Skipton, N. Yorks, *BD23 5LJ*.
Large house in own grounds.
Tel: **01756 752385**

Mr Lockyer.
Rates fr: *£15.00-£15.00*.
Open: All Year (not Xmas)
Beds: 3F 1T
Baths: 2 Ensuite 1 Shared
🖢⊉(6)⊬◻►✗▥Ⅵ⊬

(0.25m) *Burtree Cottage*, Hebden Road, Grassington, Skipton, N. Yorks, *BD23 5LH*.
Attractive C18th cottage.
Tel: **01756 752442**
Mrs Marsden.
Rates fr: *£13.50-£20.00*.
Open: Easter to Oct
Beds: 1D 1T
Baths: 1 Shared
🖢(10)⊉(3)⊬◻▥Ⅵ⊬

(0.25m 🚍) *Mayfield Bed & Breakfast*, Low Mill Lane, Grassington, Skipton, North Yorkshire, *BD23 5BX*.
Dales long house.
Tel: **01756 753052**
Mr & Mrs Trewartha.
Rates fr: *£16.00-£18.00*.
Open: All Year
Beds: 1F 1T 1D
Baths: 1 Ensuite 1 Shared
🖢⊉(10)⊬►✗▥Ⅵê⊬

Threshfield 10

National Grid Ref: SD9863

|⊙| ◫ The Old Hall

(1.5m 🚍) *3 Wharfeside Avenue*, Threshfield, Skipton, N. Yorks, *BD23 5BS*.
Large Victorian private house.
Grades: ETB 2 Cr
Tel: **01756 752115**
Mr & Mrs Cahill.
Rates fr: *£18.00-£18.50*.
Open: All Year (not Xmas)
Beds: 1F 1D 1T 1S
Baths: 4 Ensuite
🖢⊉(4)⊬◻▥Ⅵê⊬

don't leave your footprint behind !

footprint
map - guides

Kettlewell 11

National Grid Ref: SD9772

|●| ◀ Races Horses Hotel, Kings Head Inn, Blue Bell, Fox Hounds

(On Path) *Lynburn, Kettlewell, Skipton, N. Yorks, BD23 5RF*.
Modern Dales cottage with excellent views.
Tel: **01756 760803**
Mrs Thornborrow.
Rates fr: *£17.50*-**£20.00**.
Open: Feb to Dec
Beds: 1D 1T
Baths: 1 Shared
🛏 (11) 🅿 (2) 🖵 🎹 Ⓥ 🗈 ≉

(On Path) *The Elms, Middle Lane, Kettlewell, Skipton, N. Yorks, BD23 5QX*.
Large Victorian private house.
Grades: ETB 2 Cr, High Comm
Tel: **01756 760224** Mr Cuthbert.
Rates fr: *£19.00*-**£26.50**.
Open: All Year (not Xmas)
Beds: 2D 1T
Baths: 3 Ensuite
🅿 (1) ⅍ 🖵 🎹 Ⓥ ≉

(▲ On Path) *Kettlewell Youth Hostel, Whernside House, Kettlewell, Skipton, N. Yorks, BD23 5QU*.
Actual grid ref: SD9772
Warden: Mr G Chamberlain.
Tel: **01756 760232**
Under 18: £5.00 **Adults:** £7.45
Family Bunk Rooms, Centrally Heated, Showers, Evening Meal (7.00 pm), Shop, Television
Large house right in the middle of the pretty Wharfedale village of Kettlewell, ideal for families and small groups

(On Path 🚌) *Cam Lodge, Kettlewell, Skipton, N. Yorks, BD23 5QU*.
Large private house.
Tel: **01756 760276** Miss Lister.
Rates fr: *£20.00*-**£20.00**.
Open: Easter to Oct
Beds: 1D 2T
Baths: 2 Shared
🅿 (6) ⅍ ✗ 🎹 Ⓥ 🗈 ≉

(On Path) *High Fold, Kettlewell, Skipton, N. Yorks, BD23 5RJ*.
Converted Dales barn.
Grades: ETB 4 Cr, High Comm
Tel: **01756 760390** Mr Earnshaw.

Rates fr: *£25.00*-**£30.00**.
Open: Feb to Dec
Beds: 1F 2D 1T
Baths: 4 Ensuite
🛏 (2) 🅿 (4) 🖵 🎹 ✗ 🎹 Ⓥ 🗈 ≉

Starbotton 12

National Grid Ref: SD9574

|●| ◀ Fox & Hounds

(0.25m) *Fox & Hounds Inn, Starbotton, Skipton, N. Yorks, BD23 5HY*.
Traditional cosy Dales Inn.
Tel: **01756 760269**
Mr & Mrs McFadyen.
Rates fr: *£22.00*-**£30.00**.
Open: Mid Feb to Dec
Beds: 1D 1T
Baths: 2 Private
🅿 (10) 🖵 🎹 ✗ 🎹 Ⓥ 🗈

(0.5m 🚌) *Hill Top Country Guest House, Starbotton, Skipton, N. Yorks, BD23 5HY*.
C17th listed farmhouse..
Grades: ETB 2 Cr, High Comm, AA 5 Q, Prem Select
Tel: **01756 760321** Mr Rathmell.
Rates fr: *£25.00*-**£35.00**.
Open: Easter to Nov
Beds: 1F 3D 1T
Baths: 5 Ensuite
🛏 (6) 🅿 (6) 🖵 ✗ 🎹 Ⓥ 🗈 ≉

Buckden 13

National Grid Ref: SD9477

|●| ◀ Village Restaurant, Buck Inn

(0.25m 🚌) *Beck Cottage, Buckden, Skipton, N. Yorks, BD23 5JA*.
Actual grid ref: SD943773
Tel: **01756 760340**
Mr & Mrs Leach.
Rates fr: *£15.00*-**£20.00**.
Open: All Year (not Xmas)
🛏 🅿 (2) ⅍ 🎹 🗈 ≉
Dales cottage. Central. Peaceful situation. Walkers welcome at all times. Ideal base for touring. Special breakfast diets catered for. Friendly welcome.

(On Path 🚌) *Whimsical Cottage, Clifford House, Buckden, Skipton, N. Yorks, BD23 5JA*.
Modern comfortable rooms.
Tel: **01756 760827** Mr Horseman.
Rates fr: *£15.00*-**£20.00**.
Open: All Year (not Xmas)
Beds: 2D
Baths: 1 Shared
🅿 ⅍ 🖵 🎹 🗈 ≉

All rates are subject to alteration at the owners' discretion.

Hubberholme 14

National Grid Ref: SD9278

|●| ◀ George Inn

(On Path 🚌) *Church Farm, Hubberholme, Skipton, N. Yorks, BD23 5JE*.
Actual grid ref: SD935773
Comfortable farmhouse bed and breakfast.
Tel: **01756 760240** Mrs Huck.
Rates fr: *£15.00*-**£15.00**.
Open: All Year
Beds: 1F 1T
Baths: 1 Shared
🛏 🅿 🖵 🎹 Ⓥ 🗈 ≉

(On Path 🚌) *Kirkgill Manor Guest House, Hubberholme, Skipton, N. Yorks, BD23 5JE*.
Comfortable detached converted old vicarage.
Tel: **01756 760800** Mrs Jowsey.
Rates fr: *£23.00*-**£28.00**.
Open: All Year
Beds: 1F 3D 2T
Baths: 6 Private
🅿 (10) ⅍ 🖵 ✗ 🎹 & 🗈 ≉

(On Path) *The George Inn, Hubberholme, Skipton, N. Yorks, BD23 5JE*.
C16th stone-flagged country inn.
Grades: ETB Reg
Tel: **01756 760223** Mr Lanchbury.
Rates fr: *£17.00*-**£18.00**.
Open: All Year
Beds: 3D 3T
Baths: 1 Ensuite 2 Shared
🛏 (8) 🅿 ⅍ 🖵 ✗ 🎹 Ⓥ 🗈 ≉

Raisgill 15

National Grid Ref: SD9079

(0.25m) *Low Raisgill Cottage, Raisgill, Yockenthwaite, Skipton, N. Yorks, BD23 5JQ*.
Actual grid ref: SD906786
Converted C17th cottage, quiet location.
Tel: **01756 760351** Mrs Middleton.
Rates fr: *£8.50*-**£17.00**.
Open: All Year (not Xmas)
Beds: 1F 1D 1T 1S
Baths: 3 Ensuite 1 Shared
🛏 (12) 🅿 (3) 🖵 🎹 Ⓥ 🗈 ≉

Cam Houses 16

National Grid Ref: SD8282

(On Path) *Cam Farm, Cam Houses, Oughtershaw, Skipton, N. Yorks, BD23 5JT*.
Actual grid ref: SD823821
Typical Dales hill farm.
Tel: **0860 648045** Mrs Smith.
Rates fr: *£16.00*-**£16.00**.
Open: All Year
Beds: 3T
Baths: 1 Shared
🛏 🅿 ⅍ 🖵 🎹 ✗ 🎹 Ⓥ 🗈 ≉
Also ▲ *Also bunkhouse, £5.00 per bunk, Open: All Year* 🔥 Ⓣ 🔥 ✗ ≉

Ribblehead 17

National Grid Ref: SD7880

(On Path ⌂) Station Inn, *Ribblehead, Ingleton, Carnforth, Lancs, LA6 3AS.*
Actual grid ref: SD763792
Comfortable country inn, fantastic views.
Grades: ETB Listed, Approv
Tel: **015242 41274** Mr Coates.
Rates fr: *£17.50*-**£16.00**.
Open: All Year
Beds: 1F3D 1T
Baths: 3 Ensuite 1 Shared
🛏 🅿 (50) ⌷ ✕ Ⅲ. Ⅴ 🛊 ✦
Also ▲ *Also bunkhouse, £4.00 per bunk,*
Open: All Year 🏠 Ⅱ ✕ 👶

Dent Head 18

National Grid Ref: SD7785

🍴 🍺 Sportsman Inn

(▲ On Path) Dentdale Youth Hostel, *Dent Head, Cowgill, Sedbergh, Cumbria, LA10 5RN.*
Actual grid ref: SD7785
Warden: Mr M Tracy.
Tel: **015396 25251**
Under 18: £5.00 **Adults:** £7.45
Family Bunk Rooms, Centrally Heated, Showers, Evening Meal (7.00 pm)
Former shooting lodge, now a Listed building, beside the River Dee in the upper reaches of the magnificent Dentdale Valley

Lea Yeat 19

National Grid Ref: SD7686

🍴 🍺 Sports Man Inn

(On Path) River View, *Lea Yeat, Cowgill, Sedbergh, Cumbria, LA10 5RF.*
Actual grid ref: SD761869
Converted Quaker meeting house.
Tel: **015396 25592**
Mr & Mrs Playfoot.
Rates fr: *£14.50*-**£14.50**.
Open: All Year (not Xmas)
Beds: 1D 1T
Baths: 1 Shared
🛏 (12) 🅿 (2) ⌁ ⌷ Ⅲ. 🛊 ✦

Cowgill 20

National Grid Ref: SD7587

🍴 🍺 Sportsmans Inn

(On Path ⌂) Scow Cottage, *Cowgill, nr Dent, Sedbergh, Cumbria, LA10 5RN.*
Actual grid ref: SD853774
Attractive and comfortable Dales Way cottage.
Tel: **015396 25445** Mrs Ferguson.
Rates fr: *£16.00*-**£19.00**.
Open: All Year
Beds: 1D 1T
🛏 (7) 🅿 ⌁ ✝ ✕ Ⅲ. 🛊 ✦

(On Path ⌂) The Sportsman's Inn, *Cowgill, Dent, Sedbergh, Cumbria, LA10 5RG.*
300-year-old Listed building, quiet country inn.
Grades: ETB Registered
Tel: **015396 25282**
Mr & Mrs Martin.
Rates fr: *£19.00*.
Open: All Year
Beds: 1F 3D 2T
Baths: 3 Shared
🛏 🅿 ✝ ✕ Ⅲ. Ⅴ 🛊

Whernside Manor 21

National Grid Ref: SD7285

🍴 🍺 Sun Inn (Whernside Manor)

(On Path) Smithy Fold, *Whernside Manor, Dent, Sedbergh, Cumbria, LA10 5RE.*
Actual grid ref: SD725859
Small C18th country house.
Tel: **015396 25368**
Mrs Cheetham.
Rates fr: *£15.00*-**£15.00**.
Open: All Year (not Xmas)
Beds: 1F 1D 1T
Baths: 1 Shared
🛏 🅿 ⌷ ✝ ✕ Ⅲ. Ⅴ 🛊
Also ▲ *£1.50 per person.*
Open: All Year 👶

Dent 22

National Grid Ref: SD7188

🍴 🍺 The Sun Inn, The George and Dragon

(0.25m) Stone Close Tea Shop, *Main Street, Dent, Sedbergh, Cumbria, LA10 5QL.*
C17th cottage tea-shop with exposed beams.
Tel: **015396 25231**
Mr Hudson.
Rates fr: *£14.75*-**£16.75**.
Open: Mar to Dec
Beds: 1F 1D 1S
Baths: 1 Shared
🛏 ⌁ ✝ Ⅲ. Ⅴ 🛊 ✦

(0.5m ⌂) Slack Cottage, *Dent, Sedbergh, Cumbria, LA10 5QU.*
Actual grid ref: SD716859
Comfortable old cottage.
Tel: **015396 25439**
Mrs Gunson.
Rates fr: *£13.00*-**£13.00**.
Open: All Year (not Xmas)
Beds: 1D
Baths: 1 Shared
🛏 🅿 ⌁ ⌷ ✝ Ⅲ. 🛊 ✦

(0.5m) The Sun Inn, *Dent, Sedbergh, Cumbria, LA10 5TE.*
Actual grid ref: SD7188
C17th inn.
Grades: ETB Listed
Tel: **015396 25208** Mrs Winn.
Rates fr: *£16.50*-**£16.50**.
Open: All Year (not Xmas)
Beds: 1F 1D 1T
🛏 🅿 (20) ⌁ ⌷ ✕ Ⅲ. Ⅴ 🛊

All rooms full and nowhere else to stay? Ask the owner if there's anywhere nearby

Gawthrop 23

National Grid Ref: SD6987

🍴 🍺 Sun Inn (Gawthrop)

(On Path) Ivy Dene, *Gawthrop, Dentdale, Sedbergh, Cumbria, LA10 5TA.*
Oak-beamed cottage.
Tel: **015396 25353**
Mrs Williamson.
Rates fr: *£16.00*.
Open: Mar to Oct
Beds: 1F 2D **Baths:** 1 Shared
🛏 🅿 ⌁ ⌷ ✕ Ⅴ 🛊 ✦

Dent Foot 24

National Grid Ref: SD6791

(On Path ⌂) Rash House, *Dent Foot, Sedbergh, Cumbria, LA10 5SU.*
Actual grid ref: SD6690
C18th farmhouse.
Grades: ETB Reg
Tel: **015396 20113** Mrs Hunter.
Rates fr: *£15.00*-**£16.00**.
Open: All Year (not Xmas)
Beds: 1F 1D
Baths: 1 Shared
🛏 🅿 (2) ⌷ ✝ ✕ Ⅲ. Ⅴ 🛊 ✦

Sedbergh 25

National Grid Ref: SD6592

🍴 🍺 The Dalesman, The Red Lion

(0.5m) The Moss House, *Garsdale Road, Sedbergh, Cumbria, LA10 5JL.*
Actual grid ref: SD672918
Tel: **015396 20940** Mrs Jarvis.
Rates fr: *£16.99*-**£21.00**.
Open: Mar to Nov
Beds: 1F 1D 1T
Baths: 2 Shared
🛏 🅿 (5) ⌁ ⌷ ✕ Ⅲ. Ⅴ 🛊 ✦
Situated just outside Sedbergh on A684 in Yorkshire Dales National Park, just off Dales Way and Howgills. Ideal walking, touring. Home cooking, high standard, friendly.

(On Path) Stable Antiques, *15 Back Lane, Sedbergh, Cumbria, LA10 5AQ.*
17th Century wheelwright's cottage.
Tel: **015396 20251** Miss Thurlby.
Rates fr: *£16.00*-**£16.00**.
Open: All Year
Beds: 1D 1T **Baths:** 1 Shared
🛏 (10) ✝ Ⅲ. Ⅴ 🛊 ✦

(0.5m) *Holmecroft, Station Road, Sedbergh, Cumbria, LA10 5DW*.
Actual grid ref: SD650919
Lovely detached house with fell views.
Tel: **015396 20754**
Mrs Sharrocks.
Rates fr: *£15.50-£15.50*.
Open: All Year (not Xmas)
Beds: 2D 1T
Baths: 1 Shared
⛇ 🅿 (6) 🚶 ❏ 📁 🛏 Ⅲ 🅥 🖩 ⚡

(0.5m) *Sun Lea, Joss Lane, Sedbergh, Cumbria, LA10 5AS*.
Actual grid ref: SD658922
Large, Victorian private house.
Tel: **015396 20828**
Mr & Mrs Ramsden.
Rates fr: *£15.00-£15.00*.
Open: All Year (not Xmas)
Beds: 2D 1T
Baths: 2 Shared
⛇ 🅿 (3) 🚶 ❏ Ⅲ 🅥 🖩 ⚡

(0.5m 🚐) *Randall Hill, Sedbergh, Cumbria, LA10 5HJ*.
Actual grid ref: SD649917
Country house in 3 acres.
Tel: **015396 20633** Mrs Snow.
Rates fr: *£15.00-£16.00*.
Open: All Year
Beds: 1D 2T **Baths:** 1 Shared
⛇ 🅿 (6) 🚶 ❏ 🛏 Ⅲ 🅥 🖩 ⚡

(0.75m 🚐) *Marshall House, Main Street, Sedbergh, Cumbria, LA10 5BL*.
Actual grid ref: SD658922
Lovingly restored townhouse with walled garden.
Tel: **015396 21053** Mrs Kerry.
Rates fr: *£20.00-£28.00*.
Open: All Year (not Xmas)
Beds: 1D 2T
Baths: 3 Private
⛇ (12) 🅿 (5) ❏ ✕ Ⅲ ♿ 🅥 🖩 ⚡

Howgill 26

National Grid Ref: SD6396

(On Path) *Ash-Hining Farm, Howgill, Sedbergh, Cumbria, LA10 5HU*.
Modernised C16th farmhouse.
Tel: **015396 21595** Mrs Mattinson.
Rates fr: *£16.00-£16.00*.
Open: Mar to Oct
Beds: 1D 1T **Baths:** 2 Shared
⛇ 🅿 🚶 ❏ 🛏 Ⅲ 🖩 ⚡

🚐 sign means that, given due notice, owners will pick you up from the path and drop you off within reason.

Beck Foot 27

National Grid Ref: SD6196

(On Path 🚐) *Tarnclose, Beck Foot, Lowgill, Kendal, Cumbria, LA8 0BL*.
Old pay-master's cottage, large garden.
Tel: **01539 824658** Mrs Hogg.
Rates fr: *£20.50 (inc dinner)-£16.50*.
Open: Easter to Oct
Beds: 1D 1T
Baths: 1 Ensuite 1 Shared
⛇ (6) 🅿 (2) 🚶 ❏ 🛏 ✕ Ⅲ 🅥 🖩 ⚡

Grayrigg 28

National Grid Ref: SD5797

(0.5m) *Grayrigg Hall Farm, Grayrigg, Kendal, Cumbria, LA8 9BU*.
C18th comfortable farmhouse.
Tel: **01539 824689** Mrs Bindloss.
Rates fr: *£14.00-£14.00*.
Open: Easter to Oct
Beds: 1F 1D 1S
Baths: 1 Shared
⛇ 🅿 (2) ❏ 🛏 ✕ Ⅲ 🅥 🖩 ⚡

Docker 29

National Grid Ref: SD5695

(1.25m) *Myers Farm, Docker, Grayrigg, Kendal, Cumbria, LA8 0DF*.
Working hill/sheep farm.
Grades: ETB Listed
Tel: **01539 824610** Mrs Knowles.
Rates fr: *£17.00-£17.00*.
Open: All Year
Beds: 1F 1D 1T
Baths: 1 Shared
⛇ 🅿 🚶 ❏ ✕ Ⅲ 🖩 ⚡

Lambrigg 30

National Grid Ref: SD5696

(On Path 🚐) *Holme Park Hall, Lambrigg, Kendal, Cumbria, LA10 0SJ*.
Family run. Large country house.
Grades: ETB Listed
Tel: **015394 84336** Mrs Boardley.
Rates fr: *£14.00-£16.00*.
Open: Feb to Nov
Beds: 3F
Baths: 1 Private 1 Shared
⛇ 🅿 (10) ❏ 🛏 ✕ Ⅲ 🅥 🖩

Patton 31

National Grid Ref: SD5597

(On Path) *High Barn, Shaw End, Patton, Kendal, Cumbria, LA8 9DU*.
Actual grid ref: SD558972
Beautiful barn conversion - peaceful setting.
Tel: **01539 824625** Mrs Sanderson.
Rates fr: *£14.50-£14.50*.
Open: All Year (not Xmas)
Beds: 2D **Baths:** 2 Private
⛇ (5) 🅿 (4) 🚶 ❏ 🛏 Ⅲ 🅥 🖩 ⚡

Skelsmergh 32

National Grid Ref: SD5395

(0.5m) *Hollin Root Farm, Garth Row, Skelsmergh, Kendal, Cumbria, LA8 9AW*.
Peaceful farmhouse with warm welcome.
Grades: ETB Listed
Tel: **01539 823638** Mrs Metcalfe.
Rates fr: *£15.00-£16.00*.
Open: All Year (not Xmas)
Beds: 1F 1D 1T
Baths: 1 Ensuite 1 Shared
⛇ 🅿 (6) 🚶 ❏ 🛏 Ⅲ

High season, bank holidays and special events mean low availability *everywhere*.

Kendal 33

National Grid Ref: SD5192

🍴 🍺 Castle Pub, Kendal Arms, Wheatsheaf Inn, The Fleece, The Phoenix, The Rainbow, The Brewery, The Bridge, Gateway Hotel

(4m 🚐) *Bridge House, 65 Castle Street, Kendal, Cumbria, LA9 7AD*.
Actual grid ref: SD5293
Grades: ETB 1 Cr
Tel: **01539 722041**
Mrs Brindley.
Rates fr: *£15.00-£18.00*.
Open: All Year
Beds: 1F 1T
Baths: 1 Shared
⛇ ❏ 🛏 Ⅲ 🅥 🖩 ⚡
Beautiful "Listed" building, former station master's house (close to Kendal bus and train stations). Ample drying room. Will collect and deliver to Dales Way Path.

(2m) *Newlands Guest House, 37 Milnthorpe Road, Kendal, Cumbria, LA9 5QG*.
Actual grid ref: SD515916
Comfortable, friendly Victorian house.
Grades: ETB 2 Cr, Approv
Tel: **01539 725340**
Mrs Horsley.
Rates fr: *£15.00-£15.00*.
Open: All Year (not Xmas)
Beds: 1F 2D 1T 1S
Baths: 2 Private, 1 Shared
⛇ 🅿 (5) ❏ 🛏 ✕ Ⅲ 🅥 🖩 ⚡

(0.5m) *Sundial House,*
51 Milnthorpe Road, Kendal,
Cumbria, LA9 5QG.
Actual grid ref: SD515916
Large Victorian family house.
Grades: ETB 2 Cr
Tel: **01539 724468** Mrs Bowker.
Rates fr: *£15.50*-**£15.50**.
Open: All Year
Beds: 1F 2D 2T
Baths: 1 Ensuite 3 Shared
ॐ P (8) ⌷ ★ ▥ Ⅴ ▯ ✦

(0.5m) *Fairways, 102 Windermere*
Road, Kendal, Cumbria, LA9 5EZ.
Traditional Victorian guesthouse.
Grades: ETB 2 Cr, Comm
Tel: **01539 725564** Mrs Paylor.
Rates fr: *£17.00*.
Open: All Year
Beds: 1F 3D
Baths: 3 Ensuite
ॐ (2) P ⊬ ⌷ ▥ Ⅴ ✦

(▲ On Path) *Kendal Youth*
Hostel, 118 Highgate, Kendal,
Cumbria, LA9 4HE.
Actual grid ref: SD515924
Warden: Mr Butcher.
Tel: **01539 724066**
Under 18: £5.35 **Adults:** £8.00
Meals available, Self-Catering,
Central Heating, Shop, Car Park
Converted Georgian townhouse,
adjoining Brewery Arts Centre, in
a prime postion in the centre of
Kendal

(1.5m) *Da Francos, 101 Highgate,*
Kendal, Cumbria, LA9 4EN.
Three-storey town house.
Grades: ETB 2 Cr
Tel: **01539 722430** Mr Messina.
Rates fr: *£20.00*-**£25.00**.
Open: All Year
Beds: 3F 4D 1T 2S
Baths: 10 Private
ॐ P (3) ⌷ ✕ ▥ Ⅴ

(2m) *19 Castle Street, Kendal,*
Cumbria, LA9 7AD.
Cosy cottage.
Tel: **01539 727424**
Mrs Swainbank.
Rates fr: *£15.50*-**£16.00**.
Open: All Year
Beds: 1D **Baths:** 1 Ensuite
⊬ ⌷ ▥ Ⅴ ✦

(2m 🚐) *Sonata, 19 Burnside*
Road, Kendal, Cumbria, LA9 4RL.
Friendly family run guesthouse.
Grades: ETB Listed
Tel: **01539 732290** Mr Wilkinson.
Rates fr: *£17.00*-**£17.00**.
Open: All Year
Beds: 2F 1D 1T 1S
Baths: 2 Shared
ॐ ⌷ ★ ✕ ▥ Ⅴ ▯ ✦

(2m) *Park Lea, 15 Sunnyside,*
Kendal, Cumbria, LA9 7DJ.
Actual grid ref: SD519924
Comfortable Victorian house over-
looking parkland.
Grades: ETB 2 Cr, Comm
Tel: **01539 740986** Mr Bunney.

Rates fr: *£16.00*-**£16.00**.
Open: All Year (not Xmas)
Beds: 2D 1T
Baths: 2 Ensuite 1 Private
P (2) ⌷ ★ ▥ Ⅴ ✦

(2m) *7 Thorny Hills, Kendal,*
Cumbria, LA9 7AL.
Quiet, unspoilt Georgian town
house.
Grades: ETB 1 Cr, Comm
Tel: **01539 720207**
Mr & Mrs Jowett.
Rates fr: *£17.00*-**£19.00**.
Open: Jan to Nov
Beds: 2D 1T
Baths: 3 Private
ॐ ⊬ ⌷ ✕ ▥ Ⅴ

(On Path) *Brantholme,*
7 Sedbergh Road, Kendal,
Cumbria, LA9 6AD.
Victorian house in private grounds.
Grades: ETB Listed
Tel: **01539 722340** Mrs Bigland.
Rates fr: *£18.00*-**£24.00**.
Open: Feb to Nov
Beds: 3T
Baths: 3 Private
ॐ P (5) ⊬ ⌷ ✕ ▥ Ⅴ ▯ ✦

Burnside 34

National Grid Ref: SD5095

🍴 🍺 Jolly Anglers Inn

(1m) *Hill Fold Farm, Burnside,*
Kendal, Cumbria, LA8 9AU.
Actual grid ref: SD517977
Warm friendly comfortable farm-
house.
Grades: ETB 1 Cr, Approved
Tel: **01539 722574** Mrs Bell.
Rates fr: *£14.00*.
Open: All Year
Beds: 1F 1D 1T
Baths: 1 Shared
ॐ P (3) ⌷ ✕ ▯ ✦

Please don't camp

on *anyone's* land

without first obtaining

their permission.

(0.5m) *Garnett House Farm,*
Burnside, Kendal, Cumbria,
LA9 5SF.
Actual grid ref: SD500959
C15th farmhouse.
Grades: ETB 2 Cr, Comm,
AA Listed, RAC Acclaim
Tel: **01539 724542** Mrs Beaty.
Rates fr: *£14.00*.
Open: All Year (not Xmas)
Beds: 2F 2D 1T
Baths: 3 Private 2 Shared
ॐ P (10) ⌷ ✕

Plantation Bridge 35

National Grid Ref: SD4896

(0.5m) *Burrow Hall Country*
Guesthouse, Plantation Bridge,
Kendal, Cumbria, LA8 9JR.
C17th Lakeland guesthouse.
Grades: ETB 3 Cr, High Comm,
AA 4 Q, Select
Tel: **01539 821711**
Mrs Brind.
Rates fr: *£22.50*.
Open: All Year
Beds: 1D 2T
Baths: 3 Private
ॐ (16) P (8) ⌷ ✕ ▥

Staveley 36

National Grid Ref: SD4698

🍴 🍺 Eagle & Child Inn, Duke
William, Railway Hotel

(1m) *Tarn House, 18 Danes Road,*
Staveley, Kendal, Cumbria, LA8 9PW.
Actual grid ref: SD469986
Clean, friendly home, fabulous
breakfast.
Grades: ETB 1 Cr
Tel: **01539 821656**
Mrs Porter.
Rates fr: *£14.00*-**£20.00**.
Open: Easter to Nov
Beds: 1F 2D
Baths: 1 Shared
ॐ P (3) ⊬ ⌷ ★ ▥ Ⅴ ▯ ✦

(0.5m) *17 Danes Road, Staveley,*
Kendal, Cumbria, LA8 9PW.
Actual grid ref: SD4698
Attractive Victorian country home.
Grades: ETB Listed
Tel: **01539 821148**
Mrs Crawford.
Rates fr: *£14.00*-**£20.00**.
Open: All Year (not Xmas)
Beds: 2F 1S
Baths: 1 Shared
ॐ P (2) ⊬ ⌷ ★ ▥ Ⅴ ▯ ✦

(0.25m) *Danes House, 1 Danes*
Road, Staveley, Kendal, Cumbria,
LA8 9PW.
Convenient Windermere, Lakes
and Dales.
Tel: **01539 821294**
Mr Alexander.
Rates fr: *£14.00*-**£16.00**.
Open: All Year (not Xmas)
Beds: 2F
Baths: 1 Shared
ॐ P ⌷ ▥

(On Path) *Stock Bridge Farm,*
Staveley, Kendal, Cumbria, LA8 9LP.
Actual grid ref: SD473978
Modernised, comfortable C17th
farmhouse.
Grades: ETB Listed, Comm
Tel: **01539 821580**
Mrs Fishwick.
Rates fr: *£14.50*-**£14.50**.
Open: Mar to Oct
Beds: 1F 4D 1S
Baths: 1 Shared
ॐ P (6) ⌷ ★ ▥ Ⅴ ▯ ✦

Ings 37

National Grid Ref: SD4498

|◉| ⛴ Water Mill

(1.5m 🚌) A Badger's Rest, *Ings, Nr Staveley, Kendal, Cumbria, LA8 9PY.*
Actual grid ref: SD4498
Grades: ETB Listed, Approv
Tel: **01539 821135** Mrs Badger.
Rates fr: *£13.50-£16.00.*
Open: All Year
Beds: 1F 2D 1T
Baths: 2 Ensuite 1 Shared
⛺ 🅿 (5) ⌇ ⌇ 🔥 🗙 🎞 Ⓥ 🖴 ✦
Also 🛆 *£3.50 per tent.*
Open: All Year ⊤ ⛭ 🗙 ✦ ⅃
On cycleway, bus route A591
between Windermere and Staveley.
Delightful rest stop, a home from
home. Continental breakfast in bed,
Bavarian supper by log fire.

(1.5m) St Annes Farm, *Ings, Kendal, Cumbria, LA8 9QG.*
Very clean comfortable farmhouse.
Tel: **01539 821223** Mrs Allen.
Rates fr: *£15.00-£20.00.*
Open: Easter to Oct
Beds: 2D **Baths:** 1 Shared
🅿 (4) ⌇ ⌇ Ⓥ

Bowness 38

National Grid Ref: SD4096

|◉| ⛴ Hole In the Wall, The Albert
Hotel, John Peel, Grey Walls Inn,
Village Inn, Old John Peel Pub

(0.25m 🚌) Eastbourne Hotel,
Biskey Howe Road, Bowness, Windermere, CumbriaCumbria, LA23 2JR.
Grades: ETB 2 Cr, Comm,
AA 3 Q, RAC High Acclaim
Tel: **015394 43525** Mr Whitfield.
Rates fr: *£17.00-£18.00.*
Open: All Year
Beds: 2F 4D 2S
Baths: 6 Ensuite, 2 Shared
⛺ 🅿 (6) ⌇ ⌇ 🎞 Ⓥ 🖴 ✦
A quiet family-run hotel. Easy
walking distance to Lake and all
amenities. Comfortable, spacious
and well furnished bedrooms with
private facilities and colour TV.

**(1m 🚌) Fayrer Garden House
Hotel,** *Lyth Valley Road, Bowness, Windermere, Cumbria, LA23 3JP.*
Grades: ETB 3 Cr, High Comm,
AA 2 St
Tel: **015394 88195** Mr Garside.
Rates fr: *£25.00.*
Open: All Year
Beds: 15D
Baths: 15 Private
⛺ 🅿 ⌇ 🔥 🗙 🎞 Ⓥ 🖴 ✦
Beautiful country house overlook-
ing Lake Windermere. 4 posters,
jacuzzis, free local leisure facilities.
Your reward for completing Dales
Way! Special breaks available.
Please send for colour brochure

(0.25m) Cranleigh Hotel, *Kendal Road, Bowness, Windermere, Cumbria, LA23 3EW.*
Large Edwardian private house.
Grades: ETB 3 Cr, Comm,
AA 2 St, RAC High Acclaim
Tel: **015394 43293**
Mr Wigglesworth.
Rates fr: *£18.00-£18.00.*
Open: All Year
Beds: 4F 5D 6T
Baths: 15 Ensuite
⛺ 🅿 (15) ⌇ 🗙 🎞 Ⓥ ✦

(0.5m 🚌) Above The Bay,
5, Brackenfield, Bowness, Windermere, Cumbria, LA23 3HL.
Modern with superb lake views.
Tel: **015394 88658** Mr Bell.
Rates fr: *£17.50-£20.00.*
Open: All Year
Beds: 1F 2D 1T 1S
Baths: 5 Ensuite
⛺ 🅿 (8) ⌇ ⌇ 🔥 🎞 ⅃ Ⓥ 🖴 ✦

**(On Path) Fairfield Country
House Hotel,** *Brantfell Road, Bowness, Windermere, Cumbria, LA23 3AE.*
Actual grid ref: SD967404
200-year-old Lakeland hotel.
Grades: ETB 3 Cr, Comm,
AA 3 Q, RAC High Acclaim
Tel: **015349 46565**
Mr & Mrs Hood.
Rates fr: *£24.00-£24.00.*
Open: All Year (not Xmas)
Beds: 2F 5D 1T 1S
Baths: 8 Ensuite 1 Shared
⛺ 🅿 (12) ⌇ ⌇ 🗙 🎞 🖴 ✦

(0.25m) Westbourne, *Biskey House Road, Bowness, Windermere, CumbriaCumbria, LA23 2JR.*
Small friendly hotel in peaceful
location.
Grades: ETB 3 Cr, Comm,
RAC High Acclaim
Tel: **015394 43625** Mr Wright.
Rates fr: *£17.00-£21.00.*
Open: All Year (not Xmas)
Beds: 3F 4D 2T
Baths: 9 Ensuite
⛺ 🅿 (11) ⌇ 🔥 🗙 🎞 Ⓥ 🖴 ✦

(0.25m) Lingwood, *Birkett Hill, Bowness, Windermere, CumbriaCumbria, LA23 3EZ.*
Actual grid ref: SD403964
Modern, comfortable, family guest-
house.
Grades: ETB 2 Cr
Tel: **015394 44680** Mrs Mossop.
Rates fr: *£15.00-£18.00.*
Open: All Year
Beds: 2F 3D 1T
Baths: 2 Ensuite 3 Shared
⛺ 🅿 (6) ⌇ 🎞 ✦

(On Path) Virginia Cottage,
Kendal Road, Bowness, Windermere, Cumbria, LA23 3EJ.
Two adjoining C19th cottages.
Grades: ETB 2 Cr
Tel: **015394 44891** Mr Britton.
Rates fr: *£14.00-£18.00.*
Open: All Year (not Xmas)
Beds: 2F 9D
Baths: 3 Ensuite 3 Shared
⛺ 🅿 (9) ⌇ 🎞 Ⓥ ✦

(0.5m 🚌) Nogoya, *4 Brackenfield, Kendal Road, Bowness, Windermere, Cumbria, LA23 3HL.*
Modern house overlooking lake.
Tel: **015349 44356**
Rates fr: *£17.50.*
Open: All Year
Beds: 3D 1T **Baths:** 4 Ensuite
⛺ (3) 🅿 (5) ⌇ 🔥 🎞 Ⓥ ✦

Pay B&Bs by cash or cheque and be prepared to pay up front.

Essex Way

Covering a distance of 81 miles, the **Essex Way** stretches from Epping in the south-west to Harwich, the busy sea port, in the northeast. The path is perfect for Londoners who want easy access to a good, waymarked long distance footpath. It is well-placed for public transport, which is accessible at all points of the path. You get to see a rural Essex unheard of outside the county boundaries - ancient woodland, open farmland, the tree-flanked River Colne, leafy valleys, green country lanes and saltmarshes. A good spring-time or autumn walk - the terrain is very easy going, but can be muddy after rain.

Guides: *The Essex Way* by Essex County Council (ISBN 1852810874), published by Essex County Council and available directly from their offices (Ways Through Essex, Planning Dept, County Hall, Chelmsford, Essex, CM1 1LF, tel. 01245 450777), £3.00

Maps: 1:50000 Ordnance Survey Landranger Series: 167, 168, 169

Epping   1

National Grid Ref: TL4502

¹⁰¹ 🍺 Duke of Wellington

(0.75m) *Uplands, 181a Lindsey Street, Epping, Essex, CM16 6RF.*
Comfortable family house, rural views.
Grades: ETB Listed, Approv
Tel: 01992 573733
Mrs Stacy.
Rates fr: *£16.00-£16.00.*
Open: All Year
Beds: 2F 2S
Baths: 2 Shared
🛌 🅿 (6) ½ 🗖 🛏 ⚡

Stanford Rivers   2

National Grid Ref: TL5301

¹⁰¹ 🍺 Drill House, Green Man

(0.75m) *Newhouse Farm, Mutton Row, Stanford Rivers, Chipping Ongar, Essex, CM5 9QH.*
Tudor farmhouse with disabled unit. **Grades:** ETB 1 Cr
Tel: 01277 362132
Mr & Mrs Martin.
Rates fr: *£16.00-£16.00.*
Open: All Year (not Xmas)
Beds: 1F 1D 4S
Baths: 1 Private 1 Shared
🛌 🅿 (100) 🗖 🛏 & Ⅴ 🍴

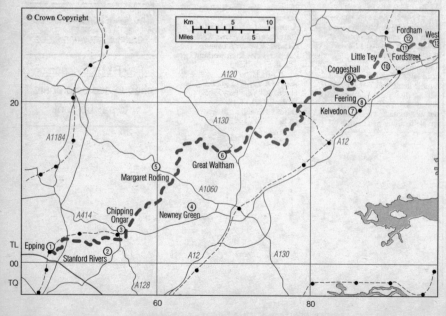

Chipping Ongar 3

National Grid Ref: TL5103

(1.75m 🚌) **Bumbles,** *Moreton Road, Chipping Ongar, Essex, CM5 0EZ.*
Actual grid ref: TL546052
Comfortable cottage plus good breakfast.
Grades: ETB Listed
Tel: 01277 362695 Mrs Withey.
Rates fr: *£17.00*-**£17.00**.
Open: All Year (not Xmas)
Beds: 3T
Baths: 2 Shared
🛇 (12) 🅿 (6) ⅍ 🖵 🎟 🖩 ⓥ 🛆 ⚡

Newney Green 4

National Grid Ref: TL6507

🅃🍴 🍺 The Duck

(4m) **Moor Hall,** *Newney Green, Writtle, Chelmsford, Essex, CM1 3SE.*
Actual grid ref: TL650065
Medieval timber-framed working farm.
Grades: ETB Listed
Tel: 01245 420814 Mrs Gemmill.
Rates fr: *£19.00*-**£21.00**.
Open: All Year (not Xmas)
Beds: 2F **Baths:** 1 Shared
🛇 🅿 (10) ⅍ 🖵 ✕ 🖩 ⓥ 🛆 ⚡

Margaret Roding 5

National Grid Ref: TL5912

🅃🍴 🍺 Hare & Hounds

(1m) **Greys,** *Ongar Road, Margaret Roding, Great Dunmow, Essex, CM6 1QR.*
Beamed cottage, amidst our farm.
Grades: ETB Listed, AA 2 Q
Tel: 01245 231509 Mrs Matthews.
Rates fr: *£19.00*-**£20.00**.
Open: All Year (not Xmas)
Beds: 2D 1T **Baths:** 1 Shared
🛇 (10) 🅿 (3) ⅍ 🖩.

The Grid Reference beneath the location heading is for the village or town - *not* for individual houses, which are shown (where supplied) in each entry itself.

Great Waltham 6

National Grid Ref: TL6913

🅃🍴 🍺 The Windmill

(0.75m) **Wildingtree,** *South Street, Great Waltham, Chelmsford, Essex, CM3 1EE.*
Actual grid ref: TL692129
Traditional, non-smoking, village house.
Grades: ETB Listed, High Comm
Tel: 01245 362369 Mrs Pyne.
Rates fr: *£20.00*-**£20.00**.
Open: All Year (not Xmas/New Year)
Beds: 1D 2S
Baths: 1 Ensuite 1 Shared
🛇 (12) 🅿 (3) ⅍ 🖵 🖩 ⓥ ⚡

Kelvedon 7

National Grid Ref: TL8618

🅃🍴 🍺 The Sun, The Railway Tavern

(2m) **Highfields Farm,** *Kelvedon, Colchester, Essex, CO5 9BJ.*
Large farmhouse on working farm.

Grades: ETB 2 Cr
Tel: 01376 570334 Mrs Bunting.
Rates fr: *£17.00*-**£20.00**.
Open: All Year
Beds: 3T
Baths: 3 Ensuite
🛇 🅿 (10) ⅍ 🖵 🛆 ⚡

Feering 8

National Grid Ref: TL8719

🅃🍴 🍺 Sun Inn

(1.25m) **Hanover House,** *The Street, Feering, Colchester, Essex, CO5 9QN.*
Unusual country house rural views.
Tel: 01376 570437 Mrs Cooke.
Rates fr: *£14.00*-**£14.00**.
Open: All Year (not Xmas)
Beds: 2T 1S
Baths: 1 Shared
🛇 (2) 🅿 (3) 🖵 🖩 ⓥ

Coggeshall 9

National Grid Ref: TL8522

🅃🍴 🍺 Cricketers Pub

(0.25m) **White Heather Guest House,** *19 Colchester Road, Coggeshall, Colchester, Essex, CO6 1RP.*
Actual grid ref: TL859228
Modern family run guesthouse.
Tel: 01376 563004 Mrs Shaw.
Rates fr: *£20.00*-**£20.00**.
Open: All Year (not Xmas)
Beds: 2D 1T 3S
Baths: 2 Ensuite, 1 Shared
🅿 (8) ⅍ 🖵 🖩 ⚡

The lowest *double* rate per person is shown in *italics*.

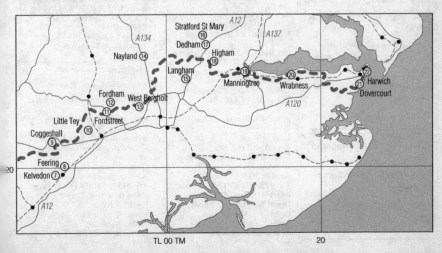

Little Tey 10

National Grid Ref: TL8923

(0.25m) *Knaves Farmhouse, Great Tey Road, Little Tey, Colchester, Essex, CO6 1JA.*
Actual grid ref: TL895240
Victorian farmhouse in rural surroundings.
Grades: ETB Listed
Tel: 01206 211039 Mrs Carr.
Rates fr: *£30.00-£20.00*.
Open: All Year
Beds: 1D 1T
Baths: 1 Ensuite 1 Shared
🛏 (2) 🅿 (4) 🗪 🏠 ⬛ ⌖

Fordstreet 11

National Grid Ref: TL9226

🍴 🍺 Coopers Arms, Queens Head, Shoulder of Mutton

(On Path) *Old House, Fordstreet, Aldham, Colchester, Essex, CO6 3PH.*
Actual grid ref: TL920270
Historic C14th oak-beamed hallhouse.
Grades: ETB 1 Cr, Comm
Tel: 01206 240456 Mrs Mitchell.
Rates fr: *£17.50-£25.00*.
Open: All Year
Beds: 1F 1T 1S
Baths: 1 Ensuite 2 Private
🛏 🅿 (8) 🗪 ⬛ ⌖

The Country Code

Enjoy the countryside and respect its life and work

Guard against all risk of fire

Fasten all gates

Keep your dogs under close control

Keep to public paths across farmland

Use gates and stiles to cross fences, hedges and walls

Leave livestock, crops and machinery alone

Take your litter home

Help to keep all water clean

Protect wild-life, plants and trees

Take special care on country roads

Make no unnecessary noise

Fordham 12

National Grid Ref: TL9228

🍴 🍺 Vulcan

(On Path 🚲) *Kings Vineyard, Fordham, Colchester, Essex, CO6 3NY.*
Actual grid ref: TL9328
Friendly farmhouse, beautiful views all around.
Grades: ETB 2 Cr, Comm
Tel: 01206 240377
Mrs Tweed.
Rates fr: *£16.00-£18.00*.
Open: All Year
Beds: 1F 1D 1T
Baths: 1 Private 1 Shared
🛏 (1) 🅿 (6) ⌖ 🗪 ⬛ Ⓥ ⌖
Also ⛺ *£1.50 per tent.*Ⓣ ⌖

West Bergholt 13

National Grid Ref: TL9627

🍴 🍺 The White Hart, The Treble Tile

(On Path) *The Old Post House, 10 Colchester Road, West Bergholt, Colchester, Essex, CO6 3JG.*
Actual grid ref: TL9527
Large Victorian private house.
Grades: ETB 2 Cr
Tel: 01206 240379
Mrs Brown.
Rates fr: *£16.00-£20.00*.
Open: All Year (not Xmas)
Beds: 1F 1D 1T
Baths: 1 Ensuite, 1 Shared
🛏 🅿 (3) 🗪 🏠 ✕ ⬛ ⌖ ⌖

Nayland 14

National Grid Ref: TL9734

🍴 🍺 The Angel, The Anchor

(0.5m 🚲) *Hill House, Gravel Hill, Nayland, Colchester, Essex, CO6 4JB.*
Actual grid ref: TL975345
C16th village house.
Grades: ETB Listed, Comm, AA 3 Q
Tel: 01206 262782 Mrs Heigham.
Rates fr: *£19.00-£20.00*.
Open: All Year (not Xmas)
Beds: 1D 1T 1S
Baths: 1 Ensuite 1 Shared
🛏 (10) 🅿 (3) 🗪 ⬛ Ⓥ ⌖ ⌖

(0.5m 🚲) *Gladwins Farm, Harpers Hill, Nayland, Colchester, Essex, CO6 4NU.*
Actual grid ref: TL961347
Modernised Suffolk farmhouse. Wonderful views.
Grades: ETB 2 Cr, Comm
Tel: 01206 262261 Mrs Dossor.
Rates fr: *£20.00-£20.00*.
Open: All Year (not Xmas)
Beds: 1F 1D 1T 1S
Baths: 2 Ensuite 1 Shared
🛏 🅿 🗪 🏠 ✕ ⬛ Ⓥ ⌖ ⌖

Langham 15

National Grid Ref: TM0231

🍴 🍺 Shepherd & Dog

(1m 🚲) *Oak Apple Farm, Greyhound Hill, Langham, Colchester, Essex, CO4 5QF.*
Actual grid ref: TM023320
Comfortable farmhouse, large attractive garden.
Grades: ETB Listed
Tel: 01206 272234 Mrs Helliwell.
Rates fr: *£17.50-£18.00*.
Open: All Year (not Xmas)
Beds: 2T 1S
Baths: 1 Shared
🛏 🅿 (6) 🗪 ⬛ Ⓥ ⌖ ⌖

Stratford St Mary 16

National Grid Ref: TM0434

🍴 🍺 The Swan, The Anchor, Black Horse

(0.75m 🚲) *Teazles, Stratford St Mary, Colchester, Essex, CO7 6LU.*
Modernised C15th weaver's house.
Grades: ETB Listed, Comm
Tel: 01206 323148 Mrs Clover.
Rates fr: *£18.00-£18.00*.
Open: All Year
Beds: 4F 1D 2T 1S
Baths: 1 Shared
🛏 🅿 (7) ⌖ 🗪 🏠 ⬛ Ⓥ ⌖ ⌖

Dedham 17

National Grid Ref: TM0533

🍴 🍺 The Anchor, The Lamb

(0.5m) *Mays Barn Farm, Mays Lane, Dedham, Colchester, Essex, CO7 6EW.*
Actual grid ref: TM0531
Tranquil secluded comfortable old farmhouse.
Grades: ETB 2 Cr, High Comm
Tel: 01206 323191 Mrs Freeman.
Rates fr: *£19.00-£22.00*.
Open: All Year (not Xmas)
Beds: 1D 1T
Baths: 2 Ensuite
🛏 (12) 🅿 (4) ⌖ 🗪 ⬛ Ⓥ

Higham 18

National Grid Ref: TM0335

🍴 🍺 Ross Inn, Thorington Street

(0.5m) *The Bauble, Higham, Colchester, Essex, CO7 6LA.*
Actual grid ref: TM031354
Quiet family home overlooking meadows.
Grades: ETB 2 Cr, High Comm, AA 4 Q, Select
Tel: 01206 337254 Mrs Watkins.
Rates fr: *£20.00-£22.00*.
Open: All Year
Beds: 2T 1S
Baths: 3 Ensuite
🛏 (12) 🅿 (4) ⌖ 🗪 ⬛ Ⓥ ⌖ ⌖

Manningtree 19

National Grid Ref: TM1031

†⊙¶ ⚑ Kings Arms, Wagon & Horses

(0.75m 🚌) *Aldhams, Bromley Road, Lawford, Manningtree, Essex, CO11 2NE.*
Actual grid ref: TM098302
Grades: ETB 2 Cr, Comm
Tel: **01206 393210** Mrs McEwen.
Rates fr: *£22.50-£25.00.*
Open: All Year (not Xmas)
Beds: 1D 1T 2S
Baths: 2 Ensuite, 1 Shared
🛏 🅿 (6) ⊬ ♌ 🛏 📺 ⚡
A Lutyens-style converted farmhouse set in beautiful gardens surrounded by farmland. Ideal base for Flatford Mill and Dedham, walking, birdwatching, sailing and visiting gardens.

Wrabness 20

National Grid Ref: TM1731

†⊙¶ ⚑ Black Boy Inn

(0.5m 🚌) *Dimbols Farm, Station Road, Wrabness, Nr Manningtree, Essex, CO11 2TH.*
Actual grid ref: TM175313
Large, comfortable, quiet Georgian farmhouse.
Grades: ETB 1 Cr

Tel: **01255 880328** Mrs Macaulay.
Rates fr: *£14.50-£16.00.*
Open: All Year
Beds: 1F 1D
Baths: 1 Shared
🛏 🅿 ⊬ ♌ 🛏 📺 ⚡

Dovercourt 21

National Grid Ref: TM2531

†⊙¶ ⚑ Kings Head, Cliff Hotel, Royal Oak, Queens Hotel

(m) *154 Fronks Road, Dovercourt, Harwich, Essex, CO12 4EF.*
Detached house in tree-lined boulevard.
Grades: ETB 3 Cr Comm
Tel: **01255 503081**
Mrs Cullen.
Rates fr: *£13.00-£15.00.*
Open: Dec to Jan
Beds: 1F 1T
🛏 🅿 (4) ⊬ ♌ 🛏

(m) *Queens Hotel, 119 High Street, Dovercourt, Harwich, Essex, CO12 3AP.*
Public house/hotel.
Grades: ETB 1 Cr
Tel: **01255 502634**
Mrs Skinner.
Rates fr: *£15.00-£15.00.*
Open: All Year
Beds: 1F 4T 2S
Baths: 1 Shared
🛏 🅿 (15) ♌ ✕ 🛏

(0.75m) *Ivy Lea Guest House, 42 Cliff Road, Dovercourt, Harwich, Essex, CO12 3PP.*
Small friendly guesthouse.
Grades: ETB 1 Cr
Tel: **01255 507816** Mrs Johnson.
Rates fr: *£12.50-£13.00.*
Open: All Year
Beds: 1D 2T **Baths:** 2 Shared
🛏 🅿 (3) ♌ ⊀ ✕ 🛏 📺

Harwich 22

National Grid Ref: TM2431

†⊙¶ ⚑ Alma Inn, Hanover Inn

(On Path 🚌) *Reids of Harwich, 3 West Street, Harwich, Essex, CO12 3DA.*
Comfortable Victorian property, historic location.
Grades: ETB 1 Cr
Tel: **01255 506796** Mr Reid.
Rates fr: *£16.00-£16.00.*
Open: Apr to Oct
Beds: 1D 1T 1S **Baths:** 2 Shared
🛏 🅿 (12) ♌ 🛏 📺 🔥 🛁 ⚡

All rates are subject
to alteration at the
owners' discretion.

Fife Coastal Walk

The **Fife Coastal Walk** is a little-known long distance footpath that deserves greater recognition and wider coverage. It follows a beautiful 94-mile stretch of the East Scottish coastline, famous for its fishing villages, golf links and silvery estuaries. It is pretty much easy going and makes for a decent week's walking. From Tentsmuir Point inland to Newburgh it's very quiet indeed. The pioneers among you will appreciate that the path is only partly waymarked and may therefore be keen to blaze the trail (not literally), perhaps even to write the first all-in-one guidebook. Hence its inclusion

here. Be careful round Fife Ness - the cliffs can be dangerous, especially where the path is unfenced.

Guide: A series of booklets with hand-drawn maps of the Fife Coastal Walk is available from the Wemyss Environmental Education Centre, East Wemyss Primary School, School Wynd, East Wemyss, Fife, KY1 4RN.

Map: 1:50000 Ordnance Survey Landranger Series: 58, 59, 65 and 66.

All rates are subject to alteration at the owners' discretion.

North Queensferry 1

National Grid Ref: NT1380

(On Path) *Bankton House, Main Street, North Queensferry, Fife, KY11 1HA.*
Self-contained basement flat.
Tel: **01383 415711** Mrs Chambers.
Rates fr: *£15.00-£20.00.*
Open: All Year (not Xmas)
Beds: 1D ▣ ⚥ ▢

Inverkeithing 2

National Grid Ref: NT1382

⊗ ◳ Queens Hotel

(On Path 🐾) *Borland Lodge Private Hotel, 31-33 Boreland Road, Inverkeithing, Fife, KY11 1DA.*
Modern hotel in quiet location.
Grades: STB 3 Cr, Comm
Tel: **01383 413792** Mr Milton.
Rates fr: *£16.00-£21.00.*
Open: All Year
Beds: 2F 7D 3T 14S
Baths: 26 Private
▻ ▤ ▢ ⼎ ✕ ▥ & �v ⓐ ✦

Hillend 3

National Grid Ref: NT1483

(1.5m) *National Activity Centre, Fordell Firs, Hillend, Dunfermline, Fife, KY11 5HQ.*
Actual grid ref: NT143854
Superb bunkhouse and campsite.
Tel: **01383 412704** Mr Barnes.
Rates fr: *£5.00-£7.00.*
Open: All Year (not Xmas)
Beds: 7F 2D
▻ (7) ▣ (100) ▢ ⼎ ▥.
Also ⛺ *£3.50 per tent. Also bunkhouse, £4.50 per bunk*
Open: All Year ⌂ Ⓣ ⚏ ✦ ⚘

The Grid Reference beneath the location heading is for the village or town - *not* for individual houses, which are shown (where supplied) in each entry itself.

Aberdour 4

National Grid Ref: NT1985

⊗ ◳ Woodside Hotel, Aberdour Hotel

(On Path) *Hawkcraig House, Hawkcraig Point, Aberdour, Burntisland, Fife, KY3 0TZ.*
Actual grid ref: NT198850
Water's edge, old ferryman's house.
Grades: STB 3 Cr, De Luxe, AA 4 Q, Select
Tel: **01383 860335** Barrie.
Rates fr: *£20.00-£26.00.*
Open: Mar to Oct
Beds: 1D 1T
Baths: 2 Private
▻ (10) ▣ (3) ⚥ ▢ ✕ ▥.Ⓥ

(On Path) *The Woodside Hotel, High Street, Aberdour, Burntisland, Fife, KY3 0SW.*
Actual grid ref: NT187853
Interesting, recently refurbished Listed building.
Grades: RAC 3 St
Tel: **01383 860328** Mr Austen.
Rates fr: *£26.50-£49.50.*
Open: All Year
Beds: 1F 15D 3T 1S
Baths: 20 Ensuite
▣ (31) ⚥ ▢ ⼎ ✕ ▥.Ⓥ ⓐ

Burntisland 5

National Grid Ref: NT2386

⊗ ◳ Smugglers Inn, Inchview Hotel, Harbour Place

(1.5m) *Inchview Hotel, 69 Kinghorn Road, Burntisland, Fife, KY3 9EB.*
Beautiful comfortable family-run hotel.
Grades: STB 4 Cr, Comm
Tel: **01592 872239**
Mr Black.
Rates fr: *£29.50-£39.50.*
Open: All Year
Beds: 1F 6D 3T 2S
Baths: 12 Ensuite
▻ ▣ (15) ▢ ⼎ ✕ ▥.Ⓥ ⓐ ✦

(1.25m 🐾) *Gleniffer, 28 Kirkton Road, Burntisland, Fife, KY3 0BY.*
Comfortable bungalow near town centre.
Tel: **01592 873903**
Mrs Lawson.
Rates fr: *£11.00-£13.00.*
Open: All Year
Beds: 1D
Baths: 1 Shared
▻ (10) ▣ ▢ ⼎ ✕ ▥.Ⓥ ⓐ ✦

(1.25m) *Inchcape Guest House, 1 South View, Lammerlaws, Burntisland, Fife, KY3 9BS.*
Large Victorian private house.
Tel: **01592 873270**
Mrs Sharp.
Rates fr: *£15.00-£15.00.*
Open: All Year
Beds: 1F 1T 1S
▻ ▣ ▢ ⼎ ▥. ✦

(1.5m) *127 Kinghorn Road, Burntisland, Fife, KY3 9JW.*
Victorian house close to beach.
Tel: **01592 873165** Mrs Chisholm.
Rates fr: *£15.00-£15.00.*
Open: All Year (not Xmas)
Beds: 1T 1S 1D 1F
Baths: 2 Shared
▻ ▣ (1) ⚥ ▢ ▥.

Kinghorn 6

National Grid Ref: NT2686

⊗ ◳ Longboat Inn

(On Path) *Craigo-Er, 45 Pettycur Road, Kinghorn, Fife, KY3 9RN.*
Large Victorian house. Sea views.
Tel: **01592 890527** Mrs Thomson.
Rates fr: *£16.00-£16.00.*
Open: All Year
Beds: 1D 2T
Baths: 2 Shared
▻ ▣ ⼎ ▥.Ⓥ ⓐ ✦

Kirkcaldy 7

National Grid Ref: NT2791

⊗ ◳ Four Ways Restauran, St. Clair Tavern, Grant Restaurant, Hoffmans, La Gondola, St. Clair Tavern, The Steadings, Betty Nicol's

(On Path) *Castleview, 17 Dysart Road, Kirkcaldy, Fife, KY1 2AY.*
Tel: **01592 269275** Mrs Dick.
Rates fr: *£14.00-£14.00.*
Open: All Year (not Xmas)
Beds: 1F 2T **Baths:** 1 Shared
▻ ▣ ⼎ ✕ ▥.Ⓥ ⓐ ✦

(0.25m) *Cameron House, 44 Glebe Park, Kirkcaldy, Fife, KY1 1BL.*
Friendly and comfortable, good food.
Tel: **01592 264531** Mrs Nicol.
Rates fr: *£13.50-£13.50.*
Open: Mar to Dec
Beds: 1F 1D **Baths:** 1 Shared
▻ (2) ⚥ ▢ ⼎ ✕ ▥.Ⓥ ✦

(0.25m) *Cherrydene, 44 Bennochy Road, Kirkcaldy, Fife, KY2 5RB.*
Large Victorian with original features.
Grades: STB 2 Cr, Comm
Tel: **01592 202147** Mrs Nicol.
Rates fr: *£16.00-£18.00.*
Open: All Year
Beds: 1F 1D 1S
Baths: 2 Ensuite 1 Shared
▻ ▣ (3) ▢ ⼎ ✕ ▥.Ⓥ ⓐ ✦

(0.25m) *Scotties B&B, 213 Nicol Street, Kirkcaldy, Fife, KY1 1PF.*
Modernised town house, all facilities.
Grades: STB 1 Cr, Comm
Tel: **01592 268596** Mrs Scott.
Rates fr: *£15.00-£17.00.*
Open: All Year (not Xmas)
Beds: 1F 3T
Baths: 3 Ensuite 1 Shared
▣ ▢ ⼎ ▥.Ⓥ ⓐ ✦

(0.25m) *143 Victoria Road,
Kirkcaldy, Fife,* KY1 1DQ.
Large former Victorian manse. Sea
views.
Grades: STB High Comm
Tel: 01592 268864 / 0585 215059
Mr & Mrs Cairns.
Rates fr: *£15.00-*£15.00.
Open: All Year
Beds: 1D 1T 1S
Baths: 1 Shared
⇖ (12) ⊇ (4) ⬓ Ⅲ, Ⓥ

(0.25m) *Crawford Hall,* 2
Kinghorn Road, Kirkcaldy, Fife,
KY1 1SU.
Large restored old vicarage.
Tel: 01592 262658 Mrs Crawford.
Rates fr: *£15.00-*£17.00.
Open: Jan to Nov
Beds: 1F 1T
Baths: 1 Shared
⇖ ⊇ (5) ⬓ 🛉 Ⅲ, ⓣ Ⓥ ✦

Dysart 8

National Grid Ref: NT3093
🍴 🍺 Royal Hotel

(0.25m) *Royal Hotel, Townhead,
Dysart, Kirkcaldy, Fife,* KY1 2XQ.
C19th friendly coaching inn.
Tel: 01592 654112 Mrs Di Marco.
Rates fr: *£16.00-*£19.00.
Open: All Year
Beds: 1F 2D 7T
Baths: 4 Ensuite 2 Shared
⇖ ⊇ (20) ⚲ ⬓ 🛉 ✗ Ⅲ, Ⓥ ◼ ✦

(On Path) *Norview, 59 Normand
Road, Dysart, Kirkcaldy, Fife,*
KY1 2XP.
Homely, comfortable, detached
stone house.
Grades: STB Approv
Tel: 01592 652804 Mrs Linton.
Rates fr: *£11.00-*£11.00.
Open: All Year **Beds:** 1D 2T
⇖ ⬓ Ⅲ, Ⓥ ◼ ✦

Leven 9

National Grid Ref: NO3800
(On Path 🚌) *Forth Bay Guest
House, Promenade, Leven, Fife,*
KY8 4HZ.
Very comfortable large Victorian
house.
Grades: STB Comm
Tel: 01333 423009 Mrs Hamilton.
Rates fr: *£12.50-*£12.50.
Open: All Year
Beds: 2F 2D
Baths: 3 Ensuite, 2 Shared
⇖ ⊇ (5) ⬓ 🛉 ✗ Ⅲ, Ⓥ ◼ ✦

Planning a longer
stay? Always ask for
any special rates.

Lundin Links 10

National Grid Ref: NO4002
🍴 🍺 Old Manor Hotel

(0.25m) *Old Manor Hotel, Leven
Road, Lundin Links, Leven, Fife,*
KY8 6AJ.
Country house hotel (12 miles St
Andrews).
Grades: STB 4 Cr, Comm,
AA 3 St
Tel: 01333 320368
Rates fr: *£25.00-*£45.00.
Open: All Year
Beds: 2F 5D 10T 2S
Baths: 19 Ensuite
⇖ ⊇ (70) ⬓ 🛉 ✗ Ⅲ, ⓣ Ⓥ

Lower Largo 11

National Grid Ref: NO4102
🍴 🍺 Railway Inn

(On Path) *Crusoe Hotel,* 2 *Main
Street, Lower Largo, Leven, Fife,*
KY8 6BT.
Actual grid ref: NO4102
Grades: STB 3 Cr, Comm
Tel: 01333 320759
Mr Jurgensen.
Rates fr: *£31.50-*£50.90.
Open: All Year
Beds: 1F 6D 4T 2S
Baths: 13 Ensuite
⇖ ⊇ (25) ⬓ ✗ Ⅲ, Ⓥ ◼ ✦
Friendly family-run hotel at waters
edge in Lower Largo, birthplace of
Alexander Selkirk, Daniel Defoe's
Robinson Crusoe (exhibition in
hotel). Bar and restaurant meals
daily

Elie 12

National Grid Ref: NO4900
🍴 🍺 Ship Inn, The Toft, The
Victoria Hotel, The Golf Hotel

(0.5m) *Milford House, 19 High
Street, Elie, Leven, Fife,* KY9 1BY.
Large Georgian private house.
Tel: 01333 330567
Mr Cowan.
Rates fr: *£15.00-*£20.00.
Open: All Year (not Xmas)
Beds: 1F 1D 1T
Baths: 3 Ensuite
⇖ ⬓ Ⅲ, ✦

(0.5m) *Ingleside, 39 Park Place,
Elie, Leven, Fife,* KY9 1DH.
Self-contained garden flat. Self-
catering available.
Grades: STB Listed
Tel: 01333 330418
Mrs Birrell.
Rates fr: *£15.00-*£20.00.
Open: All Year
Beds: 1F
Baths: 1 Private
⇖ ⬓ ⓣ Ⓥ ✦

Pay B&Bs by
cash or cheque and
be prepared to
pay up front.

St Monans 13

National Grid Ref: NO5201
🍴 🍺 The Cabin Bar, Mayview
Hotel

(0.25m) *Mayview Hotel, 40 Station
Road, St Monans, Fife,* KY10 2BN.
Family hotel. Comfortable accom-
modation.
Grades: STB 1 Cr, Approv
Tel: 01333 730564
Mr & Mrs Robb.
Rates fr: *£22.00-*£22.00.
Open: All Year
Beds: 1F 1D 1S **Baths:** 2 Shared
⇖ ⊇ ⬓ ✗ Ⅲ, Ⓥ ◼ ✦

(0.5m) *Inverforth, 20 Braehead, St
Monans, Fife,* KY10 2AN.
Comfortable homely accommoda-
tion, home baking.
Grades: STB Listed, Comm
Tel: 01333 730205 Miss Aitken.
Rates fr: *£17.00-*£17.00.
Open: Easter to Oct
Beds: 1D 2T
Baths: 1 Shared
⇖ (8) ⚲ ⬓ Ⅲ,

Easter Kellie 14

National Grid Ref: NO5405
🍴 🍺 West End Bar, Anchor Inn

(2.5m 🚌) *Lawside Cottage,
Easter Kellie Farm, Easter Kellie,
Pittenweem, Anstruther, Fife,*
KY10 2RF.
Actual grid ref: NO5206
Modernised, farm cottages, quiet,
scenic.
Tel: 01333 720249 Mrs Howden.
Rates fr: *£14.00-*£20.00.
Open: Mar to Nov
Beds: 1F
Baths: 1 Shared
⇖ ⊇ (4) ⬓ 🛉 Ⅲ, ⓣ ✦

Pittenweem 15

National Grid Ref: NO5402
(0.25m) *The Anchor Inn,* 42
*Charles Street, Pittenweem,
Anstruther, Fife,* KY10 2QJ.
Local inn.
Grades: STB Listed
Tel: 01333 311326 Miss Chung.
Rates fr: *£18.00-*£18.00.
Open: All Year (not Xmas)
Beds: 1F 1D 1T 1S
Baths: 1 Shared
⇖ ⊇ ⬓ 🛉 ✗ Ⅲ, Ⓥ ◼

Anstruther 16

National Grid Ref: NO5603

⚲ ⌔ The Old Bank, The Dreel Inn

(0.25m) *The Hermitage, Ladywalk, Anstruther, Fife, KY10 3EX.*
Actual grid ref: NO568036
Grades: STB 1 Cr, High Comm, AA 4Q Selected
Tel: **01333 310909**
Mrs McDonald.
Rates fr: *£20.00-£25.00.*
Open: All Year
Beds: 3D 1T
Baths: 2 Shared
🅿 (4) 🗅 ✕ 🏚 Ⓥ î
First class accommodation in charming "East Neuk" town house (c.1817). Delightful walled gardens. Sea views. Licensed. Ten miles from the golfing mecca of St Andrews

(On Path) *The Sheiling, 32 Glenogil Gardens, Anstruther, Fife, KY10 3ET.*
Pretty white bungalow 200m to harbour.
Grades: STB 1 Cr, Comm
Tel: **01333 310697** Mrs Ritchie.
Rates fr: *£15.00-£22.50.*
Open: Easter to Oct
Beds: 2D **Baths:** 1 Shared
🅿 (2) 🗅 🏚 & Ⓥ ✦

(On Path) *The Spindrift, Pittenweem Road, Anstruther, Fife, KY10 3DT.*
An imposing Victorian house.
Grades: STB 3 Cr, High Comm, AA 4 Q, Select,
RAC High Acclaim
Tel: **01333 310573**
Mr McFarlane.
Rates fr: *£25.00-£31.50.*
Open: All Year
Beds: 3F 2D 3T
Baths: 8 Private
🅿 (10) ✍ 🗅 ✕ 🏚 Ⓥ î ✦

Kilrenny 17

National Grid Ref: NO5704

⚲ ⌔ The Dreel, The Haven, The Golf

(0.5m) *Rennyhill House, Kilrenny, Anstruther, Fife, KY10 3JF.*
C18th farmhouse in own grounds.
Grades: STB 2 Cr, High Comm
Tel: **01333 312234**
Mrs Wotherspoon.
Rates fr: *£17.50-£24.50.*
Open: Jan to Dec
Beds: 1F 1D 1T
Baths: 3 Private
🐦 🅿 (6) 🗅 🏚 Ⓥ î ✦

**The *lowest* single
rate *is shown in* bold.**

Crail 18

National Grid Ref: NO6107

⚲ ⌔ Golf Hotel, Marine Hotel

(0.25m) *Selcraig House, 47 Nethergate, Crail, Anstruther, Fife, KY10 3TX.*
Victorian villa with antique furniture.
Grades: STB 1 Cr, Comm, AA 2 Q
Tel: **01333 450697** Ms Carstairs.
Rates fr: *£15.00-£20.00.*
Open: All Year
Beds: 1F 2D 2T **Baths:** 2 Shared
🐦 ✍ 🗅 🏚 ✕ Ⓥ î ✦

(On Path) *The Honey Pot Guesthouse, 6 High Street, Crail, Anstruther, Fife, KY10 3TD.*
Comfortable cottage with annexe.
Grades: STB Listed, Approv
Tel: **01333 450935**
Rates fr: *£16.00-£16.00.*
Open: All Year
Beds: 1F 1D 3T 1S
Baths: 1 Ensuite 1 Shared
🐦 🅿 (8) 🗅 🏚 î ✦

(0.25m) *Hazelton Guest House, 29 Marketgate, Crail, Anstruther, Fife, KY10 3TH.*
Actual grid ref: NO613077
Your comfort is our concern.
Grades: STB Comm
Tel: **01333 450250**
Mr Brown.
Rates fr: *£15.00-£15.00.*
Open: Jan to Nov
Beds: 2F 2D 2T 1S
Baths: 2 Shared
🐦 🅿 🗅 ✕ 🏚 Ⓥ î

The Country Code

Enjoy the countryside and respect its life and work

Guard against all risk of fire

Fasten all gates

Keep your dogs under close control

Keep to public paths across farmland

Use gates and stiles to cross fences, hedges and walls

Leave livestock, crops and machinery alone

Take your litter home

Help to keep all water clean

Protect wild-life, plants and trees

Take special care on country roads

Make no unnecessary noise

(0.25m) 🚗 *Woodlands Guest House, Balcomie Road, Crail, Anstruther, Fife, KY10 3TN.*
Large detached villa, half-acre garden.
Grades: STB 1 Cr, Approv
Tel: **01333 450147** Mrs Wood.
Rates fr: *£16.50-£17.50.*
Open: Feb to Nov
Beds: 1F 2D **Baths:** 2 Shared
🐦 (3) 🅿 (7) ✍ 🗅 🏚 ✕ 🏚 î ✦

(0.5m) *Golf Hotel, 4 High Street, Crail, Anstruther, Fife, KY10 3TD.*
A comfortable and friendly hotel.
Grades: STB 3 Cr, Comm
Tel: **01333 50206** Mr Guthrie.
Rates fr: *£18.00-£22.00.*
Open: All Year
Beds: 5T **Baths:** 5 Ensuite
🐦 🅿 (8) 🗅 🏚 ✕ 🏚 î

Kingsbarns 19

National Grid Ref: NO5912

⚲ ⌔ Cambo Arms Hotel

(0.5m) *Kingsbarns Bed & Breakfast, 3 Main St, Kingsbarns, St Andrews, Fife, KY16 8SL.*
Converted farmhouse, modern facilities.
Grades: STB 2 Cr, Comm
Tel: **01334 880234** Mrs Hay.
Rates fr: *£18.00-£20.00.*
Open: Apr to Oct
Beds: 2D 1T **Baths:** 3 Ensuite
🐦 🅿 (2) 🗅 🏚 Ⓥ ✦

Boarhills 20

National Grid Ref: NO5614

(1m) *Parkmill, Boarhills, St Andrews, Fife, KY16 8PS.*
C18th mill and house.
Grades: STB Reg
Tel: **01334 88254**
Mr & Mrs Frodsham.
Rates fr: *£14.00-£16.00.*
Open: All Year (not Xmas)
Beds: 2D 1S
Baths: 1 Ensuite 1 Shared
🐦 🅿 (4) ✍ 🗅 🏚 ✕ 🏚 Ⓥ î ✦

St Andrews 21

National Grid Ref: NO5116

⚲ ⌔ Russell Hotel, Playfairs Bar, Ardgowan Hotel, Links Hotel, New Inn

(0.75m) 🚗 *Amberside Guest House, 4 Murray Park, St Andrews, Fife, KY16 9AW.*
Actual grid ref: NO5116
Popular Victorian friendly guesthouse.
Grades: STB 2 Cr, Comm, AA 3 Q, RAC Listed
Tel: **01334 74644**
Mr & Mrs Wood.
Rates fr: *£19.00-£19.00.*
Open: All Year **Beds:** 2F 2D 2T 1S
Baths: 5 Private 1 Shared
🐦 🗅 🏚 🏚 Ⓥ î ✦

sign means that, given due notice, owners will pick you up from the path and drop you off with-in reason.

(0.75m) ***2 King Street,*** *St Andrews, Fife, KY16 8JQ.*
Modern semi-detached.
Grades: STB Listed, Approv
Tel: **01334 76326** Mrs Allan.
Rates fr: *£14.00*-**£18.00**.
Open: All Year (not Xmas)
Beds: 1D 1T **Baths:** 1 Shared
(12) P (1) V

(1m) ***Aslar House,*** *120 North Street, St Andrews, Fife, KY16 9AF.*
Actual grid ref: NO508168
Elegant and comfortable Victorian townhouse.
Grades: STB 2 Cr, High Comm
Tel: **01334 73460** Mrs Pardoe.
Rates fr: *£23.00*-**£23.00**.
Open: All Year
Beds: 1F 2D 1T 1S
Baths: 5 Private
(5) V

(3m) ***Parkland Hotel & Restaurant,*** *Double Dykes Road, St Andrews, Fife, KY16 9DS.*
1890 castellated building.
Grades: STB 3 Cr, Comm, AA 2 St, RAC 2 St
Tel: **01334 73620**
Mr MacLennan.
Rates fr: *£25.00*-**£30.00**.
Open: All Year (not Xmas)
Beds: 2F 2D 4T 7S
Baths: 9 Private 3 Shared
P (15) V

(1.5m) ***1 Kilrymont Place,*** *St Andrews, Fife, KY16 8DH.*
Welcoming and comfortable family home.
Tel: **01334 72335**
Mrs W J Chenery.
Rates fr: *£13.00*-**£13.00**.
Open: All Year (not Xmas)
Beds: 1T 1S
Baths: 1 Shared
(10) P (1) V

Taking your dog? Book in advance only with owners who accept dogs

(0.5m) ***12 Newmill Gardens,*** *St Andrews, Fife, KY16 8RY.*
Actual grid ref: NO5016
Modern, clean, friendly private house.
Grades: STB Reg
Tel: **01334 7552** Mrs Irvine.
Rates fr: *£13.00*-**£18.00**.
Open: All Year (not Xmas)
Beds: 1D
Baths: 1 Ensuite
P (1) V

(0.75m) ***Spinkstown Farmhouse,*** *St Andrews, Fife, KY16 8PN.*
Grades: AA 3 Q
Tel: **01334 473475**
Mrs Duncan.
Rates fr: *£17.00*-**£17.50**.
Open: All Year (not Xmas)
Beds: 2D 1T
Baths: 3 Ensuite
P (4) V

(0.75m) ***Shorecrest Guest House,*** *23 Murray Park, St Andrews, Fife, KY16 9AW.*
Closeby all amenities, clean, comfortable.
Tel: **01334 475310** Mr Leader.
Rates fr: *£25.00*-**£25.00**.
Open: All Year
Beds: 2F 4D 4T 2S
Baths: 12 Private

(1m) ***Arran House,*** *5 Murray Park, St Andrews, Fife, KY16 9AW.*
High standard family-run guest-house.
Grades: STB 3 Cr, Comm
Tel: **01334 474724** Mrs Scanlon.
Rates fr: *£20.00*-**£20.00**.
Open: Feb to Nov
Beds: 2F 1T 1S
Baths: 3 Ensuite 1 Shared
V

(0.75m) ***Number Ten,*** *10 Hope Street, St Andrews, Fife, KY16 9HJ.*
Large Georgian town house.
Grades: STB 2 Cr, Comm
Tel: **01334 474601**
Mr & Mrs Wallace.
Rates fr: *£22.00*-**£22.00**.
Open: Feb to Nov
Beds: 1F 3D 3T 3S
Baths: 10 Private
V

(1m) ***Ashleigh House Hotel,*** *37 St Marys Street, St Andrews, Fife, KY16 8AZ.*
Small friendly comfortable hotel.
Grades: STB 3 Cr, Comm
Tel: **01334 75429** Mr Pratt.
Rates fr: *£26.00*-**£30.00**.
Open: Easter to Oct
Beds: 3F 5D 3T
Baths: 9 Ensuite 2 Shared
P

(1m) ***Rockview,*** *15 The Scores, St Andrews, Fife, KY16 9AR.*
Victorian, sea view, parking.
Tel: **01334 75844** Mrs Hippisley.
Rates fr: *£17.00*-**£20.00**.
Open: Easter to Oct
Beds: 1F 1D 1T 1S
Baths: 1 Ensuite 1 Shared
P (5) V

Edenside 22

National Grid Ref: NO4518

(0.5m) ***Edenside House,*** *Edenside, St Andrews, Fife, KY16 9SQ.*
Actual grid ref: NO462189
Waterfront pre-1775 former farm-house.
Grades: AA 4 Q, Select
Tel: **01334 838108**
Dr & Mrs Mansell.
Rates fr: *£20.00*-**£25.00**.
Open: Easter to Oct
Beds: 3D 6T
Baths: 9 Private
P (10) V

Clayton 23

National Grid Ref: NO4318

Clayton Restaurant, Guardbridge Hotel

(1m) ***East Lodge,*** *Clayton, St Andrews, Fife, KY16 9YE.*
Country lodge set in own 9-acres.
Tel: **01334 870282**
Mr & Mrs Rollo.
Rates fr: *£15.00*-**£18.00**.
Open: Easter to Oct
Beds: 2D 1T
Baths: 2 Shared
P V

Guardbridge 24

National Grid Ref: NO4519

Guardbridge Hotel

(On Path) ***The Larches,*** *7 River Terrace, Guardbridge, St Andrews, Fife, KY16 0XA.*
Actual grid ref: NO448197
Large, comfortable, converted memorial hall.
Grades: STB 1 Cr, Comm, AA 2 Q, Recomm
Tel: **01334 838008**
Mrs Mayner.
Rates fr: *£16.00*-**£21.00**.
Open: All Year
Beds: 1F 1D 2T
Baths: 2 Shared
P (2) V

All rooms full and nowhere else to stay? Ask the owner if there's anywhere nearby

Leuchars 25

National Grid Ref: NO4521

(1m) *Milton Farm, Leuchars, St Andrews, Fife, KY16 0AB.*
Charming Georgian farmhouse in 500 acres.
Tel: **01334 839281** Mrs Black.
Rates fr: *£20.00.*
Open: All Year (not Xmas)
Beds: 1F 2D 1T
🛏 (10) 🅿 (6) ⅍ 🗗 ✕ Ⓥ

All details shown
are as supplied
by B&B owners in
Autumn 1995.

Newburgh 26

National Grid Ref: NO2318

🍴 🍺 Taybridge Tavern, Burnside House Hotel

(On Path) *Ninewells Farm, Newburgh, Cupar, Fife, KY14 6EY.*
Actual grid ref: NO2217
Modern, comfortable, welcoming farmhouse.
Grades: STB Listed, Comm
Tel: **01337 840307** Mrs Baird.
Rates fr: *£15.00*-**£18.00**.
Open: Easter to Oct
Beds: 1F 1D 1T
Baths: 2 Shared
🛏 (10) 🅿 ⅍ 🗗 ✕ 🎞 Ⓥ ⵁ

The lowest *double* rate per person is shown in *italics*.

(On Path 🚌) *200 High Street, Newburgh, Cupar, Fife, KY14 6DZ.*
Comfortable converted Georgian property.
Tel: **01337 840606** Mrs Menzies.
Rates fr: *£15.00*-**£15.00**.
Open: All Year
Beds: 1F 1D
Baths: 1 Shared
🛏 🅿 (1) 🗗 ★ ✕ 🎞 ♿ Ⓥ ⵁ ⵁ

Easter Clunie 27

National Grid Ref: NO2217

(1.5m) *Easter Clunie, Easter Clunie, Newburgh, Cupar, Fife, KY14 6EJ.*
Traditional, stone-built, comfortable farmhouse.
Grades: STB 2 Cr, Comm
Tel: **01337 840218** Mrs Baird.
Rates fr: *£14.00*-**£14.00**.
Open: Easter to Oct
Beds: 1D 2T
Baths: 1 Ensuite 2 Private
🛏 (3) 🅿 (3) 🗗 🎞 Ⓥ ⵁ

Glyndwr's Way

What a path - leading through 120 miles of the quietest parts of mid-Wales with its superb scenery, its wooded valleys, its lowland moors - the true hinterland of the entire country. From the Welsh Marches to Machynlleth on the River Dyfi, the path visits sites associated with the life and deeds of the Welsh national hero **Owain Glyndwr** and his campaign against the English in the early 15th century. The path was featured in a BBC radio series in 1993 and has accordingly become more popular, but you may still spend a day walking quite by yourself. Because the path begins at Knighton and ends at Welshpool, there is the opportunity to link both ends with the relevant section of **Offa's Dyke** (q.v.) and turn the trail into a circular walk.

Guides: *Owain Glyndwr's Way* by Richard Sale (ISBN 00 947131 03), published by Constable & Co. Ltd and available from all major bookshops, £9.95

Glyndwr's Way by Gillian Walker, published by Management Update and available only from Powney's Bookshop (4-5 St Alkmund's Place, Shrewsbury, SY1 1UJ, tel. 01743 369165), £4.95 (+ 95p p&p)

Comments on the path to: **Rab Jones**, Glyndwr's Way Project Officer, Powys County Council, Canolfan Owain Glyndwr, Machynlleth, Powys, SY20 8EE

Maps: 1:50000 Ordnance Survey Landranger Series: 125, 126, 135, 136 and 148.

Knighton   1

National Grid Ref: SO2872

🍴 🍺 Horse & Jockey, George & Dragon

(0.25m) *The Fleece House, Market Street, Knighton, Powys, LD7 1BB.*
Converted 18th Century coaching inn.
Grades: WTB 2 Cr, Comm
Tel: **01547 520168** Mrs Simmons.
Rates fr: *£15.50*-**£18.50**.
Open: All Year
Beds: 6T
Baths: 2 Private 2 Shared
🅿 🖵 🛏 🛆 ⚡

(0.25m 🚌) *Cwmgilla Farm, Knighton, Powys, LD7 1PG.*
Actual grid ref: SO263718
Modern, comfortable farmhouse. 1.5 miles Offa's Dyke.
Grades: WTB 1Cr, High Comm
Tel: **01547 528387** Mrs Davies.
Rates fr: *£17.00*-**£17.00**.
Open: Easter to Nov
Beds: 1D 1T 1S
Baths: 1 Shared
🐾 (10) 🅿 (5) 🖵 🛏 🛆 ⚡

> The lowest *double* rate per person is shown in *italics*.

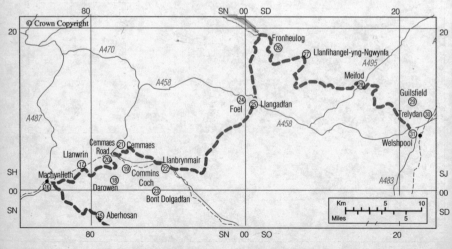

High season,
bank holidays and
special events mean
low availability
everywhere.

(On Path 🚌) *Plough Hotel*,
*40 Market Street, Knighton, Powys,
LD7 1EY.*
Actual grid ref: SO285724
Olde worlde inn on dyke.
Tel: **01547 528041**
Mrs Scotford.
Rates fr: *£26.00*-**£14.00**.
Open: All Year
Beds: 1D 3T
Baths: 2 Ensuite 1 Shared
🅿 🖵 🏃 ✕ 📺 Ⓥ ⓘ ⚡

**(0.5m) *Pilleth Court*, *Whitton,
Knighton, Powys, LD7 1NP.***
Listed Elizabethan farmhouse.
Grades: WTB 2 Cr, De Luxe
Tel: **01547 560272**
Mrs Hood.
Rates fr: *£17.00*-**£19.00**.
Open: All Year (not Xmas)
Beds: 1F 2D 1T
Baths: 1 Ensuite 1 Shared
🛏 (9) 🅿 (6) 🖵 ✕ 📺

**(On Path 🚌) *Ryelands*, *The Rhos,
Knighton, Powys, LD7 1NG.***
Actual grid ref: SO277700
Tel: **01547 520291** Ms Wells.
Rates fr: *£14.00*-**£14.00**.
Open: All Year (not Xmas)
Beds: 1D
Baths: 1 Shared
🛏 (12) 🅿 (6) ⚲ 🖵 ✕ 📺 Ⓥ ⓘ ⚡
Also ⛺ Ⓣ 🚿 ✕ ⚡ 🐾

Knucklas 2

National Grid Ref: SO2574

🍽 🍺 Castle Inn

**(1m 🚌) *The Castle Inn*, *Knucklas,
Knighton, Powys, LD7 1PW.***
Actual grid ref: SO253742
Grades: WTB 3 Cr Highly
Commended
Tel: **01547 528150**
Mr & Mrs Hughes.
Rates fr: *£17.50*-**£17.50**.
Open: All Year
Beds: 3D 3T
Baths: 5 Private
🛏 (12) 🅿 (20) 🖵 ✕ 📺 ⚲ 🐾 Ⓥ ⓘ ⚡
Family-run village inn. Oak beams,
panelling, log fires, TV, drinks tray
all rooms. Guided walking holidays
our speciality, bird watching, fish-
ing, clay shooting arranged

Llangunllo 3

National Grid Ref: SO2171

**(0.5m 🚌) *Craig Fach*, *Llangunllo,
Knighton, Powys, LD7 1SY.***
Actual grid ref: SO198739
Renovated, extended, traditional
stone cottage.
Tel: **01547 81605**
Mrs Livingstone-Lawn.
Rates fr: *£12.50*-**£12.50**.
Open: All Year (not Xmas)
Beds: 2F 1S
Baths: 1 Shared
🛏 🅿 (10) 🖵 🏃 ✕ 📺 Ⓥ ⓘ ⚡

The *lowest* **single**
rate *is shown in* **bold.**

Felindre 4

National Grid Ref: SO1681

🍽 🍺 Wharf Inn

**(On Path 🚌) *Trevland*, *Felindre,
Knighton, Powys, LD7 1YL.***
Spacious, comfortable and quiet
bungalow.
Tel: **01547 510211** Mrs Edwards.
Rates fr: *£15.00*-**£15.00**.
Open: All Year
Beds: 2F 1D 1T
Baths: 2 Ensuite 1 Shared
🛏 🅿 (4) 🖵 🏃 ✕ 📺 ⚲ Ⓥ ⓘ ⚡

Llananno 5

National Grid Ref: SO0974

**(On Path) *Bwlch Farm*, *Llananno,
Llandrindod Wells, Powys, LD1 6TT.***
C15th cruck hall house.
Grades: WTB 2 Cr, High Comm
Tel: **01597 840366**
Mr & Mrs Taylor.
Rates fr: *£17.00*-**£19.50**.
Open: Apr to Oct
Beds: 2D 1T
Baths: 3 Private
🛏 🅿 🖵 🏃 ✕ 📺 Ⓥ ⓘ ⚡

Llanbister 6

National Grid Ref: SO1073

🍽 🍺 The Lion

**(1m) *Trellwydion*, *Llanbister,
Llandrindod Wells, Powys, LD1 6TH.***
Old farmhouse, comfortable &
friendly.
Tel: **01597 840278** Mrs Bennet.
Rates fr: *£12.00*-**£12.00**.
Open: Easter to Oct
Beds: 1F 1D
🛏 🅿 🖵 🏃 ✕ 🐾 Ⓥ ⓘ ⚡

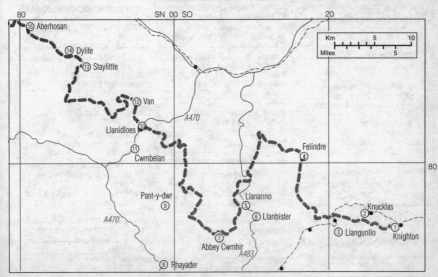

🚐 **sign means that,** *given due notice,* **owners will pick you up from the path and drop you off** *within reason.*

Abbey Cwmhir 7

National Grid Ref: SO0571

(On Path) 🚐 *Home Farm, Abbey Cwmhir, Llandrindod Wells, Powys, LD1 6PH.*
C18th working farm.
Tel: **01597 851666** Mrs Hamer.
Rates fr: *£13.00-£13.00.*
Open: All Year (not Xmas)
Beds: 3D
Baths: 1 Private 1 Shared
🛏🅿🖵📶🗙📺📺🏺✦

Rhayader 8

National Grid Ref: SN9768

🍽🍺 Cornhill Inn

(1m 🚐) *Beili Neuadd, Rhayader, Powys, LD6 5NS.*
Actual grid ref: SN994698
Grades: WTB 3 Cr, High Comm
Tel: **01597 810211** Mrs Edwards.
Rates fr: *£17.50-£17.50.*
Open: All Year (not Xmas)
Beds: 1D 1T 2S
Baths: 2 Ensuite 1 Shared
🛏(10)🅿🖵📶🗙📺📺🏺✦
Warm, comfortable C16th farmhouse run by L.D.W. members. Log fires, hot showers and Aga breakfasts. Near Glyndwr's Way (four miles), Cambrian Way (six miles), Monk's Trod (0.5 miles).

Pant-y-dwr 9

National Grid Ref: SN9874

🍽🍺 Mid-Wales Inn

(1.5m 🚐) *Mid-Wales Inn, Pant-y-dwr, Rhayader, Powys, LD6 5LL.*
Old Welsh black-and-white pub.
Grades: WTB Reg
Tel: **01597 870224**
Mr Bailey-Green.
Rates fr: *£15.00-£12.00.*
Open: All Year (not Xmas)
Beds: 1F 1D 1T
Baths: 2 Private 1 Shared
🛏🅿(8)🖵🗙🏺✦

Pay B&Bs by cash or cheque and be prepared to pay up front.

Llanidloes 10

National Grid Ref: SN9584

🍽🍺 Mount Inn, Unicorn

(On Path) *Gorphwysfa Guest House, Westgate Street, Llanidloes, Powys, SY18 6HL.*
Comfortable Victorian house.
Tel: **01686 413356** Mrs Lines.
Rates fr: *£12.50-£12.50.*
Open: All Year
Beds: 1F 1D 1T 1S
Baths: 2 Shared
🛏🅿(5)✦🖵📶🗙📺📺🏺

(On Path) *Lloyds, Cambrian Place, Llanidloes, Powys, SY18 6BX.*
Quiet, Victorian town-centre hotel.
Grades: WTB 1 Cr
Tel: **01686 412284** Mr Lines.
Rates fr: *£16.00-£15.00.*
Open: All Year
Beds: 2D 3T 5S
Baths: 2 Private 3 Shared
🛏🖵🗙📺🏺✦

(0.25m 🚐) *Dol-Llys Farm, Llanidloes, Powys, SY18 6JA.*
C17th farmhouse.
Grades: WTB 2 Cr, High CommRAC Listed
Tel: **01686 412694** Mr Evans.
Rates fr: *£15.00-£17.00.*
Open: All Year (not Xmas)
Beds: 2 D 1T
Baths: 3 Private
🖵📶🏺✦
Also 🏕 £4 per tent.
Open: All Year (not Xmas)
🏰📺🎯♿

Cwmbelan 11

National Grid Ref: SN9481

🍽🍺 Angel Mount Inn, Blue Bell

(2.25m) *Glyngynwydd, Cwmbelan, Llanidloes, Powys, SY18 6QQ.*
Beautifully restored traditional C17th farmhouse.
Grades: WTB 2 Cr, High Comm
Tel: **01686 413854**
Mrs Davies.
Rates fr: *£17.50-£20.00.*
Open: All Year
Beds: 3D
Baths: 1 Private 2 Shared
🛏🅿(12)✦🖵📶🏺📺

Van 12

National Grid Ref: SN9587

(2.5m 🚐) *Esgairmaen, Van, Llanidloes, Powys, SY18 6NT.*
Actual grid ref: SN925904
Modern comfortable farmhouse.
Grades: WTB 3 Cr
Tel: **01551 6272** Mrs Rees.
Rates fr: *£15.00-£15.00.*
Open: Easter to Oct
Beds: 1F 1D
Baths: 2 Ensuite
🛏🅿(10)🖵🗙🏺📺✦

Staylittle 13

National Grid Ref: SN8892

🍽🍺 Star Inn (Dylife)

(1m) *Maesmedrisiol Farm, Staylittle, Llanbrynmair, Powys, SY19 7BN.*
Actual grid ref: SN8894
Friendly, comfortable, stone-built farmhouse.
Grades: WTB 1 Cr
Tel: **01650 521494** Mrs Anwyl.
Rates fr: *£14.00-£14.00.*
Open: All Year (not Xmas)
Beds: 2F 2D 1T 2S
Baths: 1 Private
🛏(1)🅿(8)🖵🗙📺🏺✦

The Grid Reference beneath the location heading is for the village or town - *not* **for individual houses, which are shown (where supplied) in each entry itself.**

Dylife 14

National Grid Ref: SN8694

🍽🍺 Star Inn

(0.75m) *Star Inn, Dylife, Staylittle, Llanbrynmair, Powys, SY19 7BW.*
Traditional country inn, log fires, real ales.
Grades: WTB 2 Cr, Approv
Tel: **01650 521345**
Mrs Ward -Banks.
Rates fr: *£17.00-£17.00.*
Open: All Year
Beds: 1F 3D 1T 2S
Baths: 2 Private 1 Shared
🛏🅿✦🖵📶🗙📺📺🏺✦

Aberhosan 15

National Grid Ref: SN8097

(1m) *Bacheiddon Farm, Aberhosan, Machynlleth, Powys, SY20 8SG.*
Modern, comfortable farmhouse, lovely scenery.
Grades: WTB 2 Cr
Tel: **01654 702229** Mrs Lewis.
Rates fr: *£17.00-£20.00.*
Open: May to Oct
Beds: 3D
Baths: 3 Private
🛏🅿🖵

Machynlleth 16

National Grid Ref: SH7400

⚍ ⊄ White Horse, Dyfi Forester, Glyndwr

(1m 🚍) *Talbontdrain,* *Machynlleth, Powys, SY20 8.* **Actual grid ref:** SH777959 Remote, comfortable farmhouse, excellent food. Tel: **01654 702192** Ms Matthews. **Rates fr:** *£15.00*-**£15.00**. **Open:** All Year (not Xmas) **Beds:** 1F 1D 2T 2S **Baths:** 1 Private 2 Shared ☎ �ₚ (5) ⌇ ⅋ ⊁ ✕ ⅏ Ⅴ ⓘ ⌁

(0.25m) *Pendre Guest House,* *Maengwym Street, Machynlleth, Powys, SY20 8EF.* Georgian house, warm friendly atmosphere. **Grades:** WTB 2 Cr, Comm Tel: **01654 702088** Ms Petrie. **Rates fr:** *£14.50*-**£20.00**. **Open:** All Year (not Xmas) **Beds:** 2F 1D 1T **Baths:** 2 Private 2 Shared ☎ �ₚ (3) ⅋ ⅏ Ⅴ

(On Path) *Maenllwyd,* Newtown Road, Machynlleth, Powys, *SY20 8EY.* Large Victorian former manse. **Grades:** WTB 3 Cr, High Comm, AA 3 Q Tel: **01654 702928** Mr Vince. **Rates fr:** *£17.50*-**£22.00**. **Open:** All Year (not Xmas) **Beds:** 2F 4D 2T **Baths:** 8 Ensuite ☎ ⓟ (10) ⌇ ⌁ ⅋ ✕ ⅏ Ⅴ ⓘ ⌁

(On Path) *The Glyndwr Hotel,* Doll Street, Machynlleth, Powys, *SY20 8BQ.* Small family-run hotel. **Grades:** WTB Listed Tel: **01654 703989** Mrs Duckett. **Rates fr:** *£13.00*-**£15.00**. **Open:** All Year **Beds:** 3F 1D 2T **Baths:** 3 Shared ☎ ⓟ ⊐ ✕ ⅏ ⓘ

(0.25m) *Dyfi Forester Inn,* 4 Doll Street, Machynlleth, Powys, *SY20 8BQ.* Friendly town pub. Tel: **01654 702004** Mr Davies. **Rates fr:** *£15.00*-**£15.00**. **Open:** All Year (not Xmas) **Beds:** 1F 1D 1S **Baths:** 1 Shared ☎ ⓟ (20) ⊐ ✕ ⓘ ⌁

(On Path) *Awelon,* Heol Powys, Machynlleth, Powys, *SY20 8AY.* Small comfortable private house. Tel: **01654 702047** Ms Williams. **Rates fr:** *£13.50*-**£14.50**. **Open:** All Year (not Xmas) **Beds:** 1F 1T 1S **Baths:** 1 Shared ☎ (2) ⅋ ⅏ Ⅴ ⓘ ⌁

Llanwrin 17

National Grid Ref: SH7803

⚍ ⊄ Penrhos Arms

(1m 🚍) *Mathafarn,* Llanwrin, Machynlleth, Powys, *SY20 8QJ.* Elegant country farmhouse. **Grades:** WTB 2 Cr, High Comm, AA Listed Tel: **01650 511226** Mrs Hughes. **Rates fr:** *£16.00*-**£16.00**. **Open:** All Year (not Xmas) **Beds:** 1D 1T 1S **Baths:** 1 Private 1 Shared ☎ ⓟ ⊐ ⅋ ⅏ Ⅴ ⓘ ⌁

Darowen 18

National Grid Ref: SH8201

⚍ ⊄ The Penrhos Arms

(0.5m) *Cefn Farm,* Darowen, Machynlleth, Powys, *SY20 8NS.* Quiet, comfortable, modernised old farmhouse. **Grades:** WTB 2 Cr Tel: **01650 511336** Mr Lloyd. **Rates fr:** *£14.00*-**£14.00**. **Open:** All Year (not Xmas) **Beds:** 1F **Baths:** 1 Private ☎ ⓟ (3) ⌇ ⊐ ⅋ ⅏ Ⅴ

Commins Coch 19

National Grid Ref: SH8403

⚍ ⊄ The Penrhos Arms

(On Path) *Gwalia,* Commins Coch, Machynlleth, Powys, *SY20.* **Actual grid ref:** SH853048 Peaceful family smallholding. Tel: **01650 511377** Mrs Chandler. **Rates fr:** *£14.00*-**£14.00**. **Open:** All Year (not Xmas) **Beds:** 1F 1T **Baths:** 1 Shared ☎ ⓟ ⅋ ⅏ ✕ Ⅴ ⓘ ⌁

Cemmaes Road 29

National Grid Ref: SH8204

⚍ ⊄ Penrhos Arms

(On Path 🚍) *Cefn Coch Uchaf,* Cemmaes Road, Machynlleth, Powys, *SY20 8LU.* **Actual grid ref:** SH835033 C14th Dovey Valley farmhouse, lovely views. **Grades:** WTB Listed, Comm Tel: **01650 511552** Mrs Harris. **Rates fr:** *£14.50*-**£14.50**. **Open:** All Year (not Xmas) **Beds:** 2D 1T **Baths:** 1 Private 1 Shared ☎ ⓟ ⊐ ⅋ ⅏ ✕ ⅏ Ⅴ ⓘ ⌁

All rates are subject to alteration at the owners' discretion.

The Country Code

Enjoy the countryside and respect its life and work

Guard against all risk of fire

Fasten all gates

Keep your dogs under close control

Keep to public paths across farmland

Use gates and stiles to cross fences, hedges and walls

Leave livestock, crops and machinery alone

Take your litter home

Help to keep all water clean

Protect wild-life, plants and trees

Take special care on country roads

Make no unnecessary noise

Cemmaes 21

National Grid Ref: SH8306

⚍ ⊄ Penrhos Arms

(2m) *Penrhos Arms Hotel,* Cemmaes, Machynlleth, Powys, *SY20.* An old coaching inn. **Grades:** WTB Listed Tel: **01650 511243** Mr Astley. **Rates fr:** *£12.00*-**£12.00**. **Open:** April to Sept **Beds:** 1F 2D 3S **Baths:** 2 Shared ⓟ (15) ⌇ ⊐ ✕ Ⅴ ⓘ

Llanbrynmair 22

National Grid Ref: SH8902

⚍ ⊄ Wynnstay Arms

(On Path) *Wynnstay Arms Hotel,* Llanbrynmair, Powys, *SY19 7AA.* C14th country house. **Grades:** WTB Listed Tel: **01650 521431** Mrs Taylor. **Rates fr:** *£13.00*-**£14.00**. **Open:** All Year (not Xmas) **Beds:** 1F 2D **Baths:** 2 Shared ☎ ⓟ ⊐ ⅋ ✕ ⅏ Ⅴ ⓘ ⌁

Bont Dolgadfan 23

National Grid Ref: SH8800

(2m 🚐) *Cyfeiliog Guest House,* Bont Dolgadfan, Llanbrynmair, Powys, *SY19 7BB.*
Actual grid ref: SH885001
Comfortable licensed C18th riverside guesthouse.
Grades: WTB 2 Cr, Comm
Tel: 01650 521231 Mr & Mrs Fox.
Rates fr: £15.00-£15.00.
Open: All Year
Beds: 1F 1D 1T
Baths: 1 Private 1 Shared
🖙 🅿 (3) ⅏ 🗖 ✕ 🎞 Ⓥ 🛆 ∅

Foel 24

National Grid Ref: SH9911

🍴 🍺 The Cann Office Hotel

(0.75m 🚐) *Lluest Fach,* Foel, Llangadfan, Welshpool, Powys, *SY21 0PB.*
Actual grid ref: SH982109
Grades: WTB Listed, 3 Dragons
Tel: 01938 820351 Miss Wallace.
Rates fr: £14.00-£14.00.
Open: All Year (not Xmas)
Beds: 1F
Baths: 1 Shared
🅿 (4) ⅏ 🗖 🛏 ✕ 🎞 Ⓥ 🛆 ∅
Also 🔺 £5.00 per tent. Also
bunkhouse, £9.00 per bunk,.
Open: All Year (not Xmas)
🕮 🎿 👥 ∅ 🅰
Secluded smallholding also has
self-catering chalet, comfortable
walkers' barns, fishing and unspoilt
walks from the door. Pets very welcome. Call or write for free leaflet.

Llangadfan 25

National Grid Ref: SJ0110

🍴 🍺 Cann Office Hotel

(On Path) *Cann Office Hotel,* Llangadfan, Welshpool, Powys, *SY21 0PL.*
Historic posting inn.
Tel: 01938 820202
Mr Lewis.
Rates fr: £18.00-£20.00.
Open: All Year (not Xmas)
Beds: 3T
Baths: 2 Shared
🖙 🅿 ⅏ 🗖 ✕ 🎞 Ⓥ 🛆 ∅

Fronheulog 26

National Grid Ref: SJ0418

🍴 🍺 Lake Vyrnwy Hotel

(0.25m 🚐) *Fronheulog Bungalow,* Fronheulog, Llanwddyn, Oswestry, Salop, *SY10 0LX.*
Top of the hill, lovely views.
Tel: 01691 73662
Mrs Jones.
Rates fr: £12.50-£15.00.
Open: Easter to Oct

Beds: 1D 1T **Baths:** 1 Shared
🅿 🗖 ✕ 🎞 🛆 ∅
Also 🔺 £2.00 per person.
Open: Easter to OctⓉ ♿

Llanfihangel-yng-Ngwynfa 27

National Grid Ref: SJ0816

🍴 🍺 Royal Oak

(1m 🚐) *Cyfir Farm,* Llanfihangel-yng-Ngwynfa, Llanfyllin, Powys, *SY22 5JE.*
Traditional Welsh longhouse - food
our speciality.
Grades: WTB 3 Cr, De Luxe
Tel: 01691 648451 Mrs Jenkins.
Rates fr: £19.50-£19.50.
Open: All Year (not Xmas)
Beds: 1F 1D 1T **Baths:** 3 Private
🖙 🅿 ⅏ 🗖 ✕ 🎞 Ⓥ 🛆 ∅

Meifod 28

National Grid Ref: SJ1513

🍴 🍺 Meifod & Pontrobert, Kings
Head

(On Path) *Pentrego Farm,* Meifod, Llanfyllin, Powys, *SY22 6HP.*
Listed C16th farmhouse, working
farm.
Grades: WTB 2 Cr
Tel: 01938 500353 Mrs Watkin.
Rates fr: £15.00-£15.00.
Open: All Year (not Xmas)
Beds: 2F 1S **Baths:** 2 Private
🖙 🅿 🗖 🛏 ✕ Ⓥ 🛆 ∅

Guilsfield 29

National Grid Ref: SJ2211

🍴 🍺 Kings Head

(1m 🚐) *Lower Trelydan,* Guilsfield, Welshpool, Powys, *SY21 9PH.*
Actual grid ref: SJ2207
Award-winning black and white
farmhouse.
Grades: WTB 3 Cr, High Comm, AA 4 Q, Select
Tel: 01938 553105 Mrs Jones.
Rates fr: £18.00-£25.00.
Open: All Year
Beds: 1F 1D 1T **Baths:** 3 Private
🖙 🅿 (10) 🗖 ✕ 🎞 Ⓥ 🛆 ∅

Trelydan 30

National Grid Ref: SJ2310

🍴 🍺 Raven Inn

(2m) *Burnt House,* Trelydan, Welshpool, Powys, *SY21 9HU.*
Luxurious Tudor house!.
Grades: WTB 3 Cr, De Luxe
Tel: 01938 552827 Mrs Wykes.
Rates fr: £16.00-£16.00.
Open: Easter to Nov
Beds: 1D 1T
Baths: 1 Ensuite 1 Shared
🖙 (12) 🅿 (10) 🗖 🛏 ✕ 🎞 Ⓥ ∅

Welshpool 31

National Grid Ref: SJ2207

🍴 🍺 Royal Oak Hotel, Raven Inn

(0.5m 🚐) *Tynllwyn Farm,* Welshpool, Powys, *SY21 9BW.*
Actual grid ref: SJ214080
Comfortable farmhouse dated
1861.
Grades: WTB 1 Cr, AA 3 Q, RAC Listed
Tel: 01938 553175 Mrs Emberton.
Rates fr: £15.00-£15.00.
Open: All Year
Beds: 2F 2D 2T 1S
Baths: 2 Shared
🅿 (10) 🗖 🛏 ✕ 🎞 Ⓥ 🛆 ∅

(2.25m) *Tresi-Aur,* Brookfield Road, Welshpool, Powys, *SY21 7PZ.*
Actual grid ref: SJ224082
Modern house, warm friendly
welcome.
Grades: WTB 2 Cr
Tel: 01938 552430
Mrs Davies.
Rates fr: £14.00-£15.00.
Open: Jan to Nov
Beds: 1F 1D 1S
Baths: 1 Shared
🖙 🅿 (2) ⅏ 🗖 🎞 Ⓥ 🛆

(2.25m 🚐) *Peniarth,* 10 Cefn Hawys, (off Adelaide Drive), Red Bank, Welshpool, Powys, *SY21 7RH.*
Actual grid ref: SJ224082
Modern detached house above
town.
Grades: WTB 2 Cr
Tel: 01938 552324
Mrs Jones.
Rates fr: £15.00-£15.00.
Open: Easter to Oct
Beds: 1F 1T 1S
Baths: 1 Ensuite 1 Shared
🖙 (5) 🅿 (2) ⅏ 🗖 🎞 Ⓥ ∅

(1.75m 🚐) *Hafren Guest House,* 38 Salop Road, Welshpool, Powys, *SY21 7EA.*
Actual grid ref: SJ227076
Georgian house with modern
amenities.
Grades: WTB Listed
Tel: 01938 554112 / 0831 183152
Ms Shaw.
Rates fr: £13.00-£15.00.
Open: All Year
Beds: 1F 1D 1T
Baths: 1 Shared
🖙 🅿 (3) 🗖 🛏 🎞 Ⓥ 🛆 ∅

(0.5m 🚐) *Severn Farm,* Welshpool, Powys, *SY21 7BB.*
Actual grid ref: SJ233069
Modernised farmhouse on edge of
town.
Grades: WTB 1 Cr
Tel: 01938 553098 Ms Jones.
Rates fr: £14.50-£15.00.
Open: All Year (not Xmas)
Beds: 1F 1D 1T 1S
Baths: 2 Shared
🖙 🅿 (20) 🗖 🛏 ✕ 🎞 Ⓥ 🛆 ∅

Greensand Way

This is a lovely part of the country, kept secret by natives of Surrey and Kent. Between the great chalk ridges of the North and South Downs there runs a sandstone strip that stands out peculiarly from the ordinary clay vales of the Sussex Weald. There is sand underfoot - in dry weather it can be like walking on a beach. The full 110-mile **Greensand Way** was opened in 1989, beginning at Haslemere in Surrey and finishing at Hamstreet in Kent. The Surrey section has the more extensive Lower Greensand hills (including the two highest points, Leith Hill and Gibbet Hill); towards Dorking the path crosses farmland and cuts through villages; the North Downs are ever present. On the Kent side, much of the Greensand ridge's mature oaks and beeches were devastated by the great storm of 1987. So now the woodland floor is covered with young silver birch. The path is prone to mud at times, but much of the walk is over freely draining sand, providing firm walking ground most of the year.

Guide: *The Greensand Way in Surrey: A Walkers Guide* (ISBN 0 946840 41 5), published by Surrey County Council and available directly from their offices (Public Relations Unit, County Hall, Kingston-upon-Thames, Surrey, KT1 2DN, tel. 0181 541 9082), £2.50

The Greensand Way in Kent (ISBN 1 873010 23 0), published by Kent County Council and available directly from their offices (Planning Dept, Countryside Section, Springfield, Maidstone, Kent, ME14 2LX, tel. 01622 671411), £2.95

Map: 1:50000 Ordnance Survey Landranger Series: 186, 187, 188, 189

Haslemere   1

National Grid Ref: SU8932

(0.75m) *Town House, High Street, Haslemere, Surrey, GU27 2JY.*
Listed Georgian house.
Grades: ETB Listed, Comm
Tel: **01428 643310** Mrs Smyrk.
Rates fr: *£18.50*-£20.00.
Open: Feb to Dec **Beds:** 1D 1T 2S
Baths: 2 Private 1 Shared
🛏 (4) 🅿 (3) ⌀ 🖵 🏚

(0.75m) *Quoins, Museum Hill, Haslemere, Surrey, GU27 2JR.*
Elegant, comfortable Edwardian home.

Tel: **01428 658540** Mrs Bell.
Rates fr: *£18.00*-£20.00.
Open: All Year
Beds: 1D 1T
Baths: 2 Private
🅿 (3) 🖵 🏚

The lowest *double*

rate per person is

shown in *italics*.

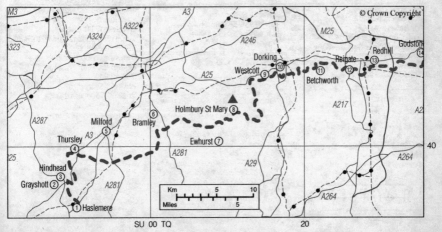

Grayshott 2

National Grid Ref: SU8735

|๏| 🍺 Fox & Pelican

(1m 🚌) *The Valleys, School Road, Grayshott, Hindhead, Surrey, GU26 6LR.*
Actual grid ref: SU869355
Hospitable, beautifully situated, comfortable house.
Grades: ETB Listed
Tel: 01428 606987 Mrs Burgess.
Rates fr: £18.50-£18.50.
Open: All Year
Beds: 1D 1S **Baths:** 1 Shared
🛇 🅿 (4) ⬚ 🛏 🖿 🎹 ♨ ✏

Hindhead 3

National Grid Ref: SU8836

(▲ 1m) *Hindhead Youth Hostel, Highcoombe Bottom, Bowlhead Green, Hindhead, Godalming, Surrey, GU1 6NS.*
Actual grid ref: SU892368
Warden: Mr M Hiles.
Tel: 01428 604285
Under 18: £3.75 **Adults:** £5.50
Family Rooms, Self Catering Facilities, Centrally Heated, No Smoking, Grounds Available for Games, Parking
A superbly simple Hostel, set in the peaceful haven of the Devil's Punchbowl, converted from three National Trust Cottages and refurbished to a good standard

Thursley 4

National Grid Ref: SU9039

|๏| 🍺 Three Horseshoes

(On Path) *Little Cowdray Farm, Thursley, Godalming, Surrey, GU8 6QJ.*
Comfortable farmhouse. Quiet location.

Grades: ETB Reg
Tel: 01428 605016 Mrs Goble.
Rates fr: £30.00-£15.00.
Open: All Year (not Xmas)
Beds: 1T
Baths: 1 Shared
🄿 ⬚ 🛏 ✗ 🖿 🎹 ♨

(0.5m 🚌) *Hindhead Hill Farm, Portsmouth Road, Thursley, Godalming, Surrey, GU8 6NN.*
Actual grid ref: SU906387
Modern farmhouse, family-run farm.
Grades: ETB Reg
Tel: 01428 684727 Mrs Roe.
Rates fr: £14.50-£14.50.
Open: All Year (not Xmas)
Beds: 1F 1T
Baths: 1 Ensuite 1 Shared
🛇 (5) 🅿 (4) ⬚ 🛏 ✗ 🖿 🎹 ♨

Milford 5

National Grid Ref: SU9442

(2m) *Coturnix House, Rake Lane, Milford, Godalming, Surrey, GU8 5AB.*
Modern house, friendly family atmosphere.
Grades: ETB 1 Cr
Tel: 01428 416897 Mrs Bell.
Rates fr: £17.00-£17.00.
Open: All Year
Beds: 1D 2T
Baths: 1 Private 1 Shared
🛇 (1) 🅿 (6) ⬚ 🛏 ✗ 🖿 🎹

Bramley 6

National Grid Ref: TQ0044

|๏| 🍺 Jolly Farmer, Grantley Arms

(1.75m) *Beevers Farm, Chinthurst Lane, Bramley, Guildford, Surrey, GU5 0DR.*
Actual grid ref: TQ0044
Modern comfortable farmhouse. Own eggs.
Grades: ETB Listed

Tel: 01483 898764 Mr Cook.
Rates fr: £13.00-£20.00.
Open: March to Nov
Beds: 1F 2T
Baths: 1 Ensuite 1 Shared
🛇 (12) ⬚ 🛏 🖿 ♨ ✏

Ewhurst 7

National Grid Ref: TQ0940

|๏| 🍺 Windmill Pub, Bull's Head

(1.5m) *Yard Farm, North Breache Road, Ewhurst, Cranleigh, Surrey, GU6 7SN.*
Actual grid ref: TQ101403
Comfortable farmhouse.
Tel: 01483 276649 Mrs Nutting.
Rates fr: £20.00-£20.00.
Open: All Year (not Xmas)
Beds: 1D 2T 1S
Baths: 2 Ensuite 1 Shared
🛇 (12) 🅿 (6) 🛏 ✗ 🖿 ♨ ✏

(1.5m 🚌) *Malricks, The Street, Ewhurst, Cranleigh, Surrey, GU6 7RH.*
Actual grid ref: TQ093401
Modern centrally-heated detached house.
Tel: 01483 277575 Mrs Budgen.
Rates fr: £16.00-£16.00.
Open: All Year
Beds: 1F 1T
Baths: 1 Ensuite 2 Shared
🛇 🅿 (4) ⬚ 🛏 🖿 🎹 ✏

(1.5m) *High Edser, Shere Road, Ewhurst, Cranleigh, Surrey, GU6 7PQ.*
16th Century family run home.
Grades: ETB Listed, Comm
Tel: 01483 278214 Mrs Franklin-Adams.
Rates fr: £20.00-£22.00.
Open: All Year (not Xmas)
Beds: 2D 1T
Baths: 1 Shared
🛇 🅿 (6) 🛏 🖿 ✏

Holmbury St Mary 8

National Grid Ref: TQ1144

🍴 🍺 Royal Oak, King's Head

(▲ 1m) *Holmbury St Mary Youth Hostel*, Radnor Lane, Holmbury St Mary, Dorking, Surrey, *RH5 6NW*.
Actual grid ref: TQ104450
Warden: Mr I Collins.
Tel: **01306 730777**
Under 18: £5.55 **Adults:** £8.25
Family Rooms, Evening Meal, Self Catering Facilities, Camping, No Smoking, Grounds Available for Games, Shop, Parking
Set in its own 4,000 acres of woodland grounds, this purpose-built Hostel offers tranquil beauty amongst the Surrey hills

(On Path) *Bulmer Farm*,
Holmbury St Mary, Dorking, Surrey, *RH5 6LG*.
Actual grid ref: TQ114441
C17th farmhouse and barn conversion.
Grades: ETB 2 Cr
Tel: **01306 730210** Mrs Hill.
Rates fr: *£18.00*-£19.00.
Open: All Year (not Xmas)
Beds: 3D 5T
Baths: 5 Ensuite 2 Shared
🛏 (12) 🅿 (12) ⌁ 🛏 🖿 ♿ Ⅴ ⚡

(0.75m 🚍) *Woodhill Cottage*,
Holmbury St Mary, Dorking, Surrey, *RH5 6NL*.
Actual grid ref: TQ108453
Comfortable country family home.
Tel: **01306 730498** Mrs McCann.
Rates fr: *£17.00*-£20.00.
Open: All Year
Beds: 1F 1D 1T
Baths: 1 Ensuite 2 Shared
🛏 🅿 (3) ⌁ 🛏 ✕ 🖿 Ⅴ ⚡

Westcott 9

National Grid Ref: TQ1448

🍴 🍺 Crown, Cricketers, Prince of Wales

(m) *The Dene*, Hole Hill, Westcott, Dorking, Surrey, *RH4 3LS*.
Large country house in seven acres.
Tel: **01306 885595** Mrs King.
Rates fr: *£15.00*-£20.00.
Open: All Year (not Xmas)
Beds: 1F 1D 2T
Baths: 2 Shared
🛏 🅿 (10) 🗗 🛏 ✕ 🖿

The lowest *double* rate per person is shown in *italics*.

Dorking 10

National Grid Ref: TQ1649

🍴 🍺 King William, Wootten Hatch, Kings Arms, The Plough, Water Mill

(2m) *The Waltons*, 5 Rose Hill, Dorking, Surrey, *RH4 2EG*.
Listed Victorian house/conservation area.
Grades: ETB Listed
Tel: **01306 883127** Mrs Walton.
Rates fr: *£15.00*-£17.50.
Open: All Year **Beds:** 1F 2D 1T
🛏 🅿 ⌁ 🗗 🛏 ✕ 🖿 Ⅴ ⓘ ⚡

(1.5m) *Shrub Hill*, 3 Calvert Road, Dorking, Surrey, *RH4 1LT*.
Convenient, comfortable, quiet family home.
Tel: **01306 885229**
Mrs Scott Kerr.
Rates fr: *£17.50*-£18.00.
Open: All Year (not Xmas)
Beds: 1T 1S
Baths: 1 Shared
🛏 (5) 🅿 (2) ⌁ 🗗 🛏 🖿 Ⅴ

(1.25m) *The Waltons*, 5 Rose Hill, Dorking, Surrey, *RH4 2EG*.
Listed Victorian house/conservation area.
Grades: ETB Listed
Tel: **01306 883127** Mrs Walton.
Rates fr: *£15.00*-£15.00.
Open: All Year
Beds: 2F 1D 1T
🛏 🅿 (3) ⌁ 🗗 🛏 ✕ 🖿 Ⅴ

(1.5m) *Highbank*, 1 Townfield Road, Dorking, Surrey, *RH4 2HX*.
Family home - central - lovely views.
Grades: ETB 1 Cr
Tel: **01306 888135** Mrs Paul.
Rates fr: *£15.00*-£15.00.
Open: All Year
Beds: 1T 1S
Baths: 1 Private 1 Shared
🗗 🖿.

Betchworth 11

National Grid Ref: TQ2150

(1m 🚍) *Gadbrook Old Farm*,
Wellhouse Lane, Betchworth, Surrey, *RH3 7HH*.
Actual grid ref: TQ200485
Comfortable old farmhouse.
Grades: ETB Listed
Tel: **01737 842183** Mrs Bibby.
Rates fr: *£15.00*-£15.00.
Open: All Year (not Xmas)
Beds: 1D 2T
Baths: 1 Ensuite 1 Shared
🛏 (4) 🅿 (4) ⌁ 🗗 🛏 ✕ 🖿 Ⅴ ⓘ ⚡

Reigate 12

National Grid Ref: TQ2649

🍴 🍺 Nutley Hall

(1m) *Norfolk Lodge Hotel*,
23-25 London Road, Reigate, Surrey, *RH2 9PY*.
Very comfortable, licensed family hotel.
Tel: **01737 248702** Mr Bowley.
Rates fr: *£15.00*-£24.00.
Open: All Year
Beds: 3F 2D 5T 6S
Baths: 2 Shared
🛏 🅿 (50) 🗗 🛏

Redhill 13

National Grid Ref: TQ2750

🍴 🍺 Red Lion, Home Cottage

(0.75m) *Lynwood Guest House*,
50 London Road, Redhill, Surrey, *RH1 1LN*.
Large Victorian modernised house.
Grades: AA 3 Q
Tel: **01737 766894**
Mrs Rao.
Rates fr: *£17.00*-£21.00.
Open: All Year
Beds: 4F 1D 2T 2S
Baths: 3 Ensuite 1 Shared
🛏 🅿 (7) 🗗 🖿.

Godstone 14

National Grid Ref: TQ3551

(1m) *Godstone Hotel*, The Green, Godstone, Surrey, *RH9 8DT*.
Tel: **01883 742461**
Mr Howe.
Rates fr: *£22.50*-£32.00.
Open: All Year
Beds: 1F 5D 2T
Baths: 8 Private
🛏 🅿 🗗 🛏 ✕ 🖿 Ⅴ
Set in the lovely old village of Godstone, this C16th coaching house is full of original timbers and inglenook fireplaces. A warm welcome awaits you.

Oxted 15

National Grid Ref: TQ3852

🍴 🍺 The Royal Oak, Staffhurst Wood, George Inn, Old Oxted

(0.5m) *Pinehurst Grange Guest House*, East Hill (Part of A25), Oxted, Surrey, *RH8 9AE*.
Actual grid ref: TQ393525
Comfortable, homely, refurbished, Victorian ex-farmhouse.
Tel: **01883 716413**
Mr Rodgers.
Rates fr: *£19.50*-£24.00.
Open: All Year (not Xmas/New Year)
Beds: 1D 1T 1S
Baths: 1 Shared
🛏 (5) 🅿 (3) ⌁ 🗗 🖿 ⓘ ⚡

(0.5m) *Rosehaven, 12 Hoskins Road, Oxted, Surrey,* RH8 9HT.
Comfortable house, quiet, residential road.
Tel: **01883 712700** Mrs Snell.
Rates fr: *£18.00-£18.00.*
Open: All Year (not Xmas)
Beds: 2T 1S
Baths: 1 Shared
🛏 🅿 (1) ⊬ 🗗 🎟 ♥

(0.5m 🚗) *Old Forge House, Merle Common, Oxted, Surrey,* RH8 0JB.
Actual grid ref: TQ416493
Comfortable home in rural surroundings.
Grades: ETB Reg
Tel: **01883 715969** Mrs Mills.
Rates fr: *£17.00-£18.00.*
Open: All Year (not Xmas)
Beds: 1D 1T 1S
Baths: 1 Shared
🛏 🅿 (3) 🗗 ⊁ 🎟 ♥ ⚕ ✦

(On Path 🚗) *The Croft, Quarry Road, Oxted, Surrey,* RH8 9HE.
Actual grid ref: TQ393521
Substantial Edwardian house in beautiful gardens.
Tel: **01883 713605** Mrs Todd.
Rates fr: *£17.50-£19.00.*
Open: All Year (not Xmas)
Beds: 1F 1D 1S
Baths: 1 Shared
🛏 (5) 🅿 (10) ⊬ 🗗 🎟 ♥ ✦

Westerham 16

National Grid Ref: TQ4454

🍴 🍺 Fox & Hounds

(On Path) *Corner Cottage, Toys Hill, Westerham, Kent,* TN16 1PY.
Actual grid ref: TQ4651
Spectacular views, extremely comfortable, self-contained.
Tel: **01732 750362**
Mrs Olszowska.
Rates fr: *£18.50-£25.00.*

Open: All Year
Beds: 1F **Baths:** 1 Ensuite
🛏 🅿 ⊬ 🗗 🎟

Brasted 17

National Grid Ref: TQ4655

🍴 🍺 The Bull Inn, The White Hart

(1m 🚗) *The Orchard House, Chart Lane, Brasted, Westerham, Kent,* TN16 1LR.
Delightful family home, rural surroundings.
Tel: **01959 563702** Mrs Godsal.
Rates fr: *£16.00-£17.00.*
Open: All Year (not Xmas)
Beds: 2T 2S
Baths: 1 Shared
🛏 🅿 (4) ⊬ 🗗 🎟 ♿ ♥ ⚕ ✦

(0.25m 🚗) *Holmesdale House, High Street, Brasted, Westerham, Kent,* TN16 1HS.
Actual grid ref: TQ469550
Large Victorian private house.
Tel: **01959 564834** Mr Jinks.
Rates fr: *£18.00-£22.00.*
Open: All Year
Beds: 1F 1D 2T 1S
Baths: 3 Ensuite 2 Shared
🛏 🅿 (6) 🗗 🎟 ♿ ♥ ⚕ ✦

Ide Hill 18

National Grid Ref: TQ4851

🍴 🍺 The Wheatsheaf, The Castle

(On Path) *Winkhurst Green, Ide Hill, Sevenoaks, Kent,* TN14 6LD.
Comfortable farmhouse with excellent cuisine.
Tel: **01732 750257** Mrs Cohen.
Rates fr: *£18.00-£18.00.*
Open: All Year (not Xmas)
Beds: 2D 1S
Baths: 1 Private
🛏 (10) 🅿 (20) ⊬ 🗶 🎟

Sevenoaks Weald 19

National Grid Ref: TQ5250

🍴 🍺 The Prince of Wales, The Windmill

(On Path) *Lambarde Hill, Glebe Road, Sevenoaks Weald, Sevenoaks, Kent,* TN14 6PD.
Actual grid ref: TQ5250
Quietly situated former vicarage.
Grades: ETB 2 Cr, Comm
Tel: **01732 463635**
Mrs Conacher.
Rates fr: *£19.00-£19.00.*
Open: All Year (not Xmas)
Beds: 1D 1T 1S
Baths: 3 Ensuite
🛏 🅿 (3) 🗗 ⊁ 🗶 🎟 ♥ ⚕ ✦

(0.5m) *Laural Cottage, Morleys Road, Sevenoaks Weald, Sevenoaks, Kent,* TN13 6QY.
Actual grid ref: TQ538512
Picturesque chalet bungalow, rural, views.
Tel: **01732 463500**
Mrs Townsend.
Rates fr: *£17.50-£20.00.*
Open: All Year
Beds: 1F 1T
Baths: 2 Ensuite
🛏 (12) 🅿 (2) ⊬ 🗗 🎟 ⚕ ✦

Fawke Common 20

National Grid Ref: TQ5553

(On Path) *Lower Fawke Farm, Fawke Common, Sevenoaks, Kent,* TN15 0JX.
Comfortable quiet working farm.
Tel: **01732 762660**
Mr Francis.
Rates fr: *£17.50-£20.00.*
Open: All Year (not Xmas or Apr)
Beds: 2D 1T
Baths: 1 Shared
🛏 🅿 ⊬ 🗗 🎟 ♥

Tonbridge 21

National Grid Ref: TQ5946

🍴 🍺 Hilden Manor Inn

(3.5m) *61 The Ridgeway, Tonbridge, Kent,* TN10 4NL.
Comfortable and convenient modern house.
Tel: **01732 353530** Mrs Bohan.
Rates fr: *£15.00-£18.00.*
Open: All Year (not Xmas)
Beds: 1T 1D 1S
🛏 🅿 🗗 🎟

(3.5m) *4 Redwood Park, Five Oak Green, Tonbridge, Kent,* TN12 6WB.
New house, rural district.
Grades: ETB Listed
Tel: **01892 838200** Mrs Prance.
Rates fr: *£15.00-£15.00.*
Open: All Year (not Xmas/New Year)
Beds: 1D 1S
Baths: 1 Shared
🅿 (3) 🗗 🎟

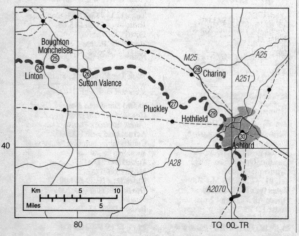

(1.25m) *Starvecrow Place,*
Shipbourne Road, Tonbridge, Kent,
TN11 9NL.
Luxury accommodation set in
woodlands.
Tel: **01732 356863** Mrs Batson.
Rates fr: *£18.00-£25.00*.
Open: All Year (not Xmas)
Beds: 1D 1T 1S
Baths: 3 Private
🛇 (14) 🅿 (6) ⅍ ⟋ 🔲 🅸 🛡 ✓

Hadlow 22

National Grid Ref: TQ6350

⭑◖ 🍺 The Harrow

(1.5m) *James House, Maidstone*
Road, Hadlow, Tonbridge, Kent,
TN11 0HP.
Actual grid ref: TQ636503
Period farmhouse.
Tel: **01732 850217** Mrs Dumbreck.
Rates fr: *£18.00-£20.00*.
Open: All Year (not Xmas)
Beds: 2T
Baths: 1 Shared
🛇 🅿 (3) ⅍ 🔲 🅸 🛡 ✓

(1.5m) *Dunsmore, Hadlow Park,*
Hadlow, Tonbridge, Kent, TN11 0HX.
Private park, ground floor accom-
modation.
Tel: **01732 850611** Mrs Tubbs.
Rates fr: *£17.00-£20.00*.
Open: All Year (not Xmas)
Beds: 1T **Baths:** 1 Private
🛇 🅿 🔲 🅸

Hunton 23

National Grid Ref: TQ7149

(0.75m) *The Woolhouse, Grove*
Lane, Hunton, Maidstone, Kent,
ME15 0SE.
Listed C16th wool house conver-
sion.
Tel: **01622 820778** Mrs Wetton.
Rates fr: *£20.00-£22.00*.
Open: All Year (not Xmas)
Beds: 1D 1T 2S
Baths: 4 Ensuite
🅿 (10) 🔲 ➤ ✗ 🅸

Linton 24

National Grid Ref: TQ7549

⭑◖ 🍺 The Bull

(On Path 🚌) *The White Lodge,*
Loddington Lane, Linton,
Maidstone, Kent, ME17 4AG.
Elegant house in parkland.
Tel: **01622 743129**
Mrs Boorman.
Rates fr: *£19.00-£19.00*.
Open: All Year
Beds: 2D 2T 2S
Baths: 1 Ensuite, 1 Shared
🛇 (A) 🅿 (20) ⅍ 🔲 ➤ 🅸 🛡 ✓

(0.25m) *Hill Place, Linton,*
Maidstone, Kent, ME17 4AL.
Actual grid ref: TQ754505
Grade II Listed family home.

Tel: **01622 743834** Mrs Johnston.
Rates fr: *£18.00-£18.00*.
Open: All Year (not Xmas)
Beds: 2D 1T 1S
Baths: 2 Ensuite 1 Shared
🛇 (7) 🅿 (6) ⅍ ⟋ ➤ 🅸 🛡 ✓

Boughton Monchelsea 25

National Grid Ref: TQ7651

⭑◖ 🍺 Cock Inn, Albion Pub

(0.5m) *Bramleys, Church Street,*
Boughton Monchelsea, Maidstone,
Kent, ME17 4HN.
Modern detached house in village.
Grades: ETB Reg
Tel: **01622 747455** Mrs Knight.
Rates fr: *£12.50-£14.00*.
Open: All Year (not Xmas)
Beds: 1D 1S
Baths: 1 Shared
🛇 🅿 (4) 🔲 ➤ 🅸 🔻 ✓

Sutton Valence 26

National Grid Ref: TQ8149

⭑◖ 🍺 The Kings Head, The Queens
Head, The Swan

(0.25m) *Coppins, Maidstone Road,*
Sutton Valence, Maidstone, Kent,
ME17 3LW.
Actual grid ref: TQ813498
Spacious detached chalet
bungalow.
Grades: ETB Recomm
Tel: **01622 842600**
Mrs Wilding.
Rates fr: *£15.00*.
Open: Mar to Oct
Beds: 1D 1T
🛇 (7) 🅿 (2) ⅍ 🔲 🅸 🔻

(On Path) *West Belringham, Chart*
Road, Sutton Valence, Maidstone,
Kent, ME17 3AW.
Large bungalow with panoramic
views.
Grades: ETB 1 Cr, Comm
Tel: **01622 843995**
Mrs King.
Rates fr: *£18.00-£23.00*.
Open: All Year (not Xmas)
Beds: 2T
Baths: 1 Shared
🛇 (7) 🅿 (6) ⅍ 🔲 🅸 🛡 ✓

Pluckley 27

National Grid Ref: TQ9245

⭑◖ 🍺 Chequers

(0.25m) *Arden, Forge Hill,*
Pluckley, Ashford, Kent, TN27 0SN.
Large country house in two acres.
Grades: ETB 2 Cr
Tel: **01233 840330**
Mrs Hummerson.
Rates fr: *£17.00-£17.00*.
Open: Easter to Oct
Beds: 1F 1D 1T 1S
Baths: 2 Ensuite
🛇 (5) 🅿 (20) ⅍ 🔲 🅸 🛡 ✓

Charing 28

National Grid Ref: TQ9549

⭑◖ 🍺 The Red Lion, Royal Oak

(2.5m 🚌) *Barnfield, Charing,*
Ashford, Kent, TN28 0BN.
Romantic welcoming family C15th
farmhouse.
Grades: ETB Listed, Comm,
AA 3 Q
Tel: **01233 712421** Mrs Pym.
Rates fr: *£18.50-£20.00*.
Open: All Year (not Xmas)
Beds: 1F 1D 1T 1S
Baths: 1 Shared
🛇 🅿 (50) ⅍ 🔲 ✗ 🅸 ✓

(3m 🚌) *Arketts Farm, Charing,*
Ashford, Kent, TN27 0HH.
Actual grid ref: TQ950517
Listed farmhouse, pasture and
woodland.
Grades: ETB Listed
Tel: **01233 712893** Mrs Okell.
Rates fr: *£14.00-£15.00*.
Open: All Year (not Xmas)
Beds: 1D 1T
Baths: 1 Shared
🛇 (4) 🅿 (5) ⅍ 🔲 ➤ ✗ 🅸 🔻 🛡 ✓
Also ⛺ *£2 per tent.* 🆃 ✗ ✓ ♿

(3m 🚌) *Timber Lodge, Charing*
Hill, Charing, Ashford, Kent,
TN27 0NG.
Comfortable house with beautiful
views. **Grades:** ETB Listed
Tel: **01233 712822** Mrs Bigwood.
Rates fr: *£16.00-£20.00*.
Beds: 2D 1S
Baths: 1 Ensuite 1 Shared
🛇 (10) ⅍ ✗ 🅸 🛡 ✓

Hothfield 29

National Grid Ref: TQ9744

(0.25m) *The Coach House, Chapel*
Road, Hothfield, Ashford, Kent,
TN25 4LN.
Large, detached, oak-beamed
house.
Tel: **01233 713878** Mr Cooke.
Rates fr: *£13.00-£15.00*.
Open: All Year
Beds: 2D **Baths:** 1 Shared
🅿 (3) ⅍ 🔲 ✗ 🅸 🔻

Ashford 30

National Grid Ref: TR0042

⭑◖ 🍺 Hare & Hound

(4m) *Quantock House, Quantock*
Drive, Ashford, Kent, TN24 8QH.
Family-run, comfortable and wel-
coming.
Grades: ETB 2 Cr, Comm
Tel: **01233 638921**
Mr & Mrs Tucker.
Rates fr: *£17.00-£18.00*.
Open: All Year (not Xmas)
Beds: 1D 1T 1S
Baths: 3 Private
🛇 (7) 🅿 (3) 🔲 ✗ 🅸 🔻

Hadrian's Wall

From Wallsend to Bowness-on-Solway, Mark Richards' route runs for 83 miles - another one to do in under a week or over a couple of long weekends. **Hadrian's Wall** is still the most impressive monument to the Romans' presence in Britain; indeed, it stands alongside the Pyramids and the Parthenon as a World Heritage Site. Its scale and presence is quite breathtaking, despite its approaching 1,900 years. As with **Offa's Dyke**, to walk along the wall is to sense an atavistic purpose in your stride; on these bleak hills, as the wall's long line leads the way ahead, you truly march in step with shadows. There is a proposed National Trail for the Wall, but the plans are controversial and the final go-ahead could be years away. This route thus has no official sanction, although one part of it coincides with the **Pennine Way**. There are no special waymarks, so for the time being you will have to rely on Mark Richard's excellent guide. Carry suitable clothing, for the northern winds still possess a cold edge even in summer. Weatherproofs and good strong boots are essential.

Guides: *Hadrian's Wall: The Wall Walk* (vol.1) by Mark Richards (ISBN 1 85284 128 1), published by Cicerone Press and available from all good map shops or directly from the publishers (2 Police Square, Milnthorpe, Cumbria, LA7 7PY, 01539 562069), £7.99

Maps: 1:50000 Ordnance Survey Landranger Series: 85, 86, 87 and 88. Also *Hadrian's Wall Historical Map & Guide* (ISBN 0319290182), from the Ordnance Survey, £4.15.

Comments on the proposed Hadrian's Wall National Trail to: **David McGlode**, Countryside Commission, 4th Floor, Warwick House, Grantham Road, Newcastle upon Tyne, NE2 1QF.

Heaton 1

National Grid Ref: NZ2766

⚑ Corner House, Coast Road

(0.5m) *Ann Stratford Guesthouse, 47 Stratford Road, Heaton, Newcastle-upon-Tyne, NE6 5PB.*
Warm, friendly, comfortable guesthouse. **Grades:** ETB Approv
Tel: **0191 265 6219** Mr Scott.
Rates fr: *£15.00-£15.00.*
Open: All Year
Beds: 1F 1D 1T 1S
Baths: 2 Shared
🛏 🅿 (4) 💷 🔭 🛏 📷 🔟 💤

Jesmond 2

National Grid Ref: NZ2566

⚑ Legendary Yorkshire Heroes

(0.25m) *Dene Hotel, 38-42 Grosvenor Road, Jesmond, Newcastle-upon-Tyne, NE2 2RP.*
Modern.
Grades: ETB 3 Cr, Comm
Tel: **0191 281 1502**
Mr Venayak.
Rates fr: *£25.50-£25.50.*
Open: Easter to Dec
Beds: 3F 5D 3T 12S
Baths: 5 Ensuite 14 Shared25.5
🛏 🅿 (10) 🔌 🔭 🗡 📷 🔟 💧 💤

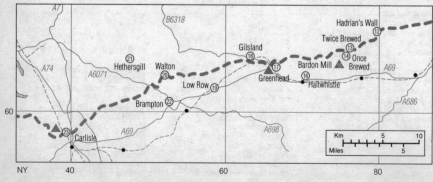

(0.25m) *Osborne Hotel, Osborne Road, Jesmond, Newcastle-upon-Tyne, NE2 2AL.*
Grades: ETB 3 Cr, AA 1 St, RAC 2 St
Tel: 0191 281 3385 Mr Curry.
Rates fr: *£20.00-£20.00.*
Open: All Year
Beds: 3T 4D 18S
Baths: 13 Ensuite 4 Shared
🛏 🅿 🕭 🗙 🏧

(0.25m) *Hansen Hotel, 131 Sandyford Road, Jesmond, Newcastle-upon-Tyne, NE2 1QR.*
Homely family business near town.
Grades: ETB Listed
Tel: 0191 281 0289 Miss Hansen.
Rates fr: *£17.00-£18.00.*
Open: All Year (not Xmas)
Beds: 2F 1T 8S
Baths: 4 Shared
🛏 🕭 🏧 Ⓥ

Newcastle-upon-Tyne 3

National Grid Ref: NZ2564

🍽 🍺 Bacchus, Broken Doll, Chapel Park, Crown Posada, Cooperage, Fitzgerald's, Rose & Crown, Newcastle Arms, Tap & Stile

(▲ On Path) *Newcastle upon Tyne Youth Hostel, 107 Jesmond Road, Newcastle-upon-Tyne, NE2 1NJ.*
Actual grid ref: NZ257656
Warden: Mr L Heslop.
Tel: 0191 281 2570
Under 18: £4.60 **Adults:** £6.75
Family Rooms, Evening Meal, Self Catering Facilities, Games Room, Shop, Parking
A large town house conveniently located for the centre of this vibrant city, the regional capital of the north east

---

The lowest *double* rate per person is shown in *italics.*

The Grid Reference beneath the location heading is for the village or town - *not* for individual houses, which are shown (where supplied) in each entry itself.

(On Path) *Chirton House Hotel, 46 Clifton Road, Newcastle-upon-Tyne, NE4 6SH.*
Large Victorian private house.
Grades: ETB 3 Cr, AA 3 Q, RAC Acclaim
Tel: 0191 273 0407
Mr Hagerty.
Rates fr: *£17.00-£23.00.*
Open: All Year
Beds: 3F 2D 3T 3S
Baths: 5 Ensuite 2 Shared
🛏 🅿 🗙 🏧 Ⓥ

Wylam 4

National Grid Ref: NZ1164

🍽 🍺 Fox & Hounds

(3m 🚌) *Wormald House, Main Street, Wylam, Northd, NE41 8DN.*
Actual grid ref: NZ1164
Very welcoming, pleasant country home.
Grades: ETB 2 Cr, High Comm
Tel: 01661 852529
Mr & Mrs Craven.
Rates fr: *£16.50.*
Open: All Year (not Xmas)
Beds: 1D 1T
Baths: 2 Ensuite
🛏 (5) 🅿 (3) 🕭 🏧 Ⓥ

Newton 5

National Grid Ref: NZ0364

🍽 🍺 Wellington, Robin Hood

(2m 🚌) *Crookhill Farm, Newton, Stocksfield, Northumberland, NE43 7UX.*
Comfortable, welcoming farm-house.
Grades: ETB Listed, Comm, AA Listed
Tel: 01661 843117
Mrs Leech.
Rates fr: *£15.00-£17.00.*
Open: Easter to Oct
Beds: 1F 1T 1S
Baths: 1 Shared
🛏 🅿 (4) 🕭 🏧 Ⓥ 🔒

Corbridge 6

National Grid Ref: NY9964

🍽 🍺 Black Bull, Lion of Corbridge, Angel Hotel, The Wheatsheaf, Fox & Hounds (Corbridge)

(2.5m) *Holmlea, Station Road, Corbridge, Northumberland, NE45 5AY.*
Grades: ETB 2 Cr, Comm
Tel: 01434 632486
Mrs Stoker.
Rates fr: *£16.00-£16.00.*
Open: All Year
Beds: 1F 1D 1S
Baths: 1 Ensuite 1 Private 1 Shared
🛏 🅿 (2) 🏧 🔒

(3m 🚌) *Fellcroft, Station Road, Corbridge, Northd, NE45 5AY.*
Large Victorian house.
Grades: ETB 2 Cr, High Comm
Tel: 01434 632384
Mr & Mrs Brown.
Rates fr: *£15.00-£19.00.*
Open: All Year (not Xmas)
Beds: 2T
Baths: 1 Ensuite 1 Private
🛏 🅿 (2) 🕭 🗙 🏧 Ⓥ 🔒

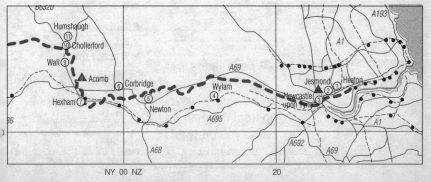

(2.5m) *The Hayes Guest House,* Newcastle Road, Corbridge, Northd, *NE45 5LP.*
Peaceful house, spacious, lovely views.
Grades: ETB 1 Cr
Tel: 01434 632010
Mr Matthews.
Rates fr: *£16.00-£15.5016.00.*
Open: All Year (not Xmas)
Beds: 2F 2D 2T 3S
☎ ▣ (12) ⌂ ⊁ ▥ ₺ Ⓥ

⊟ Pub with evening meal

▲ Youth Hostel

⊁ Children welcome
(from age shown in brackets, if specified)

🚐 Vehicle back-up
(pick up/drop off on path)

▣ Off-street car parking
(number of places shown in brackets)

⊁ No smoking

⌂ Television (either in every room or in a TV lounge)

⊁ Dogs accepted
(by prior arrangement)

✕ Evening meal available
(by prior arrangement)

Ⓥ Special diets catered for
(by prior arrangement - please check with owner to see if your particular requirements are catered for)

▥ Central heating

₺ Suitable for disabled people (please check with owner to see what level of disability is provided for)

▮ Packed lunch

▲ Campsite

☌ Shower facilities

Ⓣ Toilets

⊁ Drying facilities

♨ Washing facilities

⌂ Water tap

(2.25m) *Fellcroft,* Station Road, Corbridge, Northd, *NE45 5AY.*
Comfortable Edwardian house.
Grades: ETB 2 Cr, High Comm
Tel: 01434 632384
Mr & Mrs Brown.
Rates fr: *£15.00-£19.00.*
Open: All Year **Beds:** 2T
Baths: 1 Private 1 Ensuite
☎ ▣ (2) ⊁ ⌂ ⊁ ✕ ▥ Ⓥ

Hexham   7

National Grid Ref: NY9363

⚑ Angel, Black Bull, Boatside Inn, County Hotel, Dipton Mill, Queen Halls, Heart of England

(3m 🚐) *Dukeslea, 32 Shaws Park,* Hexham, Northd, *NE46 3BJ.*
Modern, comfortable, detached, private house.
Grades: ETB 2 Cr, High Comm, AA 3 Q
Tel: 01434 602947 Mrs Theobald.
Rates fr: *£16.00-£16.00.*
Open: All Year (not Xmas)
Beds: 2D **Baths:** 2 Ensuite
☎ ▣ (4) ⊁ ⌂ ⊁ ✕ ▥ Ⓥ ⊁

(3m) *Topsy Turvy, 9 Leazes Lane,* Hexham, Northd, *NE46 3BA.*
Pretty, chalet type home.
Tel: 01434 603152
Ms McCormick.
Rates fr: *£14.00.* **Open:** All Year
Beds: 2D
Baths: 1 Ensuite 1 Shared
☎ ▣ (3) ⊁ ⌂ ⊁ ✕ ▥ ▮ ⊁

(3.25m) *18 Hextol Terrace,* Hexham, Northd, *NE46 2DF.*
Spacious, comfortable Victorian private house.
Tel: 01434 602265 Mrs Boaden.
Rates fr: *£15.00-£15.00.*
Open: All Year (not Xmas)
Beds: 1F 1D 1S
Baths: 1 Shared
☎ ⌂ ⊁ Ⓥ ⊁

(4m 🚐) *Burncrest Guest House,* Burnland Terrace, Hexham, Northd, *NE46 3JT.*
Home from home.
Grades: ETB Listed
Tel: 01434 605163 Mr Ellery.
Rates fr: *£15.00-£18.00.*
Open: All Year
Beds: 2D **Baths:** 2 Shared
☎ (14) ⊁ ⌂ ✕ ▥ Ⓥ ▮ ⊁

🚐 sign means that, *given due notice,* owners will pick you up from the path and drop you off *within reason.*

The *lowest* **single** rate *is shown in* **bold.**

Acomb   8

National Grid Ref: NY9366

⚑ The Miners

(0.25m) *Mariner's Cottage Hotel,* Fallowfield Dene Road, Acomb, Hexham, Northd, *NE46 4RP.*
Tel: 01434 603666 Mrs Darling.
Rates fr: *£17.00-£16.00.*
Open: All Year
Beds: 1F 1D 1T 2S
Baths: 3 Private 2 Shared
☎ ▣ (60) ⌂ ⊁ ✕ ▥
Hotel set in country, 3 miles from market town of Hexham and within easy reach of Hadrian's Wall, Kielder Water, Beamish Museum, Metro Shopping Centre

(▲ 0.2m) *Acomb Youth Hostel,* Main Street, Acomb, Hexham, Northumberland, *NE46 4PL.*
Actual grid ref: NY934666
Warden: Mr P Kirsopp.
Tel: 01434 602864
Under 18: £3.75
Adults: £5.50
Family Rooms, Self Catering Facilities, No Smoking, Shop, Parking
A simple youth Hostel, converted from stable buildings in a small village in the valley of the River Tyne

Wall   9

National Grid Ref: NY9168

⚑ Hadrian Hotel (Wall)

(On Path 🚐) *St Oswalds Farm,* Wall, Hexham, Northd, *NE46 4HB.*
Actual grid ref: NY940695
Farmhouse on line of Wall.
Grades: ETB Listed
Tel: 01434 681307 Mrs Reay.
Rates fr: *£13.50-£13.50.*
Open: Feb to Nov
Beds: 1D 1T 1S
Baths: 1 Shared
☎ ▣ (4) ⌂

Chollerford   10

National Grid Ref: NY9170

⚑ Hadrian Hotel

(On Path 🚐) *Brunton Water Mill,* Chollerford, Hexham, Northumberland, *NE46 4EL.*
Beautifully converted water mill.
Tel: 01434 681002 Mrs Pesarra.
Rates fr: *£20.00-£25.00.*
Open: All Year (not Xmas)
Beds: 2D 1T
Baths: 2 Ensuite 1 Shared
☎ (12) ▣ (8) ⊁ ⌂ ▥ ▮ ⊁

Humshaugh 11

National Grid Ref: NY9171

⏹ Crown Inn

(0.25m) *Crown Inn, Humshaugh, Hexham, Northd, NE46 4AG.*
Old fashioned country inn.
Tel: **01434 681231**
Miss Buck.
Rates fr: *£15.00-£15.00.*
Open: All Year (not Xmas)
Beds: 1F 1D 1S
Baths: 1 Shared
🛇 ⌇ ⌖ ✕ ▥ Ⓥ

Hadrians Wall 12

National Grid Ref: NY7969

⏹ Milecastle Inn, Twice Brewed Inn

(On Path 🚌) *Sewingshields Farm, Hadrians Wall, Haydon Bridge, Hexham, Northd, NE47 6NW.*
Comfortable farmhouse with spectacular views.
Grades: ETB Listed, Comm
Tel: **01434 684418**
Mrs Murray.
Rates fr: *£15.00-£15.00.*
Open: All Year (not Xmas)
Beds: 1F 1D 1T
Baths: 2 Shared
🛇 🄿 ⌖ ⌇ ✕ ▥ Ⓥ

(On Path 🚌) *Crindledykes Farm, Hadrians Wall, Housesteads, Hexham, Northd, NE47 7AP.*
C17th well-maintained farmhouse.
Working stock farm.
Grades: ETB High Comm, AA 3 Q
Tel: **01434 344316**
Mrs Davidson.
Rates fr: *£15.00-£21.00.*
Open: Mar to Nov
Beds: 1D 1T
Baths: 1 Shared
🛇 🄿 ⌖ ⌇ ✕ ▥ Ⓥ

The Country Code

Enjoy the countryside and respect its life and work

Guard against all risk of fire

Fasten all gates

Keep your dogs under close control

Keep to public paths across farmland

Use gates and stiles to cross fences, hedges and walls

Leave livestock, crops and machinery alone

Take your litter home

Help to keep all water clean

Protect wild-life, plants and trees

Take special care on country roads

Make no unnecessary noise

Twice Brewed 13

National Grid Ref: NY7567

⏹ Twice Brewed Inn

(0.75m) *Vallum Lodge Hotel, Military Road, Twice Brewed, nr Bardon Mill, Hexham, Northd, NE47 7AN.*
Country hotel by Hadrian's Wall.
Grades: ETB 2 Cr, Comm, AA 1 St
Tel: **01434 344248** Mr/Mrs Wright.
Rates fr: *£20.00-£21.00.*
Open: Mar to Nov
Beds: 3D 3T 1S
Baths: 2 Private 2 Shared
🄿 (25) ⌇ ⌖ ⌇ ✕ ▥ & Ⓥ

Once Brewed 14

National Grid Ref: NY7566

⏹ The Twice Brewed Inn

(0.25m) *Winshields Farm, Once Brewed, Bardon Mill, Hexham, Northd, NE47 7AN.*
Large farmhouse on Hadrian's Wall.
Grades: ETB Listed, Comm
Tel: **01434 344243** Ms Lawson.
Rates fr: *£16.00-£16.00.*
Open: May to Sep
Beds: 1F 1D 1T
Baths: 2 Shared
🄿 ⌖ ▥ &
Also ▲ *£2.00 per person.* 🄿 Ⓣ &

Bardon Mill 15

National Grid Ref: NY7864

⏹ Twice Brewed Inn

(▲ 0.5m) *Once Brewed Youth Hostel, Military Road, Bardon Mill, Hexham, Northumberland, NE47 7AN.*
Actual grid ref: NY752668
Warden: Mr B & P Keen.
Tel: **01434 344045**
Under 18: £5.55 **Adults:** £8.25
Family Rooms, Evening Meal, Centrally Heated, Games Room, Laundry Facilities, Facilities for the disabled, Shop, Parking
A modern and comfortable Hostel, just 1/2m from Hadrian's Wall, amidst the beauty of the Northumberland National Park and North Pennines

Haltwhistle 16

National Grid Ref: NY7064

⏹ Milecastle Inn, Spotted Cow, Manor House Hotel

(2m) *Manor House Hotel, Main Street, Haltwhistle, Northd, NE49 0BS.*
Grades: ETB 2 Cr, Approv
Tel: **01434 322588**
Mr & Mrs Hind
Rates fr: *£12.50-£12.50.*
Open: All Year (not Xmas)
Beds: 1F 1D 4T
Baths: 3 Ensuite 3 Shared
🛇 🄿 (5) ⌖ ✕ ▥ Ⓥ &
Comfortable family-run hotel in small town 2 miles Hadrians Wall. Good food. Real ales. Car park at rear. Warm welcome from Kevin and Clare Hind

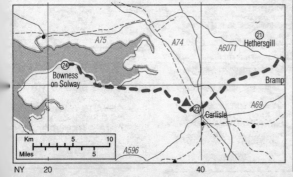

**All details shown
are as supplied
by B&B owners in
Autumn 1995.**

(2m 🚍) **Grey Bull Hotel**, *Main Street, Haltwhistle, Northd,* *NE49 0DL.*
Actual grid ref: NY706645
Grades: ETB 1 Cr, Approv
Tel: 01434 321991
Mr & Mrs Morpeth.
Rates fr: £12.50-£15.00.
Open: All Year
Beds: 2F 3D 1T 1S
Baths: 3 Shared
🛉 🖭 (20) 🗆 🛏 🛏 ✕ Ⓥ 🗎 ✦
C18th coaching inn, ideally situated for Hadrian's Wall. Superb local walks. Fishing, shooting available. Excellent touring base

(1.25m) **White Craig**, *Nr Hadrian's Wall, Shield Hill, Haltwhistle, Northd, NE49 9NW.*
Actual grid ref: NY714650
Rambling old bungalow, very comfortable.
Grades: ETB 2 Cr, High Comm, AA 4 Q, Select
Tel: 01434 320565 Ms Laidlow.
Rates fr: £18.50-£23.50.
Open: All Year
Beds: 2D 1T
Baths: 3 Ensuite
🛉 🖭 (3) ✕ 🗆 🛏 ⬟ & Ⓥ 🗎 ✦

(1.5m) **Hall Meadows**, *Main Street, Haltwhistle, Northd, NE49 0AZ.*
Large C19th Century private house.
Grades: ETB 1 Cr, Comm
Tel: 01434 321021
Mrs Humes.
Rates fr: £15.00-£15.00.
Open: All Year (not Xmas)
Beds: 1D 1T 1S
Baths: 1 Shared
🛉 🖭 (3) 🗆 ⬟ 🗎 ✦

Greenhead 17

National Grid Ref: NY6665

(▲0.5m) **Greenhead Youth Hostel**, *Greenhead, Carlisle, Cumbria, CA6 7HG.*
Actual grid ref: NY659655
Tel: 016977 47401
Under 18: £4.60 **Adults:** £6.75
Evening Meal, Self Catering Facilities, Centrally Heated, Grounds Available for Games, Parking
Complete with high beamed roof, arched windows and thick stone walls, this former Methodist chapel has a spacious yet cosy feel to it

(On Path) **Holmhead Farm**, *Licensed Guesthouse, Hadrians Wall, Greenhead, Carlisle, Cumbria, CA6 7HY.*
Actual grid ref: NY661659
Fantastic breakfasts.
Grades: ETB 3 Cr, Comm, AA 3 Q
Tel: 016977 47402
Mr & Mrs Staff.
Rates fr: £22.50-£28.00.
Open: All Year (not Xmas)
Beds: 1F 1D 2T **Baths:** 4 Ensuite
🛉 🖭 (6) ✕ 🗆 ✕ ⬟ 🗎 Ⓥ 🗎 ✦
Also ▲ Also bunkhouse, £3 per bunk🛉.

Gilsland 18

National Grid Ref: NY6366

🍴 🛏 Samson Inn

(On Path 🚍) **Alpha Mount House**, *Gilsland, Carlisle, Cumbria, CA6 7EB.*
Large family home.
Grades: ETB 1 Cr, Comm
Tel: 016977 47070 Mr Cole.
Rates fr: £13.00-£13.00.
Open: All Year
Beds: 1F 1D 1S **Baths:** 1 Shared
🛉 🖭 (2) ✕ 🗆 ✕ ⬟ Ⓥ 🗎 ✦

Low Row 19

National Grid Ref: NY5863

(On Path) **High Nook Farm**, *Low Row, Brampton, Cumbria, CA8 2LU.*
Actual grid ref: NY589644
Comfortable farmhouse built in 1857.
Grades: ETB Listed
Tel: 016977 46273 Mrs Foster.
Rates fr: £11.00-£12.00.
Open: Easter to Oct
Beds: 1F 1D
🛉 🖭 (3) 🗆 🛏 ✕ 🗎 ✦

Walton 20

National Grid Ref: NY5264

🍴 🛏 Centurion Inn

(On Path 🚍) **High Rigg Farm**, *Walton, Brampton, Cumbria, CA8 2AZ.*
C18th listed farmhouse - working farm.
Grades: ETB 1 Cr, Approv
Tel: 016977 2117 Mrs Mounsey.
Rates fr: £15.00-£15.50.
Open: All Year (not Xmas)
Beds: 1F 1S
Baths: 1 Shared
🛉 ✕ 🗆 🛏 ✕ ⬟ Ⓥ 🗎 ✦

Hethersgill 21

National Grid Ref: NY4767

🍴 🛏 Black Lion

(4m 🚍) **New Pallyards**, *Hethersgill, Carlisle, Cumbria, CA6 6HZ.*
Actual grid ref: NY4767
Country farmhouse. National award winner.
Grades: ETB 3 Cr, Comm
Tel: 01228 577308 Mr Elwen.
Rates fr: £18.50-£19.50.
Open: All Year
Beds: 1F 2D 1T 1S
Baths: 5 Ensuite
🛉 🖭 (6) 🗆 🛏 ✕ ⬟ Ⓥ 🗎 ✦

Brampton 22

National Grid Ref: NY5261

🍴 🛏 The Drove Inn, Pointer Dog Inn

(5m) **Cracrop Farm**, *Brampton, Brampton, Cumbria, CA8 2BW.*
High standard farmhouse.
Grades: ETB 3 Cr, High Comm, AA 4 Q, Select
Tel: 016977 48245 Mrs Stobart.
Rates fr: £20.00-£20.00.
Open: All Year (not Xmas)
Beds: 2D 1T 1S
Baths: 4 Private
🖭 (6) ✕ 🗆 ✕ ⬟.

(4m) **Halidon**, *Tree Road, Brampton, Cumbria, CA8 1TY.*
Comfortable, friendly, Edwardian terrace house.
Grades: ETB 1 Cr
Tel: 016977 2106 Mrs Streames.
Rates fr: £14.50-£15.00.
Open: All Year
Beds: 1F 1T **Baths:** 1 Shared
🛉 🗆 ⬟ Ⓥ

(5m) **Beechwood**, *Capon Tree Road, Brampton, Cumbria, CA8 1QL.*
Detached house in own grounds.
Grades: ETB Listed
Tel: 016977 2239
Mrs Clark.
Rates fr: £14.00-£16.00.
Open: All Year (not Xmas)
Beds: 1D 1T 1S
Baths: 1 Shared
🛉 (2) 🖭 (10) 🗆 ⬟.

Carlisle 23

National Grid Ref: NY3955

🍴 🍺The Plough Inn, Coach & Horses,The Black Lion, The White Quay, Crown Inn, Lordy's, Gianni's, Metal Bridge Inn

(On Path) *Angus Hotel, 14 Scotland Road, Stanwix, Carlisle, Cumbria, CA3 9DG.*
Clean, comfortable Victorian town house.
Grades: AA 3 Q, RAC Listed, Acclaim
Tel: 01228 23546 Mr Webster.
Rates fr: £18.00-**£22.00.**
Open: All Year
Beds: 4F 2D 4T 2S
Baths: 7 Ensuite 3 Shared
🛇 🅿 (6) ✍ 🗖 🛏 ✗ 🎞 Ⓥ 🖿 🖊

(0.75m) *Avondale, 3 St Aidans Road, Carlisle, Cumbria, CA1 1LT.*
Grades: ETB 2 Cr, High Comm, RAC Acclaim
Tel: 01228 23012
Mr & Mrs Hayes.
Rates fr: £17.00-**£20.00.**
Open: All Year (not Xmas)
Beds: 1D 2T
Baths: 1 Private 1 Shared
🅿 (3) 🗖 ✗ 🎞 Ⓥ
Attractive, comfortable Edwardian house in a quiet position, convenient for M6 (J.43), City Centre and amenities. Spacious well furnished rooms. Private parking

(🔺0.75m) *Carlisle Youth Hostel, Etterby House, Etterby, Carlisle, Cumbria, CA3 9QS.*
Actual grid ref: NY386569
Tel: 01228 23934
Under 18: £4.15 **Adults:** £6.10

Family Rooms, Evening Meal, Self Catering Facilities, Laundry Facilities, Shop, Parking
The Hostel is a Victorian house in a quiet suburb standing on the banks of River Eden, in close proximity to the historic city of Carlisle

(0.75m) *Courtfield Guest House, 169 Warwick Road, Carlisle, Cumbria, CA1 1LP.*
Large Victorian guest house.
Grades: ETB 3 Cr, High CommRAC Acclaim
Tel: 01228 22767 Mrs Dawes.
Rates fr: £17.50-**£18.00.**
Open: All Year
Beds: 1F 2D 1T **Baths:** 4 Private
🛇 🅿 🗖 🛏 ✗ 🎞 Ⓥ

(0.75m) *Howard House, 27 Howard Place, Carlisle, Cumbria, CA1 1HR.*
Elegant Victorian town house.
Grades: ETB 3 Cr, High Comm, AA 4 Q, Select
Tel: 01228 29159 / 512550
Mrs Fisher.
Rates fr: £15.00-**£15.00.**
Open: All Year **Beds:** 2F 3D 3T
Baths: 2 Private 2 Shared
🛇 🗖 🛏 ✗ 🎞 Ⓥ

(0.75m) *Howard Lodge, 90 Warwick Road, Carlisle, Cumbria, CA1 1JU.*
Grades: ETB 1 Cr, Approv
Tel: 01228 29842 Mr Hendrie.
Rates fr: £15.00-**£15.00.**
Open: All Year **Beds:** 2F 1D 2T
Baths: 3 Ensuite 1 SHared
🛇 🗖 🛏 ✗ 🎞 Ⓥ
Large Victorian house on main road, 400 metres from city centre. Recently refurbished with ensuite facilities. Satellite TV and welcome tray in all rooms

Bowness on Solway 24

National Grid Ref: NY2262

🍴 🍺Hope & Anchor, Port Carlisle

(On Path) *Maia Lodge, Bowness on Solway, Carlisle, Cumbria, CA5 5BH.*
Actual grid ref: NY217628
Modern dormer bungalow. Drinks licence.
Grades: ETB Listed, Comm
Tel: 016973 51955
Mrs Chettle.
Rates fr: £15.00-**£15.00.**
Open: All Year (not Xmas)
Beds: 1F 1D 1T
Baths: 2 Shared
🛇 (5) 🅿 (4) ✍ 🗖 ✗ 🎞 🖿 🖊

(On Path) *The Old Rectory, Bowness on Solway, Carlisle, Cumbria, CA5 5AF.*
Actual grid ref: NY224626
Large former rectory.
Grades: ETB 1 Cr, AA 2 Q
Tel: 016973 51055
Mr Simpson
Rates fr: £14.00-**£17.00.**
Open: All Year (not Xmas)
Beds: 3D 2S
Baths: 1 Shared
🅿 (4) ✍ 🗖 🛏 🎞 🖊

Many rates vary

according to season -

the lowest only are

shown here

Heart of England Way

This is a good find in the Midlands - like the North Downs Way, never far away from busy city life, but somehow keeping it at a healthy distance - a good mixture of the rural and the urban. The 100-mile **Heart of England** Way is waymarked and has easy access to public transport at most points along the route. From the Cannock Chase heathland the path heads off to Lichfield, the Tame Valley, Arden and the Avon Valley and then on to Bourton-on-the-Water in the Cotswolds. The path also usefully connects the **Staffordshire Way** with the **Cotswold Way** and the **Oxfordshire Way**. This makes it possible to walk, if you really wish, from the Cheshire border right down to Bath or London along waymarked footpaths.

Guides: *The Heart of England Way* by John Roberts (ISBN 0 947708 31 6), published by Walkways and available from good map shops or directly from the publishers (8 Hillside Close, Bartley Green, Birmingham, B32 4LT, tel: 0121 550 3158), £5.50

Maps: 1:50000 Ordnance Survey Landranger Series: 127, 128, 139, 140, 150, 151, 163

Comments about the path to: **Heart of England Way Association**, 50 George Road, Water Orton, Birmingham B46 1PE (membership £3.00).

Stafford   1

National Grid Ref: SJ9223

¶⊙¶ ⊑ The Sun Inn, Bird in Hand, Stafford Arms, Telegraph, Trumpet

(4m) *Albridge Hotel & Bridge Guest, House, 73 Wolverhampton Road, Stafford, ST17 4AW.*
Actual grid ref: SJ923225
Large converted Victorian house and annexe.
Grades: ETB 3 Cr, RAC 2 St
Tel: **01785 54100** Mrs Pinhorn.
Rates fr: £14.00-£20.00.
Open: All Year (not Xmas)
Beds: 3F 3D 5T 8S
Baths: 10 Ensuite 3 Shared
⌂ ℙ (20) ⊓ ⋔ ✕ ⅢⅢ ♥ ≬ ✄

(3m) *Leonards Croft Hotel, 80 Lichfield Road, Stafford, ST17 4LP.*
Large Victorian private house.
Grades: AA 3 Q
Tel: **01785 223676**
Mr & Mrs Johnson.

Rates fr: £18.00-£18.00.
Open: All Year (not Xmas)
Beds: 3F 4D 3T 2S
Baths: 4 Ensuite 4 Shared
⌂ ℙ (12) ⊓ ⋔ ✕ ⅢⅢ.

(3m) *The Albany Guest House, 49 Lichfield Road, Stafford, ST17 4LL.*
Comfortable, family run guesthouse.
Grades: ETB 1 Cr
Tel: **01785 56285**
Mr & Mrs Bradley.
Rates fr: £14.00-£14.00.
Open: All Year (not Xmas)
Beds: 1F 1D 1T 1S
Baths: 1 Shared
⌂ ℙ (4) ⋔ ⅢⅢ ♥ ≬

(3m) *Furtherhill Guest House, 55 Lichfield Road, Stafford, ST17 4LL.*
Large clean comfortable house.
Grades: ETB 1 Cr
Tel: **01785 58723** Mrs Payne.
Rates fr: £13.50-£16.00.
Open: All Year (not Xmas)
Beds: 1F 1D 2T 1S
Baths: 1 Ensuite 1 Shared
⌂ (1) ℙ (6) ⊓ ⅢⅢ.

Rugeley   2

National Grid Ref: SK0418

¶⊙¶ ⊑ Ash Tree, Plum Pudding, Red Lion

(3m 🚌) *Parks Farm, Hawksyard, Armitage Lane, Rugeley, Staffs, WS15 1ED.*
Actual grid ref: SK0616
Old quiet comfortable farmhouse.
Grades: ETB 2 Cr
Tel: **01889 583477** Mrs Lewis.
Rates fr: £15.00-£15.00.
Open: All Year (not Xmas)
Beds: 2F **Baths:** 2 Ensuite
⌂ ℙ (10) ⊓ ⋔ ✕ ⅢⅢ ♥ ≬ ✄

(2.75m) *The Cedar Tree Hotel, Main Road, Brereton, Rugeley, Staffs, WS15 1DY.*
Centrally situated, comfortable historic building.
Grades: ETB 3 Cr, AA 2 St, RAC 2 St
Tel: **01889 584241** Mrs Elderkin.
Rates fr: £22.00-£29.00.
Open: All Year (not Xmas)
Beds: 1F 10D 10T 9S
Baths: 15 Private 4 Shared
⌂ ℙ ⊓ ✕ ⅢⅢ.

Longdon Green   3

National Grid Ref: SK0813

¶⊙¶ ⊑ Red Lion, Swan with Two Necks

(3m) *Rookery Field Cottage, Longdon Green, Rugeley, Staffs, WS13 4QF.*
Large Victorian private country house.
Tel: **01543 492026** Mr Popp.
Rates fr: £15.00-£15.00.
Open: All Year (not Xmas)
Beds: 1D 1T **Baths:** 1 Shared
⌂ ℙ (4) ⊓ ⋔ ⅢⅢ. ⓥ

Farewell   4

National Grid Ref: SK0811

¶⊙¶ ⊑ Nelson Inn

(1.5m) *Little Pipe Farm, Little Pipe Lane, Farewell, Lichfield, Staffs, WS13 8BS.*
Old comfortable farmhouse, superb views.
Grades: ETB Listed
Tel: **01543 683066** Mrs Clewley.
Rates fr: £15.00-£15.00.
Open: All Year
Beds: 1F 1D 1S **Baths:** 2 Shared
⌂ ℙ (10) ⊓ ✕ ⅢⅢ. ⓥ

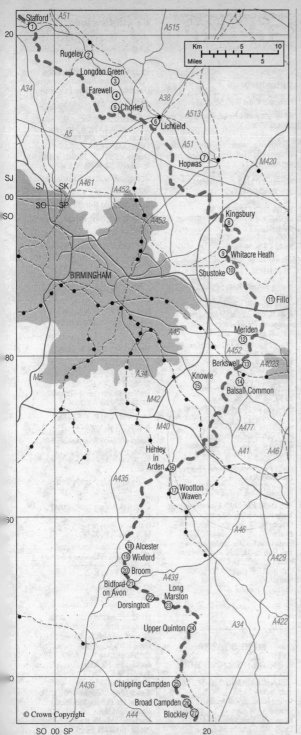

Chorley 5

National Grid Ref: SK0710

(0.25m) **The Stone House,**
Farewell, Chorley, Lichfield,
Staffs, WS13 8DS.
Actual grid ref: SK076115
360-year-old stone cottage.
Grades: ETB Reg
Tel: **01543 682575** Mrs Cowell.
Rates fr: *£15.00*-**£15.00**.
Open: All Year (not Xmas)
Beds: 2D 1S
Baths: 2 Shared
⌛ (5) 🅿 ⊬ ⊡ ⋔ ✕ Ⅲ ♥ 🗎 ♦

Lichfield 6

National Grid Ref: SK1109

🍴 🍺 Pig & Truffle, Kings Head,
Horse & Jockey, George Hotel,
Angel Croft Hotel, Greyhound,
Shoulder of Mutton, Trent Valley
Inn

(0.5m) **21-23 Dam Street,**
Lichfield, Staffs, WS13 6AE.
Listed large C18th town house.
Tel: **01543 264303** Mrs Duval.
Rates fr: *£18.00*-**£20.00**.
Open: All Year (not Xmas)
Beds: 1D 1T 1S
Baths: 1 Ensuite 3 Shared
⌛ 🅿 (2) ⊬ ⊡ ⋔ Ⅲ 🗎 ♦

(0.5m) **Old Rectory Cottage,**
21 Gaia Lane, Lichfield, Staffs,
WS13 7LW.
C18th beamed cottage.
Grades: ETB Listed
Tel: **01543 254941** Mrs Zavou.
Rates fr: *£17.00*-**£22.00**.
Open: All Year
Beds: 1D 1T
Baths: 1 Shared
⌛ (5) 🅿 (2) ⊬ ⊡ Ⅲ 🗎 ♦

(0.75m) **35 Broad Lane,** *Boley*
Park, Lichfield, Staffs, WS14 9SZ.
Modern comfortable house.
Tel: **01543 262301** Mrs Shipley.
Rates fr: *£14.00*-**£17.00**.
Open: All Year (not Xmas)
🅿 ⊡ Ⅲ

(0.25m) **Copper's End,** *Walsall*
Road, Muckley Corner, Lichfield,
Staffs, WS14 0BG.
Attractive, comfortable, rural,
detached house.
Grades: ETB 2 Cr, Comm,
AA 2 Q, Listed, RAC Listed
Tel: **01543 372910** Mr Lumb.
Rates fr: *£17.50*-**£20.00**.
Open: All Year (not Xmas)
Beds: 2D 3T 1S
Baths: 1 Private 1 Shared
⌛ 🅿 (8) ⊡ ⋔ ✕ Ⅲ ♿ Ⅴ

The lowest *double* rate per
person is shown in *italics.*

(0.25m) *Netherstowe House North*, Netherstowe Lane, Off Eastern Avenue, Lichfield, Staffs, WS13 6AY.
Grade II Listed Georgian house.
Grades: ETB Listed
Tel: 01543 254631 Mrs Marshall.
Rates fr: £18.00-£16.00.
Open: All Year (not Xmas)
Beds: 1F 1T
Baths: 1 Private 1 Shared
ॐ (1) ▣ (6) ✱ ⌷ ▥.

Hopwas 7

National Grid Ref: SK1705

† ⌷ Chequers, Red Lion

(1.5m) *Oak Tree Farm*, Hints Road, Hopwas, Tamworth, Staffs, B79 3AA.
Luxuriously renovated farmhouse; all comforts.
Tel: 01827 56807 Mrs Purkis.
Rates fr: £20.00-£20.00.
Open: All Year
Beds: 1F 3D 2T **Baths:** 6 Ensuite
▣ (10) ✱ ⌷ ┢ ✕ ▥. Ⓥ

Kingsbury 8

National Grid Ref: SP2196

† ⌷ Kingsbury Country Club

(On Path) *67 Tamworth Road*, Kingsbury, Tamworth, Staffs, B78 2HH.
Modern bungalow in country village.
Tel: 01827 873880 Mrs Painter.
Rates fr: £15.00-£15.00.
Open: All Year
Beds: 1F 1D 1S **Baths:** 1 Shared
ॐ (5) ▣ (2) ⌷ ▥. &

Whitacre Heath 9

National Grid Ref: SP2192

† ⌷ Swan Inn

(1m) *Heathland Farm*, Birmingham Road, Whitacre Heath, Coleshill, W. Midlands, B46 2ER.
Rural quiet farmhouse.
Grades: RAC 3 St
Tel: 01675 462129
Rates fr: £18.00-£22.00.
Open: All Year (not Xmas)
Beds: 4T 2S
Baths: 4 Ensuite 1 Shared
ॐ ▣ (10) ✱ ⌷ ▥. Ⓥ ✦

Shustoke 10

National Grid Ref: SP2290

† ⌷ The Bulls Head, Furnace

(0.25m) *The Old Vicarage*, Shustoke, Coleshill, Birmingham, B46 2LA.
Actual grid ref: SP243909
Country house opposite homebrew pub.

Tel: 01675 481331 Mrs Hawkins.
Rates fr: £19.00-£19.00.
Open: All Year (not Xmas)
Beds: 3D
Baths: 2 Shared
ॐ ▣ (4) ⌷ ✕ ▥. Ⓥ 🛈 ✦

Fillongley 11

National Grid Ref: SP2887

† ⌷ Saracens Head, Horse & Jockey

(2m) *Rangemoor*, Coventry Road, Fillongley, Coventry, W. Mids, CV7 8BZ.
Large garden, excellent views.
Grades: ETB 1 Cr, Approv
Tel: 01676 542197
Mr Hawkins.
Rates fr: £17.50-£17.50.
Open: All Year
Beds: 1F 2T
Baths: 1 Ensuite 1 Shared
ॐ ▣ ⌷ ┢ ✕ ▥.

Meriden 12

National Grid Ref: SP2482

(On Path 🚲) *Cooperage Farm B & B*, Old Road, Meriden, Coventry, W. Mids, CV7 7JP.
Actual grid ref: SP2482
Tel: 01676 523493
Mrs Simonds.
Rates fr: £22.50-£25.00.
Open: All Year (not Xmas)
Beds: 2F 2D 2T
Baths: 4 Ensuite 2 Shared
ॐ ▣ ⌷ ┢ ✕ ▥. Ⓥ 🛈 ✦
Also ▲ £5.00 per tent. ☏ Ⓣ ✕ &
In the attractive village of Meriden on Heart of England Way. Tea/coffee facilities. Cooperage Farm is a 300-year-old Listed farmhouse.
Tel. Lucy on 01676 523493.

Berkswell 13

National Grid Ref: SP2479

(On Path) *Elmcroft Country Guest House*, Hodgetts Lane, Berkswell, Coventry, W. Mids, CV7 7DH.
Charming C18th country cottage.
Tel: 01676 535204 Mrs Weston.
Rates fr: £20.00-£20.00.
Open: All Year (not Xmas)
Beds: 2D 1T
Baths: 3 Private
ॐ ▣ (6) ⌷ ┢ ✕ ▥. Ⓥ

High season,
bank holidays and
special events mean
low availability
everywhere.

Balsall Common 14

National Grid Ref: SP2377

† ⌷ Ye Old Saracens Head

(0.25m 🚲) *Blythe Paddocks*, Barston Lane, Balsall Common, Coventry, W. Midlands, CV7 7BT.
Actual grid ref: SP218779
Detached house in four acres.
Grades: ETB 1 Cr
Tel: 01676 533050 Mrs Marshall.
Rates fr: £18.00-£18.00.
Open: All Year
Beds: 1D 1T 2S **Baths:** 1 Shared
ॐ ▣ (10) ⌷ ┢ ▥. Ⓥ 🛈 ✦

Knowle 15

National Grid Ref: SP1876

† ⌷ Black Boy, Bridge Water Hotel

(On Path) *Ivy House*, Warwick Road, Knowle, Solihull, W. Mids, B93 0EB.
Large family country residence.
Grades: ETB 3 Cr, AA 3 Q
Tel: 01564 770247
Mr & Mrs Townsend.
Rates fr: £22.00-£28.00.
Open: All Year (not Xmas)
Beds: 1F 2D 3T 2S
Baths: 8 Ensuite
ॐ ▣ (20) ✱ ⌷ ┢ ✕ ▥. & Ⓥ ✦
Also ▲ £3 per tent.
Open: All Year (not Xmas)
Ⓣ ⚏ ✕ ✦ &

Henley-in-Arden 16

National Grid Ref: SP1565

(On Path) *Irelands Farm*, Irelands Lane, Henley-in-Arden, Solihull, W. Mids, B95 5SA.
Farmhouse surrounded by countryside.
Grades: ETB 2 Cr, Comm
Tel: 01564 792476 Mrs Shaw.
Rates fr: £17.50-£20.00.
Open: All Year (not Xmas)
Beds: 2D 1T
Baths: 3 Private
▣ (6) ✱ ⌷ ┢ ▥. Ⓥ

Wootton Wawen 17

National Grid Ref: SP1563

† ⌷ Navigation Inn, Bulls Head, The White Swan

(1.5m) *Wootton Park Farm*, Alcester Road, Wootton Wawen, Solihull, W. Mids, B95 6HJ.
Delightful C16th half-timbered farmhouse.
Grades: ETB 2 Cr
Tel: 01564 792673
Mrs McCall.
Rates fr: £19.00-£24.00.
Open: All Year (not Xmas)
Beds: 2F 1D
Baths: 1 Private 1 Shared
(A) ▣ (6) ⌷ ▥. Ⓥ

Alcester 18

National Grid Ref: SP0857

|●| ◀ Green Dragon

(0.25m) *Sambourne Hall Farm,*
Sambourne, Alcester, Warks.
B96 6NZ.
Beautiful C16th farmhouse. Idyllic
setting.
Grades: AA Listed, High Comm
Tel: 01527 852151
Mrs Hammersley.
Rates fr: *£17.50-£22.00*.
Open: All Year (not Xmas)
Beds: 1F 1D 1T
Baths: 1 Ensuite 1 Private
⛺ 🅿 (6) ⊬ 🖵 🐾 📺 Ⓥ

Wixford 19

National Grid Ref: SP0854

|●| ◀The Fish Pub

(On Path) *Orchard Lawns,*
Wixford, Alcester, Warks, B49 6DA.
Actual grid ref: SP087547
Edwardian style detached village
house.
Grades: ETB 2 Cr, High Comm
Tel: 01789 772668
Mrs Kember.
Rates fr: *£16.00-£16.00*.
Open: All Year (not Xmas)
Beds: 1D 1T 1S
Baths: 1 Ensuite 1 Shared
⛺ (5) 🅿 (6) ⊬ 🖵 🐾 📺 Ⓥ

Broom 20

National Grid Ref: SP0953

(On Path) *Broom Hall Inn,*
Bidford Road, Broom, Alcester,
Warks, B50 4HE.
16th Century country inn.
Grades: ETB 3 Cr, Approv
Tel: 01789 773757
Mrs Tavener.
Rates fr: *£20.00-£20.00*.
Open: All Year
Beds: 2F 2D 4T 4S
Baths: 12 Ensuite
⛺ 🅿 (100) 🖵 🐾 ✗ 📺 Ⓥ ♿

Bidford-on-Avon 21

National Grid Ref: SP1051

|●| ◀ The Golden Cross Inn

(0.25m) *Fosbroke House, 4 High*
Street, Bidford-on-Avon, Alcester,
Warks, B50 4BU.
Comfortable Georgian house in
village.
Grades: ETB 2 Cr, Comm
Tel: 01789 772327 Mr Newbury.
Rates fr: *£17.50-£20.00*.
Open: Feb to Nov
Beds: 1F 2D 1T 1S
Baths: 5 Ensuite
⛺ (3) 🅿 (6) 🖵 🐾 ✗ 📺 Ⓥ ♿

(0.25m 🚗) *Huit Barn, Tower*
Croft, Tower Hill, Bidford-on-
Avon, Alcester, Warks, B50 4DY.
Delightful Victorian barn conver-
sion. **Tel: 01789 778516**
Mrs Pugh. **Rates fr:** *£17.50-£16.00*
Open: All Year (not Xmas)
Beds: 1D 1S
Baths: 1 Ensuite 1 Shared
⛺ (5) 🅿 (4) ⊬ 🖵 🐾 📺 Ⓥ ♿

Dorsington 22

National Grid Ref: SP1349

|●| ◀ Cottage of Content

(On Path) *Church Farm,*
Dorsington, Stratford upon Avon,
Warks, CV37 8AX.
Friendly Georgian farmhouse.
Quiet, peaceful.
Grades: ETB 2 Cr, Comm
Tel: 01789 720471 / 0831 504194
Mrs Walters.
Rates fr: *£14.50-£18.00*.
Open: All Year **Beds:** 2F 3D 2T
Baths: 4 Ensuite 3 Shared
⛺ 🅿 (12) 🖵 🐾 📺 ♿ Ⓥ ♿

Long Marston 23

National Grid Ref: SP1548

|●| ◀ Masons Arms

(0.25m) *Kings Lodge, Long*
Marston, Stratford upon Avon,
Warks, CV37 8RL.
Actual grid ref: SP152480

Historic country house.
Grades: ETB 2 Cr, Comm
Tel: 01789 720705
Mrs Jenkins.
Rates fr: *£19.00-£20.00*.
Open: Feb to Nov
Beds: 2D 1T 1S
Baths: 1 Ensuite 3 Shared
⛺ 🅿 (11) 🖵 🐾 ✗ 📺 Ⓥ ♿ ♿

(On Path) *Church Farm, Long*
Marston, Stratford upon Avon,
Warks, CV37 8RH.
Actual grid ref: SP153484
Homely comfortable farmhouse,
high standards.
Grades: ETB 2 Cr, Comm
Tel: 01789 720275
Mrs Taylor.
Rates fr: *£17.50-£17.50*.
Open: All Year
Beds: 1F 1T
Baths: 1 Ensuite
⛺ 🅿 (4) 🖵 🐾 📺 Ⓥ ♿ ♿

Upper Quinton 24

National Grid Ref: SP1746

(On Path) *Winton House, The*
Green, Upper Quinton, Stratford
upon Avon, Warks, CV37 8SX.
Actual grid ref: SP178464
Large Victorian farmhouse.
Grades: ETB High Comm
Tel: 01789 720500 / 0831 485483
Mrs Lyon.
Rates fr: *£21.00*.
Open: All Year
Beds: 1F 1D 1T
Baths: 3 Ensuite
⛺ 🅿 ⊬ 🖵 📺 Ⓥ ♿

Chipping Campden 25

National Grid Ref: SP1539

|●| ◀ The Eight Bells, The Lygon
Arms, Volunteer Pub , King Arms,
Butcher Arms

(0.25m 🚗) *The Bank House,*
Mickleton, Chipping Campden,
Glos, GL55 6RX.
Period stone built village house.
Grades: ETB 2 Cr, Comm
Tel: 01386 438302 Mrs Billington.
Rates fr: *£17.50-£27.00*.
Open: All Year (not Xmas)
Beds: 1D 2T **Baths:** 3 Ensuite
🅿 (3) ⊬ 🖵 📺 ♿

(On Path) *Haydon House, Church*
Street, Chipping Campden, Glos,
GL55 6JG.
Converted dairy and bakehouse.
Grades: ETB 2 Cr, Comm
Tel: 01386 840275 Mrs Gilmour.
Rates fr: *£22.00-£22.00*.
Open: Easter to Nov
Beds: 1D 1T 1S
Baths: 2 Ensuite 1 Private
⊬ 🖵 📺 Ⓥ ♿ ♿

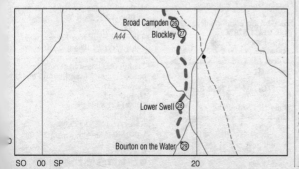

SO   00   SP   20

(On Path) *Weston Park Farm,
Dovers Hill, Chipping Campden,
Glos, GL55 6UW.*
Traditional Cotswold stone beamed
farmhouse.
Grades: ETB 2 Cr
Tel: 01386 840835
Mr Whitehouse.
Rates fr: *£19.00-£25.00.*
Open: All Year
Beds: 1F 1D
Baths: 2 Ensuite
ﾋ P ⌂ ﾐ V ✦

(On Path) *Sandalwood House,
Back Ends, Chipping Campden,
Glos, GL55 6AU.*
Actual grid ref: SP143387
Traditional Cotswold house.
Peacefully located.
Grades: ETB 2 Cr, Approv
Tel: 01386 840091
Mrs Bendall.
Rates fr: *£20.00-£25.00.*
Open: All Year (not Xmas)
Beds: 1F 1T
Baths: 2 Private
ﾋ (6) P (5) ✂ ⌂ ﾐ V ✦

Broad Campden   26
National Grid Ref: SP1537

⋔ ▦ Bakers Arms

(1m) *The Malt House, Broad
Campden, Chipping Campden,
Glos, GL55 6UU.*
C16th Cotswold home.
Grades: AA 5 Q, Prem
Tel: 01386 840295
Mr Brown.
Rates fr: *£39.50.*
Open: All Year
Beds: 1F 4D
Baths: 5 Ensuite
P (8) ⌂ ﾔ ✕ ﾐ V ▮ ✦

(On Path) *Wyldlands, Broad
Campden, Chipping Campden,
Glos, GL55 6UR.*
Highly recommended comfortable
home.
Grades: ETB Comm
Tel: 01386 840478
Mrs Wadey.
Rates fr: *£17.00-£20.00.*
Open: All Year (not Xmas)
Beds: 2D 1T
Baths: 1 Ensuite 1 Shared
ﾋ P (3) ✂ ⌂ ﾐ V ✦

(1m) *Marnic, Broad Campden,
Chipping Campden, Glos, GL55 6UR.*
Actual grid ref: SP159378
Family cottage in Cotswold village.
Grades: ETB 2 Cr, High Comm
Tel: 01386 840014
Mrs Rawlings.
Rates fr: *£17.00-£20.00.*
Open: All Year (not Xmas)
Beds: 1F 1D 1T
Baths: 2 Ensuite
ﾋ (5) P (4) ✂ ⌂ ﾐ V ✦

Blockley   27
National Grid Ref: SP1634

⋔ ▦ Greast Western Arms, Crown
Hotel

(On Path) 🚍 *Park Farm,
Blockley, Moreton in Marsh, Glos,
GL56 9TA.*
C16th farmhouse.
Grades: ETB Listed
Tel: 01386 700266 Mr & Mrs Dee.
Rates fr: *£16.00-£16.00.*
Open: Easter to Oct
Beds: 1D 1T 2S
Baths: 1 Shared
ﾋ P (6) ⌂ ﾔ V ▮ ✦

(On Path) 🚍 *Tudor House, High
Street, Blockley, Moreton in
Marsh, Glos, GL56 9EX.*
Actual grid ref: SP1634
Peaceful, unspoilt village, warm
welcome.
Tel: 01386 700356 Mrs Thompson.
Rates fr: *£18.00-£20.00.*
Open: All Year (not Xmas)
Beds: 1D 1T
Baths: 1 Shared
ﾋ (12) ⌂ ﾐ

Lower Swell   28
National Grid Ref: SP1725

⋔ ▦ Golden Ball Public House,
Old Farmhouse Hotel

(On Path) *Wendover, 2 Rectory
Close, Lower Swell, Stow On The
Wold, Cheltenham, Glos, GL54 1LH.*
Cotswold stone house.
Grades: ETB Listed, Comm
Tel: 01451 831310 Mrs Worker.
Rates fr: *£16.00-£18.00.*
Open: All Year (not Xmas)
Beds: 1F 1D 1S
Baths: 1 Shared
ﾋ (7) P (3) ✂ ⌂ ﾐ V

Bourton on the Water   29
National Grid Ref: SP1620

⋔ ▦ The Mousetrap Inn,
Lansdowne, Mouse Trap, Plough
Inn, Old Manse Hotel

(On Path) *6 Moore Road, Bourton
on the Water, Cheltenham, Glos,
GL54 2AZ.*
Modern and comfortable, quiet.
Tel: 01451 820767
Mrs Mustoe.
Rates fr: *£15.00-£17.00.*
Open: All Year (not Xmas)
Beds: 1D 1T
Baths: 1 Shared
ﾋ (8) P (2) ✂ ⌂ ﾔ ﾐ V

(On Path) *Broadlands Guest
House, Clapton Row, Bourton on
the Water, Cheltenham, Glos,
GL54 2DN.*
Actual grid ref: SP168204
C17th traditional Cotswold stone
guest house.

Grades: ETB 3 Cr, Comm
Tel: 01451 822002 Mr Ferrari.
Rates fr: *£19.75-£30.00.*
Open: All Year
Beds: 3F 6D 2T
Baths: 11 Ensuite
ﾋ P (12) ⌂ ﾔ ✕ ﾐ ✦

(On Path) *Lansdowne Villa Guest
House, Bourton on the Water,
Cheltenham, Glos, GL54 2AT.*
Large refurbished stone village.
Grades: ETB 3 Cr, High Comm
Tel: 01451 820673
Rates fr: *£20.00-£20.00.*
Open: Easter to Dec
Beds: 8D 2T 2S
Baths: 12 Ensuite
ﾋ P (14) ✂ ⌂ ✕ ﾐ V ▮ ✦

(On Path) *Fosseside, Lansdowne,
Bourton on the Water, Cheltenham,
Glos, GL54 2AT.*
Comfortable accommodation in
lovely location.
Grades: ETB High Comm
Tel: 01451 820574
Mrs Waterworth.
Rates fr: *£16.50-£26.50.*
Open: All Year (not Xmas)
Beds: 3D
Baths: 2 Ensuite 1 Private
ﾋ (10) P (3) ⌂ ﾐ V ▮ ✦

(On Path) *Lansdowne House,
Lansdowne, Bourton on the Water,
Cheltenham, Glos, GL54 2AT.*
Tastefully furnished period stone
house.
Grades: ETB 1 Cr, Comm
Tel: 01451 820812
Mrs Garwood.
Rates fr: *£14.50-£18.00.*
Open: All Year (not Xmas)
Beds: 1F 1D 1T
Baths: 3 Private
ﾋ P (5) ⌂ ﾐ V

(On Path) *Sycamore Guest House,
Lansdowne, Bourton on the Water,
Cheltenham, Glos, GL54 2AR.*
Comfortable, homely guesthouse.
Grades: ETB 2 Cr, Comm
Tel: 01451 821647
Mr Norman.
Rates fr: *£17.00-£22.00.*
Open: All Year
Beds: 1F 3D 1T
Baths: 5 Private
ﾋ (6) ⌂ ✕ ﾐ ♿ V

(On Path) *Windrush Farm,
Bourton on the Water, Cheltenham,
Glos, GL54 3BY.*
Traditional Cotswold stone farm-
house 1.5 miles from Bourton-on-
the-water village.
Grades: ETB 2 Cr, Comm
Tel: 01451 820419
Mrs Burrough.
Rates fr: *£17.50-£25.00.*
Open: Mar to Dec
Beds: 1D 1T
Baths: 2 Private
P (4) ✂ ⌂ ﾐ V

STILWELL'S
B&B PHONELINE

0891-515696

Cost per minute: 39p (cheap) / 49p (otherwise).

Touring? On business? Just plain stuck? Is there a mountain you wish to walk up? A historic house or a beautiful church you wish to see, an art gallery or a special museum you wish to visit? Perhaps a path not featured in this book?

We suggest superb, low-cost, Bed & Breakfasts EXACTLY where you want to stay (not 20 miles away) anywhere in Britain or Ireland.

Wherever you are or whatever you are doing, we can locate a B&B right on the doorstep offering overnight accommodation at under £25 per person per night (average £16 per person in a double room).

Just ring us up and we'll look it up for you on our computer. And if your request is elaborate (an itinerary requiring special research), we'll take down the details, do the work and phone you back or fax you with the results.

Hereward Way

Here is a curious path - it runs for most of its length below sea-level. The **Hereward Way** is the waymarked 'path across the fens', named after the English hero **Hereward the Wake**, who eluded the Normans in this area for so long. Its flatness clearly makes for easy walking. Starting at Oakham near Rutland Water, it heads off through the Fens to Ely with its lovely cathedral, before heading off to Brandon and the Brecklands of West Norfolk. The mountaineers among you will be bored; the naturalists and historians will be fascinated. The path links up with the **Viking Way** and the **Peddars Way** and, via the latter, the **Icknield Way**.

Guides: *Hereward Way* by Trevor Noyes (ISBN 0 900613 57 2), published by Peterborough RA Group and available from Trevor Noyes (8 Welmore Road, Glinton, Peterborough, Cambs, PE6 7LU), £1.50 (+50 p&p)

Maps: 1:50000 Ordnance Survey Landranger Series: 141, 142, 143, 144

Oakham 1

National Grid Ref: SK8509

¶⊙¶ ⚑ White Lion, Whipper Inn, White Hart Inn, Crown Walk Complex, Melton Road

(On Path) *The Merry Monk,*
12 Church St, Oakham, Leics,
LE15 6AA.
Town centre pub.
Tel: **01572 722094** Mr Riordam.
Rates fr: *£28.00*.
Open: All Year (not Xmas)
Beds: 3T
Baths: 1 Shared
🄿 ⏁

(On Path) *Angel House,*
20 Northgate, Oakham, Leics,
LE15 6QS.
Large Victorian private house.
Grades: ETB Reg
Tel: **01572 756153** Mrs Weight.
Rates fr: *£15.00*-£15.00.
Open: All Year
Beds: 1F 1D **Baths:** 3 Ensuite
🕭 🄿 (1) ⛒ ▣ ⓥ ⓘ ⚡

(On Path) *Westgate Lodge,*
9 Westgate, Oakham, Leics,
LE15 6BH.
Large friendly family period property.
Grades: ETB Listed
Tel: **01572 757370** Mrs Baines.
Rates fr: *£18.50*-£18.50.
Open: All Year
Beds: 1F 1D 1T
Baths: 3 Ensuite
🕭 (3) 🄿 (3) ⚻ ⛒ ⏁ ⓥ ⚡

(On Path) *27 Northgate, Oakham,*
Leics, LE15 6QR.
Victorian private house. Very homely.
Tel: **01572 755057** Mrs George.
Rates fr: *£13.00*-£13.00.
Open: All Year (not Xmas)
🕭 ⚻ ⛒ ⏁ ⏁

Whitwell 2

National Grid Ref: SK9208

¶⊙¶ ⚑ Noel Arms

(On Path) *Noel Arms, Main St,*
Whitwell, Oakham, Leics, LE15 8BW.
Farmhouse and public house.
Tel: **01780 460334** Mr Healey.
Rates fr: *£19.00*-£17.50.
Open: All Year
Beds: 1F 3D 9T 1S
Baths: 4 Private 2 Shared
🕭 🄿 ⛒ ⏁ ✕ ⏁ ⚻ ⓥ

The lowest *double* rate per person is shown in *italics*.

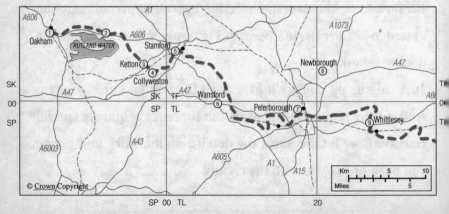

© Crown Copyright

Ketton 3

National Grid Ref: SK9704

!●! 🍺 The Railway, Royal Oak, The Crown, Wheatsheaf, Edith Weston

(On Path) *Church House,*
21 Church Road, Ketton, Stamford,
Rutland, PE9 3RD.
Grade II Listed country house.
Tel: 01780 720746 Mrs Connolly.
Rates fr: *£15.00-£15.00.*
Open: All Year (not Xmas)
Beds: 1D 2T
Baths: 1 Ensuite 1 Shared
🛏 (10) 🅿 (2) ⊬ 🖵 🛏.

Collyweston 4

National Grid Ref: SK9902

!●! 🍺 Exeter Arms, The Cavalier, The Oak

(1.25m) *The Manor Cottage,*
Collyweston, Stamford,
Lincolnshire, PE9 3PN.
Georgian house with panoramic views.
Grades: ETB Listed, High Comm
Tel: 01780 444209
Mr & Mrs Mitchell.
Rates fr: *£15.00-£20.00.*
Open: All Year
Beds: 1F 1D 2T
Baths: 2 Private 2 Shared
🛏 🅿 (15) 🖵 🛏. Ⓥ

Stamford 5

National Grid Ref: TF0207

!●! 🍺 The Plough Inn, Great Casterton, Danish Invader, Anchor, The Bull & Swan, The Dolphin, Daniel Lambert, Hole in the Wall, St Peter's Inn, The Crown

(1.5m 🚌 **)** *176 Casterton Road,*
Stamford, Lincolnshire, PE9 2XX.
Actual grid ref: TF013078
Modern detached house. On B1081.
Grades: ETB Listed, Comm

Tel: 01780 63368 Mrs Ford.
Rates fr: *£15.00-£16.00.*
Open: All Year (not Xmas)
Beds: 1D 2S
Baths: 1 Shared
🛏 (1) 🅿 (3) ⊬ 🖵 🛏 🛏. 🛅 ⚡

(3.25m) *Birch House, 4 Lonsdale*
Road, Stamford, Lincs, PE9 2RW.
Established well-presented family-run B&B.
Grades: ETB Listed, Comm
Tel: 01780 54876 Mrs Headland.
Rates fr: *£15.00-£15.00.*
Open: All Year (not Xmas)
Beds: 2D 2S
Baths: 1 Shared
🛏 (5) 🅿 (2) ⊬ 🖵 🛏. Ⓥ ⚡

(2.5m) *10 Stirling Road, Stamford,*
Lincs, PE9 2XG.
1960's private town house.
Grades: ETB Listed
Tel: 01780 63065
Mrs Nichols.
Rates fr: *£14.00-£14.00.*
Open: All Year
Beds: 1F 1D 1T 1S
Baths: 1 Shared
🛏 (4) 🅿 (1) ⊬ 🖵 🛏 🛏. Ⓥ 🛅

(2.25m) *Rock Lodge, 1*
Empingham Road, Stamford, Lincs,
PE9 2RH.
Large Victorian private house.
Grades: ETB 2 Cr
Tel: 01780 64211 Mrs Hermann.
Rates fr: *£20.00-£25.00.*
Open: All Year
Beds: 2D 1T
Baths: Ensuite
🛏 (10) 🅿 (3) 🖵 🛏 🛏. Ⓥ

(2m) *10 Luffenham Close,*
Stamford, Lincs, PE9 2SE.
Large, modern, comfortable bungalow, parking.
Grades: ETB Listed
Tel: 01780 63354 Mrs McKittrick.
Rates fr: *£12.00-£12.00.*
Open: All Year
Beds: 2D or Single
Baths: 1 Shared
🅿 🖵 🛏. ⅙ Ⓥ

(2m) *Cringleford, 7 Exeter*
Gardens, Stamford, Lincs, PE9 2RN.
Updated private house.
Grades: ETB Listed
Tel: 01780 62136
Mrs Webster.
Rates fr: *£15.00-£15.00.*
Open: All Year (not Xmas)
Beds: 1D 1S
Baths: 1 Shared
🅿 (2) 🖵 🛏. Ⓥ

Wansford 6

National Grid Ref: TL0799

!●! 🍺 Papermills Inn, Haycock, Cross Keys

(1.75m) *Stoneacre, Elton Road,*
Wansford, Peterborough, Cambs,
PE8 6JT.
Modern country house, large grounds.
Grades: ETB 2 Cr
Tel: 01780 783283
Mr Wilkinson.
Rates fr: *£14.00-£22.00.*
Open: All Year
Beds: 1F 4D 1T
Baths: 3 Private 1 Shared
🛏 (5) 🅿 (12) ⊬ 🖵 🛏 🛏. Ⓥ

Peterborough 7

National Grid Ref: TL1999

!●! 🍺 Coach & Horses, Botolph Arms, Gordon Arms

(5m) *St Margarets Guest House,*
187 London Road, Peterborough,
Cambs, PE2 9DS.
Small, Victorian, family run business.
Grades: ETB Reg
Tel: 01733 555008
Mr & Mrs Atkins.
Rates fr: *£15.00-£15.00.*
Open: All Year (not Xmas)
Beds: 2T 1S
Baths: 1 Shared
🅿 (3) 🖵 🛏 🛏. 🛅 ⚡

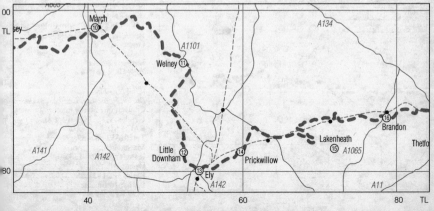

(2.5m) *Aragon House, 75/77 London Road, Peterborough, Cambs, PE2 9BS.*
Friendly family-run guesthouse.
Grades: ETB 2 Cr
Tel: **01733 63718**
Mr & Mrs Spence.
Rates fr: *£15.00-£18.00*.
Open: All Year (not Xmas)
Beds: 1F 3D 2T 6S
Baths: 3 Private 2 Shared
⛺ 🅿 (8) 🛏 ✕ 📷 Ⓥ

Newborough 8

National Grid Ref: TF2005

🍴 🍺 The Decoy

(2.5m) *Hill Farm & Dexter Centre, Thorney Road, Newborough, Peterborough, Cambs, PE5 7RW.*
Traditional fenland farmhouse with livestock.
Tel: **01733 810321**
Mrs Chamberlain.
Rates fr: *£12.00-£12.00*.
Open: All Year
Beds: 1F 2D 1T
Baths: 1 Shared
⛺ ✄ 🛏 ✕ Ⓥ

Whittlesey 9

National Grid Ref: TL2797

🍴 🍺 Boat Inn

(On Path 🚌) *Cobwebs Guest House, 21 The Delph, Whittlesey, Peterborough, Cambs, PE7 1QH.*
Modern comfortable rooms with H&C.
Grades: ETB Listed
Tel: **01733 350960**
Mrs Ekins.
Rates fr: *£15.00-£15.00*.
Open: All Year (not Xmas)
Beds: 5T
Baths: 3 Shared
🅿 (5) 🛏 ✕ 📷 & Ⓥ ⓘ

March 10

National Grid Ref: TL4197

🍴 🍺 White House Inn, West End

(On Path) *The Old Brew House, 52 West End, March, Cambs, PE15 8DL.*
Listed 17th Century cottage.
Grades: ETB Reg
Tel: **01354 53793**
Mr Vawser.
Rates fr: *£17.00-£17.00*.
Open: All Year
Beds: 1D 1T 1S
Baths: 2 Shared
⛺ (1) 🅿 (2) 🛏 ✕ 📷 ⓘ ✦

Welney 11

National Grid Ref: TL5294

🍴 🍺 Lamp, Flag, Old Mill

(0.5m) *Stockyard Farm, Wisbeck Road, Welney, Wisbech, Cambs, PE14 9RQ.*
Actual grid ref: TL529945
Comfortable former Fenland farmhouse.
Tel: **01354 610433**
Mrs Bennett.
Rates fr: *£16.00-£20.00*.
Open: All Year (not Xmas)
Beds: 1D 1T
Baths: 1 Shared
🅿 (2) ✄ 🛏 📷 Ⓥ ⓘ ✦

(On Path) *Welney House, Wisbech Road, Welney, Wisbech, Cambs, PE14 9QA.*
Classic Georgian farmhouse, beautiful garden.
Grades: ETB Comm
Tel: **01354 610207**
Mrs Gerrard Wright.
Rates fr: *£17.00-£17.00*.
Open: All Year (not Xmas)
Beds: 2T
⛺ 🅿 (4) ✄ 🛏 📷

Little Downham 12

National Grid Ref: TL5283

🍴 🍺 The Plough, Main Street

(On Path) *Bury House, 11 Main Street, Little Downham, Ely, Cambs, CB6 2ST.*
Actual grid ref: TL526841
Comfortable friendly home.
Tel: **01353 699386** Mrs Ambrose.
Rates fr: *£16.00-£16.00*.
Open: All Year (not Xmas)
Beds: 1F 1D 1T **Baths:** 2 Shared
⛺ 🅿 ✄ 📷 ⓘ ✦

Ely 13

National Grid Ref: TL5480

🍴 🍺 High Flyer, Newkham Street, The Lamb Hotel, King's Arms, Cutter Inn

(⛰ 0.25m) *Ely Youth Hostel, Sixth Form Centre, St Audreys, Downham Road, Ely, Cambridgeshire, CB6 1BD.*
Actual grid ref: TL538812
Warden: Mr B Lee.
Tel: **01353 667423**
Under 18: £4.60 **Adults:** £6.75
Centrally Heated, Games Room, Facilities for the Disabled, Grounds Available for Games, Parking
A summer-only hostel within the Downham Road College Campus, with limited cooking facilities but spacious dining area

(2m 🚌) *Greenways, Prickwillow Road, Queen Adelaide, Ely, Cambs, CB7 4TZ.*
Ground floor modern comfortable accommodation.
Tel: **01353 666706**
Mr Spring.
Rates fr: *£16.00-£18.00*.
Open: All Year
Beds: 1F 1D 1T 1S
Baths: 2 Shared
⛺ 🅿 (6) 🛏 📷 & ⓘ ✦

(1m 🚌) *84 Broad Street, Ely, Cambs, CB7 4BE.*
Newly refurbished Victorian cottage.
Tel: **01353 666862** Mrs Collins.
Rates fr: *£14.00-£14.00*.
Open: All Year
Beds: 1F
Baths: 1 Shared
⛺ ✄ 📷 ✕ 📷 Ⓥ ⓘ ✦

(On Path) *The Nyton Hotel, 7 Barton Road, Ely, Cambs, CB7 4HZ.*
Comfortable family hotel.
Grades: ETB 3 Cr, AA 1 St, RAC 1 St
Tel: **01353 662459**
Mr Setchell.
Rates fr: *£25.00-£33.00*.
Open: All Year
Beds: 3F 3D 2T 2S
Baths: 10 Ensuite
⛺ 🅿 📷 ✕ 📷 &

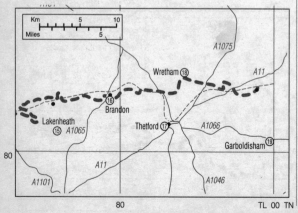

(0.25m) *The Black Hostelry, The College, The Cathedral Close, Ely, Cambs,* CB7 4DL.
Norman/medieval house cathedral house.
Grades: ETB Listed
Tel: 01353 662612
Mrs Green.
Rates fr: £24.50-£49.00.
Open: All Year (not Xmas)
Beds: 2F
Baths: 2 Ensuite
🛏🅿🛄🖚🎍📺🏊

(0.5m) *71 Fleetwood, Northwold, Ely, Cambs,* CB6 1BH.
Large, centrally situated, modern bungalow.
Grades: ETB Listed
Tel: 01353 662149
Mrs Bradford.
Rates fr: £19.00-£20.00.
Open: All Year (not Xmas)
Beds: 2D 1T
Baths: 1 Private 1 Shared
🅿 (4)🎍📺🛄.

(0.5m) *84 Broad Street, Ely, Cambs,* CB7 4BE.
Private cottage near river/cathedral.
Grades: ETB Listed
Tel: 01353 666862
Mrs Collins.
Rates fr: £14.00-£14.00.
Open: All Year
Beds: 1F 1D
Baths: 1 Shared
🛏🎍📺🛄📺

Prickwillow 14

National Grid Ref: TL5982

(On Path) *The Old School, Prickwillow, Ely, Cambs,* CB7 4UN.
Actual grid ref: TL596825
Converted Victorian school in Fenland.
Grades: ETB 2 Cr, Comm
Tel: 01353 688325 / 0589 260166
Mrs Roberts.
Rates fr: £18.00-£22.00.
Open: All Year
Beds: 2F 2D 1T
Baths: 5 Ensuite
🛏🅿 (20)🎍📺🛄🖚📷

Lakenheath 15

National Grid Ref: TL7182

🍴🍺 Plough

(3m 🚗) *Bell Inn, 20 High Street, Lakenheath, Brandon, Suffolk,* IP27 9DS.
Old haunted coaching inn.
Tel: 01842 860308
Mr Guy.
Rates fr: £10.00-£15.00.
Open: All Year
Beds: 3F 3D 3T 1S
Baths: 2 Shared
🛏🅿 (20)🛄🖚📺🏊
*Also ⛺ £5 per tent.,
Open: All Year* 🍴🍽🗙🚿

Brandon 16

National Grid Ref: TL7886

🍴🍺 Five Bells

(⛺ 0.5m) *Brandon Youth Hostel, Heath House, Off Waren Close, Bury Road, Brandon, Suffolk,* IP27 0BU.
Actual grid ref: TL786864
Warden: Ms S Howarth.
Tel: 01842 812075
Under 18: £5.55
Adults: £8.25
Family Room, Evening Meal, Self Catering Facilities, Centrally Heated, Grounds Available for Games, Study Room Available, Parking
A charming Edwardian house provides a relaxed stay, while surrounded by the largest forested area in England - Thetford Chase

(1m) *Bridge House Hotel, 79 High Street, Brandon, Suffolk,* IP27 0AX.
Privately owned Victorian riverside hotel.
Tel: 01842 813137
Mrs Gordon.
Rates fr: £25.00-£25.00.
Open: All Year
Beds: 1F 1T 1D 1S
Baths: 4 Ensuite
🛏🅿 (15)🛄🖚🗙🛄📺

Thetford 17

National Grid Ref: TL8783

🍴🍺 Black Horse, The Ark, Bridge Inn, Anchor Hotel, Albion

(4m) *Wereham House Hotel, 24 White Hart Street, Thetford, Norfolk,* IP24 1AD.
Comfortable family-run hotel.
Grades: ETB 2 Cr, AA 1 Q
Tel: 01842 761956
Rates fr: £24.50-£39.00.
Open: All Year
Beds: 1F 4D 2T 1S
🛏🅿🛄🗙🛄📺

(5m 🚗) *29 Priory Park, Thetford, Norfolk,* IP24 1AU.
Large comfortable family home.
Tel: 01842 752656
Mrs Atkinson.
Rates fr: £14.00-£14.00.
Open: All Year (not Xmas)
Beds: 1D 1T 2S
Baths: 1 Shared
🛏🅿 (2)🎍📺🖚🛄📺

(3.75m) *The Wilderness, Earls Street, Thetford, Norfolk,* IP24 2AF.
Tudor house in large gardens.
Grades: ETB Reg
Tel: 01842 764646
Mrs Pomorski.
Rates fr: £17.00-£19.00.
Open: All Year
Beds: 1D 1T 1S
Baths: 1 Shared
🛏 (6)🅿 (5)🎍📺🛄📺

(4m) *43 Magdalen Street, Thetford, Norfolk,* IP24 2BP.
200-year-old cottage, near station.
Grades: ETB East Anglian T.B
Tel: 01842 764564
Mrs Findlay.
Rates fr: £17.00-£17.00.
Open: All Year (not Xmas)
Beds: 2T 1S
Baths: 1 Shared
📺🛄.

Wretham 18

National Grid Ref: TL9190

(On Path 🚗) *Dog & Partridge, Watton Road, Wretham, Thetford, Norfolk,* IP24 1QS.
Actual grid ref: LM928907
C18th flint public house.
Tel: 01953 498245
Mrs Nicholls.
Rates fr: £14.00-£16.00.
Open: All Year
Beds: 1F 3D
🛏🅿🛄🖚🗙🛄📺📷🏊

Garboldisham 19

National Grid Ref: TM0081

🍴🍺 White Horse

(3.5m) *Swan House B&B, Hopton Road, Garboldisham, Diss, Norfolk,* IP22 2RQ.
Comfortable converted C17th coaching inn.
Grades: ETB Listed, Comm
Tel: 01953 688221
Mr Eldridge.
Rates fr: £17.00-£22.00.
Open: Feb to Dec
Beds: 1D 1T 1S
Baths: 1 Shared
🛏 (12)🅿 (5)🎍📺🛄📺

(3.5m 🚗) *Ingleneuk Lodge, Hopton Road, Garboldisham, Diss, Norfolk,* IP22 2RQ.
Actual grid ref: TM002801
Modern family run. Friendly atmosphere.
Grades: ETB 3 Cr, Comm, AA 3 Q, RAC High Acclaim
Tel: 01953 681541
Mr & Mrs Atkins.
Rates fr: £25.00-£33.00.
Open: All Year (not Xmas)
Beds: 1F 2D 2T 2S
Baths: 6 Private 1 Shared
🛏🅿 (20)🛄🖚🗙🛄📺

Please don't camp
on anyone's land
without first obtaining
their permission.

Icknield Way

The **Icknield Way** proper is a series of pre-historic pathways, ancient even when the Romans came, following the great chalk ridges of southern England. The **Icknield Way** long distance footpath covers only part of this long road, but it links the **Ridgeway** and the **Peddars Way** National Trails, which between them cover the rest of the old way. This is a good path for restless Londoners, with easy access back to the capital. From the Ivinghoe Beacon, the route passes through rural Hertfordshire and up into South Cambridgeshire, before heading off to the open heath of the Breckland in West Norfolk.

Guides: *The Icknield Way - A Walker's Guide* (ISBN 0 9521819 0 8), published by the by the Icknield Way Association and available from the Rambler's Association National Office (1/5 Wandsworth Road, London, SW8 2XX, tel. 0171 582 6878), £4.50 (+ 70p p&p).

Maps: 1:50000 Ordnance Survey Landranger Series: 144, 153, 154, 155, 165, 166

Cheddington   1

National Grid Ref: SP9217

⊙ ⊈ The Old Swan

(0.5m) *Rose Cottage, 68 High Street, Cheddington, Leighton Buzzard, Beds, LU7 0RQ.*
Victorian house, garden. Open NGS. **Grades:** ETB 1 Cr
Tel: **01296 668693** Mrs Jones.
Rates fr: *£18.00-£20.00.*
Open: All Year (not Xmas)
Beds: 1D 1T 1S **Baths:** 2 Ensuite
🛌 (10) 🅿 (3) ✠ ⛔ 📺 Ⓥ ✦

Ivinghoe   2

National Grid Ref: SP9416

⊙ ⊈ Rose & Crown

(▲ 1m) *Ivinghoe Youth Hostel, The Old Brewery House, Ivinghoe, Leighton Buzzard, Beds, LU7 9EP.*
Actual grid ref: SP945161
Warden: Mr J Chaplin.
Tel: **01296 668251**
Under 18: £5.00
Adults: £7.45
Family Bunk Rooms, Centrally Heated, Showers, Evening Meal (6.30 pm), Shop
Georgian mansion, once the home of a local brewer, next to the village church in the Chilterns Area of Outstanding Natural Beauty

Edlesborough   3

National Grid Ref: SP9719

⊙ ⊈ Travellers Rest, The Bell

(1m 🚌) *Ridgeway End, 5 Ivinghoe Way, Edlesborough, Dunstable, Beds, LU6 2EL.*
Actual grid ref: SP975183
Bungalow in quiet location.
Tel: **01525 220405** Mrs Lloyd.

Rates fr: *£18.00-£18.00.*
Open: All Year (not Xmas)
Beds: 1D 1T 1S
Baths: 1 Ensuite 1 Shared
🛌 🅿 (4) ⛔ 📺 Ⓥ 🚼 ✦

Totternhoe   4

National Grid Ref: SP9821

⊙ ⊈ The Old Farm Inn, The Old Bell, The Cross Keys

(0.5m) *Gower Cottage, 5 Brightwell Avenue, Totternhoe, Dunstable, Beds, LU6 1QT.*
Actual grid ref: SP994210
Executive style, peaceful country position.
Tel: **01582 601287**
Mrs Mardell.
Rates fr: *£16.00-£16.00.*
Open: All Year (not Xmas)
Beds: 1F 1T 1S
Baths: 1 Shared
🛌 🅿 (3) ✠ ⛔ 📺 ✦

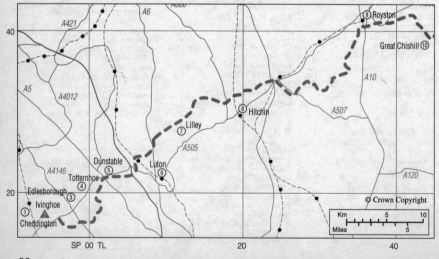

© Crown Copyright

Pay B&Bs by
cash or cheque and
be prepared to
pay up front.

Dunstable 5

National Grid Ref: TL0121

⚫ Priory, Sugar Loaf, The
Hungry Horse

(On Path) *10 St Peters Road,
Dunstable, Beds, LU5 4HY.*
Actual grid ref: TL023218
Centrally placed, cosy comfortable
house.
Grades: ETB Listed
Tel: 01582 699470
Mrs Drinkwater.
Rates fr: £15.00-£17.00.
Open: All Year (not Xmas)
Beds: 1T 2S **Baths:** 1 Shared
🛇 🖵 �🖭 ⚡

(1m) *Regent House Guest House,
79a High St North, Dunstable, LU6 1JF*
Close to town centre.
Grades: ETB Listed
Tel: 01582 660196 Mr Woodhouse
Rates fr: £14.00-£16.00.
Open: All Year
Beds: 3T 2S **Baths:** 2 Shared
🛇 🖻 ⚡🖵 🖮 ⚭ 🖭 ♥ 👁 ⚡

(1m) *23 Priory Road, Dunstable,
Beds, LU5 4HR.*
Large Georgian private house.
Grades: ETB Listed
Tel: 01582 667396 Mrs Reavey.
Rates fr: £15.00-£20.00.
Open: All Year (not Xmas)
Beds: 1F 1D 1T 1S
Baths: 1 Private 1 Shared
🛇 🖻 (4) 🖵 🖭

Luton 6

National Grid Ref: TL0921

⚫ O'Shea's, The Barn Owl, Bird
& Bush

(1.25m) *Belzayne, 70 Lalleford
Road, Luton, Beds, LU2 9JH.*
Small, friendly guesthouse, conve-
nient airport.

Grades: ETB Listed
Tel: 01582 36591 Mrs Bell.
Rates fr: £11.00-£18.00.
Open: All Year (not Xmas)
Beds: 1D 2T
Baths: 2 Shared
🛇 (6) 🖻 (5) 🗡 🖭

(1.25m) *Stockwood Hotel, 41-43
Stockwood Crescent, Luton, Beds,
LU1 3SS.*
Tudor-style town centre premises.
Tel: 01582 21000 Mr Blanchard.
Rates fr: £20.00-£20.00.
Open: All Year (not Xmas)
Beds: 1F 2D 6T 9S
Baths: 4 Private 3 Shared
🛇 🖻 (12) 🗡 🖭

Lilley 7

National Grid Ref: TL1126

(1m) *Lilley Arms, West Street,
Lilley, Luton, Beds, LU2 8LN.*
Early C18th coaching inn.
Tel: 01462 768371 Mrs Brown.
Rates fr: £16.25-£18.50.
Open: All Year
Beds: 1F 1D 1T
Baths: 2 Ensuite 1 Shared
🛇 🖻 ⚡🖵 🗡 🖭 ♥ 👁 ⚡

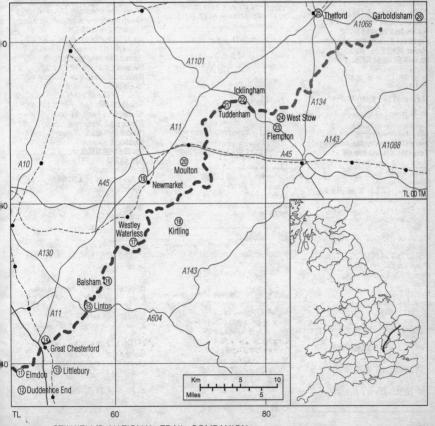

Hitchin 8

National Grid Ref: TL1930

(1m) **Long Ing,** *64 Fishponds Road, Hitchin, Herts, SG5 1NU.*
Actual grid ref: TL182298
Warm, comfortable and dry.
Tel: **01462 458050** Mr Rollason.
Rates fr: *£15.00-*£17.00.
Open: All Year (not Xmas)
Beds: 1F 2T 1S
Baths: 1 Shared
🖵 📟 🔥

Royston 9

National Grid Ref: TL3541

🍴 🍺 Old Bull Inn

(0.25m) **Middle Brooklands,**
44 Kneesworth Street, Royston, Herts, SG8 5AQ.
Late Regency town house.
Tel: **01763 245750** Mrs King.
Rates fr: *£14.00-*£15.00.
Open: Easter to OCt
Beds: 1T 1S
Baths: 1 Shared
📟 (1) 🔥

(0.25m) **White Bear Lodge,**
53 Kneesworth Street, Royston, Herts, SG8 5AQ.
Victorian lodge, adjacent pub/restaurant.
Tel: **01763 242458**
Rates fr: *£19.00-*£20.00.
Open: All Year
Beds: 4F 3D 4T 4S
Baths: 3 Shared
🍺 📟 (20) 🖵 🔥 ✕ 📟 Ⓥ 🛆

(0.25m 🚗) **The White Bear Lodge,** *49/53 Kneesworth Street, Royston, Herts, SG8 5AQ.*
Comfortable lodge adjacent pub/restaurant.
Tel: **01763 243398** Mrs Smeeton.
Rates fr: *£19.00-*£20.00.
Open: All Year
Beds: 4F 4T 4S
Baths: 2 Shared
🍺 📟 (30) 🔥 🖵 🔥 ✕ 📟 Ⓥ 🛆 🔥

(On Path) **Pilgrim's Sojourn,**
7 Garden Lane, Royston, Herts, SG8 9EH.
Clean, comfortable, warm, unique townhouse.
Tel: **01763 241656** Mrs Waites.
Rates fr: *£17.00-*£17.00.
Open: All Year
Beds: 1D 1T
Baths: 1 Shared
📟 (2) 🔥 🖵 ✕ 📟 Ⓥ 🛆

The lowest *double*
rate per person is
shown in *italics*.

Great Chishill 10

National Grid Ref: TL4238

🍴 🍺 Pheasant

(1.25m) **Hall Farm,** *Great Chishill, Royston, Herts, SG8 8SH.*
Homely, comfortable, Georgian farmhouse.
Grades: ETB Listed
Tel: **01763 838263** Mrs Wiseman.
Rates fr: *£17.50-*£20.00.
Open: All Year
Beds: 1F 1D 1T
Baths: 1 Shared
🍺 📟 (4) 🔥 🖵 🔥 📟 Ⓥ

Elmdon 11

National Grid Ref: TL4639

(On Path) **Elmdon Bury,** *Elmdon, Saffron Walden, Essex, CB11 4NF.*
Actual grid ref: TL4640
Peaceful, spacious, comfortable, refurbished farmhouse.
Grades: ETB 2 Cr, High Comm
Tel: **01763 838220**
Mrs Pearson.
Rates fr: *£20.00-*£28.00.
Open: All Year (not Xmas)
Beds: 2D 1T
Baths: 3 Private
🍺 (10) 📟 (12) 🔥 🔥 ✕ 📟 🔥

Duddenhoe End 12

National Grid Ref: TL4636

🍴 🍺 The Bell, The Axe & Compass

(2m) **Rockells Farm,** *Duddenhoe End, Saffron Walden, Essex, CB11 4UY.*
Comfortable farm in Essex countryside.
Grades: ETB 2 Cr, Comm
Tel: **01763 838053**
Mrs Westerhuis.
Rates fr: *£17.00-*£17.00.
Open: All Year
Beds: 1F 1T 1S
Baths: 3 Ensuite
🍺 📟 (8) 🖵 🔥

Littlebury 13

National Grid Ref: TL5139

🍴 🍺 The Queens Head Inn

(2.25m) **The Queens Head Inn,** *High Street, Littlebury, Saffron Walden, Essex, CB11 4TD.*
Actual grid ref: TL4353
Best pub in Essex 1995.
Grades: ETB 3 Cr, Comm
Tel: **01799 522251**
Mr & Mrs O'Gorman.
Rates fr: *£25.00-*£27.95.
Open: All Year
Beds: 1F 3D 1T 1S
Baths: 6 Ensuite
🍺 📟 (30) 🖵 ✕ 📟 Ⓥ 🛆 🔥

The *lowest* **single**
rate *is* shown in **bold.**

Great Chesterford 14

National Grid Ref: TL5042

🍴 🍺 Crown & Thistle

(On Path) **July Cottage,** *Carmel Street, Great Chesterford, Saffron Walden, Essex, CB10 1PH.*
Actual grid ref: TL507429
Fully modernised period cottage.
Grades: ETB Listed, Comm
Tel: **01799 530315** Mrs Dey.
Rates fr: *£17.00-*£17.00.
Open: All Year (not Xmas)
Beds: 2T
Baths: 1 Shared
🍺 (6) 📟 (2) 🔥 🔥 📟 🔥

Linton 15

National Grid Ref: TL5646

🍴 🍺 The Crown

(0.5m) **Linton Heights,**
36 Wheatsheaf Way, Linton, Cambridge, CB1 6XB.
Modern, comfortable and friendly.
Tel: **01223 892516**
Mr & Mrs Peake.
Rates fr: *£15.00-*£15.00.
Open: All Year (not Xmas)
Beds: 1T 1S
Baths: 1 Shared
🍺 (6) 📟 (2) 🔥 🖵 📟 🛆 🔥

(On Path 🚗) **Springfield House,**
14-16 Horn Lane, Linton, Cambridge, CB1 6HT.
Peaceful riverside Regency family home.
Grades: ETB 2 Cr
Tel: **01223 891383**
Mrs Rossiter.
Rates fr: *£16.50-*£20.00.
Open: All Year
Beds: 1F 2D
Baths: 1 Ensuite 2 Private
🍺 📟 (4) 🔥 🖵 📟 Ⓥ 🛆 🔥

Balsham 16

National Grid Ref: TL5850

🍴 🍺 The Bull

(On Path 🚗) **Yole Farm,** *Linton Road, Balsham, Cambridge, CB1 6HB.*
Actual grid ref: TL5849
Modern, comfortable farmhouse, very quiet.
Tel: **01223 893280** Mrs Kiddy.
Rates fr: *£14.00-*£14.00.
Open: All Year (not Xmas)
Beds: 1D 1T
Baths: 1 Shared
🍺 📟 (6) 🔥 🖵 📟 Ⓥ 🛆 🔥
Also 🅰 *£2.50 per tent.*
Open: Easter to Oct Ⓣ 🅰

Westley Waterless 17

National Grid Ref: TL6256

(0.75m) *Westley House, Westley Waterless, Newmarket, Suffolk, CB8 0RQ.*
Actual grid ref: TL6256
Georgian style former rectory.
Grades: ETB Listed
Tel: **01638 508112** Mrs Galpin.
Rates fr: £20.00-£20.00.
Open: All Year
Beds: 2T 2S **Baths:** 2 Shared
🅿 (6) ❑ 🛏 ✕ 🎞 Ⅴ ≠

Kirtling 18

National Grid Ref: TL6856

🍴 🍺 Three Blackbirds

(2.75m) *Hill Farm Guest House, Kirtling, Newmarket, Suffolk, CB8 9HQ.*
Comfortable old farmhouse.
Grades: ETB 3 Cr, AA 2 St
Tel: **01638 730253** Mrs Benley.
Rates fr: £20.00-£22.00.
Open: All Year
Beds: 1D 1T 1S
Baths: 2 Ensuite
🅿 (4) ❑ 🛏 ✕ 🎞 Ⅴ

Newmarket 19

National Grid Ref: TL6463

🍴 🍺 The Bushel

(7m) *Derby House, 27 Exeter Road, Newmarket, Suffolk, CB8 8LL.*
Large restored Victorian house.
Tel: **01638 662887** Mr & Mrs Kay.
Rates fr: £17.50-£22.50.
Open: All Year (not Xmas)
Beds: 1F 1D 3T **Baths:** 2 Shared
🛏 🅿 (10) ❑ 🎞 🛉

(4.5m) *Falmouth House, Falmouth Avenue, Newmarket, Suffolk, CB8 0NB.*
Large, comfortable, modern, detached house.
Grades: ETB Listed
Tel: **01638 660409** Mrs Shaw.
Rates fr: £18.00-£24.00.
Open: All Year (not Xmas)
Beds: 1D 2T
Baths: 1 Shared
🛏 (10) 🅿 (6) ❑ ✕ 🎞 Ⅴ

Moulton 20

National Grid Ref: TL6964

🍴 🍺 The Kings Head

(0.75m) *Flint End House, 6 The Street, Moulton, Newmarket, Suffolk, CB8 8RZ.*
Actual grid ref: TL695644
Comfortable Victorian private house.
Tel: **01638 750966** Mrs Bolus.
Rates fr: £18.50-£18.50.
Open: All Year (not Xmas)
Beds: 1D 1S **Baths:** 2 Shared
🛏 🅿 (2) 🛶 ❑ 🎞 🛉

(On Path) *Handsell House, The Street, Moulton, Newmarket, Suffolk, CB8 8RZ.*
Unusually attractive and artistic home.
Tel: **01638 751803** Mrs Perry.
Rates fr: £18.50-£18.50.
Open: All Year (not Xmas)
Beds: 1D 1T 1S
Baths: 2 Shared
🛏 (14) 🅿 (4) 🛶 ❑ ✕ 🎞 ♿ ▮

Tuddenham 21

National Grid Ref: TL7471

🍴 🍺 White Hart

(0.25m 🚌) *Oakdene, Higham Road, Tuddenham, Bury St Edmunds, Suffolk, IP28 6SG.*
Modern house offering friendly accommodation.
Grades: ETB Listed
Tel: **01638 718822** Mrs Titcombe.
Rates fr: £16.50-£17.50.
Open: All Year (not Xmas)
Beds: 2F 1T
Baths: 1 Ensuite 1 Shared
🛏 🅿 (4) 🛶 ❑ ✕ 🎞 Ⅴ ▮ 🛉

Icklingham 22

National Grid Ref: TL7772

🍴 🍺 Red Lion, The Plough

(On Path) *Weatherhill Farm, Icklingham, Bury St Edmunds, Suffolk, IP28 6PP.*
C18th farmhouse on working arable farm.
Tel: **01284 728839** Mr Browning.
Rates fr: £12.50-£12.50.
Open: All Year
Beds: 1F 1T 2S
Baths: 2 Shared
🛏 🅿 (8) ❑ 🛏 🎞 Ⅴ

Flempton 23

National Grid Ref: TL8169

🍴 🍺 Greyhound

(1.5m) *School House, Flempton, Bury St Edmunds, Suffolk, IP28 6EG.*
Converted Victorian school and house.
Tel: **01284 728792** Mrs Lindsay.
Rates fr: £11.50-£12.00.
Open: All Year **Beds:** 1F 1T
🛏 🅿 (6) 🛏 🎞 Ⅴ

West Stow 24

National Grid Ref: TL8170

(1.25m) *Eastleigh, West Stow, Bury St Edmunds, Suffolk, IP28 6EZ.*
Cottage in village. Homely welcome.
Grades: ETB Listed
Tel: **01284 728264** Mrs Cooke.
Rates fr: £13.00-£13.00.
Open: All Year
Beds: 1D 1S **Baths:** 1 Shared
🛏 ✕

Thetford 25

National Grid Ref: TL8783

🍴 🍺 Black Horse, The Ark, Bridge Inn

(5m 🚌) *29 Priory Park, Thetford, Norfolk, IP24 1AU.*
Large comfortable family home.
Tel: **01842 752656**
Mrs Atkinson.
Rates fr: £14.00-£14.00.
Open: All Year (not Xmas)
Beds: 1D 1T 2S
Baths: 1 Shared
🛏 🅿 (2) 🛶 ❑ 🛏 🎞 🛉

(5m) *The Wilderness, Earls Street, Thetford, Norfolk, IP24 2AF.*
Tudor-style house, landscaped
Tel: **01842 764646**
Mrs Pomorski.
Rates fr: £17.00-£19.00.
Open: All Year (not Xmas)
Beds: 3D 1S
Baths: 1 Shared
(6) 🅿 (6) 🛶 ❑ 🎞

(5m) *43 Magdalen Street, Thetford, Norfolk, IP24 2BP.*
200-year-old cottage, near station.
Grades: ETB East Anglian T.B
Tel: **01842 764564**
Mrs Findlay.
Rates fr: £17.00-£17.00.
Open: All Year (not Xmas)
Beds: 2T 1S
Baths: 1 Shared
❑ 🎞

Garboldisham 26

National Grid Ref: TM0081

🍴 🍺 White Horse

(3.5m 🚌) *Ingleneuk Lodge, Hopton Road, Garboldisham, Diss, Norfolk, IP22 2RQ.*
Actual grid ref: TM002801
Modern family run. Friendly atmosphere.
Grades: ETB 3 Cr, Comm, AA 3 Q, RAC High Acclaim
Tel: **01953 681541**
Mr & Mrs Atkins.
Rates fr: £25.00-£33.00.
Open: All Year (not Xmas)
Beds: 1F 2D 2T 2S
Baths: 6 Private 1 Shared
🛏 🅿 (20) ❑ 🛏 ✕ 🎞 Ⅴ

(3m) *Swan House B&B, Hopton Road, Garboldisham, Diss, Norfolk, IP22 2RQ.*
Comfortable converted C17th coaching inn.
Grades: ETB Listed, Comm
Tel: **01953 688221** Mr Eldridge.
Rates fr: £17.00-£22.00.
Open: Feb to Dec
Beds: 1D 1T 1S
Baths: 1 Shared
🛏 (12) 🅿 (5) 🛶 ❑ 🎞 Ⅴ

North Downs Way

For 141 miles you walk through the woodland and downland of Surrey and Kent, along the northern chalk escarpment up to the Medway and then right down to Dover. Much of the route coincides with the old **Pilgrim's Way** from Winchester and there is a loop link that will take you via the historic cathedral city of Canterbury, should you so wish. For a path that cuts right through the South East commuter belt, only a few hedges away from the motorway, it's remarkably rural and peaceful, a glorious breath of fresh air. In fact, the proximity of the roads and railway makes this a great one for Londoners seeking a trail they can do at weekends - every stretch of the walk has a railway line bisecting it or running alongside it. The terrain is easy, the main gradients occurring as you come onto the escarpment itself and off again. Parts of the walk can be muddy in winter, while on some stretches in summer the nettles are tall, the brambles thick and the hedgerows overgrown: so dress accordingly.

Guides: *A Guide to the Pilgrims Way & North Downs Way* by C J Wright, published by Constable & Co Ltd and available from all good map shops, £10.95

Discovering the North Downs Way by David Allen & Patrick Imrie, published by Shire Publications and available by post from the publishers (Cromwell House, Church Street, Princes Risborough, Bucks, HP27 9AA), £2.50 (+ 70p p&p)

North Downs Way by Neil Curtis (ISBN 1 85410 187 0), published by Aurum Press in association with the Countryside Commission and Ordnance Survey and available from all major bookshops, £9.99.

Maps: 1:50000 Ordnance Survey Landranger Series: 177, 178, 179, 186, 187, 188, 189 Comments on the path to: North Downs Way Project Officer, c/o Planning Dept, Kent County Council, Springfield, Maidstone, Kent ME14 2LX

Wimble Hill   1

National Grid Ref: SU8046

🍴 🍺 Plume of Feathers

(3m 🚌) *The School House, Wimble Hill, Crondall, Farnham, Surrey, GU10 5HL.*
Actual grid ref: SU802467
Comfortable family house, friendly welcome.
Grades: ETB Registered
Tel: 01252 850824
Mr & Mrs Collet.
Rates fr: *£17.50-£17.50*.
Open: All Year (not Xmas)
Beds: 1T 1S
Baths: 1 Shared
🛏 (8) 🅿 (6) ⊬ 🖵 🕮 ✦

Lower Bourne   2

National Grid Ref: SU8446

🍴 🍺 Bat & Ball (Lower Bourne)

(1m) *High Wray, 73 Lodge Hill Road, Lower Bourne, Farnham, Surrey, GU10 3RB.*
Actual grid ref: SU856453
Family home in large garden.
Grades: ETB Listed, Comm
Tel: 01252 715589
Mrs Crawford.
Rates fr: *£20.00-£16.00*.
Open: All Year
Beds: 1D 3T 2S
Baths: 1 Ensuite, 3 Shared
🛏 🅿 (6) 🖵 🏋 ✕ ♿ 🆅 🎒 ✦

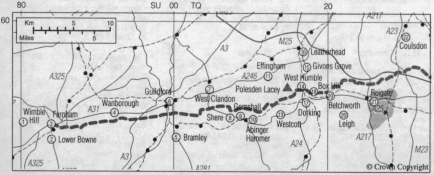

Farnham   3

National Grid Ref: SU8446

🍴 🍺 Cherry Tree, Bat & Ball, Hare & Hounds, The Waverley Arms, Lamb

(1m) *High Wray, 73 Lodge Hill Road, Farnham, Surrey, GU9 3RB.*
Actual grid ref: SU856453
Family home in large garden.
Grades: ETB Listed, Comm
Tel: **01252 715589** Mrs Crawford.
Rates fr: £20.00-£16.00.
Open: All Year
Beds: 1D 3T 2S
Baths: 1 Ensuite, 3 Shared
🛇 🅿 (6) 🛏 🏋 ✗ & Ⅴ ▮ ✤

Pay B&Bs by
cash or cheque and
be prepared to
pay up front.

(2m) *Orchard House, 13 Applelands Close, Boundstone, Farnham, Surrey, GU10 4TL.*
Actual grid ref: SU835438
Quiet, overlooking beautiful countryside.
Grades: ETB Listed
Tel: **01252 793813** Mrs Warburton.
Rates fr: £16.00-£16.00.
Open: All Year (not Xmas)
Beds: 1T 1S **Baths:** 1 Shared
🛇 🅿 (3) ✤ 🖵 🛏

(0.25m) *20 Red Lion Lane, Farnham, Surrey, GU9 7QN.*
Attractive country cottage.
Tel: **01252 712981** Mrs Mothersele.
Rates fr: £16.00-£22.00.
Open: All Year
Beds: 1D 1S **Baths:** 1 Private
🛇 (12) ✤ 🖵 🛏

(1m) *Hawridge, 20 Upper Old Park Lane, Farnham, Surrey, GU9 0AT.*
Large private house.
Tel: **01252 722068**
Mr & Mrs Ackland.
Rates fr: £17.50-£22.50.
Open: All Year
Beds: 1D 1T 1S
Baths: 1 Shared
🅿 ✤ 🖵 ✗ 🛏 Ⅴ ▮ ✤

(0.5m) *The Croft, 2 Trebor Avenue, Farnham, Surrey, GU9 8JH.*
Comfortable family 'home from home'.
Tel: **01252 715054** Mr Rose.
Rates fr: £18.00-£20.00.
Open: All Year
Beds: 1T 1S
Baths: 1 Ensuite 1 Shared
🅿 (2) ✤ 🖵 🛏 🛏

(0.25m) *1 Broomleaf Corner, Farnham, Surrey, GU9 8BG.*
Secluded house, walking distance town.
Tel: **01252 721930** Mrs Diment.
Rates fr: £16.00-£18.00.
Open: All Year (not Xmas)
Beds: 2T 1S **Baths:** 1 Shared
🛇 🅿 (3) ✤ 🖵 ✗ 🛏

(0.25m) *Heath Lodge, 91a Shortheath Road, Farnham, Surrey, GU9 8SF.*
Victorian, private, very comfortable house.
Grades: ETB Listed
Tel: **01252 722918** Mrs Jones.
Rates fr: £20.00-£25.00.
Open: All Year
Beds: 2T **Baths:** 1 Shared
🛇 🅿 (4) ✤ 🖵 ✗ 🛏 Ⅴ ▮ ✤

Wanborough   4

National Grid Ref: SU9348

🍴 🍺 Harrow Inn, Cross Keys, Brewers Arms, Plough Inn, Black Horse

(0.5m) *Little Flexford, Flexford Road, Wanborough, Guildford, Surrey, GU3 2EE.*
Modernised Elizabethan farmhouse.

Tel: **01483 811179** Mr & Turner.
Rates fr: £20.00-£22.00.
Open: Mar to Oct
Beds: 1D 1T
Baths: 1 Private 1 Shared
🛇 🅿 (2) ✤ 🖵 🛏

Bramley   5

National Grid Ref: TQ0044

🍴 🍺 Jolly Farmer, The Wheatsheaf

(1.5m) *Beevers Farm, Chinthurst Lane, Bramley, Guildford, Surrey, GU5 0DR.*
Quiet position, homemade preserves.
Grades: ETB Listed
Tel: **01483 898764** Mr Cook.
Rates fr: £13.00-£20.00.
Open: Mar to Nov
Beds: 1F 2T
Baths: 1 Private 1 Shared
🛇 🅿 (10) ✤ 🖵 🛏 ▮ ✤

Guildford   6

National Grid Ref: SU9949

🍴 🍺 Sea Horse, The Parrot, King's Head

(0.5m) *Mulberry Corner, East Shalford Lane, Guildford, Surrey, GU4 8AE.*
Actual grid ref: SU999478
Private house, lovely walled garden.
Tel: **01483 573885**
Mrs Webb.
Rates fr: £16.00-£18.00.
Open: All Year (not Xmas)
Beds: 2D 1T
Baths: 1 Shared
🛇 (3) 🅿 (3) ✤ 🖵 🛏 ▮ ✤

(1m) *Atkinsons Guest House, 129 Stoke Road, Guildford, Surrey, GU1 1ET.*
Comfortable Victorian guesthouse.
Grades: ETB Listed, Comm
Tel: **01483 38260**
Rates fr: £17.50-£20.00.
Open: All Year
Beds: 2T 2S
🛇 (6) 🅿 (2) 🖵 🛏

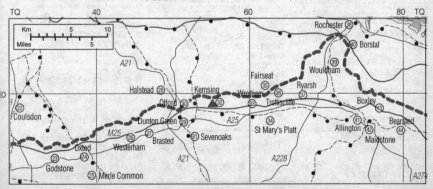

(1m) *Weybrook House, 113 Stoke Road, Guildford, Surrey, GU1 1ET.*
Actual grid ref: SU998504
Quiet and friendly atmosphere.
Grades: ETB Listed
Tel: **01483 302394**
Mr & Mrs Bourne.
Rates fr: *£14.00*-£18.00.
Open: All Year (not Xmas)
Beds: 1F 1D 1S **Baths:** 2 Shared
⛺ 🅿 (2) 🛏 🗡 📷 Ⓥ 📖 ∦

(1m) *25 The Chase, Guildford, Surrey, GU2 5UA.*
Private family home.
Grades: ETB Listed
Tel: **01483 69782** Mrs Ellis.
Rates fr: *£14.50*-£14.50.
Open: All Year (not Xmas)
Beds: 2S
∦ 🗡 📷

West Clandon 7

National Grid Ref: TQ0452

🍴 🍺 The Queens Head, The Bulls Head

(2.5m 🚍) *Ways Cottage, Lime Grove, West Clandon, Guildford, Surrey, GU4 7UT.*
Actual grid ref: TQ045521
Detached, rural family home.
Grades: ETB Comm
Tel: **01483 222454** Mrs Hughes.
Rates fr: *£16.50*-£17.00.
Open: All Year **Beds:** 1T 1S
Baths: 1 Private 1 Shared
⛺ 🅿 (3) ∦ 🗡 ✕ 📷 📖

Shere 8

National Grid Ref: TQ0747

🍴 🍺 White Horse, Prince of Wales

(0.5m) *Manor Cottage, Shere, Guildford, Surrey, GU5 9JE.*
Actual grid ref: TQ0747
C16th cottage in beautiful village.
Grades: ETB Listed
Tel: **01483 202979** Mrs James.
Rates fr: *£16.00*-£18.00.
Open: Easter to Oct
Beds: 1D 1S **Baths:** 1 Shared
⛺ (6) 🅿 (2) ∦ Ⓥ ∦

Gomshall 9

National Grid Ref: TQ0847

🍴 🍺 ▣✕✪ White Horse, Prince of Wales

(On Path) *Cherry Trees, Gomshall, Guildford, Surrey, GU5 9HE*
Actual grid ref: TQ072487
Quiet comfortable home, beautiful garden.
Grades: ETB 2 Cr, Comm
Tel: **01483 202288** Mrs Warren.
Rates fr: *£18.50*-£18.50.
Open: Jan to Nov
Beds: 1D 2T 1S
Baths: 2 Private 1 Shared
⛺ 🅿 (4) ∦ 🗡 📷 Ⓥ 📖 ∦

Abinger Hammer 10

National Grid Ref: TQ0947

🍴 🍺 Wootton Hatch

(1.75m) *Crossways Farm, Raikes Lane, Abinger Hammer, Dorking, Surrey, RH5 6PZ.*
Listed C17th farmhouse.
Tel: **01306 730173** Mrs Hughes.
Rates fr: *£14.00*-£21.00.
Open: All Year
Beds: 1F 1D 1T
Baths: 1 Private 1 Shared
⛺ 🅿 (3) ∦ 🗡 📷

Effingham 11

National Grid Ref: TQ1153

🍴 🍺 The Plough, Sir Douglas Haig

(3m) *Chalklands, Beech Avenue, Effingham, Surrey, KT24 5PJ.*
Large detached house overlooking golfcourse.
Grades: ETB Listed
Tel: **01372 454936** Mrs Reilly.
Rates fr: *£20.00*-£20.00.
Open: All Year (not Xmas)
Beds: 1F 1D 1T
Baths: 2 Ensuite 1 Shared
⛺ 🅿 (5) ∦ 🗡 🛏 ✕ 📷 Ⓥ 📖 ∦

Polesden Lacey 12

National Grid Ref: TQ1451

(🔺 0.25m) *Tanners Hatch Youth Hostel, Polesden Lacey, Dorking, Surrey, RH5 6BE.*
Actual grid ref: TQ1451
Warden: Mr G Peddie.
Tel: **01372 452528**
Under 18: £4.15 **Adults:** £6.10
Family Bunk Rooms
Simple conditions only in isolated cottages amid 1,000 acres of the Surrey Hills Area of Outstanding Natural Beauty

Westcott 13

National Grid Ref: TQ1448

🍴 🍺 Crown, Cricketers

(0.5m 🚍) *The Dene, Hole Hill, Westcott, Dorking, Surrey, RH4 3LS.*
Large country house on slopes of Ranmore. Aviary, amenities near.
Grades: ETB Registered
Tel: **01306 885595** Mrs King.
Rates fr: *£15.00*-£20.00.
Open: All Year (not Xmas)
Beds: 1F 1D 2T
Baths: 2 Shared
⛺ 🅿 (10) 🗡 🛏 ✕ 📷 ∦

The lowest *double* rate per person is shown in *italics*.

Westhumble 14

National Grid Ref: TQ1651

🍴 🍺 Stepping Stones

(0.25m 🚍) *Treetops, Pilgrims Way, Westhumble, Dorking, Surrey, RH5 6AP.*
Quiet, friendly, detached house overlooking Box Hill.
Tel: **01306 883905** Miss Wood.
Rates fr: *£15.00*-£23.00.
Open: All Year (not Xmas)
Beds: 1D 1S
Baths: 1 Private 1 Shared
🅿 ∦ 🗡 ✕ 📷 Ⓥ 📖 ∦

Givons Grove 15

National Grid Ref: TQ1754

(On Path 🚍) *Bronwen, Crabtree Drive, Givons Grove, Leatherhead, Surrey, KT22 8LJ.*
Large attractive house, close to farmland.
Grades: ETB Listed
Tel: **01372 372515** Mrs Harris.
Rates fr: *£18.00*-£18.00.
Open: All Year
Beds: 1F 1D 1T 2S
Baths: 1 Ensuite 1 Shared
⛺ 🅿 (4) 🗡 📷 ♿ 📖 ∦

Leatherhead 16

National Grid Ref: TQ1656

🍴 🍺 Plough

(3m) *20 Melvinshaw, Leatherhead, Surrey, KT22 8SX.*
Clean, comfortable family house.
Tel: **01372 373786** Mrs Pearce.
Rates fr: *£15.00*-£15.00.
Open: All Year
Beds: 1T 1S **Baths:** 1 Shared
⛺ (12) 🅿 (2) ∦ 🗡 📷

Dorking 17

National Grid Ref: TQ1649

🍴 🍺 King William, Wootton Hatch, Kings Arms, The Plough, Water Mill

(2m 🚍) *The Waltons, 5 Rose Hill, Dorking, Surrey, RH4 2EG.*
Large Listed Victorian house.
Grades: ETB Listed
Tel: **01306 883127** Mrs Walton.
Rates fr: *£15.00*-£17.50.
Open: All Year
Beds: 2F 1T
Baths: 2 Shared
⛺ 🅿 (3) ∦ 🗡 🛏 📷 Ⓥ 📖 ∦

(2m) *Shrub Hill, 3 Calvert Road, Dorking, Surrey, RH4 1LT.*
Convenient, comfortable, quiet family home.
Tel: **01306 885229** Mrs Scott Kerr.
Rates fr: *£17.50*-£18.00.
Open: All Year (not Xmas)
Beds: 1T 1S **Baths:** 1 Shared
⛺ 🅿 (5) 🅿 (2) ∦ 🗡 🛏 📷 Ⓥ

(2m) **Highbank,** *1 Townfield Road, Dorking, Surrey, RH4 2HX.*
Family home - central - lovely views.
Grades: ETB 1 Cr
Tel: 01306 888135 Mrs Paul.
Rates fr: *£15.00-***£15.00**.
Open: All Year
Beds: 1T 1S
Baths: 1 Private 1 Shared
🖵 🛏,

Box Hill 18

National Grid Ref: TQ2051

🍴 🍺 Hand in Hand, Box Hill Tavern

(0.5m) 🐾) **Merrow,** *Box Hill Road, Box Hill, Tadworth, Surrey, KT20 7PS.*
Actual grid ref: TQ202518
Modern comfortable chalet bungalow.
Tel: 01737 842855 Mrs Durant.
Rates fr: *£15.00-***£18.00**.
Open: All Year (not Xmas)
Beds: 2D 1S
Baths: 1 Ensuite 1 Shared
🅿 (3) ⅍ 🖵 🛏 ▪

Betchworth 19

National Grid Ref: TQ2150

(1m 🐾) **Gadbrook Old Farm,** *Wellhouse Lane, Betchworth, Surrey, RH3 7HH.*
Actual grid ref: TQ208502
Comfortable old farmhouse.
Grades: ETB Listed
Tel: 01737 842183 Mrs Bibby.
Rates fr: *£15.00-***£15.00**.
Open: All Year (not Xmas)
Beds: 1D 2T
Baths: 1 Ensuite 1 Shared
🐕 (4) 🅿 (4) ⅍ 🖵 🛏 🗙 🛏 ♥ ▪ ✦

Leigh 20

National Grid Ref: TQ2246

🍴 🍺 The Plough, The Seven Stars

(1m 🐾) **Barn Cottage,** *Church Road, Leigh, Reigate, Surrey, RH2 8RF.*
Converted C17th barn, beautiful gardens.
Grades: ETB Listed
Tel: 01306 611347 Mrs Comer.
Rates fr: *£22.00-***£22.00**.
Open: All Year
Beds: 1D 1T
Baths: 2 Shared
🐕 🅿 (3) 🖵 🗙 🛏 ♥ ▪ ✦

The lowest *double* rate per person is shown in *italics*.

Reigate 21

National Grid Ref: TQ2649

🍴 🍺 Nutley Hall, Yew Tree

(2.5m) **Norfolk Lodge Hotel,** *23-25 London Road, Reigate, Surrey, RH2 9PY.*
Very comfortable, licensed family hotel.
Tel: 01737 248702 Mr Bowley.
Rates fr: *£15.00-***£24.00**.
Open: All Year
Beds: 3F 2D 5T 6S
Baths: 2 Shared
🐕 🅿 (50) 🖵 🛏

Coulsdon 22

National Grid Ref: TQ3058

(3m) **512 Chipstead Valley Road,** *Coulsdon, Surrey, CR5 2BN.*
Modern, homely, comfortable.
Tel: 01737 553155 Mrs Bateman.
Rates fr: *£17.50-***£17.00**.
Open: All Year (not Xmas)
Beds: 1D 1S **Baths:** 1 Shared
🅿 🖵 🗙 🛏,

Godstone 23

National Grid Ref: TQ3551

🍴 🍺 Old Surrey

(1.5m) **Godstone Hotel,** *The Green, Godstone, Surrey, RH9 8DT.*
C16th oak-beamed hotel, inglenook fireplaces.
Tel: 01883 742461 Mr Howe.
Rates fr: *£22.50-***£32.00**.
Open: All Year
Beds: 1F 5D 2T **Baths:** 8 Private
🐕 🅿 (40) 🖵 🛏 🗙 🛏 ♥ ▪ ✦

Oxted 24

National Grid Ref: TQ3852

🍴 🍺 George, Crown, The Royal Oak

(1m) **Pinehurst Grange Guest House,** *East Hill (Part of A25), Oxted, Surrey, RH8 9AE.*
Actual grid ref: TQ393525
Comfortable, homely, refurbished, Victorian ex-farmhouse.
Tel: 01883 716413 Mr Rodgers.
Rates fr: *£19.50-***£24.00**.
Open: All Year (not Xmas/New Year)
Beds: 1D 1T 1S
Baths: 1 Shared
🐕 (5) 🅿 (3) ⅍ 🖵 🛏 ▪ ✦

(1m) **Rosehaven,** *12 Hoskins Road, Oxted, Surrey, RH8 9HT.*
Comfortable house, quiet, residential road.
Tel: 01883 712700 Mrs Snell.
Rates fr: *£18.00-***£18.00**.
Open: All Year (not Xmas)
Beds: 2T 1S
Baths: 1 Shared
🐕 🅿 (1) ⅍ 🖵 🛏, ♥

The Croft, Quarry Road

(2m 🐾) **The Croft,** *Quarry Road, Oxted, Surrey, RH8 9HE.*
Actual grid ref: TQ393521
Substantial Edwardian house. Peaceful location.
Tel: 01883 713605 Mrs Todd.
Rates fr: *£17.50-***£19.00**.
Open: All Year (not Xmas)
Beds: 1F 1T 1S
Baths: 1 Shared
🐕 (5) 🅿 (8) ⅍ 🖵 🛏 ✦

Merle Common 25

National Grid Ref: TQ4049

(3.5m) **Old Forge House,** *Merle Common, Oxted, Surrey, RH8 0JB.*
Comfortable home in rural surroundings.
Grades: ETB Listed
Tel: 01883 715969
Mrs Mills.
Rates fr: *£15.00-***£17.00**.
Open: All Year (not Xmas)
Beds: 1D 1T 1S
🐕 🅿 (3) 🛏 🛏, Ⓥ

Westerham 26

National Grid Ref: TQ4454

🍴 🍺 Fox & Hounds

(1.5m) **Corner Cottage,** *Toys Hill, Westerham, Kent, TN16 1PY.*
Self-contained very comfortable room, spectacular views.
Grades: ETB Memb
Tel: 01732 750362
Mrs Olszowska.
Rates fr: *£18.50-***£25.00**.
Open: All Year
Beds: 1F
🐕 🅿 (2) ⅍ 🖵 🗙 🛏, Ⓥ ▪

Brasted 27

National Grid Ref: TQ4653

🍴 🍺 Bull Inn, The White Hart

(2.5m 🐾) **The Orchard House,** *Chart Lane, Brasted, Westerham, Kent, TN16 1LR.*
Actual grid ref: TQ469537
Family home, quiet, rural surroundings.
Tel: 01959 563702
Mrs Godsal.
Rates fr: *£16.00-***£17.00**.
Open: All Year (not Xmas)
Beds: 2T 1S
Baths: 2 Shared
🐕 🅿 (4) ⅍ 🖵 🗙 🛏, ♿ Ⓥ ▪ ✦

(1.25m 🐾) **Holmesdale House,** *High Street, Brasted, Westerham, Kent, TN16 1HS.*
Actual grid ref: TQ469550
Large Victorian private house.
Tel: 01959 564834 Mr Jinks.
Rates fr: *£18.00-***£22.00**.
Open: All Year
Beds: 1F 1D 2T 1S
Baths: 3 Ensuite 2 Shared
🐕 🅿 (6) 🖵 🛏, Ⓥ ▪ ✦

Halstead 28

National Grid Ref: TQ4861

(1.5m) *April Cottage, Otford Lane, Halstead, Sevenoaks, Kent, TN14 7EG.*
Late C18th cottage, rural, convenient.
Tel: **01959 533082** Mrs Crawford.
Rates fr: *£17.50-£20.00*.
Open: Easter to Oct
Beds: 2D 1T 2S
Baths: 2 Private 1 Shared
P (6) ⊬ ⛌ ✗ Ⓥ

Dunton Green 29

National Grid Ref: TQ5157

¶ ⛲ Rose and Crown, Harvesters

(0.25m) *Glebe House, London Road, Dunton Green, Sevenoaks, Kent, TN13 2TE.*
Large Victorian house, lovely garden.
Grades: ETB Reg
Tel: **01732 462604** Mrs Stanley.
Rates fr: *£20.00-£20.00*.
Open: All Year (not Xmas)
Beds: 2T 1S
Baths: 1 Private 1 Shared
➳ P (6) ⛌ ⼍ Ⅲ. ▮ ⼂

Otford 30

National Grid Ref: TQ5159

¶ ⛲ The Crown, The Horns, The Bull

(On Path 🚲) *Whitesides, 24a Pilgrims Way East, Otford, Sevenoaks, Kent, TN14 5QN.*
Modern house directly on route.
Grades: ETB Approved
Tel: **01959 523743** Mrs Hord.
Rates fr: *£18.00-£18.00*.
Open: Easter to Nov
Beds: 1T 1S **Baths:** 1 Shared
➳ (12) P (4) ⊬ ⛌ ✗ Ⅲ. Ⓥ ▮ ⼂

Sevenoaks 31

National Grid Ref: TQ5255

¶ ⛲ George & Dragon, Rose & Crown, White Hart, Halfway House

(3.5m) *33 Chipstead Lane, Riverhead, Sevenoaks, Kent, TN13 2AH.*
Chalet/bungalow with large garden.
Tel: **01732 461612** Mrs Davies.
Rates fr: *£15.00-£15.00*.
Open: Apr to Oct
Beds: 1D 1T **Baths:** 1 Shared
➳ (6) P ⊬ Ⅲ.

All rates are subject
to alteration at the
owners' discretion.

(2.5m) *Green Tiles, 46 The Rise, Sevenoaks, Kent, TN13 1RJ.*
Quiet ground floor garden annexe.
Grades: ETB Comm
Tel: **01732 451522** Mrs Knoops.
Rates fr: *£15.00-£20.00*.
Open: All Year (not Xmas)
Beds: 1F
Baths: 1 Private
➳ P (2) ⛌ Ⅲ.

Kemsing 32

National Grid Ref: TQ5558

¶ ⛲ The Bell, Rising Sun

(On Path) *16 Copperfields, Kemsing, Sevenoaks, Kent, TN15 6QG.*
Modern, comfortable, quiet, private house.
Grades: ETB Listed
Tel: **01732 761607**
Mr & Mrs Swales.
Rates fr: *£15.00-£15.00*.
Open: All Year (not Xmas)
Beds: 1D
Baths: 1 Private
➳ (8) P (2) ⛌ Ⅲ. Ⓥ ▮ ⼂

(⛺ On Path) *Kemsing Youth Hostel, Church Lane, Kemsing, Sevenoaks, Kent, TN15 6LU.*
Actual grid ref: TQ5558
Warden: Ms J Dock.
Tel: **01732 761341**
Under 18: £5.55 **Adults:** £8.25
Family Bunk Rooms, Partially Heated, Showers, Evening Meal (7.00 pm), Shop, Television
Imposing Victorian vicarage in its own grounds at the foot of the North Downs

Wrotham 33

National Grid Ref: TQ6059

¶ ⛲ The Bull, Rose and Crown, Three Post Boys, Three Post Boys, Geaorge & Dragon

(On Path) *Hillside House, Gravesend Road, Wrotham, Sevenoaks, Kent, TN15 7JH.*
Family home on wooded hillside.
Tel: **01732 822564** Mrs Thomas.
Rates fr: *£16.00-£16.00*.
Open: All Year (not Xmas)
Beds: 2D 1S
Baths: 1 Shared
➳ ⊬ P ⛌ ⼍ ✗ Ⅲ. Ⓥ ▮ ⼂

(On Path) *Green Hill House, High Street, Wrotham, Sevenoaks, Kent, TN15 7AH.*
Actual grid ref: TQ611592
Quietly situated comfortable family house.
Grades: ETB Reg
Tel: **01732 883069** Mrs Jolliffe.
Rates fr: *£16.00-£20.00*.
Open: All Year
Beds: 1F 1T
Baths: 1 Shared
➳ ⊬ ⛌ Ⅲ. ▮ ⼂

St Mary's Platt 34

National Grid Ref: TQ6257

(1.75m) *Holmes, Boneashe Lane, St Mary's Platt, Sevenoaks, Kent, TN15 8NW.*
C15th Listed beamed hall farmhouse.
Grades: ETB Reg
Tel: **01732 882502**
Mrs Hickey.
Rates fr: *£15.00*.
Open: Apr to Oct
Beds: 1D 1T
Baths: 1 Shared
➳ (12) P (4) ⊬ ⛌ ✗ Ⅲ. Ⓥ

Fairseat 35

National Grid Ref: TQ6261

¶ ⛲ Plough

(0.5m) *The Old Post House, Fairseat, Sevenoaks, Kent, TN15 7LU.*
Actual grid ref: TQ632612
Pretty C18th house, lovely gardens.
Grades: ETB Listed
Tel: **01732 822444**
Mrs Gray.
Rates fr: *£16.00-£17.00*.
Open: All Year (not Xmas)
Beds: 1D 1T
Baths: 2 Shared
P (2) ⊬ ⛌ ✗ Ⅲ. Ⓥ

Trottiscliffe 36

National Grid Ref: TQ6460

¶ ⛲ The Plough, The George

(0.75m) *Bramble Park, Church Lane, Trottiscliffe, West Malling, Kent, ME19 5EB.*
Actual grid ref: TQ644563
Secluded, tranquil, Victorian rectory.
Grades: ETB Memb
Tel: **01732 822397**
Mrs Towler.
Rates fr: *£18.00-£18.00*.
Open: All Year
Beds: 1F 1T 1S
Baths: 2 Shared
➳ P (6) ⛌ Ⅲ. ▮ ⼂

Ryarsh 37

National Grid Ref: TQ6759

¶ ⛲ Duke of Wellington

(0.5m 🚲) *Heavers Farm, Ryarsh, West Malling, Kent, ME19 5JU.*
Actual grid ref: TQ665603
C17th comfortable farmhouse.
Tel: **01732 842074**
Mrs Edwards.
Rates fr: *£16.00-£20.00*.
Open: All Year (not Xmas)
Beds: 1D 2T
Baths: 1 Shared
➳ P (3) ⊬ ⛌ ⼍ ✗ Ⅲ. Ⓥ ▮ ⼂

Rochester 38

National Grid Ref: TQ7268

⎚⊆ Ship Inn, Man of Kent, Greyhound, Granville Arms, Coopers Arms, Queen Charlotte

(2.5m) *255 High Street, Rochester, Kent, ME1 1HQ.*
Actual grid ref: TQ748681
Victorian family house near station, French spoken.
Tel: **01634 842737** Mrs Thomas.
Rates fr: £13.00-£15.00.
Open: All Year (not Xmas)
Beds: 1F 1D 1T
Baths: 1 Private 1 Shared
⌂ ▣ (1) ⌷ ♿ ✦

(1m) *St Martin, 104 Borstal Road, Rochester, Kent, ME1 3BD.*
Actual grid ref: TQ737674
Comfortable Victorian home overlooking river.
Tel: **01634 848192** Mrs Colvin.
Rates fr: £14.00-£15.00.
Open: All Year (not Xmas)
Beds: 2T
Baths: 1 Shared
⌂ ⌷ ⽧ ✕ ▥ Ⓥ ♿ ✦

(0.5m) *St Ouen, 98 Borstal Road, Rochester, Kent, ME1 3BD.*
Victorian family house overlooking river.
Tel: **01634 843528** Mrs Beggs.
Rates fr: £15.00-£16.00.
Open: All Year
Beds: 1D 1T
Baths: 1 Shared
⌂ ⽧ ⌷ ⽧ ▥ ♿ ✦

Wouldham 39

National Grid Ref: TQ7164

(0.5m) *Wouldham Court Farmhouse, 246 High Street, Wouldham, Rochester, Kent, ME1 3TY.*
Actual grid ref: TQ714643
Beamed C16th house, inglenook fireplace.
Tel: **01634 683271** Ms Parnell.
Rates fr: £15.00-£15.00.
Open: All Year
Beds: 1F 1D 1S
Baths: 2 Shared
⌂ ▣ (1) ⽧ ⌷ ⽧ ✕ ▥ Ⓥ ♿ ✦

Borstal 40

National Grid Ref: TQ7366

⎚⊆ Inner Dowsing Light Ship

(0.25m) *Walnut Tree House, 21 Mount Road, Borstal, Rochester, Kent, ME1 3NQ.*
Comfortable, friendly, family house.
Tel: **01634 849355** Mrs Hext.
Rates fr: £15.00-£15.00.
Open: All Year (not Xmas)
Beds: 2T 1S
Baths: 1 Shared
⌂ ⽧ ⌷ ⽧ ▥ ✦

Allington 41

National Grid Ref: TQ7457

⎚⊆ Sir Thomas Wyatt, The Malta

(2m) *Conway House, 12 Conway Road, Allington, Maidstone, Kent, ME16 0HD.*
Comfortable family home.
Grades: ETB 2 Cr, Comm
Tel: **01622 688287** Mrs Backhouse.
Rates fr: £17.00-£20.00.
Open: All Year
Beds: 1F 1T 1S
Baths: 1 Shared
⌂ ▣ (5) ⌷ ✕ ▥ ♿ ♿ ✦

Maidstone 42

National Grid Ref: TQ7655

⎚⊆ Greyhound, Hare & Hounds, Hogshead, Pilot, Wheeler's Arms, Walnut Tree, Kings Arms, Chequers, The Old Plantation, Admiral Gordon

(2m) *Willington Court, Willington Street, Maidstone, Kent, ME15 8JW.*
Charming Tudor style listed building.
Grades: ETB 2 Cr, High Comm, AA 4 Q, Select
Tel: **01622 738885** Mrs Waterman.
Rates fr: £19.00-£25.00.
Open: All Year (not Xmas)
Beds: 2D 1T
Baths: 2 Ensuite 1 Private
▣ (6) ⌷ ▥ Ⓥ

(3m) *Wits End Guest House, 78 Bower Mount Road, Maidstone, Kent, ME16 8AT.*
Edwardian licensed guest house.
Grades: ETB 3 Cr
Tel: **01622 752684** Mrs King.
Rates fr: £17.00-£18.00.
Open: All Year
Beds: 2F 1D 2T 2S
Baths: 3 Ensuite 2 Shared
⌂ ▣ (10) ⌷ ⽧ ✕ ▥ ♿ Ⓥ

(1m) *Emmaus, 622 Loose Road, Maidstone, Kent, M E15 9UW.*
Large family house, originally post-office.
Tel: **01622 745745** Mrs Hodgson.
Rates fr: £16.00-£16.00.
Open: All Year
Beds: 2T 2S
⌂ (5) ▣ (3) ⽧ ⌷ ✦

(3m) *25 Holland Road, Maidstone, Kent, ME14 1UN.*
Victorian town house, warm welcome.
Tel: **01622 678606** Ms Davies-Wheeler.
Rates fr: £15.00-£16.00.
Open: All Year (not Xmas)
Beds: 1D 2T
⌂ ⽧ ⌷ ▥ Ⓥ ♿

Boxley 43

National Grid Ref: TQ7757

(1m) *Barn Cottage, Harbourland, Boxley, Maidstone, Kent, ME14 3DN.*
Listed converted C16th barn.
Tel: **01622 675891** Mrs Munson.
Rates fr: £15.00-£15.00.
Open: All Year (not Xmas)
Beds: 1D 2T
Baths: 1 Shared
⌂ (10) ▣ (6) ⽧ ⌷ ✕ ▥ Ⓥ ♿ ✦

Bearsted 44

National Grid Ref: TQ7955

⎚⊆ The White Horse, The Old Plantation, The Bell

(1.75m) *The Hazels, 13 Yeoman Way, Bearsted, Maidstone, Kent, ME15 8PQ.*
Large, comfortable family home.
Tel: **01622 737943** Mr & Mrs Buse.
Rates fr: £16.00-£16.00.
Open: All Year (not Xmas)
Beds: 2T
Baths: 1 Shared
⌂ (2) ▣ (2) ⽧ ⌷ ▥ ♿ ✦

Hollingbourne 45

National Grid Ref: TQ8455

⎚⊆ The Sugar Loaves, The Windmill, The Dirty Habit

(0.5m) *Woodhouses, 49 Eyhorne Street, Hollingbourne, Maidstone, Kent, ME17 1TR.*
Actual grid ref: TQ833546
Two inter-connected C17th cottages.
Grades: ETB Listed
Tel: **01622 880594** Mr & Mrs Woodhouse.
Rates fr: £17.00-£17.50.
Open: All Year
Beds: 3D
Baths: 3 Private
⌂ ▣ (2) ⽧ ⌷ ▥ Ⓥ ♿ ✦

(1m) *The Limes, 53 Eyhorne Street, Hollingbourne, Maidstone, Kent, ME17 1TS.*
Actual grid ref: TQ835545
Comfortable Georgian family home.
Tel: **01622 880554** Mrs Reed.
Rates fr: £16.00-£16.00.
Open: Jan to Nov
Beds: 1T 1S
Baths: 1 Ensuite 1 Shared
⌂ (10) ▣ (5) ⽧ ⌷ ▥ ♿ ✦

All rates are subject to alteration at the owners' discretion.

All paths are popular: you are well-advised to book ahead

Harrietsham 46

National Grid Ref: TQ8752

¶ ◖ The Roebuck

(On Path) *Mannamead*, *Pilgrims Way, Harrietsham, Maidstone, Kent, ME17 1BT*.
Actual grid ref: TQ8752
Quiet comfortable private house.
Grades: ETB 2 Cr
Tel: **01622 859336** Mrs Atkins.
Rates fr: *£16.00*-**£18.00**.
Open: All Year (not Xmas)
Beds: 1D 1T 1S
Baths: 1 Ensuite 1 Shared
ॐ ₽ (4) ⅏⌑⊁

Charing 47

National Grid Ref: TQ9549

¶ ◖ The Bowl, Queens Head, Royal Oak

(0.5m ⚘) *Arketts Farm*, *Charing, Ashford, Kent, TN27 0HH*.
Actual grid ref: TQ9552
C17th Listed farmhouse, woodlands, pasture.
Grades: ETB Listed
Tel: **01233 712893** Mrs Okell.
Rates fr: *£14.00*-**£15.00**.
Open: All Year (not Xmas)
Beds: 1D 1T **Baths:** 1 Shared
ॐ (3) ₽ (4) ⅏⌑⊁⋔✕▥Ⅵ⛯⊁
Also ⚊ *£2 per tent.*[T]⛭

(2.5m ⚘) *Barnfield*, *Charing, Ashford, Kent, TN27 0BN*.
Actual grid ref: TQ923484
Comfortable, quiet, C15th hall farmhouse.
Grades: ETB Listed, Comm, AA 3 Q
Tel: **01233 712421** Mrs Pym.
Rates fr: *£19.00*-**£21.00**.
Open: All Year
Beds: 2D 1T 1S
Baths: 1 Shared
ॐ ₽ (20) ⅏⌑⋔✕▥⊁

(0.5m ⚘) *Armada House*, 9 The High Street, *Charing, Ashford, Kent, TN27 0HU*.
Actual grid ref: TQ9549
Lovely house with wonderful views.
Grades: ETB Listed
Tel: **01233 712822** Mrs Bigwood.
Rates fr: *£16.50*-**£18.00**.
Open: Easter to Feb
Beds: 2D 1S
Baths: 2 Ensuite 1 Private
ॐ ₽ (4) ⅏⌑✕▥Ⅵ⛯⊁

Westwell 48

National Grid Ref: TQ9847

(0.25m) *Dean Court Farm*, *Challock Lane, Westwell, Ashford, Kent, TN25 4NH*.
Actual grid ref: TQ989488
Period farmhouse with modern comforts. **Grades:** ETB Listed
Tel: **01233 712924** Mrs Lister.
Rates fr: *£16.00*-**£17.00**.
Open: All Year
Beds: 2T **Baths:** 1 Shared
₽ (5) ⌑✕▥Ⅵ⊁
Also ⚊ *£4 per tent.*,
Open: All Year [T] ⛭

Kennington 49

National Grid Ref: TR0144

(1m ⚘) *Stone House*, *Faversham Road, Kennington, Ashford, Kent, TN25 4PQ*.
Actual grid ref: TR015456
Jacobean-style Listed building.
Tel: **01233 623776**
Mr & Mrs Buckler.
Rates fr: *£15.00*-**£15.00**.
Open: All Year (not Xmas)
Beds: 3T **Baths:** 2 Shared
ॐ (5) ₽ (4) ⅏⌑✕▥Ⅵ⛯⊁

Ashford 50

National Grid Ref: TR0042

¶ ◖ Hare & Hound

(3.75m) *Vickys Guest House*, *38 Park Road North, Ashford, Kent, TN24 8LY*.
Large Victorian private house.
Tel: **01233 631061** Mrs Ford.
Rates fr: *£17.00*-**£15.00**.
Open: All Year
Beds: 1F 1T **Baths:** 2 Ensuite
ॐ ₽ (4) ⌑✕▥⛯⊁

(4m) *Quantock House*, *Quantock Drive, Ashford, Kent, TN24 8QH*.
Family-run, comfortable and welcoming.
Grades: ETB 2 Cr, Comm
Tel: **01233 638921**
Mr & Mrs Tucker.
Rates fr: *£17.00*-**£18.00**.
Open: All Year (not Xmas)
Beds: 1D 1T 1S **Baths:** 3 Private
ॐ (7) ₽ (3) ⌑✕▥Ⅵ

Boughton Aluph 51

National Grid Ref: TR0348

¶ ◖ Flying Horse Inn (Boughton Aluph)

(0.25m ⚘) *Warren Cottage*, *Boughton'Aluph, Ashford, Kent, TN25 4HS*.
All home comforts, true Kentish hospitality.
Tel: **01233 740483** Mrs Fearne.
Rates fr: *£12.00*-**£15.00**.
Open: All Year (not Xmas)
Beds: 2D **Baths:** 1 Shared
ॐ ₽ (6) ⅏⌑⋔▥⛯⊁

(On Path) *Flying Horse Inn*, *Boughton Aluph, Ashford, Kent, TN25 4HS*.
Open fires, beams, comfortable, friendly reception.
Grades: ETB Listed
Tel: **01233 620914** Ms Smith.
Rates fr: *£17.50*-**£20.00**.
Open: All Year (not Xmas)
Beds: 3D 1T
Baths: 2 Shared
ॐ (14) ₽ (60) ⌑✕▥Ⅵ⛯⊁
Also ⚊ *£5 per tent.*,
Open: All Year (not Xmas)
[T] ⛭ ✕⛷

If you are walking the Canterbury Loop alternative, please see p.107

Wye 52

National Grid Ref: TR0546

¶ ◖ New Flying Horse

(0.25m) *The New Flying Horse*, *Upper Bridge Street, Wye, Ashford, Kent, TN25 5AN*.
Traditional country pub.
Grades: ETB 3 Cr
Tel: **01233 812297** Mrs Evans.
Rates fr: *£22.50*-**£35.00**.
Open: All Year (not Xmas)
Beds: 1F 4D 4T 1S
Baths: 10 Private
ॐ ₽ ⌑⋔✕▥Ⅵ⛯

Hastingleigh 53

National Grid Ref: TR0944

(0.5m) *Hazel Tree Farm*, *Hassell Street, Hastingleigh, Ashford, Kent, TN25 5JE*.
C15th farmhouse in pretty garden.
Grades: ETB Listed
Tel: **01233 750324**
Mrs Gorell Barnes.
Rates fr: *£16.00*-**£16.00**.
Open: Easter to Oct
Beds: 2D 2T
Baths: 2 Shared
ॐ ₽ (6) ⌑⋔✕▥Ⅵ

Stowting 54

National Grid Ref: TR1241

¶ ◖ The Tiger Inn

(On Path) *Water Farm*, *Stowting, Ashford, Kent, TN25 6BA*.
Actual grid ref: TR1241
Homely, comfortable lakeside farmhouse.
Grades: ETB Listed
Tel: **01303 862401** Mrs Cole.
Rates fr: *£17.00*-**£17.00**.
Open: All Year (not Xmas)
Beds: 1F 1T
Baths: 1 Ensuite, 1 Private
ॐ (8) ₽ (2) ⅏⌑▥Ⅵ⛯⊁

> Many rates vary according to season - the lowest only are shown here

Farthing Common 55

National Grid Ref: TR1340

|◎| 🍺 Drum Inn

(On Path 🚐) *Southfields, Farthing Common, Lyminge, Folkestone, Kent, CT18 8DH.*
Actual grid ref: TR138404
Home comfort with panoramic views.
Tel: **01303 862391** Ms Wadie.
Rates fr: *£15.00-£15.00.*
Open: May to Sept
Beds: 1F 1T
Baths: 1 Shared
🛇 ℗ (6) ⅃✓☐✗⛟ Ⓥ 🛈 ✏

Newington 56

National Grid Ref: TR1737

(2.75m 🚐) *Beachborough Park, Newington, Folkestone, Kent, CT18 8BW.*
Converted barn accommodation.
Grades: ETB 3 Cr, Approv
Tel: **01303 275432** Mr Wallis.
Rates fr: *£20.00-£25.00.*
Open: All Year
Beds: 2F 3D 3T
Baths: 8 Ensuite
🛇 ℗ (30) ☐ 🛏 ✗ ⛟ Ⓥ 🛈 ✏

Hythe 57

National Grid Ref: TR1634

|◎| 🍺 Duke's Head

(3.5m 🚐) *Nyanza Lodge Hotel, 87 Seabrook Road, Hythe, Kent, CT21 5RB.*
Large Edwardian, one acre, parking, seaviews.
Grades: ETB 2 Cr, Approv
Tel: **01303 267315**
Rates fr: *£20.00-£25.00.*
Open: All Year (not Xmas)
Beds: 2F 3D 1T
Baths: 4 Ensuite 2 Shared
🛇 ℗ (6) ⅃✓☐ 🛏 ✗ ⛟ Ⓥ 🛈 ✏

Densole 58

National Grid Ref: TR2141

(5m 🚐) *Garden Lodge, 324 Canterbury Road, Densole, Folkestone, Kent, CT18 7BB.*
Home cooking, all meals.
Washbasins, central heating, TV lounge, garden.
Grades: ETB 1 Cr
Tel: **01303 893147**
Mrs Cooper, MCFA.

Rates fr: *£16.00-£16.00.*
Open: All Year
Beds: 3F 1D 2S
Baths: 2 Shared
🛇 ℗ (10) ⅃✓☐✗⛟ Ⓥ 🛈 ✏

Folkestone 59

National Grid Ref: TR2136

|◎| 🍺 Wards Bistro, Ship Inn, Metropole Bar, Burlington Bar, Clifton Hotel, Harveys Wine Bar, Richmond Tavern

(1.5m 🚐) *Abbey House Hotel, 5-6 Westbourne Gardens, Off Sandgate Road, Folkestone, Kent, CT20 2JA.*
Actual grid ref: TR217355
Friendly comfortable fully licensed hotel.
Grades: ETB 2 Cr
Tel: **01303 255514**
Mr Donoghue.
Rates fr: *£17.00-£18.00.*
Open: All Year
Beds: 4F 4D 4T 4S
Baths: 3 Private 3 Shared
🛇 ☐ 🛏 ✗ Ⓥ 🛈 ✏

(1.5m 🚐) *Wycliffe Hotel, 63 Bouverie Road West, Folkestone, Kent, CT20 2RN.*
Clean, comfortable, friendly family hotel.
Tel: **01303 252186**
Mr & Mrs Shorland.
Rates fr: *£15.00-£15.00.*
Open: All Year
Beds: 2F 4D 5T 2S
Baths: 3 Shared
🛇 ℗ (5) ☐ 🛏 ✗ Ⓥ 🛈 ✏

(2m 🚐) *Normandie Guest House, 39 Cheriton Road, Folkestone, Kent, CT20 1DD.*
Comfortable family-run guest house.
Grades: ETB Listed
Tel: **01303 256233**
Mrs Watts.
Rates fr: *£14.50-£14.50.*
Open: All Year (not Xmas)
Beds: 2F 1D 2T 1S
Baths: 1 Shared
🛇 (4) ☐ ⛟ 🛈

Capel-le-Ferne 60

National Grid Ref: TR2538

|◎| 🍺 Valiant Salor, Dove Hill

(On Path) *Xaipe, 18 Alexandra Road, Capel-le-Ferne, Folkestone, Kent, CT18 7LD.*
Actual grid ref: TR2539
Modern comfortable bungalow.
Tel: **01303 257956**
Mrs Strutt.
Rates fr: *£12.50-£12.00.*
Open: Mar to Oct
Beds: 1D 1T
Baths: 1 Shared
℗ (2) ⅃✓☐✗⛟ Ⓥ 🛈 ✏

South Alkham 61

National Grid Ref: TR3141

(0.5m) *Hopton Manor, Alkham Valley Road, South Alkham, Dover, Kent, CT15 7EL.*
Small manorhouse, parts dated C14th.
Grades: ETB 2 Cr, Comm
Tel: **01303 892481**
Mrs Walk.
Rates fr: *£18.00-£20.00.*
Open: All Year (not Xmas)
Beds: 2D 1T
Baths: 3 Ensuite
℗ (6) ⅃✓☐✗⛟

Chilham 62

National Grid Ref: TR0653

|◎| 🍺 The George, The White Horse, The Woolpack

(0.5m) *Cutlers Farmhouse, Chilham, Canterbury, Kent, CT4 8EU.*
Quiet, rural, flintstone farmhouse.
Tel: **01233 740349**
Mrs Dixon.
Rates fr: *£15.00-£18.00.*
Open: Apr to Oct
Beds: 1F 1D 1T
Baths: 1 Shared
🛇 ℗ (4) ☐ ⛟ 🛈

Canterbury 63

National Grid Ref: TR1457

|◎| 🍺 Bishops Anger, Kings Head, White Hart, Canterbury Tales,

(0.25m) *London Guest House, 14 London Road, Canterbury, Kent, CT2 8LR.*
Spacious Victorian town house.
Grades: ETB Listed
Tel: **01227 765860**
Mrs Harris.
Rates fr: *£17.50-£18.00.*
Open: All Year
Beds: 1F 1D 2T 2S
Baths: 2 Shared
🛇 ☐ ⛟ Ⓥ ✏

> The Grid Reference beneath the location heading is for the village or town - *not* for individual houses, which are shown (where supplied) in each entry itself.

Please don't camp on anyone's land without first obtaining their permission.

(On Path 🚍) *Alicante Guest House,* 4 Roper Road, Canterbury, Kent, *CT2 7EH.*
Victorian, good value, clean, comfortable.
Grades: ETB Listed, Comm
Tel: **01227 766277**
Rates fr: *£16.00-£20.00.*
Open: All Year
Beds: 2F 2D 1T 1S
🛏🍽🖾Ⅴ⅊✦

(▲ 0.5m) *Canterbury Youth Hostel,* 'Ellerslie', 54 New Dover Road, Canterbury, Kent, *CT1 3DT.*
Actual grid ref: TR1557
Warden: Ms S Hunter.
Tel: **01227 462911**
Under 18: £6.15 **Adults:** £9.10
Family Bunk Rooms, Centrally Heated, Showers, Evening Meal (6.30 pm), Shop, Security Lockers
A Victorian villa close to the centre of the principal cathedral city of England

(0.25m) *Abbey Lodge Guest House,* 8 New Dover Road, Canterbury, Kent, *CT1 3AP.*
Large Victorian family house.
Tel: **01227 462878**
Mrs Gardener.
Rates fr: *£15.00-£19.00.*
Open: All Year
Beds: 1F
Baths: 2 Ensuite
🛏🅿(16)⅊🖾Ⅴ

(1m) *Milton House,* 9 South Canterbury Road, Canterbury, Kent, *CT1 3LH.*
Quiet, comfortable, Edwardian family house.
Grades: ETB Reg
Tel: **01227 765531** Mrs Wright.
Rates fr: *£15.00-£17.00.*
Open: All Year (not Xmas)
Beds: 1D 1T **Baths:** 1 Shared
🅿🍽🖾Ⅴ

(On Path) *Oriel Lodge,* 3 Queens Avenue, Canterbury, Kent, *CT2 8AY.*
Actual grid ref: TR143580
Comfortable Edwardian family house.
Grades: ETB 2 Cr, Highly Comm, AA 3 Q, RAC Acclaim
Tel: **01227 462845**
Mr & Mrs Rishworth.
Rates fr: *£17.50-£20.00.*
Open: All Year
Beds: 1F 3D 1T 1S
Baths: 2 Private 2 Shared
🛏(6)🅿(6)⅊🖾

(0.25m) *Maynard Cottage,* 106 Wincheap, Canterbury, Kent, *CT1 3RS.*
C17th, excellent food, value and hospitality!.
Grades: ETB 1 Cr
Tel: **01227 454991 / 0850 315558**
F S Bianks.
Rates fr: *£17.50-£25.00.*
Open: All Year
Beds: 1F 1D 1T **Baths:** 1 Shared
🛏⅊🖾Ⅴ

(0.25m) *Clare Ellen Guest House,* 9 Victoria Rd, Canterbury, Kent, *CT1 3SG.*
Large elegant Victorian guest house.
Grades: ETB 2 Cr, High Comm
Tel: **01227 760205** Mr Williams.
Rates fr: *£22.00-£22.00.*
Open: All Year **Beds:** 1F 2D 2T 2S
Baths: 5 Ensuite 2 Shared
🛏🅿🖾Ⅴ✦

(0.5m 🚍) *Little Courtney Guest House,* 5 Whitstable Road, St Dunstans, Canterbury, Kent, *CT2 8DG.*
Grades: ETB Listed
Tel: **01227 454207** Mrs Sheath.
Rates fr: *£16.00-£17.00.*
Open: All Year
Beds: 2T 1S
Baths: 1 Shared
🅿(1)⅊🖾✦

Adisham 64

National Grid Ref: TR2253

🍽🍺 Moors Head

(2.25m) *Moors Head Hotel,* Station Approach, Adisham, Canterbury, Kent, *CT3 3JE.*
Large Victorian country house.
Grades: ETB Listed
Tel: **01304 840935** Mr Tovee.
Rates fr: *£17.50-£25.00.*
Open: All Year
Beds: 2F 3D 2T 1S
Baths: 2 Shared
🛏🅿(30)🍽🖾Ⅴ

Shepherdswell 65

National Grid Ref: TR2547

🍽🍺 The Bell Courage, Village Green

(On Path 🚍) *Sunshine Cottage,* The Green, Shepherdswell, Dover, Kent, *CT15 7LQ.*
Actual grid ref: TR262478
C17th cottage on village green.
Grades: ETB 2 Cr, Comm
Tel: **01304 831359 / 831218**
Mrs Popple.
Rates fr: *£16.00-£20.00.*
Open: All Year
Beds: 1F 3D 2T
Baths: 2 Private, 4 Shared
🛏🅿(6)⅊🖾Ⅶ& Ⅴ⅊✦

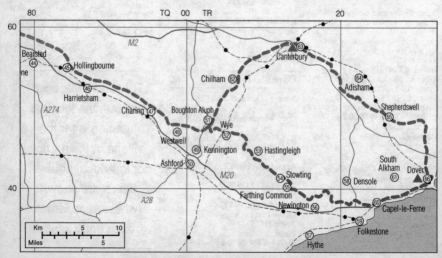

Dover 66

National Grid Ref: TR3141

⁅●⁆ ⛢ White Horse, Red Lion, Park Inn

(0.25m) *Pennyfarthing,*
109 Maison Dieu Road, Dover,
Kent, CT16 1RT.
Old Victorian guesthouse.
Grades: ETB 2 Cr,
RAC High Acclaim
Tel: **01304 205563**
Mrs McPherson.
Rates fr: *£17.00-£20.00.*
Open: All Year (not Xmas)
Beds: 2F 2D 1T 1S
Baths: 5 Private 1 Shared
ప 🅿 ⌖ ▥ ⓘ ⚡

(▲ 0.5m) *Dover Youth Hostel,*
306 London Road, Dover, Kent,
CT17 0SY.
Actual grid ref: TR311421
Warden: Mr S Martin.
Tel: **01304 201314**
Under 18: £6.15 **Adults:** £9.10

Family Bunk Rooms, Centrally Heated, Showers, Evening Meal (7.00 pm), Shop, Television, Security Lockers, Games Room *There are two buildings for hostel accommodation in historic Dover, both recently refurbished*

(0.25m) *Bleriot's Guest House,*
47 Park Avenue, Dover, Kent,
CT16 1HE.
Family-run, quiet, central location.
Grades: ETB 2 Cr
Tel: **01304 203643**
Mr Casey.
Rates fr: *£14.00-£18.00.*
Open: All Year (not Xmas)
Beds: 5F 1D 1T 1S
Baths: 5 Ensuite 3 Shared
ప 🅿 (8) ⌖ ✗ ▥

(On Path) *Gladstone Guest House,*
3 Laureston Place, Dover, Kent,
CT16 1QX.
Large Victorian house.
Grades: ETB 2 Cr
Tel: **01304 208457** Mrs Davies.
Rates fr: *£16.00-£18.00.*

Open: All Year (not Xmas)
Beds: 2D 2T 1S
Baths: 3 Ensuite 2 Shared
ప (10) ⌫ ⌖ ▥ Ⓥ ⓘ ⚡

(2m) *Longfield Guest House,*
203 Folkestone Road, Dover, Kent,
CT17 9SL.
Family-run guest house.
Grades: ETB Listed
Tel: **01304 204716** Mrs Elson.
Rates fr: *£14.00-£14.00.*
Open: All Year (not Xmas)
Beds: 1F 1D 1T 6S
Baths: 1 Ensuite 2 Shared
ప (2) 🅿 (8) ⌖ ✗ ▥ ⓘ

(1.25m) *Elmo Guest House, 120*
Folkestone Road, Dover, Kent,
CT17 9SP.
Family run guest house.
Grades: ETB 1 CrRAC Listed
Tel: **01304 206236** Mr Christo.
Rates fr: *£24.00-£12.00.*
Open: All Year
Beds: 3F 2D 1S
Baths: 2 Ensuite 1 Shared
ప 🅿 (7) ⌖ ✗ ▥ Ⓥ ⓘ ⚡

Offa's Dyke Path

This is a splendid 168-mile trail through the Welsh Marches, roughly following the line of a large wall and ditch built as a border by an Anglo-Saxon king. From Chepstow to Prestatyn, the terrain changes every 15 miles or so - riverside walk, castle country, the Black Mountains, lonely moorland, canal towpath, old mining land and the Clwydian Hills - making the trail different every day. The ancient Dyke itself is prominent at many points of the walk, giving that strange feeling that you are walking where others, too, paced with purpose hundreds of years ago. The walking is for the most part moderately easy, with the main obstacle the extraordinary number of stiles. It can, however, be difficult on the hills in mist and wet weather, so make sure you have the right kit with you.

The path is supported by the **Offa's Dyke Association** (Offa's Dyke Centre, West St, Knighton, Powys, LD7 1EW) who promote the path with great verve and application; its prime movers, Ernie and Kathy Kay, wrote the Aurum Press/OS book mentioned below with Mark Richards. The association sells a large range of books, maps and branded merchandise and your membership would certainly help in the conservation of the path. There is also a taxi-based service, handling luggage delivery, safe car-parking and passenger back-up along the entire path - **White Knight** (tel. 01903 766475, please see advertisement). It provides a useful fallback for weary or injured walkers or just those who do not wish to carry a large pack.

Guides (available from all good map shops, unless stated)

Offa's Dyke North (ISBN 1 85410 2958) and *Offa's Dyke South* (ISBN 1 85410 3229) by Ernie & Kathy Kay and Mark Richards, published by Aurum Press in association with the Countryside Commission and Ordnance Survey, £9.99

Langton's Guide to the Offa's Dyke Path by Andrew Durham (ISBN 1 899242 02 3), published by Langton's Guides and also available directly from the publishers (Ashleigh, Radley Road, Halam, Newark, Notts, NG22 8AQ, tel. 01636 813883), £12.99

Through Welsh Border Country (following Offa's Dyke Path) by Mark Richards, published by Thornhill Press and also available from the Rambler's Association National Office (1/5 Wandsworth Road, London, SW8 2XX, tel. 0171 582 6878), £4.50 (+70p p&p)

Walking Offa's Dyke Path by David Hunter, published by Cicerone Press and available from all good map shops or directly from the publishers (2 Police Square, Milnthorpe, Cumbria, LA7 7PY, 01539 562069), £8.99 (+ 75p p&p)

A Guide to Offa's Dyke Path by C J Wright, published by Constable & Co Ltd and available from all good bookshops, £8.95

Maps: 1:50000 Ordnance Survey Landranger Series: 116, 117, 126, 137, 148, 161 and 162.

Comments on the path to: **Jim Saunders**, Offa's Dyke Development Officer, Offa's Dyke Centre, West St, Knighton, Powys, LD7 1EW.

Sedbury 1

National Grid Ref: ST5493

📶 Live & Let Live

(0.5m 🚌) **Upper Sedbury House,** Sedbury Lane, Sedbury, Chepstow, Gwent, NP6 7HN.
Actual grid ref: ST547943
Quaint, cottagey, superior country house.
Grades: WTB 2 Cr •
Tel: **01291 627173** Mrs Potts.
Rates fr: £16.50-£18.00.
Open: All Year (not Xmas)
Beds: 1F 1D 1T
Baths: 1 Ensuite 1 Shared
🛏 🅿 (10) 🗗 🛏 ✕ 🖩 🔽 🅸 ✦
Also 🅰 £2.00 per tent.,
Open: Easter to Oct🅃 🎚 ✕ ✦ 🕭

Chepstow 2

National Grid Ref: ST5393

📶 Rising Sun, Bridge Inn, Castle View Hotel

(0.3m 🚌) **Lower Hardwick House,** Mount Pleasant, Chepstow, Gwent, NP6 5PT.
Beautiful Georgian house, walled garden.
Tel: **01291 622162**
Mrs Grassby.
Rates fr: £14.00-£14.00.
Open: All Year
Beds: 2F 1D 1T 1S
Baths: 1 Private, 2 Shared
🛏 🅿 (12) 🗗 🛏 ✕ 🖩 🅸 ✦
Also 🅰 £5.00 per tent.
Open: All Year ⓡ 🅃 ✦ 🕭

(0.5m) *Castle Guest House,* 4 Bridge Street, Chepstow, Gwent, NP6 5EY.
Actual grid ref: ST435941
Large Georgian house.
Tel: **01291 622040**
Mr & Mrs Cherrington.
Rates fr: £17.50-£17.50.
Open: All Year **Beds:** 1F 1D 1T 1S
Baths: 4 Ensuite 🛏 🅿 (3) 🛏 🖩 🔽

(1m 🚌) *Langcroft,* 71 St Kingsmark Avenue, Chepstow, Gwent, NP6 5LY.
Actual grid ref: ST529938
Modern comfortable family friendly home. **Grades:** WTB Listed
Tel: **01291 625569** Mrs Langdale.
Rates fr: £15.00-£15.00.
Open: All Year **Beds:** 1D 1T 1S
Baths: 1 Shared
🛏 🅿 (3) 🗗 🛏 🖩 🔽 🅸 ✦

(1.25m) *Cobweb Cottage, Belle Vue Place, Streep Street, Chepstow, Monmouthshire, NP6 5PL.* Quiet, secluded, comfortable period cottage.
Grades: WTB 1 Cr
Tel: **01291 626643**
Mrs Warren.
Rates fr: *£16.50-£18.00.*
Open: All Year (not Xmas)
Beds: 1D 1T
Baths: 1 Shared
🛏 (5) 🅿 (6) 🗇 🖵 🏠 🎞

Pwllmeyric 3

National Grid Ref: ST5192

🍴 🍷 New Inn

(2m) *Bridge House, Pwllmeyric, Chepstow, Monmouthshire, NP6 6LF.* Comfortable friendly home.
.**Grades:** WTB Listed
Tel: **01291 622567** Mrs Gleed.
Rates fr: *£15.00-£16.00.*
Open: All Year
Beds: 1F 1D
🅿 (4) 🖵 🎞,

Tutshill 4

National Grid Ref: ST5494

🍴 🍷 Live & Let Live

(0.25m) 🚌 *The Vicarage, Gloucester Road, Tutshill, Chepstow, Gwent, NP6 7DH.*
Actual grid ref: ST543947
Large house in large gardens.
Tel: **01291 622442** Mrs Green.
Rates fr: *£16.00-£16.00.*
Open: Feb to Oct
Beds: 1D 2S
Baths: 1 Shared
🛏 🅿 (4) 🗇 🗙 🎞 Ⓥ 🔥 🍴

Tintern 5

National Grid Ref: SO5300

🍴 🍷 Wye Valley Hotel, Rose & Crown

(0.75m) *The Old Rectory, Tintern, Gwent, NP6 6SG.*
Actual grid ref: SO529008
Welcoming, comfortable early Victorian house.

Grades: WTB 1 Cr
Tel: **01291 689519**
Mrs Newman.
Rates fr: *£14.50-£14.50.*
Open: All Year
Beds: 1F 1D 2T 1S
Baths: 1 Shared
🛏 🅿 (8) 🗇 🏠 🗙 🎞 Ⓥ 🔥 🍴

Bigsweir 6

National Grid Ref: SO5305

(0.25m) 🚌 *Blue Barn, The Hudnalls, Bigsweir, St Briavels, Lydney, Glos, GL15 6RT.*
Actual grid ref: S05203
New Continental design house.
Grades: WTB 3 Cr
Tel: **01594 530252**
Ms Parker.
Rates fr: *£18.50-£18.50.*
Open: All Year
Beds: 3D 2T 2S
Baths: 7 Ensuite
🅿 (15) 🗇 🖵 🗙 🎞 Ⓥ 🔥 🍴
Also ⛺ *£5 per person. Also bunkhouse, £5 per bunk*
Open: All Year 🔥 🎞 🌡 🗙 🍴 🛏

St Briavels   7

National Grid Ref: SO5604

⭑ ◧ The George, Crown Inn

(On Path 🚗) *Tyersall*, *St Briavels, Lydney, Glos, GL15.*
Actual grid ref: SO537037
Wisteria covered period farmhouse.
Tel: **01594 530215** Mrs Morgan.
Rates fr: £15.50-£15.50.
Open: Easter to Nov
Beds: 1D 1T 1S
Baths: 1 Ensuite, 1 Shared
⛻ ▣ (4) ⠀⤬ ⠀⤬ ▥ ▤ ⓥ ▮ ✦

(⛰ 1m) *St Briavels Castle Youth Hostel*, The Castle, St Briavels, Lydney, Glos, GL15 6RG.
Actual grid ref: SO5504
Warden: J & E Cotterill.
Tel: **01594 530272**
Under 18: £5.55 Adults: £8.25
Partially Heated, Showers, Evening
Meal (7.00 pm)
800-year-old moated Norman castle used by King John as a hunting lodge, in the centre of a quiet village above the River Wye

(1m) *Ghyll House Farm*, St Briavels, Lydney, Glos, GL15 6UQ.
Grade II Listed Edwardian working farm.
Tel: **01594 530341** Mrs Price.
Rates fr: £14.00-£14.00.
Open: Easter to Oct
Beds: 1F 1D
Baths: 1 Shared
⛻ (3) ▣ ▢ ▥ ▮ ✦

(0.5m) *Woodcroft*, Lower Meend, St Briavels, Lydney, Glos, GL15 6RW.
Actual grid ref: SO552042
Stone house set in 5-acre small-holding.
Tel: **01594 530083** Mrs Allen.
Rates fr: £15.00-£15.00.
Open: All Year (not Xmas)
Beds: 2F
Baths: 2 Private
⛻ ▣ (7) ⤬ ▢ ▥ ▥ ▮ ✦

(On Path 🚗) *Offas Mead*, The Fence, St Briavels, Lydney, Glos, GL15 6QG.
Actual grid ref: SO544056
Spacious country house, superb views.
Grades: ETB 1 Cr
Tel: **01594 530229** Mrs Lacey.
Rates fr: £14.50-£16.00.
Open: All Year (not Xmas)
Beds: 2F 1T
Baths: 2 Private 1 Shared
⛻ (8) ▣ (5) ⤬ ▢ ▥ ▥ ⓥ ▮ ✦

(On Path) *Oak Cottage*, St Briavels Common, St Briavels, Lydney, Glos, GL15 6SJ.
Actual grid ref: SO538035
Comfortable country cottage, lovely views.
Tel: **01594 530440**
Mr & Mrs Watts.
Rates fr: £15.00-£15.00.

Open: Easter to Nov
Beds: 1T 1S **Baths:** 1 Shared
▣ (2) ⤬ ▢ ⤬ ▥ ▮
Also ⛺ £3.00 per tent.,
Open: Easter to Sep ⓡ ⓣ ⤬ ⓰

Llandogo   8

National Grid Ref: SO5204

⭑ ◧ The Sloop Inn

(1.5m) *The Sloop Inn*, Llandogo, Monmouth, Gwent, NP5 4TW.
Actual grid ref: SO526042
Grades: WTB 3 Cr, AA Recomm,
RAC Listed
Tel: **01594 530291** Mr Morgan.
Rates fr: £19.50-£22.50.
Open: All Year
Beds: 1F 2D 1T
Baths: 4 Ensuite
⛻ (8) ▣ (30) ▢ ⤬ ⤬ ▥ ⓥ ▮ ✦
Traditional hostelry with ensuite character bedrooms. Wholesome food at realistic prices and a cheerful atmosphere make this award winning inn a popular place to stay.

Trellech   9

National Grid Ref: SO5005

⭑ ◧ Lion Inn

(3.25m) *Woodfields*, Trellech, Monmouth, Monmouthshire, NP5 4PF.
Country bungalow, large garden, swimming pool.
Grades: WTB 1 Cr
Tel: **01600 860220** Mrs Smith.
Rates fr: £14.00-£14.00.
Open: All Year
Beds: 1D 1T 1S **Baths:** 1 Shared
⛻ ▣ (5) ▢ ▥ � ⓥ

Redbrook   10

National Grid Ref: SO5310

⭑ ◧ Bush Inn

(On Path) *Tresco*, Redbrook, Monmouth, Gwent, NP5 4LY.
Actual grid ref: SO536101
All ground floor bedrooms.
Tel: **01600 712325** Mrs Evans.
Rates fr: £14.00-£14.00.
Open: All Year
Beds: 1D 1T 2S **Baths:** 2 Shared
⛻ ▣ ▢ ⤬ ⤬ ▥ ⓰ ⓥ ▮ ✦

Penallt   11

National Grid Ref: SO5210

(1m 🚗) *Cherry Orchard Farm*, Lone Lane, Penallt, Monmouth, Gwent, NP5 4AJ.
Actual grid ref: SO5210
C18th stone farmhouse.
Grades: WTB Listed
Tel: **01600 714010** Mrs Beale.
Rates fr: £15.00-£15.00.
Open: All Year
Beds: 1D 1T **Baths:** 2 Shared
⛻ ▣ (6) ⤬ ⤬ ⤬ ▥ ⓥ ▮ ✦

Monmouth   12

National Grid Ref: SO5012

⭑ ◧ The Riverside Hotel Pub, Robin Hood, Britannia Inn, Punch House, Vine Tree, Somerset Arms, Queens Head

(On Path) *Burton House*, St James Square, Monmouth, Gwent, NP5 3DN.
Actual grid ref: SO512129
Large Georgian town house.
Grades: WTB Listed
Tel: **01600 714958**
Mrs Banfield.
Rates fr: £16.50-£16.50.
Open: All Year (not Xmas)
Beds: 1F 1D 1T
▣ (3) ▢ ⤬ ▥ ▮ ✦

(⛰ 0.5m) *Monmouth Youth Hostel*, Priory School, Priory Street, Monmouth, Gwent, NP5 3NX.
Actual grid ref: SO5013
Warden: Ms B Elias.
Tel: **01600 715116**
Under 18: £4.60
Adults: £6.75
Family Bunk Rooms, Partially Heated, Showers, Self-Catering Only, Shop
In the remains of a late C15th priory, this building, alongside the River Monnow was used as a school for 200 years until 1970

(On Path) *Red Lion House*, 16 Drybridge Street, Monmouth, Gwent, NP5 3AD.
C17th private town house.
Tel: **01600 713633**
Mrs Frost.
Rates fr: £12.50-£14.00.
Open: All Year (not Xmas)
Beds: 1D 2T
Baths: 2 Shared
▣ ▢ ▥

(0.5m 🚗) *Troy Lodge*, Monmouth, Gwent, NP5 4HX.
Actual grid ref: SO509116
Comfortable annexe with own sitting-room.
Tel: **01600 715098**
Mr & Mrs Bennett.
Rates fr: £17.50-£17.50.
Open: All Year (not Xmas)
Beds: 1D 1T
Baths: 1 Private 1 Shared
⛻ (5) ▣ (2) ⤬ ▢ ⤬ ▥ ⓥ ✦
Also ⛺ £1.50 per person.
Open: Apr - Oct ⓡ ⓣ ⤬ ⤬ ✦ ⓰

(0.25m 🚗) *Riverside Hotel,*
Cinderhill Street, Monmouth,
Gwent, NP5 3EY.
Outstanding converted C17th
coaching inn.
Grades: WTB 4 Cr, High Comm,
AA 2 St
Tel: 01600 715577
Mr Dodd.
Rates fr: *£20.00-£25.00.*
Open: All Year
Beds: 2F 6D 9T
Baths: 17 Private
🛏 (1) 🅿 (50) 🎽 🗗 🛏 ✕ 🛍 ⓖ ♉ ⓥ ▮
♉

(0.25m) *Wye Avon, Dixton Road,*
Monmouth, NP5 3PR.
Large Victorian private house.
Tel: 01600 713322
Mrs Cantrell.
Rates fr: *£14.00-£14.00.*
Open: All Year (not Xmas)
Beds: 1F 1D 1T 1S
Baths: 1 Shared
🛏 🅿 🎽 🛍.

(0.75m 🚗) *Caseta Alta,*
15 Toynbee Close, Osbaston,
Monmouth, Gwent, NP5 3NU.
Actual grid ref: SO505140
Comfortable "upside-down" house.
Welcome-Host Certificate.
Grades: WTB Listed
Tel: 01600 713023
Mrs Allcock.
Rates fr: *£16.50-£18.50.*
Open: All Year (not Xmas)
Beds: 2D 1T 1S
Baths: 1 Ensuite 1 Shared
🛏 (8) 🅿 (2) 🗗 ✕ 🛍 ⓥ ▮ ♉

Osbaston 13

National Grid Ref: SO5014

(1m 🚗) *Caseta Alta, 15 Toynbee*
Close, Osbaston, Monmouth,
Gwent, NP5 3NU.
Grades: WTB Listed
Tel: 01600 713023
Mrs Allcock.
Rates fr: *£13.00-£18.50.*
Open: All Year (not Xmas)
Beds: 2D 1T 1S
Baths: 1 Private 1 Shared
🛏 (8) 🅿 (2) 🗗 ✕ 🛍 ⓥ ▮ ♉
Comfortable 'upside-down' house.
Glorious views. Colour TV, radio,
tea/coffee facilities in bedrooms.
Evening meals by arrangement.
Wye Valley Walk 1/2 mile away.
Welcome Host certificate

> **All paths are**
> **popular: you are**
> **well-advised to**
> **book ahead**

Mitchel Troy 14

National Grid Ref: SO4910

(2m 🚗) *Church Farm Guest*
House, Mitchel Troy, Monmouth,
Gwent, NP5 4HZ.
Actual grid ref: SO492103
C16th beamed former farmhouse.
Grades: WTB 2 Cr Comm,
AA 2 Q
Tel: 01600 712176 Mrs Ringer.
Rates fr: *£17.00-£17.00.*
Open: All Year
Beds: 2F 3D 2T 1S
Baths: 6 Private, 2 Shared
🛏 🅿 (8) 🎽 🗗 🛏 ✕ 🛍 ⓥ ▮ ♉

Dingestow 15

National Grid Ref: SO4510

🍴 🍺 Somerset Arms

(1.5m 🚗) *The Lilacs, Dingestow,*
Monmouth, Gwent, NP5 4DZ.
Actual grid ref: SO435103
Country cottage off beaten track.
Tel: 01600 740686 Mrs Clark.
Rates fr: *£12.50-£12.50.*
Open: All Year (not Xmas)
Beds: 1D 2S **Baths:** 1 Shared
🛏 🅿 (1) 🗗 🛏 ✕ 🛍 ⓥ ▮ ♉

(0.5m 🚗) *Upper Llantrothy*
Farm, Dingestow, Monmouth,
Gwent, NP5 4EB.
Secluded working farm, warm
welcome.
Grades: WTB Listed
Tel: 01600 740685 Mrs Adamson.
Rates fr: *£15.00-£20.00.*
Open: All Year **Beds:** 1F 1D 1T
Baths: 1 Private 1 Shared
🛏 🅿 (4) 🗗 ✕ 🛍 ⓥ ▮ ♉

(2.5m) *New House Farm,*
Dingestow, Monmouth, Gwent,
NP5 4EB.
Comfortable farmhouse on work-
ing farm.
Grades: WTB Listed
Tel: 01600 83245 Mrs Smith.
Rates fr: *£15.00-£18.00.*
Open: All Year **Beds:** 3F 1D
🛏 🅿 ✕ 🛏 🛍 ⓥ ▮

(5m 🚗) *Lower Pen-y-Clawdd*
Farm, Dingestow, Monmouth,
Gwent, NP5 4BG.
Old converted cider mill.
Grades: WTB 1 Cr
Tel: 01600 83223 Mrs Bayliss.
Rates fr: *£15.00-£16.00.*
Open: All Year **Beds:** 1F 1D 1T
Baths: 1 Shared
🛏 (1) 🅿 (10) 🎽 🗗 🛏 🛍.

Penrhos 16

National Grid Ref: SO4111

(1.5m 🚗) *Bottom Farm, Penrhos,*
Raglan, Gwent, NP5 2DE.
Actual grid ref: SO394122
C15th farmhouse, working farm.
Grades: WTB Listed
Tel: 01600 780216 Mrs Watkins.

Rates fr: *£13.00.*
Open: Feb to Nov
Beds: 1D 1T
Baths: 1 Shared
🛏 🅿 (10) 🎽 🗗 ✕ 🛍. ⓥ ▮ ♉

Tregaer 17

National Grid Ref: SO4110

(3m 🚗) *Court Robert, Tregaer,*
Raglan, Gwent, NP5 2BZ.
Actual grid ref: SO401098
C16th country house, large rooms.
Grades: WTB Listed
Tel: 01291 690709 Ms Paxton.
Rates fr: *£13.00-£15.00.*
Open: All Year (not Xmas)
Beds: 2F
Baths: 1 Shared
🛏 🅿 🛏 🛍. ⓥ ▮ ♉

Llanvihangel Ystern Llewern 18

National Grid Ref: SO4313

🍴 🍺 Halfway House, Taly Coed

(0.25m) *Mill House Farm,*
Llanvihangel Ystern Llewern,
Monmouth, Monmouthshire,
NP5 4HN.
Tradional C17th Welsh farmhouse.
Tel: 01600 780468
Mr & Mrs Anders.
Rates fr: *£15.00-£15.00.*
Open: All Year
Beds: 1F 1D 1T 1S
Baths: 1 Ensuite 1 Shared
🛏 🅿 🎽 ✕ 🛍. ⓥ

Norton 19

National Grid Ref: SO4420

🍴 🍺 The Bell Inn

(0.75 m from Castles Alternative 🚗)
Brook Cottage, Norton, Skenfrith,
Abergavenny, Gwent,
NP7 8UB.
Actual grid ref: SO443201
Converted chapel in rural Wales.
Grades: WTB Listed
Tel: 01600 750319 Miss Finn.
Rates fr: *£13.00-£13.00.*
Open: All Year (not Xmas)
Beds: 1F 1D 1S
Baths: 1 Shared
🛏 🅿 (3) 🗗 🛍. ⓥ ▮ ♉

Llantilio Crossenny 20

National Grid Ref: SO3914

🍴 💷 Three Salmon, Hunter's Moon, Halfway

(0.5m) *Treloyvan Farm, Llantilio Crossenny, Abergavenny, Gwent, NP7 8UE.*
Actual grid ref: SO385172
Converted C17th farmhouse.
Grades: WTB 1 Cr
Tel: **01600 780478**
Mr & Mrs Watkins.
Rates fr: *£12.00-£14.00.*
Open: Mar to Nov
Beds: 1F 1T **Baths:** 2 Ensuite
🛇 🅿 (4) ⅊ 🗆 🛏 ✗ ⅏ 🎰 🗑 ♦ ⚯

Llanvetherine 21

National Grid Ref: SO3617

(0.5m 🚌) *Great Tre-Rhew Farm, Llanvetherine, Abergavenny, Gwent, NP7 8RA.*
Actual grid ref: SO377177
Ancient farmhouse on working farm. **Grades:** WTB Listed
Tel: **01873 821268** Ms Beavan.
Rates fr: *£13.00-£13.00.*
Open: All Year (not Xmas)
Beds: 1F 1D 1T **Baths:** 2 Shared
🛇 🅿 (8) 🗆 🛏 ✗ ⅏ 🗑 ♦ ⚯
Also ▲ *£1.00 per tent.*

Grosmont 22

National Grid Ref: SO4024

🍴 💷 Skirrid Mountain Inn

(4m but on Castles Alternative)
Lawns Farm, Grosmont, Abergavenny, Monmouthshire, NP7 8ES.
Beautiful old C17th farmhouse.
Grades: WTB 2 Cr, Comm
Tel: **01981 240298**
Mr & Mrs Ferneyhough.
Rates fr: *£18.00-£15.00.*
Open: Mar to Oct
Beds: 1F 1D1T **Baths:** 3 Ensuite
🛇 🅿 ⅊ 🗆 ⅏

Abergavenny 23

National Grid Ref: SO2914

🍴 💷 Walnut Tree Inn, Nanty-fyn Cider Mill, The Bear, Drum & Money

(5m) *The Guest House & Mansel Rest, 2 Oxford Street, Abergavenny, Gwent, NP7 5RP.*
Licensed restaurant, central to town.
Grades: WTB 1 Cr
Tel: **01873 854823** Mr & Mrs Cook.
Rates fr: *£16.00-£18.50.*
Open: All Year
Beds: 3F 5D 4T 2S
Baths: 4 Shared
🛇 🅿 🗆 ✗ ⅏ 🗑 ♦

(5m 🚌) *Pentre House, Brecon Road, Abergavenny, Gwent, NP7 7EW.*
Actual grid ref: SO283151
Delightful small Georgian country house.
Grades: WTB 1 Cr, High Comm
Tel: **01873 853435**
Mrs Reardon-Smith.
Rates fr: *£15.00-£18.00.*
Open: All Year
Beds: 3F 2D 1T **Baths:** 2 Shared
🛇 🅿 (4) 🗆 🛏 ✗ ⅏ 🗑 ♦ ⚯

(1m) *Lower House Farm, Old Hereford Road, Abergavenny, Gwent, NP7 7HR.*
Actual grid ref: SO304178
Recently converted bunk house.
Tel: **01873 853432** Mrs Smith.
Also ▲ *£3.00 per tent. Also bunkhouse, £3.00 per bunk.*
Open: All Year 🏠 🎰 ✗ ♿

(3m) *Ty'r Morwydd House, Pen-y-Pound, Abergavenny, Monmouthshire, NP7 5UD.*
Grades: WTB 1 Cr
Tel: **01873 855959** Mrs Senior.
Rates fr: *£12.50-£17.00.*
Open: All Year (not Xmas)
Beds: 19T 31S
Baths: 19 Shared
🛇 🅿 (30) ⅊ 🗆 🛏 ✗ ⅏ 🗑
Group training and conference bookings welcome. Georgian house wedded to modern accommodation. Most bedrooms H/C ensuite

Llantilio Pertholey 24

National Grid Ref: SO3116

🍴 💷 Red Hart, Halfway House, Mitre Inn, Walnut Tree Inn

(2.5m) *Wern Gochlyn Farm, Llantilio Pertholey, Abergavenny, Monmouthshire, NP7 8DB.*
Working farm with C12th farmhouse.
Tel: **01873 857357**
Mr Sage.
Rates fr: *£15.00-£18.00.*
Open: All Year
Beds: 1F 1D
Baths: 2 Private
🛇 (1) 🅿 (7) 🗆 🛏 ⅏

Llanvihangel Crucorney 25

National Grid Ref: SO3220

🍴 💷 Skirnd Inn

(0.5m) *The Skirrid Mountain Inn, Llanvihangel Crucorney, Abergavenny, Gwent, NP7 8DH.*
Actual grid ref: SO3220
Unique character C12th country inn.
Grades: WTB 3 Cr, Comm
Tel: **01873 890258**
Mrs Gant.
Rates fr: *£25.00-£25.00.*
Open: All Year
Beds: 1F 1D **Baths:** 2 Ensuite
🛇 🅿 (20) 🗆 🛏 ✗ ⅏ 🗑 ♦ ⚯

The lowest *double* rate per person is shown in *italics*.

(1.5m 🚌) *Penyclawdd Farm, Llanvihangel Crucorney, Abergavenny, Gwent, NP7 7LB.*
Comfortable farmhouse in Black Mountains.
Grades: WTB Listed, Comm, AA 3 Q
Tel: **01873 890591**
Mrs Davies.
Rates fr: *£15.00-£15.00.*
Open: All Year
Beds: 1F 1D
Baths: 1 Shared
🛇 🅿 (4) ⅊ 🗆 🛏 ⅏ 🗑 ♦ ⚯

Pandy 26

National Grid Ref: SO3322

🍴 💷 Pandy Inn, Park Hotel, Lancaster Arms, Offas Tavern, Skirrid Inn

(On Path) *Llanerch Farm, Pandy, Abergavenny, Gwent, NP7 8EW.*
Actual grid ref: SO345208
Georgian farmhouse, beautiful views, comfortable.
Grades: WTB 1 Cr
Tel: **01873 890432** Ms Ikin.
Rates fr: *£17.00-£17.00.*
Open: Easter to Nov
Beds: 1F **Baths:** 1 Ensuite
🛇 (1) 🅿 (6) 🗆 ✗ ⅏ 🗑 ♦ ⚯

(On Path 🚌) *Rhos Rhudd, Pandy, Abergavenny, Gwent, NP7 8DW.*
Actual grid ref: SO333218
Old Welsh stone cottage.
Tel: **01873 890703** Mrs Bray.
Rates fr: *£12.00-£12.00.*
Open: All Year (not Xmas)
Beds: 1F 1D 1T **Baths:** 1 Shared
🛇 (5) 🅿 (3) 🗆 🛏 ⅏ ♿ 🗑 ♦ ⚯

(0.25m) *Brynhonddu, Pandy, Abergavenny, Gwent, NP7 7PD.*
Actual grid ref: SO326224
Large C16th-C19th country house.
Grades: WTB Listed
Tel: **01873 890535** Mrs White.
Rates fr: *£13.50-£15.50.*
Open: All Year
Beds: 1D 1T **Baths:** 1 Shared
🛇 (5) 🅿 (6) 🗆 🛏 ⅏ 🗑 ♦ ⚯

Taking your dog?
Book in advance only with owners who accept dogs (🐕)

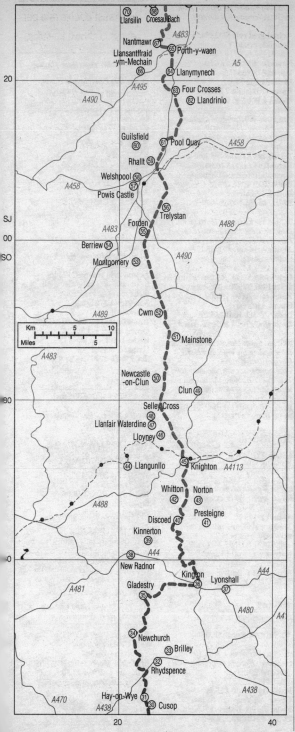

(0.25m 🚌) *Ty Newydd Farm,*
Pandy, Abergavenny, Gwent,
NP7 8DW.
Actual grid ref: SO335220
Victorian farmhouse.
Grades: WTB Listed
Tel: **01873 890235** Mrs Evans.
Rates fr: £14.00-£15.00.
Open: All Year (not Xmas)
Beds: 1D 2T
🛇 🅿 (20) 🖵 🍽 ✗ 🁢 Ⓥ ⚡
Also ⛺ *£2.00 per person.,*
Open: All Year 🏠 Ⓣ ✗ ⚡ ♿

Llanthony   27

National Grid Ref: SO2827

🍽 🍺 The Half Moon

(1m) *The Half Moon, Llanthony,*
Abergavenny, Gwent, NP7 7NN.
Actual grid ref: SO286278
Small, friendly country hotel.
Grades: WTB 1 Cr
Tel: **01873 890611** Mrs Smith.
Rates fr: £17.00-£20.00.
Open: All Year (not Xmas)
Beds: 1F 4D 2T **Baths:** 3 Shared
🛇 🅿 (5) 🍽 ✗ 🁢 Ⓥ ⚡

Longtown   28

National Grid Ref: SO3228

🍽 🍺 Crown Inn

(0.5m 🚌) *Olchon Cottage Farm,*
Turnant Road, Longtown,
Hereford, Herefordshire, HR2 0NS.
Actual grid ref: SO311294
Small working farm.
Grades: WTB 1 Cr, Comm
Tel: **01873 860233** Mrs Pritchard.
Rates fr: £15.00-£15.00.
Open: All Year (not Xmas)
Beds: 2F **Baths:** 1 Shared
🛇 🅿 🖵 🍽 ✗ Ⓥ ⚡

Capel-y-Ffin   29

National Grid Ref: SO2531

(⛰ 1.5m) *Capel-y-Ffin Youth*
Hostel, Capel-y-Ffin,
Abergavenny, Gwent, NP7 7NP.
Actual grid ref: SO2532
Warden: Ms D Evans.
Tel: **01873 890650**
Under 18: £4.60 **Adults:** £6.75
Partially Heated, Showers, Evening
Meal (7.30 pm), Shop, No
Smoking
An old hill farm set in 40-acre
grounds on the mountainside in the
Brecon Beacons National Park

(0.5m 🚌) *The Grange, Capel-y-*
Ffin, Abergavenny, Gwent, NP7 7NP.
Actual grid ref: SO251315
Small family farm guesthouse.
Grades: WTB 1 Cr
Tel: **01873 890215** Miss Griffiths.
Rates fr: £20.00-£20.00.
Open: Easter to Oct
Beds: 1F 1D 1T 1S
Baths: 1 Shared
🛇 (5) 🅿 (10) 🍽 ✗ 🁢 Ⓥ ⚡

Cusop 30

National Grid Ref: SO2341

⊯🍺Swan Hotel, Old Black Lion

(0.25m 🚐) *Fernleigh, Hardwick Road, Cusop, Hay-on-Wye, Hereford, Herefordshire, HR3 5QX.*
Large Victorian private house.
Tel: **01497 820459**
Mr Hughes.
Rates fr: *£14.00-£18.00.*
Open: Easter to Oct
Beds: 2D 1T
Baths: 1 Shared
🅿⊬🖵📖

Hay-on-Wye 31

National Grid Ref: SO2242

⊯🍺Black Lion, Pinocchios, The Swan, Blue Boar, Bull Ring

(On Path 🚐) *Tinto House, Broad Street, Hay-on-Wye, Hereford, Herefordshire, HR3 5DB.*
Comfortable Georgian town house.
Grades: WTB 2 Cr, Comm
Tel: **01497 820590**
Mrs Ratcliffe.
Rates fr: *£16.00.*
Open: Easter to Nov
Beds: 1F 1D 1T
Baths: 3 Ensuite
🛏🅿(2)🖵📖,🗹🛊⊬

(On Path) *Rosedale, Cusop, Hay-on-Wye, Hereford, Herefordshire, HR3 5RF.*
Actual grid ref: SO234417
Large Victorian house.
Tel: **01497 820804**
Mrs Jenkins.
Rates fr: *£14.50-£14.50.*
Open: All Year
Beds: 1F 2D 1T 2S
Baths: 1 Shared
🛏🅿(4)🖵📖,🗹🛊⊬
Also ⛺ *£2.50 per person.*
Open: All Year 🔥🆃🗙⊬♿

(0.2m 🚐) *Lansdowne, Cusop, Hay-on-Wye, Hereford, Herefordshire, HR3 5RF.*
Actual grid ref: SO237417
Large Victorian stone house.
Tel: **01497 820125**
Ms Flack.
Rates fr: *£15.00-£20.00.*
Open: All Year (not Xmas)
Beds: 1D 1T
Baths: 2 Ensuite
🛏🅿⊬🖵🗙📖♿🛊⊬

(On Path 🚐) *La Fosse Guest House, Oxford Road, Hay-on-Wye, Hereford, Herefordshire, HR3 5AJ.*
Period cottage with walled garden.
Grades: WTB 2 Cr
Tel: **01497 820613** Mr Crook.
Rates fr: *£16.00-£25.00.*
Open: All Year
Beds: 4D 1T
Baths: 5 Private
🛏🅿(5)🖵🛉📖,🗹🛊⊬

(On Path) *Belmont House, Hay-on-Wye, Hereford, Herefordshire, HR3 5DA.*
Actual grid ref: SO229426
Georgian house.
Tel: **01497 820718** Mr Gwynns.
Rates fr: *£12.50-£17.50.*
Open: All Year
Beds: 1F 2D 2T
Baths: 1 Ensuite 2 Shared
🛏🅿🖵🛉📖,🗹🛊⊬

(On Path 🚐) *Jasmine Cottage, Brook Street, Hay-on-Wye, Hereford, Herefordshire, HR3 5BQ.*
Pretty stone cottage.
Tel: **01497 821168** Mr Jones.
Rates fr: *£14.00-£16.00.*
Open: All Year (not Xmas)
Beds: 2D 1T
Baths: 1 Shared
🛏(12)🅿⊬🖵📖,🗹🛊⊬

(0.5m) *York House, Hardwicke Road, Cusop, Hay-on-Wye, Hereford, Herefordshire, HR3 5QX.*
Actual grid ref: SO233422
Quietly situated, late Victorian house.
Grades: AA 3 Q, RAC Acclaim
Tel: **01497 820705** Mr Roberts.
Rates fr: *£20.00-£20.00.*
Open: All Year
Beds: 2F 3D **Baths:** 5 Private
🛏(8)🅿(6)⊬🖵🛉🗙📖,🗹🛊⊬

(0.25m) *Cwm Dulais House, Heol Y Dwr, Hay-on-Wye, Hereford, Herefordshire, HR3 5AT.*
Converted police house and cells.
Tel: **01497 820640** Ms Knights.
Rates fr: *£15.00-£20.00.*
Open: All Year
Beds: 1F 2D 2T **Baths:** 3 Ensuite
🛏(8)🅿(5)⊬🖵📖,🛊⊬

Rhydspence 32

National Grid Ref: SO2447

⊯🍺Rhydspence Inn

(1.5m 🚐) *Rhydspence Cottage, Rhydspence, Whitney-on-Wye, Hereford, Herefordshire, HR3 6EU.*
Actual grid ref: SO241472
Traditional stone-built cottage, wonderful views.
Tel: **01497 831595** Mrs Phillips.
Rates fr: *£14.00-£14.00.*
Open: All Year (not Xmas)
Beds: 1T 1S **Baths:** 1 Shared
🛏🅿(3)🖵🛉📖,🗹🛊⊬

Brilley 33

National Grid Ref: SO2649

⊯🍺Rhydspence Inn (Brilley)

(0.25m) *Pentwyn Farm, Brilley, Hereford, Herefordshire, HR3 6HW.*
Working farm.
Tel: **01497 831337** Mrs Price.
Rates fr: *£15.00-£15.00.*
Open: All Year (not Xmas)
Beds: 2D 2S **Baths:** 1 Shared
🛏🅿🖵🛉🗙📖,🗹🛊⊬

Newchurch 34

National Grid Ref: SO2150

⊯🍺Royal Oak (Newchurch)

(On Path 🚐) *The Great House, Newchurch, Kington, Herefordshire, HR5 3QF.*
Actual grid ref: SO216506
Listed C14th medieval cruck hall..
Tel: **01544 22257**
Mrs Lloyd.
Rates fr: *£16.00.*
Open: Easter to Oct
Beds: 1F 1T
Baths: 1 Shared
🛏🅿⊬🖵🛉🗙📖,🗹🛊⊬

Gladestry 35

National Grid Ref: SO2355

⊯🍺Royal Oak

(1.25m 🚐) *Wain Wen Farm, Gladestry, Kington, Herefordshire, HR5 3NT.*
Actual grid ref: SO217546
Comfortable farmhouse, warm welcome assured.
Tel: **01544 370226**
Mrs Lloyd.
Rates fr: *£15.00-£15.00.*
Open: Easter to Oct
Beds: 1F 1T
Baths: 2 Shared
🅿🖵🗙🛊⊬

Kington 36

National Grid Ref: SO2956

⊯🍺Swan Inn, Royal Oak, Burton Hotel

(0.25m) *Royal Oak Inn, Church Street, Kington, Herefordshire, HR5 3BE.*
Tel: **01544 230484**
Mrs Thompson.
Rates fr: *£18.00-£18.00.*
Open: All Year
Beds: 1F 2T 1S
Baths: 1 Shared
🛏(5)🅿(4)🗙📖,🗹⊬
Traditional friendly family run inn, on Offa's Dyke Path, offering comfortable centrally heated accommodation. Hot/cold. Tea/coffee. Bar snacks, real ales. Attractive beer garden.

(On Path) *Cambridge Cottage, 19 Church Street, Kington, Herefordshire, HR5 3BE.*
Actual grid ref: SO295567
17th Century cottage.
Tel: **01544 231300**
Mr & Mrs Hooton.
Rates fr: *£12.50-£12.50.*
Open: All Year (not Xmas)
Beds: 1F 1S
Baths: 1 Ensuite, 1 Shared
🛏🅿(2)⊬🖵🛉📖,🛊⊬
Also ⛺ *£2 per person.* 🔥🆃♿

(0.1m) *Burton Hotel, Mill Street, Kington, Herefordshire, HR5 3BQ.*
Actual grid ref: SO295568
Converted coaching inn.
Grades: WTB 4 Cr, Approved, AA 2 St, RAC 2 St
Tel: 01544 230323
Mrs Richardson.
Rates fr: £27.50-£40.00.
Open: All Year
Beds: 6F 5D 3T 1S
Baths: 15 Private
🛇 🅿 (30) 🛏 🍴 ✕ Ⅲ Ⅵ ♿ ⚕

(On Path) *26 Church Street, Kington, Herefordshire, HR5 3BE.*
Actual grid ref: SO295567
Tel: 01544 231103
Mr & Mrs Price.
Rates fr: £13.00-£16.00.
Open: All Year (not Xmas)
Beds: 1D 1T **Baths:** 1 Shared
🍽 🛏 Ⅲ Ⅵ ⚕

(On Path) *2 Bradnor View Close, Kington, Herefordshire, HR5 3UA.*
Actual grid ref: SO295569
Modern bungalow with lovely views.
Tel: 01544 231208 Mrs Condon.
Rates fr: £11.00-£11.00.
Open: All Year (not Xmas)
Beds: 1D 1T 1S
Baths: 1 Private 1 Shared
🛇 (10) 🅿 (1) 🍽 Ⅲ Ⅵ ♿ ⚕

Lyonshall   37

National Grid Ref: SO3356

(2.5m 🚌) *Church House, Lyonshall, Kington, Herefordshire, HR5 3HR.*
Actual grid ref: SO333562
Grades: ETB 2 Cr
Tel: 01544 340350
Mr & Mrs Dilley.
Rates fr: £15.00-£20.00.
Open: All Year (not Xmas)
Beds: 2D 1T
Baths: 1 Ensuite 1 Shared
🛇 🅿 (8) 🍽 🛏 Ⅲ Ⅵ ♿ ⚕
Fascinating small Georgian country house, quietly located in 10 acres of gardens and fields. Home-cooked food. Large bedrooms. Handy buses

New Radnor   38

National Grid Ref: SO2160

🍴 🍺 Red Lion

(3m 🚌) *Eagle Hotel, Broad Street, New Radnor, Presteigne, Powys, LD8 2SN.*
Actual grid ref: SO213609
Village hotel, excellent walking country. **Grades:** WTB 1 Cr
Tel: 01544 350208 Mr Charters.
Rates fr: £17.00-£20.00.
Open: All Year **Beds:** 3D 3T
Baths: 2 Private, 2 Shared
🛇 🅿 (8) 🛏 🍴 ✕ Ⅲ ⚕
Also 🏕 £5.00 per tent.
Open: All Year 🔥 🔟 🍴 ✕ ♿ 🅿

Kinnerton   39

National Grid Ref: SO2463

(2m 🚌) *Corner House, Kinnerton, Presteigne, Powys, LD8 2PE.*
Actual grid ref: SO243633
Delightful self-catering cottage.
Grades: WTB 3 Cr
Tel: 01547 560 207 Mrs Jones.
Rates up to: £220 per week.
Open: All Year (not Xmas)
Beds: 1F 1T
Baths: 1 Shared
🛇 🅿 (3) 🛏 🍴 ✕ Ⅲ ⚕

Discoed   40

National Grid Ref: SO2764

(0.2m 🚌) *Woodwinds, Discoed, Presteigne, Powys, LD8 2NW.*
Actual grid ref: SO276648
Clean modern house in superb location.
Grades: WTB Comm
Tel: 01547 560302 Mrs Ambridge.
Rates fr: £15.00-£18.00.
Open: All Year (not Xmas)
Beds: 1F 1D 2T
Baths: 2 Private 1 Shared
🅿 (3) 🍽 🛏 ✕ Ⅲ Ⅵ ♿ ⚕

Presteigne   41

National Grid Ref: SO3164

(2.5m) *The Cabin Restaurant, High Street, Presteigne, Powys, LD8 2BA.*
Actual grid ref: SO314645
C16th licensed restaurant.
Tel: 01544 267068
Mr & Mrs Duggan.
Rates fr: £14.00-£14.00.
Open: All Year
Beds: 2T
Baths: 1 Shared
🛇 🛏 🍴 ✕ Ⅲ Ⅵ ♿ ⚕

Whitton   42

National Grid Ref: SO2767

(1m 🚌) *Pilleth Court, Whitton, Knighton, Powys, LD7 1NP.*
Actual grid ref: SO257683
Elizabethan house offering quality accommodation.
Grades: WTB 2 Cr, High Comm
Tel: 01547 560272 Mrs Hood.
Rates fr: £17.00-£20.00.
Open: All Year (not Xmas)
Beds: 1F 1D 1T
Baths: 1 Ensuite 1 Shared
🛇 (9) 🅿 (6) 🍽 ✕ Ⅲ Ⅵ ♿ ⚕

Norton   43

National Grid Ref: SO3067

🍴 🍺 Farmers Arms, The Bull

(3m) *Wellingtonia Cottage, Norton, Presteigne, Powys, LD8 2EU.*
Extended late-Victorian farm worker's cottage.
Tel: 01544 260255 Mrs Hobley.

Rates fr: £13.00-£13.00.
Open: All Year (not Xmas)
Beds: 1D 1T 1S
Baths: 1 Private 1 Shared
🛇 🅿 (3) 🍽 🛏 ✕ Ⅲ Ⅵ

Llangunllo   44

National Grid Ref: SO2171

(6m 🚌) *Craig Fach, Llangunllo, Knighton, Powys, LD7 1SY.*
Actual grid ref: SO198739
Renovated, extended, traditional stone cottage.
Tel: 01547 81605
Mrs Livingstone-Lawn.
Rates fr: £12.50-£12.50.
Open: All Year (not Xmas)
Beds: 2F 1S
Baths: 1 Shared
🛇 🅿 (10) 🍽 🛏 🍴 ✕ Ⅲ Ⅵ ♿ ⚕

(3m 🚌) *Cernsuran Farm, Llangunllo, Knighton, Powys, LD7 1SY.*
Actual grid ref: SO228711
C16th Welsh farmhouse, superb views.
Grades: WTB 2 Cr, High Comm
Tel: 01547 550219
Mrs Morgan.
Rates fr: £16.00-£17.00.
Open: All Year (not Xmas)
Beds: 1F 1D 2T
Baths: 4 Private
🛇 (10) 🅿 (8) 🍽 🛏 ✕ Ⅲ Ⅵ ♿ ⚕

Knighton   45

National Grid Ref: SO2872

🍴 🍺 Horse & Jockey, George & Dragon

(On Path 🚌) *Plough Hotel, 40 Market Street, Knighton, Powys, LD7 1EY.*
Actual grid ref: SO285724
Olde worlde inn on dyke.
Tel: 01547 528041 Mrs Scotford.
Rates fr: £26.00-£14.00.
Open: All Year
Beds: 1D 3T
Baths: 2 Ensuite 1 Shared
🅿 🛏 🍴 ✕ Ⅲ Ⅵ ♿ ⚕

(0.25m) *The Fleece House, Market Street, Knighton, Powys, LD7 1BB.*
Converted 18th Century coaching inn.
Grades: WTB 2 Cr, Comm
Tel: 01547 520168 Mrs Simmons.
Rates fr: £15.50-£18.50.
Open: All Year
Beds: 6T
Baths: 2 Private 2 Shared
🅿 🍽 Ⅲ ♿ ⚕

Pay B&Bs by cash or cheque and be prepared to pay up front.

(On Path 🚐) *Ryelands, The Rhos,*
Knighton, Powys, LD7 1NG.
Actual grid ref: SO277700
Tel: 01547 520291
Ms Wells.
Rates fr: *£14.00-£14.00*.
Open: All Year (not Xmas)
Beds: 1D
Baths: 1 Shared
🛏 (12) 🅿 (6) ✍ 🗙 📺 ⊠ ▮ ✦
Also ▲ Ⓣ ♨ 🗙 ✦ ♿

(m) *Cwmgilla Farm, Knighton,*
Powys, LD7 1PG.
Modern comfortable farmhouse.
Grades: WTB 1 Cr, High Comm
Tel: 01547 528387
Mrs Davies.
Rates fr: *£17.00-£18.00*.
Open: Easter to Nov
Beds: 2D 1S
Baths: 1 Shared
🛏 (10) 🅿 (5) ▢ 📺

Lloyney 46

National Grid Ref: SO2475
🍴 🍺 The Horse & Jockey

(1.5 m 🚐) *The Mill, Lloyney,*
Knighton, Powys, LD7 1RG.
Actual grid ref: SO245759
Old mill, cozy beds, log fires.
Tel: 01547 528049
Mr & Mrs Davies.
Rates fr: *£13.50-£13.50*.
Open: All Year
Beds: 1D 2T
Baths: shared
🛏 🅿 (6) ✍ ▢ 🛏 🗙 📺 ⊠ ▮ ✦

Llanfair Waterdine 47

National Grid Ref: SO2476

(0.5m 🚐) *Cwm Cole, Llanfair*
Waterdine, Knighton, Powys,
LD7 1TU.
Actual grid ref: SO243778
Comfortable cottage amid peaceful
hills.
Tel: 01547 520357
Ms Lewis.
Rates fr: *£16.00-£16.00*.
Open: All Year (not Xmas)
Beds: 2D 1T
Baths: 2 Shared
🛏 ▢ 🛏 🗙 📺 ⊠ ▮ ✦

Selley Cross 48

National Grid Ref: SO2676
🍴 🍺 Red Lion

(3m) *Selley Hall, Selley Cross,*
Knighton, Powys, LD7 1TR.
Large comfortable farmhouse,
quiet situation.
Tel: 01547 528429
Mr Morgan.
Rates fr: *£16.00*.
Open: May to Oct
Beds: 2D 1S
Baths: 1 Ensuite
🅿 (4) ✍ 🗙

Clun 49

National Grid Ref: SO3080
🍴 🍺 White Horse Inn, The
Buffalo Head Hotel

(3m 🚐) *Crown House, Church*
Street, Clun, Craven Arms, Salop,
SY7 8JW.
Actual grid ref: SO305805
Self-contained accommodation in
converted stables.
Grades: ETB 2 Cr
Tel: 01588 640780 Mr Maund.
Rates fr: *£15.75-£16.75*.
Open: All Year (not Xmas)
Beds: 1D 1T
Baths: 2 Private
🛏 (8) 🅿 (2) ✍ ▢ 🛏 📺 ⊠ ▮ ✦

(4m 🚐) *Woodside Old*
Farmhouse, Woodside, Clun,
Craven Arms, Salop, SY7 0JB.
Actual grid ref: SO310802
300-year-old stone farmhouse.
Grades: ETB 1 Cr
Tel: 01588 640695 Mr Wall.
Rates fr: *£15.00-£15.00*.
Open: Easter to Oct
Beds: 1F 1D **Baths:** 1 Shared
🛏 🅿 (3) ✍ ▢ 🛏 🗙 📺 ⊠ ✦

(3m 🚐) *Clun Farm, High Street,*
Clun, Craven Arms, Salop, SY7 8JB.
C16th double cruck farmhouse.
Grades: ETB Listed
Tel: 01588 640432 Mrs Lewis.
Rates fr: *£14.00-£14.00*.
Open: All Year
Beds: 1F 1T 2S
Baths: 1 Private 1 Shared
🛏 (1) 🅿 (6) ▢ 🛏 📺 ⊠ ✦

(2.5m) *Llanhedric Farm, Clun,*
Craven Arms, Salop, SY7 8NG.
Characteristic old stone farmhouse.
Grades: ETB Listed, Comm
Tel: 01588 640203 Mrs Jones.
Rates fr: *£14.00-£15.00*.
Open: Easter to Nov
Beds: 1F 1D
🛏 🅿 (5) ▢ 🗙 📺 ⊠ ▮

Newcastle-on-Clun 50

National Grid Ref: SO2482

(0.5m) *The Quarry House,*
Newcastle-on-Clun, Craven Arms,
Salop, SY7 8QJ.
Converted barn, fantastic views,
peaceful.
Grades: WTB Listed
Tel: 01588 640774 Mr Woodward.
Rates fr: *£19.00-£19.00*.
Open: All Year (not Xmas)
Beds: 2T
Baths: 1 Private 1 Shared
🅿 (20) ✍ ▢ 📺 ⊠

The *lowest* single
rate *is shown in* bold.

Mainstone 51

National Grid Ref: SO2787

(1m 🚐) *New House Farm,*
Mainstone, Clun, Craven Arms,
Salop, SY7 8NJ.
Actual grid ref: SO275863
C18th farmhouse set in Clun hills.
Grades: WTB 2 Cr, High Comm,
AA 4 Q, Select
Tel: 01588 638314
Mr & Mrs Ellison.
Rates fr: *£18.00*.
Open: Mar to Oct
Beds: 1D 1T
Baths: 1 Ensuite 1 Private
🛏 🅿 (6) ✍ ▢ 🛏 🗙 📺 ⊠ ✦

Cwm 52

National Grid Ref: SO2590

🍴 🍺 Boars Head, Dragon Hotel,
Cottage Inn

(On Path 🚐) *The Drewin Farm,*
Cwm, Church Stoke, Montgomery,
Powys, SY15 6TW.
C17th farm with panoramic views.
Grades: WTB 3 Cr, High Comm,
AA 4 Q, Select
Tel: 01588 620325
Mrs Richards.
Rates fr: *£14.00-£15.00*.
Open: Easter to Oct
Beds: 2F
Baths: 1 Private 1 Shared
🛏 🅿 (6) ✍ ▢ 🛏 🗙 📺 ⊠ ✦

Montgomery 53

National Grid Ref: SO2494

🍴 🍺 Dragon Hotel, Cottage Inn

(On Path 🚐) *Little Brompton*
Farm, Montgomery, Powys,
SY15 6HY.
Actual grid ref: SO244941
C17th farmhouse on working farm.
Grades: WTB 3 Cr, High Comm,
AA 4 Q, Select
Tel: 01686 668371
Mrs Bright.
Rates fr: *£18.00-£20.00*.
Open: All Year
Beds: 1F 1D 1T
Baths: 3 Private
🛏 🅿 ✍ ▢ 🛏 🗙 📺 ⊠ ✦
Also ▲ *£2.00 per person.,*
Open: All Year 🔥 Ⓣ ♨ 🗙 ✦ ♿

(0.75m 🚐) *The Manor House,*
Pool Road, Montgomery, Powys,
SY15 6QY.
Actual grid ref: SO223968
Friendly private house.
Tel: 01686 668736
Mrs Williams.
Rates fr: *£15.00-£15.00*.
Open: All Year (not Xmas)
Beds: 1F 1D 1T 1S
Baths: 1 Private
🛏 (5) 🅿 (2) ▢ 🛏 📺 ⊠ ▮ ✦

Berriew 54

National Grid Ref: SJ1800

(4m) *Plasdwpa Farm, Berriew, Welshpool, Powys, SY21 8PS*.
Actual grid ref: SJ1800
Very comfortable farmhouse.
Grades: WTB 1 Cr
Tel: 01686 640298
Mrs Hughes.
Rates fr: *£14.00*-£14.00.
Open: Easter to Oct
Beds: 1F 1D 1T
Baths: 1 Shared
🖤 🅿 🍴 🗆 ✕ 🛉 ⚡

Forden 55

National Grid Ref: SJ2200

🍴 🍺 Railway Inn, Cork Hotel

(1m) *Railway Inn, Forden, Welshpool, Powys, SY21 8NN*.
Black-and-white country inn.
Grades: WTB 2 Cr
Tel: 01938 580237
Mr & Mrs Thomas.
Rates fr: *£15*-£15.
Open: All Year (not Xmas)
Beds: 2D 3T
Baths: 2 Private 3 Shared
🖤 🅿 (20) 🗆 ✕ 🛏 🆅 🛉 ⚡

(0.5m 🚗) *Church House, Forden, Welshpool, Powys, SY21 8NE*.
Large private house and garden.
Tel: 01938 580353
Mrs Bright.
Rates fr: *£14.00*-£14.00.
Open: All Year
Beds: 1F 1D 1T
Baths: 2 Shared
🖤 🅿 (3) 🍴 🗆 ✕ 🛉 ⚡
Also ⛺ *£2 per person.* 🏕 🆃 🎣

Trelystan 56

National Grid Ref: SJ2603

(0.5m 🚗) *Chapel House, Trelystan, Leighton, Welshpool, Powys, SY21 8HX*.
Old house with smallholding.
Tel: 01938 580476
Mr & Mrs Owens.
Rates fr: *£14.00*-£14.00.
Open: All Year (not Xmas)
Beds: 1F 2D
Baths: 1 Shared
🖤 (7) 🅿 (2) 🍴 🗆 ✕ 🛏 🆅 🛉 ⚡

Many rates vary according to season - the lowest only are shown here

Powis Castle 57

National Grid Ref: SJ2106

(3m) *Dysserth Hall, Powis Castle, Welshpool, Powys, SY21 8RQ*.
Peaceful late-Georgian family home.
Grades: WTB Listed
Tel: 01938 552153
Mrs Marriott.
Rates fr: *£17.00*-£17.00.
Open: Easter to Nov
Beds: 1D 2T 1S
Baths: 2 Private 1 Shared
🖤 (8) 🅿 (12) 🍴 🗆 ✕ 🛏 🆅 ⚡

Welshpool 58

National Grid Ref: SJ2207

🍴 🍺 Royal Oak Hotel, Raven Inn, Corn Store

(2.5m 🚗) *Tynllwyn Farm, Welshpool, Powys, SY21 9BW*.
Actual grid ref: SJ214080
Farmhouse.
Grades: WTB 1 Cr, AA 3 Q, RAC Listed
Tel: 01938 553175 Mrs Emberton.
Rates fr: *£14.50*-£14.50.
Open: All Year
Beds: 2F 2D 2T
Baths: 2 Shared
🖤 🅿 (20) 🗆 🛏 ✕ 🛏 🆅 🛉 ⚡

(2.25m 🚗) *Peniarth, 10 Cefn Hawys, (off Adelaide Drive), Red Bank, Welshpool, Powys, SY21 7RH*.
Actual grid ref: SJ224082
Modern detached house above town.
Grades: WTB 2 Cr
Tel: 01938 552324 Mrs Jones.
Rates fr: *£15.00*-£15.00.
Open: Easter to Oct
Beds: 1F 1T 1S
Baths: 1 Ensuite 1 Shared
🖤 (5) 🅿 (2) 🍴 🗆 🛏 🆅 🛉 ⚡

(2m 🚗) *Tresi-Aur, Brookfield Road, Welshpool, Powys, SY21 7PZ*.
Actual grid ref: SJ224082
Delightful, quiet guesthouse.
Grades: WTB 2 Cr
Tel: 01938 552430
Mrs Davies.
Rates fr: *£14.00*-£15.00.
Open: Jan to Nov
Beds: 1F 1D 1T
Baths: 1 Private
🖤 🅿 (2) 🍴 🗆 🛏 🆅 🛉 ⚡

(1.75m 🚗) *Hafren Guest House, 38 Salop Road, Welshpool, Powys, SY21 7EA*.
Actual grid ref: SJ227076
Georgian house with modern amenities.
Grades: WTB Listed
Tel: 01938 554112 / 0831 183152
Ms Shaw.
Rates fr: *£13.00*-£15.00.
Open: All Year
Beds: 1F 1D 1T
Baths: 1 Shared
🖤 🅿 (3) 🗆 🛏 🛏 🆅 🛉 ⚡

All rates are subject to alteration at the owners' discretion.

(1.5m 🚗) *Severn Farm, Welshpool, Powys, SY21 7BB*.
Actual grid ref: SJ233069
Modernised farmhouse on edge of town.
Grades: WTB 1 Cr
Tel: 01938 553098
Ms Jones.
Rates fr: *£14.50*-£15.00.
Open: All Year (not Xmas)
Beds: 1F 1D 1T 1S
Baths: 2 Shared
🖤 🅿 (20) 🗆 🛏 ✕ 🛏 🆅 🛉 ⚡

Rhallt 59

National Grid Ref: SJ2409

🍴 🍺 Green Dragon

(0.5m) *Gyngrog House, Rhallt, Welshpool, Powys, SY21 9HS*.
C17th house on hill.
Grades: AA 4 Q, Select
Tel: 01938 553381
Mrs Jones.
Rates fr: *£19.00*-£21.00.
Open: Apr to Nov
Beds: 1F 1D
Baths: 2 Private
🖤 🅿 🍴 🗆 🛏 🛉 ⚡

Guilsfield 60

National Grid Ref: SJ2211

(1m 🚗) *Lower Trelydan, Guilsfield, Welshpool, Powys, SY21 9PH*.
Actual grid ref: SJ2207
Award-winning black and white farmhouse.
Grades: WTB 3 Cr, High Comm, AA 4 Q, Select
Tel: 01938 553105
Mrs Jones.
Rates fr: *£18.00*-£25.00.
Open: All Year
Baths: 3 Ensuite
🖤 🅿 (10) 🗆 🛏 ✕ 🛏 🆅 🛉 ⚡

Pool Quay 61

National Grid Ref: SJ2511

(On Path) *Severn View, Pool Quay, Welshpool, Powys, SY21 9JS*.
Actual grid ref: SJ255115
Georgian manor house, C18th annexe.
Tel: 01938 75464
Mrs Kellaway.
Rates fr: *£17.50*-£16.50.
Open: All Year (not Xmas)
Beds: 1F 2D
Baths: 1 Private 1 Shared
🖤 🅿 (6) 🍴 🗆 🛏 ✕ 🛏 🆅 🛉 ⚡

Llandrinio 62

National Grid Ref: SJ2817

⑩ ◖ Punchbowl

(3m ☎) *Haimwood*, Llandrinio, *Llanymynech, Powys, SY22 6SQ.*
C18th farmhouse on bank of River Severn.
Tel: **01691 830764** Mrs Nixon.
Rates fr: £13.00-**£13.00**.
Open: All Year (not Xmas)
Beds: 1D 1T 1S **Baths:** 1 Shared
🛏 🅿 ⌷ ✕ Ⓥ ▮ ⋠

Four Crosses 63

National Grid Ref: SJ2718

(On Path ☎) *Ty-Coch Bungalow, Four Crosses, Llanymynech, Powys, SY22 6QZ.*
Actual grid ref: SJ26199
Extensive bungalow in 5-acre grounds.
Grades: WTB Listed
Tel: **01691 830361** Mrs Lee.
Rates fr: £14.00-**£14.00**.
Open: All Year (not Xmas)
Beds: 1D 1T 1S
🛏 🅿 (6) ⍂ ⌷ ☎ ✕ 🏧 ⅊ Ⓥ ▮ ⋠
Also ⛺ £1.75 per tent.
Open: All Year (not Xmas) ⌂ Ⓣ ♨
✕ ⋠ ⅋

Llanymynech 64

National Grid Ref: SJ2620

(0.4m ☎) *Vyrnwy Bank, Llanymynech, Powys, SY22 6LG.*
Actual grid ref: ST274209
C18th house on Welsh borders.
Grades: WTB Listed
Tel: **01691 830427** Mrs Fahey.
Rates fr: £15.00-**£15.00**.
Open: Feb to Dec
Beds: 1D 1T 1S
🅿 (6) ⌷ ☎ ✕ 🏧 Ⓥ ▮ ⋠

(On Path) *Lion Hotel, Llanymynech, Llanfyllin, Powys, SY22 6EJ.*
Family-run hotel.
Grades: WTB Listed
Tel: **01691 830234**
Mr & Mrs Beeston.
Rates fr: £17.00-**£17.00**.
Open: All Year (not Xmas)
Beds: 1F 3D 3T 3S
Baths: 4 Private 2 Shared
🛏 🅿 ⌷ ☎ ✕ 🏧 ▮ ⋠
Also ⛺ £1.50 per person. ⌂ Ⓣ ♨
✕ ⋠

Order your packed lunch the *evening before* you need them. Not at breakfast!

Porth-y-waen 65

National Grid Ref: SJ2623

⑩ ◖ Red Lion

(On Path) *Red Lion Inn, Porth-y-waen, Oswestry, Salop, SY10 8LX.*
Traditional old country pub.
Tel: **01691 830219**
Mrs Jones.
Rates fr: £15.00-**£15.00**.
Open: All Year (not Xmas)
Beds: 2D 2T
Baths: 1 Shared
🛏 🅿 ⌷ ☎ ✕ 🏧 ▮ ⋠

Llansantffraid-ym-Mechain 66

National Grid Ref: SJ2120

(2m ☎) *Penygarreg, Winllan Road, Llansantffraid-ym-Mechain, Llanfyllin, Powys, SY22 6TS.*
C17th black and white hillside house.
Grades: WTB 2 Cr, High Comm
Tel: **01691 828452**
Mrs Mills.
Rates fr: £17.00-**£17.00**.
Open: All Year (not Xmas)
Beds: 1D 2T
Baths: 1 Ensuite 1 Private 1 Shared
🛏 ⍂ ⌷ ✕ 🏧 Ⓥ ▮ ⋠

Nantmawr 67

National Grid Ref: SJ2424

⑩ ◖ Royal Oak

(On Path) *April Spring Cottage, Nantmawr, Oswestry, Salop, SY10 9HL.*
Quiet, secluded old cottage.
Grades: WTB 1 Cr
Tel: **01691 828802**
Mrs Richardson.
Rates fr: £15.50-**£31.00**.
Open: All Year (not Xmas)
Beds: 1D 1T
Baths: 1 Shared
🛏 (8) 🅿 ⍂ ⌷ ✕ 🏧 ▮ ⋠

Croesau Bach 68

National Grid Ref: SJ2428

(0.75m) *Pant Hir, Croesau Bach, Oswestry, Salop, SY10 9BH.*
Grades: WTB 2 Cr
Tel: **01691 791457**
Mrs Werry.
Rates fr: £16.00-**£24.00**.
Open: Feb to Nov
Beds: 1F 1D 1T
Baths: 3 Private
🅿 ⌷ ☎ ✕ 🏧 ▮ ⋠
Pretty country house on Shropshire/Welsh border. Views truly beautiful. 26 acres grazed by our miniature ponies. Peaceful. Ideal for exploring historic towns and countryside

---

Candy 69

National Grid Ref: SJ2528

(On Path) *The Old Llanforda Mill Inn*, Candy , Oswestry, Salop, SY10 9AZ.
Actual grid ref: SJ2528
Picturesque pub with excellent food.
Grades: WTB 1 Cr
Tel: **01691 657058** Mrs Atkinson.
Rates fr: £15.00-**£15.00**.
Open: All Year
Beds: 1D 2T 2S
Baths: 1 Shared
🛏 (3) 🅿 (100) ⌷ ✕ 🏧 Ⓥ ▮ ⋠

Llansilin 70

National Grid Ref: SJ2028

⑩ ◖ Wynstay

(3m) *Lloran Ganol, Llansilin, Oswestry, Salop, SY10 7QX.*
Dairy and sheep farm. Modern farmhouse.
Grades: WTB 1 Cr
Tel: **01691 791287** Mrs Jones.
Rates fr: £13.50-**£13.50**.
Open: Easter to Jan
Beds: 1D 1T
✕

Oswestry 71

National Grid Ref: SJ2929

⑩ ◖ Bear Hotel, Golden Lion

(2.5m ☎) *Bear Hotel, Salop Road, Oswestry, Salop, SY11 2NR.*
Town centre, family run, friendly.
Grades: WTB 3 Cr, Comm
Tel: **01691 652093**
Mr & Mrs Lucks.
Rates fr: £20.00-**£24.00**.
Open: All Year (not Xmas)
Beds: 1F 4D 2T 3S
Baths: 5 Ensuite, 5 Shared
🛏 🅿 (25) ⌷ ☎ ✕ 🏧 Ⓥ ▮ ⋠

(3m ☎) *Montrose, Weston Lane, Oswestry, Salop, SY11 2BG.*
Actual grid ref: SJ289288
Large Victorian private house.
Grades: WTB Listed
Tel: **01691 652063** Mrs Leggatt.
Rates fr: £14.00-**£14.00**.
Open: All Year
Beds: 2T
Baths: 1 Shared
🛏 🅿 (3) ⍂ ⌷ 🏧 Ⓥ ▮ ⋠

(1m ☎) *Elgar House, 16 Elgar Close, Oswestry, Salop, SY11 2LZ.*
Actual grid ref: SJ299299
Modern, comfortable elevated guesthouse.
Grades: WTB 2 Cr, High Comm
Tel: **01691 661323 / 0585 171112**
Mr Harding.
Rates fr: £17.50-**£20.00**.
Open: All Year
Beds: 2F 3D 3S
Baths: 1 Private 1 Shared
🛏 🅿 (3) ⌷ ✕ 🏧 Ⓥ ▮ ⋠

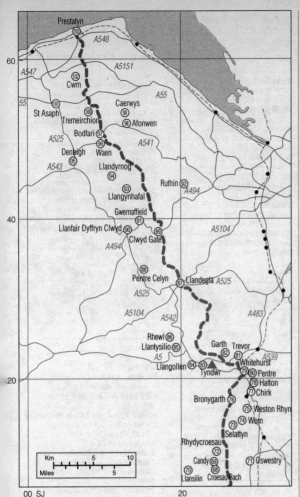

Wern   74

National Grid Ref: SJ2734

🍴 🍺 Last Inn

(2m 🚐) *Spring Cottage, Wern, Weston Rhyn, Oswestry, Clwyd, SY10 7LH.*
Actual grid ref: SJ2734
Detached modernised country cottage.
Tel: **01961 650293**
Mr & Mrs Andrews.
Rates fr: *£15.00-£15.00.*
Open: All Year
Beds: 4D 1T
Baths: 1 Shared
🅿 (2) 🍴 ⛔ 💻 📷 🛂 ⚡

Weston Rhyn   75

National Grid Ref: SJ2835

🍴 🍺 The Plough

(2m 🚐) *Rhoswiel Lodge, Weston Rhyn, Oswestry, Salop, SY10 7TG.*
Pleasantly situated Victorian country house.
Grades: WTB 2 Cr
Tel: **01691 777609**
Mrs Plunkett.
Rates fr: *£15.00-£18.00.*
Open: All Year (not Xmas)
Beds: 1D 1T
Baths: 2 Private
🛏 🅿 (6) 🍴 ⛔ 💻 📺 📷 ⚡

Bronygarth   76

National Grid Ref: SJ2637

(0.25m 🚐) *Old School, Bronygarth, Oswestry, Salop, SY10 7NB.*
Actual grid ref: SJ267370
Modernised Victorian schoolhouse.
Tel: **01691 772546**
Mr & Mrs Bampfield.
Rates fr: *£14.00-£14.00.*
Open: All Year (not Xmas)
Beds: 2T 1S
Baths: 2 Shared
🛏 (10) 🅿 (2) 🍴 ⛔ 💻 📺 📷 ⚡
Also ⛺ *£1.00 per tent.,*
Open: All Year 🍴 🛂 ⚡ ♿

Chirk   77

National Grid Ref: SJ2937

🍴 🍺 Stanton House Hotel, Holy Head Road, Chirk

(1.5m 🚐) *Pedlar Corner, Colliery Road, Chirk, Clwyd, LL14 5PB.*
Actual grid ref: SJ292379
Edwardian cottage, with warm welcome.
Tel: **01691 772903**
Mrs Berry.
Rates fr: *£14.00-£14.00.*
Open: All Year (not Xmas)
Beds: 2T
Baths: 1 Shared
🛏 (5) 🅿 (3) 💻 🛂 📷 ⚡

Rhydycroesau   72

National Grid Ref: SJ2430

(0.75m 🚐) *Pen-y-Dyffryn Hall Hotel, Tattenhall, Rhydycroesau, Oswestry, Salop, SY10 7DT.*
Actual grid ref: SJ242306
Peaceful, homely, licensed country hotel.
Grades: WTB 3 Cr, High Comm, AA 2 St
Tel: **01691 653700** Mr Hunter.
Rates fr: *£26.00-£35.00.*
Open: All Year
Beds: 1F 3D 2T 1S **Baths:** 7 Private
🛏 🅿 (20) 💻 🛏 ✕ 💻 🛂 📷 ⚡

Selattyn   73

National Grid Ref: SJ2633

(1m 🚐) *The Old Rectory, Selattyn, Oswestry, Salop, SY10 7DH.*
Attractive period stone house, secluded grounds.
Grades: WTB 2 Cr
Tel: **01691 659708** Mrs Barnes.
Rates fr: *£15.00-£15.00.*
Open: All Year (not Xmas)
Beds: 1F 1D 1S **Baths:** 3 Private
🛏 🅿 ⛔ ⛔ ✕ 💻 🛂 ⚡

(On Path) *Carreg y Big, Selattyn, Oswestry, Salop, SY10 7HX.*
Actual grid ref: SJ252322
Stone building, luxuriously converted.
Tel: **01691 654754** Mrs Brown.
Rates fr: *£12.50-£12.50.*
Open: Sep to Jun
Beds: 3T **Baths:** 2 Private
🛏 🅿 (20) 💻 🛏 ✕ 💻 ♿ 🛂 ⚡

All rates are subject to alteration at the owners' discretion.

Halton 78

National Grid Ref: SJ3039

(2m 🚌) *The Lodge, Halton, Chirk, Wrexham, Clwyd, LL14 5AU.*
Secluded Georgian country house.
Grades: WTB 3 Cr
Tel: 01691 774424 Mrs Davenport.
Rates fr: *£17.50-£20.00.*
Open: All Year (not Xmas)
Beds: 1F 4D 1T 4S
Baths: 3 Ensuite
🛇 🅿 (20) 🛋 ⠀🛏️✕ 🎆 Ⓥ 🛆 ⚡

Whitehurst 79

National Grid Ref: SJ2840

(On Path) *Plas Offa Farm, Whitehurst, Chirk, Wrexham, Clwyd, LL14 5AN.*
C17th farmhouse, inglenook fireplace.
Grades: WTB 3 Cr, Comm
Tel: 01691 773760
Ms Mullen.
Rates fr: *£15.00-£20.00.*
Open: All Year (not Xmas)
Beds: 2F 2D
Baths: 4 Private 2 Shared
🛇 🅿 🛋 ✕ 🎆 Ⓥ 🛆 ⚡

Pentre 80

National Grid Ref: SJ2940

🍴 🍺 Waterside Bar/Restaurant, Chirk Golf Club and Marina

(0.25m 🚌) *Sun Cottage, Pentre, Chirk, Wrexham, Clwyd, LL14 5AW.*
Actual grid ref: SJ289409
Homely C18th former coaching inn.
Tel: 01691 774542 Mrs Little.
Rates fr: *£15.00-£15.00.*
Open: All Year (not Xmas)
Beds: 2F 1S
Baths: 2 Shared
🛇 (10) 🅿 (2) 🛋 🛏️ 🎆 🛆 ⚡

(On Path 🚌) *Pentre Cottage, Pentre, Chirk, Wrexham, Clwyd, LL14 5AW.*
Actual grid ref: SJ288404
Extrovert household - dog-lover's paradise!
Tel: 01691 774265 Mrs Vant.
Rates fr: *£15.00.*
Open: All Year (not Xmas)
Beds: 1F 1D
Baths: 1 Shared
🅿 🛋 🛏️ ✕ 🎆 Ⓥ 🛆 ⚡

Trevor 81

National Grid Ref: SJ2141

🍴 🍺 Telford Inn

(On Path) *The Old Vicarage Guest House, Bryn Howel Lane, Trevor, Llangollen, Clwyd, LL20 7YR.*
Actual grid ref: SJ266418
Spacious comfortable Georgian country house.
Grades: WTB 2 Cr
Tel: 01978 823018 Mrs Woolley.

Rates fr: *£15.00-£25.00.*
Open: Mar to Oct
Beds: 2F 1D 1T
Baths: 4 Ensuite
🅿 (6) 🛋 🛏️ 🎆 Ⓥ 🛆 ⚡

Garth 82

National Grid Ref: SJ2542

🍴 🍺 Sun Trevor, Australia Arms

(0.75m) *Cefn y Fedw Farm, Panorama Walk, Garth, Trevor, Llangollen, Clwyd, LL14 1UA.*
Actual grid ref: SJ247439
Working hill farm. Also campsite.
Grades: WTB 2 Cr
Tel: 01978 823403
Mrs Roberts.
Rates fr: *£16.00.*
Open: May to Feb
Beds: 1F 2D 2T
Baths: 2 Private 1 Shared
🅿 (6) 🛋 ✕ 🎆 Ⓥ 🛆 ⚡ *£3.00 per person.*

Tyndwr 83

National Grid Ref: SJ2341

🍴 🍺 Tynywern Hotel

(▲ 2.5m) *Llangollen Youth Hostel, Tyndwr Hall, Tyndwr Road, Tyndwr, Llangollen, Clwyd, LL20 8AR.*
Actual grid ref: SK2341
Warden: Ms B Bamber.
Tel: 01978 860330
Under 18: £5.55
Adults: £8.25
Centrally Heated, Showers, Evening Meal (6.00 - 7.30 pm), Shop, Parking
Victorian half-timbered manor house and coach house, extensively refurbished, set in 5 acres of wooded grounds in the Vale of Llangollen

(1.5m 🚌) *Tyn Celyn Farmhouse, Tyn Celyn, Tyndwr, Llangollen, Clwyd, LL20 8AR.*
Actual grid ref: SJ234408
Comfortable oak beamed farmhouse.
Grades: WTB 3 Cr
Tel: 01978 861117 Mrs Bather.
Rates fr: *£17.50-£22.00.*
Open: All Year
Beds: 1F 1D 1T **Baths:** 3 Ensuite
🛇 🅿 (3) 🛋 🎆 Ⓥ 🛆 ⚡

Llangollen 84

National Grid Ref: SJ2141

🍴 🍺 Jenny Jones, Bryn Derwen, Bridgend, Wynstay Arms, Abbey Grange, Bensons

(1.5m 🚌) *Glanafon, Abbey Road, Llangollen, Clwyd, LL20 8SS.*
Actual grid ref: SJ210424
Family run Victorian guesthouse.
Grades: WTB 2 Cr
Tel: 01978 860725 Mrs Collinge.

Rates fr: *£15.00-£15.00.*
Open: All Year (not Xmas)
Beds: 1F 1S
Baths: 2 Private
🛇 🅿 (2) 🛋 🛏️ 🎆 Ⓥ 🛆 ⚡

(3m) *Hillcrest Guest House, Hill Street, Llangollen, Clwyd, LL20 8EU.*
Large Victorian private guesthouse.
Grades: WTB 3 Cr, AA 3 Q, RAC Acclaim
Tel: 01978 860208 Mrs Lloyd.
Rates fr: *£19.00.*
Open: All Year (not Xmas)
Beds: 2F 3D 2T
Baths: 7 Private
🛇 🅿 (10) 🛋 ✕ 🎆 Ⓥ 🛆

(1m) *The Grange, Grange Road, Llangollen, Clwyd, LL20 8AP.*
Attractive country house in town.
Grades: WTB 2 Cr, High Comm
Tel: 01978 860366 Mrs Evans.
Rates fr: *£17.50-£22.00.*
Open: All Year (not Xmas)
Beds: 1F 1D 1T
Baths: 3 Private
🛇 🅿 (3) 🛋 🎆 🛆 ⚡

(2m) *Hendy Isa, Valle Crucis Road, Llangollen, Clwyd, LL20 8DE.*
Actual grid ref: SJ201445
Peaceful, spacious, modernised country house.
Grades: WTB 2 Cr
Tel: 01978 861232
Mrs Jeffreys.
Rates fr: *£15.00.*
Open: All Year
Beds: 4F **Baths:** 4 Private
🛇 🅿 (8) 🛋 🎆 Ⓥ ⚡

(3m) *1 Bodwen Villas, Hill Street, Llangollen, Clwyd, LL20.*
Friendly family run business.
Grades: WTB 1 Cr, Comm
Tel: 01978 860882 Mrs Lewis.
Rates fr: *£13.50-£15.00.*
Open: All Year (not Xmas)
Beds: 2D 1T
Baths: 1 Ensuite 1 Shared
🛇 🛋 🛏️ 🎆 Ⓥ

(1m) *Ty'n-Y-Wern Hotel, Maesmawr Road, Llangollen, Clwyd, LL20 7PH.*
Converted farmhouse with superb views.
Grades: WTB 3 CrRAC 2 St
Tel: 01978 860252 Mr Sargeant.
Rates fr: *£21.00-£32.00.*
Open: All Year
Beds: 1F 4D 5T
Baths: 10 Private
🛇 🅿 (30) 🛏️ ✕ 🎆 ♿ Ⓥ 🛆

(0.25m) *Dinbren House, Dinbren Road, Llangollen, Clwyd, LL20 8TF.*
Large country house in large gardens.
Grades: WTB 2 Cr
Tel: 01978 860593 Ms Lewis.
Rates fr: *£15.00-£15.00.*
Open: All Year
Beds: 1F 1D 1T 1S
Baths: 2 Shared
🛇 🅿 🛋 🛏️ 🎆 Ⓥ

(On Path) *Tower Farm,*
Llangollen, Clwyd, LL20 8TE.
Happy, comfortable farmhouse and
camping.
Tel: **01978 860798** Mrs Davies.
Rates fr: *£15.00-£15.00*.
Open: All Year
Beds: 1F 2D 1S
Baths: 1 Shared
🖵 🕭 🛋 🛢 ♦
Also ▲ *£2.50 per person.* 🐾 T 🎿
♦ ⓑ

(0.5m 🚅**)** *Oakmere, Regent Street,*
Llangollen, Clwyd, LL20 8HS.
Actual grid ref: SJ216419
Large Victorian country house.
Grades: WTB 2 Cr, High Comm
Tel: **01978 861126**
Mr & Mrs Knibbs.
Rates fr: *£19.00.*
Open: All Year
Beds: 2F 2D 2T
Baths: 6 Ensuite
P (10) ⒦ 🖵 🛋 V 🛢 ♦

(2m 🚅**)** *The Hollies, Birch Hill,*
Llangollen, Clwyd, LL20 8LN.
Quiet detached house, scenic
views. **Grades:** WTB 2 Cr
Tel: **01978 861418** Mrs Pugh.
Rates fr: *£15.00-£15.00.*
Open: All Year (not Xmas)
Beds: 2D 1T
Baths: 2 Shared
ⓑ (5) P ⒦ 🖵 🗙 🛋 V ♦

Llantysilio   85

National Grid Ref: SJ1943

(2m 🚅**)** *Bryn Hyfryd, School*
Lane, Llantysilio, Llangollen,
Clwyd, LL20 7YU.
Actual grid ref: SJ1944
Grades: WTB 2 Cr
Tel: **01978 860011** Mrs Davies.
Rates fr: *£15.00-£15.00.*
Open: All Year
Beds: 1F 1D 1T
Baths: 3 Ensuite
ⓑ (3) P (4) ⒦ 🖵 🗙 🛋 ♦
Magnificently situated villa over-
looking Dee Valley in the tiny
hamlet of Llantysilio. Lovely
walks. Llangollen Steam Railway
Canal Museum 2.5 miles. Stroll to
local inn.

Rhewl   87

National Grid Ref: SJ1844

🍴 🍺 Sun Inn

(6m 🚅**)** *Dee Farm, Rhewl,*
Llangollen, Clwyd, LL20 7YT.
Actual grid ref: SJ180448
Quiet and very comfortable farm-
house.
Grades: WTB 2 Cr, Comm
Tel: **01978 861598** Mrs Harman.
Rates fr: *£16.00-£16.00.*
Open: Feb to Nov
Beds: 2T 1S
Baths: I Private 1 Shared
ⓑ (7) P (6) ⒦ 🖵 🕭 🛋 ♦

The Country Code

Enjoy the countryside and
respect its life and work

Guard against all risk of fire

Fasten all gates

Keep your dogs under close
control

Keep to public paths across
farmland

Use gates and stiles to cross
fences, hedges and walls

Leave livestock, crops and
machinery alone

Take your litter home

Help to keep all water clean

Protect wild-life, plants and
trees

Take special care on country
roads

Make no unnecessary noise

Llandegla   87

National Grid Ref: SJ1952

🍴 🍺 Crown Hotel, Plough Inn

(On Path) *Raven Farm, Llandegla,*
Wrexham, Clwyd, LL11 3AW.
Actual grid ref: SJ198517
Restored C17th farmhouse/ex-
drovers inn.
Tel: **01978 790224**
Mrs Surrey.
Rates fr: *£14.00-£14.00.*
Open: Easter to Sep
Beds: 1F 3D 1T 2S
Baths: 1 Private 1 Shared
ⓑ (10) P (6) ⒦ 🖵 🛋 V 🛢 ♦

(1m) *Saith Daran Farm,*
Llandegla, Wrexham, Clwyd,
LL11 3BL.
Working dairy farm near
Horseshoe Pass.
Grades: WTB 2 Cr
Tel: **01978 790685**
Mrs Thompson.
Rates fr: *£18.00-£18.00.*
Open: Mar to Nov
Beds: 1D 1T
ⓑ (3) P (4) 🖵 🛋 🛢 ♦

(On Path) *The Hand, Llandegla,*
Wrexham, Clwyd, LL11 3AW.
Actual grid ref: SJ198522
C16th former drovers' inn.
Grades: WTB Reg
Tel: **01978 790337**
Mr & Mrs Carlisle.
Rates fr: *£15.50-£15.50.*
Open: All Year (not Xmas)
Beds: 1F 2D 1S
Baths: 1 Private 1 Shared
ⓑ P (10) ⒦ 🖵 🗙 🛋 V 🛢 ♦

Pentre Celyn   88

National Grid Ref: SJ1453

(2 m) *Llainwen Uchaf, Pentre*
Celyn, Ruthin, Clwyd, LL15 2HL.
Modern, comfortable farmhouse.
Sleeps 6.
Grades: WTB Listed,Comm
Tel: **01978 790253** Mrs Parry.
Rates fr: *£13.00-£14.00.*
Open: All Year (not Xmas)
Beds: 1F 1D 1S
Baths: 1 Shared
ⓑ P (3) ⒦ 🖵 🗙 🛋 V 🛢 ♦

Clwyd Gate   89

National Grid Ref: SJ1658

🍴 🍺 Clwyd Gate Inn, Druid Inn

(0.75m 🚅**)** *Ffynnon Y Berth,*
Clwyd Gate, Llanarmon yn Ial,
Mold, Clwyd, CH7 5TA.
Actual grid ref: SJ176580
Working farm in idyllic setting.
Tel: **01824 780298** Ms Davies.
Rates fr: *£15.00-£15.00.*
Open: Apr to Oct
Beds: 1F 1T
Baths: 1 Private 1 Shared
ⓑ 🖵 🕭 🛋 V 🛢 ♦

Llanfair Dyffryn Clwyd 90

National Grid Ref: SJ1355

🍴 🍺 White Horse

(1.5m 🚅**)** *Eyarth Station, Llanfair*
Dyffryn Clwyd, Ruthin, Clwyd,
LL15 2EE.
Old railway station.
Grades: WTB 3 Cr, High Comm,
AA 5 Q, Select
Tel: **01824 703643** Mrs Spencer.
Rates fr: *£19.50-£27.00.*
Open: All Year
Beds: 2F 2D 2T
Baths: 6 Ensuite
ⓑ P 🖵 🕭 🗙 🛋 V 🛢 ♦

(1.5m 🚅**)** *Gorffwysfa, Llanfair*
Dyffryn Clwyd, Ruthin, Clwyd,
LL15 2UN.
Actual grid ref: SJ145567
Large Victorian private country
house.
Grades: WTB 3 Cr
Tel: **01824 702432** Mrs Horrocks.
Rates fr: *£16.00-£16.00.*
Open: All Year (not Xmas)
Beds: 1F 1D 1T
Baths: 2 Ensuite
ⓑ P ⒦ 🕭 🗙 🛋 V 🛢 ♦
Also ▲ ,
Open: All Year (not Xmas) T ♦ ⓑ

Planning a longer

stay? Always ask for

any special rates.

(1m ♠) *Plas Uchaf,*
Graigadwywynt, Llanfair Dyffryn
Clwyd, Ruthin, Clwyd, LL15 2TF.
C15th manor house, beams,
panelling.
Grades: WTB 2 Cr, High Comm
Tel: 01824 705794 Mr Jones.
Rates fr: *£15.00*-**£15.00**.
Open: All Year
Beds: 1F 1D 1T
Baths: 3 Ensuite
🛏 (1) 🅿 (4) ◻ 🛏 ▪

Gwernaffield 91

National Grid Ref: SJ2064

(4.5m) *Maes Garmon Farm,*
Gwernaffield, Mold, Clwyd,
CH7 5DB.
Actual grid ref: SJ215641
C17th farmhouse, beautiful
secluded setting.
Grades: WTB 2 Cr, High Comm
Tel: 01352 759887 Mrs Cook.
Rates fr: *£16.00*-**£18.00**.
Open: All Year (not Xmas)
Beds: 2D 1T 3S
Baths: 3 Ensuite
🛏 (7) 🅿 (12) ⬥ ◻ ✕ 🛏 Ⓥ ▪ ⚡

Ruthin 92

National Grid Ref: SJ1258

🍴 ◁ Anchor Inn, Golden Lion

(4m) *Argoed Guest House,*
Llanfwrog, Ruthin, Denbighshire,
LL15 1LG.
WTB Commended guesthouse,
rural location.
Grades: WTB 2 Cr, Comm
Tel: 01824 703407
Mr Mottram-Smale.
Rates fr: *£15.00*-**£17.50**.
Open: All Year
Beds: 1F 1D 1T
Baths: 1 Private 1 Shared
🛏 🅿 (4) ⬥ ◻ ✕ 🛏

Llangynhafal 93

National Grid Ref: SJ1263

🍴 ◁ Golden Lion (Llangynhafal)

(1.5m ♠) *Esgairlygain,*
Llangynhafal, Ruthin, Clwyd,
LL15 1RT.
Actual grid ref: SJ135625
Converted stone barn.
Grades: WTB 3 Cr
Tel: 01824 704047
Mrs Henderson.
Rates fr: *£16.00*-**£16.00**.
Open: Apr to Oct
Beds: 1F 1D **Baths:** 3 Private
🛏 🅿 ◻ 🛏 ✕ 🛏 Ⓥ ⚡

Bringing children with
you? Always ask for
any special rates.

All rates are subject
to alteration at the
owners' discretion.

Llandyrnog 94

National Grid Ref: SJ1065

(2m ♠) *Pentre Bach, Llandyrnog,*
Denbigh, LL16 4LA.
C18th farmhouse.
Grades: WTB 2 Cr
Tel: 01824 790725
Mr & Mrs Carrington-Sykes.
Rates fr: *£16.00*-**£20.00**.
Open: All Year (not Xmas)
Beds: 1D 1T **Baths:** 2 Private
🛏 🅿 (6) ◻ 🛏 ✕ 🛏 Ⓥ ▪ ⚡

Denbigh 95

National Grid Ref: SJ0566

(3m ♠) *Cayo Guest House,*
74 Vale Street, Denbigh, LL16 3BW.
Long-established comfortable
Victorian townhouse, good
reputation.
Grades: WTB 3 Cr, AA 2 Q
Tel: 01745 812686
Mrs MacCormack.
Rates fr: *£15.00*-**£15.00**.
Open: All Year (not Xmas)
Beds: 2D 3T
Baths: 5 Private 1 Shared
🛏 ◻ 🛏 ✕ 🛏 ▪

Waen 96

National Grid Ref: SJ0969

🍴 ◁ Dinorben Arms, Downing
Arms

(0.25m) *Bryn Clwyd, Waen,*
Bodfari, Denbigh, LL16 4BT.
Actual grid ref: SJ096692
Quaint cottages combined into one.
Tel: 01745 710357 Mrs Parry.
Rates fr: *£14.00*-**£14.00**.
Open: Feb to Nov
Beds: 1D 1T 1S
Baths: 1 Shared
🛏 🅿 ◻ 🛏 ▪ ⚡

Bodfari 97

National Grid Ref: SJ0970

(0.25m ♠) *Fron-Haul, Bodfari,*
Denbigh, LL16 4DY.
Actual grid ref: SJ099717
Breathtaking scenery, good whole-
some food.
Grades: WTB 2 Cr
Tel: 01745 710301 Ms Edwards.
Rates fr: *£16.00*-**£16.00**.
Open: All Year
Beds: 1F 2D 1T
Baths: 1 Private 2 Shared
🛏 🅿 (10) ◻ 🛏 ✕ 🛏 ▪ ⚡
Also ▲ *£2.00 per tent.*
Open: All Year

Afonwen 98

National Grid Ref: SJ1371

🍴 ◁ Pwll Gwyn

(2.25m ♠) *Ddol Ucha, Afonwen,*
Mold, Clwyd, CH7 5UN.
C17th coach house by nature
reserve.
Grades: WTB Listed
Tel: 01352 720125
Mrs Morris.
Rates fr: *£16.00*-**£16.00**.
Open: Feb to Dec
Beds: 1D 1T
🛏 (5) 🅿 (6) ⬥ ◻ 🛏 🛏 ▪ ⚡

Caerwys 99

National Grid Ref: SJ1272

🍴 ◁ Travellers Inn

(1.5m ♠) *Plas Penucha,*
Caerwys, Mold, Clwyd, CH7 5BH.
Actual grid ref: SJ332857
Grades: WTB 3 Cr, High Comm
Tel: 01352 720210 Mrs Price.
Rates fr: *£17.50*-**£17.50**.
Open: All Year
Beds: 2D 2T
Baths: 2 Private
🛏 🅿 ⬥ ◻ ✕ 🛏 Ⓥ ▪ ⚡
Large comfortable farmhouse with
extensive gardens overlooking
Clwydian Hills. Ideal for walking
and touring North Wales. Packed
lunches and evening meals, drying
facilities. Brochure available.

Tremeirchion 100

National Grid Ref: SJ0873

🍴 ◁ The Salisbury Arms

(0.75m ♠) *Pen Y Graig,*
Tremeirchion, St Asaph, Clwyd,
LL17 0UR.
Actual grid ref: SJ088719
Large, modern, comfortable
country house.
Grades: WTB Listed
Tel: 01745 710253
Mr & Mrs Jackson.
Rates fr: *£15.00*-**£15.00**.
Open: All Year (not Xmas)
Beds: 3T
🅿 (10) ◻ 🛏 ✕ 🛏 Ⓥ ⚡
Also ▲ *£2.00 per person. Also*
bunkhouse, £6.00 per bunk
Open: All Year 🄽 ♨ ✕ ⚡ ♿

(0.75m ♠) *Ffynnon Beuno,*
Tremeirchion, St Asaph, Clwyd,
LL17 0UE.
Actual grid ref: SJ084724
Farmhouse of great historical
interest.
Tel: 01745 710475
Ms Pierce.
Rates fr: *£15.00*-**£12.00**.
Open: All Year (not Xmas)
Beds: 1D 1S
Baths: 1 Private 1 Shared
🛏 🅿 ◻ 🛏 Ⓥ ▪ ⚡

St Asaph   101

National Grid Ref: SJ0374

(4m) *Pen-Y-Bryn Farm, Boderw, St Asaph, Denbighshire, LL17 0LF.*
Comfortable farmhouse in peaceful surroundings.
Grades: WTB 1 Cr
Tel: **01745 583213** Mrs Williams.
Rates fr: *£13.00-£13.00.*
Open: All Year (not Xmas)
Beds: 1F 1D 1S **Baths:** 2 Private
🛏 🅿 (6) 🛒 🕿 🎟 Ⓥ

Cwm   102

National Grid Ref: SJ0677

(1m 🚄) *Two Hoots, 4 Bod Hamer, Cwm, Dyserth, Rhyl, Clwyd, LL18 5SL.*
Modern, small, comfortable, homely. **Grades:** WTB Listed
Tel: **01745 570226** Tong B&B.
Rates fr: *£12.50-£12.50.*
Open: All Year (not Xmas)
Beds: 1D **Baths:** 1 Private
🛏 ⚡ 🛒 🕿 🗙 🎟 Ⓥ 🍴 ✂

Prestatyn   103

National Grid Ref: SJ0682

🍽 🍷 Cross Foxes, Offa's Tavern

(0.1m) *Roughsedge House, 26/28 Marine Road, Prestatyn, Clwyd, LL19 7HG.*
Family-run guesthouse.
Grades: WTB 2 Cr, Comm, AA 2 Q, Recomm
Tel: **01745 887359** Mrs Kubler.
Rates fr: *£13.50-£13.50.*
Open: All Year
Beds: 2F 4D 2T 2S
Baths: 3 Private 3 Shared
🛏 🅿 (3) ✂ 🛒 🗙 🎟 Ⓥ 🍴

All details shown are as supplied by B&B owners in Autumn 1995.

(0.1m) *Traeth Ganol Hotel, 41 Beach Road West, Prestatyn, Clwyd, LL19 7LL.*
Actual grid ref: SJ059836
Seafront location, special winter breaks.
Grades: WTB 3 Cr, High Comm
Tel: **01745 853594**
Mr & Mrs Groves.
Rates fr: *£23.00-£30.00.*
Open: All Year
Beds: 6F 1D 1T 1S
Baths: 9 Private
🛏 🅿 (9) 🛒 🗙 🎟 ♿ Ⓥ 🍴 ✂

(On Path) *Bryngele, 4 Ash Grove, Prestatyn, Clwyd, LL19 9DW.*
Small, friendly guesthouse.
Tel: **01745 886514**
Mrs Roberts.
Rates fr: *£15.00-£20.00.*
Open: All Year (not Xmas)
Beds: 1D 1T
Baths: 1 Shared
🛏 (10) 🛒 🍴 ✂

Oxfordshire Way

The **Oxfordshire Way** is only 65 miles long but takes the walker through the best bits of Oxfordshire from the Cotswolds down to the Chilterns. You start in beautiful Bourton-on-the-Water (actually in Gloucestershire) and head off through the pretty 'Wychwoods', near Blenheim Palace to the deserted villages of Otmoor, before heading south-east to chalk hills, beech woods and noble Henley-on-Thames on the banks of the river. The county looks after its paths well - the **Oxfordshire Way** is very well waymarked and in our opinion, the walking literature that comes from Oxfordshire County Council is the best in the country. This path links up with the **Cotswold Way** (via the **Heart of England** extension - q.v.) and the **Thames Footpath**.

Guides: *The Oxfordshire Way* by Oxfordshire County Council (ISBN 0 7509 0356 2), published by O.C.C., in association with Alan Sutton Publishing Ltd and available directly from their offices (Countryside Services, Dept for Leisure & Arts, Library HQ, Holton, Oxford, OX9 1QQ), £5.99

Maps: 1:50000 Ordnance Survey Landranger Series: 163, 164, 165, 175

Bourton on the Water   1

National Grid Ref: SP1620

🍴 🍺 Mouse Trap, Plough Inn, Old Manse Hotel, Lansdowne

(On Path) **Broadlands Guest House**, Clapton Row, Bourton on the Water, Cheltenham, Glos, *GL54 2DN*.
Actual grid ref: SP168204
C17th traditional Cotswold stone guesthouse.
Grades: ETB 3 Cr, Comm
Tel: 01451 822002 Mr Ferrari.
Rates fr: *£19.75*-**£30.00**.
Open: All Year
Beds: 3F 6D 2T
Baths: 11 Ensuite
🛏 🅿 (12) 🛇 🍽 🗙 ⛁ ⚕

(On Path) **6 Moore Road**, Bourton on the Water, Cheltenham, Glos, *GL54 2AZ*.
Modern and comfortable, quiet.
Tel: 01451 820767 Mrs Mustoe.
Rates fr: *£15.00*-**£17.00**.
Open: All Year (not Xmas)
Beds: 1D 1T
Baths: 1 Shared
🛏 (8) 🅿 (2) ✂ 🛇 🍴 ⛁ Ⓥ ⚕

(0.25m) **Windrush Farm**, Bourton on the Water, Cheltenham, Glos, *GL54 3BY*.
Traditional Cotswold stone farmhouse 1.5 miles from Bourton-on-the-Water village.
Grades: ETB 2 Cr, Comm
Tel: 01451 820419 Mrs Burrough.
Rates fr: *£17.50*-**£25.00**.
Open: Mar to Dec
Beds: 1D 1T **Baths:** 2 Private
🅿 (4) ✂ 🛇 ⛁ Ⓥ

(0.25m) **Lansdowne Villa Guest House**, Bourton on the Water, Cheltenham, Glos, *GL54 2AT*.
Spacious rooms, completely refurbished.

Grades: ETB 3 Cr, High Comm
Tel: 01451 820673
Mr & Mrs Baker.
Rates fr: *£21.50*-**£26.00**.
Open: All Year
Beds: 8D 2T 2S
Baths: 12 Ensuite
🛏 🅿 (14) 🛇 🗙 ⛁ Ⓥ

(0.25m) **Sycamore Guest House**, Lansdowne, Bourton on the Water, Cheltenham, Glos, *GL54 2AR*.
Comfortable, homely guesthouse.
Grades: ETB 2 Cr, Comm
Tel: 01451 821647
Mr Norman.
Rates fr: *£17.00*-**£22.00**.
Open: All Year
Beds: 1F 3D 1T
Baths: 5 Private
🛏 🅿 (6) 🛇 🗙 ⛁ & Ⓥ

(On Path) **Fosseside**, Lansdowne, Bourton on the Water, Cheltenham, Glos, *GL54 2AT*.
Comfortable accommodation in lovely location.
Grades: ETB High Comm
Tel: 01451 820574
Mrs Waterworth.
Rates fr: *£16.50*-**£26.50**.
Open: All Year (not Xmas)
Beds: 3D
Baths: 2 Ensuite 1 Private
🛏 (10) 🅿 (3) 🛇 ⛁ Ⓥ ⚕ ⚕

(On Path) **Lansdowne House**, Lansdowne, Bourton on the Water, Cheltenham, Glos, *GL54 2AT*.
Tastefully furnished period stone house.
Grades: ETB 1 Cr, Comm
Tel: 01451 820812
Mrs Garwood.
Rates fr: *£14.50*-**£18.00**.
Open: All Year (not Xmas)
Beds: 1F 1D 1T
Baths: 3 Private
🛏 🅿 (5) 🛇 ⛁ Ⓥ

Little Rissington   2

National Grid Ref: SP1919

🍴 🍺 The Lamb, The Mouse Trap, The Parrot & Alligator, The Wellington, The New Inn

(1m) **Hill Farm**, Little Rissington, Bourton on the Water, Cheltenham, Glos, *GL54 2ND*.
Large Cotswold farmhouse, quiet position. **Grades:** ETB 2 Cr
Tel: 01451 820330 Mrs Sweeting.
Rates fr: *£15.00*-**£18.00**.
Open: All Year **Beds:** 1F 1D 1T
Baths: 1 Private 1 Shared
🛏 🅿 (6) 🛇 🍴 ⛁ Ⓥ

Nether Westcote   3

National Grid Ref: SP2220

(0.5m) **Cotswold View Guest House**, Nether Westcote, Chipping Norton, Oxon, *OX7 6SD*.
Actual grid ref: SP222202
Converted farmyard.
Grades: ETB 2 Cr, AA 2 Q
Tel: 01993 830699 Mr Gibson.
Rates fr: *£17.50*-**£20.00**.
Open: All Year (not Xmas)
Beds: 4D 2T 2S
Baths: 6 Ensuite 2 Shared
🅿 (8) ✂ 🛇 🍴 🗙 ⛁ ⚕ ⚕

Finstock 4

National Grid Ref: SP3616

⊓❄ The Plough

(1.5m) *Well Cottage, High Street, Finstock, Chipping Norton, Oxon, OX7 3BY.*
C17th cottage in small village.
Tel: **01993 868201**
Mrs Breakell.
Rates fr: *£14.00*-**£14.00**.
Open: All Year (not Xmas)
Beds: 1D 1S
Baths: 1 Shared
🅿 (1) ⟺ ▥

Combe 5

National Grid Ref: SP4115

⊓❄ Cock Inn

(0.5m) *Mayfield Cottage, West End, Combe, Witney, Oxon, OX8 8NP.*
Actual grid ref: SP407157
Comfortable old Cotswold stone cottage.
Grades: ETB Listed, High Comm
Tel: **01993 898298**
Mrs Fox.
Rates fr: *£16.00*-**£18.00**.
Open: Mar to Oct
Beds: 1D 1T 1S
Baths: 1 Shared
🐾 (12) 🅿 (2) ⚡ ✦

Wootton 6

National Grid Ref: SP4319

⊓❄ Duke of Marlborough, Killingworth Castle

(0.25m) *Hillside, Chapel Hill, Wootton, Woodstock, Oxon, OX20 1DX.* **Grades:** ETB Listed
Tel: **01993 811979** Mrs Hirsch.
Rates fr: *£15.00*-**£18.00**.
Open: All Year (not Xmas)
Beds: 1D 1T
Baths: 1 Ensuite 1 Shared
🐾 🅿 (4) ⚡ ⟺ ▥ ✦
Comfortable Georgian farmhouse in own grounds of 1.5 acres of orchard and hill meadow bordered by millstream. In centre of historic Cotswold stone village

(0.5m) *8 Manor Court, Wootton, Woodstock, Oxon, OX20 1EU.*
Actual grid ref: SP438199
Modern friendly village house.
Grades: ETB Comm
Tel: **01993 811186** Mrs Fletcher.
Rates fr: *£16.00*-**£16.00**.
Open: Feb to Nov
Beds: 1T 2S **Baths:** 2 Shared
🐾 (12) 🅿 (2) ⚡ ⟺ ▥ Ⓥ ♦ ✦

The lowest *double* rate per person is shown in *italics*.

The *lowest* **single** rate *is shown in* **bold.**

(2m) *Killingworth Castle, Wootton, Woodstock, Oxon, OX20 1EJ.*
Actual grid ref: SP438204
C17th coaching inn.
Tel: **01993 811401** Mrs Brooks.
Rates fr: *£14.25*-**£18.50**.
Open: All Year
Beds: 2D 1T
Baths: 1 Ensuite 1 Shared
🅿 (50) ⚡ ✕ ▥ Ⓥ ♦ ✦

Bletchingdon 7

National Grid Ref: SP5017

⊓❄ Chequers, Rock of Gibraltar, Blacks Head

(1.75m) *Stonehouse Farm, Weston Road, Bletchingdon, Kidlington, Oxon, OX5 3EA.*
C17th farmhouse.
Grades: ETB Listed
Tel: **01869 350585** Mrs Hedges.
Rates fr: *£17.50*-**£20.00**.
Open: All Year (not Xmas)
Beds: 1F 1D 1T 1S
Baths: 2 Shared
🐾 🅿 (6) ⚡ ⟺ Ⓥ

© Crown Copyright

Horton cum Studley 8

National Grid Ref: SP6012

(2m) *Kings Arms Hotel, Horton cum Studley, Oxford, OX33 1AY*.
Actual grid ref: SP6012
Friendly, relaxed country village hotel.
Grades: ETB 4 St, ETB
Tel: 01865 351235
Rates fr: *£24.00-£28.00*.
Open: All Year
Beds: 1F 4D 2T 2D
Baths: 9 Ensuite
⌂ (1) ▣ (35) ▢ ✕ 圖 Ⓥ 🛆

Tetsworth 9

National Grid Ref: SP6802

†⊙⌿ ▄ Lion on the Green, Swan Restaurant

(On Path 🚌) *Little Acre, 4 High Street, Tetsworth, Thame, OX9 7AT*.
Actual grid ref: SP682022
Tel: 01844 281423 Ms Tanner.
Rates fr: *£13.00-£15.00*.
Open: All Year
Beds: 1F 1D 3T
Baths: 2 Ensuite, 2 Shared
⌂ ▣ (5) ▢ ▟ ✕ 圖 ╧ Ⓥ 🛆 ⚡
Very popular country guest house. Just 200 yards Oxfordshire Way and 3 miles Ridgeway Path. We offer a full traditional English breakfast and every comfort can be assured.

Lewknor 10

National Grid Ref: SU7197

†⊙⌿ ▄ Olde Leathern Bottle, Lambert Arms

(0.5m) *Peel Guest House, London Road, Lewknor, Watlington, Oxon, OX9 5SA*.
Detached house overlooking Chiltern escarpment.
Grades: ETB Listed
Tel: 01844 351310
Ms Hunt.
Rates fr: *£18.00-£20.00*.
Open: All Year
Beds: 5T 1S
Baths: 3 Private 1 Shared
⌂ (10) ▣ (7) ▢ 圖 Ⓥ 🛆 ⚡

Pishill 11

National Grid Ref: SU7289

†⊙⌿ ▄ The Crown Inn

(On Path 🚌) *Bank Farm, Pishill, Henley-on-Thames, Oxon, RG9 6HJ*.
Actual grid ref: SU724898
Quiet working farmhouse.
Tel: 01491 638601 Mrs Lakey.
Rates fr: *£15.00-£12.00*.
Open: All Year
Beds: 1F 1S
Baths: 1 Ensuite, 1 Shared
⌂ ▣ (10) ▢ ▟ 圖 ⚡
(On Path) *Old Rectory, Pishill,*

Henley-on-Thames, Oxon, RG9 6HJ.
Comfortable Victorian family home.
Tel: 01491 638243 Mrs Godfrey.
Rates fr: *£17.50-£20.00*.
Open: All Year (not Xmas)
Beds: 1T **Baths:** 1 Ensuite
⌂ ▣ (6) ▟ ▢ 圖 🛆 ⚡

Nettlebed 12

National Grid Ref: SU6986

†⊙⌿ ▄ Crown Inn

(1.75m) *Park Corner Farm House, Nettlebed, Henley-on-Thames, Oxon, RG9 6DR*.
Queen Anne brick-and-flint farmhouse.
Tel: 01491 641450 Mrs Rutter.
Rates fr: *£16.00-£18.00*.
Open: All Year (not Xmas)
Beds: 2T **Baths:** 1 Shared
⌂ ▣ ▟ ▄ 圖

Henley-on-Thames 13

National Grid Ref: SU7682

†⊙⌿ ▄ Ye Olde Bell, Anchor Hotel, Bottle & Glass, Little Angel, The Bull, Golden Ball, Little White Hart, The Tuns, Argyll, Anchor, Saracen's Head

(0.5m 🚌) *New Lodge, Henley Park, Henley-on-Thames, Oxon, RG9 6HU*.
Actual grid ref: SU758847
Victorian lodge cottage in parkland. **Grades:** ETB 1 Cr, Comm
Tel: 01491 576340 Mrs Warner.
Rates fr: *£14.50-£22.00*.
Open: All Year
Beds: 2D **Baths:** 2 Ensuite
⌂ ▣ (5) ▟ ▢ 圖 ♿ 🛆 ⚡

(0.25m 🚌) *Ledard, Rotherfield Road, Henley-on-Thames, Oxon, RG9 1NN*.
Well appointed Victorian family home.
Tel: 01491 575611 Mrs Howard.
Rates fr: *£16.00-£18.00*.
Open: All Year (not Xmas)
Beds: 1F 1D **Baths:** 1 Private
⌂ ▣ (3) ▢ 圖 Ⓥ 🛆 ⚡

(0.25m) *The Jolly Waterman, 291 Reading Road, Henley-on-Thames, Oxon, RG9.*
Comfortable family-run public house.
Tel: 01491 573055 Mrs Scott.
Rates fr: *£17.50-£20.00*.
Open: All Year (not Xmas)
Beds: 1F 1D 2T **Baths:** 1 Shared
⌂ ▣ (6) ▟ ▢ ✕ 圖 Ⓥ

(0.5m) *The Saracens Head, 129 Greys Road, Henley-on-Thames, Oxon, RG9 1QW*.
Friendly, local pub on outskirts.
Tel: 01491 575929 Mrs Sumner.
Rates fr: *£18.00-£28.00*.
Open: All Year (not Xmas)

Beds: 1D 1T
Baths: 1 Shared
⌂ (10) ▣ (20) ▢ ✕ 圖 Ⓥ 🛆 ⚡

(0.5m 🚌) *Lenwade, 3 Western Road, Henley-on-Thames, Oxon, RG9 1JL*.
Large beautifully decorated Victorian house.
Grades: ETB 1 Cr, High Comm, AA 3 Q
Tel: 01491 573468 Mrs Williams.
Rates fr: *£17.00-£25.00*.
Open: All Year **Beds:** 2D 1T
Baths: 1 Ensuite 2 Shared
⌂ ▣ (1) ▢ ▄ 圖 Ⓥ ⚡

(0.5m) *Mervyn House, 4 St Marks Road, Henley-on-Thames, Oxon, RG9 1LJ*.
Actual grid ref: SU6878
Victorian house, close to town centre.
Grades: ETB 1 Cr, Comm
Tel: 01491 575331 Mrs Ely.
Rates fr: *£16.00-£21.50*.
Open: All Year (not Xmas)
Beds: 2D 1T
Baths: 1 Ensuite 1 Shared
⌂ (12) ▢ ▄ 圖

(0.5m 🚌) *The Laurels, 107 St Marks Road, Henley-on-Thames, Oxon, RG9 1LP*.
Large, comfortable, friendly and quiet home.
Tel: 01491 572982 Mrs Bridekirk.
Rates fr: *£16.50-£20.00*.
Open: All Year
Beds: 1F 1D 1T 1S
Baths: 1 Ensuite 1 Shared
⌂ ▣ (2) ▢ 圖 Ⓥ ⚡

(On Path) *Old Bell House, Northfield End, Henley-on-Thames, Oxon, RG9 2JG*.
Large townhouse built 1650, Georgian addition.
Tel: 01491 574350 Mrs Duckett.
Rates fr: *£17.00-£19.00*.
Open: All Year
Beds: 2F
Baths: 2 Ensuite
⌂ ▣ (3) ▟ ▢ ▄ 圖 🛆 ⚡

(1m) *Alftrudis, 8 Norman Avenue, Henley-on-Thames, Oxon, RG9 1SG*.
Large detached Victorian private house.
Grades: ETB 1 Cr, High Comm
Tel: 01491 573099 Mrs Lambert.
Rates fr: *£16.00-£25.00*.
Open: All Year
Beds: 2D 1T
Baths: 2 Ensuite 1 Shared
⌂ ▣ (1) ▢ 圖

(m 🚌) *107 St Marks Road, Henley-on-Thames, Oxon, RG9 1LP*.
Large, comfortable, friendly and quiet home.
Tel: 01491 572982 Mrs Bridekirk.
Rates fr: *£16.50-£20.00*.
Open: All Year
Beds: 1F 1D 1T 1S
Baths: 1 Ensuite 1 Shared
⌂ ▣ (2) ▢ 圖 Ⓥ ⚡

STILWELL'S BRITAIN: BED & BREAKFAST 1996

Bed & breakfast accommodation is a British institution. It's a great value alternative to expensive hotels and a world away from camping and caravanning. You may be touring, travelling or pursuing a hobby. You may just wish to get away from it all. Whatever the reason, the British bed & breakfast is the great value answer to all your accommodation needs.

There's such a wide range to choose from - private houses, country halls, farms, cottages, inns, small hotels and guest houses. Stilwell's Britain Bed & Breakfast 1996 publishes by far and away the most extensive list of bed & breakfasts available. The book is thus ideal for planning trips and short stays in every part of the country.

Arranged by country, county and location with local maps alongside, Stilwell's Britain Bed & Breakfast 1996 is the indispensable reference work for bed & breakfast accommodation in Britain.

- **Plan your trips with no fuss!**

- **All official grades shown!**

- **Local maps - see where you want to stay at a glance!**

- **Pubs serving evening meals shown too!**

- **The largest choice ever - a massive 8,500 entries!**

- **Good value only - from £10 to £25 a night!**

- **Handy size for easy packing!**

Peddars Way and Norfolk Coast Path

Two paths - one ancient and the other brand new - provide a easy-going 98-mile walk through flat but very different landscapes. The **Peddar's Way** is a flinty old Roman road, running straight as a die through the heaths, forest and military training grounds of Breckland in West Norfolk up to the sea. At Hunstanton it joins the **Norfolk Coast Path**, which leads among the famous dunes, salt marshes, creeks and shingle ridges of North Norfolk, rich in birds and wild-life. A good path to cut your teeth on over a couple of long weekends or on a week's break in winter or summer. There is also a path association -membership details from the **Peddars Way Association**, 150 Armes Street, Norwich, NR2 4EG.

Guides (available from all good map shops)
Walking the Peddars Way & Norfolk Coast Path with the Weavers Way, published by Peddars Way Association and available only from them by post (150 Armes Street, Norwich, NR2 4EG), £1.80

Langton's Guide to the Peddars Way & Norfolk Coast Path by Andrew Durham (ISBN 1 899242 00 7), published by Langton's Guides and available directly from the publishers (Ashleigh, Radley Road, Halam, Newark, Notts, NG22 8AQ, tel. 01636 813883), £6.95

Peddars Way & Norfolk Coast Path by Bruce Robinson (ISBN 1 85410 408 X), published by Aurum Press in association with the Countryside Commission and Ordnance Survey, £9.99. Maps: 1:50000 Ordnance Survey Landranger Series: 132, 133 and 134

Maps: 1:50000 Ordnance Survey Landranger Series: 132, 133 and 134

Comments on the path to the association and to: **Tim Lidstone-Scott**, Peddar's Way Officer, Norfolk Coast Project, 6 Station Road, Wells next the Sea, Norfolk, NR23 1AE.

Thetford 1

National Grid Ref: TL8783

|O| ▥ The Ark, The Anchor, Black Horse, Albion

(6m) *The Wilderness, Earls Street, Thetford, Norfolk, IP24 2AF.*
Tudor-style house, landscaped garden.
Grades: ETB Reg
Tel: 01842 764646 Mrs Pomorski.
Rates fr: £17.00-£19.00.
Open: All Year (not Xmas)
Beds: 3D 1S **Baths:** 1 Shared
┣ (8) ▣ ⅍ ▭ ▥ ⓐ ✦

(5.5m) *43 Magdalen Street, Thetford, Norfolk, IP24 2BP.*
200-year-old cottage, near station.
Tel: 01842 764564 Mrs Findlay.
Rates fr: £17.00-£17.00.
Open: All Year (not Xmas)
Beds: 2T 1S **Baths:** 1 Shared
▭ ▥ ✦

(7m 🚗) *29 Priory Park, Thetford, Norfolk, IP24 1AU.*
Large, comfortable, friendly walkers' home.
Tel: 01842 752656 Mrs Atkinson.
Rates fr: £14.00-£14.00.
Open: All Year (not Xmas)
Beds: 1D 1T 2S **Baths:** 1 Shared
┣ ▣ (2) ⅍ ▭ ⅍ ▥ ✦

(5.5m) *Wereham House Hotel, 24 White Hart Street, Thetford, Norfolk, IP24 1AD.*
Comfortable family-run hotel.
Grades: ETB 2 Cr, AA 1 Q
Tel: 01842 761956
Rates fr: £24.50-£39.00.
Open: All Year **Beds:** 1F 4D 2T 1S
┣ ▣ ▭ ✕ ▥ ▦

Garboldisham 2

National Grid Ref: TM0081

|O| ▥ White Horse

(3.5m 🚗) *Ingleneuk Lodge, Hopton Road, Garboldisham, Diss, Norfolk, IP22 2RQ.*
Actual grid ref: TM002801
Modern family run. Friendly atmosphere.
Grades: ETB 3 Cr, Comm, AA 3 Q, RAC High Acclaim
Tel: 01953 681541 Mr/Mrs Atkins.
Rates fr: £25.00-£33.00.
Open: All Year (not Xmas)
Beds: 1F 2D 2T 2S
Baths: 6 Private 1 Shared
┣ ▣ (20) ▭ ⅍ ✕ ▥ ▦

(3.5m) *Swan House B&B, Hopton Road, Garboldisham, Diss, Norfolk, IP22 2RQ.*
Comfortable converted C17th coaching inn.

Grades: ETB Listed, Comm
Tel: 01953 688221 Mr Eldridge.
Rates fr: £17.00-£22.00.
Open: Feb to Dec
Beds: 1D 1T 1S **Baths:** 1 Shared
┣ (12) ▣ (5) ⅍ ▭ ▥ ▦

Wretham 3

National Grid Ref: TL9190

(On Path 🚗) *Dog & Partridge, Watton Road, Wretham, Thetford, Norfolk, IP24 1QS.*
Actual grid ref: TL928907
C18th flint public house.
Tel: 01953 498245 Mrs Nicholls.
Rates fr: £14.00-£16.00.
Open: All Year **Beds:** 1F 3D
┣ ▣ ▭ ⅍ ✕ ▥ ⓐ ✦

Thompson 4

National Grid Ref: TL9196

|O| ▥ Chequers

(2m) *College Farm, Thompson, Thetford, Norfolk, IP24 1QG.*
Actual grid ref: TL933966
600 year old farmhouse.
Grades: ETB Listed
Tel: 01953 483318 Mrs Garnier.
Rates fr: £18.00-£18.00.
Open: All Year **Beds:** 1D 2T 1S
Baths: 2 Private 2 Shared
┣ (7) ▣ (10) ▭ ▥ ▦ ⓐ ✦

(1.5m) *The Thatched House,*
Pockthorpe Corner, Thompson,
Thetford, Norfolk, IP24 1PJ.
400-year-old thatched house.
Tel: **01953 483577**
Mrs Mills.
Rates fr: *£17.50-£17.50.*
Open: All Year (not Xmas)
Beds: 3T 1S
Baths: 2 Shared
🛏 (12) ▣ (8) ⅏ ⬛ 🛏 ⊞ ⓘ ∦

Watton 5

National Grid Ref: TF9100

🍴 ⬛ Crown Hotel, Willow House,
Hare & Barrel

(1.25m) *The Hare & Barrel,* 80
Brandon Road, Watton, Thetford,
Norfolk, IP25 6LB.
Converted Victorian house and out-
houses.

Grades: ETB 2 Cr
Tel: **01953 882752**
Rates fr: *£18.00-£23.00.*
Open: All Year
Beds: 2 F 2D 12T 2S
Baths: 18 Private
🛏 ▣ (40) ⬛ 🛏 ✕ ⊞ Ⓥ ⓘ ∦

Little Cressingham 6

National Grid Ref: TF8700

🍴 ⬛ White Horse Inn

(On Path) *Sycamore House, Little*
Cressingham, Thetford, Norfolk,
IP25 6NE.
Modern, comfortable private
house.
Tel: **01953 881887**
Mrs Wittridge.
Rates fr: *£16.00-£16.00.*
Open: All Year
Beds: 2D 1T 1S
Baths: 1 Private 2 Shared
🛏 ▣ (4) ⬛ 🛏 ⊞ ⓘ ∦

Great Cressingham 7

National Grid Ref: TF8501

🍴 ⬛ The Windmill Inn

(0.75m) *The Vines, The Street,*
Great Cressingham, Thetford,
Norfolk, IP25 6NL.
Comfortable, friendly, C16th
house.
Tel: **01760 756303** Mrs Wymer.
Rates fr: *£12.50-£12.50.*
Open: All Year (not Xmas)
Beds: 2D 1T
Baths: 1 Shared
🛏 ▣ ⬛ ⊞ ⓘ ∦

The Country Code

Enjoy the countryside and
respect its life and work

Guard against all risk of fire

Fasten all gates

Keep your dogs under close
control

Keep to public paths across
farmland

Use gates and stiles to cross
fences, hedges and walls

Leave livestock, crops and
machinery alone

Take your litter home

Help to keep all water clean

Protect wild-life, plants and
trees

Take special care on country
roads

Make no unnecessary noise

North Pickenham 8

National Grid Ref: TF8606

⊮ ▥ Blue Lion

(0.25m) *Riverside House, Meadow Lane, North Pickenham, Swaffham, Norfolk, PE37 8LE.*
Flintstone house. Large secluded garden.
Tel: **01760 440219**
Mrs Norris.
Rates fr: *£15.00*-**£16.00**.
Open: All Year (not Xmas)
Beds: 2T
Baths: 2 Shared
🛏 🅿 (4) 🖵 🕇 🎟 ▪ ✦

Swaffham 9

National Grid Ref: TF8109

⊮ ▥ White Hart, Red Lion, George Hotel

(0.5m) *Hill View, 15 Norwich Road, Swaffham, Norfolk, PE37 8DF.*
Modern, comfortable house.
Tel: **01760 723306**
Mrs Johnstone.
Rates fr: *£14.00*-**£14.00**.
Open: All Year (not Xmas)
Beds: 1D 2T 1S
Baths: 1 Shared
🛏 (5) 🅿 (8) 🖵 🕇 🎟 ▪ ✦

(0.25m) *Purbeck House, Whitsands Road, Swaffham, Norfolk, PE37 7BJ.*
Family-run detached house in large garden.
Tel: **01760 721805 / 725345**
Mrs Webster.
Rates fr: *£15.00*-**£15.00**.
Open: All Year (not Xmas)
Beds: 2F 2T 2S
Baths: 1 Private 2 Shared
🛏 🅿 (3) 🖵 🎟 ▪ ✦

Sporle 10

National Grid Ref: TF8411

⊮ ▥ George & Dragon

(0.25m) *Cambridge Cottage, Love Lane, Sporle, Kings Lynn, Norfolk, PE32 2EP.*
200-year-old converted cottages in 4 acres.
Tel: **01760 723718**
Mr & Mrs Anderson.
Rates fr: *£15.00*-**£15.00**.
Open: All Year (not Xmas)
Beds: 2T
Baths: 1 Shared
🛏 🅿 🖵 🕇 🎟 ▥ ✦

(1m) *Corfield House, Sporle, Kings Lynn, Norfolk, PE32 2EA.*
Family-run country guesthouse.
Grades: ETB 3 Cr, High Comm, AA 4 Q, Select
Tel: **01760 723636**
Mr & Mrs Hickey.
Rates fr: *£18.50*-**£23.00**.

Open: Apr to Nov
Beds: 2D 2T 1S
Baths: 5 Private
🛏 🅿 🖵 🕇 🗙 🎟 ▥ ▪ ✦

Castle Acre 11

National Grid Ref: TF8115

⊮ ▥ Ostrich Inn, Albert Victor, George & Dragon

(On Path 🚌) *Willow Cottage, Stocks Green, Castle Acre, Kings Lynn, Norfolk, PE32 2AE.*
Listed Flint cottage, tea room.
Tel: **01760 755551** Mrs Johnson.
Rates fr: *£15.00*-**£18.00**.
Open: Easter to Dec
Beds: 2D 2T
Baths: 1 Shared
🛏 🖵 🕇 🗙 🎟 ▥ ▪ ✦

(On Path) *Gemini House, Pyes Lane, Castle Acre, Kings Lynn, Norfolk, PE32 2XB.*
Modern, well situated for walkers.
Tel: **01760 755375** Mrs Clark.
Rates fr: *£15.00*-**£15.00**.
Open: All Year
Beds: 2D 2T
Baths: 1 Private 2 Shared
🛏 🅿 (4) 🖵 🕇 🎟 ▪ ✦

(0.5m 🚌) *Home Farm, Castle Acre, Kings Lynn, Norfolk, PE32 2BW.*
Actual grid ref: TF794184
Pretty old farmhouse.
Tel: **01760 755342** Miss Bannister.
Rates fr: *£17.50*-**£17.50**.
Open: Easter to Oct
Beds: 1D 1T 1S
Baths: 1 Shared
🛏 🅿 (3) 🖵 🗙 ✦

(On Path 🚌) *The Old Red Lion, Bailey Street, Castle Acre, Kings Lynn, Norfolk, PE32 2AG.*
Converted pub, unique historic village.
Tel: **01760 755557** Mrs Loughlin.
Rates fr: *£10.00*-**£12.50**.
Open: All Year
Beds: 1F 2T
Baths: 2 Shared
🛏 (0) 🅿 (10) 🖵 🕇 🗙 🎟 ▥ ▪ ✦
Also 🅰 Also bunkhouse,
£10.00 per bunk
Open: All Year 🏠 🔲 ⚏ 🗙 ✦ 🕭

🚌 sign means that,
given due notice,
owners will pick you
up from the path
and drop you off *within reason.*

The lowest *double* rate per person is shown in *italics*.

Great Massingham 12

National Grid Ref: TF7922

⊮ ▥ Rose & Crown

(0.25m 🚌) *Pleasant House, Great Massingham, Kings Lynn, Norfolk, PE32 2HN.*
Georgian red Norfolk brick country house.
Tel: **01485 520259** Mr Rae.
Rates fr: *£16.00*-**£16.00**.
Open: All Year (not Xmas)
Beds: 1F 1T
Baths: 1 Shared
🛏 🅿 🖵 🕇 🗙 🎟 ▥ ▪ ✦

Harpley 13

National Grid Ref: TF7825

⊮ ▥ Rose & Crown (Harpley)

(1.25m) *Manor Farm Barn, 11 Rudham Road, Harpley, Kings Lynn, Norfolk, PE31 6TJ.*
Actual grid ref: TF793265
Converted barn, quiet village setting.
Grades: ETB Listed
Tel: **01485 520708** Mrs Thomas.
Rates fr: *£17.50*-**£17.50**.
Open: All Year
Beds: 2D 1T
Baths: 1 Private 2 Shared
🛏 (4) 🅿 (5) 🖵 🕇 🗙 🎟 ▥ ▪ ✦

Sedgeford 14

National Grid Ref: TF7136

⊮ ▥ King William

(0.5m) *Dove Hill Cottage, Cole Green, Sedgeford, Hunstanton, Norfolk, PE36 5LS.*
Actual grid ref: TF713366
Family home in Conservation Area.
Tel: **01485 571642** Mrs Lyle.
Rates fr: *£15.00*-**£15.00**.
Open: All Year (not Xmas)
Beds: 1F 1T
Baths: 1 Shared
🛏 🅿 🖵 🕇 🎟 ▪ ✦

Ringstead 15

National Grid Ref: TF7040

⊮ ▥ Gin Trap

(1m) *Courtyard Farm, Bunkhouse Barn, Ringstead, Hunstanton, Norfolk, PE36 5LQ.*
Farm building converted to bunkhouse.
Tel: **01485 25369** Mrs Calvert.
Price per person £4.00
Open: All Year 🏠 🔲

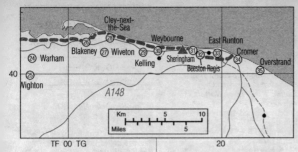

Hunstanton 16

National Grid Ref: TF6740

🍴 🍺 Gin Trap Inn, Lodge Hotel, Ancient Mariner, King William, The Marine Bar, The Golden Lion

(On Path 🚍) Pinewood House, 26 Northgate, Hunstanton, Norfolk, PE36 6AP.
Actual grid ref: TF673413
Grades: ETB 2 Cr, AA 3 Q
Tel: 01485 533068
Mrs Morison.
Rates fr: £16.50-£16.50.
Open: All Year (not Xmas)
Beds: 2F 4D 2T
Baths: 4 Ensuite 2 Shared
🛏 (6) 🅿 🏃 🛄 Ⓥ ⬛ ✦
Comfortable Victorian house offering bed and breakfast. 8 bedrooms, some ensuite with sea views. Ideal for Peddars Way/Coastal Path birdwatching. Groups welcome

(0.25m) Northgate House, 46 Northgate, Hunstanton, Norfolk, PE36 6DR.
Actual grid ref: TF6740
Comfortable spacious guesthouse, quietly located.
Tel: **01485 533269**
Mrs Bamfield.
Rates fr: £15.50-£15.50.
Open: All Year (not Xmas)
Beds: 1F 3D 2T 1S
Baths: 3 Private 1 Shared
🛏 ✦ 🅿 🏃 🛄 Ⓥ ⬛ ✦

(2m) Gate Lodge Guest House, 2 Westgate, Hunstanton, Norfolk, PE36 5AL.
Warm, comfortable, Victorian property.
Grades: ETB 2 Cr, Comm
Tel: **01485 533549**
Mr & Mrs Wellard.
Rates fr: £18.00-£23.00.
Open: Mar to Nov
Beds: 3D 3T
Baths: 6 Ensuite
🛏 (5) 🅿 (6) 🏃 🗙 🛄 Ⓥ ⬛ ✦

(🔺 1m) Hunstanton Youth Hostel, 15 Avenue Road, Hunstanton, Norfolk, PE36 5BW.
Actual grid ref: TF6740
Warden: Ms C Warner.
Tel: **01485 532061**
Under 18: £5.55 **Adults:** £8.25

Family Bunk Rooms, Centrally Heated, Showers, Evening Meal (7.00 pm), Shop, Television *Victorian Carrstone house in seaside resort with Blue Flag beach, famous for birdwatching and ecology studies*

(On Path) Caltofts, 15 Austin Street, Hunstanton, Norfolk, PE36 6AJ.
Family-run guesthouse.
Tel: **01485 533759**
Mr & Mrs Vass.
Rates fr: £15.00-£15.00.
Open: All Year
Beds: 2F 2D 1T 1S
Baths: 2 Private 1 Shared
🛏 🅿 (3) ✦ 🗙 🛄 ⬛

(1m) Rosamaly Guest House, 14 Glebe Avenue, Hunstanton, Norfolk, PE36 6BS.
Relaxed atmosphere, warm friendly guesthouse.
Grades: ETB Listed, Approv
Tel: **01485 534187**
Mr & Mrs Duff Dick.
Rates fr: £15.00-£15.00.
Open: All Year
Beds: 2F 1D 1T 1S
Baths: 1 Shared
🛏 🏃 🗙 🛄 Ⓥ ⬛ ✦

(0.75m 🚍) Fieldsend, Homefields Road, Hunstanton, Norfolk, PE36 5HL.
Large Edwardian country house style.
Grades: ETB 2 Cr, Comm
Tel: **01485 532593**
Mrs Tweedy Smith.
Rates fr: £17.50-£20.00.
Open: All Year (not Xmas)
Beds: 1F 1D 1T
Baths: 2 Ensuite 1 Private
🛏 🅿 🛄 Ⓥ ✦

(2m 🚍) Sutton House Hotel, 24 Northgate, Hunstanton, Norfolk, PE36 6AP.
Edwardian house near town/sea.
Grades: AA 3 Q
Tel: **01485 532552**
Mr Emsden.
Rates fr: £19.00-£24.00.
Open: All Year
Beds: 2F 3D 2T 1S
Baths: 8 Private
🛏 🅿 (6) 🏃 🗙 🛄 Ⓥ ⬛ ✦

(2m) Burleigh Hotel, 7 Cliff Terrace, Hunstanton, Norfolk, PE36 6DY.
Small family run hotel.
Grades: ETB 3 Cr, Comm
Tel: **01485 533080**
Mr & Mrs Abos.
Rates fr: £22.00-£30.00.
Open: All Year
Beds: 4F 4D 2T 1S
Baths: 9 Ensuite
🛏 (5) 🅿 🗙 🛄 Ⓥ ⬛ ✦

(1.5m) Kiama Cottage, 23 Austin Street, Hunstanton, Norfolk, PE36 6AN.
Small family guesthouse.
Grades: ETB 2 Cr, Comm
Tel: **01485 533615**
Mr & Mrs Flowerdew.
Rates fr: £15.00-£17.00.
Open: Mar to Oct
Beds: 1F 2D 1T
Baths: 4 Private
🛏 🅿 (1) 🏃 🗙 🛄 Ⓥ

Old Hunstanton 17

National Grid Ref: TF6842

🍴 🍺 Ancient Mariner

(1m) Lakeside, Waterworks Road, Old Hunstanton, Norfolk, PE36 6JE.
Converted waterworks, overlooking private lake.
Grades: ETB 3 Cr
Tel: **01485 533763**
Mr Diamant.
Rates fr: £18.00-£17.50.
Open: All Year
Beds: 3D 1T 2S
Baths: 4 Private 1 Shared
🛏 (13) 🅿 (10) 🗙 🛄 Ⓥ

Thornham 18

National Grid Ref: TF7343

🍴 🍺 The Lifeboat, King's Head, Chequers

(0.25m) Kings Head Hotel, High Street, Thornham, Hunstanton, Norfolk, PE36 6LY.
C16th inn, open log fires.
Tel: **01485 512213**
Mrs John.
Rates fr: £18.00-£18.00.
Open: All Year (not Xmas)
Beds: 2D 1T
Baths: 1 Shared
🛏 🅿 🗙 Ⓥ ⬛ ✦

(On Path 🚍) Ilex Cottage, High Street, Thornham, Hunstanton, Norfolk, PE36 6QY.
Fully modernised traditional style property.
Grades: ETB Listed Commended
Tel: **01485 512310**
Miss Leary.
Rates fr: £17.50-£20.00.
Open: All Year
Beds: 1D 2T
Baths: 2 Private ! Shared
🛏 (8) 🅿 (5) ✦ 🏃 🛄 Ⓥ ⬛ ✦

(On Path 🐾) *Orchard House, Thornham, Hunstanton, Norfolk, PE36 6LY.*
Quiet, select, detached residence.
Grades: ETB Registered
Tel: 01485 512259
Mrs Rutland.
Rates fr: *£18.00-£28.00.*
Open: All Year (not Xmas)
Baths: 2 Private 1 Shared
🛏 (8) 🅿 (4) ⅍⛒✕▥Ⓥⓘ✦

Brancaster   19

National Grid Ref: TF7743
🍴 ◖ Ship Hotel

(On Path) *Barmstone House, Brancaster, Kings Lynn, Norfolk, PE31 8AZ.*
Edwardian family house, warm welcome guaranteed!
Tel: 01485 210501
Mrs Townshend.
Rates fr: *£17.50-£20.00.*
Open: All Year (not Xmas)
Beds: 2D 1T 1S
Baths: 2 Shared
🛏 🅿 (3) ⛒▥ⓘ✦

Burnham Market   20

National Grid Ref: TF8342
🍴 ◖ Hoste Arms, Fishes Restaurant, Lord Nelson

(1m) *Holmesdale, Church Walk, Burnham Market, Kings Lynn, Norfolk, PE31 8DH.*
1930's extended chalet/bungalow.
Tel: 01328 738699
Mr & Mrs Groom.
Rates fr: *£16.00-£16.00.*
Open: All Year (not Xmas)
Beds: 1F
Baths: 1 Shared
🛏 🅿 ⛒🛏🛏▥Ⓥⓘ✦

(0.5m) *Millwood, Herrings Lane, Burnham Market, Kings Lynn, Norfolk, PE31 8DW.*
Actual grid ref: TF8343
Peaceful, luxurious, coastal country house.
Tel: 01328 730152
Mrs Leftley.
Rates fr: *£20.00-£23.00.*
Open: All Year (not Xmas)
Beds: 1D 1T 1S
Baths: 1 Ensuite 1 Shared
🛏 (8) 🅿 (8) ⅍⛒🛏▥ Ⓥ

Burnham Overy Staithe   21

National Grid Ref: TF8444
🍴 Hoste Arms, Lord Nelson, The Hero

(0.25m) *Domville Guest House, Glebe Lane, Burnham Overy Staithe, Kings Lynn, Norfolk, PE31 8JQ.*
Quietly situated, family-run guesthouse.
Grades: ETB 1 Cr, Comm
Tel: 01328 738298
Mr & Mrs Smith.
Rates fr: *£16.00-£16.00.*
Open: All Year (not Xmas)
Beds: 2D 2T 4S
Baths: 2 Private 2 Shared
🛏 (6) 🅿 (10) ⅍⛒✕Ⓥ✦

Holkham   22

National Grid Ref: TF8943
🍴 ◖ The Victoria

(0.75m) *Victoria Hotel, Holkham, Wells-next-the-Sea, Norfolk, NR23 1RG.*
Comfortable Victorian family-run hotel.
Grades: RAC Listed
Tel: 01328 710469
Mr Hoskins.
Rates fr: *£25.00-£27.50.*
Open: All Year (not Xmas)
Beds: 4D 2T 1S
Baths: 7 Private
🛏 🅿 (50) ⛒🛏✕▥Ⓥⓘ✦

Wells-next-the-Sea   23

National Grid Ref: TF9143
🍴 ◖ The Ark Royal Pub, Freeman Street, Wells, The Edinburgh Hotel

(On Path 🐾) *Eastdene Guest House, Northfield Lane, Wells-next-the-Sea, Norfolk, NR23 1LH.*
Grades: ETB 2 Cr
Tel: 01328 710381
Mrs Court.
Rates fr: *£16.00-£17.50.*
Open: All Year
Beds: 1D 2T 1S
Baths: 3 Ensuite, 1 Shared
🛏 (10) 🅿 (6) ⅍⛒🛏▥ⓘ✦
Central for Cley and Titchwell.
Close to Coastal Path. Bed and
breakfast. All ensuite with TV, tea
and coffee facilities. pets welcome.

(On Path 🐾) *The Old Police House, Polka Road, Wells-next-the-Sea, Norfolk, NR23 1ED.*
Actual grid ref: TF918436
Purpose built B&B extension.
Grades: ETB 2 Cr, Comm
Tel: 01328 710630 Mr Ashworth.
Rates fr: *£18.00-£20.00.*
Open: All Year
Beds: 3T
Baths: 3 Ensuite
🛏 (12) 🅿 (6) 🛏🛏▥Ⓥⓘ✦

All paths are popular: you are well-advised to book ahead

(0.5m) *Blenheim House, Theatre Road, Wells-next-the-Sea, Norfolk, NR23 1DJ.*
Comfortable C17th house.
Tel: 01328 711368 Mrs Court.
Rates fr: *£19.00.*
Open: Jan to Nov
Beds: 2F 1T **Baths:** 3 Ensuite
🛏 (10) 🅿 (4) ▥ⓘ✦

(0.5m 🐾) *St Heliers Guest House, Station Road, Wells-next-the-Sea, Norfolk, NR23 1EA.*
Large Georgian house, centrally located.
Tel: 01328 710361 Mrs Kerr.
Rates fr: *£14.00-£18.00.*
Open: All Year
Beds: 1F 1D 1T **Baths:** 2 Shared
🅿 (5) ⅍⛒🛏▥Ⓥⓘ✦

(0.5m) *Whimbrels, 31 Burnt Street, Wells-next-the-Sea, Norfolk, NR23 1HP.*
Charming beamed 250-year-old house.
Tel: 01328 710768 Mrs Wykes.
Rates fr: *£14.00-£18.00.*
Open: All Year (not Xmas)
Beds: 1F 1D
Baths: 1 Shared
🛏 (7) 🅿 (2) ⅍⛒▥.

(0.25m 🐾) *The Normans Guest House, Invaders Court, Standard Road, Wells-next-the-Sea, Norfolk, NR23 1JW.*
Large Georgian house.
Grades: ETB 2 Cr
Tel: 01328 710657
Mrs MacDonald.
Rates fr: *£23.50-£30.00.*
Open: All Year (not Xmas)
Beds: 6D 1T
Baths: 2 Ensuite
🅿 (10) ⅍⛒🛏✕▥Ⓥ✦

The Grid Reference beneath the location heading is for the village or town - *not* for individual houses, which are shown (where supplied) in each entry itself.

Taking your dog? Book in advance only with owners who accept dogs (🐾)

(On Path 🚲) *East House, East Quay, Wells-next-the-Sea, Norfolk, NR23 1LE.*
Actual grid ref: TF921437
Old home overlooking coastal marsh.
Tel: 01328 710408 Mrs Scott.
Rates fr: *£18.50-£22.00.*
Open: All Year (not Xmas)
Beds: 2T
Baths: 2 Private
🛏 (7) 🅿 (2) 🍽 🖾 Ⅴ ✦

(On Path) *Hideaway, Red Lion Yard, Wells-next-the-Sea, Norfolk, NR23 1AX.*
Actual grid ref: TF924344
Annex onto private house.
Grades: ETB 2 Cr, Approv
Tel: 01328 710524 Miss Higgs.
Rates fr: *£16.00-£16.00.*
Open: Jan to Nov
Beds: 1D 2T
Baths: 3 Ensuite
🅿 (3) 🍽 🖙 ✕ 🖾 Ⅴ 🛈 ✦

(1.5m 🚲) *The Edinburgh, Station Road, Wells-next-the-Sea, Norfolk, NR23.*
Old refurbished inn. Very comfortable.
Tel: 01328 710210 Mrs Bailey.
Rates fr: *£20.00-£20.00.*
Open: All Year (not Xmas)
Beds: 1D 2T 1S
Baths: 4 Ensuite
🛏 🍽 ✕ 🖾 Ⅴ 🛈 ✦

(On Path) *Mill House, Northfield Lane, Wells-next-the-Sea, Norfolk, NR23 1JZ.*
Actual grid ref: TF918435
Secluded former mill-owner's house.
Tel: 01328 710739 Mrs Fisher.
Rates fr: *£17.50-£17.50.*
Open: All Year
Beds: 1F 4D 2T 2S
Baths: 7 Private 1 Shared
🛏 (10) ⚡ 🍽 🖙 ✕ 🖾 ♿ Ⅴ ✦

(0.5m 🚲) *Greengates, Stiffkey Road, Wells-next-the-Sea, Norfolk, NR23 1QB.*
Actual grid ref: TF9243
Very comfortable C17th cottage.
Tel: 01328 711040 Mrs Jarvis.
Rates fr: *£18.00-£18.00.*
Open: All Year (not Xmas)
Beds: 1D 1T
Baths: 2 Shared
🅿 (2) 🍽 🖾

Warham 24

National Grid Ref: TF9441

🍽 🍺 Three Horseshoes

(1m 🚲) *Three Horseshoes/Old Post Office, 69 The Street, Warham, Wells-next-the-Sea, Norfolk, NR23 1NL.*
Dream country cottage adjoining village pub.
Grades: ETB 2 Cr
Tel: 01328 710547 Mr Salmon.

Rates fr: *£20.00-£18.00.*
Open: All Year (not Xmas)
Beds: 3D 1S
Baths: 1 Private 1 Shared
🛏 (14) 🅿 (20) 🍽 🖙 ✕ 🖾 Ⅴ 🛈 ✦

Wighton 25

National Grid Ref: TF9439

🍽 🍺 Sandpiper

(3m) *The Sandpiper Inn, 57 High Street, Wighton, Wells-next-the-Sea, Norfolk, NR23 1PF.*
Modernised C18th country inn.
Grades: ETB Listed
Tel: 01328 820752 Mrs Bridge.
Rates fr: *£15.00-£20.00.*
Open: All Year
Beds: 1D 2T
Baths: 1 Shared
🛏 (7) 🅿 (30) 🍽 🖾 Ⅴ 🛈

Blakeney 26

National Grid Ref: TG0243

🍽 🍺 Kings Arms, White Horse, Manor Hotel

(On Path) *Dallinga, 71 Morston Road, Blakeney, Holt, Norfolk, NR25 7BD.*
Modern, comfortable, private house.
Grades: ETB Registered
Tel: 01263 740943
Mr & Mrs Ward.
Rates fr: *£15.00-£20.00.*
Open: All Year (not Xmas)
Beds: 1D 1T
Baths: 2 Private
🅿 (6) 🍽 🖾 Ⅴ

(0.25m 🚲) *55 New Road, Off Coast Road, Blakeney, Holt, Norfolk, NR25 7PA.*
Modern, comfortable, detached family home.
Tel: 01263 740103 Mrs Buckey.
Rates fr: *£16.00-£17.50.*
Open: All Year (not Xmas)
Beds: 1T
Baths: 1 Private
🛏 🅿 (3) ⚡ 🍽 ✕ 🖾 Ⅴ 🛈 ✦

(On Path) *Bramble Lodge, 3 Morston Road, Blakeney, Holt, Norfolk, NR25 7PF.*
Comfortable, modern guesthouse.
Tel: 01263 740191 Mrs Gray.
Rates fr: *£17.50-£20.00.*
Open: All Year (not Xmas)
Beds: 1D 2T **Baths:** 3 Private
🛏 (10) 🅿 (3) 🍽 ✕ 🖾 🛈 ✦

Wiveton 27

National Grid Ref: TG0443

🍽 🍺 George & Dragon (Wiveton)

(1m) *Flintstones Guest House, Wiveton, Holt, Norfolk, NR25 7TL.*
Actual grid ref: TG0443
Grades: ETB Listed, Comm, AA 3 Q, RAC Acclaim
Tel: 01263 740337
Mr Ormerod.
Rates fr: *£17.50-£22.50.*
Open: All Year (not Xmas)
Beds: 3F 1D 1S
Baths: 5 Private
🛏 🅿 (5) ⚡ 🍽 🖙 ✕ 🖾 Ⅴ 🛈 ✦

Cley-next-the-Sea 28

National Grid Ref: TG0544

🍽 🍺 George & Dragon Hotel, Three Swallows,

(On Path) *Cley Windmill, Cley-next-the-Sea, Holt, Norfolk, NR25 7NN.*
Actual grid ref: TG045441
Converted C18th Windmill.
Grades: ETB 2 Cr
Tel: 01263 740209 Mr Mallam.
Rates fr: *£24.50-£29.00.*
Open: Mar to Dec **Beds:** 3D 2T 1S
Baths: 4 Private 2 Shared
🛏 (6) 🅿 (8) 🍽 🖙 ✕ 🖾 Ⅴ 🛈 ✦

(On Path) *The George & Dragon, Cley-next-the-Sea, Holt, Norfolk, NR25 7RN.*
Centrally-heated, comfortable Edwardian inn.
Grades: ETB 3 Cr, Comm
Tel: 01263 740652
Mr Sewell.
Rates fr: *£20.00-£30.00.*
Open: All Year (not Xmas)
Beds: 1F 4D 2T 1S
Baths: 6 Private 1 Shared
🛏 🅿 (30) 🍽 🖙 ✕ 🖾 Ⅴ 🛈 ✦

(On Path 🚲) *Marshlands, High Street, Cley-next-the-Sea, Holt, Norfolk, NR25 7RB.*
Actual grid ref: TG045438
Victorian old town hall house.
Grades: ETB Registered
Tel: 01263 740284
Mr & Mrs Kinsella.
Rates fr: *£14.00-£18.00.*
Open: All Year (not Xmas)
Beds: 1D 2T
Baths: 1 Shared
🛏 (5) ⚡ 🍽 🖾 Ⅴ 🛈 ✦

(On Path) *Whalebone House, High Street, Cley-next-the-Sea, Holt, Norfolk, NR25 7RN.*
Charming Georgian Listed building.
Tel: **01263 740336**
Mr & Mrs Bragg.
Rates fr: *£16.00*-**£20.00**.
Open: All Year
Beds: 2D 2T 1S
Baths: 1 Ensuite 2 Shared
📷 (10) ⒀ 🖵 🛏 Ⅴ ⓐ ✦

Kelling 29

National Grid Ref: TG0942

🅗 🍴 The Pheasant

(0.5m) *The Pheasant Hotel, Weybourne Road (A 149), Kelling, Holt, Norfolk, NR25 7EG.*
Actual grid ref: TG098428
Outstanding value, friendly country hotel.
Grades: ETB 2 Cr, Comm, AA 2 St, RAC 2 St
Tel: **01263 588382** Percival.
Rates fr: *£22.00*-**£28.00**.
Open: All Year
Beds: 1F 15D 13T
Baths: 29 Private
📷 (10) 🅿 (80) ⒀ 🖵 🛏 ✕ Ⅲ Ⅴ ⓐ ✦

Weybourne 30

National Grid Ref: TG1142

(0.5m) *The Maltings Hotel, The Street, Weybourne, Holt, Norfolk, NR25 7SY.*
Actual grid ref: TG1043
Tel: **01263 70731** Mr Mears.
Rates fr: *£25.00*-**£28.00**.
Open: All Year
Beds: 3F 8D 7T 2S
Baths: 20 Ensuite
📷 🅿 (150) 🖵 ✕ Ⅲ Ⅴ ⓐ ✦

Sheringham 31

National Grid Ref: TG1543

🅗 🍴 Windham Arms, Dunstable Arms, Crown, Two Lifeboats, Robin Hood

(0.25m) *The Bay-Leaf Guest House, 10 St Peters Road, Sheringham, Norfolk, NR26 8QY.*
Charming Victorian guesthouse.
Grades: ETB 1 Cr, Approv
Tel: **01263 823779** Mr Pigott.
Rates fr: *£17.00*-**£17.00**.
Open: All Year (not Xmas)
Beds: 2F 3D 2T
Baths: 7 Ensuite
📷 🅿 (4) 🖵 🛏 ✕ Ⅲ Ⅴ ⓐ ✦

Many rates vary according to season - the lowest only are shown here

---

(0.25m 🚗) *Anser Guest House, 18 New Street, Sheringham, Norfolk, NR26 8EE.*
Actual grid ref: TG158431
Centrally situated quiet guesthouse.
Grades: ETB Listed
Tel: **01263 823861** Mr Rose.
Rates fr: *£16.00*-**£16.00**.
Open: All Year (not Xmas)
Beds: 2F 1D 1T 1S
Baths: 2 Private, 1 Shared
📷 🅿 (4) 🖵 🛏 ✕ Ⅲ & Ⅴ ⓐ ✦

(0.25m) *Montague Lodge, 1 Montague Road, Sheringham, Norfolk, NR26 8LN.*
Large house in quiet road.
Grades: ETB Listed
Tel: **01263 822267**
Mrs Childs.
Rates fr: *£15.50*-**£15.50**.
Open: All Year
Beds: 2F 3D 2T 2S
Baths: 3 Private 2 Shared
📷 (10) 🅿 🖵 🛏 ✕ Ⅲ & Ⅴ

(On Path 🚗) *Beeston Hills Lodge, 64 Cliff Road, Sheringham, Norfolk, NR26 8BJ.*
Edwardian Lodge, superb sea-views, near beach/cliff path.
Tel: **01263 825936** Mr Rowan.
Rates fr: *£15.50*-**£24.00**.
Open: Easter to Oct
Beds: 1F 1D
Baths: 2 Private 1 Shared
📷 🅿 (3) ⒀ 🛏 Ⅲ Ⅴ ⓐ ✦

(▲0.25m) *Sheringham Youth Hostel, 1 Cremer's Drift, Sheringham, Norfolk, NR26 8HX.*
Actual grid ref: TG1542
Warden: Ms J Cooper.
Tel: **01263 823215**
Under 18: £5.55 **Adults:** £8.25
Family Bunk Rooms, Centrally Heated, Showers, Evening Meal (7.00 pm), Shop, Television, Games Room, Facilities for the Disabled
Victorian building with modern annexe and facilities for disabled. Wide sandy beaches, good bird-watching and a seal colony on this coast.

(0.25m 🚗) *The Old Vicarage, Sheringham, Norfolk, NR26 8NH.*
Turn of century, comfortable, spacious house.
Tel: **01263 822627** Mrs O'Connor.
Rates fr: *£20.00*-**£20.00**.
Open: All Year (not Xmas)
Beds: 1F 1D 1T
Baths: 3 Private
🅿 (5) 🖵 ✕ Ⅲ Ⅴ ⓐ ✦

(0.25m) *The Birches, 27 Holway Road, Sheringham, Norfolk, NR26 8HW.*
Late Victorian private house.
Tel: **01263 823550** Ms Pearce.
Rates fr: *£20.00*-**£25.00**.
Open: Easter to Oct
Beds: 1D 1T
Baths: 2 Ensuite
📷 (12) 🅿 (2) ⒀ 🖵 ✕ Ⅲ ⓐ ✦

(On Path) *Camberley Guest House, 62 Cliff Road, Sheringham, Norfolk, NR26 8BJ.*
Comfortable spacious, ideally situated, quiet.
Grades: ETB 2 Cr, Comm
Tel: **01263 823101**
Mr & Mrs Simmons.
Rates fr: *£18.00*-**£18.00**.
Open: All Year (not Xmas)
Beds: 2F 4D 2T
Baths: 4 Private
🅿 (8) 🖵 Ⅲ ✦

(0.25m) *Holly Cottage, The Rise, Sheringham, Norfolk, NR26 8QB.*
Small, modern cottage, sea view.
Grades: ETB Listed
Tel: **01263 822807** Mrs Perkins.
Rates fr: *£15.00*-**£16.00**.
Open: All Year (not Xmas)
Beds: 1F 1S
Baths: 1 Ensuite 1 Shared
📷 (3) 🅿 ⒀ 🖵 Ⅲ Ⅴ ⓐ ✦

(2m) *Sans Souci, 19 Waterbank Road, Sheringham, Norfolk, NR26 8RB.*
Victorian family guesthouse.
Tel: **01263 824436** Mrs Majewski.
Rates fr: *£15.00*-**£15.00**.
Open: Easter to Oct
Beds: 1D 1T 1S
Baths: 1 Shared
📷 ⒀ 🖵 🛏 Ⅲ

(0.5m) *Wykeham Guest House, Morley Road North, Sheringham, Norfolk, NR26 8JB.*
Quiet family home, centrally located.
Tel: **01263 823818**
Mrs Meakin.
Rates fr: *£15.00*-**£15.00**.
Open: Apr to Oct
Beds: 1F 1D 1T 1S
Baths: 1 Private 1 Shared
📷 🅿 (6) ⒀ 🖵 Ⅲ Ⅴ ⓐ ✦

(0.25m) *Honeylands, 22 South Street, Sheringham, Norfolk, NR26 8LL.*
Large comfortable private house.
Tel: **01263 823209**
Mr & Mrs Allwood.
Rates fr: *£18.00*-**£18.00**.
Open: All Year
Beds: 2D 1T
Baths: 1 Shared
📷 (6) ⒀ 🖵 Ⅲ ⓐ ✦

Beeston Regis 32

National Grid Ref: TG1742

(1m 🚗) *Hilltop, Old Wood, Beeston Regis, Sheringham, Norfolk, NR26 8TS.*
Actual grid ref: TG162204
Modern comfortable outdoor centre.
Tel: **01263 824514** Mr Read.
Rates fr: *£16.00*-**£16.00**.
Open: All Year (not Xmas)
Beds: 5F 6T 2S
Baths: 7 Ensuite 6 Shared
📷 🅿 (20) ⒀ 🖵 Ⅲ Ⅴ ⓐ ✦

East Runton 33

National Grid Ref: TG1942

(1m) *Dalkeith, Lower Green, East Runton, Cromer, Norfolk, NR27 9PG.*
Comfortable, friendly, family home.
Tel: **01263 514803**
Mr & Mrs Slater.
Rates fr: *£16.50-£22.00.*
Open: All Year (not Xmas)
Beds: 1T 2D
Baths: 2 Shared
ᗧ �P (5) ⚡ ☐ ☆ ✕ ▦ Ⓥ

Cromer 34

National Grid Ref: TG2142

⊫ ▨ Bath House, Red Lion, Adnams

(0.25m 🚐) *Morden House, 20 Cliff Avenue, Cromer, Norfolk, NR27 0AN.*
Elegant Victorian house - user friendly.
Grades: ETB 2 Cr, Comm, AA 3 Q, Recomm
Tel: **01263 513396** Mrs Votier.

Rates fr: *£21.00.*
Open: All Year **Beds:** 4D 1T 1S
Baths: 4 Private 1 Shared
ᗧ P (2) ⚡ ☐ ☆ ✕ ▦ Ⓥ ⓐ ✔

(0.25m) *Cambridge House, Sea Front, Cromer, Norfolk, NR27 9HD.*
Charming Victorian house on seafront.
Grades: ETB 2 Cr
Tel: **01263 512085** Mrs Wass.
Rates fr: *£18.50-£18.50.*
Open: Easter to Sept
Beds: 3F 1D 1S
Baths: 2 Private 2 Shared
ᗧ P (5) ⚡ ☐ ☆ ✕ ▦ Ⓥ ⓐ ✔

(1m) *The Grove Guest House, 95 Overstrand Road, Cromer, Norfolk, NR27 0DS.*
Actual grid ref: TG2241
Beautifully situated Georgian house.
Grades: ETB 2 Cr, Comm
Tel: **01263 512412** Mrs Graveling.
Rates fr: *£17.50-£21.50.*
Open: Easter to Sep
Beds: 2F 3D 3T 2S
Baths: 8 Private 1 Shared
ᗧ P (10) ✕ ▦ Ⓥ ⓐ

(1m 🚐) *Crowmere Guest House, 4 Vicarage Road, Cromer, NR27 9DQ.*
Large Victorian house near sea.
Grades: ETB Listed
Tel: **01263 513056** Ms Marriott.
Rates fr: *£18.00-£18.00.*
Open: All Year (not Xmas)
Beds: 2F 3D 2T
Baths: 5 Ensuite 1 Shared
ᗧ P (6) ⚡ ☐ ☆ ▦ Ⓥ ⓐ ✔

Overstrand 35

National Grid Ref: TG2440

(0.5m) *Danum House, 22 Pauls Lane, Overstrand, Cromer, Norfolk, NR27 0PE.*
Modernised old Norfolk house.
Tel: **01263 579327** Mrs Sim.
Rates fr: *£18.00-£18.00.*
Open: Easter to Oct
Beds: 2F 2D 1T **Baths:** 5 Private
ᗧ P (4) ☐ ☆ ▦ Ⓥ

The *lowest* **single**
rate *is shown in* **bold.**

Pembrokeshire Coast Path

The **Pembrokeshire Coast Path** runs for 186 miles around a beautiful Welsh National Park. Although more popular than it used to be, this part of the country still has relatively few visitors (compared, let's say, with Cornwall) and walkers will encounter unspoilt, quiet beaches, dramatic clifftops and superb sea-views all to themselves, even during summer. The bird-life is rich, with many seabirds breeding here - watch out for the rare chough. Between Bosherston and Pembroke you will encounter the Army's tank firing ranges. Please avoid these during firing times, which are published locally and by the **Pembrokeshire National Park Office** (01437 764591). The walking can prove exerting, especially when the wind is up and where the path regularly dips, bends and climbs to follow the cliffs. **Menter Preseli** also offer a luggage transfer service along this path in addition to their accommodation network (see advertisement). Phone 01437 763110 for more details.

Guides (available from all good map shops)
Pembrokeshire Coast Path by Dr Brian S. John

(ISBN 1 85410 023 8), published by Aurum Press in association with the Countryside Commission and Ordnance Survey, £9.99
A Guide to the Pembrokeshire Coast Path by C J Wright, published by Constable & Co Ltd, (ISBN 09 469260 2) and available from all good bookshops, £9.95
The Pembrokeshire Coast Path by John Merrill, published by Footprint Press Ltd, (ISBN 0 907496 69 5) and also available directly from the publishers (19 Moseley Street, Ripley, Derbyshire, DE5 3DA, tel. 01773 512143), £4.95 (+ 70p p&p)
The Pembrokeshire Coastal Path by Dennis Kelsall, published by Cicerone Press and also available directly from the publishers (2 Police Square, Milnthorpe, Cumbria, LA7 7PY, 01539 562069), £7.99 (+ 75p p&p)

Maps: 1:50000 Ordnance Survey Landranger Series: 145, 157 and 158.
All comments on the path to: **Tom Goodall**, Pembrokeshire Coast National Park, County Offices, Haverfordwest, Dyfed, SA61 1QZ.

Cardigan 1

National Grid Ref: SN1746

🍽 🕮 Eagle Inn

(3m 🚍) *Maes-A-Mor,* Park Place, Gwbert Road, Cardigan, Dyfed, SA43 1AE.
Edwardian family-run Welsh guesthouse.
Tel: **01239 614929**
Mr Jones.
Rates fr: £14.00.
Open: All Year
Beds: 2F 3D 2T
Baths: 3 Ensuite
🅿 (4) ✦ 🗆 🎹 🛢 ✦

St Dogmaels 2

National Grid Ref: SN1645

🍽 🕮 Ferry Inn, Teifi Netpool Inn, The Webley

(2.5m) *Briar Bank,* Poppit Sands, St Dogmaels, Cardigan, SA43 3LR.
Spacious, comfortable bungalow.
Tel: **01239 612339**
Mrs Thomas.
Rates fr: £12.50-£12.50.
Open: Easter to Oct
Beds: 1F
Baths: 1 Shared
🏠 🅿 (2) ✦ 🗆 🎋 ✕ 🎹 Ⓥ

Poppit Sands 3

National Grid Ref: SN1548

🍽 🕮 Webley Hotel

(🔺On Path) *Poppit Sands Youth Hostel,* Sea View, Poppit Sands, Cardigan, Dyfed, SA43 3LP.
Actual grid ref: SN1448
Warden: Mr M Hennessey.
Tel: **01239 612936**
Under 18: £4.60 **Adults:** £6.75
Family Bunk Rooms, Partially Heated, Showers, Shop
Former inn set in 5 acres reaching down to the estuary and sea, designated a Site of Special Scientific Interest

(On Path) *Glan-y-Mor,* Poppit Sands, St Dogmaels, Cardigan, Dyfed, SA43 3LP.
Actual grid ref: SN147487
Large character seaside ex-farmhouse.
Tel: **01239 612329** Mrs Sharp.
Rates fr: £12.50-£12.50.
Open: All Year (not Xmas)
Beds: 1F 1D 🏠 🅿 🎋 🎹 Ⓥ 🛢 ✦

Moylegrove 4

National Grid Ref: SN1144

(0.5m) *Cwm Connell,* Moylegrove, Cardigan, Dyfed, SA43 3BX.
Actual grid ref: SN119461
Heritage conversion of traditional farm buildings.

Grades: WTB Grade 5
Tel: **01239 881691**
Mr & Mrs Jenkins.
Rates fr: £14.50-£14.50.
Open: Jan to May, Sep to Dec
Beds: 2D 2T **Baths:** 2 Private
🏠 🅿 (4) 🗆 🎋 ✕ 🎹 Ⓥ 🛢 ✦

Newport 5

National Grid Ref: SN0539

🍽 🕮 Llwyngwair Arms, Royal Oak

(On Path 🚍) *Grove Park Guest House,* Pen y Bont, Newport, Dyfed, SA42 0LT.
Scenic setting close to mountains.
Grades: WTB 3 Cr
Tel: **01239 820122** Mrs King.
Rates fr: £18.00-£23.00.
Open: All Year (not Xmas)
Beds: 3D 1T
Baths: 2 Private 1 Shared
🏠 🅿 (3) ✦ 🗆 🎋 ✕ 🎹 Ⓥ 🛢 ✦

(0.25m 🚍) *Llysmeddyg Guest House,* East Street, Newport, Pembrokeshire, SA42 0SY.
House and self-catering mews flat.
Grades: WTB 2 Cr
Tel: **01239 820008**
Mr & Mrs Ross.
Rates fr: £17.50-£17.50.
Open: All Year **Beds:** 2D 2T 2S
🏠 🅿 (5) ✦ 🗆 ✕ 🎹 Ⓥ 🛢 ✦

(0.25m) 🚲 *Cnapan Country House, East Street, Newport, Dyfed, SA42 0WF.*
Fine Listed Georgian town house.
Grades: WTB 3 Cr
Tel: **01239 820575** Mrs Cooper.
Rates fr: *£24.00-£29.00.*
Open: Mar to Jan
Beds: 2D 3T **Baths:** 5 Ensuite
🛇 🅿 (6) ⊟ ✕ Ⅲ. Ⓥ ♠ ⚡

(0.25m) 🚲 *2 Springhill, Parrog Road, Newport, Dyfed, SA42 0RH.*
Actual grid ref: SN054394
Listed comfortable house, coastal path.
Grades: WTB 1 Cr
Tel: **01239 820626** Mr Inman.
Rates fr: *£14.00-£14.00.*
Open: All Year
Beds: 1F 1D 1T
Baths: 2 Shared
🛇 🅿 (2) ⊟ ★ ✕ Ⅲ. Ⓥ ♠ ⚡

(0.25m) *Hafan Deg, Long Street, Newport, Dyfed, SA42 0TN.*
Actual grid ref: SN057393
Quiet, central, modern and warm.
Grades: WTB 2 Cr
Tel: **01239 820301**
Mr & Mrs Joseph.
Rates fr: *£15.00-£15.00.*
Open: All Year (not Xmas)
Beds: 1D 1S 2T
Baths: 2 Ensuite 2 Shared
🛇 🅿 (6) ⚡ ⊟ ★ Ⅲ. Ⓥ ♠ ⚡

Dinas Cross   6

National Grid Ref: SN0039

🍴 🍺 The Freemasons Arms

(1.25m) 🚲 *Fron Isaf Farm, Dinas Cross, Newport, Dyfed, SA42 0SW.*
Actual grid ref: SN018384
Comfortable, homely farmhouse, overlooking sea.

Tel: **01348 811339** Mr/Mrs Urwin.
Rates fr: *£18.00-£18.00.*
Open: All Year (not Xmas)
Beds: 1D 1T
Baths: 1 Shared
🛇 (3) 🅿 (5) ⊟ ★ Ⓥ ♠ ⚡

Fishguard   7

National Grid Ref: SM9537

🍴 🍺 Old Coach House, Royal Oak

(0.25m) *Manor House Hotel, Main Street, Fishguard, Dyfed, SA65 9HH.*
Georgian town house.
Grades: WTB 3 Cr, High Comm, RAC Acclaim
Tel: **01348 873260** Mr Davies.
Rates fr: *£18.00-£18.00.*
Open: All Year (not Xmas)
Beds: 1F 2D 2T 2S
Baths: 5 Ensuite, 1 Shared
🛇 ⊟ ★ ✕ Ⅲ. Ⓥ ♠

© Crown Copyright

The lowest *double* rate per person is shown in *italics*.

(On Path 🚍) **Seaview Hotel,** *Seafront, Fishguard, Dyfed, SA65 9BL.*
Super family-run hotel on seafront.
Grades: WTB 3 Cr
Tel: **01348 874282** Mrs Wren.
Rates fr: *£19.00*-**£23.50**.
Open: All Year
Beds: 3F 7D 8T 5S
Baths: 23 Private
🛏 🅿 (50) 🍴 ⛄ 🗙 📺 🎖 ♿

(On Path) **Cartref Hotel,** *13-19 High Street, Fishguard, Dyfed, SA65 9AW.*
Convenient and friendly town hotel.
Grades: WTB 3 Cr, AA 2 St, RAC 2 St
Tel: **01348 872430**
Rates fr: *£22.50*-**£17.00**.
Open: All Year
Beds: 2F 2D 2T 6S
Baths: 6 Ensuite 2 Shared
🛏 🅿 (5) 🗙 ⛄ 🗙 📺 🎖 ♿

(0.5m 🚍) **Cri'r Wylan,** *Pen Wallis, Fishguard, Dyfed, SA65 9HR.*
Peaceful, fantastic view, good breakfast.
Grades: WTB 1 Cr, High Comm
Tel: **01348 873398** Mrs Nicholas.
Rates fr: *£13.00*-**£14.00**.
Open: All Year (not Xmas)
Beds: 1F 1D 1T 1S
Baths: 1 Shared
🛏 🅿 (4) 🗙 ⛄ 🗙 📺 🎖 ♿

(0.5m) **Inglewood,** *13 Vergam Terrace, Fishguard, Dyfed, SA65 9DD.*
Comfortable mid-terrace dwelling house.
Grades: WTB 1 Cr, High Comm
Tel: **01348 873475**
Mrs Lewis.**Rates fr:** *£13.00*.
Open: All Year (not Xmas)
Beds: 2D 1T **Baths:** 1 Shared
🛏 (12) 🅿 🗙 📺

Goodwick 8

National Grid Ref: SM9438
🍴 🍺 The Farmhouse Kitchen, Fishguard Bay Hotel

(0.75m 🚍) **Ivybridge,** *Drim Mill, Dyffryn, Goodwick, Dyfed, SA64 0FT.*
Actual grid ref: SM942372
Grades: WTB 3 Cr, High Comm
Tel: **01348 875366 / 872623**
Mrs Davies.
Rates fr: *£19.50*-**£19.50**.
Open: All Year (not Xmas)
Beds: 1F 3D 1T 1S
Baths: 6 Ensuite
🛏 🅿 🗙 ⛄ 🗙 📺 🎖 ♿
Ivybridge is conveniently placed for Pembrokeshire Coastal Path and other rural walks. After walking, relax in our heated indoor pool and whirlpool spa.

(On Path 🚍) **Villa Calabria,** *New Hill, Goodwick, Dyfed, SA64 0DU.*
Actual grid ref: SM947388
Modern homely villa - sea views.
Tel: **01348 874175** Mrs Trueman.
Rates fr: *£13.50*-**£13.50**.
Open: All Year (not Xmas)
Beds: 1D 1T **Baths:** 2Shared
🛏 🅿 (2) 🗙 ⛄ 🎖 ♿

(On Path) **Hope & Anchor,** *Goodwick, Dyfed, SA64 0BP.*
Actual grid ref: SM945383
Grades: WTB 2 Cr
Tel: **01348 872314** Mr McDonald.
Rates fr: *£18.00*-**£18.00**.
Open: All Year
Beds: 1D 2T **Baths:** 3 Ensuite
🅿 🗙 ⛄ 🗙 📺 🎖 ♿
Family-run inn overlooking Fishguard Bay. Restaurant: sea food, vegetarian meals. Pets by arrangement. Two minutes from Sealink to Ireland. WTB. Les Routiers

(On Path) **Stanley House,** *Quay Road, Goodwick, Dyfed, SA64 0BS.*
Comfortable village, lovely views.
Grades: WTB 1Cr, Comm
Tel: **01348 873024** Mrs Hendrie.
Rates fr: *£13.00*-**£13.00**.
Open: All Year **Beds:** 1F 2D 1T 1S
Baths: 1Private
🛏 🅿 🗙 ⛄ 📺 🎖

(On Path 🚍) **Bryntirion Guest House,** *Glan-y-mor Road, Goodwick, Fishguard, Dyfed, SA64 0ER.*
Large Victorian private house.
Tel: **01348 872189** Mr Grace.
Rates fr: *£13.00*-**£13.00**.
Open: All Year (not Xmas)
Beds: 1F 1T 1S **Baths:** 2 Shared
🛏 🅿 (2) 🗙 ⛄ 🗙 📺 🎖 ♿

Tref Asser 9

National Grid Ref: SM8938
(⛰ On Path) **Pwll Deri Youth Hostel,** *Castell Mawr, Tref Asser, Goodwick, Dyfed, SA64 0LR.*
Actual grid ref: SM8938
Warden: Ms A Griffiths.
Tel: **01348 891233**
Under 18: £4.60 **Adults:** £6.75
Family Bunk Rooms, Partially Heated, Showers, Evening Meal (7.00 pm)
Former private house perched atop 400ft cliffs next to an ancient hill fort, overlooking Pwll Deri Bay

Tregwynt 10

National Grid Ref: SM8834

(0.25m 🚍) **New Mill,** *Tregwynt, Castlemorris, Haverfordwest, Dyfed, SA62 5UX.*
Family-run working organic farm.
Tel: **01348 891637** Mrs Holloway.
Rates fr: *£16.00*-**£19.00**.
Open: Easter to Sep
Beds: 1D 2T
Baths: 2 Shared
🛏 🅿 (4) 🗙 ⛄ 🗙 📺 🎖 ♿

(0.5m 🚍) **Tregwynt Mansion,** *Tregwynt, Castlemorris, Haverfordwest, Pembrokeshire, SA62 5UU.*
Actual grid ref: SM889346
Historic C18th mansion.
Grades: WTB Listed
Tel: **01348 891685** Mrs Sayer.
Rates fr: *£18.00*-**£24.00**.
Open: All Year
Beds: 2D 1T
Baths: 1 Ensuite 2 Private
🛏 🅿 (10) 🗙 ⛄ 🗙 📺 🎖 ♿

Trefin 11

National Grid Ref: SM8332
🍴 🍺 Ship Inn

(⛰ 0.5m) **Trefin Youth Hostel,** *11 Ffordd-yr-Afon, Trefin, Haverfordwest, Dyfed, SA62 5AU.*
Actual grid ref: SM840324
Warden: Mr S Pinner.
Tel: **01348 831414**
Under 18: £4.35 **Adults:** £6.50
Family Bunk Rooms, Centrally Heated, Showers, Self-catering, No Smoking
Recently refurbished to high standard, this hostel is a former school in the centre of a small village half a mile from the sea

(0.5m) *Bryngarw, Abercastle Road, Trefin, Trevine, Haverfordwest, Dyfed, SA62 5AR.*
Actual grid ref: SM842325
Sea views, modern bungalow, 2.5 acres.
Grades: WTB 3 Cr, High Comm
Tel: **01348 831211** Mr/Mrs Gratton
Rates fr: *£20.00-£23.00.*
Open: Easter to Oct
Beds: 1F 2D 2T **Baths:** 5 Ensuite
🅿 (10) ⌇□✕▥♿Ⓥ🌙✦

Croesgoch 12

National Grid Ref: SM8230

🍴🍺 Artramont Arms, Ship Inn, Square & Compass, Sloop Inn

(2.25m 🚌) *Trearched Farm, Croesgoch, Haverfordwest, Dyfed, SA62 5JP.*
Actual grid ref: SM8230
Grades: WTB High Comm
Tel: **01348 831310** Mrs Jenkins.
Rates fr: *£15.00-£15.00.*
Open: All Year **Beds:** 2D 2T 2S
🅿 ⌇▥,✦
C18th listed farmhouse on arable farm down Long Drive off A487 in village. Spacious grounds to relax in. Small lake ideal for birdwatching and walking.

(1.25m 🚌) *Maes y Ffynnon, Penygroes, Croesgoch, Haverfordwest, Dyfed, SA62 5JN.*
Actual grid ref: SM8431
Modern large bungalow, private grounds.
Grades: WTB 1 Cr, Comm
Tel: **01348 831319** Mrs Evans.
Rates fr: *£15.50-£17.50.*
Open: Apr to Sep
Beds: 1F 1T **Baths:** 2 Ensuite
🐾🅿⌇□🏠▥,Ⓥ✦

(1.5m) *Bank House Farm, Abereiddy Road, Croesgoch, Haverfordwest, Dyfed, SA62 6XZ.*
Actual grid ref: SM8230
Comfortable, Welsh speaking farming family.
Grades: WTB Listed
Tel: **01348831305** Mrs Lloyd.
Rates fr: *£13.50-£15.00.*
Open: All Year (not Xmas)
Beds: 1D 1T **Baths:** 1 Shared
🐾 (10) 🅿 (2) □✕▥,Ⓥ🌙✦

Cwmdwig Water 13

National Grid Ref: SM8030

(0.5m) *Cwmdwig Water Guesthouse, Berea, Cwmdwig Water, Haverfordwest, Dyfed, SA62 6DW.*
Converted old oak-beamed farmhouse.
Grades: WTB High Comm
Tel: **01348 831434** Mr Evans.
Rates fr: *£18.00-£18.00.*
Open: All Year (not Xmas)
Beds: 5D 5T 2S
Baths: 5 Private 3 Shared
🐾🅿□🏠✕▥,Ⓥ🌙✦

Llaethdy 14

National Grid Ref: SM7327

(🔺0.5m) *St David's Youth Hostel, Llaethdy, St David's, Haverfordwest, Dyfed, SA62 6PR.*
Actual grid ref: SM7327
Warden: Ms A Davies.
Tel: **01437 720345**
Under 18: £4.15 **Adults:** £6.10
Family Bunk Rooms, Partially Heated, Showers, Evening Meal (7.00 pm - Self-catering Thurs)
White painted National Trust farmhouse with red painted doors beneath the summit of Carn Llidi

St Davids 15

National Grid Ref: SM7525

🍴🍺 Farmers Arms, Grove Hotel, The Cartref

(1m) *Y Gorlan, 77 Nun Street, St Davids, Haverfordwest, Dyfed, SA62 6NU.*
Grades: WTB 3 Cr, Comm, RAC Acclaim
Tel: **01437 720837** Mrs Dyson.
Rates fr: *£17.50-£18.50.*
Open: All Year
Beds: 1F 2D 1T 1S
Baths: 5 Ensuite
🐾🅿 (2) □✕▥,🎣
Family run guest house. Close to cathedral. Beautiful Pembrokeshire coast, golf course, coastal paths, local attractions, licensed restaurant. Guest lounge with panoramic views.

(1m) *Felin Isaf, Old Bishops Mill, St Davids, Haverfordwest, Dyfed, SA62 6QB.*
Converted C16th corn mill.
Grades: WTB Listed
Tel: **01437 720853**
Mrs Lloyd.
Rates fr: *£15.50.*
Open: All Year (not Xmas)
Beds: 2D 1T
Baths: 1 Shared
🅿 (3) □🏠▥,Ⓥ

(0.75m 🚌) *Grove Hotel, High Street, St Davids, Haverfordwest, Dyfed, SA62 6SB.*
Regency hotel/bars/restaurant.
Grades: WTB 3 Cr
Tel: **01437 720341** Mrs Pengelly.
Rates fr: *£22.00-£22.00.*
Open: All Year
Beds: 5D 5T 1S
🐾🅿 (20) ⌇□🏠✕▥,Ⓥ🌙✦

(1m) *Swn-Y-Don, 18 Cross Square, St Davids, Haverfordwest, Dyfed, SA62 6SE.*
Victorian house, central but quiet.
Tel: **01437 720744**
Mrs Gudgeon.
Rates fr: *£16.50-£16.50.*
Open: May to Sep
Beds: 1T 2S
Baths: 2 Private
🐾 (1) □Ⓥ✦

(0.75m) *Ramsey House, Lower Moor, St Davids, Haverfordwest, Dyfed, SA62 6RP.*
Actual grid ref: SM747250
Delightful rooms, memorable meals, licensed.
Grades: WTB 3 Cr, High Comm, AA 4 Q, Select, RAC High Acclaim **Tel:** **01437 720321**
Mr & Mrs Thompson.
Rates fr: *£22.00-£25.00.*
Open: All Year
Beds: 4D 3T
Baths: 7 Ensuite
🅿 (10) ⌇□🏠✕▥,Ⓥ🌙✦

(1m 🚌) *Ty Olaf, Mount Gardens, St Davids, Haverfordwest, Dyfed, SA62 6BS.*
Actual grid ref: SM757258
Quiet bungalow.
Grades: WTB High Comm
Tel: **01437 720885** Mrs Liggitt.
Rates fr: *£13.00-£13.00.*
Open: Easter to Oct
Beds: 1F 1D 1T 1S
Baths: 1 Shared
🅿 (6) ⌇□▥,Ⓥ✦

Solva 16

National Grid Ref: SM8024

🍴🍺 Royal George, Cambrian Inn, Square & Compass Inn

(3m 🚌) *Llanddinog Old Farmhouse, Solva, Haverfordwest, Dyfed, SA62 6NA.*
C16th traditional Welsh farmhouse.
Grades: WTB 3 Cr
Tel: **01348 831224** Mrs Griffiths.
Rates fr: *£16.00-£16.00.*
Open: All Year (not Xmas)
Beds: 1F 1D **Baths:** 2 Ensuite
🐾🅿 (20) □🏠✕▥,Ⓥ✦

(On Path) *Pendinas, St Brides View, Solva, Haverfordwest, Dyfed, SA62 6TB.*
Actual grid ref: SM798243
Modern comfortable house, sea views. **Grades:** WTB Listed
Tel: **01437 721283** Miss Davies.
Rates fr: *£15.00-£15.00.*
Open: All Year (not Xmas)
Beds: 2D 1T **Baths:** 1 Shared
🐾 (10) 🅿 (3) ▥,Ⓥ🌙✦

Penycwm 17

National Grid Ref: SM8525

(🔺2m) *Solva (Penycwm) Youth Hostel, Hafod Lodge, Whitehouse, Penycwm, Newgale, Haverfordwest, Dyfed, SA62 6LA.*
Actual grid ref: SM8525
Tel: **01437 720959**
Under 18: £5.00 **Adults:** £7.45
Family Bunk Rooms, Centrally Heated, Showers, Evening Meal (6.30 pm), Shop, Television, Security Lockers
Purpose-built hostel with excellent facilities, set in 2 acres of lawned grounds

Nolton Haven 18

National Grid Ref: SM8618

(On Path 🚐) *Nolton Haven Farm,*
Nolton Haven, Haverfordwest,
Dyfed, SA62 3NH.
Actual grid ref: SM849187
Large modernised farmhouse.
Beach 30 yds.
Grades: WTB Listed
Tel: **01437 710263** Mr Canton.
Rates fr: *£14.00-£14.00.*
Open: All Year (not Xmas)
Beds: 3F 2D 1T 1S
Baths: 2 Private 4 Shared
ॐ ☑ (20) ◻ ⅄ ✕ ▥ ♥ ♥ ⅏

Broad Haven 19

National Grid Ref: SM8613

⚭ ◧ The Royal

(▲ On Path) *Broad Haven Youth*
Hostel, Broad Haven,
Haverfordwest, Dyfed, SA62 3JH.
Actual grid ref: SM8614
Warden: J & L Garner.
Tel: **01437 781688**
Under 18: £5.55 **Adults:** £8.25
Family Bunk Rooms, Centrally
Heated, Showers, Evening Meal
(18.30 pm), Shop, Television,
Games Room, Facilities for the
Disabled
Purpose-built, award-winning hos-
tel, close to beach with fine views
of the coastal headlands.

(On Path) *Ringstone Guest House,*
Haroldston Hill, Haroldston,
Broad Haven, Haverfordwest,
Dyfed, SA62 3JP.
Magnificent seaviews, patio/lounge
access all day.
Grades: WTB 2 Cr, High Comm
Tel: **01437 781051** Mrs Morgan.
Rates fr: *£16.00.*
Open: All Year (not Xmas)
Beds: 1F 2D **Baths:** 3 Ensuite
ॐ (3) ☑ (6) ◻ ▥ ♥ ⅏

Little Haven 20

National Grid Ref: SM8512

⚭ ◧ Littlehaven Hotel, Swan Inn,
The Castle

(On Path 🚐) *Whitegates,*
Settlands Hill, Little Haven,
Haverfordwest, Dyfed, SA62 3LA.
Country house, spectacular sea
views.
Grades: WTB 3 Cr, Comm
Tel: **01437 781552**
Mr & Mrs Llewellyn.
Rates fr: *£16.00-£22.50.*
Open: All Year **Beds:** 1F 2D 2T
Baths: 3Private 1Shared
ॐ ☑ ◻ ⅄ ✕ ▥ ♥ ⅏
Also ▲

(0.25m) *The Bower Farm, Little*
Haven, Haverfordwest, Pembs,
SA62 3TY.
Friendly farmhouse, fantastic sea
views.
Grades: WTB 3 Cr, High Comm

Tel: **01437 781554**
Mr Birt-Llewellin.
Rates fr: *£19.00-£23.00.*
Open: All Year (not Xmas)
Beds: 1F 1D 1T 1S
Baths: 4 Private
ॐ ☑ (12) ◻ ⅄ ✕ ▥ ♿ ☑

St Brides 21

National Grid Ref: SM8010

(1m) *Fopston Farm, St Brides,*
Haverfordwest, Dyfed, SA62 3.
Actual grid ref: SM788093
Spacious C17th comfortable farm-
house.
Grades: WTB Listed
Tel: **01646 636271** Mrs Price.
Rates fr: *£15.00-£15.00.*
Open: All Year (not Xmas)
Beds: 1F 1D 1T 1S
Baths: 1 Shared
ॐ ☑ (6) ⅏ ◻ ⅄ ▥ ☑ ♥ ⅏

Marloes 22

National Grid Ref: SM7908

⚭ ◧ Lobster Pot, Foxes Inn

(1m 🚐) *Foxdale, Glebe Lane,*
Marloes, Haverfordwest, Dyfed,
SA62 3AX.
Actual grid ref: SM796083
Large detached family house.
Grades: WTB 2 Cr, Highly Comm
Tel: **01646 636243**
Mrs Roddam-King.
Rates fr: *£16.00-£18.00.*
Open: All Year
Beds: 3F 3D 3T
Baths: 1 Ensuite 4 Shared 4 Shared
☑ (6) ◻ ⅄ ▥ ☑
Also ▲ *£5.00 per tent.*
Open: All Year (not Xmas)
♠ ⊤ ⩍ ✕ ⅃

Runwayskiln 23

National Grid Ref: SM7707

(▲ On Path) *Marloes Sands*
Youth Hostel, Runwayskiln,
Marloes, Haverfordwest, Dyfed,
SA62 3BH.
Actual grid ref: SM7708
Warden: Mr J Garner.
Tel: **01437 781688**
Under 18: £4.60 **Adults:** £6.75
Family Bunk Rooms, Partially
Heated, Showers, Self-catering
Only, Parking, No Smoking
Delightful cluster of farm buildings
on National Trust property, over-
looking Marloes Sands Bay

Dale 24

National Grid Ref: SM8205

⚭ ◧ Griffin Inn

(On Path 🚐) *Point Farm, Dale,*
Haverfordwest, Dyfed, SA62 3RD.
Actual grid ref: SM814054
Large period farmhouse, overlook-
ing sea.
Grades: WTB 2 Cr

Tel: **01646 636254** Mrs Webber.
Rates fr: *£15.00-£15.00.*
Open: All Year (not Xmas)
Beds: 4D 1S
Baths: 5 Private
☑ ◻ ⅄ ▥ ♥ ⅏

St Ishmaels 25

National Grid Ref: SM8307

⚭ ◧ Brook Inn, Foxes Inn (St
Ishmaels)

(1m) *Whiteholme Farm, St*
Ishmaels, Haverfordwest, Pembs,
SA62 3TL.
Friendly working farmhouse.
Tel: **01646 636357** Mrs Watts.
Rates fr: *£12.00-£12.00.*
Open: All Year
Beds: 1D 1S
Baths: 1 Shared
☑ ✕ ▥ ☑

Bicton 26

National Grid Ref: SM8407

⚭ ◧ Brook Inn

(1m 🚐) *Bicton Farm, Bicton, St*
Ishmaels, Haverfordwest, Dyfed,
SA62 3DR.
Actual grid ref: SM843078
Warm welcome in comfortable
farmhouse.
Grades: WTB Listed
Tel: **01646 636215** Mrs Llewellyn.
Rates fr: *£15.00-£15.00.*
Open: March to Oct
Beds: 2D 1T
Baths: 1Private 1Shared
ॐ ☑ ◻ ⅄ ✕ ▥ ☑ ♥ ⅏

Sandy Haven 27

National Grid Ref: SM8507

(On Path 🚐) *Skerryback*
Farmhouse, Sandy Haven, St
Ishmaels, Haverfordwest, Dyfed,
SA62 3DN.
Actual grid ref: SM852074
Pembrokeshire farmhouse on
coastal path.
Grades: WTB 1 Cr, High Comm
Tel: **01646 636598**
Mrs Williams.
Rates fr: *£15.00-£15.00.*
Open: Jan to Nov
Beds: 1D 1T 1S
ॐ ☑ ⅏ ◻ ✕ ▥ ♥ ⅏

Milford Haven 28

National Grid Ref: SM9005

(On Path) *Kings Arms, Hakin*
Point, Milford Haven, Dyfed, SA73
3DG.
Public house, comfortable, sea
views.
Tel: **01646 693478** Mrs Hutchings.
Rates fr: *£15.00-£15.00.*
Open: All Year (not Xmas)
Beds: 2F 1D 3T
Baths: 3 Private
ॐ ☑ ◻ ✕ ☑ ♥ ⅏

(On Path) *Belhaven House Hotel,*
29 Hamilton Terrace, Milford
Haven, Dyfed, SA73 3JJ.
Large Georgian surgeon's private
house. **Grades:** RAC Listed
Tel: **01646 695983** Mr Henricksen.
Rates fr: *£16.00-£16.00.*
Open: All Year (not Xmas)
Beds: 4F 1D 2T 4S
Baths: 2 Ensuite
🛏 🅿 ⬜ ⼊ ✕ ▥ Ⓥ ▮

Llanstadwell 29

National Grid Ref: SM9404

🍽 ⼕ Ferry Inn

(On Path) *Ferry Inn, Hazelbeach,*
Llanstadwell, Milford Haven,
Dyfed, SA73 1EG.
Modern riverside village inn.
Grades: WTB 1 Cr
Tel: **01646 600270** Mr Philips.
Rates fr: *£15.00-£15.00.*
Open: All Year (not Xmas)
Beds: 1F 2T 3S
Baths: 1Ensuite, 2 Shared
🛏 🅿 ⬜ ✕ ▥ Ⓥ ▮

(On Path) *The Old Mill,*
Hazelbeach, Llanstadwell, Milford
Haven, Dyfed, SA73 1EG.
Converted old mill, comfortable.
Tel: **01646 600150** Mr Johnson.
Rates fr: *£10.00-£10.00.*
Open: All Year (not Xmas)
Beds: 1F 2D 5T **Baths:** 4 Shared
🛏 🅿 ⼥ ⬜ ⼊ ✕ Ⓥ ▮ ⼀

Neyland 30

National Grid Ref: SM9605

🍽 ⼕ Oddfellows Arms

(On Path) *Y Ffynnon,*
45 Honeyborough Road, Great
Honeyborough, Neyland, Milford
Haven, Dyfed, SA73 1RF.
Comfortable private house, friendly
welcome.
Grades: WTB Listed
Tel: **01646 601369**
Mr & Mrs Hawley.
Rates fr: *£14.00-£14.00.*
Open: All Year (not Xmas)
Beds: 1D 1T 1S
🅿 (1) ⬜ ▥ ▮

Pembroke Dock 31

National Grid Ref: SM9603

🍽 ⼕ Navy Inn, Ferry Inn
(Pembroke Dock)

(On Path) *Roxana, Victoria Road,*
Pembroke Dock, Dyfed, SA72 6XU.
Family-run guesthouse, quiet loca-
tion.
Grades: WTB 3 Cr
Tel: **01646 683116** Mr Etherington.
Rates fr: *£17.00-£17.50.*
Open: All Year
Beds: 4F 1T 1S
Baths: 6 Ensuite
🛏 🅿 ⬜ ✕ ▥ Ⓥ ▮ ⼀

Cosheston 32

National Grid Ref: SN0003

(2m) *The Old Rectory, Cosheston,*
Pembroke, Dyfed, SA72 4UJ.
Large former rectory.
Grades: WTB 1 Cr
Tel: **01646 684960** Mrs Bailey.
Rates fr: *£15.00-£15.00.*
Open: All Year (not Xmas)
Beds: 1F 1D 1T 1S
Baths: 2 Shared
🛏 🅿 (4) ⬜ ⼊ ✕ Ⓥ

Pembroke 33

National Grid Ref: SM9801

🍽 ⼕ The Dial, The Kings Arms,
Watermans Arms

(On Path) *Merton Place, 3 East*
Back, Pembroke, Dyfed, SA71 4HL.
Lovely old merchant house, walled
garden. Full of books.
Grades: WTB Approv
Tel: **01646 684796** Mrs Pearce.
Rates fr: *£12.50-£14.00.*
Open: All Year
Beds: 2D 2S **Baths:** 1 Shared
🛏 (10) ⬜ ▥ ⼀

(0.5m) *High Noon Guest House,*
Lower Lamphey Road, Pembroke,
Dyfed, SA71 4AB.
Cosy, homely, rural hotel, good
views.
Grades: WTB 3 Cr, Comm
Tel: **01646 683736** Mrs Barnikel.
Rates fr: *£17.00-£15.00.*
Open: All Year (not Xmas) 2F 5D 1T 3S
Baths: 5 Private 2 Shared
🛏 🅿 ⬜ ⼊ ✕ ▥ Ⓥ ▮ ⼀

Angle 34

National Grid Ref: SM8602

🍽 ⼕ The Hibernia

(On Path) *Timothy Lodge,*
39 Angle, Angle, Pembroke, Dyfed,
SA71 5AT.
C18th family-run house, large
garden.
Tel: **01646 641342** Mrs Reece.
Rates fr: *£13.00-£13.00.*
Open: All Year
Beds: 2T **Baths:** 1 Shared
🅿 ⬜ ⼊ Ⓥ ▮ ⼀

Castlemartin 35

National Grid Ref: SR9198

🍽 ⼕ Welcome Inn

(0.25m) *Gupton Farm,*
Castlemartin, Pembroke, Dyfed,
SA71 5HW.
Actual grid ref: SR894989
Friendly comfortable farmhouse.
Grades: WTB Listed
Tel: **01646 661268** Mrs Watkins.
Rates fr: *£14.00-£14.00.*
Open: All Year (not Xmas)
Beds: 1F 1D **Baths:** 1 Shared
🛏 🅿 (6) ⼥ ⬜ ⼊ ▮ ⼀

(On Path) *Chapel Farm,*
Castlemartin, Pembroke, Dyfed,
SA71 5HW.
Actual grid ref: SR907986
Comfortable farmhouse with sea
views.
Tel: **01646 661312** Mrs Smith.
Rates fr: *£15.00-£15.00.*
Open: All Year (not Xmas)
Beds: 1F 1T **Baths:** 1 Shared
🛏 🅿 (5) ⬜ ✕ ▥ Ⓥ ▮

Corston 36

National Grid Ref: SR9299

(1.25m 🚗 **)** *Corston House Hotel,*
Axton Hill, Corston, Hundleton,
Pembroke, Dyfed, SA71 5HB.
Comfortable, spacious, homely
Georgian house.
Tel: **01646 661220**
Mrs Remmington.
Rates fr: *£15.00-£17.00.*
Open: All Year
Beds: 3F 5D 1T 4S
🛏 🅿 ⬜ ✕ ▥ Ⓥ ▮

Bosherston 37

National Grid Ref: SR9694

🍽 ⼕ St Govan's Inn

(On Path) *School House,*
Bosherston, Pembroke, Dyfed,
SA71 5DN.
Victorian village cottage.
Tel: **01646 661269**
Mrs Strudwick.
Rates fr: *£13.00-£13.00.*
Open: All Year (not Xmas)
Beds: 1D 1T **Baths:** 1 Shared
🅿 (2) ▥ ▮ ⼀

East Trewent 38

National Grid Ref: SS0097

(On Path 🚗 **)** *East Trewent Farm,*
East Trewent, Freshwater East,
Pembroke, Dyfed, SA71 5LR.
Beautifully converted stone-built
farm buildings.
Grades: WTB 1 Cr
Tel: **01646 672127** Mr Ireland.
Rates fr: *£15.50-£15.50.*
Open: All Year
Beds: 2D 2T 1S **Baths:** 2 Shared
🛏 🅿 ⼊ ✕ ▥ Ⓥ ▮ ⼀

Freshwater East 39

National Grid Ref: SS0198

🍽 ⼕ Freshwater Inn

(0.5m) *Seahorses, Freshwater*
East, Pembroke, Dyfed, SA71 5LA.
Modern, comfortable house. Sea
view.
Grades: WTB 1 Cr, Comm
Tel: **01646 672405** Miss Philips.
Rates fr: *£13.00-£13.00.*
Open: Easter to Sep
Beds: 1D 1T
Baths: 1 Shared
🅿 (2) ⬜ ▥ Ⓥ ▮

Hodgeston 40

National Grid Ref: SS0399

(1.5m 🚅) *Rosedene, Hodgeston, Pembroke, Dyfed, SA71 5JU.*
Actual grid ref: SS029994
Picturesque guesthouse adjacent to village green.
Grades: WTB 2 Cr
Tel: 01646 672586 Mrs Fallon.
Rates fr: *£16.00-***£20.00***.*
Open: Easter to Oct
Beds: 3D 1T
Baths: 4 Ensuite
🛇 🅿 (5) 🌫 🗙 🎟 🕭 Ⓥ 🅰

Manorbier 41

National Grid Ref: SS0697

🍴 🍺 Castle Inn

(0.5m 🚅) *Hillgarth, Manorbier, Tenby, Dyfed, SA70 7TN.*
Actual grid ref: SS077980
Country house in delightful gardens.
Tel: 01834 871266 Mrs Bell.
Rates fr: *£16.00-***£16.00***.*
Open: All Year (not Xmas)
Beds: 1F 1D 1T 1S
Baths: 1 Ensuite, 1 Shared
🛇 🅿 (10) 🌫 🖵 🅰 ✦

(0.25m 🚅) *The Old Vicarage, Manorbier, Tenby, Dyfed, SA70 7TN.*
Victorian Gothic old vicarage.
Tel: 01834 871452 / 0421 595858
Mrs McHugh.
Rates fr: *£19.00-***£19.00***.*
Open: All Year (not Xmas)
Beds: 1D 1T
Baths: 1 Ensuite 1 Private
🛇 (10) 🅿 🌫 🖵 🅰 ✦

Skrinkle 42

National Grid Ref: SS0797

(🔺 On Path) *Manorbier Youth Hostel, Skrinkle, Manorbier, Tenby, Dyfed, SA70 7TT.*
Actual grid ref: SR0897
Warden: Mr E Audige.
Tel: 01834 871803
Under 18: £5.55 **Adults:** £8.25
Family Bunk Rooms, Centrally Heated, Showers, Evening Meal (7.00 pm), Shop, Television, Games Room, Facilities for the Disabled, Parking
Attractively refurbished building, modern and bright, with award-winning sandy beach less than 200 yards away, between Manorbier and Lydstep

Pay B&Bs by
cash or cheque and
be prepared to
pay up front.

Penally 43

National Grid Ref: SS1199

🍴 🍺 Cross Inn

(On Path) *Myrtle House, Penally, Tenby, Dyfed, SA70 7PU.*
Friendly old terraced cottage, sea view.
Tel: 01834 843623 Mrs Penn.
Rates fr: *£12.50-***£12.50***.*
Open: All Year (not Xmas)
Beds: 1F 1D 1T
Baths: 1 Shared
🛇 🖵 🎟 Ⓥ

(On Path) *Crossing Cottage, Penally, Tenby, Dyfed, SA70 7PP.*
Actual grid ref: SS122995
Secluded house, village outskirts.
Tel: 01834 842291
Mr & Mrs Watts.
Rates fr: *£12.50-***£12.50***.*
Open: All Year (not Xmas)
Beds: 1F 2D
Baths: 1Shared
🛇 🅿 (5) 🌫 🎟

Tenby 44

National Grid Ref: SN1300

🍴 🍺 Five Arches Tavern, Normandie Hotel, Mews Bistro, Coach & Horses

(0.25m) *Clarence House Hotel, Esplanade, Tenby, Dyfed, SA70 7DL.*
Actual grid ref: SN135002
Grades: WTB 3 Cr, Comm, AA 3 Q
Tel: 01834 844371 Mr Phillips.
Rates fr: *£13.00-***£16.00***.*
Open: Easter to Oct
Beds: 25D 25T 18S
Baths: 68 Ensuite, 5 Shared
🌫 🖵 🕭 🗙 🎟 Ⓥ 🅰 ✦
South centre seafront, resident licensed. Near mediaeval walled town entrance. Ten minutes walk to coach, train, harbour. Lift. All ensuite bedrooms. Phone/fax free colour brochure.

(0.25m) *Weybourne, 14 Warren Street, Tenby, Dyfed, SA70 7JU.*
Popular, clean, private hotel.
Grades: WTB 1 Cr
Tel: 01834 843641 Mr Parfitt.
Rates fr: *£13.00-***£13.00***.*
Open: Feb to Sep **Beds:** 3F 1D 2S
🛇 (5) 🖵 🕭 🗙 🎟 Ⓥ 🅰 ✦

(0.25m) *Belgrave Hotel, The Esplanade, Tenby, Dyfed, SA70 7DU.*
Tel: 01834 842377 Mr Thomas.
Rates fr: *£17.50-***£17.50***.*
Open: All Year
Beds: 25F 10D 3T 7S
Baths: 37 Private
🛇 🅿 (12) 🖵 🕭 🗙 🎟 Ⓥ 🅰 ✦
Superb position overlooking South Beach and Caldey Island. Licensed bar. Good food. Choice menus. Special midweek breaks and 'Over 50's' discounts. Nightly entertainment May - October.

The *lowest* **single**
rate *is shown in* **bold.**

(On Path 🚅) *Glenholme, Picton Terrace, Tenby, Dyfed, SA70 7DR.*
Actual grid ref: SN133003
Large comfortable homely Victorian house.
Grades: WTB 2 Cr
Tel: 01834 843909 Ms Milward.
Rates fr: *£12.50-***£15.00***.*
Open: All Year (not Xmas)
Beds: 3F 3D 1T 1S
Baths: 5 Ensuite, 3 Shared
🛇 (2) 🖵 🕭 🗙 🎟 Ⓥ 🅰 ✦

(On Path 🚅) *Paragon Hotel, The Paragon, Tenby, Dyfed, SA70 7HL.*
Family-run, overlooking sea, carpark.
Grades: WTB 3 Cr, Comm
Tel: 01834 843022
Rates fr: *£15.00-***£15.00***.*
Open: All Year (not Xmas)
Beds: 4F 2D 2T 2S
Baths: 9 Ensuite
🛇 (2) 🅿 (10) 🖵 🕭 🗙 🎟 Ⓥ 🅰 ✦

(0.25m) *Ashby House Hotel, Victoria Street, Tenby, Dyfed, SA70 7DY.*
Large Victorian private house.
Grades: WTB 2 Cr, Comm, RAC Acclaim
Tel: 01834 842867
Mr Sarrionandia.
Rates fr: *£16.00-***£20.00***.*
Open: Easter to Oct
Beds: 3F 3D 3T **Baths:** 9 Ensuite
🛇 🅿 🖵 🎟 Ⓥ 🅰 ✦

(0.25m) *Glenthorne, 9 Deer Park, Tenby, Dyfed, SA70 7LE.*
Comfortable clean friendly guesthouse.
Grades: WTB 2 Cr
Tel: 01834 842300 Mr Hughes.
Rates fr: *£12.50-***£13.00***.*
Open: All Year (not Xmas)
Beds: 3F 3D 2T 1S
Baths: 5 Ensuite 4 Shared
🛇 🅿 (4) 🖵 🕭 🗙 🎟 Ⓥ 🅰 ✦

New Hedges 45

National Grid Ref: SN1302

🍴 🍺 New Hedges Tavern

(0.5m) *Pen Mar Guest House, New Hedges, Tenby, Dyfed, SA70 8TL.*
Homely, situated between Saundersfoot/Tenby.
Grades: WTB 3 Cr, High Comm, RAC Acclaim
Tel: 01834 842435 Mr Romeo.
Rates fr: *£16.00-***£16.00***.*
Open: All Year (not Nov)
Beds: 3F 5D 2T
Baths: 6 Private 4 Shared
🛇 🅿 (10) 🖵 🗙 🎟 Ⓥ 🅰 ✦

(1m) *Red House Farm, New Hedges, Saundersfoot, Dyfed, SA69 9DP.*
Actual grid ref: SN126035
Tel: 01834 813918
Also ▲ *£4.00 per tent.*
Open: Easter to Oct
⋔ ⊤ ⚹

Saundersfoot 46

National Grid Ref: SN1304

⏱⛵ The Woodridge Inn, Royal Oak

(1.5m) *The Grange Hotel, Wooden, Saundersfoot, Dyfed, SA69 9DY.*
Small family-run licensed hotel.
Grades: WTB 2 Cr, Comm
Tel: 01834 812809 Mrs Griffin.
Rates fr: *£14.00-£21.00.*
Open: Easter to Sep
Beds: 1F 5D
Baths: 2 Ensuite 2 Shared
⚹ (3) ₽ (10) ⬜ ▥.

(0.25m 🚌**)** *The Harbour Light, 2 High Street, Saundersfoot, Pembs, SA69 9EJ.*
Actual grid ref: SN1304
Close to beach & harbour.
Grades: WTB 2 Cr, AA Comm
Tel: 01834 813496 Mrs Wadey.
Rates fr: *£15.00-£15.00.*
Open: Mar to Oct
Beds: 5F 3D 1T 1S
Baths: 3 Private 7 Shared
⚹ ₽ (9) ⬜ ⼞ ✕ Ⓥ ⓐ ⚡

Pentlepoir 47

National Grid Ref: SN1105

(▲ 1.5m) *Pentlepoir Youth Hostel, The Old School, Pentlepoir, Saundersfoot, Dyfed, SA69 9BJ.*
Actual grid ref: SM1106
Warden: Ms J Liddle.
Tel: 01834 812333
Under 18: £4.60 Adults: £6.75

Family Bunk Rooms, Partially Heated, Showers, Evening Meal (7.00 pm), No Smoking
Old village school just inland from Saundersfoot in the Pembrokeshire Coast National Park

Wiseman's Bridge 48

National Grid Ref: SN1405

⏱⛵ Wisemans Bridge Inn

(On Path) *Wisemans Bridge Inn, Wiseman's Bridge, Narberth, Dyfed, SA67 9AU.*
Olde worlde pub. Log fires.
Tel: 01834 813236
Mrs Kemble.
Rates fr: *£12.50-£12.50.*
Open: All Year
Beds: 1F 3D
Baths: 1 Shared
⚹ ⬜ ⼞ ✕ ▥. ⓐ

(On Path 🚌**)** *Pinewood, Cliff Road, Wiseman's Bridge, Narberth, Dyfed, SA67 8NU.*
Actual grid ref: SN149065
Quiet house overlooking Saundersfoot Bay.
Grades: WTB 2 Cr, High Comm
Tel: 01834 811082 Mrs Grecian.
Rates fr: *£16.00-£16.00.*
Open: All Year (not Xmas)
Beds: 1D 1T
Baths: 2 Ensuite
₽ (3) ⬜ ▥. ⓐ ⚡

Pleasant Valley 49

National Grid Ref: SN1406

⏱⛵ Wiseman's Bridge, Stepaside Inn

(0.25m) *Pleasant Valley House, Pleasant Valley, Stepaside, Narberth, Dyfed, SA67 8NY.*
Small detached hotel, own grounds.
Grades: WTB 2 Cr, High Comm
Tel: 01834 813607 Mrs Holmes.
Rates fr: *£13.50-£13.50.*

Open: Easter to Sep
Beds: 1F 5D 1T 1S
Baths: 3 Private 5 Shared
⚹ (4) ₽ ⬜ ✕ ▥. Ⓥ ⓐ ⚡

Stepaside 50

National Grid Ref: SN1307

⏱⛵ Stepaside Inn

(1m 🚌**)** *Merrixton Bungalow, Stepaside, Narberth, Pembs, SA67 8PJ.*
Comfortable bungalow, panoramic sea views.
Tel: 01834 812002 Mrs Carlan.
Rates fr: *£12.50-£15.00.*
Open: Easter to Sept
Beds: 1T
Baths: 1Ensuite
₽ (2) ⼀ ⬜ ⼞ ▥. Ⓥ ⓐ ⚡

Amroth 51

National Grid Ref: SN1607

⏱⛵ Amroth Arms, Temple Bar, New Inn

(On Path) *Ashdale Guest House, Amroth, Narberth, Dyfed, SA67 8NA.*
Family-run licensed guesthouse.
Excellent food.
Tel: 01834 813853
Mrs Williamson.
Rates fr: *£12.00-£12.00.*
Open: All Year (not Xmas)
Beds: 4F 1T 1S
Baths: 2 Shared
⚹ ₽ ⬜ ⼞ ✕ ▥. Ⓥ ⓐ ⚡

(0.25m) *Beach Haven, Amroth, Narberth, SA67 8NG.*
Family-run guesthouse/Post Office.
Tel: 01834 813310
Miss Evans.
Rates fr: *£14.00-£14.00.*
Open: Easter to Nov
Beds: 2F 2D 1T
Baths: 2 Shared
⚹ ⼞ ▥. Ⓥ

Pennine Way

This is the great-grandfather of all the National Trails in Britain, running for 256 miles along Britain's backbone, the great upland mass of hills and dales that divides the East and West of the country. Officially opened in 1965, the path has actually been developing since the 1930s: it runs from Edale in Derbyshire right the way up to Kirk Yetholm, just inside the Scottish border. It is still probably the toughest trail of the lot and should be attempted only by fit, experienced fell-walkers, fully equipped for rough weather, boggy conditions and mist. There are stretches, especially towards the North, where accommodation is very sparse and well off the beaten track. Take care therefore with the logistics of your route-planning - this is not a path to be under-estimated; many set out only to have their resolve broken by the testing conditions after a couple of days! This said, the walking is superb, passing bare moors, bogs, industrial landscape, limestone country, dales and meadowland, rugged valleys with racing rivers, Hadrian's Wall, conifer forest and the bleak, dramatic Border ridge of the Cheviot massif. To get an idea of the first-class walking country in the North of England, it can't be beaten. Why attempt the path all in one go? Spend a summer doing it bit by bit. There are stretches that make ideal weekend walks, which test the stamina less and make the walk more memorable. That's part of the reason for this book - to show that you don't have to yomp the whole trail at once.

The Youth Hostel Association run a useful Accommodation Booking Bureau for the **Pennine Way**, based on their hostels and local B&Bs along the path. Ring 01629 825850 and ask for the Pennine Way Booking Bureau Pack and they can sort out your entire itinerary without further ado.

Guides (available from all major bookshops unless stated)

Pennine Way South: Edale to Bowes (ISBN 1 85410 3210) and *Pennine Way North: Bowes to Kirk Yetholm* (ISBN 1 85410 0181), both by Tony Hopkins and published by Aurum Press in association with the Countryside Commission and Ordnance Survey, £9.99

The Pennine Way Companion by A. Wainwright available from the Rambler's Association National Office (1/5 Wandsworth Road, London, SW8 2XX, tel. 0171 582 6878), £9.99

A Guide to the Pennine Way by C J Wright (ISBN 09 470640 9), published by Constable & Co Ltd, £8.95

Maps: 1:50000 Ordnance Survey Landranger Series: 74, 80, 86, 87, 91, 92, 98, 103, 109 and 110. *The Pennine Way, Part One - South*, ISBN 1 871149 01 0 (4-colour linear route map) and *The Pennine Way, Part Two - North*, ISBN 1 871149 02 9 (4-colour linear route map), both published by Footprint and available from all good map shops or directly from their offices (Unit 87, Stirling Enterprise Park, Stirling, FK7 7RP), £2.95 (+ 40p p&p) each.

All comments on the path to: **Tony Philpin**, Pennine Way Coordinator, Area Countryside Office, Clegg Nook, Cragg Road, Mytholmroyd, W. Yorks, HX7 5EB.

Edale   1

National Grid Ref: SK1285

🍴 🍺 Nags Head Inn, Grindsbrook Booth, Rambler Inn

(0.5m) *Brookfield, Barber Booth, Edale, Sheffield, S30 2ZL.*
Actual grid ref: SK113847
Beautiful Victorian private house.
Tel: **01433 670227**
Mrs Chapman.
Rates fr: £14.00-£16.00.
Open: Easter to Nov
Beds: 1D 1T
Baths: 1 Shared
🅿 (4) ⅙ 🛏 🎱 ⬛ ⅙

(On Path) *Stonecroft, Grindsbrook, Edale, Sheffield, S30 2ZA.*
Lovely family home with pretty, well-equipped rooms.
Grades: ETB 2 Cr, Comm
Tel: **01433 670262** Mrs Reid.
Rates fr: £21.00-£26.00.
Open: All Year (not Xmas)
Beds: 1D 1T
Baths: 1 Ensuite 1 Private
🛏 (12) 🅿 (5) ⅙ 🛏 ✕ ⬛ 📺 🎱 ⅙

(On Path) *The Old Parsonage, Grindsbrook, Edale, Sheffield, S30 2ZD.*
Secluded C17th house and garden.
Grades: ETB Reg
Tel: **01433 670232** Mrs Beney.

Rates fr: £12.50-£12.50.
Open: March to Nov
Beds: 1D 1T 1S **Baths:** 1Shared
🅿 (2) ⅙ 🎱 ⅙

(▲ 1.5m) *Edale Youth Hostel, Rowland Cote, Nether Booth, Edale, Sheffield, S30 2ZH.*
Actual grid ref: SJ1386
Warden: Mr J Hardy.
Tel: **01433 670302**
Under 18: £6.15 **Adults:** £9.10
Family Bunk Rooms, Centrally Heated, Showers, Evening Meal in Cafeteria (5.30 - 7.15pm), Shop, Television, Games Room
Large former private house set in extensive grounds on the hillside below Kinder Scout Plateau

Chinley 2

National Grid Ref: SK0482

⊪ ⌨ Squirrels Hotel, Old Hall

(2m) *Mosley House Farm,*
Maynestone Road, Chinley,
Stockport, Cheshire, SK12 6AH.
Actual grid ref: SK0482
Working farm, peaceful attractive
surroundings.
Grades: ETB Listed
Tel: 01663 750240 Mrs Goddard.
Rates fr: *£15.00-£17.00.*
Open: All Year (not Xmas)
Beds: 1F 1D **Baths:** 1 Private
🛏 🅿 (3) 🖵 🛏

Hayfield 3

National Grid Ref: SK0387

⊪ ⌨ The Sportsman, The Pack
Horse

(1m 🚌) *The Old Bank House,*
Hayfield, Stockport, Cheshire,
SK12 5EP.
Family home, beautiful decor.
Tel: **01663 747354**
Mrs Collier-Johnson.
Rates fr: *£18.50-£20.00.*
Open: All Year
Beds: 1F 1D 1T
Baths: 2 Shared
🛏 🅿 🖵 🛏 ⚲ 🗙 🛒 🎔 Ⓥ 🎔 ✦

Little Hayfield 4

National Grid Ref: SK0388

⊪ ⌨ The Grouse, Lantern Pike

(2.5m) *Stet Barn Farm, Lane*
Head Road, Little Hayfield,
Stockport, Cheshire, SK12 5NS.
Actual grid ref: SK0389
Comfortable converted farmhouse,
beautiful gardens.
Grades: ETB Listed, Comm
Tel: **01663 745970** Mrs Isaacs.
Rates fr: *£17.00-£17.00.*
Open: All Year (not Xmas)
Beds: 1D 1T
Baths: 1Shared
🛏 (2) 🅿 (4) ⚲ 🖵 🛒 ✦

Chunal 5

National Grid Ref: SK0491

⊪ ⌨ Grouse Inn

(3m 🚌) *Stanley Farm*
Bunkhouse, Chunal, Glossop,
Derbyshire, SK15 9JY.
Grades: ETB Listed
Tel: **01457 863727** Mrs Brown.
Rates fr: *£15.00-£18.00.*
Open: All Year (not Xmas)
Beds: 1D 1T **Baths:** 1 Shared
🛏 🅿 (10) ⚲ 🖵 🗙 🛒 Ⓥ 🎔 ✦
Also ⛺ *Also bunkhouse,*
£8.00 per bunk.
Open: All Year 🔥 🛏 ♨ 🗙 ✦ ♿
Private farmhouse on 26 acres.
B&B in peaceful surroundings.
Warm welcome, superb views.
Brilliant bunkerbarn on same site
accommodating 14. First class
facilities, safe parking, self
catering.

Moorfield 6

National Grid Ref: SK0492

⊪ ⌨ The Grouse Inn

(1m 🚌) *Moorfield Barn,*
Derbyshire Level, Moorfield,
Glossop, Derbyshire, SK13 9PR.
Actual grid ref: SK048928
Moorfield Barn, panoramic views.
Peaceful, convenient for Pennine
Way.
Tel: **01457 862853** Mrs Bamford.
Rates fr: *£15.00-£14.00.*
Open: All Year (not Xmas)
Beds: 2T 1S
Baths: 1 Private 1 Shared
🛏 🅿 (4) ⚲ 🖵 🛒 Ⓥ 🎔 ✦

Glossop 7

National Grid Ref: SK0394

⊪ ⌨ Crown Inn, Prince of Wales,
Friendship

(4m) *Birds Nest Cottage, 40*
Primrose Lane, Glossop,
Derbyshire, SK13 8EW.
Actual grid ref: SK0394
Relaxed and friendly atmosphere.
Grades: ETB 3 Cr
Tel: **01457 853478** Mills.
Rates fr: *£15.00-£15.00.*
Open: All Year (not Xmas)
Beds: 1F 3T 1S
Baths: 3 Shared
🛏 ⚲ 🖵 🛏 🗙 🛒 Ⓥ 🎔 ✦

© Crown Copyright

Padfield 8

National Grid Ref: SK0296

¶ ⌕ Peels Arms

(3.5m) *Whitehouse Farm,*
Padfield, Hyde, Cheshire, SK14 7ET.
Comfortable working farmhouse.
Grades: ETB Listed, Comm
Tel: 01457 854695 Mrs Wynne.
Rates fr: *£15.00-£18.00.*
Open: All Year
Beds: 2T
✿ **P** (6) ⌑ ⭢ ⛬ �V

(3m) *The Peels Arms, Temple*
Street, Padfield, Hyde, Cheshire,
SK14 7ET.
Family-run inn in picturesque village.
Grades: ETB Listed, Approv
Tel: 01457 852719
Mrs Murray.
Rates fr: *£15.00-£21.00.*
Open: All Year (not Xmas)
Beds: 1F 2D 2T
Baths: 3 Ensuite
✿ **P** (20) ⌑ ⭢ ✕ ⛬ �V

Crowden-in-Longdendale 9

National Grid Ref: SK0799

(▲ On Path) *Crowden Youth*
Hostel, Crowden-in-Longdendale,
Hayfield, Hyde, Cheshire, SK14 7HZ.
Actual grid ref: SJ0799
Warden: Mr M Norris.
Tel: 01457 852135
Under 18: £4.60 **Adults:** £6.75
Family Bunk Rooms, Centrally
Heated, Showers, Evening Meal
(7.30 pm)
Formerly a row of railwaymen's
cottages, right on the Pennine Way
in a remote part of Longdendale.

Holme 10

National Grid Ref: SE1005

(2m ⌖) *Holme Castle Country*
Hotel, Holme, Holmfirth,
Huddersfield, W. Yorks, HD7 1QG.
Actual grid ref: SE1106
Conservation area. BBC Green
Award.
Grades: AA 4 Q, Select
Tel: 01484 686764
Ms Hayfield.
Rates fr: *£20.00-£20.00.*
Open: All Year
Beds: 1F 4D 2T 1S
Baths: 5 Private 3 Shared
✿ **P** (12) ⍿ ⌑ ✕ ⛬ �V ⓘ ✦

Holmfirth 11

National Grid Ref: SE1408

¶ ⌕ Shoulder of Mutton, Victoria
Inn, Post Card

(4.5m) *Springfield House, 95*
Huddersfield Road, Holmfirth,
Huddersfield, W. Yorks, HD7 1JA.
Large Victorian guesthouse.

Tel: 01484 683031 Mr Brook.
Rates fr: *£14.50-£19.00.*
Open: All Year
Beds: 2F 1D 1T
Baths: 2 Ensuite 1 Shared
✿ **P** (3) ⌑ ⭢ ⛬ �V ⓘ ✦

Netherthong 12

National Grid Ref: SE1309

¶ ⌕ Clothiers Arms

(4m) *Westwood, 7 St Marys*
Crescent, Netherthong, Holmfirth,
W. Yorks, HD7 2XP.
Detached bungalow with swimming pool.
Tel: 01484 685695 Mrs Dickinson.
Rates fr: *£16.00-£16.00.*
Open: All Year
Beds: 1T 1S
Baths: 1 Private 1 Shared
P (2) ⍿ ⌑ ⛬

Standedge 13

National Grid Ref: SE0110

(0.25m) *Globe Farm Guest House*
& Bunkhouse, Huddersfield Road,
Standedge, Delph, Oldham, Lancs,
OL3 5LU.
Actual grid ref: SE012097
Warm, comfortable, friendly farmhouse.
Grades: ETB 1 Cr, Comm,
AA 2 Q
Tel: 01457 873040 Mrs Mayall.
Rates fr: *£18.00-£18.50.*
Open: All Year (not Xmas)
Beds: 2D 2T 3S
Baths: 7 Ensuite
✿ **P** (20) ⌑ ✕ ⛬ �V ⓘ ✦
Also ▲ £1.75 per person. Also
bunkhouse, £6.00 per bunk.
Open: All Year ⋔ ⍿ ⛺ ✕ ✦ ⛭

Diggle 14

National Grid Ref: SE0008

¶ ⌕ Diggle Hotel, Navigation Inn,
Church Inn

(0.5m) *New Barn, Harrop Green*
Farm, Diggle, Oldham, Lancs,
OL3 5LW.
Modern farmhouse on working
sheep farm.
Tel: 01457 873937 Mr Rhodes.
Rates fr: *£14.00-£14.50.*
Open: All Year (not Xmas)
Beds: 1F 1D 1T 1S
Baths: 1 Private 1 Shared
✿ **P** ⌑ ⭢ ⛬ �V

(1.5m ⌖) *Sunfield, Diglea,*
Diggle, Oldham, Lancs, OL3 5LA.
Comfortable farmhouse with
ensuite rooms.
Tel: 01457 874030
Mr & Mrs Francis.
Rates fr: *£15.00-£17.50.*
Open: All Year
Beds: 1F 2D 3T
Baths: 3 Ensuite 3 Shared
✿ **P** (6) ⌑ ⭢ ⛬ ⛬ �V ✦

Dobcross 15

National Grid Ref: SD9906

¶ ⌕ Swan Inn, Navigation Inn

(2.5m ⌖) *Fold Guest House, 18*
Woods Lane, Dobcross, Oldham,
Lancs, OL3.
Friendly, family-run village guest-
house/stores. **Grades:** ETB Reg
Tel: 01457 876491 Mr Hodgkinson
Rates fr: *£15.00-£15.00.*
Open: All Year (not Xmas)
Beds: 2D 1T **Baths:** 1 Shared
✿ ⌑ ⛬ �V ⓘ

Delph 16

National Grid Ref: SD9807

¶ ⌕ Old Bell Inn, Bulls Head

(4m) *Globe Farm Bunkhouse,*
Huddersfield Road, Standedge,
Delph, Oldham, Lancs, OL3 5LU.
Independent youth hostel. Self-
catering/catered.
Tel: 01457 873040
Rates fr: *£6.50-£6.50.*
Open: All Year
Beds: 4F 1D **Baths:** 2 Shared
✿ **P** (20) ⌑ ⭢ ✕ ⛬ �V

Marsden 17

National Grid Ref: SE0411

¶ ⌕ Tunnel End Inn

(2m ⌖) *Tomar Cottage, 5 Clough*
Lea, Marsden, Huddersfield, W.
Yorks, HD7 6DN.
Actual grid ref: SE0411
Weaver's cottage in village centre.
Tel: 01484 845578 Ms Kyle.
Rates fr: *£16.00-£16.00.*
Open: All Year (not Xmas)
Beds: 1D 1T **Baths:** 1 Shared
✿ ⌑ ✕ ⛬ �V ⓘ

(3.5m) *Forest Farm, Mount Road,*
Marsden, Huddersfield, W. Yorks,
HD7 6NN.
300-year-old farmhouse and supe-
rior bunkhouse.
Tel: 01484 842687 Mrs Fussey.
Rates fr: *£14.00-£14.00.*
Open: All Year
Beds: 1F 1D 1T **Baths:** 2 Shared
✿ **P** (6) ⌑ ⭢ ✕ ⛬ �V ⓘ ✦

Slaithwaite 18

National Grid Ref: SE0813

¶ ⌕ Rose & Crown, Cop Hill

(3.5m ⌖) *Oakmere, 44 Longlands*
Road, Slaithwaite, Huddersfield,
W. Yorks, HD7 5DR.
Detached family house overlooking
reservoir.
Tel: 01484 843323 Mrs Campbell.
Rates fr: *£15.00-£15.00.*
Open: All Year (not Xmas)
Beds: 1D 1T **Baths:** 2 Ensuite
✿ (12) **P** (1) ⍿ ⌑ ⭢ ⛬ �V ⓘ

Denshaw 19

National Grid Ref: SD9710

⏹ 🍺 Junction Inn, Printers Arms

(3m 🚌) **Boothstead Farm,**
Rochdale Road, Denshaw, Oldham,
Lancs, *OL3 5UE*.
Pretty, C18th farmhouse, log fires.
Grades: ETB Comm
Tel: **01457 878622** Mrs Hall.
Rates fr: £17.00-£17.50.
Open: All Year (not Xmas)
Beds: 1F 1D 1T
Baths: 1 Shared
🛇 🅿 ⅃ ⌷ ✕ 🎆 Ⓥ 🛉 ✦

Littleborough 20

National Grid Ref: SD9316

⏹ 🍺 Stubley Old Hall, Spinning
Wheel Restaurant

(2.5m) **16 Laburnum Way,**
Littleborough, Lancs, *OL15 8LS*.
Actual grid ref: SD925164
Semi-detached bungalow.
Tel: **01706 379170** Mrs Hill.
Rates fr: £13.50-£13.50.
Open: All Year (not Xmas)
Beds: 1S
Baths: 1 Shared
🅿 (3) ⅃ ⌷ 🎆

(2.5m) **Kenmoor House,**
Smithybridge Road, Hollingworth
Lake, Littleborough, Lancs,
OL15 0BQ.
Rooms in annexe to main house.
Tel: **01706 378203**
Mr Craven.
Rates fr: £17.50-£30.00.
Open: All Year
Beds: 1F 1D 2T
Baths: 4 Private
🛇 🅿 (6) ⌷ 🐾 🎆 ⅃ Ⓥ

Soyland 21

National Grid Ref: SE0320

(3m 🚌) **Wood End,** Lighthazels
Road, Soyland, Ripponden,
Sowerby Bridge, W. Yorks, *HX6 4NP*.
Actual grid ref: SE032209
C17th converted farmhouse, idyllic
setting.
Tel: **01422 822135** Mrs Eccles.
Rates fr: £20.00-£15.00.
Open: All Year (not Xmas)
Beds: 1F 2D 1S
Baths: 3 Ensuite 1 Shared
🛇 🅿 (4) ⅃ ⌷ ✕ 🎆 Ⓥ 🛉 ✦

Ripponden 22

National Grid Ref: SE0319

⏹ 🍺 The Bridge Inn, The Butchers
Apron, Blue Ball Inn, White Hart

(2.25m) **Blue Ball Inn,** Blue Ball
Lane, Ripponden, Sowerby Bridge,
W. Yorks, *HX6 4LR*.
C18th moorland inn, good food.
Tel: **01422 823603** Mrs Foster.

Rates fr: £17.60-£17.60.
Open: All Year
Beds: 3D 1T
Baths: 1 Private 1 Shared
🛇 🅿 ⌷ ✕ 🎆 Ⓥ 🛉 ✦

(3m 🚌) **Dove Dale,** 14 Small
Lees, Ripponden, Sowerby Bridge,
W. Yorks, *HX6 4DZ*.
Hillside home with Ryburn Valley
views.
Grades: ETB Listed, Comm
Tel: **01422 823611**
Mr & Mrs Sands.
Rates fr: £14.50-£15.00.
Open: All Year
Beds: 2D 1T
Baths: 1 Shared
🛇 🅿 (4) ⅃ ⌷ ✕ 🎆 Ⓥ 🛉 ✦

Mankinholes 23

National Grid Ref: SD9623

⏹ 🍺 Fountain

(⛺ 0.5m) **Mankinholes Youth
Hostel,** Mankinholes, Todmorden,
W. Yorks, *OL14 6HR*.
Actual grid ref: SD9623
Warden: Mr R Jones.
Tel: **01706 812340**
Under 18: £4.60
Adults: £6.75
Family Bunk Rooms, Centrally
Heated, Showers, Evening Meal
(7.00 pm), Shop
Listed ancient manor house in a
conservation village with typical
South Pennine architecture, sur-
rounded by moorland

Cragg Vale 24

National Grid Ref: SE0023

⏹ 🍺 Hinchliffe Arms

(2m) **Springfield,** Cragg Road,
Cragg Vale, Hebden Bridge, W.
Yorks, *HX7 5SR*.
Peaceful, modern stone-built
house.
Tel: **01422 882029** Mrs Nelson.
Rates fr: £16.00-£16.00.
Open: All Year (not Xmas)
Beds: 1D 1T 2S
Baths: 1 Private 1 Shared
🛇 🅿 (4) ⅃ ⌷ 🎆 🛉 ✦

Todmorden 25

National Grid Ref: SD9424

⏹ 🍺 Rose & Crown, Woodman,
Fountain

(1.5m 🚌) **Calder Bank House,**
Shaw Wood Road, Todmorden, W.
Yorks, *OL14 6DA*.
Millowner's house set in 1.5 acres.
Grades: ETB Listed
Tel: **01706 816188** Ms Wardroper.
Rates fr: £17.00-£17.00.
Open: All Year
Beds: 1F 1D 2T 2S
Baths: 1 Private
🛇 🅿 (10) ⌷ 🐾 ✕ 🎆 ⅃ Ⓥ 🛉 ✦

(1.5m) **The Berghof Hotel,** Cross
Stone Road, Todmorden, W. Yorks,
OL14 8RQ.
Authentic Austrian hotel and
restaurant.
Grades: ETB 3 Cr, Comm
Tel: **01706 812966** Mrs Brandstatter
Rates fr: £22.00-£28.00.
Open: All Year
Beds: 6D 1T **Baths:** 7 Ensuite
🛇 🅿 (30) ⌷ 🐾 ✕ 🎆 Ⓥ

Mytholmroyd 26

National Grid Ref: SE0126

⏹ 🍺 Shoulder of Mutton, White
House, Travellers Rest, Hinchliffe
Arms

(2.75m) **Reedacres,** Mytholmroyd,
Hebden Bridge, W. Yorks, *HX7 5DQ*.
Detached modern house.
Tel: **01422 884423** Mr/Mrs Boggis.
Rates fr: £16.00-£20.00.
Open: All Year (not Xmas)
Beds: 1D 1P **Baths:** 1 Private
🅿 ⅃ ⌷ 🐾 🎆

Blackshawhead 27

National Grid Ref: SD9527

⏹ 🍺 Shoulder of Mutton,
Sportsman

(1m 🚌) **Higher Earnshaw,**
Blackshawhead, Hebden Bridge,
W. Yorks, *HX7 7JB*.
Comfortable warm stone-built
farmhouse.
Tel. **01422 844117**
Mr/Mrs Redmond
Rates fr: £15.00-£16.00.
Open: All Year (not Xmas)
Beds: 1F 1D 1S **Baths:** 1 Shared
🛇 🅿 (5) ⅃ 🐾 🎆 🛉 ✦

(On Path) **Badger Fields Farm,**
Badger Lane, Blackshawhead,
Hebden Bridge, W. Yorks, *HX7 7JX*.
Actual grid ref: SD274968
Modern, comfortable farmhouse.
Grades: ETB Listed
Tel: **01422 845161** Mrs Whitaker.
Rates fr: £15.00-£15.00.
Open: Apr to Oct
Beds: 1F 1D **Baths:** 1 Shared
🛇 🅿 (3) ⅃ 🎆 Ⓥ 🛉

Hebden Bridge 28

National Grid Ref: SD9827

⏹ 🍺 Nutclough House, White
Lion, Nelsons Wine Bar, White
Swan

(1m) **1 Primrose Terrace,** Hebden
Bridge, W. Yorks, *HX6 6HN*.
Actual grid ref: SD990271
Stonebuilt house with canalside
location.
Tel: **01422 844747** Ms McNamee.
Rates fr: £13.00-£13.00.
Open: All Year
Beds: 1D 1T 1S **Baths:** 1 Shared
🅿 (1) 🎆 Ⓥ ✦

(1m) *Prospect End, 8 Prospect Terrace, Savile Road, Hebden Bridge, W. Yorks, HX7 6NA.*
Actual grid ref: SD982273
Victorian house, Pennine Way 1 mile.
Grades: ETB 1 Cr, Comm
Tel: **01422 843586** Ms Anthon.
Rates fr: *£17.00-£20.00.*
Open: All Year
Beds: 1D 1T
Baths: 2 Ensuite
⊬⌂✕▥.Ⅴ🛈✦

(0.25m) *Old Civic Hall Hotel, Crown Street, Hebden Bridge, W. Yorks, HX7 8EH.*
Friendly, busy, town centre hotel.
Tel: **01422 842814** Mr Midgley.
Rates fr: *£19.50-£28.00.*
Open: All Year
Beds: 3F 3D 2T 1S
Baths: 9 Ensuite
ਠ⌂✕▥.Ⅴ🛈

(2m) *8 Birchcliffe, (off Sandy Gate), Hebden Bridge, W. Yorks, HX7 8JA.*
Large, stone cottage own entrance.
Tel: **01422 844777** Ms Handley.
Rates fr: *£13.50-£15.00.*
Open: All Year
Beds: 1D **Baths:** 1 Private
🅿(1)⌂▥.&✦

Colden 29

National Grid Ref: SD9628

(0.25m 🚌) *New Delight Inn, Jack Bridge, Colden, Hebden Bridge, W. Yorks, HX7 7HT.*
Tel: **01422 842795** Mr Marigold.
Rates fr: *£13.00-£13.00.*
Open: All Year
Beds: 3 **Baths:** 3 Ensuite
ਠ🅿(50)⊬⌂ⵜ✕▥.Ⅴ🛈✦
Also ▲ *£2.00 per person.*
Open: All Year ⊤ ⚡ ♿

Heptonstall 30

National Grid Ref: SD9728

⊮| 🍺 White Lion, New Delight

(0.5m) *29 Slack Top, Heptonstall, Hebden Bridge, W. Yorks, HX7 7HA.*
Actual grid ref: SD978287
Guest wing to private house.
Grades: ETB Listed
Tel: **01422 843636** Mrs Morley.
Rates fr: *£16.00-£16.00.*
Open: All Year
Beds: 1F 1D
ਠ🅿(4)⌂▥.Ⅴ🛈✦

(0.5m) *White Lion Hotel, 58 Towngate, Heptonstall, Hebden Bridge, W. Yorks, HX7 7NB.*
C17th village inn.
Tel: **01422 842027**
Rates fr: *£18.00-£18.00.*
Open: All Year (not Xmas)
Beds: 2F 1D
Baths: All Ensuite
ਠ(4)🅿(4)⌂ⵜ✕▥.&Ⅴ

Stanbury 31

National Grid Ref: SE0037

⊮| 🍺 Old Silent Inn, Friendly Inn, Wuthering Heights

(On Path) *Ponden Hall, Stanbury, Haworth, Keighley, W. Yorks, BD22 0HR.*
Actual grid ref: SD991371
Grades: ETB Reg
Tel: **01535 644154** Mrs Taylor.
Rates fr: *£17.00-£15.00.*
Open: All Year (not Xmas)
Beds: 1F 1D 1T
ਠⵜ✕Ⅴ🛈✦
Also ▲ *£1.00 per tent.*⊤
Welcoming relaxed Elizabethan farmhouse. Are you into good food, log fires, family chaos, animals and the peace and tranquillity of another era? Do come.

(On Path 🚌) *Buckley Green, Stanbury, Haworth, Keighley, W. Yorks, BD22 0HL.*
Actual grid ref: SD998367
Large moorland cottage.
Grades: ETB 1 Cr
Tel: **01535 645095** Mrs Archer.
Rates fr: *£14.00-£15.00.*
Open: All Year (not Xmas)
Beds: 2D 1T **Baths:** 1 Shared
ਠ🅿(6)⌂ⵜ✕▥.Ⅴ🛈✦

(0.25m) *Wuthering Heights Inn, 26 Main Street, Stanbury, Keighley, W. Yorks, BD22 0HB.*
Warm and friendly country inn.
Tel: **01535 643332** Mrs Mitchell.
Rates fr: *£13.00-£14.00.*
Open: All Year (not Xmas)
Beds: 1F 1D 1T 1S
Baths: 2 Shared
ਠ🅿(20)⌂ⵜ✕▥.Ⅴ✦

Oxenhope 32

National Grid Ref: SE0337

⊮| 🍺 The Dog and Gun, The Three Sisters

(On Path) *West View, Jew Lane, Oxenhope, Haworth, Keighley, W. Yorks, BD22 9HS.*
Large Victorian semi in countryside.
Tel: **01535 642779** Mrs Pawson.
Rates fr: *£14.00-£16.00.*
Open: Easter to Oct
Beds: 2T **Baths:** 1 Shared
ਠ(8)🅿(2)⊬⌂▥.🛈

Haworth 33

National Grid Ref: SE0337

⊮| 🍺 Old White Lion, Three Sisters, Old Hall, The Weavers, Royal Oak, Black Bull

(2.5m 🚌) *Moorfield Guest House, 80 West Lane, Haworth, Keighley, W. Yorks, BD22 8EN.*
Large Victorian private house..
Grades: ETB Listed

Tel: **01535 643689**
Mrs Hargreaves.
Rates fr: *£16.00-£16.00.*
Open: All Year (not Xmas)
Beds: 1F 2D 2T 1S
Baths: 5 Private 1 Shared
ਠ🅿(6)⌂✕▥.Ⅴ✦

(2m) *Roos Cottage, 1 Belle Isle Road, Haworth, Keighley, W. Yorks, BD22 8QQ.*
Tel: **01535 642594** Mrs Dickson.
Rates fr: *£15.00-£15.00.*
Open: All Year
Beds: 1F 1D 1S
Baths: 1 Shared
ਠ🅿(1)⊬⌂ⵜ✕▥.Ⅴ
A warm welcome awaits our guests. Enjoy delicious food in a cosy atmosphere. Little luxuries included eg. bathrobes, toiletries. Brontë Parsonage, Steam Railway nearby

(2m) *Meltham House, 3 Belle Isle Road, Haworth, Keighley, W. Yorks, BD22 8QQ.*
Modern, comfortable, detached house.
Tel: **01535 645282** Mrs Ingham.
Rates fr: *£15.00-£15.00.*
Open: All Year
Beds: 1D 1T 1S
Baths: 1 Shared 1 Private
ਠ(5)🅿(3)⌂ⵜ▥.🛈✦

(2.5m) *Woodlands Grange Guest House, Woodlands Grange, Belle Isle, Haworth, Keighley, W. Yorks, BD22 8PB.*
Secluded detached house.
Grades: ETB 2 Cr, Comm
Tel: **01535 646814** Ms Harker.
Rates fr: *£16.00-£22.00.*
Open: All Year
Beds: 2F 4D 1T
Baths: 5 Private 1 Shared
ਠ🅿(12)⌂ⵜ✕▥.Ⅴ🛈✦

(3m) *The Manor House, Changegate, Haworth, Keighley, W. Yorks, BD22 8EB.*
C17th manor house, like parsonage.
Tel: **01535 642911** Mrs Lambert.
Rates fr: *£17.00.*
Open: Easter to Xmas
Beds: 2D 1T
Baths: 3 Private
🅿(3)⌂▥.

(▲ 4m) *Haworth Youth Hostel, Longlands Hall, Longlands Drive, Lees Lane, Haworth, Keighley, W. Yorks, BD22 8RT.*
Actual grid ref: SD0337
Warden: Mr A Head.
Tel: **01535 642234**
Under 18: £5.55 **Adults:** £8.25
Family Bunk Rooms, Centrally Heated, Showers, Evening Meal (6.30 pm), Shop, Television, Games Room
Victorian mill-owner's mansion with interesting architectural features, set in extensive grounds. Good home-cooked meals

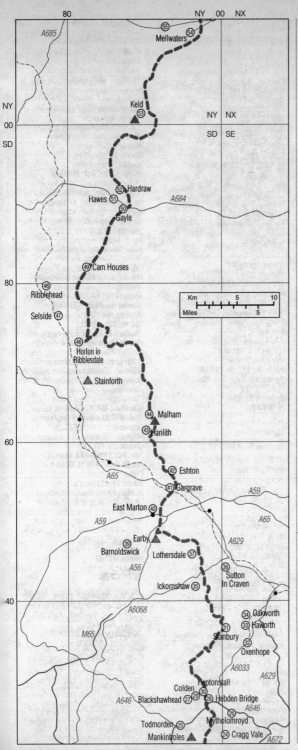

(1.25m) *Bronte Cottage, 4 Park Top Row, Main Street, Haworth, Keighley, W. Yorks, BD22 8DN.*
Modern terrace cottage with view.
Grades: ETB Listed
Tel: 01535 647012 Mrs Gray.
Rates fr: *£17.50*-£17.50.
Open: All Year (not Xmas)
Beds: 1F 1D 1S
Baths: 3 Ensuite
⌂ (10) P (3) ⚹ ⬚ ⭐ ▦ ≠

(0.25m) *The Apothecary Guest House, 86 Main Street, Haworth, Keighley, W. Yorks, BD22 8DA.*
Comfortable family-run guest-house.
Grades: ETB Listed, Approv
Tel: 01535 643642 Mrs Sisley.
Rates fr: *£17.00*-£17.00.
Open: All Year
Beds: 1F 4D 2T 1S
Baths: 7 Ensuite
⌂ P (5) ⬚ ⭐ ▦ Ⓥ

Oakworth   34

National Grid Ref: SE0338

(3m) *Greenways, 30 Goose Cote Lane, Oakworth, Keighley, W. Yorks, BD22 7NQ.*
Large house in large gardens.
Tel: 01535 667959 Mrs Cowling.
Rates fr: *£15.50*-£11.00.
Open: All Year
Beds: 1D 1S **Baths:** 1 Private
⌂ P (3) ⬚ ✕ ▦ Ⓥ

(3m) *Newsholme Manor Hotel, Slaymaker Lane, Slack Lane, Oakworth, Keighley, W Yorks, BD22 0RQ.*
Delightful country hotel, enjoying panoramic views.
Grades: ETB Listed
Tel: 01535 642964 Mr Sexton.
Rates fr: *£16.50*-£19.50.
Open: All Year
Beds: 1F 3D 1T 1S
Baths: 6 Private
⌂ P (40) ⬚ ✕ ▦ Ⓥ ▮

Ickornshaw   35

National Grid Ref: SD9642

🍽 ⌑ Black Bull

(On Path 🚌) *The Hawthorns, Ickornshaw, Cowling, Keighley, W. Yorks, BD22 0DH.*
Bungalow 'Hilton of Ickornshaw'.
Grades: ETB Reg
Tel: 01535 633299 Mrs Sawley.
Rates fr: *£14.50*-£20.00.
Open: All Year (not Xmas)
Beds: 1F 2D 1T
Baths: 2 Private 1 Shared
⌂ (5) P (6) ⬚ ✕ ▦ Ⓥ ▮ ≠

The lowest *double* rate per person is shown in *italics*.

Sutton in Craven 36

National Grid Ref: SE0043

(3.5m ⊞) *Ravenshill,* Holme Lane, Sutton in Craven, Keighley, W. Yorks, *BD20 7LN.*
Tel: **01535 633276** Mrs Barwick Nicholson.
Rates fr: *£16.00-£16.00.*
Open: All Year (not Xmas)
Beds: 1T 1S
Baths: 1 Shared
🏃 (5) 🅿 (2) 🖵 ✗ 🎹 Ⅴ ▮ ⌇

Lothersdale 37

National Grid Ref: SD9645

🍴 🍺 Hare & Hounds

(On Path) *Burlington House,*
Lothersdale, Keighley, W. Yorks, *BD20 8EL.*
Old mill-owner's house.
Grades: ETB Reg
Tel: **01535 634635** Mrs Wood.
Rates fr: *£12.00-£12.00.*
Open: All Year (not Xmas)
Beds: 1D 1T **Baths:** 1Shared
🏃 🅿 (2) 🖵 🛏 🎹 Ⅴ ▮ ⌇

Earby 38

National Grid Ref: SD9046

🍴 🍺 White Lion, Red Lion

(1m) *Grange Fell,* Skipton Road, Earby, Colne, Lancs, *BB8 6JL.*
Apartment-style accommodation in Edwardian home.
Tel: **01282 843621** Mrs Eden.
Rates fr: *£15.00.*
Open: Easter to Oct
Beds: 1F
Baths: 1 Shared
🏃 🅿 🖵 🛏 🎹 Ⅴ ▮

(▲ 1m) *Earby Youth Hostel,* Glen Cottage, Birch Hall Lane, Earby, Colne, Lancs, *BB8 6JX.*
Actual grid ref: SD9146
Warden: Ms D Swift.
Tel: **01282 842349**
Under 18: £4.15 Adults: £6.10
Family Bunk Rooms, Partially Heated, Showers, Shop
Attractive cottage with own picturesque garden and waterfall, on the NE outskirts of Earby

Barnoldswick 39

National Grid Ref: SD8746

🍴 🍺 Rolls Royce Social Club

(On Path ⊞) *Monks House,*
5 Manchester Road, Barnoldswick, Colne, Lancs, *BB8 5NZ.*
Centrally situated Georgian house.
Grades: ETB 3 Cr
Tel: **01282 814423** Mrs Robinson.
Rates fr: *£15.00-£15.00.*
Open: All Year
Beds: 2T 2S **Baths:** 2 Shared
🏃 🅿 (3) 🖵 ✗ 🎹 Ⅴ ▮ ⌇

East Marton 40

National Grid Ref: SD9050

🍴 🍺 Cross Keys

(On Path) *Sawley House,* East Marton, Skipton, N. Yorks, *BD23 3LP.*
Actual grid ref: SD9050
Grades: ETB Reg
Tel: **01282 843207**
Mrs Pilling.
Rates fr: *£17.00-£17.00.*
Open: All Year
Beds: 2T 1S
Baths: 1Shared
🏃 (8) 🅿 (10) 🖵 🛏 ✗ Ⅴ ▮ ⌇
Also ▲ *£2.50 per person.*
Open: All Year 🏃 Ⅵ ✗ ⌇ ♿
C12th farmhouse situated on Pennine Way adjacent Leeds-Liverpool canal. On A59 Yorkshire/Lancashire border. Ideally placed for touring the North of England

Gargrave 41

National Grid Ref: SD9354

🍴 🍺 Old Swan Inn

(2m) *2 Westville Gardens,* Eshton Road, Gargrave, Skipton, N. Yorks, *BD23 3SG.*
New comfortable bungalow.
Tel: **01756 748084**
Mrs Moorhouse.
Rates fr: *£15.00-£15.00.*
Open: All Year (not Xmas)
Beds: 1D 1T
Baths: 1 Shared
🏃 🅿 🖵 🎹

Eshton 42

National Grid Ref: SD9356

🍴 🍺 The Angel, Mason's Arms, Old Swan Inn

(1m) *Eshton Grange,* Eshton, Gargrave, Skipton, N. Yorks, *BD23 3QE.*
Family run, 14 acre farm.
Tel: **01756 749383**
Mr & Mrs Shelmerdine.
Rates fr: *£20.00-£25.00.*
Open: All Year
Beds: 1F 1D 1T
Baths: 2 Ensuite 1 Private
🏃 🅿 (6) 🖵 ✗ 🎹 Ⅴ

Hanlith 43

National Grid Ref: SD9061

(On Path) *Coachmans Cottage,*
Hanlith, Malham, Skipton, N. Yorks, *BD23 4BP.*
Tranquil C17th cottage, every comfort.
Tel: **01729 830538** Mrs Jenkins.
Rates fr: *£17.00-£18.00.*
Open: All Year (not Xmas)
Beds: 2D 1T 1S
Baths: 4 Private
🏃 (10) 🅿 (3) 🖂 🖵 🎹

Malham 44

National Grid Ref: SD9062

🍴 🍺 The Buck Inn, The Listers Arms

(On Path ⊞) *Eastwood House,*
Malham, Skipton, N. Yorks, *BD23 4DA.*
Comfortable large semi-detached country house.
Tel: **01729 830409** Mr Calvert.
Rates fr: *£16.00-£18.00.*
Open: All Year
Beds: 3F 2D 1T 1S
Baths: 3 Shared
🏃 🅿 (3) 🖂 🖵 🛏 ✗ Ⅴ ▮ ⌇

(On Path ⊞) *Hill Top Farm,*
Malham, Skipton, N. Yorks, *BD23 4DJ.*
Actual grid ref: SD899631
Tel: **01729 830320**
Mr & Mrs Heseltine.
Bunk Barn. £6.00 per person

(▲ On Path) *Malham Youth* ***Hostel,*** John Dower Memorial Hostel, Malham, Skipton, N. Yorks, *BD23 4DE.*
Actual grid ref: SD9062
Warden: Mr M Peryer.
Tel: **01729 830321**
Under 18: £6.15 Adults: £9.10
Family Bunk Rooms, Centrally Heated, Showers, Evening Meal (7.00 pm), Shop, Television
Superbly located purpose-built hostel close to the centre of the picturesque Malham village

(On Path ⊞) *Miresfield Farm,*
Malham, Skipton, N. Yorks, *BD23 4DA.*
Malham farmhouse, excellent food.
Grades: ETB 3 Cr
Tel: **01729 830414** Mrs Sharp.
Rates fr: *£18.00-£28.00.*
Open: All Year
Beds: 2F 6D 6T 1S
Baths: 12 Private 2 Shared
🏃 🅿 (20) 🖵 🛏 ✗ 🎹 & Ⅴ ▮ ⌇
Also ▲
Open: All Year 🏃 Ⅵ 🎯 ✗ ⌇ ♿

Stainforth 45

National Grid Ref: SD8266

🍴 🍺 Craven Heifer

(▲ 4m) *Stainforth Youth Hostel,* Taitlands, Stainforth, Settle, N. Yorks, *BD24 9PA.*
Actual grid ref: SD8266
Warden: D & D McGuiness.
Tel: **01729 823577**
Under 18: £5.00 Adults: £7.45
Family Bunk Rooms, Centrally Heated, Showers, Evening Meal (7.00 pm), Shop, Television
Victorian Listed building with fine interior, much refurbished recently, set in extensive grounds with grazing paddock. DISCOUNT TAXI SERVICE TO/FROM HORTON AVAILABLE

Horton in Ribblesdale 46

National Grid Ref: SD8072

🍴 🛏 Helwith Bridge Hotel, Golden Lion, Crown Hotel

(1.5m 🚌) *Studfold House, Horton in Ribblesdale, Settle, N. Yorks, BD24 0ER.*
Georgian house in own grounds.
Tel: **01729 860200**
Mr & Mrs Horsfall.
Rates fr: *£15.00-£15.00.*
Open: All Year (not Xmas)
Beds: 1F 2D 1T
Baths: 2 Shared
🛏 🅿 (8) 🛋 🛏 ✗ 🏘 Ⅴ 🖄 ⚡

(0.25m) *Townend Cottage, Townend, Horton in Ribblesdale, Settle, N. Yorks, BD24 0EX.*
Actual grid ref: SD811799
Converted farm/barn, quiet.
Tel: **01729 860320** Mrs Wagstaff.
Rates fr: *£18.00-£18.00.*
Open: All Year **Beds:** 1D 2T
Baths: 1 Ensuite 2 Shared
🛏 🅿 (6) 🛋 🛏 ✗ 🏘 Ⅴ 🖄 ⚡

(0.25m) *The Golden Lion Hotel, Horton in Ribblesdale, Settle, N. Yorks, BD24 0HB.*
Friendly, comfortable village hotel.
Grades: ETB Listed
Tel: **01729 860206** Mrs Johnson.
Rates fr: *£16.25-£16.25.*
Open: All Year (not Xmas)
Beds: 2D 2T 1S
Baths: 1 Private 4 Shared
🅿 (30) ✗ 🏘 Ⅴ

(0.25m) *The Willows, Horton in Ribblesdale, Settle, N. Yorks, BD24 0.*
Large house with lovely views.
Tel: **01729 860373** Mrs Barker.
Rates fr: *£17.00-£17.00.*
Open: Easter to Oct
Beds: 1F 1D 1T
Baths: 1 Ensuite 1 Shared
🛏 🅿 (6) 🛋 🛏 ✗ 🏘 Ⅴ 🖄 ⚡

(0.25m 🚌) *The Rowe House, Horton in Ribblesdale, Settle, N. Yorks, BD24 0HT.*
Charming large country house.
Tel: **01729 860212**
Mr & Mrs Jones.
Rates fr: *£17.95-£21.95.*
Open: March to October
Beds: 3D 3T
Baths: 4 Ensuite 1 Shared
🅿 (6) 🛋 🛏 ✗ 🏘 Ⅴ 🖄 ⚡

(0.25m) *Burnside, Horton in Ribblesdale, Settle, N. Yorks, BD24 0EX.*
Actual grid ref: SD811721
Private house in beautiful surroundings.
Tel: **01729 860223**
Mr & Mrs Jowett.
Rates fr: *£15.00-£15.00.*
Open: All Year (not Xmas)
Beds: 2D 1T 1S
Baths: 1 Private 2 Shared
🛏 🖄 🛋 🛏 🏘 Ⅴ 🖄

Selside 47

National Grid Ref: SD7875

(3m 🚌) *South House Farm, Selside, Settle, N. Yorks, BD24 0HU.*
Modern, comfortable farmhouse.
Tel: **01729 860271** Ms Kenyon.
Rates fr: *£15.00-£15.00.*
Open: All Year (not Xmas)
Beds: 1F 2D 1T
Baths: 1 Shared
🛏 (1) 🅿 🛋 🛏 ✗ 🏘 🖄 ⚡

Ribblehead 48

National Grid Ref: SD7880

🍴 🛏 Station Inn

(2m) *Station Inn, Ribblehead, Ingleton, Carnforth, Lancs, LA6 3AS.*
Comfortable country inn, fantastic views.
Grades: ETB Listed, Approv
Tel: **015242 41274** Mr Coates.
Rates fr: *£17.50-£16.00.*
Open: All Year
Beds: 1F 3D 1T
Baths: 3 Ensuite, 1 Shared
🛏 🅿 (50) 🛋 ✗ 🏘 Ⅴ

Cam Houses 49

National Grid Ref: SD8282

(0.5m) *Cam Farm, Cam Houses, Oughtershaw, Skipton, N. Yorks, BD23 5JT.*
Actual grid ref: SD823821
Typical Dales hill farm.
Tel: **0860 648045** Mrs Smith.
Rates fr: *£16.00-£16.00.*
Open: All Year
Beds: 3T
Baths: 1 Shared
🛏 🅿 (6) 🛋 🛏 ✗ 🏘 Ⅴ 🖄 ⚡
Also ⛺ Also bunkhouse, £5.00 per bunk.
Open: All Year 🏚 🖀 🚿 ✗ ⚡

Gayle 50

National Grid Ref: SD8789

🍴 🛏 The Board, The Fountain, The Whitehart, The Crown, The Wensleydale Pantry, The Bulls Head

(On Path 🚌) *Rookhurst Hotel, West End, Gayle, Hawes, N. Yorks, DL8 3RT.*
Family-run hotel beside Pennine Way. **Grades:** AA 2 St
Tel: **01969 667454**
Mrs Vandersteen.
Rates fr: *£30.00-£30.00.*
Open: Feb to Dec
Beds: 4D 1T **Baths:** 5 Private
🛏 (12) 🅿 (10) 🛋 🛋 ✗ 🏘 Ⅴ 🖄 ⚡

(0.25m) *East House, Gayle, Hawes, N. Yorks, DL8 3RZ.*
Peaceful comfortable private house.
Grades: ETB 2 Cr
Tel: **01969 667405** Mrs Ward.

Rates fr: *£16.00-£16.00.*
Open: Easter to Oct
Beds: 1F 1D 1T 1S
Baths: 1 Ensuite 1 Shared
🛏 (5) 🅿 (3) 🛋 🛋 🏘 Ⅴ 🖄 ⚡

(On Path) *Ivy House, Gayle, Hawes, N. Yorks, DL8 3RZ.*
Quiet, comfortable house, beautiful views.
Tel: **01969 667476**
Mrs Chapman.
Rates fr: *£13.00-£13.00.*
Open: All Year (not Xmas)
Beds: 1D **Baths:** 1 Shared
🛏 🅿 🛋 🛏 🏘 ⚡

(On Path) *Gayle Laithe, Gayle, Hawes, N. Yorks, DL8 3RR.*
Modern, comfortable, converted barn.
Tel: **01969 667397**
Mrs McGregor.
Rates fr: *£15.00-£15.00.*
Open: Mar to Nov
Beds: 1D 1T 1S
Baths: 1 Shared
🅿 🛋 🏘 Ⅴ 🖄

Hawes 51

National Grid Ref: SD8789

🍴 🛏 White Hart (Hawes), The Crown (Hawes), Fountain (Hawes), The Board (Hawes)

(On Path 🚌) *White Hart Inn, Hawes, N. Yorks, DL8 3.*
Grades: ETB 1 Cr
Tel: **01969 667259**
Mr & Mrs Sleightholme.
Rates fr: *£16.50-£17.50.*
Open: All Year (not Xmas)
Beds: 4D 2T 1S
Baths: 2 Shared
🛏 🅿 (6) 🛋 🛏 ✗ Ⅴ 🖄 ⚡
Small country inn with a friendly welcome, offering home cooked meals. Open fires, hand pulled ales. Ideally situated.

(On Path) *Herriots Hotel, Main Street, Hawes, N. Yorks, DL8 3QX.*
Relaxed, informal and friendly.
Grades: ETB 3 Cr
Tel: **01969 667536**
Mr Evans.
Rates fr: *£20.00-£20.00.*
Open: Mar to Nov
Beds: 1F 4D 1T 1S
Baths: 7 Ensuite
🛏 🛋 🛏 ✗ 🏘 Ⅴ 🖄 ⚡

(On Path 🚌) *Cocketts Hotel & Restaurant, Market Place, Hawes, N. Yorks, DL8 3RD.*
C17th hotel with modern facilities.
Grades: ETB 3 Cr, High Comm, AA 2 St
Tel: **01969 667312**
Mr Bedford.
Rates fr: *£27.00-£30.00.*
Open: All Year
Beds: 6D 2T
Baths: 8 Ensuite
🛏 (10) 🅿 (8) 🛋 🛋 ✗ 🏘 ♿ Ⅴ 🖄 ⚡

(0.25m) *East House, Gayle Lane, Hawes, N. Yorks, DL8 3RZ.*
Actual grid ref: SD871892
Spacious country private house.
Grades: ETB 2 Cr
Tel: 01969 667405 Mrs Ward.
Rates fr: *£15.00-£15.00.*
Open: Easter to Nov
Beds: 1F 1D 1T 1S
Baths: 1 Ensuite 1 Shared
🛁 🅿 (3) 🛏 🏧 Ⓥ 🛒 ⊁

(0.25m) *Board Hotel, Market Place, Hawes, N. Yorks, DL8 3RQ.*
A friendly traditional Dales pub.
Grades: ETB 2 Cr
Tel: 01969 667223
Mr Barron.
Rates fr: *£17.00-£18.00.*
Open: All Year
Beds: 2D 1T
Baths: 3 Private
🛁 🅿 ⊁ 🛏 ✕ 🏧 Ⓥ 🛒

(▲ 0.25m) *Hawes Youth Hostel, Lancaster Terrace, Hawes, N. Yorks, DL8 3LQ.*
Actual grid ref: SD8689
Warden: C & P Harman.
Tel: 01969 667368
Under 18: £5.55
Adults: £8.25
Family Bunk Rooms, Centrally Heated, Showers, Evening Meal (7.00 pm), Shop, Television, Games Room
Friendly and attractively refurbished purpose-built hostel overlooking Hawes and Wensleydale beyond. Good home cooking

(On Path) *Ebor House, Burtersett Road, Hawes, N. Yorks, DL8 3NT.*
Family-run, central, friendly.
Grades: ETB 2 Cr
Tel: 01969 667337 Mrs Clark.
Rates fr: *£15.00-£15.00.*
Open: All Year (not Xmas)
Beds: 2D 1T 1S
Baths: 2 Private 1 Shared
🛁 🅿 (4) ⊁ 🛏 🛏 🏧 Ⓥ 🛒 ⊁

(0.75m) *Halfway House, Hawes, N. Yorks, DL8 3LL.*
Actual grid ref: SD865902
Homely secluded farmhouse, firm beds.
Tel: 01969 667442 Mrs Guy.
Rates fr: *£16.00-£20.00.*
Open: Easter to Nov
Beds: 1D 1T
Baths: 1 Shared
🛁 🅿 (4) ⊁ Ⓥ ⊁

Hardraw   52

National Grid Ref: SD8691

🍽 🍺 Green Dragon

(On Path) *The Green Dragon Inn, Hardraw, Hawes, N. Yorks, DL8 3.*
Olde worlde inn/hotel, fully modernised.
Tel: 01969 667392 Mr Stead.
Rates fr: *£17.00-£18.00.*
Open: All Year (not Xmas)
Beds: 1F 11D 1T 3S
Baths: 16 Private
🛁 🅿 🛏 🛏 ✕ 🏧 Ⓥ 🛒 ⊁

Keld   53

National Grid Ref: NY8901

(On Path) *Frith Lodge, Keld, Richmond, N. Yorks, DL11 6EB.*
Actual grid ref: NY891031
Family-run farmhouse accommodation.
Tel: 01748 886489 Mrs Pepper.
Rates fr: *£14.00-£14.00.*
Open: All Year
Beds: 2T **Baths:** 1 Shared
🛁 🛏 🛏 ✕ 🏧 Ⓥ 🛒 ⊁

(▲ 0.25m) *Keld Youth Hostel, Keld Lodge, Keld, Upper Swaledale, Richmond, N. Yorks, DL11 6LL.*
Actual grid ref: NY8900
Warden: Mr L Roe.
Tel: 01748 886259
Under 18: £4.60
Adults: £6.75

Family Bunk Rooms, Centrally Heated, Showers, Evening Meal (7.00 pm), Shop, Television
Former shooting lodge located at the head of Swaledale, surrounded by moorland and waterfalls

Mellwaters   54

National Grid Ref: NY9612

(On Path 🐾) *East Mellwaters Farm, Mellwaters, Bowes, Barnard Castle, Co Durham, DL12 9RH.*
Actual grid ref: NZ968128
Modernised comfortable C17th farmhouse.
Grades: ETB 3 Cr, Comm, AA 3 Q, Recomm
Tel: 01833 28269 Mrs Milner.
Rates fr: *£17.50-£18.00.*
Open: All Year (not Xmas)
Beds: 1F 2D 1T 1S
Baths: 5 Private
🛁 🅿 (10) 🛏 🛏 ✕ 🏧 Ⓥ 🛒 ⊁
Also ▲ *£2.00 per tent.*
Open: Easter to Oct
🏠 Ⓣ ✕ ⊁ ♿

Bowes Moor   55

National Grid Ref: NY9211

(2m 🐾) *Bowes Moor Hotel, Bowes Moor, Barnard Castle, Co Durham, DL12 9RH.*
300-year-old former hunting lodge.
Grades: ETB 3 Cr
Tel: 01833 628331
Mrs Luscombe.
Rates fr: *£19.75-£27.50.*
Open: All Year
Beds: 5D 2T 3S
Baths: 8 Ensuite 2 Private
🛁 🅿 (60) 🛏 🛏 ✕ 🏧 Ⓥ 🛒 ⊁

Bowes   56

National Grid Ref: NY9913

🍽 🍺 Ancient Unicorn

(On Path) *West End Farm, Bowes, Barnard Castle, Co Durham, DL12 9LH.*
Traditional old working farm, camping, caravans.
Tel: 01833 628239 Mrs Foster.
Rates fr: *£12.00.*
Open: May to Oct
Beds: 1F
Baths: 1 Shared
🛁 🅿 🛏
Also ▲ 🏠 Ⓣ ♿

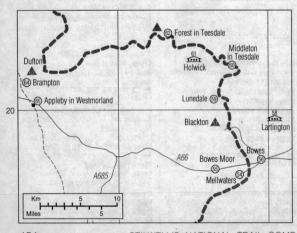

Blackton 57

National Grid Ref: NY9317

(▲ 0.25m) *Baldersdale Youth Hostel*, Blackton, Baldersdale, Barnard Castle, Co Durham, *DL12 9UP*.
Actual grid ref: NY9317
Warden: Mr C Chadwick.
Tel: **01833 50629**
Under 18: £4.60 **Adults:** £6.75
Family Bunk Rooms, Centrally Heated, Showers, Evening Meal (6.00 - 10.00pm), Shop, Television, Games Room, Parking
Fully modernised farmhouse at mid-point of the Pennine Way

Lartington 58

National Grid Ref: NZ 0217

(▲ 4m) *Lartington Camping Barn*, Pecknell Farm, Lartington, Barnard Castle, Co Durham, .
Actual grid ref: NZ029177
Tel: **01629 825850** *Simple barn, sleeps 15. Excellent for exploring Teesdale. ADVANCE BOOKING ESSENTIAL* Mr & Mrs Dent.
£3.00 per person.

Lunedale 59

National Grid Ref: NY9221

(On Path) *Wythes Hill Farm*, Lunedale, Middleton in Teesdale, Barnard Castle, Co Durham, *DL12 0NX*.
Farmhouse with panoramic views.
Grades: ETB 1 Cr, Comm
Tel: **01833 40349** Mrs Dent.
Rates fr: £15.00-£15.00.
Open: Easter to Oct
Beds: 1F 1T
Baths: 1 Ensuite 1 Shared
🛏 🅿 (3) ❑ ✕ ▥ Ⓥ ⓘ ✦

Middleton in Teesdale 60

National Grid Ref: NY9425

🍴 🍺 Talbot Hotel, Bridge Inn, Teesdale Hotel, Chatterbox

(On Path 🚗) *Talbot Hotel*, Market Place, Middleton in Teesdale, Barnard Castle, Co Durham, *DL12 0*.
Old village inn. Tel: **01833 40273**
Rates fr: £12.50-£13.50.
Open: All Year
Beds: 2D 1T 1S
🛏 ❑ 🛏 ✕ ▥ Ⓥ ⓘ ✦

don't leave your footprint behind !

footprint
map - guides

(0.5m 🚗) *Teesdale Hotel*, Middleton in Teesdale, Barnard Castle, Co Durham, *DL12 0QG*.
C17th coaching inn.
Grades: ETB 4 Cr, Comm, AA 2 St, RAC 2 St
Tel: **01833 40264** Mr Streit.
Rates fr: £30.25-£49.50.
Open: All Year
Beds: 1F 7D 2S
Baths: 10 Ensuite
🛏 🅿 ❑ 🛏 ✕ ▥ Ⓥ ✦

(0.25m 🚗) *Kingsway Adventure Centre*, Alston Road, Middleton in Teesdale, Barnard Castle, Co Durham, *DL12 0UU*.
Actual grid ref: NY945255
Friendly-run Christian outdoor activity centre.
Tel: **01833 40881** Mr Hearn.
Rates fr: £11.00-£11.00.
Open: All Year
Beds: 1F 2T
Baths: 2 Private 2 Shared
🛏 🅿 (10) ✕ ▥ Ⓥ ⓘ ✦
Also ▲ *£2.00 per person. Also bunkhouse, £11.00 per bunk.*
Open: All Year 🛏 Ⓣ ✕ ✦ ♿

(0.5m) *Lonton South Farm*, Middleton in Teesdale, Barnard Castle, Co Durham, *DL12 0PL*.
Modern comfortable farmhouse.
Tel: **01833 640409** Mrs Watson.
Rates fr: £15.00-£15.00.
Open: Mar to Oct
Beds: 1D 1T 1S
Baths: 1 Shared
🛏 ▥ ✦

(On Path) *25 Bridge Street*, Middleton in Teesdale, Barnard Castle, Co Durham, *DL12 0QB*.
Large Victorian terrace house.
Tel: **01833 640549** Mrs Sowerby.
Rates fr: £16.50-£16.50.
Open: All Year
Beds: 1D 4T 1S
Baths: 1 Shared
❑ 🛏 ▥ Ⓥ ⓘ ✦

(0.25m) *Brunswick House*, 55 Market Place, Middleton in Teesdale, Barnard Castle, Co Durham, *DL12 0QH*.
Actual grid ref: NY945255
Charming C18th guesthouse, excellent food.
Grades: ETB 3 Cr, Comm, AA 3 Q
Tel: **01833 640393**
Mr & Mrs Milnes.
Rates fr: £20.00-£27.50.
Open: All Year
Beds: 1F 2D 1T
Baths: 4 Private
🛏 🅿 (4) 🛏 ❑ ✕ ▥ Ⓥ ⓘ ✦

Holwick 61

National Grid Ref: NY 9127

(▲ On Path) *Holwick Camping Barn*, Low Way Farm, Holwick, Barnard Castle, Co Durham.
Actual grid ref: NY914270

Tel: **01629 825850** *Simple barn, sleeps 20 and 8. A field bunkhouse barn near the River Tees. ADVANCE BOOKING ESSENTIAL* Mr & Mrs Scott.
£4.00 per person

Forest in Teesdale 62

National Grid Ref: NY8629

🍴 🍺 High Force Hotel

(0.25m) *High Force Hotel*, Forest in Teesdale, Barnard Castle, Co Durham, *DL12 0XH*.
Family-run country hotel in Teesdale. **Grades:** ETB 3 Cr
Tel: **01833 22222** Mrs Baxter.
Rates fr: £21.00-£19.00.
Open: All Year **Beds:** 2F 3D 2T 2S
Baths: 8 Private 1 Shared
🛏 🅿 (10) ❑ ✕ ▥ Ⓥ ⓘ ✦

(1.5m) *Langdon Beck Hotel*, Forest in Teesdale, Barnard Castle, Co Durham, *DL12 0XP*.
Friendly, comfortable hotel - good food. **Grades:** ETB Listed
Tel: **01833 622267** Mrs Collin.
Rates fr: £19.00-£19.00.
Open: All Year (not Xmas)
Beds: 1F 2D 1T 3S
Baths: 2 Ensuite 1 Shared
🛏 🅿 (15) ❑ 🛏 ✕ ▥ Ⓥ ⓘ

(0.25m) *High Force Training Centre*, The Old Vicarage, Forest in Teesdale, Barnard Castle, Co Durham, *DL12 0HA*.
Actual grid ref: NY854307
Comfortable old vicarage.
Tel: **01833 22302** Mr Hosey.
Rates fr: £13.50-£13.50.
Open: All Year
Beds: 5F 2T **Baths:** 4 Shared
🛏 🅿 (20) ❑ ✕ ▥ Ⓥ ⓘ ✦

(▲ On Path) *Langdon Beck Youth Hostel*, Forest in Teesdale, Barnard Castle, Co Durham, *DL12 0XN*.
Actual grid ref: NY8630
Warden: Mr S Neal.
Tel: **01833 22228**
Under 18: £5.55 **Adults:** £8.25
Family Bunk Rooms, Centrally Heated, Showers, Evening Meal (7.00 pm), Shop
A purpose-built hostel in Upper Teesdale with an excellent standard of accommodation

Dufton 63

National Grid Ref: NY6825

🍴 🍺 Stag Inn

(On Path) *Ghyll View*, Dufton, Appleby in Westmorland, Cumbria, *CA16 6DF*.
Large Victorian private house.
Tel: **017683 51855** Mrs Hullock.
Rates fr: £14.00-£14.00.
Open: Easter to Oct
Beds: 3T 1S **Baths:** 2 Shared
🅿 (4) ❑ ✕

National Grid Ref: NY6723

|◎| 🍺 New Inn

(1.5m 🚌) *New Inn*, *Brampton,
Appleby in Westmorland, Cumbria,
CA16 6JS.*
C18th traditional oak-beamed
country pub.
Grades: ETB Listed
Tel: **017683 51231** Mrs Cranswick.
Rates fr: *£18.00-£18.00.*
Open: All Year (not Xmas)
Beds: 1F 1D 1T
Baths: 2 Shared
🛇 🅿 🖵 🛉 ✕ 🖫 Ⅴ 🛉 ✦

Appleby in Westmorland 65

National Grid Ref: NY6820

|◎| 🍺 The Royal Oak, The Gate

(2.5m) *Wemyss House, 48
Boroughgate, Appleby in
Westmorland, Cumbria, CA16 6XG.*
Georgian house in small country
town.
Tel: **017683 51494** Mrs Hirst.
Rates fr: *£14.00-£14.00.*
Open: Easter to Nov
Beds: 1D 1T 1S
Baths: 2 Shared
🛇 🅿 (3) 🖵 🖫 Ⅴ ✦

(4.25m) *Appleby Manor Ctry Hse
Hotel, Roman Road, Appleby in
Westmorland, Cumbria, CA16 6JD.*
Actual grid ref: NY693206
Victorian country manor, wooded
grounds.
Grades: ETB 4 Cr, High Comm,
AA 3 St, RAC 3 St
Tel: **017683 51571** Mr Swinscoe.
Rates fr: *£44.00-£59.00.*
Open: All Year (not Xmas)
Beds: 8F 14D 8T
Baths: 30 Private
🛇 🅿 (50) 🖵 🛉 ✕ 🖫 Ⅴ 🛉 ✦

(2.5m) *Bongate House, Appleby in
Westmorland, Cumbria, CA16 6UE.*
Large Georgian guesthouse.
Grades: ETB 3 Cr, Comm,
AA 3 Q
Tel: **017683 51245**
Mrs Dayson.
Rates fr: *£16.00-£16.00.*
Open: All Year (not Xmas)
Beds: 2F 3D 2T 1S
Baths: 5 Private
🛇 (7) 🅿 (8) 🖵 🛉 ✕ 🖫 Ⅴ 🛉

(2m) *Church View, Bongate,
Appleby in Westmorland, Cumbria,
CA16 6UN.*
C18th Listed character house.
Grades: ETB Listed
Tel: **017683 51792**
Mrs Kemp.
Rates fr: *£13.50-£15.00.*
Open: All Year (not Xmas)
Beds: 1F 1D 1S
Baths: 1 Shared
🛇 (1) 🅿 (4) ⅍ 🖵 🖫 Ⅴ 🛉 ✦

(🔺 On Path) *Dufton Youth
Hostel, Redstones, Dufton, Appleby
in Westmorland, Cumbria, CA16 6DB.*
Actual grid ref: NY6825
Warden: Ms H Moore.
Tel: **017683 51236**
Under 18: £5.00 **Adults:** £7.45
Family Bunk Rooms, Centrally
Heated, Showers, Evening Meal
(7.00 pm), Shop
*Large stone-built house with log
fire in attractive C18th village sur-
rounded by the fine scenery of the
Eden Valley*

(On Path) *Bow Hall, Dufton,
Appleby in Westmorland, Cumbria,
CA16 6DE.*
Fellside sandstone farmhouse,
walkers paradise.
Grades: ETB Listed
Tel: **017683 51835** Mrs Burrows.

Rates fr: *£15.00-£15.00.*
Open: Mar to Oct
Beds: 1F 1D 1T
Baths: 1 Shared
🛇 🅿 🖵 ✕ Ⅴ 🛉 ✦

(On Path) *Dufton Hall Farm,
Dufton, Appleby in Westmorland,
Cumbria, CA16 6DD.*
Actual grid ref: NY6825
Large, comfortable C18th farm-
house.
Grades: ETB 1 Cr, AA Approv
Tel: **017683 51573** Mrs Howe.
Rates fr: *£15.00-£18.00.*
Open: Mar to Oct
Beds: 1F 1D 1T
Baths: 3 Private
🛇 🅿 (6) ⅍ 🖵 Ⅴ 🛉 ✦
Also 🔺 *£2.00 per person.*
🏠 🕾 ⚒ ✦ ♿

(2.5m) *Howgill House, Bongate, Appleby in Westmorland, Cumbria, CA16 6UW.*
Old farmhouse, now private house.
Grades: ETB 1 Cr, Comm
Tel: **017683 51574 / 51240**
Mrs Pigney.
Rates fr: *£13.50-£15.00.*
Open: May to Oct
Beds: 2F 1T 1S
Baths: 2 Shared
🛇 🅿 🛏 Ⓥ ✦

Garrigill 66

National Grid Ref: NY7441

🍴 🍺 George & Dragon

(On Path 🚍) *The Post Office, Garrigill, Alston, Cumbria, CA9 3DS.*
C17th village post office.
Tel: **01434 381257**
Mrs Bramwell.
Rates fr: *£14.00-£14.00.*
Open: Easter to Oct
Beds: 1F 2D 1T
Baths: 1 Shared
🛇 🅿 ⊬ 🖵 🛏 Ⓥ ✦

(On Path) *Ivy House Farm, Garrigill, Alston, Cumbria, CA9 3DU.*
C17th farmhouse.
Grades: ETB Listed, Comm
Tel: **01434 382079**
Mrs Dent.
Rates fr: *£13.00-£13.00.*
Open: All Year (not Xmas)
Beds: 1F 1D 1T 2S
Baths: 1 Shared
🛇 🅿 (2) ⊬ 🖵 🛏 Ⓥ ✦

(0.5m 🚍) *High Windy Hall Hotel, Middleton In Teesdale Road, Garrigill, Alston, Cumbria, CA9 3EZ.*
Actual grid ref: NY7441
Panoramic views, good food, peaceful.
Grades: ETB 2 Cr, High Comm
Tel: **01434 381547**
Mrs Platts.
Rates fr: *£20.00-£30.00.*
Open: All Year
Beds: 1F 2D 1T
Baths: 4 Private
🛇 (1) 🅿 (5) 🖵 ✕ 🖾 Ⓥ 🛆 ✦

Nenthead 67

National Grid Ref: NY7843

🍴 🍺 The Miners Arms, The Crown Inn

(On Path 🚍) *Cherry Tree, Nenthead, Alston, Cumbria, CA9 3PD.*
Converted stone cottages, modern amenities.
Tel: **01434 381434**
Mrs Sherlock.
Rates fr: *£15.00-£15.00.*
Open: All Year
Beds: 2F 1D 1T
Baths: 3 Shared
🛇 🅿 (6) ⊬ 🖵 🖾 🛆 ✦

Alston 68

National Grid Ref: NY7146

🍴 🍺 Angel Inn, Blue Bell Inn

(1m) *Middle Bayles Farm, Penrith Road, Alston, Cumbria, CA9 3BS.*
Actual grid ref: NY707451
C17th traditional farmhouse.
Grades: ETB 2 Cr, Comm
Tel: **01434 381383** Mrs Dent.
Rates fr: *£15.00-£18.00.*
Open: All Year (not Xmas) or April
Beds: 1F 1D
Baths: 2 Private
🛇 🅿 (2) ⊬ 🖵 ✕ 🖾 Ⓥ 🛆

(0.25m 🚍) *Nentholme B&B, The Butts, Alston, Cumbria, CA9 3JQ.*
Actual grid ref: NY719467
Modern comfortable quiet bed and breakfast.
Grades: ETB 2 Cr
Tel: **01434 381523** Mrs Thompson.
Rates fr: *£19.00-£17.00.*
Open: All Year
Beds: 1F 4D 4T 2S
Baths: 2 Ensuite 1 Shared
🛇 🅿 (8) ⊬ 🖵 🛏 ✕ 🖾 Ⓥ 🛆 ✦

(0.25m) *Bridge End Farm, Alston, Cumbria, CA9 3BJ.*
Actual grid ref: NY7146
Warm, friendly, comfortable farmhouse.
Grades: ETB 2 Cr, Comm
Tel: **01434 381261** Mrs Williams.
Rates fr: *£14.50-£17.50.*
Open: All Year
Beds: 1F 1D 1T
Baths: 1 Ensuite 1 Shared
🛇 (1) 🅿 (4) ⊬ 🖵 🛏 ✕ 🖾 Ⓥ 🛆 ✦

(0.5m 🚍) *Harbut Law, Brampton Road, Alston, Cumbria, CA9 3BD.*
Large Victorian former farmhouse.
Tel: **01434 381950** Mrs Younger.
Rates fr: *£13.00-£13.00.*
Open: All Year **Beds:** 2D 1T
Baths: 1 Private 2 Shared
🛇 🅿 (3) 🖵 🖾 Ⓥ 🛆 ✦

(🔺 On Path) *Alston Youth Hostel, The Firs, Alston, Cumbria, CA9 3RW.*
Actual grid ref: NY7146
Warden: Mr R Richardson.
Tel: **01434 381509**
Under 18: £5.00 **Adults:** £7.45
Family Bunk Rooms, Centrally Heated, Showers, Evening Meal (7.00 pm), Shop
A purpose-built hostel overlooking the South Tyne river, on outskirts of Alston, the highest market town in England

Knarsdale 69

National Grid Ref: NY6753

🍴 🍺 Kirk Style Inn

(0.25m) *Stonehall Farm, Knarsdale, Slaggyford, Carlisle, Cumbria, CA6 7PB.*
C18th farmhouse.

Tel: **01434 381349** Mrs Graham.
Rates fr: *£15.00-£15.00.*
Open: All Year (not Xmas)
Beds: 2F 1T
Baths: 1 Private 1 Shared
🛇 🅿 🖵 🛏 🖾 🛆 ✦

Featherstone Park 70

National Grid Ref: NY6862

🍴 🍺 Wallace Arms

(2m 🚍) *Park Burnfoot Farm, Featherstone Park, Haltwhistle, Northd, NE49 0JP.*
Comfortable C18th riverside farmhouse.
Grades: ETB Listed
Tel: **01434 320378**
Mrs Dawson.
Rates fr: *£14.50-£16.00.*
Open: All Year
Beds: 1D 1T
Baths: 1 Shared
🛇 (3) 🅿 ⊬ 🖵 🛆 ✦

Gilsland 71

National Grid Ref: NY6366

🍴 🍺 Samson Inn, Station Hotel

(1m 🚍) *Alpha Mount House, Gilsland, Carlisle, Cumbria, CA6 7EB.*
Large family home.
Grades: ETB 1 Cr, Comm
Tel: **016977 47070**
Mrs Cole.
Rates fr: *£13.00-£13.00.*
Open: All Year
Beds: 1F 1D 1S
Baths: 1 Shared
🛇 🅿 (2) 🖵 ✕ 🖾 Ⓥ 🛆 ✦

(2m) *Howard House Farm, Gilsland, Carlisle, Cumbria, CA6 7AN.*
Comfortable farmhouse on Roman wall.
Grades: ETB 2 Cr, High Comm
Tel: **016977 47285**
Mrs Woodmass.
Rates fr: *£16.00-£20.00.*
Open: All Year (not Xmas)
Beds: 1F 1T
Baths: 1 Private 1 Shared
🛇 (5) 🅿 🖵 ✕ 🖾 🛆 ✦

Greenhead 72

National Grid Ref: NY6665

(On Path) *Holmhead Farm, Licensed Guesthouse, Hadrians Wall, Greenhead, Carlisle, CA6 7HY.*
Actual grid ref: NY661659
Former farm on Pennine Way.
Grades: ETB 3 Cr, Comm, AA 3 Q
Tel: **016977 47402** Mr Staff.
Rates fr: *£22.50-£31.00.*
Open: All Year (not Xmas)
Beds: 1F 1D 2T
Baths: 4 Private
🛇 🅿 (6) ⊬ 🖵 ✕ 🖾 🛆 Ⓥ 🛆 ✦

(▲On Path) *Greenhead Youth Hostel, Greenhead, Carlisle, Cumbria, CA6 7HG.*
Actual grid ref: NY6565
Warden: Mr G Metcalfe.
Tel: 016977 47401
Under 18: £4.60
Adults: £6.75
Family Bunk Rooms, Centrally Heated, Showers, Evening Meal (7.00 pm), Shop
Pleasantly converted Methodist Chapel in a small village, close to some of the most dramatic parts of Hadrian's Wall

Haltwhistle 73

National Grid Ref: NY7064

╏◉╏ ◖ Manor House Hotel, Spotted Cow

(1.5m) *Hall Meadows, Main Street, Haltwhistle, Northd, NE49 0AZ.*
Large C19th private house.
Grades: ETB 1 Cr, Comm
Tel: 01434 321021 Mrs Humes.
Rates fr: £15.00-£15.00.
Open: All Year (not Xmas)
Beds: 1D 1T 1S
Baths: 1 Shared
☎ ₽ (3) ⌑ ▥ ▮ ✦

(1.25m) 🚐 *White Craig, Haltwhistle, Northd, NE49 9NW.*
Actual grid ref: NY713649
Snug old rambling single storey farmhouse.
Grades: ETB 2 Cr, High Comm, AA 4 Q, Select
Tel: 01434 320565
Ms Laidlow.
Rates fr: £19.25-£25.00.
Open: All Year (not Xmas)
Beds: 2D 1T
Baths: 3 Private
₽ (3) ⅍ ⌑ ▥ ▵ ▮ ✦

(2m) *Manor House Hotel, Main Street, Haltwhistle, Northd, NE49 0BS.*
Comfortable family-run hotel.
Grades: ETB 2 Cr, Approv
Tel: 01434 322588
Mr & Mrs Hind.
Rates fr: £12.50-£12.50.
Open: All Year
Beds: 1F 1D 4T
Baths: 3 Ensuite 3 Shared
☎ ₽ (5) ⌑ ✕ ▥ ▮ ✦

Bardon Mill 74

National Grid Ref: NY7864

╏◉╏ ◖ Twice Brewed, Mile Castle

(0.5m) *The Craws Nest, East Twice Brewed Farm, Bardon Mill, Hexham, Northd, NE47 7AL.*
Actual grid ref: NY759671
Converted farmhouse with spectacular views.
Grades: ETB Listed
Tel: 01434 344348 Mrs Wanless.

Rates fr: £15.00.
Open: All Year
Beds: 2F 1D 1T
Baths: 1 Shared
☎ ₽ ⅍ ⌑ ✕ ▥ ▮

Once Brewed 75

National Grid Ref: NY7566

╏◉╏ ◖ The Twice Brewed Inn

(▲0.5m) *Once Brewed Youth Hostel, Military Road, Once Brewed, Bardon Mill, Hexham, North'd, NE47 7AN.*
Actual grid ref: NY7566
Warden: Mr B & P Keen.
Tel: 01434 344360
Under 18: £5.55 **Adults:** £8.25
Family Bunk Rooms, Centrally Heated, Showers, Evening Meal (7.00 pm), Shop, Television, Games Room, Facilities for the Disabled
Excellent residential accommodation with small bedrooms and superb range of facilities

Twice Brewed 76

National Grid Ref: NY7567

╏◉╏ ◖ Twice Brewed Inn

(0.3m) 🚐 *Vallum Lodge Hotel, Military Road, Twice Brewed, Bardon Mill, Hexham, Northd, NE47 7AN.*
Actual grid ref: NY748669
Quiet country hotel.
Grades: ETB 2 Cr, Comm, AA 1 St
Tel: 01434 344248
Mr & Mrs Wright.
Rates fr: £20.00-£21.00.
Open: Mar to Nov
Beds: 3D 3T 1S
Baths: 2 Private 2 Shared
₽ (25) ⅍ ⌑ ⸚ ✕ ▥ ▵ ▮ ✦

Hetherington 77

National Grid Ref: NY8278

╏◉╏ ◖ Battlesteads Hotel

(On Path) *Hetherington Farm, Hetherington, Wark, Hexham, Northd, NE48 3DR.*
Actual grid ref: NY824782
Very comfortable farmhouse in country.
Tel: 01434 230260 Mrs Nichol.
Rates fr: £14.00-£14.00.
Open: Easter to Nov
Beds: 2D 1T
Baths: 1 Shared
☎ (10) ₽ (3) ⌑ ✕ ▥

All paths are popular: you are well-advised to book ahead

Pay B&Bs by cash or cheque and be prepared to pay up front.

Bellingham 78

National Grid Ref: NY8383

╏◉╏ ◖ Cheviot, Rose & Crown, Boyds

(On Path) 🚐 *Lyndale Guest House, Off The Square, Bellingham, Hexham, Northd, NE48 2AW.*
Grades: ETB 3 Cr, High Comm, RAC Acclaim
Tel: 01434 220361
Mrs Gaskin.
Rates fr: £20.00-£20.00.
Open: Jan to Nov
Beds: 1F 2D 1T 1S
Baths: 3 Private 2 Shared
☎ ₽ (5) ⅍ ⌑ ▾ ✕ ▥ ▵ ▮ ✦
Relax, enjoy panoramic views. A free glass of wine. Delicious home-cooking. Colour TV's. Hairdryers. Ensuite rooms. Non-smoking. Private parking. Good walking. Pennine Way. Historic houses. Quiet roads. A warm welcome awaits. Pretty Dorma bungalow. 'Home from home'.

(On Path) 🚐 *Bank Cottage, Off The Square, Bellingham, Hexham, Northd, NE48 2AW.*
Panoramic views, home from home
Grades: ETB 4 Keys, Comm
Tel: 01434 220361 Mrs Gaskin.
Rates fr: £20.00-£20.00.
Open: Jan to Nov
Beds: 1F 2D 1T 1S
Baths: 3 Private 2 Shared
☎ ₽ (5) ⅍ ⌑ ▾ ✕ ▥ ▵ ▮ ✦

(On Path) 🚐 *Westfield House, Bellingham, Hexham, Northd, NE48 2DP.*
Large, friendly Victorian house.
Grades: ETB 2 Cr, High Comm, AA 4 Q, Select
Tel: 01434 220340
Mr & Mrs Minchin.
Rates fr: £18.00-£18.00.
Open: All Year (not Xmas)
Beds: 1F 2D 2T
Baths: 2 Private 1 Shared
☎ ₽ (8) ⅍ ▾ ✕ ▥ ▮ ✦

(On Path) 🚐 *Crofters End, The Croft, Bellingham, Hexham, Northd, NE48 2JY.*
Family house overlooking beautiful countryside.
Tel: 01434 220034
Mrs Forster.
Rates fr: £14.00-£14.00.
Open: Easter to Oct
Beds: 1F 1D 1S
Baths: 1 Shared
☎ (4) ₽ (3) ⅍ ▥ ▵ ▮ ✦

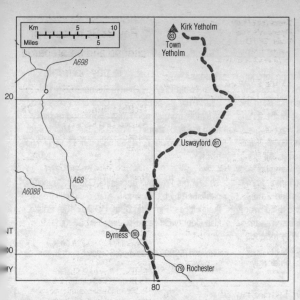

(▲ On Path) *Bellingham Youth Hostel, Woodburn Road, Bellingham, Hexham, North'd, NE48 2ED.*
Actual grid ref: NY8483
Warden: Ms A Fuller.
Tel: **01434 220313**
Under 18: £4.15 **Adults:** £6.10
Family Bunk Rooms, Centrally Heated, Showers, No Smoking
Single-storey building of cedarwood overlooking Bellingham in beautiful Border country

Rochester 79

National Grid Ref: NY8398

⊷ ⊞ Queen Charlotte

(3m) *Redesdale Arms Hotel, Rochester, Otterburn, Tyne & Wear, NE19 1TA.*
600-year-old coaching inn.
Grades: ETB 3 Cr, Comm
Tel: **01830 520668**
Mrs Wright.
Rates fr: £25.00-£33.00.
Open: All Year
Beds: 4F 3D 5T
Baths: 10 Ensuite
🛏 (0) 🅿 (30) ⬜ ⫟ ✕ ▥ ⱽ 🗎 ✦

Byrness 80

National Grid Ref: NT7602

⊷ ⊞ Byrness Hotel

(▲ 0.25m) *Byrness Youth Hostel, 7 Otterburn Green, Byrness, Newcastle-upon-Tyne, NE19 1TS.*
Actual grid ref: NT7602
Warden: Mr D Christon.
Tel: **01830 520519**
Under 18: £4.15 **Adults:** £6.10
Family Bunk Rooms, Partially Heated, Showers, Self-catering Only
Two adjoining houses in a peaceful Forestry Commission village 5 miles from the Scottish border

Uswayford 81

National Grid Ref: NT8814

(1.5m) *Uswayford Farm, Uswayford, Harbottle, Morpeth, Northumberland, NE65 7BU.*
Actual grid ref: NT887145
Tel: **01669 50237** Mrs Buglass.
Rates fr: £14.00-£14.00.
Open: All Year
Beds: 1F 1D 1T
Baths: 1 Shared
🛏 🅿 ⬜ ⫟ ✕ ▥ ⱽ 🗎 ✦

Kirk Yetholm 82

National Grid Ref: NT8228

⊷ ⊞ Border Hotel

(▲ On Path) *Kirk Yetholm Youth Hostel, Kirk Yetholm, Kelso, Roxburghshire, TD5 8PG.*
Actual grid ref: NT8228
Warden: Mr A Murphy.
Tel: **01573 420631**
Under 18: £4.15 **Adults:** £6.10

Family Bunk Rooms, Self-Catering Facilities, Shop
Stone-built house and a warm welcome at the end of the Pennine Way

(0.25m ⇌) *Blunty's Mill, Kirk Yetholm, Kelso, Roxburghshire, TD5 8PG.*
Quiet rural cottage in 6 acres.
Grades: ETB 1 Cr, Comm
Tel: **01573 420288** Mrs Brooker.
Rates fr: £16.00-£16.00.
Open: All Year (not Xmas)
Beds: 1D 1T
Baths: 1 Private 1 Shared
🛏 (2) 🅿 (6) ⬜ ⫟ ✕ ⱽ 🗎 ✦

Town Yetholm 83

National Grid Ref: NT8128

⊷ ⊞ The Plough Inn, The Border Hotel

(2m) *Lochside, Town Yetholm, Kelso, Roxburghshire, TD5 8PD.*
Actual grid ref: NT802829
Victorian country house, beautiful setting.
Grades: ETB 2 Cr, Comm
Tel: **01573 420349** Mrs Hurst.
Rates fr: £20.00-£22.00.
Open: Easter to Oct
Beds: 1D 1T **Baths:** 2 Ensuite
🛏 🅿 (2) ⬜ ⫟ ✕ ▥ ⱽ 🗎 ✦

(0.75m ⇌) *Greenside, Main Street, Town Yetholm, Kelso, Roxburghshire, TD5 8RG.*
Large Victorian home offers warm welcome in conservation village.
Tel: **01573 420249** Mrs Gowers.
Rates fr: £15.00-£15.00.
Open: All Year (not Xmas)
Beds: 1F 1D 1T 1S
Baths: 2 Shared
🛏 🅿 (4) ⬜ ⫟ ✕ ▥ ⱽ 🗎 ✦

The Country Code

Enjoy the countryside and respect its life and work

Guard against all risk of fire

Fasten all gates

Keep your dogs under close control

Keep to public paths across farmland

Use gates and stiles to cross fences, hedges and walls

Leave livestock, crops and machinery alone

Take your litter home

Help to keep all water clean

Protect wild-life, plants and trees

Take special care on country roads

Make no unnecessary noise

Ribble Way

This is a first class river walk leading through excellent Lancashire walking country up into the Yorkshire Dales, past caves and potholes, to the source of the Ribble (should you so wish). It runs for 70 miles from the sea marshes west of Preston, past lovely Ribchester and Giggleswick right up to Ribblehead in the Pennines. All along the route the river is ever present, changing character the further upstream you move, from the broad river plain to rushing gills and water-falls. The **Ribble Way** is a good one to do over a couple of long weekends and it meets up with the **Dales Way** and the **Pennine Way** for good measure. The path is well waymarked in Lancashire, although it loses out to other way-marks once into Yorkshire.

Guides:
The Ribble Way by Gladys Sellers (ISBN 1 85284 107 9), published by Cicerone Press and available from all good map shops or directly from the publishers (2 Police Square, Milnthorpe, Cumbria, LA7 7PY, 01539 562069), £5.95 (+ 75p p&p).

The Ribble Way by Lancashire County Council, published by L.C.C. and available directly from their offices (Planning Dept, PO Box 160, East Cliff County Offices, Preston, PR1 3EX), £0.90p.

Maps: 1:50000 Ordnance Survey Landranger Series: 98, 102, 103

Hutton 1

National Grid Ref: SD4926

🍴 🍺 The Anchor, The Fleece, The Farmers, The Black Bull

(2m) *The Anchor, Liverpool Road, Hutton, Preston, Lancs, PR4 5SL.*
Clean, comfortable, pub accommo-dation.
Tel: **01772 612962** Mrs Mccarthy.
Rates fr: *£15.00*-**£18.00**.
Open: All Year
Beds: 1F 2D 2T 3S
Baths: 4 Shared
🛏 🅿 ⊬ 🗕 🛉 🎟.

The *lowest* **single** rate *is shown in* **bold.**

Preston 2

National Grid Ref: SD5329

🍴 🍺 Fleece Inn

(0.25m) *Butler's Guest House, (Formerly Stanley House Hotel), 6 Stanley Terrace, Off Fishergate Hill, Preston, Lancs, PR1 8JE.*
Tel: **01772 254486**
Mrs Reynolds-Butler.
Rates fr: *£14.50*-**£17.00**.
Open: All Year (not Xmas)
Beds: 2F 1T 3S
Baths: 2 Ensuite
🛏 🅿 (5) 🗕 🛉 🎟. 🎟 ⧫
Family-run town centre guest-house, Grade II Listed. Five min-utes from rail and bus stations. Easy access to M6. Ground floor ensuite rooms

(On Path) *County Hotel, 1 Fishergate Hill, Preston, Lancs, PR1 8UL.*
Listed Victorian building, 120 yds from station.
Grades: ETB 2 Cr
Tel: **01772 253188** Mr Hunt.
Rates fr: *£17.00*-**£20.00**.
Open: All Year **Beds:** 1F 3D 4T 6S
Baths: 7 Private 2 Shared
🛏 🅿 (7) 🗕 🛉 ✗ 🗕 🎟. 🎟

Ribchester 3

National Grid Ref: SD6435

🍴 🍺 Black Bull, White Bull, Ribchester Arms, Halls Arms

(0.5m) *New House Farm, Preston Road, Ribchester, Preston, Lancs, PR3 3XL.*
Luxurious renovated 1820s farm-house.

Grades: ETB Comm
Tel: **01254 878954**
Mr & Mrs Bamber.
Rates fr: *£16.00*-**£20.00**.
Open: All Year
Beds: 1F 1D 1T
Baths: 3 Ensuite
🛏 (3) 🅿 (5) ⊬ 🗕 🎟. 🎟 ⧫

(1.5m 🐾) *Smithy Farm, Huntingdon Hall Lane, Dutton, Ribchester, Preston, Lancs, PR3 2ZT.*
Comfortable, homely, helpful.
Grades: ETB Listed
Tel: **01254 878250** Mrs Jackson.
Rates fr: *£12.50*-**£15.00**.
Open: All Year (not Xmas)
Beds: 1F 1D 1T
Baths: 1 Shared
🛏 🅿 🗕 🛉 ✗ 🗕 ⧫ ⧫

Hurst Green 4

National Grid Ref: SD6738

(▲ 2m) *Hurst Green Camping Barn, Greengore Farm, Hurst Green , Blackburn, Lancashire.*
Actual grid ref: SD674389
Tel: **01200 28366** *Simple Barn, sleeps 12. Henry VII is reputed to have stayed in the hunting lodge at Greengore Farm.*
ADVANCE BOOKING ESSENTIAL

Pay B&Bs by cash or cheque and be prepared to pay up front.

Great Mitton 5

National Grid Ref: SD7138

🍴 🍺 Owd Ned's River View Tavern

(On Path) *Mitton Green Barn, Church Lane, Great Mitton, Clitheroe, Lancs, BB7 9PJ.*
Newly-converted barn offering luxury accommodation.
Tel: **01245 826673**
Mrs Hargreaves.
Rates fr: *£17.00-£22.00.*
Open: All Year
Beds: 2D 1T
Baths: 2 Private 1 Shared
🛏 🅿 (6) 🍽 💷 Ⓥ

Clitheroe 6

National Grid Ref: SD7441

🍴 🍺 Victoria Hotel, Shireburn Arms, Swan Inn, Calf's Head, Three Millstones, Moorcock Inn, Edisford Bridge Hotel, Red Pump Inn

(On Path) *Springfield Cottage, 18 Nelson Street, Low Moor, Clitheroe, Lancs, BB7 2NQ.*
Terraced home of character.
Tel: **01200 442237** Mrs Whitfield.
Rates fr: *£15.00-£15.00.*
Open: All Year
Beds: 1F 1D
Baths: 1 Shared
🛏 🗝 🍽 💷 Ⓥ ✦

(0.75m �) *Brooklands, 9 Pendle Road, Clitheroe, Lancs, BB7 1JQ.*
Actual grid ref: 750414
Warm welcome, comfortable Victorian home.
Tel: **01200 22797** Mrs Lord.
Rates fr: *£15.00-£15.00.*
Open: All Year
Beds: 1D 2T
Baths: 1 Ensuite 1 Shared
🛏 🅿 (5) 🍽 🍴 💷 Ⓥ ∎ ✦

The *lowest* **single** rate *is shown in* **bold.**

(0.25m) *Selborne House, Back Commons, Clitheroe, Lancs, BB7 2DX.*
Quiet lane, short walk to town.
Tel: **01200 23571 / 22236**
Mrs Barnes.
Rates fr: *£15.00-£17.50.*
Open: All Year
Beds: 1F 2D 1T
Baths: 1 Private 1 Shared
🛏 🅿 (6) 🍽 🍴 🗡 💷 ♿ Ⓥ

Waddington 7

National Grid Ref: SD7243

🍴 🍺 Lower Buck Inn, Waddington Arms

(1m) *Waddington Arms, Clitheroe Road, Waddington, Clitheroe, Lancs, BB7 3HP.*
Character inn with modern facilities.
Tel: **01200 22636**
Mr Warburton.
Rates fr: *£22.50-£32.50.*
Open: All Year
Beds: 3D 1T **Baths:** 4 Ensuite
🛏 🅿 (50) 🍽 🗡 💷 Ⓥ ∎

(1m 🚍) *Backfold Cottage, The Square, Waddington, Clitheroe, Lancs, BB7 3HZ.*
Luxury mini-hotel. Outstanding value.
Tel: **01200 22367** Mrs Forbes.
Rates fr: *£18.00-£18.00.*
Open: All Year (not Xmas)
Beds: 1F 1D 1T 1S
Baths: 4 Ensuite
🛏 🅿 🍽 🍴 🗡 💷 Ⓥ ∎ ✦

West Bradford 8

National Grid Ref: SD7444

🍴 🍺 Three Millstones

(0.25m) *Old Hall, West Bradford, Clitheroe, Lancs, BB7 4SN.*
Actual grid ref: SD745444
Comfortable family home, extensive grounds.
Tel: **01200 23282**
Mr & Mrs Gretton.
Rates fr: *£14.00-£16.00.*
Open: All Year (not Xmas)
Beds: 2D 2T
Baths: 2 Shared
🛏 🅿 🗝 🍽 🍴 💷 ✦

Grindleton 9

National Grid Ref: SD7545

🍴 🍺 Duke of York

(0.5m) *Fellside Farm, Grindleton, Clitheroe, Lancs, BB7 4RX.*
Beautiful farmhouse with fantastic views.
Tel: **01200 441359**
Mrs MacGregor.
Rates fr: *£13.00-£20.00.*
Open: All Year (not Xmas)
Beds: 1D
Baths: 1 Private
🅿 (6) 🗝 🍽 🗡 💷

Downham 10

National Grid Ref: SD7944

(⛺ 2.5m) *Downham Camping Barn, Downland Estate, Downham, Clitheroe, Lancashire.*
Actual grid ref: SD795445
Tel: **01200 28366** *Simple barn, sleeps 12. Near the foot of Pendle Hill. ADVANCE BOOKING ESSENTIAL*

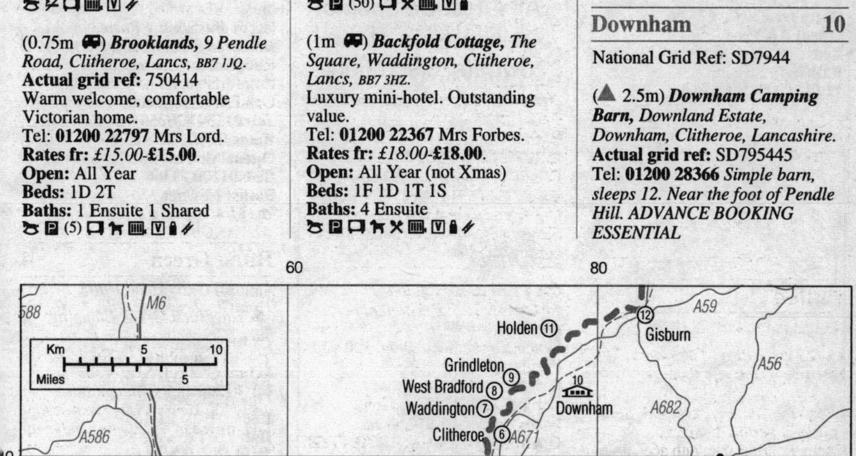

60   80

© Crown Copyright

All paths are popular: you are well-advised to book ahead

Holden 11

National Grid Ref: SD7749

๒| ◥Copy Nook Pub

(2.5m) *Baygate Farm, Holden, Bolton-By-Bowland, Clitheroe, Lancs, BB7 4PQ.*
Actual grid ref: SD758498
Modern comfortable farmhouse.
Grades: ETB Listed
Tel: **01200 447643** Ms Townson.
Rates fr: *£14.00-£14.00.*
Open: Easter to Nov
Beds: 3T **Baths:** 1 Shared
と (4) 回 (3) ❏ ★ ▮ ∻

Gisburn 12

National Grid Ref: SD8248

(0.5m 🐾) *The Stirk House Hotel, Gisburn, Clitheroe, Lancs, BB7 4LJ.*
Actual grid ref: SD812482
Country house hotel.
Grades: ETB 4 Cr, AA 3 St, RAC 3 St
Tel: **01200 445581**
Mrs MacMillan.
Rates fr: *£20.00-£25.00.*
Open: All Year
Beds: 1F 4D 31T 13S
Baths: 48 Ensuite
と 回 (75) ❏ ✕ ▥ ▾ ▮ ∻

Hellifield 13

National Grid Ref: SD8556

๒| ◥Black Horse Hotel

(3m) *Black Horse Hotel, Hellifield, Skipton, N. Yorks, BD23 4HT.*
Comfortable country public house, hotel.
Grades: ETB 3 Cr, Comm
Tel: **01729 850223** Mr/Mrs Langlois
Rates fr: *£20.00-£20.00.*
Open: All Year
Beds: 1F 3D 2T 1S
Baths: 7 Private
と 回 (40) ❏ ✕ ▥ ▾

Wigglesworth 14

National Grid Ref: SD8056

๒| ◥Plough Inn

(0.75m) *The Plough Inn, Wigglesworth, Skipton, N. Yorks, BD23 4RJ.*
Dales country inn.
Grades: ETB 4 Cr, Comm, RAC 3 St
Tel: **01729 840243** Mr Goodhall.
Rates fr: *£22.50-£31.50.*
Open: All Year **Beds:** 2F 7D 3T
Baths: 12 Private
と 回 (50) ✔ ❏ ✕ ὖ ▾

All rates are subject to alteration at the owners' discretion.

Long Preston 15

National Grid Ref: SD8358

๒| ◥Maypole Inn

(0.5m 🐾) *Maypole Inn, Long Preston, Skipton, N. Yorks, BD23 4PH.*
Actual grid ref: SD834582
Traditional 17th Century village inn.
Grades: ETB 3 Cr, Comm
Tel: **01729 840219**
Mr & Mrs Palmer.
Rates fr: *£19.50-£26.00.*
Open: All Year
Beds: 2F 2D 1T 1S
Baths: 6 Ensuite
と 回 (25) ✔ ❏ ★ ✕ ▥ ▾ ▮ ∻

Giggleswick 16

National Grid Ref: SD8063

๒| ◥Harts Head, Black Horse

(0.25m 🐾) *Yorkshire Dales Field Centre, Church Street, Giggleswick, Settle, N. Yorks, BD24 0BE.*
Actual grid ref: SD813641
Tel: **01729 824180** Mrs Barbour.
Rates fr: *£12.00-£12.00.*
Open: All Year
Beds: 2F 1D 5T 1S
Baths: 2 Shared
と 回 (8) ✔ ❏ ★ ✕ ▥ ▾ ▮ ∻
Dales Way and Pennine Way - 4 miles. Renowned for cuisine and accommodation. Situated in quiet corner of Dales village by village pub. Group bookings only.

(▲1.5m) *Giggleswick Camping Barn, Grain House, Giggleswick, Settle, N. Yorkshire.*
Actual grid ref: SD795632
Tel: **01200 28366** *Simple barns, sleeps 12. Built 1761, situated in the farm opposite Grain House.*
ADVANCE BOOKING ESSENTIAL

(1.25m) *Harts Head Hotel, Belle Hill, Giggleswick, Settle, N. Yorks, BD24 0BA.*
C17th freehouse/hotel.
Tel: **01729 822086** Mr Pearson.
Rates fr: *£19.00-£20.00.*
Open: All Year
Beds: 1F 2D 2T 1S
Baths: 4 Private 2 Shared
と 回 (20) ❏ ★ ✕ ▥ ▾

Taking your dog? Book in advance only with owners who accept dogs (★)

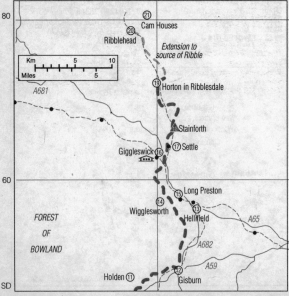

80

Settle   17

National Grid Ref: SD8163

|o| ⊈ Royal Oak, Golden Lion, Fisherman's Restaurant, Falcon Hotel

(On Path) *Whitebeam Croft, Duke Street, Settle, N. Yorks, BD24 9AN.*
Modern chalet bungalow off road.
Grades: ETB Listed
Tel: 01729 822824 Mrs Houlton.
Rates fr: *£15.00-£17.00.*
Open: All Year (not Xmas)
Beds: 1F 1T
Baths: 2 Shared
☎ 🅿 (3) ⅓ ⊡ ☼ 🎟 ⅏ 🔲 ⅘

(On Path 🚌**)** *Langcliffe Lodge, Langcliffe Road, Settle, N. Yorks, BD24 9LT.*
Attractive cosy Victorian country lodge.
Grades: ETB Reg
Tel: 01729 823362 Mrs Barton.
Rates fr: *£15.00-£15.00.*
Open: All Year
Beds: 2F 1D 1T
Baths: 1 Ensuite 1 Shared
☎ 🅿 ⊡ ☼ 🎟 & 🔲 ⅘

(0.5m) *Liverpool House, Chapel Square, Settle, N. Yorks, BD24 9HR.*
Comfortable C17th Listed guesthouse.
Grades: AA 2 Q
Tel: 01729 822247 Mrs Duerden.
Rates fr: *£15.00-£15.00.*
Open: All Year
Beds: 2D 2T 4S
Baths: 2 Shared
☎ 🅿 (8) ⅓ ⊡ ☼ 🎟 🔲 ⅘

(0.5m) *Chalimbana Cottage, 3 Ribble Terrace, Settle, N. Yorks, BD24 9DE.*
Homely accommodation in private house.
Tel: 01729 823988 Mrs Jarvis.
Rates fr: *£14.50-£16.00.*
Open: All Year (not Xmas)
Beds: 1F 1D 1T
Baths: 1 Shared
☎ ⅓ ⊡ 🎟 🔲

Stainforth   18

National Grid Ref: SD8266

(▲ 0.25m) *Stainforth Youth Hostel, 'Taitlands' Stainforth, Stainforth, Settle, North Yorkshire, BD24 9PA.*
Actual grid ref: SD8266
Tel: 01729 823577
Under 18: £5.00 **Adults:** £7.45
Family Rooms, Evening Meal, Centrally Heated, Grounds Available for Games, Shop, Study Room Available, Parking
A handsome, stone-built Listed Victorian house still retaining its original character of a large country house, in its own attractively walled gardens

Horton in Ribblesdale   19

National Grid Ref: SD8072

|o| ⊈ Golden Lion, Crown Hotel

(1.5m 🚌**)** *Middle Studfold Farm, Horton in Ribblesdale, Settle, N. Yorks, BD24 0ER.*
Actual grid ref: SD813704
C18th farmhouse.
Tel: 01729 860236 Mrs Pilkington.
Rates fr: *£32.00-£16.00.*
Open: All Year
Beds: 1F 1D 1T 1S
Baths: 1 Shared
☎ 🅿 (10) ⅓ ⊡ ☼ ✕ 🎟 🔲 ⅘

(0.5m) *Townend Cottage, Townend, Horton in Ribblesdale, Settle, N. Yorks, BD24 0EX.*
Actual grid ref: SD811799
Converted barn/farm, quiet.
Tel: 01729 860320 Mrs Wagstaff.
Rates fr: *£18.00-£18.00.*
Open: All Year
Beds: 1D 2T
Baths: 1 Ensuite 2 Shared
🅿 (6) ⊡ ☼ ✕ 🎟 🔲 ⅘

(0.5m) *The Golden Lion Hotel, Horton in Ribblesdale, Settle, N. Yorks, BD24 0HB.*
Welcoming country hotel, ideal for walkers.
Tel: 01729 860206 Mrs Johnson.

Rates fr: *£16.25-£16.25.*
Open: All Year (not Xmas)
Beds: 2D 2T 1S
Baths: 1 Ensuite 1 Shared
🅿 ✕ 🎟 🔲 ⅃

(0.25m) *Studfold House, Horton in Ribblesdale, Settle, N. Yorks, BD24 0ER.*
Actual grid ref: SD814702
Georgian house in own grounds.
Tel: 01729 860200
Mr & Mrs Horsfall.
Rates fr: *£15.00-£15.00.*
Open: All Year (not Xmas)
Beds: 1F 1D 1T
Baths: 2 Shared
☎ 🅿 (8) ⊡ ☼ ✕ 🎟 🔲 ⅃ ⅘

Ribblehead   20

National Grid Ref: SD7880

(On Path 🚌**)** *Station Inn, Ribblehead, Ingleton, Carnforth, Lancs, LA6 3AS.*
Actual grid ref: SD763792
Comfortable country inn, fantastic views.
Grades: ETB Listed, Approv
Tel: 015242 41274 Mr Coates.
Rates fr: *£17.50-£16.00.*
Open: All Year
Beds: 1F 3D 1T
Baths: 3 Ensuite, 1 Shared
☎ 🅿 (50) ⊡ ✕ 🎟 🔲 ⅃ ⅘
Also ▲ *Also bunkhouse, £24.00 per bunk.*
Open: All Year 🏠 🔲 ✕ &

Cam Houses   21

National Grid Ref: SD8282

(0.75m) *Cam Farm, Cam Houses, Oughtershaw, Skipton, N. Yorks, BD23 5JT.*
Comfortable self-catering accommodation.
Tel: 0860 648045 Mrs Smith.
Rates fr: *£6.50-£6.50.*
Open: All Year
Beds: 3T
Baths: 1 Shared
☎ (1) 🅿 (6) ☼ ✕ 🔲 ⅘
Also ▲ *Also bunkhouse, £6.50 per bunk* 🏠 🔲 ⅘ &

The Ridgeway

The **Ridgeway** is the name for a series of ancient pathways following the line of a chalk escarpment that extends for 85 miles from Avebury in Wiltshire, with its famous stone circle, up to the Ivinghoe Beacon in Buckinghamshire. You head over the beacons to Goring, where the River Thames bisects the path and then you turn east to cross the Thames Valley to the Chilterns. The western part is all open downland, following the ancient track on the ridge, while the eastern part is largely through leafy woods. In the height of a hot summer the hard, broken chalk track of the western section will test the ankles; and after rain the surface becomes awkward, so look after your feet. There are links with four other paths featured in this book: the **Wessex Ridgeway**, the **Thames Footpath**, the **Oxfordshire Way** and the **Icknield Way**. An excellent series of information leaflets can be had from the Ridgeway Officer at the **Oxfordshire County Council** address given below.

Guides (available from all good bookshops, unless stated)
The Ridgeway by Neil Curtis (ISBN 1 85410 268

0), published by Aurum Press in association with the Countryside Commission and Ordnance Survey, £9.99.
Exploring The Ridgeway by Alan Charles (ISBN 1 853060 09 7), published by Countryside Books and available by post from the publishers (Highfield House, 2 Highfield Avenue, Newbury, Berks, RG14 5DS, tel. 01635 43816), £4.95 (+ 75p p&p).
Discovering the Ridgeway by Vera Burden (ISBN 0-7478026-7-X), published by Shire Publications and available by post from the publishers (Cromwell House, Church Street, Princes Risborough, Bucks, HP27 9AA, tel. 01844 344301), £3.95 (+ £1 p&p).
Maps: 1:50000 Ordnance Survey Landranger Series: 165, 173, 174 and 175. Also The Ridgeway, ISBN 1 871149 03 7, (4-colour linear route map) published by Footprint and available directly from their offices (Unit 87, Stirling Enterprise Park, Stirling, FK7 7RP), £2.95 (+ 40p p&p).

All comments on the path to: **Jos Joslin**, Ridgeway Officer, O.C.C. Countryside Service, Library HQ, Holton, Oxford, OX33 1QQ.

Avebury   1

National Grid Ref: SU1069

¶◀ Red Lion

(1.25m) **6 Beckhampton Road, Avebury, Marlborough, Wilts,** *SN8 1QT.*
Semi-detached house near the Stones.
Tel: **01672 539588** Mrs Dixon.
Rates fr: *£15.00-£18.00.*
Open: All Year (not Xmas)
Beds: 1D 1T
Baths: 1 Shared
🕭 🅿 ♿ 🛏 🛎 🍴

West Kennett   2

National Grid Ref: SU1168

(0.75m) **Silbury Hill Cottage, West Kennett, Marlborough, Wilts,** *SN8 1QH.*
Actual grid ref: SU103683
Charming thatched cottage, warm welcome.
Grades: ETB Listed
Tel: **01672 539416**
Mr & Mrs Rendle.
Rates fr: *£16.00-£18.00.*
Open: Mar to Nov
Beds: 1D 1T
Baths: 1 Shared
🕭 🅿 ♿ ✕ 🛏 🛎 🍴

Lockeridge   3

National Grid Ref: SU1467

¶◀ The Who'd A' Thought It

(3m 🚗) **The Taffrail, Rhyls Lane, Lockeridge, Marlborough, Wilts,** *SN8 4ED.*
Unusual and delightful modern house.
Tel: **01672 861266** Mrs Spencer.
Rates fr: *£15.00-£18.00.*
Open: All Year (not Xmas)
Beds: 1D 1T 1S
Baths: 1 Shared
🕭 (8) 🅿 (3) 🛏 🛎 🍴

Broad Hinton   4

National Grid Ref: SU1076

¶◀ Bell Inn, Crown Inn

(0.75m 🚗) **Weir Farm, Broad Hinton, Swindon, Wilts,** *SN4 9NE.*
Actual grid ref: SU113772
Lovely period farmhouse, warm welcome.
Grades: ETB Listed, Comm, AA 3 Q
Tel: **01793 731207**
Mr & Mrs Hussey.
Rates fr: *£16.00-£20.00.*
Open: All Year (not Xmas or Feb)
Beds: 1D 2T
Baths: 1 Shared
🕭 (8) 🅿 (4) ♿ 🛏 🛎 🍴

Taking your dog?
Book in advance
only with owners who
accept dogs (🐕)

(0.75m) *Damar Guest House, Post Office Lane, Broad Hinton, Swindon, Wilts, SN4 9PB.*
Large modern house, lovely views.
Grades: ETB 1 Cr
Tel: 01793 731442 Mrs Baker.
Rates fr: *£15.00-£17.50.*
Open: All Year (not Xmas)
Beds: 1F 1T 1S
Baths: 1 Shared
Ȣ (8) ▣ (5) ⏆ ☐ ▥ Ⅴ ▮ ⌇

Broad Town 5

National Grid Ref: SU0977

|●| ◖ The Crown, The Bell

(4.5m) *Little Cotmarsh Farm, Broad Town, Wootton Bassett, Swindon, Wilts, SN4 7RA.*
Actual grid ref: SU0979
Comfortable, cosy farmhouse with character.
Grades: ETB Listed, Comm
Tel: 01793 731322 Mrs Richards.
Rates fr: *£16.00-£17.00.*
Open: All Year (not Xmas)
Beds: 1F 1D 1T
Baths: 1 Ensuite, 1 Shared
Ȣ ▣ (10) ⏆ ☐ ▥ ▮ ⌇

Chiseldon 6

National Grid Ref: SU1879

|●| ◖ Patriots Arms, Plough Inn

(0.75m 🚍) *Norton House, 46 Draycott Road, Chiseldon, Swindon, Wilts, SN4 0LS.*
Actual grid ref: SU185789
Country house, quiet location, open countryside.
Grades: ETB Reg
Tel: 01793 741210 Mrs Dixon.
Rates fr: *£17.00-£18.00.*
Open: Jan to Nov
Beds: 1D 1T
Baths: 1 Shared
Ȣ (5) ▣ (3) ⏆ ☐ ▥ ▮ ⌇

(0.25m 🚍) *Courtleigh House, 40 Draycott Road, Chiseldon, Swindon, Wilts, SN4 0LS.*
Actual grid ref: SU184791
Large, welcoming, comfortable family home.
Tel: 01793 740246 Ms Hibberd.
Rates fr: *£15.00-£18.00.*
Open: All Year (not Xmas)
Beds: 1T **Baths:** 1 Private
Ȣ ▣ (4) ☐ ▥ ▮

Manton 7

National Grid Ref: SU1768

|●| ◖ Oddfellows Arms, Up the Garden Path

(3m) *Sunrise Farm, Manton, Marlborough, Wilts, SN8 4HL.*
Actual grid ref: SU168682
Modern, comfortable, spacious chalet/bungalow.
Grades: ETB Reg
Tel: 01672 512878 Mrs Couzens.
Rates fr: *£16.00-£20.00.*
Open: Easter to Sep
Beds: 1D 2T
Baths: 1Private 1 Shared
▣ (3) ⏆ ☐ ▥ ▮

Marlborough 8

National Grid Ref: SU1869

|●| ◖ Green Dragon, Wellington Arms

(3.5m) *Cartref, 63 George Lane, Marlborough, Wilts, SN8 4BY.*
Actual grid ref: SU1969
Family home near town and restaurants.
Grades: ETB Listed
Tel: 01672 512771 Mrs Harrison.
Rates fr: *£15.00-£15.00.*
Open: All Year (not Xmas)
Beds: 1F 1D 1T
Baths: 1 Shared
Ȣ (1) ▣ (2) ⌇ ▥ Ⅴ ▮ ⌇

(4m) *Kennet Beeches, 54 George Lane, Marlborough, Wilts, SN8 4BY.*
Comfortable house, central, no smoking.
Grades: ETB Reg
Tel: 01672 512579
Mr & Mrs Young.
Rates fr: *£15.00-£15.00.*
Open: All Year (not Xmas)
Beds: 2T 2S **Baths:** 1Shared
▣ (2) ⏆ ▥ Ⅴ ⌇

(3.5m) *The Royal Oak, Wootton Rivers, Marlborough, Wilts, SN8 4NQ.*
C16th free house.
Grades: ETB 1 Cr
Tel: 01672 810322 J C Jones.
Rates fr: *£15.00-£22.50.*
Open: All Year
Beds: 1F 4D 1T 1S
Baths: 3 Private 1 Shared
Ȣ ▣ ☐ ⌇ ✕ ▥ Ⅴ ▮ ⌇

Mildenhall 9

National Grid Ref: TL7174

(4m) *Watersedge, Werg Lane, Mildenhall, Marlborough, Wilts, SN8 2LY.*
Riverside position in beautiful Kennet Valley.
Tel: 01672 511590 Mrs Hodder.
Rates fr: *£15.00-£15.00.*
Open: All Year (not Xmas)
Beds: 1D 1S
Baths: 1 Shared
Ȣ (11) ▣ (3) ☐ ▥

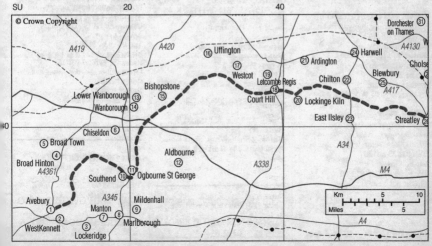

Southend 10

National Grid Ref: SU1974

¶⊙| ⊄ The Old Crown

(On Path) *Laurel Cottage, Southend, Ogbourne St George, Marlborough, Wilts, SN8 1SG.*
Actual grid ref: SU198735
C16th thatched farm cottage.
Grades: ETB 2 Cr, High Comm, AA 4 Q, Select
Tel: **01672 841288**
Mrs Francis.
Rates fr: *£16.50*-**£26.00**.
Open: Easter to Oct
Beds: 1F 2D 1T
Baths: 2 Private 1 Shared
⛺ (8) ₽ (5) ⊬ ⬜ 🎹 ⓥ ⓐ ✦

Ogbourne St George 11

National Grid Ref: SU2074

¶⊙| ⊄ The Old Crown

(On Path) 🚕 *The Parklands Hotel, Ogbourne St George, Marlborough, Wilts, SN8 1SL.*
Tel: **01672 841555**
Mrs Naffine.
Rates fr: **£30.00**-**£30.00**.
Open: All Year
Beds: 2D 6T 2S
Baths: 10 Ensuite
⛺ ₽ (20) ⊬ ⊁ 🎹 🎹 ⓥ ⓐ ✦
£4 per tent.
Open: May to Sep
Charming village inn at the foot of the Ridgeway Path, tastefully converted to offer comfortable ensuite bedrooms with hotel facilities (tea/coffee making, television, telephone).

(0.5m) 🚕 *The Old Crown, Marlborough Road, Ogbourne St George, Marlborough, Wilts, SN8 1SQ.*
Actual grid ref: SU202743
C18th coaching inn with restaurant.
Tel: **01672 841445**
Mr & Mrs Shaw.
Rates fr: *£15.00*-**£25.00**.
Open: Easter to Sep
Beds: 2T
Baths: 2 Private
⛺ (5) ₽ (15) ⬜ ⊁ 🎹 ⓐ ✦

(0.25m) 🚕 *Foxlynch, Bytham Road, Ogbourne St George, Marlborough, Wilts, SN8 1TD.*
Family bunkroom with double bed.
Tel: **01672 841307**
Mr Edwins.
Rates fr: *£12.50*-**£12.50**.
Open: All Year
Beds: 1F
Baths: 1Private
⛺ ₽ ⬜ ⊁ 🎹 ⓥ ⓐ ✦
Also ⛺ *£2.50 per tent.*
Open: All Year ⟨ ⓣ 🎹 ✗ ✦ ⛺

Aldbourne 12

National Grid Ref: SU2675

(2.5m) *Burney Farm, Aldbourne, Marlborough, Wilts, SN8 2NN.*
Informal accommodation in beautiful setting.
Grades: ETB Listed
Tel: **01672 520272** Mrs Ewing.
Rates fr: *£13.00*-**£15.00**.
Open: All Year
Beds: 1D 2T
Baths: 1 Shared
⛺ ₽ ⬜ ⊁ 🎹

Lower Wanborough 13

National Grid Ref: SU2183

(2m) 🚕 *Iris Cottage, Lower Wanborough, Swindon, Wilts, SN4 0AP.*
Comfortable cottage. Swindon 4 miles.
Tel: **01793 790591** Mrs Rosier.
Rates fr: *£18.00*-**£19.00**.
Open: All Year
Beds: 1D 1S
Baths: 1 Shared
₽ (2) ⬜ ✗ 🎹 ⓐ ✦

Wanborough 14

National Grid Ref: SU2082

¶⊙| ⊄ Harrow Inn, Cross Keys, Brewers Arms, Plough Inn, Black Horse

(3m) *Ducksbridge, Bury Croft, Wanborough, Swindon, Wilts, SN4 0AP.*
Large house, lawns and lake.
Tel: **01793 790338**
Mr & Mrs Sadler.
Rates fr: *£18.00*-**£20.00**.
Open: All Year (not Xmas)
Beds: 1D 1T 2S
Baths: 1 Shared
⛺ ₽ ⊬ ⬜ ⊁ 🎹 ⓥ

Bishopstone 15

National Grid Ref: SU2483

¶⊙| ⊄ The True Heart

(1m) 🚕 *Prebendal Farm, Bishopstone, Swindon, Wilts, SN6 8PT.*
Actual grid ref: SU244836
Farmhouse in beautiful Downland village.
Tel: **01793 790485** Mrs Selbourne.
Rates fr: *£19.00*-**£20.00**.
Open: All Year (not Xmas)
Beds: 2D 1T 1S
Baths: 2 Shared
⛺ ₽ (12) ⬜ ⊁ ✗ 🎹 ⓥ ⓐ ✦

The lowest *double* rate per person is shown in *italics*.

---

don't leave your footprint behind !

footprint
map - guides

Uffington 16

National Grid Ref: SU3089

¶⊙| ⊄ The Fox & Hounds

(1.5m) 🚕 *Norton House, Broad Street, Uffington, Faringdon, Oxon, SN7 7RA.*
Actual grid ref: SU305895
Friendly C18th family home.
Tel: **01367 820230** Mrs Oberman.
Rates fr: *£16.00*-**£17.00**.
Open: All Year (not Xmas)
Beds: 1F 1D 1T 1S
Baths: 1 Private, 1 Shared
⛺ ₽ (3) ⊬ ⊁ 🎹 ⓥ ⓐ ✦

(1.5m) *Shotover House, Uffington, Faringdon, Oxon, SN7 7RH.*
Actual grid ref: SU304889
Romantic country cottage, rose-filled garden.
Grades: ETB 2 Cr, High Comm
Tel: **01367 820351** Mrs Shaw.
Rates fr: **£25.00**-**£25.00**.
Open: All Year (not Xmas)
Beds: 1D 1T 1S
Baths: 3 Private
⛺ ₽ (3) ⊬ ⬜ ⊁ ✗ 🎹 ⓥ ⓐ ✦

(1m) 🚕 *Sower Hill Farm, Uffington, Faringdon, Oxon, SN7 7QH.*
Actual grid ref: SU3087
Modern farmhouse with brilliant views.
Grades: ETB Listed
Tel: **01367 820758** Mrs Cox.
Rates fr: *£17.00*-**£17.00**.
Open: All Year (not Xmas)
Beds: 2D 1T
Baths: 2 Shared
⛺ (10) ₽ (6) ⊬ ⬜ ⊁ 🎹 ⓐ ✦

Westcot 17

National Grid Ref: SU3387

¶⊙| ⊄ Star Inn

(1m) *Westcot Lodge, Westcot, Sparsholt, Wantage, Oxon, OX12 9QA.*
Actual grid ref: SU338874
Comfortable modern country house.
Tel: **01235 751251** Mrs Upton.
Rates fr: **£20.00**-**£20.00**.
Open: All Year (not Xmas)
Beds: 1D 1T
Baths: 1 Shared
⛺ ₽ (3) ⊬ ⬜ ✗ 🎹 ⓥ ⓐ ✦

Court Hill 18

National Grid Ref: SU3985

(▲0.5m) *The Ridgeway Youth Hostel*, Court Hill Ridgeway Centre, Court Hill, Wantage, Oxon, *OX12 9NE*.
Actual grid ref: SU3985
Warden: Mr S Bunyard.
Tel: **012357 60253**
Under 18: £5.00
Adults: £7.45
Family Bunk Rooms, Centrally Heated, Showers, Evening Meal (7.00 pm), Shop
Modern hostel, beautifully reconstructed from five barns, with beechwood grounds, panoramic views and stabling for 4 horses

Letcombe Regis 19

National Grid Ref: SU3886

(1m) *The Greyhound*, Main Street, Letcombe Regis, Wantage, Oxon, *OX12 9JL*.
C18th historic village pub.
Tel: **01235 763052**
Mr Smithard.
Rates fr: £17.50-£17.50.
Open: All Year (not Xmas)
Beds: 2T
Baths: 1 Shared
⛨ (1) 🅿 (30) 🗗 🛏 ✗ 🏢 🛆

Lockinge Kiln 20

National Grid Ref: SU4283

🍴 🍺 The Boars Head

(0.5m) *Lockinge Kiln Farm*, Lockinge Kiln, Wantage, Oxon, *OX12 8PA*.
Actual grid ref: SU424834
Comfortable farmhouse, working mixed farm.
Tel: **01235 763308** Mrs Cowan.
Rates fr: £16.00-£17.00.
Open: All Year (not Xmas)
Beds: 1F 1T
⛨ 🅿 🗗 ✗ 🏢 🛆 ⚡

Ardington 21

National Grid Ref: SU4188

🍴 🍺 Boars Head

(2m) *Orpwood House*, Ardington, Wantage, Oxon, *OX12 8PN*.
Spacious farmhouse in picturesque village location.
Tel: **01235 833300** Mrs Haigh.
Rates fr: £19.00-£19.00.
Open: All Year (not Xmas)
Beds: 1F 2T 1S
Baths: 1 Private 1 Shared
⛨ (15) 🗗 ✗ 🏢 🛆 ⚡
Also ▲ £6.00 per tent.,
Open: Apr to Sep 🎣 🅃 ♨ ♿

Chilton 22

National Grid Ref: SU4885

🍴 🍺 Rose & Crown, Red Lion, George & Dragon

(1m) *The Workshop*, South Road, Chilton, Didcot, Oxon, *OX11 0RT*.
Large modern bungalow set in 1.75 acres.
Tel: **01235 834130**
Mrs Young.
Rates fr: £20.00-£25.00.
Open: All Year (not Xmas)
Beds: 2T
Baths: 2 Private
🅿 🗗 🏢 🆅 🛆 ⚡

East Ilsley 23

National Grid Ref: SU4981

🍴 🍺 The Swan

(1m) *The Swan*, East Ilsley, Newbury, Berks, *RG16 0LF*.
County inn, open log fires.
Tel: **01635 281238**
Mr & Mrs Connolly.
Rates fr: £22.50-£32.50.
Open: All Year
Beds: 2F 4D 2T 2S
Baths: 10 Ensuite
⛨ (3) 🅿 (20) 🛏 ✗ 🏢 🆅 🛆

Harwell 24

National Grid Ref: SU4989

¶¶ 🍺 The White Hart

(2m) *The Old Brewery, High Street, Harwell, Didcot, Oxon, OX11 0EQ.*
Coverted C17th brewery.
Tel: **01235 832880** Mrs Howes.
Rates fr: £20.00-£22.00.
Open: All Year (not Xmas)
Beds: 2T 2S
Baths: 4 Ensuite
🛏 🅿 (6) ⊬ 🗗 🎟 & 🅥 🛊 ≉

Blewbury 25

National Grid Ref: SU5385

¶¶ 🍺 The Load of Mischief

(On Path) *The Load of Mischief, South Street, Blewbury, Didcot, Oxon, OX11 9PX.*
Comfortable C17th village inn.
Tel: **01235 850281** Mrs Welch.
Rates fr: £17.50-£17.50.
Open: All Year (not Xmas)
Beds: 2F 1S
Baths: 1 Shared
🛏 🅿 (20) 🗗 ✕ 🎟 🛊

Streatley 26

National Grid Ref: SU5980

(🔺 0.5m) *Streatley -on-Thames Youth Hostel, Hill House, Reading Road, Streatley, Reading, Berks, RG8 9JJ.*
Actual grid ref: SU591806
Warden: Mr A Wilson.
Tel: **01491 872278**
Under 18: £6.15 **Adults:** £9.10
Family Bunk Rooms, Centrally Heated, Showers, Evening Meal (7.00 pm), Shop, Television
Homely Victorian family house, completely refurbished, in a beautiful riverside village

Goring 27

National Grid Ref: SU6081

¶¶ 🍺 John Barley Corn, Catherine Wheel, Miller of Mansfield, Bull, Perch & Pike

(On Path 🚍) *14 Mountfield, Wallingford Road, Goring, Reading, Berks, RG8 0BE.*
Modern home in riverside village.
Grades: ETB Listed
Tel: **01491 872029** Mrs Ewen.
Rates fr: £15.00-£17.00.
Open: All Year
Beds: 1D 1T 1S
🛏 🅿 (4) 🗗 🎟 ✕ 🎟 🛊 ≉

(0.5m) *The John Barleycorn, Manor Road, Goring, Reading, Berks, RG8 9DP.*
C17th inn near Thames.
Grades: ETB 1 Cr
Tel: **01491 872509** Mr Fincham.

Rates fr: *£19.50-£23.00.*
Open: All Year
Beds: 1F 1D 1T 1S
Baths: 1 Shared
🛏 🗗 🎟 ✕ 🛊 ≉

(0.5m 🚍) *Queens Arms, Reading Road, Goring, Reading, Berks, RG8 0ER.*
200-year-old country pub.
Tel: **01491 872825** Mrs Carter.
Rates fr: £19.00-£19.00.
Open: All Year (not Xmas)
Beds: 1T 2S
Baths: 1 Shared
🛏 🅿 (30) 🗗 🎟 🎟 🛊 ≉

North Stoke 28

National Grid Ref: SU6186

¶¶ 🍺 The White House

(On Path 🚍) *The Old Farm House, North Stoke, Wallingford, Oxon, OX10 6BL.*
C17th farmhouse in Oxfordshire village.
Tel: **01491 837079** Mrs Lucey.
Rates fr: £17.00-£18.00.
Open: All Year
Beds: 2T 1S
Baths: 1 Shared
🅿 (4) ⊬ 🗗 ✕ 🎟 🅥 🛊 ≉

(On Path) *Footpath Cottage, The Street, North Stoke, Wallingford, Oxon, OX10 6BJ.*
Comfortable 200-year-old cottage.
Grades: ETB Listed
Tel: **01491 839763** Mrs Tanner.
Rates fr: £18.00-£18.00.
Open: All Year
Beds: 1D 1S
Baths: 1 Shared
🛏 🅿 (2) 🗗 🎟 ✕ 🎟 🅥 🛊 ≉

Cholsey 29

National Grid Ref: SU5886

¶¶ 🍺 Red Lion, Walnut Tree

(2m) *Old Blackalls, Old Blackalls Drive, Cholsey, Wallingford, Oxon, OX10 9HD.*
Friendly, family house in rural position.
Tel: **01491 652864** Mrs Robson.
Rates fr: £17.50-£17.50.
Open: All Year (not Xmas)
Beds: 1D
Baths: 1 Private
🛏 🅿 (5) ⊬ 🗗 ✕ 🎟 & 🅥

Wallingford 30

National Grid Ref: SU6089

¶¶ 🍺 Town Arms, Shillingford Bridge Hotel

(2.5m) *North Farm, Shillingford Hill, Wallingford, Oxon, OX10 8ND.*
Actual grid ref: SU586924
Quiet farmhouse near River Thames.
Grades: ETB 2 Cr, High Comm

Tel: **01865 858406** Mrs Warburton.
Rates fr: £19.00-£25.00.
Open: All Year
Beds: 1D 1T
Baths: 2 Ensuite
🛏 (8) 🅿 (4) ⊬ 🗗 ✕ 🎟 🅥 🛊 ≉

(0.5m) *The Nook, 2 Thames Street, Wallingford, Oxon, OX10 0BH.*
Character house, close to town/river.
Tel: **01491 834214** Mrs Colclough.
Rates fr: £17.50-£25.00.
Open: All Year (not Xmas)
Beds: 1F 1D 1T
Baths: 2 Shared
🛏 🅿 (3) 🗗 🎟 🛊

Dorchester-on-Thames 31

National Grid Ref: SU5794

¶¶ 🍺 Plough, Fleur-de-Lis

(4.5m) *Willowmour, 24 Martins Lane, Dorchester-on-Thames, Wallingford, Oxon, OX10 7JE.*
Quiet, modern detached house.
Tel: **01865 340444** Mrs Taylor.
Rates fr: £21.00-£21.00.
Open: All Year (not Xmas)
Beds: 1T
Baths: 1 Private
🛏 🅿 ⊬ 🗗 🎟 🎟

Benson 32

National Grid Ref: SU6191

¶¶ 🍺 Three Horseshoes

(2m 🚍) *Fyfield Manor, Brook Street, Benson, Wallingford, Oxon, OX10 6HA.*
Comfortable C12th manor house.
Grades: ETB 2 Cr
Tel: **01491 835184** Mrs Brown.
Rates fr: £19.00-£25.00.
Open: All Year (not Xmas)
Beds: 1F 1D 1T
Baths: 3 Ensuite
🛏 (10) 🅿 (10) ⊬ 🗗 🎟 🛊 ≉

(0.5m 🚍) *Hale Farm, Benson, Wallingford, Oxon, OX10 6NE.*
Large Victorian farmhouse.
Tel: **01491 836818** Mrs Belcher.
Rates fr: £15.00-£15.00.
Open: Easter to Oct
Beds: 1D 1T 1S
Baths: 1 Shared
🛏 🅿 🗗 🎟 🛊 ≉

Ewelme 33

National Grid Ref: SU6491

¶¶ 🍺 Shepherd's Hut

(2m) *Fords Farm, Ewelme, Wallingford, Oxon, OX10 6HU.*
Part-15th century farmhouse.
Grades: ETB Listed
Tel: **01491 839272** Miss Edwards.
Rates fr: £17.50-£17.50.
Open: All Year
Beds: 2T **Baths:** 1 Shared
🛏 (6) 🅿 (4) ⊬ 🗗 🎟

Nuffield 34

National Grid Ref: SU6687

|O| ⊈Crown Inn

(On Path 🚌) *The Rectory,*
Nuffield, Henley-on-Thames, Oxon,
RG9 5SN.
Working rural Rectory.
Tel: **01491 641305** Mr Shearer.
Rates fr: *£18.00-£18.00.*
Open: All Year
Beds: 1T 1S
Baths: 1Shared
⛨ 🅿 ⅛ ✕ 🎨 🛢 ⚡
Also ⛺ *£2.00 per tent.*
Open: All Year 🆃 ⛌ ⅋

Nettlebed 35

National Grid Ref: SU6986

|O| ⊈Crown Inn (Nettlebed)

(0.5m 🚌) *Park Corner Farm*
House, Nettlebed, Henley-on-
Thames, Oxon, RG9 6DR.
Queen Anne brick-and-flint farm-
house.
Tel: **01491 641450** Mrs Rutter.
Rates fr: *£16.00-£18.00.*
Open: All Year (not Xmas)
Beds: 2T
Baths: 1 Shared
⛨ 🅿 ⅛ ⅄ 🎨 ⚡

Pishill 36

National Grid Ref: SU7289

|O| ⊈Crown Inn, Five Horseshoes

(2m) *Bank Farm, Pishill, Henley-*
on-Thames, Oxon, RG9 6HJ.
Tel: **01491 638601**
Mrs Lakey.
Rates fr: *£14.00-£14.00.*
Open: All Year
Beds: 1F 1S
Baths: 1 Ensuite 1 Shared
⛨ 🅿 (10) ⌺ ⅄ 🎨.
Quiet comfortable farmhouse,
beautiful countryside. Well placed
for Oxford, Windsor and London
(by train). Ideal for ramblers, River
Thames 6 miles. Large tasty break-
fasts

Aston Rowant 37

National Grid Ref: SU7298

(0.75m 🚌) *Libra, Chinnor Road,*
Aston Rowant, Chinnor, Oxon,
OX9 5SH.
Actual grid ref: SU728985
Detached family house, open coun-
try surrounding.
Tel: **01844 351856**
Mrs Trotman.
Rates fr: *£16.00-£17.00.*
Open: All Year (not Xmas)
Beds: 2T
Baths: 1 Shared
⛨ (8) 🅿 (4) ⅛ ⌺ ⅄ ✕ 🎨 🆅 🛢 ⚡

Lodge Hill 38

National Grid Ref: SU7899

|O| ⊈The Lions of Bledlow, The
Boot

(0.25m) *Old Callow Down Farm,*
Wigans Lane, Lodge Hill, Bledlow,
High Wycombe, Bucks, HP14 4BH.
Actual grid ref: SU787000
Early C16th farmhouse, large
garden.
Grades: ETB 2 Cr
Tel: **01844 344416** Mr & Mrs Gee.
Rates fr: *£18.00-£20.00.*
Open: All Year
Beds: 1T **Baths:** 1 Private
⛨ 🅿 ⅛ ⌺ ⅄ ✕ 🎨 🆅

Princes Risborough 39

National Grid Ref: SP8003

|O| ⊈Rose & Crown, Black Prince,
Black Horse, Red Lion, Three
Crowns

(0.25m) *The Rose & Crown Hotel,*
Wycombe Road, Princes
Risborough, Bucks, HP27.
Georgian style family run inn.
Grades: ETB 3 Cr, AA 2 St,
RAC 2 St
Tel: **01844 345299** Mr Watson.
Rates fr: *£27.50-£39.95.*
Open: All Year (not Xmas/New
Year) **Beds:** 10D 1T 6S
Baths: 14 Ensuite 1 Shared
⛨ 🅿 ⌺ ✕ 🎨 🛢 ⚡

Whiteleaf 40

National Grid Ref: SP8204

|O| ⊈Red Lion

(0.25m) *The Red Lion, Upper*
Icknield Way, Whiteleaf, Princes
Risborough, Bucks, HP27 0LL.
C17th inn off the beaten track.
Tel: **01844 344476** Mr Howard.
Rates fr: *£14.75-£29.50.*
Open: All Year (not Xmas)
Beds: 2D 2T
Baths: 4 Ensuite
⛨ 🅿 (10) ⌺ ⅄ ✕ 🎨 🆅 🛢 ⚡

The Grid Reference
beneath the location
heading is for the
village or town - *not*
for individual houses,
which are shown
(where supplied) in
each entry itself.

All rates are subject
to alteration at the
owners' discretion.

Great Kimble 41

National Grid Ref: SP8205

|O| ⊈Bernard Arms

(1m) *Bernard Arms, Risborough*
Road, Great Kimble, Aylesbury,
Bucks, HP27 0XS.
Small, friendly inn - wonderful
breakfasts.
Grades: ETB 1 Cr
Tel: **01844 346172** Mrs Page.
Rates fr: *£22.50-£30.00.*
Open: All Year (not Xmas)
Beds: 1F 2D 1T 1S
Baths: 2 Shared
⛨ 🅿 ⌺ ✕ 🎨 🆅 🛢 ⚡

Stoke Mandeville 42

National Grid Ref: SP8310

|O| ⊈The Harrow

(2.75m) *Marsh Hill Farm, Marsh,*
Stoke Mandeville, Aylesbury,
Bucks, HP17 8ST.
Modern comfortable farmhouse.
Excellent view.
Tel: **01296 613460** Mrs Mason.
Rates fr: *£15.00-£15.00.*
Open: All Year
Beds: 1D 1T
⛨ 🅿 ⌺ ⅄ 🎨 🆅

Wendover 43

National Grid Ref: SP8607

|O| ⊈Red Lion, Shoulder of
Mutton, The Swan & Brewer, The
Marquis of Granby, The Swan

(0.25m) *3 Lionel Avenue,*
Wendover, Aylesbury, Bucks,
HP22 6LL.
Excellent accommodation, many
facilities available.
Grades: ETB Comm
Tel: **01296 624115** Mrs Bocca.
Rates fr: *£15.00-£15.00.*
Open: All Year
Beds: 2T 1S
Baths: 1 Shared
⛨ 🅿 (2) ⌺ ⅄ ✕ 🎨 🆅

(On Path) *26 Chiltern Road,*
Wendover, Aylesbury, Bucks,
HP22 6DB.
Large Victorian private house.
Tel: **01296 622351** Mrs Condie.
Rates fr: *£12.00-£12.00.*
Open: All Year
Beds: 2F 1S
Baths: 1 Shared
⛨ ⅛ ⌺ ⅄

(0.5m) *46 Lionel Avenue,
Wendover, Aylesbury, Bucks,
HP22 6LP.*
Actual grid ref: SP863087
Private house with large garden.
Tel: **01296 623426** Mrs
MacDonald.
Rates fr: *£16.00-***£16.00.**
Open: All Year (not Xmas)
Beds: 1T 3S
🛇 🅿 (3) 🖵 🖢 🗉 ⅏ ✓

Aston Clinton   44

National Grid Ref: SP8712

🍴 🍺 Rising Sun

(2.5m) *The Haven, Lower Icknield
Way, Aston Clinton, Aylesbury,
Bucks, HP22 5JS.*
Comfortable, homely bungalow.
Grades: ETB Listed
Tel: **01296 630751** Mrs Hall.
Rates fr: *£16.00-***£16.00.**
Open: All Year (not Xmas)
Beds: 1T 1S
Baths: 1 Shared
🅿 (1) ⅏ 🖵 🗉 ⬧ ✓

Tring   45

National Grid Ref: SP9211

🍴 🍺 Crows Nest

(0.5m) *Terriers End, Tring, Herts,
HP23 6JT.*
Actual grid ref: SP912098
C17th country cottage.
Grades: ETB Listed
Tel: **01442 822274** Mrs Dixon.
Rates fr: *£16.00-***£15.00.**
Open: All Year
Beds: 1D 1T 1S
Baths: 1 Shared
🛇 (8) ⅏ 🖵 🖢 🗉 🗉 ⬧ ✓

The *lowest* **single**

rate *is shown in* **bold.**

Cheddington   46

National Grid Ref: SP9217

(2m) *Rose Cottage, 68 High Street,
Cheddington, Leighton Buzzard,
Beds, LU7 0RQ.*
Victorian house, garden N.G.S.
Grades: ETB Reg
Tel: **01296 668693**
Mrs Jones.
Rates fr: *£18.00-***£20.00.**
Open: All Year
Beds: 1T 1S
Baths: 2 Shared
🛇 (7) 🅿 (2) ⅏ 🖵 🗉 ✓

Ringshall   47

National Grid Ref: SP9814

🍴 🍺 Bridgwater Arms

(1.5m) *12/13 Ringshall, Ringshall,
Berkhamsted, Herts, HP4 1ND.*
C18th cottage in NT woodland.
Tel: **01442 843396**
Mrs Martin.
Rates fr: *£13.00-***£13.00.**
Open: All Year (not Xmas)
Beds: 1F 1T
Baths: 1 Private 1 Shared
🛇 🅿 (4) 🖵 🖢 ✗ 🗉 🖢 ✓

Ivinghoe   48

National Grid Ref: SP9416

🍴 🍺 Rose & Crown

(⚠ 1m) *Ivinghoe Youth Hostel,
The Old Brewery House, Ivinghoe,
Leighton Buzzard, Beds, LU7 9EP.*
Actual grid ref: SP9416
Warden: Mr J Chaplin.
Tel: **01296 668251**
Under 18: £5.00 **Adults:** £7.45
Family Bunk Rooms, Centrally
Heated, Showers, Evening Meal
(6.30 pm), Shop
*Georgian mansion, once the home
of a local brewer, next to the vil-
lage church in the Chilterns Area
of Outstanding Natural Beauty*

Edlesborough   49

National Grid Ref: SP9719

🍴 🍺 The Travellers Rest, The Bell

(1m 🚭) *Ridgeway End, 5
Ivinghoe Way, Edlesborough,
Dunstable, Beds, LU6 2EL.*
Actual grid ref: SP975183
Bungalow set in quiet location.
Tel: **01525 220405** Mrs Lloyd.
Rates fr: *£18.00-***£18.00.**
Open: All Year (not Xmas)
Beds: 1F 1D 1T 1S
Baths: 1 Private 3 Shared
🛇 🅿 (3) 🖵 🗉 🗉 🖢 ✓

Totternhoe   50

National Grid Ref: SP9821

🍴 🍺 The Old Farm Inn, The Old
Bell, The Cross Keys

(6m) *5 Brightwell Avenue,
Totternhoe, Dunstable, Beds,
LU6 1QT.*
Actual grid ref: SP994210
Executive-style house in peaceful
country position.
Tel: **01582 601287** Mrs Mardell.
Rates fr: *£16.00-***£16.00.**
Open: All Year (not Xmas)
Beds: 1F 1T 1S
Baths: 1 Shared
🅿 (3) ⅏ 🖵 🖢 🗉 ✓

(0.5m) *Gower Cottage, 5
Brightwell Avenue, Totternhoe,
Dunstable, Beds, LU6 1QT.*
Actual grid ref: SP994210
Executive style, peaceful country
position.
Tel: **01582 601287** Mrs Mardell.
Rates fr: *£16.00-***£16.00.**
Open: All Year (not Xmas)
Beds: 1F 1T 1S
Baths: 1 Shared
🛇 🅿 (3) ⅏ 🖵 🗉 ✓

Shropshire Way

The **Shropshire Way** is a 140-mile way-marked circular walk starting in Shrewsbury and is well worth coming a long way for. Shropshire is an extraordinary county. Its strange hills - the Stiperstones, the Long Mynd, Wenlock Edge and the Wrekin; the classical English market town of Ludlow; those little villages near the Welsh Border that begin with 'Clun'- the 'quietest places under the sun'; the relics of the Industrial Revolution at Ironbridge - all make for a walk which you will remember for a long time. The local **Rambler's Association** have done an excellent job on

this path together with their county council. Buy the book and walk it now!

Guides: *Rambler's Guide to the Shropshire Way* by the Shropshire Area RA (ISBN 0 94667 94 44), published by Management Update and available from Powney's Bookshop (4-5 St Alkmund's Place, Shrewsbury, SY1 1UJ, tel. 01743 369165), £5.99

Maps: 1:50000 Ordnance Survey Landranger Series: 117, 126, 127, 137, 138

Shrewsbury   1

National Grid Ref: SJ4912

|o| 🥢 Three Fishes, Bird in Hand, The Beacon, Stiperstones Inn, Dun Cow, White Horse Inn, Peacock Hotel, The Boathouse, The Wheatsheaf, The Oxen

(0.25m) *Bancroft Guest House, 17 Coton Crescent, Shrewsbury, Shropshire, SY1 2NY.*
Actual grid ref: SJ490134
Comfortable, clean, friendly guest-house.
Grades: ETB Listed
Tel: **01743 231746**
Mrs Oldham-Malcolm.
Rates fr: *£15.00*-£16.00.
Open: All Year (not Xmas)
Beds: 1F 1T 2S
Baths: 2 Shared
🛏 🅿 (4) 🔲 🔭 ✕ Ⅲ. Ⅵ 🛢 ⚒

The lowest *double* rate per person is shown in *italics*.

(▲ On Path) *Shrewsbury Youth Hostel, The Woodlands, Abbey Foregate, Shrewsbury, Shropshire, SY2 6LZ.*
Actual grid ref: SJ505120
Warden: Mr M Roberts.
Tel: **01743 360179**
Under 18: £5.55
Adults: £8.25
Family Rooms, Evening Meal, Self Catering Facilities, Centrally Heated, Games Room, Laundry Facilities, Secure Lockers, Grounds Available for Games, Shop, Parking
A former Victorian ironmaster's house built in a distinct Red Sandstone, the Hostel is set in its own attractive grounds just on the outskirts of Shrewsbury

(0.25m) *The Stiperstones, 18 Coton Crescent, Coton Hill, Shrewsbury, Shropshire, SY1 2NZ.*
Tastefully furnished, comfortable, quality accommodation.
Grades: ETB 1 Cr, Comm
Tel: **01743 246720 / 350303**
Mrs Coomby.
Rates fr: *£15.00*-£17.00.
Open: All Year
Beds: 1F 3D 1T 1S
Baths: 3 Shared
🛏 🅿 (4) ⚡ 🔲 ✕ Ⅲ. Ⅵ 🛢

(0.25m) *Roseville, 12 Berwick Road, Shrewsbury, Shropshire, SY1 2LN.*
Comfortable detached Victorian town house.
Grades: ETB 2 Cr, High Comm, AA 3 Q, Recomm
Tel: **01743 236470**
Mr & Mrs Stening-Rees.
Rates fr: *£20.00*-£30.00.
Open: Feb to Dec
Beds: 1D 1T 1S
Baths: 2 Ensuite 1 Private
🛏 (12) 🅿 (3) ⚡ 🔲 ✕ Ⅲ. Ⅵ ⚒

(0.5m) *Abbey Court House, 134 Abbey Foregate, Shrewsbury, Shropshire, SY2 6AU.*
Substantial well-appointed guest-house.
Grades: ETB 2 Cr, Comm
Tel: **01743 364416** Mrs Turnock.
Rates fr: *£16.50*-£19.00.
Open: All Year (not Xmas)
Beds: 21F 3D 3T 2S
Baths: 4 Private 6 Shared
🛏 (10) 🅿 (10) 🔲

(0.5m) *Merevale House, 66 Ellesmere Road, Shrewsbury, Shropshire, SY1 2QP.*
Grades: ETB Listed, Comm
Tel: **01743 243677** Mrs Spooner.
Rates fr: *£15.00*-£15.00.
Open: All Year
Beds: 3D 1S **Baths:** 1 Shared
🛏 🅿 (4) 🔲 🔭 Ⅲ. Ⅵ
Comfortable Victorian house, 10 minutes from town. Lovely bedrooms with washbasin, TV, hairdryer, drinks and biscuits. Many extra home comforts. Vegetarians welcome. Private parking

(0.5m) *Anton House, 1 Canon Street, Monkmoor, Shrewsbury, Shropshire, SY2 5HG.*
Comfortable, large Victorian private house.
Grades: ETB 2 Cr, Comm
Tel: **01743 359275** Mrs Sandford.
Rates fr: *£16.00*-£18.00.
Open: All Year (not Xmas)
Beds: 1F 2D 1T
Baths: 2 Shared
🛏 🅿 (3) ⚡ 🔲 Ⅲ. Ⅵ

Bringing children with you? Always ask for any special rates.

The *lowest* **single** rate *is shown in* **bold**.

Ratlinghope   2

National Grid Ref: SO4096

(0.5m) *Lower Stitt Farm,*
Ratlinghope, Shrewsbury, Salop,
SY5 0SN.
Actual grid ref: SO403986
Comfortable warm and friendly
farmhouse.
Grades: ETB 1 Cr
Tel: **01588 650640** Mrs Betton.
Rates fr: *£14.00-*£15.00.
Open: All Year (not Xmas)
Beds: 1D 1T
Baths: 1 Shared
🛌 🅿 (2) ⊬ 🗖 ✗ 🎟 Ⓥ ⓘ ✦

Stiperstones   3

National Grid Ref: SO3599

🍴 🍺 Stiperstones Inn

(1m) *Tankerville Lodge,*
Stiperstones, Minsterley,
Shrewsbury, Shropshire, SY5 0NB.
Actual grid ref: SO355995
Cosy country house, quiet, friendly.
Grades: ETB 1 Cr, Comm,
AA 2 Q, Recomm
Tel: **01743 791401**
Mr & Mrs Anderson.
Rates fr: *£15.75-*£18.25.
Open: All Year
Beds: 1D 3T **Baths:** 2 Shared
🛌 (5) 🅿 (4) 🗖 ✗ 🎟 ⓘ ✦

Church Stoke   4

National Grid Ref: SO2794

🍴 🍺 Boars Head, Dragon Hotel,
Cottage Inn

(3m) *The Drewin Farm, Church*
Stoke, Montgomery, Powys,
SY15 6TW.
C17th farmhouse with panoramic
views.
Grades: ETB 3 Cr, High Comm,
AA 4 Q, Select, RAC Listed
Tel: **01588 620325** Mrs Richards.
Rates fr: *£15.00-*£16.00.
Open: Easter to Oct
Beds: 2F
Baths: 1 Private 1 Shared
🛌 🅿 (6) ⊬ 🗖 ✗ ✗ 🎟 Ⓥ

Many rates vary according to season - the lowest only are shown here

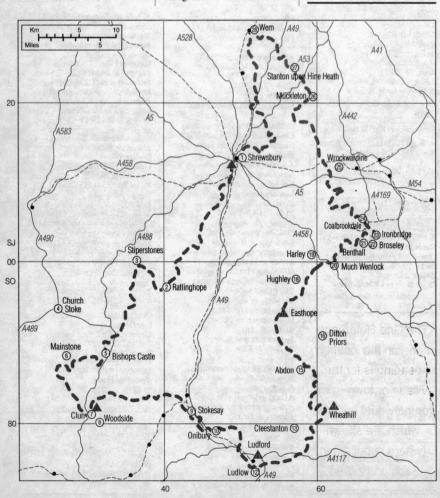

Bishops Castle 5

National Grid Ref: SO3288

� Three Tuns, Boars Head

(On Path 🚌) *Old Brick Guest House, 7 Church Street, Bishops Castle, Salop, SY9 5AA.*
C18th guesthouse in historic town.
Grades: ETB 2 Cr, AA 3 Q
Tel: **01588 638471** Mr Hutton.
Rates fr: *£17.50-£19.00.*
Open: All Year (not Xmas)
Beds: 1F 2D 2T 1S
Baths: 3 Ensuite, 1 Shared
🛏 🅿 (5) 🖵 🛉 ✕ 📖 Ⓥ ⬩ ✦

Mainstone 6

National Grid Ref: SO2787

(1m 🚌) *New House Farm, Mainstone, Clun, Craven Arms, Salop, SY7 8NJ.*
Actual grid ref: SO275863
C18th farmhouse set in Clun hills.
Grades: ETB 2 Cr, High Comm, AA 4 Q, Select
Tel: **01588 638314**
Mr & Mrs Ellison.
Rates fr: *£18.00.*
Open: Mar to Oct
Beds: 1F 1D 1T
Baths: 1 Ensuite 1 Private
🛏 🅿 (6) ⚡ 🖵 🛉 ✕ Ⓥ ⬩ ✦

Clun 7

National Grid Ref: SO3080

⚑ Buffalo Head Hotel, White Horse Inn

(On Path 🚌) *Crown House, Church Street, Clun, Craven Arms, Salop, SY7 8JW.*
Actual grid ref: SO305805
Self-contained accommodation in converted stables.
Grades: ETB 2 Cr
Tel: **01588 640780** Mr Maund.
Rates fr: *£15.75-£16.75.*
Open: All Year (not Xmas)
Beds: 1D 1T
Baths: 2 Ensuite
🛏 (8) 🅿 (2) ⚡ 🖵 🛉 📖 ⬩ ✦

The Grid Reference beneath the location heading is for the village or town - *not* for individual houses, which are shown (where supplied) in each entry itself.

(▲ On Path) *Clun Mill Youth Hostel, The Mill, Clun, Craven Arms, Shropshire, SY7 8NY.*
Actual grid ref: SO303812
Warden: Ms R Pinder.
Tel: **01588 640582**
Under 18: £4.60
Adults: £6.75
Self Catering Facilities, Centrally Heated, Camping, No Smoking, Grounds Available for Games, Shop, Parking
Former watermill (workings still visible) upgraded yet unspoilt by modern development, set in stone-built town (C16th humpbacked bridge) and Norman castle

(0.25m 🚌) *Clun Farm, High Street, Clun, Craven Arms, Salop, SY7 8JB.*
Actual grid ref: SO302808
C16th double cruck farmhouse.
Grades: ETB Listed
Tel: **01588 640432**
Mrs Lewis.
Rates fr: *£15.00-£15.00.*
Open: All Year (not Xmas)
Beds: 1F 1T 2S
Baths: 1 Ensuite 1 Shared
🛏 (1) 🅿 (6) 🖵 🛉 📖 Ⓥ ⬩ ✦

Woodside 8

National Grid Ref: SO3180

(2.5m) *Llanhedric Farm, Clun, Craven Arms, Salop, SY7 8NG.*
Characteristic old stone farmhouse.
Grades: ETB Listed, Comm
Tel: **01588 640203**
Mrs Jones.
Rates fr: *£14.00-£15.00.*
Open: Easter to Nov
Beds: 1F 1D
🛏 🅿 (5) 🖵 ✕ 📖 Ⓥ ⬩

(4m 🚌) *Woodside Old Farmhouse, Woodside, Clun, Craven Arms, Salop, SY7 0JB.*
Actual grid ref: SO310802
300-year-old stone farmhouse.
Grades: ETB 1 Cr
Tel: **01588 640695**
Mr Wall.
Rates fr: *£15.00-£15.00.*
Open: Easter to Oct
Beds: 1F 1D
Baths: 1 Shared
🛏 🅿 (3) ⚡ 🖵 🛉 ✕ 📖 Ⓥ ⬩ ✦

(1m 🚌) *The Old Farmhouse, Woodside, Clun, Craven Arms, Salop, SY7 0JB.*
Actual grid ref: SO310802
300-year-old stone farmhouse.
Grades: ETB 1 Cr
Tel: **01588 640695**
Mr Wall.
Rates fr: *£15.00-£15.00.*
Open: Easter to Oct
Beds: 1F 1D
Baths: 1 Shared
🛏 🅿 (3) ⚡ 🖵 🛉 ✕ 📖 Ⓥ ⬩ ✦

Stokesay 9

National Grid Ref: SO4381

⚑ Craven Arms

(On Path) *Castle View B & B, Stokesay, Craven Arms, Salop, SY7 9AL.*
Large Victorian stone-built house.
Grades: ETB Listed
Tel: **01588 673712** Mrs Grizzell.
Rates fr: *£15.00-£15.00.*
Open: All Year
Beds: 1D 1T 1S
Baths: 1 Private 1 Shared
🛏 (3) 🅿 (4) 🖵 🛉 📖.

Onibury 10

National Grid Ref: SO4579

⚑ Engine & Tender

(1.25m 🚌) *Fairview, Green Lane, Onibury, Craven Arms, Salop, SY7 9BL.*
Actual grid ref: SO433785
Grades: ETB 2 Cr, High Comm
Tel: **01584 856505** Mrs Coates.
Rates fr: *£16.50-£20.50.*
Open: Apr to Oct
Beds: 2D 1T
Baths: 1 Ensuite, 1 Shared
🛏 (10) 🅿 (6) ⚡ 🖵 ✕ 📖 Ⓥ ⬩ ✦
A smallholding in the Shropshire Hills with good home cooking using own or local produce. Leave Way at Stokesay Crossing to reach us via Aldon.

Ludford 11

National Grid Ref: SO5174

(▲ 0.5m) *Ludlow Youth Hostel, Ludford Lodge, Ludford, Ludlow, Shropshire, SY8 1PJ.*
Actual grid ref: SO513741
Warden: Ms L Cox.
Tel: **01584 872472**
Under 18: £4.60 **Adults:** £6.75
Family Rooms, Evening Meal, Self Catering Facilities, Centrally Heated, Shop, Parking
Standing on the banks of the River Teme, the Hostel faces the town across the medieval Ludford bridge

Ludlow 12

National Grid Ref: SO5174

⚑ Ye Olde Bull Ring, Unicorn Hotel, Salway Arms Hotel, Temeside Hotel

(0.5m) *Arran House, 42 Gravel Hill, Ludlow, Salop, SY8 1QR.*
Large comfortable Victorian house.
Grades: ETB 1 Cr
Tel: **01584 873764** Mrs Bowen.
Rates fr: *£15.00-£15.00.*
Open: All Year
Beds: 1D 1T 2S
Baths: 1 Shared
🛏 (3) 🅿 (4) 🖵 🛉 ✕ 📖 ⬩ ✦

(0.5m) *Cecil Guest House, Sheet Road, Ludlow, Salop, SY8 1LR.*
Modern, comfortable guesthouse.
Grades: ETB 3 Cr, Comm,
AA 3 Q, RAC Acclaim
Tel: **01584 872442** Mrs Phillips.
Rates fr: *£18.00-£22.00.*
Open: All Year (not Xmas)
Beds: 1F 1D 3S
Baths: 3 Ensuite 2 Shared
⛌ ▣ (8) ⊬ ⌷ ⍐ ✕ ▥ Ⅴ ⓘ ∦

(0.5m) *Pengwern, 5 St Julians Avenue, Ludlow, Shropshire, SY8 1ET.*
Quiet Edwardian town house.
Grades: ETB Listed
Tel: **01584 872587** Mrs Styles.
Rates fr: *£15.00-£15.50.*
Open: All Year (not Xmas)
Baths: 1 Shared
▣ (1) ⊬ ⌷ ▥ Ⅴ

Cleestanton   13

National Grid Ref: SO5779

⦀ ⌘ Royal Oak

(1m) *The Bank Farm, Cleestanton, Ludlow, Salop, SY8 3EL.*
Modernised Victorian farmhouse near Ludlow.
Grades: ETB 2 Cr
Tel: **01584 823368** Mrs Campbell.
Rates fr: *£12.00-£12.00.*
Open: Easter to Oct
Beds: 1F 1T 1S
Baths: 1 Ensuite 1 Private 1 Shared
⛌ (A) ▣ (6) ⊬ ⌷ ✕ ▥ Ⅴ

Wheathill   14

National Grid Ref: SO6181

(▲ 0.1m) *Wheathill Youth Hostel, Malthouse Farm, Wheathill, Bridgnorth, Shropshire, WV16 6QT.*
Actual grid ref: SO613818
Warden: Mr F Powell.
Tel: **01746 787236**
Under 18: £3.75 **Adults:** £5.50
Self Catering, Camping, No Smoking, Grounds Available for Games, Shop, Parking
Excellent rural setting in the Clee Hills for this simple Hostel, part of a Malthouse Farm dating back to the C17th

Abdon   15

National Grid Ref:

⦀ ⌘ Tally Ho, Howard Arms

(0.1m) *Spring Cottage, Cockshutford Road, Abdon, Craven Arms, Shropshire, SY7 9HU.*
Modernised C18th house.
Grades: ETB 2 Cr, High Comm
Tel: **01746 712551** Mrs Langholm.
Rates fr: *£18.00-£23.00.*
Open: All Year (not Xmas)
Beds: 1D 1T 1S
Baths: 3 Ensuite
⛌ (A) ▣ ⊬ ⌷ ✕ ▥ Ⅴ ⓘ ∦

Ditton Priors   16

National Grid Ref: SO6089

⦀ ⌘ Howard Arms, The Tally Ho

(2m) *Court House, South Road, Ditton Priors, Bridgnorth, Shropshire, WV16 6SJ.*
Converted C18th beamed 'dhustone' barn.
Grades: ETB 2 Cr
Tel: **01746 712554** Mrs Tipton.
Rates fr: *£21.00.*
Open: Mar to Nov
Beds: 2D
Baths: 2 Ensuite
▣ ⌷ ▥ ⓘ ∦

Easthope   17

National Grid Ref: SO5492

(▲ On Path) *Wilderhope Manor Youth Hostel, The John Cadbury Memorial Hostel, Easthope, Much Wenlock, Shropshire, TF13 6EG.*
Actual grid ref: SO544928
Warden: Mr A Smith.
Tel: **01694 771363**
Under 18: £5.55 **Adults:** £8.25
Family Room, Evening Meal, Camping, Games Room, No Smoking, Grounds Available for Games, Shop, Study Room Available, Parking
Exquisite Elizabethan Manor House owned by the National Trust, idyllically situated on top of Wenlock Edge

Hughley   18

National Grid Ref: SO5697

(0.5m 🚐) *Mill Farm, Hughley, Shrewsbury, Salop, SY5 6NT.*
Victorian farmhouse with own riding centre.
Grades: ETB 2 Cr
Tel: **01746 785645** Mrs Bosworth.
Rates fr: *£18.00-£20.00.*
Open: All Year (not Xmas)
Beds: 1F 1D
⛌ ▣ ⊬ ⌷ ⓘ ∦

Harley   19

National Grid Ref: SJ5901

⦀ ⌘ Feathers Inn

(1m) *Rowley Farm, Harley, Shrewsbury, Shropshire, SY5 6LX.*
Actual grid ref: SJ505
Clean, comfortable Georgian farmhouse.
Grades: ETB Listed
Tel: **01952 727348** Ms Munslow.
Rates fr: *£29.00-£20.00.*
Open: May to Oct
Beds: 1D 1T **Baths:** 1 Shared
▣ ⌷ ⍐ ∦

(0.5m 🚐) *The Plume of Feathers, Harley, Shrewsbury, Salop, SY5 6LP.*
Actual grid ref: SJ600009
C17th coaching inn.
Grades: ETB 3 Cr, Comm,

AA 3 Q, Recomm
Tel: **01952 727360**
Mr & Mrs Hitchin.
Rates fr: *£18.00-£24.00.*
Open: All Year
Beds: 6F 2D 1T
Baths: 9 Ensuite
⛌ ▣ ⌷ ✕ ▥ Ⅴ ⓘ

Much Wenlock   20

National Grid Ref: SO6299

⦀ ⌘ Weatland Fox

(On Path) *31 Oakfield Park, Much Wenlock, Salop, TF13 6HH.*
Modern comfortable bungalow.
Grades: ETB Listed
Tel: **01952 727473** Mrs Stevenson.
Rates fr: *£26.00-£13.00.*
Open: All Year
Beds: 2D 1S
Baths: 1 Shared
⛌ ▣ (3) ⊬ ⌷ ▥ ⛟ ⓘ ∦

Benthall   21

National Grid Ref: SJ6602

⦀ ⌘ Cumberland Hotel (Benthall)

(1.75m) *Hill Top House, Bridge Road, Benthall, Broseley, Shropshire, TF12 5RL.*
Large detached private house.
Grades: ETB Listed
Tel: **01952 882150** Mrs Tacchi.
Rates fr: *£15.00-£15.00.*
Open: All Year
Beds: 1F 1T 1S
Baths: 1 Ensuite, 1 Shared
⛌ ▣ (6) ⌷ ⍐ ▥ ⓘ ∦

Broseley   22

National Grid Ref: SJ6701

⦀ ⌘ Cumberland Hotel, Duke of York

(0.75m) *Annscroft, 25 King Street, Broseley, Shropshire, TF12 5NA.*
Actual grid ref: SJ672025
Converted Victorian shop - comfortable, flexible.
Grades: ETB Listed
Tel: **01952 882670** Mrs Beddow.
Rates fr: *£15.00-£18.00.*
Open: All Year (not Xmas)
Beds: 1F 1D 2T
Baths: 2 Shared
⛌ ⌷ Ⅴ ⓘ ∦

🚐 sign means that, given due notice, owners will pick you up from the path and drop you off within reason.

(1m 🚐) *Cumberland Hotel,*
Jackson Avenue, Broseley,
Shropshire, TF12 5NB.
Was large Victorian private house.
Grades: ETB 3 CrRAC Listed
Tel: **01952 882301** Mr Southorn.
Rates fr: *£17.50*-**£28.00**.
Open: All Year
Beds: 3F 5D 3T 3S
Baths: 7 Ensuite 3 Shared
🏠 🅿 (30) 🗡 ❏ ⛳ ✕ 🛏 Ⓥ 🛍 ⚡

(1m) *Lord Hill Guest House, Duke*
Street, Broseley, Salop, TF12 5LU.
Renovated public house, comfort-
able, friendly.
Grades: ETB Listed
Tel: **01952 884270 / 580792**
Mr Ryan.
Rates fr: *£15.00*-**£15.00**.
Open: All Year
Beds: 1D 4T 2S
Baths: 3 Private 1 Shared
🏠 🅿 (9) ❏ ⛳ ✕ 🛏 ♿ Ⓥ

Ironbridge 23

National Grid Ref: SJ6703

🍴 🍺 The Old Vaults, Olivers
Vegetarian Restaurant

(On Path) *Post Office House, 6*
The Square, Ironbridge, Telford,
Shropshire, TF8 7AQ.
Elegant 18th Century residence.
Grades: ETB 1 Cr
Tel: **01952 433201** Mrs Jones.
Rates fr: *£16.50*-**£20.00**.
Open: All Year
Beds: 1F 2D
Baths: 1 Ensuite, 1 Shared
🏠 ❏ 🛏 Ⓥ 🛍 ⚡

Coalbrookdale 24

National Grid Ref: SJ6604

🍴 🍺 The Coalbrookdale Inn,
Wellington Road

(On Path) *Paradise House,*
Coalbrookdale, Telford,
Shropshire, TF8 7NR.
Large comfy Georgian private
house.

Grades: ETB 1 Cr, Approv
Tel: **01952 433379**
Mrs Gilbride.
Rates fr: *£19.00*-**£20.00**.
Open: Feb to Nov
Beds: 1F 1D 1T
Baths: 2 Ensuite, 1 Shared
🏠 🅿 (1) ❏ 🛏 Ⓥ 🛍 ⚡

(On Path) *Springhill, 2 School*
Road, Coalbrookdale, Telford,
Salop, TF8 7DY.
Georgian family house.
Grades: ETB 2 Cr
Tel: **01952 432210** Mrs Clegg.
Rates fr: *£18.00*-**£25.00**.
Open: All Year (not Xmas)
Beds: 2D 2T
Baths: 4 Ensuite
🏠 🅿 🗡 ❏ ✕ 🛏 Ⓥ 🛍 ⚡

Wrockwardine 25

National Grid Ref: SJ6211

(0.5m 🚐) *Church Farm,*
Wrockwardine, Wellington,
Telford, Salop, TF6 5DG.
Actual grid ref: SJ624120
Georgian village farmhouse, lovely
garden.
Grades: ETB 3 Cr, High Comm,
AA 4 Q, Select
Tel: **01952 244917**
Mrs Savage.
Rates fr: *£20.00*-**£25.00**.
Open: All Year
Beds: 3D 3T
Baths: 3 Ensuite 3 Shared
🏠 (12) 🅿 (20) ❏ ⛳ ✕ 🛏 Ⓥ 🛍 ⚡

Muckleton 26

National Grid Ref: SJ5921

🍴 🍺 Elephant & Castle

(On Path) *New Farm, Muckleton,*
Shawbury, Telford, Salop, TF6 6RJ.
Modern, comfortable farmhouse.
Grades: ETB 2 Cr, Comm
Tel: **01939 250358** Mr Evans.
Rates fr: *£16.00*-**£16.00**.
Open: All Year (not Xmas)
Beds: 1F 1D 2T 1S

Baths: 3 Ensuite 1 Shared
🏠 🅿 (6) ❏ 🛏 ⚡
Also 🏕 *£2 per tent.*
Open: All Year ♿

Stanton-upon-Hine Heath 27

National Grid Ref: SJ5624

(0.25m 🚐) *The Sett, Stanton-*
upon-Hine Heath, Shrewsbury,
Shropshire, SY4 4LR.
Actual grid ref: SJ569240
Farmhouse in converted barn.
Grades: ETB 3 Cr, High Comm
Tel: **01939 250391** Mr Grumdey.
Rates fr: *£20.00*-**£20.00**.
Open: All Year (not Xmas)
Beds: 3D **Baths:** 3 Ensuite
🏠 🅿 (3) 🗡 ❏ ⛳ ✕ 🛏 Ⓥ 🛍 ⚡

Wem 28

National Grid Ref: SJ5129

🍴 🍺 The Raven, The Dicken
Arms

(0.75m) *Lowe Hall Farm, The*
Lowe, Wem, Shrewsbury,
Shropshire, SY4 5UE.
Actual grid ref: SJ501306
C16th historically famous Listed
farmhouse.
Grades: ETB 2 Cr, RAC Listed
Tel: **01939 232236** Mrs Jones.
Rates fr: *£16.00*-**£17.50**.
Open: All Year
Beds: 1F 1D 1T **Baths:** 1 Ensuite
🏠 🅿 (6) ❏ ✕ 🛏 🛍

(0.75m 🚐) *Foxleigh House,*
Foxleigh Drive, Wem, Shrewsbury,
Shropshire, SY4 5BP.
Actual grid ref: SJ516296
Interesting comfortable
Georgian/Victorian house.
Grades: ETB 2 Cr, Comm,
AA 4 Q
Tel: **01939 233528** Mrs Barnes.
Rates fr: *£16.00*-**£18.00**.
Open: All Year (not Xmas)
Beds: 1F 1T 1S
Baths: 1 Private 1 Shared
🏠 (10) 🅿 (4) ❏ ⛳ ✕ 🛏 🛍 ⚡

South Downs Way

The **South Downs Way** runs for 106 miles from Eastbourne to Winchester along the line of famous chalk hills that dominates the Sussex skyline. The Way is a bridleway, too, and is thus open to horse-riders and cyclists, although only walkers may take the Seven Sisters alternative out of Eastbourne. The downlands are very popular; from Eastbourne to Buriton you will rarely be alone. On hot days you will see hang-gliders, balloonists and para-gliders; the forests and the hilltops are favourite spots for picnickers. And there are many walkers, too. The path itself makes up for any lack of solitude, though. On a early summer day, with larks rising and with views far out to sea and across the Sussex Weald, the walk defies superlatives. The terrain is principally chalk path which, wet or dry, will test the ankles. The path is well way-marked up until the Hampshire border, at which point your map-reading skills will be tested, for this last section of the Way has only recently been approved. An excellent feature of the **South Downs Way** is its accessibility by rail. Eastbourne, Brighton, Worthing, Chichester, Portsmouth and Winchester are all termini for lines that bisect the downs. This is therefore another good path to walk in weekend stretches. There is also a taxi-based service handling luggage delivery, safe car-parking and passenger back-up along the entire path - **White Knight** (tel. 01903 766475, please see advertisement). It provides a useful fallback for weary or injured walkers or just those who do not wish to carry a large pack.

Guides (all available from good bookshops unless stated):
South Downs Way by Paul Millmore (ISBN 1 854 10 40 71), published by Aurum Press in association with the Countryside Commission and Ordnance Survey, £9.99.
Along the South Downs Way to Winchester by the Society of Sussex Downsmen and available from the RA's National Office (1/5 Wandsworth Road, London, SW8 2XX, tel. 0171 582 6878), £5.00 (+ £1.00 p&p).
A Guide to the South Downs Way by Miles Jebb (ISBN 09 471170 4), published by Constable & Co Ltd, £10.95.
South Downs Way & The Downs Link by Kev Reynolds (ISBN 1 85284 023 4), published by Cicerone Press and also available from the publishers (2 Police Square, Milnthorpe, Cumbria, LA7 7PY, 01539 562069), £5.99 (+75p p&p).

Maps: 1:50000 Ordnance Survey Landranger Series: 185, 197, 198 and 199

Comments on the path to: **Russell Robson**, South Downs Way Officer, Sussex Downs Conservation Board, Chanctonbury House, Church St, Storrington, W. Sussex, RH20 4LT.

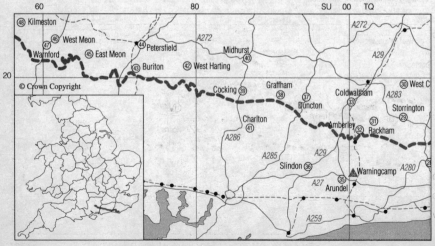

Eastbourne   1

National Grid Ref: TQ5900

🍴 🍺 Lamb Inn, The Pilot, New Inn, Dolphin

(1m) *Edelweiss Hotel, 10-12 Elms Avenue, Eastbourne, E. Sussex, BN21 3DN.*
Grades: ETB 2 Cr
Tel: **01323 732071**
Mr & Mrs Butler.
Rates fr: *£14.00-£14.00.*
Open: All Year
Beds: 1F 6D 5T 2S
Baths: 3 Ensuite, 4 Shared
🛇 🗕 🗙 📖 Ⅵ 🕯
Small friendly family-run hotel 50 yards from seafront. Comfortable rooms, guests' lounge and bar. Open all year. Excellent value for money. Ring for brochure.

(2m) *Cambridge House, 6 Cambridge Road, Eastbourne, E. Sussex, BN22 7BS.*
Family-run seaside guesthouse.
Grades: ETB 2 Cr, Comm
Tel: **01323 721100** Mr Blackman.
Rates fr: *£15.00-£15.00.*
Open: All Year (not Xmas)
Beds: 2F 3D 1T 1S
Baths: 4 Private 1 Shared
🛇 (2) 🗕 🙀 🗙 📖 Ⅵ 🕯

(1m) *Heatherdene Hotel, 26-28 Elms Avenue, Eastbourne, E. Sussex, BN21 3DN.*
Tel: **01323 723598**
Mrs Mockford.
Rates fr: *£14.50-£12.00.*
Open: All Year
Beds: 1F 3D 8T 3S
Baths: 5 Ensuite, 4 Shared
🛇 🗕 🙀 🗙 📖 🕭 Ⅵ
The Heatherdene is a friendly licensed hotel, popular with walkers on the South Downs. Comfortable rooms and good food ensure your stay will be enjoyable.

(0.5m) *Seagulls Guest House, 12 South Cliff Avenue, Eastbourne, E. Sussex, BN20 7AH.*
Large Victorian house.
Tel: **01323 737831**
Mrs Rogers.
Rates fr: *£17.50-£17.50.*
Open: All Year
Beds: 3D 2T 1S
Baths: 2 Ensuite, 2 Shared
🛇 (3) 🗲 🗕 🗙 📖 🕯

(🔺 On Path) *Eastbourne Youth Hostel, East Dean Road, Eastbourne, E. Sussex, BN20 8ES.*
Actual grid ref: TV5899
Warden: Mr M Featherstone.
Tel: **01323 721081**
Under 18: £5.00
Adults: £7.45
Family Bunk Rooms, Partially Heated, Showers, Shop
Former golf clubhouse on South Downs 450 ft above sea level with sweeping views across Eastbourne and Pevensey Bay

(1m) *Grange Guest House, 3 Grange Road, Eastbourne, E. Sussex, BN21 4EU.*
Friendly family-run guesthouse.
Grades: ETB Reg
Tel: **01323 734046** Mrs Brennan.
Rates fr: *£15.00-£15.00.*
Open: All Year
Beds: 3F 2D 2T 1S
Baths: 2Shared
🛇 🗕 🙀 🗙 📖 🕯 🗲

(1m) *Pevensey Lodge, 27 Pevensey Road, Eastbourne, E. Sussex, BN21 3HR.*
7-bedroom guesthouse near town centre.
Grades: ETB 2 Cr
Tel: **01323 649539**
Mrs Chapman.
Rates fr: *£14.00-£14.00.*
Open: Mar to Nov
Beds: 1F 2D 2T 2S
Baths: 3 Ensuite 2 Shared
🛇 (3) 🗕 🗙 📖 🕯

(2.5m) *Bay Lodge Hotel, 61 62 Royal Parade, Eastbourne, E. Sussex, BN20.*
Small seafront Victorian hotel.
Grades: ETB 3 Cr, Comm, AA 3 Q, Recomm, RAC Acclaim
Tel: **01323 732515**
Mr Hunt.
Rates fr: *£19.00-£19.00.*
Open: Mar to Oct
Beds: 5D 4T 3S
Baths: 9 Ensuite
🛇 (7) 🗕 🗙 📖 Ⅵ 🕯

Jevington   2

National Grid Ref: TQ5601

🍴 🍺 Eight Bells

(0.25m 🚗**)** *Ash Farm, Filching, Jevington, Polegate, E. Sussex, BN26 5QA.*
Actual grid ref: TQ565002
150-year-old Downland farmhouse.
Grades: ETB Reg
Tel: **01323 484474**
Mr Steer.
Rates fr: *£15.00-£16.00.*
Open: All Year
Beds: 1F 1D 1T
Baths: 2 Ensuite 1 Shared
🛇 🅿 (20) 🗲 🗕 🙀 🗙 📖 Ⅵ 🕯 🗲
Also 🛆 *£2.50 per person.*
Open: All Year 🍵 ⚌ 🗙 🗲 ♿

Wilmington   3

National Grid Ref: TQ5404

🍴 🍺 Giants Rest

(0.5m) *Fairview, Wilmington, Polegate, E. Sussex, BN26 5SQ.*
Small country cottage.
Tel: **01323 870210**
Mrs Forrest.
Rates fr: *£14.00-£14.00.*
Open: Apr to Oct
Beds: 2T
Baths: 1 Shared
🅿 (2) 🗲 🙀 📖

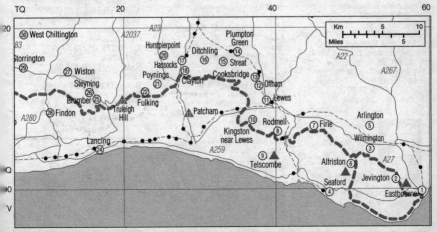

Seaford   4

National Grid Ref: TV4899

¶⊙¶ ⊲ White Lion Hotel

(2m) *Silverdale, 21 Sutton Park Road, Seaford, E. Sussex, BN25 1RH.*
Grades: AA 2 Q, Recomm
Tel: 01323 491849 Mr Cowdrey.
Rates fr: *£13.00*-**£13.00.**
Open: All Year
Beds: 4F 4D 3T 2S
Baths: 2 Ensuite, 2 Shared
� ⊞ (4) ⬜ ⊁ ✕ Ⅷ. Ⅵ 🖥
Friendly family-run licensed guesthouse with home cooking. Clean catering award. Single rooms up to group rooms sleeping 5. Some rooms with kitchen facilities.

Arlington   5

National Grid Ref: TQ5407

¶⊙¶ ⊲ Old Oak, Yew Tree

(2.5m) *Bates Green, Arlington, Polegate, E. Sussex, BN26 6SH.*
Actual grid ref: TQ553077
Tile-hung farmhouse, originally gamekeeper's cottage.
Grades: AA 5 Q, Prem Select
Tel: 01323 482039
Mrs McCutchan.
Rates fr: *£21.00*-**£30.00.**
Open: All Year (not Xmas)
Beds: 1D 2T
Baths: 3 Private
⊞ (3) ⊁ ⬜ ✕ Ⅷ. Ⅵ 🖥 ⚡

Alfriston   6

National Grid Ref: TQ5103

¶⊙¶ ⊲ George, Smugglers, Market Cross, Star, Sussex Ox, Moonrakers

(▲ 2.5m) *Alfriston Youth Hostel, Frog Firle, Alfriston, Polegate, E. Sussex, BN26 5TT.*
Actual grid ref: TQ518019
Warden: Ms W Nicholls.
Tel: 01323 870423
Under 18: £5.55
Adults: £8.25
Family Bunk Rooms, Centrally Heated, Showers, Evening Meal (6.30 pm), Shop, Television
A comfortable Sussex country house, dating from 1530, set in the Cuckmere Valley with views over the river and Litlington

South Downs Way
Safe • Flexible • Door to Door • Any Direction
Tel: 0193 766 475
Mobile: 0850 007 062

The lowest *double* rate per person is shown in *italics*.

(On Path) *Pleasant Rise Farm, Alfriston, Polegate, E. Sussex, BN26 5TN.*
Very quiet, beautiful house - lovely views.
Tel: **01323 870545**
Mrs Savage.
Rates fr: *£16.50*-**£16.50.**
Open: All Year (not Xmas)
Beds: 2D 1T 1S
Baths: 2 Private
going (8) ⊞ ⊁ ⬜ Ⅷ. Ⅵ 🖥 ⚡

(0.5m) *Winton Street Farm Cottage, Winton Street, Alfriston, Polegate, E. Sussex, BN26 5UH.*
Pretty village, historic buildings.
Tel: **01323 870118** Mrs Fitch.
Rates fr: *£13.50*-**£13.50.**
Open: All Year
Beds: 1D 1T 1S
Baths: 1 Shared
going (5) ⊞ (2) ⊁ ⬜ ⊁ Ⅷ. Ⅵ

Firle   7

National Grid Ref: TQ4607

¶⊙¶ ⊲ Ram Inn

(1.5m 🚌) *Gibraltar Farm, Firle, Lewes, E. Sussex, BN8 6NB.*
Large comfortable C17th farmhouse.
Grades: ETB Reg
Tel: **01273 858225** Mrs Yallowley.
Rates fr: *£20.00*-**£17.50.**
Open: All Year
Beds: 2D 1T
Baths: 2 Private
going ⊞ (12) ⬜ ⊁ ✕ Ⅷ. Ⅵ 🖥 ⚡
Also ▲

Rodmell   8

National Grid Ref: TQ4105

¶⊙¶ ⊲ Abergavenny Arms

(On Path) *Bankside, Rodmell, Lewes, E. Sussex, BN7 3EZ.*
Actual grid ref: TQ410198
Converted cart lodge.
Tel: **01273 477058**
Mrs Burnaby Davies.
Rates fr: *£16.50*-**£20.00.**
Open: All Year (not Xmas)
Beds: 1F
Baths: 1 Private
going ⬜ Ⅷ. Ⅵ 🖥 ⚡

(On Path) *Barn House, Rodmell, Lewes, E. Sussex, BN7 3HE.*
Converted C18th barn.
Grades: ETB 3 Cr
Tel: **01273 477865** Mr Fraser.
Rates fr: *£20.00*-**£20.00.**
Open: Mar to Feb
Beds: 4D 3T 1S
Baths: 7 Ensuite
going ⊞ (10) ⬜ ✕ Ⅷ. Ⅵ 🖥 ⚡

Telscombe   9

National Grid Ref: TQ4003

¶⊙¶ ⊲ The Jug

(▲ 1.5m) *Telscombe Youth Hostel, Bank Cottages, Telscombe, Lewes, E. Sussex, BN7 3HZ.*
Actual grid ref: TQ4003
Tel: **01273 301357**
Under 18: £5.00
Adults: £7.45
Family Bunk Rooms, Centrally Heated, Showers, Self-catering Only, Shop, No Smoking
Three 200-year-old cottages combined into one hostel, next to the Norman church in a small unspoilt village in the Sussex Downs AONB

(1.5m) *Stud Farm House, Telscombe, Lewes, E. Sussex, BN7 3HZ.*
Large C16th stud farm house.
Tel: **01273 302486** Mrs Armour.
Rates fr: *£16.50*-**£18.50.**
Open: All Year (not Xmas)
Beds: 1F 1D 2T
Baths: 1 Shared
going ⊞ (20) ⊁ ✕ Ⅷ. Ⅵ

Kingston near Lewes   10

National Grid Ref: TQ3908

¶⊙¶ ⊲ Juggs Pub, The Street

(0.5m) *Hyde Cottage, The Street, Kingston near Lewes, Lewes, E. Sussex, BN7 3PB.*
Actual grid ref: TQ393081
Oak beamed flint cottage.
Tel: **01273 472709**
Mrs Maddock.
Rates fr: *£20.00*-**£15.00.**
Open: All Year (not Xmas)
Beds: 2T 1S
Baths: 1 Ensuite 1 Shared
going ⊞ (2) ⊁ ⬜ ⊁ Ⅷ. 🖥 ⚡

(0.25m) *Nightingales, The Avenue, Kingston near Lewes, Lewes, E. Sussex, BN7 3LL.*
Actual grid ref: TQ389083
Marvellous breakfast, lovely garden, quiet.
Grades: AA 4 Q, Select
Tel: **01273 475673**
Mr Hudson.
Rates fr: *£20.00*-**£25.00.**
Open: All Year
Beds: 1D 1T
Baths: 1 Ensuite 1 Private
going ⊞ (2) ⊁ ⬜ ⊁ Ⅷ. ♿ Ⅵ 🖥 ⚡

All paths are popular: you are well-advised to book ahead

Lewes 11

National Grid Ref: TQ4110

ᵀᵒᴵ 🍺 Stewards Enquiry, Cock Inn, Halfway House, Royal Oak, Pelham Arms, Kings Head, Cock Inn, Chalk Pit, Blacksmiths Arms

(1m) *Hillside, Rotten Row, Lewes, E. Sussex, BN7 1TN.*
Victorian house on quiet road.
Tel: **01273 473120**
Miss Hollins.
Rates fr: *£20.00-£20.00.*
Open: All Year
Beds: 1D 1T 1S
Baths: 1 Ensuite, 1 Shared
🛏 (1) 🅿 (3) ⅋ 🗙 🔲 ⚡

(1.5m) *Number Four, Castle Bank, Lewes, E. Sussex, BN7 1UZ.*
Large pretty room in period cottage.
Tel: **01273 476291**
Mrs Wigglesworth.
Rates fr: *£15.00-£17.50.*
Open: All Year
Beds: 1T
Baths: Shared
🛏 ⅋ 🗙 🔲 Ⓥ ⚡

(2m) *Millers, 134 High Street, Lewes, E. Sussex, BN7 1XS.*
Actual grid ref: TQ411100
Attractive C16th town house.
Tel: **01273 475631**
Mrs Tammar.
Rates fr: *£24.00-£43.00.*
Open: All Year (not Xmas)
Beds: 2D
Baths: 2 Ensuite
⅋ 🗙 🔲

(2m) *Felix Gallery, 2 Sun Street, Lewes, E. Sussex, BN7 2QB.*
Modernised period house, town centre.
Grades: ETB Listed
Tel: **01273 472668**
Mrs Whitehead.
Rates fr: *£18.00-£23.00.*
Open: All Year
Beds: 1T 1S
Baths: 1 Shared
🛏 (8) 🗙 🔲 Ⓥ ⚡

(0.25m) *Grey Tiles, 12 Gundreda Road, Lewes, E. Sussex, BN7 1PX.*
Large detached house near downs.
Tel: **01273 471805**
Rates fr: *£17.00-£19.00.*
Open: All Year
Beds: 2T
Baths: 2 Shared
🛏 (5) 🅿 (2) ⅋ 🗙 🔲 Ⓥ ⚡

(0.5m) *Crink House, Barcombe Mills, Lewes, E. Sussex, BN8 5BJ.*
Welcoming rural family home.
Grades: ETB 3 Cr, Comm
Tel: **01273 400625** Mrs Gaydon.
Rates fr: *£20.00-£25.00.*
Open: All Year (not Xmas)
Beds: 2D 1T
Baths: 3 Private
🛏 🅿 (10) ⅋ 🗙 🔲 Ⓥ

Offham 12

National Grid Ref: TQ3912

ᵀᵒᴵ 🍺 Chalk Pit Inn, Blacksmith Arms

(1.5m 🚲) *Ousedale House, Offham, Lewes, E. Sussex, BN7 3QF.*
Victorian country house in 3.5-acre garden.
Grades: ETB 2 Cr, High Comm
Tel: **01273 478680**
Mrs Gough.
Rates fr: *£22.00-£24.00.*
Open: All Year
Beds: 1F 1D 1T
Baths: 2 Private 1 Shared
🅿 (17) ⅋ 🗙 🔲 Ⓥ 🛄 ⚡

Cooksbridge 13

National Grid Ref: TQ4013

ᵀᵒᴵ 🍺 Pump House

(2m) *Lower Tulleys Wells Farm, East Chiltington Road, Cooksbridge, Lewes, E. Sussex, BN7 3QU.*
C17th farmhouse.
Grades: ETB Listed
Tel: **01273 472622**
Mrs Thomas.
Rates fr: *£13.50-£13.50.*
Open: All Year (not Xmas)
Beds: 2T
Baths: 1 Shared
🅿 (4) ⅋ 🗙 🔲 Ⓥ

Plumpton Green 14

National Grid Ref: TQ3616

ᵀᵒᴵ 🍺 Half Moon

(3m 🚲) *Farthings, Station Road, Plumpton Green, Lewes, E. Sussex, BN7 3BY.*
Actual grid ref: TQ365172
Grades: ETB Highly Comm
Tel: **01273 890415**
Mrs Baker.
Rates fr: *£18.00-£20.00.*
Open: All Year (not Xmas)
Beds: 1F 1D 1T
Baths: 1 Private 1Shared
🛏 🅿 (Yes) ⅋ 🗙 🗙 🔲 Ⓥ 🛄 ⚡

Streat 15

National Grid Ref: TQ3515

ᵀᵒᴵ 🍺 Half Moon (Streat)

(1.5m 🚲) *North Acres, Streat, Hassocks, E. Sussex, BN6 8RX.*
Large, comfortable Victorian house.
Tel: **01273 890278**
Mr & Mrs Eastwood.
Rates fr: *£15.00-£15.00.*
Open: All Year (not Xmas)
Beds: 1F 2T
Baths: 1 Shared
🛏 🅿 ⅋ 🗙 🔲 🛄 ⚡

Ditchling 16

National Grid Ref: TQ3215

ᵀᵒᴵ 🍺 White Horse

(1.75m) *Longcroft, Beacon Road, Ditchling, Hassocks, West Sussex, BN6 8UZ.*
Beautiful South Downs country house.
Tel: **01273 842740**
Mr & Mrs Scull.
Rates fr: *£19.50-£25.00.*
Open: All Year
Beds: 2D 1T
Baths: 2 Ensuite 1 Private
🛏 🅿 ⅋ 🗙 🔲 Ⓥ

Hassocks 17

National Grid Ref: TQ3015

ᵀᵒᴵ 🍺 Greyhound, Thatched Inn

(1.5m 🚲) *26 Kymer Gardens, Hassocks, W. Sussex, BN6 8QZ.*
Quiet, friendly, views to Downs.
Grades: ETB Reg
Tel: **01273 844537**
Mrs Davies.
Rates fr: *£12.00-£16.00.*
Open: All Year (not Xmas)
Beds: 1F 1D
Baths: 1 Shared
🛏 ⅋ 🔲 Ⓥ ⚡

Clayton 18

National Grid Ref: TQ3014

(0.25m) *Dower Cottage, Underhill Lane, Clayton, Hassocks, W. Sussex, BN6 9PL.*
Tel: **01273 843363**
Mrs Bailey.
Rates fr: *£17.50-£20.00.*
Open: All Year
Beds: 1F 3D 1S
Baths: 2 Private 1 Shared
🛏 🅿 (8) ⅋ 🗙 🗙 🔲 Ⓥ 🛄 ⚡
Lovely country house with large attractive rooms, all with wonderful views over Sussex Weald. Library for guests, garage for bikes, stables for horses

Patcham 19

National Grid Ref: TQ3008

(🔺 3.5m) *Brighton Youth Hostel, Patcham Place, London Road, Patcham, Brighton, E. Sussex, BN1 8YD.*
Actual grid ref: TQ3008
Warden: Mr G Holdsworth/Ms V Schotman.
Tel: **01273 556196**
Under 18: £5.00
Adults: £7.45
Family Bunk Rooms, Centrally Heated, Showers, Cafeteria, Shop, Security Lockers, Games Room, Television, Parking
Splendid old country house with Queen Anne front, on the edge of Brighton and the South Downs

Hurstpierpoint 20

National Grid Ref: TQ2816

¶●¶ ◐ The Hassocks, New Inn

(2.5m) *Wickham Place, Wickham Drive, Hurstpierpoint, Hassocks, W. Sussex, BN6 9AP.*
Tel: **01273 832172**
Mrs Moore.
Rates fr: *£18.50-£22.00.*
Open: All Year (not Xmas)
Beds: 1D 2T
Baths: 1 Shared
⛵ ⚟ (5) ⅙⌷≒↟⊞.
For a pleasant relaxed stay, our home is ideally situated in a pretty village. All rooms have hand basins. There is a separate shower room.

Poynings 21

National Grid Ref: TQ2612

¶●¶ ◐ Royal Oak

(0.25m) *Manor Farm, Poynings, Brighton, E. Sussex, BN45 7AG.*
Comfortable farmhouse on working farm.
Grades: ETB 1 Cr
Tel: **01273 857371**
Mrs Revell.
Rates fr: *£19.00-£25.00.*
Open: Mar to Dec
Beds: 1D 2T
Baths: 2 Shared
⛵ ⚟ ⅙⌷✕⊞.≜⊘

Fulking 22

National Grid Ref: TQ2411

¶●¶ ◐ Shepherd and Dog

(1.75m) *Downers Vineyard, Clappers Lane, Fulking, Henfield, W. Sussex, BN5 9NH.*
Actual grid ref: TQ247128
Panoramic view of South Downs.
Grades: ETB Listed, Approv
Tel: **01273 857484**
Mrs Downer.
Rates fr: *£16.50-£19.00.*
Open: All Year (not Xmas)
Beds: 1D 1T
Baths: 2 Shared
⚟ (6) ⌷≒⊞.⊘

Truleigh Hill 23

National Grid Ref: TQ2210

(▲ On Path) *Truleigh Hill Youth Hostel, Tottington Barn, Truleigh Hill, Shoreham-by-Sea, W. Sussex, BN43 5FB.*
Actual grid ref: TQ2210
Warden: Mr A Harris.
Tel: **01903 813419**
Under 18: £5.55 **Adults:** £8.25
Family Bunk Rooms, Centrally Heated, Showers, Evening Meal (6.30 pm), Shop, Television
Modern hostel in the Sussex Downs AONB with conservation project and old dew pond in grounds

---

The lowest *double* rate per person is shown in *italics.*

Lancing 24

National Grid Ref: TQ1804

¶●¶ ◐ Three Horseshoes, The Sussex

(3m) *The Moorings, 71 Brighton Road, Lancing, W. Sussex, BN15 8RB.*
1930's house on seafront.
Tel: **01903 755944** Mr Stuart.
Rates fr: *£14.00-£15.00.*
Open: All Year
Beds: 1F 1D 1T 1S
Baths: 1 Shared
⛵ ⚟ ⌷↟⊞.⊻≜⊘

Bramber 25

National Grid Ref: TQ1810

¶●¶ ◐ The Castle Hotel

(1m) *Castle Hotel, The Street, Bramber, Steyning, W. Sussex, BN44 3WE.*
Tel: **01903 812102**
Mr & Mrs Mitchell.
Rates fr: *£17.00-£22.00.*
Open: All Year
Beds: 2F 4D 2T
Baths: 4 Private 2 Shared
⛵ ⚟ (30) ⅙⌷↟✕⊞.≜⊘

Steyning 26

National Grid Ref: TQ1711

(0.75m) *5 Coxham Lane, Steyning, W. Sussex, BN44 3LG.*
Comfortable house in quiet lane.
Tel: **01903 812286** Mrs Morrow.
Rates fr: *£14.00-£14.00.*
Open: All Year (not Xmas)
Beds: 2T 1S
Baths: 1Shared
⚟ (4) ⌷↟✕⊞.⊻≜⊘

(1m) *Milestones, 25 High Street, Steyning, W. Sussex, BN44 3YE.*
Location edge of South Downs.
Tel: **01903 812338** Mrs Wood.
Rates fr: *£18.50.*
Open: All Year (not Xmas)
Beds: 1T
Baths: 1 Private
⛵ (12) ⅙⌷✕⊞.⊻≜

All rates are subject to alteration at the owners' discretion.

Wiston 27

National Grid Ref: TQ1414

¶●¶ ◐ Star Inn

(1m ☎) *Buncton Manor Farm, Steyning Road, Wiston, Steyning, W. Sussex, BN44 3DD.*
Actual grid ref: TQ146136
C15th moated farmhouse on working farm.
Grades: ETB Listed
Tel: **01903 812736**
Mrs Rowland.
Rates fr: *£17.00-£20.00.*
Open: All Year
Beds: 1F 1T
Baths: 1 Shared
⛵ ⚟ (6) ⅙⌷✕⊞.⊻≜⊘
Also ▲ *£3.00 per tent.*
Open: All Year⊤⛵

Findon 28

National Grid Ref: TQ1208

¶●¶ ◐ Village House Hotel, The Zoo

(2m ☎) *Findon Tower, Cross Lane, Findon, Worthing, W. Sussex, BN14 0UG.*
Actual grid ref: TQ123083
Elegant Edwardian country house.
Grades: ETB 2 Cr, Comm
Tel: **01903 873870**
Mr & Mrs Smith.
Rates fr: *£17.50-£20.00.*
Open: All Year (not Xmas)
Beds: 2D 1T
Baths: 3 Private
⛵ ⚟ (10) ⅙⌷↟⊞.⊻≜⊘

(2.5m) *Racehorse Cottage, Nepcote, Findon, Worthing, W. Sussex, BN14 0SN.*
Actual grid ref: TQ128083
Comfortable cottage under Cissbury Ring.
Tel: **01903 873783**
Mr Lloyd.
Rates fr: *£15.00-£20.00.*
Open: All Year (not Xmas)
Beds: 2T
Baths: 2 Private
⛵ (5) ⚟ (2) ⌷↟⊞.⊘

Storrington 29

National Grid Ref: TQ0814

¶●¶ ◐ Franklands Arms, White Horse, The Square

(2m ☎) *Heathcroft, Merrywood Lane, Storrington, Pulborough, W. Sussex, RH20 3HD.*
Actual grid ref: TQ103156
Rural, pleasant family house.
Tel: **01903 744814**
Mrs Churcher.
Rates fr: *£15.00-£15.00.*
Open: All Year (not Xmas)
Beds: 1D 1S
Baths: 2 Shared
⛵ ⚟ (4) ⅙⌷↟⊞.⊘

(1.5m 🚶) *Greenacres Farm, Washington Road, Storrington, Pulborough, W. Sussex, RH20 4AF.* Comfortable modern country house.
Tel: **01903 742538** Ms Greenyer.
Rates fr: £22.00-£25.00.
Open: All Year
Beds: 3F 2D 2T
Baths: 7 Ensuite
⛵🅿✂🗂🟆✕🟔Ⓥ♟✦
Also ⛺ £2.50 per tent.
Open: All Year 🟆🔲♨✕✦⛷

(2.25m 🚶) *Oakfield House, Merrywood Lane, Thakeham, Storrington, Pulborough, W. Sussex, RH20 3HD.*
Actual grid ref: TQ1015
Modern, comfortable, friendly, delightful house.
Tel: **01903 740843** Mrs Arter.
Rates fr: £17.50-£16.50.
Open: All Year (not Xmas)
Beds: 1D 1S
Baths: 2 Shared
🅿(2)✂🟆♟✦

West Chiltington 30

National Grid Ref: TQ0918

🟆🟥 Queens Head, Elephant & Castle

(3m 🚶) *New House Farm, Broadford Bridge Road, West Chiltington, Pulborough, W. Sussex, RH20 2LA.*
C15th oak-beamed farmhouse.
Grades: ETB 2 Cr, Comm, AA 3 Q
Tel: **01798 812215** Mrs Steele.
Rates fr: £20.00-£25.00.
Open: All Year (not Xmas)
Beds: 1D 2T
Baths: 2 Ensuite 1 Private
⛵(10)🅿(6)🗂🟆🟔Ⓥ✦

Rackham 31

National Grid Ref: TQ0413

🟆🟥 The Sportsman

(0.25m) *Sparright Farm, Rackham, Pulborough, W. Sussex, RH20 2EY.*
C17th, peacefully situated, homely.
Grades: ETB Listed
Tel: **01798 872132** Mrs West.
Rates fr: £15.00-£16.00.
Open: All Year (not Xmas)
Beds: 1F 1D
Baths: 2 Shared
⛵(2)🗂🟆🟔

Pay B&Bs by cash or cheque and be prepared to pay up front.

Amberley 32

National Grid Ref: TQ0313

🟆🟥 Black Horse, Sportsman

(1m) *Bacons, Amberley, Arundel, W. Sussex, BN18 9NJ.*
Pretty old cottage.
Tel: **01798 831234** Mrs Jollands.
Rates fr: £16.00-£16.00.
Open: All Year (not Xmas)
Beds: 2T
Baths: 1 Shared
⛵🟔

Coldwaltham 33

National Grid Ref: TQ0216

🟆🟥 Labouring Man

(3m) *Barn Owls, London Road, Coldwaltham, Pulborough, W. Sussex, RH20 1LR.*
Victorian farmhouse converted to restaurant.
Tel: **01798 872498**
Mrs Hellenberg.
Rates fr: £23.00-£33.00.
Open: All Year **Beds:** 2D 1T
🅿(17)🗂🟆✕🟔Ⓥ

Warningcamp 34

National Grid Ref: TQ0307

🟆🟥 Swan

(⛺ 3.5m) *Arundel Youth Hostel, Warningcamp, Arundel, W. Sussex, BN18 9QY.*
Actual grid ref: TQ0307
Warden: Mr M Hiles.
Tel: **01903 882204**
Under 18: £5.00 **Adults:** £7.45
Family Bunk Rooms, Partially Heated, Showers, Evening Meal (7.00 pm), Shop, Television, Games Room
Georgian building 1.5 miles from the ancient town of Arundel, dominated by its castle and the Sussex Downs

Arundel 35

National Grid Ref: TQ0107

🟆🟥 The White Hart, Swan

(3m) *Portreeves Acre, The Causeway, Arundel, W. Sussex, BN18 9JL.*
Actual grid ref: TQ0207
Modern house in own grounds.
Tel: **01903 883277** Mr Rogers.
Rates fr: £16.00-£18.00.
Open: All Year (not Xmas)
Beds: 2D 1T
Baths: 3 Private
⛵(8)🅿(7)🗂🟆🟔Ⓥ✦

(3m) *Bridge House, 18 Queen Street, Arundel, W. Sussex, BN18 9JG.*
Actual grid ref: TQ020069
C18th family-run guesthouse.
Grades: ETB 3 Cr, AA 2 Q

Tel: **01903 882142** Mr Hutchinson.
Rates fr: £15.00-£20.00.
Open: All Year (not Xmas)
Beds: 7F 8D 2T 2S
Baths: 15 Ensuite 2 Shared
⛵🅿(10)🗂🟆✕🟔🟔Ⓥ✦

Slindon 36

National Grid Ref: SU9608

(2.75m 🚶) *Mill Lane House, Mill Lane, Slindon, Arundel, W. Sussex, BN18 0RP.*
Actual grid ref: SU964084
C18th house in National Trust village.
Grades: ETB 2 Cr
Tel: **01243 814440** Mrs Fuente.
Rates fr: £18.00-£23.50.
Open: All Year
Beds: 1F 2D 3T 1S
Baths: 7 Ensuite
⛵🅿(10)🗂🟆✕🟔🟔Ⓥ♟✦

Duncton 37

National Grid Ref: SU9517

🟆🟥 Cricketers

(1.5m) *Drifters, Duncton, Petworth, W. Sussex, GU28 0JZ.*
Lovely friendly modern country house.
Tel: **01798 342706** Mrs Folkes.
Rates fr: £16.00-£20.00.
Open: All Year
Beds: 1D 2T
Baths: 1 Ensuite 1 Private
🅿✂🗂✕🟔♟✦

Graffham 38

National Grid Ref: SU9217

🟆🟥 White Horse

(On Path 🚶) *Eastwood Farm, Graffham, Petworth, W. Sussex, GU28 0QF.*
Actual grid ref: SU940168
Large country house, lovely surroundings.
Tel: **01798 867317** Mrs Allen.
Rates fr: £19.00-£19.00.
Open: All Year
Beds: 1D 1T 2S
Baths: 1 Private 1 Shared
⛵(5)🅿(6)🗂🟔♟✦

Cocking 39

National Grid Ref: SU8717

🟆🟥 Bluebell Inn

(0.25m) *Cocking Village Tea Garden, Chichester Road, Cocking, Midhurst, W. Sussex, GU29 0HN.*
1815 house with tea garden.
Tel: **01730 813336** Mrs Thomas.
Rates fr: £16.00-£20.00.
Open: All Year (not Xmas)
Beds: 2D 1T
Baths: 1 Shared
⛵🅿(5)🟆🟔Ⓥ♟✦

Midhurst 40

National Grid Ref: SU8821

⏣ The Bricklayers Arms, The Swan

(3m) *The Crown Inn, Edinburgh Square, Midhurst, W. Sussex, GU29 9NL.*
Actual grid ref: SU887215
C16th free house.
Grades: ETB Listed
Tel: **01730 813462** Mr Stevens.
Rates fr: *£12.50-£15.00.*
Open: All Year
Beds: 1D 1T 1S
Baths: 1 Shared
⿴⿻⿴⿻⿴⿻⿴⿻

Charlton 41

National Grid Ref: SU8812

⏣ Fox Goes Free

(On Path) *The Charlton Fox, Charlton, Chichester, W. Sussex, PO18 0HU.*
Lovely C16th South Downs inn.
Tel: **01243 811461** Mr Dudeney.
Rates fr: *£15.00-£30.00.*
Open: All Year
Beds: 1F 3D 1T
Baths: 3 Ensuite 2 Shared
⿴⿻(1) ⿴⿻(6) ⿴⿻⿴⿻⿴⿻

West Harting 42

National Grid Ref: SU7821

⏣ The Ship

(1.75m) *3 Quebec, West Harting, Petersfield, Hants, GU31 5PG.*
Actual grid ref: SU780214
Peaceful secluded private country house.
Grades: ETB Reg
Tel: **01730 825386** Mrs Stevens.
Rates fr: *£15.00-£17.00.*
Open: All Year
Beds: 1F 1S
Baths: 1 Ensuite, 1 Shared
⿴⿻(2) ⿴⿻⿴⿻⿴⿻

Buriton 43

National Grid Ref: SU7320

⏣ The Five Bells, The Master Robert

(0.5m) *The Old Hop Kiln, Bones Lane, Buriton, Petersfield, Hants, GU31 5SE.*
In centre of picturesque village.
Tel: **01730 266822** Mrs Beeson.
Rates fr: *£20.00-£20.00.*
Open: All Year (not Xmas)
Beds: 2T 1S
Baths: 1 Private 1 Shared
⿴⿻(3) ⿴⿻⿴⿻⿴⿻

Petersfield 44

National Grid Ref: SU7423

⏣ Five Bells, Master Robert, Good Intent, Royal Oak

(4m) *Heath Farmhouse, Sussex Road, Petersfield, Hants, GU31 4HU.*
Actual grid ref: SU7522
Pretty Georgian farmhouse near town.
Grades: ETB 2 Cr, Comm
Tel: **01730 264709** Mrs Scurfield.
Rates fr: *£15.00-£16.00.*
Open: All Year (not Xmas)
Beds: 1D 1T
Baths: 1 Private 1 Shared
⿴⿻(4) ⿴⿻⿴⿻

(0.25m) *Pilmead House, North Lane, Petersfield, Hants, GU31 5RS.*
Victorian family house.
Tel: **01730 266795** Mrs Moss.
Rates fr: *£38.00-£20.00.*
Open: All Year (not Xmas)
Beds: 1D 1T **Baths:** 2 Ensuite
⿴⿻(2) ⿴⿻⿴⿻⿴⿻⿴⿻⿴⿻

(4m) *Riverside Guest House, 4 The Causeway, Petersfield, Hants, GU31 4JS.*
Modern house, overlooking open countryside. **Grades:** ETB Listed
Tel: **01730 261246** Mrs Andrews.
Rates fr: *£14.00-£16.00.*
Open: All Year
Beds: 1F 1D 1T 2S
Baths: 1 Private 1 Shared
⿴⿻(5) ⿴⿻⿴⿻⿴⿻

East Meon 45

National Grid Ref: SU6822

⏣ The Isaac Walton, George & Falcon

(On Path) *Coombe Cross House & Stables, Coombe Road, East Meon, Petersfield, Hants, GU32 1HQ.*
Georgian country house with superb views.
Grades: ETB Listed
Tel: **01730 823298** Mrs Bulmer.
Rates fr: *£20.00-£20.00.*
Open: All Year (not Xmas)
Beds: 1D 2T
Baths: 2 Private 1 Shared
⿴⿻(8) ⿴⿻(12) ⿴⿻⿴⿻⿴⿻⿴⿻⿴⿻

(0.75m) *Drayton Cottage, East Meon, Petersfield, Hants, GU32 1PW.*
Period cottage overlooking river.
Tel: **01730 823472** Mrs Rockett.
Rates fr: *£18.00-£20.00.*
Open: All Year
Beds: 1T 1D
Baths: 2 Shared
⿴⿻(9) ⿴⿻(3) ⿴⿻⿴⿻⿴⿻⿴⿻

West Meon 46

National Grid Ref: SU6424

⏣ Thomas Lord

(2.25m) *Brocklands Farm, West Meon, Petersfield, Hants, GU32 1JG.*
Actual grid ref: SU639237
Modern comfortable farmhouse.
Grades: ETB Listed, Comm
Tel: **01730 829228** Mrs Wilson.
Rates fr: *£17.00-£17.00.*
Open: All Year (not Xmas)
Beds: 2D 1T
Baths: 2 Shared
⿴⿻(6) ⿴⿻⿴⿻⿴⿻⿴⿻

Warnford 47

National Grid Ref: SU6223

⏣ The George & Falcon

(1m) *Hayden Barn Cottage, Warnford, Southampton, Hants, SO32 3LF.*
Actual grid ref: SU634228
Tel: **01730 829454**
Mrs Broadbent.
Rates fr: *£18.50-£18.50.*
Open: All Year (not Xmas)
Beds: 2T 1S
Baths: 1 Ensuite 1 Private 1 Shared
⿴⿻(5) ⿴⿻⿴⿻⿴⿻⿴⿻

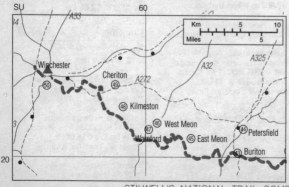

Kilmeston 48

National Grid Ref: SU5925

(1.75m 🚌) *Dean Farm, Kilmeston, Alresford, Hants, SO24 0NL.*
Comfortable C18th farmhouse in peaceful surroundings.
Grades: ETB Listed
Tel: 01962 771286 Mrs Warr.
Rates fr: *£17.00-£17.00.*
Open: All Year (not Xmas)
Beds: 3D
Baths: 1 Shared
🛏 (10) 🅿 🏖 ❑ 🎟 Ⅴ 🗡 ⚡

Cheriton 49

National Grid Ref: SU5828

🍴 🍺 Flowerpot, Tichborne Arms, Millburys

(2.5m) *Brandy Lea, Cheriton, Alresford, Hants, SO24 0QQ.*
Friendly semi-detached next to pub.
Tel: 01962 771534 Mrs Hoskings.
Rates fr: *£13.50-£13.50.*
Open: All Year
Beds: 1T
Baths: 1 Private
🛏 🅿 ❑ 🎟 🎟

(0.25m) *Flower Pots Inn, Cheriton, Alresford, Hants, SO24 0QQ.*
Converted byre next to inn/brew-house.
Tel: 01962 771318
Rates fr: *£22.00-£26.00.*
Open: All Year (not Xmas)
Beds: 2D 3T
Baths: 5 Ensuite
🅿 ❑ 🎟 🎟

All rooms full and
nowhere else to stay?
Ask the owner if
there's anywhere
nearby

Winchester 50

National Grid Ref: SU4829

🍴 🍺 Green Man, St Cross Hotel (Cellar Bar), Wykeham Arms, Golden Lion, The Roebuck, The Chimney's, The Jolly Farmer

(1.5m) *Sycamores, 4 Bereweeke Close, Winchester, Hants, SO22 6AR.*
Actual grid ref: SU472304
Detached family house, peaceful residential area.
Grades: ETB Listed, Comm
Tel: 01962 867242
Mrs Edwards.
Rates fr: *£16.00.*
Open: All Year
Beds: 2D 1T **Baths:** 3 Private
🛏 (10) 🅿 (3) 🏖 ❑ 🎟

(1m 🚌) *Dellbrook, Hubert Road, St Cross, Winchester, Hants, SO23 9RG.*
Actual grid ref: SU474278
Spacious welcoming Edwardian family home.
Grades: ETB 2 Cr, Comm
Tel: 01962 865093
Mrs Leonard.
Rates fr: *£18.00-£25.00.*
Open: All Year
Baths: 2 Ensuite, 1 Shared
🛏 🅿 (4) ❑ 🎟 ✕ 🎟 Ⅴ ⚡

(1m) *5 Ranelagh Road, Winchester, Hants, SO23 9TA.*
Actual grid ref: SU476287
Charming Victorian villa.
Grades: ETB 2 Cr, Comm
Tel: 01962 869555 Mr Farrell.
Rates fr: *£15.00-£15.00.*
Open: All Year (not Xmas)
Beds: 1F 1D 1T 1S
Baths: 2 Private 2 Shared
🛏 (5) 🅿 (1) ❑ 🎟 🗡 ⚡

(🔺 On Path) *Winchester Youth Hostel, The City Mill, 1 Water Lane, Winchester, Hants, SO23 8EJ.*
Warden: Mr L Garvin.
Tel: 01962 853723
Under 18: £5.00 **Adults:** £7.45
Family Bunk Rooms, Partially Heated, Showers, Evening Meal (7.00), No Smoking

Charming C18th watermill (National Trust) straddling the River Itchen at the East end of King Alfred's capital

(0.1m 🚌) *Brambles, Northbrook Avenue, Winchester, Hants, SO23 8JW.*
Actual grid ref: SU492294
Delightful, self contained studio flat.
Grades: ETB Listed, High Comm
Tel: 01962 856387 Mrs Meadows.
Rates fr: *£18.00-£25.00.*
Open: All Year
Beds: 1F
Baths: 1 Private
🛏 🅿 (2) 🏖 ❑ 🎟 Ⅴ 🗡 ⚡

(3m 🚌) *The Lilacs, 1 Harestock Close, Andover Road North, Winchester, Hants, SO22 6NP.*
Actual grid ref: SU468321
Georgian-style family home, clean accommodation.
Grades: ETB Reg
Tel: 01962 884122 Mrs Pell.
Rates fr: *£15.00-£18.00.*
Open: All Year (not Xmas)
Beds: 1F 1D 1T
Baths: 1 Private 1 Shared
🛏 🅿 (2) 🏖 ❑ 🎟 🎟 Ⅴ 🗡 ⚡

(1m) *32 Hyde Street, Winchester, Hants, SO23 7DX.*
Actual grid ref: SU481301
Attractive C18th town house.
Grades: ETB 1 Cr
Tel: 01962 851621 Mrs Tisdall.
Rates fr: *£14.00-£17.00.*
Open: All Year (not Xmas)
Beds: 1F 1D
Baths: 1 Shared
🛏 (3) 🏖 ❑ 🎟

(1m) *85 Christchurch Road, Winchester, Hants, SO23 9QY.*
Actual grid ref: SU473282
Comfortable detached Victorian family house.
Grades: ETB 2 Cr, Comm
Tel: 01962 868661
Mrs Fetherston Dilke.
Rates fr: *£18.00-£18.00.*
Open: All Year (not Xmas)
Beds: 1D 1T 1S
Baths: 1 Ensuite 2 Shared
🛏 🅿 (3) 🏖 ❑ 🎟 ⚡

Southern Upland Way

Of all the paths in this book, the **Southern Upland Way** is the most remote, rivalling the northernmost parts of the **Pennine Way**, the Fermanagh and Derry sections of the **Ulster Way** and the Rhinogs stretch of the **Cambrian Way**. The walking, especially in the western half of this coast-to-coast route, is certainly as tough - if not tougher - providing a challenge that brings its own particular rewards. The path runs for 202 miles through Scottish Border country, from the seaside village of Portpatrick, over the exposed moorland of the West, across the Nithsdale Valley and then past the smoother, more rounded hills and moors of the East, finishing on the cliffs at Cockburnspath in Berwickshire. It is a path for fit, experienced fell-walkers, fully equipped for rough weather, boggy conditions and mist. A quick glance at the map here will show the paucity of accommodation along the route. Some judicious planning, however, renders the walk quite manageable without resorting to canvas or bothy, although neither should be ruled out in the event of an emergency.

Guides (available from all good bookshops)
The Southern Upland Way (maps & book set) by Roger Smith (ISBN 0 11495 17 05), published by HMSO, £17.50

A Guide to the Southern Upland Way by David Williams (ISBN 09 467910 X), published by Constable & Co Ltd, £8.95

Maps: Ordnance Survey 1:50,000 Landranger series: 67, 73, 76, 77, 78, 79 and 82.

Portpatrick   1

National Grid Ref: NW9954

🍴 🍺 The Crown Hotel, The Crown Golf Hotel, The Downshire Hotel, The Mount Stewart Hotel

(On Path 🚐) *Melvin Lodge Guest House, South Crescent, Portpatrick, Stranraer, Wigtownshire, DG9 8LE.*
Large detached Victorian private villa.
Grades: STB 2 Cr, Comm
Tel: 01776 810238
Mr & Mrs Pinder.
Rates fr: *£17.00*-£18.00.

Open: All Year (not Xmas)
Beds: 3F 3D 2T 2S
Baths: 4 Ensuite, 2 Shared
🛇 🅿 (10) ⊬ ⬜ 🏲 ✕ 🛏 📶 Ⅵ ⓘ ⚡

(On Path) *Blinkbonnie Guest House, Portpatrick, Stranraer, Wigtownshire, DG9 8LG.*
Actual grid ref: NX001543
Modern coastal villa, panoramic views.
Grades: STB 3 Cr, Comm, AA 3 Q, Recomm
Tel: **01776 810282** Mrs Robinson.
Rates fr: *£17.00*-£17.00.
Open: All Year **Beds:** 4D 2T
Baths: 3 Private 1 Shared
🛇 🅿 (10) ⊬ ⬜ ✕ 🛏 & Ⅵ ⓘ ⚡

(On Path) *Ard Choille Guest House, 1 Blair Terrace, Portpatrick, Stranraer, Wigtownshire, DG9 8SY.*
Comfortable, family run guesthouse.
Tel: **01776 810313** Mrs Black.
Rates fr: *£15.00*-£15.00.
Open: All Year **Beds:** 1F 1D 1T 1S
Baths: 1 Ensuite
🛇 🅿 (2) ⬜ 🏲 ✕ 🛏 Ⅵ ⓘ ⚡

> The lowest *double* rate per person is shown in *italics*.

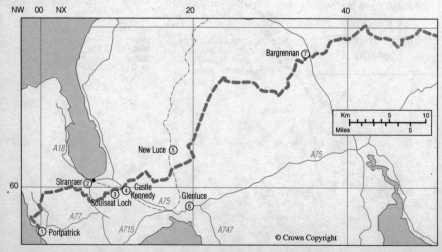

(0.25m 🚌) **Bendochy,** *Heugh Road, Portpatrick, Stranraer, Wigtownshire, DG9 8TD.*
Large private house.
Grades: STB Listed
Tel: **01776 810318** Mrs Campbell.
Rates fr: *£17.00-£19.00.*
Open: All Year (not Xmas)
Beds: 1F 2D 1T **Baths:** 3 Shared
🛇 (1) 🅿 (6) 🍴 ⬛ 🛄 ⚡

Stranraer 2

National Grid Ref: NX0560

🍴 ◻ L'Aperitif

(1m) **Fernlea Guest House,** *Lewis Street, Stranraer, Wigtownshire, DG9 7AQ.*
Comfortable, friendly guesthouse.
Close transport.
Grades: STB 3 Cr, Comm
Tel: **01776 703037** Mrs Spiers.
Rates fr: *£15.00-£20.00.*
Open: All Year (not Xmas)
Beds: 2D 2T
Baths: 2 Private 2 Shared
🛇 (10) 🅿 (5) ⚡ ◻ ✕ ⬛ Ⓥ 🛄

(1m) **Auld Ayre,** *4 Park Lane, Stranraer, Wigtownshire, DG9 0DS.*
Private house.
Grades: STB 3 Cr, Comm
Tel: **01776 704500** Mrs McDonald.
Rates fr: *£17.00-£20.00.*
Open: All Year (not Xmas)
Beds: 1F 1D 1T
Baths: 3 Ensuite
🛇 🅿 (3) ◻ 🍴 ✕ ⬛ Ⓥ 🛄

(1.5m) **Jan Da Mar,** *1 Ivy Place, London Road, Stranraer, Wigtownshire, DG9 8ER.*
Victorian town house.
Grades: STB 2 Cr, Comm
Tel: **01776 706194** Mrs Bewley.
Rates fr: *£13.00-£15.00.*
Open: All Year **Beds:** 3F 3T 2S
Baths: 2 Ensuite 2 Shared
🛇 ◻ 🍴 ⬛ Ⓥ 🛄

(5m) **2 Birnam Place,** *Station Street, Stranraer, Wigtownshire, DG9 7HN.*
Tel: **01776 703935** Mrs Jameson.
Rates fr: *£17.00-£14.00.*
Open: All Year **Beds:** 1F 1D 1T 1S
Baths: 2 Ensuite 1 Shared
🛇 🅿 (4) ◻ 🍴 ✕ ⬛ 🛄 ⚡

Soulseat Loch 3

National Grid Ref: NX1059

(0.5m 🚌) **Meadowsweet,** *Soulseat Loch, Castle Kennedy, Stranraer, Wigtownshire, DG9.*
Large house on loch.
Tel: **01776 820288** Mrs McKinlay.
Rates fr: *£16.00-£16.00.*
Open: All Year (not Xmas)
Beds: 1F 1D 1T 1S
Baths: 1 Shared
🛇 (10) 🅿 (5) ⚡ ✕ Ⓥ 🛄 ⚡

The *lowest* **single**
rate *is shown in* **bold.**

Castle Kennedy 4

National Grid Ref: NX1160

🍴 ◻ Eynhallow Hotel

(On Path) **Serendipity Cottage,** *(Old Railway Station), Castle Kennedy, Stranraer, Wigtownshire, DG9 8RY.*
Former station-master's house.
Tel: **01776 705206**
Mrs Tait.
Rates fr: *£12.50-£12.50.*
Open: Easter to Sep
Beds: 1D 1T
Baths: 1 Private 1 Shared
🛇 🅿 ◻ 🍴 ⬛ Ⓥ ⚡

New Luce 5

National Grid Ref: NX1764

🍴 ◻ Kenmuir Arms

(1m) **Kenmuir Arms Hotel,** *New Luce, Newton Stewart, Wigtownshire, DG8 0AJ.*
Small, comfortable country inn.
Tel: **01581 600218**
Mrs Green.
Rates fr: *£18.00-£18.00.*
Open: All Year (not Xmas)
Beds: 1F 1D 2T
Baths: 1 Shared
🛇 🅿 ◻ 🍴 ✕ ⬛ Ⓥ 🛄 ⚡
Also ⛺ *£2.00 per tent.*
Open: All Year (not Xmas)

Glenluce 6

National Grid Ref: NX1957

⓪ ◨ Kelvin Hotel, Glen Bay Hotel, Glenby House

(3.5m ⌂) Kelvin House Hotel, 53 Main Street, Glenluce, Newton Stewart, Wigtownshire, DG8 0PP.
Grades: STB 3 Cr, Comm
Tel: 01581 300303 Mr Holmes.
Rates fr: £20.00-£25.00.
Open: All Year
Beds: 3F 1D 1T
Baths: 4 Ensuite 1 Shared
⓫ ☐ ◨ ⋔ ✕ ▦ Ⓥ ▮ ✦
Comfortable C19th hotel in tranquil village. Noted for food and hospitality. Close to five golf courses, and fishing. Ideal base for touring the area.

(2m ⌂) Torwood House Hotel, Glenluce, Newton Stewart, Wigtownshire, DG8 0PB.
Outdoor activity specialists, 40-acre grounds.
Grades: STB Listed
Tel: 01581 300469
Mr Canning.
Rates fr: £20.00-£20.00.
Open: All Year
Beds: 3F 2D 4T 1S
Baths: 4 Shared
⓫ ☐ (30) ⤢ ☐ ⋔ ✕ ▦ Ⓥ ▮ ✦

(5m ⌂) Grayhill Farm, Glenluce, Newton Stewart, Wigtownshire, DG8 0NS.
Actual grid ref: NX198571
Working beef farm, very comfortable.
Grades: STB Listed, Comm
Tel: 01581 300400
Mrs Marshall.
Rates fr: £14.00-£15.00.
Open: Easter to Oct
Beds: 1D 1T
Baths: 1 Shared
☐ (3) ☐ ▦ ▮ ✦

(3m) Bankfield Farm, Glenluce, Newton Stewart, Wigtownshire, DG8 0JF.
Large, friendly working farm.
Grades: STB 1 Cr, Comm
Tel: 01581 300281
Mrs Stewart.
Rates fr: £16.00-£15.00.
Open: Easter to Oct
Beds: 1F 1D 1T
Baths: 2 Ensuite 1 Shared
⓫ ☐ ▦ ▮ ✦

All paths are popular: you are well-advised to book ahead

(3m ⌂) Belgrano, 81 Main Street, Glenluce, Newton Stewart, Wigtownshire, DG8 0PP.
Very large modernised town house.
Tel: 01581 300554 Mr Walker.
Rates fr: £16.00-£18.00.
Open: All Year
Beds: 2F 1D 1T 1S
Baths: 2 Ensuite 1 Shared
⓫ ☐ (4) ☐ ⋔ ▦ ▮ ✦

Bargrennan 7

National Grid Ref: NX3576

⓪ ◨ House O'Hill Hotel

(On Path) House O'Hill Hotel, Bargrennan, Newton Stewart, Wigtownshire, DG8 6RN.
Small, family-run C19th hotel.
Tel: 01671 840243 Mrs Allwood.
Rates fr: £17.00-£17.00.
Open: All Year (not Xmas)
Beds: 2F
Baths: 2 Private
⓫ ☐ ◨ ⋔ ✕ ▮ ✦
Also ⛺ £Free! per tent.

St John's Town of Dalry 8

National Grid Ref: NX6281

⓪ ◨ Clachan Inn, Lochinvar

(On Path) 59 Main Street, St John's Town of Dalry, Castle Douglas, Kirkcudbrightshire, DG7 3UP.
Comfortable, friendly accommodation.
Tel: 01644 430420 Mrs Findlay.
Rates fr: £13.00-£13.00.
Open: Easter to Oct
Beds: 1D 1T
Baths: 1 Shared
⓫ ☐ ⤢ ☐ ✕ ▦ Ⓥ ▮ ✦

(On Path ⌂) Lochinvar Hotel, St John's Town of Dalry, Castle Douglas, Kirkcudbrightshire, DG7 3UP.
C18th ivy-clad hotel.
Grades: STB 3 Cr, Comm
Tel: 01644 430210
Mrs Pennington.
Rates fr: £15.00-£17.50.
Open: All Year **Beds:** 3F 6D 5T 1S
Baths: 7 Private 2 Shared
⓫ ☐ (30) ☐ ⋔ ✕ ▦ Ⓥ ▮ ✦

Balmaclellan 9

National Grid Ref: NX6579

(2.5m) High Park, Balmaclellan, Castle Douglas, Kirkcudbrightshire, DG7 3PT.
Comfortable, traditional farmhouse.
Grades: STB 1 Cr, Comm
Tel: 01644 420298 Mrs Shaw.
Rates fr: £14.00-£14.00.
Open: Easter to Oct
Beds: 2D 1T
Baths: 1 Shared
⓫ ☐ (3) ⤢ ☐ ✕ ▦ ⓖ Ⓥ

New Galloway 10

National Grid Ref: NX6377

(2m) Kenmure Arms Hotel, High Street, New Galloway, Castle Douglas, Kirkcudbrightshire, DG7 3RL.
Actual grid ref: NX6378
Comfortable family run hotel.
Grades: RAC 1 St
Tel: 01644 420240 Mrs Swain.
Rates fr: £14.50-£14.50.
Open: All Year
Beds: 3F 1D 6T 2S
Baths: 5 Ensuite 3 Shared
⓫ (1) ☐ (12) ☐ ⋔ ✕ ▦ Ⓥ ▮ ✦

(2m) Leamington Hotel, High Street, New Galloway, Castle Douglas, Kirkcudbrightshire, DG7 3RN.
Comfortable hotel and licensed restaurant.
Grades: STB 3 Cr, Comm
Tel: 01644 420327
Mr & Mrs Dolan.
Rates fr: £16.00-£14.00.
Open: Dec to Oct
Beds: 3F 3D 1T 2S
Baths: 6 Private 2 Shared
⓫ ☐ (9) ☐ ✕ ▦ Ⓥ ▮ ✦

High Bridge of Ken 11

National Grid Ref: NX6191

(2.5m) 2 Muirdrochwood, High Bridge of Ken, Carsphairn, Castle Douglas, Kircudbrightshire, DG7 1SW.
Friendly small holding.
Tel: 01644 460226 Mrs Burnie.
Rates fr: £14.00.
Open: All Year (not Xmas)
Beds: 1F
Baths: 1 Shared
⓫ ☐ ✕ ▦ Ⓥ

Sanquhar 12

National Grid Ref: NS7809

(0.25m ⌂) 28 High Street, Sanquhar, Dumfriesshire, DG4 6BL.
Large, comfortable, informal family flat.
Grades: STB Listed, Approv
Tel: 01659 58143 Mrs Turnbull.
Rates fr: £12.50-£12.50.
Open: All Year
Beds: 1D 1T
Baths: 1 Shared
⓫ ☐ ⋔ ✕ ▦ Ⓥ ▮ ✦

(0.25m) Penhurst, Townhead Street, Sanquhar, Dumfriesshire, DG4 6DA.
Actual grid ref: NS781091
Large sandstone family house.
Grades: STB Reg
Tel: 01659 50751
Mrs McDowall.
Rates fr: £12.00-£12.00.
Open: All Year
Beds: 1F 1D 1T
Baths: Shared
⓫ ☐ ⋔ ✕ ▦ Ⓥ ▮ ✦

All rates are subject to alteration at the owners' discretion.

Wanlockhead   13
National Grid Ref: NS8712

(▲ On Path) *Wanlockhead Youth Hostel, Lotus Lodge, Wanlockhead, Biggar, Lanarkshire, ML12 6UT.*
Actual grid ref: NS874131
Warden: Mr Evered.
Tel: **01659 74252**
Under 18: £5.25 **Adults:** £4.30
Family Bunk Rooms, Shop, Car Park
Lovely old white house in Scotland's highest village, famous for god-panning, silver and lead-mining

---

Daer   14
National Grid Ref: NS9512

(2m ☎) *Nunnerie Farm, Daer, Elvanfoot, Biggar, Lanarkshire, ML12 6TJ.*
Actual grid ref: NT9612
Friendly working farm.
Tel: **01864 505224** Mrs MacArthur.
Rates fr: *£20.00 (inc meal)*-**£20.00 (inc meal)**.
Open: Mar to Oct
Beds: 1D 1T
Baths: 1 Shared
🛇 🅿 🖵 ✕ 🖳 Ⓥ ⅰ ∥

Beattock   15
National Grid Ref: NT0702

🍽 🍸 Beattock House Hotel

(1m) *Auchen Castle Hotel, & Restaurant, Beattock, Moffat, Dumfriesshire, DG10 9P.*
Actual grid ref: NT062049
Country hotel in 50 acres.
Grades: STB 4 Cr, Comm, AA 3 St, RAC 3 St
Tel: **01683 300407** Mrs Beckh.
Rates fr: *£30.00*-**£46.00**.
Open: All Year (not Xmas)
Beds: 1F 12D 10T 3S
Baths: 26 Ensuite
🛇 🅿 (40) 🍴 ✕ 🖳 Ⓥ ⅰ ∥

(0.5m) *Craigielands Mill, Beattock, Moffat, Dumfriesshire, DG10 9RD.*
Actual grid ref: NT077020
Old converted saw-mill, beautiful grounds.
Tel: **01683 300677** Mr Henry.
Rates fr: *£16.00*-**£16.00**.
Open: All Year
Beds: 1D 2T
Baths: 1 Shared
🛇 (8) 🅿 🍴 🖵 🖳 ∥

Newton Wamphray   16
National Grid Ref: NY1094

(6m ☎) *The Red House Hotel, Newton Wamphray, Moffat, Dumfriesshire, DG10 9NF.*
Actual grid ref: NY106948
Country hotel.
Tel: **01564 470470** Mrs Wilson.
Rates fr: *£20.00*-**£20.00**.
Open: All Year (not Xmas)
Beds: 1D 1T 1S
Baths: 1 Shared
🛇 🅿 (6) 🖵 ✕ 🖳 ⅰ ∥

Woodhead   17
National Grid Ref: NT1003

(0.25m ☎) *Woodhead Farm, Woodhead, Moffat, Dumfriesshire, DG10 9LU.*
Luxuriously furnished farmhouse, wonderful views.
Grades: STB 3 Cr, High Comm
Tel: **01683 20225** Mrs Jackson.
Rates fr: *£22.50*-**£25.00**.
Open: All Year (not Xmas)
Beds: 1D 2T
Baths: 3 Private
🛇 🖵 ✕ 🖳 Ⓥ ⅰ ∥

Coxhill   18
National Grid Ref: NT0904

(On Path) *Coxhill Farm, Old Carlisle Road, Coxhill, Moffat, Dumfriesshire, DG10 9QN.*
Modern, comfortable farmhouse, outstanding views.
Grades: STB 2 Cr, High Comm
Tel: **01683 220471** Mrs Long.
Rates fr: *£16.00*-**£20.00**.
Open: All Year (not Xmas)
Beds: 2D 1T
Baths: 2 Shared
🛇 🅿 🍴 🖵 🖳 Ⓥ ⅰ ∥

Moffat   19
National Grid Ref: NT0805

(1m ☎) *Hartfell House, Hartfell Crescent, Moffat, Dumfriesshire, DG10 9AL.*
Splendid Victorian manor house.
Grades: STB 3 Cr, High Comm
Tel: **01683 220153**
Mr Daniel.
Rates fr: *£17.00*-**£22.50**.
Open: Mar to Nov
Beds: 2F 3D 2T 2S
Baths: 5 Ensuite, 2 Shared
🛇 🅿 (9) 🍴 ✕ 🖳 Ⓥ ⅰ ∥

(1.5m) *The Arden House Guest House, Moffat, Dumfriesshire, DG10 9HG.*
Converted bank.
Grades: RAC Acclaim
Tel: **01683 20220**
Mr Standingford.
Rates fr: *£15.50*-**£18.50**.
Open: Easter to Oct
Beds: 2F 2D 2T 1S
Baths: 4 Ensuite 2 Shared
🛇 🅿 (10) 🖵 ✕ 🖳 ⅰ

(2m ☎) *Wellview Hotel, Ballplay Road, Moffat, Dumfriesshire, DG10 9JU.*
Actual grid ref: NT092054
Large Victorian country house conversion.
Grades: STB 3 Cr, De Luxe, AA 1 St, 2 Rosettes, RAC High Acclaim
Tel: **01683 20184** Mr Schuckardt.
Rates fr: *£26.00*-**£35.00**.
Open: All Year
Beds: 4D 2T
Baths: 6 Ensuite
🛇 🅿 (8) 🍴 🖵 🍴 ✕ 🖳 Ⓥ ⅰ ∥

Ericstane   20
National Grid Ref: NT0711

(6m ☎) *Ericstane, Ericstane, Moffat, Dumfriesshire, DG10 9LT.*
Tastefully renovated period farmhouse.
Grades: STB 2 Cr, Comm
Tel: **01683 20127** Mr Jackson.
Rates fr: *£16.00*-**£20.00**.
Open: All Year
Beds: 1D 1T   **Baths:** 2 Private
🅿 🖵 🖳 ⅰ ∥

Tushielaw   21
National Grid Ref: NT3018

🍽 🍸 Tushielaw Inn

(4m ☎) *Kirkbrae House, Tushielaw, Ettrick Valley, Selkirk, Selkirkshire, TD7 5HT.*
Ideal base for walking, touring.
Grades: STB Approv
Tel: **01750 62208** Mrs Hannay.
Rates fr: *£13.00*-**£15.00**.
Open: April to October
Beds: 1F 1D 1T
🅿 (3) 🖵 ✕ 🖳 Ⓥ ⅰ ∥

The Country Code

Enjoy the countryside and respect its life and work

Guard against all risk of fire

Fasten all gates

Keep your dogs under close control

Keep to public paths across farmland

Use gates and stiles to cross fences, hedges and walls

Leave livestock, crops and machinery alone

Take your litter home

Help to keep all water clean

Protect wild-life, plants and trees

Take special care on country roads

Make no unnecessary noise

(3.5m 🚐) **Tushielaw Inn,**
Tushielaw, Ettrick Valley, Selkirk,
Roxburghshire, TD7 5HT.
Actual grid ref: NT306184
Traditional country pub, idyllic
location.
Grades: STB 2 Cr, Comm
Tel: **01750 62205**
Mr Osbourne.
Rates fr: *£19.00-£19.00.*
Open: All Year
Beds: 2D 1F
Baths: 3 Private
⛺ 🏱 ✕ 🏢 Ⓥ 🛆 ⚡

St Mary's Loch 22

National Grid Ref: NT2420

🍴 🍺 Tibbieshiels Inn

(On Path) **Tibbieshiels Inn,** *St*
Mary's Loch, Selkirk, Selkirkshire,
TD7 5.
Actual grid ref: NT205241
Very comfortable C19th inn.
Grades: STB 3 Cr, Comm,
AA 3 Q, Recomm
Tel: **01750 42231**
Mr Brown.
Rates fr: *£23.00-£26.00.*
Open: All Year
Beds: 2F 2D 1T
Baths: 5 Ensuite
⛺ 🏱 (30) 🏱 ✕ 🏢 Ⓥ 🛆
Also ⛺ *£1.00 per person.*
Open: All Year Ⓣ ♨ ✕

Mountbenger 23

National Grid Ref: NT3025

🍴 🍺 Gordon Arms

(3m 🚐) **Gordon Arms Hotel,**
Mountbenger, Yarrow Valley,
Selkirk, Selkirkshire, TD7 5LE.
200-year-old hotel, great views.
Tel: **01750 82232**
Mr Mitchell.
Rates fr: *£20.00-£25.00.*
Open: All Year (not Xmas)
Beds: 3D 3T
Baths: 4 Shared
⛺ 🏱 🏱 🏱 ✕ 🏢 Ⓥ 🛆 ⚡
Also ⛺ *Also bunkhouse, £4.50 per*
bunk.
Open: All Year (not Xmas) ☗ Ⓣ ⚡

Traquair 24

National Grid Ref: NT3334

🍴 🍺 Traquair Arms Hotel, River
Bank Restaurant

(0.75m) **Traquair Bank,** *Traquair,*
Innerleithen, Peebleshire, EH44 6PH.
Grades: STB Listed, Comm
Tel: **01896 830425**
Mrs Caird.
Rates fr: *£16.00-£16.00.*
Open: May to Feb
Beds: 1F 1D 1T
Baths: 2 Shared
⛺ 🏱 🏱 🏱 ✕ 🏢 Ⓥ 🛆 ⚡

(On Path 🚐) **Traquair Mill**
House, *Traquair, Innerleithen,*
Peebleshire, EH44 6PT.
Actual grid ref: NT328345
C18th mill house in beautiful
location.
Grades: STB Listed, Comm
Tel: **01896 830515**
Mrs Hamilton.
Rates fr: *£18.00-£25.00.*
Open: Easter to October
Beds: 1F
Baths: 1 Private
⛺ 🏱 (4) 🏱 ✕ 🏢 🛆 ⚡
Also ⛺ *Also bunkhouse, £10.00*
per bunk.
Open: All Year ☗ Ⓣ ♨ ✕ ⚡ ♿

Walkerburn 25

National Grid Ref: NT3537

🍴 🍺 Tweed Valley Hotel

(2m) **George Hotel,** *Galashiels*
Road, Walkerburn, Innerleithen,
Peebleshire, EH43 6.
Family run, overlooking River
Tweed.
Grades: STB 3 Cr, Comm
Tel: **01896 870336**
Mrs Forsyth.
Rates fr: *£20.00-£24.00.*
Open: All Year
Beds: 1F 4D 3T
Baths: 5 Ensuite, 3 Private
⛺ 🏱 (30) ✂ 🏱 🏱 ✕ 🏢 Ⓥ 🛆 ⚡

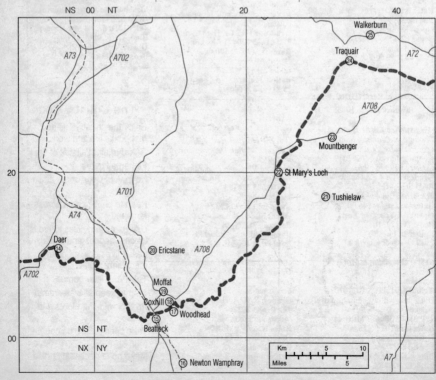

(2m) *Tweed Valley Hotel,*
Walkerburn, Innerleithen,
Peebleshire, EH43 6.
Actual grid ref: NT366374
Edwardian country house hotel.
Grades: STB 4 Cr, Comm,
AA 3 St, RAC 3 St
Tel: 01896 870636 Mr Miller.
Rates fr: *£25.00-£35.00.*
Open: All Year (not Xmas)
Beds: 1F 5D 6T 4S
☺ (16) ₽ (30) ⌷ ㅏ ✕ Ⅲ Ⅵ 🛈 ♦

Selkirk   26

National Grid Ref: NT4728

╏●╏ ⬗ County Hotel, Cross Keys
Inn, Queens Head Inn

(3m) 🚗 *Ivy Bank, Hillside*
Terrace, Selkirk, Selkirkshire, TD7 2LT.
Actual grid ref: NT4728
Grades: STB 1 Cr, Comm
Tel: 01750 21270 Mrs MacKenzie.
Rates fr: *£15.00-£15.00.*
Open: All Year (not Xmas)
Beds: 1D 1T **Baths:** 1 Shared
☺ ₽ (4) ⅊ ⌷ ㅏ Ⅲ Ⅵ 🛈 ♦
Ivy Bank sits in its own grounds
with beautiful views of the local
Linglie Hills. Superior accommo-
dation with all amenities including
private parking. Most friendly wel-
come.

(3m) *Alwyn, Russell Place, Selkirk,*
Selkirkshire, TD7 4NF.
Large bungalow in quiet street.
Grades: STB 2 Cr, Comm
Tel: 01750 22044 Mrs Donaldson.
Rates fr: *£16.00-£16.00.*
Open: Easter to Oct
Beds: 1D 1T
Baths: 1 Shared
₽ (2) ⌷ Ⅲ ♿ ♦

(2m) *County Hotel, 35 High Street,*
Selkirk, Selkirkshire, TD7 4BZ.
Friendly, family-run old coach-
house.
Grades: STB 3 Cr, Comm
Tel: 01750 21233 Mr Muir.
Rates fr: *£20.00-£22.50.*
Open: All Year
Beds: 1F 2D 2T 1S
Baths: 6 Ensuite
☺ ₽ (12) ⅊ ⌷ ㅏ ✕ Ⅲ Ⅵ 🛈 ♦

(2m) *Hillholm, 36 Hillside*
Terrace, Selkirk, Selkirkshire,
TD7 4ND.
Elegant Victorian private home.
Grades: STB 2 Cr, Comm, AA 4 Q
Tel: 01750 21293 Mrs Hannah.
Rates fr: *£15.00-£20.00.*
Open: Easter to Oct
Beds: 2D 2T
Baths: 2 Private 1 Shared
☺ (10) ₽ (3) ⅊ ⌷ ✕ Ⅲ 🛈 ♦

Galashiels   27

National Grid Ref: NT4936

╏●╏ ⬗ Hedges Bistro, Kings Knowe
Hotel, Abbotsford Arms Hotel

(0.25m) *Island House, 65 Island*
Street, Galashiels, Selkirkshire,
TD1 1PA.
Large Victorian private house.
Grades: STB Listed, Comm,
AA 3 Q
Tel: 01896 752649
Mr Brown.
Rates fr: *£14.00-£14.00.*
Open: All Year
Beds: 1D 2T
Baths: 2 Ensuite, 1 Shared
☺ ₽ (2) ⌷ ㅏ Ⅲ Ⅵ ♦

(0.5m) *Ettrickvale, 33 Abbotsford*
Road, Galashiels, Selkirkshire,
TD1 3HW.
Comfortable, modern semi-
detached bungalow.
Grades: STB 1 Cr, Comm
Tel: 01896 755224
Mrs Field.
Rates fr: *£13.00-£16.00.*
Open: All Year (not Xmas)
Beds: 1D 2T
Baths: 1 Shared
☺ ₽ (2) ⌷ ㅏ ✕ Ⅲ ♿ Ⅵ 🛈

NT 40   60   80   NT

STILWELL'S NATIONAL TRAIL COMPANION

🚐 sign means that, given due notice, owners will pick you up from the path and drop you off within reason.

(On Path 🚐) *Wakefield Bank, 9 Abbotsford Road, Galashiels, Selkirkshire, TD1 3DP.*
Actual grid ref: NT496356
Award-winning B&B in large Victorian house.
Grades: STB 2 Cr, High Comm
Tel: 01896 752641 Mrs Platt.
Rates fr: £16.00.
Open: Easter to Oct
Beds: 2D 1T **Baths:** 2 Shared
▣ (2) ⅍⌷✕Ⅲ.Ⅴ🛆✦

(0.25m) *Kings Hotel, Galashiels, Selkirkshire, TD1 3AN.*
Town centre family-run hotel.
Grades: STB 3 Cr, Comm, AA 2 St
Tel: 01896 755497 Mr MacDonald.
Rates fr: £26.00-£35.00.
Open: All Year (not Xmas)
Beds: 1F 1D 4T 1S
Baths: 7 Private
⌂ ▣ (6) ⌷✕Ⅲ.Ⅴ🛆✦

(0.25m) *Abbotsford Arms Hotel, Stirling Street, Galashiels, Selkirkshire, TD1 1BY.*
Recently refurbished family-run hotel.
Grades: STB 3 Cr, Comm, AA 2 St, RAC 2 St
Tel: 01896 752517
Rates fr: £22.00-£28.00.
Open: All Year (not Xmas)
Beds: 3F 3D 5T 3S
Baths: 10 Private 2 Shared
⌂ ▣ (10) ⌷✕Ⅲ.Ⅴ🛆✦

(0.25m 🚐) *Keranalt, 3 Bridge Street, Galashiels, Selkirkshire, TD1 1SW.*
Comfortable homely central terraced house.
Grades: STB Listed, Comm
Tel: 01896 754859 Mrs Lowe.
Rates fr: £15.00-£15.00.
Open: All Year (not Xmas)
Beds: 1F 1T 1S **Baths:** 2 Shared
⌂ ⅍⌷✕Ⅲ.Ⅴ🛆✦

Planning a longer stay? Always ask for any special rates.

Melrose 28
National Grid Ref: NT5434

🍴 🍺 Burts Hotel

(⌂ On Path) *Melrose Youth Hostel, Priorwood, Melrose, Roxburghshire, TD6 9EF.*
Actual grid ref: NT549339
Warden: Mr Christison.
Tel: 01896 822521
Under 18: £5.65 **Adults:** £6.75
Family Rooms, Shower Room, Shop, Car Park, Laundry, Drying Facilities
Imposing stone-built Georgian mansion surrounded by own grounds, overlookingMelrose Abbey, the Museum and the Gardens

(0.25m 🚐) *Dunfermline House, Buccleuch Street, Melrose, Roxburghshire, TD6 9LB.*
Highly commended Victorian town house.
Grades: STB 2 Cr, High Comm, AA 4 Q, Select
Tel: 01896 822148 Mrs Graham.
Rates fr: £21.00-£21.00.
Open: All Year
Beds: 2D 2T 1S **Baths:** 5 Ensuite
⌂⅍⌷Ⅲ.🛆✦

(0.25m) *Kings Arms Hotel, High St, Melrose, Roxburghshire, TD6 9PB.*
Former C18th coaching inn.
Grades: STB 3 Cr, Comm
Tel: 01896 822143 Mr Dalgetty.
Rates fr: £24.75-£30.50.
Open: All Year
Beds: 1F 1D 3T 1S
Baths: 6 Private
⌂ ▣ (10) ⌷🛏✕Ⅲ.Ⅴ🛆

Gattonside 29
National Grid Ref: NT5435

🍴 🍺 Kings Arms, Burts Hotel

(0.5m) *Treetops, Gattonside, Melrose, Roxburghshire, TD6 9NH.*
Actual grid ref: NT543354
Modern house with magnificent view. **Grades:** STB Listed, Comm
Tel: 01896 823153 Mrs Davison.
Rates fr: £15.00-£18.00.
Open: Easter to October
Beds: 1T **Baths:** 1 Private
⌂ ▣ (4) ⅍⌷🛏Ⅲ.🛆✦

Langshaw 30
National Grid Ref: NT5139

(0.5m) *Over Langshaw Farm, Langshaw, Galashiels, Selkirkshire, TD1 2PE.*
Actual grid ref: NT523402
Comfortable farmhouse accommodation.**Grades:** STB 1 Cr, Comm
Tel: 01896 860244 Mrs Bergius.
Rates fr: £16.00-£25.00.
Open: All Year
Beds: 1F 1D
Baths: 1 Ensuite 1 Private
⌂ ▣ ⅍⌷🛏✕Ⅲ.Ⅴ🛆✦

The Grid Reference beneath the location heading is for the village or town - *not* for individual houses, which are shown (where supplied) in each entry itself.

Lauder 31
National Grid Ref: NT5347

🍴 🍺 Lauderdale Hotel, Eagle Hotel, Black Bull

(On Path) *The Grange, 6 Edinburgh Road, Lauder, Berwickshire, TD2 6TW.*
Grades: STB 1 Cr, Comm
Tel: 01578 722649
Mr Gilardi.
Rates fr: £14.00-£14.00.
Open: All Year (not Xmas)
Beds: 1D 2T
Baths: 1 Shared
⌂ ▣ (4) ⅍⌷Ⅲ.Ⅴ🛆✦
Large comfortable detached house in own grounds overlooking rolling Lammermuir Hills. Walkers always welcome.

(2m) *Lauderdale Hotel, Lauder, Berwickshire, TD2 6.*
Traditional country sporting hotel.
Grades: AA 2 St
Tel: 01578 722231
Mrs Van Sloten.
Rates fr: £26.00-£35.00.
Open: All Year
Beds: 2D 7T
Baths: 9 Ensuite
⌂ ▣ (40) ⌷🛏✕Ⅲ.Ⅴ🛆✦

(On Path 🚐) *Ripeth, 25 Eas High Street, Lauder, Berwickshire, TD2 6SS.*
Actual grid ref: NT604583
Grades: STB 1 Cr
Tel: 01578 718795
Mrs Christie.
Rates fr: £7.00-£15.00.
Open: All Year
Beds: 1F 1D 1T
Baths: 2 Shared
⌂ ▣ ⅍⌷🛏Ⅲ.🛆✦
Also ⛺ *Also bunkhouse, £4 per bunk.*
Open: All Year 📺 🎱 ✦ ♿
Bright comfortable family home on Southern Upland Way. Lauder town centre. Fishing on Rivers Tweed and Leader. Good touring base close to Edinburgh and borders

---

Longformacus 32

National Grid Ref: NT5769

(On Path) *Eildon Cottage,*
Longformacus, Duns,
Berwickshire, TD11 3PB.
Large, friendly house. Great breakfasts.
Tel: **01361 890230** Mrs Amos.
Rates fr: *£15.00-*£16.00.
Open: All Year (not Xmas)
Beds: 1F 1D 1T
Baths: 3 Private
さ🅿🏲✕Ⓥⓐ⅍

Abbey St Bathans 33

National Grid Ref: NT7562

(▲ On Path) *Abbey St Bathans*
Youth Hostel, Abbey St Bathans,
Duns, Berwickshire, TD11 3TX.
Actual grid ref: NT7562
Tel: **01361 840245**
Under 18: £5.50 **Adults:** £6.95
Shower, Self-Catering
A modern stone-built single-storey
building, this hostel lies beside the
Whiteadder River in a beautiful,
unspoilt valley

Grantshouse 34

National Grid Ref: NT8065

🍽🍷 Grantshouse Inn

(1m 🚌) *Haggerston House Hotel,*
Grantshouse, Duns, Berwickshire,
TD11 3RW.
Quiet, family-run hotel. Good food.
Grades: STB 3 Cr, Comm
Tel: **01361 850229** Mr Baty.
Rates fr: *£30.00-*£20.00.
Open: All Year (not Xmas)
Beds: 2D 3T
Baths: 3 Private 1 Shared
さ🅿 (20) 🏲🏴✕🎖Ⓥⓐ⅍

Cockburnspath 35

National Grid Ref: NT7770

🍽🍷 Cockburnspath Hotel, Pease
Bay Restaurant, Haggerston House
Hotel, Grantshouse Inn

(On Path) *Townhead Farm,*
Cockburnspath, Berwickshire,
TD13 5YR.
Traditional Berwickshire working
farm.

Grades: STB Listed, Comm
Tel: **01368 830465** Mrs Russell.
Rates fr: *£14.00-*£14.00.
Open: Easter to Oct
Beds: 1F 1D
Baths: 1 Shared
さ🅿🏲🎖ⓐ⅍

(On Path) *Cockburnspath Hotel,*
Cockburnspath, Berwickshire,
TD13 5YG.
Family-run C17th coach house.
Tel: **01368 830217** Mr Redpath.
Rates fr: *£16.00-*£17.00.
Open: All Year
Beds: 1F 5D 1T 1S
Baths: 3 Shared
さ⅍🏲🏴✕🎖Ⓥⓐ⅍

Please don't camp

on anyone's land

without first obtaining

their permission.

The coast of Britain's South Western peninsular is rightly famous for its scenery which ranks among the best in Europe. Spectacular cliffs, lonely beaches, wide river estuaries, buzzing resorts and tranquil coves - all are bounded by the Atlantic as its pushes up the English Channel on the South and into the Irish Sea and the Bristol Channel to the North. In the summer the coast is crowded with holiday-makers and the path is popular, but there are still long stretches where you will keep your own company. The **South West Coast Path** is by far and away the longest of Britain's National Trails. It combines the **Somerset & North Devon, Cornwall, South Devon** and **Dorset Coastal Paths**, running up a total of some 613 miles. Not many walkers will complete the path in one go. In fact, it's a natural candidate for walking in sections. Take the prevailing wind (a south-westerly) into consideration when planning your walk, for this path is certainly exposed. Do you wish to walk into the wind or to have it at your back? Squalls and gales can blow up unexpectedly and cliff-walking can be become

quite dangerous in these conditions, so take care to listen to the right forecasts. One of the most enjoyable features of the **South West Coast Path** is the number of estuaries one must cross. While some are fordable, it is strongly recommended that ferries are used wherever possible, as river conditions may prove unpredictable, if not perilous. If there is no ferry, allowances for a detour must be made. Details of ferries can be had locally, but to plan the route properly, there is an excellent book published by the **South West Way Association**. Called simply *The South West Way*, it publishes both tide and ferry timetables, public transport details and suggested itineraries. Ring 01803 873061 for more details. There is also a taxi-based service, handling luggage delivery, safe car-parking and passenger back-up along the Somerset & North Devon and Cornwall stretches only - **White Knight** (tel. 01903 766475, please see advertisement)
Comments on the path to: **David Venner**, South West Coast Path Project, Luscombe House, County Hall, Exeter, EX2 4QW.

Somerset & North Devon

This section of the **South West Coast Path** runs for only a short way in Somerset from Minehead, then past the North Devon resorts of Ilfracombe and Woolacombe and the major towns of Barnstaple and Bideford, to the border with Cornwall.

Guides: *South West Way: Vol I (Minehead to Penzance)* by Martin Collins (ISBN 1 85284 025 0), published by Cicerone Press and also available from the publishers (2 Police Square, Milnthorpe, Cumbria, LA7 7PY, 01539 562069), £8.99
South West Way: Minehead to Padstow by Roland Tarr (ISBN 1 85410 4152), published by

Aurum Press in association with the Countryside Commission and Ordnance Survey, £9.99
South West Way: Padstow to Falmouth by John Macadam (ISBN 1 85410 3873), published by Aurum Press in association with the Countryside Commission and Ordnance Survey, £9.99.

There is also invaluable local information in *The South West Way* 1996 by the South West Way Association, available directly from them (1 Orchard Drive, Kingskerswell, Newton Abbot, Devon, TQ12 5DG, tel 01803 873061), £3.99 (+ 70p p&p).

Maps: Ordnance Survey 1:50,000 Landranger series: 180, 181 and 190

Dunster   1

National Grid Ref: SS9943

|o| ◖ Dunster Castle Hotel, Luttrel Arms, Stables Restaurant

(1.5m 🚍) *Spears Cross Hotel, West Street, Dunster, Minehead, Somerset, TA24 6SN.*
Actual grid ref: SS990439
Small 15th Century licensed hotel.
Grades: ETB 2 Cr
Tel: **01643 821439** Mr Rathbone.

Rates fr: *£20.00*-**£20.00**.
Open: Feb to Dec
Beds: 1F 2D 1T
Baths: 4 Ensuite
(A) 🅿 (4) ⊬☐🛏⛺🍽 Ⅴ 🛉 ✔

Alcombe Combe   2

National Grid Ref: SS9744

(▲ 2m) *Minehead Youth Hostel, Alcombe Combe, Minehead, Somerset, TA24 6EW.*
Actual grid ref: SS9744

Warden: Mr R Moss.
Tel: **01643 702595**
Under 18: £5.00 **Adults:** £7.45
Family Room,Partially Heated, Showers, Evening Meal (7.00 pm)
In a secluded position up a wooded combe on the edge of Exmoor

The lowest *double* rate per person is shown in *italics*.

The
*White
Knight*
Luggage Link

Somerset/N Devon
Safe • Flexible • Door to Door • Any Direction
Tel: 0193 766 475
Mobile: 0850 007 062

Minehead 3

National Grid Ref: SS9646

⚑ 🍴 The Wellington Hotel, The Beach Hotel, Kildare Lodge, York House Inn, Salworthy, Old Ship Aground

(0.25m) *Gascony Hotel, 50 The Avenue, Minehead, Somerset, TA24 5BB*.
Grades: ETB 3 Cr, Highly Comm, AA 4 Q, Select, RAC Listed, High Acclaim. Tel: **01643 705939**
Rates fr: *£21.00-£22.00*.
Open: Mar to Oct
Beds: 2F 4D 4T 3S
Baths: 13 Ensuite
🛏 (A) 🅿 (14) 🗖 🛉 ✕ 🎟 Ⓥ 🛢 ✦
Friendly and well appointed hotel, situated only 0.25 miles from South West Way. Ensuite bedrooms. Home cooked food with choice of menu. Licensed. Car park.

(On Path) *Beaconswood Hotel, Church Road, North Hill, Minehead, Somerset, TA24 5SB*.
Edwardian hotel with panoramic views.
Grades: ETB 4 Cr, AA 2 St, RAC 2 St
Tel: **01643 702032** Mr Roberts.
Rates fr: *£28.00-£36.00*.
Open: Mar to Nov
Beds: 3F 6D 5T **Baths:** 14 Ensuite

(0.25m) *Armadale, 11 Tregonwell Rd, Minehead, Somerset, TA24 5DU*.
Small guesthouse near coastal path.
Grades: ETB Listed
Tel: **01643 702931** Mrs Pile.
Rates fr: *£15.00-£15.00*.
Open: March to Nov
Beds: 1F 2D 1T 1S
Baths: 3 Private 🛏 (A) 🅿 🗖 🎟,

(On Path) 🚐 *Hindon Farm, Minehead, Somerset, TA24 8SH*.
Superbly situated C18th lovely farmhouse.
Grades: ETB Listed, Comm
Tel: **01643 705244** Mrs Webber.
Rates fr: *£18.00-£22.00*.
Open: Oct to Nov
Beds: 2D 1T **Baths:** 1 Shared
(A) 🅿 (6) 🗖 🛉 ✕ 🎟 Ⓥ ✦

(0.25m) *Kildare Lodge, Townsend Road, Minehead, Somerset, TA24 5RQ*.
Outstanding Lutyens-style hotel, inn and pub.
Grades: ETB 3 Cr, Comm, AA 3 Q, Recomm
Tel: **01643 702009** Mr Beckett.
Rates fr: *£20.00-£20.00*.
Open: All Year
Beds: 2F 4D 2T 1S
Baths: 9 Ensuite
(A) 🅿 (26) ✕ 🗖 🛉 ✕ 🎟 🚹 Ⓥ 🛢 ✦

(0.25m) *Fernside, The Holloway, Minehead, Somerset, TA24 5PB*.
200-year-old cottage.
Grades: ETB 2 Cr, Comm
Tel: **01643 707594** Mrs Smith.
Rates fr: *£14.00-£15.00*.
Open: All Year (not Xmas)
Beds: 1F 2D
Baths: 1 Ensuite 1 Shared
(A) 🗖 ✕ 🎟 Ⓥ ✦

(1m) *Tranmere House, 24 Tregonwell Road, Minehead, Somerset, TA24 5DU*.
Modern comfortable guest house.
Grades: ETB 1 Cr
Tel: **01643 702647** Mr Doyle.
Rates fr: *£14.00-£15.00*.
Open: All Year
Beds: 3F 3D 2S
Baths: 6 Ensuite
(A) 🅿 (6) 🗖 🛉 ✕ 🎟 Ⓥ 🛢

(0.5m) *Avill House, Townsend Road, Minehead, Somerset, TA24 5RG*.
Large comfortable Victorian house.
Grades: ETB 2 Cr, AA 3 Q
Tel: **01643 704370** Mr Pooley.
Rates fr: *£14.50-£16.00*.
Open: All Year (not Xmas)
Beds: 4F 4D 1S
Baths: 3 Ensuite 2 Shared
(A) 🅿 (7) 🗖 🛉 ✕ 🎟 Ⓥ 🛢 ✦

(0.25m) *Glen View, 39 Summerland Road, Minehead, Somerset, TA24 5BS*.
Small, quiet, friendly private house.
Tel: **01643 705025** Miss Tame.
Rates fr: *£12.50-£13.50*.
Open: Easter to Nov
Beds: 1F 1D 1S
Baths: 1 Shared
🛏 (A) 🅿 (1) ✕ 🗖 🛉 🎟 Ⓥ 🛢 ✦

(0.5m) *Mentone Hotel, The Parks, Minehead, Somerset, TA24 8BS*.
Actual grid ref: SS966463
Victorian villa: 55 years hotel.
Grades: ETB 3 Cr
Tel: **01643 705229**
Mr & Mrs Ravenscroft.
Rates fr: *£19.00-£19.00*.
Open: Easter to Oct
Beds: 4D 3T 1S
Baths: 7 Ensuite 1 Shared
(A) 🅿 (7) ✕ 🗖 🎟 Ⓥ

Porlock 4

National Grid Ref: SS8846

⚑ 🍴 Culbone Inn, Royal Oak, The Ship Inn

(1m) *Lorna Doone Hotel, High Street, Porlock, Minehead, Somerset, TA24 8PS*.
Village centre hotel.
Grades: ETB 3 Cr, AA 3 Q, RAC Acclaim
Tel: **01643 862404**
Mr Thornton.
Rates fr: *£19.00-£22.50*.
Open: All Year (not Xmas)
Beds: 2 F 5D 6T 2S
Baths: 15 Ensuite
(A) 🅿 (8) 🗖 🛉 ✕ 🎟 Ⓥ ✦

(On Path) 🚐 *Silcombe Farm, Porlock, Minehead, Somerset, TA24 8JN*.
Actual grid ref: SS8348
Secluded Exmoor farmhouse on SW Way.
Grades: ETB Listed
Tel: **01643 862248**
Mrs Richards.
Rates fr: *£15.50-£14.50*.
Open: All Year (not Xmas)
Beds: 1D 1T 1S
Baths: 1 Private 2 Shared
🛏 (A) 🅿 (10) 🗖 🛉 ✕ 🎟 Ⓥ 🛢 ✦

80

SS 00 ST

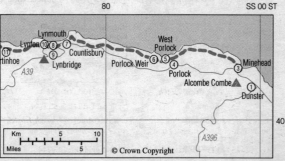

40

© Crown Copyright

Bringing children with you? Always ask for any special rates.

(1m 🚐) *Leys, The Ridge, Bossington Lane, Porlock, Minehead, Somerset, TA24 8HA.*
Actual grid ref: SS892469
Comfortable spacious house, beautiful garden.
Tel: **01643 862477** Mrs Stiles-Cox.
Rates fr: *£15.00-£15.00*.
Open: All Year (not Xmas)
Beds: 1D 1T 2S
Baths: 1 Shared
(A) 🅿 (4) 🛏 ▥ 🛊 ⚡

(0.5m) *Myrtle Cottage, High Street, Porlock, Minehead, Somerset, TA24 8PU.*
C17th thatched cottage.
Tel: **01643 862978** Mr Thorne.
Rates fr: *£16.00-£17.00*.
Open: All Year
Beds: 2D 1T
Baths: 1 Shared
🛏 (A) 🅿 (4) ⚡ 🛏 ▥ Ⓥ ⚡

(0.25m) *Doverhay Place, Porlock, Minehead, Somerset, TA24 8EX.*
Actual grid ref: SS891468
Tastefully refurbished characterful country house.
Tel: **01643 862398**
Mr & Mrs Bower.
Rates fr: *£18.00-£18.00*.
Open: All Year
Beds: 6D 12T 9S
Baths: 20 Private 5 Shared
(A) 🅿 (20) ✕ ▥ Ⓥ 🛊 ⚡

(2.5m 🚐) *West Luccombe Farm, Porlock, Minehead, Somerset, TA24 8HT.*
Large farmhouse on 340-acre working farm.
Tel: **01643 862478**
Rates fr: *£15.00-£16.00*.
Open: All Year (not Xmas)
Beds: 1F 2D
(A) 🅿 (4) 🛏 🛏 ✕ ▥ Ⓥ ⚡

(1m) *Glenlea, Doverhay, Porlock, Minehead, Somerset, TA24 8AJ.*
Actual grid ref: SS888467
Edwardian cottage, comfortable accommodation.
Tel: **01643 862760** Mrs Roy.
Rates fr: *£14.50-£14.50*.
Open: Mar to Oct
Beds: 1D 1T
Baths: 1 Private 1 Shared
⚡ ▥ 🛊 ⚡

(0.25m 🚐) *The Ship Inn, High Street, Porlock, Minehead, Somerset, TA24 8QT.*
C13th thatched inn.
Grades: RAC 1 St
Tel: **01643 862507** Mr Robinson.
Rates fr: *£16.50-£16.50*.
Open: All Year
Beds: 2F 5D 2T 2S
Baths: 7 Private 2 Shared
(A) 🅿 (20) 🛏 🛏 ✕ ▥ Ⓥ ⚡

(0.5m) *The Cottage, High Street, Porlock, Minehead, Somerset, TA24 8PU.*
Tel: **01643 862687** Mrs Dunn.
Rates fr: *£19.00-£19.00*.
Open: All Year
Beds: 5D 2T
Baths: 7 Ensuite
(A) 🅿 (20) ⚡ 🛏 🛏 ✕ ▥ Ⓥ 🛊 ⚡

(1m) *Culbone Inn, Porlock, Minehead, Somerset, TA24 8JW.*
Actual grid ref: SS8347
Highest free house on Exmoor.
Tel: **01643 862259**
Mrs Baker-Gill.
Rates fr: *£15.00-£17.50*.
Open: All Year
Beds: 1D 2T
Baths: 1 Private 1 Shared
🅿 (100) 🛏 🛏 ▥ Ⓥ 🛊

West Porlock   5
National Grid Ref: SS8747

🍴 🍺 Ship Inn, Royal Oak, Castle

(On Path) *West Porlock House, Country House Hotel, West Porlock, Minehead, Somerset, TA24 8NX.*
Actual grid ref: SS870470
Small, elegant, secluded country house.
Grades: ETB 2 Cr, High Comm
Tel: **01643 862880**
Mrs Dyer.
Rates fr: *£23.00-£27.50*.
Open: Feb to Nov
Beds: 1F 2D 2T
Baths: 5 Private
🛏 (A) 🅿 (8) ⚡ 🛏 ✕ ▥ 🛊 ⚡

(0.25m 🚐) *Lavender Cottage, West Porlock, Minehead, Somerset, TA24 8NX.*
Cottage with panoramic sea views.
Tel: **01643 862678**
Mrs Cox.
Rates fr: *£16.50-£16.50*.
Open: Feb to Nov
Beds: 1D 1T 1S
Baths: 1 Shared
🛏 (A) 🅿 (8) 🛏 🛏 ▥ Ⓥ 🛊 ⚡

The Country Code

Enjoy the countryside and respect its life and work

Guard against all risk of fire

Fasten all gates

Keep your dogs under close control

Keep to public paths across farmland

Use gates and stiles to cross fences, hedges and walls

Leave livestock, crops and machinery alone

Take your litter home

Help to keep all water clean

Protect wild-life, plants and trees

Take special care on country roads

Make no unnecessary noise

Porlock Weir 6

National Grid Ref: SS8647

|⚓| ⛴ Ship Inn

(On Path) *Sea View Cottage,*
Porlock Weir, Porlock, Minehead,
Somerset, TA24 8.
Actual grid ref: SS864478
Lovely old cottage, homely atmosphere.
Tel: **01643 862523**
Mrs Starr.
Rates fr: *£15.00-£15.00.*
Open: All Year
Beds: 1T 1S
Baths: 1 Shared
(A) 🅿 (2) 🗔 🏋 📺 📺 🛡 ✦

Countisbury 7

National Grid Ref: SS7457

|⚓| ⛴ Hunter's Lodge, Floyd's Inn,
Red Lion, Durant Arms

(0.5m) *Coombe Farm,*
Countisbury, Lynton, Devon,
EX35 6NF.
C17th farmhouse.
Grades: ETB 2 Cr, Comm,
AA 3 Q
Tel: **01598 741236**
Mrs& Mrs Pile.
Rates fr: *£16.00-£18.00.*
Open: Mar to Nov
Beds: 2F 2D 1T
Baths: 2 Private 2 Shared
(A) 🅿 (6) 🗲 🗔 🏋 📺 📺 📺

Lynmouth 8

National Grid Ref: SS7249

|⚓| ⛴ Village Inn

(0.25m) *Glenville House, 2 Tors*
Road, Lynmouth, Devon, EX35 6ET.
Comfortable, licensed, riverside
Victorian house.
Tel: **01598 752202**
Mr & Mrs Francis.
Rates fr: *£16.50-£16.50.*
Open: Mar to Nov
Beds: 1F 4D 1T 1S
Baths: 3 Private, 2 Shared
🐾 (A) 🗔 🗙 📺 📺 🛡 ✦

(0.25m) *The Heatherville,*
Lynmouth, Lynton, Devon, EX35 6.
Licenced country house.
Magnificent views.
Grades: ETB 3 Cr, Comm,
AA 4 Q, Select, RAC Acclaim
Tel: **01598 752327** Mrs Davis.
Rates fr: *£23.00-£22.50.*
Open: Easter to Nov
Beds: 2F 5D 3T
Baths: 5 Private 2 Shared
🐾 (A) 🅿 (10) 🗔 🏋 🗙 📺 📺

(On Path) *Ferndale House,*
Watersmeet Road, Lynmouth,
Lynton, Devon, EX35 6EP.
Large Victorian house.
Tel: **01598 753431** Mr Burns.
Rates fr: *£17.50.*
Open: Easter to Nov
Baths: 3 Ensuite
🐾 (A) 🗲 🗔 📺 📺 🛡 ✦

(0.25m) *Oakleigh, 4 Tors Road,*
Lynmouth, Lynton, Devon, EX35 6ET.
Small friendly comfortable guesthouse.
Tel: **01598 752220** Mr & Mrs Pile.
Rates fr: *£16.50-£16.50.*
Open: All Year (not Xmas)
Beds: 5D 2T 2S **Baths:** 2 Shared
(A) 🅿 (9) 🗔 🏋 🗙 🛡 ✦

Lynbridge 9

National Grid Ref: SS7248

(🏠 1m) *Lynton Youth Hostel,*
Lynbridge, Lynton, Devon, EX35 6AZ.
Actual grid ref: SS7248
Warden: Mr S Hayes.
Tel: **01598 53237**
Under 18: £5.00 **Adults:** £7.45
Family Bunk Rooms, Centrally
Heated, Showers, Evening Meal
(7.00 pm)
Homely Victorian house in the
steep wooded gorge of the West
Lyn river, where Exmoor meets the
sea

All paths are popular: you are well-advised to book ahead

(1m) *Top of the World, Lynbridge,*
Lynton, Devon, EX35 6BE.
Grades: ETB Listed
Tel: **01598 753693** Mrs Champion.
Rates fr: *£14.50-£17.00.*
Open: Feb to Oct
Beds: 1D 1T
Baths: 1 Shared
(A) 🅿 (2) 🗔 🏋 🗙 📺 📺 📺
Character Victorian cottage on high
ground, glorious views across the
West Lyn Valley, ten mins beach,
3/4 mile from Lynton at Lynbridge,
home cooking.

Lynton 10

National Grid Ref: SS7149

|⚓| ⛴ Royal Castle

(0.5m) *Woodlands Hotel,*
Lynbridge, Lynton, Devon, EX35 6AX.
Actual grid ref: SS721488
Grades: ETB 3 Cr, Comm
Tel: **01598 752324** Mrs Christian.
Rates fr: *£16.00-£16.00.*
Open: Mar to Nov
Beds: 5D 2T 1S
Baths: 5 Ensuite, 2 Shared
🐾 (A) 🅿 (8) 🗔 🗙 📺 📺 🛡 ✦
Warm welcome for walkers.
Peaceful location in a beautiful setting overlooking N.T. woodland.
Spacious rooms. Delicious homemade food including vegetarian
choice and hearty breakfast.

(0.25m 🚲) *Lynhurst Hotel,*
Lynton, Devon, EX35 6AX.
Charming Victorian residence,
amazing views.
Grades: ETB 3 Cr, AA 4 Q, Select
Tel: **01598 752241**
Mr Townsend.
Rates fr: *£18.00-£25.00.*
Open: All Year (not Xmas)
Beds: 2F 4D 2T 1S
Baths: 7 Ensuite
(A) 🅿 (2) 🗔 🏋 🗙 📺 📺 ✦

(On Path) *Rockvale Hotel, Lee*
Road, Lynton, Devon, EX35 6HW.
Spacious Victorian building, central location.
Grades: ETB 3 Cr, Comm,
AA 3 Q, RAC 1 St
Tel: **01598 752279**
Mr Woodland.
Rates fr: *£22.00-£18.00.*
Open: Mar to Oct
Beds: 2F 5D 1S
Baths: 8 Ensuite
🐾 (A) 🅿 (10) 🗲 🗔 🗙 📺 📺 🛡 ✦

(0.5m) *The Denes Guest House,*
Longmead, Lynton, Devon,
EX35 6DQ.
Actual grid ref: SS7149
Victorian style family home.
Tel: **01598 753573**
Mr & Mrs Gay.
Rates fr: *£15.00-£15.00.*
Open: All Year (not Xmas)
Beds: 3F 2D 2S
Baths: 2 Shared
(A) 🅿 (7) 🗲 🗔 🗙 📺 🛡 ✦

(0.5m) *Gable Lodge Hotel, Lee Road, Lynton, Devon, EX35 6BS.* Large Victorian Listed private house.
Tel: **01598 752367** Mr Bowman.
Rates fr: *£15.00*-**£15.00**.
Open: All Year
Beds: 1F 5D 1T 1S
Baths: 6 Ensuite 1 Shared
(A) ▣ (8) ⊬⌷ ⊩ ⨯ Ⅲ, Ⓥ

(0.25m) *Victoria Lodge, Lee Road, Lynton, Devon, EX35 6BP.* Comfortable Victorian house.
Grades: ETB 3 Cr, High Comm, AA 5 Q, Prem Select, RAC High Acc
Tel: **01598 53203**
Mr & Mrs Bennett.
Rates fr: *£20.00*-**£25.00**.
Open: All Year (not Xmas)
Beds: 1F 8D 1T
Baths: 10 Private 1 Shared
(A) ⊬⌷ ⊩ Ⅲ, Ⓥ

Martinhoe   11

National Grid Ref: SS6648

⑩ ⓠ The Hunters Inn, The Fox

(0.25m) *Mannacott Farm, Martinhoe, Parracombe, Barnstaple, Devon, EX31 4QS.* Bar meals obtainable nearby inn.
Tel: **01598 763227** Mrs Dallyn.
Rates fr: *£13.00*-**£14.00**.
Open: Apr - Nov
Beds: 1D 1T
⌂ (A) ▣ (2) ⊬⌷ ⊩ Ⅲ,

Combe Martin   12

National Grid Ref: SS5846

⑩ ⓠ Dolphin, Focastle, Royal Marine, Devon Fayre Cafe

(On Path) *Hillview Guest House, Woodlands, Combe Martin, Ilfracombe, Devon, EX34 0AT.* **Actual grid ref:** SS575469 Stone-built turn of century house.
Grades: ETB Reg
Tel: **01271 882331**
Mrs Bosley.
Rates fr: *£13.00*-**£14.00**.
Open: Easter to Sep
Beds: 4D 1T
Baths: 2 Private 1 Shared
▣ (6) ⊬⌷ Ⅲ, Ⓥ

(0.25m) *The Firs, Woodlands, Combe Martin, Ilfracombe, Devon, EX34 0A.* Family friendly guesthouse.
Tel: **01271 883404**
Mr & Mrs Perkin.
Rates fr: *£13.50*-**£13.50**.
Open: Easter to Oct
Beds: 2F 4D 1T 2S
Baths: 1 Ensuite 2 Shared
(A) ▣ (10) ⌷ ⨯ Ⅲ, Ⓥ

(On Path) *Glendower, King Street, Combe Martin, Ilfracombe, Devon, EX34 0AL.* Large Victorian private house.

Tel: **01271 883449**
Mr & Mrs Barry.
Rates fr: *£12.00*-**£15.00**.
Open: Easter to Nov
Beds: 1F 1D 1T 1S
Baths: 1 Shared
⌂ (A) ▣ (3) ⌷ ⊩ Ⓥ

Ilfracombe   13

National Grid Ref: SS5147

⑩ ⓠ Coach House Inn, Wheel House, Britannia Inn, George & Dragon, Waverley Inn

(0.25m) *Combe Lodge Hotel, Chambercombe Park, Ilfracombe, Devon, EX34 9QW.*
Actual grid ref: SS530473
Tel: **01271 864518**
Mr & Mrs Cath.
Rates fr: *£18.00*-**£18.75**.
Open: All Year (not Xmas)
Beds: 3F 4D 1S
Baths: 5 Ensuite, 2 Shared
⌂ (A) ▣ (8) ⊬⌷ ⊩ ⨯ Ⅲ, Ⓥ
Small no-smoking hotel specialising in walking and cycling holidays. Opposite public swimming baths. Very close to South-West Way and Tarka Trail.

(0.75m) *Cairn House Hotel, 43 St Brannocks Road, Ilfracombe, Devon, EX34 8EH.* Comfortable family hotel. Super views.
Grades: ETB 3 Cr, RAC 1 St
Tel: **01271 863911**
Mrs Tupper.
Rates fr: *£18.00*-**£20.00**.
Open: All Year
Beds: 3F 6D 1S
⌂ (A) ▣ (10) ⊬⌷ ⊩ ⨯ Ⅲ,

(1m) *Sunnymeade Hotel, Dean Cross, West Down, Ilfracombe, Devon, EX34 8NT.* Comfortable country house.
Grades: ETB 3 Cr, Approv, AA 3 Q
Tel: **01271 863668**
Mrs Hunt.
Rates fr: *£18.50*-**£20.50**.
Open: All Year
Beds: 2F 6D 1T 1S
Baths: 8 Ensuite, 2 Shared
(A) ▣ (14) ⌷ ⊩ ⨯ Ⅲ, Ⓥ

(▲ On Path) *Ilfracombe Youth Hostel, Ashmour House, 1 Hillsborough Terrace, Ilfracombe, Devon, EX34 9NR.*
Actual grid ref: SS5247
Warden: Mr M Jenkins.
Tel: **01271 865337**
Under 18: £5.55
Adults: £8.25
Family Bunk Rooms, Centrally Heated, Showers, Evening Meal (7.30 pm), Shop, Television, Games Room
End house on a fine Georgian terrace, overlooking the picturesque harbour and the Bristol Channel

(0.25m) *Highland Hotel, Fortescue Road, Ilfracombe, Devon, EX34 9AD.* Licensed family hotel near sea.
Tel: **01271 865004** Mr Foster.
Rates fr: *£15.00*-**£14.00**.
Open: All Year (not Xmas)
Beds: 2F 5D 1T 2S
Baths: 8 Ensuite 2 Shares
(A) ▣ (4) ⌷ ⨯ Ⅲ, ⦿ ⊬

(On Path) *Floyde Hotel, Brookdale Avenue, Ilfracombe, Devon, EX34 8DB.* Victorian, homely atmosphere, peaceful surroundings.
Grades: ETB Listed
Tel: **01271 862594**
Mr & Mrs Whitmore.
Rates fr: *£13.00*-**£13.00**.
Open: Easter to Oct
Beds: 4F 4D 2T
Baths: 1 Ensuite 9 Shared
⌂ (A) ▣ (10) ⊬⌷ ⨯ Ⓥ ⦿ ⊬

(On Path) *Rainbow Ridge, 53 St Brannocks Road, Ilfracombe, Devon, EX34 8E.* Delightful Victorian house.
Tel: **01271 863817** Miss Higgs.
Rates fr: *£13.00*-**£13.00**.
Open: All Year
Beds: 2F 2D 2T 1S
Baths: 5 Ensuite 2 Shared
▣ (7) ⌷ ⊩ ⨯ Ⅲ, Ⓥ ⦿ ⊬

(On Path) *The Epchris Hotel, Torrs Park, Ilfracombe, Devon, EX34 8.*
Actual grid ref: SS512475
Small, comfortable period hotel.
Grades: ETB 3 Cr
Tel: **01271 862751**
Rates fr: *£17.00*-**£17.00**.
Open: Feb to Dec
Beds: 6F 1D 1S **Baths:** 1 Shared
(A) ▣ (7) ⌷ ⨯ Ⅲ, Ⓥ ⦿ ⊬

(On Path) *2 Capstone Place, Ilfracombe, Devon, EX34 9BT.* Converted fisherman's cottage.
Tel: **01271 865201** Mrs Howard.
Rates fr: *£13.50*-**£13.50**.
Open: Easter to Oct
Beds: 1D 1T
Baths: 1 Shared
⌷ ⨯ Ⅲ, Ⓥ ⦿ ⊬

Mortehoe   14

National Grid Ref: SS4545

⑩ ⓠ Ship Aground

(On Path) *Lundy House Hotel, Chapel Hill, Mortehoe, Woolacombe, Devon, EX34 7RZ.*
Actual grid ref: SS4545
Friendly hotel with magnificent seaviews.
Grades: ETB 3 Cr, Comm
Tel: **01271 870372** Mr Sells.
Rates fr: *£17.50*-**£17.50**.
Open: Feb to Oct
Beds: 5F 2D 2S
Baths: 6 Private 1 Shared
⌂ (A) ▣ (10) ⊬⌷ ⊩ ⨯ Ⅲ, Ⓥ ⦿ ⊬

Woolacombe 15

National Grid Ref: SS4543

|O| 🍴 Hartland House, Gema Restaurant, Stables Inn

(0.5m) *Camberley, Beach Road, Woolacombe, Ilfracombe, Devon,* EX34 7AA.
Actual grid ref: SS465437
Large Victorian private house.
Grades: ETB 3 Cr, AA 3 Q, Recomm
Tel: 01271 870231
Mr & Mrs Riley.
Rates fr: £15.00-£16.00.
Open: All Year
Beds: 1F 3D 2T Baths: 6 Ensuite
(A) �P (6) ☐ 🍴 ✕ Ⅲ. ♣ ∕

(On Path) *Ocean View, The Esplanade, Woolacombe, Devon,* EX34 7DJ.
Detached gentleman's residence.
Tel: 01271 870359 Mrs Gyles.
Rates fr: £15.00-£17.00.
Open: Easter to Nov
Beds: 2F 4D 1T 3S
Baths: 10 Ensuite
☐ ☐ Ⅲ. ♣ ∕

(On Path) *Clyst House, Rockfield Road, Woolacombe, Devon,* EX34 7DH.
Friendly comfortable guesthouse.
Tel: 01271 870220 Mrs Braund.
Rates fr: £16.00-£16.00.
Open: Feb to Nov
Beds: 2D 1T Baths: 1 Shared
⛵ (A) ☐ (3) ☐ ✕ Ⅲ. Ⅴ ∕

(0.5m 🚗) *Headlands Hotel, Beach Road, Woolacombe, Devon,* EX34 7BT.
Welcoming family-run hotel.
Grades: ETB 3 Cr, RAC 2 St
Tel: 01271 970320 Mr Millichope.
Rates fr: £19.50-£19.50.
Open: Easter to Oct
Beds: 3F 8D 2T
Baths: 10 Ensuite 2 Shared
⛵ (A) ☐ (16) ⚄ 🍴 ✕ Ⅲ. Ⅴ ♣ ∕

(0.25m 🚗) *Barton Lea Guest House, Beach Road, Woolacombe, Devon,* EX34 7BT.
Modern private house with seaviews.
Tel: 01271 870928 Mrs Vickery.
Rates fr: £14.00-£18.00.
Open: All Year (not Xmas)
Beds: 1F 1D 1T
Baths: 3 Ensuite
(A) ☐ (7) ☐ ✕ Ⅲ. Ⅴ ♣ ∕

(0.25m 🚗) *Holmesdale Hotel, Bay View Road, Woolacombe, Devon,* EX34 7DQ.
Family-run hotel with sea views.
Grades: ETB 3 Cr, AA 3 Q
Tel: 01271 870335 Mr Oyarzabal.
Rates fr: £18.00-£18.00.
Open: All Year
Beds: 11D 2T 2S
Baths: 15 Ensuite
(A) ☐ 🍴 ✕ Ⅲ. Ⅴ ♣ ∕

Croyde 16

National Grid Ref: SS4439

|O| 🍴 Thatched Barn Freehouse

(On Path) *Chapel Farm, Hobbs Hill, Croyde, Braunton, Devon,* EX33 1NE.
Actual grid ref: SS444390
C16th thatched farmhouse, 10 minutes to beach.
Tel: 01271 890429 Mrs Windsor.
Rates fr: £16.00-£18.00.
Open: Easter to Oct Beds: 2D 1S
Baths: 1 Private, 1 Shared
(A) ☐ ⚄ ☐ Ⅲ. Ⅴ ∕

(0.75m 🚗) *Combas Farm, Croyde, Braunton, Devon,* EX33 1PH.
Actual grid ref: SS449396
Old world C17th farmhouse.
Grades: ETB Listed, Comm
Tel: 01271 890398 Ms Adams.
Rates fr: £15.00-£18.50.
Open: Easter to Dec
Beds: 2F 2D 1T 1S
Baths: 2 Shared
(A) ☐ (8) ☐ 🍴 ✕ Ⅴ ♣ ∕
Also ⛺ £3.50 per tent.
Open: Easter to Nov 🏠 ⛺ ✕ ♿

(On Path) *West Winds Guest House, Moor Lane, Croyde Bay, Croyde, Braunton, Devon,* EX33 1PA.
Small guesthouse, waters edge location.
Grades: ETB 3 Cr, AA 3 Q, Recomm
Tel: 01271 890489 Mrs Gedling.
Rates fr: £21.00-£19.00.
Open: All Year (not Xmas)
Beds: 3D 1T
Baths: 3 Ensuite 1 Shared
(A) ☐ (6) ⚄ ☐ 🍴 ✕ Ⅲ. Ⅴ ♣

Saunton 17

National Grid Ref: SS4537

|O| 🍴 The Skipper

(0.25m) *2 Linksview, Saunton, Braunton, Devon,* EX33.
Very comfortable, homely welcome.
Tel: 01271 812233 Mrs Dale.
Rates fr: £13.00-£13.00.
Open: All Year (not Xmas)
Beds: 1F 1D 1T Baths: 1 Shared
(A) ☐ (2) ⚄ ☐ 🍴 ✕ Ⅴ ♣ ∕

Braunton 18

National Grid Ref: SS4836

|O| 🍴 Mariners Arms

(0.25m) *North Cottage, 14 North Street, Braunton, Devon,* EX33 1AJ.
Actual grid ref: SS486367
Old picturesque cottage near village.
Tel: 01271 812703 Mrs Watkins.
Rates fr: £12.50-£12.50.
Open: All Year Beds: 1F 2D 1S
Baths: 1 Ensuite, 1 Shared
(A) ☐ (3) ⚄ ☐ 🍴 Ⅲ. Ⅴ ♣ ∕

Wrafton 19

National Grid Ref: SS4935

|O| 🍴 Williams Arms

(On Path) *Poyers Farm Hotel, Wrafton, Braunton, Devon,* EX33 2DN.
Actual grid ref: SS492355
Thatched Devon longhouse.
Tel: 01271 812149
Mr & Mrs Gross.
Rates fr: £20.00-£20.00.
Open: All Year (not Xmas)
Beds: 1F 3D 3T 2S
Baths: 9 Ensuite
(A) ☐ (15) ☐ 🍴 Ⅲ.

Barnstaple 20

National Grid Ref: SS5633

|O| 🍴 North Countryman, Windsor Arms, Rolle Quay

(0.25m) *Crossways, Braunton Road, Barnstaple, Devon,* EX31 1JY.
Actual grid ref: SS555333
Detached house - town centre 150 yds.
Tel: 01271 79120 Mr & Mrs Capp.
Rates fr: £13.50-£15.50.
Open: All Year (not Xmas)
Beds: 1F 1D 1T
Baths: 2 Private 1Shared
(A) ☐ (6) ⚄ ☐ Ⅲ. ♣

(0.75m) *Yeo Dale Hotel, Pilton Bridge, Barnstaple, Devon,* EX31 1PG.
Spacious Georgian town house.
Grades: ETB 3 Cr, Comm, RAC Acclaim
Tel: 01271 42954 Mr/Mrs Smith.
Rates fr: £19.00-£19.00.
Open: All Year
Beds: 3F 1D 3T 3S
Baths: 6 Private 2 Shared
(A) ☐ 🍴 ✕ Ⅲ. Ⅴ ♣

Fremington 21

National Grid Ref: SS5132

|O| 🍴 New Inn, Fox & Hounds

(1m) *Oakwood, 34 Yelland Road, Fremington, Barnstaple, Devon,* EX31 3DS.
Run like a family home - very friendly.
Tel: 01271 73884 Mrs George.
Rates fr: £11.00-£11.00.
Open: All Year
Beds: 1F 2D Baths: 1 Shared
(A) ☐ ☐ 🍴 ✕ Ⅲ. Ⅴ ♣ ∕

All rates are subject to alteration at the owners' discretion.

Bringing children with
you? Always ask for
any special rates.

Instow 22

National Grid Ref: SS4730
†◎! ⌖ The Quay Inn, Wayfarer,
Boathouse

(▲ On Path) *Instow Youth Hostel,*
Worlington House, New Road,
Instow, Bideford, Devon, EX39 4LW.
Actual grid ref: SS4830
Warden: Mr D Stuart.
Tel: 01271 860394
Under 18: £5.55
Adults: £8.25
Family Bunk Rooms, Partially
Heated, Showers, Evening Meal
(7.00 pm), Shop, Television
Large Victorian country house with
fine views across the Torridge estu-
ary

(On Path) *Pilton Cottage, Victoria*
Terrace, Marine Parade, Instow,
Bideford, Devon, EX39 4JW.
Victorian house, beautiful estuary
view.
Tel: 01271 860202 Mrs Gardner.
Rates fr: *£16.00-£16.00.*
Open: Easter to Oct
Beds: 1F 2D 1T 1S
Baths: 1 Private 1 Shared
🅿 (3) ⍢ ⌸ Ⅲ.

East-The-Water 23

National Grid Ref: SS4626
†◎! ⌖ The Swan

(On Path 🚐) *Kumba, Chudleigh*
Road, East-The-Water, Bideford,
Devon, EX39 4AR.
Large Edwardian residence.
Lovely gardens, views.
Tel: 01237 47 1526
Mr & Mrs Doughty.
Rates fr: *£37.00-£33.00.*
Open: All Year (not Xmas)
Beds: 3F 3D 2T
Baths: 3 Ensuite 1 Shared
(A) 🅿 (8) ⍢ ⌸ Ⅲ. ⌖ Ⅵ ⚱ ⋆

Bideford 24

National Grid Ref: SS4426
†◎! ⌖ Swan Inn, Tanton's Hotel,
Black Horse, Hunters Inn, Pig on
the Hill, Heavitree Inn, Custom
House, The Quay, Appledore Inn

(2m) *14 The Strand, Bideford,*
Devon, EX39 2ND.
Large, comfortable house.
Tel: 01237 473722 Mrs Faulkner.
Rates fr: *£14.00-£16.00.*

Open: All Year (not Xmas)
Beds: 1F 2D 1T 1S
Baths: 1 Shared
(A) ⌸ Ⅲ.

(1m - if no ferry) *Sunset Hotel,*
Landcross, Bideford, Devon,
EX39 5JA.
Actual grid ref: SS239461
Grades: ETB 3 Cr, AA 3 Q,
RAC Acclaim
Tel: 01237 472962 Mrs Lamb.
Rates fr: *£22.50-£25.00.*
Open: Feb to Dec
Beds: 2F 2D 2T
Baths: 4 Private
(A) 🅿 (8) ⍢ ⌸ ⌖ ✕ Ⅲ. Ⅵ ⚱ ⋆
Small country hotel, peaceful pic-
turesque location overlooking the
Tarka Trail. Highly recommended
quality accommodation. Ensuite,
CTV, beverages. Superb home
cooking, everything homemade.
Non-smoking establishment. AA
QQQ.

(0.5m) *Ellerton, Glenburnie Road,*
Bideford, Devon, EX39 2LW.
Modern, comfortable, homely fam-
ily house.
Tel: 01237 473352 Mrs Garnsey.
Rates fr: *£13.50-£13.50.*
Open: All Year
Beds: 1D 2T
Baths: 2 Shared
(A) ⍢ ⌖ Ⅲ. ⚿ Ⅵ ⚱ ⋆

(0.5m) *The Mount Hotel,*
Northdown Road, Bideford, Devon,
EX39 3LP.
Georgian house in own garden.
Grades: ETB 3 Cr, AA 3 Q
Tel: 01237 473748
Mr & Mrs Taylor.
Rates fr: *£19.00-£21.00.*
Open: All Year (not Xmas)
Beds: 1F 2D 3T 2S
Baths: 7 Ensuite
(A) 🅿 (4) ⌸ ✕ Ⅲ. Ⅵ ⚱ ⋆

(0.5m) *Orchard Hill Hotel,*
Orchard Hill, Bideford, Devon,
EX39 2QY.
Regency house in one acre.
Grades: ETB 2 Cr, AA 2 St
Tel: 01237 472872 Mr Lynch.
Rates fr: *£22.50-£30.00.*
Open: Feb to Dec
Beds: 2F 3D 3T 1S
Baths: 9 Ensuite
(A) 🅿 (12) ⍢ ⌸ ✕ Ⅲ. Ⅵ ⚱ ⋆

(3m) *The Mount Hotel,*
Northdown Road, Bideford, Devon,
EX39 3LP.
Quiet, Georgian, edge-of-town
hotel.
Grades: ETB 3 Cr, AA 3 Q
Tel: 01237 473748
Mr & Mrs Taylor.
Rates fr: *£18.50-£22.00.*
Open: All Year
Beds: 1F 3D 2T 2S
Baths: 7 Private 1 Shared
(A) 🅿 (4) ⌸ ✕ Ⅲ. Ⅵ

Huntshaw 25

National Grid Ref: SS5022

(1m 🚐) *The Roundhouse,*
Huntshaw Water, Huntshaw,
Bideford, Devon, EX38 7HE.
Actual grid ref: SS503237
Splendid roundhouse amidst beau-
tiful countryside.
Tel: 01271 858626 Mrs Smith.
Rates fr: *£15.00-£15.00.*
Open: All Year
Beds: 1F 2D
Baths: 3 Ensuite
(A) 🅿 (6) ⌸ ⌖ ✕ Ⅲ. Ⅵ ⚱ ⋆

Appledore 26

National Grid Ref: SS4630
†◎! ⌖ Appledore Inn

(On Path) *The Seagate Hotel, The*
Quay, Appledore, Bideford, Devon,
EX39 1QS.
C17th quayside tavern.
Tel: 01237 472589
Mr & Mrs Gent.
Rates fr: *£19.00-£25.00.*
Open: All Year
Beds: 1F 5D 1T 2S
Baths: 8 Ensuite
(A) 🅿 (20) ⌸ ⌖ ✕ Ⅲ.

Westward Ho! 27

National Grid Ref: SS4329
†◎! ⌖ Grenville Arms, The Pig on
the Hill, Elizabethan

(On Path 🚐) *Brockenhurst,*
11 Atlantic Way, Westward Ho!,
Bideford, Devon, EX39 1HX.
Actual grid ref: SS432290
Warm, clean, comfortable,
detached house.
Grades: ETB 2 Cr, Comm
Tel: 01237 423346 Mrs Snowball.
Rates fr: *£19.50-£24.00.*
Open: All Year (not Xmas)
Beds: 2D 1T
Baths: 3 Ensuite
🅿 (4) ⌸ ⌖ Ⅲ. Ⅵ ⚱ ⋆

(0.5m 🚐) *Four Winds,*
Cornborough Road, Westward
Ho!, Bideford, Devon, EX39 1AA.
Unrivalled breakfast, friendliness,
value for money.
Tel: 01237 421741 Mr Evers.
Rates fr: *£17.00-£20.00.*
Open: All Year
Beds: 1F 2D 2T
Baths: 2 Private 3 Shared
(A) 🅿 (6) ⍢ ⌸ Ⅲ. ⚱ ⋆

(1m) *72 Atlantic Way, Westward*
Ho!, Bideford, Devon, EX39 1JG.
Comfortable old house, sea views.
Tel: 01237 421174 Ms Michalak.
Rates fr: *£13.00-£13.00.*
Open: All Year
Beds: 2D 1T
Baths: 1 Shared
(A) ⌸ ⌖ Ⅲ. ⚱ ⋆

Horns Cross 28

National Grid Ref: SS3823

⊙ ◖ The Hoops Inn, Coach & Horses

(0.5m 🚌) *The Hoops Inn, Horns Cross, Bideford, Devon, EX39 5DL.*
Actual grid ref: SS373232
C13th Historic thatched Inn/Hotel.
Grades: ETB 3 Crowns, Comm, RAC XX
Tel: 01237 451222 Mrs Marriott.
Rates fr: *£26.00-£35.00.*
Open: All Year
Beds: 8D 4T 4S
Baths: 12E 2S
ॐ (A) 🅿 (100) ⊬ ▢ ★ ✕ Ⅲ. Ⅴ ▪ ⌁

(0.25m) *The Holt, (on A39), Horns Cross, Bideford, Devon.*
Breathtaking views across Bideford Bay to Lundy Island.
Tel: 01237 451342 Mrs McNeil.
Rates fr: *£12.00-£12.00.*
Open: All Year
Beds: 1F 1D 1T
Baths: 1 Shared
(A) 🅿 (6) ▢ Ⅴ ▪ ⌁

(On Path 🚌) *Northway House, Horns Cross, Bideford, Devon, EX39 5EA.*
C17th farmhouse.
Tel: 01237 451899 Mr Sanders.
Rates fr: *£16.00-£18.00.*
Open: All Year
Beds: 2F 1D
Baths: 2 Shared
(A) 🅿 ▢ ★ ✕ Ⅲ. Ⅴ ▪ ⌁

Clovelly 29

National Grid Ref: SS3124

⊙ ◖ New Inn (Clovelly), Red Lion (Clovelly)

(0.25m 🚌) *Red Lion Hotel, The Quay, Clovelly, Bideford, Devon, EX39 5TF.*
Sensitively renovated C18th harbourside hotel.
Tel: 01237 431237 Mrs Grant.
Rates fr: *£31.50-£39.00.*
Open: All Year
Beds: 2F 8D 2T
Baths: 12 Private
(A) 🅿 (12) ▢ ✕ Ⅴ ▪ ⌁

🚌 sign means that, given due notice, owners will pick you up from the path and drop you off within reason.

Higher Clovelly 30

National Grid Ref: SS3123

⊙ ◖ New Inn, Red Lion

(0.50m 🚌) *The Old Smithy, Slerra Hill, Higher Clovelly, Bideford, Devon, EX39 5ST.*
Actual grid ref: SS3124
Converted C17th blacksmith's forge.
Tel: 01237 431202 Mrs Vanstone.
Rates fr: *£14.50.*
Open: All Year
Beds: 3F 3D 2T
Baths: 2 Ensuite, 1 Shared
🅿 (3) ▢ ★ Ⅴ ▪ ⌁

(0.25m) *The Boat House, 148 Slerra Hill, Higher Clovelly, Bideford, Devon, EX39 5ST.*
C17th cottage.
Tel: 01237 431209 Mrs May.
Rates fr: *£13.50-£15.00.*
Open: All Year (not Xmas)
Beds: 1F 1D 1T 1S
Baths: 1 Shared
(A) 🅿 (3) ▢ ★ ✕ Ⅲ. ▪ ⌁

(0.25m) *Dyke Green Farm, Higher Clovelly, Bideford, Devon, EX39 5RU.*
Actual grid ref: SS311237
Beautiful converted barn, every comfort.
Tel: 01237 431279 / 431699
Mrs Johns.
Rates fr: *£14.00-£18.00.*
Open: All Year (not Xmas)
Beds: 2D 1T
Baths: 2 Ensuite 1 Shared
(A) 🅿 ⊬ ▢ ★ Ⅲ. Ⅴ ⌁
Also ▲ *£6.50 per tent.*
Open: Mar to Oct 🔥 Ⓣ

Titchberry 31

National Grid Ref: SS2427

(0.25m 🚌) *West Titchberry Farm, Titchberry, Hartland Point, Bideford, Devon, EX39 6AU.*
C18th coastal farmhouse.
Tel: 01237 441287 Mrs Heard.
Rates fr: *£13.50-£13.50.*
Open: All Year (not Xmas)
Beds: 1F 1D 1T
Baths: 1 Shared
(A) 🅿 ▢ ✕ Ⅲ. Ⅴ ▪ ⌁

Stoke 32

National Grid Ref: SS2324

⊙ ◖ Hartland Quay Hotel, Kings Arms

(0.5m 🚌) *Homeleigh, Stoke, Hartland, Bideford, Devon, EX39 6DU.*
Secluded dormer bungalow, warm welcome.
Tel: 01237 441465 Mrs Slee.
Rates fr: *£14.50-£15.00.*
Open: March to Oct
Beds: 1D 1T
Baths: 1Shared
ॐ (A) 🅿 (2) ⊬ ▢ Ⅲ. Ⅴ ▪ ⌁

Hartland Quay 33

National Grid Ref: SS2224

⊙ ◖ Hartland Quay Hotel

(On Path 🚌) *Hartland Quay Hotel, Hartland Quay, Hartland, Bideford, Devon, EX39 6DU.*
Former Corn Exchange, family home. **Grades:** ETB 2 Cr
Tel: 01237 441218 Mrs Johns.
Rates fr: *£19.00-£19.00.*
Open: Easter to Nov
Beds: 2F 6D 6T 2S
Baths: 8 Private 3 Shared
(A) 🅿 ▢ ★ ✕ Ⅲ. Ⅴ ▪ ⌁

Hartland 34

National Grid Ref: SS2524

⊙ ◖ The Hartland Quay Hotel

(2.5m 🚌) *Anchor Inn, Fore Street, Hartland, Bideford, Devon, EX39 6BD.*
Friendly 16th Century inn.
Grades: ETB 1 Cr
Tel: 01237 441414 Mr Hodges.
Rates fr: *£15.00.*
Open: All Year (not Xmas)
Beds: 2F 4D 2T 1S
Baths: 5 Ensuite, 2 Shared
(A) 🅿 (15) ▢ ✕ Ⅲ. ▪ ⌁

(1.5m) *Greenlake Farm, Hartland, Bideford, Devon, EX39 6DN.*
Actual grid ref: SS245227
Old comfortable farmhouse.
Tel: 01237 441251 Mrs Heard.
Rates fr: *£12.00-£12.00.*
Open: Easter to Nov
Beds: 1F 1D **Baths:** 1 Shared
(A) 🅿 (3) ▢ ★ ✕

Elmscott 35

National Grid Ref: SS2524

(▲ 0.5m) *Elmscott Youth Hostel, Elmscott, Hartland, Bideford, Devon, EX39 6ES.*
Warden: Ms A Tooby.
Tel: 01237 441367
Under 18: £3.75 **Adults:** £5.50
Family Bunk Rooms, Partially Heated, Showers, Self-Catering Only
Former Victorian schoolhouse and enclosed garden in a remote Area of Outstanding Natural Beauty with views of Lundy Island

Welcombe 36

National Grid Ref: SS2218

(1.25m) *Old Smithy Inn, Welcombe, Hartland, Bideford, Devon, EX39 6HG.*
C13th thatched inn.
Tel: 01288 331305 Mr Marshall.
Rates fr: *£17.50-£19.50.*
Open: All Year **Beds:** 1F 1D
Baths: 1 Ensuite 1 Shared
(A) 🅿 (50) ▢ ★ ✕ Ⅲ. Ⅴ ▪ ⌁

Cornwall

This section of the **South West Coast Path** covers the entire Cornish coast, from the exposed and rugged cliffs of the North, past Lands End and the Lizard to the quieter creeks and bold promontories of the South (see beginning of chapter for more **South West Coast Path** details).

Guides: *South West Way: Vol I* (Minehead to Penzance) ISBN 1 85284 025 0, and *South West Way: Vol II* (Penzance to Poole), ISBN 1 85284 026 9, both by Martin Collins and published by Cicerone Press and available from the publishers (2 Police Square, Milnthorpe, Cumbria, LA7 7PY, 01539 562069), £8.99 (+75p p&p) each

South West Way: Padstow to Falmouth by John Macadam (ISBN 1 85410 3873), published by Aurum Press in association with the Countryside Commission and Ordnance Survey, £9.99

South West Way: Falmouth to Exmouth by Brian Le Messuarier (ISBN 1 85410 3881), published by Aurum Press in association with the Countryside Commission and Ordnance Survey, £9.99.

There is also invaluable local information in *The South West Way 1996* by the **South West Way Association**, available directly from them (1 Orchard Drive, Kingskerswell, Newton Abbot, Devon, TQ12 5DG, tel 01803 873061), £3.99 (+ 70p p&p).

Maps: Ordnance Survey 1:50,000 Landranger series: 190, 200, 201, 203 and 204.

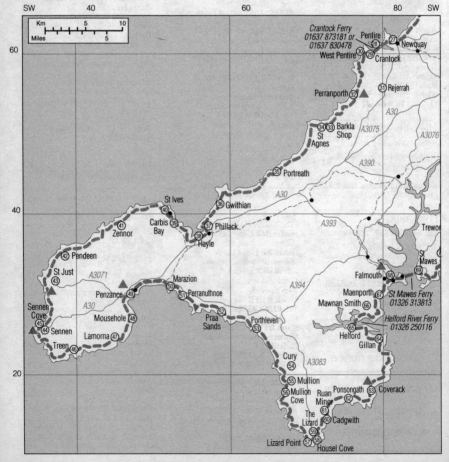

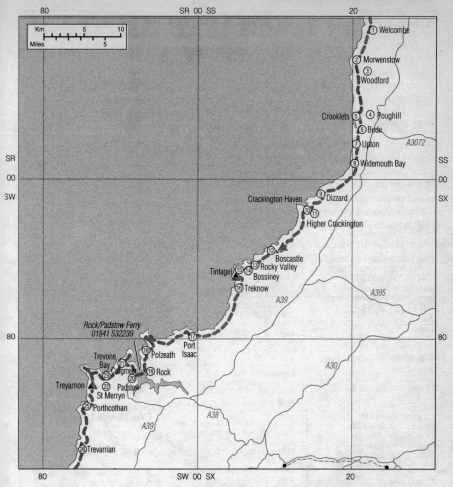

① Welcombe
② Morwenstow
③ Woodford
Crooklets ⑤ ④ Poughill
⑥ Bude
⑦ Upton
A3072
⑧ Widemouth Bay
Crackington Haven ⑨ Dizzard
⑩
⑪
Higher Crackington
⑫
Boscastle
⑬ Rocky Valley
Tintagel ⑮ ⑭ Bossiney
⑯ Treknow
A39   A395
Rock/Padstow Ferry
01841 532239
⑰
⑱ Polzeath
Trevone Port
Bay ㉑ Isaac
Tregmeer ㉓ ㉒㉔ ⑲ Rock
Treyarnon ㉒ ㉔ ㉑ Padstow
St Merryn
㉕ Porthcothan
A39   A38
㉖ Trevarrian
A30

Welcombe 1

National Grid Ref: SS2218

(1.25m) *Old Smithy Inn,*
Welcombe, Hartland, Bideford,
Devon, EX39 6HG.
C13th thatched inn.
Tel: **01288 331305** Mr Marshall.
Rates fr: *£17.50-£19.50.*
Open: All Year
Beds: 1F 1D
Baths: 1 Ensuite 1 Shared
(A) 🅿 (50) 🛏 ✕ ▥ ⓥ ♪

Please take muddy

boots off before

entering premises

Morwenstow 2

National Grid Ref: SS2015

(1.5m) *Dene Farm,*
Morwenstow, Bude, Cornwall,
EX23 9SL.
Comfortable farmhouse surrounded
with gardens.
Grades: ETB Comm
Tel: **01288 83330**
Mrs Heard.
Rates fr: *£15.00-£15.00.*
Open: All Year (not Xmas)
Beds: 1F 3D
Baths: 1 Ensuite, 1 Shared
(A) 🅿 (6) ✕ 🛏 ✕ ▥ ⓥ ♪

(1m) *Meadow Park, Lee*
Barton, Morwenstow, Bude,
Cornwall, EX23 9ST.
Actual grid ref: SS2212
Large farm bungalow, scenic
views.
Grades: ETB Listed

Tel: **01288 331499** Mrs Hobbs.
Rates fr: *£13.00-£13.00.*
Open: All Year (not Xmas)
Beds: 1F 1D 1T
Baths: 2 Private 1 Shared
(A) 🅿 (3) 🛏 ✕ ▥ ♪

Woodford 3

National Grid Ref: SS2113

(2m) *Darzle Farm, Woodford,*
Morwenstow, Bude, Cornwall,
EX23 9HY.
Grades: ETB 2 Cr, Comm
Tel: **01288 331222** Mrs Cholwill.
Rates fr: *£17.00-£17.00.*
Open: All Year
Beds: 3F 1D
Baths: 4 Private
🅿 (8) 🛏 ✕ ⓥ ♪
Warm, homely welcome, quiet
countryside, lovely walks, beach 2
miles, colour TV, coffee & tea-
making facilities in all bedrooms,
all ensuite.

Poughill 4

National Grid Ref: SS2207

(0.25m 🚗) *Lower Northcott Farm, Poughill, Bude, Cornwall, EX23 7EL.*
Actual grid ref: SS2207
Georgian farmhouse with spectacular views.
Grades: ETB 2 Cr, Comm, AA 3 Q, Recomm
Tel: **01288 352350** Mrs Trewin.
Rates fr: *£17.00.*
Open: All Year **Beds:** 2F 2D 1T 1S
Baths: 6 Ensuite 1 Shared
(A) ▣ (5) ⅍ ⊐ ⻗ ✕ ⅏ ⓥ ⋒ ⥹

Crooklets 5

National Grid Ref: SS2007

†⊙† 🍴 Crooklets Inn (Crooklets)

(On Path) *Crooklets Inn, Crooklets, Bude, Cornwall, EX23 8NF.*
Friendly family-run inn, sea views.
Tel: **01288 352335** Mrs Warburton.
Rates fr: *£12.50-£12.50.*
Open: All Year (not Xmas)
Beds: 2F 7D 2T **Baths:** 6 Private
(A) ▣ ⊐ ⻗ ✕ ⅏ ⓥ ⋒ ⥹

Bude 6

National Grid Ref: SS2106

†⊙† 🍴 Crooklets Inn, Globe Hotel, Brendon Arms

(On Path) *Inn On The Green, Crooklets Beach, Bude, Cornwall, EX23 8NF.*
Tel: **01288 356013** Mr Bellward.
Rates fr: *£16.00-£16.00.*
Open: All Year (not Xmas)
Beds: 2F 9D 9T 5S
Baths: 14 Ensuite, 3 Shared
⛵ (A) ▣ (6) ⊐ ⻗ ✕ ⅏ ⓥ ⋒ ⥹
Comfortable family run hotel superbly situated at Crooklets Beach, Bude, in an area of majestic Cornish cliffs and unspoilt sandy beaches midway between Hartland Point and Boscastle. Bar and restaurant open daily.

(On Path 🚗) *Kisauni, 4 Downs View, Bude, Cornwall, EX23 8.*
Bright and airy Victorian house.
Tel: **01288 352653** Mrs Kimpton.
Rates fr: *£13.00-£13.00.*
Open: All Year (not Xmas)
Beds: 2F 3D 1T 1S
Baths: 1 Ensuite, 2 Shared
(A) ▣ (5) ⊐ ⻗ ✕ ⓥ ⋒ ⥹

(1.5m 🚗) *Marhamrise Guest House, 50 Kings Hill, Bude, Cornwall, EX23 8QH.*
Large Victorian house, warm and comforting.
Tel: **01288 354713** Mrs Thornton.
Rates fr: *£12.00-£12.00.*
Open: Easter to Oct
Beds: 1F 1D
⛵ (A) ▣ (3) ⊐ ✕ ⅏ ⅋ ⋒ ⥹

(0.5m) *Travellers Friend, 8 Downs View, Bude, Cornwall, EX23 8RF.*
Clean, comfortable, friendly, good breakfast.
Grades: ETB Reg
Tel: **01288 355059** Mrs Stock.
Rates fr: *£12.00-£12.00.*
Open: All Year (not Xmas)
Beds: 2F 1D 2T 1S
Baths: 2 Ensuite 4 Shared
(A) ▣ (2) ⊐ ⅏ ⓥ ⋒ ⥹

(On Path) *Mornish Hotel, 20 Summerleaze Crescent, Bude, Cornwall, EX23 8HJ.*
Actual grid ref: SS221140
Best situated hotel in Bude.
Grades: ETB Memb
Tel: **01288 352972**
Mr Hilder.
Rates fr: *£18.00-£18.00.*
Open: Mar to Nov
Beds: 3F 5D 2T
Baths: 10 Private
(A) ▣ (4) ⊐ ⻗ ✕ ⅏ ⓥ ⋒ ⥹

(On Path) *Sea Jade, 15 Burn View, Bude, Cornwall, EX23 8BZ.*
Licensed comfortable guest house.
Grades: ETB Reg
Tel: **01288 353404**
Mrs Lloyd.
Rates fr: *£12.50-£12.50.*
Open: All Year
Beds: 2F 2D 2T 1S
Baths: 1 Shared
(A) ⊐ ⅏ ⓥ ⋒ ⥹

Upton 7

National Grid Ref: SS2004

†⊙† 🍴 Brendon Arms, Falcon Hotel

(On Path) *The Meva Gwin Hotel, Upton, Bude, Cornwall, EX23 0LY.*
Actual grid ref: SS202049
Modern spacious hotel, breathtaking views.
Grades: ETB 3 Cr, Comm, AA 1 St, RAC 1 St
Tel: **01288 352347**
Mrs Ball.
Rates fr: *£18.00-£18.00.*
Open: Easter to Oct
Beds: 7D 3T 3S
Baths: 13 Private
(A) ▣ (44) ⊐ ✕ ⅏ ⋒ ⥹

Widemouth Bay 8

National Grid Ref: SS2002

†⊙† 🍴 Widemouth Manor, Brocksmoor Hotel, Bay View

(On Path) *Seaspray, 1 The Crescent, Widemouth Bay, Bude, Cornwall, EX23 0AD.*
Actual grid ref: SS2002
Modern comfortable bungalow.
Tel: **01288 361459**
Mr & Mrs Golby-Green.
Rates fr: *£14.00-£15.00.*
Open: All Year
Beds: 2D 1T
Baths: 3 Ensuite
▣ (4) ⅍ ⊐ ⅏ ⓥ ⋒ ⥹

(On Path) *The Bay View Inn, Widemouth Bay, Bude, Cornwall, EX23 0AW.*
Actual grid ref: SS201028
Family freehouse pub, overlooking sea.
Grades: ETB Listed
Tel: **01288 361273** Mr Gooder.
Rates fr: *£12.00-£12.00.*
Open: All Year
Beds: 3F 3D 1T 2S
Baths: 4 Private, 2 Shared
(A) ▣ (30) ⊐ ⻗ ✕ ⅏ ⓥ ⥹

(0.25m) *Penhalt Farm, Widemouth Bay, Bude, Cornwall, EX23 0.*
Panoramic sea views.
Grades: ETB 3 Cr
Tel: **01288 361210**
Mrs Marks.
Rates fr: *£12.50-£15.00.*
Open: All Year (not Xmas)
Beds: 1F 1D 1T
Baths: 2 Shared
(A) ▣ ⻗ ⥹
Also ⛺ *£5 (2) per tent.*
Open: Easter to Oct ⋒ ⊤ ⊞ ⥹ �

Dizzard 9

National Grid Ref: SX1698

(0.25m 🚗) *Penrose, Dizzard, St Gennys, Bude, Cornwall, EX23 0NX.*
C17th cosy comfortable cottage.
Tel: **01840 230318**
Mrs Joyner.
Rates fr: *£15.00-£15.00.*
Open: All Year
Beds: 1F 4D 1T
Baths: 2 Ensuite, 1 Shared
(A) ▣ (8) ⅍ ⊐ ✕ ⅏ ⓥ ⋒

Crackington Haven 10

National Grid Ref: SX1496

†⊙† 🍴 Coombe Barton Inn

(0.75m 🚗) *Hallagather, Crackington Haven, Bude, Cornwall, EX23 0LA.*
Actual grid ref: SX146956
C15th listed farm house.
Grades: ETB 2 Cr, Comm
Tel: **01840 230276**
Mrs Anthony.
Rates fr: *£12.50-£14.00.*
Open: All Year (not Xmas)
Beds: 1F 1D 1S
Baths: 3 Private
⛵ (A) ▣ (5) ⊐ ⻗ ⅏ ⓥ ⥹

(0.25m 🚗) *Tregather, Crackington Haven, Bude, Cornwall, EX23 0LQ.*
Actual grid ref: SX138957
Delightful accommodation, welcoming atmosphere.
Grades: ETB Listed, Comm
Tel: **01840 230667**
Mrs Crocker.
Rates fr: *£14.00-£16.00.*
Open: Feb to Nov
Beds: 2D 1T
Baths: 1 Private 1 Shared
(A) ▣ (4) ⊐ ✕ ⓥ ⋒ ⥹

**Pay B&Bs by
cash or cheque and
be prepared to
pay up front.**

(0.25m) *Trevigue, Crackington
Haven, Bude, Cornwall, EX23 0LQ.*
C16th farmhouse with courtyard.
Grades: AA 5 Q
Tel: 01840 230418 Mrs Crocker.
Rates fr: *£20.00-£25.00.*
Open: Mar to Oct
Beds: 5D 1T **Baths:** 6 Private
🛏 (A) 🅿 (20) 🖵 ✗ Ⅴ

(On Path) *Coombe Barton Inn,
Crackington Haven, Bude, ·
Cornwall, EX23 0L.*
Fully licensed free-house next to
beach.
Grades: ETB 3 Cr, AA 3 Q,
RAC Listed
Tel: 01840 230345 Mr Cooper.
Rates fr: *£17.50-£19.50.*
Open: March to Oct
Beds: 1F 3D 1T 3S
Baths: 3 Private 2 Shared
🛏 (A) 🅿 (40) 🖵 🛏 ✗ 🖵 Ⅴ 🗎 ✓

Higher Crackington 11
National Grid Ref: SX1595

🍴 🍷 The Coombe Barton Inn

(1m 🚌) *5 Penkenna Close,
Higher Crackington, St Gennys,
Bude, Cornwall, EX23 0PF.*
Actual grid ref: SX155956
Private bungalow with sea view.
Tel: 01840 230648 Mrs Short.
Rates fr: *£11.50-£11.50.*
Open: All Year (not Xmas)
Beds: 2T
(A) 🅿 (2) ✗ 🖵 🖵 Ⅴ 🗎 ✓

(1m 🚌) *8 Penkenna Close,
Higher Crackington, St Gennys,
Bude, Cornwall, EX23 0PF.*
Actual grid ref: SX155956
Homely comfortable, easy parking,
garden.
Tel: 01840 230413 Mrs Redman.
Rates fr: *£12.50-£13.50.*
Open: All Year (not Xmas)
Beds: 1D 1T 1S
Baths: 1 Shared
(A) 🅿 (3) 🖵 ✗ 🖵 🗎 ✓

**Always telephone
to get directions to
the B&B - you will
save time!**

Boscastle 12
National Grid Ref: SX0990

🍴 🍷 The Wellington Hotel,
Napoleon Inn, Long Bar

(0.25m 🚌) *Tolcarn Hotel,
Tintagel Road, Boscastle,
Cornwall, PL35 0AS.*
Actual grid ref: SX098905
Grades: ETB 3 Cr, Comm,
AA 4 Q, Select
Tel: 01840 250654
Mr & Mrs Crown.
Rates fr: *£20.00-£24.00.*
Open: Feb to Nov
Beds: 6D 2T 1S
Baths: 8 Private 1 Shared
🛏 (A) 🅿 (15) ✗ 🖵 🛏 ✗ 🖵 🗎 ✓
A character Victorian house with
large grounds and spectacular
views of the NT owned coastline.
Family-run, warm atmosphere.
Licensed restaurant and bar. Ample
parking.

(0.25m 🚌) *The Wellington Hotel,
The Harbour, Boscastle, Cornwall,
PL35 0AQ.*
Actual grid ref: SX009913
Historic listed C16th coaching inn.
Grades: ETB 3 Cr, Comm,
AA 2 St, RAC 2 St
Tel: 01840 250202
Mr & Mrs Tobutt.
Rates fr: *£21.00-£12.00.*
Open: All Year
Beds: 8D 5T 8S
Baths: 16 Private 5 Shared
🛏 (A) 🅿 (20) 🖵 🛏 ✗ 🖵 Ⅴ 🗎 ✓

(0.5m 🚌) *Bottreaux House Hotel,
Boscastle, Cornwall, PL35 0BG.*
Grades: ETB 3 Cr
Tel: 01840 250231 Mr Mee.
Rates fr: *£18.00-£23.00.*
Open: All Year **Beds:** 1F 4D 2T
Baths: 7 Ensuite
🛏 (A) 🅿 (9) 🖵 🛏 ✗ 🖵 Ⅴ 🗎 ✓
Georgian hotel set in conservation
area of harbour village. Candlelit
restaurant and bar, superb quality
rooms, free use of mountain bikes,
complete key freedom.

(🚶 On Path) *Boscastle Harbour
Youth Hostel, Palace Stables,
Boscastle, Cornwall, PL35 0HD.*
Actual grid ref: SX0991
Warden: Ms L Masters.
Tel: 01840 250287
Under 18: £5.00 **Adults:** £7.45
Family Bunk Rooms, Partially
Heated, Showers, Evening Meal
(7.00 pm)
*In a superb position right on the
harbour edge where the River
Valency enters the National Trust
fishing harbour*

(0.5m) *The Old Coach House,
Boscastle, Cornwall, PL35.*
Actual grid ref: SX096906
Beautiful former coach-house.
Grades: ETB 2 Cr, AA 3 Q,
RAC Listed

Tel: 01840 250398 Mrs Miller.
Rates fr: *£15.00-£15.00.*
Open: March to Oct
Beds: 1F 2D 2T 1S
Baths: 6 Private
🛏 (A) 🅿 (9) 🖵 🖵 🗎 ✓

Rocky Valley 13
National Grid Ref: SX0789

🍴 🍷 Cornishman

(0.25m) *Trevillett Mill Trout
Farm, Rocky Valley, Tintagel,
Cornwall, PL34 0.*
Actual grid ref: SX073892
C15th working watermill in idyllic
setting.
Tel: 01840 770564 Mr Read.
Rates fr: *£14.00-£14.00.*
Open: All Year (not Xmas)
Beds: 1F 4T
Baths: 2 Shared
(A) 🅿 (6) 🖵 🛏 ✗ 🖵 Ⅴ 🗎 ✓

Bossiney 14
National Grid Ref: SX0688

(On Path) *Willapark Manor Hotel,
Bossiney, Tintagel, Cornwall,
PL34 0BA.*
Character house, spectacular
clifftop setting.
Grades: ETB 3 Cr, Comm
Tel: 01840 770782
Mr Leeds.
Rates fr: *£23.00-£23.00.*
Open: All Year (not Xmas)
Beds: 2F 7D 2T 2S
Baths: 13 Private
(A) 🅿 (20) 🖵 🛏 ✗ 🖵 Ⅴ 🗎 ✓

(0.25m) *The Old Borough House,
Bossiney, Tintagel, Cornwall,
PL34 0AY.*
Charming licensed C17th guest-
house.
Grades: ETB 3 Cr, Comm
Tel: 01840 770475 Mrs Rayner.
Rates fr: *£15.50-£25.50.*
Open: All Year
Beds: 1F 3D 1T
Baths: 2 Private 2 Shared
🛏 (A) 🅿 (10) 🖵 ✗ 🖵 Ⅴ 🗎

Tintagel 15
National Grid Ref: SX0588

🍴 🍷 Tintagel Arms, Cornishman,
Port William

(0.25m) *Polkerr Guest House,
Tintagel, Cornwall, PL34.*
Grades: ETB High Comm
Tel: 01840 770382
Mrs Fry.
Rates fr: *£17.00-£17.00.*
Open: All Year (not Xmas)
Beds: 2F 2D 2T 1S
Baths: 6 Ensuite
(A) 🅿 (8) 🖵 ✗ 🖵
Family-run modernised country
house. Off road parking close to
village, King Arthurs Castle and
Coastal Path.

(0.25m) *The Wharncliffe Arms,* Fore Street, Tintagel, Cornwall, *PL34 0DA*.
Hotel for over 100 years.
Tel: **01840 770393**
Mrs Williamson.
Rates fr: £14.00-**£15.00**.
Open: All Year
Beds: 7F 13D 5T 4S
Baths: 2 Ensuite, 4 Shared
(A) 🅿 (30) ⌷ ⊁ ✕ Ⅴ 🛆 ⚡

(▲ On Path) *Tintagel Youth Hostel,* Dunderhole Point, Tintagel, Cornwall, *PL34 0DW*.
Actual grid ref: SX0488
Warden: Mr J Daniels.
Tel: **01840 770334**
Under 18: £5.00 **Adults:** £7.45
Family Bunk Rooms, Partially Heated, Showers, No Smoking
150-year-old slate quarry cottage now owned by the National Trust, in a spectacular clifftop setting, with extensive views across Port Isaac Bay

(0.25m) *The Old Malt House,* Fore Street, Tintagel, Cornwall, *PL34 0DA*.
C14th hotel and licensed restaurant.
Grades: ETB 2 Cr, Comm
Tel: **01840 770461**
Mr & Mrs Ridgewell.
Rates fr: £14.00-**£14.00**.
Open: Easter to Oct
Beds: 1F 5D 1T 1S
Baths: 3 Private 2 Shared
🛏 (A) 🅿 (12) ⌷ ✕ 🛆 ▮

(0.25m) *Tintagel Arms Hotel,* Fore Street, Tintagel, Cornwall, *PL34 0DB*.
Warm family run inn.
Grades: AA 3 Q
Tel: **01840 770780** Mr Hunter.
Rates fr: £17.50-**£25.00**.
Open: All Year
Baths: 7 Ensuite
(A) 🅿 (8) ⌷ ⌷ ✕ 🛆 ▮ ⚡

(0.25m 🚗) *Bossiney House Hotel,* Tintagel, Cornwall, *PL34 0AX*.
Actual grid ref: SX065888
Comfortable family run licensed hotel.
Grades: ETB 3 Cr, AA 2 St, RAC 2 St
Tel: **01840 770240** Mr Savage.
Rates fr: £24.00-**£29.00**.
Open: Easter to Oct
Beds: 1F 9D 9T
Baths: 19 Ensuite
(A) 🅿 (30) ⌷ ⌷ ✕ 🛆 & Ⅴ ▮ ⚡

(On Path) *Grange Cottage,* Bossiney, Tintagel, Cornwall, *PL34 0AX*.
Actual grid ref: SX885065
400-year-old Cornish cottage.
Grades: ETB Reg
Tel: **01840 77 0487** Mrs Jones.
Rates fr: £15.00-**£15.00**.
Open: Easter to Oct
Beds: 1F 1D 1S
Baths: 1 Shared
🛏 (A) 🅿 (4) ⊁ ⌷ ⌷ ✕ 🛆 Ⅴ ▮ ⚡

(0.75m) *Min Pinn,* Tregatta Corner, Tintagel, Cornwall, *PL34*.
Former inn farmhouse.
Tel: **01840 770241** Mrs Hall.
Rates fr: £16.00-**£16.00**.
Open: Easter to Oct
Beds: 1D 1T
Baths: 2 Ensuite
🅿 (20) ⌷ ⌷ ✕ 🛆

(0.25m) *Ferny Park,* Bossiney Hill, Tintagel, Cornwall, *PL34 0BB*.
Actual grid ref: SX073890
Comfortable warm house. Country situation.
Grades: ETB 2 Cr
Tel: **01840 770523**
Mrs Mendoza.
Rates fr: £15.00-**£18.00**.
Open: All Year (not Xmas)
Beds: 1F 1T
Baths: 1 Shared
(A) 🅿 (2) ⊁ 🛆 Ⅴ ⚡

(0.75m) *Trevillett Parc Farm,* Tintagel, Cornwall, *PL34*.
Modern comfortable farmhouse.
Tel: **01840 770662**
Rates fr: £12.50-**£12.50**.
Open: All Year
Beds: 1F 1D 1S
Baths: 3 Ensuite

Treknow 16

National Grid Ref: SX0586

(0.25m) *Stonecroft,* Trelake Lane, Treknow, Tintagel, Cornwall, *PL34 0EW*.
Comfortable bungalow, coastal rural views.
Tel: **01840 770875** Mrs Vernon.
Rates fr: £13.00-**£13.00**.
Open: All Year (not Xmas)
Beds: 2D
Baths: 1 Shared
🛏 (A) 🅿 (2) ⊁ ⌷ ✕ 🛆

Port Isaac 17

National Grid Ref: SW9980

🍴 🍷 Golden Lion, Wheelhouse

(0.25m) *Dunoon Guest House,* 12 Tintagel Terrace, Port Isaac, Cornwall, *PL29 3SE*.
Actual grid ref: SX999808
Overlooking the Atlantic.
Tel: **01208 880383**
Mrs Castle.
Rates fr: £12.00-**£12.00**.
Open: All Year
Beds: 2D 1T
(A) 🅿 ⌷ Ⅴ ▮ ⚡

(On Path 🚗) *St Andrews Hotel,* Port Isaac, Cornwall, *PL29 3SG*.
Clean, comfortable, value for money.
Tel: **01208 880240** Mr Slack.
Rates fr: £17.00-**£16.00**.
Open: All Year
Beds: 1F 5D 1T 2S
Baths: 5 Ensuite 2 Shared
(A) 🅿 (8) ⌷ ⌷ 🛆 ▮ ⚡

Polzeath 18

National Grid Ref: SW9378

(On Path) *Pentire View,* Polzeath, Cornwall, *PL27 6TB*.
Large Victorian house near beach.
Tel: **01208 862484** Mrs Pashley.
Rates fr: £12.00-**£12.00**.
Open: All Year (not Xmas)
Beds: 1F 3T 2S
Baths: 1 Shared
(A) 🅿 ⌷ ⌷ ✕ Ⅴ ⚡

Rock 19

National Grid Ref: SW9476

(0.5m) *Roskarnon House Hotel,* Rock, Wadebridge, Cornwall, *PL27 6LD*.
Large Edwardian house.
Grades: ETB 3 CrRAC 2 St
Tel: **01208 862785** Mr Veall.
Rates fr: £20.00-**£22.50**.
Open: Mar to Oct
Beds: 2F 2D 2T **Baths:** 6 Ensuite
(A) 🅿 (15) ⌷ ⌷ ✕ 🛆 & 🛆 ▮ ⚡

(On Path) *Silvermead,* Rock, Wadebridge, Cornwall, *PL27 6LB*.
Family-run guesthouse.
Tel: **01208 862425** Mrs Martin.
Rates fr: £15.00-**£15.00**.
Open: All Year
Beds: 2F 2D 2T 3S
Baths: 5 Private 1 Shared
(A) 🅿 (9) ⌷ ⌷ ✕ 🛆 Ⅴ ▮ ⚡

Padstow 20

National Grid Ref: SW9175

(0.5m) *Cross House Hotel,* Church Street, Padstow, Cornwall, *PL28 8BG*.
Comfortable, friendly, family run hotel.
Tel: **01841 532391** Miss Gidlow.
Rates fr: £20.00-**£25.00**.
Open: All Year
Beds: 1F 5D 1T
Baths: 4 Ensuite, 3 Shared
🛏 (A) 🅿 (4) ⌷ ⌷ ✕ 🛆 Ⅴ ▮ ⚡

(On Path 🚗) *Newlands Hotel,* Trevone Bay, Padstow, Cornwall, *PL28 8QJ*.
Small friendly licensed hotel.
Tel: **01841 520469** Mrs Philpott.
Rates fr: £18.50-**£18.50**.
Open: All Year
Beds: 1F 6D 3T 1S
Baths: 9 Ensuite
(A) 🅿 (15) ⌷ ⌷ ✕ 🛆 Ⅴ ▮ ⚡

Crugmeer 21

National Grid Ref: SW9076

🍴 ⊄ Old Ship Hotel

(0.75m) *Homeleigh House,*
Crugmeer, Padstow, Cornwall,
PL28.
Actual grid ref: SW903765
Warm, comfortable private house.
Grades: ETB Reg
Tel: **01841 532203** Mrs Jones.
Rates fr: *£16.00-£16.00.*
Open: Mar to Nov
Beds: 1T
Baths: 1 Ensuite
🅿 (2) ⊬ ⊐ Ⅶ 🛈 ✦

St Merryn 22

National Grid Ref: SW8874

🍴 ⊄ Farmers Arms

(1m 🚍) *Well Away, St Merryn,*
Padstow, Cornwall, PL28 8NR.
Bungalow with spacious garden,
friendly atmosphere.
Tel: **01841 520534** Ms Ridgers.
Rates fr: *£12.00-£12.00.*
Open: All Year
Beds: 2D 1T
Baths: 2 Shared
(A) 🅿 (20) ⊬ ⊐ ✕ ▥ Ⅶ 🛈 ✦

Trevone Bay 23

National Grid Ref: SW8876

(0.25m) *Well Parc Hotel, Trevone*
Bay, Padstow, Cornwall, PL28 8QN.
Small family run hotel.
Tel: **01840 520318** Mrs Mills.
Rates fr: *£20.00.*
Open: All Year (not Xmas)
Beds: 4F 4D 1T 1S
(A) 🅿 🛈 ✕ Ⅶ 🛈 ✦

Treyarnon 24

National Grid Ref: SW8673

(▲ On Path) *Treyarnon Bay*
Youth Hostel, Tregonnan,
Treyarnon, Padstow, Cornwall,
PL28 8JR.
Actual grid ref: SW8574
Warden: Ms H Willis.
Tel: **01841 520322**
Under 18: £5.00 **Adults:** £7.45
Family Bunk Rooms, Partially
Heated, Showers, Evening Meal
(7.00 pm)
Overlooking a sandy cove in a des-
ignated Area of Outstanding
Natural Beauty

Porthcothan 25

National Grid Ref: SW8572

🍴 ⊄ Tredrea Inn

(On Path) *Bay House Hotel,*
Porthcothan Bay, Porthcothan,
Padstow, Cornwall, PL28 8L.
Comfortable family hotel, daytime
cafe.

Grades: ETB Listed, AA 2Q
Tel: **01841 520472** Mr & Mrs
Coombes.
Rates fr: *£17.00-£17.00.*
Open: Easter to Nov
Beds: 1F 7D 4T 2S
Baths: 5 Ensuite 4 Shared
(A) 🅿 (15) ⊐ ✕ ▥ Ⅶ 🛈 ✦

Trevarrian 26

National Grid Ref: SW8566

(On Path) *Double K Hotel,*
Trevarrian, Mawgan Porth,
Newquay, Cornwall, TR8 4AQ.
Family-run hotel, warm welcome.
Grades: ETB Listed
Tel: **01637 860422** Mrs Lambert.
Rates fr: *£12.00-£12.00.*
Open: All Year
Beds: 3F 4D 2T
Baths: 5 Private 1 Shared
(A) 🅿 ✕ ▥ Ⅶ 🛈 ✦

Newquay 27

National Grid Ref: SW8161

🍴 ⊄ Famous Firkin

(On Path) *Cliffside Hotel, The*
Crescent, Newquay, Cornwall,
TR7 1DT.
Comfortable modern family hotel.
Tel: **01637 872897** Mrs Machin.
Rates fr: *£15.00-£15.00.*
Open: Easter to Jan
Beds: 5F 15D 15T 5S
Baths: 37 Ensuite 1 Shared
(A) 🅿 (10) ⊐ ✕ ▥ Ⅶ 🛈

(0.25m) *Hemick Lodge, 33 Pentire*
Avenue, Newquay, Cornwall,
TR7 1PB.
Large 1920's semi-detached, non-
smoking.
Tel: **01637 872592** Mrs Schofield.
Rates fr: *£13.50-£15.00.*
Open: May to Oct
Beds: 2F 2D 1T 1S
Baths: 1 Shared
(A) 🅿 (6) ⊬ ⊐ ✕ ▥ Ⅶ 🛈 ✦

(0.3m 🚍) *Chichester Guest*
House, 14 Bay View Terrace,
Newquay, Cornwall, TR7 2LR.
Actual grid ref: SW814613
Comfortable, centrally situated
guesthouse.
Grades: ETB 1 Cr, Comm
Tel: **01637 874216** Miss Harper.
Rates fr: *£13.00-£13.00.*
Open: Mar to Nov
Beds: 1F 2D 2T 2S
Baths: 1 Shared
☺ (A) 🅿 (6) ⊐ ✕ ▥ Ⅶ 🛈 ✦
Also 🏕

All paths are popular:
you are well-advised to
book ahead

Pay B&Bs by
cash or cheque and
be prepared to
pay up front.

(0.25m) *Gainsborough Hotel,*
Mount Wise, Newquay, Cornwall,
TR7 2BT.
Family run hotel.
Tel: **01637 852020**
Mr & Mrs Jackson.
Rates fr: *£15.00-£15.00.*
Open: Easter to Oct
Beds: 10F 5D 1T 2S
Baths: 18 Ensuite
(A) 🅿 (8) ⊬ ⊐ ✕ ▥ Ⅶ 🛈 ✦

Pentire 28

National Grid Ref: SW7961

(On Path) *Corisande Manor Hotel,*
Riverside Avenue, Pentire,
Newquay, Cornwall, TR7 1PL.
Actual grid ref: SW794613
Austrian Victorian turreted
building.
Grades: ETB 3 Cr, Comm,
AA 2 St, RAC 2 St
Tel: **01637 872042** Mr Painter.
Rates fr: *£20.00-£20.00.*
Open: May to Oct
Beds: 3F 8D 3T 5S
Baths: 17 Private 4 Shared
☺ (A) 🅿 (30) ⊐ ✕ ✕ ▥ Ⅶ 🛈 ✦

Crantock 29

National Grid Ref: SW7960

🍴 ⊄ Old Albion

(0.25m) *The Malt House,*
Crantock, Newquay, Cornwall,
TR8 5RB.
Tel: **01637 830662** Mrs Cann.
Rates fr: *£18.00-£18.00.*
Open: All Year (not Xmas)
Beds: 1F 1D 1T **Baths:** 3 Ensuite
☺ (A) 🅿 (3) ⊬ ⊐ ✕ ▥ Ⅶ
Crantock village surrounded by
spectacular coastline is perfect for
walking, surfing, relaxing. Eight
minutes walk from magnificent
beach. Warm welcome, total com-
fort, unbeatable breakfasts assured!

West Pentire 30

National Grid Ref: SW7760

(0.5m) *Goose Rock Hotel, West*
Pentire, Crantock, Newquay,
Cornwall, TR8 5SE.
Actual grid ref: SW774607
Friendly bungalow/hotel, fantastic
views. **Grades:** ETB Reg
Tel: **01637 830755**
Mr & Mrs Somerville.
Rates fr: *£19.00-£26.00.*
Open: March to Nov
Beds: 4F 2D 1T **Baths:** 7 Private
(A) 🅿 (20) ⊐ ✕ ✕ ▥ Ⅶ 🛈 ✦

Rejerrah 31
National Grid Ref: SW8056

(2m) *Lower Treludderow Farm,*
Rejerrah, Newquay, Cornwall,
TR8 5QE.
Comfortable, homely farmhouse.
Grades: ETB Listed
Tel: 01637 830392
Rates fr: £12.00-£16.00.
Open: Jun to Sep
Beds: 1F 1D **Baths:** 1 Shared
(A) **P** (3) ⬜ V

Perranporth 32
National Grid Ref: SW7554

🍴 🍺 Seiners Arms, Tywarnhale
Inn, Bolingey Inn

(0.5m 🚍) *The Morgans of*
Perranporth, Grannys Lane,
Perranporth, Cornwall, TR6 0HB.
Actual grid ref: SW758538
Superior guesthouse overlooking
Atlantic Ocean.
Grades: ETB 3 Cr
Tel: 01872 573904 Mrs Morgan.
Rates fr: £17.50-£20.00.
Open: All Year (not Xmas)
Beds: 2F 4D 2T 1S
Baths: 3 Private, 1 Shared
🛏 (A) **P** (6) ✑ ⬜ 🛏 ✕ 🛁 V 🍴 ⬥

(⚑ On Path) *Perranporth Youth*
Hostel, Droskyn Point,
Perranporth, Cornwall, TR6 0DS.
Actual grid ref: SW7554
Warden: Ms S Kennedy.
Tel: 01872 573812
Under 18: £4.60 **Adults:** £6.75
Family Bunk Rooms, Partially
Heated, Showers, Self-Catering
Only, No Smoking
Single storey hostel high up on the
cliffs, with spectacular views along
3 miles of surf beach, looking
across to Ligger Point

(On Path 🚍) *Cliffside Hotel, Cliff*
Road, Perranporth, Cornwall,
TR6 0DR.
Small comfortable family-run hotel
overlooking beach.
Grades: ETB Reg
Tel: 01872 573297 Mrs Doyle.
Rates fr: £16.00-£14.50.
Open: All Year (not Xmas)
Beds: 2F 2D 3T 3S
(A) **P** ⬜ ✕ 🛁 V 🍴 ⬥

(0.25m 🚍) *Tremore, Liskey Hill*
Crescent, Perranporth, Cornwall,
TR6 0HP.
Friendly non-smoking guesthouse.
Tel: 01872 573537 Mrs Crofts.
Rates fr: £14.00-£14.00.
Open: All Year
Beds: 3D 1T **Baths:** 3
P (6) ✑ ⬜ ✕ 🛁 V 🍴 ⬥

(On Path) *Cellar Cove Hotel,*
Droskyn Way, Perranporth,
Cornwall, TR6 0DS.
Family-run, friendly licenced hotel.
Grades: ETB Reg

Tel: 01872 572110 Mr Hurley.
Rates fr: £15.00-£15.00.
Open: All Year
Beds: 7F 4D 1T 2S
Baths: 14 Ensuite
(A) **P** (20) ⬜ 🛏 ✕ 🛁 V 🍴 ⬥

Barkla Shop 33
National Grid Ref: SW7350

🍴 🍺 Victory Cross, Towan Cross

(0.25m 🚍) *The Grange Farm,*
Barkla Shop, St Agnes, Cornwall,
TR5 0XN.
Actual grid ref: SW7350
Comfortable, modern farmhouse.
Warm welcome.
Tel: 01872 552332 Mrs Shine.
Rates fr: £17.50-£17.50.
Open: All Year
Beds: 1F 1D 1T
Baths: 2 Shared
(A) **P** (6) ✑ ⬜ 🛏 ✕ 🛁 V 🍴 ⬥

St Agnes 34
National Grid Ref: SW7250

🍴 🍺 Driftwood Spars Hotel, St
Agnes Hotel

(On Path) *Beach Cottage, Quay*
Road, St Agnes, Cornwall, TR5 0.
200-year-old cottage - lots of
character.
Tel: 01872 553802
Mrs Glover.
Rates fr: £13.00.
Open: All Year (not Xmas)
Beds: 3D
Baths: 1 Private 1 Shared
(A) **P** ✑ ⬜ 🛁 V 🍴 ⬥

(On Path) *Driftwood Spars Hotel,*
Trevaunance Cove, St Agnes,
Cornwall, TR5 0RT.
Delightful old inn, enormous
beams.
Grades: ETB 3 Cr
Tel: 01872 552428
Mrs Treleaven.
Rates fr: £29.00-£29.00.
Open: All Year
Beds: 1F 7D 1T
Baths: 9 Ensuite
(A) **P** ⬜ 🛏 ✕ V 🍴 ⬥

Portreath 35
National Grid Ref: SW6545

🍴 🍺 Tabbs Restaurant, Bassett
Arms

(On Path) *Cliff House, The Square,*
Portreath, Redruth, Cornwall,
TR16 4LB.
200-year-old whitewashed cottage.
Grades: AA 2 Q
Tel: 01209 842008
Mrs Healan.
Rates fr: £15.00-£15.00.
Open: All Year (not Xmas)
Beds: 1D 1T 2S
Baths: 4 Private
🛏 (A) **P** (5) ✑ ⬜ 🛁 V 🍴 ⬥

(On Path 🚍) *Suhaili, 14 Forth-*
an-Nance, Portreath, Redruth,
Cornwall, TR16 4NQ.
Friendly and comfortable accom-
modation.
Tel: 01209 842110 Mrs Symonds.
Rates fr: £14.00-£16.00.
Open: All Year (not Xmas)
Beds: 2D 1T **Baths:** 3 Private
(A) ✑ ⬜ 🛏 🛁 V 🍴 ⬥

(0.25m 🚍) *Portreath Sycamore*
Lodge, Guest House, Primrose
Terrace, Portreath, Redruth,
Cornwall, TR16 4JS.
Actual grid ref: SW661452
Delightful old house, peaceful
situation.
Tel: 01209 842784
Mr & Mrs Pattinson.
Rates fr: £16.00-£16.00.
Open: Apr to Oct
Beds: 2D 1T 2S
Baths: 2 Shared
🛏 (A) **P** (6) ✑ ⬜ ✕ 🛁 V 🍴 ⬥

(0.25m 🚍) *Glenfeadon House*
Hotel, Portreath, Redruth,
Cornwall, TR16 4JU.
Private licensed hotel.
Grades: ETB Reg
Tel: 01209 842650
Mr Crudgington.
Rates fr: £17.50-£17.50.
Open: Easter to Oct
Beds: 1F 4D 3T 2S
Baths: 4 Ensuite 1 Shared
🛏 (A) **P** ⬜ 🛏 ✕ V 🍴 ⬥

(On Path 🚍) *Bensons, 1 The*
Hillside, Portreath, Redruth,
Cornwall, TR16 4LL.
Actual grid ref: SW658453
Quality B&B, perfect setting.
Grades: AA 4 Q
Tel: 01209 842534 Mrs Benson.
Rates fr: £17.50-£25.00.
Open: All Year
Beds: 2D 2T **Baths:** 4 Private
P (5) ✑ ⬜ 🛁 V 🍴 ⬥

Gwithian 36
National Grid Ref: SW5841

🍴 🍺 Pendarvis Arms

(0.25m) *Orchard Close, 3 Church*
Town Road, Gwithian, Hayle,
Cornwall, TR27 5.
Lovely 200-year-old fisherman's
cottage.
Tel: 01736 753077 Mr/Mrs Eddy.
Rates fr: £12.50-£12.50.
Open: All Year (not Xmas)
Beds: 2D 1T **Baths:** 2 Shared
(A) **P** 🛏 ⬜ V 🍴 ⬥

(On Path) *Calize Country House,*
Prosper Hill, Gwithian, Hayle,
Cornwall, TR27 5BW.
Friendly, family-run guesthouse.
Tel: 01736 753268 Mrs Mayho.
Rates fr: £15.00-£15.00.
Open: All Year **Beds:** 4D
Baths: 2 Private 1 Shared
(A) **P** ⬜ 🛏 ✕ 🛁 V 🍴 ⬥

Phillack 37

National Grid Ref: SW5638

⏶⏶ Bucket of Blood

(On Path) *Penellen Hotel, The Towans, Phillack, Hayle, Cornwall, TR27 5AF.*
Small family-run hotel, sea views.
Grades: ETB 2 Cr
Tel: **01736 753777** Mrs Beare.
Rates fr: *£18.00*-**£18.00**.
Open: All Year (not Xmas)
Beds: 5F 2D 5T
Baths: 12 Private
(A) ▣ ☐ ⌇ ✕ �📖 ☑ ⓘ ✦

Hayle 38

National Grid Ref: SW5537

⏶⏶ Royal Standard

(0.25m 🚐) *54 Penpol Terrace, Hayle, Cornwall, TR27 4BQ.*
Large Victorian private house.
Tel: **01736 752855** Mrs Cooper.
Rates fr: *£15.00*-**£17.50**.
Open: All Year (not Xmas)
Beds: 1D 1T 1S
Baths: 2 Shared
(A) ▣ (2) ⌇ ☐ 📖 ♿ ☑ ⓘ ✦

(0.25m) *White Hart Hotel, 10 Foundry Square, Hayle, Cornwall, TR27 4HQ.*
Tel: **01736 752322**
Mrs Moyle.
Rates fr: -**£29.50**.
Open: All Year
Beds: 3F 4D 5T 3S
Baths: 15 Ensuite
(A) ▣ (6) ☐ ✕ 📖 ☑ ⓘ

Carbis Bay 39

National Grid Ref: SW5238

(On Path 🚐) *Chineside Guest House, Boskerris Road, Carbis Bay, St Ives, Cornwall, TR26 2N.*
Comfortable home, close to beach.
Grades: ETB Reg
Tel: **01736 795659**
Mrs Branton.
Rates fr: *£12.00*-**£12.00**.
Open: Easter to Oct
Beds: 2F 4D 1T 1S
Baths: 4 Ensuite 3 Shared
(A) ▣ (9) ☐ ✕ 📖 ✦

🚐 **sign means that, given due notice, owners will pick you up from the path and drop you off within reason.**

(On Path 🚐) *Monowai Hotel, Headland Road, Carbis Bay, St Ives, Cornwall, TR26 2NR.*
Actual grid ref: SW533387
Delightful hotel, views, bar, swimming.
Grades: ETB 2 Cr, Comm, AA 4 Q
Tel: **01736 795733** Mr Whyte.
Rates fr: *£20.00*-**£18.00**.
Open: Mar to Oct
Beds: 2F 4D 1T 1S
Baths: 8 Ensuite
♨ (A) ▣ (7) ⌇ ⌇ ✕ 📖 ☑ ⓘ ✦

(On Path) *Headland House, Headland Road, Carbis Bay, St Ives, Cornwall, TR26 2NS.*
Panoramic seaviews, good food and accommodation.
Grades: ETB 2 Cr
Tel: **01736 796647** Mrs Antonini.
Rates fr: *£14.00*-**£14.00**.
Open: All Year
Beds: 3F 3D 1T
Baths: 5 Private 2 Shared
(A) ▣ (10) ☐ ⌇ ✕ 📖 ☑ ⓘ ✦

St Ives 40

National Grid Ref: SW5140

⏶⏶ Queen's Taverm, Sloop Inn, The Wharf, Cornishman (St Ives), The Croft Inn

(0.5m) *Chy-Roma Guest House, 2 Sea View Terrace, St Ives, Cornwall, TR26 2DH.*
Tel: **01736 797539**
Mrs Shackleton.
Rates fr: *£13.00*-**£13.00**.
Open: All Year
Beds: 2F 3D 1T 1S
Baths: 1 Ensuite 2 Shared
♨ (A) ▣ (5) ☐ ⌇ ✕ 📖 ☑ ⓘ
Family guesthouse with superb sea views overlooking town/harbour three/four minutes bus/rail/beaches. Ideal base coastal walking/bird watching. Good home cooking.

(On Path) *Kandahar, The Warren, St Ives, Cornwall, TR26 2EA.*
Actual grid ref: SW519403
Water's edge and town centre location.
Grades: AA 3 Q
Tel: **01736 796183**
Mr & Mrs Mason.
Rates fr: *£17.00*-**£19.00**.
Open: All Year (not Xmas)
Beds: 1F 6D 1T 1S
Baths: 4 Private, 3 Shared
☐ 📖 ☑

(0.25m) *Rivendell, 7 Porthminster Terrace, St Ives, Cornwall, TR26 2DQ.*
Friendly hospitality/excellent food.
Grades: ETB Comm
Tel: **01736 794923** Ms Walker.
Rates fr: *£14.00*-**£14.00**.
Open: All Year
Beds: 1F 4D 1T 2S
Baths: 1 Ensuite 1 Shared
(A) ▣ (6) ☐ ✕ 📖 ☑ ⓘ

(0.25m 🚐) *The Old Vicarage Hotel, Parc-An-Creet, St Ives, Cornwall, TR26 2ES.*
Actual grid ref: SW515404
Large Victorian vicarage, beautifully converted.
Grades: AA 4 Q
Tel: **01736 796124**
Mr & Mrs Sykes.
Rates fr: *£17.00*-**£19.00**.
Open: Easter to Oct
Beds: 3F 4D 1T
Baths: 4 Private 2 Shared
(A) ▣ (10) ☐ ⌇ 📖 ⓘ ✦

(0.5m 🚐) *Chy-An-Creet Hotel, The Stennack, St Ives, Cornwall, TR26 2HA.*
Cosy, parking, bar, good food.
Grades: AA 3 Q
Tel: **01736 796559**
Mr & Mrs Crowston.
Rates fr: *£15.00*-**£15.00**.
Open: All Year
Beds: 3F 4D 2T 1S
Baths: 10 Ensuite
(A) ▣ (14) ☐ ⌇ ✕ ☑ ✦

(On Path) *Kynance, The Warren, St Ives, Cornwall, TR26 2EA.*
Originally a C19th tin-miner's cottage.
Grades: AA 4 Q, Select
Tel: **01736 796636**
Mr & Mrs Norris.
Rates fr: *£16.00*-**£18.50**.
Open: Feb to Nov
Beds: 5D 2T
Baths: 5 Ensuite 2 Shared
♨ (A) ▣ (4) ☐ 📖 ☑

(On Path) *Blue Hayes, Trelyon Avenue, St Ives, Cornwall, TR26 2AD.*
Actual grid ref: SW5240
Comfortable former gentleman's residence.
Grades: ETB 3 Cr, High Comm
Tel: **01736 797129** Mr Shearn.
Rates fr: *£26.50*-**£28.50**.
Open: Easter to Oct
Beds: 2F 5D 2S
Baths: 5 Private 4 Shared
♨ (A) ▣ (10) ☐ ⌇ ✕ 📖 ☑

(0.25m) *Ren Roy Guest House, 2 Ventnor Terrace, St Ives, Cornwall, TR26 1DY.*
Small family-run guesthouse.
Grades: ETB Listed
Tel: **01736 796971**
Mrs McPherson.
Rates fr: *£14.00*-**£14.00**.
Open: All Year (not Xmas)
Beds: 1F 1D 1T 2S
Baths: 1 Shared
(A) ☐ ✕ ☑ ⓘ

All rates are subject to alteration at the owners' discretion.

Zennor 41

National Grid Ref: SW4538

¶ ◀ The Tinners Arms, The
Gurnards Head

(0.5m ⌁) *Boswednack Manor,*
Zennor, St Ives, Cornwall, TR26 3DD.
Actual grid ref: SW442378
Sea and moorland views, small-
holding.
Tel: **01736 794183** Mr Gynn.
Rates fr: *£14.00-£14.00.*
Open: All Year (not Xmas)
Beds: 3F 1T 1S
Baths: 2 Private 1 Shared
(A) **P** (10) ⊬ ✕ Ⅴ ⓐ ✦

(0.5m ⌁) *Tregeraint House,*
Zennor, St Ives, Cornwall, TR26 3DB.
Actual grid ref: SW451378
Beautiful Cornish cottage, out-
standing views.
Tel: **01736 797061**
Mr & Mrs Wilson.
Rates fr: *£14.50-£16.00.*
Open: All Year (not Xmas)
Beds: 1F 2D 1T **Baths:** 1 Shared
(A) **P** (4) ⊬ ☐ ▦ Ⅴ ✦

Pendeen 42

National Grid Ref: SW3834

¶ ◀ North Inn

(0.5m) *The Old Count House,*
Boscaswell Downs, Pendeen,
Penzance, Cornwall, TR19 7ED.
Actual grid ref: SW383344
Lovely old granite detached house.
Tel: **01736 788058** Mrs Dymond.
Rates fr: *£13.00-£13.00.*
Open: May to Oct
Beds: 1F 1D **Baths:** 1 Shared
ⓨ (A) **P** (2) ☐ ▦ ⓐ ✦

The Country Code

Enjoy the countryside and
respect its life and work

Guard against all risk of fire

Fasten all gates

Keep your dogs under close
control

Keep to public paths across
farmland

Use gates and stiles to cross
fences, hedges and walls

Leave livestock, crops and
machinery alone

Take your litter home

Help to keep all water clean

Protect wild-life, plants and
trees

Take special care on country
roads

Make no unnecessary noise

St Just 43

National Grid Ref: SW3631

¶ ◀ Star Inn, Wellington Hotel

(▲ On Path) *Lands End Youth
Hostel,* Letcha Vean, St Just,
Penzance, Cornwall, TR19 7NT.
Actual grid ref: SW3630
Warden: Ms T Wright.
Tel: **01736 788437**
Under 18: £5.00 **Adults:** £7.45
Family Bunk Rooms, Partially
Heated, Showers, Evening Meal
(7.00 pm), Camping, Parking
*A house with sea views in the
peaceful Cot Valley with a path
leading to the cove*

(0.5m) *Bosavern House,* St Just,
Penzance, Cornwall, TR19 7RD.
C17th Cornish guesthouse in
walled gardens.
Grades: ETB 2 Cr
Tel: **01736 788301**
Mr & Mrs Hartley.
Rates fr: *£14.00-£15.60.*
Open: Mar to Nov
Beds: 4F 2D 2T 1S
Baths: 5 Ensuite 5 Shared
(A) **P** (15) ☐ ⌁ ✕ ▦ Ⅴ ⓐ ✦

(0.33m ⌁) *Coy Manor,* Cot
Valley, St Just, Penzance,
Cornwall, TR19 7NT.
Actual grid ref: SW365305
500 year old manor house.
Grades: ETB Reg
Tel: **01736 787764**
Mrs Jay.
Rates fr: *£14.50-£18.00.*
Open: All Year (not Xmas)
Beds: 1F 2D
Baths: 1 Ensuite 1 Shared
(A) **P** (4) ⊬ ☐ ▦ Ⅴ ✦

(0.25m) *Boscean Country Hotel,*
St Just, Penzance, Cornwall, TR19.
Lovely quiet country hotel.
Grades: ETB 3 Cr Comm
Tel: **01736 788748**
Mr & Mrs Lee.
Rates fr: *£19.00-£22.50.*
Open: Easter to Oct
Beds: 3F 4D 4T
Baths: 11 Private
(A) **P** (12) ☐ ⌁ ✕ ▦ Ⅴ ⓐ ✦

Sennen 44

National Grid Ref: SW3525

¶ ◀ First & Last Inn

(0.5m) *Sunny Bank Hotel,*
Seaview Hill, Sennen, Penzance,
Cornwall, TR19 7AR.
Actual grid ref: SW365263
Large house in own grounds.
Grades: AA 2 Q, RAC Listed
Tel: **01736 871278**
Mr & Mrs Comber.
Rates fr: *£14.00-£14.00.*
Open: Jan to Nov
Beds: 2F 5D 2T 2S
Baths: 2 Ensuite 2 Shared
(A) **P** (20) ☐ ✕ ▦ Ⅴ ⓐ ✦

(0.25m) *Lyonesse Guest House,*
Sennen, Penzance, Cornwall,
TR19 7AD.
Large old rectory, own grounds.
Tel: **01736 871207 / 871564**
Mrs Harrison.
Rates fr: *£12.50-£12.50.*
Open: All Year
Beds: 3F 2D 2T 1S
Baths: 3 Private 2 Shared
(A) **P** (20) ☐ ⌁ ▦ Ⅴ ⓐ ✦

Sennen Cove 45

National Grid Ref: SW3526

(On Path) *Old Success Inn,* Sennen
Cove, Lands End, Penzance,
Cornwall, TR19 7DG.
C17th fisherman's inn.
Grades: ETB 3 Cr, AA 2 St,
RAC 2 St
Tel: **01736 871232** Mr Thorne.
Rates fr: *£30.00-£20.00.*
Open: All Year
Beds: 1F 7D 2T 2S
Baths: 10 Private
(A) **P** ☐ ⌁ ✕ ▦ Ⅴ ⓐ

Please take muddy

boots off before

entering premises

Treen 46

National Grid Ref: SW3923

¶ ◀ Logan Rock Inn

(On Path) *Penver,* Treen,
Penzance, Cornwall, TR19 6.
Homely, friendly bungalow, near
Minack Theatre.
Tel: **01736 810778**
Mrs Jilbert.
Rates fr: *£12.50-£15.00.*
Open: All Year (not Xmas)
Beds: 1D 1T
Baths: 1 Private 1 Shared
P ⊬ ⌁ ▦ Ⅴ ⓐ ✦

Lamorna 47

National Grid Ref: SW4425

¶ ◀ Tremeneth Hotel

(0.25m ⌁) *Tremeneth Hotel,*
Lamorna, Penzance, Cornwall,
TR19 6XL.
Family-run hotel overlooking beau-
tiful valley.
Grades: ETB Reg
Tel: **01736 731367**
Mr & Mrs Richards.
Rates fr: *£15.00-£16.00.*
Open: All Year
Beds: 5D 3T 1S
Baths: 6 Private, 2 Shared
(A) **P** ☐ ⌁ ✕ ▦ Ⅴ ⓐ ✦

Mousehole 48

National Grid Ref: SW4626

🍴 🍺 Old Coastguard Hotel

(On Path 🐾) *The Lobster Pot,* Mousehole, Penzance, Cornwall, *TR19.*
Actual grid ref: SW469263
Grades: ETB 4 Cr, Comm, AA 2 St
Tel: 01736 731251 Mrs Deakin.
Rates fr: *£21.00-£21.00.*
Open: Mar to Dec
Beds: 5F 9D 9T 2S
Baths: 22 Ensuite, 3 Shared
(A) 🗔 🗙 🖳 🆅 🛍 ⚡
Literally perching on the harbour wall in Mousehole, with the South West Way on its front doorstep, this internationally famous hotel and restaurant is a must for those seeking comfort and relaxation at the end of the day.

(On Path) *The Old Coastguard Hotel,* Mousehole, Penzance, Cornwall, *TR19 6PR.*
Freehouse and seafood restaurant with gardens.
Grades: AA 3 Q
Tel: 01736 731222 Mr Wood.
Rates fr: *£18.00-£18.00.*
Open: All Year
Beds: 1F 7D 2T 22S
Baths: 10 Private 2 Shared
(A) 🅿 (4) 🗔 🍴 🗙 🖳 🆅 🛍 ⚡

(On Path 🐾) *Carn Du Hotel,* Mousehole, Penzance, Cornwall, *TR19 6SS.*
Actual grid ref: SW468258
Licensed hotel with magnificent views.
Grades: ETB 3 Cr, AA 2 St
Tel: 01736 731233 Mr Field.
Rates fr: *£25.00-£25.00.*
Open: All Year
Beds: 3D 3T 1S **Baths:** 7 Private
(A) 🅿 (12) 🗔 🗙 🖳 🆅 🛍 ⚡

Penzance 49

National Grid Ref: SW4630

🍴 🍺 Turks Head, Navy Inn, The Coldstreamer, Admiral Benbow, Tolcarne, Mounts Bay Inn

(0.25m) *Woodstock Guest House,* 29 Morrab Road, Penzance, Cornwall, *TR18 4EZ.*
Actual grid ref: SW472299
Large Victorian private guesthouse.
Grades: ETB 2 Cr, RAC Listed
Tel: 01736 69049 Mrs Hopkins.
Rates fr: *£11.00-£11.00.*
Open: All Year
Beds: 2F 2D 2T 1S
Baths: 2 Private 2 Shared
(A) 🗔 🍴 🖳 🆅 🛍

(On Path 🐾) *Lynwood Guest House,* 41 Morrab Road, Penzance, Cornwall, *TR18 4EX.*
Large comfortable Victorian private house.

Grades: ETB 1 Cr, RAC Listed.
Tel: 01736 65871 Mrs Stacey.
Rates fr: *£11.50-£15.00.*
Open: All Year
Beds: 2F 1D 2T 1S
Baths: 2 Ensuite 2 Shared
(A) 🗔 🍴 🖳 🆅 ⚡
Also ⛺

(On Path) *Carnson House Private Hotel,* East Terrace, Market Jew Street, Penzance, Cornwall, *TR18 2TD.*
Friendly small hotel, near station.
Grades: ETB 2 Cr, RAC Listed
Tel: 01736 65589
Mr & Mrs Hilder.
Rates fr: *£15.00-£16.00.*
Open: All Year (not Xmas)
Beds: 3D 2T 3S
Baths: 2 Ensuite, 1 Shared
🛌 (A) 🖋 🗔 🗙 🖳 🛍

(▲ 0.5m) *Penzance Youth Hostel,* Castle Horneck, Alverton, Penzance, Cornwall, *TR20 8TF.*
Actual grid ref: SW4530
Warden: P & M Kavanagh.
Tel: 01736 62666
Under 18: £6.15
Adults: £9.10
Family Bunk Rooms, Partially Heated, Showers, Evening Meal (7.00 pm), Camping, Parking
Mansion rebuilt in 18th century on site of ancient fortification, just outside the busy market town of Penzance

---

Taking your dog?
Book in advance only
with owners who
accept dogs (🐾)

(1.5m) *Glencree Private Hotel,* 2 Mennaye Road, Penzance, Cornwall, *TR18 4NG.*
Comfortable Victorian guesthouse.
Grades: ETB 2 Cr
Tel: 01736 62026 Mr Hodgetts.
Rates fr: *£13.00-£16.00.*
Open: Mar to Oct
Beds: 2F 4D 1T 2S
Baths: 6 Ensuite 1 Shared
🛌 (A) 🗔 🍴 🗙 🖳 🛍 ⚡

(0.25m) *Ocean View,* Chayndour Cliffe, Penzance, Cornwall, *TR18 3LQ.*
C17th seafront guesthouse.
Grades: ETB Listed
Tel: 01736 51770
Mr & Mrs Mayes.
Rates fr: *£12.000-£15.00.*
Open: All Year (not Xmas)
Beds: 1F 1D 1T **Baths:** 2 Shared
🛌 (A) 🅿 (3) 🗔 🗙 🖳 ♿ 🆅 ⚡

(1m) *The Tarbert Hotel,* Clarence Street, Penzance, Cornwall, *TR18 2NU.*
Georgian town house hotel.
Grades: ETB 3 Cr, Comm, AA 1 St, RAC High Acclaim
Tel: 01736 63758 Mrs Evans.
Rates fr: *£23.00-£25.50.*
Open: All Year (not Xmas)
Beds: 6D 4T 2S
Baths: 12 Private 1 Shared
(A) 🅿 (5) 🗔 🗙 🖳 🆅 ⚡

(1m) *Ashton House,* 14 Mennaye Road, Penzance, Cornwall, *TR18 4NG.*
Friendly well run guesthouse.
Tel: 01736 62546
Mr & Mrs Lomas.
Rates fr: *£13.00-£13.00.*
Open: All Year
Beds: 2F 2D 1T 1S
Baths: 3 Ensuite 2 Shared
(A) 🍴 🗙 🖳 🆅 🛍 ⚡

(1m) *Kimberley House,* 10 Morrab Road, Penzance, Cornwall, *TR18 4EZ.*
Large Victorian converted house.
Grades: AA Listed, RAC Listed
Tel: 01736 62727
Mr & Mrs Mudway.
Rates fr: *£14.00-£14.00.*
Open: All Year (not Xmas)
Beds: 2F 2D 3T 2S
Baths: 3 Shared
🛌 (A) 🅿 (4) 🗔 🗙 🖳

(0.25m) *The Georgian House Hotel,* 20 Chapel Street, Penzance, Cornwall, *TR18 4AN.*
360-year-old Georgian house.
Grades: ETB 2 Cr, AA 3 Q, Recomm
Tel: 01736 65664 Ms Craver.
Rates fr: *£16.00-£18.00.*
Open: All Year (not Xmas)
Beds: 2F 5D 4T 1S
Baths: 6 Private 3 Shared
(A) 🅿 (11) 🗔 🍴 🗙 🖳 🆅 🛍

(1m) *Glencree Private Hotel,* 2 Mennaye Road, Penzance, Cornwall, *TR18 4NG.*
Grades: ETB 2 Cr
Tel: 01736 62026 Mr Hodgetts.
Rates fr: *£12.00-£15.00.*
Open: Mar to Oct
Beds: 3F 4D 2S
Baths: 6 Private 1 Shared
🛌 (A) 🗔 🍴 🗙 🖳 🆅
Victorian Hotel 100 yards off seafront. Spacious rooms, some with sea views and fourposter beds. Highly recommended for its comfort, cleanliness, excellent food and friendly personal service.

The *lowest* **single**
rate *is shown in* **bold.**

Marazion 50

National Grid Ref: SW5130

(On Path) Cutty Sark Hotel, Marazion, Cornwall, TR18.
Tel: **01736 710334** Mrs Stevens.
Rates fr: *£15.00-£20.00.*
Open: All Year
Beds: 2F 4D 4T 1S
Baths: 11 Ensuite
(A) ⴲ (20) ⌷ ✕ ⅲ ⅴ ⌶ ⅋
Small family run hotel with public bar. Renowned for our excellent food (home cooking/fish speciality). Log fires in winter. Warm friendly welcome awaits you.

(On Path) Anneth Lowen, Leys Lane, Marazion, Cornwall, TR17 0AQ.
Comfortable, picturesque house, sea 50 yards.
Tel: **01736 710211** Mrs Glover.
Rates fr: *£12.00-£12.00.*
Open: All Year (not Xmas)
Beds: 1D 2T **Baths:** 2 Shared
ⴲ (A) ⴲ (2) ⌂ ⅲ ⌶ ⅋

Perranuthnoe 51

National Grid Ref: SW5329

⍩⍙ Victoria Inn

(On Path) Ednovean House, Perranuthnoe, Penzance, Cornwall, TR20 9LZ.
Actual grid ref: SW5329
Grades: ETB 3 Cr, AA 3 Q
Tel: **01736 711071**
Mr & Mrs Compton.
Rates fr: *£18.00-£20.00.*
Open: All Year
Beds: 1F 4D 2T 2S
Baths: 6 Ensuite 3 Shared
ⴲ (A) ⴲ (12) ⌂ ⅲ ⅲ ⌶ ⅋
Lovely Victorian house set in its own peaceful gardens with wonderful views over Mounts Bay and St. Michaels Mount. An ideal base for walking and exploring the many footpaths in this legendary part of Cornwall.

(0.25m ☎) Ednovean Farm, Perranuthnoe, Penzance, Cornwall, TR20 9LZ.
Actual grid ref: SW5430
Delightful, tranquil, elegant, memorable.
Grades: AA 4 Q, Select
Tel: **01736 711883** Mrs Taylor.
Rates fr: *£15.00-£20.00.*
Open: All Year
Beds: 2D 1T
Baths: 2 Private 1 Shared
ⴲ (A) ⴲ (6) ⅟ ⌷ ⅲ ✕ ⅲ ⅋

Pay B&Bs by cash or cheque and be prepared to pay up front.

Praa Sands 52

National Grid Ref: SW5827

⍩⍙ Welloe Rock Inn

(On Path) Boslowen-Mor, Castle Drive, Praa Sands, Penzance, Cornwall, TR20 9TF.
Modern bungalow.
Tel: **01736 762223** Mrs Jennings.
Rates fr: *£12.50-£14.50.*
Open: Easter to Oct
Beds: 2D 1T
Baths: 1 Private 2 Shared
ⴲ (3) ⌷ ⌶ ⅋

Porthleven 53

National Grid Ref: SW6225

(On Path) Tye Rock Hotel, & Holiday Apartments, Porthleven, Helston, Cornwall, TR13 9EW.
Tel: **01326 572695**
Mr & Mrs Palmer.
Rates fr: *£28.00-£35.00.*
Open: All Year
Beds: 4D 3T **Baths:** 7 Ensuite
(A) ⴲ (10) ⌷ ✕ ⅲ ⌶
Surrounded by National Trust land, Tye Rock Hotel has an air of seclusion, yet the fishing village of Porthleven is only a short walk away.

(On Path ☎) Seefar, Peverell Terrace, Porthleven, Helston, Cornwall, TR13 9DZ.
Traditional Cornish Victorian mine captain's house.
Grades: ETB 1 Cr
Tel: **01326 573778**
Mr & Mrs Hallam.
Rates fr: *£14.00-£14.00.*
Open: All Year
Beds: 3D 1T 2S
Baths: 3 Shared
(A) ⌷ ⅲ ⌂ ⅲ ⅴ ⌶ ⅋

(On Path) An Mordros Hotel, Porthleven, Cornwall, TR13 9DZ.
Family-run hotel.
Tel: **01326 562236** Mr Kelynack.
Rates fr: *£14.50-£17.50.*
Open: All Year (not Xmas)
Beds: 3F 4D 1T 1S
Baths: 1 Shared
(A) ⌷ ⅲ ✕ ⅲ ⅴ ⌶ ⅋

Cury 54

National Grid Ref: SW6721

⍩⍙ Wheel Inn

(3m) Tregaddra Farmhouse, Cury, Helston, Cornwall, TR12 7BB.
Working farm, beautiful garden, friendly atmosphere.
Grades: ETB 3 Cr, High Comm
Tel: **01326 240235** Mrs Lugg.
Rates fr: *£17.50-£17.50.*
Open: All Year
Beds: 2F 2D 1T 1S
Baths: 5 Private 1 Shared
(A) ⴲ (10) ⅟ ⌷ ✕ ⌶ ⅋

Mullion 55

National Grid Ref: SW6719

⍩⍙ Old Inn, Mounts Bay Inn

(0.5m ☎) Campden House, The Commons, Mullion, Helston, Cornwall, TR12 7HZ.
Actual grid ref: SW673195
Family run guesthouse.
Tel: **01326 240365**
Mr & Mrs Hyde.
Rates fr: *£14.00-£14.00.*
Open: All Year
Beds: 1F 3D 1T 2S
Baths: 2 Shared
ⴲ (A) ⴲ (9) ⌷ ⅲ ✕ ⅴ ⌶ ⅋

(1.25m) Alma House Hotel & Restaurant, Mullion, Helston, Cornwall, TR12 7BZ.
Small hotel with restaurant and bar.
Grades: ETB Reg
Tel: **01326 240509** Mrs Richards.
Rates fr: *£16.25-£20.00.*
Open: Easter to Oct
Beds: 2D 1T
Baths: 1 Ensuite 1 Shared
(A) ⴲ (18) ⌷ ⅲ ✕ ⅲ ⅴ ⌶

(0.25m) Parc Cres, 15 La Flouder Fields, Mullion, Helston, Cornwall, TR12 7EL.
Modern home near village centre.
Grades: ETB Reg
Tel: **01326 240653**
Mr Minns.
Rates fr: *£14.50-£15.00.*
Open: Feb to Oct
Beds: 1D 1T
Baths: 1 Ensuite
ⴲ (A) ⴲ (4) ⌷ ⅲ ⅴ ⌶ ⅋

(0.25m) Trenance Farmhouse, Mullion, Helston, Cornwall, TR12 7HB.
Large Victorian farmhouse.
Grades: ETB 2 Cr, Comm
Tel: **01326 240639**
Mr & Mrs Tyler-Street.
Rates fr: *£15.00-£15.00.*
Open: Easter to Oct
Beds: 3D 1T
Baths: 4 Ensuite
ⴲ (A) ⴲ (8) ⌷ ⅲ ⅲ ⅴ ⅋

Mullion Cove 56

National Grid Ref: SW6617

(On Path ☎) Criggan Mill, Mullion Cove, Helston, Cornwall, TR12 7EU.
Actual grid ref: SW667180
Self-contained suites in timber lodge.
Grades: ETB 5 Cr
Tel: **01326 240496** Mrs Storey.
Rates fr: *£13.00-£15.00.*
Open: Easter to Oct
Beds: 1F 1D 1T
Baths: 3 Ensuite
(A) ⴲ ⅟ ⌷ ✕ ⅲ ⅴ ⌶ ⅋
Also ▲ *£6/couple per tent.*
Open: Apr to Oct ⍩ ⏢ ⛺ ✕ ⅋ ⅗

Lizard Point 57

National Grid Ref: SW6911
🍴 ⬛ Top House, The Lizard

(On Path 🚌) *The Most Southerly House*, Lizard Point, Helston, Cornwall, *TR12 7NU*.
Actual grid ref: SW702115
Detached clifftop house, fantastic views.
Tel: **01326 290300**
Mrs Sowden.
Rates fr: *£13.00*-**£15.00**.
Open: All Year (not Xmas)
Beds: 2D **Baths:** 1Shared
🛇 (A) ⬛ (4) 乄⬛📗🖋

Housel Cove 58

National Grid Ref: SW7011

(On Path 🚌) *Housel Bay Hotel*, Housel Cove, Helston, Cornwall, *TR12 7PG*.
Elegant Victorian hotel.
Grades: ETB 3 Cr, High Comm, AA 2 St, RAC 2 St
Tel: **01326 290417** Mrs Oswald.
Rates fr: *£24.00*-**£24.00**.
Open: All Year
Beds: 1F 8D 8T 4S
Baths: 21 Ensuite
(A) ⬛ (25) 乄⬛🐓✕▥Ⓥ📗🖋

The Lizard 59

National Grid Ref: SW7012
🍴 ⬛ Top House, Witchball, Lizard Village

(0.25m) *Trethvas Farm*, The Lizard, Helston, Cornwall, *TR12 7AR*.
Actual grid ref: SW709136
Comfortable farmhouse.
Tel: **01326 290720** Mrs Rowe.
Rates fr: *£14.50*-**£15.00**.
Open: Easter to Oct
Beds: 1D 1T
Baths: 1 Private 1 Shared
🛇 (A) ⬛ (3) ⬛🖋

(0.5m) *Parc Brawse House*, Penmenner Road, The Lizard, Helston, Cornwall, *TR12 7NR*.
Lovely old Cornish house with seaviews.
Grades: ETB 2 Cr, Comm, RAC Acclaim
Tel: **01326 290466** Mrs Kilmister.
Rates fr: *£14.50*-**£14.50**.
Open: All Year
Beds: 1F 3D 2T 1S
Baths: 2 Private 2 Shared
(A) ⬛ (6) ⬛🐓✕▥Ⓥ📗🖋

(On Path 🚌) *Caerthillian Farm*, The Lizard, Helston, Cornwall, *TR12 7NX*.
Perfick!
Tel: **01326 290596** Mrs Lyne.
Rates fr: *£15.00*-**£15.00**.
Open: Mar to Oct
Beds: 1F 3D 1T 1S
Baths: 1 Shared
(A) ⬛ (4) 乄⬛Ⓥ📗🖋

(On Path) *Penmenner House Hotel*, Penmenner Road, The Lizard, Helston, Cornwall, *TR12 7NR*.
Actual grid ref: SW702121
Beautiful detached Victorian house.
Grades: AA 3 Q
Tel: **01326 290370** Mr Timperley.
Rates fr: *£21.00*-**£23.00**.
Open: All Year (not Xmas)
Beds: 5D 1T 2S
Baths: 5 Ensuite 2 Shared
🛇 (A) ⬛ (10) 乄⬛✕▥📗🖋

(0.5m) *Mounts Bay House Hotel*, The Lizard, Helston, Cornwall, *TR12 7NP*.
Tranquil and comfortable.
Grades: ETB 2 Cr, Comm
Tel: **01326 290305**
Mr Crossley.
Rates fr: *£18.00*-**£18.00**.
Open: Dec to Oct
Beds: 5D 1T 1S
Baths: 2 Private 1 Shared
⬛ (10) ⬛🐓✕▥Ⓥ📗🖋

Cadgwith 60

National Grid Ref: SW7214
🍴 ⬛ Cadgwith Cove Inn, Cellars Restaurant

(On Path 🚌) *High Massetts*, Cadgwith, Helston, Cornwall, *TR12 7L*.
Welcoming Edwardian house, overlooking cove.
Tel: **01326 290571** Mrs Betty.
Rates fr: *£16.50*.
Open: All Year (not Xmas)
Beds: 2D
Baths: 1 Shared
⬛⬛✕▥Ⓥ📗🖋

(On Path) *Cadgwith Hotel*, Cadgwith, Helston, Cornwall, *TR12 7*.
Actual grid ref: SW722145
C17th inn.
Tel: **01326 290513** Mr Chesters.
Rates fr: *£17.50*-**£17.50**.
Open: All Year (not Xmas)
Beds: 2D 2T 1S
Baths: 2 Shared
🛇 (A) ⬛ (4) ✕Ⓥ

Ruan Minor 61

National Grid Ref: SW7115
🍴 ⬛ Cadgwith Cove Inn, Top House

(0.5m 🚌) *Treworder Farm*, Ruan Minor, Helston, Cornwall, *TR12 7JL*.
Actual grid ref: SW722153
Quiet, friendly, comfortable converted barn.
Grades: ETB Reg
Tel: **01326 290970**
Mr & Mrs Rosindale.
Rates fr: *£14.50*-**£18.00**.
Open: Mar to Oct
Beds: 1D 1T
Baths: 1 Shared
🛇 (A) ⬛ (6) ⬛▥📗🖋

High season,
bank holidays and
special events mean
low availability
everywhere.

Ponsongath 62

National Grid Ref: SW7517

(0.75m) *Wych Elm*, Ponsongath, Helston, Cornwall, *TR12 6SQ*.
Modern comfortable bungalow.
Tel: **01326 280576** Mrs Whitaker.
Rates fr: *£14.00*-**£14.00**.
Open: All Year (not Xmas)
Beds: 1T
Baths: 1 Private
⬛ (2) 乄⬛🐓✕▥Ⓥ📗🖋
Also ⛺ *£3.00 per tent.,*
Open: All Year 📷Ⓣ🚾♿

Coverack 63

National Grid Ref: SW7818
🍴 ⬛ Paris Hotel

(On Path 🚌) *Boak House*, Coverack, Helston, Cornwall, *TR12 6SH*.
Seaside guesthouse.
Grades: ETB Listed
Tel: **01326 280608** Mrs Watters.
Rates fr: *£14.00*-**£14.00**.
Open: All Year (not Xmas)
Beds: 3D 1T 1S
(A) ⬛🐓✕Ⓥ🖋

(On Path) *Bakery Cottage*, Coverack, Helston, Cornwall, *TR12 6TD*.
Comfortable accommodation in lovely fishing village.
Grades: ETB Listed
Tel: **01326 280474** Mrs Daw.
Rates fr: *£13.80*-**£13.50**.
Open: All Year (not Xmas)
Beds: 1F 1D
Baths: 1 Shared
(A) ⬛ (3) ⬛🐓📗🖋

The Grid Reference
beneath the location
heading is for the
village or town - *not*
for individual houses,
which are shown
(where supplied) in
each entry itself.

(▲ 0.25m) *Coverack Youth Hostel*, Park Behan, School Hill, Coverack, Helston, Cornwall, *TR12 6SA*.
Actual grid ref: SW7818
Warden: Mr M Hammond.
Tel: **01326 280687**
Under 18: £5.00 **Adults:** £7.45
Family Bunk Rooms, Partially Heated, Showers, Evening Meal (7.00 pm), Shop, Games Room, Camping, Parking
Large country house situated above an old fishing village, with views of the bay and the coastline

(On Path) *Tamarisk Cottage*, Coverack, Helston, Cornwall, *TR12 6TG*.
Cottage overlooking bay, built 1720.
Tel: **01326 280638** Mrs Carey.
Rates fr: *£13.50*-**£13.50**.
Open: Easter to Oct
Beds: 1D 1T
Baths: 1 Shared
⌂ (A) ₽ (1) ⌖ Ⅳ ▮ ⚡

Gillan   64
National Grid Ref: SW7825

⁑ ◗ The New Inn

(0.25m) *Porthvean*, Gillan, Manaccan, Helston, Cornwall, *TR12 6HL*.
Self-contained annexe.
Tel: **01326 231204** Mrs Whale.
Rates fr: *£15.00*-**£15.00**.
Open: All Year (not Xmas)
Beds: 1T
Baths: 1 Private
₽ (4) ⚘ ⌖ Ⅲ ⚡

Helford   65
National Grid Ref: SW7526

⁑ ◗ Shipwrights' Arms

(0.25m) *Heronsway*, Orchard Lane, Helford, Helston, Cornwall, *TR12 6LA*.
Actual grid ref: SW755260
Friendly modern bungalow, lovely garden.
Grades: ETB Listed
Tel: **01326 231424** Mrs Chambers.
Rates fr: *£15.00*.
Open: All Year (not Xmas)
Beds: 1D 1T
Baths: 1 Private 1 Shared
⌂ (A) ₽ (4) ⌷ Ⅲ Ⅳ ▮ ⚡

(On Path) *Pengwedhen*, Helford, Helston, Cornwall, *TR12 6*.
Actual grid ref: SW755265
Wonderful views from 1920's verandahs.
Tel: **01326 231481** Mrs Davies.
Rates fr: *£15.00*-**£15.00**.
Open: All Year
Beds: 1F 1T
Baths: 1 Shared
(A) ₽ (4) ⌷ ⌖ Ⅲ ▮ ⚡

All rooms full and nowhere else to stay? Ask the owner if there's anywhere nearby

---

Mawnan Smith   66
National Grid Ref: SW7728

⁑ ◗ Red Lion

(1m ⌂) *The White House*, 28 Castle View Park, Mawnan Smith, Falmouth, Cornwall, *TR11 5HB*.
Comfortable, modern family guesthouse. **Grades:** ETB Reg
Tel: **01326 250768** Mrs Grant.
Rates fr: *£17.00*-**£17.00**.
Open: All Year
Beds: 1F 1D 1T 1S
Baths: 1 Ensuite 3 Shared
⌂ (A) ₽ (4) ⚘ ⌷ Ⅲ Ⅳ ▮ ⚡

(0.75m) *Carwinion Vean*, Grove Hill, Mawnan Smith, Falmouth, Cornwall, *TR11 5ER*.
Large comfortable country house.
Tel: **01326 250513** Mrs Spike.
Rates fr: *£17.50*-**£17.50**.
Open: All Year (not Xmas)
Beds: 2F 2D 1T
Baths: 1 Ensuite 2 Shared
⌂ (A) ₽ (7) ⌷ ⌖ Ⅲ ▮ ⚡

Maenporth   67
National Grid Ref: SW7929

⁑ ◗ Sea Horse Inn

(On Path ⌂) *West Bay Hotel*, Maenporth, Falmouth, Cornwall, *TR11 5HP*.
Actual grid ref: SW7929
Small family run hotel.
Tel: **01326 250447**
Mr & Mrs Skelley.
Rates fr: *£18.50*-**£17.50**.
Open: All Year (not Xmas)
Beds: 1F 3D 1T 2S
Baths: 5 Ensuite 1 Shared
(A) ₽ ⌷ ⌖ Ⅲ Ⅳ ▮ ⚡

Falmouth   68
National Grid Ref: SW8032

⁑ ◗ Chain Locker,Trelowarren Arms, Clipper Way, Cross Keys,Four Winds, Boslowick Inn, Quayside Inn

(On Path ⌂) *The Grove Hotel*, Grove Place, Falmouth, Cornwall, *TR11 4AU*.
Harbourside Georgian hotel.
Grades: ETB 3 Cr, Approv

Tel: **01326 319577** Mrs Cork.
Rates fr: *£20.00*-**£20.00**.
Open: All Year (not Xmas)
Beds: 5F 5D 3T 2S
Baths: 13 Private 2 Shared
(A) ⌷ ⌖ Ⅲ Ⅳ ▮ ⚡

(0.25m ⌂) *Dolvean Hotel*, 50 Melvill Road, Falmouth, Cornwall, *TR11 4DQ*.
Actual grid ref: SW809319
Warm friendly family-run hotel.
Grades: AA 3 Q, Recomm
Tel: **01326 313658** Mrs Crocker.
Rates fr: *£16.00*-**£16.00**.
Open: All Year (not Xmas)
Beds: 1F 4D 3T 4S
Baths: 9 Ensuite 3 Shared
⌂ (A) ₽ (10) ⌷ ⌖ Ⅲ Ⅳ ▮ ⚡

(On Path) *Kentina Hotel*, 2 Emslie Road, Falmouth, Cornwall, *TR11 4BG*.
Actual grid ref: SW810310
Large Edwardian house.
Tel: **01326 313232**
Mr Morgan.
Rates fr: *£14.00*-**£14.00**.
Open: All Year (not Xmas)
Beds: 3F 5D 1T 3S
Baths: 4 Ensuite
(A) ⌖ ⌷ Ⅲ Ⅳ ⚡

(▲ 0.5m) *Pendennis Castle Youth Hostel*, Falmouth, Cornwall, *TR11 4LP*.
Actual grid ref: SW8231
Warden: Mr F Lawson.
Tel: **01326 311435**
Under 18: £5.55
Adults: £8.25
Family Bunk Rooms, Partially Heated, Showers, Evening Meal (7.00 pm), Shop, Television
A Victorian barracks building, floodlit at night, in the grounds of a C16th castle on the promontory beyond Falmouth town

(On Path) *Selwood Cottage Guest House*, 38 Melvill Road, Falmouth, Cornwall, *TR11 4DQ*.
Actual grid ref: SW811320
Excellent accommodation. Highly recommended.
Grades: ETB Reg
Tel: **01326 314135**
Mrs Trezise.
Rates fr: *£14.00*-**£14.00**.
Open: Feb to Oct
Beds: 1F 1D 2T
Baths: 2 Ensuite 1 Shared
⌂ (A) ₽ (6) ⌷ Ⅲ Ⅳ

(0.5m) *Tudor Court Hotel*, 55 Melvill Road, Falmouth, Cornwall, *TR11 4DF*.
Tudor-style, modern family home.
Grades: ETB Reg, RAC Listed
Tel: **01326 312807**
Mrs Swade.
Rates fr: *£17.50*-**£18.50**.
Open: All Year
Beds: 1F 6D 1T 3S
Baths: 9 Private 2 Shared
⌂ (A) ⌖ ⌷ ✕ Ⅲ Ⅳ ▮ ⚡

(On Path) *Esmond, 5 Emslie Road, Falmouth, Cornwall, TR11 4BG.*
Quiet, comfortable, licensed guesthouse.
Tel: **01326 313214**
Mr Harmer.
Rates fr: *£14.00-£14.00.*
Open: All Year (not Xmas)
Beds: 1F 3D 2T 1S
Baths: 4 Private 2 Shared
(A) ⌂ ✕ ▥ ≜ ⊁

(0.25m 🐾) *Ambleside Guest House, 9 Marlborough Road, Falmouth, Cornwall, TR11 3LP.*
Victorian guesthouse.
Grades: ETB Reg
Tel: **01326 319630**
Mr Walker.
Rates fr: *£14.00-£14.00.*
Open: All Year
Beds: 1F 2D 1T 1S
(A) 🐾 ✕ ▥ ≜ ⊁

(0.25m) *Melvill House Hotel, 52 Melvill Road, Falmouth, Cornwall, TR11 4DQ.*
Modernised, elegant Victorian hotel.
Grades: ETB Approv, AA 3Q
Tel: **01326 316645**
Mrs Jones.
Rates fr: *£14.95-£17.50.*
Open: All Year
Beds: 3F 2D 2T
Baths: 7 Private
☼ (A) ℗ (9) ⊁ ⌂ ✕ ▥.

(0.25m) *The Grove Hotel, Grove Place, Falmouth, Cornwall, TR11 4AU.*
Harbourside Georgian hotel, friendly atmosphere.
Grades: ETB 3 Cr, Approv
Tel: **01326 319577**
Mrs Cork.
Rates fr: *£20.00-£20.00.*
Open: All Year (not Xmas)
Beds: 5F 5D 3T 2S
Baths: 13 Private 2 Shared
(A) ⌂ ✕ ▥ ▣

St Mawes 69

National Grid Ref: SW8433

(0.5m) *Idle Rocks Hotel, Harbourside, 1 Tredenham Road, St Mawes, Truro, Cornwall, TR2 5AN.*
Harbourside hotel. Excellent restaurant.
Grades: ETB 4 Cr, High Comm, AA 3 St, RAC 3 St
Tel: **01326 270771** Miss Vicary.
Rates fr: *£30.00-£42.00.*
Open: All Year
Beds: 5F 11D 5T 3S
Baths: 24 Private
(A) ℗ ⊁ ⌂ 🐾 ✕ ▥ ▣

Gerrans 70

National Grid Ref: SW8735

🍴 🍺 The Plume of Feathers, The Royal Standard

(0.5m 🐾) *Harberton House, Churchtown Road, Gerrans, Portscatho, Truro, Cornwall, TR2 5DZ.*
Large traditionally built family home. **Grades:** ETB Reg
Tel: **01872 580598**
Mr & Mrs Davis.
Rates fr: *£16.00-£16.00.*
Open: Apr to Oct
Beds: 1D 1T **Baths:** 2 Shared
(A) ℗ (3) ⌂ ▥ ▣ ≜ ⊁

Treworlas 71

National Grid Ref: SW8938

(On Path 🐾) *Penhallow Coombe Farm, Treworlas, Ruan High Lanes, Truro, Nr St Mawes, Cornwall, TR2 5LR.*
Farmhouse breakfast in comfortable farmhouse.
Grades: ETB Comm
Tel: **01872 501105** Mrs Palmer.
Rates fr: *£12.00-£14.00.*
Open: All Year
Beds: 1F 1T 1S
(A) ℗ (10) ⌂ 🐾 ✕ ▥ ≜ ⊁

Ruan High Lanes 72

National Grid Ref: SW9039

(0.5m 🐾) *The Old Stables, Crugsillick, Ruan High Lanes, Truro, Cornwall, TR2 5LJ.*
Actual grid ref: SW904394
Barn conversion, 2-acre gardens, own produce.
Tel: **01872 501783** Mrs Moore.
Rates fr: *£12.50-£13.00.*
Open: All Year (not Xmas)
Beds: 1F 1D
Baths: 1 Shared
(A) ℗ (4) ⊁ ⌂ ✕ ▥ ▣ ≜ ⊁

(0.5m) *Treluggan Farm Cottage, Ruan High Lanes, Truro, Cornwall, TR2 5LP.*
Character Cornish cottage. Home cooking.
Tel: **01872 580733** Mrs Symons.
Rates fr: *£12.00-£13.00.*
Open: Apr to Oct
Beds: 2D
Baths: 1 Shared
(A) ℗ (2) ⊁ ⌂ ▥ ▣ ⊁

(0.75m 🐾) *Trenestall Farm, Ruan High Lanes, Truro, Cornwall, TR2 5LX.*
Recently converted 200-year-old barn.
Grades: ETB Listed
Tel: **01872 501259** Mrs Palmer.
Rates fr: *£13.00-£13.00.*
Open: Feb to Nov
Beds: 1D 2T
Baths: 2 Shared
(A) ℗ (6) ⌂ 🐾 ✕ ▥ ♿ ▣ ≜ ⊁

Portloe 73

National Grid Ref: SW9339

(On Path) *Tregain , Portloe, Truro, Cornwall, TR2 5QU.*
Actual grid ref: SW935395
Friendly cottage accommodation near sea.
Tel: **01872 501252**
Mrs Holdsworth.
Rates fr: *£18.50-£18.50.*
Open: All Year
Beds: 1T 1S
Baths: 1 Shared
(A) 🐾 ✕ ▣ ≜ ⊁

Boswinger 74

National Grid Ref: SW9941

(⛺ 0.25m) *Boswinger Youth Hostel, Boswinger, Gorran, St Austell, Cornwall, PL26 6LL.*
Actual grid ref: SX9941
Warden: Ms S Roberts.
Tel: **01726 843234**
Under 18: £5.00 **Adults:** £7.45
Family Bunk Rooms, Centrally Heated, Showers, Evening Meal (7.00 pm)
Stone-built cottages and a converted barn in an area of outstanding coastal scenery. Sandy bathing beaches nearby

Gorran Haven 75

National Grid Ref: SX0041

🍴 🍺 Llawnroc Inn, Barley Sheaf

(On Path) *Llawnroc Inn, Gorran Haven, St Austell, Cornwall, PL26 6NU.*
Family-run pub overlooking picturesque harbour.
Grades: ETB 3 Cr, Comm, AA 1Q
Tel: **01726 843461** Mr Gregory.
Rates fr: *£18.00-£20.00.*
Open: All Year
Beds: 1F 3D 3T
Baths: 6 Private 1 Shared
(A) ℗ (40) ⊁ ⌂ 🐾 ✕ ▥ ▣ ≜ ⊁

(On Path) *Piggys Pantry, The Willows, Gorran Haven, St Austell, Cornwall,* PL26 6JG.
Family bungalow, beach 200 yards.
Tel: **01726 843545** Mrs Mott.
Rates fr: *£16.00-£16.00.*
Open: All Year
Beds: 1F 1D
Baths: 1 Shared
(A) ▣ ⊁ ⟤ ⭲ ⚹ ▥ 🗄 & Ⓥ ⋔ ✦

Portmellon 76

National Grid Ref: SX0143

(On Path) *The Rising Sun Inn, Portmellon, Mevagissey, St Austell, Cornwall,* PL26 6NU.
Superb C17th inn on beach.
Tel: **01726 843235** Mr Neale.
Rates fr: *£17.50-£19.50.*
Open: Mar to Sep
Beds: 1F 2D 2T
Baths: 5 Ensuite
⤳ (A) ▣ (60) ⟤ ⚹ ▥ Ⓥ ⋔ ✦

Mevagissey 77

National Grid Ref: SX0145

|◉| ⚑ Fountain Inn

(On Path) *Honeycomb House, Polkirt Hill, Mevagissey, St Austell, Cornwall,* PL26 6UR.
Large Victorian house, superb views.
Grades: ETB 1 Cr
Tel: **01726 842200** Mrs Pannell.
Rates fr: *£14.00-£16.00.*
Open: All Year
Beds: 1F 1D 1T 1S
Baths: 2 Shared
(A) ⟤ ⚹ ▥ Ⓥ ✦

(On Path) *Polrudden Farm, Mevagissey, St Austell, Cornwall,* PL26 6BJ.
Actual grid ref: SX0247
Modern comfortable farmhouse on coast.

Grades: ETB Listed
Tel: **01726 843213**
Mrs Bainbridge.
Rates fr: *£16.50-£18.00.*
Open: All Year
Beds: 1F 1T
Baths: 1 Ensuite 1 Shared
(A) ▣ (12) ⊁ ⟤ ⚹ ▥ ⋔ ✦
Also ⚊ *£7.50 per tent.* ⌂ ⊺ ✦ ⚶

(0.25m ⭐) *Tregorran Guest House, Cliff Street, Mevagissey, St Austell, Cornwall,* PL26 6QW.
Actual grid ref: SX015450
Modern detached split-level house.
Grades: ETB Listed
Tel: **01726 842319** Mrs Lawrence.
Rates fr: *£15.00-£15.00.*
Open: Easter to Oct
Beds: 3F 2D 1T
Baths: 3 Shared
⤳ (A) ▣ (6) ⟤ ⭲ ⚹ ▥ Ⓥ ⋔ ✦

(0.25m) *Rosedale, Valley Park, Tregoney Hill, Mevagissey, St Austell, Cornwall,* PL26 6RS.
Quiet modern farmhouse, superb views.
Tel: **01726 842769** Mrs Rowe.
Rates fr: *£15.00-£15.00.*
Open: Easter to Sep
Beds: 1D 1T
Baths: 1 Shared
⤳ (A) ▣ (3) ⟤ ✦

Pentewan 78

National Grid Ref: SX0147

(1m) *Peruppa Farm, Pentewan, St Austell, Cornwall,* PL26 6EJ.
Modern comfortable farmhouse near sea.
Tel: **01726 843286** Mrs Nancarrow.
Rates fr: *£15.00-£20.00.*
Open: All Year
Beds: 1F 3D 1T
Baths: 1 Shared
⤳ (A) ▣ (4) ⟤ ⭲ ▥.

St Austell 79

National Grid Ref: SX0252

|◉| ⚑ Britannia Inn

(1.5m) *Poltarrow Farm, St Mewan, St Austell, Cornwall,* PL26 7DR.
Comfortable farmhouse, centrally positioned.
Grades: ETB 2 Cr, High Comm, AA 4 Q
Tel: **01726 67111** Mrs Nancarrow.
Rates fr: *£18.00-£19.00.*
Open: All Year (not Xmas)
Beds: 1F 3D 1T **Baths:** 5 Private
(A) ▣ ⟤ ⚹ ▥ &

Charlestown 80

National Grid Ref: SX0352

|◉| ⚑ Rashleigh Arms Hotel

(On Path) *Rashleigh Arms Hotel, Charlestown, St Austell,* PL25.
Pub-hotel, charming Cornish port.
Grades: ETB Listed, Comm, AA Listed
Tel: **01726 73635** Mr Caithness.
Rates fr: *£30.00-£24.00.*
Open: All Year
Beds: 2D 2T 1S **Baths:** 5 Private
(A) ▣ (100) ⟤ ⚹ ▥ Ⓥ ⋔

Carlyon Bay 81

National Grid Ref: SX0552

(On Path) *Porth Avallen Hotel, Sea Road, Carlyon Bay, St Austell, Cornwall,* PL25 3.
Family-owned country house hotel.
Grades: AA 3 St
Tel: **01726 812802** Mrs Sim.
Rates fr: *£36.00-£48.50.*
Open: All Year (not Xmas)
Beds: 6F 11D 4T 3S
Baths: 24 Ensuite
(A) ▣ (70) ⊁ ⟤ ⚹ ▥ Ⓥ ⋔ ✦

SW 00 SX   20

High season,
bank holidays and
special events mean
low availability
everywhere.

(0.25m) *Amberley, Crinnis Close,
Carlyon Bay, St Austell, Cornwall,
PL25 3SE*.
Modern Spanish-style detached
house.
Tel: **01726 815174** Mrs Pipe.
Rates fr: *£14.00-£14.00*.
Open: All Year
Beds: 2T 1S
Baths: 1 Shared
(A) ▣ (3) ⌇⌷ ⊶ ▥, Ⓥ ⚡

Par 82

National Grid Ref: SX0753

|o| ◀ Rashleigh Inn, Ship Inn

(On Path) *Colwith Farm, Par,
Cornwall, PL24 2TU*.
200-acre family-run working farm.
Tel: **01208 872201**
Mrs Dustow.
Rates fr: *£14.00-£18.00*.
Open: Easter to Sep
Beds: 2D 1T **Baths:** 1 Shared
⌇ (A) ▣ ⌷ ▥, Ⓥ

Coombe 83

National Grid Ref: SX1151

|o| ◀ Ship Inn (Coombe)

(On Path 🚐) *Coombe Farm,
Coombe, Fowey, Cornwall,
PL23 1HW*.

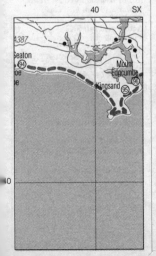

Actual grid ref: SX115071
Farmhouse overlooking sea, near
Fowey.
Tel: **01726 833123** Mrs Paull.
Rates fr: *£15.50-£17.50*.
Open: All Year
Beds: 2D 1T
Baths: 1 Shared
(A) ▣ ⌷ ⊶ ▮ ⚡

Fowey 84

National Grid Ref: SX1251

|o| ◀ The Ship, The Lugger, Sams,
Galleon

(On Path) *Marina Hotel, Fowey,
Cornwall, PL23 1HY*.
200-year-old bishops's summer
residence.
Grades: ETB 4 Cr, AA 2 St,
RAC 2 St
Tel: **01726 833315** Mr Roberts.
Rates fr: *£26.00-£26.00*.
Open: Mar to Jan
Baths: 11 Ensuite
⌷ ⊶ ✕ ▥, Ⓥ ▮

(0.75m) *Trevanion, 70 Lostwithiel
Street, Fowey, Cornwall, PL23*.
Actual grid ref: SX124517
Comfortable 16th Century mer-
chant's house.
Grades: ETB Listed, Comm,
AA 3 Q, Recomm
Tel: **01726 832602** Mr Bullock.
Rates fr: *£15.00-£16.00*.
Open: Mar to Dec
Beds: 1F 3D 1S
Baths: 2 Shared
⌇ (A) ▣ (3) ⌇⌷ ⊶ ▥, ⚡

(0.25m) *Fowey Hall, Fowey,
Cornwall, PL23 1ET*.
Actual grid ref: SX121521
Grand Victorian manor house.
Tel: **01726 833104** Mrs Rayment.
Rates fr: *£18.00-£18.00*.
Open: All Year
Beds: 8F 22T 11S
(A) ▣ (50) ⌇⌷ ✕ ▥, Ⓥ ▮ ⚡

(0.5m 🚐) *11 Park Road, Fowey,
Cornwall, PL23 1EB*.
1930's private house with river
views.
Tel: **01726 833559** Mrs Dorkins.
Rates fr: *£12.50-£13.50*.
Open: Easter to Nov
Beds: 1D 1T **Baths:** 1 Shared
(A) ▣ (2) ⌇⌷ ⊶ ▥, Ⓥ ▮ ⚡

(0.25m) *Panorama, Daglands
Road, Fowey, Cornwall, PL23 1JY*.
Modern home with superb views.
Tel: **01726 833153**
Rates fr: *£15.00-£15.00*.
Open: Easter to Oct
Beds: 1D 1T 1S **Baths:** 1 Shared
▣ (3) ⌇⌷ Ⓥ ⚡

(On Path) *Wheelhouse,
60 Esplanade, Fowey, Cornwall,
PL23 1JA*.
Welcoming Victorian house overlooking harbour.

Grades: AA 3 Q
Tel: **01726 832452** Mrs Sixton.
Rates fr: *£16.00-£16.00*.
Open: Mar to Oct
Beds: 1F 3D 2T 1S
Baths: 2 Private 3 Shared
(A) ⌷ ⊶ ▥, ▮ ⚡

(On Path) *The Ship Hotel,
Trafalgar Square, Fowey,
Cornwall, PL23 1AZ*.
Actual grid ref: SX125515
C16th inn.
Tel: **01726 833751**
Mr Barnicle.
Rates fr: *£18.50-£18.50*.
Open: All Year
Beds: 2F 2D 2T
Baths: 1 Ensuite 2 Shared
(A) ⌇⌷ ⊶ ✕ ▥, ▮ ⚡

Polruan 85

National Grid Ref: SX1250

|o| ◀ The Lugger, The Russell

(0.5m) *Holly House, 18 Fore
Street, Polruan, Fowey, Cornwall,
PL23 1PQ*.
Actual grid ref: SX124506
4 minutes from ferry to Fowey.
Tel: **01726 870478**
Mr & Mrs Blamey.
Rates fr: *£13.50-£13.50*.
Open: All Year (not Xmas)
Beds: 3T
Baths: 1 Shared
(A) ⌷ ▥, ▮

Lansallos 86

National Grid Ref: SX1751

|o| ◀ Blue Peter, Crumplehorn Inn

(0.5m) *Lansallos Barton Farm,
Lansallos, Polperro, Looe,
Cornwall, PL13 2PU*.
380-year-old farmhouse overlook-
ing NT coastland.
Grades: ETB Reg
Tel: **01503 272192**
Mrs Talling.
Rates fr: *£11.50-£15.00*.
Open: All Year (not Xmas)
Beds: 1F 1D
Baths: 1 Shared
(A) ▣ (4) ⌷ ⊶ ▥, Ⓥ ▮ ⚡

🚐 sign means that,
given due notice,
owners will pick you
up from the path
and drop you off with-
in reason.

Polperro 87

National Grid Ref: SX2050

¶⚫ The Three Pilchards, Noughts & Crosses

(0.25m ⊕) *Claremont Hotel, The Coombes, Polperro, Looe, Cornwall, PL13 2RG.*
Actual grid ref: SX207511
Grades: ETB 3 Cr, AA 1 St, RAC 1 St
Tel: 01503 272241
Mr Couturier.
Rates fr: *£17.00-£17.00.*
Open: All Year
Beds: 2F 7D 1T 1S
Baths: 10 Private 1 Shared
(A) ⓟ (16) ⌨ ⊁ ✕ ⊞ ⓥ ⓐ ⚡
Family-run hotel close to Harbour. Private car-park. Fully ensuite, CTV, T.m.f. Seafood restaurant. Secluded beaches, superb walks and places of interest nearby. Off-season and Christmas breaks.

(On Path) *Corner Ways, Landaviddy Lane, Polperro, Looe, Cornwall, PL13 2RT.*
Homely accommodation 400 yards from harbour.
Grades: ETB Reg
Tel: 01503 272324
Mrs Puckey.
Rates fr: *£14.00-£15.00.*
Open: All Year
Beds: 1F 1D 1T
Baths: 2 Shared
(A) ⓟ (3) ⌨ ⊞ ⓥ

(0.25m) *Penryn House Hotel, The Coombes, Polperro, Looe, Cornwall, PL13.*
Grades: ETB 3 Cr, AA Listed, RAC Listed
Tel: 01503 272157
Rates fr: *£18.00-£19.00.*
Open: All Year
Beds: 10D 2T
Baths: 10 Ensuite 2 Shared
⛵ (A) ⓟ ⌨ ⊁ ✕ ⊞ ⓥ ⓐ ⚡
Charming victorian hotel, village centre location close to path. Comfortable ensuites, cosy bar and lounge. Excellent standard of cuisine. Murder mystery weekends, watercolour weekends, etc.

(0.2m ⊕) *Landaviddy Manor, Landaviddy Lane, Polperro, Looe, Cornwall, PL13 2RT.*
C18th manor-house set in beautiful gardens.
Grades: AA 4 Q
Tel: 01503 272210
Mr Rowe.
Rates fr: *£22.00-£26.00.*
Open: March to Nov
Beds: 6D 1T
Baths: 5 Ensuite 2 Private
⛵ (A) ⓟ (8) ⌨ ⊞ ⓥ ⓐ ⚡

Hannafore 88

National Grid Ref: SX2552

¶⚫ Tom Sawyers, Marine Drive

(0.25m) *Stonerock Cottage, Portuan Road, Hannafore, Looe, Cornwall, PL13 2DN.*
Very charming modernised old world cottage.
Grades: ETB 2 Cr, Comm
Tel: 01503 263651 Mrs Tymm.
Rates fr: *£15.00-£15.00.*
Open: Easter to Nov
Beds: 1F 2D 1S
Baths: 1 Private 2 Shared
⛵ (A) ⓟ (4) ⌨ ⊞ ⓥ ⓐ

Portlooe Barton 89

National Grid Ref: SX2452

(0.25m) *The Duchy, Top Of West Looe Hill, Portlooe Barton, Looe, Cornwall, PL13 2HY.*
Comfortable family-run guest-house.
Grades: ETB Listed
Tel: 01503 262664
Mrs Robinson.
Rates fr: *£13.50-£13.50.*
Open: All Year
Beds: 3F 1D 1T 1S
Baths: 2 Private 1 Shared
(A) ⓟ (10) ⊁ ⌨ ⊁ ✕ ⊞ ⓖ ⓥ ⓐ ⚡

Watergate 90

National Grid Ref: SX2354

(1m) *Harescombe Lodge Country, Guest House, Watergate, Looe, Cornwall, PL13 2NE.*
Actual grid ref: SX253554
Converted shooting lodge, idyllic location.
Grades: AA 4 Q, Select
Tel: 01503 263158 Mr Wynn.
Rates fr: *£17.00.*
Open: All Year
Beds: 2D 1T
Baths: 3 Ensuite
ⓟ (10) ✕ ⊞

West Looe 91

National Grid Ref: SX2553

¶⚫ Harbour Moon

(On Path) *Trevanion Hotel, Hannafore Road, West Looe, Cornwall, PL13 2DE.*
Victorian licensed hotel.
Grades: ETB 3 Cr, Comm
Tel: 01503 262003 Mr French.
Rates fr: *£22.00-£25.00.*
Open: All Year (not Xmas)
Beds: 2F 6D 1T 2S
Baths: 11 Ensuite
(A) ⌨ ⊁ ✕ ⊞ ⓥ ⓐ ⚡

(On Path) *Schooner Point Guest House, 1 Trelawney Terrace, Polperro Road, West Looe, Cornwall, PL13 2AG.*
Friendly family run guesthouse.
Grades: ETB Reg

Tel: 01503 262670
Mr & Mrs Neaves.
Rates fr: *£12.00-£12.00.*
Open: All Year (not Xmas)
Beds: 1F 3D 2S
Baths: 2 Private 1 Shared
(A) ⓟ (2) ⌨ ✕ ⊞ ⓥ ⓐ ⚡

East Looe 92

National Grid Ref: SX2654

¶⚫ Oats, Ye Olde Salutation Inn

(On Path) *Sea Breeze Guest House, Lower Chapel Street, East Looe, Cornwall, PL13 1AT.*
Comfortable and friendly guest-house.
Tel: 01503 263131 Mr Miles.
Rates fr: *£14.00-£15.00.*
Open: All Year (not Xmas)
Beds: 4D 1T
Baths: 3 Ensuite, 2 Shared
⛵ (A) ⓟ (2) ⌨ ⊁ ⊞ ⚡

(On Path) *Rivercroft Hotel, Station Road, East Looe, Cornwall, PL13 1HL.*
Comfortable family hotel with bar.
Grades: ETB 3 Cr, Comm
Tel: 01503 262251 Mr Cairns.
Rates fr: *£15.00.*
Open: All Year
Beds: 4F 5D 1T 3S
(A) ⓟ (2) ✕ ⊞ ⓐ ⚡

(0.25m) *Grasmere Guest House, St Martins Road, East Looe, Cornwall, PL13 1LP.*
Actual grid ref: SX254542
Clean, comfortable, splendid river views.
Tel: 01503 262556
Mr Eveleigh.
Rates fr: *£12.00-£13.00.*
Open: All Year (not Xmas)
Beds: 2F 3D
Baths: 1 Shared
(A) ⓟ (5) ⌨ ✕ ⊞ ⓐ

(0.5m) *Woodlands Guest House, St Martins Road, East Looe, Cornwall, PL13 1LP.*
Actual grid ref: SX254542
Victorian house overlooking East Looe River.
Grades: AA 4 Q, Select
Tel: 01503 264405
Mr & Mrs Chapman.
Rates fr: *£18.00-£18.00.*
Open: Easter to Dec
Beds: 2F 4D 1T 1S
Baths: 8 Private
(A) ⓟ (7) ⊁ ⌨ ✕ ⊞ ⓥ ⓐ ⚡

(0.5m ⊕) *Leeward House, Shutta Road, East Looe, Cornwall, PL13 1LT.*
Quiet modern house, ample parking.
Tel: 01503 262032
Rates fr: *£13.00.*
Open: All Year
Beds: 3D
Baths: 1 Ensuite 1 Shared
ⓟ (5) ⊁ ⌨ ⊞ ⓐ

(On Path) *Marwinthy Guest House, East Cliff, East Looe, Cornwall, PL13 1DE.*
Friendly Edwardian house over-looking beach.
Grades: ETB Reg
Tel: **01503 264382**
Mr & Mrs Mawby.
Rates fr: *£15.00-£16.00.*
Open: All Year
Beds: 1F 2D 1T
Baths: 2 Private 1 Shared
⏃ (A) ⌷ ★ ✕ ▥ Ⅴ ▮ ✦

St Martin 93

National Grid Ref: SX2655

(1m ⛟) *Tregoad Farm Touring Caravan & Camping Park, St Martin, Looe, Cornwall, PL13 1PB.*
Actual grid ref: SX273559
Tel: **01503 262718**
Mr Werkmeister.
Also ⚑ *£6.00 per tent.*
Open: April to Sept
⏃ Ⓣ ✦ ⚏ ⏃

Seaton 94

National Grid Ref: SX3054

⫴⫷ ◀ Smuggler's Inn

(On Path ⛟) *Blue Haven Hotel, Looe Hill, Seaton, Torpoint, Cornwall, PL11 3JQ.*
Small select hotel, panoramic sea-views.

Tel: **01503 250310** Mrs White.
Rates fr: *£15.00-£15.00.*
Open: All Year
Beds: 1F 2D 1T
Baths: 4 Private
🅿 (4) ⌷ ✕ ▥ Ⅴ ▮ ✦

Kingsand 95

National Grid Ref: SX4350

⫴⫷ ◀ Old Ship Inn, Halfway House Inn

(On Path) *Clarendon, Garrett Street, Cawsand, Kingsand, Torpoint, Cornwall, PL10 1PD.*
C18th seafront village property.
Tel: **01752 823460**
Mrs Goodwright.
Rates fr: *£14.00-£14.00.*
Open: All Year (not Xmas)
Beds: 1D 1T 1S
Baths: 1 Shared
⏃ (A) ▥.

(On Path ⛟) *The Halfway House Inn, Fore Street, Kingsand, Cawsand Bay, Torpoint, Cornwall, PL10 1NA.*
Actual grid ref: SX435505
Inn and fish speciality restaurant.
Grades: ETB 3 Cr, High Comm
Tel: **01752 822279**
Mr Riggs.
Rates fr: *£19.50-£19.50.*
Open: All Year
Beds: 1F 3D 1S
Baths: 5 Private
(A) 🅿 ⌷ ★ ✕ ▥ Ⅴ ▮ ✦

(On Path) *The Haven, Market Street, Kingsand, Torpoint, Cornwall, PL10 1ND.*
Country cottage overlooking sea.
Tel: **01752 823860** Mrs Taylor.
Rates fr: *£16.00-£16.00.*
Open: All Year (not Xmas)
Beds: 2D 1S **Baths:** 1 Shared
(A) ⌷ ▮ ✦

Mount Edgcumbe 96

National Grid Ref: SX4552

(On Path) *Friary Manor Hotel, Maker Heights, Mount Edgcumbe, Millbrook, Torpoint, Cornwall, PL10 1JB.*
Family-run C18th hotel.
Grades: ETB 3 Cr
Tel: **01752 822112**
Mr & Mrs Wood.
Rates fr: *£21.00-£25.00.*
Open: All Year
Beds: 3F 3D 3T 2S
Baths: 1 Private
(A) 🅿 (25) ⌷ ★ ✕ ▥ Ⅴ ▮ ✦

All rooms full and
nowhere else to stay?
Ask the owner if
there's anywhere
nearby

South Devon

This section of the **South West Coast Path** runs from the great sprawl of Plymouth, past numerous river estuaries and inlets to the border with Dorset, just before Lyme Regis (see beginning of chapter for more **South West Coast Path** details).

Guides: *South West Way: Vol II* (Penzance to Poole) by Martin Collins (ISBN 1 85284 026 9), published by Cicerone Press and available from the publishers (2 Police Square, Milnthorpe, Cumbria, LA7 7PY, 01539 562069), £8.99 *South West Way: Falmouth to Exmouth* by Brian Le Messurier (ISBN 1 85410 3881), published by

Aurum Press in association with the Countryside Commission and Ordnance Survey, £9.99 *South West Way: Exmouth to Poole* by Roland Tarr (ISBN 1 85410 389X), published by Aurum Press in association with the Countryside Commission and Ordnance Survey, £9.99. There is also invaluable local information in The *South West Way 1996* by the **South West Way Association**, available directly from them (1 Orchard Drive, Kingskerswell, Newton Abbot, Devon, TQ12 5DG, tel 01803 873061), £3.99 (+ 70p p&p).

Maps: Ordnance Survey 1:50,000 Landranger series: 192, 193, 201 and 202

Plymouth 1

National Grid Ref: SX4756

|●| ◖ Walrus Pub, The Hoe, The China House, Newmarket Inn, Frog & Frigate, The Tap & Barrel

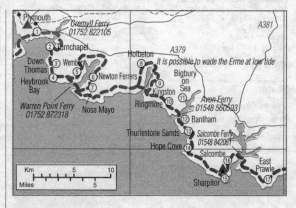

(1m) *Berkeleys Of St James,* 4 St James Place East, The Hoe, Plymouth, Devon, *PL1 3AS*. Large Victorian town house. **Grades:** ETB Comm **Tel: 01752 221654** Mrs Coon. **Rates fr:** *£15.00*-**£16.00**. **Open:** All Year **Beds:** 1F 1D 2T 1S **Baths:** 3 Ensuite, 1 Shared (A) 🅿 (2) ⊬ 🗖 🖮 🎞 ⅙ Ⓥ ✦

(▲ 0.5m) *Plymouth Youth Hostel,* Belmont House, Devonport Road, Stoke, Plymouth, Devon, *PL3 4DW*. **Actual grid ref:** SX4655 Warden: Mr R Thorpe. **Tel: 01752 562189** **Under 18:** £5.55 **Adults:** £8.25 Family Rooms, Centrally Heated, Showers, Evening Meal (6.30 pm), Shop, Television, Games Room *Classical Grecian-style house built in 1820 for a wealthy banker, set in own grounds, within easy walking distance of the city centre*

(1m) *The Churston,* 1 Apsley Road, Plymouth, Devon, *PL4 6PJ*. Family-run guesthouse. **Grades:** ETB 2 Cr **Tel: 01752 664850** D J Tiley. **Rates fr:** *£15.00*-**£15.00**. **Open:** All Year (not Xmas) **Beds:** 1F 2D 2T 3S **Baths:** 2 Private 2 Shared 🗖 ✕ 🖮 🛢

(2.5m 🚅) *Teviot Guest House,* 20 North Road East, Plymouth, Devon, *PL4 6AS*. Early Victorian town house. **Tel: 01752 262656** Mrs Fisher. **Rates fr:** *£15.00*-**£16.00**. **Open:** All Year (not Xmas) **Beds:** 2F 2D 1T 1S **Baths:** 2 Ensuite 2 Shared ⛵ (A) 🅿 (2) ⊬ 🗖 🖮 🛢 ✦

(0.5m) *Sea Breezes,* 28 Grand Parade, West Hoe, Plymouth, Devon, *PL1 3DJ*. **Actual grid ref:** SX483538 Victorian town house on seafront. **Tel: 01752 667205** Mr/Mrs Lake. **Rates fr:** *£14.00*-**£16.00**. **Open:** All Year **Beds:** 3F 2D 2T 1S **Baths:** 1 Private 4 Shared (A) 🗖 🎝 ✕ 🖮 Ⓥ 🛢

(5m) *West Winds Hotel,* 99 Citadel Road, The Hoe, Plymouth, Devon, *PL1 2RH*. Large Victorian house, friendly welcome. **Grades:** ETB 3 Cr **Tel: 01752 662158** **Rates fr:** *£12.50*-**£15.00**. **Open:** All Year **Beds:** 2F 6D 3T 4S **Baths:** 2 Ensuite 6 Shared (A) 🅿 (3) 🗖 🖮 Ⓥ ✦

(0.5m) *Kildare,* 82 North Road East, Plymouth, Devon, *PL4 6AN*. Large Edwardian end terrace house. **Tel: 01752 229375** Mr Churchill. **Rates fr:** *£14.00*-**£15.00**. **Open:** All Year **Beds:** 3F 2D 1T 1S **Baths:** 6 Ensuite 1 Shared ⛵ (A) 🗖 🎝 🖮.

(On Path 🚅) *Osmond Guest House,* 42 Pier Street, West Hoe, Plymouth, Devon, *PL1 3BT*. Victorian house just off seafront. **Grades:** ETB 2 Cr **Tel: 01752 229705** Mrs Richards. **Rates fr:** *£15.00*-**£15.00**. **Open:** All Year **Beds:** 1F 2D 2T 1S **Baths:** 3 Ensuite 2 Shared (A) 🅿 (2) 🗖 🎝 🖮 🛢 ✦

(0.5m 🚅) *Rigsby's Guest House,* 35 North Road East, Plymouth, Devon, *PL4 6AY*. Home from home. **Tel: 01752 669161** Mr Preece. **Rates fr:** *£18.00*-**£15.00**. **Open:** All Year (not Xmas) **Beds:** 1F 1D 3T 1S **Baths:** 1 Shared (A) 🅿 ⊬ 🗖 ✕ 🖮 Ⓥ 🛢 ✦

(0.5m) *Furzehill Hotel,* 41-43 Furzehill Road, Mutley, Plymouth, Devon, *PL4 7JZ*. Large Victorian private hotel. **Grades:** ETB 2 Cr **Tel: 01752 662625** Mr Holman. **Rates fr:** *£14.50*-**£14.50**. **Open:** Jun to Sep **Beds:** 1F 6D 1T 1S **Baths:** 4 Ensuite 2 Shared (A) 🅿 (4) 🗖 🎝 🖮 ✦

(1m) *The Rosaland Hotel,*
32 Houndscombe Road, Plymouth,
Devon, PL4 6HQ.
Beautiful large Victorian town
house.
Grades: ETB 3 Cr, Comm,
AA 3 Q, RAC Listed
Tel: **01752 664749** Mrs Shaw.
Rates fr: £16.00-£16.00.
Open: All Year
Beds: 2F 1D 2T 4S
Baths: 5 Private 2 Shared
(A) ▣ (2) ◻ ✕ 🛏, Ⓥ

(0.5m) *Rainbow Lodge,*
29 Athenaeum Street, The Hoe,
Plymouth, Devon, PL1 2RQ.
Elegant Victorian town house.
Grades: ETB Listed
Tel: **01752 229699** Mrs Graham.
Rates fr: £12.00-£13.00.
Open: All Year (not Xmas)
Beds: 5F 4T 2S
Baths: 7 Ensuite
(A) ▣ (5) ◻ 🛏 🛏,

(0.5m) *Sunray Hotel, 3/5 Alfred*
Street, The Hoe, Plymouth, Devon,
PL1 2RP.
Large Victorian private house.
Tel: **01752 669113**
Mr Sutton.
Rates fr: £17.50-£18.95.
Open: All Year
Beds: 6F 8D 3T 2S
Baths: 13 Ensuite 6 Shared
(A) ▣ (6) ◻ 🛏 🛏 ✕ 🛏, Ⓥ ♠ ✦

(1m) *The Dudley, 42 Sutherland*
Road, Mutley, Plymouth, Devon,
PL4 6BN.
Small comfortable family-run
hotel.
Grades: ETB 2 Cr, Comm,
AA 3 Q, RAC Listed
Tel: **01752 668322**
Mr Folland.
Rates fr: £16.00-£18.00.
Open: All Year
Beds: 2F 3D 2S
Baths: 5 Private 1 Shared
(A) ▣ ◻ 🛏 ✕ 🛏, Ⓥ ♠ ✦

(0.5m) *Allington House, 6 St*
James Place East, The Hoe,
Plymouth, Devon, PL1 3AS.
Clean, comfortable Victorian town
house.
Tel: **01752 221435**
Mrs Budziak.
Rates fr: £15.00-£16.00.
Open: All Year
Beds: 3D 2T 1S
Baths: 3 Ensuite 1 Shared
▣ (2) ◻ 🛏, Ⓥ

(0.5m) *Highbury Guest House,*
21 Mount Gould Road, Lipson,
Plymouth, Devon, PL4 7PT.
Large Victorian guesthouse.
Tel: **01752 665957**
Mr Hammett.
Rates fr: £13.00-£15.00.
Open: All Year
Beds: 2F 2T 1S
Baths: 4 Private 1 Shared
(A) ▣ (8) ◻ 🛏 ✕ 🛏, Ⓥ ♠ ✦

(1m) *Benvenuto Guest House, 69*
Hermitage Road, Mannamead,
Plymouth, Devon, PL3 4RZ.
Large Victorian private house.
Grades: RAC Listed
Tel: **01752 667030**
Mr & Mrs Milton.
Rates fr: £14.00-£14.00.
Open: All Year (not Xmas)
Beds: 1F 3D 2T 2S
Baths: 2 Ensuite 2 Shared
(A) ◻ ✕ 🛏, ♠ ✦

(0.5m) *Mount Batten Hotel, 52*
Exmouth Road, Stoke, Plymouth,
Devon, PL4 4QH.
Large Victorian property overlook-
ing parkland.
Grades: ETB 2 Cr
Tel: **01752 563843**
Rates fr: £14.50-£15.00.
Open: All Year
Beds: 3F 6D 2T 4S
Baths: 6 Ensuite 2 Shared
(A) ▣ (4) ◻ 🛏 ✕ 🛏, Ⓥ ♠

(0.5m) *Sea Breezes, 28 Grand*
Parade, West Hoe, Plymouth,
Devon, PL1 3DJ.
Tel: **01752 667205**
Mr & Mrs Lake.
Rates fr: £15.00-£15.00.
Open: All Year
Beds: 3F 2D 2T 1S
Baths: 1 Ensuite,3 Private
2 Shared
(A) ◻ 🛏 ✕ 🛏, Ⓥ
A warm welcome assured in our
elegant Victorian town-house on
sea front. Theatres, shopping cen-
tre, historic Hoe and Barbican close
by. Ideal touring centre for South-
West Peninsula.

(0.5m) *Teviot Guest House,*
20 North Road East, Plymouth,
Devon, PL4 6AS.
Comfort, quality in Victorian town-
house.
Tel: **01752 262656**
Mrs Fisher.
Rates fr: £15.00-£16.00.
Open: All Year (not Xmas)
Beds: 2F 2D 1T 1S
Baths: 5 Private 1 Shared
🐾 (A) ▣ (2) ✗ ◻ 🛏, Ⓥ

(0.5m) *Bowling Green Hotel, 9-10*
Osborne Place, Lockyer Street,
Plymouth, Devon, PL1 2PU.
Grades: ETB 2 Cr, High Comm,
AA 4 Q, Select, RAC Listed
Tel: **01752 667485**
Mr Dawkins.
Rates fr: £18.00-£28.00.
Open: All Year (not Xmas)
Beds: 3F 6D 2T 1S
Baths: 8 Private
🐾 (A) ▣ ◻ 🛏 🛏, Ⓥ
Extensively refurbished Georgian
property overlooking Drake's
famous bowling green. En-suites
with pocket-sprung beds. Colour/
Satellite TV. Direct dial telephone,
hairdryers, CH, radio, tea & coffee
facilities.

Turnchapel   2

National Grid Ref: SX4952

🍴 🍺 Boringdon Arms

(On Path) *Boringdon Arms,*
Boringdon Terrace, Turnchapel,
Plymouth, Devon, PL9 9TQ.
Award-winning real ale pub.
Grades: ETB Listed
Tel: **01752 402053**
Mrs Rayne.
Rates fr: £14.00-£14.00.
Open: All Year
Beds: 2F 2D 2T
(A) ▣ ◻ 🛏 ✕ 🛏, Ⓥ ♠

Down Thomas   3

National Grid Ref: SX5050

🍴 🍺 Langdow Hotel, Mussel Inn,
The Eddystone

(0.5m 🚌) *Gabber Farm, Down*
Thomas, Plymouth, Devon, PL9 0AW.
Comfortable working farm, friend-
ly welcome.
Grades: ETB 2 Cr, Comm
Tel: **01752 862269**
Mrs MacBean.
Rates fr: £15.50-£15.50.
Open: All Year (not Xmas)
Beds: 2F 1D 2T
Baths: 2 Private 1 Shared
(A) ▣ ✗ ◻ 🛏 🛏, Ⓥ ♠ ✦

Heybrook Bay 4

National Grid Ref: SX4948

⚑ ⌕ The Eddystone

(On Path) *Heybrook Bay Private Hotel*, Beach Road, Heybrook Bay, Plymouth, Devon, *PL9 0BS*.
Comfortable, friendly 1920's hotel.
Grades: ETB Reg
Tel: 01752 862345 Mrs Shelford.
Rates fr: *£13.50*-£17.00.
Open: All Year (not Xmas)
Beds: 6D **Baths:** 2 Shared
�P (12) ⏰ ✗ ⊞ 🖾 Ⅴ 🛈 ⚡

Wembury 5

National Grid Ref: SX5248

⚑ ⌕ Odd Wheel

(0.75m ⚘) *Willowhayes*, (near Post Office), Ford Road, Wembury, Plymouth, Devon, *PL9 0JA*.
Actual grid ref: SX524495
3 minutes from village pub.
Tel: 01752 862581 Mrs Mills.
Rates fr: *£12.50*-£12.50.
Open: All Year (not Xmas)
Beds: 1F 3D 1T 1S
Baths: 1 Shared
(A) P (4) ✔ ⏰ ⊞ Ⅴ 🛈

(On Path ⚘) *Bay Cottage*, 150 Church Road, Wembury, Plymouth, Devon, *PL9 0HR*.
Actual grid ref: SX520486
Victorian cottage by the sea.
Tel: 01752 862559 Mrs Farrington.
Rates fr: *£21.00*-£21.00.
Open: All Year (not Xmas)
Beds: 2D 1T
Baths: 3 Private 1 Shared
(A) P (1) ✔ ⏰ ✗ ⊞ Ⅴ 🛈 ⚡

Newton Ferrers 6

National Grid Ref: SX5448

⚑ ⌕ Dolphin Inn, Swan Inn, Ship Inn

(On Path ⚘) *Melbury*, Church Park Road, Newton Ferrers, Plymouth, Devon, *PL8 1AZ*.
Accommodation in twin and double rooms.
Grades: ETB 3 Cr, High Comm
Tel: 01752 872755 Mrs Hemming.
Rates fr: *£15.00*-£17.00.
Open: All Year
Beds: 1D 2T **Baths:** 1 Private
(A) ⏰ ⊞ Ⅴ 🛈 ⚡

(1m) *Crown Yealm*, Bridgend Hill, Newton Ferrers, Plymouth, Devon, *PL8 1AW*.
Actual grid ref: SX5447
All guest rooms overlook estuary.
Grades: ETB Listed
Tel: 01752 872365 Mrs Johnson.
Rates fr: *£18.50*-£21.00.
Open: All Year
Beds: 1F 1D 1T
Baths: 1 Ensuite 1 Shared
⚑ (A) P (9) ⊞ ⏰ 🛈

Noss Mayo 7

National Grid Ref: SX5447

⚑ ⌕ Old Ship Inn, Swan Inn

(1m ⚘) *Chesnut Cottage*, Noss Mayo, Plymouth, Devon, *PL8 1JA*.
Detached cottage in walled garden.
Tel: 01752 872939 Mrs Knebel.
Rates fr: *£15.00*-£15.00.
Open: All Year (not Xmas)
Beds: 1D 1T
Baths: 1 Ensuite 1 Shared
⚑ (A) P (4) ✔ ⏰ ⊞ Ⅴ 🛈 ⚡

(0.5m ⚘) *Rowden House*, Stoke Road, Noss Mayo, Plymouth, Devon, *PL8 1JG*.
Listed Victorian farmhouse.
Actual grid ref: SX555472
Tel: 01752 872153 Mrs Hill.
Rates fr: *£14.00*-£14.00.
Open: Apr to Oct
Beds: 1F 1T
Baths: 1 Private
(A) P (3) ⊞ ⏰ ⊞ 🛈 ⚡

(0.25m ⚘) *Rookery Nook*, Noss Mayo, Plymouth, Devon, *PL8 1EJ*.
Country house, rural location.
Tel: 01752 872296 Mrs Steer.
Rates fr: *£15.00*-£15.00.
Open: All Year
Beds: 1F 1D **Baths:** 2 Shared
(A) P (4) ✔ ⏰ ✗ ⊞ ⚒ Ⅴ 🛈 ⚡

Holbeton 8

National Grid Ref: SX6150

⚑ ⌕ Mildmay Colours

(0.3m) *The Mildmay Colours Inn*, Holbeton, Plymouth, Devon, *PL8 1NA*.
Traditional village inn with brewery.
Tel: 01752 830248 Mrs Patrick.
Rates fr: *£20.00*-£20.00.
Open: All Year
Beds: 1F 1D 6T
Baths: 8 Private
(A) P (25) ⏰ ✗ ⊞ Ⅴ

Kingston 9

National Grid Ref: SX6347

⚑ ⌕ Dolphin (Kingston)

(1m ⚘) *Torr House*, Kingston, Kingsbridge, Devon, *TQ7 4PT*.
Actual grid ref: SX640480
Georgian style country farmhouse.
Tel: 01548 810723 Mr & Mrs Kies.
Rates fr: *£15.00*-£15.00.
Open: All Year
Beds: 2D 1T 1S
Baths: 2 Shared
(A) P (2) ✔ ⏰ ⊞ Ⅴ 🛈 ⚡

(1m ⚘) *Trebles Cottage Hotel*, Kingston, Kingsbridge, Devon, *TQ7 4PT*.
Actual grid ref: SX640480
Converted 1801 country cottage.

Grades: AA 4 Q, Select, RAC Acclaim
Tel: 01548 810268 Mr Kinder.
Rates fr: *£22.50*-£36.00.
Open: All Year
Beds: 3D 2T
Baths: 5 Private
⚑ (A) P (10) ⏰ ⏰ ✗ ⊞ Ⅴ 🛈 ⚡

Ringmore 10

National Grid Ref: SX6545

⚑ ⌕ Journeys End Inn

(0.5m) *Cliff Path*, Ringmore, Kingsbridge, Devon, *TQ7 4HR*.
Actual grid ref: SX651456
Bungalow on Coast Path link.
Tel: 01548 810654 Mrs Brunskill.
Rates fr: *£15.00*-£15.00.
Open: All Year (not Xmas)
Beds: 1T
Baths: 1 Shared
P (2) ✔ ⏰ ⊞ Ⅴ ⚡

(1m) *Journeys End Inn*, Ringmore, Kingsbridge, Devon, *TQ7 4H*.
Actual grid ref: SX652459
C13th inn offers warm welcome.
Grades: ETB 4 Cr
Tel: 01548 810205 Mr Parkin.
Rates fr: *£20.00*-£20.00.
Open: All Year
Beds: 1F 3D 1T
Baths: 4 Ensuite
(A) P (30) ⏰ ⏰ ✗ ⊞ Ⅴ 🛈 ⚡

Bigbury on Sea 11

National Grid Ref: SX6544

⚑ ⌕ Royal Oak Pub, Bay Cafe in summer, Pickwick Pub

(On Path) *Merrylees*, Ringmore Drive, Bigbury on Sea, Kingsbridge, Devon, *TQ7 4AU*.
Every guest made very welcome.
Tel: 01548 810247 Mrs Evans.
Rates fr: *£15.00*-£15.00.
Open: All Year (not Xmas)
Beds: 2D 1S
Baths: 3 Shared
P (2) ⏰ ⊞ Ⅴ ⚡

(On Path) *The Atlantic*, Marine Drive, Bigbury on Sea, Kingsbridge, Devon, *TQ7 4AS*.
Licensed restaurants, spectacular sea views.
Tel: 01548 810 682
Mrs Richardson.
Rates fr: *£16.00*-£18.00.
Open: Easter to Oct
Beds: 3D
Baths: 3 Private
P ⏰ ✗ ⊞ 🛈 ⚡

The lowest *double* rate per person is shown in *italics*.

Bantham 12

National Grid Ref: SX6643

⚐ Sloop Inn

(On Path) , *Sloop Inn, Bantham, Kingsbridge, Devon, TQ7 3AJ.*
Actual grid ref: SX668438
C16th village pub.
Grades: ETB 2 Cr, Comm, AA Listed
Tel: **01548 560489** Mr Girling.
Rates fr: £25.00-**£30.00**.
Open: All Year (not Xmas)
Beds: 2F 3D
Baths: 5 Private
(A) ⅌ (25) ⌷ ⇞ ✕ 皿 Ⅵ ⓘ ✧

Thurlestone Sands 13

National Grid Ref: SX6742

(On Path 🚗) *La Mer Hotel, Thurlestone Sands, Kingsbridge, Devon, TQ7 3JY.*
Actual grid ref: SX675412
Family run hotel, all modern conveniences.
Tel: **01548 561207** Mr Upsdale.
Rates fr: £16.00-**£16.00**.
Open: Easter to Oct
Beds: 3F 3D 2T
Baths: 4 Ensuite, 1 Shared
(A) ⅌ (10) ⌷ ⇞ ✕ 皿 Ⅵ ⓘ ✧

Hope Cove 14

National Grid Ref: SX6739

⚐ Hope & Anchor, Lobster Pot

(On Path 🚗) *5, Coastguard Cottages, Hope Cove, Kingsbridge, Devon, TQ7 3HW.*
Actual grid ref: SX677397
Very comfortable Victorian private cottage.
Tel: **01548 561543** Mrs Nunn.
Rates fr: £12.50-**£12.50**.
Open: All Year (not Xmas)
Beds: 1T 1S
Baths: 1 Shared
⛺ (A) ⅌ (2) ⼌ ⌷ ⇞ ✕ 皿 ⓘ ✧

(On Path 🚗) *Hope Cove Hotel, Hope Cove, Kingsbridge, Devon, TQ7 3HH.*
Hotel with spectacular sea views.
Grades: ETB 2 Cr, RAC 1 St
Tel: **01548 561233** Mr Clarke.
Rates fr: £22.50-**£32.50**.
Open: Easter to Oct
Beds: 7T
Baths: 7 Ensuite
⛺ (A) ⅌ (15) ⌷ ✕ 皿 ⓘ ✧

(On Path) *Rockcliffe, Hope Cove, Kingsbridge, Devon, TQ7 3HE.*
Modern comfortable detached house.
Tel: **01548 560061**
Mrs Hewitt.
Rates fr: £16.50.
Open:
Beds: 1F 2D
Baths: 3 Ensuite
(A) ⅌ ⌷ ⇞ 皿

(On Path) *Hope & Anchor Inn, Hope Cove, Kingsbridge, Devon, TQ7 3HF.*
Family-run public house.
Tel: **01548 561294** Mr Hall.
Rates fr: £18.00-**£18.00**.
Open: All Year
Beds: 9D 3T
Baths: 12 Private
(A) ⅌ ⌷ ⇞ ✕ 皿 Ⅵ ⓘ ✧

Sharpitor 15

National Grid Ref: SX7237

(🔺 On Path) *Salcombe Youth Hostel, Overbecks, Sharpitor, Salcombe, Devon, TQ8 8LW.*
Actual grid ref: SX7237
Warden: Ms j Phillips.
Tel: **0154884 2856**
Under 18: £5.00 **Adults:** £7.45
Family Bunk Rooms, Showers, Evening Meal (7.00 pm)
Large house in National Trust semi-tropical gardens on the cliff just before Sharpitor Rocks, overlooking the estuary and the sea

Salcombe 16

National Grid Ref: SX7339

⚐ Fortescue Inn, Kings Arms, Victoria Inn, Ferry Inn, Shipwright, Victoria Inn

(On Path) *Torre View Hotel, Devon Road, Salcombe, Devon, TQ8 8HJ.*
Actual grid ref: SX7439
Cosy licensed hotel, excellent views.
Grades: ETB 3 Cr, Comm, AA 3 Q, RAC Acclaim
Tel: **01548 842633** Mrs Bouttle.
Rates fr: £22.00-**£25.00**.
Open: Feb to Nov
Beds: 1F 4D 2T 1S
Baths: 8 Private
⛺ (A) ⅌ (4) ⼌ ⌷ ✕ 皿 ⓘ ✧

(1m 🚗) *Lyndhurst Hotel, Bonaventure Road, Salcombe, Devon, TQ8 8BG.*
Former Edwardian harbour-master's residence.
Grades: ETB 3 Cr, AA 3 Q, RAC High Acclaim
Tel: **01548 842481**
Mr & Mrs Sharp.
Rates fr: £18.50-**£18.50**.
Open: Feb to Nov
Beds: 1F 3D 4T 1S
Baths: 8 Ensuite
⛺ (A) ⅌ ⼌ ⌷ ✕ 皿 Ⅵ ⓘ ✧

(0.5m 🚗) *Suncroft, Fortescue Road, Salcombe, Devon, TQ8 8AP.*
Spacious home, spectacular coastal views.
Tel: **01548 843975**
P V Sherlock.
Rates fr: £18.00-**£24.00**.
Open: All Year (not Xmas)
Beds: 3D
Baths: 1 Ensuite 1 Shared
⛺ (A) ⅌ (2) ⌷ 皿 ✧

(0.5m) *Dell House, Dell Court, Onslow Road, Salcombe, Devon, TQ8 8BW.*
Actual grid ref: SX735391
Large family home, quiet position.
Tel: **01548 843215** Mrs Pritchard.
Rates fr: £11.50-**£11.50**.
Open: Feb to Nov
Beds: 1F 1D 1T 1S
Baths: 2 Shared
(A) ⅌ (3) ⌷ ✕ 皿 Ⅵ ✧

(0.5m) *The Lodge, Devon Road, Salcombe, Devon, TQ8 8HL.*
Large Victorian house/panoramic views.
Tel: **01548 844008** Mrs Daw.
Rates fr: £14.50-**£13.50**.
Open: All Year
Beds: 4D 1T 1S
(A) ⅌ (6) ⌷ ⇞ 皿 Ⅵ ⓘ ✧

East Prawle 17

National Grid Ref: SX7836

⚐ Pigs Nose Inn, Providence Inn

(0.3m) , *Stures Court, East Prawle, Kingsbridge, Devon, TQ7 2BY.*
C17th thatched cottage, C20th comfort.
Grades: ETB Listed, High Comm
Tel: **01548 511261** Ms Benson.
Rates fr: £15.00-**£15.00**.
Open: All Year
Beds: 2D 2S
Baths: 1 Shared
⛺ (A) ⼌ ⌷ 皿 Ⅵ ⓘ ✧

(On Path 🚗) *Maelcombe House, East Prawle, Kingsbridge, Devon, TQ7 2DE.*
Actual grid ref: SX791364
Coastguard officer's house by the sea.
Tel: **01548 511300**
Mr & Mrs Davies.
Rates fr: £16.50-**£16.50**.
Open: Easter to Oct
Beds: 3F 4D 1S
Baths: 5 Shared
(A) ⅌ (10) ⇞ ✕ 皿 Ⅵ ⓘ ✧
Also 🔺 £3.50 per tent.
Open: All Year ⛺

(0.5m 🚗) *Migrants Rest, East Prawle, Kingsbridge, Devon, TQ7 2DB.*
Naturalists' comfortable private home.
Tel: **01548 511443** Mr Catt.
Rates fr: £14.50-**£14.50**.
Open: All Year
Beds: 1D 1T
Baths: 1 Shared
(A) ⅌ (6) ⼌ ⌷ ✕ ⓘ ✧

The *lowest* **single**
rate *is shown in* **bold.**

Slapton 18

National Grid Ref: SX8245

¶¶ ⌂ Queens Arms, Tower Inn

(0.5m 🚋) *Old Walls, Slapton,*
Kingsbridge, Devon, TQ7 2QN.
Listed C18th house.
Grades: ETB Reg
Tel: **01548 580516** Mrs Mercer.
Rates fr: *£14.00*-**£14.00**.
Open: All Year (not Xmas)
Beds: 2D 1T 1S
Baths: 2 Shared
(A) ⅛⌀🐾⬛.V⌂✦

(1.5m 🚋) *Start House, Start,*
Slapton, Kingsbridge, Devon,
TQ7 2QD.
Comfortable house in quiet valley.
Grades: ETB 2 Cr, Comm
Tel: **01548 580254**
Mrs Ashby.
Rates fr: *£19.50*-**£18.00**.
Open: All Year (not Xmas)
Beds: 2D 1T 1S
Baths: 2 Ensuite, 1 Shared
(A) 🅿 (4) ⅛⌀🐾🛱✕⬛.V✦

Stoke Fleming 19

National Grid Ref: SX8648

¶¶ ⌂ Green Dragon, London Inn,
Endsleigh Hotel, Stoke Lodge,
Flemings

(On Path) *Southfield House, Stoke*
Fleming, Dartmouth, Devon,
TQ6 0NR.
Superior B&B in elegant Georgian
house.
Tel: **01803 770359**
Ms Nixon.
Rates fr: *£18.00*-**£20.00**.
Open: All Year (not Xmas)
Beds: 1D 2T
Baths: 2 Ensuite 1 Private
🅿⅛⌀⬛.V⌂✦

Dartmouth 20

National Grid Ref: SX8751

¶¶ ⌂ George & Dragon, Royal
Castle, Windjammer, Seale Arms,
Bayards Restaurant

(On Path) *The Captains House, 18*
Clarence Street, Dartmouth,
Devon, TQ6 9NW.
Grades: ETB 2 Cr, High Comm,
AA 4 Q, RAC Acclaim
Tel: **01803 832133**
Mr Jestico.
Rates fr: *£18.00*-**£24.00**.
Open: All Year
Beds: 1F 2D 1T 1S
Baths: 5 Ensuite
🛏 (A) 🐾⬛.✦
Georgian Listed house built 1730.
Quiet street close town centre/river.
All rooms TV, hairdryer, etc.
Guests' fridge. Choice breakfasts
with homemade produce.

(On Path) *Regency House, 30*
Newcomen Road, Dartmouth,
Devon, TQ6 9BN.
Actual grid ref: SX879510
Overlooking Bayards Cove and
The River Dart.
Tel: **01803 832714** Mrs Shalders.
Rates fr: *£20.00*.
Open: All Year (not Xmas)
Beds: 1F 2D
Baths: 3 Private
(A) ⅛⌀⬛.&V✦

(1m) , *75 Victoria Road,*
Dartmouth, Devon, TQ6 9RX.
Large Victorian house.
Tel: **01803 833415** Mrs Bruckner.
Rates fr: *£12.50*-**£12.50**.
Open: Easter to Dec
Beds: 2F 1D 1T 1S
Baths: 2 Shared
🛏 (A) ⅛⌀🐾⬛.V✦

(1m 🚋) *Britannia, 19 Clarence*
Street, Dartmouth, Devon, TQ6 9NW.
Modern conversion of Listed
building.
Tel: **01803 833069** Mrs Dash.
Rates fr: *£15.00*-**£15.00**.
Open: All Year (not Xmas)
Beds: 1F 1D 1S
Baths: 1 Private 1 Shared
🛏 (A) ⌀🐾⬛.V⌂✦

(0.75m) *Valley House, 46 Victoria*
Road, Dartmouth, Devon, TQ6.
Comfortable small friendly guest-
house.
Tel: **01803 834045** Mr & Mrs Ellis.
Rates fr: *£18.00*-**£24.00**.
Open: All Year (not Xmas)
Beds: 2D 2T **Baths:** 4 Ensuite
🅿 (4) ⌀✕⬛.V✦

(0.25m) *Victoria Cote, 105*
Victoria Road, Dartmouth, Devon,
TQ6 9DY.
Comfortable detached Victorian
house.
Tel: **01803 832997** Mr Fell.
Rates fr: *£19.00*-**£25.00**.
Open: All Year (not Xmas)
Beds: 2D 1T
Baths: 3 Ensuite
(A) 🅿 (4) ⌀🐾✕⬛.V

(0.5m) *2 Charles Street,*
Dartmouth, Devon, TQ6 8QG.
Comfortable friendly Victorian
cottage.
Tel: **01803 833823** Mrs Hayes.
Rates fr: *£15.00*-**£12.50**.
Open: All Year (not Xmas)
Beds: 1D 1S
Baths: 1 Shared
🛏 (A) 🐾⬛.⌂✦

(On Path) *Bayards, 28 Lower*
Street, Dartmouth, Devon, TQ6 9AN.
Comfortable C16th converted pub-
lic house.
Tel: **01803 833523** Mrs Scribbins.
Rates fr: *£13.50*-**£15.50**.
Open: All Year
Beds: 2D 1T
Baths: 1 Shared
(A) ⅛⌀🐾✕V⌂✦

(0.75m) *Brenec House, 73 South*
Ford Road, Dartmouth, Devon,
TQ6 9QT.
Comfortable and friendly guest-
house.
Grades: ETB Listed
Tel: **01803 834788**
Mr & Mrs Culley.
Rates fr: *£13.50*-**£12.50**.
Open: All Year (not Xmas)
Beds: 1F 1D 1S
Baths: 1 Shared
(A) 🅿⅛✕⬛.V⌂✦

(0.25m) *Three Feathers,*
51 Victoria Road, Dartmouth,
Devon, TQ6 9RT.
Early Victorian town house.
Tel: **01803 834694**
Mrs George.
Rates fr: *£14.50*-**£15.00**.
Open: All Year (not Xmas)
Beds: 4F 1T
(A) ⌀🐾⬛.V✦

All paths are
popular: you are
well-advised to
book ahead

Kingswear 21

National Grid Ref: SX8851

¶¶ ⌂ Ship Inn

(On Path) *Carlton House, Higher*
Street, Kingswear, Dartmouth,
Devon, TQ6 0AG.
Superb views over River Dart
estuary.
Tel: **01803 752244**
Mr & Mrs Congdon.
Rates fr: *£14.00*-**£15.00**.
Open: All Year
Beds: 2F 2D 1T 1S
Baths: 2 Shared
(A) ⌀🐾✕⬛.V⌂✦

Maypool 22

National Grid Ref: SX8754

(▲ 4m) *Maypool Youth Hostel,*
Maypool, Galmpton, Brixham,
Devon, TQ5 0ET.
Actual grid ref: SX8754
Warden: D & J Rowe.
Tel: **01803 842444**
Under 18: £5.00 **Adults:** £7.45
Family Bunk Rooms, Partially
Heated, Showers, Evening Meal
(7.00 pm), Shop, Television,
Games Room
Victorian house, set in 4-acre
grounds, originally built for local
boatyard owner, with views of
Kingswear, Dartmouth and the
Dart Estuary

Brixham 23

National Grid Ref: SX9255

|ⓞ| 🍴 Manor Inn

(0.5m) *Smugglers Haunt Hotel, & Restaurant, Church Hill, Brixham, Devon, TQ5 8HH.*
Grades: ETB 3 Cr, AA 1 St
Tel: 01803 853050
Mr Hudson.
Rates fr: *£18.00*-**£18.00**.
Open: All Year
Beds: 2F 7D 3T 4S
Baths: 4 Ensuite, 2 Shared
(A) 🖵 ✗ 🎞 Ⓥ 📶
Friendly, private 300-year-old hotel situated in the centre of old Brixham, only 400 metres from the "old world" harbour. Very well known restaurant.

(0.25m 🚗**)** *Mimosa Cottage, 75 New Road, Brixham, Devon, TQ5 8NL.*
Spacious, well-furnished Georgian house.
Tel: 01803 855719
Mr Kershaw.
Rates fr: *£13.50*-**£15.00**.
Open: All Year (not Xmas)
Beds: 2D 1T 1S
Baths: 2 Private 1 Shared
ਠ (A) 🅿 (4) 🖵 ⼦ 🎞 Ⓥ 📶 ✦

(On Path) *Sampford House, 57-59 King Street, Brixham, Devon, TQ5 9TH.*
Harbourside Georgian house, stunning views.
Grades: AA 2 Q, RAC Listed
Tel: 01803 857761
Mrs Hunter.
Rates fr: *£15.00*-**£18.00**.
Open: Mar to Nov
Beds: 5D
Baths: 4 Ensuite 1 Private
🖵 🎞 📶 ✦

(0.25m) *Melville Hotel, 45 New Road, Brixham, Devon, TQ5 8NL.*
A welcome home from home.
Tel: 01803 852033
Mr & Mrs Hancock.
Rates fr: *£13.50*-**£14.50**.
Open: Mar to Dec
Beds: 3F 2D 2T 2S
Baths: 2 Ensuite 2 Shared
(A) 🅿 (9) 🖵 ✗ Ⓥ 📶 ✦

(0.25m) *Richmond House Hotel, Higher Manor Road, Brixham, Devon, TQ5 8HA.*
Quiet, detached, Victorian family house.
Grades: ETB 2 Cr, Comm
Tel: 01803 882391
Mr Hayhurst.
Rates fr: *£16.00*-**£16.00**.
Open: All Year (not Xmas)
Beds: 2F 3D 1T 1S
Baths: 2 Private 2 Shared
(A) 🅿 (4) 🖵 ⼦ 🎞

Paignton 24

National Grid Ref: SX8960

|ⓞ| 🍴 Inn on the Green, Quaywest, Cutt Inn

(On Path) *South Sands Hotel, Alta Vista Road, Paignton, Devon, TQ4 6BZ.*
Actual grid ref: SX895599
Grades: ETB 3 Cr, Comm, AA 1 St
Tel: 01803 557231 Mr Cahill.
Rates fr: *£20.00*-**£20.00**.
Open: Mar to Oct
Beds: 12F 3D 2T 2S
Baths: 19 Private
(A) 🅿 (18) 🖵 ⼦ ✗ 🎞 ♿ Ⓥ ✦
Licensed family-run hotel in peaceful location overlooking beach/park. Close harbour. Superb cuisine. Outstanding value for money. All rooms ensuite with televisions, telephones, teamakers.

(0.33m) *Cheltor Private Hotel, 20 St Andrews Road, Paignton, Devon, TQ4 6HA.*
Actual grid ref: SX891602
Large comfortable Victorian private hotel.
Grades: ETB 2 Cr
Tel: 01803 551507 Mrs Whitlam.
Rates fr: *£12.00*-**£12.00**.
Open: All Year (not Xmas)
Beds: 5F 2D 1T 1S
Baths: 5 Ensuite 2 Shared
(A) 🅿 (6) 🖵 ⼦ ✗ 🎞 Ⓥ 📶 ✦

(0.5m 🚗**)** *Sunnybank Private Hotel, 2 Cleveland Road, Paignton, Devon, TQ4 6EN.*
Modern, comfortable hotel.
Licenced.
Grades: RAC Listed
Tel: 01803 525540
Mrs Blount.
Rates fr: *£13.00*-**£13.00**.
Open: All Year
Beds: 4F 4D 2T 3S
Baths: 3 Private 2 Shared
ਠ (A) 🅿 (8) ✦ 🖵 ⼦ ✗ 🎞 Ⓥ 📶 ✦

(1m) *Commodore Hotel, 14 Esplanade Road, Paignton, Devon, TQ4 6EB.*
Sea front licensed hotel.
Tel: 01803 553107
Mr Langmaid.
Rates fr: *£15.00*-**£15.00**.
Open: All Year
Beds: 5F 8D 1S
Baths: 12 Ensuite
(A) 🅿 (12) 🖵 ⼦ ✗ 🎞 📶 ✦

(On Path) *Arden House Licensed Hotel, 10 Youngs Park Road, Paignton, Devon, TQ4 6BU.*
Homely, family-run, seaside hotel.
Tel: 01803 558443
Mr Tyler.
Rates fr: *£11.00*-**£11.00**.
Open: Easter to Oct
Beds: 6F 2D 1T 1S
Baths: 2 Shared
(A) 🅿 (6) 🖵 ⼦ ✗ 🎞 Ⓥ 📶

(0.25m) *Bruce Lodge Guest House, 2 Elmsleigh Road, Paignton, Devon, TQ4 5AU.*
Comfortable, level, own carpark.
Grades: ETB 1 Cr, Comm
Tel: 01803 550972 Mrs Kingdon.
Rates fr: *£12.00*-**£12.00**.
Open: Easter to Sep
Beds: 1F 1D 1T 1S
🅿 (5) ✗ 🎞 Ⓥ 📶 ✦

(1.5m 🚗**)** *Carlton House Hotel, 62 Dartmouth Road, Paignton, Devon, TQ4 5AN.*
Family run, good food, clean.
Tel: 01803 551055 Mrs Jackson.
Rates fr: *£13.00*-**£13.00**.
Open: All Year
Beds: 3F 3D 2T 2S
Baths: 5 Ensuite 2 Shared
(A) 🅿 (6) 🖵 ✗ 🎞 Ⓥ

(0.25m) *Worcester House Hotel, 33 New Street, Paignton, Devon, TQ3 3HL.*
Family-run hotel.
Tel: 01803 553103 Mr Willcocks.
Rates fr: *£12.00*-**£12.00**.
Open: All Year
Beds: 2F 8D 1T
Baths: 2 Ensuite 8 Shared
(A) 🖵 ⼦ ✗ Ⓥ 📶

(0.25m) *Adelphi Hotel, 14 Queens Road, Paignton, Devon, TQ4 6AT.*
Large homely run hotel.
Tel: 01803 558022 Mr Elnor.
Rates fr: *£10.00*-**£10.00**.
Open: All Year
Beds: 5F 4D 1T 2S
Baths: 2 Shared
ਠ (A) 🖵 ⼦ ✗ Ⓥ 📶

(1m) *The Barbican, 5 Beach Road, Paignton, Devon, TQ4 6AY.*
Licensed, spotless family-run hotel.
Grades: ETB Listed
Tel: 01803 551332
Mr & Mrs Bunting.
Rates fr: *£11.00*-**£11.00**.
Open: All Year (not Xmas)
Beds: 4F 3D 2T 1S
Baths: 4 Shared
(A) ✦ 🖵 ⼦ ✗ 🎞 Ⓥ 📶

(On Path) *The Look Out Hotel, Marine Parade, Paignton, Devon, TQ3 2NU.*
Friendly seafront hotel.
Tel: 01803 525 638
Rates fr: *£15.00*-**£15.00**.
Open: Easter to Oct
Beds: 1F 5D 2T 2S
Baths: 10 Ensuite
ਠ (A) 🅿 (8) 🖵 ⼦ ✗ 🎞 Ⓥ 📶 ✦

(0.25m) *Concorde Lodge Private Hotel, 57 Dartmouth Road, Paignton, Devon, TQ4 5AE.*
Genuine Budget accommodation.
Tel: 01803 551087
Mr Allen.
Rates fr: *£8.50*-**£10.00**.
Open: All Year (not Xmas)
Beds: 3F 6D 3T 2S
Baths: 7 Ensuite 7 Shared
(A) 🅿 (12) 🖵 ⼦ ✗ 🎞 ♿ ✦

(0.25m) *Norbeck Guest House,*
35 New Street, Paignton, Devon,
TQ3 3HL.
Large family run guesthouse.
Tel: **01803 558033**
Mr & Mrs Edworthy.
Rates fr: *£10.00-£10.00.*
Open: All Year
Beds: 5F 1D 1T 1S
Baths: 2 Ensuite
(A) ⌷ ⊁ ✕ ▥ Ⓥ

Cockington 25

National Grid Ref: SX8963

(0.25m 🐾) *Courtlands Hotel &*
Cellar Bar, Rawlyn Road,
Cockington, Chelston, Torquay,
Devon, TQ2 6PL.
Large Victorian mansion. Public
bar.
Tel: **01803 605506** Mr Cooper.
Rates fr: *£14.15-£14.15.*
Open: All Year
Beds: 7F 2D 6T 3S
Baths: 13 Private 1 Shared
(A) Ⓟ (30) ⌷ ✕ ▥ Ⓥ ₤ ⧸

Chelston 26

National Grid Ref: SX8964

(0.75m 🐾) *Fairmount House*
Hotel, Herbert Road, Chelston,
Torquay, Devon, TQ2 6RW.
Actual grid ref: SX898639
Grades: ETB 3 Cr, High Comm,
AA 1 St, RAC 1 St
Tel: **01803 605446** Mrs Tolkien.
Rates fr: *£26.50-£26.50.*
Open: Mar to Oct
Beds: 1F 4D 2T 2S
Baths: 8 Ensuite
(A) Ⓟ (8) ⌷ ⊁ ✕ ▥ Ⓥ ₤ ⧸
Treat yourself at our small, friendly
hotel in peaceful setting near
Cockington Country Park. Enjoy
comfort, hospitality and delicious
home-cooking. Cosy licensed bar.

(0.5m 🐾) *Acacia Hotel, Old Mill*
Road, Chelston, Torquay, Devon,
TQ2 6HJ.
Actual grid ref: SX9063
Friendly modernised Victorian
licensed hotel.
Grades: ETB 3 Cr
Tel: **01803 605492** Mr Palmer.
Rates fr: *£16.00-£16.00.*
Open: All Year
Beds: 4F 8D
Baths: 9 Ensuite 1 Shared
(A) Ⓟ (10) ⌷ ✕ ▥ Ⓥ

(0.75m) *Cedar Court Hotel,*
3 St Matthews Road, Chelston,
Torquay, Devon, TQ2 6JA.
Victorian house offering superior
B&B.
Tel: **01803 607851** Mr Abbott.
Rates fr: *£14.00-£14.00.*
Open: All Year
Beds: 2F 6D 1T 1S
Baths: 10 Ensuite
(A) Ⓟ (5) ⌷ ▥.

Torquay 27

National Grid Ref: SX9165
🍴 🍺 Devon Dumpling

(0.25m) *Claver Guest House,*
119 Abbey Road, Torquay, Devon,
TQ2 5NP.
Grades: ETB Listed
Tel: **01803 297118**
Mr & Mrs Pearce.
Rates fr: *£12.50-£12.50.*
Open: Easter to Oct
Beds: 3F 3D 1T 1S
Baths: 2 Ensuite 2 Shared
(A) Ⓟ (4) ⌷ ✕ ▥ Ⓥ ₤ ⧸
Warm welcome awaits you after a
good day's walking. Excellent
home cooked evening meal and full
English breakfast sets you up for
next day's hike.

(0.5m) *Shirley Hotel, Braddons*
Hill Road East, Torquay, Devon,
TQ1 1HF.
Licensed, outdoor swimming pool,
sauna, jacuzzi.
Grades: ETB 3 Cr, RAC Acclaim
Tel: **01803 293016** Mrs Stephens.
Rates fr: *£15.00-£15.00.*
Open: All Year
Beds: 2F 9D 1T 2S
Baths: 11 Private 1 Shared
🐾 (A) Ⓟ (4) ⌷ ✕ ▥ Ⓥ ₤ ⧸

(0.25m 🐾) *Hotel Fluela,*
15-17 Hatfield Road, Torquay,
Devon, TQ1 3BW.
Award winning, family-run hotel.
Grades: ETB 3 Cr, AA 1 St,
RAC 1 St
Tel: **01803 297512** Mrs Jarvis.
Rates fr: *£14.50-£14.50.*
Open: All Year
Beds: 3F 9D 1T
(A) Ⓟ (20) ⌷ ✕ ▥ Ⓥ ₤ ⧸

(3m) *Hotel Fiesta, St Marychurch*
Road, Torquay, Devon, TQ1 3JE.
Elegant Neo-Georgian Listed
building.
Tel: **01803 292388** Mr James.
Rates fr: *£14.00-£14.00.*
Open: All Year (not Xmas)
Beds: 2F 5D 1T 1S
Baths: 5 Ensuite 4 Shared
🐾 (A) Ⓟ ⌷ ✕ ▥ Ⓥ ₤

(2.5m) *Romney Court Hotel,*
30 Ash Hill Road, Torquay, Devon,
TQ1 3HZ.
Detached Victorian house.
Tel: **01803 213830** Mr Green.
Rates fr: *£17.00-£17.00.*
Open: Easter to Nov
Beds: 3F 5D 2T 2S
Baths: 12 Ensuite
(A) Ⓟ (15) ⌷ ⊁ ✕ ▥ Ⓥ ₤ ⧸

(2.5m) *Durlstone Guest House,*
156 Avenue Road, Torquay, Devon,
TQ2 5LQ.
Large 1930 guesthouse.
Grades: ETB Reg
Tel: **01803 212307**
Mr & Mrs Evans.

Rates fr: *£10.00-£11.00.*
Open: All Year
Beds: 1F 3D 1T 1S
(A) Ⓟ (6) ⌷ ⊁ ✕ ▥ Ⓥ ₤ ⧸

(1m 🐾) *Clovelly Guest House,*
91 Avenue Road, Torquay, Devon,
TQ2 5LH.
Actual grid ref: SX904647
Speciality - good food and comfort.
Grades: ETB 1 Cr, AA 2 Q
Tel: **01803 292286**
Mr & Mrs Ledward.
Rates fr: *£12.00-£12.00.*
Open: All Year
Beds: 2F 2D 1T 2S
Baths: 1 Private 1 Shared
(A) Ⓟ (4) ⌷ ⊁ ✕ ▥ Ⓥ ₤ ⧸

(2m) *Westwood Hotel, 111 Abbey*
Road, Torquay, Devon, TQ2 5NP.
AA 1-Star licensed family hotel.
Grades: ETB 3 Cr, AA 1 St
Tel: **01803 293818**
Mrs Ainsley.
Rates fr: *£16.00-£16.00.*
Open: All Year
Baths: 26 Ensuite
(A) Ⓟ (12) ⌷ ✕ ▥ Ⓥ ₤

(2m) *Sunleigh Hotel, Livermead*
Hill, Torquay, Devon, TQ2 6QY.
Family hotel overlooking sea.
Grades: ETB 3 Cr, AA 1 St,
RAC 1 St
Tel: **01803 607137**
Mr & Mrs Smith.
Rates fr: *£17.00-£17.00.*
Open: Easter to Oct
Beds: 3F 11D 4T 2S
Baths: 20 Ensuite
(A) Ⓟ (14) ⌷ ⊁ ✕ ▥ Ⓥ ₤

(2m) *Palm Tree House, 93 Avenue*
Road, Torquay, Devon, TQ2 5LH.
Home from home, good food.
Tel: **01803 299141**
Ms Barnett.
Rates fr: *£12.00-£12.00.*
Open: All Year (not Xmas)
Beds: 2F 3D 1T
Baths: 1 Shared
🐾 (A) Ⓟ (3) ⌷ ✕ ▥ Ⓥ

(2m 🐾) *Garway Lodge,*
79 Avenue Road, Torquay, Devon,
TQ2 5LL.
Large comfortable Victorian guest-
house.
Tel: **01803 293126**
Mr Robinson.
Rates fr: *£10.00-£10.00.*
Open: All Year
Beds: 2F 3D 1T 1S
Baths: 5 Ensuite 2 Shared
🐾 (A) Ⓟ (7) ⌷ ⊁ ✕ ▥ ⧸

(1m) *Carysfort, 13 Warren Road,*
Torquay, Devon, TQ2 5TQ.
Friendly central area guesthouse.
Tel: **01803 294160**
Mr Tanner.
Rates fr: *£12.00-£13.00.*
Open: All Year (not Xmas)
Beds: 2F 1D 2T 1S
Baths: 2 Ensuite 2 Shared
(A) Ⓟ (4) ⌷ ⊁ ✕ ▥ Ⓥ ₤

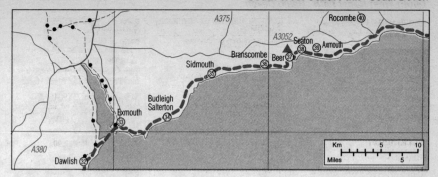

(0.5m) *Albaston House Hotel,* 27 *St Marychurch Road, Torquay, Devon, TQ1 3JF.*
Luxury hotel..
Grades: AA 2 St
Tel: 01803 296758
Rates fr: *£30.00-£30.00.*
Open: All Year (not Xmas)
Beds: 2F 6D 2T 3S
Baths: 13 Ensuite
(A) 🅿 (10) ⌷ ⊷ ✕ ▥ Ⅵ 🗋 ✔

(0.5m 🐾) *Hantwell Guest House,* 487 *Babbacombe Road, Torquay, Devon, TQ1 1HL.*
Homely, friendly, Victorian guesthouse.
Grades: ETB Listed
Tel: 01803 293990 Mrs Williams.
Rates fr: *£10.00-£10.00.*
Open: All Year **Beds:** 3F 1S
Baths: 1 Ensuite 1 Shared
(A) ⌷ ⊷ ✕ ▥ Ⅵ 🗋 ✔
Also ⛺

Babbacombe 28

National Grid Ref: SX9265

(0.2m) *Sandhurst Hotel,* 8 *Manor Road, Babbacombe, Torquay, Devon, TQ1 3XJ.*
Detached licensed hotel.
Tel: 01803 329722
Mr & Mrs Proles.
Rates fr: *£14.00-£14.00.*
Open: May to Oct
Beds: 2F 10D 3T 1S
Baths: 12 Ensuite 3 Shared
🛏 (A) 🅿 (20) ⌷ ⊷ ✕ ▥ 🕭 🗋

Maidencombe 29

National Grid Ref: SX9268

🍴 🍺 Thatched Tavern

(0.75m 🐾) *Parkfield Hotel,* *Claddon Lane, Maidencombe, Torquay, Devon, TQ1 4TB.*
Friendly, comfortable family-run hotel.
Tel: 01803 328952 Mrs Jones.
Rates fr: *£12.50-£12.50.*
Open: Easter to Oct
Beds: 4F 6D
Baths: 10 Private
(A) 🅿 ⌷ ⊷ ✕ Ⅵ 🗋 ✔

Shaldon 30

National Grid Ref: SX9372

🍴 🍺 Shipwrights Arms

(1.5m) *Glenside Hotel, Ringmore Road, Shaldon, Teignmouth, Devon, TQ14 0EP.*
Olde worlde waterside cottage hotel. **Grades:** ETB 3 Cr, Comm, AA 1 St **Tel: 01626 872448** Mr & Mrs Newbold.
Rates fr: *£18.00-£18.00.*
Open: All Year
Beds: 1F 6D 3T
Baths: 8 Private 1 Shared
(A) 🅿 ⌷ ⊷ ✕ ▥ Ⅵ 🗋 ✔

Teignmouth 31

National Grid Ref: SX9473

🍴 🍺 Trade Winds

(0.25m) *Seafield Guest House,* 21 *Higher Brimley Road, Teignmouth, Devon, TQ14 8JS.*
Attractive Georgian guesthouse.
Tel: 01626 773550 Mrs Field.
Rates fr: *£11.00-£12.00.*
Open: All Year (not Xmas)
Beds: 2F 4D 2T 3S
Baths: 7 Ensuite, 4 Shared
(A) 🅿 (4) ⌷ ⊷ ▥ Ⅵ 🗋 ✔

(0.25m) *London Hotel, Bank Street, Teignmouth, Devon, TQ14 8AW.*
Comfortable and family run hotel.
Grades: ETB 4 Cr
Tel: 01626 776336 Tsoi.
Rates fr: *£29.00-£34.00.*
Open: All Year
Beds: 11F 19D 2T
Baths: 32 Ensuite
🛏 (A) 🅿 (8) ⌷ ⊷ ✕ ▥ Ⅵ 🗋

(0.25m) *Beachley Guest House,* 3 *Brunswick Street, Teignmouth, Devon, TQ14 8AE.*
Grades: ETB Listed
Tel: 01626 774249
Rates fr: *£14.00-£14.00.*
Open: All Year (not Xmas)
Beds: 3F 2D 1T 1S
Baths: 3 Shared
(A) ⌷ ✕ ▥ Ⅵ

Dawlish 32

National Grid Ref: SX9676

🍴 🍺 Marine Tavern, Smugglers Inn, Prince Albert

(On Path) *West Hatch Hotel,* 34 *West Cliff, Dawlish, Devon, EX7 9DN.*
Actual grid ref: SX962763
Quality homely hotel near sea.
Grades: ETB 3 Cr, High Comm, RAC Acclaim
Tel: 01626 864211
Mr & Mrs Badcock.
Rates fr: *£20.00-£25.00.*
Open: All Year
Beds: 2F 8D 1T
Baths: 10 Ensuite 1 Private
(A) 🅿 (11) ⌷ ✕ ▥ 🕭 Ⅵ 🗋 ✔

Exmouth 33

National Grid Ref: SY0081

🍴 🍺 Carlton Lodge, Carlton Hill, The Barn, The Grove

(0.5m) *The Sandpiper,* 59 *St Andrews Road, Exmouth, Devon, EX8 1AS.*
Comfortable traditional seaside guesthouse.
Tel: 01395 277254
Rates fr: *£14.00-£14.00.*
Open: Easter to Oct
Beds: 1F 2D 2T 1S
Baths: 2 Ensuite, 1 Shared
🛏 (A) 🅿 (2) ✂ ⌷ ⊷ ▥ Ⅵ 🗋 ✔

(0.5m 🐾) *Pendennis Guest House,* 84 *St Andrews Road, Exmouth, Devon, EX8 1AS.*
Actual grid ref: SX996807
Comfortable family-run guesthouse.
Grades: ETB 1 Cr
Tel: 01395 271458
Mr & Mrs Field.
Rates fr: *£13.50-£13.50.*
Open: All Year (not Xmas)
Beds: 2F 2D 1T 2S
Baths: 2 Shared
🛏 (A) 🅿 (2) ✂ ⌷ ⊷ ✕ ▥ Ⅵ 🗋 ✔

(2m) *Blenheim Guest House,*
39 Morton Road, Exmouth, Devon,
EX8 1BA.
Comfortable house near beach and
shops.
Tel: **01395 223123**
Mr Dormer.
Rates fr: *£12.50*-**£12.50**.
Open: All Year
Beds: 2F 3D 2T
Baths: 1 Shared
(A) 🅿 (1) 🖵 ⇞ ✕ Ⅲ, Ⓥ

(0.5m) *Clifton House, 51 St*
Andrews Road, Exmouth, Devon,
EX8 1AS.
Actual grid ref: SX997807
Friendly family run house.
Grades: ETB 1 Cr
Tel: **01395 266072**
Mrs Keen.
Rates fr: *£14.50*-**£16.50**.
Open: All Year
Beds: 1F 2D 1T 3S
Baths: 2 Ensuite 1 Shared
(A) ⚡ 🖵 ✕ Ⅲ, Ⓥ ⓐ ⚹

(On Path) *Barn Hotel, Foxholes*
Hill, Exmouth, Devon, EX8 2DF.
Character Listed building over-
looking sea.
Grades: ETB 3 Cr, Comm,
AA 2 St, RAC 2 St
Tel: **01395 224411**
Mr Palfreman.
Rates fr: *£28.00*-**£28.00**.
Open: All Year (not Xmas)
Beds: 4F 5D 1T 1S
Baths: 11 Ensuite
(A) 🅿 (20) 🖵 ✕ Ⅲ, Ⓥ ⓐ ⚹

(0.5m 🚗) *Sandrevin, 59 Salterton*
Road, Exmouth, Devon, EX8 2EQ.
Large detached Victorian private
house.
Tel: **01395 266898**
Mr & Mrs Cooper.
Rates fr: *£16.00*-**£16.00**.
Open: All Year (not Xmas)
Beds: 1F 1D 2T 1S
Baths: 2 Ensuite 1 Shared
(A) 🅿 (10) 🖵 ⇞ Ⅲ, Ⓥ ⓐ ⚹

(On Path 🚗) *Spindrift, Maer*
Road, Exmouth, Devon, EX8 2DB.
Private, quiet, end of seafront.
Tel: **01395 271295**
Mrs Marshall-Lee.
Rates fr: *£20.00*-**£20.00**.
Open: All Year
Beds: 1D 1S
Baths: 1 Private
(A) 🅿 (4) 🖵 ⇞ Ⅲ, ⓐ ⚹

(0.25m) *Murray Court Guest*
House, 43 Imperial Road,
Exmouth, Devon, EX8 1DQ.
Clean attractive guest house.
Grades: ETB Listed
Tel: **01395 272492**
Mr Daniels.
Rates fr: *£13.00*-**£13.00**.
Open: All Year (not Xmas)
Beds: 1F 1D 1T 1S
Baths: 1 Shared
(A) ⚡ 🖵 ✕ Ⅲ, Ⓥ ⓐ ⚹

(0.5m) *St Andrews, 15 Elvis Road,*
Exmouth, Devon, EX8 2QB.
Pleasant family guesthouse.
Tel: **01395 270726**
Mrs Tilbury.
Rates fr: *£12.00*-**£12.00**.
Open: All Year (not Xmas)
Beds: 1F 1D 1T 1S
Baths: 2 Shared
(A) 🅿 (3) 🖵 ⇞ ✕ Ⅲ, Ⓥ ⓐ ⚹

Budleigh Salterton   34
National Grid Ref: SY0682

🍴 🍺 Salterton Arms

(1m) *Glendale, 11 Clinton Terrace,*
Budleigh Salterton, Devon, EX9 6RX.
Quietly located, spacious detached
house.
Tel: **01395 443565** Mrs Long.
Rates fr: *£12.50*-**£15.00**.
Open: All Year (not Xmas)
Beds: 2F
Baths: 1 Shared
(A) 🅿 (2) 🖵 Ⅲ,

(0.5m 🚗) *Long Range Hotel,*
Budleigh Salterton, Devon, EX9 6HS.
Comfortable family run modern
hotel.
Grades: AA 4 Q, RAC Acclaim
Tel: **01395 443321**
Mr & Mrs Morton.
Rates fr: *£21.50*-**£21.50**.
Open: All Year
Beds: 1F 1D 3T 1S
Baths: 5 Ensuite 1 Private
(A) 🅿 (6) 🖵 ⇞ ✕ Ⅲ, Ⓥ ⓐ ⚹

(0.5m) *The White Cottage, 25 East*
Budleigh Road, Budleigh Salterton,
Devon, EX9 6EJ.
Quiet family home.
Tel: **01395 443574**
Mrs Fletcher.
Rates fr: *£16.00*-**£18.00**.
Open: Easter to Oct
Beds: 1D 1T
Baths: 1 Shared
🅿 (4) ⚡ ✕ Ⅲ, ⚹

(0.25m 🚗) *Chapter House,*
6 Westbourne Terrace, Budleigh
Salterton, Devon, EX9 6BR.
Cliff walks near town.
Grades: ETB Listed
Tel: **01395 444100**
Ms Summons.
Rates fr: *£15.00*-**£16.00**.
Open: All Year
Beds: 4F 2D 2T
Baths: 1 Shared
(A) 🅿 (4) ⚡ 🖵 ⇞ Ⅲ, Ⓥ ⓐ ⚹

(0.75m 🚗) *Millroy, Budleigh*
Salterton, Devon, EX9.
Cosy farmhouse overlooking Otter
Valley.
Tel: **01395 445699** Mrs Orchard.
Rates fr: *£15.00*-**£15.00**.
Open: All Year
Beds: 1T 2S
Baths: 1 Shared
(A) 🅿 (3) 🖵 ⇞ ✕ Ⅲ, Ⓥ ⓐ ⚹

Sidmouth   35
National Grid Ref: SY1287

🍴 🍺 The Old Ship, Rising Sun,
Tudor Rose, Radway Volunteer
Inn, The Swan, The Black Horse

(On Path 🚗) *Barrington Villa*
Guest House, Salcombe Road,
Sidmouth, Devon, EX10 8PU.
Grades: ETB 2 Cr, Comm
Tel: **01395 514252**
Mr & Mrs Carr.
Rates fr: *£13.00*-**£13.00**.
Open: Jan to Oct
Beds: 1F 3D 1T 3S
Baths: 4 Private, 1 Shared
(A) 🅿 (10) 🖵 ⇞ ✕ Ⅲ, Ⓥ ⓐ ⚹
A charming Regency Gothic villa,
set in beautiful gardens on the bank
of the River Sid in the heart of glo-
rious East Devon.

(0.5m 🚗) *Cheriton Guest House,*
1 Elysian Villas, Vicarage Road,
Sidmouth, Devon, EX10 8.
Large Victorian house.
Grades: ETB 2 Cr, Comm
Tel: **01395 513810**
Mrs Lee.
Rates fr: *£12.00*-**£12.00**.
Open: All Year
Beds: 2F 4D 1T 3S
Baths: 9 Ensuite, 1 Shared
(A) 🅿 (8) ⚡ 🖵 ⇞ ✕ Ⅲ, Ⓥ ⓐ ⚹

(0.25m) *Fortfield Place Guest*
House, 1 Fortfield Place, Station
Road, Sidmouth, Devon, EX10 8NX.
Large comfortable Victorian guest-
house.
Tel: **01395 514588**
Mr & Mrs Bavington.
Rates fr: *£15.00.*
Open: Feb to Nov
Beds: 4D 2T
Baths: 3 Ensuite, 2 Shared
(A) 🅿 🖵 ⇞ Ⅲ, ⓐ

(On Path) *Bramley Lodge,*
Vicarage Road, Sidmouth, Devon,
EX10 8UQ.
Friendly family-run guesthouse.
Tel: **01395 515710** Mrs Bracey.
Rates fr: *£14.00*-**£14.00**.
Open: All Year
Beds: 3F 1D 1T 2S
Baths: 2 Private 3 Shared
(A) 🅿 (6) ⚡ 🖵 ⇞ ✕ Ⅲ, 🚻 Ⓥ ⓐ

(0.25m) *Ryton Guest House,*
52-54 Winslade Road, Sidmouth,
Devon, EX10 9EX.
Actual grid ref: SY1288
Large Victorian private house.
Grades: ETB 2 Cr, Comm,
AA 2 Q
Tel: **01395 513981**
Mr & Mrs Williams.
Rates fr: *£15.00*-**£16.00**.
Open: Mar to Nov
Beds: 4F 3D 1T 2S
Baths: 8 Ensuite 2 Shared
🛏 (A) 🅿 (8) ⚡ 🖵 ⇞ ✕ Ⅲ, Ⓥ ⓐ ⚹

(0.25m) *Sidling Field, 105 Peaslands Road, Sidmouth, Devon, EX10 8XE.*
Large comfortable centally heated bungalow.
Tel: **01395 513859**
Rates fr: *£13.00-£15.50.*
Open: Jan to Nov
Beds: 1D 1T
Baths: 1 Shared
🛎 (A) ⓟ (4) ⌷ ⌆ Ⅲ, 🛆 ≠

(0.5m) *Lynstead, Lynstead Vicarage Road, Sidmouth, Devon, EX10 8UQ.*
Comfortable friendly family-run guesthouse.
Grades: ETB 2 Cr
Tel: **01395 514635** Mrs Jump.
Rates fr: *£16.00-£16.00.*
Open:
Beds: 2F 2D 1T 1S
Baths: 2 Ensuite 2 Shared
(A) ⓟ (8) ⅍⌷⌆✕Ⅲ,Ⓥ ≠

(0.5m) *Enstone Guest House, Lennox Avenue, Sidmouth, Devon, EX10 8TX.*
Delightful, quietly situated guest-house.
Grades: ETB 1 Cr
Tel: **01395 514444** Mrs Osswald.
Rates fr: *£14.00.*
Open: Easter to Sep
Beds: 1F 3D 1T
Baths: 1 Shared
🛎 (A) ⓟ (5) ⌷✕Ⓥ

(0.5m) *Number Four, Fortfield Place, Station Road, Sidmouth, Devon, EX10 8NX.*
Large Victorian private house.
Grades: AA 4 Q, Select
Tel: **01395 578733** Mrs Barnes.
Rates fr: *£15.00-£15.00.*
Open: All Year (not Xmas)
Beds: 1F 1D 1T
Baths: 3 Private
(A) ⓟ (4) ⅍⌷⌆✕Ⅲ,🛆≠

(0.5m) *The Blue Ball Inn,* Sidmouth, Devon, EX10.
Comfortable old world inn.
Grades: ETB Listed
Tel: **01395 514062** Mr Newton.
Rates fr: *£18.00-£22.00.*
Open: All Year
Beds: 1D 2T
(A) ⓟ (100) ⌷⌆✕Ⓥ🛆

Branscombe 36

National Grid Ref: SY1988

⑩⏷ 🍺 Masons Arms, Fountain Head

(1.25m 🚌) *Hole Mill, Branscombe, Seaton, Devon, EX12 3BX.*
Actual grid ref: SY192895
Old converted water mill.
Tel: **01297 680314** Mr & Mrs Hart.
Rates fr: *£15.00-£18.00.*
Open: All Year
Beds: 2D 1T
Baths: 2 Shared
🛎 (A) ⓟ (6) ⅍⌷⌆Ⅲ,Ⓥ ≠

Beer 37

National Grid Ref: SY2289

⑩⏷ 🍺 The Anchor

(0.25m) *Pamber House, Clapps Lane, Beer, Seaton, Devon, EX12 3HD.*
Tel: **01297 20722** Mrs Cummins.
Rates fr: *£16.00.*
Open: All Year
Beds: 1F 4D
Baths: 2 Private 1 Shared
🛎 (A) ⓟ (3) ⅍⌷Ⅲ,
Three minutes walking from fish-ing village centre and beach. Quiet position with beautiful views. Ideal base for walking, etc. Three course breakfast, cooked to order.

(0.25m 🚌) *Garlands, Stovar Long Lane, Beer, Seaton, Devon, EX12 3EA.*
Actual grid ref: SY232895
Edwardian character house on 1 acre.
Tel: **01297 20958** Ms Harding.
Rates fr: *£18.00-£18.00.*
Open: Easter to OctLarge
Edwardian house
Beds: 2F 3D 1T
Baths: 6 Private
(A) ⓟ (10) ⅍⌷⌆✕Ⅲ,Ⓥ🛆≠

(🔺 0.5m) *Beer Youth Hostel, Bovey Combe, Beer, Seaton, Devon, EX12 3LL.*
Actual grid ref: SY2289
Warden: Mr G Kopanyua.
Tel: **01297 20296**
Under 18: £5.00 Adults: £7.45

Family Bunk Rooms, Partially Heated, Showers, Evening Meal (7.00 pm)
Large house standing in land-scaped grounds on the hillside to the west of a picturesque 'old world' fishing village

Seaton 38

National Grid Ref: SY2489

(On Path 🚌) *Tors Guest House, 55 Harbour Road, Seaton, Devon, EX12 2LX.*
Large Victorian private house.
Tel: **01297 20531** Mrs Tawse.
Rates fr: *£17.00-£17.00.*
Open: All Year (not Xmas)
Beds: 4D 2T 2S Baths: 8 Ensuite
ⓟ (6) ⌷⌆🛆≠

(On Path) *Mariners Hotel,* Esplanade, Seaton, Devon, EX12 2NP.
Small private hotel.
Grades: ETB 3 Cr, RAC Acclaim
Tel: **01298 20560** Mr Christopher.
Rates fr: *£19.00-£23.00.*
Open: All Year
Beds: 1F 6D 2T 1S
Baths: 10 Ensuite
(A) ⓟ (10) ⌷⌆✕Ⅲ,🛆

(On Path) *The Kettle Restaurant, 15 Fore Street, Seaton, Devon, EX12 2LE.*
Comfortable, friendly, very good food.
Tel: **01297 20428** Mr Thomas.
Rates fr: *£15.00-£18.00.*
Open: Feb to Dec
Beds: 1F 1D 1T Baths: 3 Ensuite
(A) ⓟ (2) ⅍⌷⌆✕Ⅲ,Ⓥ🛆≠

Axmouth 39

National Grid Ref: SY2591

⑩⏷ 🍺 Harbour Inn, Ship Inn (Axmouth)

(0.25m) *Stepps House, Axmouth, Seaton, Devon, EX12 4AR.*
Beautifully preserved medieval hall house.
Tel: **01297 20679** Mrs Trezise.
Rates fr: *£15.00-£30.00.*
Open: All Year (not Xmas)
Beds: 1D 1T Baths: 1 Shared
(A) ⓟ (10) Ⅲ,Ⓥ🛆

Dorset

This section of the **South West Coast Path** is the shortest, leading from Lyme Regis in the West to Studland Point (opposite Poole) in the East. Part of the path, between West Bay and Weymouth, runs slightly inland.

Guides: *South West Way: Vol II (Penzance to Poole)* by Martin Collins (ISBN 1 85284 026 9), published by Cicerone Press and available from the publishers (2 Police Square, Milnthorpe, Cumbria, LA7 7PY, 01539 562069), £8.99 *South West Way: Exmouth to Poole* by Roland

Tarr (ISBN 1 85410 389X), published by Aurum Press in association with the Countryside Commission and Ordnance Survey, £9.99. There is also invaluable local information in *The South West Way 1996* by the South West Way Association, available directly from them (1 Orchard Drive, Kingskerswell, Newton Abbot, Devon, TQ12 5DG, tel 01803 873061), £3.99 (+ 70p p&p).

Maps: Ordnance Survey 1:50,000 Landranger series: 193, 194 and 195.

Lyme Regis 1

National Grid Ref: SY3492

|●| ◼ Mad Hatter Restaurant, Nags Head, Pilot Boat, Royal Standard, Volunteer Inn

(0.25m) *Willow Cottage, Ware Lane, Lyme Regis, Dorset, DT7 3EL.*
Actual grid ref: SY332921
Tel: **01297 443199** Mr Griffin.
Rates fr: *£20.00-£20.00.*
Open: March to Nov
Beds: 1D 1S
Baths: 1 Private
⛲ (A) 🅿 (1) ☐ ⌾ �📺 ≉
Overlooking pastureland and Coast Path. Bedrooms (single adjacent main bedroom for third member of party) command sea views. Main room opens onto private balcony.

(0.25m) *The White House, 47 Silver Street, Lyme Regis, Dorset, DT7 3HR.*
Actual grid ref: SY339923
Small C18th Georgian guesthouse.
Grades: ETB 2 Cr, Comm, AA 3 Q

Tel: **01297 443420**
Mrs Edmondson.
Rates fr: *£16.00-£18.00.*
Open: Easter to Oct
Beds: 5D 2T
Baths: 7 Ensuite
🅿 (6) ☐ ⌾ �📺 ▮ ≉

(0.5m) *Coverdale Guest House, Woodmead Road, Lyme Regis, Dorset, DT7 3AB.*
Actual grid ref: SY339925
Spacious comfortable non-smoking guesthouse.
Grades: ETB 2 Cr, Comm, AA 3 Q, Recomm
Tel: **01297 442882**
Mr & Mrs Harding.
Rates fr: *£13.00-£15.00.*
Open: Feb to Nov
Beds: 4D 2T 2S
Baths: 6 Private 1 Shared
(A) 🅿 (9) ⅋ ☐ ⌾ ⤬ 📺 ▮ ≉

(0.5m) *Southernhaye, Pound Road, Lyme Regis, Dorset, DT7 3HX.*
Edwardian house with sea views.
Grades: ETB 1 Cr, Comm
Tel: **01297 443077**
Mr Garrard.

Rates fr: *£16.00-£18.00.*
Open: All Year (not Xmas)
Beds: 1D 1T
Baths: 1 Shared
⛲ (A) 🅿 (2) ☐ ⌾ 📺 ≉

(0.5m) 🍴 *New Haven Hotel, 1 Pound Street, Lyme Regis, Dorset, DT7 3HZ.*
Warm welcome at C17th town-house.
Tel: **01297 442499** Mrs Petitt.
Rates fr: *£14.50-£14.50.*
Open: All Year
Beds: 1F 3D 1T 2S
Baths: 1 Shared
(A) ☐ ⌾ 📺 ▮ ≉

(0.25m) 🍴 *Whitsbury, 38 Silver Street, Lyme Regis, Dorset, DT7 3HS.*
Actual grid ref: SY338923
Victorian house, magnificent sea views.
Tel: **01297 443753**
Mr Jones.
Rates fr: *£14.00-£14.00.*
Open: All Year
Beds: 1D 1T
Baths: 2 Private
(A) 🅿 (6) ☐ ⌾ 📺 ▮ ≉

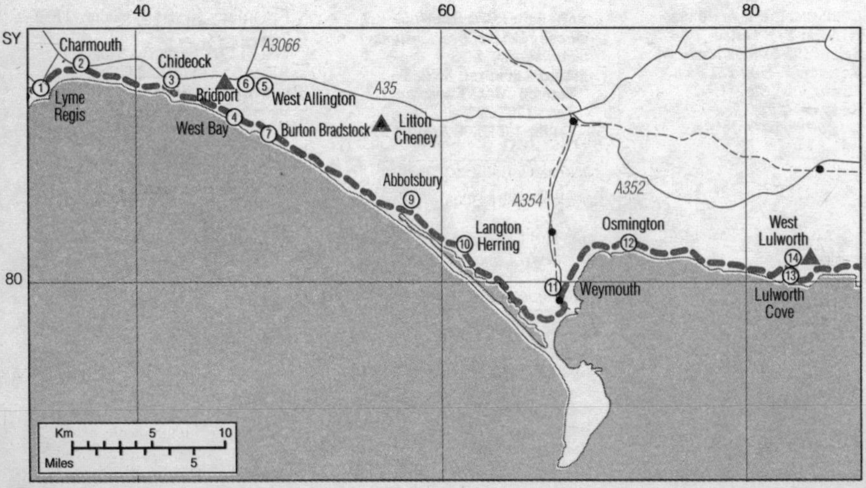

(On Path 🚍) *Kersbrook Hotel,*
Pound Road, Lyme Regis, Dorset,
DT7.
C18th thatched hotel in grounds.
Grades: ETB 3 Cr, High Comm,
AA 2 St, 1 Rosette, RAC 2 St
Tel: 01297 442596
Mr Stephenson.
Rates fr: £30.00-£45.00.
Open: All Year (not Xmas)
Beds: 7D 3T 2S
Baths: 12 Ensuite
(A) 🅿 ⌷ ⍭ ✕ 🎞 Ⅴ ⌷ ✦

(On Path) *Rotherfield Guest*
House, View Road, Lyme Regis,
Dorset, DT7 3AA.
Actual grid ref: SY3492
Clean, comfortable, with spacious
rooms.
Tel: 01297 445585 Mr Hall.
Rates fr: £13.50-£16.00.
Open: All Year
Beds: 1F 3D 2T 1S
Baths: 3 Ensuite 2 Shared
(A) 🅿 (7) ⌷ ⍭ ✕ 🎞 Ⅴ ⌷

Charmouth 2

National Grid Ref: SY3693

🍴 ⌸ Charmouth House Hotel, The
Street, The George

(0.25m) *Springfield House,*
Axminster Road, Charmouth,
Bridport, Dorset, DT6 6PB.
Actual grid ref: SY361937
Tel: 01297 560509
Mrs Ward.
Rates fr: £17.50-£17.50.
Open: All Year
Beds: 2D 1T
Baths: 3 Ensuite
(A) 🅿 (3) ⌷ ⍭ 🎞 Ⅴ ⌷ ✦
Wet and muddy boots welcome.
17th Century cottage. Residents'
TV lounge. Tea making facilities in
dining room. Smoking restricted to
tea area. Rooms ensuite.

SY 00 SZ

A35

A351
Kimmeridge
Worth
Matravers
Studland 18
Swanage
Kimmeridge 15
16
17

(On Path) *Fernhill Hotel,*
Charmouth, Bridport, Dorset,
DT6 6BX.
Hotel, large manor house.
Grades: ETB 3 Cr
Tel: 01297 560492 Mr Bridges.
Rates fr: £22.50-£30.00.
Open: Easter to Oct
Beds: 3F 6D 6T 6S
Baths: 21 Ensuite
(A) 🅿 (50) ⌷ ⍭ 🎞 ✦

(0.25m) *Hensleigh Hotel, Lower*
Sea Lane, Charmouth, Bridport,
Dorset, DT6 6P.
Comfortable, Georgian-style house,
large conservatory.
Grades: ETB 3 Cr, High Comm,
AA 2 St, RAC 2 St
Tel: 01297 60830 Mrs Macnair.
Rates fr: £23.00-£23.00.
Open: Mar to Oct
Beds: 2F 3D 4T 2S
Baths: 11 Ensuite
(A) 🅿 ⌷ ⍭ ✕ 🎞 Ⅴ ⌷

(0.25m 🚍) *Charleston House,*
The Street, Charmouth, Bridport,
Dorset, DT6 6NX.
Comfortable former inn.
Tel: 01297 60347
Mr & Mrs Charge.
Rates fr: £12.50-£12.50.
Open: All Year
Beds: 2F 1D
Baths: 1 Ensuite 1 Shared
(A) 🅿 ⍭ ⌷ ⍭ ✕ 🎞 Ⅴ ⌷ ✦

Chideock 3

National Grid Ref: SY4292

🍴 ⌸ George Inn, Clock House

(0.5m) *Betchworth House,*
Chideock, Bridport, Dorset,
DT6 6JW.
Lovely C17th cottage in gardens.
Grades: AA Listed
Tel: 01297 489478
Mr Wagstaff.
Rates fr: £15.00-£15.00.
Open: All Year
Beds: 1F 2D 2T 1S
Baths: 3 Private 3 Shared
(A) 🅿 (15) ⌷ 🎞 Ⅴ ⌷ ✦

West Bay 4

National Grid Ref: SY4690

🍴 ⌸ West Bay Hotel

(On Path) *Egdon, Third Cliff Walk,*
West Bay, Bridport, Dorset,
DT6 4HX.
Quiet house, panoramic views of
Lyme Bay.
Grades: ETB Listed
Tel: 01308 422542
Mrs Vallard.
Rates fr: £12.50.
Open: All Year
Beds: 1F 1D 1T
Baths: 2 Shared
(A) 🅿 (4) ⍭ ⌷ ⍭ 🎞 Ⅴ ⌷ ✦

West Allington 5

National Grid Ref: SY4693

(▲ 1.5m) *Bridport Youth Hostel,*
West Rivers House, West Allington,
Bridport, Dorset, DT6 5BW.
Actual grid ref: SY4693
Warden: Ms C Simpson.
Tel: 01308 422655
Under 18: £5.00 **Adults:** £7.45
Family Bunk Rooms, Partially
Heated, Showers, Evening Meal
(7.00 pm), Shop, Television,
Games Room
Former flax warehouse and rope
works on the edge of Bridport, sur-
rounded by rolling hills and fine
coastal scenery

Bridport 6

National Grid Ref: SY4692

🍴 ⌸ Crown Inn, The Greyhound
Hotel

(0.75m 🚍) *Britmead House, West*
Bay Road, Bridport, Dorset,
DT6 4EG.
Actual grid ref: SY465912
Grades: ETB 3 Cr, High Comm,
AA 4 Q, RAC Acclaim
Tel: 01308 422941 Mr Walker.
Rates fr: £19.00-£24.00.
Open: All Year
Beds: 1F 4D 2T **Baths:** 7 Private
🛏 (A) 🅿 (8) ⌷ ⍭ ✕ 🎞 Ⅴ ⌷ ✦
Twixt Bridport & West Bay.
Lounge, dining room overlooking
garden. Delicious meals, optional
dinner and putting guests' comfort
first mean that visitors return time
after time.

(1.5m) *107 South Street, Bridport,*
Dorset, DT6 3PA.
Listed Victorian cosy terraced
cottage.
Grades: ETB Listed
Tel: 01308 420907 Mrs Webber.
Rates fr: £14.00-£15.50.
Open: All Year (not Xmas)
Beds: 1F **Baths:** 1 Ensuite
🛏 (A) ⍭ ⌷ ⍭ 🎞 Ⅴ ✦

Burton Bradstock 7

National Grid Ref: SY4889

🍴 ⌸ Three Horseshoes

(0.25m) *Three Horseshoes, Mill*
Street, Burton Bradstock, Bridport,
Dorset, DT6 4QZ.
Grades: ETB 1 Cr
Tel: 01308 897259
Mr & Mrs Attrill.
Rates fr: £15.50-£17.50.
Open: All Year (not Xmas)
Beds: 2D 1T
🅿 (16) ⍭ ⌷
Three Horseshoes, one of West
Dorset's finer inns, situated in
Burton Bradstock, a picturesque
coastal village on the scenic
Bridport to Weymouth Coast Road.
Adjacent to Chesil Beach.

(On Path 🚍) *Burton Cliff Hotel,
Cliff Road, Burton Bradstock,
Bridport, Dorset, DT6 4RB.*
Grades: ETB 3 Cr, Approv
Tel: 01308 897205 Mr Barnikel.
Rates fr: *£18.00-***£18.00***.*
Open: Feb to Dec
Beds: 15D 3S
Baths: 11 Private 3 Shared
(A) 🅿 (40) 🖵 🔭 ✗ 📖 Ⅵ 🛇 ∻
Unique cliff-top position, set in
Heritage Coast countryside. South
West Coast Path on our doorstep.
Group facilities available, large
lounge, dining/bar areas. Owner a
trekker and photographer.

Litton Cheney   8
National Grid Ref: SY5590

🍴 🍺 White Horse

(🔺3.5m) *Litton Cheney Youth
Hostel, Litton Cheney, Dorchester,
Dorset, DT2 9AT.*
Actual grid ref: SY5490
Warden: Mr P Chubb.
Tel: 01308 482340
Under 18: £3.75 **Adults:** £5.50
Partially Heated, Showers, Evening
Meal (7.30 pm)
*Traditional Dutch Barn in the
Bride Valley, once a cheese and
milk factory*

Abbotsbury   9
National Grid Ref: SY5785

🍴 🍺 Ilchester Arms, Swan Inn

(0.5m) *Swan Lodge, Abbotsbury,
Weymouth, Dorset, DT3 4JL.*
Modern guest house - opposite inn.
Grades: ETB 2 Cr, Comm
Tel: 01305 871249 Mr Roper.
Rates fr: *£20.00-***£20.00***.*
Open: All Year
Beds: 4D 3T
Baths: 2 Ensuite 3 Shared
(A) 🅿 🖵 🔭 ✗ 📖 🛇 ∻

(0.5m) *Swan Lodge, Abbotsbury,
Weymouth, Dorset, DT3 4JL.*
Modern guest house.
Grades: ETB 2 Cr
Tel: 01305 871249 Mr Roper.
Rates fr: *£20.00-***£28.00***.*
Open: All Year
Beds: 2F 4D 2T
Baths: 2 Private 3 Shared
(A) 🅿 🖵 🔭 ✗ 📖 Ⅵ

Langton Herring   10
National Grid Ref: SY6182

🍴 🍺 Elm Tree Inn

(On Path) *Lower Farmhouse,
Langton Herring, Weymouth,
Dorset, DT3 4JB.*
Actual grid ref: SY8261
Homely C16th character farm-
house.
Grades: ETB 2 Cr
Tel: 01305 871187 Ms Mayo.

Rates fr: *£17.00-***£20.00***.*
Open: All Year (not Xmas)
Beds: 1D 2T
Baths: 3 Ensuite
(A) 🅿 (4) 🖵 🔭 📖 Ⅵ ∻

Weymouth   11
National Grid Ref: SY6769

🍴 🍺 Spa Hotel, Radipole

(0.75m) *Rosedale Guest House,
217 Dorchester Road, Weymouth,
Dorset, DT3 5EQ.*
Clean comfortable friendly guest-
house.
Tel: 01305 784339 Mrs Nixey.
Rates fr: *£14.00-***£14.00***.*
Open: All Year (not Xmas)
Beds: 4F 3D 1T
Baths: 2 Ensuite 3 Shared
(A) 🅿 (8) 🖵 🔭 📖 🛇 ∻

Osmington   12
National Grid Ref: SY7283

🍴 🍺 Sun Ray, Smugglers Inn

(On Path) *Rosedale, Church Lane,
Osmington, Weymouth, Dorset,
DT3 6EW.*
Grades: ETB Listed
Tel: 01305 832056 Mrs Legg.
Rates fr: *£14.00*.
Open: March to Nov
Beds: 1D 1T
Baths: 2 Private
🛏 (A) 🅿 (3) 📖 ∻
Very attractive cottage situated in
village of Osmington. Large com-
fortable rooms, warm friendly
atmosphere.

Lulworth Cove   13
National Grid Ref: SY8279

🍴 🍺 Castle Inn

(0.25m) *The Old Barn, Lulworth
Cove, West Lulworth, Wareham,
Dorset, BH20 5RL.*
Actual grid ref: SY822802
Picturesque barn conversion.
Grades: ETB Listed
Tel: 01929 400305 Mrs Else.
Rates fr: *£17.00-***£17.00***.*
Open: All Year
Beds: 2F 2D 2T 2S
Baths: 3 Shared
(A) 🅿 (8) 🔭 📖 Ⅵ ∻

West Lulworth   14
National Grid Ref: SY8280

🍴 🍺 Shirly Hotel, Castle Inn,
Bishop Cottage, Mill House

(🔺0.5m) *Lulworth Cove Youth
Hostel, School Lane, West
Lulworth, Wareham, Dorset,
BH20 5SA.*
Actual grid ref: SY8380
Warden: Ms A Roberts.
Tel: 01929 400564

Under 18: £4.60 **Adults:** £6.75
Family Bunk Rooms, Centrally
Heated, Showers, Evening Meal
(7.00 pm), Parking
*Purpose-built hostel, constructed
from cedarwood, recently refurbished*

(0.25m) *Graybank Guest House,
Main Road, West Lulworth,
Wareham, Dorset, BH20 5RL.*
Comfortable Victorian guesthouse.
Grades: ETB Listed
Tel: 01929 400256
Mr & Mrs Burrill.
Rates fr: *£17.00*.
Open: Feb to Nov
Beds: 2F 2D 2T 1S
Baths: 3 Shared
🛏 (A) 🅿 (7) 🖵 🔭 📖 Ⅵ 🛇

(0.5m) *Elads Nevar, West Road,
West Lulworth, Wareham, Dorset,
BH20 5RZ.*
Large modern house.
Tel: 01929 400467
Mrs Ravensdale.
Rates fr: *£13.00-***£15.00***.*
Open: All Year (not Xmas)
Beds: 1F 1D 1T
Baths: 1 Shared·
🛏 (A) 🅿 (3) 🖵 🔭 📖 Ⅵ 🛇

(0.25m) *Shirley Hotel, West
Lulworth, Wareham, Dorset,
BH20 5RL.*
Actual grid ref: SY823806
Comfortable hotel, indoor heated
pool.
Grades: ETB 3 Cr, High Comm,
AA 1 St
Tel: 01929 400358
Tony Williams.
Rates fr: *£27.50-***£27.50***.*
Open: Feb to Nov
Beds: 3F 8D 4T 3S
Baths: 18 Ensuite
(A) 🅿 (22) 🖵 🔭 ✗ 📖 Ⅵ 🛇 ∻

(0.25m 🚍) *The Orchard, West
Road, West Lulworth, Wareham,
Dorset, BH20 5RY.*
Actual grid ref: SY824807
Comfortable accommodation in old
vicarage orchard.
Tel: 01929 400592
Mr & Mrs Aldridge.
Rates fr: *£12.50-***£12.50***.*
Open: Easter to Oct
Beds: 1D 1T
Baths: 1 Shared
🛏 (A) 🅿 (3) Ⅵ 🛇 ∻

(On Path) *Tewkesbury Cottage, 28
Main Road, West Lulworth,
Wareham, Dorset, BH20 5RL.*
Converted 16th Century thatched
cottage.
Tel: 01929 400561
Mrs Laing.
Rates fr: *£15.00-***£16.00***.*
Open: All Year (not Xmas)
Beds: 2D 1T
Baths: 1 Ensuite 2 Shared
🛏 (A) 🅿 (6) 🔭 Ⅵ ∻

Kimmeridge   15

National Grid Ref: SY9179

¶| ⊄ The Seven Taps

(0.5m) *Kimmeridge Farmhouse,*
Kimmeridge, Wareham, Dorset,
BH20 5PE.
Large attractive C16th farmhouse.
Grades: ETB Listed
Tel: 01929 480990 Mrs Hole.
Rates fr: *£16.00-£20.00*.
Open: All Year (not Xmas)
Beds: 2D 1T
Baths: 1 Private 1 Shared
(A) **P** (3) ⊡ ⊞ V ⓘ ≉

Worth Matravers   16

National Grid Ref: SY9777

(1m) *Belros, Worth Matravers,*
Swanage, Dorset, BH19 3LW.
Comfortable house, warm
welcome, good food.
Tel: 01929 439259 Ms Prior.
Rates fr: *£18.00-£18.00*.
Open: All Year (not Xmas)
Beds: 3D 1T
Baths: 1 Private 2 Shared
(A) **P** ⊡ ⊁ ⊞ V ≉

Swanage   17

National Grid Ref: SZ0278

¶| ⊄ Black Swan, Durlston Castle,
The Ship Hotel, Red Lion,
Tawneys Wine Bar, Purbeck Inn,
The Crows Nest

(0.5m) *Cluny Croft Hotel,*
19 Cluny Crescent, Swanage,
Dorset, BH19 2BP.
Friendly family run private hotel.
Grades: ETB 2 Cr
Tel: 01929 424322 Mr Dack.
Rates fr: *£17.50-£17.50*.
Open: All Year (not Xmas)
Beds: 3F 3D 1T
Baths: 3 Ensuite, 2 Shared
(A) **P** (6) ⊡ ⊁ ✕ ⊞ V ⓘ ≉

(0.25m) *Skelmorlie House,*
50 Queens Road, Swanage, Dorset,
BH19 2EU.
Actual grid ref: SZ030784
Small comfortable welcoming
guesthouse.
Grades: ETB 2 Cr, Comm
Tel: 01929 424643 Mrs Rudd.
Rates fr: *£17.00-£15.00*.
Open: Apr to Sep
Beds: 1F 1D 2S
Baths: 2 Ensuite 1 Shared
⚲ (A) **P** (2) ⊁ ⊡ ✕ ⊞ ⓘ

(▲ On Path) *Swanage Youth*
Hostel, Cluny, Cluny Crescent,
Swanage, Dorset, BH19 2BS.
Actual grid ref: SZ0378
Warden: Mr D Pearson.
Tel: 01929 422113
Under 18: £6.15 **Adults:** £9.10
Family Bunk Rooms, Centrally
Heated, Showers, Evening Meal
(6.30 pm), Shop, Security Lockers,

Television, Games Room, Parking
Large refurbished house built on
the site of a Cluny monastery in the
well-known seaside resort of the
Isle of Purbeck

(0.5m) *West Country Hotel,*
12 Rempstone Road, Swanage,
Dorset, BH19 1DW.
Close to sea-front, town, railway.
Tel: 01929423271
Mrs Pettitt.
Rates fr: *£18.50-£18.50*.
Open: All Year (not Xmas)
Beds: 3D 2T 1S
Baths: 5 Ensuite 1 Private
⚲ (A) **P** (11) ⊞

(0.75m ⊞) *Pennyfarthings,*
124 Kings Road West, Swanage,
Dorset, BH19 1HS.
Actual grid ref: SZ023789
Comfortable, friendly Edwardian
guesthouse.
Tel: 01929 422256
Mr & Mrs Davison.
Rates fr: *£14.00-£16.00*.
Open: All Year
Beds: 1F 1D 1T
Baths: 1 Private 1 Shared
⚲ (A) **P** (2) ⊁ ⊡ ⊁ ✕ ⊞ ⓘ ≉

(On Path ⊞) *Easter Cottage,*
9 Eldon Terrace, Swanage, Dorset,
BH19 1HA.
C19th friendly stone cottage.
Grades: ETB 2 Cr
Tel: 01929 427782 Mrs Needham.
Rates fr: *£13.00*.
Open: All Year
Beds: 1D 1T
Baths: 1 Ensuite 1 Shared
⊡ ⊞ V ≉

(On Path) *Hermitage Guest*
House, 1 Manor Road, Swanage,
Dorset, BH19 2BH.
Quietly situated friendly guest
house.
Tel: 01929 423014 Mrs Pickering.
Rates fr: *£15.00-£16.50*.
Open: Easter to Nov
Beds: 4F 2D 1T
Baths: 2 Shared
(A) **P** (7) ⊁ ⊞ V ≉

(0.25m) *The Corner House,*
4 Manor Road, Swanage, Dorset,
BH19 2BJ.
Actual grid ref: SZ031786
Large private house near beach.
Tel: 01929 424410 Mrs Preston.
Rates fr: *£13.00*.
Open: Easter to Nov
Beds: 1F 1T
Baths: 1 Shared
⚲ (A) **P** (1) ⊁ ⊡ V ≉

(0.25m) *The Oxford Hotel,*
3-5 Park Road, Swanage, Dorset,
BH19 2AA.
Friendly run hotel with all
amenities.
Grades: ETB 3 Cr, Comm,
AA 3 Q, Recomm, RAC Acclaim
Tel: 01929 422247
Mr & Mrs Taylor.

Rates fr: *£15.00-£15.00*.
Open: All Year
Beds: 3F 9D 1T 2S
Baths: 8 Ensuite 7 Shared
(A) ⊡ ⊁ ⊞ V ≉

(0.5m) *Ingleston Hotel,* *2 Victoria*
Road, Swanage, Dorset, BH19 1LY.
Large Victorian house.
Grades: ETB Listed
Tel: 01929 422391
Mrs McLintic.
Rates fr: *£16.00-£16.00*.
Open:
Beds: 4F 2D 2T 2S
Baths: 3 Private 2 Shared
(A) **P** (9) ⊁ ⊡ ⊁ ⊞ V ⓘ

(0.75m ⊞) *Newton Manor*
House, High Street, Swanage,
Dorset, BH19 2PQ.
Historic building. Guided walking
holidays.
Tel: 01929 427222
Mr King.
Rates fr: *£15.00-£17.50*.
Open: All Year
Beds: 1D 1T 4S
Baths: 2 Ensuite 2 Shared
P (6) ⊁ ⊡ ✕ ⊞ V ⓘ ≉

Studland   18

National Grid Ref: SZ0382

¶| ⊄ Bankes Arms, Manor House
Hotel

(On Path) *Purbeck Down Guest*
House, The Glebe, Studland,
Swanage, Dorset, BH19 3AS.
Spacious/secluded, with 40ft pool.
Tel: 01929 450257
Mrs Rose.
Rates fr: *£17.50-£22.00*.
Open: Feb to Dec
Beds: 1F 1D1T
Baths: 2 Ensuite 1 Private
⚲ (A) **P** (3) ⊡ ⊁ ⊞ V ≉

The Grid Reference
beneath the location
heading is for the
village or town - *not*
for individual houses,
which are shown
(where supplied) in
each entry itself.

Speyside Way

At 45 miles, this is not a very long path and much of it is at low level, running alongside the River Spey, making it an excellent choice for a long weekend's walk. It runs from where the Spey joins the North Sea at Spey Bay, down to Aberlour with a spur running off to Dufftown, joins a former railway track, reaches Glenlivet and then climbs Carn Daimh before descending to the old military town of Tomintoul in the South. Besides the beautiful scenery, one great attraction is the number of distilleries the route passes (it's also called the 'Whisky Trail'), each offering its own distinctive malt. Should you care to drop in at each one, that weekend may well turn out to be a bit longer.

Guides: S*peyside Way Leaflet* published by Moray District Council and available free of charge from the M.D.C. Ranger Service (Dept of Leisure & Libraries, High Street, Elgin, Moray, IV30 1BX, tel. 01340 881266).

Maps: Ordnance Survey 1:50,000 Landranger series: 28 and 36.

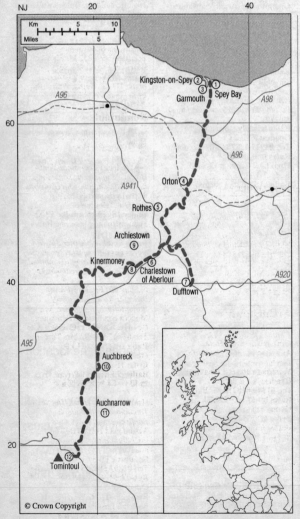

© Crown Copyright

Spey Bay 1

National Grid Ref: NJ3565

|O| ⬛ Grant Arms Hotel

(On Path) *Spey Bay Hotel, Spey Bay, Fochabers, Morayshire, IV32 7PY.*
All rooms with bath or shower.
Grades: ETB Approv
Tel: **01343 820424** Mr Dann.
Rates fr: *£24.00-£27.00*.
Open: All Year
Beds: 3F 3D 2T 2S
Baths: 10 Ensuite
⛺ 🅿 🏠 🏃 ✕ 🛏 🔥 🏃 🍴
Also ▲ *£6.50 per tent.*
Open: Apr to Oct 🏠 T 🏕 ✕

Kingston-on-Spey 2

National Grid Ref: NJ3365

|O| ⬛ Garmouth Hotel

(2m) *Sunnybank, Lein Road, Kingston-on-Spey, Fochabers, Morayshire, IV32 7NW.*
Large 1800s family house on coast.
Tel: **01343 870362**
Mrs Anderson.
Rates fr: *£10.00-£10.00*.
Open: All Year (not Xmas)
Beds: 1F 1D
Baths: 1 Shared
⛺ (0.5) 🅿 (3) ⊁ 🏠 🏃 ✕ 🛏 🔥

Garmouth 3

National Grid Ref: NJ3364

(0.25m) *Rowan Cottage, Station Road, Garmouth, Fochabers, Morayshire, IV32 7LZ.*
C18th Speyside cottage.
Tel: **01343 870267**
Mrs Bingham.
Rates fr: *£13.00-£13.00*.
Open: Jan to Nov
Beds: 1D 1S
Baths: 1 Shared
⛺ 🅿 (5) 🏠 ✕ 🛏 V 🔥

Orton 4

National Grid Ref: NY6208

|O| 🦪 George Hotel

(1m) *Berwyn House, Orton,
Penrith, Cumbria, CA10 3RQ.*
Family home catering for walkers.
Tel: **015396 24345** Mrs Dunford.
Rates fr: *£15.00*-**£15.00.**
Open: All Year
Beds: 1D 2T **Baths:** 1 Shared
🛇 (8) 🖵 ✕ 🛒 Ⅵ

Rothes 5

National Grid Ref: NJ2749

|O| 🦪 Eastbank Hotel, Speyside
Restaurant

(3m) 🚌 *Eastbank Hotel, 15/17
High Street, Rothes, Banffshire,
AB38 7AU.*
Friendly, comfortable 'Whisky
Trail' hotel.
Grades: ETB 3 Cr, Comm
Tel: **01340 831564**
Mrs Humphreys.
Rates fr: *£15.00*-**£16.50.**
Open: All Year
Beds: 2F 3D 3T 2S
Baths: 3 Private 3 Shared
🛇 🅿 (10) 🖵 ⛰ ✕ 🛒 🛱 Ⅵ
Also ▲

Charlestown of Aberlour 6

National Grid Ref: NJ2642

|O| 🦪 Aberlour Hotel

(On Path) *The Station Bar, 7-8
Broomfield Square, Charlestown of
Aberlour, Banffshire, AB38 9QP.*
Actual grid ref: NJ267429
Comfortable inn on River Spey.
Tel: **01340 871858** Mrs Booth.
Rates fr: *£14.00*-**£14.00.**
Open: All Year
Beds: 1D 2T
Baths: 1 Shared
🅿 (20) 🖵 ⛰ ✕ 🛒 Ⅵ 🛱 ⤧

(On Pathm) *83 High Street,
Charlestown of Aberlour,
Banffshire, AB38 9QB.*
Attatched to Leather Craft Shop.
Tel: **01340 871319** Mrs Gammack.
Rates fr: *£11.50*-**£11.50.**
Open: All Year **Beds:** 1F 1D 1S
🛇 🅿 (2) 🖵 Ⅵ

Dufftown 7

National Grid Ref: NJ3240

|O| 🦪 Taste of Speyside, Fife Arms
Hotel, Commercial Hotel, The
Mason Arms

(On Path) *Fife Arms Hotel, 2 The
Square, Dufftown, Keith,
Banffshire, AB55 4AD.*
Small modern town centre hotel.
Grades: ETB 1 Cr, Approv,
AA 2 Q, Recomm

Tel: **01340 820220**
Mr Widdowson.
Rates fr: *£20.00*-**£25.00.**
Open: All Year
Beds: 1F 2D 3T **Baths:** 6 Private
🛇 🅿 (10) 🖵 ⛰ ✕ 🛒 🛱 Ⅵ 🛱 ⤧

(On Pathm) 🚌 *Errolbank,
134 Fife Street, Dufftown, Keith,
Banffshire, AB55 4DP.*
Large Victorian private house.
Tel: **01340 820229** Mrs Smart.
Rates fr: *£12.50*-**£12.50.**
Open: All Year
Beds: 3F 1D 1S
🛇 🅿 (5) 🖵 ⛰ ✕ 🛒 Ⅵ 🛱 ⤧

(1.25m) *43 Fife Street, Dufftown,
Keith, Banffshire, AB55.*
Stone built house on street.
Tel: **01340 820408** Mrs Souter.
Rates fr: *£12.50*-**£12.50.**
Open: Easter to Oct
Beds: 1F 1D
Baths: 1 Shared
🛇 ⤧ 🖵 🛒 ⤧

(1.25m) *Fife Arms Hotel, 2 The
Square, Dufftown, Keith,
Banffshire, AB55 4AD.*
Small modern town centre hotel.
Grades: ETB Listed, Approv,
AA 2 Q
Tel: **01340 820220**
Mr Widdowson.
Rates fr: *£21.00*-**£26.00.**
Open: All Year
Beds: 1F 2D 3T
Baths: 6 Private
🛇 (1) 🅿 (8) 🖵 ⛰ ✕ 🛒 🛱 Ⅵ

Kinermoney 8

National Grid Ref: NJ2541

(0.5m) 🚌 *Kinermoney Farm,
Kinermoney, Charlestown of
Aberlour, Banffshire, AB38 9LX.*
200-year-old white farmhouse.
Tel: **01340 871818** Mrs Thom.
Rates fr: *£12.50*-**£12.50.**
Open: All Year (not Xmas)
Beds: 3T **Baths:** 2 Shared
🛇 🅿 🖵 ⛰ ✕ 🛱 ⤧

Archiestown 9

National Grid Ref: NJ2344

(3m) *Archiestown Hotel,
Archiestown, Aberlour, Moray,
AB38 7QX.*
Victorian village fishing hotel.
Grades: AA 2 St
Tel: **01340 810218** Mr Bulger.
Rates fr: *£18.75*-**£30.00.**
Open: Feb to Oct
Beds: 1D 5T 2S
Baths: 6 Ensuite 1 Shared
🛇 🅿 🖵 ⛰ ✕ 🛒 Ⅵ 🛱 ⤧

The lowest *double* rate per
person is shown in *italics*.

Auchbreck 10

National Grid Ref: NJ2028

(1m) 🚌 *Deepdale, Auchbreck,
Glenlivet, Ballindalloch,
Banffshire, AB37 9EJ.*
Actual grid ref: NJ208285
Warm comfortable farming family
hospitality.
Grades: ETB 1 Cr, Comm
Tel: **01807 590364** Mrs Durno.
Rates fr: *£14.00*-**£14.00.**
Open: All Year (not Xmas)
Beds: 1D 1T
Baths: 1 Shared
🛇 🅿 (3) ⤧ ✕ 🛒 Ⅵ 🛱 ⤧

Auchnarrow 11

National Grid Ref: NJ2123

|O| 🦪 Pole Inn

(2m) 🚌 *Pole Inn, Auchnarrow,
Glenlivet, Ballindalloch,
Banffshire, AB37 9JN.*
Traditional Scottish pub.
Tel: **01807 590252** Mr Shewan.
Rates fr: *£14.00*-**£12.50.**
Open: All Year (not Xmas)
Beds: 1D 1T **Baths:** 1 Shared
🛇 🅿 (15) 🖵 ⛰ ✕ 🛒 🛱 ⤧

Tomintoul 12

National Grid Ref: NJ1618

|O| 🦪 Glenavon Hotel

(▲ On Path) *Tomintoul Youth
Hostel, Main Street, Tomintoul,
Ballindalloch, Banffshire, AB37 9HA.*
Actual grid ref: NJ1619
Tel: **(No Telephone)**
Under 18: £3.15 **Adults:** £3.85
Shower Room, Shops and Buses
nearby
*Green weather-boarded single-
storey hut with a picket fence, on
the main road through Tomintoul.
Great fishing and great whisky.*

(1.75m) 🚌 *Findron Farm,
Braemar Road, Tomintoul,
Ballindalloch, Banffshire, AB37 9ER.*
Modern comfortable farmhouse.
Grades: ETB 2 Cr, Comm
Tel: **01807 580382** Mrs Turner.
Rates fr: *£14.00*-**£14.00.**
Open: All Year
Beds: 1F 2D
Baths: 2 Ensuite 1 Private
🛇 🅿 (3) 🖵 ⛰ ✕ 🛒 Ⅵ 🛱 ⤧

(1m) *Glenavon Hotel, The Square,
Tomintoul, Ballindalloch,
Banffshire, AB37 9ET.*
Actual grid ref: NJ188168
Friendly informal comfortable
hotel.
Grades: ETB 3 Cr, Comm
Tel: **01807 580218** Mr Kennedy.
Rates fr: *£18.00*-**£18.00.**
Open: All Year
Beds: 2F 2D 1T 2S
Baths: 5 Ensuite 1 Shared
🛇 🅿 ⤧ 🖵 ⛰ ✕ 🛒 Ⅵ 🛱 ⤧

Staffordshire Way

Here is a 93 mile path that straddles a county of true contrast, a county that belongs at the heart of England's industrial heritage. In a landscape criss-crossed by motorways, suburbia and manu-facturing sites, this path gracefully picks its way southwards from the gritstone hills at the edge of the **Peak District**, along canals and wooded river valleys to the open heaths of Cannock Chase, then heading off through the landscaped park-lands of Chillington, Wrottesley and Enville, before finishing at the soft sandstone ridge of Kinver Edge. The **Staffordshire Way** links with the **Heart of England Way** and thence to the **Cotswold** or the **Oxfordshire Ways**.

Guides: *The Staffordshire Way*, published by Staffordshire County Council and available directly from their offices (County Buildings, Planning & Economic Dev, Martin Street, Stafford, ST16 2LE, tel. 01785 223121), £3.00

The Staffordshire Way by Les Lumsdon and Chris Rushton (ISBN 1 850583153), published by Sigma Leisure and available from all good map shops or directly from the publishers (1 South Oak Lane, Wilmslow, Cheshire, SK9 6AR), £6.95 (+ 75p p&p)

Maps: Ordnance Survey 1:50,000 Landranger series: 118, 119, 127, 128, 138, 139

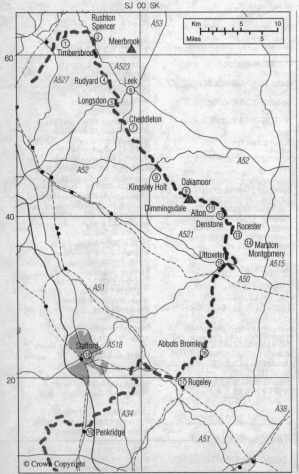

Timbersbrook   1

National Grid Ref: SJ8962

🍴 🍺 Coach & Horses

(0.5m 🚌) *Pedley House Farm*, *Pedley Lane, Timbersbrook, Congleton, Cheshire, CW12 3QD.* Warm, comfortable old stone farm-house.
Tel: **01260 273650** Mrs Gilman.
Rates fr: *£15.00*-**£16.00**.
Open: All Year (not Xmas)
Beds: 1F 1D **Baths:** 1 Shared
🛇 🅿 🖵 ✕ ⦸ Ⓥ ⏷ ✦

Rushton Spencer   2

National Grid Ref: SJ9362

🍴 🍺 The Royal Oak, The Knott

(1m) *Barnswood Farm*, *Rushton Spencer, Macclesfield, Cheshire, SK11 0RA.*
Large comfortable farmhouse.
Grades: ETB Listed
Tel: **01260 226261** Mrs Brown.
Rates fr: *£14.00*-**£16.00**.
Open: All Year (not Xmas)
Beds: 1F 3D
🛇 🅿 🖵 ⦸ Ⓥ ⏷ ✦

Meerbrook 3

National Grid Ref: SJ9960

(▲ 4.5m) *Meerbrook Youth Hostel*, Old School, Meerbrook, Leek, Staffordshire, ST13 8SJ.
Actual grid ref: SJ989608
Warden: Ms I Carline.
Tel: 01629 650394
Under 18: £4.15 Adults: £6.10
Self Catering Facilities, Centrally Heated, No Smoking, Shop, Parking (cars only)
A former school house in the centre of Meerbrook village, within sight of The Roaches - a long ridge of millstone grit

Rudyard 4

National Grid Ref: SJ9458

🍴 🍺 Royal Oak, The Knot

(2m 🚐) *Fairboroughs Farm*, Rudyard, Leek, Staffs, ST13 8PR.
Spacious, comfortable 16th/17th Century farmhouse.
Grades: ETB 1 Cr
Tel: 01260 226341
Mrs Lowe.
Rates fr: £15.00-£15.00.
Open: Easter to Oct
Beds: 1F 1D
Baths: 1 Shared
🛏 🅿 (4) ⛽ 🐕 ✕ 🎷 📖 Ⅵ 🛁 ⅋

Longsdon 5

National Grid Ref: SJ9655

(0.25m) *Micklea Farm*, Micklea Lane, Longsdon, Stoke on Trent, Staffs, ST9 9QA.
Actual grid ref: SJ961539
Grades: ETB Listed, Comm
Tel: 01538 385006
Mrs White.
Rates fr: £16.00-£16.00.
Open: All Year (not Xmas)
Beds: 2D 2S
Baths: 2 Shared
🛏 🅿 (4) ⛽ ⌷ ✕ 🎷 Ⅵ 🛁 ⅋
Delightful Staffordshire stone house with a homely welcome, good home cooking, open fires. Ideal walking country or visiting the potteries or Alton Towers.

Leek 6

National Grid Ref: SJ9856

🍴 🍺 Royal Oak, Raymonds Restaurant

(1m 🚐) *Warrington House*, 108 Buxton Road, Leek, Staffs, ST13 6EJ.
Large Victorian private house.
Grades: ETB 1 Cr
Tel: 01538 399566
Mr Whone.
Rates fr: £14.00-£17.00.
Open: All Year
Beds: 2F 1D 1T
Baths: 1 Shared
🛏 🅿 (3) ⌷ ✕ 🎷 Ⅵ 🛁 ⅋

(1.25m) *The Hatcheries,* Church Lane, Mount Pleasant, Leek, Staffs, ST13 5ET.
Adapted farm buildings, fully modernised.
Grades: ETB Listed
Tel: 01538 383073
Rates fr: £17.50-£20.50.
Open: All Year
Beds: 11F 3D 2T 2S
Baths: 3 Shared
🛏 (4) 🅿 (12) ⌷ ✕ 🎷 🛁 ⅋

Cheddleton 7

National Grid Ref: SJ9752

(0.5m) *Choir Cottage*, Ostlers Lane, Cheddleton, Leek, Staffs, ST13 7HS.
Accommodation in C17th cottage.
Grades: ETB 4 Cr, High Comm, AA 4 Q, RAC High Acclaim
Tel: 01538 360561
Mr & Mrs Sutcliffe.
Rates fr: £22.50-£30.00.
Open: All Year (not Xmas)
Beds: 1F 1D
Baths: 2 Ensuite
🛏 (5) 🅿 (6) ⛽ ⌷ ✕ 🎷 Ⅵ 🛁

All rooms full and nowhere else to stay? Ask the owner if there's anywhere nearby

---

Kingsley Holt 8

National Grid Ref: SK0246

(On Path 🚐) *The Holt Guest House*, Churnet Valley Road, Kingsley Holt, Stoke on Trent, Staffs, ST10 2BQ.
Homely, welcoming, relaxing guesthouse.
Grades: ETB Listed, Comm, RAC Acclaim
Tel: 01538 757221
Mr & Mrs Barrow.
Rates fr: £15.00-£20.00.
Open: All Year (not Xmas)
Beds: 1F 1D **Baths:** 1 Shared
🛏 🅿 (2) ⛽ ⌷ ✕ 🎷 Ⅵ 🛁 ⅋

High season, bank holidays and special events mean low availability everywhere.

The lowest *double* rate per person is shown in *italics*.

Oakamoor 9

National Grid Ref: SK0544

🍴 🍺 Cross, Star, Green Man, Crown, George, Crickets, Lord Nelson

(1m) *Tenement Farm*, Ribden, Oakamoor, Stoke on Trent, Staffs, ST10 3BW.
Modern comfortable guesthouse in Staffordshire Moorlands.
Grades: ETB 2 Cr, Comm
Tel: 01538 702333 Ms Miller.
Rates fr: £17.50-£25.00.
Open: Easter to Nov
Beds: 3F 2D 3T
Baths: 8 Ensuite
🛏 (5) 🅿 (10) ⛽ ⌷ 🎷 ⅋

(1m 🚐) *Bank House*, Farley Road, Oakamoor, Stoke on Trent, Staffs, ST10 3BD.
Elegant, luxurious licensed country house.
Grades: ETB 2 Cr, High Comm, AA 5 Q, Prem Select
Tel: 01538 702810
Mrs Orme.
Rates fr: £25.00-£38.00.
Open: All Year
Beds: 2F 1D 1S
Baths: 2 Ensuite 1 Shared
🛏 🅿 (8) ⛽ ⌷ 🐕 ✕ 🎷 Ⅵ ⅋

(1m) *The Beehive Guest House*, Churnet View Road, Oakamoor, Stoke on Trent, Staffs, ST10 3AE.
Comfortable family guesthouse.
Grades: ETB 2 Cr
Tel: 01538 702420
Mr & Mrs Beard.
Rates fr: £15.00-£20.00.
Open: Easter to Nov
Beds: 2F 2D 1T
Baths: 2 Ensuite 3 Shared
🛏 🅿 ⌷ 🎷 Ⅵ ⅋

Dimmingsdale 10

National Grid Ref: SK0543

(▲ 0.5m) *Dimmingsdale Youth Hostel*, Little Ranger, Dimmingsdale, Oakamoor, Stoke on Trent, Staffordshire, ST10 3AS.
Actual grid ref: SK052436
Warden: Ms S Bennett.
Tel: 01538 702304
Under 18: £4.15 Adults: £6.10
Self Catering Facilities, Centrally Heated, Shop, Parking (no coaches)
A simple Hostel in secluded woods overlooking the Churnet Valley, in a corner of the relatively undiscovered Staffordshire Moorlands

Alton 11

National Grid Ref: SK0742

|○|🍺 Blacksmiths Arms, Royal Oak

(On Path) *Bulls Head Inn, High Street, Alton, Stoke on Trent, Staffs, ST10 4AR.*
Actual grid ref: SK074425
C18th village inn.
Grades: ETB 3 Cr, AA 2 St
Tel: **01538 702307** Mr Harvey.
Rates fr: *£20.00-£30.00.*
Open: All Year
Beds: 2F 3D 1T **Baths:** 6 Ensuite
🛏 🅿 (15) 🗖 ✕ 🎹 Ⅴ 🏃 🌂

(0.25m) *The Hawthorns, 8 Tythe Barn, Alton, Stoke on Trent, Staffs, ST10 4AZ.*
Cosy, comfortable, homely private house.
Grades: ETB 1 Cr
Tel: **01538 702197** Mrs Callear.
Rates fr: *£15.00-£20.00.*
Open: All Year (not Xmas)
Beds: 1F 1D
Baths: 1 Ensuite 1 Shared
🛏 (5) 🅿 (4) 🗖 🎹 Ⅴ 🌂

(On Path 🚫) *Dale Farm, The Dale, Alton, Stoke on Trent, Staffs, ST10 4BG.*
6 Upgraded period farmhouse - secluded location.
Tel: **01538 702012** Mrs Gregory.
Rates fr: *£14.50-£20.00.*
Open: All Year (not Xmas)
Beds: 1F 1D 1T
Baths: 1 Shared
🛏 (5) 🅿 (6) ✂ 🎹 Ⅴ 🌂

Denstone 12

National Grid Ref: SK0940

(0.25m) *Denstone Hall Farm, Denstone, Uttoxeter, Staffs, ST14 5HF.*
Tel: **01889 590253** Mrs Boden.
Rates fr: *£14.00-£16.00.*
Open: Easter to Nov
Beds: 1F 1T
🛏 🅿 (3) 🗖 🎹 Ⅴ 🌂

Rocester 13

National Grid Ref: SK1039

(On Path) *The Leeze Guest House, 63 High Street, Rocester, Uttoxeter, Staffs, ST14 5JU.*
Actual grid ref: SK109394
Comfortable 18th Century guesthouse.
Grades: ETB 2 Cr
Tel: **01889 591146** Mr Venn.
Rates fr: *£15.00-£17.00.*
Open: All Year
Beds: 2F 1D 2T
Baths: 1 Ensuite, 2 Shared
🛏 🅿 (6) 🗖 🍴 ✕ 🎹 🏃 🌂

Marston Montgomery 14

National Grid Ref: SK1337

|○|🍺 The Crown Inn

(0.75m) *Waldley Manor, Marston Montgomery, Doveridge, Ashbourne, Derbyshire, DE6 5LR.*
C16th manor farmhouse.
Grades: ETB 1 Cr, High Comm
Tel: **01889 590287** Ms Whitfield.

Rates fr: *£17.00-£18.00.*
Open: All Year (not Xmas)
Beds: 1F 1D **Baths:** 2 Ensuite
🛏 🗖 🎹 Ⅴ

Uttoxeter 15

National Grid Ref: SK0933

(On Path) *Old Royd Guest House, 18-20 Bridge Street, Uttoxeter, Staffs, ST14 8AP.*
Tel: **01889 562763** Mrs Butterworth.
Rates fr: *£15.00-£15.00.*
Open: All Year
Beds: 4F 1D 1T 2S
Baths: 4 Shared
🛏 🅿 (14) 🗖 🍴 ✕ 🎹 Ⅴ 🏃 🌂
A very comfortable family run guesthouse offering first class accommodation and excellent food. Ideally situated for the Staffordshire Way and the Peak District.

Abbots Bromley 16

National Grid Ref: SK0824

|○|🍺 Bagot Arms

(On Path 🚫) *Crown Inn, Market Place, Abbots Bromley, Rugeley, Staffs, WS15 3BS.*
Grades: ETB 1 Cr, Approv, AA 2 Q
Tel: **01283 840227** Mr Barford.
Rates fr: *£20.00-£20.00.*
Open: All Year
Beds: 1F 2D 2T 1S
Baths: 2 Shared
🛏 🅿 (40) 🗖 🍴 ✕ 🎹 Ⅴ 🏃 🌂
Traditional inn overlooking ancient Butter Cross 60 yards from Staffordshire Way. Home cooked food, fine ales, warm, comfortable and welcoming. Ring for a brochure.

Rugeley 17

National Grid Ref: SK0418

|○|🍺 Ash Tree, Plum Pudding

(2m 🚫) *Park Farm, Hawksyard, Armitage Lane, Rugeley, Staffs, WS15 1ED.*
Quiet old working farm.
Grades: ETB 2 Cr
Tel: **01889 583477** Mrs Lewis.
Rates fr: *£15.00-£15.00.*
Open: All Year
Beds: 2F 1T
Baths: 3 Ensuite
🛏 🅿 (10) 🗖 🍴 ✕ 🎹 Ⅴ 🏃 🌂

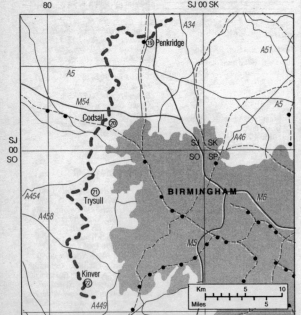

Pay B&Bs by cash or cheque and be prepared to pay up front.

Stafford 18

National Grid Ref: SJ9223

⦿ 🍺 The Sun Inn

(4m) *Albridge Hotel & Bridge Guest, House*, 73 Wolverhampton Road, Stafford, *ST17 4AW*.
Actual grid ref: SJ923225
Large converted Victorian house and annexe.
Grades: ETB 3 Cr, RAC 2 St
Tel: **01785 54100** Mrs Pinhorn.
Rates fr: *£14.00*-**£20.00**.
Open: All Year (not Xmas)
Beds: 3F 3D 5T 8S
Baths: 10 Ensuite 3 Shared
🛏 🅿 (20) 🛏 🍴 ✕ 📺 Ⓥ ⓘ ✦

(3m) *The Albany Guest House*, 49 Lichfield Road, Stafford, Staffs, *ST17 4LL*.
Comfortable, family run guesthouse.
Grades: ETB 1 Cr
Tel: **01785 56285**
Mr & Mrs Bradley.
Rates fr: *£14.00*-**£14.00**.
Open: All Year (not Xmas)
Beds: 1F 1D 1T 1S
Baths: 1 Shared
🛏 🅿 (4) 🍴 📺 Ⓥ ⓘ

(3m) *Leonards Croft Hotel*, 80 Lichfield Road, Stafford, *ST17 4LP*.
Large Victorian private house.
Grades: AA 3 Q
Tel: **01785 223676**
Mr & Mrs Johnson.
Rates fr: *£18.00*-**£18.00**.
Open: All Year (not Xmas)
Beds: 3F 4D 3T 2S
Baths: 4 Ensuite 4 Shared
🛏 🅿 (12) 🍴 ✕ 📺

Penkridge 19

National Grid Ref: SJ9213

⦿ 🍺 Vaughan Arms

(0.5m) *Bickford Grange*, Bickford, Penkridge, Stafford, *ST19 5QJ*.
Large Georgian country private house.
Grades: ETB Listed
Tel: **01785 840257** Mrs Bryant.
Rates fr: *£17.50*-**£18.00**.
Open: All Year (not Xmas)
Beds: 1F 1D 3T 2S
Baths: 1 Ensuite 2 Shared
🛏 🅿 (6) ✕ 🍴 ✕ 📺 ⓘ ✦

Codsall 20

National Grid Ref: SJ8703

(0.25m) *Moors Farm & Country Restaurnt*, Chillington Lane, Codsall, Wolverhampton, Staffs, *WV8 1QF*.
Actual grid ref: SJ8703
Cosy picturesque farmhouse, quiet valley.
Grades: ETB 3 Cr, AA 3 Q, RAC Acclaim
Tel: **01902 842330** Mrs Moreton.
Rates fr: *£21.00*-**£25.00**.
Open: All Year
Beds: 2F 2D 2T
Baths: 3 Ensuite 2 Shared
🛏 (4) 🅿 (20) 🍴 ✕ 📺 Ⓥ ⓘ ✦

The *lowest* single rate *is shown in* bold.

Trysull 21

National Grid Ref: SO8594

⦿ 🍺 Plough Inn

(On Path 🚌) *Park Farm*, Trysull, Wolverhampton, W. Mids, *WV5 7HT*.
Farmhouse in delightful setting.
Tel: **01902 324797** Mrs Baker.
Rates fr: *£13.00*-**£13.00**.
Open: All Year
Beds: 1D 1T
Baths: 2 Shared
🛏 🅿 (10) ✕ 🍴 🍴 📺 ⓘ ✦

Kinver 22

National Grid Ref: SO8483

⦿ 🍺 Vine Inn

(0.75m) *Anchor Hotel*, Dark Lane, Kinver, Stourbridge, W. Mids, *DY7 6NR*.
Converted pub and cottages.
Grades: ETB 2 Cr
Tel: **01384 872085** Mr Olivieri.
Rates fr: *£17.00*-**£21.00**.
Open: All Year (not Xmas)
Beds: 1F 4D 3T 2S
Baths: 10 Ensuite
🛏 🅿 (20) 🍴 🍴 ✕ 📺 ⓘ ✦

(0.25m) *The Old Vicarage*, Vicarage Drive, Kinver, Stourbridge, W. Mids, *DY7 6HJ*.
Victorian old vicarage.
Tel: **01384 872784**
Mr & Mrs Harris.
Rates fr: *£17.50*-**£17.50**.
Open: All Year (not Xmas)
Beds: 2T
Baths: 1 Shared
🛏 (10) 🅿 (10) 🍴 🍴 📺 Ⓥ ✦

Thames Path

The **Thames Path** runs for 175 miles along the banks of the River Thames from the great Thames Barrier near Woolwich in London, through the heartland of England, to the river's source at the Thames Head near Cirencester in Gloucestershire. It is, of course, a walk with no hills - bliss for some, anathema to others. Above all, the walk offers a rolling social picture of Southern England today, starting near what used to be the old London Docklands, moving through genteel South West London, out through the affluent commuter belt of Royal Berkshire, on to the city of Oxford (half ancient university, half busy industry) and beyond through the deserted pastures south of the Cotswolds. The Thames itself, with its boats, bridges, locks and weirs, shifts character accordingly. The towpaths are quite busy in the lower reaches, but beyond Oxford it goes quiet. After rain, the path stays muddy, but apart from flooding, there are no real hazards. We have left out accommodation in central London (apart from Youth Hostels), as the usual hotels tend to be rather expensive. If the Thames Barrier to Kew stretch is too much for you, our suggestion is to make use of the Underground and stay at the same place two nights running.

Guides: *The Thames Walk* by David Sharp, published by the Rambler's Association and available from their National Office (1/5 Wandsworth Road, London, SW8 2XX, tel. 0171 582 6878), £2.95 (+ 70p p&p).

Thames Path by David Sharp (ISBN 1 85410 4063), published by Aurum Press in association with the Countryside Commission and Ordnance Survey and available from all major bookshops, £9.99

Maps: Ordnance Survey 1:50,000 Landranger series: 163, 164, 174, 175 and 176

Comments on the path to: **Karen Groeneveld**, Thames Path Project Officer, c/o Leisure Services, Reading Borough Council, Civic Centre, Reading, Berks, RG1 7TD

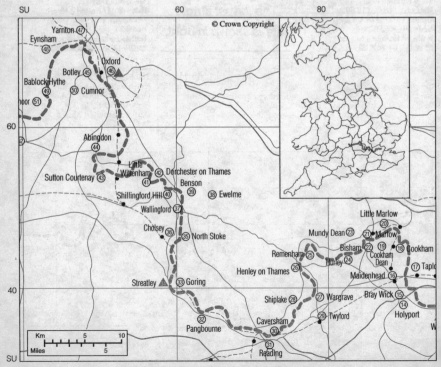

Blackheath 1

National Grid Ref: TQ3976

⊛ ◫ Fox under the Hill, The Brook, Sun in the Sands, Princess of Wales

(0.2m) *78 Vanbrugh Park, Blackheath, Greenwich, London, SE3 7JQ.*
Beautiful Victorian house, near Heath.
Grades: ETB Listed
Tel: 0181 858 0338 Mrs Mattey.
Rates fr: *£15.00-£15.00.*
Open: All Year (not Xmas)
Beds: 1F 2T
Baths: 2 Private
(A) ☐ (3) ☐ ▥.

Greenwich 2

National Grid Ref: TQ3977

⊛ ◫ Ashburnham Arms

(0.5m) *Dover House, 155 Shooters Hill, Greenwich, London, SE18 3HP.*
Victorian family house opposite Oxleas Wood.
Tel: 0181 856 9892 Mrs Araniello.
Rates fr: *£15.00-£15.00.*
Open: All Year
Beds: 2F 2T 2S
(A) ☐ ▥.

(0.5m ⊕) *4 Egerton Drive, Greenwich, London, SE10 8JS.*
Listed building (1829), conservation area.
Tel: 0181 691 5587 Mrs Courtney.
Rates fr: *£18.00-£18.00.*
Open: All Year
Beds: 1F 2T 3S
Baths: 2 Shared
(A) ⅍ ☐ ▥. Ⓥ ⧸

(0.5m) *Greenwich Parkhouse Hotel, 1 & 2 Nevada Street, Greenwich, London, SE10 9JL.*
Small hotel facing Greenwich Park.
Tel: 0181 305 1478 Mrs Bryan.

Rates fr: *£17.50-£27.50.*
Open: All Year (not Xmas)
Beds: 2F 3D 1T 3S
Baths: 3 Private, 2 Shared
(A) ☐ (8) ⅍ ☐ ▥.

Rotherhithe 3

National Grid Ref: TQ3680

(▲ 0.25m) *Rotherhithe Youth Hostel, Salter Road, Rotherhithe, London, SE16 1PP.*
Actual grid ref: TQ3680
Warden: Mr R Stackhouse.
Tel: 0171 232 2114
Under 18: £16.55 **Adults:** £19.75
Family Rooms, Centrally Heated, Showers, Evening Meal (5.30 - 8.30 pm), Shop, Facilities for the Disabled, Security Lockers, Television
New purpose-built hostel in a striking modern design on four floors, all bedrooms ensuite

St Pauls 4

National Grid Ref: TQ3181

(▲ 1m) *City of London Youth Hostel, 36 Carter Lane, St Pauls, London, EC4V 5AD.*
Actual grid ref: TQ3181
Warden: Mr Peter Clarke.
Tel: 0171 236 4965
Under 18: £16.55 **Adults:** £19.75
Family Rooms and Bunk Rooms, Centrally Heated, Showers, Evening Meal (7.00 pm), Shop, Security Lockers, Television
The former Choir school for St Paul's Cathedral, fully refurbished, while retaining the character of the old building

Kew 5

National Grid Ref: TQ1977

(0.25m) *1 Chelwood Gardens, Kew, Richmond, Surrey, TW9 4JG.*
Large Edwardian, friendly family house.

Grades: ETB Comm
Tel: 0181 876 8733 Mrs Gray.
Rates fr: *£20.00-£20.00.*
Open: All Year
Beds: 2T 2S **Baths:** 2 Shared
⌂ (A) ☐ (6) ⅍ ☐ ▥. ⧸

(0.25m) *8 Taylor Avenue, Kew, Richmond, Surrey, TW9 4ED.*
Spacious, modernised period family home.
Tel: 0181 876 3930 Mrs Allen.
Rates fr: *£19.00-£19.00.*
Open: All Year (not Xmas)
Beds: 1T 1S **Baths:** 1 Private
⌂ (A) ☐ ▥. 🛈 ⧸

Richmond 6

National Grid Ref: TQ1874

⊛ ◫ The White Horse Pub

(0.5m) *136 Sheen Road, Richmond, Surrey, TW9 1UR.*
Large Victorian private house.
Tel: 0181 948 5608 Mrs Bates.
Rates fr: *£17.50-£25.00.*
Open: All Year (not Xmas)
Beds: 2T 2S
Baths: 3 Shared
☐ ⅍ ▥. ⧸

(1m) *4 Church Road, Richmond, Surrey, TW9 2QA.*
Bright, spacious, comfortable Victorian house
Tel: 0181 948 5852 Mrs Bird.
Rates fr: *£22.50-£35.00.*
Open: All Year
Beds: 1F 1D **Baths:** 2 Ensuite
(A) ☐ ▥. Ⓥ ⧸

(1m) *Anna Guest House, 37 Church Road, Richmond, Surrey, TW9 1UA.*
Large Victorian private house.
Tel: 0181 940 5237 Mr Delgado.
Rates fr: *£20.00-£25.00.*
Open: All Year (not Xmas)
Beds: 1F 3D 1T 1S
Baths: 3 Ensuite 1 Shared
⌂ (A) ☐ ▥.

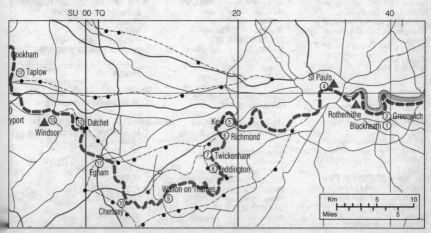

Twickenham 7

National Grid Ref: TQ1573

(1.5m) *11 Spencer Road,*
Twickenham, Middx, TW2 5TH.
Elegant Edwardian private house.
Grades: ETB Approv
Tel: **0181 894 5271** Mrs Duff.
Rates fr: *£17.00-£17.00.*
Open: All Year
Beds: 1D 1T **Baths:** 1 Shared
‍(A) ▣ (all) ⊬ ⌷ ▥.

Teddington 8

National Grid Ref: TQ1670

▯ ◗ King's Arms

(0.5m) *Bushy Park Lodge Hotel,*
6 Sandy Lane, Teddington, Middx,
TW11 0DR.
Lodge style, 5 years old.
Grades: ETB 2 Cr
Tel: **0181 943 5428** Mr Bosher.
Rates fr: *£22.50-£35.00.*
Open: All Year
Beds: 5D 1T 6S
Baths: 12 Ensuite
‍(A) ▣ (8) ⌷ ⌘ ▥.

Walton on Thames 9

National Grid Ref: TQ1066

▯ ◗ Old Colonial, Wellington,
Anglers & Swan

(1.25m) *Beech Tree Lodge,*
7 Rydens Avenue, Walton on
Thames, Surrey, KT12 3JB.
Large Edwardian private house,
friendly.
Grades: ETB Listed
Tel: **01932 242738** Mrs Spiteri.
Rates fr: *£16.00-£17.00.*
Open: All Year
Beds: 1F 2T **Baths:** 2 Shared
(A) ▣ (6) ⊬ ⌷ ▥, ▮

(0.75m) *Oak Tree Lodge, 11*
Hersham Road, Walton on Thames,
Surrey, KT12 1LQ.
Mock Tudor family home.
Tel: **01932 221907** Mrs Hall.
Rates fr: *£15.00-£16.00.*
Open: All Year
Beds: 1F 1D
Baths: 1 Shared
▣ (3) ⊬ ⌷ ▥.

Chertsey 10

National Grid Ref: TQ0466

▯ ◗ Coach & Horses, Crown

(0.75m) *Brambles, Stonehill,*
Chertsey, Surrey, KT16 0EW.
Quiet country cottage, woodland
setting.
Tel: **01932 873523** Mrs Fletcher.
Rates fr: *£20.00-£24.00.*
Open: All Year (not Xmas)
Beds: 2D
Baths: 2 Private
(A) ▣ (2) ⊬ ⌷ ⌘ ▥, ▣

Egham 11

National Grid Ref: TQ0071

▯ ◗ Crown

(1m) *Beau Villa, 44 Grange Road,*
Egham, Surrey, TW20 9QP.
Friendly, clean, comfortable family
house.
Tel: **01784 435115** Mrs Wilding.
Rates fr: *£17.00-£18.00.*
Open: All Year (not Xmas)
Beds: 1D 1S
Baths: 1 Ensuite
‍(A) ▣ (4) ⌷ ▥.

Datchet 12

National Grid Ref: SU9877

(0.25m) *55 London Road, Datchet,*
Slough, Berks, SL3 9JY.
Conveniently located, near
Heathrow, M25.
Grades: ETB Listed, AA Listed
Tel: **01753 580401** Mrs Greenham.
Rates fr: *£20.00-£25.00.*
Open: All Year
Beds: 1F 2D 1T **Baths:** 2 Private
(A) ▣ ⊬ ⌷ ▥, ▣

Windsor 13

National Grid Ref: SU9676

▯ ◗ Harvester Restaurant,
Wheatsheaf Pub, Oxford Blue,
Bees & Barts, Red Lion, Belgium
Arms,The George

(0.25m) *13 Keppel Spur, Old*
Windsor, Windsor, Berks, SL4 2LU.
Clean, comfortable, homely private
house.
Grades: ETB Reg
Tel: **01753 868757** Mr Wren.
Rates fr: *£16.00-£16.00.*
Open: All Year
Beds: 1F 1D 1T **Baths:** 1 Shared
(A) ▣ (4) ⌷ ▥, ▣ ⚡

(▲ 0.25m) *Windsor Youth Hostel,*
Edgeworth House, Mill Lane,
Windsor, Berks, SL4 5JE.
Actual grid ref: SU9577
Warden: Mr C Thomas.
Tel: **01753 861710**
Under 18: £6.15 **Adults:** £9.10
Family Bunk Rooms, Centrally
Heated, Showers, Evening Meal
(7.00 pm), Shop, Games Room
Queen Anne residence in the old
Clewer Village quarter of historic
Windsor

(1m) *Trinity Guest House,*
18 Trinity Place, Windsor, Berks,
SL4 3AT.
Town centre, large Victorian
house.
Grades: ETB 2 Cr
Tel: **01753 864186** Mrs Jackson.
Rates fr: *£22.00-£28.00.*
Open: All Year
Beds: 2F 3D 2T 1S
Baths: 4 Ensuite 2 Shared
(A) ⌷ ⌘ ▥, ▣ ▮ ⚡

(1.75m) *62 Buckland Crescent,*
Windsor, Berks, SL4 5JS.
25 minutes walk to town.
Tel: **01753 859109**
Mrs Hutson.
Rates fr: *£14.00-£14.00.*
Open: All Year (not Xmas)
Beds: 1T 1S
Baths: 1 Shared
‍(A) ⌷ ▥.

(1m) *57 Grove Road, Windsor,*
Berks, SL4 1JD.
Victorian town house.
Grades: ETB Listed
Tel: **01753 853600** Mrs Ford.
Rates fr: *£17.00-£20.00.*
Open: All Year (not Xmas)
Beds: 1F 1T
Baths: 1 Ensuite
(A) ▣ ⌷ ▥.

(0.5m) *Tanglewood, Oakley Green,*
Windsor, Berks, SL4 4PZ.
Chalet style house. Beautiful gar-
den. Quiet.
Grades: ETB Listed, High Comm
Tel: **01753 860034**
Mrs Salter.
Rates fr: *£18.00-£21.00.*
Open: May to Sep
Beds: 2T
Baths: 1 Shared
(A) ▣ (2) ⊬ ⌷ ▥, ▣

(1m) *62 Queens Road, Windsor,*
Berks, SL4 3BH.
Excellent reputation,quiet and con-
venient.
Tel: **01753 866036**
Mrs Hughes.
Rates fr: *£18.00-£20.00.*
Open: All Year
Beds: 1F 1T
Baths: 2 Private
(A) ▣ (1) ⊬ ⌷ ▥, ▣

(1m) *2 Benning Close, St Leonards*
Park, Windsor, Berks,
SL4 4YS.
Modern detached large private
house.
Tel: **01753 852294** Mrs Hume.
Rates fr: *£17.00-£17.00.*
Open: All Year
Beds: 1F 1D
Baths: 2 Shared
‍(A) ▣ (2) ⊬ ⌷ ⌘ ▥, ⚿ ▣

Holyport 14

National Grid Ref: SU8977

▯ ◗ Belgian Arms

(1.75m) *Moor Farm, Holyport,*
Maidenhead, Berks, SL6 2HY.
Medieval manor, near pretty
village.
Grades: ETB 2 Cr, High Comm
Tel: **01628 33761**
Mrs Reynolds.
Rates fr: *£19.00-£35.00.*
Open: All Year
Beds: 1D 2T
Baths: 3 Private
(A) ▣ (3) ⊬ ⌷ ▥.

Bray Wick 15

National Grid Ref: SU8979

¶ ◖ The Pig in Hiding

(2m) *The Old Coach House*,
3 Windsor Road, Bray Wick,
Maidenhead, Berks, *SL6 1UX*.
Lovely 200-year-old house.
Tel: **01628 71244** Mrs Collier.
Rates fr: £20.00-**£20.00**.
Open: All Year
Beds: 1D 1T 1S
Baths: 1 Ensuite 2 Shared
P (3) ⊬ ▥ Ⅴ

Maidenhead 16

National Grid Ref: SU8781

¶ ◖ Elva Lodge

(0.5m) *Laburnham Guest House*,
31 Laburnham Road, Maidenhead,
Berks, *SL6 4DB*.
Fine Edwardian guesthouse.
Tel: **01628 76748** Mrs Stevens.
Rates fr: £19.00-**£20.00**.
Open: All Year
Beds: 1F 2D 1T 1S
Baths: All Ensuite
(A) P (4) ⊬ ▭ ▥ ▮

(0.5m) *Sheephouse Manor*,
Sheephouse Road, Maidenhead,
Berks, *SL6 8HJ*.
Actual grid ref: SU8878
Charming C16th farmhouse.
Grades: ETB 2 Cr, Comm
Tel: **01628 776902** Mrs Street.
Rates fr: £19.00-**£28.00**.
Open: All Year (not Xmas)
Beds: 2D 1T 2S
Baths: 5 Private
ॐ (A) P (6) ▭ ⼞ ▥ Ⅴ ✦

(0.5m) *Copperfields Guest House*,
54 Bath Road, Maidenhead, Berks,
SL6 4JY.
Comfortable accommodation.
Tel: **01628 74941** Mrs Lindsay.
Rates fr: £20.00-**£20.00**.
Open: All Year
Beds: 2D 3T 3S
Baths: 5 Ensuite
(A) P (5) ▭ ⼞ ▥

(0.5m) *Clifton Guest House*,
21 Craufurd Rise, Maidenhead,
Berks, *SL6 7LR*.
Family guesthouse.
Grades: ETB 3 Cr, RAC Listed
Tel: **01628 23572** Mr Arora.
Rates fr: £24.00-**£28.00**.
Open:
Beds: 3F 4D 7T 3S
Baths: 7 Ensuite 3 Shared
(A) P (11) ✕ ▥ Ⅴ

**The *lowest* single
rate *is shown in* bold.**

Taplow 17

National Grid Ref: SU9182

(1m) *Bridge Cottage Guest House*,
Bath Road, Taplow, Maidenhead,
Berks, *SL6 0AR*.
Family-run, characteristic cottage,
cosy rooms.
Grades: ETB 2 Cr
Tel: **01628 26805** Mrs Staszewski.
Rates fr: £18.00-**£20.00**.
Open: All Year
Beds: 3F 1T 2S
Baths: 2 Private 1 Shared
(A) P (6) ⊬ ▭ ▥ Ⅴ

Cookham 18

National Grid Ref: SU8985

¶ ◖ Spencers

(1m) *Koala*, Vivien Close,
Cookham, Maidenhead, Berks,
SL6 9DQ.
Actual grid ref: SU885845
Family home 1 mile from Thames.
Grades: ETB Listed
Tel: **01628 523031** Mrs Gibbings.
Rates fr: £14.00-**£15.00**.
Open: All Year
Beds: 1F 1T
Baths: 2 Shared
ॐ (A) P (3) ⊬ ▭ ▥ Ⅴ ▮

(On Path) *Wylie Cottage*, School
Lane, Cookham, Maidenhead,
Berks, *SL6 9QJ*.
Actual grid ref: SU897851
Comfortable large Victorian house.
Tel: **01628 520106** Mrs Crowe.
Rates fr: £17.00-**£17.00**.
Open: All Year (not Xmas)
Beds: 1D 1T
Baths: 1 Shared
(A) P (2) ⊬ ▭ ⼞ ▥ ✦

Cookham Dean 19

National Grid Ref: SU8684

¶ ◖ Chequers, Inn on the Green,
Uncle Tom's Cabin, Jolly Farmer

(1.5m ⊕) *Primrose Hill*,
Bradcutts Lane, Cookham Dean,
Maidenhead, Berks, *SL6 9TL*.
Actual grid ref: SU879862
Large Edwardian private house.
Grades: ETB Listed
Tel: **01628 528179** Mrs Benson.
Rates fr: £17.50-**£17.50**.
Open: All Year (not Xmas)
Beds: 1F 1S **Baths:** 1 Shared
(A) P (3) ⊬ ▭ ⼞ ✕ ▥ ▮ ✦

(1.25m) *Primrose Hill*, Bradcutts
Lane, Cookham Dean,
Maidenhead, Berks, *SL6 9TL*.
Easy access Heathrow. Rural
location.
Grades: ETB Listed
Tel: **01628 528179** Mrs Benson.
Rates fr: £17.50-**£17.50**.
Open: All Year (not Xmas)
Beds: 1F 1S **Baths:** 1 Shared
(A) P (3) ⊬ ▭ ⼞ ▥

Little Marlow 20

National Grid Ref: SU8788

¶ ◖ Three Horseshoes, King's
Head

(1m) *Monkton Farm*, Little
Marlow, Marlow, Bucks, *SL7 3RF*.
C14th cruck farmhouse.
Grades: ETB Listed, Comm
Tel: **01494 521082** Ms Kimber.
Rates fr: £20.00-**£20.00**.
Open: All Year
Beds: 1F 1T 1S
Baths: 1 Shared
ॐ (A) P (3) ⊬ ▭ ▥

Marlow - 21

National Grid Ref: SU8586

¶ ◖ Chequers Inn, Royal Oak,
George & Dragon, Coach & Horses

(1.25m ⊕) *Acha Pani*, Bovingdon
Green, Marlow, Bucks, *SL7 2JL*.
Actual grid ref: SU836869
Modern private house quiet garden.
Grades: ETB Listed, Comm
Tel: **01628 483435**
Mrs Cowling.
Rates fr: £15.00-**£15.00**.
Open: All Year
Beds: 1D 1T 1S
Baths: 1 Private 1 Shared
ॐ (A) P (3) ▭ ✕ ▥ Ⅴ ▮ ✦

(1.25m ⊕) *Merrie Hollow*,
Seymour Court Hill, Marlow,
Bucks, *SL7 3DE*.
Actual grid ref: SU840889
Secluded quiet country cottage.
Tel: **01628 485663**
Mr Wells.
Rates fr: £16.00-**£20.00**.
Open: All Year
Beds: 1D 1T
Baths: 1 Shared
(A) P (4) ⊬ ▭ ⼞ ▥ Ⅴ ✦

(1m) *29 Oaktree Road*, Marlow,
Bucks, *SL7 3ED*.
Close to shops and river.
Grades: ETB Listed
Tel: **01628 472145**
Mr & Mrs Lasenby.
Rates fr: £16.50-**£18.00**.
Open: All Year (not Xmas)
Beds: 1T 1S
Baths: 1 Ensuite 1 Shared
(A) ⊬ ▭ ▥

(0.25m ⊕) *5 Pound Lane*,
Marlow, Bucks, *SL7 2AE*.
Actual grid ref: SU848861
Comfortable house near River
Thames.
Grades: ETB Listed
Tel: **01628 482649**
Mrs Bendall.
Rates fr: £25.00-**£25.00**.
Open: All Year (not Xmas)
Beds: 1D 1T
Baths: 1 Shared
(A) P (2) ⊬ ▭ ⼞ ▥ Ⅴ ▮ ✦

Bisham 22
National Grid Ref: SU8585

¶¶ ⬛ The Bull

(0.5m) *Warren Cottage, Bisham,*
Marlow, Bucks, SL7 1RR.
Tel: **01628 475199** Mrs Hodgson.
Rates fr: *£18.00-£18.00*.
Open: All Year (not Xmas)
Beds: 1D 1T 1S
Baths: 1 Shared
(A) **P** (4) ⅃⊬ ⬛ ▥ **V** ▮ ⅃

Munday Dean 23
National Grid Ref: SU8488

(1.25m) *The Venture, Munday*
Dean, Marlow, Bucks, SL7 3BU.
Home from home. Quiet location.
Grades: ETB Listed
Tel: **01628 472195** Mrs Whittle.
Rates fr: *£12.50-£20.00*.
Open: All Year
Beds: 2D **Baths:** 1 Shared
🛏 (A) **P** (4) ⅃⊬ ⬛ ✗ ▥ **V**

Hurley 24
National Grid Ref: SU8283

¶¶ ⬛ The Black Boy Inn

(0.25m) *The Black Boy Inn,*
Hurley, Maidenhead, Berks,
SL6 5NQ.
Famous C16th beamed rural inn.
Tel: **01628 824212** Mr Wymark.
Rates fr: *£20.00-£20.00*.
Open: All Year (not Xmas)
Beds: 1T 1S
P (20) ⅃ ✗ ▥ **V**

Remenham 25
National Grid Ref: SU7784

¶¶ ⬛ Two Brewers, Five
Horseshoes

(On Path) *The Two Brewers,*
Wargrave Road, Remenham,
Henley-on-Thames, Oxon, RG9 2LT.
Friendly public house.
Tel: **01491 574375** Mr Godmon.
Rates fr: *£22.00-£22.00*.
Open: All Year
Beds: 2F 1D 2T 1S
Baths: 1 Private 1 Shared
(A) **P** (18) ⅃ ⚲ ✗ ▥ **V**

Henley-on-Thames 26
National Grid Ref: SU7682

¶¶ ⬛ Ye Olde Bell, Anchor Hotel,
Bottle & Glass, Little Angel, The
Bull, Golden Ball, Little White
Hart, The Tuns, Argyll, Anchor,
Saracen's Head, Angel on the
Bridge

(0.25m 🚗) *Ledard, Rotherfield*
Road, Henley-on-Thames, Oxon,
RG9 1NN.
Actual grid ref: SU761814

Large well appointed Victorian
house.
Tel: **01491 575611**
Mr & Mrs Howard.
Rates fr: *£16.00-£16.00*.
Open: All Year (not Xmas)
Beds: 1F 1D **Baths:** 1 Private
(A) **P** (4) ⅃ ▥ ▮ ⅃

(0.5m) *The Saracens Head, 129*
Greys Road, Henley-on-Thames,
Oxon, RG9 1QW.
Friendly, local pub on outskirts.
Tel: **01491 575929** Mrs Sumner.
Rates fr: *£18.00-£28.00*.
Open: All Year (not Xmas)
Beds: 1D 1T **Baths:** 1 Shared
🛏 (A) **P** (20) ⅃ ✗ ▥ **V** ▮ ⅃

(0.25m) *The Jolly Waterman, 291*
Reading Road, Henley-on-Thames,
Oxon, RG9.
Comfortable family-run public
house.
Tel: **01491 573055** Mrs Scott.
Rates fr: *£17.50-£20.00*.
Open: All Year (not Xmas)
Beds: 1F 1D 2T
Baths: 1 Shared
(A) **P** (6) ⅃⊬ ⅃ ✗ ▥ **V**

(0.5m) *Mervyn House, 4 St Marks*
Road, Henley-on-Thames, Oxon,
RG9 1LJ.
Victorian house, close to town
centre. **Grades:** ETB 1 Cr, Comm
Tel: **01491 575331** Mrs Ely.
Rates fr: *£16.00-£21.50*.
Open: All Year (not Xmas)
Beds: 2D 1T
Baths: 1 Ensuite 1 Shared
🛏 (A) ⅃ ⚲ ▥

(0.5m 🚗) *107 St Marks Road,*
Henley-on-Thames, Oxon, RG9 1LP.
Large, comfortable, friendly and
quiet home.
Tel: **01491 572982** Mrs Bridekirk.
Rates fr: *£16.50-£20.00*.
Open: All Year
Beds: 1F 1D 1T 1S
Baths: 1 Ensuite 1 Shared
(A) **P** (2) ⅃ ▥ **V** ⅃

(0.25m) *Old Bell House,*
Northfield End, Henley-on-Thames,
Oxon, RG9 2JG.
Large townhouse built 1650,
Georgian facade.
Tel: **01491 574350** Mrs Duckett.
Rates fr: *£17.00-£19.00*.
Open: All Year
Beds: 2F
Baths: 2 Ensuite
(A) **P** (3) ⅃⊬ ⅃ ⚲ ▥ ▮ ⅃

(0.5m) *Alftrudis, 8 Norman*
Avenue, Henley-on-Thames, Oxon,
RG9 1SG.
Large Victorian private house.
Grades: ETB 1 Cr, High Comm
Tel: **01491 573099** Mrs Lambert.
Rates fr: *£16.00-£22.00*.
Open: All Year
Beds: 2D 1T
Baths: 1 Private 1 Shared
(A) **P** (2) ⅃ ▥

(0.5m 🚗) *Lenwade, 3 Western*
Road, Henley-on-Thames, Oxon,
RG9 1JL.
Large beautifully decorated
Victorian house.
Grades: ETB 1 Cr, High Comm,
AA 3 Q
Tel: **01491 573468** Mrs Williams.
Rates fr: *£17.00-£25.00*.
Open: All Year
Beds: 2D 1T
Baths: 1 Ensuite 2 Shared
(A) **P** (1) ⅃ ⚲ ▥ **V** ⅃

(1m) *43 Valley Road, Henley-on-*
Thames, Oxon, RG9 1RL.
Modern 3 storey town house.
Tel: **01491 573545** Mrs Williams.
Rates fr: *£15.00-£15.00*.
Open: All Year (not Xmas)
Beds: 1T 2S
Baths: 1 Shared
🛏 (A) **P** (2) ⅃⊬ ▥

(0.75m) *4 Coldharbour Close,*
Henley-on-Thames, Oxon, RG9 1QP.
Quiet bungalow in large garden.
Tel: **01491 575297** Mrs Bower.
Rates fr: *£15.00-£17.50*.
Open: Easter to Nov
Beds: 2T
Baths: 1 Private 1 Shared
(A) **P** (2) ⅃⊬ ⅃ ✗ ▥ **V**

(0.5m 🚗) *New Lodge, Henley*
Park, Henley-on-Thames, Oxon,
RG9 6HU.
Actual grid ref: SU758847
Victorian lodge cottage in park-
land.
Grades: ETB 1 Cr, Comm
Tel: **01491 576340** Mrs Warner.
Rates fr: *£14.50-£22.00*.
Open: All Year
Beds: 2D
Baths: 2 Ensuite
(A) **P** (5) ⅃⊬ ⅃ ▥ ⅃ ▮ ⅃

Wargrave 27
National Grid Ref: SU7878

¶¶ ⬛ The Bull

(0.5m 🚗) *Windy Brow, 204*
Victoria Road, Wargrave, Reading,
Berks, RG10 8AJ.
Large Victorian house overlooking
fields.
Grades: ETB Listed
Tel: **01734 403336** Mrs Carver.
Rates fr: *£18.50-£18.50*.
Open: All Year
Beds: 1F 3D 3T 2S
Baths: 1 Private 2 Shared
(A) **P** (6) ⅃⊬ ⅃ ⚲ ▥ ⅃ **V** ⅃

**Bringing children with
you? Always ask for
any special rates.**

Shiplake 28

National Grid Ref: SU7678

⊶ ◧ Baskerville Arms

(2.5m) *Baskerville Arms, Station Road, Shiplake, Henley-on-Thames, Oxon, RG9 3NY.*
Built 1937, friendly & comfortable.
Tel: **01734 403332** Mr Tomlin.
Rates fr: *£18.00-£20.00.*
Open: All Year
Beds: 1F 1D 2T
Baths: 1 Shared
(A) �🅿 (10) ⌿ ⼌ 圳.

Twyford 29

National Grid Ref: SU7975

(2m) *Chesham House, 79 Wargrave Road, Twyford, Reading, Berks, RG10 9PE.*
Ensuite beverage facilities, television, refrigerator.
Grades: ETB Listed
Tel: **01734 320428**
Mr & Mrs Ferguson.
Rates fr: *£18.00-£24.00.*
Open: All Year (not Xmas)
Beds: 1D 1T
Baths: 2 Private
(A) ⅌ (6) ⌂ 圳. ♿

Caversham 30

National Grid Ref: SU7175

(1m) *10 Greystoke Road, Caversham, Reading, Berks, RG4 0EL.*
Family home in private road.
Grades: ETB Listed, Comm
Tel: **01734 475784** Mrs Tyler.
Rates fr: *£15.00-£18.00.*
Open: All Year (not Xmas)
Beds: 1D 2S
Baths: 2 Shared
⅌ (1) ⌿ ⌂ 圳.

Reading 31

National Grid Ref: SU7173

⊶ ◧ The Mansion House, Blagrave Arms

(On Path ☎) *Crescent Hotel, 35 Coley Avenue, Reading, Berks, RG1 6LL.*
Tel: **01734 507980** Ms Evans.
Rates fr: *£17.50-£20.00.*
Open: All Year (not Xmas)
Beds: 1F 5D 5T 5S
Baths: 2 Ensuite, 4 Shared
(A) ⅌ ⌂ ⼌ ✕ 圳. ♦
All rooms with TV and tea/coffee facility. Close to town centre. Free parking. Bar. Games room. Evening meals.

(1.5m) *Dittisham Guest House, 63 Tilehurst Road, Reading, Berks, RG3.*
Renovated Edwardian house.
Ensuite rooms.
Grades: ETB Listed, Comm
Tel: **01734 569483** Mr Harding.

Rates fr: *£15.00-£19.00.*
Open: All Year
Beds: 1F 1D 3S **Baths:** 5 Ensuite
(A) ⅌ ⌂ 圳. ♦

(2m) *The Berkeley Guest House, 32 Berkeley Avenue, Reading, Berks, RG1 6JE.*
Friendly family, town centre home.
Grades: ETB Listed
Tel: **01734 595699** Mr Hubbard.
Rates fr: *£16.00-£18.00.*
Open: All Year
Beds: 2F
Baths: 2 Private
(A) ⅌ (6) ⌿ ⌂ ⼌ ✕ 圳. Ⓥ

Pangbourne 32

National Grid Ref: SU6376

⊶ ◧ Swan Inn, Cross Keys

(0.25m) *Weir View House, 9 Shooters Hill, Pangbourne, Reading, Berks, RG8 7BJ.*
Superb views overlooking weir and river.
Grades: ETB 2 Cr
Tel: **01734 842120** Mrs King.
Rates fr: *£19.00-£22.00.*
Open: All Year (not Xmas)
Beds: 2D 1T 1S
Baths: 1 Private 1 Shared
⌂ (A) ⅌ ⌿ ⌂ 圳. ♦

Goring 33

National Grid Ref: SU6081

⊶ ◧ John Barley Corn, Catherine Wheel, Miller of Mansfield, Bull, Perch & Pike

(0.25m ☎) *14 Mountfield, Wallingford Road, Goring, Reading, Berks, RG8 0BE.*
Modern home in riverside village.
Grades: ETB Listed
Tel: **01491 872029** Mrs Ewen.
Rates fr: *£15.00-£17.00.*
Open: All Year
Beds: 1D 1T 1S
(A) ⅌ (4) ⌂ ⼌ ✕ 圳. ♦ ♦

(0.25m ☎) *Queens Arms, Reading Road, Goring, Reading, Berks, RG8 0ER.*
200-year-old country pub.
Tel: **01491 872825** Mrs Carter.
Rates fr: *£19.00-£19.00.*
Open: All Year (not Xmas)
Beds: 1T 2S
Baths: 1 Shared
(A) ⅌ (30) ⌂ ⼌ ✕ ♦ ♦

(On Path) *The John Barleycorn, Manor Road, Goring, Reading, Berks, RG8 9DP.*
C17th inn close to Thames.
Grades: ETB 1 Cr
Tel: **01491 872509** Mr Fincham.
Rates fr: *£19.50-£23.00.*
Open: All Year
Beds: 1F 2D 1T 1S
Baths: 1 Shared
(A) ⅌ (2) ⌂ ⼌ ✕ Ⓥ ♦

Streatley 34

National Grid Ref: SU5980

(▲ 0.5m) *Streatley -on-Thames Youth Hostel, Hill House, Reading Road, Streatley, Reading, Berks, RG8 9JJ.*
Actual grid ref: SU5980
Warden: Mr A Wilson.
Tel: **01491 872278**
Under 18: £6.15 **Adults:** £9.10
Family Bunk Rooms, Centrally Heated, Showers, Evening Meal (7.00 pm), Shop, Television
Homely Victorian family house, completely refurbished, in a beautiful riverside village

North Stoke 35

National Grid Ref: SU6186

⊶ ◧ The White House

(On Path) *Footpath Cottage, The Street, North Stoke, Wallingford, Oxon, OX10 6BJ.*
C18th cottage, exquisite village.
Grades: ETB Listed
Tel: **01491 839763** Mrs Tanner.
Rates fr: *£16.00-£18.00.*
Open: All Year
Beds: 2D 1S
Baths: 1 Private 1 Shared
(A) ⌂ ⼌ ✕ 圳. Ⓥ ♦ ♦

(On Path) *The Old Farm House, North Stoke, Wallingford, Oxon, OX10 6BL.*
Actual grid ref: SU610863
Listed C17th farmhouse.
Tel: **01491 837079** Mrs Lucey.
Rates fr: *£17.00-£18.00.*
Open: All Year (not Xmas)
Beds: 2T 1S **Baths:** 1 Shared
(A) ⅌ (44) ⌿ ⌂ ✕ 圳. Ⓥ ♦ ♦

Cholsey 36

National Grid Ref: SU5886

⊶ ◧ Red Lion, Walnut Tree

(2m) *Old Blackalls, Old Blackalls Drive, Cholsey, Wallingford, Oxon, OX10 9HD.*
Friendly, family house in rural position.
Tel: **01491 652864** Mrs Robson.
Rates fr: *£17.50-£17.50.*
Open: All Year (not Xmas)
Beds: 1D **Baths:** 1 Private
(A) ⅌ (5) ⌿ ⌂ ✕ 圳. ♿ Ⓥ

Wallingford 37

National Grid Ref: SU6089

⊶ ◧ Stoweys Restaurant

(0.25m ☎) *The Nook, 2 Thames Street, Wallingford, Oxon, OX10 0BH.*
Character house close to river/town.
Tel: **01491 834214** Mrs Colclough.
Rates fr: *£17.50-£25.00.*
Open: All Year **Beds:** 1D 2T
(A) ⅌ 圳. Ⓥ ♦ ♦

Ewelme 38

National Grid Ref: SU6491

ioi ⚓ Shepherd's Hut

(2m) *Fords Farm*, *Ewelme,
Wallingford, Oxon, OX10 6HU*.
Part-C15th farmhouse.
Grades: ETB Listed
Tel: **01491 839272** Miss Edwards.
Rates fr: *£17.50-£17.50*.
Open: All Year
Beds: 2T **Baths:** 1 Shared
☎ (A) 🅿 (4) ⊬ 🖵 🛏.

Benson 39

National Grid Ref: SU6191

ioi ⚓ Three Horseshoes

(0.5m 🚲) *Hale Farm*, *Benson,
Wallingford, Oxon, OX10 6NE*.
Large Victorian farmhouse.
Tel: **01491 836818** Mrs Belcher.
Rates fr: *£15.00-£15.00*.
Open: Easter to Oct
Beds: 1D 1T 1S **Baths:** 1 Shared
(A) 🅿 🖵 🛏 🛉 🥄

(1m 🚲) *Fyfield Manor*, *Brook
Street, Benson, Wallingford, Oxon,
OX10 6HA*.
Comfortable C12th manor house.
Grades: ETB 2 Cr
Tel: **01491 835184** Mrs Brown.
Rates fr: *£19.00-£25.00*.
Open: All Year (not Xmas)
Beds: 1F 1D 1T
Baths: 3 Ensuite
☎ (A) 🅿 (10) ⊬ 🛏 🛉 🥄

Shillingford Hill 40

National Grid Ref: SU5892

ioi ⚓ Shillingford Bridge Hotel

(0.5m 🚲) *North Farm*,
*Shillingford Hill, Wallingford,
Oxon, OX10 8ND*.
Actual grid ref: SU586924
Quiet farmhouse near River
Thames.
Grades: ETB 2 Cr, High Comm
Tel: **01865 858406** Mrs Warburton.
Rates fr: *£19.00-£25.00*.
Open: All Year (not Xmas)
Beds: 1D 1T
Baths: 2 Private
☎ (A) 🅿 ⊬ 🖵 🛏 🛉 🥄

Little Wittenham 41

National Grid Ref: SU5693

(0.25m 🚲) *Rooks Orchard*, *Little
Wittenham, Abingdon, Oxon,
OX14 4QY*.
Actual grid ref: SU563927
Pretty Listed C17th family house.
Grades: ETB 2 Cr, High Comm
Tel: **01865 407765** Mrs Welfare.
Rates fr: *£19.00-£20.00*.
Open: All Year (not Xmas)
Beds: 1D 1S
Baths: 1 Shared
(A) 🅿 (4) ⊬ 🖵 🛏 🗶 🛏 🛉 🥄

Dorchester-on-Thames 42

National Grid Ref: SU5794

ioi ⚓ Plough, Fleur-de-Lis

(0.5m) *Willowmour*, *24 Martins
Lane, Dorchester-on-Thames,
Wallingford, Oxon, OX10 7JE*.
Quiet, modern detached house.
Tel: **01865 340444** Mr Taylor.
Rates fr: *£22.00-£22.00*.
Open: All Year (not Xmas)
Beds: 1T
Baths: 1 Private
(A) 🅿 ⊬ 🛏 🛏 🛉 🥄

Sutton Courtenay 43

National Grid Ref: SU5093

ioi ⚓ The Swan Pub, The George
& Dragon, The Fish

(0.25m) *Bekynton House*,
*7 The Green, Sutton Courtenay,
Abingdon, Oxon, OX14 4AE*.
Traditional house on village green.
Tel: **01235 848630** Ms Cornwall.
Rates fr: *£20.00-£20.00*.
Open: All Year (not Xmas)
Beds: 1D 1T 1S **Baths:** 2 Shared
(A) 🅿 (1) ⊬ 🖵 🗶 🛏 🔻 🛉 🥄

Abingdon 44

National Grid Ref: SU4997

ioi ⚓ Ox, Boundary House

(1.25m 🚲) *Pastures Green*,
*46 Picklers Hill, Abingdon, Oxon,
OX14 2BB*.
Actual grid ref: SU501988
Comfortable friendly and quiet
home.
Tel: **01235 521369** Mrs White.
Rates fr: *£15.00-£16.00*.
Open: All Year (not Xmas)
Beds: 1D 1T 1S
Baths: 2 Shared
☎ (A) 🅿 (3) ⊬ 🖵 🛏 🔻 🥄

(0.75m) *42a Oxford Road*,
Abingdon, Oxon, OX14 2DZ.
Small family-run B&B close to
Thames.
Tel: **01235 522066** Mrs Woodford.
Rates fr: *£17.50-£24.00*.
Open: All Year
Beds: 1F 1D 3T 1S
(A) 🅿 (8) 🖵 🛏 🔻 🛉 🥄

(0.25m) *1 The Copse*, *Abingdon,
Oxon, OX14 3YW*.
Large modern detached house.
Tel: **01235 527158** Mrs Shaw.
Rates fr: *£17.00-£17.00*.
Open: All Year
Beds: 1F 1D 3S
Baths: 2 Ensuite 1 Shared
☎ (A) 🅿 (7) ⊬ 🖵 🛏 🥄

(1.5m) *5 Galley Field*, *Radley
Road, Abingdon, Oxon, OX14 3RU*.
Detached 1960 house in quiet cul-
de-sac.
Tel: **01235 521088** Mrs Bird.

Rates fr: *£15.00-£18.00*.
Open: All Year
Beds: 3T
Baths: 2 Shared
(A) 🅿 (2) ⊬ 🖵 🛏.

(0.5m) *22 East St Helen Street*,
Abingdon, Oxon, OX14 5EB.
Elegant Georgian town house.
Tel: **01235 533278** Mrs Howard.
Rates fr: *£16.00-£20.00*.
Open: All Year
Beds: 1D 1T 1S
Baths: 1 Ensuite 2 Shared
(A) ⊬ 🖵 🛏 🔻 🥄

(2m) *9 Gravel Lane*, *Drayton,
Abingdon, Oxon, OX14 4HY*.
Actual grid ref: SU478952
Old groom's cottage in village.
Tel: **01235 533194** Mrs Bird.
Rates fr: *£16.00-£18.00*.
Open: All Year (not Xmas)
Beds: 2T **Baths:** 1 Shared
🅿 (2) ⊬ 🖵 🛏 🥄

Botley 45

National Grid Ref: SP4805

ioi ⚓ The Sea Court Bridge Hotel

(On Path 🚲) *Conifer Lodge*,
*159 Eynsham Road, Corner Nobles
Lane, Botley, Oxford, Oxon,
OX2 9NE*.
Modern, comfortable, 1/2 acre gar-
den.. **Grades:** ETB 2 Cr
Tel: **01865 862280** Mr Underwood.
Rates fr: *£19.00-£23.00*.
Open: All Year
Beds: 1F 1D 1T 1S
Baths: 2 Ensuite
🅿 (8) 🖵 🛏 🛏 🔻 🛉 🥄

All details shown
are as supplied
by B&B owners in
Autumn 1995.

Oxford 46

National Grid Ref: SP5106

ioi ⚓ Anchor Inn, Kings Arms,
Carpenters Arms, The Fox &
Hounds

(0.25m 🚲) *Combermere House*,
*11 Polstead Road, Oxford, Oxon,
OX2 6TW*.
Victorian house in quiet road.
Grades: ETB Listed, AA Listed
Tel: **01865 56971**
Mr & Mrs Welding.
Rates fr: *£20.00-£22.00*.
Open: All Year **Beds:** 2F 1D 2T 4S
(A) 🅿 (3) 🛏 🔻 🛏 🔻 🛉 🥄

🔥 1.75m) *Oxford Youth Hostel,*
32 Jack Straw's Lane, Oxford,
Oxon, OX3 0DW.
Actual grid ref: SP5307
Warden: Mr M Stanley.
Tel: **01865 62997**
Under 18: £6.15 **Adults:** £9.10
Centrally Heated, Showers,
Evening Meal (7.00 pm), Shop,
Television, Games Room
*Victorian mansion surrounded by
trees in the conservation area of
this historic university city*

(1m) *58 St John Street,* Oxford,
Oxon, OX1 2QR.
Tall Victorian house.
Grades: ETB Listed
Tel: **01865 515454** Mrs Old.
Rates fr: £16.00-£16.00.
Open: All Year
Beds: 1F 1T 1S
Baths: 1 Shared
🛏 (A)

(1m) *Gables Guest House,*
6 Cumnor Hill, Oxford, Oxon,
OX2 9HA.
Gabled attractive detached guest-
house.
Grades: ETB 2 Cr, Comm, AA 3
Q, Recomm, RAC High Acclaim
Tel: **01865 862153**
Mrs Tompkins.
Rates fr: £20.00-£24.00.
Open: All Year (not Xmas)
Beds: 1F 2D 1T 2S
Baths: 6 Ensuite
(A) 🅿 (6) 🖵 🛏, 📺

(0.5m) *Walton Guest House,*
169 Walton Street, Oxford, Oxon,
OX1 2HD.
Centrally located and comfortable.
Grades: ETB Listed
Tel: **01865 52137** Mr Durrant.
Rates fr: £35.00-£18.00.
Open: All Year
Beds: 1F 2D 3T 3S
Baths: 2 Shared
(A) 🖵 🛏 🛏, 📺 ▮ ✦

(1m) *Cornerways Guest House,*
282 Abingdon Road, Oxford, Oxon,
OX1 4TA.
Attractive house with comfortable
rooms.
Grades: ETB 2 Cr, Comm
Tel: **01865 240135**
Mrs Jeakings.
Rates fr: £20.00-£25.00.
Open: All Year (not Xmas)
Beds: 1F 1D 1T 1S
Baths: 4 Ensuite
(A) 🅿 (2) 🖵 🛏, 📺

(1m) *302 Banbury Road,* Oxford,
Oxon, OX2 7ED.
B&B close to city centre.
Grades: ETB 1 Cr
Tel: **01865 56118**
Mr Strange.
Rates fr: £19.00-£25.00.
Open: All Year
Beds: 2F 2D 2T 1S
Baths: 6 Ensuite
🛏 (A) 🅿 (2) 🖵 🛏, 📺 ✦

(0.5m) *Green Gables, 326*
Abingdon Road, Oxford, Oxon,
OX1 4TE.
Characterful, secluded, Edwardian
house.
Grades: ETB 2 Cr, Comm,
AA 3 Q
Tel: **01865 725870** Mrs Ellis.
Rates fr: £18.00-£23.00.
Open: All Year
Beds: 3F 3D 1T 1S
Baths: 5 Private 1 Shared
(A) 🅿 (6) 🖵 🛏, 📺

(1m) *Arden Lodge, 34 Sunderland
Avenue,* Oxford, Oxon, OX2 8DX.
Modern detached house in select
area.
Grades: ETB Listed
Tel: **01865 52076** Mr & Mrs Price.
Rates fr: £20.00-£26.00.
Open: All Year
Beds: 1D 1T 1S
Baths: 3 Ensuite
🛏 (A) 🅿 (6) 🛏, 📺

Yarnton 47
National Grid Ref: SP4712

🍴 🍺 The Grapes

(2m 🚌) *Eltham Villa, 148
Woodstock Road, Yarnton,
Kidlington,* Oxon, OX5 1PW.
Converted 100 year old house.
Grades: ETB 3 Cr, Comm,
AA 3 Q, RAC Acclaim
Tel: **01865 376037**
Mrs Willoughby.
Rates fr: £15.00-£20.00.
Open: All Year (not Xmas)
Beds: 2F 2D 1T 2S
Baths: 7 Ensuite
(A) 🅿 (8) 🖵 🛏 🛏, 📺 ▮ ✦

(2m) *Kings Bridge Guest House,*
Woodstock Road, Yarnton,
Kidlington, Oxon, OX5 1PH.
Friendly welcome in modern bun-
galow.
Grades: ETB Listed
Tel: **01865 841748** Ms Shaw.
Rates fr: £17.50-£25.00.
Open: All Year
Beds: 1F 1D 1T
Baths: 3 Private
(A) 🅿 (6) ✦ 🖵 🛏, ▮

Eynsham 48
National Grid Ref: SP4309

🍴 🍺 The Talbot

(On Path) *Swinford Park,*
Eynsham, Witney, Oxon, OX8 1BY.
Modern, comfortable country
house.
Tel: **01865 881212**
Mrs Tapper.
Rates fr: £12.00-£15.00.
Open: All Year (not Xmas)
Beds: 1D 1T 1S
Baths: 1 Private 1 Shared
🛏 (A) 🅿 (2) ✦ 🖵 🛏, ▮

Bablock Hythe 49
National Grid Ref: SP4304

🍴 🍺 Ferryman Inn

(On Path 🚌) *The Ferryman Inn,*
Bablock Hythe, Northmoor,
Witney, Oxon, OX8 1BL.
Recently renovated Thames river-
side inn.
Tel: **01865 880028** Mr Kelland.
Rates fr: £17.50-£30.00.
Open: All Year
Beds: 2F 2D 2T 2S
Baths: 8 Private
(A) 🅿 (100) ✦ 🖵 ✕ 🛏, 📺 ▮ ✦
Also ▲ *£5.00 per tent.*
Open: Easter to October 🔥 🕐 ⛳
✕ ✦ ♿

Cumnor 50
National Grid Ref: SP4604

🍴 🍺 The Vine Inn

(2m 🚌) *Beinn Bheag, 96 Oxford
Road, Cumnor,* Oxford, Oxon,
OX2 9PQ.
Actual grid ref: SP465043
Spacious detached bungalow, vil-
lage setting.
Grades: ETB Listed
Tel: **01865 864020** Mrs Tricker.
Rates fr: £19.50-£19.00.
Open: All Year (not Xmas)
Beds: 1F 1D 1T
Baths: 2 Ensuite 1 Shared
(A) 🅿 (3) ✦ 🛏, 📺 ▮ ✦

Northmoor 51
National Grid Ref: SP4202

🍴 🍺 Red Lion

(0.75m) *Rectory Farm,*
Northmoor, Witney, Oxon, OX8 1SX.
C16th semi-moated working farm.
Grades: ETB 2 Cr, High Comm
Tel: **01865 300207**
Mrs Florey.
Rates fr: £20.00-£30.00.
Open: Feb to Nov
Beds: 1D 1T
Baths: 2 Private
🅿 ✦ 🖵 🛏, ▮ ✦

Southmoor 52
National Grid Ref: SU3998

🍴 🍺 The Rose Revived

(2m 🚌) *Alpenhaus, Faringdon
Road, Southmoor,* Abingdon, Oxon,
OX13 5AF.
Actual grid ref: SU402981
Large modern house with lovely
garden.
Tel: **01865 820666**
Mrs Curtis.
Rates fr: £16.00-£23.00.
Open: All Year (not Xmas)
Beds: 1D 2T
Baths: 2 Shared
🛏 (A) 🅿 (3) ✦ 🖵 🛏, ▮

The Grid Reference beneath the location heading is for the village or town - *not* for individual houses, which are shown (where supplied) in each entry itself.

Bampton   53

National Grid Ref: SP3103

⑩ ⬛ Romany Inn, Elephant & Castle

(2m) *Romany Inn, Bridge Street, Bampton, Oxon, OX18 2HA*.
C17th Georgian building, just refurbished.
Grades: ETB Listed
Tel: 01993 850237 Mr Booth.
Rates fr: *£15.00-£21.00*.
Open: All Year
Beds: 2F 6D 4T
Baths: 8 Private
(A) ▣ (7) ⬛ ⼞ ✕ ▥ ▣

Clanfield   54

National Grid Ref: SP2801

⑩ ⬛ Clanfield Tavern

(1m) *The Granary, Clanfield, Bampton, Oxon, OX18 2SH*.
Actual grid ref: SP284018
1 ground-floor room ensuite.
Grades: ETB 2 Cr
Tel: 01367 810266 Mrs Payne.
Rates fr: *£16.00-£16.00*.
Open: All Year (not Xmas)
Beds: 1D 1T 1S
Baths: 1 Private 1 Shared
▣ (4) ⼢ ⼞ ▥ ◈

(1m ⬛) *Chestnut Grove, Clanfield, Bampton, Oxon, OX18 2RG*.
Modern, newly-built house.
Tel: 01367 81249 Miss Pocock.
Rates fr: *£16.00-£16.00*.
Open: All Year
Beds: 1D 2S **Baths:** 1 Private
(A) ▣ (3) ⼢ ⼞ ⼤ ▥ ◈ ◈
Also ⛺ ⼦ ⼯ ▦ ◈ ♿

Kelmscott   55

National Grid Ref: SU2599

⑩ ⬛ The Plough Inn

(0.25m) *The Plough Inn, Kelmscott, Lechlade, Glos, GL7 3HG*.
Actual grid ref: SU249992
C17th inn. Recently refurbished.
Grades: ETB 3 Cr
Tel: 01367 253543
Mr & Mrs Pardoe.
Rates fr: *£22.50-£25.00*.
Open: All Year
Beds: 2F 3D 2T 1S
Baths: 8 Ensuite
(A) ▣ (14) ⼞ ⼯ ✕ ▦ ▣ ◈

Buscot   56

National Grid Ref: SU2397

⑩ ⬛ Trout Inn

(0.25m ⬛) *Apple Tree House, Buscot, Faringdon, Oxon, SN7 8DA*.
Listed building in NT village.
Grades: ETB 2 Cr
Tel: 01367 252592 Mrs Reay.
Rates fr: *£16.00-£22.00*.
Open: All Year **Beds:** 2D 1T 1S
Baths: 1 Private 1 Shared
(A) ▣ (10) ⼢ ⼞ ✕ ▥ ◈

Lechlade   57

National Grid Ref: SU2199

⑩ ⬛ New Inn, Red Lion, Crown, Trout

(On Path) *Cambrai Lodge Guest House, Oak Street, Spring Gardens, Lechlade, Glos, GL7 3AH*.
Modern comfortable house off the road.

Grades: ETB Listed
Tel: 01367 253173 / 0860 150467
Mr Titchener.
Rates fr: *£15.00-£20.00*.
Open: All Year
Beds: 1F 1D 1T 1S
Baths: 2 Private 1 Shared
(A) ▣ (9) ⼞ ⼯ ▦ ◈ ◈

(On Path) *The New Inn Hotel, Market Square, Lechlade, Glos, GL7 3AB*.
C17th fully modernised coaching inn.
Grades: ETB 3 Cr
Tel: 01367 252296
Mr Sandhu.
Rates fr: *£20.00-£40.00*.
Open: All Year
Beds: 2F 10D 10T 4S
Baths: 26 Ensuite
▣ (40) ⼢ ⼞ ⼯ ✕ ▦ ▣ ◈ ◈

(On Path ⬛) *The Travellers Inn, Market Square, Lechlade, Glos, GL7 3AB*.
Fully refurbished C18th coaching inn.
Grades: ETB 3 Cr
Tel: 01367 252296
Mr Sandhu.
Rates fr: *£20.00-£35.00*.
Open: All Year
Beds: 2F 10D 7T 4S
Baths: 23 Private
▣ (40) ⼞ ⼯ ✕ ▦ ▣ ◈ ◈

Leigh   58

National Grid Ref: SU0692

⑩ ⬛ Foresters Arms

(On Path) *Waterhay Farm, Leigh, Swindon, Wilts, SN6 6QY*.
Actual grid ref: SU061931
Working farm in peaceful surroundings.
Grades: ETB 2 Cr, Comm
Tel: 01285 861253
Mrs Rumming.
Rates fr: *£17.00-£17.00*.
Open: All Year
Beds: 1F 1D 1T
Baths: 3 Private
⛺ (A) ▣ (4) ⼢ ⼞ ✕ ▦ ◈ ◈

Kemble 59

National Grid Ref: ST9897

᭡ ᒻ Wild Duck, Thames Head

(0.75m) *Smerrill Barns, Kemble, Cirencester, Glos, GL7 6BW.*
Actual grid ref: ST998988
Comfortable converted barns - friendly atmosphere.
Grades: ETB 2 Cr, Comm, AA 3 Q, RAC Acclaim
Tel: **01285 770907** Mrs Benson.
Rates fr: *£22.50-£17.50.*
Open: All Year
Beds: 1F 4D 1T 1S
Baths: 7 Private, 1 Shared
ﾅ (A) �P (8) ½ ロ 皿 ⋔ ⌁

Rodmarton 60

National Grid Ref: ST9497

(3m ⊕) *The Old Rectory, Rodmarton, Cirencester, Glos, GL7 6PE.*
C16th Listed building in own grounds.
Grades: ETB 2 Cr, Comm
Tel: **01285 841246** Mrs FitzGerald.
Rates fr: *£17.50-£23.50.*
Open: All Year (not Xmas)
Beds: 2T **Baths:** 2 Private
(A) �P (6) ½ ロ ⋔ ✕ 皿 Ⓥ ⌁

Planning a longer
stay? Always ask for
any special rates.

Cirencester 61

National Grid Ref: SP0201

᭡ ᒻ Wagon & Horses Inn, Talbot, Odd Fellows, Plough Stratton

(3m) *58 Queen Elizabeth Road, Cirencester, Glos, GL7 1DJ.*
Modern comfortable home, rural outlook.
Tel: **01285 652782**
Mrs Biggs.
Rates fr: *£13.00-£15.00.*
Open: All Year (not Xmas)
Beds: 1D 1T 2S
Baths: 2 Shared
ﾅ (A) �P (2) ½ ロ ⋔ ✕ 皿 Ⓥ ⋔ ⌁

(3m ⊕) *The Golden Cross Inn, Black Jack Street, Cirencester, Glos, GL7 2AA.*
Early C18th inn.
Grades: ETB 1 Cr
Tel: **01285 652137**
Mr & Mrs Smith.
Rates fr: *£15.00-£18.00.*
Open: All Year
Beds: 1F 1T
Baths: 1 Shared
(A) ロ ✕ 皿 Ⓥ ⋔ ⌁

(3m) *26 Victoria Road, Cirencester, Glos, GL7 1ES.*
Large Victorian private house.
Grades: ETB 2 Cr
Tel: **01285 656440**
Mrs Cremin.
Rates fr: *£11.00-£15.00.*
Open: All Year (not Xmas)
Beds: 1F 1D 1T
Baths: 1 Private 1 Shared
(A) �P (2) ロ 皿 Ⓥ ⌁

(3m) *Ivy House, 2 Voctoria Road, Cirencester, Gloucestershire, GL7 1ER.*
Lovely Victorian town house.
Grades: ETB Listed
Tel: **01285 656626** Mrs Goldsbury.
Rates fr: *£19.00-£25.00.*
Open: All Year (not Xmas)
Beds: 3D 1T
Baths: 4 Ensuite
ﾅ (A) �P (4) ½ ロ 皿 Ⓥ ⋔ ⌁

(3m) *Clonsilla Guest House, 7 Victoria Road, Cirencester, Glos, GL7 1EN.*
Five minutes from town centre.
Grades: ETB Listed
Tel: **01285 652621** Mr Sullivan.
Rates fr: *£14.00-£18.00.*
Open: All Year
Beds: 1F 3D 3T 1S
Baths: 4 Private 2 Shared
(A) �P (6) ロ ⋔ ✕ 皿 ⅋ Ⓥ ⋔ ⌁

(3.5m) *The Leauses, 101 Victoria Road, Cirencester, Glos, GL7 1EU.*
Attractive Victorian guesthouse.
Grades: ETB 2 Cr, Comm
Tel: **01285 653643** Mrs Richens.
Rates fr: *£15.00.*
Open: All Year
Beds: 2F 2D 1T **Baths:** 5 Ensuite
(A) �P ½ ロ ⋔ ✕ 皿 ⅋ Ⓥ ⋔ ⌁

(4.5m ⊕) *Sunset, Baunton Lane, Cirencester, Glos, GL7 2NQ.*
Quietly situated detached friendly guesthouse.
Grades: ETB Listed
Tel: **01285 654822** Mrs Castle.
Rates fr: *£13.50-£13.50.*
Open: All Year (not Xmas)
Beds: 1T 2S **Baths:** 1 Shared
ﾅ (A) �P (4) ½ ロ 皿 Ⓥ ⋔ ⌁

Two Moors Way

The **Two Moors Way** runs northwards for 103 miles from Ivybridge over Devon's two famous moors, **Dartmoor** and **Exmoor**, up to Lynmouth on the north coast. You pass through fabulous terrain; misty and uninhabited moorlands with prehistoric sites, the rich, undulating farmlands of mid-Devon; sudden combes with little rivers. Between Hawkridge and Withypool you follow the River Barle through a beautiful wooded valley to the ancient Tarr Steps. This is a walk with a lot of hills, wilderness, great horizons and a sense of mystery - a great introduction to one of England's largest counties. After exceptionally wet weather, some sections can become impassable but alternative routes can be found in the guidebooks. Please take protective clothing, food, and a compass, for much of the Devon hinterland is not sign-posted and these moors are not to be underestimated.

Guides: *Two Moors Way* by RA Devon Area (ISBN 0 900613 43 2), published by the Two Moors Way Association and available from the Rambler's Association National Office (1/5 Wandsworth Road, London, SW8 2XX, tel. 0171 582 6878), £2.70 (+ 70 p p&p)
The Two Moors Way by James Roberts (ISBN 1 85 284 159 10 90), published by Cicerone Press and available from all good map shops or directly from the publishers (2 Police Square, Milnthorpe, Cumbria, LA7 7PY, 01539 562069), £5.99 (+75p p&p)

Maps: Ordnance Survey 1:50,000 Landranger series: 180, 181, 191, 202

Holbeton   1

National Grid Ref: SX6150

ᵗᵒᵗ ⌕ Mildmay Colours, Dartmoor Union

(3m) *The Mildmay Colours Inn, Holbeton, Plymouth, Devon, PL8 1NA.*
Traditional village inn with brewery.
Tel: **01752 830248** Mrs Patrick.
Rates fr: *£20.00-£20.00.*
Open: All Year
Beds: 1F 1D 6T **Baths:** 8 Private
ⓢ 🅿 (25) ⬜ 🛏 ✕ 🖾 Ⓥ

Ivybridge   2

National Grid Ref: SX6356

ᵗᵒᵗ ⌕ Imperial Inn

(0.25m) *The Toll House, Exeter Road, Ivybridge, Devon, PL21 0DE.*
1850's house with beautiful gardens.
Tel: **01752 893522** Mrs Hancox.
Rates fr: *£13.00-£16.00.*
Open: All Year **Beds:** 2T 1S
Baths: 1 Ensuite, 1 Shared
ⓢ 🅿 (5) ⊬ ⬜ 🛏 🖾 Ⓥ 🛆 ⋌

(3m 🚍) *Hillhead Farm, Ugborough, Ivybridge, Devon, PL21 0HQ.*
Actual grid ref: SX674563
Comfortable old family farmhouse.
Grades: ETB 1 Cr, Comm
Tel: **01752 892674** Mrs Johns.
Rates fr: *£14.00-£14.00.*
Open: All Year (not Xmas)
Beds: 2D 1T
Baths: 1 Shared
ⓢ 🅿 (5) ⊬ ⬜ 🛏 ✕ 🖾 Ⓥ 🛆 ⋌

(1m 🚍) *East Highlands, Blachford Road, Ivybridge, Devon, PL21 0AD.*
Wine of Georgian mansion.
Grades: ETB Reg
Tel: **01752 893121**
Mr/Mrs Lucas.
Rates fr: *£14.00-£14.00.*
Open: All Year (not Xmas)
Beds: 1F 1D 1T
Baths: 1 Ensuite 1 Shared
ⓢ 🅿 (5) ⬜ 🖾 Ⓥ 🛆 ⋌

Harford   3

National Grid Ref: SX6359

ᵗᵒᵗ ⌕ The Imperial Inn

(On Path) *Stowford House, Harford, Ivybridge, Devon, PL21 0JD.*
Actual grid ref: SX642572
Spacious elegant Georgian family home. Tel: **01752 698088**
Mr & Mrs Kneen.
Rates fr: *£15.00-£20.00.*
Open: All Year
Beds: 1F
Baths: 1 Ensuite
ⓢ 🅿 ⊬ ⬜ 🖾 Ⓥ

Watercombe   4

National Grid Ref: SX6261

(⌂ 1m) *Watercombe Camping Barn, Watercombe, Dorchester, Dorset.*
Actual grid ref: SX625613
Tel: **01271 24420** *Simple barn, sleeps 12. on the southern tip of Dartmoor. ADVANCE BOOKING ESSENTIAL. £3.00 per bunk.*
Open: All Year

Scorriton   5

National Grid Ref: SX7068

ᵗᵒᵗ ⌕ Tradesman's Arms

(0.5m 🚍) *Newcombe Farm, Scorriton, Buckfastleigh, Devon, TQ11 0JE.*
Modern comfortable farmhouse.
Tel: **01364 643734** Mr Pearse.
Rates fr: *£18.00-£15.00.*
Open: All Year (not Xmas)
Beds: 1D 1T 1S **Baths:** 2 Ensuite
ⓢ 🅿 (6) ⊬ ⬜ 🖾 Ⓥ 🛆 ⋌

Holne   6

National Grid Ref: SX7069

ᵗᵒᵗ ⌕ Old Forge, Church House Inn

(On Path 🚍) *Church House Inn, Holne, Ashburton, Newton Abbot, Devon, TQ13 7R.*
14th Century village inn.
Grades: ETB 3 Cr, Comm
Tel: **01364 631208** Mrs Bevan.
Rates fr: *£19.50-£22.50.*
Open: All Year **Beds:** 1F 2D 2T 1S
Baths: 4 Ensuite, 2 Shared
ⓢ 🅿 (5) ⬜ 🛏 ✕ 🖾 Ⓥ 🛆 ⋌

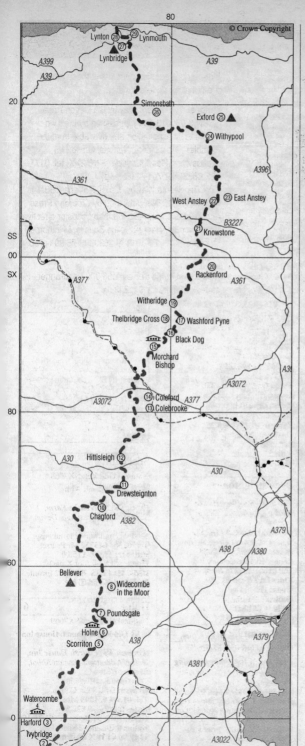

© Crown Copyright

80

(0.33m) *Mill Leat Farm, Holne, Ashburton, Newton Abbot, Devon, TQ13 7RZ.*
Actual grid ref: SX713685
Off the beaten track.
Grades: ETB Listed, Approv
Tel: 01364 631283 Mrs Cleave.
Rates fr: *£15.00-£17.00.*
Open: All Year (not Xmas)
Beds: 2F
Baths: 1 Ensuite, 1 Shared
⛧ 🅿 (2) 🗆 🖙 ✕ Ⅵ 🛋 ✦

(On Path) *Hunters Reach, Michelcombe Lane, Holne, Newton Abbot, Devon, TQ13 7WR.*
Actual grid ref: SX703693
Modern comfortable bungalow.
Peaceful location.
Tel: 01364 631300
Mr & Mrs Dance.
Rates fr: *£14.00-£15.00.*
Open: All Year (not Xmas)
Beds: 2D 1S
Baths: 1 Shared
🅿 (4) 🏃 🗆 🛏.

(🏕 On Path) *Holne Camping Barn, Holne, Newton Abbot, Devon.*
Actual grid ref: SX706696
Tel: 01271 24420 *Simple barn, sleeps 14, and part of a 200 acre working farm. ADVANCE BOOKING ESSENTIAL. £3.00 per bunk.*
Open: All Year

(On Path 🚍) *Chase Gate Farm, Holne, Newton Abbot, Devon, TQ13 7RX.*
Comfortable friendly farmhouse.
Tel: 01364 631261 Mr Adnitt.
Rates fr: *£11.00-£11.00.*
Open: All Year
Beds: 1F 1D 1T
Baths: 1 Shared
⛧ 🅿 ✕ Ⅵ 🛋 ✦

(0.5m) *Middle Stoke Farm, Holne, Newton Abbot, Devon, TQ13 7SS.*
Stone barn conversion on
Dartmoor.
Tel: 01364 631444 Miss Neal.
Rates fr: *£15.00-£15.00.*
Open: All Year (not Xmas)
Beds: 1D **Baths:** 1 Ensuite
⛧ 🅿 (2) 🏃 🗆 🖙 🛏. 🛋 ✦

The Grid Reference
beneath the location
heading is for the
village or town - *not*
for individual houses,
which are shown
(where supplied) in
each entry itself.

Poundsgate 7

National Grid Ref: SX7072

⑪ ⌕ Tavistock Inn

(1.5m) *New Cott Farm,*
Poundsgate, Newton Abbot, Devon,
TQ13 7PD.
Actual grid ref: SX701729
Working farm with modern bunga-
low.
Grades: ETB 2 Cr, Comm,
AA 3 Q
Tel: **01364 631421** Mrs Phipps.
Rates fr: £17.00-£21.00.
Open: All Year
Beds: 1F 2D 1T
Baths: 4 Ensuite
🛏 (3) ⒫ (4) ⊬⌷✗▥ⓥ⌨♦

(1.5m) *Lower Aish Guest House,*
Poundsgate, Ashburton, Newton
Abbot, Devon, TQ13 7NY.
C17th house on Dartmoor.
Grades: ETB Listed
Tel: **01364 631229** Mrs Wilkinson.
Rates fr: £15.00-£18.00.
Open: Easter to Oct
Beds: 1F 3D 1S
🛏 ⒫ (8) ⌷↻▥

Widecombe in the Moor 8

National Grid Ref: SX7176

⑪ ⌕ Old Inn

(0.25m 🚍) *Langworthy,*
Widecombe in the Moor, Newton
Abbot, Devon, TQ13 7UB.
Luxurious, friendly, comfortable
farmhouse.
Tel: **0136 621242** Mrs Baker.
Rates fr: £16.00-£23.00.
Open: All Year
Beds: 1F 1D 1T
Baths: 1 Ensuite 1 Shared
🛏 ⒫ (6) ⊬⌷✗▥⌨♦
Also ▲ *£3.00 per tent.,*
Open: Summer ⛺ 🛖 ✗ ♦ ♿

Bellever 9

National Grid Ref: SX6577

(▲ 4m) *Bellever Youth Hostel,*
Bellever, Postbridge, Yelverton,
Devon, PL20 6TU.
Actual grid ref: SX654773
Warden: Mr I Harris.
Tel: **01822 88227**
Under 18: £5.55 **Adults:** £8.25
Family Rooms, Evening Meal, Self
Catering Facilities, No Smoking,
Grounds Available for Games,
Parking
Recently refurbished converted
barn, idyllically situated at the
heart of Dartmoor National Park

The lowest *double* rate per
person is shown in *italics.*

Chagford 10

National Grid Ref: SX7087

⑪ ⌕ Ring O' Bells, Bullers Arms,
Globe, Three Crowns

(0.25m 🚍) *Glendarah House,*
Lower Street, Chagford, Newton
Abbot, Devon, TQ13 8BZ.
Actual grid ref: SX703879
Grades: ETB 2 Cr, High Comm,
AA 4 Q, Select
Tel: **01647 433270** Mrs Bellenger.
Rates fr: £22.00-£22.50.
Open: All Year (not Xmas)
Beds: 3D 3T
Baths: 6 Ensuite
🛏 (10) ⒫ (7) ⊬⌷▥⌨♦
Spoil yourselves along the Way!
Comfortable spacious rooms, all
ensuite baths. Peaceful location 5
minutes walk from village centre
pubs. Huge breakfasts from friend-
ly hosts.

(0.25m) *Lawn House, 24 Mill*
Street, Chagford, Newton Abbot,
Devon, TQ13 7AW.
C18th thatched house.
Tel: **01647 433329** Mrs Law.
Rates fr: £15.00-£20.00.
Open: All Year
Beds: 1F 2D
Baths: 1 Shared
🛏 (7) ⊬⌷↻▥⌨

(0.25m) *The Globe Inn, High*
Street, Chagford, Newton Abbot,
Devon, TQ13 8AJ.
C16th historic coaching inn.
Tel: **01647 433485**
Mrs Ashpool.
Rates fr: £21.00-£26.25.
Open: All Year
Beds: 2D 1T
Baths: 3 Ensuite
⌷✗

Drewsteignton 11

National Grid Ref: SX7390

⑪ ⌕ Drewe Arms

(On Path) *The Old Inn, The*
Square, Drewsteignton, Exeter,
Devon, EX6 6QR.
Converted 18th Century inn.
Tel: **01647 281276** Mr Butcher.
Rates fr: £17.50-£17.50.
Open: Feb to Dec
Beds: 2D 1T
Baths: 1 Ensuite, 1 Shared
⒫ (3) ⊬⌷↻✗ⓥ⌨♦

(On Path 🚍) *The Old Rectory,*
Drewsteignton, Exeter, Devon,
EX6 6QT.
Actual grid ref: SX737908
Georgian house in two acres.
Grades: AA 2 Q
Tel: **01647 281269** Mrs Emanuel.
Rates fr: £15.00-£22.50.
Open: All Year (not Xmas)
Beds: 1D 1T
Baths: 1 Ensuite 1 Shared
🛏 ⒫ (3) ⊬✗▥ⓥ♦

(0.5m 🚍) *East Fingle Farm,*
Drewsteignton, Exeter, Devon,
EX6 6NJ.
Actual grid ref: SX744914
Devon farm longhouse.
Tel: **01647 281639** Mrs Bond.
Rates fr: £15.00-£15.00.
Open: Easter to Oct
Beds: 1D 1T
Baths: 1 Shared
🛏 ⒫ (10) ⌷✗ⓥ⌨♦

Hittisleigh 12

National Grid Ref: SX7395

(On Path) *Hill Farm, Hittisleigh,*
Exeter, Devon, EX6 6LQ.
C17th farmhouse - heated pool -
seclusion.
Grades: ETB Listed
Tel: **01647 24149** Mrs Howell.
Rates fr: £15.00-£15.00.
Open: All Year (not Xmas)
Beds: 1D 1T
Baths: 1 Shared
🛏 ⒫ (10) ⌷✗▥ⓥ

Colebrooke 13

National Grid Ref: SS7700

(0.25m) *Birchmans Farm,*
Colebrooke, Crediton, Devon,
EX17 5BL..
Actual grid ref: SS743983
All bedrooms ensuite, tea/coffee
facilities.
Grades: ETB 2 Cr, Comm
Tel: **01363 82393** Mrs Hill.
Rates fr: £15.00-£15.00.
Open: All Year (not Xmas)
Beds: 2D 1T
Baths: 3 Ensuite
🛏 ⒫ ✗▥ⓥ♦

(0.75m 🚍) *The Oyster,*
Colebrooke, Crediton, Devon,
EX17 5JQ.
Modern bungalow in central
Devon.
Tel: **01363 84576**
Mrs Hockridge.
Rates fr: £14.00-£14.00.
Open: All Year
Beds: 2D 1T
Baths: 2 Ensuite
🛏 ⒫ (5) ⌷▥♿⌨♦

Coleford 14

National Grid Ref: SS7701

⑪ ⌕ New Inn

(1.5m) *Coombe House Country*
Hotel, Coleford, Crediton, Devon,
EX17 5BY.
Georgian country house hotel.
Grades: ETB 4 Cr
Tel: **01363 84487**
Mr Wirrich.
Rates fr: £26.50-£30.00.
Open: All Year
Beds: 4F 4D 2T 2S
Baths: 12 Ensuite
🛏 ⒫ (90) ⌷↻✗▥ⓥ⌨♦

Morchard Bishop 15

National Grid Ref: SS7607

¶ ⌺ London Inn

(2.75m 🚐) *Wigham, Morchard Bishop, Crediton, Devon, EX17 6RJ.*
Actual grid ref: SS756087
Grades: AA 5 Q, Prem Select
Tel: **01363 877350**
Mr & Mrs Chilcott.
Rates fr: £25.50-**£25.50**.
Open: All Year
Beds: 1F 2D 2T
Baths: 5 Ensuite
🛏 (8) 🖪 ⅏⌷✗🕮Ⅵ🔥
Delightful C16th thatched longhouse in superb setting. Super views. Complete quiet. Heated pool. Barbecue. Snooker. Bar. 30 acre farm. Lovely garden. AA: 5 Q, Premier Selected.

(On Path 🚐) *Kantara, Church Street, Morchard Bishop, Crediton, Devon, EX17 6PH.*
Actual grid ref: SS771075
En-route, welcoming, comfortable, modern home.
Tel: **01363 877259**
Mrs Hutchings.
Rates fr: £16.00-**£17.50**.
Open: Mar to Oct
Beds: 1D 1T
Baths: 1 Shared
🛏 (10) 🖪 (2) ⅏⌷🕇🕮Ⅵ🔥

(⌂ On Path) *Beech Hill Camping Barn, Morchard Bishop, Crediton, Devon, .*
Actual grid ref: SS781087
Tel: **01271 24420** *Simple barn, sleeps 12, located in quiet, rural countryside. ADVANCE BOOKING ESSENTIAL. £3.00 per bunk.*

(0.5m 🚐) *Oldborough Fishing Retreat, Morchard Bishop, Crediton, Devon, EX17 6JQ.*
Actual grid ref: SS774061
Modern house, by lakes/woods.
Tel: **01363 877437**
Mrs Wilshaw.
Rates fr: £15.00-**£19.00**.
Open: All Year (not Xmas)
Beds: 1F 2T
Baths: 1 Shared
🛏 🖪 (10) ⅏⌷🕇✗🕮🔥

Black Dog 16

National Grid Ref: SS8009

¶ ⌺ The Black Dog Inn

(On Path 🚐) *Lower Brownstone Farm, Black Dog, Crediton, Devon, EX17 4QE.*
Spacious Georgian comfortable farmhouse.
Tel: **01363 877256**
Mrs Wedlake.
Rates fr: £12.00-**£12.00**.
Open: All Year
Beds: 1F 1D
Baths: 1 Shared
🛏 🖪 (10) ⅏⌷🕇✗Ⅵ🔥

(0.5m 🚐) *Sentrys, Black Dog, Crediton, Devon, EX17 4RA.*
Modern comfortable farmhouse.
Tel: **01884 860288** Mrs Crang.
Rates fr: £15.00-**£15.00**.
Open: Easter to Oct
Beds: 1F 1D 1T **Baths:** 1 Shared
🛏 (3) 🖪 ⅏⌷✗🔥

Washford Pyne 17

National Grid Ref: SS8111

¶ ⌺ The Black Dog Inn, Thelbridge Inn

(On Path 🚐) *Cobscombe Farm, Washford Pyne, Black Dog, Crediton, Devon, EX17 4QJ.*
Actual grid ref: SS798101
Tel: **01884 860075** Mrs Ayre.
Rates fr: £15.00-**£15.00**.
Open: Easter to Oct
Beds: 1F 1D 1T 1S
Baths: Ensuite Shared
🛏 (1) 🖪 (6) ⅏⌷🕇✗🕮🔥
Chris and Merv welcome you to their lovely home, on a working farm. Set in a very picturesque area - central Devon good touring base.

(0.5m) *Harbourford House, Washford Pyne, Crediton, Devon, EX17 4RA.*
Spacious, comfortable old farmhouse.
Tel: **01884 861250** Mrs Truss.
Rates fr: £15.00-**£15.00**.
Open: All Year (not Xmas)
Beds: 1D 1S
Baths: 1 Ensuite 1 Shared
🖪 (8) ⌷🕮🔥

Thelbridge Cross 18

National Grid Ref: SS7911

¶ ⌺ Thelbridge Cross Inn

(2m 🚐) *Marchweeke Farm, Thelbridge Cross, Witheridge, Tiverton, Devon, EX16 8NY.*
Modernised old farmhouse.
Grades: ETB 2 Cr, Comm, AA 4 Q, Select
Tel: **01884 860418** Ms Webber.
Rates fr: £16.00-**£16.00**.
Open: Feb to Nov
Beds: 1D 1T
Baths: 1 Ensuite 1 Private
🛏 🖪 (2) ⅏⌷🕇✗🕮🔥

Witheridge 19

National Grid Ref: SS8014

¶ ⌺ Mitre Inn, The Square

(0.75m 🚐) *Hole Farm, Witheridge, Tiverton, Devon, EX16 8QD.*
Actual grid ref: SS814152
Grade II Listed Devon longhouse.
Tel: **01884 860265** Mrs Knapton.
Rates fr: £18.00-**£12.00**.
Open: All Year (not Xmas)
Beds: 1F 1D 1S
Baths: 2 Ensuite 1 Shared
🛏 🖪 (3) ⌷🕇🕮Ⅵ🔥

(On Path) *Hope House, 6 The Square, Witheridge, Tiverton, Devon, EX16 8AE.*
Actual grid ref: SS804146
Spacious Victorian rectory in village.
Tel: **01884 860012**
Mr & Mrs Childs.
Rates fr: £14.00-**£14.00**.
Open: All Year
Beds: 1F 2D 1T 1S
Baths: 2 Shared
🛏 🖪 (3) ⅏🕮🔥

Rackenford 20

National Grid Ref: SS8518

¶ ⌺ The Stag Inn

(1m 🚐) *The Stag Inn, Rackenford, Tiverton, Devon, EX16 8DT.*
800 year old, thatched inn. Inglenook fireplace.
Tel: **01884 881369**
Rates fr: £15.50-**£15.50**.
Open: All Year (not Xmas day)
Beds: 1F 1D 2S
Baths: 2 Shared
🛏 🖪 (15) ⌷🕇✗🕮Ⅵ🔥

Knowstone 21

National Grid Ref: SS8223

(On Path) *The Masons Arms Inn, Knowstone, South Molton, Devon, EX36 4RY.*
Tel: **01398 341231**
Mr & Mrs Todd.
Rates fr: £24.00-**£27.50**.
Open: All Year (not Xmas)
Beds: 4D **Baths:** 4 Ensuite
🛏 🖪 (12) ⌷🕇✗Ⅵ🔥
Charming thatched inn with garden overlooking Exmoor. Renowned home cooked food, charming bedrooms. Real ales served straight from cask. Log fires in winter. Warm welcome all seasons.

West Anstey 22

National Grid Ref: SS8426

¶ ⌺ Jubilee Inn

(On Path 🚐) *The Old Vicarage, West Anstey, South Molton, Devon, EX36 3PE.*
Actual grid ref: SS851274
Manor house, peaceful, all comforts.
Tel: **01398 341529** Lady Loram.
Rates fr: £18.00-**£15.00**.
Open: All Year
Beds: 1D 4S
Baths: 1 Ensuite, 2 Shared
🛏 🖪 (7) ⌷🕇✗🕮Ⅵ🔥

The *lowest* single rate *is shown* in bold.

(On Path 🚌) *Partridge Arms Farm,* Yeo Mill, West Anstey, South Molton, Devon, EX36 3NU.
Actual grid ref: SS841262
Licensed olde-worlde farmhouse. Formerly inn.
Grades: ETB 2 Cr, Comm
Tel: 01398 341217 Mrs Milton.
Rates fr: *£17.50-£17.50.*
Open: All Year (not Xmas)
Beds: 2F 3D 2T
Baths: 4 Ensuite 1 Shared
🛏 🅿 (10) 🔲 📺 ✕ 🎴 Ⓥ 🛢 ♿
Also ▲ *£2 per tent.,*
Open: All Year ✕ ⚫

(On Path 🚌) *The Jubilee Inn,* West Anstey, South Molton, Devon, EX36 3PH.
Country inn set in three acres.
Tel: 01398 341401
Mr Wraight.
Rates fr: *£17.50-£17.50.*
Open: All Year
Beds: 1D 1T 1S
Baths: 2 Ensuite 1 Shared
🛏 (1) 🅿 (80) 🔲 🎴 📺 Ⓥ 🛢
£1.00 per tent.
Open: All Year

(On Path 🚌) *Lands Farm,* West Anstey, South Molton, Devon, EX36 3PD.
Comfortable farmhouse.
Tel: 01398 341309
Mrs Maude.
Rates fr: *£12.50-£12.50.*
Open: All Year
Beds: 2D
🛏 🅿 🔲 🎴 ✕ 🎴 🛢 ♿

East Anstey 23

National Grid Ref: SS8626

🍴 🍺 Jubilee Inn, London Inn

(0.75m) *Threadneedle,* East Anstey, Tiverton, Devon, EX16 9JH.
Modern comfortable accommodation with character.
Tel: 01398 341598
Mr & Mrs Webb.
Rates fr: *£16.00-£17.50.*
Open: All Year (not Xmas)
Beds: 1F 1T
Baths: 2 Ensuite
🅿 (3) ✁ 🔲 🎴 🎴 Ⓥ

Withypool 24

National Grid Ref: SS8435

🍴 🍺 Royal Oak Inn

(On Path) *The Old Rectory,* Withypool, Minehead, Somerset, TA24 7QP.
Large comfortable bungalow. Lovely views.
Tel: 01643 831553
Mr Clatworthy.
Rates fr: *£14.00-£14.00.*
Open: All Year
Beds: 1D 1T 1S
Baths: 1 Shared
🛏 🅿 (3) ✁ 🔲 🎴 🎴 🛢 ♿

(On Path) *Fir Tree Cottage,* Withypool, Minehead, Somerset, TA24 7RA.
Spacious and comfortable detached cottage.
Tel: 01643 831453 Mrs Bennett.
Rates fr: *£14.00-£14.00.*
Open: All Year (not Xmas)
Beds: 2T
Baths: 1 Shared
🛏 🅿 (6) 🔲 🎴 🎴 Ⓥ ♿

Exford 25

National Grid Ref: SS8538

🍴 🍺 Exmoor White Horse Inn

(2.5m 🍺) *Exmoor House Hotel,* Chapel Street, Exford, Minehead, Somerset, TA24 7PY.
Actual grid ref: SS854383
Grades: ETB 2 Cr
Tel: 01643 831304 Mr Dolmam.
Rates fr: *£15.00-£18.00.*
Open: All Year
Beds: 1F 6D 4T 2S
Baths: 8 Ensuite 2 Shared
🛏 🅿 (20) 🔲 🎴 🎴 ✕ 🎴 Ⓥ 🛢 ♿
Village hotel situated in central Exmoor. Comfortable and homely accommodation. Rooms with TVs, most ensuite, beverage and drying facilities. Good touring base (ideal for walkers).

(▲ 2m) *Exford Youth Hostel,* Exe Mead, Exford, Minehead, Somerset, TA24 7PU.
Actual grid ref: SS853383
Warden: Mr R Fisher.
Tel: 01643 831650
Under 18: £5.55 **Adults:** £8.25
Family Rooms, Evening Meal, Self Catering, Centrally Heated, Camping, Laundry Facilities, Grounds Available for Games, Shop, Parking
Very attractive Victorian house, refurbished, in lovely grounds with River Exe flowing through the gardens, and beyond an idyllic village setting

(2m) *Edgcott House,* Exford, Minehead, Somerset, TA24 7QG.
Actual grid ref: SS848388
Spacious peaceful C17th country house.
Grades: ETB 2 Cr, Comm
Tel: 01643 831495 Ms Lamble.
Rates fr: *£18.00-£18.00.*
Open: All Year **Beds:** 1D 1T 1S
Baths: 1 Ensuite 2 Shared
🅿 (4) 🔲 🎴 ✕ 🎴 ♿ Ⓥ 🛢 ♿

(On Path 🚌) *Court Farmhouse,* Exford, Minehead, Somerset, TA24 7LY.
Actual grid ref: SS856380
Lovely, comfortable C16th farmhouse.
Tel: 01643 831207 Mrs Mole.
Rates fr: *£16.00-£17.00.*
Open: All Year **Beds:** 1F 2D 1T
Baths: 2 Shared
🎴 🎴 Ⓥ 🛢 ♿

Simonsbath 26

National Grid Ref: SS7739

(2m 🚌) *Warren Farm,* Simonsbath, Minehead, Somerset, TA24 7LN.
Actual grid ref: SS795408
Traditional, beautiful, uniquely situated farmhouse.
Tel: 01643 831283 Mrs Hawkins.
Rates fr: *£15.00-£18.00.*
Open: All Year
Beds: 1F 1T
Baths: 1 Shared
🛏 🅿 (4) 🔲 🎴 ✕ 🎴 Ⓥ 🛢 ♿

(0.75m 🚌) *Moorland Cottage,* Simonsbath, Minehead, Somerset, TA24 7LQ.
Actual grid ref: SS735401
Comfortable renovated character farm cottage.
Tel: 01643 831458 Mrs Pile.
Rates fr: *£15.00-£15.00.*
Open: All Year (not Xmas)
Beds: 1D 2S
Baths: 1 Private
🛏 🅿 (4) ✁ 🔲 🎴 ✕ 🎴 Ⓥ 🛢 ♿

Lynbridge 27

National Grid Ref: SS7248

🍴 🍺 The Rock House Inn, Royal Castle

(▲ 0.5m) *Lynton Youth Hostel,* Lynbridge, Lynton, Devon, EX35 6AZ.
Actual grid ref: SS720487
Warden: Mr D Matthews.
Tel: 01598 53237
Under 18: £5.00 **Adults:** £7.45
Family Bunk Rooms, Centrally Heated, Showers, Evening Meal (7.00 pm)
Homely Victorian house in the steep wooded gorge of the West Lyn river, where Exmoor meets the sea

(0.5m) *Top of the World,* Lynbridge, Lynton, Devon, EX35 6BE.
Grades: ETB Listed
Tel: 01598 753693 Mrs Champion.
Rates fr: *£14.50-£17.00.*
Open: Feb to Oct
Beds: 1D 1T
Baths: 1 Shared
🛏 🅿 (2) 🔲 🎴 ✕ 🎴 Ⓥ
Character Victorian cottage on high ground, glorious views across the West Lyn Valley, ten mins beach, 3/4 mile from Lynton at Lynbridge, home cooking.

Pay B&Bs by
cash or cheque and
be prepared to
pay up front.

Lynton 28

National Grid Ref: SS7149

◻◻ Rock House Inn, Royal Castle

(0.25m) *Rockvale Hotel*, Lee Road, Lynton, Devon, *EX35 6HW*.
Spacious Victorian building, central location.
Grades: ETB 3 Cr, Comm, AA 3 Q, RAC 1 St
Tel: 01598 752279 Mr Woodland.
Rates fr: £22.00-£18.00.
Open: Mar to Oct
Beds: 2F 5D 1S **Baths:** 8 Ensuite
◻ (4) ◻ (10) ◻◻✕◻◻◻◻◻

(0.5m) *Woodlands Hotel*, Lynbridge, Lynton, Devon, *EX35 6AX*.
Actual grid ref: SS721488
Grades: ETB 3 Cr, Comm
Tel: 01598 752324 Mrs Christian.
Rates fr: £16.00-£16.00.
Open: Mar to Nov
Beds: 5D 2T 1S
Baths: 5 Ensuite, 2 Shared
◻ (12) ◻ (8) ◻◻✕◻◻◻◻◻
Warm welcome for walkers. Peaceful location in a beautiful setting overlooking N.T. woodland. Spacious rooms. Delicious home-made food including vegetarian choice and hearty breakfast.

(0.5m) *Sandrock*, Longmead, Lynton, Devon, *EX35 6DH*.
Fully licensed hotel.
Grades: ETB 3 Cr, Comm, AA 2 St, RAC 2 St
Tel: 01598 753307
Mr & Mrs Harrison.
Rates fr: £21.00-£19.50.
Open: Feb to Nov **Beds:** 4D 3T 2S
Baths: 7 Ensuite 1 Shared
◻ (5) ◻ (9) ◻◻✕◻◻◻◻◻

(0.5m) *Gable Lodge Hotel*, Lee Road, Lynton, Devon, *EX35 6BS*.
Large Victorian Listed private house.
Tel: 01598 752367
Mr Bowman.
Rates fr: £15.00-£15.00.
Open: All Year
Beds: 1F 5D 1T 1S
Baths: 6 Ensuite 1 Shared
◻ ◻ (8) ◻◻✕◻✕◻◻

(0.5m) *Sylvia House Hotel*, Lydiate Lane, Lynton, Devon, *EX35 6HE*.
Delightful Georgian house.
Grades: ETB 3 Cr Comm
Tel: 01598 752391
Mr Channing.
Rates fr: £17.00-£15.00.
Open: Feb - Dec
Beds: 5D 1T 1S 1F
Baths: 6 Private 1 Shared
◻◻✕◻✕◻◻◻

(0.5m) *The Denes Guest House*, Longmead, Lynton, Devon, *EX35 6DQ*.
Quiet comfortable, friendly Victorian home.
Tel: 01598 753573
Mr & Mrs Gay.
Rates fr: £15.00-£15.00.
Open: All Year (not Xmas)
Beds: 3F 2D 2S
Baths: 2 Shared
◻ ◻ (7) ◻◻✕◻

Lynmouth 29

National Grid Ref: SS7249

◻◻ Village Inn

(On Path) *Ferndale House*, Watersmeet Road, Lynmouth, Lynton, Devon, *EX35 6EP*.

Large Victorian house.
Tel: 01598 753431
Mr Burns.
Rates fr: £17.50.
Open: Easter to Nov
Baths: 3 Ensuite
◻ (5) ◻◻◻◻◻◻◻

(On Path) *Glenville House*, 2 Tors Road, Lynmouth, Lynton, Devon, *EX35 6ET*.
Comfortable, licensed, Victorian riverside house.
Tel: 01598 752202
Mr & Mrs Francis.
Rates fr: £16.50-£16.50.
Open: Mar to Nov
Beds: 1F 4D 1T 1S
Baths: 3 Ensuite 2 Shared
◻ (7) ◻◻✕◻◻◻

(0.25m) *Oakleigh*, 4 Tors Road, Lynmouth, Lynton, Devon, *EX35 6ET*.
Small friendly comfortable guest-house.
Tel: 01598 752220
Mr & Mrs Pile.
Rates fr: £16.50-£16.50.
Open: All Year (not Xmas)
Beds: 5D 2T 2S
Baths: 2 Shared
◻ ◻ (9) ◻◻✕◻◻◻

(0.25m) *The Heatherville*, Lynmouth, Lynton, Devon, *EX35 6*.
Licenced country house. Magnificent views.
Grades: ETB 3 Cr, Comm, AA 4 Q, Select, RAC Acclaim
Tel: 01598 752327
Mrs Davis.
Rates fr: £23.00-£22.50.
Open: Easter to Nov
Beds: 2F 5D 3T
Baths: 5 Private 2 Shared
◻ (7) ◻ (10) ◻◻✕◻◻◻

Ulster Way

Someone suggested that outside the **South West Coast Path**, none of our paths can actually lay claim to being truly long distance. The **Ulster Way**, although not on the mainland, proves them wrong. Running for 560 miles through each of the Six Counties, this path is another candidate for completion in several trips. And it's certainly worth the effort. This path is very special. It visits places famed throughout the world for their beauty - the unspoilt North Antrim Coast, the extraordinary basalt formations of the **Giant's Causeway**, the remote Sperrin Mountains, Lough Erne with its multitude of islands, the deserted **Mountains of Mourne** and the bird sanctuaries of **Strangford Lough**. Now, Northern Ireland is an enormous place with a small population. Consequently, this path takes the walker past the true outposts of these islands, a rare privilege afforded mainly to Ulstermen and Irishmen alike, as most walkers stick to the mainland. Our advice is to make the plunge, plan the trip and set out - your walking will be memorable. You will see from the map here that certain stretches of the **Ulster Way** are not well served by accommodation - notably from Dungiven down to Belleek. Logistics thus mean that you may have to double up on accommodation - ie., return to your previous port of call or arrange transport to your next destination, to return in the morning to the point where you left the path. You will need to be well-versed in map and compass work (signposting along the **Ulster Way** leaves a lot to be desired) and you should be prepared for all weathers.

Guides: *Walking the Ulster Way - A Journal and a Guide* by Alan Warner (ISBN 086 281 2275), published by Appletree Press (Belfast) and available from all major bookshops, £6.95

Maps: Ordnance Survey of Northern Ireland 1:50,000 Discoverer series: 4, 5, 7, 8, 9, 12, 13, 15, 17, 18, 19, 20, 26, 27 and 29.

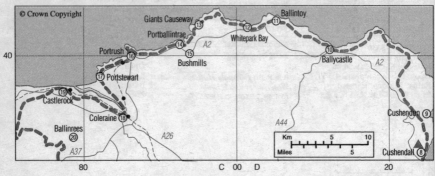

Newtownabbey	1

National Grid Ref: J3480

[icon] Bellevue Arms

(0.5m) *Iona, 161 Antrim Road, Newtownabbey, Belfast, BT36 7QR.*
5 minutes from Cave Hill Mountain.
Tel: **01232 842256** Mrs Kelly.
Rates fr: *£16.00*-**£18.00**.
Open: All Year (not Xmas)
Beds: 1F 1D 2S
Baths: 2 Shared
[icons]

The lowest *double* rate per person is shown in *italics*.

Ballynure	2

National Grid Ref: J3193

[icon] Corrs Corner, Henrys, Ballyboe

(1m) *Rockbank, 40 Belfast Road, Ballynure, Ballyclare, Co Antrim, BT39 9TZ.*
Actual grid ref: J314921
Farmhouse accommodation on working dairy farm.
Tel: **019603 52261**
Mrs Park.
Rates fr: *£15.00*-**£15.00**.
Open: All Year
Beds: 1F 1T
Baths: 1 Shared
[icons]

Kilwaughter	3

National Grid Ref: D3500

(2m) *Kilwaughter House Hotel, 61 Shanes Hill Road, Kilwaughter, Larne, County Antrim, BT40 2TQ.*
Peaceful family-run hotel, lovely grounds.
Tel: **01574 272591** Mr Dobbin.
Rates fr: *£20.00*-**£20.00**.
Open: All Year
Beds: 4D 4S
Baths: 3 Shared
[icons]

The *lowest* **single** rate *is shown in* **bold**.

Cairncastle 4

National Grid Ref: D3307

⑩ ◀ The Meeting House

(0.25m) *Meeting House, 120 Brustinbrae Road, Cairncastle, Larne, Co Antrim, BT40 2RL.*
Modern comfortable home situated 1 mile inland from famous Antrim coast.
Tel: **01574 583252** Mrs Moore.
Rates fr: *£16.00-£17.00.*
Open: Jan to Nov
Beds: 1D 2T **Baths:** 3 Ensuite
⛺ (4) 🅿 ✁ 🗙 🍴 🗙 🖿 ▯ ≠

Glenarm 5

National Grid Ref: D3215

⑩ ◀ Meeting House

(On Path) *10 Altmore Street, Glenarm, Ballymena, Co Antrim, BT44 0AR.*
Comfortable guest house in first of

Nine Glens of Antrim.
Grades: NITB Approv
Tel: **01574 841307** Mrs Morrow.
Rates fr: *£14.00-£14.00.*
Open: All Year
Beds: 2F 3D
Baths: 1 Shared
⛺ 🅿 (10) 🗙 🍴 🖿 ▯

Carnlough 6

National Grid Ref: D2817

⑩ ◀ Bridge Inn

(On Path) *Bridge Inn (McAuleys), 2 Bridge Street, Carnlough, Ballymena, County Antrim, BT44 0ET.*
Traditional, family-run pub.
Grades: NITB Grade B
Tel: **01574 885669**
Mr Davidson.
Rates fr: *£16.00-£16.00.*
Open: All Year (not Xmas)
Beds: 1F 3D 1T
Baths: 1 Shared
⛺ 🗙 🗙 🖿 ▯ ≠

Glenariff 7

National Grid Ref: D2425

⑩ ◀ Miner's, Glenariff Inn, Manor Lodge

(0.5m) *Dieskirt Farm, 104 Glen Road, Glenariff, Ballymena, County Antrim, BT44 0RG.*
Tel: **012667 71308 / 58769 / 71796**
Mrs McHenry.
Rates fr: *£13.00-£17.00.*
Open: May to Oct
Beds: 1F 2D
Baths: 1 Shared
⛺ 🅿 (10) ✁ 🗙 🍴 🗙 🖿 ▯ ▯
Also ▲
Enjoy the tranquillity of this working 2,000-acre hill farm on the wild and beautiful Antrim Plateau, near the Ulster and Moyle Ways. Dine well at our Glenariffe Forest Park restaurant. 'Switzerland in miniature', said Thackeray - come and see for yourself!

(0.25m) *4 Lurig View, Glenariff, Ballymena, Co Antrim, BT44 0RD.*
Friendly family bungalow, sea views.
Tel: **012667 71618**
Mrs Ward.
Rates fr: *£14.00-£15.00.*
Open: All Year (not Xmas)
Beds: 2F 1D
Baths: 1 Shared
⛺ 🅿 🖿 ▯ ≠

Cushendall 8

National Grid Ref: D2427

⑩ ◀ Harry's Restaurant, Thornlea Hotel

(On Path) 🚐 *Ardclinis Activity Centre, 11 High Street, Cushendall, Ballymena, County Antrim, BT44 0NB.*
Actual grid ref: D236277
Outdoor activity centre, weekend breaks.
Grades: NITB Listed
Tel: **012667 71340**
Mrs Bowen.
Rates fr: *£12.50-£13.00.*
Open: All Year (not Xmas)
Beds: 1F
Baths: 1 Shared
⛺ (8) 🅿 (2) 🗙 🗙 ▯ ≠

(3m) *Cullentra House, 16 Cloghs Road, Cushendall, Ballymena, County Antrim, BT44 0SP.*
Modern country home.
Breathtaking views.
Grades: NITB Approv
Tel: **012667 71762**
Mrs McAuley.
Rates fr: *£14.00-£20.00.*
Open: All Year (not Xmas)
Beds: 1F 1D 1T
Baths: 2 Ensuite 1 Shared
⛺ (4) 🅿 (6) ✁ 🗙 🖿 ♿

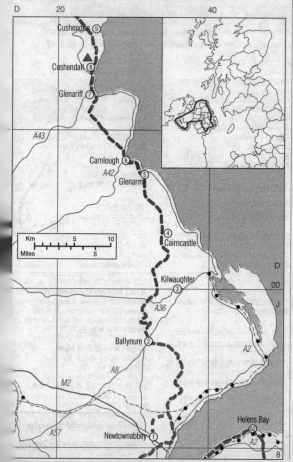

(0.5m 🚍) *The Burn, 63 Ballyeamon Road, Cushendall, Ballymena, County Antrim, BT44 0SN.*
Actual grid ref: D2327
Home-cooking, friendly Irish welcome.
Grades: NITB Approv
Tel: 012667 71733 / 011266 46111
Mrs McAuley.
Rates fr: *£13.00*-**£15.00.**
Open: All Year
Beds: 1D 1T 1S
Baths: 1 Ensuite 2 Shared
🛏 🅿 (6) ⅙ ⅗ 🏲 🛆 🎇 🛆 Ⓥ 🛆 ⸜

(0.75m) *Riverside, 14 Mill Street, Cushendall, Ballymena, County Antrim, BT44 0RR.*
Situated in centre of village.
Tel: 012667 71655
Mr & Mrs McKeegan.
Rates fr: *£14.00*-**£16.00.**
Open: All Year (not Xmas)
Beds: 1F 1D 1T
Baths: 2 Shared
🛏 🅿 (3) ⅙ ⅗ 🏲

Cushendun   9

National Grid Ref: D2533

(On Path) *The Burns, 116 Torr Road, Cushendun, Ballycastle, County Antrim, BT44 0PY.*
Actual grid ref: D245374
Large old comfortable picturesque farmhouse.
Grades: NITB 3 Cr
Tel: 012657 62709
Mrs McKendry.
Rates fr: *£15.00*-**£15.00.**
Open: All Year
Beds: 1F 2D 1T
Baths: 1 Ensuite 1 Shared
🛏 🅿 (12) ⅗ 🏲 🎇 Ⓥ 🛆

Ballycastle   10

National Grid Ref: D1241

🍴 🍺 Central Bar, McCarroll's Pub, Strand Restaurant

(On Path) *Ardmara, 34 Whitepark Road, Ballycastle, County Antrim, BT54 6LJ.*
Actual grid ref: D095416
Charming villa on coast road.
Tel: 012657 69533
Mr & Mrs Herron.
Rates fr: *£15.00*-**£19.00.**
Open: Easter to Sep
Beds: 1D 2T
Baths: 1 Ensuite 1 Private 1 Shared
🛏 🅿 (4) 🏲 🎇 Ⓥ

(0.2m) *Fragrens, 34 Quay Road, Ballycastle, County Antrim, BT54 6BH.*
Modernised C17th private house.
Grades: NITB Approv
Tel: 012657 62168 Mrs McCook.
Rates fr: *£14.00*-**£15.00.**
Open: All Year (not Xmas)
Beds: 5F 2D 1T
Baths: 5 Ensuite 2 Shared
🛏 🅿 (5) ⅗ ⅙ 🏲 🎇 🛆 Ⓥ 🛆 ⸜

(On Path) *Fragrens, 34 Quay Road, Ballycastle, Co Antrim, BT54 6BH.*
Modernised C17th private guest house. Family-run. Good food a priority.
Grades: NITB Approv
Tel: 012657 62168 Mrs McCook.
Rates fr: *£14.00*-**£15.00.**
Open: All Year (not Xmas)
Beds: 5F 2D 1T
Baths: 5 Ensuite 2 Private 1 Shared
🛏 🅿 (4) ⅗ ⅙ 🏲 🎇 Ⓥ

(On Path) *Glenhaven, 10 Beechwood Avenue, Ballycastle, Co Antrim, BT54 6BL.*
Family run B&B close to all amenities. Warm welcome.
Grades: NITB Approv
Tel: 012657 63612
Mr Gormley.
Rates fr: *£15.00*-**£18.00.**
Open: All Year (not Xmas)
Beds: 2D 1T
Baths: 1 Ensuite 1 Shared
🛏 🅿 (3) ⅗ ⅙ 🎇 Ⓥ

Ballintoy   11

National Grid Ref: D0444

(On Path) *Fullerton Arms Hotel, 22 Main Street, Ballintoy, Ballycastle, County Antrim, BT54 6LX.*
Licensed guesthouse and restaurant, public bar.
Grades: NITB Grade B
Tel: 012657 69613
Mrs McCaughan.
Rates fr: *£18.00*-**£22.00.**
Open: All Year
Beds: 1F 4D 1S
Baths: 6 Private
🛏 🅿 ⅙ 🏲 🎇 Ⓥ 🛆

Whitepark Bay   12

National Grid Ref: D0243

🍴 🍺 Fullerton Arms

(0.25m) *Whitepark House, 150 Whitepark Road, Whitepark Bay, Ballintoy, Ballycastle, County Antrim, BT54 6NH.*
C18th house, spacious rooms, log fire.
Grades: NITB Approv
Tel: 012657 31482 Mr & Mrs Isles.
Rates fr: *£20.00*-**£26.00.**

All rooms full and nowhere else to stay? Ask the owner if there's anywhere nearby

---

Open: All Year (not Xmas)
Beds: 2D 1T
Baths: 1 Shared
🛏 🅿 ⅙ ⅗ 🎇 🛆 ⸜

Giants Causeway   13

National Grid Ref: C9443

(On Path) *Lochaber, 107 Causeway Road, Giants Causeway, Bushmills, Co Antrim, BT57 8SX.*
Modern farm bungalow. Lovely coastal walks.
Tel: 012657 31385 Mrs Ramage.
Rates fr: *£13.00*-**£15.00.**
Open: All Year **Beds:** 1D 1T
🛏 (2) 🅿 ⅙ ⅗ 🎇

Portballintrae   14

National Grid Ref: C9241

🍴 🍺 Sweeneys Wine Bar, Bayview Hotel, Beach Hotel

(0.25m) *Keeve Na, 62 Ballaghmore Road, Portballintrae, Bushmills, County Antrim, BT57 8RL.*
Modern, detached house.
Grades: NITB Approv
Tel: 012657 32184 Mrs Wilkinson.
Rates fr: *£14.00*-**£14.00.**
Open: All Year (not Xmas)
Beds: 1F 1D 1S
Baths: 1 Shared
🛏 🅿 (3) 🎇 🛆 ⸜

(0.25m) *Bayhead Guest House, 8 Bayhead Road, Portballintrae, Bushmills, County Antrim, BT57 8RZ.*
Large period house overlooking bay.
Tel: 012657 31441 Mr Cooke.
Rates fr: *£19.50*-**£19.50.**
Open: All Year
Beds: 2F 3D 2T
Baths: 7 Ensuite
🛏 🅿 (7) ⅗ 🏲 🎇 🛆 ⸜

Bushmills   15

National Grid Ref: C9440

(0.5m) *Ahimsa, 243 Whitepark Road, Bushmills, Co Antrim, BT57 8SP.*
Traditional, tastefully modernised, Irish cottage with organic garden.
Tel: 012657 31383 Miss Reynolds.
Rates fr: *£12.00*-**£15.00.**
Open: All Year (not Xmas)
Beds: 1D 1T
Baths: 1 Shared
🛏 🅿 (2) ⅙ ⅗ 🏲 🎇 Ⓥ

(0.5m) *Knocklayde View, 90 Causeway Road, Bushmills, Co Antrim, BT57 8SX.*
Country house with lovely view of the countryside and so near to the beauty of the Giant's Causeway.
Grades: NITB Approv
Tel: 012657 32099 Mrs Wylie.
Rates fr: *£13.00*-**£15.00.**
Open: All Year
Beds: 2D
🛏 🅿 ⅗ 🎇

(0.5m) *Pineview, 111 Castlecatt Road, Bushmills, Co Antrim,* *BT53 8AP.*
Beautiful countryside with quiet surroundings on family farm, small bungalow, ample space.
Grades: NITB Approv
Tel: **01265 41527** Mrs Simpson.
Rates fr: *£13.50-£14.50.*
Open: Easter to Oct
Beds: 1F 1T
Baths: 1 Shared
🗄 🛏️ ᵍ

Portrush   16

National Grid Ref: C8540

🍴 🍷 Ramore Wine Bar, The Harbour

(On Path) *Casa A La Mar Guest House, 21 Kerr Street, Portrush, County Antrim,* *BT56 8DG.*
Small family-run guesthouse.
Grades: NITB Grade B
Tel: **01265 822617**
Mrs Larner.
Rates fr: *£13.00-£13.00.*
Open: All Year (not Xmas)
Beds: 2F 3D 2S
Baths: 2 Ensuite 1 Shared
🛏️🗄🛏️✗🖾Ⓥ🛈

(0.25m 🚘) *Atlantic View, 103 Eglinton Street, Portrush, County Antrim,* *BT56 8DZ.*
Friendly stay guaranteed, centrally located.
Tel: **01265 823647**
Mrs McIntyre.
Rates fr: *£14.00-£14.00.*
Open: All Year
Beds: 2F 6D 1T
Baths: 2 Shared
🛏️🗄🖾

(0.25m 🚘) *The Old Manse Guest House, 3 Main Street, Portrush, County Antrim,* *BT56 8BL.*
Large Victorian rectory.
Grades: NITB Grade B
Tel: **01265 824118**
Miss Owler.
Rates fr: *£16.50-£20.00.*
Open: All Year
Beds: 2D 2T
Baths: 2 Ensuite
🛏️ P (10) 🗄🛏️✗🖾Ⓥ🖉

(0.25m) *Clarmont, 10 Lansdowne Crescent, Portrush, County Antrim,* *BT56 8AY.*
Large Victorian seaview guest-house.
Grades: NITB Grade B
Tel: **01265 822397**
Mr & Mrs Duggan.
Rates fr: *£14.00-£18.00.*
Open: All Year (not Xmas)
Beds: 5F 8D 5T 1S
Baths: 7 Private
🗄🖾

Portstewart   17

National Grid Ref: C8138

(0.25m) *Edgewater Hotel, 88 Strand Road, Portstewart, Co Londonderry,* *BT55 7LZ.*
Modern hotel at edge of sea with magnificent views.
Grades: NITB 2 St
Tel: **01265 833314** Mr O'Malley.
Rates fr: *£25.00-£35.50.*
Open: All Year
Beds: 8F 9D 10T 4S
Baths: 31 Ensuite
🛏️ P (100) 🗄✗🖾Ⓥ

Coleraine   18

National Grid Ref: C8432

🍴 🍷 Wine Bar, Silver Sands

(0.75m) *Coolbeg, 2e Grange Road, Coleraine, County Londonderry,* *BT52 1NG.*
Comfortable modern bungalow.
Tel: **01265 44961** Mrs Chandler.
Rates fr: *£18.00-£20.00.*
Open: All Year
Beds: 1F 3T 1S
Baths: 3 Ensuite, 2 Shared
P (6) 🗄🗄🛏️🛈🖉

(3m 🚘) *Tullans Farm B &b Caravan Park, 46 Newmills Road, Coleraine, Co Londonderry,* *BT52 2JB.*
Homely and welcoming farmhouse.
Tel: **01265 42309** Mrs McClelland.
Rates fr: *£15.00-£17.00.*
Open: All Year (not Xmas)
Beds: 1F 2D
Baths: 1 Ensuite 1 Shared
🛏️P🗄🛏️🖾Ⓥ🛈🖉
Also ⛺ *£6 - 10.00 per tent.,*
Open: All Year ⛺ Ⓣ 🍳 🖉 🛁

(2.75m 🚘) *Ballylagan House, 31 Ballylagan Road, Coleraine, County Londonderry,* *BT52 2PQ.*
Traditional farmhouse on working farm.
Grades: NITB Listed
Tel: **01265 822487** Mrs Lyons.
Rates fr: *£16.00-£18.00.*
Open: All Year (not Xmas)
Beds: 2F 3D
Baths: All Ensuite
🛏️ (0) P (8) 🗄🛏️🖾Ⓥ🖉

Castlerock   19

National Grid Ref: C7735

(0.5m) *Carneety House, 120 Mussenden Road, Castlerock, Coleraine, Co Londonderry,* *BT51 4TX.*
300-year-old farmhouse in beautiful countryside by the sea..
Tel: **01265 848640** Mrs Henry.
Rates fr: *£15.00-£16.00.*
Open: All Year (not Xmas)
Beds: 2D 1T
Baths: 1 Ensuite 1 Shared
🛏️ (5) P (4) 🗄🛏️🖾

Ballinrees   20

National Grid Ref: C7829

(0.75m) *Rockmount, 241 Windyhill Road, Ballinrees, Coleraine, Co Londonderry,* *BT51 4JN.*
Comfortable, detached old farmhouse.
Grades: NITB Approv
Tel: **01265 42914**
Mrs Kerr.
Rates fr: *£12.50-£12.50.*
Open: Easter to Sep
Beds: 2D
Baths: 1 Shared
🛏️P🖉🗄🛏️✗🖾Ⓥ🛈🖉

Dungiven   21

National Grid Ref: C6809

🍴 🍷 Castle Inn

(0.5m 🚘) *Bradagh, 132 Main Street, Dungiven, Londonderry, Co Londonderry,* *BT47 4LG.*
Detached town centre house.
Grades: NITB Approv
Tel: **015047 41346**
Mrs McMackens.
Rates fr: *£12.00-£12.00.*
Open: All Year (not Xmas)
Beds: 1F 1T 1S
Baths: 2 Shared
🛏️P(3)🗄🛏️🖾Ⓥ🛈🖉

Ballynatubbrit Foot   22

National Grid Ref: H4585

(3.5m) *Woodbrook Farm, 21 Killymore Road, Ballynatubbrit Foot, Newtonstewart, Co Tyrone,* *BT78 4DT.*
Modern working farm.
Tel: **016626 61432**
Mrs McFarland.
Rates fr: *£12.50-£12.50.*
Open: All Year (not Xmas)
Beds: 1F 1D 1S
Baths: 1 Private 1 Shared
🛏️P🖉🗄🛏️🖾🛈🖉

Lislap   23

National Grid Ref: H4782

(0.5 - 1.0m 🚘) *Hillcrest Farm, Lislap, Gortin Glen, Omagh, County Tyrone,* *BT79 7UE.*
Actual grid ref: H475827
Comfortable farmhouse on working dairy farm.
Tel: **016626 48284**
Mrs McFarland.
Rates fr: *£12.00-£13.00.*
Open: All Year (not Xmas)
Beds: 1F 1D
Baths: 2 Shared
🛏️P(6)🖉🗄🛏️✗🖾Ⓥ🛈🖉

Mountjoy 24

National Grid Ref: H4277

(1m) *Camphill Farm, 5 Mellon Road, Mountjoy, Omagh, Co Tyrone, BT78 5QU.*
Comfortable two storey farmhouse. Adjacent to Ulster-American Folk Park.
Tel: **01662 245400** Mrs Fulton.
Rates fr: *£14.00-£14.00.*
Open: All Year (not Xmas)
Beds: 2D 1T **Baths:** 1 Shared
🅿 (6) ⊬ 🗖 🛏

Baronscourt 25

National Grid Ref: H3583

(0.75m) *Hunting Lodge Hotel, Letterbin Road, Baronscourt, Newtownstewart, Omagh, County Tyrone, BT78 4HR.*
Hotel in converted C19th schoolhouse.
Grades: NITB 1 St
Tel: **016626 61679 / 61122**
Mr Clarke.
Rates fr: *£25.00-£25.00.*
Open: All Year
Beds: 6D 6T 4S
Baths: 16 Ensuite
🌟 🅿 (100) 🗖 🛏 ✕ 🛏 Ⓥ 🛂 ✦

Gortnacullion 26

National Grid Ref: H1868

(2m) *Hollyfield House, Gortnacullion, Kesh, Co Fermanagh, BT93 1BT.*
Detached house, south of the path.
Tel: **013656 32072** Mrs Loane.
Rates fr: *£12.00-£12.00.*
Open: All Year (not Xmas)
Beds: 1D 1T
Baths: 1 Shared
🌟 🅿 ⊬ 🗖 🛏 🛂 ✦

Aughnablaney 27

National Grid Ref: H0763

(On Path) *Manville House, Aughnablaney, Letter, Kesh, Enniskillen, Co Fermanagh, BT93 2BF.*
Comfortable old house in beautiful setting overlooking Lough Erne Sligo Hills.
Grades: NITB Grade A
Tel: **013656 31668** Mrs Graham.
Rates fr: *£15.00-£15.00.*
Open: Easter to Oct
Beds: 1F 2D 1T 1S
Baths: 2 Shared
🌟 (5) 🅿 (6) ⊬ 🗖 🛏 🛏

Belleek 28

National Grid Ref: G9459

📶 🍴 Moohans Fiddlestone

(2m) *Moohans Fiddlestone Inn, 15-17 Main Street, Belleek, Enniskillen, Co Fermanagh, BT74 7JY.*

Traditional Irish pub and guesthouse in the centre of Belleek, beside Belleek Pottery & River Erne.
Tel: **013656 58008** Mr McCann.
Rates fr: *£15.00-£15.00.*
Open: All Year
Beds: 1F 1D 3T **Baths:** 5 Private
🌟 (1) 🗖 🛏 🛏 ⚄

Meenacloybane 29

National Grid Ref: H0053

(1m 🚗) *Heathergrove, Meenacloybane, Garrison, Kesh, Co Fermanagh, BT93 4AT.*
Family-run farm guesthouse.
Tel: **013656 58362** Mrs Duffy.
Rates fr: *£15.00-£20.00.*
Open: All Year (not Xmas)
Beds: 4D 3T **Baths:** 7 Private
🌟 🅿 🗖 🛏 ✕ 🛏 Ⓥ 🛂 ✦

Derrygonnelly 30

National Grid Ref: H1252

(1.75m 🚗) *Meadow View, Sandhill, Derrygonnelly, Enniskillen, Co Fermanagh, BT93 6G.*

Modern, comfortable house. Peaceful setting.
Tel: **013656 41233**
Mrs Wray.
Rates fr: *£13.50-£13.50.*
Open: All Year (not Xmas)
Beds: 1F 1D
Baths: 1 Private 1 Shared
🌟 🅿 🗖 🛏 ✕ 🛏 Ⓥ 🛂 ✦

Belcoo 31

National Grid Ref: H0838

📶 🍴 Leo's Bar

(2.5m) *Corralea Forest Lodge, Belcoo, Enniskillen, County Fermanagh, BT93 5DZ.*
Actual grid ref: H0838
All rooms ensuite with patio doors.
Grades: NITB Grade A
Tel: **01365 86325**
Mr Catterall.
Rates fr: *£18.00-£21.00.*
Open: Mar to Sep
Beds: 1D 3T
Baths: 4 Ensuite
🌟 🅿 (4) 🗖 ✕ 🛏 🛂 ✦

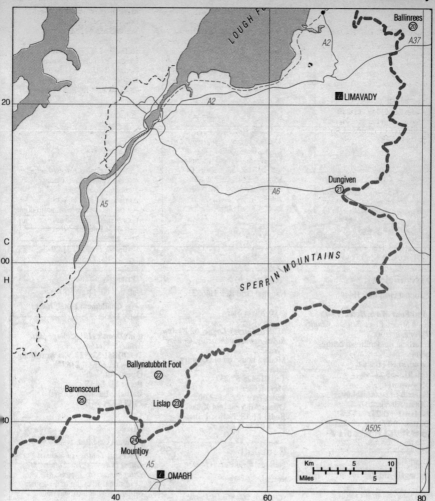

Florencecourt   32

National Grid Ref: H1734

(0.5m 🚍) *Tullyhona House, Marble Arch Road, Florencecourt, Enniskillen, County Fermanagh,* BT92 1DE.
Actual grid ref: H166347
Award-winning purpose-built quiet farmhouse.
Grades: NITB Grade A
Tel: **01365 348452** Mrs Armstrong
Rates fr: £16.00-£18.50.
Open: All Year **Beds:** 4F 2D 1T
Baths: 5 Ensuite 2 Shared
⏰ 🅿 ⅄ 🛏 🛏 ✕ 🖳 ⅃ 🚲 Ⅴ 📷 ✦

Derrylin   33

National Grid Ref: H2728

(1.25m) *Hollytree Farm, Drumanybeg, Knockaraven PO, Derrylin, Enniskillen, Co Fermanagh,* BT92 9QN.
Comfortable working farm on the shores of Upper Lough Erne.
Grades: NITB Approv
Tel: **013657 48319**
Mrs Whittendale
Rates fr: £16.00-£16.00.
Open: All Year **Beds:** 1F 2D
Baths: 2 Ensuite 1 Shared
⏰ 🅿 ⅄ 🛏 🖳

Ports   34

National Grid Ref: H3927

(1.5m 🚍) *Ports House, Ports, Newtownbutler, Co Fermanagh,* BT92 8DT.
Old house and converted stables.
Tel: **013657 38528**
Mr Mewes.
Rates fr: £12.50-£13.50.
Open: All Year (not Xmas)

Beds: 3D
Baths: 1 Private 1 Shared
⏰ 🅿 🛏 🛏 ✕ 🖳 Ⅴ 📷 ✦

Corcreevy   35

National Grid Ref: H4347

🍽 🍺 Valley Hotel, Four Ways Hotel

(2.75m) *Valley Villa, 92 Colebrook Road, Corcreevy, Fivemiletown, County Tyrone,* BT75 0SA.
Collection and drop-off near Ulster Way.
Tel: **013655 21553**
Mrs Malone.
Rates fr: £15.00-£15.00.
Open: All Year (not Xmas)
Beds: 2D
Baths: 2 Ensuite
⏰ 🅿 (5) ⅄ 🛏 🛏 🖳 📷 ✦

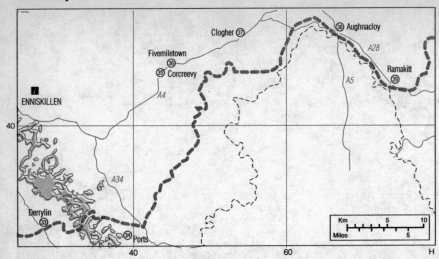

Fivemiletown 36

National Grid Ref: H4448

(3m) *Four Ways Hotel, 41-45 High Street, Fivemiletown, County Tyrone, BT75 0LE.*
Excellent modern town centre hotel.
Grades: NITB 1 Cr
Tel: 013655 21260
Mr Armstrong.
Rates fr: *£20.00-£24.00.*
Open: All Year
Beds: 1F 7D 2T
Baths: 10 Private
🛏 🅿 (20) 🖵 🟊 ✗ 📠 Ⓥ 🛉 ∥

Clogher 37

National Grid Ref: H4442

(On Path) *Ashfield Park, 8 Ashfield Road, Clogher, County Tyrone, BT76 0HF.*
Large Victorian house - self-catering flats.
Tel: 016625 48684
Mrs Beatty.
Rates fr: *£200.00/wk (sleeps 6-8).*
Open: All Year
Beds: 2F
Baths: 1 Shared
🛏 🅿 (6) 🖵 🟊 📠 ∥

(3.5m) 🚜 *Ratory, Clogher, County Tyrone, BT76 0UT.*
Victorian farmhouse on Fintona road.
Tel: 016625 48288
Mr & Mrs Johnston.
Rates fr: *£12.50-£12.50.*
Open: All Year (not Xmas)
Beds: 1D
Baths: 1 Private
🅿 (6) ✓ 🖵 🟊 ✗ 📠 🛉 ∥

Aughnacloy 38

National Grid Ref: H6652

🍽 🍲 Silver Star

(0.25m) *Garvey Lodge, 62 Favour Royal Road, Aughnacloy, County Tyrone, BT69 6BR.*
Modern house on old country estate.
Tel: 016625 57 239
Mrs McClements.
Rates fr: *£12.50-£12.00.*
Open: All Year (not Xmas)
Beds: 1T 1S **Baths:** 1 Shared
🛏 🅿 🖵 🟊 ✗ 📠 🛉 ∥

Ramakitt 39

National Grid Ref: H7445

🍽 🍲 Deer Park

(On Path 🚜) *Model Farm, Derrycourtney Road, Ramakitt, Caledon, County Tyrone, BT68 4UQ.*
Working farm.
Tel: 01861 568247 Mrs Agnew.
Rates fr: *£30.00-£16.50.*
Open: Easter to Oct
Beds: 2D **Baths:** 1 Shared
🛏 🅿 ✓ 🖵 🟊 ✗ 📠 Ⓥ 🛉 ∥

Benburb 40

National Grid Ref: H8151

(On Path) *Benburb Conference Centre, 10 Main Street, Benburb, Dungannon, Co Tyrone, BT71 7LA.*
Converted C19th stables and coachroom located in breathtaking grounds.
Tel: 01861 548170 Mrs Mullin.
Rates fr: *£10.50-£12.00.*
Open: All Year
Beds: 1F 2D 8T 17S
Baths: 4 Shared
🛏 🅿 🖵 ✗ Ⓥ

Armagh 41

National Grid Ref: H8745

🍽 🍲 Charlemont Hotel, Jodies, Harry Hoots

(3m) *Dean's Hill, College Hill, Armagh, BT61 9DF.*
Tel: 01861 524923 Mrs Armstrong.
Rates fr: *£22.00-£16.00.*
Open: All Year
Beds: 1D 1T 1S
Baths: 2 Ensuite 1 Shared
🛏 🅿 🖵 🟊 📠 Ⓥ

Moy 42

National Grid Ref: H8556

(On Path) *Tomneys Licensed Guest Inn, 9-10 The Square, Moy, Dungannon, Co Tyrone, BT71 7SG.*
Traditional Irish inn in Georgian Square. Irish traditional music home.
Tel: 01868 784895
Mrs McNeice.
Rates fr: *£15.00-£18.00.*
Open: All Year
Beds: 1F 1D 1S
🛏 🅿 (3) ✓ 🖵 🟊 ✗ 📠 Ⓥ

Ardress West 43

National Grid Ref: H9055

(3m) *125 Summerisland Road, Ardress West, Portadown, Craigavon, Co Armagh, BT62 1SJ.*
Modern home in lovely rural countryside in the Apple County Armagh.
Tel: 01762 851437
Mrs Neville.
Rates fr: *£12.50-£12.50.*
Open: All Year
Beds: 1D 1T
Baths: 1 Shared
🅿 🖵 ✗ 📠 🛉

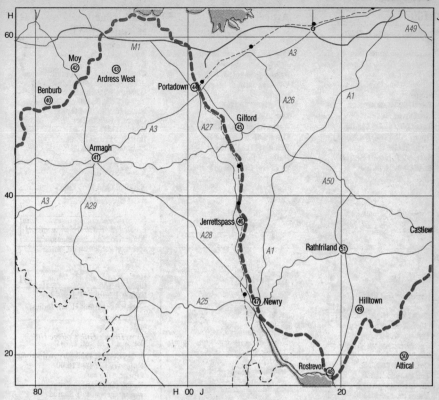

Portadown   44

National Grid Ref: J0053

(On Path 🚧) *Bannview Squash Club, 60 Portmore Street, Portadown, Craigavon, County Armagh,* BT62 3NF.
Luxury ensuite bedroom accommodation. **Grades:** NITB Listed
Tel: **01762 33 6666** Mr Black.
Rates fr: *£19.00-£24.00.*
Open: All Year (not Xmas)
Beds: 10T **Baths:** 10 Ensuite
🛇 🅿 (17) 🗂 ✕ 🎇 V 🔒 ✦

(0.25m) *Redbrick Country House, Corbracky Lane, Portadown, Craigavon, County Armagh,* BT62 1PQ.
Modern luxury house. Rural setting. Tel: **01762 335268** Mrs Stephenson.
Rates fr: *£15.00-£15.00.*
Open: All Year (not Xmas)
Beds: 3D 3T 1S
Baths: 4 Private 2 Shared
🅿 (14) 🗂 ✕ 🎇 V

Gilford   45

National Grid Ref: J0648

(2m) *Mount Pleasant, 38 Banbridge Road, Gilford, Craigavon, Co Armagh,* BT63 6DJ.

Approved country house in beautiful countryside central for touring Northern Ireland.
Grades: NITB Approv
Tel: **01762 831522** Mrs Buller.
Rates fr: *£12.50-£14.00.*
Open: All Year
Beds: 1F 2D 1T 1S
Baths: 2 Shared
🛇 🅿 (10) ✦ 🗂 🏡 🎇

Jerrettspass   46

National Grid Ref: J0534

🍴 🍺 Brass Monkey

(0.25m) *Deerpark, 177 Tandragee Rd, Drumbanagher, Jerrettspass, Newry, Co Down,* BT35 6LP.
C17th stone built farmhouse in beautiful countryside.
Tel: **01693 821409** Mrs Thompson.
Rates fr: *£15.00-£15.00.*
Open: All Year (not Xmas)
Beds: 1F 1D 1S
Baths: 1 Ensuite 2 Private
🛇 🅿 ✦ 🗂 🎇

Newry   47

National Grid Ref: J0828

(On Path) *Drumconrath, 28 Ballymacdermot Road, Newry, Co Down,* BT35 8AZ.

Modern, centrally heated home in scenic area, good home cooking.
Grades: NITB Approv
Tel: **01693 63508**
Mrs Magennis.
Rates fr: *£15.00-£15.00.*
Open: All Year
Beds: 2F 1D
Baths: 2 Shared
🛇 🅿 (10) 🗂 🏡 ✕ 🎇 V

Rostrevor   48

National Grid Ref: J1818

🍴 🍺 Top of the Town

(0.5m) *Forestbrook House, 11 Forestbrook Road, Rostrevor, Newry, County Down,* BT34 3BT.
Listed C18th house in Fairy Glen.
Grades: NITB Approv
Tel: **016937 38105** Mrs Henshaw.
Rates fr: *£15.00-£16.00.*
Open: All Year (not Xmas)
Beds: 1F 3D 1T
Baths: 2 Shared
🛇 🅿 🗂 🏡 ✕ 🎇 🔒 ✦

The *lowest* **single**
rate *is shown in* **bold.**

Hilltown 49

National Grid Ref: J2226

(0.5m) *Mountain Pass, 49
Sandbank Road, Hilltown, Newry,
Co Down, BT34 5XX.*
Modern bungalow, gateway to
Mournes.
Tel: **018206 38002**
Mrs Devlin.
Rates fr: £15.00-£15.00.
Open: All Year (not Xmas)
Beds: 2D 2T
Baths: 2 Private 1 Shared
ॐ ▣ ◻ ☆ ✕ ▥ ▮ ∥

Attical 50

National Grid Ref: J2819

(5m ☎) *Hillview, 18 Bog Road,
Attical, Newry, Co Down, BT34 4HT.*
Actual grid ref: J283201
Working farm in Mourne moun-
tains.
Tel: **016937 64269**
Mrs Trainor.
Rates fr: £12.50-£15.50.
Open: All Year (not Xmas)
Beds: 1F 1D 1T 1S
Baths: 3 Private
ॐ ▣ (16) ◻ ✕ ▥ ▯ ▮ ∥

Rathfriland 51

National Grid Ref: J1933

(3m) *Rathglen Villa, 7 Hilltown
Road, Rathfriland, Newry,
Co Down, BT34 5EN.*
Country house. Panoramic views
of the Mourne Mountains..
Grades: ETB Grade A
Tel: **018206 38090** Mrs Magine.
Rates fr: £15.00-£16.00.
Open: Easter to Oct
Beds: 1F 1D 2T
Baths: 1 Ensuite 1 Shared
ॐ ▣ (10) ◻ ✕ ▥ ▯

Castlewellan 52

National Grid Ref: J3435

†❍† ⊌ Chestnut Inn

(1.5m) *Treetops, 39 Circular Road,
Castlewellan, Co Down, BT31 9ED.*
Attractive modern bungalow in
spacious gardens with ample
parking facilities..
Tel: **013967 78132** Mrs King.
Rates fr: £13.00-£17.00.
Open: All Year **Beds:** 1F 1D 3T
Baths: 1 Ensuite 1 Shared
ॐ ▣ ◻ ☆ ▥ ⅋ ▯

Newcastle 53

National Grid Ref: J3731

†❍† ⊌ Pavilion, Donard Hotel,
Percy French

(▲ On Path) *Newcastle Youth
Hostel, 30 Downs Road,
Newcastle, Co Down, BT33 0AG.*
Actual grid ref: J379315
Warden: Mrs Spiers.
Tel: **013967 22133**
Under 18: £5.50
Adults: £6.50
Family Rooms, Shower, Self-
Catering
*Converted 3-storey town-house,
looking directly out onto the beach
and sea*

(1m ☎) *Beverley, 72 Tollymore
Road, Newcastle, County Down,
BT33 0JN.*
Actual grid ref: J366329
Other self catering cottages avail-
able.
Grades: NITB Listed
Tel: **013967 22018**
Mrs McNeilly.
Rates fr: £17.50-£22.00.
Open: All Year (not Xmas)
Beds: 1D **Baths:** 1 Ensuite
ॐ ▣ ◻ ☆ ✕ ▥ ▮ ∥

(1m) *Homeleigh, 7 Slievemoyne
Park, Newcastle, County Down,
BT33 0JD.*
Central heating, electric blankets.
Tel: **013967 22305** Mrs McBride.
Rates fr: £12.00-£13.00.
Open: All Year (not Xmas)
Beds: 1F 1D 1S **Baths:** 1 Shared
ॐ (4) ▣ (2) ⅋ ◻ ▥

(On Path) *Ashmount,*
19 Bryansford Road, Newcastle,
County Down, BT33 0HJ.
TV and tea-making facilities in
rooms.
Tel: **013967 25074**
Mr & Mrs Biggerstaff.
Rates fr: *£12.50-£15.00.*
Open: All Year (not Xmas)
Beds: 3D
ㅂ ₽ (3) ☐ ⅋ ⅋ ⅏ 🕮 Ⓥ 🖩 ⅋

(On Path) *Brook Cottage Hotel,*
58 Bryansford Road, Newcastle,
County Down, BT33 0LD.
Actual grid ref: J372313
Historical building in own grounds.
Grades: NITB 1 CrRAC Acclaim
Tel: **013967 22204**
Rates fr: *£30.00-£40.00.*
Open: All Year (not Xmas)
Beds: 7F 1T 1S
Baths: 7 Ensuite 1 Shared
ㅂ ₽ (40) ☐ ✕ 🕮 Ⓥ 🖩 ⅋

(On Path) *Harbour House Inn,*
4 South Promenade, Kilkeel Road,
Newcastle, County Down, BT33 0EX.
Actual grid ref: J380298
Situated on seawall beside harbour.
Grades: NITB B Grade
Tel: **013967 23445**
Rates fr: *£17.00-£25.00.*
Open: All Year
Beds: 1F 3D **Baths:** 4 Ensuite
ㅂ ₽ ⅋ ☐ ✕ 🕮 🖩

Ardglass 54

National Grid Ref: J5637

(On Path 🚍**)** *Strand Farm,*
231 Ardglass Road, Ardglass,
Downpatrick, County Down,
BT30 7UL.
Modernised old farmhouse (work-
ing farm).
Tel: **01396 841446** Mrs Donnan.
Rates fr: *£13.00.*
Open: Mar to Oct
Beds: 1F 1T **Baths:** 1 Shared
ㅂ ₽ (12) ☐ ✕ 🖩 ⅋

Portaferry 55

National Grid Ref: J5950

🍴 🍺 Portaferry Hotel

(0.5m by Ferry) *22 The Square,*
Portaferry, Co Down, BT22 1LW.
Comfortable town house.
Tel: **012477 28412** Mrs Adair.
Rates fr: *£14.00-£26.00.*
Open: All Year (not Xmas)
Beds: 1F 1D 1S
Baths: 1 Ensuite, 1 Shared
ㅂ ☐ 🕮 🖩 ⅋

(▲0.5m by Ferrym) *Portaferry*
Youth Hostel, Barholm, 11 The
Strand, Portaferry, Co Down,
BT22 1PS.
Warden: Mr Poots.
Tel: **012477 29598**
Under 18: £6.75 **Adults:** £8.95
Family Rooms, Double Rooms,
Single Rooms, Linen Service,

Evening Meal, Self-Catering
Facilities, Showers, Television
Room
Large Victorian house (former
Hall of Residence) with walled gar-
den backing onto the Castle, direct-
ly opposite the ferry terminal, with
the best views across the Straits in
Portaferry!

Downpatrick 56

National Grid Ref: J4844

(1m) *Abbey Lodge Hotel,*
38 Belfast Road, Downpatrick,
County Down, BT30 9AV.
Grades: NITB Grade A, AA 2 St,
RAC 2 St
Tel: **01396 614511**
Miss Mulvenna
Rates fr: *£30.00-£44.00.*
Open: All Year (not Xmas)
Beds: 1D 20T 1S
Baths: 22 Ensuite
ㅂ ₽ ☐ ✕ 🕮 Ⓥ 🖩 ⅋

Ballintogher 57

National Grid Ref: J5147

(0.5m) *Hillcrest, 157 Strangford*
Road, Ballintogher, Downpatrick,
Co Down, BT30 7JZ.
Family-run farmhouse in the heart
of Down. Overlooking Strangford
Lough.
Grades: NITB Approv
Tel: **01396 612583**
Mrs Fitzsimons.
Rates fr: *£14.00-£16.00.*
Open: All Year (not Xmas)
Beds: 2D 1T
Baths: 1 Ensuite 1 Shared
ㅂ ₽ (6) ☐ ✕ 🕮

Whiterock 58

National Grid Ref: J5261

(0.25m) *Tides Reach,*
107 Whiterock Road, Whiterock,
Killinchy, Newtownards, Co Down,
BT23 6PU.
On shores of Stranford Lough in
area of outstanding beauty.
Grades: NITB Approv
Tel: **01238 541347**
Mrs Booth.
Rates fr: *£19.00-£20.00.*
Open: All Year
Beds: 1D 2T
Baths: 2 Ensuite 1 Private
ㅂ ₽ (5) ☐ ✕ 🕮 Ⓥ 🖩 ⅋

Ardmillan 59

National Grid Ref: J5062

(On Path) *Barnageeha, 90*
Ardmillan Road, Ardmillan,
Killinchy, Newtownards, County
Down, BT23 6QN.
Actual grid ref: J509629
Peaceful Lough-shore farm, award-
winning food.
Tel: **01238 541011**
Mr & Mrs Crawford.
Rates fr: *£20.00-£20.00.*

Open: All Year (not Xmas)
Beds: 3D
Baths: 3 Private
₽ ☐ ⅋ ✕ 🕮 Ⓥ 🖩 ⅋

Comber 60

National Grid Ref: J4568

🍴 🍺 TT Lounge

(1.25m) *Flax Mill House, 117*
Glen Road, Comber, Newtownards,
County Down, BT23 5QT.
Tel: **01247 873253** Mrs McEntee.
Rates fr: *£17.00-£17.00.*
Open: All Year (not Xmas)
Beds: 1D 1T **Baths:** 1 Shared
ㅂ ₽ ⅋ ☐ 🕮

Newtownards 61

National Grid Ref: J4874

🍴 🍺 Ballyharry Road House,
Roma Hamill, Strangford Arms
Hotel

(4m 🚍**)** *Beechill Farm,*
10 Loughries Road, Newtownards,
County Down, BT23 3RN.
Modern farmhouse with central
heating.
Tel: **01247 818404** Mrs McKee.
Rates fr: *£14.50-£14.50.*
Open: All Year (not Xmas)
Beds: 1F 1D 1S **Baths:** 2 Shared
ㅂ ₽ (15) ☐ ⅋ ✕ 🕮 Ⓥ 🖩 ⅋

(1m 🚍**)** *Ard Cuan, 3 Manse Road,*
Newtownards, County Down,
BT23 4TP.
Victorian home in 1-acre garden.
Grades: NITB Approv
Tel: **01247 811302** Mrs Kerr.
Rates fr: *£15.00-£15.00.*
Open: All Year (not Xmas)
Beds: 1F 1T **Baths:** 1 Shared
₽ ☐ 🕮 🖩 ⅋

Helens Bay 62

National Grid Ref: J4582

(0.5m) *Carrig Gorm, 27 Bridge*
Road, Helens Bay, Bangor, County
Down, BT19 1TS.
Old country house.
Tel: **01247 853680** Mrs Eves.
Rates fr: *£20.00-£25.00.*
Open: All Year (not Xmas)
Beds: 1F 1T **Baths:** 2 Private
₽ ☐ 🕮 🖩 ⅋

Dunmurry 63

National Grid Ref: J2968

🍴 🍺 Balmoral Hotel

(0.5m) *Manor House, 12 The*
Manor, Blacks Road, Dunmurry,
Belfast, BT10 0PD.
Modern detached villa.
Tel: **01232 600807** Mrs Tully.
Rates fr: *£17.50-£15.00.*
Open: All Year (not Xmas)
Beds: 1D 1S **Baths:** 1 Private
ㅂ (16) ₽ ⅋ ☐ 🕮 🖩 ⅋

Vanguard Way

A relaxing walk, ideal for Londoners wanting to finish a path over a couple of weekends. The 62-mile **Vanguard Way** leaves the skyscrapers of Croydon behind in a matter of minutes, heading off for the North Downs escarpment and then the Greensand Ridge. You then cross the Weald, with its low pastures, to the edge of Ashdown Forest, before heading off to Cuckmere Haven, with its majestic view of the Seven Sisters cliffs rearing beyond. The **Vanguard Way** links the **North Downs Way**, the **Greensand Way** and the **South Downs Way**. There are excellent rail connections.

Guides: *The Vanguard Way*, published by the Vanguards Rambling Club and available directly from them (109 Selsdon Park Road, South Croydon, Surrey, CR2 8JJ), £1.35
The Wealdway and the Vanguard Way by Kev Reynolds (ISBN 0 9 023 63859), published by Cicerone Press and available from all good map shops or directly from the publishers (2 Police Square, Milnthorpe, Cumbria, LA7 7PY, 01539 562069), £4.99 (+ 75p p&p)

Maps: Ordnance Survey 1:50,000 Landranger series: 177, 187, 188, 199

Oxted 1

National Grid Ref: TQ3852

|●| ◀ The Old Bell, The Crown, George Inn, The Royal Oak, Staffhurst Wood

(1m) Pinehurst Grange Guest House, *East Hill (Part of A25), Oxted, Surrey, RH8 9AE.*
Actual grid ref: TQ393525
Comfortable, homely, refurbished, Victorian ex-farmhouse.
Tel: **01883 716413** Mr Rodgers.
Rates fr: *£19.50-£24.00.*
Open: All Year (not Xmas/New Year)
Beds: 1D 1T 1S
Baths: 1 Shared
🛏 (5) 🅿 (3) ⌧ ▭ ▥ 🖤 ⚡

Pay B&Bs by cash or cheque and be prepared to pay up front.

(1m 🚍) Rosehaven, *12 Hoskins Road, Oxted, Surrey, RH8 9HT.*
Actual grid ref: TQ3952
Comfortable house, quiet residential road.
Tel: **01883 712700** Mrs Snell.
Rates fr: *£18.00-£18.00.*
Open: All Year (not Xmas)
Beds: 2T 1S **Baths:** 1 Shared
🛏 🅿 (1) ⌧ ▭ ▥ 🖤 ⚡

(2m 🚍) The Croft, *Quarry Road, Oxted, Surrey, RH8 9HE.*
Actual grid ref: TQ393521
Substantial Edwardian house. Peaceful location.
Tel: **01883 713605** Mrs Todd.
Rates fr: *£17.50-£19.00.*
Open: All Year (not Xmas)
Beds: 1F 1T 1S **Baths:** 1 Shared
🛏 (5) 🅿 (8) ⌧ ▭ ▥ ⚡

(1.5m 🚍) Old Forge House, *Merle Common, Oxted, Surrey, RH8 0JB.*
Actual grid ref: TQ416493
Comfortable home in rural surroundings.
Grades: ETB Reg
Tel: **01883 715969** Mrs Mills.
Rates fr: *£17.00-£18.00.*
Open: All Year (not Xmas)
Beds: 1D 1T 1S **Baths:** 1 Shared
🛏 🅿 (3) ▭ 🍴 ▥ 🖤 ⚡

Westerham 2

National Grid Ref: TQ4454

|●| ◀ Fox & Hounds

(On Path) Corner Cottage, *Toys Hill, Westerham, Kent, TN16 1PY.*
Actual grid ref: TQ4651
Spectacular views, extremely comfortable, self-contained.
Tel: **01732 750362**
Mrs Olszowska.
Rates fr: *£18.50-£25.00.*
Open: All Year
Beds: 1F **Baths:** 1 Ensuite
🛏 🅿 (1) ⌧ ▭ ▥

Edenbridge 3

National Grid Ref: TQ4446

|●| ◀ Four Elms Public House

(0.75m) Knowlands, Five Fields Lane, *Four Elms, Edenbridge, Kent, TN8 6NA.*
Actual grid ref: TQ469478
Large Edwardian private house.
Grades: AA 3 Q
Tel: **01732 700314**
Mr & Mrs Haviland.
Rates fr: *£25.00-£35.00.*
Open: All Year (not Xmas)
Beds: 2D 1S
Baths: 1 Shared
🅿 (3) ⌧ ▭ ⌧ ▥ 🖤 ⚡

The Country Code

Enjoy the countryside and respect its life and work

Guard against all risk of fire

Fasten all gates

Keep your dogs under close control

Keep to public paths across farmland

Use gates and stiles to cross fences, hedges and walls

Leave livestock, crops and machinery alone

Take your litter home

Help to keep all water clean

Protect wild-life, plants and trees

Take special care on country roads

Make no unnecessary noise

Colemans Hatch 4

National Grid Ref: TQ4533

⚑ ◗ The Haywagon Inn

(On Path 🐾) **Gospel Oak,** *Sandy Lane, Colemans Hatch, Hartfield, E. Sussex, TN7 4ER.*
Actual grid ref: TQ447325
Converted C17th crofters cottage.
Grades: ETB Listed
Tel: 01342 823840 Mrs Hawker.
Rates fr: *£17.00-£18.00.*
Open: All Year

Beds: 1D 1T
Baths: 1 Ensuite 1 Shared
🛏 🅿 (5) 🍴✗ 🖳 Ⓥ 🛆 ✦

High Hurstwood 5

National Grid Ref: TQ4926

⚑ ◗ Crow & Gate Pub,

(0.75m) **Chillies Granary,** *High Hurstwood, Crowborough, E. Sussex, TN6 3TB.*
Actual grid ref: TQ497278

Converted granary, warm and cheerful!
Tel: 01892 655560
Mr & Mrs Peck.
Rates fr: *£15.00-£20.00.*
Open: Mar to Dec
Beds: 1F 1D 1T
Baths: 2 Shared
🛏 🅿 (6) 🍴✗ 🖳 🛆 ✦

(0.75m) **Old Mill Farm,** *High Hurstwood, Uckfield, E. Sussex, TN22 4AD.*
Converted Sussex barn, picturesque setting.
Grades: ETB 2 Cr
Tel: 01825 732279
Mrs Sharpe.
Rates fr: *£17.00-£17.00.*
Open: All Year
Beds: 1F 2T
Baths: 3 Private
🛏 🅿 (6) 🍴✗ 🖵 🐾 ✗ 🖳 Ⓥ

Blackboys 6

National Grid Ref: TQ5221

(⛺ 0.75m) **Blackboys Youth Hostel,** *Blackboys, Uckfield, East Sussex, TN22 5HU.*
Actual grid ref: TQ521215
Tel: 01825 890607
Under 18: £4.60
Adults: £6.75
Self Catering, Camping, No Smoking, Grounds Available for Games, Parking
This rustic wooden cabin in a deciduous sylvan setting offers good basic accomodation with a cosy open fire, spacious lounge/dining room, kitchen

Halland 7

National Grid Ref: TQ5016

⚑ ◗ Black Lion

(1.75m) **Black Lion,** *Lewes Road, Halland, Lewes, E. Sussex, BN8 6PN.*
Tel: 01825 840304
Mrs Sumers.
Rates fr: *£15.00-£19.50.*
Open: All Year
Beds: 1F 2D 1T 2S
Baths: 4 Ensuite 2 Shared
🛏 🅿 (40) 🖵 🐾 ✗ 🖳 ♿

Gun Hill 8

National Grid Ref: TQ5614

(1m) **The Gun,** *Gun Hill, Horam, Heathfield, E. Sussex, TN21 0JU.*
Actual grid ref: TQ543143
Idyllic C16th inn, excellent food.
Tel: 01825 872361
Mr & Mrs Brockway.
Rates fr: *£16.00-£26.00.*
Open: All Year (not Xmas)
Beds: 1F 1D 1T
Baths: 1 Ensuite 1 Shared
🛏 🅿 (60) 🍴✗ 🖵 🐾 ✗ 🖳 Ⓥ ✦

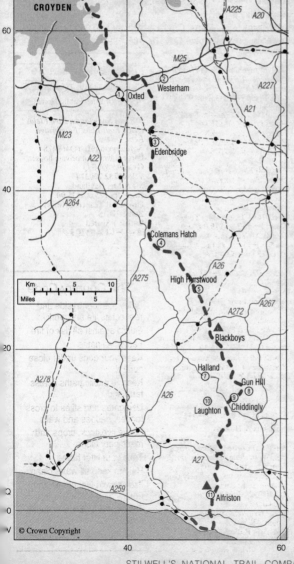

(1m 🚌) *Pedlars Cottage, Gun
Hill, Horam, Heathfield, E. Sussex,
TN21 0JS.*
Actual grid ref: TQ567149
C18th country cottage.
Tel: **01825 873107** Mrs Winter.
Rates fr: *£15.50-***£15.50**.
Open: Easter to Oct
Beds: 2D
Baths: 1 Shared
🛏 🅿 🍴 🗄 ✕

Chiddingly   9

National Grid Ref: TQ5414

🍴 🍺 Golden Cross Inn

(On Path) *Holmes Hill, (off
Holmes Hill), Chiddingly, Lewes,
E. Sussex, BN8 6JA.*
Actual grid ref: TQ533127
Sussex-style cottage.
Tel: **01825 872746** Mr & Mrs
Farrier.
Rates fr: *£17.50-***£17.50**.
Open: All Year (not Xmas)
Beds: 2D 1S
Baths: 1 Shared
🛏 🅿 (2) 🗄 🗄 🍺 ⟋

Laughton   10

National Grid Ref: TQ5013

🍴 🍺 The Gun

(1m) *Holly Cottage, Lewes Road,
Laughton, Lewes, E. Sussex,
BN8 6BL.*
Actual grid ref: TQ503131
Country cottage with modern facil-
ities.
Tel: **01323 811309** Mrs Clarke.
Rates fr: *£17.50-***£20.00**.
Open: All Year (not Xmas)
Beds: 1F 1T **Baths:** 2 Ensuite
🛏 🅿 (4) 🗄 🍺 🗄 🚿 🛁

Alfriston   11

National Grid Ref: TQ5103

🍴 🍺 George, Smugglers, Market
Cross, Star, Sussex Ox,
Moonrakers

(▲ 1m) *Alfriston Youth Hostel,
Frog Firle, Alfriston, Polegate, E.
Sussex, BN26 5TT.*
Actual grid ref: TQ518019
Warden: Ms W Nicholls.

Tel: **01323 870423**
Under 18: £5.55 **Adults:** £8.25
Family Bunk Rooms, Centrally
Heated, Showers, Evening Meal
(6.30 pm), Shop, Television
*A comfortable Sussex country
house, dating from 1530, set in the
Cuckmere Valley with views over
the river and Litlington*

(1m) *Pleasant Rise Farm,
Alfriston, Polegate, E. Sussex,
BN26 5TN.*
Very quiet, beautiful house - lovely
views.
Grades: ETB Listed
Tel: **01323 870545** Mrs Savage.
Rates fr: *£16.50-***£16.50**.
Open: All Year (not Xmas)
Beds: 2D 1T 1S
Baths: 2 Private
🅿 🗄 🗄 🍺 Ⓥ

The *lowest* **single**
rate *is shown in* **bold.**

STILWELL'S IRELAND: BED & BREAKFAST 1996

Now that serious steps have been taken towards peace in Northern Ireland, more and more people have been making their way to this great island, steeped in history, full of wild and beautiful countryside. Getting over to Ireland has never been cheaper in real terms. Some of the fly/drive deals offered by the airlines are not to be missed. And what better way to travel the island, seeing the sights, than staying in bed & breakfast accommodation. Irish hospitality is renowned throughout the world and the B&B is the best place to find it.

If you like Stilwell's Britain: Bed & Breakfast, then our Irish book will suit you down to the ground, too. It is arranged in exactly the same way. Listed in county order, with county maps at the head of each chapter, it's the most practical B&B book on Ireland that there is, with a massive 1,500 entries, North and South. All the entries listed charge no more than £25 (punt or sterling) per person per night (the average is £16 per person per night in a double room). All official grades or notices of Tourist Board approval are shown.

Stilwell's Ireland: Bed & Breakfast 1996
is available from all good bookshops
(ISBN No 0-9521909-5-8) or direct from Stilwell Publishing Ltd
(see order form) @ £6.95 (inc £1 p&p - UK only).

Viking Way

The **Viking Way** runs for 140 miles through a quiet, sparsely populated area of Eastern England that stretches from the Humber down to the Fens - the heart of the historic 'Danelaw' area, once ruled by Scandinavian kings. Beginning in Barton-upon-Humber, the path follows the scarp of the Lincolnshire Wolds, then along the River Witham to the cathedral city of Lincoln, before cutting south along the Lincoln 'Cliff' to head along the Roman Ermine Street, skirting Grantham and finishing in pretty Oakham alongside Rutland Water. It is easy going and makes for an excellent introduction to long distance walking, linking with the **Wolds Way** (q.v.) via the Humber Bridge and with the **Hereward Way** at Oakham in Rutland.

Guide: *The Viking Way* by John Stead (ISBN 185 284 057 9), published by Cicerone Press and available from all good map shops or directly from the publishers (2 Police Square, Milnthorpe, Cumbria, LA7 7PY, 01539 562069), £5.99 (+75p p&p).

The Viking Way, published by Lincolnshire County Council and available from their offices (Recreational Services Dept, County Offices, Newland, Lincoln, LN1 1YL, 01522 552222), £1.50

A useful alternative route to the river walk between Bardney and Lincoln can be had for 30p (plus a stamped, addressed envelope) from the indefatigable Lincolnshire walker **Brett Collier** at Chloris House, 208 Nettleham Road, Lincoln, LN2 4DH.

Maps: 1:50000 Ordnance Survey Landranger Series: 112, 113, 121, 130 and 141.

Barton-upon-Humber 1

National Grid Ref: TA0322

|O| ⌨ Thornton Hunt, Wheatsheaf

(1m) *Southgarth Guest House*, 2 Caistor Road, Barton-upon-Humber, *DN18 5AH*.
Originally a gatekeepers lodge.
Tel: **01652 632833** Mrs Havercroft.
Rates fr: *£14.00-£16.00*.
Open: All Year (not Xmas)
Beds: 3T
Baths: 2 Shared
> (5) 🅿 (5) ❐ ⅙ ✕ Ⅲ. Ⅵ ᐃ

Deepdale 2

National Grid Ref: TA0418

|O| ⌨ Wheatsheaf, The Old Mill

(1.5m 🚐) *West Wold Farmhouse*, Deepdale, Barton-upon-Humber, S Humberside, *DN18 6ED*.
8 Friendly comfortable farmhouse, home-cooking.
Tel: **01652 633293**
Mrs Atkin.
Rates fr: *£16.00-£16.00*.
Open: All Year
Beds: 1D 1T
Baths: 1 Private 1 Shared
> (5) 🅿 (5) ⅙ ❐ ⅙ ✕ Ⅲ. Ⅵ ᐃ ✦

Barnetby 3

National Grid Ref: TA0509

(On Path) *Holcombe Guest House*, 34 Victoria Road, Barnetby, S Humberside, *DN38 6JR*.
Very comfortable, modern, guest-house.
Grades: ETB 3 Cr, Comm
Tel: **01850 764002** Ms Vera.
Rates fr: *£15.00-£17.50*.
Open: All Year
Beds: 4T 4S
Baths: 3 Private 2 Shared
> 🅿 (7) ❐ ✕ Ⅲ. ᐃ Ⅵ ᐃ ✦

Caistor 4

National Grid Ref: TA1101

(On Path) *The White Guest House*, Market Place, Caistor, Lincs, *LN7 6TR*.
Old Victorian town house.
Tel: **01472 851459** Mrs Wilkin.
Rates fr: *£15.00-£15.00*.
Open: All Year (not Xmas)
Beds: 3D 1S **Baths:** 1 Shared
> 🅿 ❐ ✕ ᐃ ✦

Market Rasen 5

National Grid Ref: TF1089

|O| ⌨ The Chase, The Gordon

(2.5m 🚐) *The Waveney Guest House*, Willingham Road, Market Rasen, Lincs, *LN8 3DN*.
Tudor-style cottage in attractive gardens.
Grades: ETB 2 Cr, Comm
Tel: **01673 843236** Mrs Dawson-Margrave.
Rates fr: *£15.00-£17.00*.
Open: All Year
Beds: 1F 2T
Baths: 3 Ensuite
> 🅿 (6) ⅙ ❐ ⅙ ✕ Ⅲ. Ⅵ ᐃ ✦

White Swan Hotel

(1m 🚐) *White Swan Hotel*, Queen Street, Market Rasen, Lincs, *LN8 3*.
Main street, market town, inn.
Tel: **01673 843356**
Rates fr: *£12.50-£15.00*.
Open: All Year
Beds: 1F 1D 1T 2S
Baths: 1 Shared
> 🅿 ❐ ✕ Ⅲ. Ⅵ ᐃ ✦

Ludford 6

National Grid Ref: TF1989

(On Path) *The White Hart*, Ludford, Lincoln, Lincs, *LN3 6*.
Actual grid ref: TF1989
18th Century coaching inn.
Tel: **01507 313489**
Mrs Johnson.
Rates fr: *£15.00-£18.00*.
Open: All Year
Beds: 1D 3T
Baths: 4 Ensuite
> 🅿 (30) ❐ ⅙ ✕ Ⅲ. Ⅵ ᐃ ✦

Hainton 7

National Grid Ref: TF1884

(3m 🚐) *The Old Vicarage*, Hainton, Burgh-on-Bain, Lincoln, Lincs, *LN3 6LW*.
Peaceful C19th house in charming gardens.
Grades: AA 3 Q, Recomm
Tel: **01507 313660** Mrs Ashton.
Rates fr: *£15.00-£15.00*.
Open: All Year
Beds: 2T 1D
Baths: 2 Shared
> (12) 🅿 (6) ⅙ ❐ ✕ Ⅲ. Ⅵ ᐃ ✦

Donington-on-Bain 8

National Grid Ref: TF2382

(On Path) *The Black Horse,*
Donington-on-Bain, Louth, Lincs,
LN11 9TJ.
18th Century inn and motel.
Tel: **01507 343640** Mrs Pacey.
Rates fr: *£20.00-***£25.00**.
Open: All Year (not Xmas)
Beds: 1D 8T **Baths:** 8 Ensuite
🛏 🅿 (100) ½ 🗙 ⚒ 🗙 🎦 🖳 ⚕ 🗓 🛎
Also 🅰 🐾

The *lowest* **single**
rate *is shown in* **bold.**

Benniworth 9

National Grid Ref: TF2081

🍴 🍺 Black Horse

(1.5m 🚐) *Skirbeck Farm,*
Benniworth, Lincoln, Lincs, LN3 6JN.
Secluded farmhouse, gardens, fish-
ing lakes.
Grades: ETB 2 Cr
Tel: **01507 313682**
Mrs Olivant.
Rates fr: *£16.00-***£17.50**.
Open: Easter to Nov
Beds: 1F 1T
Baths: 1 Private 1 Shared
🛏 🅿 (10) ½ 🗙 🖳 🎦 🛎 ⚕

Scamblesby 10

National Grid Ref: TF2778

(On Path) *Old Vicarage,*
Scamblesby, Louth, Lincs, LN11 9XL.
Victorian vicarage in secluded
grounds.
Tel: **01507 343790** Mrs Duncumb.
Rates fr: *£13.00-***£18.00**.
Open: All Year
Beds: 1F 1D 1T
Baths: 3 Private
🛏 🅿 (6) 🎦

Horncastle 11

National Grid Ref: TF2669

🍴 🍺 Fighting Cocks

(0.25m) *The Admiral Rodney*
Hotel, North Street, Horncastle,
Lincs, LN9 5DX.
Actual grid ref: TF2669
Central location.
Grades: ETB 4 Cr, Comm,
AA 2 St
Tel: **01507 523131** Mrs Young.
Rates fr: *£24.00-***£35.50**.
Open: All Year
Beds: 3F 16D 12T
Baths: 31 Ensuite
🛏 🅿 (70) 🎦 🗙 ⚒ 🖳 🎦 🛎 ⚕

(0.25m) *Fighting Cocks, West*
Street, Horncastle, Lincs, LN9 5JF.
Traditional C17th inn.
Tel: **01507 527307**
Mr Butler.
Rates fr: *£17.50-***£17.50**.
Open: All Year (not Xmas)
Beds: 2F 1T
Baths: 1 Shared
🛏 🅿 🎦 🗙 🖳 🎦 🛎 ⚕

(0.25m) *Red Lion Hotel, 1 The*
Bull Ring, Horncastle, Lincs,
LN9 5HT.
Old coaching inn.
Tel: **01507 523338**
Mrs Benson.
Rates fr: *£17.00-***£17.00**.
Open: Apr to Dec
Beds: 1F 1D 2T 1S
Baths: 1 Shared
🛏 🅿 (8) 🎦 🖳 🎦 🛎

Woodhall Spa 12

National Grid Ref: TF1963

🍴 🍺 The Mall, Broadway, Dower
House Hotel

(On Path 🚐) *Claremont Guest*
House, 9-11 Witham Road,
Woodhall Spa, Lincs, LN10 6RW.
Homely, traditional Victorian
guesthouse.
Grades: ETB 2 Cr, AA 2 Q
Tel: **01526 352000**
Mr & Mrs Brennan.
Rates fr: *£15.00-***£13.50**.
Open: All Year
Beds: 1F 3D 2T 2S
Baths: 2 Private 2 Shared
🛏 🅿 (3) 🎦 🛎 ⚕

Barton upon Humber
① A1077
② Deepdale
A15
M180
③ Barnetby
A1084
A11
SE TA
SK TF
Caistor ④ A46
A18
© Crown Copyright
Km 5 10
Miles 5
A631
⑤ Market Rasen
⑥ Ludford
A157
A46
Hainton ⑦
⑧ Donington on Bain
⑨ Benniworth
Scamblesby ⑩
A158
▲ ⑮ Lincoln
Bardney
⑭
⑬ Southrey
Horncastle ⑪
A15
⑫ Woodhall Spa
SK 00 TF
20

(0.25m 🚌) *Pitchaway Guest House, The Broadway, Woodhall Spa, Lincs, LN10 6SQ.*
A friendly, family-run guesthouse.
Grades: ETB 2 Cr, AA 2 Q, Recomm
Tel: **01526 352969** Miss Leggate.
Rates fr: *£15.00*-**£15.00**.
Open: All Year
Beds: 2F 2D 2T 2S
Baths: 2 Private
🛇 (1) 🅿 (10) 🖵 🏠 ✕ 🎐 Ⓥ ⚡

(On Path) *The Golf Hotel, The Broadway, Woodhall Spa, Lincs, LN10 6.*

Tudor-style hotel set in 7-acre gardens.
Grades: ETB 4 Cr, AA 3 St
Tel: **01526 353535** Miss Marshall.
Rates fr: *£37.50*-**£47.50**.
Open: All Year
Beds: 16D 28T 6S
Baths: 50 Ensuite
🛇 🅿 (100) 🖵 🏠 ✕ 🎐 Ⓥ ⚡

The lowest *double* rate per person is shown in *italics*.

Southrey   13

National Grid Ref: TF1366

(0.25m 🚌) *Riverside Inn, Ferry Road, Southrey, Lincoln, Lincs, LN3 5TA.*
Actual grid ref: TF1366
Peaceful country inn by river.
Tel: **01526 398374** Mrs Walley.
Rates fr: *£15.00*-**£18.00**.
Open: All Year
Beds: 1F
Baths: 1 Shared
🛇 🅿 (10) 🖵 🏠 ✕ 🎐 Ⓥ ⚡
Also ⛺ *£3 per tent.,*
Open: All Year ✕ 🛇

Bardney   14

National Grid Ref: TF1169

🍴 🚂 Railway

(On Path) *Railway Inn, Station Road, Bardney, Lincoln, Lincs, LN3 5UF.*
Riverside pub.
Tel: **01526 398313**
Rates fr: *£12.50*-**£12.50**.
Open: All Year (not Xmas)
Beds: 2D 1S
Baths: 1 Shared
🛇 🅿 🖵 ✕ Ⓥ ⚡

Lincoln   15

National Grid Ref: SK9771

🍴 🚂 Lord Tennyson Inn, Ye Olde Crown

(1m) *Mayfield Guest House, 213 Yarborough Road, Lincoln, Lincs, LN1 3NQ.*
Warm, comfortable Victorian walkers' rest.
Grades: ETB 2 Cr, Comm
Tel: **01522 533732** Mrs Richland.
Rates fr: *£16.00*-**£16.00**.
Open: All Year (not Xmas)
Beds: 1F 2D 1T 1S
Baths: 5 Ensuite
🛇 (5) 🅿 (5) ⚲ 🖵 🎐 Ⓥ ⚡

(On Path 🚌) *Eardleys Hotel, 21 Cross O'Cliff Hill, Lincoln, Lincs, LN5 8PN.*
Large rooms, very comfortable, Edwardian-style.
Tel: **01522 523050** Mr Joyce.
Rates fr: *£17.50*-**£25.00**.
Open: All Year
Beds: 2F 3D 2T 5S
Baths: 2 Ensuite, 3 Shared
🛇 🅿 (10) 🖵 🏠 ✕ 🎐 ⚡

High season, bank holidays and special events mean low availability *everywhere*.

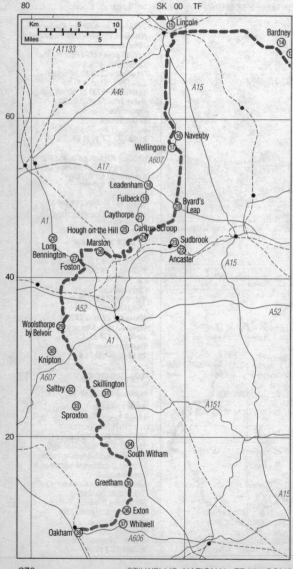

(1m) *Aaron Whisby Guest House*, 262 West Parade, Lincoln, Lincs, LN1 1LY.
Large Victorian end terraced house.
Grades: ETB 2 Cr
Tel: 01522 526930 Mr Harley.
Rates fr: £18.00-**£20.00**.
Open: All Year
Beds: 2F 2D 2T 2S
🛏 🅿 (8) ⅊ 🗙 Ⅲ Ⅴ ⅋ ✦

(▲ On Path) *Lincoln Youth Hostel*, 77 South Park, Lincoln, Lincs, LN5 8ES.
Actual grid ref: SK9870
Warden: Mr P Griffin.
Tel: 01522 522076
Under 18: £5.55 **Adults:** £8.25
Family Rooms, Centrally Heated, Showers, Evening Meal (7.00 pm), Shop, Television
Victorian villa in a quiet road opposite South Common open parkland

(0.5m) *Admiral Guest House*, 16 Nelson Street, Lincoln, Lincs, LN1 1PJ.
100-year-old cosy converted cottages.
Grades: ETB Listed, RAC Listed
Tel: 01522 544467 Mr Robertson.
Rates fr: £16.00-**£16.00**.
Open: All Year (not Xmas)
Beds: 3F 3D 3T 3S
Baths: 9 Ensuite
🛏 🅿 (12) 🗙 Ⅲ Ⅴ ⅋ ✦

(1m) *Westlyn Guest House*, 67 Carholme Road, Lincoln, Lincs, LN1 1RT.
Victorian town house with garden.
Tel: 01522 537468 Mr Kaye.
Rates fr: £15.00-**£16.00**.
Open: All Year (not Xmas)
Beds: 2F 1D 1T 1S
Baths: 3 Shared
🛏 🅿 (3) 🗙 Ⅲ ⅋

The Country Code

Enjoy the countryside and respect its life and work

Guard against all risk of fire

Fasten all gates

Keep your dogs under close control

Keep to public paths across farmland

Use gates and stiles to cross fences, hedges and walls

Leave livestock, crops and machinery alone

Take your litter home

Help to keep all water clean

Protect wild-life, plants and trees

Take special care on country roads

Make no unnecessary noise

(1m) *Edward King House*, The Old Palace, Minster Yard, Lincoln, Lincs, LN2 1PU.
Superb views over the City.
Tel: 01522 528778 Rev Adkins.
Rates fr: £17.50-**£18.00**.
Open: All Year (not Xmas)
Beds: 1F 11T 5S
Baths: 7 Shared
🛏 🅿 (12) ⅊ 🗙 Ⅲ Ⅴ ⅋

Navenby 16

National Grid Ref: SK9857

(0.25m) *The Lion & Royal*, 57 High Street, Navenby, Lincoln, Lincs, LN5 0DZ.
Grade II Listed public house.
Tel: 01522 810288 Mr Parrish.
Rates fr: £12.50-**£17.50**.
Open: All Year
Beds: 1F 1D 1T
Baths: 1 Private 1 Shared
🛏 🅿 🗙 Ⅲ Ⅴ

Wellingore 17

National Grid Ref: SK9856

⚍ Marquis of Granby

(On Path) *Marquis of Granby*, High Street, Wellingore, Lincoln, Lincs, LN5 0HW.
Tel: 01522 810442 Mrs Justice.
Rates fr: £17.50-**£20.00**.
Open: All Year (not Xmas)
Beds: 1F 1D 3T 1S
Baths: 3 Private 1 Shared
🛏 🅿 🗙 Ⅲ Ⅴ ⅋
Friendly village inn on the Viking Way. Wide range of ales and lagers. Excellent restaurant. Bar meals available lunchtimes and evenings.

Leadenham 18

National Grid Ref: SK9552

⚍ George Hotel

(1.5m 🚌) *George Hotel*, High Street, Leadenham, Lincoln, Lincs, LN5 0PN.
Old country coaching inn.
Tel: 01400 272251 Mrs Willgoose.
Rates fr: £12.50-**£18.00**.
Open: All Year
Beds: 2D 3T 2S
Baths: 2 Private 2 Shared
🛏 🅿 (100) 🗙 Ⅲ Ⅴ ⅋

Fulbeck 19

National Grid Ref: SK9450

⚍ Hare & Hounds

(3m) *Hare & Hounds*, Fulbeck, Grantham, Lincs, NG32 3JJ.
Converted coaching inn.
Tel: 01400 272090 Mr Skinner.
Rates fr: £14.00-**£18.00**.
Open: All Year
Beds: 2D 4T **Baths:** 6 Private
🛏 (5) 🅿 (60) 🗙 Ⅲ Ⅴ

Byard's Leap 20

National Grid Ref: SK9949

(On Path) *Byard's Leap Cottage*, Byard's Leap, Cranwell, Sleaford, Lincs, NG34 8EY.
Actual grid ref: SK9949
Comfortable, stone-built cottage. Warm welcome.
Tel: 01400 261537 Mrs Wood.
Rates fr: £15.00-**£15.00**.
Open: All Year (not Xmas)
Beds: 1F 1T
Baths: 1 Shared
🛏 🅿 (6) ⅊ 🗙 Ⅲ Ⅴ ⅋

Caythorpe 21

National Grid Ref: SK9348

(2.5m) *Kings Hill Farm*, Gorse Hill Lane, Caythorpe, Grantham, Lincs, NG32 3DY.
Modern comfortable farmhouse.
Grades: ETB Listed
Tel: 01400 272371 Mrs Siddans.
Rates fr: £15.00-**£17.00**.
Open: All Year
Beds: 2T
Baths: 1 Private
🛏 (8) 🅿 (4) ⅊ Ⅲ Ⅴ

Ancaster 22

National Grid Ref: SK9643

(2m) *Woodlands*, West Willoughby, Ancaster, Grantham, Lincs, NG32 3SH.
Peaceful Victorian farmhouse.
Grades: ETB Listed, AA 1 Q
Tel: 01400 230340 Mrs Mival.
Rates fr: £16.00-**£18.00**.
Open: Easter to Dec
Beds: 1F 1T
Baths: 1 Shared
🛏 (1) 🅿 (6) 🗙 Ⅲ Ⅴ

Sudbrook 23

National Grid Ref: SK9744

(1.5m 🚌) *Willoughby Lodge*, Sudbrook, Grantham, Lincs, NG32 3SQ.
Peaceful, rural Victorian lodge.
Tel: 01400 230258 Ms Bagnald.
Rates fr: £13.00-**£13.00**.
Open: All Year (not Xmas)
Beds: 1D 1T
Baths: 1 Shared
🅿 🗙 Ⅲ Ⅴ ⅋

Carlton Scroop 24

National Grid Ref: SK9545

(On Path 🚌) *Stonehorse Farm*, Hough Lane, Carlton Scroop, Grantham, Lincs, NG32 3BB.
Farmhouse in quiet country area.
Grades: ETB Listed
Tel: 01400 250147 Mrs Hutchins.
Rates fr: £13.00-**£15.00**.
Open: All Year (not Xmas)
Beds: 1D 1T
Baths: 1 Shared
🛏 🅿 ⅊ 🗙 Ⅲ Ⅴ ⅋

Hough-on-the-Hill 25

National Grid Ref: SK9246

¶◄ ⌨ Brownlow Arms

(1m) *Brownlow Arms*, *Hough-on-the-Hill, Grantham, Lincs*, NG32 2AZ. Lovely C17th stone-built country inn.
Grades: ETB 4 Cr, Comm
Tel: 01400 250234 Mrs Willoughby.
Rates fr: £21.00-£30.00.
Open: All Year (not Xmas)
Beds: 2D 1T 1S
Baths: 64Private
⌂ (5) 🅿 ⌨ ✕ 📖 Ⓥ

Marston 26

National Grid Ref: SK8943

¶◄ ⌨ Thorold Arms

(1.5m 🍴) *Gelston Grange*, *Marston, Grantham, Lincs*, NG32 2AQ.
Quiet, comfortable, working farm.
Grades: ETB 2 Cr
Tel: 01400 250281 Mrs Sharman.
Rates fr: £16.00-£16.00.
Open: All Year (not Xmas)
Beds: 2D 1T
Baths: 1 Private 1 Shared
⌂ 🅿 ⌿ ⌨ 📖 Ⓥ ⓐ ⌀

(0.25m) *The Pinfold*, *Pinfold Lane, Marston, Grantham, Lincs*, NG32 2.
Large house, site of old pinfold.
Tel: 01400 250571 Mrs Hartwell.
Rates fr: £15.00-£15.00.
Open: All Year (not Xmas)
Beds: 1D
Baths: 1 Private
🅿 ⌿ ⌨ 📖 ⓐ ⌀

(On Path) *Thorold Arms*, *Marston, Grantham, Lincs*, NG32 2HH.
Large Victorian pub.
Tel: 01400 250899 Mr Bryan.
Rates fr: £25.00-£25.00.
Open: All Year
Beds: 1F 1D
Baths: 2 Ensuite
⌂ 🅿 ⌿ ⌨ ✕ 📖 Ⓥ ⓐ ⌀

Foston 27

National Grid Ref: SK4582

¶◄ ⌨ Coopers Arms

(0.5m) *Hillcrest*, *Foston, Grantham, Lincs*, NG32 2LF.
Large detached house.
Tel: 01400 281339 Mrs Cooper.
Rates fr: £11.00-£15.00.
Open: All Year (not Xmas)
Beds: 2D 2S
Baths: 1 Shared
🅿 (4) ⌨ 📖 ⓐ ⌀

Long Bennington 28

National Grid Ref: SK8344

(2m) *Springfield*, *15 Main Road, Long Bennington, Newark, Notts*, NG23 5EH.
Detached house in 1 acre garden.
Tel: 01400 281445 Mrs Richardson.
Rates fr: £12.50-£12.50.
Open: All Year
Beds: 1F 1D 1T 1S
Baths: 1 Shared
⌂ 🅿 (6) ⌿ ⌨ 📖 ⓐ ⌀

Woolsthorpe-by-Belvoir 29

National Grid Ref: SK8334

¶◄ ⌨ Chequers Inn

(0.5m) *1 Rosey Row*, *Woolsthorpe-by-Belvoir, Grantham, Lincs*, NG32 1LZ.
Two converted old village cottages.
Tel: 01476 870239 Ms McClary.
Rates fr: £15.00-£15.00.
Open: All Year (not Xmas)
Beds: 2D 1T
Baths: 1 Private 1 Shared
⌂ 🅿 ⌿ ⌨ 📖 ⓐ ⌀

Knipton 30

National Grid Ref: SK8231

¶◄ ⌨ Red House

(1.5m 🍴) *The Red House*, *Knipton, Grantham, Lincs*, NG32 1RH.
C18th ex-hunting lodge near Belvoir Castle.
Grades: ETB 3 Cr, Approv
Tel: 01476 870352 Mr Newport.
Rates fr: £16.25-£18.00.
Open: All Year (not Xmas)
Beds: 1F 6D 2S
Baths: 3 Private 1 Shared
⌂ 🅿 ⌨ ⋔ ✕ 📖 Ⓥ ⓐ ⌀

Skillington 31

National Grid Ref: SK8925

¶◄ ⌨ Blue Horse, Cross Swords

(On Path) *Sproxton Lodge*, *Skillington, Grantham, Lincs*, NG33 5HJ.
Grades: ETB Listed
Tel: 01476 860307 Mrs Whatton.
Rates fr: £14.00-£15.00.
Open: All Year (not Xmas)
Beds: 1F 1D 1S **Baths:** 1 Shared
⌂ 🅿 (4) ⌿ ⌨ 📖 Ⓥ ⓐ ⌀

(0.5m 🍴) *Beeches*, *Park Lane, Skillington, Grantham, Lincs*, NG33 5HH.
Modern well appointed bungalow.
Tel: 01476 860271 Mrs Black.
Rates fr: £16.00-£16.00.
Open: All Year (not Xmas)
Beds: 1D 1T 2S
Baths: 2 Ensuite 1 Shared
⌂ (5) 🅿 (6) ⌿ ⌨ ✕ 📖 Ⓥ ⓐ ⌀

Saltby 32

National Grid Ref: SK8526

¶◄ ⌨ Nag's Head

(1.5m 🍴) *The Nags Head Inn*, *1 Back Street, Saltby, Melton Mowbray, Leics*, LE14 4QD.
200-year-old inn, open fires.
Tel: 01476 860491 Mr Mannion.
Rates fr: £16.00-£16.00.
Open: All Year (not Xmas)
Beds: 2D 2T
Baths: 2 Private 1 Shared
⌂ 🅿 ⌨ ⋔ ✕ 📖 Ⓥ ⓐ ⌀

Sproxton 33

National Grid Ref: SK8524

¶◄ ⌨ Crown Inn

(1.75m 🍴) *Appletree Cottage*, *The Green, 19 Main St, Sproxton, Melton Mowbray, Leics*, LE14 4QS.
Actual grid ref: SK8524
Converted C19th Ironstone barn.
Tel: 01476 860435 Mrs Slack.
Rates fr: £18.00-£19.00.
Open: All Year
Beds: 1D 1S
Baths: 1 Shared
⌂ 🅿 (1) ⌿ ⌨ 📖 Ⓥ

South Witham 34

National Grid Ref: SK9219

¶◄ ⌨ Blue Cow

(1m) *Corner Cottage*, *Water Lane, South Witham, Grantham, Lincs*, NG33 5PH.
Old stone cottage in 1 acre.
Tel: 01572 767258 Mrs Williamson.
Rates fr: £12.50 (inc dinner)-£12.50.
Open: All Year (not Xmas)
Beds: 2D 1S
Baths: 2 Shared
🅿 ⌿ ⌨ ⋔ ✕ Ⓥ ⓐ ⌀

Greetham 35

National Grid Ref: SK9214

(On Path 🍴) *Priestwells*, *Main Street, Greetham, Oakham, Leics*, LE15 7HU.
Comfortable and peaceful family house.
Tel: 01572 812660 Mrs Wilson.
Rates fr: £15.00-£15.00.
Open: All Year (not Xmas)
Beds: 1F 1D 1S
Baths: 2 Shared
⌂ 🅿 (6) ⌨ ⋔ 📖 ⓐ

Pay B&Bs by cash or cheque and be prepared to pay up front.

Exton 36

National Grid Ref: SK9211

⦿ ◧ Fox and Hounds

(0.5m) *Fox & Hounds, Exton,
Oakham, Leics, LE15 8AP.*
C17th inn.
Grades: ETB Listed
Tel: 01572 812403
Mr Hillier.
Rates fr: *£18.00-£22.00.*
Open: All Year
Beds: 1D 1T 1S
⛺ (8) ▣ (2) ✗ ▥ ▮

(On Path) *Church Farmhouse,
5 Oakham Road, Exton, Oakham,
Leics, LE15 8AX.*
Listed homely farmhouse.
Grades: ETB Listed
Tel: 01572 813435
Mr & Mrs Hudson.
Rates fr: *£15.00-£15.00.*
Open: All Year
Beds: 1D 1T
Baths: 1 Private
⛺ (5) ▣ (1) ⚲ ▢ ▥ Ⓥ ▮ ✦

Whitwell 37

National Grid Ref: SK9208

⦿ ◧ Noel Arms

(1m) *Noel Arms, Main Street,
Whitwell, Oakham, Leics, LE15 8BW.*
Farmhouse and public house.
Tel: 01780 460334 Mr Healey.
Rates fr: *£19.00-£17.50.*
Open: All Year **Beds:** 1F 3D 9T 1S
Baths: 4 Private 2 Shared
⛺ ▣ ▢ ⼊ ✗ ▥ ⅋ Ⓥ

Oakham 38

National Grid Ref: SK8509

⦿ ◧ White Lion, Whipper Inn

(0.5m) *27 Northgate, Oakham,
Leics, LE15 6QR.*
Large Victorian private house.
Tel: 01572 755057 Mrs George.
Rates fr: *£12.50-£12.50.*
Open: All Year
Beds: 1F 1D 1T 1S
Baths: 1 Shared
⛺ ▣ ⚲ ▢ ⼊ ▥ ▮ ✦

(0.25m) *Westgate Lodge, 9
Westgate, Oakham, Leics, LE15 6BH.*
Spacious and friendly family home.
Grades: ETB Listed
Tel: 01572 757370 Mrs Baines.
Rates fr: *£18.50-£18.50.*
Open: All Year
Beds: 1F 1D 1T **Baths:** 3 Private
⛺ (5) ▣ (3) ⚲ ▢ ⼊ ▥ Ⓥ ✦

(On Path) *Angel House, 20
Northgate, Oakham, Leics, LE15 6QS.*
Large Victorian private house,
converted out-buildings.
Grades: ETB Reg
Tel: 01572 756153 Mrs Weight.
Rates fr: *£15.00-£15.00.*
Open: All Year
Beds: 1F 1D 2T 1S
Baths: 3 Ensuite 1 Shared
⛺ ▣ ▢ Ⓥ ▮ ✦

(0.5m) *The Merry Monk,
12 Church Street, Oakham, Leics,
LE15 6AA.*
Town centre pub.
Tel: 01572 722094 Mr Riordam.
Rates fr: *£28.00.*
Open: All Year (not Xmas)
Beds: 3T **Baths:** 1 Shared
▣ ▥

Wayfarers Walk

Another pleasant 70 miles in the South of England, readily accessible by train, showing off the chalklands of Hampshire with its rolling hills and those peaceful brooks much-loved by fly fishermen throughout the world. Between a medieval drover's track, a riverside path, a classic steep beech 'hanger' and the lonely mudflats at Langstone Harbour, you discover some classic English villages, including the reputed birthplace of cricket - Hambledon. Be prepared for heavy mud on this path after rain.

Guides:

Along and Around the Wayfarers Walk (ISBN 0 948176 04 0), published by Hampshire County Council. and available directly from their offices (Countryside & Community Dept, Mottisfont Court, High Street, Winchester, SO23 8ZF, tel. 01962 841841), £4.95

Maps: Ordnance Survey 1:50,000 Landranger series: 174, 185, 196, 197

Inkpen 1

National Grid Ref: SU3764

(1m 🚍) *Beacon House*, Bell Lane, Upper Green, Inkpen, Hungerford, Berks, *RG17 9QJ*.
Interesting '30s comfortable country house.
Tel: **01488 668640**
Mr & Mrs Cave.
Rates fr: *£16.00-£16.00*.
Open: All Year
Beds: 1T 2S **Baths:** 2 Shared
🛌 (7) 🅿 🛏 🗙 🎕 🎬 V 🍴 ♿

Woolton Hill 2

National Grid Ref: SU4261

🍴 🍺 Furze Bush, Rampant Cat, Carnarvon Arms

(2.5m) *Tile Barn House*, Woolton Hill, Newbury, Berks, *RG15 9UZ*.
Part large Victorian country house.
Tel: **01635 254677** Mrs Mitchell.
Rates fr: *£16.00-£16.00*.

Open: All Year **Beds:** 1 F 1D
Baths: 1 Ensuite 1 Shared
🛌 (0) 🅿 (10) 🛏 🎕 🍴 ♿

(2.5m) *The Coach House*, Tile Barn, Goose Hill, Woolton Hill, Newbury, Hants, *RG15 9UZ*.
Large Victorian converted coach house.
Grades: ETB Listed
Tel: **01635 253572** Mrs Keates.
Rates fr: *£16.00-£20.00*.
Open: All Year (not Xmas)
Beds: 2D 1T
Baths: 2 Shared
🛌 🅿 (4) ⚡ 🗙 🎬 V

Highclere 3

National Grid Ref: SU4360

🍴 🍺 The Red House

(2m) *Westridge Open Centre*, Andover Road, Highclere, Newbury, Berks, *RG20 9PJ*.
Country house with gardens.
Tel: **01635 253322** Miss Gribble.
Rates fr: *£10.00-£10.00*.

Open: All Year (not Xmas or public holidays) **Beds:** 2T 2S
Baths: 2 Shared 🅿 (2) 🗙 🎬 ♿

Crux Easton 4

National Grid Ref: SU4256

🍴 🍺 Furze Bush

(1m 🚍) *Manor House*, Crux Easton, Newbury, Hants, *RG20 9QF*.
Comfortable historic farmhouse.
Tel: **01635 254314** Mrs O'Shaughnessy.
Rates fr: *£16.50-£16.50*.
Open: All Year (not Xmas)
Beds: 3T **Baths:** 2 Shared
🛌 🅿 (6) 🗙 🎬 🍴 ♿

Kingsclere 5

National Grid Ref: SU5258

🍴 🍺 The Swan

(1.5m 🚍) *Cleremede*, Foxs Lane, Kingsclere, Newbury, Hants, *RG15 8SL*.
Secluded house with large garden.
Grades: ETB 2 Cr, Comm
Tel: **01635 297298** Mrs Salm.
Rates fr: *£18.00-£20.00*.
Open: All Year **Beds:** 2T 1S
Baths: 1 Ensuite, 1 Shared
🛌 (10) 🅿 (7) ⚡ 🛏 🎬 V 🍴 ♿

Dummer 6

National Grid Ref: SU5845

🍴 🍺 The Sun Inn

(On Path 🚍) *Oakdown Farm*, Dummer, Basingstoke, Hants, *RG23 7LR*.
Actual grid ref: SU5845
Secluded modern farm bungalow.
Grades: ETB 1 Cr, Comm
Tel: **01256 397218** Mrs Hutton.
Rates fr: *£15.00-£15.00*.
Open: All Year **Beds:** 1D 2T
Baths: 1 Shared
🛌 (12) 🅿 (4) 🗙 🎬 V ♿

Itchen Stoke 7

National Grid Ref: SU5532

(1m) *The Parsonage, Itchen Stoke, Alresford, Hants, SO24 0QU.*
Modern house, quiet rural setting.
Tel: **01962 732123** Mrs Pitt.
Rates fr: *£14.00-£14.00*.
Open: All Year
Beds: 1T
Baths: 1 Shared
🅿 (20) 📟 ✦

Cheriton 8

National Grid Ref: SU5828

🍴 🍺 Flowerpot, Tichborne Arms, Millburys

(0.25m) *Flower Pots Inn, Cheriton, Alresford, Hants, SO24 0QQ.*
Actual grid ref: SU582283
Converted byre next to inn/brew-house.
Tel: **01962 771318**
Rates fr: *£22.00-£26.00*.
Open: All Year (not Xmas)
Beds: 2D 3T
Baths: 5 Ensuite
🅿 🗠 🏨 📟

(0.25m) *Brandy Lea, Cheriton, Alresford, Hants, SO24 0QQ.*
Friendly semi-detached next to pub.
Tel: **01962 771534** Mrs Hoskings.
Rates fr: *£13.50-£13.50*.
Open: All Year
Beds: 1T **Baths:** 1 Private
🏃 🅿 🗠 🏨 📟

Kilmeston 9

National Grid Ref: SU5926

(On Path 🚲) *Dean Farm, Kilmeston, Alresford, Hants, SO24 0NL.*
Warm, comfortable C18th farmhouse.
Grades: ETB Listed
Tel: **01962 771286** Mrs Warr.
Rates fr: *£17.00-£20.00*.
Open: All Year (not Xmas)
Beds: 3D
Baths: 2 Shared
🏃 (10) 🅿 (3) ✦ 🗠 📟 Ⓥ ♦ ✦

West Meon 10

National Grid Ref: SU6424

🍴 🍺 Thomas Lord

(2.25m) *Brocklands Farm, West Meon, Petersfield, Hants, GU32 1JG.*
Actual grid ref: SU639237
Modern comfortable farmhouse.
Grades: ETB Listed, Comm
Tel: **01730 829228** Mrs Wilson.
Rates fr: *£17.00-£17.00*.
Open: All Year (not Xmas)
Beds: 2D 1T
Baths: 2 Shared
🅿 (6) ✦ 🗠 🏨 📟 Ⓥ ♦

Warnford 11

National Grid Ref: SU6223

🍴 🍺 The George & Falcon

(4m 🚲) *Hayden Barn Cottage, Warnford, Southampton, Hants, SO32 3LF.*
Actual grid ref: SU634228
Real hospitality, stunning country location.
Tel: **01730 829454** Mrs Broadbent.
Rates fr: *£18.50-£18.50*.
Open: All Year (not Xmas)
Beds: 2T 1S
Baths: 1 Ensuite 1 Private 1 Shared
🏃 🅿 (5) ✦ 🗠 📟 Ⓥ ♦ ✦

Hambledon 12

National Grid Ref: SU6414

🍴 🍺 Vine, George

(On Path) *Cams, Hambledon, Waterlooville, Hants, PO7 4SP.*
Comfortable C17th house.
Grades: ETB 2 Cr
Tel: **01705 632865** Mrs Fawcett.
Rates fr: *£16.00-£17.00*.
Open: All Year (not Xmas)
Beds: 1D 2T
Baths: 1 Ensuite 1 Shared
🏃 (10) 🅿 (6) ✦ 🗠 🏨 🗡 📟 ✦

Denmead 13

National Grid Ref: SU6511

🍴 🍺 The White Hart, The Fox & Hounds

(0.25m) *Forest Gate, Hambledon Road, Denmead, Waterlooville, Hants, PO7 6EX.*
Large Georgian private house.

Grades: ETB Listed
Tel: **01705 255901** Mrs Cox.
Rates fr: *£16.00-£20.00*.
Open: All Year (not Xmas)
Beds: 2T **Baths:** 2 Ensuite
🏃 (10) 🅿 (2) ✦ 🗠 🗡 🏨 ✦

Bedhampton 14

National Grid Ref: SU7006

🍴 🍺 Rusty Cutter

(0.5m) *High Towers, 14 Portsdown Hill Road, Bedhampton, Havant, Hants, PO9 3JY.*
Large modern detached house.
Tel: **01705 471748** Mrs Boulton.
Rates fr: *£18.00-£18.00*.
Open: All Year
Beds: 1F 1D 1T 2S
Baths: 4 Ensuite 1 Shared
🏃 (5) 🅿 (6) ✦ 🗠 🏨 ♦ ✦

(0.5m) *Holland House, 33 Bedhampton Hill, Bedhampton, Havant, Hants, PO9 3JN.*
Tel: **01705 475913** Mrs Brighton.

Emsworth 15

National Grid Ref: SU7406

🍴 🍺 King's Head

(0.5m) *Strathfield Guest House, 99 Havant Road, Emsworth, Hants, PO10 7LF.*
Actual grid ref: SU737060
Non-smoking large Victorian house. **Grades:** ETB Reg
Tel: **01243 377351** Mrs Stamp.
Rates fr: *£17.00-£17.00*.
Open: All Year (not Xmas)
Beds: 1D 1T 1S
Baths: 3 Ensuite
🏃 (11) 🅿 (5) ✦ 🗠 🗡 🏨 Ⓥ ♦ ✦

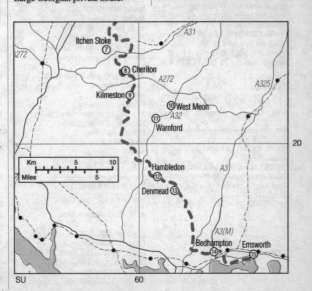

Wealdway

Gravesend is the starting point of this delightful 80-mile walk across Kent and Sussex. You leave the Thames Estuary and cross the North Downs, exploring the valleys round Luddesdown, to gain panoramic views of Kent's 'Garden of England' at Gover Hill on the Greensand Ridge, before wandering through orchards to join the Medway into Tonbridge. Once in Sussex, the path passes through thick woods to emerge onto the high open heathland of Ashdown Forest, and then heads off to the South Downs and the sea at Beachy Head. The **Wealdway** is fully way-marked with the initials WW on a yellow arrow.

Guides: *The Wealdway and the Vanguard Way* by Kev Reynolds (ISBN 0 9 023 63859), published by Cicerone Press and available directly from the publishers (2 Police Square, Milnthorpe, Cumbria, LA7 7PY, 01539 562069), £4.99 (+ 75p p&p).
A Guide to the Wealdway by John H N Mason (ISBN 09 464820 4), published by Constable & Co. Ltd, £6.95
The Wealdway by Geoffrey King (ISBN 0 951 6006 05), published by RA Kent & Sussex Areas and available from the Rambler's Association National Office (1/5 Wandsworth Road, London, SW8 2XX, tel. 0171 582 6878), £3.50 (+70p p&p).
Maps: Ordnance Survey 1:50,000 Landranger series: 177, 188, 199

Meopham 1

National Grid Ref: TQ6465

(1m) **The Croft**, Hook Green, Meopham, Gravesend, *DA13 0HT*.
Character house in acre gardens.
Grades: ETB Reg
Tel: **01474 813502** Mr/Mrs Russell
Rates fr: *£15.00-£15.00*.
Open: All Year (not Xmas)
Beds: 1T 1S **Baths:** 1 Shared
🛏 (12) 🅿 (2) ⊬⌨ 🖳 Ⓥ ✔

Trottiscliffe 2

National Grid Ref: TQ6460
🍴 🍺 The Plough

(0.5m) **Bramble Park**, Church Lane, Trottiscliffe, West Malling, Kent, *ME19 5EB*.
Actual grid ref: TQ644563
Secluded, tranquil, spacious Victorian rectory.
Tel: **01732 822397** Mrs Towler.
Rates fr: *£18.00-£18.00*.
Open: All Year **Beds:** 1F 1T 1S
Baths: 2 Shared 🛏 🅿 (6) ⌨ 🖳 � ✔

Ryarsh 3

National Grid Ref: TQ6759
🍴 🍺 Duke of Wellington

(2m) **Heavers Farm**, Ryarsh, West Malling, Kent, *ME19 5JU*.
House in quiet location.
Grades: ETB 3 Cr
Tel: **01732 842074** Mrs Edwards.
Rates fr: *£15.00-£20.00*.
Open: All Year (not Xmas)
Beds: 1D 2T
🛏 (Birth) 🅿 (3) ⊬⌨ 🛏 ✕ 🖳 Ⓥ

Leybourne 4

National Grid Ref: TQ6858
🍴 🍺 King & Queen

(2m) **20 Rectory Lane South**, Leybourne, West Malling, *ME19 5HB*. Comfortable, secluded bungalow, private sitting-room.
Tel: **01732 848020** Mrs Pragnell.
Rates fr: *£18.00-£20.00*.
Open: All Year (not Xmas)
Beds: 1D **Baths:** 1 Private
🅿 (2) ⊬⌨ 🖳 Ⓥ

Wrotham 5

National Grid Ref: TQ6059
🍴 🍺 The Bull, Rose and Crown, Three Post Boys

(On Path) **Hillside House**, Gravesend Road, Wrotham, Sevenoaks, Kent, *TN15 7JH*.
Family home on wooded hillside.
Tel: **01732 822564** Mrs Thomas.
Rates fr: *£16.00-£16.00*.
Open: All Year (not Xmas)
Beds: 2D 1S
Baths: 1 Shared
🛏 🅿 ⌨ 🛏 ✕ 🖳 Ⓥ æ ✔

(On Path) **Green Hill House**, High Street, Wrotham, Sevenoaks, Kent, *TN15 7AH*.
Actual grid ref: TQ611592
Quietly situated comfortable family house.
Grades: ETB Reg
Tel: **01732 883069** Mrs Jolliffe.
Rates fr: *£16.00-£20.00*.
Open: All Year
Beds: 1F 1T
Baths: 1 Shared
🛏 ⊬⌨ 🖳 æ ✔

Borough Green 6

National Grid Ref: TQ6057
🍴 🍺 Brickmakers Arms

(On Path 🚗) **Holmes**, Boneashe Lane, St Marys Platt, Borough Green, Sevenoaks, Kent, *TN15 8NW*.
Luxurious spacious peaceful medieval farmhouse.
Tel: **01732 882502** Mrs Hickey.

Rates fr: *£15.00*.
Open: Mar to Nov
Beds: 1F 1T **Baths:** 1 Shared
🛏 (12) 🅿 (6) ⊬⌨ ✕ 🖳 Ⓥ æ ✔

St Mary's Platt 7

National Grid Ref: TQ6257
🍴 🍺 Blue Anchor, Brickmakers Arms

(On Path) **Holmes**, Potash Lane, St Mary's Platt, Sevenoaks, Kent, *TN15 8NW*.
Actual grid ref: TQ626568
Beautiful peaceful comfortable C15th farmhouse.
Grades: ETB Reg
Tel: **01732 882502** Mrs Hickey.
Rates fr: *£15.00*.
Open: Apr to Nov
Beds: 1F 1T **Baths:** 1 Shared
🛏 (12) 🅿 (4) ⊬⌨ 🖳 Ⓥ æ ✔

(0.25m) **Langleys**, Long Mill Lane, St Mary's Platt, Sevenoaks, Kent, *TN15 8QE*.
Quiet, comfortable country house.
Grades: ETB Reg
Tel: **01732 884652** Mrs Guilliard.
Rates fr: *£18.00-£20.00*.
Open: All Year (not Xmas)
Beds: 2D 1T **Baths:** 3 Ensuite
🛏 (6) 🅿 (3) ⊬⌨ 🖳 Ⓥ ✔

Hadlow 8

National Grid Ref: TQ6350
🍴 🍺 The Harrow

(1.5m) **James House**, Maidstone Road, Hadlow, Tonbridge, Kent, *TN11 0HP*.
Period farmhouse.
Tel: **01732 850217** Mrs Dumbreck.
Rates fr: *£18.00-£20.00*.
Open: All Year (not Xmas)
Beds: 2T **Baths:** 1 Shared
🛏 🅿 (3) ⊬⌨ 🛏 æ ✔

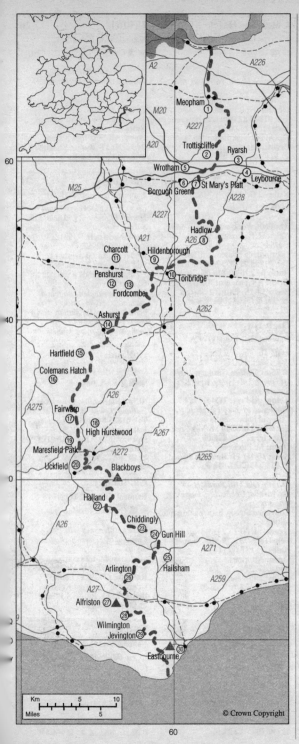

(1.5m) *Dunsmore, Hadlow Park, Hadlow, Tonbridge, Kent,* TN11 0HX.
Private park, ground floor accommodation.
Tel: **01732 850611** Mrs Tubbs.
Rates fr: *£17.00-£20.00.*
Open: All Year (not Xmas)
Beds: 1T
Baths: 1 Private
🛇 🅿 ❑ 🖃

Hildenborough 9

National Grid Ref: TQ5648

(0.3m) *150 Tonbridge Road, Hildenborough, Tonbridge, Kent,* TN11 9HW.
Spacious Victorian house.
Grades: ETB Listed
Tel: **01732 838894** Mrs Romney.
Rates fr: *£12.50-£15.00.*
Open: All Year (not Xmas)
Beds: 1T 1S
Baths: 1 Shared
🛇 🅿 (2) ⊬ ❑ 🖃

Tonbridge 10

National Grid Ref: TQ6053

🍴 🍺 Hilden Manor Inn

(On Path) *Chequers Inn, 122 High Street, Tonbridge, Kent,* TN9 1AS.
Historic inn.
Tel: **01732 358957** Mrs Evans.
Rates fr: *£18.00-£18.00.*
Open: All Year
Beds: 3T 1S
Baths: 1 Shared
🛇 🅿 (7) ❑ 🐕 ✕ 🛉 ⚡

(On Path) *4 Redwood Park, Five Oak Green, Tonbridge, Kent,* TN12 6WB.
New house, rural district.
Grades: ETB Listed
Tel: **01892 838200**
Mrs Prance.
Rates fr: *£15.00-£15.00.*
Open: All Year (not Xmas/New Year)
Beds: 1D 1S
Baths: 1 Shared
🅿 (3) ❑ 🖃

Charcott 11

National Grid Ref: TQ5247

🍴 🍺 Greyhound, Castle Inn, Little Brown Jug

(2.75m) *Charcott Farmhouse, Charcott, Leigh, Tonbridge, Kent,* TN11 8LG.
Listed farmhouse in peaceful surroundings.
Tel: **01892 870024**
Mr & Mrs Morris.
Rates fr: *£17.50-£22.00.*
Open: All Year
Beds: 3 T
Baths: 1 Private 2 Ensuite
🛇 🅿 (4) ⊬ ❑ 🐕 🖃

Penshurst 12

National Grid Ref: TQ5243

|o| ◖ Bottle House, Leicester Arms Hotel, Spotted Dog Pub, Chafford Arms

(2.5m) *2 Keymer Court, Penshurst, Tonbridge, Kent, TN11 8BU.*
Large double room, village centre.
Tel: **01892 870280** Mrs Day.
Rates fr: £17.50-£35.00.
Open: All Year (not Xmas)
Beds: 1T **Baths:** 1 Shared
▣ (1) **⊬ Ⅲ.**

Fordcombe 13

National Grid Ref: TQ5240

|o| ◖ The Chafford Arms

(0.25m) *Lockerbie, Chafford Lane, Fordcombe, Tunbridge Wells, Kent, TN3 0SH.*
Actual grid ref: TQ523403
Modern comfortable private house.
Tel: **01892 740278** Mrs McRow.
Rates fr: £15.00-£15.00.
Open: All Year
Beds: 1D **Baths:** 1 Ensuite
▣ (2) **⊡ Ⅲ. ⌁**

Ashurst 14

National Grid Ref: TQ5138

(On Path) *Manor Court Farm, Ashurst, Tunbridge Wells, Kent, TN3 9TB.*
Spacious Georgian farmhouse.
Grades: ETB 2 Cr
Tel: **01892 740279** Mrs Soyke.
Rates fr: £18.00-£18.00.
Open: All Year (not Xmas)
Beds: 1D 2T **Baths:** 2 Shared
☎ ▣ (10) **⊡ ⼇ Ⅲ. Ⅴ ▯ ⌁**
Also **Å** *£3.50 per person.*
Open: All Year **⋒ Ⅱ ⚓**

Hartfield 15

National Grid Ref: TQ4735

(0.5m) *Stairs Farm House, & Tea Room, High Street, Hartfield, E. Sussex, TN7 4AB.*
Comfortable modernised 17th Century farmhouse.
Grades: ETB Listed, Comm
Tel: **01892 770793** Mrs Pring.
Rates fr: £20.00-£25.00.
Open: All Year
Beds: 1F 1D 1T 1S
Baths: 4 Ensuite
☎ ▣ (10) **⊬ ⊡ ⼇ ✕ Ⅲ. ▯ ⌁**
Also **Å** *£3 per tent.* **Ⅱ ✕ ⚓**

(0.5m) *Anchor Inn, Church Street, Hartfield, E. Sussex, TN7 4AG.*
Large comfortable cosy rooms.
Tel: **01892 770424** Mr Thompson.
Rates fr: £17.50-£25.00.
Open: All Year
Beds: 1D 1T
Baths: 2 Ensuite
☎ ▣ ⊡ ⼇ ✕ Ⅲ. Ⅴ

Colemans Hatch 16

National Grid Ref: TQ4533

|o| ◖ Haywagon Inn

(1.75m) *Gospel Oak, Sandy Lane, Colemans Hatch, Hartfield, E. Sussex, TN7 4ER.*
Converted C17th crofters cottage.
Grades: ETB Listed
Tel: **01342 823840** Mrs Hawker.
Rates fr: £17.00-£18.00.
Open: All Year **Beds:** 1D 1T
Baths: 1 Ensuite 1 Shared
☎ ▣ (5) **⊬ ✕ Ⅲ. Ⅴ**

Fairwarp 17

National Grid Ref: TQ4626

|o| ◖ The Foresters

(On Path) *Rock-a-Nore, Fairwarp, Uckfield, E. Sussex, TN22 3BP.*
Comfortable house in village.
Tel: **01825 712373** Mrs Anderson.
Rates fr: £16.00-£16.00.
Open: All Year (not Xmas)
Beds: 1T 1S **Baths:** 1 Shared
☎ (12) **▣** (3) **⊡ ✕ Ⅲ. Ⅴ ▯ ⌁**

High Hurstwood 18

National Grid Ref: TQ4926

|o| ◖ The Crow & Gate

(0.75m) *Chillies Granary, High Hurstwood, Crowborough, E. Sussex, TN6 3TB.*
Actual grid ref: TQ497278
Converted granary/carthouse.
Cheerful household!.
Tel: **01892 655560** Mr/Mrs Peck.
Rates fr: £15.00-£20.00.
Open: Mar to Dec
Beds: 1F 1D 1T **Baths:** 2 Shared
☎ ▣ (6) **⊬ ⊡ Ⅲ. Ⅴ ▯ ⌁**

(0.75m) *Old Mill Farm, High Hurstwood, Uckfield, E. Sussex, TN22 4AD.*
Converted Sussex barn, picturesque setting.
Grades: ETB 2 Cr
Tel: **01825 732279** Mrs Sharpe.
Rates fr: £17.00-£17.00.
Open: All Year
Beds: 1F 2T
Baths: 3 Private
☎ ▣ (6) **⊬ ⊡ ⼇ ✕ Ⅲ. Ⅴ**

Maresfield Park 19

National Grid Ref: TQ4624

(On Path) *South Paddock, Maresfield Park, Uckfield, E. Sussex, TN22 2HA.*
Country house set in 3.5 acres.
Grades: ETB 2 Cr, High Comm, AA 4 Q, Select
Tel: **01825 762335** Mr Allt.
Rates fr: £25.00-£24.00.
Open: All Year
Beds: 1D 2T 1S **Baths:** 2 Shared
☎ (10) **▣** (6) **⊡ Ⅲ. Ⅴ**

Uckfield 20

National Grid Ref: TQ4721

|o| ◖ Coach & Horses, The Griffin

(0.2m) *Sliders Farmhouse, Furners Green, Uckfield, E. Sussex, TN22 3RT.*
Lovely Tudor farmhouse, mature gardens. **Grades:** AA 3 Q
Tel: **01825 790258** Mr Salmon.
Rates fr: £19.00-£28.00.
Open: All Year (not Xmas)
Beds: 2D 1T **Baths:** 3 Ensuite
☎ ▣ (10) **⊡ ✕ Ⅲ. Ⅴ**

Blackboys 21

National Grid Ref: TQ5220

(**▲** 0.75m) *Blackboys Youth Hostel, Blackboys, Uckfield, East Sussex, TN22 5HU.*
Actual grid ref: TQ521215
Tel: **01825 890607**
Under 18: £4.60 **Adults:** £6.75
Self Catering, Camping, No Smoking, Grounds Available for Games, Parking
This rustic wooden cabin in a deciduous sylvan setting offers good basic accomodation with a cosy open fire, spacious lounge/dining room, kitchen

Halland 22

National Grid Ref: TQ5016

|o| ◖ Black Lion

(0.5m) *Black Lion, Lewes Road, Halland, Lewes, E. Sussex, BN8 6PN.*
Tel: **01825 840304** Mrs Sumers.
Rates fr: £15.00-£19.50.
Open: All Year **Beds:** 1F 2D 1T 2S
Baths: 4 Ensuite 2 Shared
☎ ▣ (40) **⊡ ⼇ ✕ Ⅲ. ⚲**

Chiddingly 23

National Grid Ref: TQ5414

|o| ◖ Golden Cross Inn

(On Path) *Holmes Hill, Chiddingly, Lewes, E. Sussex, BN8 6JA.*
Modernised C18th cottage.
Tel: **01825 872746** Mr/Mrs Farrier.
Rates fr: £17.50-£17.50.
Open: All Year (not Xmas)
Beds: 1D 1S **Baths:** 1 Private
☎ ▣ (2) **⊬ ⊡ Ⅲ.**

Gun Hill 24

National Grid Ref: TQ5614

(0.5m **🚌**) *Pedlars Cottage, Gun Hill, Horam, Heathfield, E. Sussex, TN21 0JS.*
Actual grid ref: TQ567149
C18th country cottage.
Tel: **01825 873107** Mrs Winter.
Rates fr: £15.50-£15.50.
Open: Easter to Oct **Beds:** 2D
Baths: 1 Shared **☎ ▣ ⊬ ⊡ ✕**

(On Path) **The Gun,** *Gun Hill,*
Horam, Heathfield, E. Sussex,
TN21 0JU.
Actual grid ref: TQ543143
Idyllic C16th inn, excellent food.
Tel: **01825 872361**
Mr & Mrs Brockway.
Rates fr: *£16.00-£26.00.*
Open: All Year (not Xmas)
Beds: 1F 1D 1T
🛏 🅿 (60) ⅍ 🖵 🕆 ✕ 🎹 Ⓥ ✔

Hailsham   25

National Grid Ref: TQ5909

(3m) **Sandy Banks,** *Magham*
Down, Hailsham, E. Sussex,
BN27 1PW.
Well appointed rooms - cottage
extension.
Grades: ETB 2 Cr, Comm
Tel: **01323 842488** Miss Burridge.
Rates fr: *£19.00-£22.00.*
Open: All Year (not Xmas)
Beds: 3T
Baths: 3 Ensuite
🛏 🅿 (3) 🖵 ✕ 🎹 ✔

Arlington   26

National Grid Ref: TQ5407

🍴 🍺 Old Oak, Yew Tree

(0.25m) **Bates Green,** *Arlington,*
Polegate, E. Sussex, BN26 6SH.
Old tile-hung farmhouse.
Grades: AA 5 Q, Prem Select
Tel: **01323 482039**
Mrs McCutchan.
Rates fr: *£21.00-£30.00.*
Open: All Year (not Xmas)
Beds: 1D 2T
Baths: 3 Ensuite
🅿 (3) ⅍ 🖵 ✕ 🎹 Ⓥ 🛎 ✔

Alfriston   27

National Grid Ref: TQ5103

🍴 🍺 George, Smugglers, Market
Cross, Star, Sussex Ox,
Moonrakers

(▲ 2.5m) **Alfriston Youth Hostel,**
Frog Firle, Alfriston, Polegate, E.
Sussex, BN26 5TT.
Actual grid ref: TQ518019
Warden: Ms W Nicholls.
Tel: **01323 870423**
Under 18: £5.55 **Adults:** £8.25
Family Bunk Rooms, Centrally
Heated, Showers, Evening Meal
(6.30 pm), Shop, Television
A comfortable Sussex country
house, dating from 1530, set in the
Cuckmere Valley with views over
the river and Litlington

(2.5m) **Pleasant Rise Farm,**
Alfriston, Polegate, E. Sussex,
BN26 5TN.
Very quiet, beautiful house - lovely
views.
Grades: ETB Listed
Tel: **01323 870545** Mrs Savage.

Rates fr: *£16.50-£16.50.*
Open: All Year (not Xmas)
Beds: 2D 1T 1S **Baths:** 2 Private
🅿 ⅍ 🖵 🎹 Ⓥ

Wilmington   28

National Grid Ref: TQ5404

🍴 🍺 Giant's Rest

(0.25m) **Crossways Hotel,**
Wilmington, Polegate, E. Sussex,
BN26 5SG.
Georgian house in two acres.
Grades: AA 4 Q, Select
Tel: **01323 482455** Mr Stott.
Rates fr: *£32.00-£40.00.*
Open: All Year (not Xmas)
Beds: 3D 2T 2S
Baths: 7 Ensuite
🅿 (20) 🖵 ✕ 🎹 Ⓥ 🛎 ✔

(On Path) **The Giants Rest,**
Wilmington, Polegate, E. Sussex,
BN26 5SQ.
Edwardian country pub.
Actual grid ref: TQ545048
Tel: **01323 870207** Mr Jones.
Rates fr: *£17.00-£17.00.*
Open: All Year (not Xmas)
Beds: 1F 1T **Baths:** 1 Shared
🛏 🅿 (16) ⅍ 🕆 ✕ 🎹 Ⓥ ✔

Jevington   29

National Grid Ref: TQ5601

🍴 🍺 Eight Bells

(0.25m 🚲) **Ash Farm,** *Filching,*
Jevington, Polegate, E. Sussex,
BN26 5QA.
150-year-old Downland farmhouse.
Grades: ETB Reg
Tel: **01323 484474** Mr Steer.
Rates fr: *£15.00-£16.00.*
Open: All Year
Beds: 1F 1D 1T
Baths: 2 Ensuite 1 Shared
🛏 🅿 (20) ⅍ 🖵 🕆 ✕ 🎹 Ⓥ 🛎 ✔
Also ▲ *£2.50 per person.,*
Open: All Year 🅣 🎁 ✕ ✔ 🛏

Eastbourne   30

National Grid Ref: TQ5900

🍴 🍺 The Pilot, The Meads,
Terminus Pub, Lamb Inn, The
Beach, The Town House, The
Marine, Lamb Inn

(1.5m) **Heatherdene Hotel,** *26-28*
Elms Avenue, Eastbourne, E.
Sussex, BN21 3DN.
Tel: **01323 723598** Mrs Mockford.
Rates fr: *£14.50-£12.00.*
Open: All Year
Beds: 1F 3D 8T 3S
Baths: 5 Ensuite, 4 Shared
🛏 🖵 🕆 ✕ 🎹 🛇 ✔
The Heatherdene is a friendly
licensed hotel, popular with walk-
ers on the South Downs.
Comfortable rooms and good food
ensure your stay will be enjoyable.

(1m) **Edelweiss Hotel,** *10-12 Elms*
Avenue, Eastbourne, E. Sussex,
BN21 3DN.
Grades: ETB 2 Cr
Tel: **01323 732071**
Mr & Mrs Butler.
Rates fr: *£14.00-£14.00.*
Open: All Year
Beds: 1F 6D 5T 2S
Baths: 3 Ensuite, 4 Shared
🛏 🖵 🎹 Ⓥ ✔
Small friendly family-run hotel 50
yards from seafront. Comfortable
rooms, guests' lounge and bar.
Open all year. Excellent value for
money. Ring for brochure.

(2m) **Cambridge House,**
6 Cambridge Road, Eastbourne,
E. Sussex, BN22 7BS.
Actual grid ref: TQ6299
Family-run seaside guesthouse.
Grades: ETB 2 Cr, Comm
Tel: **01323 721100** Mr Blackman.
Rates fr: *£15.00-£15.00.*
Open: All Year (not Xmas)
Beds: 2F 3D 1T 1S
Baths: 4 Private 1 Shared
🛏 (2) 🖵 🕆 ✕ 🎹 Ⓥ 🛎

(0.5m) **Seagulls Guest House,**
12 South Cliff Avenue, Eastbourne,
E. Sussex, BN20 7AH.
Large Victorian house.
Tel: **01323 737831** Mrs Rogers.
Rates fr: *£17.50-£17.50.*
Open: All Year
Beds: 3D 2T 1S
Baths: 2 Ensuite, 2 Shared
🛏 (3) ⅍ 🖵 ✕ 🎹 ✔

(▲ 1m) **Eastbourne Youth Hostel,**
East Dean Road, Eastbourne,
E. Sussex, BN20 8ES.
Actual grid ref: TQ588990
Tel: **01323 721081**
Under 18: £5.00 **Adults:** £7.45
Family Bunk Rooms, Partially
Heated, Showers, Shop
Former golf clubhouse on South
Downs 450 ft above sea level with
sweeping views across Eastbourne
and Pevensey Bay

(0.5m) **Cherry Tree Hotel,**
15 Silverdale Road, Eastbourne,
E. Sussex, BN20 7AJ.
Family-run quality hotel.
Grades: ETB 3 Cr, Comm
Tel: **01323 722406** Mr Clarke.
Rates fr: *£22.00-£22.00.*
Open: All Year
Beds: 2F 3D 3T 2S
Baths: 10 Ensuite
✕ 🎹 🛎 ✔

(0.5m) **Falcondale House Private**
Hotel, *5 South Cliff Avenue,*
Eastbourne, E. Sussex, BN20 7AH.
Superb family run guesthouse.
Grades: ETB 3 Cr
Tel: **01323 643633** Mr Wilson.
Rates fr: *£17.00-£18.00.*
Open: Easter to Oct/Nov
Beds: 2D 3T 1S
Baths: 4 Ensuite 2 Shared
🅿 🖵 ✕ 🎹 Ⓥ

Wessex Ridgeway

The **Wessex Ridgeway** should be seen as part of the Ramblers' Association's great project to establish a long distance route along 'The Great Ridgeway', an ancient highway that probably ran from Devon to the East Anglian coast. This path thus links up with the **Ridgeway** National Trail itself, which meets the **Icknield Way**, which in turn touches the **Peddars Way** to create a 250-mile route from the South Coast up to Norfolk. The **Wessex Ridgeway** has just been waymarked with support from the **Countryside Commission** and the county councils. From Avebury with its massive stone circle you skirt Salisbury Plain to pass through the great hinterland of Hardy's Wessex - prehistoric sites, hill forts, high chalk downland, lonely coombes and the Cerne Abbas giant before heading off to the English Channel at Lyme Regis.

Guides:

Walk the Wessex Ridgeway in Dorset by Priscilla Houstoun (ISBN 0 948 699 37 X), published by Dorset Publishing Company and available from all good map shops or directly from the publishers (c/o Wincanton Press, National School, North Street, Wincanton, Somerset, BA9 9AT, tel. 01963 32583), £7 (inc p&p).

The Wessex Ridgeway by Alan Proctor, published by the Rambler's Association and available from the RA's National Office (1/5 Wandsworth Road, London, SW8 2XX, tel. 0171 582 6878), £2.50 (+ 70p p&p).

Maps: Ordnance Survey 1:50,000 Landranger series: 173, 183, 184, 193, 194, 195

Marlborough　　　　1

National Grid Ref: SU1869

|●| 🍷 Gallaghers Wine Bar, The Bear, Bentley's Wine Bar, The Sun, Tudor Tea Rooms

(3m) *Paddocks, Cardigan Road, Marlborough, Wilts, SN8 1LB*.
Large character private house.
Tel: **01672 515280** Mrs Brockwell.
Rates fr: £16.50.
Open: All Year (not Xmas)
Beds: 2D
Baths: 2 Ensuite
🄿 (4) 🍼 🖵 🏬 Ⓥ ⊬

(3.5m 🚗) *Cartref, 63 George Lane, Marlborough, Wilts, SN8 4BY*.
Actual grid ref: SU1969
Family home near town and restaurants.
Tel: **01672 512771** Mrs Harrison.
Rates fr: £15.00-£15.00.
Open: All Year (not Xmas)
Beds: 1F 1D 1T
Baths: 1 Shared
🛇 (1) 🄿 (2) 🐾 🏬 Ⓥ ⊬

(6m) *Kennet Beeches, 54 George Lane, Marlborough, Wilts, SN8 4BY*.
Comfortable home in town centre.
Tel: **01672 512579**
Mr & Mrs Young.
Rates fr: £16.00-£16.00.
Open: All Year
Beds: 1T 2S　**Baths:** 1 Shared
🄿 (2) ⊬ 🖵 🏬 Ⓥ ⊬

Lockeridge　　　　2

National Grid Ref: SU1467

|●| 🍷 Who'd a Thought It

(3m) *The Taffrail, Rhyls Lane, Lockeridge, Marlborough, Wilts, SN8 4ED*.
Spacious modern house, large garden.
Grades: ETB Listed
Tel: **01672 861266** Mrs Spencer.
Rates fr: £17.50-£20.00.
Open: Jan to Nov
Beds: 1D 1T 1S　**Baths:** 1 Shared
🛇 (8) 🄿 (3) 🖵 🏬 Ⓥ

West Kennett　　　　3

National Grid Ref: SU1168

(0.75m) *Silbury Hill Cottage, West Kennett, Marlborough, Wilts, SN8 1QH*.
Actual grid ref: SU103683
Charming thatched cottage, warm welcome.
Grades: ETB Listed
Tel: **01672 539416**
Mr & Mrs Rendle.
Rates fr: £16.00-£18.00.
Open: Easter to Nov
Beds: 1D 1T
🛇 🄿 (3) ⊬ ✕ 🏬 Ⓥ ≀ ⊬

Avebury　　　　4

National Grid Ref: SU1069

|●| 🍷 Red Lion, Wagon & Horses

(On Path) *6 Beckhampton Road, Avebury, Marlborough, Wilts, SN8 1QT*.
Semi-detached house near the Stones.

Tel: **01672 539588** Mrs Dixon.
Rates fr: £15.00-£18.00.
Open: All Year (not Xmas)
Beds: 1D 1T
Baths: 1 Shared
🛇 🄿 🖵 🏬

Bishops Cannings　　　　5

National Grid Ref: SU0364

|●| 🍷 Crown Inn

(2m) *Partacre, Horton, Bishops Cannings, Devizes, Wilts, SN10 3NB*.
Welcoming family house.
Relaxing.
Tel: **01380 860261** Mrs Jones.
Rates fr: £13.00-£14.00.
Open: All Year
Beds: 1D 1T 1S
Baths: 1 Shared
🛇 (2) 🄿 (3) ⊬ 🖵 🏬

(2m) *Blackwells Farm, Bishops Cannings, Devizes, Wilts, SN10 2JZ*.
C16th comfortable thatched house.
Grades: ETB 2 Cr
Tel: **01380 860438** Mrs Quinlan.
Rates fr: £17.50-£20.00.
Open: All Year (not Xmas)
Beds: 1F 1D 1S
Baths: 1 Private 1 Shared
🛇 🄿 (8) ⊬ 🖵 🐾 🏬 Ⓥ

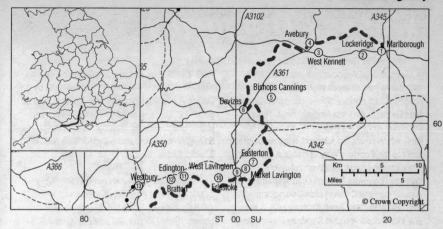

© Crown Copyright

Devizes 6

National Grid Ref: SU0061

🍴 🍺 The Elm Tree, Bear Hotel, Crown Inn, The Bridge, Castle Hotel, Royal Oak, The Bell

(0.5m) 🚗 *Pinecroft*, Potterne Road (A360), Devizes, Wilts, *SN10 5DA*.
Actual grid ref: SU006607
Spacious Georgian home, close to centre.
Grades: ETB 2 Cr, AA 3 Q
Tel: **01380 721433** Mr/Mrs Linton.
Rates fr: *£16.00*-**£20.00**.
Open: All Year **Beds:** 1F 2D 2T
Baths: 4 Ensuite, 1 Shared
🛏 🅿 (7) 🖵 ✕ 🎬 🕭 🎥 🛋 ⚡

(0.5m) *Glenholme Guest House*, 77 Nursteed Road, Devizes, Wilts, *SN10 3AJ*.
Comfortable family house.
Grades: ETB 1 Cr
Tel: **01380 723187** Mrs Bishop.
Rates fr: *£30.00*-**£17.00**.
Open: All Year
Beds: 1F 1T **Baths:** 1 Shared
🛏 🅿 (2) 🖵 🛏 ✕ 🎬 🎥 🛋

(0.5m) 🚗 *Rathlin Guest House*, Wick Lane, Devizes, Wilts, *SN10 5DP*.
Elegant, comfortable and quiet.
Grades: ETB 3 Cr, Comm
Tel: **01380 721999** Mr Fletcher.
Rates fr: *£20.00*-**£25.00**.
Open: All Year (not Xmas)
Beds: 2D 2T **Baths:** 4 Ensuite
🛏 🅿 (6) ✍ 🖵 ✕ 🎬 🎥 🛋 ⚡

(On Path) 🚗 *Kenavon*, London Road, Devizes, Wilts, *SN10 2DS*.
Modern house backing onto Kennet/Avon Canal.
Grades: ETB Listed
Tel: **01380 721494** Mr Fry.
Rates fr: *£17.00*-**£15.00**.
Open: All Year (not Xmas)
Beds: 1F 1D 2T 1S
Baths: 1 Ensuite 2 Shared
🛏 🅿 (4) 🖵 🛏 ✕ 🎬 🎥 ⚡

(0.5m) *Traquair*, 2 Bricksteed Avenue, Devizes, Wilts, *SN10 3AE*.
Comfortable house, good parking.
Quiet situaton.
Tel: **01380 722014**
Mr Forbes Peebles.
Rates fr: *£15.00*-**£15.00**.
Open: All Year (not Xmas)
Beds: 1T 1S
Baths: 1 Ensuite 1 Shared
🛏 (12) 🅿 (3) 🖵 🎬

Easterton 7

National Grid Ref: SU0255

🍴 🍺 Royal Oak

(1m) 🚗 *Eastcott Manor*, Easterton, Devizes, Wilts, *SN10 4PL*.
Actual grid ref: SU027358
Tel: **01380 813313** Mrs Firth.
Rates fr: *£20.00*-**£18.00**.
Open: All Year (not Xmas)
Beds: 2T 2S
Baths: 2 Ensuite, 2 Private
🛏 🅿 (20) 🖵 🛏 ✕ 🛋 ⚡
Eastcott Manor is an Elizabethan manor house. Wessex Ridgeway 1 mile. Fully modernised, quiet and comfortable. Convenient for Bath and Salisbury. Good food a speciality.

Market Lavington 8

National Grid Ref: SU0154

🍴 🍺 The Royal Oak

(0.75m) *The Old Coach House*, 21 Church Street, Market Lavington, Devizes, Wilts, *SN10 4DU*.
Actual grid ref: SU014541
Comfortable, spacious C18th house.
Grades: ETB 2 Cr, Comm, AA 3 Q
Tel: **01380 812879**
Mr & Mrs Mattingly.
Rates fr: *£20.00*-**£22.00**.
Open: All Year **Beds:** 1D 2T 1S
Baths: 3 Ensuite, 1 Private
🛏 🅿 (5) ✍ 🖵 ✕ 🎬 🎥 🛋 ⚡

West Lavington 9

National Grid Ref: ST8920

🍴 🍺 The Bridge Inn

(1m) *Parsonage House*, West Lavington, Devizes, Wilts, *SN10 4LT*.
C17th old parsonage.
Tel: **01380 813345**
Mrs West.
Rates fr: *£15.00*-**£17.50**.
Open: All Year
Beds: 1F 1T
🛏 🅿 (4) ✍ 🖵 ✕ 🎬 🛋 🥾 ⚡

Erlestoke 10

National Grid Ref: ST9653

🍴 🍺 George & Dragon

(1m) *Longwater*, Lower Road, Erlestoke, Devizes, Wilts, *SN10 5UE*.
Actual grid ref: ST965543
Modern comfortable farmhouse.
Grades: ETB 3 Cr, Comm, AA 3 Q
Tel: **01380 830095** Mrs Hampton.
Rates fr: *£20.00*-**£25.00**.
Open: All Year (not Xmas)
Beds: 1F 2D 2T
Baths: 5 Ensuite
🅿 (8) 🖵 🛏 ✕ 🎬 🕭 🛋 ⚡

Edington 11

National Grid Ref: ST9253

🍴 🍺 Lamb

(0.75m) *Hillside Farm*, Edington, Westbury, Wilts, *BA13 4PG*.
Secluded farmhouse with delightful gardens.
Grades: ETB 1 Cr, Comm
Tel: **01380 830437**
Mrs Mussell.
Rates fr: *£15.00*-**£16.00**.
Open: Feb to Dec
Beds: 1F 1T
Baths: 1 Shared
🛏 🅿 (3) 🖵 🎬 🛋

Bratton 12

National Grid Ref: ST9152

(0.5m) *The Duke At Bratton,*
Melbourne Street, Bratton,
Westbury, Wilts, BA13 4RW.
Actual grid ref: ST880540
Traditional village inn, fresh food.
Tel: **01380 830242**
Rates fr: *£17.50*-**£25.00**.
Open: All Year
Beds: 2D 2T **Baths:** 2 Shared
⌂ (14) ▣ (30) ⌷ ✕ Ⅲ ▣ ▮

Westbury 13

National Grid Ref: ST8650

⎰⎱ ◨ Full Moon

(0.75m) *Brokerswood House,*
Brokerswood, Westbury, Wilts,
BA13 4EH.
Situated in woodland park.
Tel: **01373 823428** Mrs Phillips.
Rates fr: *£14.00*-**£14.00**.
Open: All Year (not Xmas)
Beds: 1F 1T 1S
Baths: 1 Ensuite 1 Shared
⌂ (1) ▣ (6) ⌷ ⅓

Warminster 14

National Grid Ref: ST8745

⎰⎱ ◨ Yew Tree, The Old Bell,
Farmers Arms, The Ship

(0.25m) *Farmers Hotel, 1 Silver*
Street, Warminster, Wilts, BA12 8PS.
B&B premises with bar and restaurant.
Tel: **01985 213815** Mr Brandani.
Rates fr: *£17.00*-**£17.00**.
Open: All Year
Beds: 4F 4D 4T 8S
Baths: 16 Ensuite
⌂ ▣ (6) ⌷ ⅓ ✕ Ⅲ ▣ ▮ ⅄

(0.25m) *32a George Street,*
Warminster, Wilts, BA12 8QB.
Listed Grade 2 terrace.
Tel: **01985 212188** Mrs Brandon.

Rates fr: *£15.00*-**£23.00**.
Open: Easter to Oct
Beds: 1D
Baths: 1 Ensuite
▣ (2) ⅄ ⌷ ✕

**All details shown
are as supplied
by B&B owners in
Autumn 1995.**

Hindon 15

National Grid Ref: ST9132

⎰⎱ ◨ Grosvenor, Lamb Inn

(On Path 🚌) *Ellandee, High*
Street, Hindon, Salisbury, Wilts,
SP3 6DJ.
Actual grid ref: ST9032
Homely bungalow. Quiet situation.
Tel: **01747 820332**
Mrs Dyke.
Rates fr: *£12.50*-**£12.50**.
Open: All Year
Beds: 1D 1T
Baths: 1 Shared
⌂ ▣ (4) ⌷ ⅓ Ⅲ ▮ ⅄

East Knoyle 16

National Grid Ref: ST8830

⎰⎱ ◨ Fox & Hounds

(1m) *Moors Farmhouse, East*
Knoyle, Salisbury, Wilts, SP3 6BU.
C17th farmhouse, self-contained
suite.
Tel: **01747 830385**
Mrs Reading.
Rates fr: *£20.00*-**£25.00**.
Open: All Year (not Xmas)
Beds: 1T
Baths: 1 Ensuite
⌂ (8) ▣ ⌷ Ⅲ

Semley 17

National Grid Ref: ST8926

(2.5m 🚌) *The Benett Arms,*
Semley, Shaftesbury, Dorset,
SP7 9AS.
Actual grid ref: ST892269
C17th stone built inn.
Grades: ETB 2 Cr, AA 2 Q
Tel: **01747 830221** Mr Duthie.
Rates fr: *£22.00*-**£29.00**.
Open: All Year (not Xmas)
Beds: 4D 1T
⌂ ▣ (30) ⌷ ⅓ ✕ Ⅲ ⅙ ▣ ▮ ⅄

Ludwell 18

National Grid Ref: ST9122

⎰⎱ ◨ The Grove Arms

(On Path) *Birdbush Farm,*
Ludwell, Shaftesbury, Dorset,
SP7 9NH.
Comfortable farmhouse in quiet
position.
Tel: **01747 828252** Mrs Rossiter.
Rates fr: *£15.50*-**£16.00**.
Open: Easter to Oct
Beds: 1D 1S
Baths: 1 Shared
⌂ ▣ (6) ⅄ ⌷

(On Path) *Charnwood Cottage,*
Charlton, Ludwell, Shaftesbury,
Dorset, SP7 9LZ.
C17th thatched cottage.
Tel: **01747 828310**
Mr & Mrs Morgan.
Rates fr: *£15.00*-**£20.00**.
Open: All Year (not Xmas)
Beds: 1F 1D **Baths:** 1 Shared
⌂ (5) ▣ (2) ⌷ Ⅲ

**Pay B&Bs by cash or
cheque and be prepared
to pay up front.**

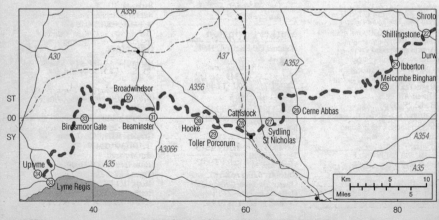

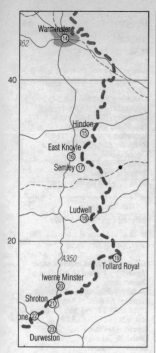

Shroton 21

National Grid Ref: ST8512

📵 🍴 The Cricketers

(0.2m) *Lattemere, Frog Lane, Shroton, Blandford Forum, Dorset, DT11 8QL.*
Comfortable house in picturesque village.
Tel: **01258 860115** Mrs Wright.
Rates fr: *£15.00*-**£16.00**.
Open: All Year
Beds: 1D 1T
Baths: 1 Private 1 Shared
🛏 🅿 (3) 🛏 🛋 Ⓥ

Shillingstone 22

National Grid Ref: ST8211

📵 🍴 Fiddleford Inn, Old Ox, Silent Whistle

(On Path) *The Willows Tea Rooms, 5 Blandford Road, Shillingstone, Blandford Forum, Dorset, DT11 0SG.*
C18th tea rooms with accommodation.
Tel: **01258 861167** Mrs Auckland.
Rates fr: *£15.00*-**£17.00**.
Open: Feb to Nov
Beds: 1D
Baths: 1 Ensuite
🛏 🅿 (8) ⚡ 🛋 ✕ 🛋 ♿ Ⓥ ♟

Durweston 23

National Grid Ref: ST8508

(2m) *Portman Lodge, Durweston, Blandford Forum, Dorset, DT11 0QA.*
Comfortable, warm Georgian private house.
Grades: ETB Listed
Tel: **01258 452168** Ms Portman.
Rates fr: *£18.00*-**£18.00**.
Open: All Year (not Xmas)
Beds: 1F 1D 1T
Baths: 2 Private 1 Shared
🛏 🅿 (20) ⚡ 🛋 ✕ 🛋 Ⓥ

Ibberton 24

National Grid Ref: ST7807

📵 🍴 The Crown Inn

(0.75m) *Manor House Farm, Ibberton, Blandford Forum, Dorset, DT11 0EN.*
C16th comfortable farmhouse.
Tel: **01258 817349** Mrs Old.
Rates fr: *£12.00*-**£14.00**.
Open: All Year
Beds: 2D 1T
Baths: 1 Ensuite 1 Shared
🛏 🅿 🛏 🛋

Melcombe Bingham 25

National Grid Ref: ST7602

(1.25m) *Badgers Sett, Cross Lanes, Melcombe Bingham, Dorchester, Dorset, DT2 7NY.*
Actual grid ref: ST759022

Converted C17th cottages.
Grades: ETB 1 Cr, Comm
Tel: **01258 880697** Ms Dowsett.
Rates fr: *£18.00*-**£19.00**.
Open: All Year (not Xmas)
Beds: 1F 1D 1T
Baths: 2 Ensuite
🛏 🅿 (4) ⚡ 🛋 🛏 ✕ 🛋 Ⓥ ♟ ♟

Cerne Abbas 26

National Grid Ref: ST6601

📵 🍴 New Inn

(0.75m) *New Inn, 14 Long Street, Cerne Abbas, Dorchester, Dorset, DT2 7JF.*
Historic C13th converted abbey.
Tel: **01300 341274** Mr Parsons.
Rates fr: *£15.00*-**£25.00**.
Open: All Year
Beds: 4D 1T
🛏 🅿 (12) 🛋 🛏 ✕ 🛋 Ⓥ

Sydling St Nicholas 27

National Grid Ref: SY6399

📵 🍴 The Greyhound

(On Path) *Lamperts Cottage, Sydling St Nicholas, Dorchester, Dorset, DT2 9NU.*
C16th Grade II Listed cottage.
Grades: ETB Listed, AA 3 Q
Tel: **01300 341659** Mr Willis.
Rates fr: *£18.00*-**£18.00**.
Open: All Year
Beds: 2D 2T
Baths: 2 Shared
🛏 (8) 🅿 (3) 🛏 🛋 Ⓥ ♟ ♟

(On Path) *City Cottage, Sydling St Nicholas, Dorchester, Dorset, DT2 9NX.*
Comfortable cottage.
Tel: **01300 341300** Mrs Wareham.
Rates fr: *£15.00*-**£15.00**.
Open: All Year (not Xmas)
Beds: 1D 1S **Baths:** 1 Shared
🅿 (3) 🛋 🛋 ♟

(On Path) *Lamperts Farmhouse, 11 Dorchester Road, Sydling St Nicholas, Dorchester, Dorset, DT2 9NU.*
C17th thatched family farmhouse.
Grades: ETB 2 Cr
Tel: **01300 341790** Mrs Bown.
Rates fr: *£18.00*-**£22.00**.
Open: All Year
Beds: 1D 1T **Baths:** 2 Ensuite
🛏 🅿 (4) 🛋 🛏 ✕ 🛋 Ⓥ ♟ ♟

(On Path) *Magiston Farm, Sydling St Nicholas, Dorchester, Dorset, DT2 9NR.*
Actual grid ref: SY6398
C16th comfortable farmhouse.
Grades: ETB Listed
Tel: **01300 320295** Mrs Barraclough.
Rates fr: *£15.50*-**£15.50**.
Open: All Year (not Xmas)
Beds: 1D 2T 1S
Baths: 1 Ensuite 1 Shared
🛏 (10) 🅿 (10) 🛏 ✕ 🛋 ♿ Ⓥ ♟ ♟

Tollard Royal 19

National Grid Ref: ST9417

📵 🍴 King John Inn

(0.2m) *King John Inn, Tollard Royal, Salisbury, Wilts, SP5 5PS.*
Large Victorian freehouse.
Tel: **01725 516207**
Mr Woodhouse.
Rates fr: *£22.50*-**£30.00**.
Open: All Year
Beds: 1D 2T **Baths:** 3 Private
🅿 🛋 ✕ 🛋 Ⓥ

Iwerne Minster 20

National Grid Ref: ST8614

(1m 🚌) *The Talbot Hotel, Blandford Road, Iwerne Minster, Blandford Forum, Dorset, DT11 8QN.*
Actual grid ref: ST865144
Large Victorian coaching inn.
Tel: **01747 811269**
Mr & Mrs Richardson.
Rates fr: *£13.75*-**£18.75**.
Open: All Year
Beds: 2F 2D 1T 1S
Baths: 2 Private 2 Shared
🛏 🅿 (30) 🛋 ✕ 🛋 Ⓥ ♟ ♟

The *lowest* **single** rate *is* shown in **bold**.

Cattistock 28

National Grid Ref: SY5999

🍴 🍺 Fox & Hound

(2m) *Sandhills Cottage, Cattistock, Dorchester, Dorset, DT2 0HQ.*
Comfortable country cottage.
Tel: **01300 321146** Mrs Willis.
Rates fr: *£18.00.*
Open: All Year (not Xmas)
Beds: 1F 1D 1T
Baths: 1 Ensuite, 1 Shared
🛇 🅿 ⅍ ☐ 🖈 🛏 Ⅲ 🗓 🛉 ⋄

Toller Porcorum 29

National Grid Ref: SY5698

🍴 🍺 The Swan

(On Path) *The Kingcombe Centre, Toller Porcorum, Dorchester, Dorset, DT2 0EQ.*
Actual grid ref: SY554991
Converted barns beside River
Hooke.
Grades: ETB Listed
Tel: **01300 320684** Mr Spring.
Rates fr: *£14.00-£15.00.*
Open: All Year
Beds: 1F 6T 4S
🛇 🅿 (25) ⅍ ☐ 🖈 ✕ Ⅲ 🗓 🛉 ⋄
Also ▲ *£2.50 per tent.*
Open: All Year 🐾 Ⓣ 🍳 ✕ ♨ ⅋

(0.75m) *Colesmoor Farm, Toller Porcorum, Dorchester, Dorset, DT2 0DU.*
Actual grid ref: SY556971
Small family farm, quiet setting.
Grades: ETB 1 Cr, Comm
Tel: **01300 320812** Mrs Geddes.
Rates fr: *£15.00-£18.00.*
Open: May to Dec
Beds: 1D 1T
Baths: 1 Ensuite 1 Private
🛇 🅿 (3) ⅍ ☐ ✕ Ⅲ 🗓 🛉 ⋄

Hooke 30

National Grid Ref: ST5300

(0.25m) *Watermeadow House, Bridge Farm, Hooke, Beaminster, Dorset, DT8 3PD.*
Large Georgian style farmhouse.
Grades: ETB 2 Cr
Tel: **01308 862619** Mrs
Wallbridge.
Rates fr: *£18.00-£24.00.*
Open: Easter to Oct
Beds: 1F 1D 1T
🛇 🅿 (4) ⅍ ☐ 🖈 Ⅲ 🗓 ⋄

(0.5m) 🚍 *Hooke Court, Hooke, Beaminster, Dorset, DT8 3NY.*
Actual grid ref: ST531004
C17th manor house.
Tel: **01308 862260**
Rates fr: *£18.00-£23.00.*
Open: All Year
Beds: 3F 6T 2S
Baths: 8 Ensuite 1 Shared
🛇 🅿 (50) ⅍ ☐ ✕ Ⅲ 🗓 ⋄

Beaminster 31

National Grid Ref: ST4701

🍴 🍺 Pickwicks

(On Path) *Kitwhistle Farm, Beaminster Down, Beaminster, Dorset, DT8 3SG.*
Comfortable farmhouse, quiet
location.
Grades: ETB Listed, 2 Cr
Tel: **01308 862458** Mrs Hasell.
Rates fr: *£15.00-£18.00.*
Open: Easter to Oct
Beds: 1D 1T
Baths: 1 Private
🛇 🅿 ☐

(On Path) *Beam Cottage, 16 North Street, Beaminster, Dorset, DT8 3DZ.*
Very attractive Listed (Grade II)
cottage.
Grades: ETB 1 Cr
Tel: **01308 863639** Mrs Standeven.
Rates fr: *£17.50-£20.00.*
Open: All Year (not Xmas)
Beds: 1D 1T
Baths: 2 Ensuite
🛇 🅿 (2) ☐ ✕ Ⅲ

Broadwindsor 32

National Grid Ref: ST4302

(0.75m) 🚍 *White Lion Inn, The Square, Broadwindsor, Beaminster, Dorset, DT8 3QD.*
Actual grid ref: ST437025
Grade 2 Listed village inn.
Tel: **01308 868855**
Mr Corbett.
Rates fr: *£13.75-£17.50.*
Open: All Year
Beds: 2F 1D 1T
Baths: 1 Shared
🛇 ☐ 🖈 ✕ Ⅲ 🛉 ⋄

Birdsmoor Gate 33

National Grid Ref: ST3900

🍴 🍺 Rose & Crown

(On Path) *Rose & Crown, Birdsmoor Gate, Marshwood, Bridport, Dorset, DT6 5QG.*
Country pub.
Tel: **01297 678527** Mr Cornock.
Rates fr: *£12.50-£12.50.*
Open: All Year
Beds: 3F 1D 1T 1S
Baths: 1 Shared
🛇 🅿 (20) ✕ 🗓 ⋄
Also ▲ *£Free per tent.*
Open: All Year Ⓣ 🍳 ✕ ♨

Uplyme 34

National Grid Ref: SY3293

🍴 🍺 Pilot Boat

(0.25m) *Lydwell House, Lyme Road, Uplyme, Lyme Regis, Dorset, DT7 3TJ.*
Charming Edwardian house with
gardens.
Grades: ETB 2 Cr, Comm
Tel: **01297 443522** Mrs
Greenhalgh.
Rates fr: *£14.50-£15.50.*
Open: All Year
Beds: 2F 1D 1T 1S
Baths: 2 Private 1 Shared
🛇 🅿 (7) ☐ 🖈 Ⅲ 🗓

Lyme Regis 35

National Grid Ref: SY3492

🍴 🍺 Mad Hatter Restaurant, Pilot
Boat, Talbot Arms

(0.25m) 🚍 *Ilex Cottage Guest House, View Road, Lyme Regis, Dorset, DT7.*
Modern comfortable guesthouse.
Grades: ETB 2 Cr, Approv
Tel: **01297 442891** Mrs Forrester.
Rates fr: *£15.00-£15.00.*
Open: All Year
Beds: 2F 3D 1T
Baths: 6 Ensuite
🛇 🅿 (6) ☐ 🖈 ✕ Ⅲ 🗓 🛉 ⋄

(0.25m) *Devonia Guest House, 2 Woodmead Road, Lyme Regis, Dorset, DT7 3AB.*
Family-run friendly comfortable
accommodation.
Tel: **01297 442869**
Mrs Gapper.
Rates fr: *£18.00-£16.00.*
Open: All Year (not Xmas)
Beds: 1F 1D 1T 1S
Baths: 3 Ensuite 1 Shared
🛇 🅿 (6) ☐ Ⅲ 🛉 ⋄

(0.5m) *The Red House, Sidmouth Road, Lyme Regis, Dorset, DT7 3ES.*
Actual grid ref: SY330922
Lovely coastal and rural views.
Grades: ETB 2 Cr, High Comm
Tel: **01297 442055** Mr Norman.
Rates fr: *£18.00-£30.00.*
Open: Mar to Nov
Beds: 1F 2T
Baths: 3 Ensuite
🛇 (8) 🅿 (3) ⅍ ☐ Ⅲ ⋄

(On Path) *Coverdale Guest House,*
Woodmead Road, Lyme Regis,
Dorset, DT7 3AB.
Actual grid ref: SY339925
Spacious comfortable non-smoking
guesthouse.
Grades: ETB 2 Cr, Comm,
AA 3 Q, Recomm
Tel: 01297 442882
Mr & Mrs Harding.
Rates fr: *£13.00-£15.00.*
Open: Feb to Nov
Beds: 4D 2T 2S
Baths: 6 Ensuite 1 Shared
⛄ P (9) ✄ ⛌ ⊁ ✕ Ⅲ, Ⓥ ⓲ ✦

(On Path 🐾) *Kersbrook Hotel,*
Pound Road, Lyme Regis, Dorset,
DT7 3HX.
C18th thatched country house
hotel.
Grades: AA 2 St, RAC 2 St
Tel: 01297 442596
Rates fr: *£30.00-£45.00.*
Open: All Year
Beds: 6D 4T **Baths:** 10 Ensuite
⛄ P (14) ⛌ ⊁ ✕ Ⅲ, Ⓥ ⓲ ✦

(0.25m) *The White House, 47*
Silver Street, Lyme Regis, Dorset,
DT7 3HR.
Actual grid ref: SY339923
Small C18th Georgian guesthouse.
Grades: ETB 2 Cr, Comm,
AA 3 Q
Tel: 01297 443420
Mrs Edmondson.
Rates fr: *£16.00-£18.00.*
Open: Easter to Oct
Beds: 7D 2T
Baths: 7 Ensuite
P (6) ⛌ ⊁ Ⅲ, ⓲ ✦

(0.5m) *Southernhaye, Pound*
Road, Lyme Regis, Dorset, DT7 3HX.
Edwardian house with sea views.
Grades: ETB 1 Cr, Comm
Tel: 01297 443077
Mr Garrard.
Rates fr: *£16.00-£18.00.*
Open: All Year (not Xmas)
Beds: 1D 1T
Baths: 1 Shared
⛄ (14) P (2) ⛌ Ⅲ, Ⓥ ✦

(0.5m) *Whitsbury, 38 Silver Street,*
Lyme Regis, Dorset, DT7 3HS.
Victorian house, magnificent sea
views.
Tel: 01297 443753
Mr Jones.
Rates fr: *£14.00-£14.00.*
Open: All Year
Beds: 1D 1T
Baths: 2 Private
⛄ P (4) ⛌ ⊁ Ⅲ, Ⓥ

High season,
bank holidays and
special events mean
low availability
everywhere.

The **West Highland Way** is an excellent, well-marked path running mainly at low-level for 95 miles from Milngavie, north of Glasgow to Fort William in Inverness-shire. It is very popular, for in that relatively short distance it manages to combine some of the greatest sights in Scotland - the largest loch (**Loch Lomond**), the bleakest moorland (**Rannoch Moor**) and the highest mountain (**Ben Nevis**). The final destination, Fort William, attracts visitors from all over the world. The way itself largely follows the droves used by the Highlanders to herd their cattle to the Lowland markets, as well as the eighteenth-century military roads built to help control the Jacobites. The walking provides a mixed challenge - sometimes a woodland stroll, at other times a tough, exposed scramble. Why not do this walk over a week in early summer when it's warm and dry, the coach parties fewer, the flowers in bloom and the midges not yet hatched? You won't regret it! There may even be a foot masseuse at Crianlarich Youth Hostel to tend to weary feet (ask the warden for more details)!

Guides (available all good bookshops, unless stated)

The West Highland Way (map & book set) by Robert Aitken (ISBN 0 1149525 23), published by HMSO and available from all major bookshops, £14.95

The West Highland Way by Anthony Burton (ISBN 1 85410391 1), published by Aurum Press in association with Ordnance Survey and available from all major bookshops, £9.99

A Guide to the West Highland Way by Tom Hunter (ISBN 09 469090 1), published by Constable & Co Ltd, £8.95

Maps: Ordnance Survey 1:50,000 Landranger series: 41 50, 56, 57 and 64. Also, *The West Highland Way* (4-colour linear route map), ISBN 1 871149 00 2, published by Footprint and available from all good map shops or directly from their offices (Unit 87, Stirling Enterprise Park, Stirling, FK7 7RP), £2.95 (+ 40p p&p)

Milngavie 1

National Grid Ref: NS5574

⊙ ⌖ The Allander, The Burn Brae Hotel, The Black Bull Hotel

(0.5m) *58 Keystone Quadrant, Milngavie, Glasgow, G62 6LP*.
Actual grid ref: NS5574
Modern bungalow near village centre.
Grades: STB Listed, Comm
Tel: **0141 956 5615** Mrs Groves.
Rates fr: £15.00-**£16.00**.
Open: All Year
Beds: 1D 1T 1S
Baths: 1 Shared
❄ (5) ▣ (5) ⊬ ▢ ⼞ ✕ ⤒ ⓥ 🖝 ∜

(0.5m 🚐) *13 Craigdhu Avenue, Milngavie, Glasgow, G62 6DX*.
Traditional family house, warm welcome.
Tel: **0141 956 3439** Mrs Ogilvie.
Rates fr: £15.00-**£16.00**.
Open: Mar to Oct
Beds: 1F 1T **Baths:** 1 Shared
❄ ▣ (3) ⊬ ▢ ⼞ ⤒ ⓥ 🖝 ∜

The *lowest* single rate *is shown* in bold.

(0.5m) *Arnish, 14 Blane Drive, Milngavie, Glasgow, G62 8HG*.
Modern comfortable home.
Grades: STB Comm
Tel: **0141 956 1767** Mrs Chapman.
Rates fr: £14.00-**£14.00**.
Open: All Year
Beds: 1D 1T 1S **Baths:** 1 Shared
❄ (5) ▣ ⊬ ✕ ⤒ 🖝 ∜

(0.5m) *Graneag House, 55 Drumlin Drive, Milngavie, Glasgow, G62 6NF*.
Large, modern, family house close to village. With wooded views.
Grades: STB Highly Comm
Tel: **0141 956 6681**
Rates fr: £16.00-**£16.00**.
Open: All Year (not Xmas)
Beds: 2D 1T
Baths: 1 Private 2 Shared
❄ (0) ⤒ ⓥ 🖝

Strathblane 2

National Grid Ref: NS5679

⊙ ⌖ Kirkhouse Inn

(On Path) *The Kirkhouse Inn, Strathblane, Glasgow, G63 9AA*.
Small, friendly hotel - good food.
Grades: STB 5 Cr, Comm, AA 3 St
Tel: **01360 770621** Mr De Banzie.

Rates fr: £25.00-**£35.00**.
Open: All Year
Beds: 6D 7T 2S **Baths:** 15 Private
❄ ▣ (100) ▢ 🖝 ✕ ⤒ ⓥ 🖝 ∜

Killearn 3

National Grid Ref: NS5285

⊙ ⌖ Old Mill

(On Path 🚐) *Croy Cunningham Farm, Killearn, Glasgow, G63 9QQ*.
Lovely large redstone house, big garden.
Grades: STB Listed
Tel: **01360 50329** Mrs Campbell.
Rates fr: £16.00-**£16.00**.
Open: All Year
Beds: 1D 1T 1S **Baths:** 2 Shared
❄ ▣ ▢ 🖝 ✕ ⤒ ⓥ 🖝 ∜

Easter Drumquhassle 4

National Grid Ref: NS4887

(On Path 🚌) *East Drumquhassle Farm, Gartness Road, Easter Drumquhassle, Drymen, Glasgow, G63 0DN.*
Actual grid ref: NS486872
Peaceful, spectacular views, comfortable farmhouse.
Grades: STB Listed, Comm
Tel: 01360 660893 Mrs Cross.
Rates fr: *£16.50-£19.50.*
Open: All Year
Beds: 1F 1T
Baths: 1 Ensuite, 1 Private
🛇 **P** (6) ⊬ 🖵 ★ ✕ 🕮 **V** ⓐ ⊬
Also ▲ *£3 per person. Also bunkhouse, £6 per bunk.*
Open: All Year ⋒ 🅣 ≋ ✕ ⊬ ⚛

The Grid Reference beneath the location heading is for the village or town - *not* for individual houses, which are shown (where supplied) in each entry itself.

Gateside 5

National Grid Ref: NS4888

🍴 ◧ Clachan Inn

(On Path) *Gateside Lodge, Gateside, Drymen, Glasgow, G63 0DW.*
Comfortable C19th lodge house.
Grades: STB Reg
Tel: 01360 660215
Mrs Ford.
Rates fr: *£13.50-£18.00.*
Open: Mar to Oct
Beds: 1D 2T
Baths: 2 Shared
🛇 **P** 🖵 🕮 **V** ⓐ ⊬

Drymen 6

National Grid Ref: NS4788

🍴 ◧ Clachan Inn, Winnock Hotel

(On Path) *Buchanan Arms Hotel, Drymen, Glasgow, G63 0.*
Grades: STB 4 Cr, Comm, AA 3 St, RAC 3 St
Tel: 01360 660588 Mr Swinton.
Rates fr: *£46.00-£46.00.*
Open: All Year
Beds: 3F 10D 30T 9S
Baths: 52 Ensuite
🛇 **P** (100) 🖵 ★ ✕ 🕮 **V** ⓐ ⊬
Welcome to a charming village hotel full of character. The superb restaurant blending excellent cuisine with high quality accommodation and leisure facilities.

(On Path) *Ceardach, Gartness Road, Drymen, Glasgow, G63 0BH.*
250-year-old converted smithy.
Grades: STB Reg
Tel: 01360 660596 Mrs Robb.
Rates fr: *£15.00-£15.00.*
Open: All Year (not Xmas)
Beds: 1D 2T
Baths: 1 Shared
🛇 **P** 🖵 ★ 🕮 ૐ **V** ⓐ ⊬

(On Path 🚌) *8 Old Gartmore Road, Drymen, Glasgow, G63 8DP.*
A warm welcome. Comfortable house.
Tel: 01360 60566 Mrs Bolzicco.
Rates fr: *£16.00-£16.00.*
Open: All Year (not Xmas)
Beds: 1F 1D **Baths:** 2 Ensuite
P 🖵 🕮 **V** ⓐ ⊬

Milton of Buchanan 7

National Grid Ref: NS4490

(1m 🚌) *Dunleen, Milton of Buchanan, Balmaha, Glasgow, G63 0JE.*
Ranch-house by trout stream.
Grades: STB 1 Cr, High Comm
Tel: 01360 870274 Mrs MacFadyen.
Rates fr: *£16.00-£20.00.*
Open: May to Oct
Beds: 1D 1T
Baths: 1 Shared
🛇 **P** (4) ⊬ 🖵 🕮 **V** ⓐ ⊬

N

⑲ Tyndrum
⑱ Auchtertyre
Ewich ⑰ Portnellan A85
⑯
⑮
Crianlarich

⑭ Inverarnan

Ferry to West bank operates in summer

⑬
Ardlui

⑫ Inversnaid

© Crown Copyright

A81

A82

⑪
Rowardennan

⑩ Sallochy

A81

A811

⑨ Critreoch
⑧ Milton of Buchanan
Balmaha ⑦
⑥ Gateside
Drymen ⑥ ④ Easter Drumquhassle
③ Killearn

A811

A809 A81

② Strathblane

Km 5 10
Miles 5

① Milngavie

NN 20 40

(0.5m) *Mar Achlais*, Milton of
Buchanan, Balmaha, Glasgow,
G63 0JE.
Family home close to W.H.W.
Grades: STB 2 Cr, Comm
Tel: 01360 870300 Mr Nichols.
Rates fr: *£16.50-£26.50*.
Open: All Year (not Xmas)
Beds: 1F 1D
Baths: 2 Ensuite
⌂ 🅿 (2) ⬚ ⼗ 🛏 Ⅲ. Ⓥ ⓐ ✦

Balmaha   8

National Grid Ref: NS4290

(On Path 🚍) *Arrochoile*,
Balmaha, Drymen, Glasgow,
G63 0JG.
Actual grid ref: NS564290
Comfortable 'Loch view'
bungalow.
Grades: STB Listed
Tel: 01360 870231
Mr & Mrs Crooks.
Rates fr: *£16.00-£16.00*.
Open: All Year (not Xmas)
Beds: 1D 2T
Baths: 3 Ensuite
⌂ 🅿 (6) ⼡ ⬚ ✕ Ⅲ. Ⓥ ⓐ ✦

(On Path 🚍) *Bay Cottage*,
Balmaha, Drymen, Glasgow,
G63 0BX.
Homely cottage overlooking Loch
Lomond.
Grades: STB 3 Cr
Tel: 01360 870346 Mrs Bates.
Rates fr: *£17.50-£17.50*.
Open: Mar to Oct
Beds: 1F 2D 2T 1S
Baths: 3 Ensuite 2 Shared
⌂ 🅿 (5) ⼡ ⬚ ⼗ 🛏 ✕ Ⅲ. Ⓥ ⓐ ✦

Critreoch   9

National Grid Ref: NS4093

(On Path 🚍) *Critreoch*,
Rowardennan Road, Critreoch,
Balmaha, Glasgow, *G63 0AW*.
Actual grid ref: NS403932
Lochside family home. Beautiful
view.
Grades: STB 1 Cr, Comm
Tel: 0136087 0309 Mrs
MacLuskie.
Rates fr: *£16.00-£16.00*.
Open: Easter to October
Beds: 1D 1T 1S
Baths: 1 Shared
🅿 (6) ⼡ ⬚ ⼗ 🛏 ✕ Ⅲ. Ⓥ ⓐ ✦

**All rooms full and
nowhere else to stay?
Ask the owner if
there's anywhere
nearby**

Sallochy   10

National Grid Ref: NS3895

🍴 🍷 Rowardennan Hotel
(Sallochy)

(On Path 🚍) *5 Forest Cottage*,
Sallochy, Rowardennan, Glasgow,
G63 0AW.
Actual grid ref: NS386950
Timber house near Ben Lomond.
Tel: 01360 870320
Mrs Fraser.
Rates fr: *£16.00-£16.00*.
Open: All Year
Beds: 1D 1T
Baths: 1 Ensuite, 1 Shared
⌂ 🅿 ⬚ ⼗ ✕ 🛏 Ⓥ ⓐ ✦

Rowardennan   11

National Grid Ref: NS3598

🍴 🍷 Rowardennan Hotel

(▲ On Path) *Rowardennan Youth
Hostel*, Rowardennan, Loch
Lomond, Glasgow, *G63 0AR*.
Actual grid ref: NS3599
Warden: Mr W Scott.
Tel: 01360 870259
Under 18: £6.40
Adults: £7.80
Family Rooms, Evening Meal,
Self-Catering, Showers, Washing
Machine, Shop, Facilities for
Disabled
*A stone-built house with annexe
right on the lochside, with canoe-
ing and wind-surfing facilities*

Inversnaid   12

National Grid Ref: NN3308

🍴 🍷 Inversnaid Hotel

(On Path 🚍) *Inversnaid Hotel*,
Inversnaid, Stirling, Stirlingshire,
FK8 3TU.
Large tourist hotel.
Tel: 01877 386223
Ms Baker.
Rates fr: *£26.00-£26.00*.
Open: Mar to Dec
Beds: 113D **Baths:** 113 Private
⌂ 🅿 ⬚ ⼗ ✕ Ⓥ ⓐ
Also ▲ Also bunkhouse, *£13.00
per bunk.*
Open: Mar to Dec 🅟 🅣 ♨ ✕ ✦ 🕭

Ardlui   13

National Grid Ref: NN3115

🍴 🍷 Ardlui Hotel

(0.5m by Ferry🚍) *Ardlui Hotel*,
Ardlui, Arrochar, Dunbartonshire,
G83 7EB.
Actual grid ref: NN318157
Warm, comfortable friendly family
hotel.
Grades: STB 3 Cr, Comm
Tel: 01301 704243
Mrs Squires.

Rates fr: *£27.20-£31.45*.
Open: All Year (not Xmas)
Beds: 2F 7D 4T
Baths: 7 Private
⌂ 🅿 (50) ⬚ ⼗ ✕ Ⅲ. Ⓥ ⓐ ✦
Also ▲ *£4.00 per tent.*
Open: All Year 🅟 🅣 ♨ ✕ ✦ 🕭

Inverarnan   14

National Grid Ref: NN3118

🍴 🍷 Stagger Inn Restaurant,
Drovers Inn

(On Path 🚍) *Rose Cottage*,
Inverarnan, Glen Falloch,
Arrochar, Dunbartonshire, *G83 7DX*.
Actual grid ref: NN317185
C18th shepherd's cottage.
Tel: 01301 704255
Mr and Mrs Fletcher.
Rates fr: *£15.00-£15.00*.
Open: All Year
Beds: 2T
Baths: 1 Shared
⌂ 🅿 (2) ⬚ ⼗ Ⓥ ⓐ ✦

Crianlarich   15

National Grid Ref: NN3825

🍴 🍷 Rod & Reel, Ben More
Lodge Hotel

(0.25m) *Tigh-na-Struith*,
Crianlarich, Perthshire, *FK20 8RU*.
Friendly, peaceful house by the
river.
Tel: 01838 300235
Mr & Mrs Chisholm.
Rates fr: *£16.00-£16.00*.
Open: All Year
Beds: 2F 3D 1T
Baths: 1 Shared
⌂ 🅿 (6) ⼡ ⬚ ⼗ 🛏 Ⅲ. Ⓥ ⓐ ✦

(0.25m 🚍) *Ben More Lodge
Hotel*, Crianlarich, Perthshire,
FK20 8QS.
Actual grid ref: NN391252
Superb ensuite accommodation in
lodges.
Grades: STB 3 Cr, Comm
Tel: 01838 300210
Mr Goodale.
Rates fr: *£25.00-£30.00*.
Open: Easter to November
Beds: 2F 8D 1T
Baths: 11 Private
⌂ 🅿 (30) ⬚ ⼗ 🛏 ✕ Ⅲ. Ⓥ ⓐ ✦

(▲ On Path) *Crianlarich Youth
Hostel*, Station Road, Crianlarich,
Perthshire, *FK20 8QN*.
Actual grid ref: NN3825
Warden: Mr & Mrs A & J Leask.
Tel: 01838 300260
Under 18: £6.40
Adults: £7.80
Family Rooms (not Jun to Aug),
Washing Machine, Self-Catering,
Shop, Facilities for Disabled
*Single-storey hostel in the village
that marks the half-way point on
the West Highland Way*

(1.5m) *Glenardran Guest House, Crianlarich, Perthshire, FK20 8QS.*
Actual grid ref: NN3825
Comfortable late Victorian guest house.
Grades: STB Listed, Comm, AA 3 Q, RAC Listed
Tel: 01838 300236
Mr Champion.
Rates fr: *£17.00*-**£19.00**.
Open: All Year
Beds: 3D 2T 1S
Baths: 1 Shared
🅿 (6) ⚲ 🍴 🐾 ✗ ▥ Ⓥ 🛇 ⚡

Portnellan 16

National Grid Ref: NN4125

(1.5m 🚌) *Portnellan Lodges, Portnellan, Crianlarich, Perthshire, FK20 8QS.*
Accommodation in luxury chalets.
Grades: STB 5 Cr, De Luxe
Tel: 01838 300284
Mrs Taylor.
Rates fr: *£18.50*-**£35.00**.
Open: Mar to Oct
Beds: 7F 10D 8T
🕭 🅿 (20) ⚲ 🍴 🐾 ✗ ▥ ⚡

Ewich 17

National Grid Ref: NN3627

(0.25m) *Ewich House, Ewich, Strathfillan, Crianlarich, Perthshire, FK20 8RU.*
Actual grid ref: NN363274
Completely refurbished farmhouse (built 1811).
Grades: STB 3 Cr, Comm
Tel: 01838 300300
Mr & Mrs Walker.
Rates fr: *£25.00*-**£25.00**.
Open: All Year
Beds: 2D 3T
Baths: 5 Private
🕭 🅿 (20) 🍴 ✗ ▥ Ⓥ 🛇 ⚡

Auchtertyre 18

National Grid Ref: NN3529

(On Path) *Auchtertyre Farm, Auchtertyre, Tyndrum, Crianlarich, Perthshire, FK20 8RU.*
Actual grid ref: NN3529
Modern comfortable farm bungalow.
Tel: 01838 400251
Mrs Baillie.

Rates fr: *£15.00*-**£15.00**.
Open: All Year
Beds: 2F
Baths: 1 Shared
🕭 🅿 🐾 ▥ Ⓥ 🛇 ⚡
Also ⛺ Also bunkhouse, £7.00 per bunk.
Open: All Year 🏚 Ⓣ ♨ ✗ ⚡ ♿

Tyndrum 19

National Grid Ref: NN3330

🍽 🍺 Invervey Hotel, Highlander Restaurant

(On Path 🚌) *Dalkjell, Tyndrum, Crianlarich, Perthshire, FK20 8RY.*
Modern bungalow in 1 acre.
Tel: 01838 400285
Mrs Coffield.
Rates fr: *£17.00*.
Open: All Year (not Xmas)
Beds: 2D 1T
Baths: 1 Shared
🅿 🍴 ▥ Ⓥ 🛇 ⚡

(On Path 🚌) *Glengarry Guest House, Tyndrum, Crianlarich, Perthshire, FK20 8RY.*
Victorian villa with fabulous views.
Grades: STB 3 Cr, Comm
Tel: 01838 400224
Mrs Cunningham.
Rates fr: *£14.00*-**£17.00**.
Open: All Year
Beds: 1F 1D 1T
Baths: 1 Shared
🕭 🅿 (4) 🐾 ✗ ▥ Ⓥ 🛇 ⚡

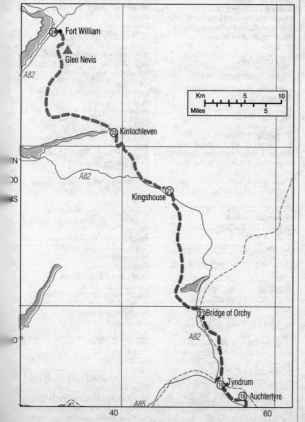

The Country Code

Enjoy the countryside and respect its life and work

Guard against all risk of fire

Fasten all gates

Keep your dogs under close control

Keep to public paths across farmland

Use gates and stiles to cross fences, hedges and walls

Leave livestock, crops and machinery alone

Take your litter home

Help to keep all water clean

Protect wild-life, plants and trees

Take special care on country roads

Make no unnecessary noise

Always telephone to get directions to the B&B - you will save time!

Bridge of Orchy 20

National Grid Ref: NN2939

🍴🛏 Bridge of Orchy Hotel, Inveroran Hotel

(On Path) *Glen Orchy Farm, Glen Orchy, Bridge of Orchy, Argyll, PA33 1BD.*
Friendly welcome on remote hill farm.
Tel: **01838 200221**
Mrs MacLennan.
Rates fr: *£13.00-£13.00.*
Open: Mar to mid-Nov
Beds: 2F
Baths: 1 Shared
🛏🖳🖈✕🛋Ⓥ

Kingshouse 21

National Grid Ref: NN2654

🍴🛏 Kingshouse Hotel

(On Path) *Kingshouse Hotel, Kingshouse, Glencoe, Argyll, PA39 4HY.*
Traditional family-run hotel.
Grades: STB 3 Cr, RAC 2 St
Tel: **01855 851259**
Mr Leitch.
Rates fr: *£20.00-£20.00.*
Open: All Year (not Xmas)
Beds: 3F 4D 10T 5S
Baths: 12 Private 2 Shared
🛏🖈✕🛋Ⓥ🛆

Kinlochleven 22

National Grid Ref: NN1861

🍴🛏 Macdonald Hotel, Tail Race Inn

(0.25m 🚐) *Mamore Lodge Hotel, Kinlochleven, Argyll, PA40 4QN.*
Grades: STB 3 Cr, Comm
Tel: **01855 831213**
Mr Bush.
Rates fr: *£16.00-£21.00.*
Open: All Year
Beds: 2F 5D 6T 1S
Baths: 15 Ensuite 2 Shared
🛏🖳(50)🖈✕Ⓥ🛆
Also ▲ *Also bunkhouse, £6 (party bookings only) per bunk.*
Open: All Year 📶Ⓣ🍴✕🛆🛆
Victorian lodge on eyrie like perch 650 foot above the village making an ideal spot for the weary walker to nestle for the night. Home cooking.

(0.25m 🚐) *Eden Coille, Garbhenn Road, Kinlochleven, Argyll, PA40 4SE.*
Family run bed and breakfast.
Grades: STB 1 Cr, Comm
Tel: **01855 831358** Mrs Robertson.
Rates fr: *£13.50-£20.00.*
Open: All Year
Beds: 3T
Baths: 2 Shared
🛏🖳(3)🖈✕🛋Ⓥ🛆

(On Path) *Macdonald Hotel and Camp Site, Fort William Road, Kinlochleven, Argyll, PA40 4QL.*
Actual grid ref: NN183623
Modern hotel - two bars, restaurant.
Grades: STB Comm
Tel: **01855 831539** Mr Macdonald.
Rates fr: *£18.00-£25.00.*
Open: March to December
Beds: 1F 4D 5T
Baths: 8 Private 2 Shared
🛏🖳(30)🖈✕Ⓥ🛆
Also ▲ *£4.00 per person.*
Open: March to January 📶Ⓣ✕🛆

(On Path) *Hermon, Kinlochleven, Argyll, PA40 4RA.*
Modern bungalow.
Tel: **01855 831383**
Miss MacAngus.
Rates fr: *£15.00-£18.00.*
Open: Easter to Oct **Beds:** 2D 1T
Baths: 1 Ensuite 1 Shared
🛏🖳(6)🖈🛋🛆🛆

Glen Nevis 23

National Grid Ref: NN1272

(▲0.25m) *Glen Nevis Youth Hostel, Glen Nevis, Fort William, Inverness-shire, PH33 6ST.*
Actual grid ref: NN1271
Warden: Mr J Adam.
Tel: **01397 702336**
Under 18: £6.40 **Adults:** £7.80
Family Rooms, Showers, Laundry Room, Self-Catering, Shop, Facilities for Disabled
Large weather-boarded hostel right at the foot of Ben Nevis

Fort William 24

National Grid Ref: NN1073

🍴🛏 Nevis Bank Hotel, Ben Nevis Bar, Nevis Bank, Food Stop, Crannog Seafood

(0.5m 🚐) *Rob Roy Hotel, High Street, Fort William, Inverness-Shire, PH33 6DH.*
Tel: **01397 700857** Mr Page.
Rates fr: *£15.00-£15.00.*
Open: All Year
Beds: 5F 10D 11T 9S
Baths: 32 Ensuite, 3 Shared
🛏🖳🖈✕🛋Ⓥ🛆🛆
Located at the end of the West Highland Way! Ideal for sightseeing, climbing and hill walking, roaming the glens and climbing the Ben

(0.5m) *Ben View Guest House, Belford Road, Fort William, Inverness-Shire, PH33 6ER.*
Grades: STB 2 Cr, Comm, AA 3 Q, Recomm
Tel: **01397 702966** Mrs Smith.
Rates fr: *£16.50-£17.00.*
Open: Mar to Nov
Beds: 1F 8D 2T 1S
Baths: 8 Ensuite, 4 Shared
🛏🖳(20)🛁🖵🛋
Centrally situated, close to all amenities, excellent base for walkers and climbers.

(1m) *Daraich Guest House, Cameron Road, Fort William, Inverness-Shire, PH33 6LQ.*
Tel: **01397 702644** Mrs Denney.
Rates fr: *£14.00-£14.00.*
Open: All Year
Beds: 1F 1D 1T 1S
Baths: 2 Shared
🖳(5)🖵🛋

(On Path) *Distillery House, Nevis Bridge, North Road, Fort William, Inverness-Shire, PH33 6LH.*
Luxury guesthouse.
Grades: STB 2 Cr, High Comm, AA 3 Q, Recomm, RAC Acclaim
Tel: **01397 700103** Mrs McLean.
Rates fr: *£18.00-£18.00.*
Open: All Year
Beds: 1F 3D 2T 1S
Baths: 7 Ensuite
🛏🖳(7)🛁🖵🖈🛋🛆

(On Path) *Glenlochy Guest House, Nevis Bridge, Fort William, Inverness-shire, PH33 6PF.*
Actual grid ref: NN1174
End of West Highland Way. Well done!
Grades: STB 2 Cr, Comm, AA 3 Q
Tel: **01397 702909** Mrs MacBeth.
Rates fr: *£15.00-£18.00.*
Open: All Year (not Xmas)
Beds: 1F 4D 5T
Baths: 8 Private 1 Shared
🛏🖳(14)🖵🛆🛆

(0.5m) *Rhu Mhor Guest House, Alma Road, Fort William, Inverness-shire, PH33 6BP.*
Actual grid ref: NN106739
Traditional guest house in secluded garden.
Grades: STB Listed, Comm, AA 1 Q, Recomm
Tel: **01397 702213**
Mr MacPherson.
Rates fr: *£16.50-£16.50.*
Open: Easter to Oct
Beds: 1F 3D 3T
Baths: 2 Shared
🛏🖳(7)🖵🖈✕🛋Ⓥ

All rates are subject to alteration at the owners' discretion.

(0.5m) *Leesholme, Cameton Road, Fort William, Inverness-shire,* *PH33 6LH.*
Modern family bungalow.
Grades: STB Listed, Comm
Tel: 01397 704204 Mrs Lee.
Rates fr: *£12.50-£15.00*.
Open: May to October
Beds: 2D 1T
Baths: 1 Shared
▣ (4) ⚲ ▥, Ⅴ

(2m) *Hillview Guest House, Achintore Road, Fort William, Inverness-Shire, PH33 6RW.*
Comfortable, modernised croft-house, family-run.
Tel: 01397 704349 Mrs Burton.
Rates fr: *£16.00-£19.00*.
Open: All Year (not Xmas)
Beds: 1F 3D 1T 1S
Baths: 4 Ensuite 1 Shared
⛄ (5) ▣ (7) ❏ ▥,

(0.5m) *Ashburn House, Achintore Road, Fort William, Inverness-shire, PH33 6RQ.*
Large Victorian private house.
Grades: STB 2 Cr, De Luxe, AA 5 Q, RAC High Acclaim
Tel: 01397 706000
Mr Henderson.
Rates fr: *£20.00-£25.00*.
Open: Feb to Nov
Beds: 1F 4D 2T 1S
Baths: 6 Private 1 Shared
⛄ ▣ (8) ⚲ ❏ ▥, Ⅴ ▮ ⚡

(On Path 🚲) *Abrach, 4 Caithness Place, Fort William, Inverness-shire, PH33 6JP.*
Actual grid ref: NN088733
Modern house in elevated position.
Grades: STB 1 Cr, Comm
Tel: 01397 702535
Mr & Mrs Moore.
Rates fr: *£14.00-£16.00*.

Open: All Year (not Xmas)
Beds: 1F 1D 1T **Baths:** 2 Shared
⛄ ▣ (6) ❏ ⓣ ▥, & Ⅴ ▮ ⚡

(0.5m) *Fort William Backpackers, Alma Road, Fort William, Inverness-shire, PH33 6HB.*
Comfortable independent hostel, 30 beds.
Tel: 01397 700711 Mr Sinclair.
£7.50 per bunk. Open all year.
⚲ Ⓣ ⚟ ✗ ⚡ ♿

All details shown are as supplied by B&B owners in Autumn 1995.

Wolds Way

The **Wolds Way** skirts the chalk hills and dry valleys of a little-known part of the former East Riding of Yorkshire. It is a quiet part of England, unspoilt by much commercial tourism. The path unwinds for 79 pleasant miles from Hessle and the muddy river beneath the Humber Bridge (the longest single-span bridge in the world) to the lofty cliffs at Filey on the North Sea coast. For the true trekker, it provides the perfect link between the **Cleveland Way** and the **Viking Way**. For the long weekender, it provides a lovely walk over rolling chalk downland - a world away from the rough moors and peat bogs usually associated with walking in Yorkshire. This is a good one for walking in autumn and winter.

Maps: Ordnance Survey 1:50,000 Landranger series: 100, 101, 106 and 107

Guide: *Wolds Way* by Roger Ratcliffe (ISBN 1 85410 189 7), published by Aurum Press in association with the Countryside Commission and Ordnance Survey and available from all major bookshops, £9.99

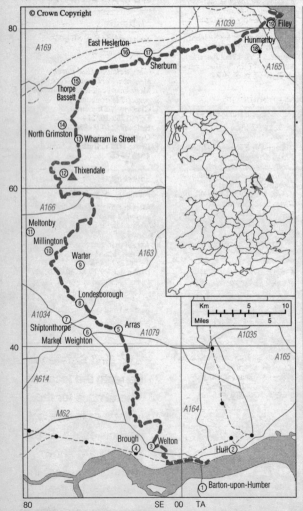

© Crown Copyright

Barton-upon-Humber   1

National Grid Ref: TA0322

⚫|⚫| 🍺 Wheatsheaf

(1m) *Southgarth Guest House,*
2 Caistor Road, Barton-upon-Humber, S Humberside, DN18 5AH.
Originally a gatekeepers lodge.
Tel: **01652 632833** Mrs Havercroft.
Rates fr: *£14.00-£16.00.*
Open: All Year (not Xmas)
Beds: 3T **Baths:** 2 Shared
🛇 (5) 🅿 (5) 🛏 🛏 ✗ 🎬 V

Hull   2

National Grid Ref: TA0929

⚫|⚫| 🍺 The Turnpike, Bay Horse, New Clarence, Olde Black Boy, Royal William, Spring Bank Tavern

(1.5m) *Acorn Guest House, 719 Beverley High Road, Hull, HU6 7JN.*
Friendly guesthouse with large garden.
Grades: ETB 2 Cr
Tel: **01482 853248** Mrs Langton.
Rates fr: *£18.00-£18.00.*
Open: All Year.
Beds: 2T 2S
Baths: 3 Ensuite 1 Shared
🛇 🅿 (6) 🛏 🛏 ✗ 🎬 V

(1.5m) *Windmill House,*
56 Witham, Hull, HU9 1AT.
Friendly Victorian inn with entertainment.
Tel: **01482 324623** Mr Binns.
Rates fr: *£12.00-£12.00.*
Open: All Year (not Xmas)
Beds: 3D 1T 3S
Baths: 1 Shared
🎬

The lowest *double* rate per person is shown in *italics*.

(1.5m) *Marlborough Hotel,*
232 Spring Bank, Hull, HU3 1LU.
Family run near city centre.
Tel: **01482 224479** Mr Stonehouse.
Rates fr: *£13.00*-**£15.00**.
Open: All Year
Beds: 3F 2D 5T 6S
Baths: 3 Shared
⛄ 🅿 (10) 🛏 ⊁ 🛏 🖳

(1.5m) *Town House, 102 Sunny*
Bank, Spring Bank West, Hull,
HU3 1LF.
Guesthouse, quiet location.
Tel: **01482 446177**
Mr Hogg.
Rates fr: *£14.00*-**£15.00**.
Open: All Year
Beds: 1D 2T 4S
Baths: 1 Shared
⛄ (8) 🛏 🖳 Ⓥ

Welton   3

National Grid Ref: SE9627

(On Path) *Hemingford House,*
Church Street, Welton, Brough,
East Yorkshire, HU15 1NH.
Large, friendly, comfortable
Georgian house.
Tel: **01482 668405**
Mr Kiddle.
Rates fr: *£18.00*-**£26.00**.
Open: All Year (not Xmas)
Beds: 1D 2T 1S
Baths: 4 Private
⛄ (7) 🅿 (6) 🗶 🛏 🖳 Ⓥ

Brough   4

National Grid Ref: SE9326

🍴 🍺 The Green Dragon, Half
Moon, Ferry Inn

(0.75m 🚗) *Elloughton Mount*
Guest House, 62 Elloughton Road,
Brough, E. Yorks, HU15 1AL.
Large Victorian house, great views.
Tel: **01482 667941**
Mrs Floyd.
Rates fr: *£16.00*-**£16.00**.
Open: All Year (not Xmas)
Beds: 1F 1T 1S
Baths: 1 Shared
⛄ 🅿 🛏 🖳 Ⓥ

Arras   5

National Grid Ref: SE9242

(On Path) *Arras Farmhouse,*
Arras, Market Weighton, York,
YO4 3RN.
Actual grid ref: SE9242
Large, traditional family farm-
house.
Grades: ETB Listed
Tel: **01430 872404**
Mrs Stephenson.
Rates fr: *£15.00*-**£18.00**.
Open: All Year
Beds: 3
Baths: 2 Private 1 Shared
⛄ 🅿 (5) 🛏 🛏 🗶 ⓐ ⌁

🚗 sign means that,
given due notice,
owners will pick you
up from the path
and drop you off *with-*
in reason.

Market Weighton   6

National Grid Ref: SE8741

🍴 🍺 Black Horse Inn

(On Path or 1m) *The Gables,*
35 Londesborough Road, Market
Weighton, York, YO4 3HS.
Lovely, friendly, comfortable
house.
Tel: **01430 872255** Mr Green.
Rates fr: *£13.50*-**£14.00**.
Open: All Year (not Xmas)
Beds: 2D 1T 2S **Baths:** 2 Shared
⛄ 🅿 (5) 🛏 🛏 🖳 Ⓥ ⓐ ⌁

Shiptonthorpe   7

National Grid Ref: SE8543

🍴 🍺 The Crown

(0.25m 🚗) *Robeanne House*
Farm, Driffield Lane,
Shiptonthorpe, York, YO4 3LB.
Modern comfortable farmhouse.
Grades: ETB Listed
Tel: **01430 873312** Mrs Wilson.
Rates fr: *£15.50*-**£15.50**.
Open: All Year
Beds: 3F 2D 1T
Baths: 6 Ensuite
⛄ 🅿 (10) 🛏 🛏 🗶 🖳 Ⓥ ⓐ ⌁
Also ⛺ £5.00 per tent.
Open: May to Sep 🏠 Ⓣ 🍽 🗶 ⌁ ♿

Londesborough   8

National Grid Ref: SE8645

(On Path) *Towthorpe Grange,*
Towthorpe Lane, Londesborough,
York, YO4 3LB.
Actual grid ref: SE869436
Comfortable working farm.
Tel: **01430 873814** Mrs Rowlands.
Rates fr: *£14.50*-**£14.50**.
Open: All Year (not Xmas)
Beds: 1F 2D 2S **Baths:** 1 Shared
⛄ 🅿 🗶 🖳 Ⓥ ⓐ ⌁

Warter   9

National Grid Ref: SE8650

🍴 🍺 Star Inn

(3m 🚗) *Rickman House, Warter,*
York, YO4 2SY.
Actual grid ref: SE875506
Secluded C17th farmhouse. Large
garden.

Grades: ETB Listed, Comm
Tel: **01759 304303** Mr Mylne.
Rates fr: *£15.00*-**£16.00**.
Open: All Year (not Xmas)
Beds: 2D 1T
Baths: 1 Ensuite 1 Private
⛄ 🅿 (4) 🛏 🛏 🗶 🖳 Ⓥ ⓐ ⌁

Millington   10

National Grid Ref: SE8351

🍴 🍺 Gate Inn

(0.5m 🚗) *Laburnum Cottage,*
Millington, York, YO4 2TX.
Actual grid ref: SE831518
Comfortable cottage with large
garden. **Grades:** ETB Reg
Tel: **01759 303055** Mrs Dykes.
Rates fr: *£15.00*-**£18.00**.
Open: Feb to Oct
Beds: 1F 1T **Baths:** 1 Shared
⛄ 🅿 (5) 🗶 🛏 🗶 🖳 Ⓥ ⓐ ⌁

Meltonby   11

National Grid Ref: SE7952

🍴 🍺 Feathers Hotel

(3m) *Meltonby Hall Farm,*
Meltonby, Pocklington, York, YO4 2PW
Modernised comfortable famhouse,
peaceful surroundings.
Grades: AA Recomm
Tel: **01759 303214**
Rates fr: *£14.00*-**£16.00**.
Open: Easter to oct
Beds: 1D 1T **Baths:** 1 Shared
⛄ 🅿 🛏 🖳

Thixendale   12

National Grid Ref: SE8461

(⛺ On Path) *Thixendale Youth*
Hostel, The Village Hall,
Thixendale, Malton, N. Yorks,
YO17 8TG.
Actual grid ref: SE8461
Warden: Ms M Smith.
Tel: **01377 288238**
Under 18: £3.75 **Adults:** £5.50
Partially Heated, Showers, Shop,
No Smoking
The old school in a quiet village,
near the foot of a remarkable chalk
dry valley

The Grid Reference
beneath the location
heading is for the
village or town - *not*
for individual houses,
which are shown
(where supplied) in
each entry itself.

(On Path) *Manor Farm,*
Thixendale, Malton, N. Yorks,
YO17 9TG.
Large Victorian working farm-
house.
Grades: ETB Listed
Tel: 01377 288315 Mrs Brader.
Rates fr: *£16.00-£16.00.*
Open: All Year (not Xmas)
Beds: 1F 1D 1T 1S
Baths: 4 Ensuite
⌂ ▣ (6) ⽅ ⌨ ⽬ ✕ ♥ ▣ ⓘ ✦

Wharram le Street   13

National Grid Ref: SE8666

(On Path 🚌) *Red House,*
Wharram le Street, Malton,
N. Yorks, YO17 9TL.
Spacious Georgian country house.
Grades: ETB 2 Cr, RAC Acclaim
Tel: 01944 768455
Mr Scott.
Rates fr: *£22.00.*
Open: All Year (not Xmas)
Beds: 1F 1D 1T
Baths: 3 Ensuite
⌂ ▣ (10) ⽅ ⌨ ⽬ ✕ ▥ ▣ ⓘ ✦
Also ⚑ *£5.00 per tent.*
Open: All Year (not Xmas)
▣ ⚎ ✕ ✦ ♿

North Grimston   14

National Grid Ref: SE8467

⊙ ◲ Middleton Arms

(1.25m) *Middleton Arms, North*
Grimston, Malton, N. Yorks,
YO17 8AX.
Country pub, at foot of escarpment.
Grades: ETB Reg
Tel: 01944 768255 Mrs Grayston.
Rates fr: *£17.50-£22.50.*
Open: All Year (not Xmas)
Beds: 2D 1T
Baths: 1 Private 1 Shared
⌂ ▣ ⌨ ✕ ▥ ▣ ⓘ ✦

**Please don't camp
on anyone's land
without first obtaining
their permission.**

Thorpe Bassett   15

National Grid Ref: SE8673

⊙ ◲ The Coach & Horses

(0.5m 🚌) *The Old School House,*
Thorpe Bassett, Rillington, Malton,
N. Yorks, YO17 8LU.
C18th converted school.
Grades: ETB Reg
Tel: 01944 758797 Mrs Baron.
Rates fr: *£16.00-£16.00.*
Open: Easter to Oct
Beds: 1D 1T 1S
Baths: 1 Shared
⌂ ▣ (2) ⌨ ⽬ ✕ ▥ ▣ ⓘ ✦

East Heslerton   16

National Grid Ref: SE9276

⊙ ◲ Dawnay Arms, Snooty Fox
Inn

(0.25m) *The Snooty Fox Inn, East*
Heslerton, Malton, N. Yorks,
YO17 8EN.
Motel, pub, restaurant, camping.
Tel: 01944 710554
Rates fr: *£19.00-£25.00.*
Open: All Year
Beds: 1F 3D 1T
Baths: 5 Ensuite
⌂ ▣ (30) ⽅ ⌨ ⽬ ✕ ▣ ⓘ ✦
Also ⚑ *£2.50 per tent.*
Open: All Year 🔥 ⚎ ⚎⚎ ✕ ✦ ♿

(0.75m 🚌) *Manor Farm, East*
Heslerton, Malton, N. Yorks,
YO17 8RN.
Actual grid ref: SE925767
Spacious farmhouse on working
farm.
Grades: ETB 2 Cr, Comm
Tel: 01944 728268 Ms Lumley.
Rates fr: *£15.00-£15.00.*
Open: Easter to Oct
Beds: 2F **Baths:** 2 Private
⌂ ▣ (4) ⽅ ⌨ ⽬ ▥ ▣ ⓘ ✦

Sherburn   17

National Grid Ref: SE9577

⊙ ◲ Pigeon Pie

(0.25m) *Pigeon Pie, Sherburn,*
Malton, N. Yorks, YO17 8QB.
Old coaching inn.
Tel: 01944 710383
Rates fr: *£17.00-£19.50.*
Open: All Year (not Xmas)
Beds: 1D 1T 2S **Baths:** 1 Shared
⌂ ▣ (100) ⌨ ✕ ▥ ▣ ⓘ ✦

Hunmanby   18

National Grid Ref: TA0977

⊙ ◲ White Swan Hotel, The
Cottage, The Buck Inn, Horse Shoe
Inn

(0.5m) *Paddock Lodge,*
25 Northgate, Hunmanby, Filey,
N. Yorks, YO14 0NT.
Comfortable guesthouse, farm-
house breakfast.
Tel: 01723 890581
Mr & Mrs Randerson.
Rates fr: *£15.00-£15.00.*
Open: All Year
Beds: 1F 1D 1T
Baths: 1 Shared
⌂ (1) ▣ (4) ⌨ ⽬ ▥ ▣ ✦

(1m) *Wrangham House,*
10 Stonelgate, Hunmanby, Filey,
N. Yorks, YO14 0NS.
Georgian vicarage in own grounds.
Grades: ETB 3 Cr
Tel: 01723 891333
Miss Shaw.
Rates fr: *£25.00-£25.00.*
Open: All Year
Beds: 7D 4T 2S
Baths: 13 Ensuite
▣ (20) ⽅ ⌨ ✕ ▥ ▣ ⓘ ✦

Filey   19

National Grid Ref: TA1180

(0.5m) *Abbots Leigh Guest House,*
7 Rutland Street, Filey, N. Yorks,
YO14 9JA.
Comfortable Victorian terrace
house.
Grades: ETB 3 Cr, Comm,
AA 3 Q
Tel: 01723 513334
Mr & Mrs Carter.
Rates fr: *£18.00-£20.00.*
Open: All Year (not Xmas)
Beds: 2F 2D 2T
Baths: 6 Ensuite
⌂ (3) ▣ (4) ⽅ ⌨ ✕ ▥ ▣

**Pay B&Bs by cash or
cheque and be prepared
to pay up front.**

STILWELL'S
B&B PHONELINE

0891-515696

Cost per minute: 39p (cheap) / 49p (otherwise).

Touring? On business? Just plain stuck? Is there a mountain you wish to walk up? A historic house or a beautiful church you wish to see, an art gallery or a special museum you wish to visit? Perhaps a path not featured in this book?

We suggest superb, low-cost, Bed & Breakfasts EXACTLY where you want to stay (not 20 miles away) anywhere in Britain or Ireland.

Wherever you are or whatever you are doing, we can locate a B&B right on the doorstep offering overnight accommodation at under £25 per person per night (average £16 per person in a double room).

Just ring us up and we'll look it up for you on our computer. And if your request is elaborate (an itinerary requiring special research), we'll take down the details, do the work and phone you back or fax you with the results.

Wye Valley Walk

This 112 mile walk leaves Rhayader in mid-Wales southwards to explore the Elan Reservoirs, the edge of the Black Mountains, the cathedral city of Hereford, through the Forest of Dean to Symonds Yat Rock with its peregrine falcons, to come to rest near Chepstow Castle at the banks of the Severn Estuary. This is river walking with a few diversions, so it is mostly flat, but the Builth to Erwood section reaches 1,300 feet. Plan your walk with a weather eye - the Wye is prone to severe flooding after lengthy rain, rendering any hopes of a walk impossible. That said, high water is rare in the summer, and that is precisely when this river is at its glorious best.

Guides: *Guide to the Wye Valley Walk* by Heather & John Hurley (ISBN 0 946 32834), published by Thornhill Press and available from all good map shops or from West Country Books, Halsgrove House, Lower Moor Way, Tiverton, Devon, EX16 6SS, tel. 01884 243242, £4.95 (+£1 p&p)

Walking Down The Wye by David Hunter (ISBN 1 85284 105 2), published by Cicerone Press, available from good map shops or directly from the publishers (2 Police Square, Milnthorpe, Cumbria, LA7 7PY, 01539 562069), £6.99 (+£75p p&p)

Wye Valley Walk (Hay-on-Wye to Rhayader) - set of 8 cards published by Powys County Council and available directly from their offices (County Hall, Planning Dept, Rights of Way, Llandrindod Wells, Powys, LD1 5LE), £2.50

Wye Valley Walk Map Pack (Chepstow to Hay-on-Wye), published by Gwent County Council and available directly from their offices (Planning & Economic Development (Monmouthshire), County Hall, Cwmbran, Gwent, NP24 2XF, tel. 01633 838838), £3.50

Maps: Ordnance Survey 1:50,000 Landranger series: 147, 148, 149, 161, 162

Rhayader   1

National Grid Ref: SN9768

¶⊙¶ ⊞ Brynafon Hotel, Bear Hotel, Crown Inn, Triangle Inn

(2.5m ⊞) *Beili Neuadd, Rhayader, Powys, LD6 5NS.*
Actual grid ref: SN994698
Grades: WTB 3 Cr, High Comm
Tel: **01597 810211**
Mrs Edwards.
Rates fr: *£17.50*-**£17.50.**
Open: All Year (not Xmas)
Beds: 1D 1T 2S
Baths: 2 Ensuite 1 Shared
⌂ (10) ⊞ ⌷ ⊁ ✕ ⅢⅢ ⓥ ⅰ ⅋
Warm, comfortable C16th farm-house run by L.D.W.A. members. Log fires, hot showers and Aga breakfasts. Near Glyndwr's Way (four miles), Cambrian Way (six miles), Monk's Trod (0.5 miles).

(1.5m) *Brynafon House, Rhayader, Powys, LD6 5BL.*
Former Victorian workhouse.
Tel: **01597 810735**
Mrs Collins.
Rates fr: *£15.50*-**£19.50.**
Open: All Year (not Xmas)
Beds: 1F 6D 6T 1S
Baths: 4 Ensuite
⌂ ⊞ ⌷ ⌷ ⊁ ✕ ⅢⅢ ⓥ ⅰ ⅋
Also ⅄ Also bunkhouse, £8 per bunk.
Open: All Year ⅏ ⊤ ⅏ ✕ ⅋ ⅍

(0.25m) *Crown Inn, North Street, Rhayader, Powys, LD6 5AB.*
C16th inn. Tel: **01597 811099**
Mr Lewis. **Rates fr:** *£15.00*-**£15.00.**
Open: All Year
Beds: 1D 2T **Baths:** 3 Ensuite
⊞ (3) ⌷ ⌷ ⊁ ✕ ⅢⅢ ⓥ ⅰ ⅋

Llanwrthwl   2

National Grid Ref: SN9763

(On Path) *Dyffryn Farm, Llanwrthwl, Llandrindod Wells, Powys, LD1 6NU.*
Peaceful, spacious C17th stone farmhouse.
Tel: **01597 811017** Mrs Tyler.
Rates fr: *£16.50*-**£18.50.**
Open: July to Oct
Beds: 1F 1D 1T
Baths: 1 Ensuite 1 Shared
⌂ (15) ⊞ (6) ⅊ ⌷ ✕

Disserth   3

National Grid Ref: SO0358

¶⊙¶ ⊞ The Hundred House Inn, Greyhound Hotel, Drovers Arms

(3m ⊞) *Disserth Mill, Disserth, Builth Wells, Powys, LD2 3TN.*
Modern comfortable guest house on farm.
Grades: WTB Listed
Tel: **01982 553217**
Mrs Worts.
Rates fr: *£14.00*-**£16.00.**

Open: All Year (not Xmas)
Beds: 1D 1T 1S
Baths: 1 Shared
⌂ ⊞ (4) ⌷ ⌷ ✕ ⅢⅢ ⅰ ⅋

Builth Wells   4

National Grid Ref: SO0350

¶⊙¶ ⊞ Hundred House Inn, Greyhound Hotel, Drovers Arms

(On Path ⊞) *The Owls, 40 High Street, Builth Wells, Powys, LD2 3AB.*
Actual grid ref: SO041510
Large Victorian, comfortable house.
Grades: WTB 3 Cr, AA 2 Q
Tel: **01982 552518**
Mrs Bond.
Rates fr: *£13.00*-**£13.00.**
Open: All Year
Beds: 1F 1D 2T 2S
Baths: 3 Ensuite
⌂ ⊞ (8) ⌷ ⌷ ✕ ⅢⅢ ⓥ ⅰ ⅋

(On Path ⊞) *Bron Wye, Church Street, Builth Wells, Powys, LD2 3BS.*
Large semi-detached Victorian house.
Grades: WTB 3 Cr, Comm
Tel: **01982 553587**
Mr & Mrs Wiltshire.
Rates fr: *£16.00*-**£16.00.**
Open: All Year
Beds: 1F 2D 1T 1S
Baths: 5 Ensuite
⌂ ⊞ ⅊ ⌷ ⌷ ✕ ⅢⅢ ⓥ ⅰ ⅋

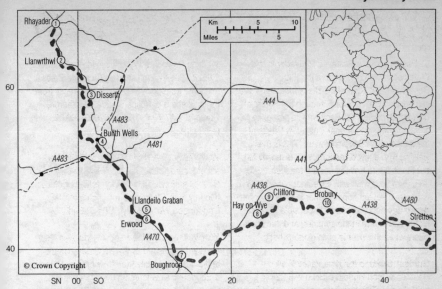

© Crown Copyright

SN 00 SO 20 40

(On Path 🚐) *The Cedar Guest House*, Hay Road, Builth Wells, Powys, *LD2 3AR*.
Actual grid ref: SO304900
Modern, good foor, bar, welcoming.
Grades: WTB 3 Cr, RAC Approv
Tel: 01982 553356 Mr Morris.
Rates fr: *£18.00*-**£20.00**.
Open: All Year
Beds: 1F 1D 3T 2S
Baths: 5 Ensuite 2 Shared
🛌 🅿 (10) ⅟ 🗗 ⅕ ⊁ 🏛 Ⅴ ⓘ ≉

Llandeilo Graban 5

National Grid Ref: SO0944

(2.5m) *Penygraig Farm*, Llandeilo Graban, Erwood, Builth Wells, Powys, *LD2 3YJ*.
Actual grid ref: SO108458
C17th Welsh farmhouse on Llandeilo Common.
Tel: 01982 560687 Mrs Carpenter.
Rates fr: *£12.00*-**£13.00**.
Open: Feb to Nov **Beds:** 2T
Baths: 1 Ensuite 1 Shared
🅿 (4) 🗗 ⅕ ⊁ 🏛 Ⅴ ≉

Erwood 6

National Grid Ref: SO0942

🍴 🍺 Erwood Inn

(On Path) *Orchard Cottage*, Erwood, Builth Wells, Powys, *LD2 3EZ*.
Tastefully modernised C18th cottage.
Grades: WTB 2 Cr, High Comm
Tel: 01982 560600 Mr/Mrs Prior.
Rates fr: *£15.50*-**£18.50**.
Open: All Year **Beds:** 1F 1D 1T
Baths: 1 Ensuite 1 Shared
🛌 🅿 (4) ⅟ 🗗 ⅕ 🏛 Ⅴ

(On Path 🚐) *The Old Vicarage*, Erwood, Builth Wells, Powys, *LD2 3DZ*.
Actual grid ref: SO0943
Spacious Edwardian former vicarage.
Grades: WTB I Cr
Tel: 01982 560680 Mrs Williams.
Rates fr: *£13.00*-**£13.00**.
Open: All Year
Beds: 1F 1D 1T 1S
Baths: 1 Shared
🛌 (0) 🅿 🗗 ⅕ ⊁ 🏛 Ⅴ ⓘ ≉

Boughrood 7

National Grid Ref: SO1339

🍴 🍺 Bridge Inn, Copper Kettle, Griffin Inn

(On Path) *Balangia*, Station Road, Boughrood, Brecon, Powys, *LD3 0YF*.
Modern house in Boughrood village.
Tel: 01874 754453
Mrs Mills Brown.
Rates fr: *£13.00*-**£13.00**.
Open: Easter to Oct
Beds: 1D 1T
Baths: 1 Shared
🛌 🅿 (1) ⅟ 🗗 ⅕ ⊁ 🏛 Ⅴ ⓘ ≉

(0.5m 🚐) *Upper Middle Road*, Boughrood, Brecon, Powys, *LD3 0BX*.
Cosy farmhouse, mountain views, peaceful.
Grades: WTB 1 Cr
Tel: 01874 754407 Mrs Kelleher.
Rates fr: *£12.50*-**£12.50**.
Open: All Year (not Xmas)
Beds: 1D 1T 1S
Baths: 1 Shared
🛌 🅿 (3) ⅟ 🗗 ⊁ 🏛 Ⅴ ⓘ ≉

Hay-on-Wye 8

National Grid Ref: SO2242

🍴 🍺 Black Lion, Pinocchios, The Swan, Kilverts, Hollybush Inn, Harp Inn, The Granary

(0.5m) *Rosedale*, Cusop, Hay-on-Wye, Hereford, Herefordshire, *HR3 5RF*.
Actual grid ref: SO234417
Large Victorian house.
Tel: 01497 820804 Mrs Jenkins.
Rates fr: *£14.50*-**£14.50**.
Open: All Year
Beds: 1F 2D 1T 2S
Baths: 1 Shared
🛌 🅿 (4) 🗗 ⅕ 🏛 Ⅴ ⓘ ≉
Also ⛺ *£2.50 per tent.*
Open: All Year 🐾 🆃 ≉ ♿

(On Path 🚐) *Tinto House*, Broad Street, Hay-on-Wye, Hereford, Herefordshire, *HR3 5DB*.
Comfortable Georgian town house.
Grades: WTB 2 Cr, Comm
Tel: 01497 820590 Mrs Ratcliffe.
Rates fr: *£16.00*.
Open: Easter to Nov
Beds: 1F 1D 1T
Baths: 3 Ensuite
🛌 🅿 (2) 🗗 🏛 Ⅴ ⓘ ≉

(On Path) *York House*, Cusop, Hay-on-Wye, Hereford, Herefordshire, *HR3 5QX*.
Victorian house in quiet situation.
Grades: AA 3 Q, RAC Acclaim
Tel: 01497 820705
Mr Roberts.
Rates fr: *£20.00*-**£20.00**.
Open: All Year
Beds: 2F 3D
Baths: 5 Ensuite
🛌 (8) 🅿 (6) ⅟ 🗗 ⅕ ⊁ 🏛 Ⅴ ⓘ ≉

(On Path) Belmont House, *Hay-on-Wye, Hereford, Herefordshire, HR3 5DA.*
Actual grid ref: SO228423
Large Georgian house.
Tel: **01497 820718**
Mr Gwynne.
Rates fr: *£15.00*-**£18.00**.
Open: All Year
Beds: 2F 3D 2T 1S
Baths: 1 Ensuite 2 Shared
🛏 🅿 🏠 ⬛ Ⅵ ⓐ ⚡

(0.25m 🚗**) Lansdowne,** *Cusop, Hay-on-Wye, Hereford, Herefordshire, HR3 5RF.*
Actual grid ref: SO237417
Large Victorian stone house.
Tel: **01497 820125**
Mrs Flack.
Rates fr: *£16.00*-**£21.00**.
Open: All Year (not Xmas)
Beds: 1D 1T
Baths: 2 Ensuite
🛏 🅿 (4) ⤢ 🏠 ✕ ⬛ 🅰 Ⅵ ⓐ ⚡

Clifford   9

National Grid Ref: SO2445

🍴 🍺 Castlefields Inn

(On Path) Cottage Farm, *Middlewood, Clifford, Hereford, HR3 5SX.*
Actual grid ref: SO288447
Working modernised farmhouse.
Families welcome.
Tel: **01497 831496**
Mrs Jones.
Rates fr: *£13.50*-**£14.00**.
Open: All Year (not Xmas)
Beds: 1F 1T
Baths: 1 Shared
🛏 🅿 (4) ⤢ ⬛ ⓐ ⚡

Brobury   10

National Grid Ref: SO3444

(On Path 🚗**) Magdalen,** *Brobury, Hereford, Herefordshire, HR3 6DX.*
Converted C13th chancel, modern extension.
Tel: **01981 500470**
Mrs Phillips.
Rates fr: *£18.50*-**£25.00**.
Open: All Year (not Xmas)
Beds: 2D
Baths: 2 Ensuite
🅿 (6) ⤢ 🏠 ✕ ⬛ Ⅵ ⓐ

Stretton Sugwas   11

National Grid Ref: SO4642

(0.2m) New Priory Hotel, *Stretton Sugwas, Hereford, Herefordshire, HR4 7AR.*
Old vicarage, 3.5 acre grounds.
Grades: WTB 3 Cr
Tel: **01432 760264** Mr Benjamin.
Rates fr: *£15.00*-**£25.00**.
Open: All Year
Beds: 1F 6D 1T
Baths: 6 Ensuite, 2 Shared
🛏 🅿 (60) 🛋 🏠 ✕ ⬛ Ⅵ ⓐ ⚡

Hereford   12

National Grid Ref: SO5140

🍴 🍺 The Imperial, Rose & Crown

(0.25m) Charades, *32 Southbank Road, Hereford, Herefordshire, HR1 2TJ.*
Comfortable accommodation.
Lovely English breakfast.
Grades: WTB 2 Cr, Comm
Tel: **01432 269444**
Rates fr: *£17.00*-**£19.50**.
Open: All Year
Beds: 4D 2T
Baths: 4 Ensuite 1 Shared
🅿 (6) 🛋 🏠 ⬛ Ⅵ

(0.25m) Somerville Hotel, *Bodenham Road, Hereford, Herefordshire, HR1 2TS.*
Large Victorian city hotel.
Grades: WTB 3 Cr, Comm,
AA 2 St
Tel: **01432 273991** Mr Westwood.
Rates fr: *£22.50*-**£16.00**.
Open: All Year (not Xmas)
Beds: 2F 4D 4S
Baths: 6 Ensuite 4 Shared
🛏 (5) 🅿 (6) 🛋 🏠 ⬛ Ⅵ ⓐ ⚡

(0.25m) Cedar Guest House, *123 Whitecross Road, Whitecross, Hereford, HR4 0LS.*
Friendly, family-run guesthouse.
Grades: WTB 1 Cr
Tel: **01432 267235**
Mr & Mrs Burrough.
Rates fr: *£15.00*-**£18.00**.
Open: All Year
Beds: 3F 1T
Baths: 1 Shared
🛏 🅿 (10) 🛋 ⬛

Dinedor   13

National Grid Ref: SO5336

🍴 🍺 Crown Inn

(1m) Dinedor Court, *Dinedor, Hereford, HR2 6LG.*
Rambling C16th farmhouse.
Grades: WTB 1 Cr
Tel: **01432 870481** Mrs Price.
Rates fr: *£17.00*-**£19.00**.
Open: Easter to Oct
Beds: 1D 1T
Baths: 1 Shared
🛏 (10) 🅿 (4) 🛋 🏠 Ⅵ

Rotherwas   14

National Grid Ref: SO5338

(1m) Sink Green Farm, *Rotherwas, Hereford, HR2 6LE.*
Picturesque C16th farmhouse.
Grades: WTB 2 Cr, Comm,
AA 3 Q
Tel: **01432 870223** Mr Jones.
Rates fr: *£18.00*-**£19.00**.
Open: All Year (not Xmas)
Beds: 2D 1T
Baths: 3 Private
🛏 🅿 (10) ⤢ 🛋 🏠 ⬛ Ⅵ

Mordiford   15

National Grid Ref: SO5737

🍴 🍺 Moon Inn, Green Man (Mordiford)

(0.5m) Orchard Farm House, *Mordiford, Hereford, Herefordshire, HR1 4EJ.*
Actual grid ref: SO575383
C17th farmhouse overlooking beautiful valley.
Grades: WTB 2 Cr, Comm
Tel: **01432 870253** Mrs James.
Rates fr: *£15.50*-**£17.00**.
Open: All Year (not Xmas)
Beds: 2D 1T **Baths:** 2 Shared
🅿 (6) ⤢ 🛋 🏠 ✕ ⬛ Ⅵ ⓐ ⚡

Fownhope   16

National Grid Ref: SO5834

🍴 🍺 Green Man Inn, Forge and Ferry Inn

(0.25m 🚗**) Tan House,** *Ferry Lane, Fownhope, Hereford, Herefordshire, HR1 4NJ.*
Actual grid ref: SO577346
C16th house, working cider mill.
Grades: WTB 2 Cr
Tel: **01432 860549** Mrs Biggs.
Rates fr: *£15.00*-**£15.00**.
Open: All Year **Beds:** 1F 1D 1S
Baths: 1 Ensuite, 1 Shared
🛏 (1) 🅿 (4) 🛋 🏠 ⬛ Ⅵ ⓐ ⚡

(0.25m) Green Man Inn, *Fownhope, Hereford, Herefordshire, HR1 4PE.*
C15th B&W coaching inn.
Grades: WTB 3 Cr, Comm,
AA 2 St, RAC 2 St
Tel: **01432 860243** Mr Williams.
Rates fr: *£25.00*-**£25.50**.
Open: All Year
Beds: 4 F 12D 2T 1S
Baths: 19 Ensuite
🛏 🅿 (70) 🛋 🏠 ✕ ⬛ Ⅵ ⓐ ⚡

(0.25m) The Squirrels, *Fownhope, Hereford, Herefordshire, HR1 4PB.*
Actual grid ref: SO573342
Modern bungalow, swimming pool, views. Tel: **01432 860413**
Rates fr: *£15.00*-**£15.00**.
Open: All Year (not Xmas)
Beds: 1D 1T **Baths:** 1 Shared
🅿 ⬛ ⓐ Ⅵ ⓐ ⚡

How Caple   17

National Grid Ref: SO6130

(3m 🚗**) White House,** *How Caple, Hereford, Herefordshire, HR4 4SR.*
Actual grid ref: SO601041
Comfortable farmhouse, also cottage.
Grades: WTB 3 Cr, High Comm
Tel: **01989 740644** Mrs Edwards.
Rates fr: *£15.00*-**£15.00**.
Open: All Year (not Xmas)
Beds: 1D 1T **Baths:** 1 Shared
🛏 🅿 (3) ⤢ 🛋 ⬛ ⓐ ⚡
Also ⛺ *£3.50 per tent.*
Open: Apr to Sep 🐾 🅣 ⚡

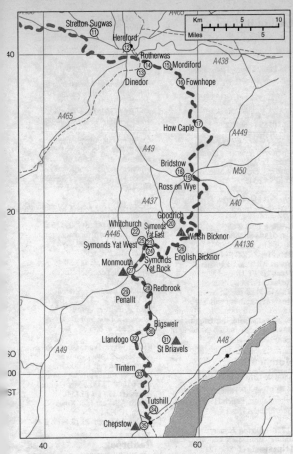

Beds: 2D 2S
Baths: 1 Shared
🐾 🅿 (6) ⛅ 📶 ∦

(0.33m) 🚗 *Sunnymount Hotel,*
Ryefield Road, Ross-on-Wye,
Herefordshire, HR9 5LU.
Actual grid ref: SO606242
Large converted Edwardian guest-
house.
Grades: ETB 3 Cr, Comm,
AA Listed, RAC Acclaim
Tel: 01989 563880
Mr & Mrs Williams.
Rates fr: *£23.00-£19.00.*
Open: All Year (not Xmas)
Beds: 3D 3T 3S
Baths: 7 Ensuite 1 Shared
🐾 🅿 (7) ⛅ ✕ 📶 Ⓥ ▮ ∦

Goodrich   20

National Grid Ref: SO5719

🍴 🍺 Ye Hostelrie

(0.5m 🚗) *Jollys, Goodrich, Ross-*
on-Wye, Herefordshire, HR9 6HX.
Actual grid ref: SO574194
Above old-fashioned village shop.
Grades: ETB 2 Cr, Comm
Tel: 01600 890135 Mrs Danby.
Rates fr: *£17.50-£21.50.*
Open: All Year (not Xmas)
Beds: 2D 1T
Baths: 1 Ensuite 2 Private
🐾 🅿 (5) ⛅ 🐾 ✕ 📶 Ⓥ ▮ ∦

Welsh Bicknor   21

National Grid Ref: SO5917

(🔺 On Path) *Welsh Bicknor*
Youth Hostel, The Rectory, Welsh
Bicknor, Goodrich, Ross-on-Wye,
Herefordshire, HR9 6JJ.
Actual grid ref: SO591177
Warden: Mr C Hawkins.
Tel: 01594 860300
Under 18: £5.55 **Adults:** £8.25
Family Rooms, Evening Meal, Self
Catering Facilities, Centrally
Heated, Camping, Games Room,
Laundry Facilities, Shop, Study
Room, Grounds available for
Games
On the banks of the River Wye, an
early Victorian Rectory surrounded
by meadows with great views
across the Forest of Dean and
Symonds Yat Rock

Whitchurch   22

National Grid Ref: SO5417

(1.5m) *The Cedars Guest House,*
Llangrove Road, Whitchurch,
Ross-on-Wye, Herefordshire,
HR9 6DQ.
Elegant, comfortable Georgian
house.
Grades: ETB 2 Cr, Comm
Tel: 01600 890351 Ms Wormser.
Rates fr: *£16.00-£17.00.*
Open: All Year **Beds:** 4D 2T 2S
Baths: 4 Private 1 Shared
🐾 🅿 (8) ⛅ ✕ 📶 Ⓥ

Bridstow   18

National Grid Ref: SO6024

🍴 🍺 Man of Ross, Kings Head

(2m 🚗) *Lavender Cottage,*
Bridstow, Ross-on-Wye,
Herefordshire, HR9 6QB.
Comfortable part 17th Century cot-
tage. **Grades:** ETB Listed
Tel: **01989 562836** Mrs Nash.
Rates fr: *£15.00-£20.00.*
Open: All Year
Beds: 1D 2T
Baths: 2 Ensuite, 1 Shared
🐾 (10) 🅿 (3) ✍ ⛅ ✕ 📶 Ⓥ ▮ ∦

Ross-on-Wye   19

National Grid Ref: SO6024

🍴 🍺 Man of Ross, Hope and
Anchor, Eagle Inn

(On Path) *Radcliffe Guest House,*
Wye Street, Ross-on-Wye,
Herefordshire, HR9 7BS.
C17th black and white guesthouse.
Grades: ETB 2 Cr, RAC Listed

Tel: **01989 563895** Mrs Sivill.
Rates fr: *£18.00-£18.00.*
Open: All Year (not Xmas)
Beds: 2D 3T 1S **Baths:** 6 Ensuite
⛅ ▮ ∦

(0.5m) *Edde Cross House, Edde*
Cross Street, Ross-on-Wye,
Herefordshire, HR9 7BZ.
Delightful Georgian no-smoking
townhouse.
Grades: ETB 2 Cr, High Comm,
AA 4 Q, Select, RAC High
Acclaim
Tel: **01989 565088**
Mrs Van Gelderen.
Rates fr: *£22.00-£30.00.*
Open: Mar to Nov **Beds:** 2D 1T
Baths: 2 Ensuite, 1 Private
🐾 (10) 🅿 (3) ✍ ⛅ 📶 Ⓥ ∦

(0.25m) *Broadlands, Ledbury*
Road, Ross-on-Wye, Herefordshire,
HR9 7AU.
Modern comfortable and friendly
home.
Tel: **01989 563663** Mrs Ryder.
Rates fr: *£15.00-£15.00.*
Open: All Year (not Xmas)

Symonds Yat East   23

National Grid Ref: SO5616

¶◖ Saracens Head Hotel

(On Path) *Rose Cottage, Symonds Yat East, Ross-on-Wye, Herefordshire, HR9 6JL.*
Elegant riverside cottage.
Grades: ETB Listed
Tel: 01600 890514 Mrs Whyberd.
Rates fr: £17.50-£33.00.
Open: All Year (not Xmas)
Beds: 3D
Baths: 2 Ensuite 1 Private
🅿 (3) ⊬ 📁 🛉 🖿 📺 🛊 ♦

Symonds Yat Rock   24

National Grid Ref: SO5615

¶◖ Rock Inn

(On Path) *The Rock Inn, Hillersland, Symonds Yat Rock, Coleford, Glos, GL16 7NY.*
Country inn - comfortable ensuite accommodation. **Grades:** ETB 2 Cr
Tel: 01594 832367 Mrs Matthews.
Rates fr: £20.00-£25.00.
Open: All year **Beds:** 1F 1D 1T
Baths: 3 Ensuite
♿ 🅿 (20) 📁 🛉 ✕ 🖿 📺 🛊 ♦

Symonds Yat West   25

National Grid Ref: SO5516

¶◖ Wye Knot Inn

(On Path 🚗) *Mountain Daisy Guest House, Symonds Yat West, Ross-on-Wye, Herefordshire, HR9 6BL.*
Actual grid ref: SO556164
Quiet cottage, superb river view.
Grades: ETB Listed
Tel: 01600 890507 Mr Smith.
Rates fr: £17.00-£17.00.
Open: All Year (not Xmas)
Beds: 1D **Baths:** 1 Ensuite
♿ 🅿 (2) ⊬ 📁 🖿 📺 ♦

(On Path 🚗) *Walnut Tree Cottage Hotel, Symonds Yat West, Ross-on-Wye, Herefordshire, HR9 6BN.*
High-standard clean and comfortable accommodation.
Grades: ETB 3 Cr
Tel: 01600 890828 Mrs Baker.
Rates fr: £23.00-£23.00.
Open: Mar to Oct
Beds: 1F 2D 1T 1S
Baths: 5 Ensuite
♿ (3) 🅿 (10) ⊬ 📁 ✕ 🖿 📺 🛊 ♦

(On Path) *Woodlea Hotel, Symonds Yat West, Ross-on-Wye, Herefordshire, HR9 6BL.*
Licensed Victorian country house hotel.
Grades: ETB 3 Cr, Comm, AA Recomm, RAC Acclaim
Tel: 01600 890206 Mrs Blunt.
Rates fr: £22.00-£22.00.
Open: All Year **Beds:** 2F 4D 2T 1S
Baths: 6 Ensuite 2 Shared
♿ 🅿 (9) 📁 🛉 ✕ 🖿 📺 🛊 ♦

English Bicknor   26

National Grid Ref: SO5815

¶◖ Courtfield Arms

(On Path) *Upper Tump Farm, East Bach, English Bicknor, Coleford, Glos, GL16 7EU.*
Actual grid ref: SO585157
C15thfarmhouse.
Grades: ETB 2 Cr, Comm
Tel: 01594 860072
Mrs Merrett.
Rates fr: £16.50-£16.50.
Open: All Year (not Xmas)
Beds: 1F 2S
Baths: 1 Ensuite 1 Shared
♿ 🅿 📁 🖿 📺 ♦

(On Path) *Oak Farm, Ross Road, English Bicknor, Coleford, Glos, GL16 7PA.*
Grades: ETB 2 Cr
Tel: 01594 860606
Mr & Mrs Edwards.
Rates fr: £1300-£14.00.
Open: All Year (not Xmas)
Beds: 1D 1T 1S
Baths: 2 Private 1 Shared
🅿 (5) 📁 ✕ 🖿 📺
Modern farmhouse with superb views from all rooms. Ideally situated for exploring the magnificent Forest of Dean and the grandeur of the Wye Valley.

Monmouth   27

National Grid Ref: SO5012

¶◖ Riverside Hotel, Robin Hood, Brittania Inn, Punch House, Vine Tree, Queens Head

(0.25m) *Burton House, St James Square, Monmouth, Gwent, NP5 3DN.*
Actual grid ref: SO512129
Large Georgian town house.
Grades: WTB Listed
Tel: 01600 714958 Mrs Banfield.
Rates fr: £16.50-£16.50.
Open: All Year (not Xmas)
Beds: 1F 1D 1T
🅿 (3) 📁 🛉 🖿 🛊 ♦

(1m 🚗) *Caseta Alta, 15 Toynbee Close, Osbaston, Monmouth, Gwent, NP5 3NU.*
Grades: WTB Listed
Tel: 01600 713023 Mrs Allcock.
Rates fr: £13.00-£18.50.
Open: All Year (not Xmas)
Beds: 2D 1T 1S
Baths: 1 Private 1 Shared
♿ (8) 🅿 (2) 📁 🖿 📺 🛊 ♦
Comfortable 'upside-down' house.
Glorious views. Colour TV, radio, tea/coffee facilities in bedrooms.
Evening meals by arrangement.
Wye Valley Walk 1/2 mile away.
Welcome Host certificate

(▲ 0.5m) *Monmouth Youth Hostel, Priory School, Priory Street, Monmouth, Gwent, NP5 3NX.*
Actual grid ref: SO508130
Warden: Ms B Elias.

Tel: 01600 715116
Under 18: £4.60 **Adults:** £6.75
Family Bunk Rooms, Partially Heated, Showers, Self-Catering Only, Shop
In the remains of a late C15th priory, this building, alongside the River Monnow was used as a school for 200 years until 1970

(On Path) *Red Lion House, 16 Drybridge Street, Monmouth, Gwent, NP5 3AD.*
C17th private town house.
Tel: 01600 713633 Mrs Frost.
Rates fr: £12.50-£14.00.
Open: All Year (not Xmas)
Beds: 1D 2T **Baths:** 2 Shared
🅿 📁 🖿

(0.5m 🚗) *Troy Lodge, Monmouth, Gwent, NP5 4HX.*
Actual grid ref: SO509116
Beautifully furnished annexe to lodge. **Tel:** 01600 715098
Mr & Mrs Bennett.
Rates fr: £17.50-£17.50.
Open: All Year (not Xmas)
Beds: 1D 1T
Baths: 1 Ensuite 1 Shared
♿ (5) 🅿 (2) ⊬ 📁 🛉 🖿 📺 ♦
Also ▲ £2 per person.
Open: All Year (not Xmas)
📶 📺 ♨ ✕ ♦ ♿

(0.25m) *Wye Avon, Dixton Road, Monmouth, Gwent, NP5 3PR.*
Actual grid ref: SO512132
Large Victorian private house.
Tel: 01600 713322 Mrs Cantrell.
Rates fr: £14.00-£14.00.
Open: All Year (not Xmas)
Beds: 1F 1D 1T 1S
Baths: 1 Shared ♿ 🅿 ⊬ 🖿 🛊 ♦

Redbrook   28

National Grid Ref: SO5310

(On Path) *Tresco, Redbrook, Monmouth, Gwent, NP5 4LY.*
Actual grid ref: SO536101
Bungalow, all ground floor bedrooms.
Tel: 01600 712325 Mrs Evans.
Rates fr: £14.00-£14.00.
Open: All Year
Beds: 1F 1D 1T 2S
Baths: 2 Shared
♿ 🅿 📁 🛉 ✕ 🖿 🛆 📺 🛊 ♦
Also ▲ £6 per person.,
Open: All Year 📶 📺 ✕ 🛆

Penallt   29

National Grid Ref: SO5210

(0.5m 🚗) *Cherry Orchard Farm, Lone Lane, Penallt, Monmouth, Gwent, NP5 4AJ.*
Actual grid ref: SO5210
C18th stone farmhouse.
Grades: WTB Listed
Tel: 01600 714010 Mrs Beale.
Rates fr: £15.00-£15.00.
Open: All Year **Beds:** 1D 1T
Baths: 2 Shared
♿ 🅿 (6) ⊬ 🛉 🖿 📺 🛊 ♦

Bigsweir 30

National Grid Ref: SO5305

(0.25m 🚌) *Blue Barn, The Hudnalls, Bigsweir, St Briavels, Lydney, Glos, GL15 6RT.*
Actual grid ref: SO5203
New Continental design house.
Grades: ETB 3 Cr
Tel: 01594 530252 Ms Parker.
Rates fr: *£18.50-£18.50.*
Open: All Year
Beds: 3D 2T 2S
Baths: 7 Ensuite
🅿 (15) ⊬🛏✗🎴🎥📖🔥
Also ⛺ *£5 per person. Also bunkhouse, £5 per bunk.*
Open: All Year 🏚🛏✗🔥♿

St Briavels 31

National Grid Ref: SO5604

🍴🍺 Crown Inn, The George

(2m 🚌) *Tyersall, St Briavels, Lydney, Glos, GL15.*
Actual grid ref: SO537037
Wisteria covered period farmhouse.
Tel: 01594 530215 Mrs Morgan.
Rates fr: *£15.50-£15.50.*
Open: Easter to Nov
Beds: 1D 1T 1S
Baths: 1 Ensuite, 1 Shared
🛏🅿 (4) ⊬🛏✗🎴🎥📖🔥

(▲ 2.5m) *St Briavels Castle Youth Hostel, The Castle, St Briavels, Lydney, Glos, GL15 6RG.*
Actual grid ref: SO558045
Warden: J & E Cotterill.
Tel: 01594 530272
Under 18: £5.55 **Adults:** £8.25
Partially Heated, Showers, Evening Meal (7.00 pm),
800-year-old moated Norman castle used by king John as a hunting lodge, in the centre of a quiet village above the River Wye

(2m 🚌) *Offas Mead, The Fence, St Briavels, Lydney, Glos, GL15 6QG.*
Actual grid ref: SO544056
Spacious country house, superb views.
Grades: WTB 1 Cr
Tel: 01594 530229
Mrs Lacey.
Rates fr: *£14.50-£16.00.*
Open: All Year (not Xmas)
Beds: 2F 1T
Baths: 2 Private 1 Shared
🛏 (8) 🅿 (5) ⊬🖵🎴🎥📖🔥

(2m) *Oak Cottage, St Briavels Common, St Briavels, Lydney, Glos, GL15 6SJ.*
Actual grid ref: SO538035
Comfortable country cottage, lovely views.
Tel: 01594 530440
Mr & Mrs Watts.
Rates fr: *£15.00-£15.00.*
Open: Easter to Nov
Beds: 1T 1S
Baths: 1 Shared
🅿 (2) ⊬🖵✗🎴📖

Also ⛺ *£3.00 per tent.*
Open: Easter to Sep 🏚🎴✗♿

Llandogo 32

National Grid Ref: SO5204

🍴🍺 The Sloop Inn

(On Path) *The Sloop Inn, Llandogo, Monmouth, Gwent, NP5 4TW.*
Actual grid ref: SO526042
Grades: WTB 3 Cr, AA Recomm, RAC Listed
Tel: 01594 530291
Mr Morgan.
Rates fr: *£19.50-£22.50.*
Open: All Year
Beds: 1F 2D 1T
Baths: 4 Ensuite
🛏 (8) 🅿 (30) 🖵🛏✗🎴🎥📖🔥
Traditional hostelry with ensuite character bedrooms. Wholesome food at realistic prices and a cheerful atmosphere make this award winning inn a popular place to stay.

Tintern 33

National Grid Ref: SO5300

🍴🍺 Wye Valley Hotel, Rose & Crown, Royal George Hotel

(0.75m) *The Old Rectory, Tintern, Chepstow, Gwent, NP6 6SG.*
Actual grid ref: SO529008
Welcoming, comfortable early Victorian house.
Grades: WTB 1 Cr
Tel: 01291 689519
Mrs Newman.
Rates fr: *£14.50-£14.50.*
Open: All Year
Beds: 1F 1D 2T 1S
Baths: 1 Shared
🛏🅿 (8) ⊬🛏✗🎴🎥📖🔥

(1.25m) *Valley House, Raglan Road, Tintern, Chepstow, Gwent, NP6 6TH.*
Actual grid ref: SO523002
Peaceful C18th detached house.
Grades: WTB 2 Cr, AA 3 Q, RAC High Acclaim
Tel: 01291 689652
Mr & Mrs Howe.
Rates fr: *£17.50-£25.00.*
Open: All Year (not Xmas)
Beds: 2D 1T
Baths: 3 Ensuite
🅿 (7) ⊬🛏🎴📖🔥

Tutshill 34

National Grid Ref: ST5494

🍴🍺 Live & Let Live

(0.25m 🚌) *The Vicarage, Gloucester Road, Tutshill, Chepstow, Gwent, NP6 7DH.*
Actual grid ref: ST543947
Private house in large garden.
Tel: 01291 622442 Mrs Green.
Rates fr: *£16.00-£16.00.*
Open: Apr to Sep

Chepstow 35

National Grid Ref: ST5393

🍴🍺 Rising Sun, Bridge Inn, Castle View Hotel, Live & Let Live

(0.25m 🚌) *Lower Hardwick House, Mount Pleasant, Chepstow, Gwent, NP6 5PT.*
Car parking for duration of walk.
Tel: 01291 622162 Mrs Grassby.
Rates fr: *£14.00-£14.00.*
Open: All Year
Beds: 2F 1D 1T 1S
Baths: 1 Ensuite 2 Shared
🛏🅿 (12) 🖵🛏🎴📖🔥
Also ⛺ *£5 per tent.* 🏚🎴

(2m) *The First Hurdle Hotel, 9-10 Upper Church Street, Chepstow, Gwent, NP6 5EX.*
Two C17th townhouses with period furnishings.
Grades: WTB 3 Cr, RAC 2 St
Tel: 01291 622189 Mrs Sleeman.
Rates fr: *£25.00-£20.00.*
Open: All Year (not Xmas)
Beds: 1F 3D 6T 2S
Baths: 7 Ensuite 5 Shared
🛏🅿 (2) 🖵🛏✗🎴♿🎥📖🔥

(On Path 🚌) *Langcroft, 71 St Kingsmark Avenue, Chepstow, Gwent, NP6 5LY.*
Actual grid ref: ST529938
Modern comfortable family friendly home.
Grades: WTB Listed
Tel: 01291 625569 Mrs Langdale.
Rates fr: *£15.00-£15.00.*
Open: All Year **Beds:** 1D 1T 1S
Baths: 1 Ensuite 1 Shared
🛏🅿 (3) 🖵🛏🎴🎥📖🔥

(0.5m) *Castle Guest House, 4 Bridge Street, Chepstow, Gwent, NP6 5EY.*
Actual grid ref: ST435941
Large Georgian house.
Tel: 01291 622040
Mr & Mrs Cherrington.
Rates fr: *£17.50-£17.50.*
Open: All Year
Beds: 1F 1D 1T 1S
Baths: 4 Ensuite
🛏🅿 (3) 🛏🎥🎴

(0.5m 🚌) *Upper Sedbury House, Sedbury Lane, Sedbury, Chepstow, Newport, Gwent, NP6 7HN.*
Actual grid ref: ST547943
Quaint, cottagey, superior country house.
Grades: WTB 2 Cr
Tel: 01291 627173 Mrs Potts.
Rates fr: *£16.50-£18.50.*
Open: All Year
Beds: 1F 2D 2T
Baths: 1 Ensuite 2 Shared
🛏🅿 (10) 🖵🛏✗🎴🎥📖🔥
Also ⛺ *£2.50 per person.,*
Open: All Year 🎴🚌✗🔥♿

ORDER A COPY FOR A FRIEND OR COLLEAGUE

Yes, I wish to order a copy of

( )   **Stilwell's Directory: Britain - Bed & Breakfast 1996 @ £11.95 (inc. £2 p&p)**

( )   **Stilwell's Directory: Ireland - Bed & Breakfast 1996 @ £6.95 (inc. £1 p&p)**

( )   **Stilwell's Directory: Scotland - Bed & Breakfast 1996 @ £6.95 (inc. £1 p&p)**

( )   **Stilwell's National Trail Companion 1996 @ £10.95 (inc. £1 p&p)**

Sterling or EC currency cheques only please, made payable to Stilwell Publishing Ltd. Please send me my copy within 21 days of receipt of this order.

Name ....

Address ....

....

.... Postcode ....

Tel No ....

Please send this order form, accompanied by your payment, to:

Copy Sales, Stilwell Publishing Ltd, The Courtyard, 59 Charlotte Road, Shoreditch, London, EC2A 3QT.
No credit card sales accepted.

ORDER A COPY FOR A FRIEND OR COLLEAGUE

Yes, I wish to order a copy of

( ) **Stilwell's Directory: Britain - Bed & Breakfast 1996 @ £11.95 (inc. £2 p&p)**

( ) **Stilwell's Directory: Ireland - Bed & Breakfast 1996 @ £6.95 (inc. £1 p&p)**

( ) **Stilwell's Directory: Scotland - Bed & Breakfast 1996 @ £6.95 (inc. £1 p&p)**

( ) **Stilwell's National Trail Companion 1996 @ £10.95 (inc. £1 p&p)**

Sterling or EC currency cheques only please, made payable to Stilwell Publishing Ltd. Please send me my copy within 21 days of receipt of this order.

Name ....

Address ....

....

.... Postcode ....

Tel No ....

Please send this order form, accompanied by your payment, to:

Copy Sales, Stilwell Publishing Ltd, The Courtyard, 59 Charlotte Road, Shoreditch, London, EC2A 3QT. No credit card sales accepted.

NOT LISTED IN STILWELL'S?

Do you know of a B&B that should be listed in these pages, but isn't? Use this form to recommend the B&B, telling us briefly why you think it merits inclusion.

I nominate the following B&B for inclusion in next years edition of Stilwell's National Trail Companion.

B&B Owner's Name ....

B&B Address ....

....

B&B Tel No ....

Reasons for Nomination ....

....

....

Nominated by ....

Nominee's Address ....

Send this form to:

National Trail Companion, Stilwell Publishing Ltd, The Courtyard, 59 Charlotte Road, Shoreditch, London, EC2A 3QT.

NOT LISTED IN STILWELL'S?

Do you know of a B&B that should be listed in these pages, but isn't? Use this form to recommend the B&B, telling us briefly why you think it merits inclusion.

I nominate the following B&B for inclusion in next years edition of Stilwell's National Trail Companion.

B&B Owner's Name ....

B&B Address ....

....

B&B Tel No ....

Reasons for Nomination ....

....

....

Nominated by ....

Nominee's Address ....

Send this form to:

National Trail Companion, Stilwell Publishing Ltd, The Courtyard, 59 Charlotte Road, Shoreditch, London, EC2A 3QT.

Key to Entries

⚬ Children welcome (from age shown in brackets, if specified)

🅿 Off-street car parking (number of places shown in brackets)

🚭 No smoking

📺 Television (either in every room or in a TV lounge)

🐾 Pets accepted (by prior arrangement)

✖ Evening meal available (by prior arrangement)

Ⓥ Special diets catered for (by prior arrangement - please check with owner to see if your particular requirements are catered for)

▥ Central heating throughout

♿ Suitable for disabled people (please check with owner to see what level of disability is provided for)

❀ Christmas breaks a speciality

☕ Coffee/Tea making facilities

▲ Youth Hostel

⌂ Camping Barn

Å Camping facilities

▮ Packed lunches available

✎ Drying facilities for wet clothes and boots

🚐 Vehicle back-up service (pick-up from path drop-off next day)

The location heading - every hamlet, village, town and city mentioned in this directory is represented on the local path map at the head of each chapter.

Use the National Grid reference with Ordnance Survey maps and any atlas that uses the National Grid. The letters refer to a 100 kilometre grid square. The first two numbers refer to a North/South grid line and the last two numbers refer to an East/West grid line. The grid reference indicates their intersection point.

Local pubs - these are the names of nearby pubs that serve food in the evening, as suggested by local B&Bs

Penny Hassett   12

National Grid Ref: PH2096.

🍽 🍺 Cat & Fiddle, The Bull

Map reference (in the order that the location appears along the route).

Distance from paths in miles

(On Path 🚐) *The Old Rectory, Main Street, Penny Hassett, Borchester, Borsetshire, BC2 3QT.* C18th former rectory, lovely garden.
Grades: ETB 2 Cr, Comm.
Tel: **01048 598464.** Mrs Smythe.
Rates fr: *£14.00*-**£16.00**.
Open: All Year
Beds: 1F 1D 1T
Baths: 1 Private 2 Shared
⚬(4) 🅿(2) 🚭 📺 🐾 ✖ ▥ Ⓥ ♿ ❀ ☕

The figure in *italics* is the lowest 1996 double or twin rate per person per night. The figure in **bold** is the lowest 1996 single rate. Some establishments do not accept single bookings.

Bedrooms
F = Family
D = Double
T = Twin
S = Single

Grades - the English, Scottish and Welsh Tourist Boards (**ETB**, **STB** and **WTB**) have the national Crown rating (**Cr**), in which the range of facilities and services an establishment provides is indicated by "Listed" or 1 to 5 Crowns in ascending order of merit. Northern Ireland has a simple approved system (**Approv**). An optional quality grading, using the terms Approved (**Approv**), Commended (**Comm**), Highly Commended (**High Comm**) and De Luxe is also used. More details of the national Crown rating and the quality grading can be had from any Tourist Information Centre. The Automobile Association (**AA**) employs two grading systems: the one for hotels uses 1 to 5 Stars (**St**) in ascending order of merit; there is also a B&B rating that uses the letter **Q** (for quality) on a scale of 1 to 4; the highest have 4 Qs and a Selected award (**Select**). For more details, telephone the AA on 01256 20123. The Royal Automobile Club (**RAC**) also uses a Star (**St**) system for large hotels; small hotels and B&Bs obtain the ratings 'Acclaimed' (**Acclaim**) or 'Highly Acclaimed' (**High Acclaim**). For more details, telephone the RAC on 0181-686 0088.